21st Century
EDUCATION
A Reference Handbook

21st Century EDUCATION
A Reference Handbook
Volume 1

Edited by

Thomas L. Good
University of Arizona, Tucson

Los Angeles • London • New Delhi • Singapore • Washington DC

A SAGE Reference Publication

For information:

SAGE Publications, Inc.
2455 Teller Road
Thousand Oaks, California 91320
E-mail: order@sagepub.com

SAGE Publications Ltd.
1 Oliver's Yard
55 City Road
London, EC1Y 1SP
United Kingdom

SAGE Publications India Pvt. Ltd.
B 1/I 1 Mohan Cooperative Industrial Area
Mathura Road, New Delhi 110 044
India

SAGE Publications Asia-Pacific Pte. Ltd.
33 Pekin Street #02-01
Far East Square
Singapore 048763

Printed in the United States of America.

Library of Congress Cataloging-in-Publication Data

21st century education : a reference handbook / Thomas L. Good, editor.
   p. cm.
 Includes bibliographical references and index.
 ISBN 978-1-4129-5011-4 (cloth : acid-free paper)
 1. Education—Study and teaching—United States. 2. Education—United
States—Philosophy. 3. Education—Research—United States. I. Good,
Thomas L., 1943- II. Title: Twenty first century education.
 LA210.A15 2009
 370.973—dc22

                        2008020266

This book is printed on acid-free paper.

08 09 10 11 12 10 9 8 7 6 5 4 3 2 1

Publisher:	Rolf A. Janke
Acquisitions Editor:	Jim Brace-Thompson
Developmental Editor:	Sara Tauber
Reference Systems Manager:	Leticia Gutierrez
Production Editor:	Belinda Thresher, Appingo Publishing Services
Cover Designer:	Candice Harman
Marketing Manager:	Amberlyn Erzinger

Contents

Volume One

PART I. TEACHERS

PART II. OTHER SCHOOL PERSONNEL

PART III. LEARNERS: DEVELOPMENTAL CONTEXT

PART VII. SOCIAL CONTEXT

PART VIII. CURRICULUM K–12

VOLUME TWO

PART XIV. ALTERNATIVE APPROACHES

PART XV. SCHOOL REFORM

PART XVI. FEDERAL, STATE, AND COMMUNITY POLICIES

PART XVII. HIGHER EDUCATION

PREFACE

American education is the cornerstone to the maintenance of our society—its safety, prosperity, health, and social good. More than 50 million students are enrolled in K–12 public education (U.S. Department of Education, 2007). The typical student spends approximately 1,000 hours in school every year, equating to almost 7,000 hours of school before entry into junior high school (Jackson, 1990). Students spend even more hours preparing homework, studying for tests, and participating in school activities. Public schools are now assuming various forms. One particular variation—charter schools—makes up 4 percent of all public schools (U.S. Department of Education, 2007). Another 11 percent of students eligible for K–12 enrollment—more than 5.1 million—are enrolled in private schools (U.S. Department of Education, 2007) and yet another 1.2 million do not attend formal, institutional schools at all but rather are home-schooled (Templeton & Johnson, this volume). At the college level and in assorted professional schools at the undergraduate and graduate levels, we have an all-time record enrollment of roughly 17.5 million students (U.S. Department of Education, 2007). In addition to the students enrolled in our schools, teachers, professors, administrators, service personnel, and others are employed in educational institutions. Parents and citizens pay large amounts of money for tuition, books, room, and board. Further, parents spend considerable time visiting schools and participating in fundraising activities. Clearly, education directly involves vast numbers of students, teachers, and educators, and—through the media, foundations, and other institutions—still more Americans are involved in the debate about our schools: What should be taught, and to what standards should students and schools be held accountable?

Purpose and Audience

With its many constituents, education has many faces. To some, it is their second-grade teacher. To others, it is an economic indicator (property values are increased on the perceived quality of nearby schools). At a micro level, schools transcend teacher-student relationships and become complex institutions around which important policy decisions and vast investments are made. Taken as a whole, the chapters contained in this book present and interpret these many faces of education. The two-volume work provides undergraduate majors and those currently in education an authoritative reference source that will serve their research needs with more information than encyclopedia entries, but not as much detail or density as journal articles or research handbook chapters. Thorough and comprehensive, these volumes offer readers a general understanding of the issues of utmost importance in education in the 21st century. The text is a combination of historical reviews, current debates, and pending issues of concern at the classroom, state, and federal levels, with sections devoted to students, their teachers, professional staff, the educational context of curriculum and learning, and current and future issues.

Students

In this collection of chapters, we provide readers with insight into a rich array of issues inherent in American education. Among those stories is an analysis of students. Who are they, how do they vary, and how can they best be educated? What percent of our students come from affluent homes or poor ones? What various languages do our students speak in their homes, and what is the general range of cultural and ethnic groups represented in our schools? Central to the thinking of many Americans is the performance level of our students. Questions abound regarding the quality of student learning. Can they calculate, think, find and solve problems, write persuasively, and work cooperatively with others on complex tasks? Are today's students better than those of a decade ago? How does student performance vary with factors such as school quality, community involvement, and the amount of money schools receive from their communities and their state?

Teachers

A second series of chapters provides an analysis of teachers. Teachers represent more than 3.2 million members of the American workforce. Their service is invaluable, with elementary teachers and high school teachers serving 650 and 6,000 students, respectively, over a typical 30-year career (Smylie, Miller, & Westbrook, this volume). We ask: Who are our teachers and what practices are representative of high-quality teaching? How and where are teachers prepared? How do teachers improve on practices? What are their perceptions of their own teaching? What are their perceptions of the profession? How do the teachers of today compare to those of the past? To what extent do teachers decide what they teach and how to measure it? To what extent are teachers viewed as professionals by the broader society?

Professional Staff

Readers are also provided with an analysis of school personnel. Who are our psychologists, school counselors, superintendents, and principals? What daily tasks and challenges do they face in the 21st century? How do they interact with teachers, students, and staff? How is leadership negotiated between superintendents and principals, and how is it negotiated between teachers and principals? How accessible are these staff members? What roles do school personnel play with parents or community leaders? What are the career opportunities for those interested in becoming a professional counselor or principal?

Context, Curriculum, and Learning

In addition to discussing the people involved in the educational enterprise, we explore the contextual factors that are important to the ways in which students and teachers interact around and within a learning environment. How do peer relationships play a role in child development? How do urban and rural schools differ from a student's, a teacher's, and an administrator's perspectives? What are the school experiences of gifted and at-risk students? Increased diversity across the nation raises questions about ways in which English language learners, immigrants, and minority students engage in educational opportunities. How do the curriculum and learning environments incorporate these contextual factors? To what extent does motivation vary within and across contexts? What topics are included in today's curriculum? How is student learning assessed?

Current Issues

Finally, we explore the considerable debate about the purpose of American schools. Some citizens, especially parents, believe schools should promote the social growth of students, as well as their academic competencies. Such citizens want students to develop leadership and cooperative skills through music, sports, and extracurricular activities. Fueled by national comparisons suggesting that students in many other countries outperform American students, policy makers tend to argue for and allocate resources toward promoting academic growth. For more than 30 years, policy reports (e.g., Nation at Risk, the Governor's Summit, and so forth) have strongly argued the need to improve American schools and students' scores on achievement tests if the United States is to avoid economic peril.

Beyond the debates on the relative amount of time and resources that should be placed on the formal curriculum versus the informal curriculum and various types of non-subject learning in school is the issue of testing. Debates at the forefront of current educational policy are exacerbated by concern over testing and accountability. Currently, $104.1 million is being allocated annually to fund the National Assessment of Educational Progress and its governing board—a figure that is expected to increase over time to extend testing to more grades and subjects (U.S. Department of Education, 2008). On just one test, states spend vast amounts of money developing, administering, scoring, and analyzing. Chapters in this volume will tackle issues related to the increase in assessment. How has the implementation of the No Child Left Behind Act shaped the past? In what ways will it shape the future of education? In what ways does testing influence the educational experiences of students, teachers, administrators, and the nation at large? The volumes conclude with an evaluation of current issues, providing readers with insight into the 22nd century: Where are we going? What is the future of education?

Acknowledgments

We thank our editorial board: Carole Ames, David Berliner, Jere Brophy, Lyn Corno, and Mary McCaslin, who helped to conceptualize the content of these volumes. Given the importance and diversity in American education, this is no easy task. Board members gave cogent advice about which issues were most important and how best to organize the topics in ways to maximize coverage and the understanding of American education. They were also helpful in identifying authors who could write both authoritatively and clearly. We thank the authors who undertook topic assignments and made important knowledge accessible and interesting.

Thomas L. Good, Editor
University of Arizona

Alyson Lavigne Dolan, Managing Editor
University of Arizona

References and Further Readings

Jackson, P. W. (1990). *Life in classrooms*. New York: Teachers College Press.

U.S. Department of Education, National Center for Education Statistics. (2007). *Fast facts*. Retrieved February 3, 2008, from http://nces.ed.gov/fastfacts/

U.S. Department of Education. (2008). *Fiscal year 2009 budget summary and background information*. Retrieved February 3, 2008, from http://www.ed.gov/

ABOUT THE EDITORS

Editor-in-Chief

Thomas L. Good is professor and department head of the Department of Educational Psychology at the University of Arizona. He received his PhD from Indiana University, and his previous appointments were at the University of Texas at Austin and the University of Missouri, Columbia. His policy interests include school and classroom improvement and youth socialization. His research interests include the communication of performance expectations in classroom settings and the analysis of effective instruction, especially in schools that serve children who reside in poverty. His teaching specialty areas are analysis of instructional behavior, theories of instruction, and the informal curriculum. His work has been supported by numerous agencies, including the National Science Foundation and the National Institute of Mental Health. He has been a Fulbright Fellow in Australia and has long served as editor of the *Elementary School Journal* (published by the University of Chicago Press). He has published numerous books, including *Looking in Classrooms*, coauthored with Jere Brophy.

Editorial Board

Carole Ames is a professor of educational psychology and dean of the College of Education at Michigan State University. She is interested in the development of social and academic motivation in children and youth. Her research focuses on the effects of classroom structure, competition, and teaching practices on children's motivation to learn. Other research interests include disadvantaged and urban children and youth, school and family relationships, and strategies for increasing parental involvement in children's learning.

David C. Berliner is Regents' Professor of Education at Arizona State University, Tempe, Arizona. He is past president of the American Educational Research Association and of the Division of Educational Psychology of the American Psychological Association and is member of the National Academy of Education. He is the author of more than 200 articles, book chapters, and books in education and psychology.

Jere Brophy is university distinguished professor of teacher education and educational psychology at Michigan State University. A clinical and developmental psychologist by training, he has conducted research on teachers' achievement expectations and related self-fulfilling prophecy effects; teachers' attitudes toward individual students and the dynamics of teacher-student relationships; students' personal characteristics and their effects on teachers; relationships between classroom processes and student achievement; teachers' strategies for managing classrooms and coping with problem students; and teachers' strategies for motivating students to learn. Recently, he has focused on curricular content and instructional method issues involved in teaching social studies for understanding, appreciation, and life application.

Lyn Corno is adjunct professor (formerly professor) at Teachers College, Columbia University, where she is also coeditor of Teachers College Record. She has been an active contributor to the field of educational psychology since receiving her doctorate from Stanford University in 1978. Professor Corno has been coeditor of the *American Educational Research Journal* and the *Educational Psychologist* and is Board Member Emeritus of the National Society for the Study of Education. She just completed a term as President of the American Psychological Association's Division of Educational Psychology (Division 15).

Mary McCaslin, PhD, Michigan State University (1981), is a professor of educational psychology at the University of Arizona. McCaslin's scholarship focuses on the relationships among cultural, social, and personal sources of influence that coregulate student adaptive learning, motivational dynamics, and emergent identity.

Managing Editor

Alyson Lavigne Dolan is a doctoral student in the Department of Educational Psychology at the University of Arizona. She received her BA in psychology at Mount Holyoke College. Prior to attending the University of Arizona she worked in the Department of Psychiatry at the Brigham and Women's Hospital in Boston, Massachusetts, researching prenatal alcohol consumption and concentration and memory in cancer patients. Her current research interests are teacher retention, student and teacher motivational dynamics, and early childhood and elementary education.

ABOUT THE CONTRIBUTORS

Maureen E. Babineau is a visiting lecturer at Mount Holyoke College. She earned her master's in psychology at Mount Holyoke College. She teaches courses in adolescent development, conducts research on development from adolescence through adulthood, and she has professional experience with residential treatment centers specializing in addiction services for adolescents and adults.

Sheri Bauman, PhD, associate professor, Department of Educational Psychology, University of Arizona, is director of the master's program in school counseling and editor of the *Journal for Specialists in Group Work*.

Thelma B. Baxter is an assistant professor of education at Manhattan College in Riverdale, New York, and a former superintendent of District 5, Central Harlem, in New York. She is the widely acclaimed former principal of Theodore Roosevelt High School in the Bronx. Under her leadership, the school was removed from New York State's failing school list (SURR) as a result of three years of positive improvement in student attendance, dropout prevention, and more positive results on Regents testing in Math and English.

Anne S. Beauchamp is a doctoral student in educational psychology at the University of Kansas. Her research foci are achievement motivation and stereotypes in the classroom. Currently, she is investigating implicit achievement goals.

Laurie Behringer is a doctoral candidate in the Higher Education Program at the Steinhardt School of Culture, Education, and Human Development at New York University. Her interests include postsecondary access and equity issues, and literacy development and practices for both youth and adults. She is currently working on a dissertation exploring remedial reading and writing education in urban community colleges.

David C. Berliner is Regents' Professor of Education at Arizona State University, Tempe, Arizona. He is past president of the American Educational Research Association, and of the Division of Educational Psychology of the American Psychological Association, and is member of the National Academy of Education. He is the author of more than 200 articles, book chapters, and books on education and psychology.

Phyllis Blumenfeld (PhD, University of California, Los Angeles) is a professor of education at the University of Michigan. Her research focuses on how teacher behavior and classroom tasks influence student motivation and learning. She engages in interdisciplinary work with education researchers and practitioners to create motivating and conceptually rich environments in both urban and suburban schools.

Cheryl Mason Bolick is an assistant professor of technology integration in the School of Education at the University of North Carolina at Chapel Hill. Her area of interest and research is the integration of technology into social studies education, specifically with digital history resources.

James H. Borland is a professor of education at Teachers College, Columbia University, where he coordinates graduate programs in gifted education. He is the author of the book *Planning and Implementing Programs for the Gifted,* edited *Rethinking Gifted Education,* and has written numerous journal articles and book chapters. He is also editor of the *Education and Psychology of the Gifted* series of books from Teachers College Press and is past coeditor of the Section on Teaching, Learning, and Human Development of the *American Educational Research Journal.* He has lectured on the education of gifted students across the United States and abroad, and he has consulted with numerous school districts, primarily as an evaluator of programs for gifted students.

Andrew M. Brantlinger is the senior research associate for MetroMath at the CUNY Graduate Center. He received his doctorate in the Learning Sciences from Northwestern University. His research interests are in the areas of mathematics education, urban education, and critical theory.

Ellen Brantlinger is Professor Emeritus of Special Education in the Curriculum and Instruction Department at Indiana University, Bloomington. She has written on social class and schooling issues and disability studies in education.

Kimberly Brenneman (PhD, University of California, Los Angeles) is an assistant research professor of psychology at Rutgers University. She is currently associated with the Cognitive Development and Learning Lab at the Rutgers Center for Cognitive Science. where she works on the development, implementation, and assessment of a research-based science program for preschoolers. Her research interests include young children's comprehension and production of notations, their understanding of the animate-inanimate distinction, and various aspects of their science learning.

Susan M. Brookhart, PhD, is an independent educational consultant and a senior research associate at the Center for Advancing the Study of Teaching and Learning (CASTL) at Duquesne University. She is the editor of the journal *Educational Measurement: Issues and Practice,* and is the author or coauthor of books and articles on classroom assessment, educational measurement, program evaluation, and teacher professional development in assessment.

Jere Brophy is University Distinguished Professor of Teacher Education and Educational Psychology at Michigan State University. A clinical and developmental psychologist by training, he has conducted research on teachers' achievement expectations and related self-fulfilling prophecy effects; teachers' attitudes toward individual students and the dynamics of teacher-student relationships; students' personal characteristics and their effects on teachers; relationships between classroom processes and student achievement; teachers' strategies for managing classrooms and coping with problem students; and teachers' strategies for motivating students to learn. His recent focus has been on curricular content and instructional method issues involved in teaching social studies for understanding, appreciation, and life application.

Jonathan E. Brown is an eight-year public schools educator and is currently a doctoral student in the Department of Educational Psychology at the University of Illinois at Chicago. His program emphasis is in measurement, evaluation, statistics, and assessment.

Heidi Legg Burross is an associate adjunct professor at the University of Arizona and research consultant on projects funded by grants from OERI and Carnegie. She earned her PhD in educational psychology in 2001. Her research interests include students' self-perceptions of performance and changes in student performances over time.

Susanna Calkins is the associate director at the Searle Center for Teaching Excellence at Northwestern University (Evanston, Illinois). She received her PhD in European History at Purdue University (West Lafayette, Indiana) in 2001. Her recent publications have focused on faculty conceptions of teaching, learning, and mentoring, and student learning in the history classroom.

Prudence L. Carter is an associate professor in the School of Education and (by courtesy) the Department of Sociology at Stanford University. She received her MA in Sociology and Education from Columbia University, Teachers College and her MPhil and PhD in Sociology from Columbia University. Dr. Carter's primary research agenda focuses on cultural explanations of academic and mobility differences among various racial and ethnic groups. She is the author of the award-winning book *Keepin' It Real: School Success beyond Black and White* (Oxford University Press, 2005), which examines the connections among achievement, culture, and identity for low-income African American and Latino students. Other publications by Dr. Carter have appeared in several journals and book volumes, including *Sociology of Education, Social Problems, Ethnic and Racial Studies, African American Research Perspectives,* and *Sociological Studies of Children and Youth.* Currently, Dr. Carter is conducting an international, comparative study of schools in South Africa and the United States, which examines strains between mobility and ethno-racial culture for disadvantaged and socially marginalized students.

Jess Castle is a graduate student in political science at Boston College and holds a BA in liberal arts from St. John's College. He has previously worked on teacher quality issues at the National Council on Teacher Quality.

Bruce S. Cooper is professor of educational leadership at the Fordham University Graduate School of Education and editor of the *Private School Monitor*; his latest book is *Better Policies, Better Schools.*

Elizabeth Covay is a sociology graduate student at the University of Notre Dame and a researcher at the Center for Research on Educational Opportunity. Her research interests include curriculum tracking, early childhood education, achievement gaps, and school community.

George Crawford is an associate professor in the Department of Teaching and Leadership at the University of Kansas, Lawrence. He holds a PhD in Education Administration from The Ohio State University and has scholarly interests in planning, leadership, the ethics of practice, and organizational behavior. Dr. Crawford is a veteran school leader in both the public schools and university.

Hugh Crethar, PhD, assistant professor, Department of Educational Psychology, University of Arizona, is the 2007–08 president of Counselors for Social Justice, a division of the American Counseling Association.

Dionne Danns is an assistant professor at Indiana University, Bloomington. She earned her PhD at the University of Illinois at Urbana-Champaign. Her research interests include African American educational history in the 20th century with special emphasis on the civil rights and Black power eras.

Linda Darling-Hammond is Charles E. Ducommun Professor of Education at Stanford University, where her research, teaching, and policy work focus on issues of teaching quality, educational equity, and school reform.

She is a member of the National Academy of Education and a former president of the American Educational Research Association. Among her recent books on teacher quality are *Preparing Teachers for a Changing World* (co-edited with John Bransford) and *Powerful Teacher Education: Lessons from Exemplary Programs.*

Heather Davis is an assistant professor at North Carolina State University in the Department of Curriculum and Instruction, where she teaches applied child and adolescent development classes for students preparing to teach in P–12 settings. In 2001, she received her PhD from the University of Georgia in applied cognition and development and has served on the faculties of University of Florida and Ohio State University. Her research interests center on the role of student–teacher relationships in promoting students' motivation, learning, and achievement.

Rheta DeVries is professor of early childhood education at the University of Northern Iowa. She was a public school teacher before studying at the University of Chicago, where she received a PhD in psychology with a specialization in developmental psychology. During subsequent faculty positions at the University of Illinois at Chicago, the Merrill-Palmer Institute, the University of Houston, and her current position, she has worked with teachers and children in classrooms to develop a constructivist approach to early education that is informed and inspired by Piaget's research and theory. Dr. DeVries has authored or coauthored eight books, three monographs, and many book chapters and journal articles. She is most well-known for her articulation of constructivist theory and practice with regard to physical-knowledge activities, group games, and the sociomoral atmosphere necessary for children's construction of knowledge/intelligence, personality, and morality.

Alyson Lavigne Dolan is a doctoral student in the Department of Educational Psychology at the University of Arizona. She received her BA in Psychology at Mount Holyoke College. Prior to attending the University of Arizona she worked in the Department of Psychiatry at the Brigham and Women's Hospital in Boston, Massachusetts, researching prenatal alcohol consumption and concentration and memory in cancer patients. Her current research interests are teacher retention, student and teacher motivational dynamics, and early childhood and elementary education.

Karen L. Drill (MA, Northwestern University, 1999) is a doctoral student in the Department of Educational Psychology at the University of Illinois at Chicago (UIC). Her research interests include moral development, adolescent development, gender, and social and emotional learning. Additionally, Drill teaches a variety of courses for current and future educators at UIC. Prior to enrolling at UIC, she worked as a program coordinator for Northwestern University's Center for Talent Development, where she oversaw a rigorous academic program for gifted youth.

Howard Ebmeier is an associate professor in the Department of Educational Leadership and Policy Studies at the University of Kansas. He holds a PhD in curriculum and instruction from the University of Missouri and has been a school administrator in several school districts. His research interests focus on employment interviews and human resource management.

Jacquelynne Eccles is the Wilbert McKeachie Collegiate Professor of Psychology, Women's Studies and Education, as well as a research scientist at the Institute for Social Research at the University of Michigan. Over the last 30 years, she has conducted research on a wide variety of topics including gender-role socialization, teacher expectancies, classroom influences on student motivation and afterschool activities. Much of this work has focused on the adolescent periods of life when health-compromising behaviors such as smoking dramatically increase. She received her PhD in developmental psychology from the University of California, Los Angeles. Dr. Eccles has served on the faculty at Smith College, the University of Colorado, and the University of Michigan.

Edmund T. Emmer is professor and chair of the Department of Educational Psychology at the University of Texas. His research career in the area of classroom management has spanned nearly 30 years. He has taught preservice teachers, teacher trainers, and educational psychologists at the university level. He has also taught at the middle school and high school levels.

Carolyn M. Evertson, PhD, is Professor of Education Emerita, Peabody College, Vanderbilt University, and director of COMP: Creating Conditions for Learning, a national program for classroom management. She has authored two textbooks on classroom management based on her research on creating supportive classrooms for students. She is the coeditor with Carol Weinstein of the *Handbook of Classroom Management: Research Practice and Contemporary Issues* (Lawrence Erlbaum Associates, 2006).

Daniel Fallon is Professor Emeritus of Psychology and Professor Emeritus of Public Policy at the University of Maryland at College Park. He was chair of the Education Division of Carnegie Corporation of New York from 2000 to 2008, and designed and directed the teacher education reform initiative, Teachers for a New Era. An experimental psychologist, he served as Dean of Arts and Sciences at the University of Colorado and Texas A&M University and as provost and academic vice president at the University of Maryland at College Park. He is the author of articles on learning, motivation, animal behavior, and education and of *The German University: A Heroic Ideal in Conflict with the Modern World,* which won the Eugene M. Kayden book prize for excellence in humanities. Fallon holds a

BA from Antioch College and a PhD from the University of Virginia.

Joyce Fienberg is a research specialist at the Learning Research and Development Center, University of Pittsburgh, where she has engaged in a variety of educational research projects for more than 20 years, including the Museum Learning Collaborative. She has collaborated with Gaea Leinhardt in the design and write-up of numerous studies, including a chapter in *Learning Conversations in Museums*.

J. D. Fletcher is a member of the senior research staff at the Institute for Defense Analyses. His research interests include "intelligent" tutoring systems, instructional simulations, wearable performance aids, analyses of skill acquisition and maintenance, and the cost-effectiveness of different instructional approaches. He has designed computer-based instruction programs used in public schools and training devices used in military training.

Ida Rose Florez, MS, NCSP, is a graduate associate at the University of Arizona, where she is completing a PhD in educational psychology. Florez teaches undergraduate child development and early childhood assessment courses. She earned a master's degree and completed requirements for certification in school psychology at Millersville University in Millersville, Pennsylvania. Florez has led preschool special education assessment teams in three states and served as clinical faculty with Penn State University's College of Medicine on the pediatric rehabilitation and child psychiatric units at the Hershey Medical Center. She currently conducts research in the areas of early childhood teacher beliefs and preparation, and early childhood assessment.

David L. Fortus, a senior scientist at the Weizmann Institute of Science in Israel and an assistant professor at Michigan State University, specializes in developing learning environments that foster the construction of scientific knowledge that can be readily applied in real-world situations. He investigates which supports teachers need to maximize the effectiveness of these environments and the ways in which learning one topic can facilitate the learning of other topics. He has received awards from the National Association for Research in Science Teaching and from the American Psychological Association for his research on the use of design in science classrooms. His publications range from science education to theoretical physics to legal economics. Before receiving a PhD in science education, he was a high school physics teacher and a project director in the aerospace industry.

Tony Frank (MA, Northwestern University, 1990; Northeastern Illinois University, 1994) is a doctoral student in educational psychology at the University of Illinois at Chicago, and has worked as an administrator and middle school teacher in private schools since 1990. He has also taught courses in adolescent development to pre- and inservice middle school teachers at the University of Illinois at Chicago. His area of research interest is adolescent identity development, particularly within the context of Jewish education.

Judith K. Franzak is an assistant professor in literacy education at New Mexico State University. A former middle and high school teacher of English language arts, she earned her PhD in language, literacy, and sociocultural studies at the University of New Mexico. Her research is in adolescent literacy policy, young adult literature, and the classroom context of secondary language arts education.

James W. Fraser is professor of history and education at New York University's Steinhardt School of Culture, Education, and Human Development. His most recent book is *Preparing America's Teachers: A History* (Teachers College Press, 2007). Earlier works include *A History of Hope: When Americans Have Dared to Dream of a Better Future* (Palgrave-Macmillan, 2002), *Between Church and State: Religion and Public Education in a Multicultural America* (Palgrave-Macmillan, 1999), and *Reading, Writing, and Justice: School Reform As If Democracy Matters* (State University of New York Press, 1997) as well as articles in several journals. Prior to coming to NYU he was professor of history and education and founding dean of the School of Education at Northeastern University in Boston, Massachusetts. Fraser holds a PhD from Columbia University.

H. Jerome Freiberg is a John and Rebecca Moores University Professor at the University of Houston in the Department of Curriculum and Instruction. His is the editor of the *Journal of Classroom Interaction* and the founder of Consistency Management and Cooperative Discipline Program. He is author or coauthor of eight books and over 100 scholarly works including: *Universal Teaching Strategies* (4th ed.), with Amy Driscoll, and *Freedom to Learn*, (3rd ed.), with psychologist Carl Rogers, which was translated into six languages and selected by the Russian Academy of Education and the Soros Foundation for translation and distribution throughout Russia.

Marilyn Friend, PhD, is professor of education in the Department of Specialized Education Services at the University of North Carolina at Greensboro, where she teaches coursework on inclusive practices and collaboration among service providers. She is the author of *Special Education: Contemporary Perspectives for School Professionals* (2nd ed., 2008), *Interactions: Collaboration Skills for School Professionals* (5th ed., 2007; with Dr. Lynne Cook), *Including Students With Special Needs: A Practical Guide for Classroom Teachers* (4th edition, 2006; with Dr. William Bursuck), and *Co-Teach! A Manual for Creating and Sustaining Classroom Partnerships* (2008). In addition, she is the coproducer on a series of videotapes about collaboration, coteaching, and inclusion, including *The Power of Two* (2nd ed., 2005), and the author of more than 50 articles on collaboration, inclusive practices, and related topics.

Douglas Fuchs is the Nicholas Hobbs Professor of Special Education and Human Development at Vanderbilt University, where he also directs the Kennedy Center Reading Clinic. Doug has conducted programmatic research on response-to-intervention as a method for preventing and identifying children with learning disabilities and on reading instructional methods for improving outcomes for students with learning disabilities. Dr. Fuchs has published more than 200 empirical studies in peer-review journals. He sits on the editorial boards of 10 journals including the *American Educational Research Journal, Journal of Educational Psychology, Elementary School Journal, Journal of Learning Disabilities,* and *Exceptional Children.*

Lynn Fuchs is the Nicholas Hobbs Professor of Special Education and Human Development at Vanderbilt University, where she also codirects the Kennedy Center Reading Clinic. She has conducted programmatic research on assessment methods for enhancing instructional planning and on instructional methods for improving reading and math outcomes for students with learning disabilities. Dr. Fuchs has published more than 200 empirical studies in peer-review journals. She sits on the editorial boards of 10 journals including the *Journal of Educational Psychology, Scientific Studies of Reading, Elementary School Journal, Journal of Learning Disabilities,* and *Exceptional Children.*

Michael Giromini is a PhD candidate at Michigan State University in K–12 educational administration exploring effective high school reform. He teaches physics and mathematics in the International Baccalaureate Diploma Programme at the International Academy in Bloomfield Hills, Michigan.

Yetta M. Goodman is Regents Professor Emerita in the Department of Language, Reading, and Culture in the College of Education at the University of Arizona. She consults with education departments and speaks at conferences throughout the United States and in many nations of the world regarding issues of language, teaching, and learning with implications for language arts curricula. In addition to her research in early literacy, miscue analysis, and in exploring reading and writing processes, she has popularized the term *kidwatching,* encouraging teachers to be professional observers of the language and learning development of their students. She is a major spokesperson for whole language and in her extensive writing shows concern for the role of democracy and social justice in the curriculum. She is past president of The National Council of Teachers of English and the Center for the Expansion of Language and Thinking. She is a member of the Reading Hall of Fame and has received numerous awards for her research, scholarship, and teaching.

A. Lin Goodwin is professor of education and associate dean for teacher education at Teachers College, Columbia University. Her research focuses on connections between teachers' identities and their development; on multicultural understandings and curriculum enactments; and on the issues facing Asian Americans in U.S. schools.

Elizabeth Graue is a professor of early childhood education in the Department of Curriculum and Instruction at the University of Wisconsin–Madison. A former kindergarten teacher, her research addresses kindergarten policy and practice, homeschool relations, and, most currently, class size reduction programs.

Teresa Greene is a doctoral student in developmental psychology/systems science at Portland State University. Her dissertation research explores the developmental progression of the dynamic relationships among perceptions of control, engagement, and coping strategies, and the contextual contributions of social partners. She also designs evaluative studies of educational programs and manages all data collection and reporting processes for the Office of Educational Improvement and Innovation at the Oregon Department of Education.

James G. Greeno is a visiting professor of education at the University of Pittsburgh and Margaret Jacks Professor of Education Emeritus at Stanford University. His research advances a situative theory of learning in classroom settings, with a particular focus on the agency and identity of students as they participate in classroom discourse and activity. Greeno is a member of the National Academy of Education and has received the Edward Lee Thorndike Award, a John Simon Guggenheim Foundation fellowship, and a fellowship from the Center for Advanced Study in Behavioral Sciences.

Douglas A. Grouws is research professor of mathematics education and William T. Kemper Fellow at the University of Missouri. His current research project, Comparing Options in School Mathematics: Investigating Curriculum (COSMIC), is funded by the National Science Foundation. The National Council of Teachers of Mathematics recently presented him with its Lifetime Achievement Award.

Thomas R. Guskey is Distinguished Service Professor and Codirector of the Center for the Advanced Study of Assessment at Georgetown College in Georgetown, Kentucky. His research focuses on educational reform, teacher change, professional development, and student assessment and grading. Dr. Guskey's publications include 14 books, 30 book chapters, and more than 100 journal articles. His most recent books include *Benjamin S. Bloom: Portraits of an Educator* (Rowman & Littlefield, 2006), *How's My Kid Doing? A Parents' Guide to Grades, Marks, and Report Cards* (Jossey-Bass, 2002), *Developing Grading and Reporting Systems for Student Learning* (Corwin Press, 2001), *Evaluating Professional Development* (Corwin Press, 2000), and *Implementing Mastery Learning, 2nd edition* (Wadsworth, 1997).

Allyson Fiona Hadwin received her PhD in psychology of education from Simon Fraser University in 2000. She is now an associate professor in educational psychology, and codirector of the Technology Integration and Evaluation Lab at the University of Victoria, Canada. Hadwin's program of research examines the design and delivery of instruction and technologies that promote self- and co-regulated learning. Hadwin is a coauthor of the *gStudy* software for supporting and researching SRL in solo and collaborative eLearning activities.

Rogers Hall is professor in the Department of Teaching and Learning, Vanderbilt University. His research interests include: the learning and teaching of mathematics, both as a school topic and as a resource for modeling and inference in scientific inquiry; studies of learning in and out of school; comparative studies of mathematical activity in school and work settings; and (most generally) the organization and development of representational practices in technical and scientific work.

Dwayne E. Ham, Sr., MSEd, is a graduate student at the University of Maryland and works as an elementary school counselor in Prince George's County (Maryland) Public Schools. He earned his master's degree from North Carolina Agricultural and Technical State University in Greensboro, North Carolina, and is interested in educational leadership/policy and counselor education.

Robert D. Hannafin is an associate professor at the University of Connecticut. His research interests include open learning environments and issues surrounding technology integration in K–12 and teacher education.

Christopher Harris (PhD, University of Michigan) is an assistant professor in the College of Education at the University of Arizona. His research focuses on science education and on designing innovative environments for science learning. Of particular interest to him is integrating science education and the learning sciences to transform classrooms into environments that promote meaningful learning for all students.

Margaret Hawkins is an associate professor of ESL and bilingual education in the Department of Curriculum and Instruction at the University of Wisconsin–Madison. Research interests include language and literacy development of young English learners in schools, homeschool relations, and community-based learning sites for immigrant and refugee youth.

Willis D. Hawley is Professor Emeritus of Education and Public Policy at the University of Maryland and Scholar-in-Residence at the American Association of School Administrators. He has been executive director of the National Partnership for Excellence and Accountability in Teaching and served as dean of the College of Education at the University of Maryland and Peabody College of Vanderbilt University. He taught at Yale and Duke Universities before going to Vanderbilt. Hawley has published numerous books, articles, and chapters dealing with the education of teachers, teacher quality, school reform,

urban politics, political learning, organizational change, race relations, school desegregation, and educational policy. In 1977–78, he served as director of Education Studies, President's Reorganization Project, Executive Office of the President of the United States. He organized and directed the Common Destiny Alliance, a national consortium of organizations and scholars committed to improving intergroup relations.

Justin Heinze (MA, University of Michigan, 2004) has worked in higher education and is currently pursuing a PhD in educational psychology. His research interests include belonging and exclusion, first year transitions to college, and moral judgments of companies and organizations.

Joan L. Herman is with the National Center for Research on Evaluation, Standards, and Student Testing. Herman is director of the National Center for Research on Evaluation, Standards, and Student Testing (CRESST), headquartered at UCLA's Graduate School of Education and Information Studies. Her research interests focus on the design and use of assessment to improve schools and student learning, teachers' formative assessment practices, and validity in new forms of testing.

Frederick M. Hess is a resident scholar and director of Education Policy Studies at the American Enterprise Institute and executive editor of *Education Next.* His work on issues related to teacher quality has appeared in publications including *Journal of Teacher Education, Teachers College Record, Phi Delta Kappan, Policy Review, Educational Policy, Urban Affairs Review, Trusteeship, American School Board Journal,* and *Boston Globe.* Dr. Hess is a former public high school teacher in Louisiana and professor of education and politics at the University of Virginia. He holds an MEd in education and an MA and PhD in government from Harvard University.

Scott R. Hinze has a master's degree in psychology and is currently pursuing his doctorate in cognitive psychology at the University of Illinois at Chicago. His research interests include the dynamic processes involved in learning and memory and the implications of cognitive science for education.

Stephanie A. Hirsh is the executive director of the National Staff Development Council. Hirsh has been recognized by the Texas Staff Development Council with a Lifetime Achievement Award; by the University of North Texas as a Distinguished Alumnae; and by the Texas Association of School Boards as Master Trustee. She serves on a number of advisory boards including Learning First Alliance, Microsoft Partners in Learning, and the National Center for Culturally Responsive Educational Systems. Dr. Hirsh's articles have appeared in most education magazines including *Educational Leadership, Phi Delta Kappan, American School Board Journal, Education Week,* and the *Journal of Staff Development.* She has coauthored more than five books including *The Learning Educator* (2008) with Joellen Killion. Dr. Hirsh spent 15 years in school district leadership positions. In 2005, she completed three terms as a school board trustee in the Richardson Independent School District.

Marcy J. Hochberg (MA, Northeastern Illinois University, 1999) is a doctoral student in educational psycholgoy at the University of Illinois at Chicago (UIC) and has worked in higher education and student affairs for a number of years. Hochberg is interested in how individuals coordinate competing types of information (scientific, religious) in making moral decisions. She also teaches courses in child and adolescent development at UIC, as well as Triton College.

John D. Hoge has taught elementary and middle school social studies in rural, urban, and suburban schools. His career in teacher education extends over 40 years and encompasses work at a variety of institutions from the South, West, and Midwest. For the past 20 years, Dr. Hoge has worked at the University of Georgia preparing graduate and undergraduate social studies educators for a variety of professional roles.

Linda Hoke-Sinex is a grants writer and adjunct instructor in the Department of Psychological and Brain Sciences at Indiana University. She received her doctorate in educational psychology from Indiana University. Dr. Hoke-Sinex's research interests include the social construction of gender and the psychological influences of gender roles on human development. Her most recent research examined the influence of college level gender studies courses on gender roles and feminist identity development.

Kathleen V. Hoover-Dempsey (PhD and MA, Michigan State University; AB, University of California, Berkeley) is associate professor of psychology and human development and education, Peabody College, Vanderbilt University. Her research focuses on parental involvement in child and adolescent education, especially parents' motivations for becoming involved and the processes through which their involvement influences student learning. She and her colleagues have also developed school-based interventions designed to increase the effectiveness of parental involvement.

Shirley M. Hord is Scholar Laureate at NSDC, the National Staff Development Council, in Boerne, Texas. She authors articles and books on school-based professional development, school change and improvement, and professional learning communities; her current publications are *Learning Together, Leading Together: Changing Schools Through Professional Learning Communities* (2004) and *Leading Professional Learning Communities: Voices from Research and Practice* (2008). She monitors and supports the Leadership for Change Networks and the Concerns-Based Adoption Model constituencies, and designs and delivers professional development that nur-

tures school leadership. Her research, development, and training efforts have taken her across the United States, Canada, Mexico, Europe, Asia, Australia, and Africa.

Stacey S. Horn (PhD, University of Maryland, 2000) is an associate professor in the Department of Educational Psychology and program coordinator for the MEd in youth development at the University of Illinois at Chicago. Dr. Horn investigates how adolescents reason about issues of peer harassment and social exclusion. She has published numerous journal articles and book chapters on adolescents' social cognition and peer relationships, prejudice related to sexual orientation and gender expression, and safe schools for lesbian, gay, bisexual, and transgender youth. She teaches a course in adolescent development to pre- and inservice middle school and high school teachers. Dr. Horn is a former high school English teacher and has been a youth advocate for more than 20 years.

Brian Hughes (EdD, Teachers College, Columbia University) is the director of the Design Center at the Gottesman Libraries at Teachers College, where he leads the development of media and production resources. His research focuses on creativity and education.

Ju Hur, MA, is a doctoral student in educational policy and administration at the University of Minnesota. Hur is currently exploring research interests in the area of school leadership and sustainability of educational innovations.

Marsha Ing is a postdoctoral fellow at Stanford University School of Education's Institute for Research on Education Policy and Practice. Her research interests focus on methods of measuring student learning ranging from large-scale surveys to teacher assessment practices.

Charles E. Jenks received his MEd from the University of South Carolina and his PhD from the University of Georgia, writing his dissertation on school desegregation in the South. He taught high school social studies for 10 years prior to completing his PhD. He taught at Penn State for 4 years and Augusta State University for the past 9 years.

Elisabeth M. Jerome, MEd, is a doctoral candidate in clinical and school psychology at the University of Virginia and a research assistant at the Center for Advanced Study of Teaching and Learning in Charlottesville, Virginia. Her research interests include child development, the role of teacher-child relationships in early developmental success, and identifying factors that promote success for ELL, refugee, and immigrant youth.

Celia E. Johnson, coordinator of special education programs, has taught in teacher education and special education programs for 36 years. The focus of her research is in the area of learning environments, particularly in the home, school, and community settings. She teaches early childhood, literacy, and special education courses. Johnson has published approximately 26 books, chapters, and articles.

Lauri Johnson is an associate professor in the Department of Educational Leadership and Policy at the University at Buffalo, where she teaches courses in multicultural education, urban education, and school leadership. She completed her PhD in multicultural education at the University of Washington in 1999. Before joining the faculty at the University at Buffalo, she was an administrator in the New York City Public Schools for many years, where she specialized in the professional development of teachers in issues of diversity. Her research interests include examining how White educators conceptualize race, multicultural policy implementation in the United States and Canada, historical and contemporary studies of community activism in urban school reform, and culturally responsive urban school leadership.

James M. Kauffman is Professor Emeritus of Education at the University of Virginia and a former classroom teacher. He received the 2002 Outstanding Leadership Award from the Council for Children with Behavioral Disorders and the 2006 Award for Effective Presentation of Behavior Analysis in the Mass Media from the Society for Applied Behavior Analysis. His primary research and publication interests are emotional and behavioral disorders, learning disabilities, and the history of special education.

Paul Kelleher is Norine R. Murchison Distinguished Professor of Education and chair of the Department of Education at Trinity University, San Antonio, Texas. Previously, he served for 35 years in public schools as a teacher, principal, and superintendent of schools. Kelleher holds a bachelor's and master's degrees from Harvard University and a doctorate from Teachers College at Columbia. He is the author of many articles and several books.

Sean Kelly is an assistant professor of sociology at the University of Notre Dame and the Center for Research on Educational Opportunity. His research has focused on several educational issues facing America's schools, including problems of student engagement, the process of matching teachers to classrooms, the assignment of diverse students to course sequences in high school, and the causes of teacher attrition.

Mary M. Kennedy is a professor at Michigan State University. Her scholarship focuses on the relationship between knowledge and teaching practice, the nature of knowledge used in teaching practice, and on how research knowledge and policy initiatives can improve practice. She has published three books addressing the relationship between knowledge and teaching and has won five awards for her work, the most recent being the Margaret B. Lindsey Award for Distinguished Research in Teacher Education.

Alesha L. Kientzler, PhD, is the principal of Re-Create Strategies, LLC, a consulting firm designed to assist businesses, schools, and youth-based organizations with the process of creating sustainable cultures of wellness. Her mission is to provide an authentic spirit of support for people to make the most out of their lives—physically, intellectually, emotionally, socially, and spiritually—through lasting improvements within and across communities.

Paul A. Kirschner is professor of educational sciences at the Department of Pedagogical and Educational Sciences at Utrecht University (as well as head of the Research Centre Interaction and Learning and dean of the research master program Educational Sciences: Learning in Interaction). He holds a master's degree in educational psychology from University of Amsterdam and a PhD from the Open University of the Netherlands. He is an internationally recognized expert in his field, having coauthored the *Ten Steps to Complex Learning* (Taylor & Francis, 2007) and edited two other recent and very successful books (*Visualizing Argumentation* [Springer Verlag, 2003] and *What We Know About CSCL* [Kluwer, 2004]).

Michael B. Krapes has been teaching art and psychology at the secondary school level since 1984. Currently teaching at Rubidoux High School in Riverside, California, he received his BA (studio art) and teaching credentials from the University of California, Irvine, his MA (psychology) from United States International University, and PhD (clinical psychology) from Alliant International University.

Timothy J. Landrum, PhD, is an associate professor and senior scientist in the Curry School of Education at University of Virginia. He serves as a member of the executive board of the Division for Research in the Council for Exceptional Children. He has been a teacher of students with emotional and behavioral disorders, and recently a teacher educator and researcher. His work focuses on classroom and behavior management and the translation of research into practice.

Suzanne Lane is a professor in the research methodology program at the University of Pittsburgh. She obtained her PhD in research methodology, measurement, and statistics at the University of Arizona. Her research has involved the design and validation of performance assessments for education reform projects as well as for state assessment programs. She has published numerous articles and chapters on technical and validity issues related to performance assessments. She was the president of the National Council on Measurement in Education.

Gaea Leinhardt, senior scientist, Learning Research and Development Center, and professor, School of Education, University of Pittsburgh, earned her PhD in educational research from the University of Pittsburgh. Her research has focused on the teaching and learning of specific subject matter, modeling instructional explanations, understanding the nature of expertise in teaching, teacher assessment, program evaluation, and recently the exploration of learning in non school settings such as museums and online initiatives. As director of the Museum Learning Collaborative, she authored journal articles and coauthored and coedited two volumes on learning in museums: *Learning Conversations in Museums* and *Listening in on Museum Conversations*.

Nonie K. Lesaux is Marie and Max Kargman Assistant Professor in Human Development and Urban Education at the Harvard Graduate School of Education. Lesaux leads a research program that focuses on reading development and difficulties of children from linguistically diverse backgrounds. Lesaux conducts developmental and instructional research that has implications for practitioners, researchers, and policy makers.

Ashley E. Lewis is a research associate at the Education Development Center's Center for Children and Technology. She currently manages a large-scale randomized controlled trial of the "Big Math for Little Kids" curriculum. Her master's degree from the University of Minnesota focused on children's comprehension within various media formats and she received her PhD in educational psychology from the same institution in 2007. In addition to her work at CCT, her diverse interests have allowed her to research a wide variety of topics, including the moral development of gifted students, the evaluation of after-school programs, the impact of domestic violence on children's development, and the symbolic understanding of young children. In addition to her research experience, Lewis has extensive teaching experience that includes both enriching student learning with online resources and designing and implementing online courses.

John S. Levin is the Bank of America Professor of Education Leadership and the director and principal investigator of the California Community College Collaborative (C4). His books in this decade include *Globalizing the Community College* (Palgrave, 2001), *Community College Faculty: At Work in the New Economy* (Palgrave MacMillan, 2006; with Susan Kater and Richard Wagoner), and *Non-Traditional Students and Community Colleges: The Conflict of Justice and Neo-Liberalism* (Palgrave MacMillan, 2007).

Guofang Li is an associate professor of literacy education in Teacher Education Department of College of Education at Michigan State University. Her research interests include second language and literacy education, family and community literacy practices of immigrant and minority groups, and the interrelationship between minority literacy practices and mainstream schooling. Li's major publications include three sole-authored books, *Culturally Contested Literacies: America's "Rainbow Underclass" and Urban Schools* (Routledge, 2008). *Culturally Contested Pedagogy: Battles of Literacy and Schooling between Mainstream Teachers and Asian Immigrant Parents* (SUNY Press, 2006, winner of 2006 Ed Fry Book Award, National Reading Conference), *"East is East, West is West"? Home Literacy, Culture, and Schooling* (Peter Lang, 2002), and a coedited volume, *"Strangers" of the Academy: Asian Women Scholars in Higher Education* (Stylus, 2006).

Greg Light is director of the Searle Center for Teaching Excellence at Northwestern University. He received his PhD in education from the University of London. His research and his publications are focused on student learning and the professional development of teaching in higher education. He is author of the book *Learning and Teaching in Higher Education: The Reflective Professional* (2001).

Francesca A. López is a former elementary teacher, and is now a doctoral candidate in the educational psychology program at the University of Arizona. Her research interests include policy influences on academic proficiency among English Language Learners, and student perceptions of academic competence.

Mary Lundeberg is a professor in the Teacher Education and Educational Psychology Departments at Michigan State University, and codirector, Literacy Achievement Research Center. Dr. Lundeberg received her PhD in educational psychology from the University of Minnesota in 1985 and joined the MSU faculty in 2003. Her research interests include cultural and gender influences in confidence, problem-based pedagogy in teacher education and science, interactive multimedia learning environments, and scientific literacy.

Douglas J. Mac Iver is principal research scientist and codirector of the Center for Social Organization of Schools at Johns Hopkins University. He directs the Talent Development Middle Grades Program and conducts research on the impact of reform efforts on middle grades student achievement. His recent articles have appeared in *Educational Psychologist, Journal of Research in Mathematics Education, Journal of Curriculum and Instruction,* and *Review of Policy Research.*

Martha Abele Mac Iver is associate research scientist at the Center for Social Organization of Schools at Johns Hopkins University. Her recent articles deal with such educational reform issues as vouchers, educational privatization, alternative certification, new teacher retention, high school reform, and other comprehensive school reform issues.

Ellen B. Mandinach is a senior research analyst at the CNA Corporation in Alexandria, VA. Previously Dr. Mandinach was the associate director for research at the Education Development Center's Center for Children and Technology and the director for research for the Northeast and Islands Regional Education Laboratory. She holds a PhD in educational psychology from Stanford University. Dr. Mandinach's research has focused on the impact of technology on teaching, learning, and social organizations. She has spent over 25 years conducting research in the area of educational technology, writing extensively on the topic. Dr. Mandinach is a member of AERA, NCME, and APA and will serve as president of APA's division of educational psychology in 2008–09.

Ronald W. Marx (PhD, Stanford University) is professor of educational psychology and dean of education at the University of Arizona. His interdisciplinary research focuses on how classrooms can be sites for learning that are highly motivating and cognitively engaging by enhancing science education and developing teacher professional development models to sustain long-term change. This work is highly collaborative with urban teachers and education leaders in order to create useable research findings that can support educational reform.

DeWayne A. Mason, after 10 years as a principal, 10 years in higher education, and 6 years as a district assistant superintendent, has returned to his roots—teaching visual arts. Currently in his fifth year at Patriot High School (Riverside, California), he received his BA (studio art), MA and educational specialist (educational administration), and PhD (curriculum and instruction) at University of Missouri, Columbia.

Christine Massey is the director of research and education at the Institute for Research in Cognitive Science at the University of Pennsylvania, where she also received her PhD in psychology. Her research interests connect basic research in developmental cognitive science with mathematics and science learning in educational settings. She has directed a number of funded projects involving research, development, and evaluation related to student learning and curriculum and instruction for PreK through high school.

Richard E. Mayer is professor of psychology at the University of California, Santa Barbara, where he has served since 1975. He received a PhD in psychology from the University of Michigan in 1973 and served as visiting assistant professor of psychology at Indiana University from 1973 to 1975. His research interests are in educational and cognitive psychology. His current research focuses on multimedia learning and computer-supported learning, with the goal of developing evidence-based principles for the design of multimedia instruction. He is the author or editor of 23 books and more than 280 journal articles and chapters, including *The Promise of Educational Psychology: Vols. 1 and 2* (1999, 2002), *Multimedia Learning* (2001), *Cambridge Handbook of Multimedia Learning* (editor, 2005), *e-Learning and the Science of Instruction* (with R. Clark, 2003, 2008), and *Learning and Instruction* (2003, 2008).

Sarah McCarthey is professor of language and literacy studies in the Department of Curriculum and Instruction at the University of Illinois at Urbana-Champaign. Her research interests include children's writing, students' literacy identities, and teachers' writing practices. She has published two books and many articles in journals including *Reading Research Quarterly, Research in the Teaching of English, Journal of Literacy Research,* and *Written Communication.* She is currently coeditor of *Research in the Teaching of English* with Mark Dressman and Paul Prior.

Mary McCaslin, PhD, Michigan State University (1981), is a professor of educational psychology at the University of Arizona. McCaslin's scholarship focuses on the relationships among cultural, social, and personal sources of influence that coregulate student adaptive learning, motivational dynamics, and emergent identity.

Kimberly A. McDuffie, PhD, is an assistant professor in the Eugene Moore School of Education at Clemson University. She was formerly a special education teacher and taught students with learning disabilities and emotional/behavioral disorders. Her research interests include instructional strategies for effective inclusive education, coteaching and collaboration, and the translation of research into practice.

Keisha McIntosh is a doctoral student in the Department of Curriculum and Teaching at Teachers College, Columbia University. She is interested in how cultural identity models may scaffold learning experiences that prepare teachers to work with culturally diverse students. She received a BA in English and an MAT from Hampton University.

Melissa D. McNaught is a PhD student in mathematics education at the University of Missouri. She is a fellow with the Center for the Study of Mathematics Curriculum, and her dissertation research focuses on mathematics curriculum implementation in high school classrooms.

Susan L. Melnick serves as assistant dean for academic outreach programs in the College of Education at Michigan State University. She teaches education policy-related courses.

Christopher L. Miller is assistant professor in the Department of Educational Policy Studies in the College of Education at the University of Illinois at Chicago. His research focuses on on how science teaching is supported at the school-district level.

Linda A. Mitchell taught social studies, language arts, and reading at the middle school level for 10 years. She received her PhD from Auburn University in Auburn, Alabama, and currently teaches secondary social studies education at Jacksonville State University in Jacksonville, Alabama.

Lindsey Mohan is a doctoral student in the educational psychology program at Michigan State University. She holds a BA from the University of Notre Dame. She taught eighth-grade science and more recently has taught undergraduate courses in the teacher education program at Michigan State University. She has worked in elementary and middle school classrooms documenting highly engaging and effective literacy and science instruction. Her research interests include teaching, learning, and motivation in science and literacy classrooms, with a special interest in the engagement and discourse practices used by exemplary teachers.

Tamera B. Murdock is an associate professor and associate chair of the Department of Psychology at University of

Missouri–Kansas City, where she teaches course in motivation, educational psychology, and statistics. Her research focuses on contextual sources of motivation and behavior in classroom settings and the application of statistical models to studying context. Most recently, she has been theoretical models from achievement motivation to understanding cheating. Her work in this area has been published in the *Journal of Educational Psychology*, the *Educational Psychologist*, *Contemporary Education*, and the *Social Psychology of Education*. She recently completed an edited book, *Psychology of Academic Cheating*, with Eric M. Anderman, which was published by Elsevier Press.

Gary Natriello (PhD, Stanford University) is the Ruth L. Gottesman Professor in Educational Research and professor of sociology and education at Teachers College, Columbia University. Natriello is the director of the Gottesman Libraries at Teachers College and the executive editor of the *Teachers College Record*. His research focuses on the social organization of educational systems.

Sharon L. Nichols received her PhD in educational psychology from the University of Arizona and is currently an assistant professor at the University of Texas at San Antonio. Her research interests merge student motivation and development, teacher-student relationships, and educational policy. Her most recent work focuses on the role and impact of high-stakes testing on teacher practice and student motivation and development. She is an editorial board member for the journal *Educational Policy Analysis Archives* and is the current chair of the Adolescence and Youth Development Special Interest Group of AERA.

Thomas Oakland is professor of educational psychology at the University of Florida. He is president of the International Foundation for Children's Education, president elect of the International Association of Applied Psychologists' Division of Psychological Assessment and Evaluation, and past president of the International School Psychology Association and the International Test Commission. He has worked in more than 40 countries. Dr. Oakland holds an honorary status of professor of psychology at the Iberoamerican University in San Jose, Costa Rica, and The University of Hong Kong.

Bridget N. O'Connor (PhD, Indiana University) is professor of higher education and business education in the Steinhardt School of Culture, Education, and Human Development at New York University, where she coordinates the MA program in business education. She has experience teaching business subjects at the high school level in Morocco, Indiana, and Brussels, Belgium. As a Peace Corps volunteer in Afghanistan (mid-1970s), she initiated a cooperative work program at Kabul University. She has served as a member of the PCBEE. Her research is centered on curriculum development and the transfer of learning. Her most recent coauthored book is *Learning at Work: How to Support Individual and Group Learning* (HRD Press, 2007).

Amy M. Olson is a graduate research associate in the Department of Educational Psychology at the University of Arizona. Olson's area of interest and research brings a measurement perspective to understanding the high school to college transition, especially for first-generation students, their families, and the social support structures available on college campuses.

Becky Wai-Ling Packard is an associate professor at Mount Holyoke College. She earned her PhD in educational psychology at Michigan State University. Her research and teaching focuses on motivation and identity development during adolescence and young adulthood with a focus on low-income, first-generation college students and women. She has worked closely with adolescent mentoring and leadership programs.

Laura Paige is a doctoral student in Teacher Education at the University of Wisconsin–Madison. Her research focuses on supporting teachers' implementation of mathematics curricula. She also works as a math specialist in a public elementary school.

Anthony D. Pellegrini is a professor of psychological foundations of education in the Department of Educational Psychology, University of Minnesota, Twin Cities Campus. He has research interests in methodological issues in the general area of human development, with specific interests in direct observations. His substantive interests are in the development of play and dominance. He is a Fellow of the American Psychological Association and has been awarded a Fellowship from the British Psychological Society.

James W. Pellegrino is Liberal Arts and Sciences Distinguished Professor of Cognitive Psychology and Distinguished Professor of Education at the University of Illinois at Chicago. He also serves as codirector of UIC's interdisciplinary Learning Sciences Research Institute. Dr. Pellegrino's research and development interests focus on children's and adult's thinking and learning and the implications of cognitive research and theory for assessment and instructional practice.

Robert C. Pianta is the dean of the Curry School of Education at the University of Virginia, as well as the Novartis U.S. Foundation Professor of Education and a professor in the Department of Psychology. He also serves as the director for both the National Center for Research in Early Childhood Education and the Center for Advanced Study of Teaching and Learning. Dr. Pianta's work has focused on the predictors of child outcomes and school readiness, particularly adult–child relationships, and the transition to kindergarten. His recent work has focused on better understanding the nature of teacher–child interactions, classroom quality, and child competence, through standardized observational assessment. Dr. Pianta has conducted research on professional development, both at the preservice and inservice levels. He has published more than 300 scholarly papers and is lead author on several influential books related to early childhood and elementary education. He has recently begun work to develop a preschool mathematics curriculum, incorporating a Web-based teacher support component. Dr. Pianta received a BS and a MA in special education from the University of Connecticut, and a PhD in psychology from the University of Minnesota, and began his career as a special education teacher.

Morgan S. Polikoff is an Institute of Education Sciences (IES)-supported doctoral fellow at the University of Pennsylvania. He is currently part of a Wallace Foundation-supported project to develop and test an education leadership performance assessment and a National Science Foundation-supported project to study middle school mathematics teacher induction. His primary research interests center on the effects of state and national policies on mathematics teaching and achievement.

Lisa S. Ponti (PhD candidate, business education, New York University) is presently at work on her dissertation, which is related to the effective learning of economics. She has an MBA from NYU's Stern School of Business and is an adjunct professor at Ramapo College in New Jersey, where she teaches macro- and microeconomics as well as personal and corporate finance. Prior to her career in academe, Lisa worked in the financial services industry as an analyst as well as a commercial lending officer.

Inge R. Poole, PhD, is an educational consultant based at Peabody College, Vanderbilt University. Her primary interest is teacher education. As a COMP National Trainer, she provides training for other workshop leaders to help teachers develop proactive classroom management.

Andrew C. Porter is dean of the Graduate School of Education at the University of Pennsylvania and George and Diane Weiss Professor of Education. He is an elected member and vice president of the National Academy of Education, member of the National Assessment Governing Board, Lifetime National Associate of the National Academies, and past president of the American Educational Research Association.

Diana C. Pullin is an attorney and educator. She teaches education law and public policy at The Lynch School of Education and the School of Law at Boston College.

Augustina Reyes, a professor at the University of Houston, has served as associate superintendent for bilingual programs at the Houston Independent School District. As an associate professor, Dr. Reyes directed the Principals' Institute at Texas A&M University. Her most current book is *Discipline, Achievement, and Race: Is Zero Tolerance the Answer?* (Rowman & Littlefield, 2006). She has published in several journals including the *Fordham University School of Law Urban Law Journal* and *St. John's School of Law Journal of Legal Commentary.*

Barak Rosenshine is an emeritus professor in the College of Education at the University of Illinois at Urbana-Champaign. His specialities are classroom instruction and cognitive strategy instruction.

Christine Rubie-Davies is currently a senior lecturer in the faculty of education at The University of Auckland in New Zealand. An elementary school teacher for more than 20 years, she was seconded into the university in 1998 to set up elementary school teacher education programs. Rubie-Davies recently received a National Tertiary Teaching Excellence Award in recognition of her teaching skills.

Frances O'Connell Rust is senior vice president for academic affairs and dean of faculty at the Erikson Institute. Between 1991 and 2007, Rust was professor of education in Steinhardt School of New York University. Her research and teaching focus on teacher education and teacher research. Rust's most recent books are *How to Do Action Research in Your Classroom: Lessons From the Teachers Network Leadership Institute* (Rust & Clark, Teachers Network, 2006), *Taking Action Through Teacher Research* (Meyers & Rust, Heinemann, 2003), and *Guiding School Change: New Understandings of the Role and Work of Change Agents* (Rust & Freidus, Teachers College Press, 2001). She was one of the contributing authors to Darling-Hammond and Bransford's *Preparing Teachers for a Changing World* (National Academies Press, 2005).

Darrell Sabers, PhD, from Iowa, is a professor of educational psychology at the University of Arizona. His research specialty is applied psychometrics, especially focused on educational testing and research.

Lawrence J. Saha is professor in the School of Social Sciences at the Australian National University (ANU). He received his PhD from the University of Texas, Austin, in sociology. He is former dean of the faculty of arts, ANU, and is currently editor of *Social Psychology of Education: An International Journal.* He has published in the fields of comparative education, education and national development, and political socialization among youth. He was editor of *The International Encyclopedia of the Sociology of Education* (Pergamon Press, 1997) and recently coauthored *The Untested Accusation: Principals, Research Knowledge, and Policy Making in Schools* (Ablex, 2002; Scarecrow Press, 2005). His teaching and research interests are in sociology of education, the sociology of social movements, and social psychology.

Susan T. Schertzer, EdD, is an educational consultant and doctoral dissertation advisor. She is a former assistant director of Diversity and Multicultural Affairs at Bowie State University, where she earned her doctorate in educational leadership.

Jill Shackelford is currently the fourth superintendent to lead the First Things First initiative in the Kansas City, Kansas, Public Schools. During the planning and beginning stages and first seven years of district-wide implementation of FTF, she was the assistant superintendent of curriculum and instruction, and instrumental in supporting the systemic change. Dr. Shackelford's knowledge is based upon 18 years as an elementary teacher and reading specialist, 5 years as an elementary principal, and 18 years in the central office working in all areas of curriculum and instruction. In addition to her elementary degree, she has a master's degree in curriculum and instruction and a doctorate in education administration—all from Oklahoma State University.

Cynthia Thrasher Shamberger, MEd, is a doctoral candidate in the Department of Specialized Education Services at the University of North Carolina at Greensboro. Her research focuses on collaboration among professional educators. She is passionate about facilitating inclusive practices which promote access to the general education curriculum for students with disabilities and other special needs. Her experience includes seven years teaching middle school students with behavioral and emotional disabilities as well as elementary students with learning disabilities.

Dorothy Shipps is associate professor of public policy and education at Baruch College, City University of New York, where she teaches urban education policy analysis to students of public affairs and prepares principals for New York City schools.

Sandra Simpkins is an assistant professor at the School of Social and Family Dynamics at Arizona State University. Her research focuses on children's participation in organized and informal afterschool activities. She was recently awarded the William T. Grant Scholar award to investigate the predictors of Mexican-origin adolescents' participation in a variety of organized afterschool activities. In addition to her empirical research, she has translated her and others' research in several articles for practitioners and policy makers in the afterschool field. She received her PhD in developmental psychology from the University of California, Riverside.

John F. Siskar is assistant to the dean of arts and humanities at Buffalo State, and recently stepped down as the interim director of the Center for Urban and Rural Education at Buffalo State. His recent research explores art education, urban education, rural education, and the role of technology in education. A former high school art teacher, he strongly believes that the best teaching takes place when sound educational theory informs effective classroom practices. He regards the public school and college partnerships he has participated in as some of his most rewarding work. He has been projector director or principal investigator on a number of grants, including work with rural schools. He has presented at national and international conferences as well as published chapters and articles on rural education.

Ellen Skinner is a professor of psychology and human development at Portland State University in Portland, Oregon. Her work focuses the development of motivation and coping in children and adolescents, with particular attention to the role of self-system processes and close relationships with parents and teachers; she has a special interest in theory development and measure construction. Trained as a life-span developmental psychologist, Dr. Skinner has also worked with the Motivation Research Group at the University of Rochester and at the Max Plank Institute for Human Development and Education in Berlin, Germany.

Robert E. Slavin is director of the Center for Data-Driven Reform in Education at Johns Hopkins University and director of the Institute for Effective Education at the University of York, England. He is also the chairman of the Success for All Foundation. Dr. Slavin's research focuses on comprehensive school reform, cooperative learning, school and classroom organization, and research review.

BetsAnn Smith is associate professor of educational administration at Michigan State University. Her research addresses school reform, urban school development, relationships between school organization and learning opportunity, and the influences of policy on school improvement.

Mark A. Smylie is professor of education at the University of Illinois at Chicago and chair of the Department of Educational Policy Studies in the College of Education. His research focuses on education organizational change, teacher and administrative leadership, and urban school improvement.

Jennifer Sommerness, MA, is a doctoral student in educational policy and administration at the University of Minnesota. She has extensive direct service and professional development experience in the area of inclusive education. She has coauthored several articles and monographs on teacher leadership in the context of inclusive education.

Christopher Span is an assistant professor at the University of Illinois at Urbana-Champaign. He is a historian of education in the department of educational policy studies. His research interests pertain to the educational history of African Americans in the 19th and 20th century.

Robert J. Sternberg is dean of the School of Arts and Sciences and professor of psychology at Tufts University, as well as honorary professor at the University of Heidelberg. His PhD is from Stanford and he also has eight honorary doctorates. His research is primarily on human abilities, including intelligence, creativity, and wisdom.

Zollie Stevenson, Jr., PhD, has managed Title I programs at the school district, state and federal education levels. In addition to serving as a Title I program manager he serves as an Adjunct Graduate Faculty member and dissertation chairman/advisor for the Educational Leadership doctoral program at Bowie State University in Maryland. He earned the PhD at the University of North Carolina at Chapel Hill.

Laura M. Stough is associate professor at Texas A&M University. Her area of research focuses on the application of educational psychology theory on individuals with disabilities. She has taught classroom management classes at the university level and currently directs a training program for special education teachers obtaining their master's degrees. She began her educational career teaching students with intellectual disabilities and autism in public schools over two decades ago.

Jessica J. Summers is an assistant professor of educational psychology at the University of Arizona. Dr. Summers earned her degree from the University of Texas at Austin in 2002 and has developed a program of research in academic motivation concerning the influence of peers and collaborative/cooperative learning methods.

Janice Templeton received her MA in general experimental psychology from Wake Forest University and is recent PhD graduate in the Combined Program in Education and Psychology at the University of Michigan. She is now an assistant professor at Fort Lewis College. Her research interests include social, emotional, and psychological factors that promote positive development in adolescence and in the transition to adulthood with an emphasis on spiritual development.

Rosalyn Anstine Templeton, executive dean of the College of Education and Human Services, has taught in teacher education and special education programs for the past 23 years. Her area of research is in learning environments, especially in the school, home and community arena. Templeton has published approximately 40 articles and book chapters and is coauthor of *How to Talk So Kids Can Learn At Home and in School.*

Robert Teranishi is assistant professor of education in the Steinhardt School of Culture, Education, and Human Development at New York University and a faculty affiliate in the Steinhardt Institute for Higher Education Policy and the Alliance for International Higher Education Policy. Prior to coming to NYU, Teranishi was a National Institute of Mental Health postdoctoral fellow at the University of Pennsylvania and received his MA and PhD from the University of California, Los Angeles.

Paul Theobald currently holds the Woods-Beals Endowed Chair in Urban and Rural Education at Buffalo State College. He is an educational historian whose work frequently crosses disciplinary boundaries and has appeared in such journals as *Educational Theory, American Journal of Education, Journal of Educational Studies, Journal of Educational Thought, Journal of Agricultural and Environmental Ethics, American Historical Review, Educational Foundations, History of Education Quarterly,* and many

others. His first book, *Call School: Rural Education in the Midwest to 1918,* is a comprehensive study of the history of rural education in this country. His second book, *Teaching the Commons: Place, Pride, and the Renewal of Community,* is an intellectual history that weaves in philosophical themes in an attempt to build a new vision for educational ends.

Sean T. Tierney is a doctoral student in the research methodology program at the University of Pittsburgh. He obtained a BA in mathematics and a BS in secondary education with a mathematics concentration at Duquesne University. His research interests are in the areas of educational measurement and statistics.

Sigmund Tobias is distinguished research scientist at the Institute for Urban and Minority Education, Teachers College, Columbia University. His research interests include metacognition, applications of technology to instruction, and adapting instruction to students' characteristics.

Vivian Tseng is program officer at the William T. Grant Foundation. She has worked to develop the Foundation's research interests in youth's everyday settings and in how research influences the policies and practices that affect youth's settings. Her theoretical and empirical work focuses on frameworks for social change and the role of immigration, race, and culture in youths' and their families' experiences in U.S. society.

Jeroen J. G. van Merriënboer is professor of educational technology and scientific director of the Netherlands Laboratory for Lifelong Learning at the Open University of the Netherlands. He holds a master's degree in experimental psychology from the Free University of Amsterdam and a PhD from the University of Twente. His prize-winning monograph *Training Complex Cognitive Skills* (1997), describes his four-component instructional design model for complex skills training and is the basis of his new book *Ten Steps to Complex Learning* (Taylor & Francis, 2007). He was declared world leader in educational technology by *Training Magazine* and received the international contributions award from the international council of the Association for Educational Communications and Technology.

Mark J. Van Ryzin is a PhD candidate at the University of Minnesota in the College of Education and Human Development. His research focuses on motivational and developmental processes in education and the potential for innovative educational environments to address the diverse range of student needs and interests that are found among today's youth. Mark received his MA in educational psychology from the University of Minnesota in 2006. Mark's work has appeared in the *Journal of Comparative Psychology,* the *Journal of School Psychology,* and the *Journal of Youth and Adolescence,* which recently accepted his master's thesis for publication. He has presented at a number of conferences, including the annual meeting of the American Educational Research Association (AREA), the biennial meeting of the Society for Research in Child Development (SRCD), and the Gates Foundation's Emerging Research Symposium.

Michael Vavrus is a professor at the Evergreen State College in Olympia, Washington, and author of *Transforming the Multicultural Education of Teachers: Theory, Research, and Practice*. He is a past president of the Association of Independent Liberal Arts Colleges for Teacher Education and the Washington state chapter of American Association of Colleges for Teacher Education. His current research focuses on the teacher autoethnographies on multicultural topics.

Jennifer R. Vermillion is an educational technologist at Springside School in Philadelphia, Pennsylvania, and has taught middle school in both private and public schools.

Joan M. T. Walker is assistant professor in the School of Education at Long Island University. Grounded in her work as a school-age child-care provider, her research examines the psychological foundations of parent-teacher interactions, and parent and teacher contributions to child development. She is also interested in teachers' attitudes toward student autonomy and family participation in children's schooling. She received her MS and PhD in developmental psychology from Vanderbilt University. She also holds undergraduate and graduate degrees in music education.

Wenxia Wang is a doctoral student in the Teacher Education Department of the College of Education at Michigan State University. Her interests include EFL/ESL pedagogies, literacy education, and teacher preparation in international and U.S. settings.

Andrew Wayne is a senior research analyst at the American Institutes for Research, where he focuses on policies affecting teachers. He currently serves as the deputy director of the Mathematics Professional Development Impact Study, a large-scale randomized field trial. He has coauthored numerous articles and reports, including two recent reports on federal programs affecting teacher quality. He holds an MA in curriculum and instruction and earned a PhD in public policy. He began his career as a middle and high school computer science teacher.

Noreen M. Webb is a professor in the Social Research Methodology Division in the Graduate School of Educa-

tion and Information Studies at the University of California, Los Angeles, with a joint appointment in the Department of Applied Linguistics and Teaching English as a Second Language. She is interested in learning and instruction, and measurement theory and applications. Her current research activities focus on classroom processes related to learning outcomes, small-group problem solving, achievement testing in mathematics and science, the role of teacher practices in student participation and learning in mathematics, and generalizability theory. She received her PhD from Stanford University.

Kyle P. Westbook is a PhD student in social foundations in the Department of Educational Policy Studies in the College of Education at the University of Illinois at Chicago. His research interests are in teacher unions and their relationship to federal authority.

Caroline R. H. Wiley is a PhD student at the University of Arizona. Her research interests are primarily classroom research, comparative research, and educational evaluation within the context of educational policy. Also of interest to her is classroom assessment and grading practices. She has served as a data analyst for various research projects, including ones sponsored by the Carnegie Foundation and the Office of Educational Research and Improvement.

Jennifer York-Barr, PhD, is a professor of educational policy and administration at the University of Minnesota. Her teaching, school development, and research interests focus on professional learning, teacher collaboration, and teacher leadership to advance student learning. Dr. York-Barr has authored more than 200 published works and is the recipient of two distinguished teaching awards.

Ken Zeichner is Hoefs-Bascom Professor of Teacher Education at the University of Wisconsin–Madison. He has published widely on issues related to teacher education and practitioner research. His books include *Reflective Teaching, Teacher Education and the Social Conditions of Schooling, Issues and Practices in Inquiry-Oriented Teacher Education, Currents of Reform in Pre-Service Teacher Education,* and *Teacher Education and the Struggle for Social Justice.*

PART I

TEACHERS

1

THE WORK OF TEACHERS

MARK A. SMYLIE, CHRISTOPHER L. MILLER, AND KYLE P. WESTBROOK

University of Illinois at Chicago

This chapter explores the work of classroom teachers. It is organized around the following questions: What is the nature of teachers' work? What are the primary goals of this work? What do teachers do in their jobs day in, day out? In what contexts is their work performed and how might those contexts shape teachers' work? Finally, what directions might teachers' work take in the future?

These questions appear easy to answer. After all, there are approximately 3.2 million elementary, middle school, and high school teachers in the United States (U.S. Department of Labor, 2007). Anyone who has completed high school has witnessed at least 45 to 50 teachers on the job. However, there is no shared public understanding of what teachers actually do (Johnson, 2005). Surprisingly, very little research has documented the full range of their work. Some aspects of teachers' work have been well documented, for example, what elementary teachers do in classroom instruction. But overall, according to Dreeben (2005), "Teaching is a prime example of . . . the limits of our knowledge of what is actually done in accomplishing a given job" (p. 60).

This chapter draws upon the available literature to map the broad contours of teachers' work. Due to space limitations, a substantial amount of nuance and detail is sacrificed (e.g., differences between elementary and secondary teachers, regular classroom and special education teachers, teachers in under-resourced and well-resourced schools and communities, etc.). We encourage the reader to consult the cited literature. Our discussion is not about who teachers are or what constitutes effective teaching; it is about the job of being a teacher. We intend to promote greater understanding of teachers' work. We hope to help persons considering becoming teachers make sound decisions. In addition, we hope to provide some insights for educational administrators and policy makers to think clearly about the problems of teachers and teaching and how to address them.

The Nature of Teachers' Work

Teachers are employees of schools and school districts, called to public service and charged with the responsibility of preparing children and youth for productive and personally satisfying lives. On average, during the course of a 30-year career, an elementary teacher will serve nearly 650 students and, depending on the assignment, a high school teacher will serve as many as 6,000 students. It is noble work, work that is crucial not only to the learning and development of children and youth but also to the vitality of society. To many, the work is extremely rewarding. To some, it is daunting and overwhelming.

Goals and Expectations

The goals and expectations for teachers' work are sometimes ambitious, broad, and dynamic. At times, they are also vague, contradictory, or in dispute (Ingersoll, 2005). They may vary substantially depending on the state, school district, and local community in which teachers are employed.

The goals for teachers' work have expanded substantially over time. At the establishment of the first publicly funded schools in New England during the mid-1600s and throughout most of the 17th and 18th centuries, a central expectation for teachers' work was the religious and moral development of children. With the growth of political liberalism and the pursuit of scientific knowledge came an increased emphasis on the political and economic utility of education. By the middle of the 19th century, expectations for teachers' work grew to include a greater emphasis on vocational education and secular instruction in the academic disciplines. Although the emphasis on overt religious training diminished, teachers were still expected to act as moral agents. Indeed, in the 19th and early 20th centuries, school boards often established "decency requirements" that governed teachers' behavior in and out of school. During the industrial period, expectations grew for teachers to develop in students the capacity for meaningful civic, economic, and intellectual life. Successive waves of immigration, rapid industrialization, and mass schooling at the turn of the 20th century further expanded expectations for teachers' work not only to prepare students for jobs but to be agents of socialization or "Americanization."

Today, the general goals and expectations for teachers' work encompass all these things. Teachers are expected to promote students' intellectual development and academic achievement as well as their personal, social, and moral development. Teachers are to prepare students for citizenship and economic productivity. Teachers are also to perform a socialization function, passing along ways of life and culture to future generations.

Occupational Status

Teachers' work is sometimes referred to as an art or a craft. It involves substantially more than the routine application of specific practices. According to Lieberman and Miller (1984), teachers' work is "a messy and highly personalized enterprise" (p. 5). It is most often considered semiprofessional work (Sykes, 1999). It reflects some qualities of professional work but differs from work of the "true" professions, such as law and medicine, in several important ways.

Teachers' work requires a substantial amount of independent judgment and discretion. Yet, it is not guided by a specialized body of knowledge that is developed and controlled by teachers themselves and that the public believes is necessary for successful job performance. There is substantial knowledge that underlies teachers' work, but that knowledge is largely tacit and "action-centered" (Pratte & Rury, 1991). It is developed in the course of, embodied in, and conveyed through practice. In the absence of an explicit technology, much of teachers'

work must be guided by their own understandings, values, beliefs, and assumptions. Unlike the "true" professions, teachers' work carries the cultural status of ordinary rather than elite work. It is a job for which relatively little formal preparation has been demanded and that many people think most anyone could do. There are few professional controls that govern teachers' work. In large measure, teachers' work is externally controlled. Criteria for entry and removal and for judging effective performance are not determined so much by teachers themselves as by others. Teachers serve at the pleasure and under the authority of state education agencies, local school boards, and school and district administrators. Since the mid-1980s, there has been substantial discussion about how to professionalize teachers and their work. A review of that discussion is beyond the scope of this chapter.

Common Properties

Teachers' work is multidimensional and remarkably complex. There are important variations associated with different job assignments (e.g., elementary or secondary, general education or special education) and classroom, school, and district work environments; however, teachers' work can be characterized by several common properties.

First, teachers' work is inherently social. It is people-centered and is enacted largely through interactions between teachers and children and among teachers, administrators, and parents. The highly interactive nature of teaching was captured years ago by Jackson (1968) who reported that elementary school teachers engage in as many as 1,000 interpersonal classroom interactions each day. Second, teachers' work is highly intellectual (Leinhardt & Greeno, 1986). It is dynamic and unpredictable, and it requires teachers to attend continuously to what is going on around them, analyze and diagnose information, draw inferences, and adjust their thinking and behavior accordingly (B. O. Smith, 1987). According to Shulman (1987), "[Teaching] begins with an act of reasoning, continues with a process of reasoning, culminates in performances of imparting, eliciting, involving, or enticing, and is then thought about some more until the process can begin again. . . ." (p. 13).

Third, teachers' work is an inherently moral enterprise. Hansen (2001) observes that it "presupposes notions of better and worse, of good and bad. . . . Teaching reflects the intentional effort to influence another human being for the good rather than for the bad" (p. 828). The moral dimension of teachers' work spans ends and means. Hansen indicates that "Any action a teacher undertakes . . . is capable of expressing moral meaning that, in turn, can influence students" (p. 826). This includes how teachers communicate with and attend to students, the subject matter they emphasize, and how they organize students and conduct classroom activity. Even the most routine and benign aspects of teachers' work can convey moral meaning as students interpret them.

Fourth, teachers' work has an important historical dimension. Teachers' work is shaped by histories of societal expectations for teaching and schooling, histories of teachers' schools and local communities, and personal histories of teachers and students. Moreover, what happens at any moment in teachers' work becomes part of the context for what happens in the future. For example, how teachers give feedback on assignments may affect how students engage in future assignments.

Contradictions and Dilemmas

Teachers' work is defined by contradictions. On one hand, teachers' work is public, and on the other, it is private and largely invisible. Teachers perform much of their work in front of students and in close proximity of other adults. Their work is performed while "living in a crowd" (Jackson, 1968, p. 8). Yet, teachers' work, especially with students, is largely out of view of other adults. And because much of it is conducted apart from other adults, it is considered largely independent, isolated, even lonely work (Lortie, 1975). Still, teachers' success with any group of students is related to the success of teachers who have previously worked with those students. Likewise, the learning and development that teachers promote in their students are likely to influence the work that other teachers do with the same students concurrently.

Teachers' work has certain constancies and regularities. It is bound by the rhythms of the school calendar and class schedule. It is contained by the walls of the classroom and the covers of textbooks and encapsulated by societal norms and expectations about teaching and schooling (Sarason, 1996). For many teachers, there is a predictable repetition in the cycles of class periods, school days, weeks, months, seasons, and years; in the rituals of assemblies and administrative work; and in seeing the same students and adults day in, day out (Lieberman & Miller, 1984; B. A. Smith, 2000).

At the same time, teachers' work is ambiguous and unpredictable (Lortie, 1975). To reiterate, the goals of teachers' work are vague, and a formal knowledge base and technology are not well developed. The complex social environments of schools and classrooms can be unpredictable. Teachers must deal with a substantial amount of nonroutine information that is often difficult to decipher. The outcomes of teachers' work are frequently hard to detect and the connections between teachers' efforts and outcomes are often not immediately evident. This is true especially with regard to student learning outcomes. This all means that teachers must make their own "translations" (Lieberman & Miller, 1984). They must improvise and devise their own solutions to complex problems (Borko & Livingston, 1989). Depending on their circumstances, teachers may become bricoleurs who can "remain creative under pressure, precisely because they routinely act in chaotic conditions and pull order out of them. . . ." (Weick, 1993, p. 639). Thus while forged in the constancies and regularities of the job, the work ultimately reflects teachers' personal knowledge, preferences, emotions, and identities (Lieberman & Miller, 1984).

Teachers' work is also defined by dilemmas. Dilemmas are conflict-filled situations that pit highly valued alternatives against one another. Most dilemmas teachers face fall within several broad areas. Some dilemmas sprout from the need to coordinate multiple purposes of schooling and expectations for teachers' work. Teachers must allocate time and energy among different aspects of their jobs. They must attend to the needs of individual students and to the needs of groups, classes, even entire schools. They must balance the need for promoting academic achievement with the need for promoting other aspects of student learning and development. They must balance work required outside the classroom with work required within. There are tensions between external organizational controls and the extent of teacher autonomy and discretion required for success in the classroom. And there are dilemmas posed by the demands of multiple, and sometimes conflicting, educational policies and reforms. Last but not least, there are dilemmas between the personal and the professional (Lieberman & Miller, 1984). These are not simply tensions between individual preferences and broader expectations for how teachers' work is to be performed, whether those expectations emanate from local communities or federal education policy, such as No Child Left Behind. These are tensions between the substantial demands that the work makes on teachers' time, energy, and emotions, and the interests that teachers have to live full and satisfying lives outside their work (Spencer, 2001). Such dilemmas are endemic. Teachers' responses can only be provisional, "good-enough compromises rather than neat solutions" (Cuban, 1992, p. 7). They make dilemma management an enduring part of teachers' work.

Work Across a Career

Teachers pass through several developmental phases in their work from entry to retirement. Although each teacher may move through them differently, these phases suggest a general way in which the work is experienced. According to Huberman (1993), teachers entering the job experience a period of initial enthusiasm, reality shock, and survival. They begin to build their practices and develop their own teaching styles largely through trial and error. During this entry phrase, teachers are typically concerned about managing classrooms and controlling students, building relationships with other teachers, and navigating school bureaucracies. They also tend to be preoccupied with concern about themselves and their own ability to succeed. This phase is usually followed by a period of stabilization during which teachers make a commitment to the job and develop an identity as a teacher. Teachers become more secure and confident personally and professionally. They hone their pedagogical skills and redirect concern about themselves toward concern about instruction and student learning. Many teachers in this phase tend to act with increased confidence and spontaneity.

Later phases are more difficult to discern as individual "routes" develop and diverge (Huberman, 1993). What often follows stabilization is a period of experimentation and diversification. Teachers may embark on personal experiments with new methods and materials. They may feel a stronger desire to increase their impact on the classroom. And they may search for new challenges outside the classroom. Diversification may give way to a period of uncertainty and reassessment. This phase usually occurs mid-career, between 15 and 25 years of teaching, but it is not experienced by all teachers in the same way.

For some teachers, reassessment leads to a period of conservation and complaint (Huberman, 1993). This period is characterized by growing disenchantment, increasing rigidity and dogmatism, greater precaution, resistance to innovation, and pronounced nostalgia for the past. Teachers in this phase may become protective of the status quo and their own self-interests. For other teachers, reassessment leads to a period of serenity and distance. Confidence and commitment return, but levels of ambition decline. There is renewed interest in doing the job well but less need to prove oneself. Whether reassessment leads to conservation and complaint or serenity and distance, both periods lead to eventual personal and professional disengagement through retirement or resignation.

Although teachers may experience different phases during the course of their careers, the structure of the career itself is usually both constant and "flat" (Lortie, 1975). For many teachers there is substantial continuity in the roles and responsibilities that teachers perform year after year. The work can look the same the year that a teacher retires as it did the year of entry. With few exceptions, the structure and nature of the job does not vary according to teachers' experience or expertise. There are no ranks associated with different levels or types of work or with accomplishment.

Historically, career advancement has meant leaving the classroom for school- or district-level administrative work. But since the mid-1980s, growing numbers of schools and districts have sought to expand and enrich teachers' work. Many early efforts came through career ladder plans. Recent efforts have focused on new leadership roles for teachers (Smylie, Conley, & Marks, 2002). While not a panacea, job expansion and enrichment are thought to increase the variety and significance of teachers' work and thus help attract, motivate, and retain teachers. Research on teacher work redesign is emergent and inconclusive, but these efforts are generally considered promising for teachers and for school improvement.

What Teachers Do

What does teachers' work look like? What do teachers do day in, day out? We consider these questions in two ways.

First, we consider the various roles that teachers perform. Second, we examine specific tasks and activities in which they engage.

Work Roles

Consistent with multiple goals and expectations, teachers perform many related roles (Heck & Williams, 1984). Their primary role is leader or facilitator of student learning. This role can be organized around any number of models for teaching and learning (e.g., student-centered, constructivist models or teacher-centered, transmission models). Teachers serve as resources of knowledge, norms, and attitudes. Teachers often function as local historians. Coupled with knowledge of contemporary community circumstance, such memory can help teachers work more effectively with students.

In addition to promoting the learning of others, teachers perform the role of learner themselves. Teachers learn through experience on the job. They also learn through interactions with other adults and participation in formal learning opportunities (e.g., professional development workshops, college and university courses, attending conferences, reading professional literature). These and other sources can help teachers develop new knowledge and skills to promote student learning. Or they may simply reinforce existing knowledge and skills.

Teachers act as gatekeepers through whom students may gain access to social and professional services inside and outside of school. Teachers often function as frontline responders when students experience social-emotional, psychological, or physical difficulties. When teachers are unable to address these needs, they may refer students to appropriate services. Teachers are often bound by state law to intervene in cases of suspected abuse or neglect.

Teachers may be partners with parents. Teachers and parents may share many interests, and they can work together to promote student learning and development. By extension, teachers may recognize shared interests with their local communities and join with individuals and organizations to garner resources and support for student success. Because there can also be competition and conflict between teachers and parents, such relationships may need to be initiated and managed by teachers. This could involve teachers helping parents and community members learn how to be effective partners in and out of school.

Teachers also perform the role of developer and implementer of programs, policies, and practices. As discussed earlier, teachers invent and improvise classroom practices. They may join with other educators to create new curriculum, programs, and policies at the school or district levels. Teachers also act as developers when they implement school- or district- or state-level programs and policies. Rarely do teachers simply administer programs and policies as they are written or even intended (Fullan, 2007). Even with prescriptive initiatives such as comprehensive school reform models, teachers often adapt programs and policies according to their own understanding, interests, skills, and classroom situations. This is not resistance or refusal (although sometimes teachers do resist and refuse); instead, such adaptation reflects the discretion that is such a key element of teachers' work (Lipsky, 1980).

In addition, teachers perform the role of colleague. Working relationships among adults in a school can make a substantial difference in the ability of the school to improve and to serve students effectively (Rosenholtz, 1989). Indeed, working relationships among adults can make a substantial difference in the opportunities available for teachers' professional learning and development. The literature suggests that the organization of adult relationships into professional communities is perhaps most conducive to school effectiveness and improvement (Fullan, 2007). Such communities and collegial relationships do not simply happen. While administrators play a crucial role in their development, teachers are the ones who must make these communities work.

Teachers may perform various leadership roles (Smylie et al., 2002). These roles may be associated with formal positions and carry titles and specific responsibilities (e.g., mentor teacher, instructional coordinator, team leader, department chair, union representative). Or they may be informal, naturally occurring, or emergent as suggested by recent conceptions of organizational leadership (e.g., distributed leadership). These roles may come on top of or in place of teachers' regular classroom responsibilities. They may focus on school governance and decision making, curricular and instructional development, and teacher professional development. Although some teachers may feel that these roles intrude on their real job in the classroom, these roles have become more focused on the work of school organizational improvement.

What connects all these particular roles is the overarching function of the teacher as an agent of change (Smylie, Bay, & Tozer, 1999). The goals and expectations for teachers' work, regardless of how vague or contradictory, call teachers to promote change. Whether it is in the learning and development of students, their own professional learning and development, the engagement of parents and community members, working with colleagues, or performing leadership work, the fundamental role of the teacher is to make things different and presumably better.

Tasks and Activities

To perform these roles, teachers engage in a large number of tasks and activities. One of the most comprehensive sources of information about these tasks and activities is the U.S. Department of Labor's *Dictionary of Occupational Titles* (*DOT*). The *DOT* identifies dozens of specific things that teachers do in their work (U.S. Department of Labor, 2007). Many are common across grade levels. Still, teachers at different levels in different contexts will devote more time and energy to some tasks and activities than to others. It is probably impossible to compile a complete inventory of the tasks and activities that teachers perform because their work is so multidimensional and complex. Nonetheless, among the many tasks and activities contained in the *DOT* are the following examples.

Teachers prepare objectives, activities, and materials for working with students, and they instruct students in groups and individually through a variety of methods, from lecture and presentation to discussion to in-class reading to group work. Teachers develop and evaluate classroom and homework assignments. They prepare and administer assessments of student learning and develop grade reports or other reports of student progress. Teachers communicate with parents and discuss curriculum and student progress with colleagues. They keep administrative records (e.g., attendance), administer standardized tests, and enforce school policies. Sometimes teachers work with students and other adults in extracurricular activities.

Other sources are also useful for identifying things that teachers do in their work. For example, Grant and Murray (1999) indicate that teachers listen to and motivate students and that they model ways of learning and of "being in the world" (p. 43). Shulman (1987) points to the tasks of managing students, discourse, and ideas: "Like a symphony conductor, posing questions, probing for alternative views, drawing out the shy while tempering the boisterous . . . , pacing and ordering, structuring and expanding, [the teacher] control[s] the rhythm of classroom life" (pp. 1–2). To this we might add that teachers perform a number of other managerial tasks, including grouping students for instruction, disciplining students, managing time and student movement in the classroom, collecting money, taking younger students to the restroom, managing fundraising activities, and keeping classroom plants and animals alive.

Beyond the School Day and Year

Teachers' work does not stop at the end of the school day. The National Education Association's 2001 national survey of public school teachers reveals that on average teachers spend 10 hours each week beyond the school day on instruction-related activities (National Education Association, 2003). They spend almost 12 hours each week performing noncompensated school-related work. Nearly 40% of teachers across the country reported that they take on additional work within their districts to supplement their incomes. Thirteen percent reported that they moonlight in jobs outside their school systems to make more money.

There are a number of tasks and activities that teachers may perform in their work beyond the school day. These can include instructional planning, reading and evaluating student work, preparing administrative reports, communicating with parents, and leading extracurricular activities (e.g., sports, clubs, performing arts). They can include tutoring, counseling, and extending other forms of extra-classroom academic and personal support to students. They can also include working with other teachers to align curriculum and coordinate instruction, planning and carrying out various school improvement activities, and engaging in one's own professional development alone or with others.

Teachers' work is often portrayed as a nine-month job. In 2001, however, nearly 30% of teachers across the county were employed during the summer within their own school systems (National Education Association, 2003). This work could involve developing new curriculum, programs, and policies; leading professional development activities; or engaging in school improvement planning and development work. It could also involve teaching summer school, an increasingly common prospect in districts where high-stakes accountability systems require attendance of low-achieving and failing students. Among other possibilities, it might involve working in school- or district-sponsored summer academic enrichment, recreational, or other nonacademic programs for children and youth. About 20% of teachers worked outside their school systems at other jobs to supplement their school year income.

These activities do not represent the totality of teachers' work beyond the school year. Most teachers use portions of their time off to plan activities and develop materials for the next school year. They also use summers for professional learning and development, often taking courses at area colleges and universities or attending workshops sponsored by school districts or professional associations.

Contexts of Teachers' Work

We have understood for some time that social and organizational contexts of work can have profound effects on the nature and structure of work and how it is performed. So too is teachers' work shaped by a constellation of contexts that extend from the most immediate workplace settings of schools and classrooms, to local communities and school districts, to state and federal policy environments, and to social institutions. Referring to schools, Johnson (1990) explains, "Workplaces are not inert boxes that house practice. Rather, they are complex sets of features that interact with practice. They convey information about what is expected. They influence what is possible. They determine what is likely" (p. 9).

The relationship between contexts and teachers' work is remarkably complex. The nature and characteristics of contexts may vary substantially from one place and one time to another, and individual teachers may interpret and respond to different contexts differently. Contexts may shape the structure of teachers' work (e.g., roles, tasks, and activities) and how teachers perform their work within that structure. Different contexts may be aligned and operate in a mutually reinforcing manner, or they may conflict. The

latter possibility was noted by Waller (1932) more than 70 years ago when he observed that the occupation of the teacher was enmeshed in a complex system of authority, with each segment having its own, often competing, agendas and demands on teachers.

The most immediate context of teachers' work is the classroom. The classroom is a "small society" (Waller, 1932) defined by structures, a social system, norms and values, and its own politics (Barr & Dreeben, 1991; Jackson, 1968). Class size and composition, particularly academic and language-cultural heterogeneity and the presence of special needs students, may shape how teachers organize classroom instruction and how they teach. So too may the quantities and qualities of curricular and instructional materials and other resources available (or unavailable) to teachers.

Classrooms are nested within the organizational contexts of schools. Schools can also be characterized by their structures, their social relationships, their politics, and their organizational cultures (Johnson, 1990; Little & McLaughlin, 1993). Structural characteristics such as range of grade levels, the size and composition of student enrollments, conditions of facilities, and adequacy of resources may affect teachers' work and how it is performed. As noted, teachers' work can be influenced by the allocation and organization of instructional time via classroom schedules and school calendars. It can be shaped by teacher assignment to particular grade levels and student groups, to particular subject areas to be taught, and to non-instructional tasks such as administrative and supervisory duties (e.g., department chair, lunchroom and hall monitoring). It can be shaped by the school's (and district's) adopted curricula, textbooks, and instructional materials and by the school's administrative systems of evaluation, supervision, and reward. Teachers' work can be influenced directly by other teachers and by building administrators, especially principals (Rosenholtz, 1989). Beliefs and expectations for what work is to be performed and how it is to be performed, sources of motivation, and mechanisms of accountability and control flow through working relationships. And through those same relationships come opportunities to exchange information and to learn.

Equally important, if not more so, are the contexts found within schools: grade-level teams, departments, and "houses." Because they are more proximal to and because they may be more tightly organized around teachers' specific job assignments and interests than the school as a whole (e.g., students at particular grade levels, different subject matters), these intermediate contexts may act as particularly potent sources of influence (McLaughlin & Talbert, 2001).

School districts can also influence teachers' work through policies and procedures concerning teachers and students; adopted curricula, textbooks, and instructional materials; teachers' assignments to particular schools; opportunities for teachers' professional learning and development; and the expectations they convey through missions, goals, and values. Districts can influence teachers' work through systems of student testing and teacher accountability. Through collective bargaining agreements with teachers unions, districts can specify various structures of teachers' work, including contract periods, work scope, evaluation policies and practices, compensation and incentives, and working conditions.

Of particular salience is the ability of school districts to raise revenue. Education in the United States is decentralized and controlled primarily at the community level. It is funded at that level primarily through local taxation, tying economic resources for school districts directly to the wealth of their local communities. This dependency is as true today as it was in an earlier century when, as needs arose, community members gathered with hammers and nails to construct one-room schoolhouses. Dependence on local revenues tends to perpetuate disparities in resources available to individual school districts, despite funding from state and federal levels that may be designed to equalize funding among districts. Funding disparities often translate into disparities in supports available to teachers, including equipment and instructional materials, work space for teachers, and the physical condition, deferred maintenance, underuse, and overcrowding of school buildings.

Among the distant contexts that shape teachers' work are state and federal policy environments. State and federal policies influence teachers' work by "bringing the resources of government—money, rules, and authority—into the service of political objectives; and by using those resources to influence the actions of individuals and institutions" (McDonnell & Elmore, 1987, p. 133). There are numerous examples of state and federal policies that might affect teachers' work. Policies at all levels—federal, state, and district—can exert direct influence on the structure of teachers' work and on its performance. Policies can also exert indirect influence by shaping other contexts in which the work is performed (e.g., the working conditions of schools). These influences can come in the form of mandates (e.g., regulations specifying instructional time in particular subject areas), inducements (e.g., grants-in-aid, merit pay), initiatives to develop capacity (e.g., training and professional development programs and policies, class size reductions, capital improvement), and initiatives to redistribute authority (e.g., decentralization and participative decision making; McDonnell & Elmore, 1987).

Among the most notable illustrations of policy influence on teachers' work are current state curriculum standards, student testing programs, and the student accountability provisions of federal No Child Left Behind legislation. There is increasing evidence that these sorts of policy mandates can significantly influence both teachers' work and their performance. They have been found to shift teachers' instruction toward subject matter tested (subject matter not tested is often sacrificed), toward more teacher-centered instruction, and toward more review and test preparation than instruction in new subject matter (Valli &

Buese, 2007). This may be because teachers find such changes more powerful than alternatives, because of a sense of care or duty to students to ensure that they do well in high-stakes testing, or because they are being held accountable for their students' performance. These mandates may also have a number of unintended consequences, including introducing new sources of stress into teachers' relationships with students and parents and disincentives for teacher performance.

The Future of Teachers' Work

There are several significant changes taking place in the contexts of teachers' work. While it is difficult to predict their effect, there is reason to believe that, as former New York Yankees catcher Yogi Berra might have put it, "The future of teaching ain't what it used to be."

One of the most significant changes is the revolutionary development of information and communications technologies (Smolin, Lawless, & Burbules, 2007). Advances in hardware and software have dramatically increased access to information and the ability to exchange it. The production of new knowledge is exponential and unprecedented. While these new technologies are opening classrooms to the world and creating unimagined opportunities for student learning, they are also making substantial demands on teachers to learn and know more, to develop new sets of technology-related skills, and to manage ever-increasing amounts of information. These advances may imply much more. They have already begun to alter the basic relationships among teachers, subject matter, and students as learners, as well as authority relations between teachers and others (e.g., administrators, students). They have substantial implications for the definition and development of learning environments, actual or virtual. Moreover, these new technologies may alter working relationships among teachers and other educators and between teachers, parents, and other members of local communities.

Another change involves the growing diversities among students and communities and concurrent increases in disparities in resources and learning opportunities. The proportion of racial and ethnic minority students in U.S. elementary and secondary schools rose from 22% to 42% between 1972 and 2005 (U.S. Census Bureau, 2007). In 2005, 41% of all fourth-grade students nationwide were eligible for free or reduced-price lunch (National Center for Educational Statistics, 2007). That year, almost three out of four African American and Hispanic fourth-graders were eligible. Growth in the numbers and proportions of racial and ethnic minority students, increases in language and cultural diversity, and accentuation of socioeconomic class differences all portend to make teachers' work more complex and challenging. More and more, teachers' work is lodged within gaps—gaps in student learning and academic achievement; gaps among classes, languages, and cultures; gaps in community wealth and resources for schooling; gaps in access to technologies and information; and gaps in visions and prospects for students' futures. These changes may introduce to teachers new social and cultural ambiguities and tensions; demands for new knowledge, skills, and commitments; and dilemmas associated with agendas for excellence and equity. For many teachers, the demands associated with increasing diversity may be made more complex and difficult to address with limited resources and heightened demands for external accountability.

There is growing specification and intensification in teachers' work (Hargreaves, 2003). In the present era of standards-based, test-driven educational policy, this is manifest in a narrowing of goals and greater accountability for student academic outcomes in a limited range of subject areas (although it is likely that most parents and community members will continue to expect that teachers achieve the broadest range of educational goals for their children). In addition, calls are coming (again) for tying teacher evaluation and compensation to student academic performance. The demands imposed by specification and intensification have already begun to conflict with demands associated with increasing diversities and disparities.

Last, but not least, is the emergence of neoliberalism and globalization. Neoliberal thinking and policy place increased emphasis on the economic and workforce development goals of education. They create prospects for expanded roles for the private sector in public services, including education. Globalization may create unimaginable opportunities for new learning. It may also promote profound shifts in notions of community. Past and present concepts of schooling within and for local community may be challenged, and perhaps supplanted, by concepts of schooling for global political and market economies. Instead of preparing students for jobs within their local communities, teachers will need to prepare students to compete worldwide for jobs unimagined.

No doubt these changes will make teachers' work even more complex, uncertain, and challenging than it is now. They will likely take teachers' work in different directions, and they will certainly introduce new tensions and dilemmas. Whether these changes will alter the basic nature and structure of the job remains to be seen. Regardless, the work of teachers will be as important as ever in years to come. It will remain necessary to ensure that those who choose this occupation will be adequately prepared and supported and that the work, whatever it might become, will be performed effectively.

References and Further Readings

Barr, R., & Dreeben, R. (1991). *How schools work.* Chicago: University of Chicago Press.

Borko, H., & Livingston, C. (1989). Cognition and improvisation: Differences in mathematics instruction by expert and novice teachers. *American Educational Research Journal, 26,* 473–498.

Cuban, L. (1992). Managing dilemmas while building professional communities. *Educational Researcher, 21*(1), 4–11.

Dreeben, R. (2005). Teaching and the competence of occupations. In L. V. Hedges & B. Schneider (Eds.), *The social organization of schooling* (pp. 51–71). New York: Russell Sage Foundation.

Elmore, R. F. (2007). Education: A "profession" in search of a practice. *Teaching in Educational Administration* (TEA SIG, Division A, American Educational Research Association), *15*(1), 1–4.

Fullan, M. (2007). *The new meaning of educational change* (4th ed.). New York: Teachers College Press.

Goodson, I. (1997). The life and work of teachers. In B. J. Biddle, T. L. Good, & I. F. Goodson (Eds.), *International handbook of teachers and teaching* (pp. 135–152). Boston: Kluwer.

Grant, G., & Murray, C. E. (1999). *Teaching in America: The slow revolution.* Cambridge, MA: Harvard University Press.

Hansen, D. T. (2001). Teaching as a moral activity. In V. Richardson (Ed.), *Handbook of research on teaching* (4th ed., pp. 826–857). Washington, DC: American Educational Research Association.

Hargreaves, A. (2003). *Teaching in the knowledge society: Education in the age of insecurity.* New York: Teachers College Press.

Heck, S. F., & Williams, C. R. (1984). *The complex role of the teacher: An ecological perspective.* New York: Teachers College Press.

Huberman, M. (1993). *The lives of teachers.* New York: Teachers College Press.

Ingersoll, R. M. (2005). The anomaly of educational organizations and the study of organizational control. In L. V. Hedges & B. Schneider (Eds.), *The social organization of schooling* (pp. 91–110). New York: Russell Sage Foundation.

Jackson, P. W. (1968). *Life in classrooms.* New York: Holt, Rinehart & Winston.

Johnson, S. M. (1990). *Teachers at work: Achieving success in our schools.* New York: Basic Books.

Johnson, S. M. (2005). The prospects for teaching as a profession. In L. V. Hedges & B. Schneider (Eds.), *The social organization of schooling* (pp. 72–90). New York: Russell Sage Foundation.

Leinhardt, G., & Greeno, J. G. (1986). The cognitive skill of teaching. *Journal of Educational Psychology, 78,* 75–95.

Lieberman, A., & Miller, L. (1984). *Teachers, their world, and their work.* Alexandria, VA: Association for Supervision and Curriculum Development.

Lipsky, M. (1980). *Street-level bureaucracy: Dilemmas of the individual in public services.* New York: Russell Sage Foundation.

Little, J. W., & McLaughlin, M. W. (Eds.). (1993). *Teachers' work: Individuals, colleagues, and contexts.* New York: Teachers College Press.

Lortie, D. C. (1975). *Schoolteacher.* Chicago: University of Chicago Press.

McDonnell, L. M., & Elmore, R. F. (1987). Getting the job done: Alternative policy instruments. *Educational Evaluation and Policy Analysis, 9,* 133–152.

McLaughlin, M. W., & Talbert, J. E. (2001). *Professional communities and the work of high school teaching.* Chicago: University of Chicago Press.

National Center for Education Statistics. (2007). *Status and trends in the education of racial and ethnic minorities* (NCES 2007–039). Washington, DC: Author.

National Education Association. (2003). *Status of the American public school teacher, 2001.* Washington, DC: Author.

Pratte, R., & Rury, J. L. (1991). Teachers, professionalism, and craft. *Teachers College Record, 93,* 59–72.

Rosenholtz, S. J. (1989). *Teachers' workplace: The social organization of schools.* New York: Longman.

Sarason, S. (1996). *Revisiting "The culture of the school and the problem of change."* New York: Teachers College Press.

Shulman, L. S. (1987). Knowledge and teaching: Foundations of the new reform. *Harvard Educational Review, 57*(1), 1–22.

Smith, B. A. (2000). Quantity matters: Annual instructional time in an urban school system. *Educational Administration Quarterly, 36,* 652–682.

Smith, B. O. (1987). Definitions of teaching. In M. J. Dunkin (Ed.), *International encyclopedia of teaching and teacher education* (pp. 11–15). New York: Pergamon.

Smylie, M. A., Bay, M., & Tozer, S. E. (1999). Preparing teachers as agents of change. In G. A. Griffin (Ed.), *The education of teachers* (99th Yearbook of the National Society for the Study of Education, Part I, pp. 29–62). Chicago: National Society for the Study of Education.

Smolin, L., Lawless, K., & Burbules, N. (Eds.) (2007). *Information and communication technologies: Considerations for current practices of teachers and teacher educators* (106th yearbook of the National Society for the Study of Education, Part II). Malden, MA: Blackwell.

Smylie, M. A., Conley, S., & Marks, H. M. (2002). Exploring new approaches to teacher leadership for school improvement. In J. Murphy (Ed.), *The educational leadership challenge: Redefining leadership for the 21st century* (102nd Yearbook of the National Society for the Study of Education, Part II, pp. 162–188). Chicago: National Society for the Study of Education.

Spencer D. A. (2001). Teachers' work in historical and social context. In V. Richardson (Ed.), *Handbook of research on teaching* (4th ed., pp. 803–825). Washington, DC: American Educational Research Association.

Sykes, G. (1999). The "new professionalism" in education: An appraisal. In J. Murphy & K. S. Louis (Eds.), *Handbook of research on educational administration* (2nd ed., pp. 227–249). San Francisco: Jossey-Bass.

U.S. Census Bureau. (2007). *Current population survey, October supplement, 1972 and 2005.* Washington, DC: Author.

U.S. Department of Labor. (2007). *Dictionary of occupational titles.* http://www.occupationalinfo.org

Valli, L., & Buese, D. (2007). The changing roles of teachers in an era of high-stakes accountability. *American Educational Research Journal, 44,* 519–558.

Waller, W. (1932). *Sociology of teaching.* New York: Russell & Russell.

Weick, K. E. (1993). The collapse of sensemaking in organizations: The Mann Gulch disaster. *Educational Administration Quarterly, 38,* 628–652.

2

TEACHER LEADERSHIP

JENNIFER YORK-BARR, JENNIFER SOMMERNESS, AND JU HUR
University of Minnesota

As we enter the new millennium, teachers are closer than ever before to realizing their critically important and rightful position as leaders in PreK–12 education. Educational practice today requires more and increasingly varied participation by teachers in the leadership work of continual school improvement and renewal. The advances in teaching and learning that are increasingly required to maximize the growth and contributions of this next generation of children will not be realized without teachers, supported by administrators and enabled in a culture of collaborative learning, who lead among their peers.

An evolution in the thinking about teacher leadership has been described by Silva, Gimbert, and Nolan (2000) as three "waves." The essence of teacher leadership in the first wave was teachers assuming formal positions, such as department chair, site committee member, or union representative, positions largely focused on increasing the efficiency of school management. Activities included scheduling, assigning classes, coordinating special events, and serving as a communication link between administrators and teachers. In this wave, conceptions of teacher-leaders focused on keeping things running smoothly.

A second wave of teacher leadership ". . . acknowledged the importance of teachers as instructional leaders and created positions that capitalized on teacher instructional knowledge" (Silva et al., 2000, p. 780). In this wave, teachers assumed formally identified leadership positions such as staff developer or curriculum specialist. Some of these instructional leadership functions were add-ons to regular classroom teaching responsibilities. Curricular and instructional leadership in the second wave was viewed as important, yet still as an extra, not central, role of teachers.

In the unfolding third wave of teacher leadership, teachers are leaders in creating and sustaining a collaborative culture of learning in the school focused on improving instructional practice (Silva et al., 2000). All teachers are viewed as potential leaders who can share the responsibility of continual professional and school development, regardless of whether they hold a formal designation of leader (Barth, 2001; Frost & Harris, 2003). An expectation for leadership is embedded within the work scope of teachers instead of being an add-on. Teachers share leadership responsibilities with the principal to shape and enact the school's vision of advancing teaching, rather than just being communicators or coordinators. Not to be construed as revisiting the quasi-administrative functions of the first wave, nor having the prepackaged curriculum feel of the second wave, teacher leadership now explicitly holds developing learning capacity as its core function—learning for the grown-ups *and* students in schools.

These three waves of teacher leadership reflect an evolution in thinking about how teachers participate in school leadership and learning. This evolution has not happened in a vacuum. Increasing educational accountability, progressive conceptions of leadership as collective, and the movement to transform schools into professional learning communities are significant contextual influences.

The educational climate in the United States has become one in which not only districts and schools, but also administrators and teachers, are held accountable for the progress of students in meeting state and district standards. One indicator of teacher accountability is the prevalence of proposals for performance- or merit-based compensation structures that tie increases in teacher pay to increases in student performance (Odden & Kelley, 1997). Federal mandates within the No Child Left Behind Act (NCLB) also create pressure for changes at the level of classroom practice, as demonstrations of adequate yearly student progress must be documented. With changes in classroom practice being the target of improvement, teachers must be centrally involved.

More inclusive conceptions of leadership have also increased attention on how teachers *can* and *do* lead. Leadership is increasingly understood as a phenomenon shared by many individuals within organizations (Lambert, 2003). A traditional view that upholds the principal as the sole source of leadership in a school is being replaced with a view that calls for administrators and teachers to share leadership. Extending the earlier work of Ogawa and Bossert (1995), who asserted that leadership was an organizational quality, Spillane, Halverson, and Diamond (2001) have introduced the concept of "distributed leadership." A distributed model of leadership suggests that leadership is influence (Yukl, 1994) and that the pathways for achieving influence in organizations are the relationships among its members (Louis, 2006; Yukl, 1994). Based on this argument, teachers are key school leaders because they are positioned to influence peers through collegial relationships.

The movement toward re-creating schools as learning communities for educators as well as students is another influence on the evolving leadership roles of teachers (Hord, 2004; Louis, 2006). Derived from the early work of Forrester (1961) and the more recent works of Senge and his colleagues (Senge et al., 2000), organizations in which learning is the cornerstone are considered more adaptable and, therefore, more viable. According to Senge and colleagues, every organization is a product of how its members think and interact. Organizations, like people, that continue to learn are better situated not only to adapt but also to thrive in the context of an ever-changing external environment. Additionally, Louis (2006) explains that understanding the learning organization involves "the creation of socially constructed interpretations of facts and knowledge that enter the organization from the environment, or are generated from within" (p. 81). Given that teachers are potentially the greatest collective force in schools, learning, adaptivity, and leadership from within the community of teachers are paramount to continual adaptation and viability.

Together, then, accountability demands, understandings about leadership as shared practice, and the transformation of schools as learning communities constitute a powerful set of forces shaping the nature of teaching and teachers. The time is right for taking a bolder and more encompassing stride toward firmly planting teacher leadership in the landscape of continual school renewal. As a field, we have grown in our understanding about what it means and what it takes to nurture teacher leadership. We have witnessed the powerful influence of teachers as they lead from the middle of the organizational hierarchy in schools and side-by-side with their colleagues.

In a comprehensive review of teacher leadership research, York-Barr and Duke (2004) offer the following definition of teacher leadership:

> Teacher leadership is the process by which teachers, individually or collectively, influence their colleagues, principals, and other members of school communities to improve teaching and learning practices with the aim of increased student learning and achievement. (pp. 287–288)

This definition is broad enough to encompass many domains of teacher leadership practice. In this chapter, however, we focus specifically on the role of teacher-leader in the domains of teacher learning and instructional practice, along with school development to support learning and practice. We identify and describe significant cultural influences on the enactment of teacher leadership, principles and practices that ground the work of teacher-leaders, and resources that encourage and support teacher-leaders in their work. Our purpose is to articulate what is known about how to most effectively and efficiently engage the talent, energy, and influence of teachers as a central resource for advancing teaching and learning in schools.

Lessons Learned About Teacher Leadership

In this third wave of teacher leadership, leadership is not restricted to a few select individuals, but is to be shared by many teachers. Numerous leading researchers advance the idea of building leadership capacity such that many people are involved in leading the learning work in schools and are supported in their own learning and growth to do so (Crowther, Kaagan, Ferguson & Hann, 2002; Fullan, 2007; Lambert, 2003; Louis, 2006). In this next section we offer 12 lessons intended to support the many or the few teachers who either step in or are invited to lead, along with those who support them in their leadership work.

Lessons About the Culture Within Which Teachers Lead

School cultures are complex webs of traditions and rituals that have been built over time as teachers, students, parents, and administrators work together and deal with various challenges and accomplishments. "Cultural patterns are highly enduring, have a powerful impact on performance, and shape the ways people think, act, and feel" (Deal & Peterson, 1998, p. 4). Existing cultures, depending on their specific nature, can either help or hinder ongoing leadership efforts for school improvement. Edward Demming, an icon of quality management, has been attributed with saying, "put a good person in a bad system and the system will win every time." This emphasizes the powerful effect of existing norms, explicit or implicit, on human behavior. It also helps explain why teachers may enter a system with one set of ideals and values but over time succumb to the prevailing ones, sometimes without awareness of the gradual shift.

Schein (2004) explains, "neither culture nor leadership, when one examines each closely, can really be understood by itself" (p. 5). Leadership and culture, he asserts, are two sides of the same coin. Fullan (2001) introduced the term "re-culturing" to capture the essence of what it means to introduce and sustain change in existing school cultures. Without a doubt, teacher leadership introduces a counter-cultural presence in many schools. It should be no surprise then that principals, teachers, and teacher-leaders themselves are not exactly sure what to think and do as the idea of teacher leadership attempts translation into practice. Wilson (1993) shares that many teacher-leaders feel that current school cultures do not reward risk taking or collaboration and may perhaps even obstruct these behaviors. Described below are several lessons about cultural and professional norms that continue to plague many schools and teacher leadership.

Beware the Effects of Isolation

One of the most enduring and counterproductive cultural norms in schools is isolation (Rosenholtz, 1991). Isolation is structured into schools architecturally and temporally (Fullan & Hargreaves, 1996). Sometimes referred to as "egg carton architecture," classrooms largely are the private practice realm of teachers and teaching. Although surrounded by students for many hours a day, teachers are separate from their colleagues. Typical school schedules leave little time during which teaching colleagues can meaningfully connect with one another about their practices. Not only does isolation diminish professional growth, but prolonged isolation reinforces a solitary orientation to one's work and often breeds defensiveness and finger pointing. This orientation further diminishes the opportunity to establish a collaborative or collective norm for the work of teaching.

Although there are a growing number of schools in which regular opportunities and expectations for collaborative learning exist, most schools continue to struggle both for structural and psychological reasons to establish such cultures. Teachers are not used to exposing their practices; to do so is a vulnerable act requiring high levels of trust. Collaborative learning and interdependent work require a different way of thinking and behaving than isolated work. Initial efforts to chip away at the culture of isolation require intentionally designed and facilitated interactions such that participants feel safe and supported as they share with colleagues.

Stepping Up Can Be Viewed as Stepping Out of Line

Many well-intended teacher leadership initiatives are thwarted by the stronghold of egalitarian norms in schools (Lieberman & Miller, 1994; Little & McLaughlin, 1993). Egalitarian norms exert invisible pressure on teachers to retain equal status and not strive to be above their teaching colleagues. Especially when teachers assume formal positions of leadership, the "all teachers are equal" culture is threatened (Smylie, 1992). Stepping up to engage in leadership work frequently has been considered stepping out of line. Teachers who do so are regarded with suspicion and distrust. The "crab-bucket" metaphor described by Duke (1994) presents a compelling image of how relationships in the schoolhouse can be challenged by teacher leadership. When crabbing, there is no need to put a lid on a bucket of crabs because in the event that a crab tries to climb out, fellow crabs will grab hold and drag it back down. This is a disturbing, yet uncomfortably familiar, portrayal of life in some traditional school cultures.

Left unacknowledged and unaddressed, egalitarian norms impede teacher leadership efforts. This is especially true amid the current wave of school development and teacher leadership, one that aims to create school cultures that are collaborative and open to learning and improvement. In school cultures that are less conducive to collaboration and learning, commitments must be made to break down resistance by creating safe places for teachers to engage in collegial conversations about teaching and learning. When relationships between teacher-leaders and their colleagues are strong, and when teacher-leaders focus on improving their own instructional knowledge and practice as well as that of their colleagues, leaders are more likely to emerge and be encouraged and valued within their schools.

The Learning Void Reinforces Cycles of Cynicism

Historically, meaningful learning in schools has not been experienced by teachers. Irrelevant, episodic, and incoherent are terms that too often have described the staff development experiences of teachers. The adage, "I hope to die in staff development because the transition would be so seamless," is not without a grounded base in teachers' reality. Although there are indications of progress, high-quality learning and sustained improvement efforts have not been standard practice in schools. Many teachers have not experienced staff development that is useful for their professional practice. Further, because specific development efforts rarely have been sustained over time, full implementation of new initiatives has rarely occurred. A lot of energy and resources have been expended but nothing much has changed. And so, the cycle of cynicism continues, reflected in comments such as: "We've tried that before and it doesn't work." . . . "Wait this one out, it will go away like all the others." . . . "It's all theory, it will never work here."

Until teachers experience the energy boost that comes from high-quality professional learning and see its positive impact on their teaching practices, and subsequently on student learning, cynicism and halfhearted engagement are well considered adaptive responses. But professional learning that is relevant to instructional practice, sustained over time, and socially supported through collaborative interactions with colleagues can begin to interrupt the cycles of cynicism that derail even valid initiatives. As cycles of cynicism decline, teachers feel more empowered in their work. The "if only" stories (that is, stories about how things could be different, if only . . .) that permeate school culture will also lose their grip.

Reframe Resistance as Cultural, Not Personal

Cultures and the people living or working therein resist being tampered with. Knowing that cultures rule much of what happens in schools, what might be some productive responses on the part of leaders seeking to advance improvements in practice? First, expect resistance or push-back to attempts to introduce new practices. Isolation, egalitarianism, irrelevant and episodic staff development, and disempowerment continue as norms in many schools. No matter how unproductive they may be, they are not easily replaced with the more productive norms of collaboration, differentiation, quality learning, and teacher empowerment. Second, reframe resistance as a cultural force, not a personal rejection. Although leadership work has relational and personal dimensions, the ways in which educators either individually or as a group respond to improvement initiatives rarely hold personal malice toward the initiators.

Finally, there is good reason to believe that change and improvement are possible. Consider this thought: "People create cultures after that, cultures shape them" (Deal & Peterson, 1998, p. 85). If people create culture, then people can re-create it. Also know that teachers, like other human beings, are wired to learn and to contribute. Most teachers enter the field because they want to make a difference in the lives of children.

Lessons About the Work of Teachers Who Lead

In this section, we offer five lessons about positioning the work of teacher-leaders and engaging the colleagues of those leaders to improve teaching and learning in schools. The effectiveness of teachers in their leadership work depends on who they are as people, as teachers, and as colleagues. The relatively robust research on the characteristics of teachers who lead yields highly consistent results (see full summary in York-Barr & Duke, 2004). Such teachers are respected and viewed as credible by teaching peers when they demonstrate in-depth curricular knowledge along with significant experience and expertise as classroom instructors. Teachers who lead well tend to be learning-oriented people who take initiative and responsi-

bility for their own learning, are effective communicators with strong interpersonal skills, and have a collaborative orientation toward working with others.

A less visible but very powerful influence on the effectiveness of teacher-leaders is a belief in the positive learning and growth potential of people, even grown-ups. Teacher resistance or reluctance to engage in new proposals about their practice can be understood as a psychological artifact of traditional school norms, as described earlier. Teacher-leaders who hold positive beliefs about the inner desire of people to learn, to feel competent, and to be socially connected are well situated to persist in making connections. Such persistence with grown-ups sometimes results in engagement and transformation, just as it does with children. Louis (2006) describes how to cultivate teacher engagement, stating that when teachers enter the profession they are engaged on various levels. Over time, demands from the profession may be stressful but can also serve to energize. She states that engagement of teachers (like students) requires "consistent *positive reinforcers* that are *meaningful, relevant, rewarding* and *enjoyable*" (emphasis in original, p. 115).

The work of teacher leadership cannot be separated from the *ways* in which individual teacher-leaders do their work. Therefore not all teachers are well suited for all types of leadership work. The many and varied leadership functions invite many and varied teachers to participate. There are, however, some lessons about the work, as well as general approaches to the work, that hold true across many areas of leadership practice.

Leading From the Middle Is a Powerful Point of Leverage

Schools and school districts, like most formal organizations, are hierarchal places. Teacher-leaders, even though most continue to be classified as teachers, are not quite positioned horizontally with teaching colleagues or with administrators. They are, organizationally speaking, "in the middle." Leading from the middle, teachers function as

> boundary spanners and networkers . . . work within and across school boundaries and structures to establish social linkages and networks among their peers and within the community . . . the influence of teachers in the system is a combination of how well they know how to work the system, their perceived expertise, [and] the influence afforded them . . . (Acker-Hocevar & Touchton, 1999, p. 26)

The great potential of leading from the middle comes from remaining connected with teachers and to ground-level practices, while at the same time developing more substantial connections with school administration and district leaders. Connected up and down, teachers have the opportunity to learn from and directly influence both other teachers and administrators. Understanding teacher culture, classroom realities, and instructional practices is necessary to inform decision making about policies, personnel, practices, and resources made at higher levels. Likewise, understanding organizational cultures, management realities, and the broad scope of development work in many schools and districts informs teachers regarding the intentional and strategic efforts to continue building organizational and professional capacities that support the work of teachers.

Some of the liabilities for teachers leading from the middle include the ambiguity of the work, a lack of transparency in some of the work, and the challenge of keeping sacred time to be present and engaged at the instructional level of practice with other teachers. First, the ambiguity of middle-level work stems from a need to grasp the complexity of instructional and organizational realities; it can be difficult to feel sure about how to progress. There are numerous variables that influence the advancement of teaching and learning. Second, a lack of full transparency occurs because there is an extraordinary amount of behind-the-scenes preparatory and follow-up work for most public leadership activities. Whether it is facilitating a workshop, presenting to the school board, or coaching a teacher after an observation, no one else sees this work. Often, work unseen is work devalued. Finally, teacher-leaders struggle to hold sacred blocks of time to be present and engaged with teachers in classrooms. Because leading from the middle involves a certain amount of flexibility in job design, such teachers are at risk for having an increasing number of responsibilities assigned to them. This results in less time for side-by-side work with other teachers, which raises questions about the notion that teacher leadership is first and foremost about the learning work for instructional improvement.

Leading from the middle of an organization can sometimes feel really big, really complex, and really lonely. Without such leadership, however, the gap between the daily life of teachers in their instructional practice and the daily life of administrators in their organizational practice is not adequately or productively bridged. Leading from the middle—serving as bridges and connectors, leveraging personnel and knowledge resources, and understanding how to advance policies and practices throughout a system—is a powerful and critically important point of leverage for continual renewal in schools.

Keep the Focus on Teaching and Learning

For teachers to be successful in the work of leadership, their core work must be significant and viewed as valid and valuable by other teachers (Little, 1988). Work that is typically valued by teachers is directly relevant to teaching and student learning. Childs-Bowen, Moller, and Scrivner (2000) explain, " . . . teachers are leaders when they function in professional learning communities to affect student learning, contribute to school improvement, inspire excellence in practice, and empower stakeholders to participate in educational improvement" (p. 28).

In collaboration with other teachers, valued teacher leadership work might include any of the following activities:

- mapping a coherent vertical curriculum
- examining student data to identify instructional goals
- designing differentiated instruction
- developing assessments to monitor student learning and guide instructional decision making
- creating a tiered set of interventions aimed at fostering constructive affective behavior
- presenting materials for teaching high student engagement strategies
- bringing attention to culturally responsive teaching principles and practices
- modeling instructional practices
- coaching teachers as they implement new teaching strategies
- mentoring new teachers during their first three years of teaching
- facilitating formal and informal professional development gatherings in which teachers reflect and learn together.

In short, the central work of teachers who lead is the ongoing work of creating instructional improvement for students and the organizational conditions that foster such improvement.

Relationships Are the Pathways for Influence

Relationships, as a defining element of school culture, significantly affect the enactment of teacher leadership. Relationships are at the core of collaborative cultures in which continuous learning is an embedded norm. They are the pathways for influencing others, especially when one does not hold a position of formal administrative authority. Teachers who influence others have the capability to establish high trust relationships with and among their teaching peers and principals (Barth, 2001; Bryk & Schneider, 2002; Tschannen-Moran, 2004).

Teacher-leaders earn the trust of their colleagues by behaving in trustworthy ways in the context of daily interactions (Bryk & Schneider, 2002). Leaders from the middle gain and maintain the trust of colleagues by being discrete in the ways they secure, interpret, use, and transmit information. Teacher-leaders often feel the tug of unstated queries, such as, "Are you one of them or one of us?" The answer is not either-or, but both-and. The challenge lies in how to negotiate the middle leadership role by building relationships with integrity and staying grounded in purpose.

Learning inherently involves a degree of humility, meaning that one does not always know what to do. Few professionals maneuver in a more complex work environment than do teachers. It is not possible to know everything there is to know about effectively teaching many and varied students or adults in a myriad of circumstances. Tapping into the experience and expertise of teaching colleagues is an invaluable resource. And yet, many teachers are not predisposed to do so. A psychologically safe place to learn requires high levels of relational trust (Bryk & Schneider, 2002; Tschannen-Moran, 2004). When trust is present, questions can be asked and challenges shared without the risk of being viewed as inadequate. Relationships can make or break the success of initiatives aimed at improvements in teaching and learning.

Get the Learning Going!

There are at least three reasons why this lesson is a cornerstone of effective leadership practice. First, learning is the catalyst for continual improvement of instructional practice. If there is no learning, expect no improvement. Second, learning by experimenting with new practices and then observing positive results is the means by which beliefs are changed. Third, introducing learning into a frozen or stuck culture is one way for these cultures to get unstuck. Learning creates momentum. Collective learning accelerates the momentum for change.

School change expert Michael Fullan (2007) asserts that educators engaged in the work of school improvement should move to implementation sooner rather than later. He notes that too much time spent planning uses huge amounts of personal and organizational energy but results in little or no skill development or change in practice. Further, he argues, until initial use of practices begin, there is no experience base from which to make well-informed decisions about what is needed to advance the work. Thomas Guskey (1985) conducted a study that showed beliefs about practice change through personal experience with the practice. To change beliefs, engage teachers in new experiences.

An implication of this lesson is for teacher-leaders to direct a large share of their focus and energy on introducing and supporting changes in practice through the provision of high-quality professional development experiences. Expending energy to convince and cajole is energy largely wasted. The validity of new practices will be discerned through experience.

Learning Side-by-Side Models Collaborative Engagement

When teacher-leaders position themselves side-by-side with other teachers, they are positioned to be colearners, to facilitate productive collegial learning experiences, and to reinforce the assertion that teaching and learning about teaching is a career-long endeavor. Further, working in authentic instructional situations allows teachers who lead to continue developing their own instructional skills and, by doing so, to remain credible as teachers.

Learning collaboratively advances the notion that leadership is vested not only in people who have formal, titled positions but also in people at every level and in every dimension of organizational life. Opportunities to influence the development of others are not restricted to scheduled events but can and do occur through interactions in the daily work of schools. Teacher-leaders who maintain close contact with their colleagues can remain firmly grounded in their positions as teachers and in their network of collegial relationships. In their capacity as supportive colleagues, teacher-leaders embed leadership through both formal and informal points of influence (Darling-Hammond, Bullmaster, & Cobb, 1995; Heller & Firestone, 1995). Learning side-by-side, teacher-leaders inspire high levels of professional engagement among colleagues.

Lessons About Support for Teachers Who Lead

The counterculture nature of teacher leadership in schools means that much attention and intention is required to realize its potential. An overarching credo for teachers who lead is "Go-eth not alone!" Leadership work is not for the faint of heart. It requires courage and support. Although many leaders have or develop a strong internal capacity for sustaining their own learning and grounding, there is much intellectual and spiritual support to be realized through connections with others. The complex and sometimes conflicted work of leadership is well supported by an inner circle of trusted and engaged colleagues with whom leaders can openly share, learn, and re-energize. We describe three areas that offer personal and professional support for growth and renewal of teachers who lead.

Create and Insist on Opportunities to Learn and Grow

The work of leadership requires an expanded set of capacities and skills, beyond those required for excellence in classroom instruction. Some of the content areas identified as supporting teacher-leaders in their work include: advanced curricular, instructional, and assessment practices; school culture and its implications for professional and organizational improvement; adult development; and facilitation, presentation, and coaching skills required to facilitate learning and collaboration for individuals as well as with small or large groups (Lambert, 2003; York-Barr & Duke, 2004). Unfortunately, teacher-leaders sometimes are not provided with a thoughtful introduction to their leadership work, nor are they offered sufficient formal and ongoing leadership development opportunities. Below we describe three types of support to be addressed as teachers begin and continue their leadership work.

First, a formal introduction to the expected work scope of the teacher-leader and to the specific contexts within which the work will take place is an appropriate and respectful place to begin. Here are some questions to frame initial conversations between teacher-leaders and those who support their work:

- What is the work that the teacher-leader is intended to support, including the desired outcomes, products, or accomplishments?

- Who, specifically, will be involved? What is their background or expectation, and how is it anticipated that they will be involved?
- What resources are available to support the work (e.g., time, materials, development opportunities)?
- What role or roles is the teacher-leader expected to assume (e.g., facilitator, consultant, presenter, coach)?
- To whom is the teacher-leader accountable and by what means will checking in be most productive?

Further supporting an introduction to the work is an opportunity to spend time in the development context (e.g., school, classrooms, meetings) to meet key people and to listen to their understandings, interests, and concerns about the work. Interactions with these people, along with observing and listening while walking through the hallways, help discern the present culture and an array of current practice.

Second, formal leadership development opportunities should be an initial and ongoing means of supporting teacher-leaders. Are there courses, institutes, graduate programs, or workshops that provide more in-depth background knowledge about the learning work or about the teacher leadership understandings and skills for advancing the work? Are there other schools, leaders, or teachers who have been engaged in such work and who could share with the teacher-leader or leaders, or even an entire faculty?

Third, ongoing learning support in the form of opportunities to reflect and learn with teachers or other education leaders doing similar work is helpful. As Judith Arin-Krupp has been quoted saying, "Adults do not learn from experience, they learn from processing experience" (cited in Garmston & Wellman, 1997, p. 1). Time to reflect and learn must be both an espoused and realized value in the work of teacher-leaders. Leaders, like teachers, continue to improve as they reflect on, make sense of, and commit to improved future action.

Administrative Support Is Essential

About two decades ago, Judith Warren Little (1988) argued that the boundaries or expectations for teacher-leaders should be clarified, the incentives and rewards articulated, and the local policy support put in place. The principal and other administrators are, in large part, responsible for enacting this set of mandates. Principals " . . . must know how to create conditions that foster empowerment and release their control over teachers, alter their roles, and engender commitment, trust, and respect" (Acker-Hocevar & Touchton, 1999, p. 26).

Strong relationships between teacher-leaders and their principals are widely acknowledged as a key determinant of the effectiveness of teacher leadership, with principals being the primary influence on how the teacher-leader–principal relationship evolves (Barth, 2001; Hart, 1994; Kahrs, 1996; Mangin, 2007; Smylie & Hart, 2000; Terry, 1999). Anderson (2004) describes three different ways in which relationships unfold among principals, teacher-leaders, and teachers. The most productive of the three is interactive, in which principals engage with teacher-leaders and other teachers about leadership work. Moller and Pankake (2006) emphasize that principals must intentionally develop trusting relationships with teacher-leaders, claiming that the building of such relationships is critical to the health and vibrancy of school culture as well as an enactment of providing support to them.

Mangin (2007) found that principals who had high levels of knowledge about teacher leadership and who demonstrated high levels of interaction with teacher-leaders were more intentionally supportive of those leaders. Such principals communicated with all teachers in their schools about expectations of instructional improvement, the roles of teacher-leaders as a resource for improvement, and expectations of teachers interacting in positive ways with the teacher-leaders. Teacher-leaders in this study acknowledged and appreciated this support from the principal as useful, although they expressed a desire for even greater support to meet challenges in their roles, including gaining acceptance by their peers.

As discussed previously, leading among peers can be risky business for teachers. Principals must not only be aware of this risk but also do what they can to minimize its impact. With this expectation set, principals can support the leadership work emotionally, financially through material means, or symbolically. They can protect the relationship between teacher-leaders and their peers, jointly and regularly check in about action plans, and support the development and understanding of skills for leading adults for themselves, as well as their teacher-leaders (Moller & Pankake, 2006).

The influence and support of teacher-leaders on their principals is equally as important to note as the influence and support of principals on teacher-leaders. Teacher-leaders support the instructional leadership work of principals in at least the following ways: (1) maintaining a proactive focus on teacher learning, (2) serving as a partner for reflecting on and refining the course of development work, (3) reinforcing and translating into practice expectations for improvement, (4) modeling targeted instructional practices, (5) embedding learning and inquiry among teachers (formally and informally), and (6) keeping principals up-to-date with new advances in teaching and learning. Acknowledging the reciprocal nature of influence and support between principals and teacher-leaders reinforces the power realized when principals and teacher-leaders lead side-by-side.

Pay Attention to Space and Stuff

This is a lesson that does not require much explanation. One way to unsettle a teacher is to mess with his or her space and stuff (too much messing around with schedules is also trying). In a work environment that is usually quite full—physically, psychologically, and emotionally—with 20 to 30 moving, living little beings, it is not possible to maintain high levels of order and control. Teachers and other in-action professionals have to be flexible and adapt, but there are limits and there are ways to help teachers thrive amid the chaotic life in schools. Being allocated a space that is one's own and that allows for reasonable order of one's stuff provides a nominal amount of steadiness that is more important than others can sometimes imagine. Attention to space and stuff is no less important for teachers who lead. Often they become the keepers of a dizzying array of resources that support the work of classroom teachers, and often they collect a large quantity of professional learning resources. In most organizations, schools among them, there is an overall press for space and usually not enough in the end. Teacher-leaders need a place to call their own with space for their stuff.

Conclusion

After reading this chapter, one could reasonably ask, why would teachers choose to lead? Teachers lead because it has the potential to matter in big and small ways. Teachers who lead well are compelled, morally and intellectually, to make a difference in the lives of students (Fullan, 1993). By positively engaging their peers, such teachers enact a larger circle of support for achieving the moral purpose of advancing the learning and development of children in their journey to adulthood. Teachers who lead also have many opportunities for learning embedded in their work. Leading and learning are inextricably linked. They learn more about instructional, collegial, and organizational practices and how to influence those practices for the benefit of students. Teachers who lead learn more about themselves. Learning and contributing are strong attractors for many teachers.

Leveraging influence from the middle of the organization and learning side-by-side with colleagues, teachers who lead can shape the future of schools such that continual learning and professional renewal are defining features of what it means to be a teacher. Experienced as teachers, knowledgeable about instruction, effective in relationships, committed to personal growth, savvy about school culture, passionate about education, and caring about children—teachers who step up to lead contribute by advancing learning for grown-ups and children in schools.

The idea of teacher leadership is not new. "What is new, [however], are increased recognition of teacher leadership, visions of expanded teacher leadership roles, and new hope for the contributions these expanded roles might make in improving schools" (Smylie & Denny, 1990, p. 237). What also is new is our field's heightened understanding about what it means and what it takes to advance teacher leadership. The time is now to apply what we know.

References and Further Readings

Acker-Hocevar, M., & Touchton, D. (1999). *A model of power as social relationships: Teacher leaders describe the phenomena of effective agency in practice.* Paper presented at the Annual Meeting of the American Educational Research Association, Montreal, Canada.

Anderson, K. (2004). Teacher leadership as reciprocal influence between teacher leaders and principals. *School Effectiveness and School Improvement, 15*(1), 97–113.

Barth, R. S. (2001). Teacher leader. *Phi Delta Kappan, 82*(6), 443–449.

Bryk, A. S., & Schneider, B. (2002). *Trust in schools: A core resource for improvement.* New York: Russell Sage Foundation.

Childs-Bowen, D., Moller, G., & Scrivner, J. (2000). Principals: Leaders of leaders. *NASSP Bulletin, 84*(616), 27–34.

Crowther, F., Kaagan, S. S., Ferguson, M., & Hann, L. (2002). *Developing teacher leaders: How teacher leadership enhances school success.* Thousand Oaks, CA: Corwin Press.

Darling-Hammond, L., Bullmaster, M. L., & Cobb, V. L. (1995). Rethinking teacher leadership through professional development schools. *The Elementary School Journal, 96*(1), 87–106.

Deal, T. E., & Peterson, K. D. (1998). *Shaping school culture: The heart of leadership.* San Francisco: Jossey-Bass.

Duke, D. L. (1994). Drift, detachment, and the need for teacher leadership. In D. R. Walling (Ed.), *Teachers as leaders: Perspectives on the professional development of teachers* (pp. 255–273). Bloomington, IN: Phi Delta Kappa Educational Foundation.

Forrester, J. W. (1961). *Industrial dynamics.* Cambridge, MA: Massachusetts Institute of Technology Press.

Frost, D., & Harris, A. (2003). Teacher leadership: Towards a research agenda. *Cambridge Journal of Education, 33,* 479–498.

Fullan, M. (1993). Why teachers must become change agents. *Educational Leadership, 50,* 12–17.

Fullan, M. (2007). *The new meaning of educational change* (4th ed.). New York: Teachers College Press.

Fullan, M., & Hargreaves, A. (1996). *What's worth fighting for in your school?* New York: Teachers College Press.

Fullan, M. G. (2001). *Leading in a culture of change.* San Francisco: Jossey-Bass.

Garmston, R., & Wellman, B. (1997). *The adaptive school: A sourcebook for developing collaborative groups.* Norwood, MA: Christopher-Gordon.

Guskey, T. (1985). The effects of staff development on teachers' perceptions about effective teaching. *Journal of Educational Research, 78*(6), 378–381.

Hart, A. W. (1994). Creating teacher leadership roles. *Educational Administration Quarterly, 30*(4), 472–497.

Heller, M. F., & Firestone, W. A. (1995). Who's in charge here? Sources of leadership for change in eight schools. *The Elementary School Journal, 96*(1), 65–86.

Hord, S. M. (2004). *Learning together, leading together: Changing school through professional learning communities.* New York: Teachers College Press.

Kahrs, J. R. (1996). Principals who support teacher leadership. *New Directions for School Leadership, 1,* 19–40.

Lambert, L. (2003). *Leadership capacity for lasting school improvement.* Alexandria, VA: Association for Supervision and Curriculum Development.

Lieberman, A., & Miller, L. (1994). Revisiting the social realities of teaching. In A. Lieberman & L. Miller (Eds.), *Staff development for education in the '90s* (pp. 92–109). New York: Teachers College Press.

Lieberman, A., & Miller, L. (2004). *Teacher leadership.* San Francisco: Jossey-Bass.

Little, J. W. (1988). Assessing the prospects for teacher leadership. In A. Lieberman (Ed.), *Building a professional culture in schools* (pp. 78–106). New York: Teachers College Press.

Little, J. W., & McLaughlin, M. W. (1993). *Teachers' work: Individuals, colleagues, and contexts.* New York: Teachers College Press.

Louis, K. S. (2006). *Organizing for school change: Contexts of learning.* New York: Routledge.

Mangin, M. (2007). Facilitating elementary principals' support for instructional teacher leadership. *Educational Administration Quarterly, 43*(3), 319–357.

Moller, G., & Pankake, A. (2006). *Lead with me: A principal's guide to teacher leadership.* Larchmont, NY: Eye on Education.

Odden, A., & Kelley, C. (1997). Paying teachers for what they know and do: New and smarter compensation strategies to improve schools. Thousand Oaks, CA: Corwin Press.

Ogawa, R. T., & Bossert, S. T. (1995). Leadership as an organizational quality. *Educational Administration Quarterly, 31*(2), 224–243.

Rosenholtz, S. J. (1991). *The teachers' workplace: The social organization of schools.* New York: Teachers College Press.

Schein, E. H. (2004). *Organizational culture and leadership* (3rd ed.) San Francisco: Jossey-Bass.

Senge, P., Cambron-McCabe, N., Lucas, T., Smith, B., Dutton, J., & Kleiner, A. (Eds.). (2000). *Schools that learn: A fifth discipline fieldbook for educators, parents, and everyone who cares about education.* New York: Doubleday.

Silva, D. Y., Gimbert, B., & Nolan, J. (2000). Sliding the doors: Locking and unlocking possibilities for teacher leadership. *Teachers College Record, 102,* 779–804.

Smylie, M. A. (1992). Teachers' reports of their interactions with teacher leaders concerning classroom instruction. *The Elementary School Journal, 93*(1), 85–98.

Smylie, M. A., & Denny, J. W. (1990). Teacher leadership: Tensions and ambiguities in organizational perspective. *Educational Administration Quarterly, 26*(3), 235–259.

Smylie, M. A., & Hart, A. W. (2000). School leadership for teacher learning and change: A human and social capital development perspective. In J. Murphy and K. S. Louis (Eds.), *Handbook of research on educational administration* (2nd ed., pp. 421–441). San Francisco: Jossey-Bass.

Spillane, J. P., Halverson, R., & Diamond, J. B. (2001). Investigating school leadership practice: A distributed perspective. *Educational Researcher, 30*(3), 23–28.

Spillane, J. P., Halverson, R., & Diamond, J. B. (2003). Forms of capital and the construction of leadership: Instructional leadership in urban elementary schools. *Sociology of Education, 76*(1), p. 1–17.

Terry, P. M. (1999). Empowering teachers as leaders. *National Forum of Teacher Education Journal, 10E*(3), 1–7.

Tschannen-Moran, M. (2004). *Trust matters: Leadership for successful schools.* San Francisco: Jossey-Bass.

Wilson, M. (1993). The search for teacher leaders. *Educational Leadership, 50*(6), 24–27.

York-Barr, J., & Duke, K. E. (2004). What do we know about teacher leadership? Findings from two decades of scholarship. *Review of Educational Research, 74*(3), 255–316.

Yukl, G. (1994). *Leadership in organizations* (3rd ed.). Englewood Cliffs, NJ: Prentice Hall.

3

TEACHERS THINKING ABOUT THEIR PRACTICE

MARY M. KENNEDY

Michigan State University

Research on teaching practice and how teachers think about their practice has existed for decades. One pervasive reason for our interest in teachers' thoughts is that thoughts are intertwined with practice, so if we want to better understand practice, we need to also understand the thoughts that guide practice. Thinking is not the same as acting, but teachers' thoughts interact with their actions every day in both large and small ways, influencing their ability to grow and improve their practice over time and influencing their responses to new policies, new curricula, and new ideas about practice as they arise.

Teacher thinking is certainly relevant to teacher learning. No one can learn if they are not intellectually engaged with the topic being studied, and many investigators now believe that teachers can learn a great deal more from their own experiences in the classroom if they take time to reflect upon those experiences (Grimmet & Erickson, 1988; Schön, 1983). Indeed, reflection has become widely valued and is now encouraged in teacher education classes and included in assessments such as those used by the National Board of Professional Teaching Standards. These programs and assessments require teachers or prospective teachers to reflect publicly, through journal entries or essays, about particular teaching experiences. The belief is that making these thoughts visible fosters more learning.

Teacher thinking is also relevant to the ability to implement new curricula, assessments, or other policies. Even when teachers are following heavily scripted programs and curricula, they make numerous ongoing adjustments to their lessons based on their own judgments and thoughts about how their lessons are working and what students are learning. Teachers do not, then, implement curricula or other instructional devices exactly as they have been prescribed.

At the same time, efforts to influence teachers' thinking have been relatively unsuccessful. Beginning with the scientific movement in education in the early 1900s and extending through the mastery learning movement in the 1960s, education experts have offered prescriptions to teachers about how to plan and design instruction. These prescriptions tend to emphasize a rational approach to planning that begins with curriculum content, moves to goals and objectives, and continues linearly to resources, materials, instructional strategies, learning activities, and so forth. Many of these prescriptions are based on either no evidence or very thin evidence. Teacher education programs continue to prescribe specific approaches to planning, believing that some are better than others, even though we now have evidence that experienced teachers rarely use these strategies in their own planning. Findings such as these add another reason to care about how teachers think about their practice.

Much of our interest in teacher thinking flows from a perception that teachers are not thinking about their practice in the way their critics think they should. Critics want to see different practices, and they assume the reason they don't is because teachers either are not thinking hard enough or are not thinking correctly. So along with articles about how teachers *do* think about their practice, we find studies of how they *should* think about their practice and some discussions about why there is a disparity between their thoughts and their critics' thoughts about practice.

Below I describe three specific lines of research on teacher thinking, each taking a slightly different approach to the issue. First, there is a body of largely descriptive research that focuses on how teachers approach specific thought processes such as planning, evaluating, or making in-the-moment decisions. For the most part, these studies do not address questions about the quality of reasoning or "rightness" of teachers' thoughts, but instead simply describe these thoughts and thought processes. These studies are reviewed in the section entitled "Teachers' Thought Processes." The second group of studies seeks to understand how the job of teaching itself influences teachers' thinking. The general focus of these studies is how teachers are affected by their chosen occupation, how they adapt to it, and how their thoughts are influenced by it. The section called "How Practice Shapes Thought" reviews some of this literature. Researchers in the third group of studies are more interested in the possibility of change. These researchers seek to understand both how teachers' thoughts arise in response to the work itself *and* how these thoughts affect the quality of teaching practice. For these authors, the question of interest is not merely how do teachers think, nor merely how do circumstances influence thinking, but how does teacher thinking affect the quality of teaching practice. These authors tend to focus on how teachers design practices that can accommodate the realities of classroom life. This line of work is examined in the third section entitled "How Thought Shapes Practices."

None of these sections presents an exhaustive rendering of the literature, but instead describes a few major contributions that give a flavor for the field as a whole.

Teachers' Thought Processes

The first line of research seeks to learn more about how teachers engage in planning and strategic decision making. This work emerged in the 1960s, peaked in the 1970s, and is very well summarized in a handful of substantial literature reviews written in the 1980s (Clark, 1983; Clark & Peterson, 1986; Shavelson, 1983; Shavelson & Stern, 1981). This chapter concentrates largely on these other reviews.

Interest in teacher thought processes arose, at least in part, as an antidote to another body of research, frequently called process-product research, that aimed to define effective teaching in terms of discrete skills that could be identified and taught in teacher education programs. The 1960s was a period of great interest in precise descriptions of teaching and in finding relationships between specific teaching acts and student learning. Much of this work assumed that knowledge of these teaching acts could eventually be directly taught to teachers (examples of articles

suggesting such an assumption include Rosenshine & Furst, 1971, and Sandefur, 1970). As emphasis on teaching skills increased, a counter-movement surfaced arguing that teaching could not be reduced to skills alone. Researchers who pursued questions about teachers' thought processes argued that teaching necessarily required judgment and thought. Their studies aimed to reveal that thought occurred and to reveal the nature of the thought processes and of the thoughts themselves.

The research methods employed in these studies are remarkably diverse, ranging from naturalistic observations and interviews to laboratory projects in which teachers are asked to think aloud as they work, view films and describe what they saw or thought, examine artifacts of classroom lessons or student work and to critique them, sort cards and engage with other devices. Shavelson, Webb, and Burstein (1986) provided an excellent review of the various methods that have been used in this body of research and a good critique of their strengths and weaknesses. Regardless of method, the goal is nearly always to reveal the contents of thoughts that are otherwise hidden from view.

This work is typically reviewed according to the type of thinking involved; that is, there is a body of literature on teacher planning, another on in-the-moment or interactive thinking, another on post hoc evaluations of events, and so forth. Researchers have found that teachers' plans focus on the sequence of events that will occur more than on the content that will be taught or what students should learn as a result of the lesson (Clark & Yinger, 1987). This approach is quite different from the kind of rational planning that is sometimes advocated. Rather than beginning with a learning goal, teachers tend to begin with an activity and then envision how that activity might unfold. They think about where students will be located and what they will be able to see, what materials will be available and how they will be distributed, and how the conversation will be organized. Lesson plans look more like scripts for a play than a deduction from goals and objectives. These scripts and images of lessons have a great deal of influence over teachers' actual teaching, and teachers rarely deviate from their scripts even when they see explicit evidence that the script is not working as they had envisioned it (Clark & Lampert, 1986; Shavelson, 1983).

With respect to interactive decision making, we have two seemingly contradictory findings. On one hand, we find that teachers rely heavily on routines in their practice. Routines can increase predictability, help students know what to expect and what to do, and reduce the number of things teachers need to attend to and the number of interactive decisions they need to make (Hargreaves, 1979). Yet despite teachers' heavy reliance on predictable routines, they still need to make numerous in-the-moment decisions. Clark and Peterson (1986) found five studies that examined the number of interactive decisions teachers made and all five concluded that teachers made more than one decision per minute. These decisions occur even after teachers have devised plans that lay out the script and orchestration of the lesson and even when they are building lessons on a structure of established operating systems and routines.

These ad hoc decisions are made in response to specific events such as an unexpected student question or comment, a complication during a transition in a lesson, missing or faulty materials, or when teachers see evidence that the lesson is not going as planned. When making specific decisions, teachers rarely consider alternative courses of action, and when they do, they don't consider very many alternatives. Once teachers are engaged in their lessons, roughly 40%–50% of all teachers' thoughts during instruction have to do with students—what they are learning or what they are doing. Goals and content comprised only 5% or less of all thoughts, and instructional procedures comprised 20%–30% of their thoughts.

Concurrent with their routines and interactive decisions, teachers are also continuously monitoring the entire class. Even while listening to one student's response to a question, a teacher may be simultaneously noticing that another student has become distracted by a fly and that two others are beginning to whisper. Kounin (1970) used the term *withitness* to refer to teachers' ability to be continuously aware of what all students are doing. Even very small deviations from the plan are likely to trigger corrective responses from teachers.

Some researchers have also looked for general principles that guide teachers' actions. For example, teachers frequently use a principle of compensation when making decisions (Clark & Peterson, 1986). Using this principle, teachers give extra attention to students who are shy or students who are less able. There is also evidence that teachers subscribe to a principle of suppressing their own emotions. A great deal of their effort goes into controlling themselves and their own emotions, so that they can maintain a particular persona and a particular classroom climate.

Most of this research has been essentially descriptive. That is, studies frequently demonstrate *that thought occurred* but rarely evaluate the quality of that thought. In fact, Berliner (1990) criticized the lack of attention to thoughts or thought processes that had some known value. He suggested that the work needed a criterion of effectiveness that would allow researchers to ascertain the value of different thoughts and thought processes. Without a criterion of effectiveness, no recommendations can follow for how to improve teaching. But I suspect that researchers at this time had no interest in improving teaching practice but instead were interested in affirming its complexity and value. Many of the practices they found could have been critiqued on normative grounds, even without a criterion of effectiveness, but they were not. For instance, teachers' tendency to build plans around events and activities rather than around learning goals could have been construed as evidence of flawed planning, but no such normative judgment was made. Similarly, teachers' inability to deviate from their plans when lessons aren't working could have been construed as evidence that teachers lack flexibility or been construed as evidence that teachers lack flexibility or

the ability to think in situ, but again no such evaluative judgments were made. Instead, researchers' interpretations of this body of work showed us that teachers are thoughtful professionals, not merely skilled laborers, and that teaching is work that requires professional judgment, not merely training in skills.

In the 1990s, research on teacher thinking shifted focus toward articulating the knowledge that teachers need to carry out their work. Again, the shift was motivated by a rejection of the notion that teaching could be defined entirely as a set of behavioral skills and a concomitant desire to highlight the intellectual demands of teaching. The need to pay more attention to the content of teaching and to the contents of teachers' knowledge was raised by Shulman (1986a, 1986b, 1987) and was followed by a number of efforts to identify categories and types of knowledge that would or could be useful in teaching (e.g., edited volumes by Reynolds, 1990, and Kennedy, 1991). Much of this work was speculative, however, and evidence for the relevance of particular bodies of knowledge tended to be limited to case studies of individual teachers. Some particularly influential studies that examined the role of knowledge in practice were Carpenter, Fennema, Peterson, Chiang, and Loef (1989); Leinhardt (1987); Ma (1999); and Stein, Baxter, and Leinhardt (1990).

The first effort to move beyond description toward a theory of teacher thinking did not occur until the late 1990s when Schoenfeld (1998) began what may be the most ambitious research program regarding how teachers' thoughts and knowledge shape their practice. Schoenfeld's goal is to go beyond description and develop models of teacher reasoning that articulate the beliefs, goals, knowledge, images, and so forth that teachers carry with them and that can account for specific interactive decisions that they make. A central feature of his model is that particular thought sequences, beliefs, ideas, and so forth, are brought into play by "triggering events" that provoke the teacher's need to draw on these elements and to generate a new idea. Shoenfeld's work is also unique because the teachers whose thought processes he models are not ordinary teachers but instead are extraordinary teachers, people whose practices look more like the kind reformers and visionaries wish to see more often.

This body of work has given us a great deal of knowledge about both the content and character of teachers' thoughts. It is distinctive in its largely descriptive orientation and its moral stance toward teachers. Virtually all authors publishing in this area subscribe to the position that teaching is not a line of work that can be reduced to a set of skills or that can be prescribed from afar; instead, it should be viewed as professional work that requires thought, judgment, and knowledge. It is this normative stance, more than a theoretical stance, that has given this work its distinctive appearance, and it is perhaps also the reason the work has not yielded any patterns of causal relationship between teachers' thoughts and their actions.

How Practice Shapes Thought

The first line of research has revealed very little about how teachers' thoughts influence their practice; this second line of research has revealed a great deal about how teachers' practices have influenced their thoughts. This line of research focuses on the unique nature of teaching as a profession and seeks to understand how the features of this work influence teachers' thoughts and actions. Whereas the first line of work was based in psychology, this one is based in sociology. And whereas the first consisted of dozens of small-scale studies, this line consists of just a handful of large studies, each of which comes to us in book-length, rather than journal article-length form.

This line of work is also the oldest of the three reviewed here; it dates back to 1932, when Willard Waller published *Sociology of Teaching* (Waller, 1932/1961). Waller focused especially on the teachers' status, both within the classroom and in the broader community, where, he said, teachers stood on such tall pedestals that it was difficult for them to have normal friendly relations with others adults. Within the school, Waller saw the teacher's authority as the central issue of classroom life. He believed that school subject matter was so tedious that teachers had to find ways to force students to learn it. He saw students as continually resisting teacher domination. Because students never fully ceded authority to the teacher, authority relationships in the classroom were inherently unstable and the balance could be upset at any moment. Waller argued that all leadership is tenuous in this way and that it easily arouses hostility. In the case of teachers, Waller thought the constant struggle to subordinate students ultimately took a toll on teachers. Subordinates—in this case students—can create problems even when they give only a small part of their own energy to the encounter. It is easy for them to challenge the teachers' authority. On the other hand, domination—in this case the teacher's—can be maintained only when the dominant personality gives its entire energy to the relationship. This difference in relative investment of energy means that it is easy for students to exhaust teachers. In classrooms, teachers try to dominate by laying down rules, but students continually diminish teachers' authority by stripping rules of their meaning, either laughing them off or overconforming to the letter of the rules but not to their spirit. Enforcement can be draining when there is a large number of students to control. Waller argued that this continuous pressure was a central aspect of teachers' work and that contending with it eventually affected the teachers' entire personality.

> Between good teaching and bad there is a great difference where students are concerned, but none in this, that *its* most pronounced effect is upon the teacher. Teaching does something to those who teach. (Waller, 1932/1961, p. 375, emphasis added)

Waller thought that the constant pressure from students forced teachers to become rigid and inflexible. Teachers are continually confronting the childish ways of their students yet are expected to always and unwaveringly represent adult norms. They must continuously defend their own authority and maintain their own dignity against student mischief, pranks, and outright challenges to their authority. In so doing, teachers forego all tendencies toward spontaneity, human responsiveness, and adaptability. Most significantly, Waller also saw a gradual deadening of the intellect as teachers grew into their profession. Tasks such as grading, which depends on fixed standards of performance, can discourage intellectual growth; similarly the sense of being continuously evaluated by others, both within and outside the classroom, can discourage inventive thinking. For Waller, then, the experience of teaching itself had a substantial influence on teachers' approach to their work, discouraging flexible thinking and intellectual engagement and encouraging rigid rule-following behavior.

Another influential study, Philip Jackson's *Life in Classrooms* (Jackson, 1968/1990), aimed mainly to describe classroom life, not to describe its effects on teachers. Yet in doing so, Jackson also showed us a great deal about how teachers think about their work. Jackson described three dominant features of classroom life: crowds, praise, and power. The presence of a crowd meant that both students and teachers were constantly being interrupted in their work and that students usually had to wait to be called on or wait to get help. Praise and power refer to teachers being in charge and evaluating students constantly, often out loud so other students are aware of the teacher's selective praise. Teachers also control what happens to students through their grouping and instructional practices, their disciplinary practices, and their grading practices. In this sense, they have great power.

When Jackson interviewed teachers, he learned that teachers often had a difficult time discerning whether their students were paying attention or not and whether they were learning or not. Teachers watched for clues such as raised hands, alert facial expressions, and the like and considered these immediate signals to be far more informative than formal tests of achievement. These ambiguities of teaching, combined with problems of crowding and interruptions, made teaching a difficult and complicated process. Jackson speculated that the job of teaching requires that teachers be able to tolerate an "enormous amount of ambiguity, unpredictability, and occasional chaos" (p. 149).

Yet, while Jackson could see the difficulties of teaching through teachers' eyes, he was nonetheless critical of teachers' nonanalytic approach to their work. He characterized teachers' language and thought as conceptually simple and lacking in technical vocabulary, in contrast to the kind of specialized vocabularies that characterize other professions. He argued that they not only avoided complex ideas but actually shunned them. Jackson chastised teachers for their reliance on intuition rather than reason when interpreting classroom events and for their simple and uncomplicated interpretation of causality, in which discrete causes yield discrete events. For instance, when seeking the reason for a complex phenomenon, teachers typically sought single sources (e.g., the parents didn't care or the student was lazy) rather than complex patterns of events. When easy solutions were not available, teachers seemed willing to accept events without question and without further probing. And when referring to potentially complex concepts such as motivation or intellectual development, teachers tended to use narrow working definitions that glossed over the nuances of these concepts. There was an immediate social and physical reality evident in teachers' language and at the same time an acceptance of classroom life as inevitable and unalterable. About teachers' habits of thought, Jackson says,

> It is easy, of course, to make fun of such oversimplifications, but the complexity underlying most classroom events is so great that the teacher's search for a quick resolution of this complexity is understandable, perhaps even forgivable. (1968/1990, p. 144)

Shortly after Jackson's examination of classroom life was published, another major treatise on teaching, Daniel Lortie's *Schoolteacher,* appeared (Lortie, 1975). Lortie was interested in teaching as a profession, and he wanted to see how the work itself hindered or enhanced the professionalization of teaching. One central feature of teaching he noticed, for instance, was that it is "career-less." That is, experienced teachers do essentially the same job that novices do, and their salaries are not substantially different. Moreover, standardized salary schedules mean that extra effort or initiative is rarely rewarded. And novices are introduced to the work virtually unaided. They enter their practice just a few months after being students themselves and are left entirely to their own devices to fashion a practice.

Lortie believed these features of the work led to a particular set of attitudes among teachers. The ease of entry into teaching means that teachers needed little commitment to the field. The egg crate structure of schools means that teachers have very little shared knowledge or experiences. Learning to teach is a private, sink-or-swim affair. Teachers' isolation leads them to adopt an attitude of individualism in which they are reluctant to work with other adults and trust only their own judgments and experiences. Indeed, most of the negative events in their lives consist of interferences from outside the classroom, thus furthering their desire to be autonomous. Moreover, the work itself is ambiguous, as Jackson had also noted, and teachers often don't understand the relationship between their own actions and their students' learning. This ambiguity, Lortie believed, adds a tendency to focus on the moment.

These circumstances of teachers' work, Lortie argued, lead to three important attitudes. One is "presentism," a tendency to focus on immediate situations more than on long-term goals. Another is "conservatism," a tendency to focus on narrow goals that are easily achievable, and to

rely on tried-and-true solutions to their problems, rather than to experiment with new ideas. The third is "individualism," a tendency to define their own private criteria for success and to prefer to work in isolation.

All three of these authors showed us a variety of ways in which the task of teaching influences teachers themselves. Teachers must work in isolation and maintain control over a large number of students, who in turn must learn to subordinate their own needs to those of the group. Teachers who can't discern how students are responding to their instruction can't know whether progress is being made. Both Waller and Jackson argued that these circumstances discourage deep analysis and ultimately deplete teachers intellectually. Lortie addded that these circumstances encourage teachers to take on only the most narrow educational goals and the most predictable instructional routines. All three authors also suggested that these effects on teachers are inevitable. Though none of them directly addressed questions about how we might try to improve teachers' practices or improve their reasoning about their practices, all implied that such improvements are unlikely to be found, for the practices we see are a direct response to the character of the work itself.

How Thought Shapes Practices

The third line of research combines elements of the first two. It acknowledges that the circumstances of teaching influence the way teachers approach their work but seeks to learn more about how teachers reason about their circumstances and devise practices that can accommodate those circumstances. With an eye toward eventually improving teaching practices, these studies are often interested in understanding why teaching practices are not more progressive, or not more intellectually rigorous, than they are and whether there are strategies we have overlooked that might help teachers raise their practices to a new level. They try to trace a path from the circumstances of teaching through teachers' thoughts, and ultimately to teachers' practices, in the hope that understanding this path may ultimately yield ideas about how to help teachers find ways to improve their practices while also accommodating the realities of their situations.

One example of this work is Walter Doyle's program of research on classroom ecology and academic tasks. Doyle began, as others had, by identifying aspects of classroom life that influenced teachers (Doyle, 1979). He identified five important features of classroom life: multidimensionality, simultaneity, immediacy, unpredictability, and history. Both teachers and students must accommodate these realities, and they do so in different ways. Students, for instance, try to reduce unpredictability by negotiating with teachers about rules and standards. Teachers also try to simplify by creating routines and operating procedures within which academic work will occur.

These observations are similar to those made by Lortie and Jackson, but Doyle went beyond them to examine the effect of the situation on the quality of teaching practice itself. Determining which academic tasks students will work on is one important decision that teachers make. Doyle argued that academic tasks provide a bridge between the student and the content. These tasks determine the content students will learn and the kind of intellectual work they will engage in with that content (Doyle, 1983). Academic tasks may require students to memorize something (say, the Gettysburg address), practice a procedure (such as subtraction with borrowing), gain an understanding of a concept (such as gravity), or express their own thoughts through an essay or poem. Academic tasks are central to student learning.

Academic tasks are also central to reform, for most reformers want academic tasks to be more intellectually demanding and to draw on more rigorous content. But Doyle argued that such tasks are not very suitable to classroom life (Doyle, 1986). He pointed out, for instance, that familiar, routine tasks go smoothly whereas novel tasks are slower, require more explanation, and engender more errors and more incompletions. To make these complicated tasks more palatable to students, teachers tend to break them into smaller pieces and to present them as work tasks rather than intellectual tasks. The alteration makes the work fit better into the classroom but also converts the task into a procedure that can be devoid of content. Ironically, the tasks that best accommodate classroom life are those that render meaning most vulnerable. For Doyle, the secret to improving teaching is to find a way for teachers to manage their students while also presenting them with more complex academic tasks.

Cuban's history of teaching practices, *How Teachers Taught* (Cuban, 1984), also seeks to learn more about how the circumstances of teaching influence practice itself. The premise for this study is that classroom practices have tended to be relatively uniform, both across time and across contexts. Cuban argued that the central reform dilemma, which has occupied reformers for many decades, is how to move teaching practices from teacher-centered to student-centered. He noted that the dominant approach to teaching has always been teacher-centered. But, he argued, it is also clear that *some* changes have occurred, so any plausible explanation of this history must be able to account *both* for the broad resistance to change *and* for the occasions when change has occurred. Over time, Cuban believes, there has been a gradual adoption of more child-centered approaches to teaching and that classrooms in the 1960s were friendlier than they had been a century earlier. Certainly the depictions of teaching that Waller provided in 1932 are different from those made decades later by other researchers.

So, Cuban asked, If teacher-centered practice is the default, when and under what circumstances are student-centered practices adopted, and what kinds of student-centered practices are adopted versus rejected? His study is essentially a history of the failures of progressive movements to change teaching practices. But he used that history to evalu-

ate alternative hypotheses about the conditions of schooling that might account for both resistance and occasional changes. For instance, the structure of schooling cannot be entirely responsible for the resistance to change because it cannot explain why changes do occasionally occur. After considering a number of hypotheses, Cuban settled on something called "situationally-constrained choice," by which he meant that both organizational constraints and teacher culture shape the practices and beliefs of teachers, but not to the point where they are entirely immutable; teachers' beliefs can and do sometimes change.

Another study that emphasized the ways in which teaching practices accommodate the circumstances of teaching is Kennedy's *Inside Teaching* (Kennedy, 2005). Like Cuban, Kennedy began with the acknowledgement that reformers have tried on numerous occasions over the past decades to alter the character and quality of teaching practices in American schools but that, for the most part, they have been unable to do so. She was particularly interested in reforms that aim to increase attention to complex subject matter, increase intellectual engagement in the classroom, and expand participation to a wider swath of the student body. She noted that such reforms have largely been unsuccessful. Instead of asking why teachers are *not* doing what reformers wished for, Kennedy asked why they are doing what they *are* doing. So she began her analysis by examining the concerns that govern teachers' decisions as they engage in their practice. She identified six overarching areas of concern: (1) identifying learning outcomes, (2) fostering student learning, (3) increasing student willingness to participate, (4) maintaining lesson momentum, (5) establishing the classroom as a community, and (6) satisfying their own personal needs. While teachers thought about most of these issues most of the time, they frequently encountered conflicts among them. If, for instance, a student becomes confused and needs to clarify some arcane point, the teacher may find that her interest in fostering this student's learning conflicts with her interest in maintaining lesson momentum. Conversely, if an enthusiastic student speaks out continually and interrupts other students, even if all remarks are substantively relevant to the lesson, the teacher may find that encouraging this student's willingness to participate conflicts with establishing a community in the classroom.

Kennedy found that teachers make decisions that involve more than one of these areas of concern simultaneously, sometimes trading one against another and sometimes choosing an action because it simultaneously satisfies multiple areas of concern. As Cuban did, Kennedy evaluated a handful of competing hypotheses that had been put forward to account for teachers' inability to engage in more rigorous and intellectually engaging practices:

- Teachers need more knowledge and instructional strategies.
- Teachers' personality traits or dispositions impede reform.

- Teachers' beliefs conflict with those of reformers, and they base their practices on their beliefs.
- The circumstances of teaching itself hinder reforms.
- Reform goals are not realistic.

Kennedy found some evidence for each of these hypotheses, but ultimately argued that the most compelling explanation is that the reforms themselves are too ambitious and do not acknowledge the realities of classroom life. Reformers, she suggested, think about only one or two of the concerns that teachers think about. They may attend only to the content being taught or only to students' intellectual engagement and do not offer teachers any help in addressing these concerns *while also* addressing teachers' other concerns, such as maintaining lesson momentum and meeting their own personal needs.

This third group of studies offers a more evaluative look at teachers' thoughts, focusing explicitly on the types of practices that result from those thoughts and comparing those practices to the practices that reformers seek. These researchers examined the relationship between teachers' thinking and their practices, but emphasized the ways in which the practices teachers devise are ultimately designed to accommodate the circumstances they encounter.

Discussion

Research on teacher thinking has not only helped us understand teachers' thoughts but helped us understand the kinds of events that teachers are trying to control. We see from these studies that teachers are trying to simultaneously establish and maintain classroom norms, respond to unwilling students, organize materials and events so that learning may occur, and converse with students about substantively abstract ideas while also conversing with them about rules and procedures. We also find that they have a difficult time ascertaining what their students are thinking or whether students understand important concepts. They work at their task in virtual isolation and have no opportunities to step away from their work long enough to recover their composure or gather their thoughts when confronting a problem.

It should not be surprising, then, to learn that teachers' plans look less like task analyses of content and instructional goals and more like envisioned sequences of events. In their visions, teachers imagine how all aspects of the lesson will work together—the discipline, the resources, the social networks, the routines and operating procedures, the needs of the more difficult students, and the needs of the more ambitious students. Nor should it be surprising to learn that teachers rely heavily on routines and standard operating procedures, nor that they still, even after students have learned all the routines, need to make interactive decisions more often than once per minute. Nor should it be surprising that their primary concern is maintaining lesson momentum and not losing any individual students as the group moves through the day's activities.

The task teachers set out for themselves is not the one reformers set for teachers. Teachers do not begin the day thinking about fascinating new ways to approach particular substantive ideas. Instead, they begin by thinking about how to get two dozen restless youngsters to cooperate on a set of activities that will be roughly educative but not so engaging that students will become overly excited (Kennedy, 2005). The task is to find a path through the curriculum that can be taken by a large group of people traveling in tandem, many of whom are not particularly interested in whether they arrive at the destination or not.

Observers who look at the classroom with a cold eye see problems of domination and subordination, of crowds and power, and of students testing the limits of rules, negotiating their workloads, and goading their friends. Those who look at the classroom with the eyes of idealists are disappointed by the difference between reality and their own visions of enthusiastic students pursuing rigorous substantive ideas—visions that don't address the question of how teachers create such classrooms while accommodating the real circumstances they face. This dilemma presents the next set of questions researchers must address.

References and Further Readings

Berliner, D. C. (1990). The place of process-product research in developing the agenda for research on teacher thinking. *Educational Psychologist, 24*(4), 325–344.

Carpenter, T. P., Fennema, E., Peterson, P. L., Chiang, C. -P., & Loef, M. (1989). Using knowledge of children's mathematics thinking in classroom teaching: An experimental study. *American Educational Research Journal, 26,* 499–531.

Clark, C. M. (1983). Research on teacher planning: An inventory of the knowledge base. In D. Smith (Ed.), *Essential knowledge for beginning teachers.* Washington, DC: American Association of Colleges of Teacher Education.

Clark, C. M., & Lampert, M. (1986). The study of teacher thinking: Implications for teacher education. *Journal of Teacher Education, 37*(5), 27–32.

Clark, C. M., & Peterson, P. L. (1986). Teachers' thought processes. In M. C. Wittrock (Ed.), *Handbook of research on teaching* (3rd ed., pp. 255–296). New York: Macmillan.

Clark, C. M., & Yinger, R. J. (1987). Teacher planning. In J. Calderhead (Ed.), *Exploring teacher thinking* (pp. 84–103). London: Cassel Educational Limited.

Cuban, L. (1984). *How teachers taught: Constancy and change in American classrooms, 1890–1980.* White Plains, NY: Longman.

Doyle, W. (1979). Classroom effects. *Theory Into Practice, 18,* 138–144.

Doyle, W. (1983). Academic work. *Review of Educational Research, 53*(2), 159–199.

Doyle, W. (1986). Content representation in teachers' definitions of academic work. *Journal of Curriculum Studies, 18*(4), 365–379.

Grimmett, P. P., & Erickson, G. L. (Eds.). (1988). *Reflection in teacher education.* New York: Teachers College Press.

Hargreaves, D. H. (1979). A phenomenological approach to classroom decision making. In J. Eggleston (Ed.), *Teacher decision making in the classroom* (pp. 74–81). London: Routledge and Kegan Paul.

Jackson, P. W. (1990). *Life in classrooms. Reissued with a new introduction.* New York: Teachers College Press. (Original work published 1968)

Kennedy, M. M. (Ed.). (1991). *Teaching academic subjects to diverse learners.* New York: Teachers College Press.

Kennedy, M. M. (2005). *Inside teaching: How classroom life undermines reform.* Cambridge, MA: Harvard University Press.

Kounin, J. (1970). *Discipline and group management in classrooms.* New York: Holt, Rinehart and Winston.

Leinhardt, G. (1987). The development of an expert explanation: An analysis of a sequence of subtraction lessons. *Cognition and Instruction, 4,* 225–282.

Lortie, D. C. (1975). *Schoolteacher: A sociological study.* Chicago: University of Chicago Press.

Ma, L. (1999). *Knowing and teaching elementary mathematics: Teachers' understanding of fundamental mathematics in China and the United States.* Mahwah, NJ: Lawrence Erlbaum Associates.

Reynolds, M. C. (Ed.). (1990). *The knowledge base for beginning teachers.* New York: Pergamon.

Rosenshine, B., & Furst, N. (1971). Research on teacher performance criteria. In B. O. Smith (Ed.), *Research on teacher education: A symposium* (pp. 37–72). Englewood Cliffs, NJ: Prentice Hall.

Sandefur, J. T. (1970). *An illustrated model for the evaluation of teacher education graduates.* Washington, DC: American Association of Colleges of Teacher Education.

Schoenfeld, A. (1998). Toward a theory of teaching-in-context. *Issues in Education, 4,* 1–94.

Schön, D. A. (1983). *The reflective practitioner: How professionals think in action.* New York: Basic Books.

Shavelson, R. J. (1983). Review of research on teachers' pedagogical judgments, plans, and decisions. *The Elementary School Journal, 83*(4), 392–413.

Shavelson, R. J., & Stern, P. (1981). Research on teachers' pedagogical thoughts, judgments, decisions and behavior. *Review of Educational Research, 51*(4), 455–498.

Shavelson, R. J., Webb, N. M., & Burstein, L. (1986). Measurement of teaching. In M. C. Wittrock (Ed.), *Handbook of research on teaching* (3rd ed., pp. 50–92). New York: Macmillan.

Shulman, L. S. (1986a). Paradigms and research programs in the study of teaching: A contemporary perspective. In M. C. Wittrock (Ed.), *Handbook of research on teaching* (3rd ed., pp. 3–36). New York: Macmillan.

Shulman, L. S. (1986b). Those who understand: Knowledge growth in teaching. *Educational Researcher, 15*(2), 4–14.

Shulman, L. S. (1987). Knowledge and teaching: Foundations of the new reform. *Harvard Educational Review, 57,* 1–22.

Stein, M. K., Baxter, J., & Leinhardt, G. (1990). Subject-matter knowledge and elementary instruction: A case from functions and graphing. *American Educational Research Journal, 27*(4), 639–663.

Waller, W. (1961). *The sociology of teaching.* New York: Russell and Russell. (Original work published 1932)

PART II

OTHER SCHOOL PERSONNEL

4

PRINCIPALS

HOWARD EBMEIER AND GEORGE CRAWFORD

University of Kansas

The principal is often viewed as the key leader of the school. Principals are expected to be master teachers, coaches, human relations experts, food managers, protectors of teachers and students, occasional bus drivers, disciplinarians, and many other things. With the advent of standardized testing emphasized by No Child Left Behind, the role has shifted toward instructional leadership where they are expected to have expertise in every subject field along with superior pedagogical skills to guide classroom teachers through systematic staff development. The principalship also represents the logical career step for classroom teachers who wish to have greater influence on the school. They are paid from two to three times the beginning teacher's salary, and the position carries some amount of prestige in the community. Principals also work long hours and are sometimes under great pressure from unions, demanding parents, unruly students, and central office administration. This chapter presents an overview of what principals actually do in schools, what they should do according to some national standards, an overview of historical research about the principal's leadership role, career advice about becoming a principal, and a slice of life as a principal. It concludes with a reference section that includes cited references and information not addressed in the chapter but of potential interest.

What Principals Do

Of the many different models that have been proposed to help understand the schooling process and the jobs of principals, Parsons' (1960) model of how organizations function seems to be the most useful tool for examining the work of principals. From Parsons' perspective, schools have four major functions and can best be understood in terms of how they address these organizational processes.

Maintenance Activities

Maintenance activities are defined as the school's ability to create and maintain its motivational and value structure. For a school to function effectively over extended periods, there must be a certain sense of client and employee loyalty to the organization—its goals and its culture. Often these values are defined as job satisfaction, staff motivation, job commitment, and central-life interests and are sometimes included under the generic label "climate."

As leaders of schools, principals must establish desirable cultures that support desirable norms in various ways. Honors banquets, teacher-of-the-week designations, student honor role, awarding of varsity letters for athletics as well as music groups, teacher recognition days, and so forth are all established and intentionally staged activities specifically designed to promote a positive school culture. Principals also do things to suppress activities that threaten climate. Suspending students for disruptive behavior, disciplining employees for reporting late to work, and establishing rules that promote positive behavior are examples of principal activities designed to curtail negative cultural influences.

Cultural maintenance is both a planned and unplanned part of the principal's day. Planned activities such as pep assemblies, awards ceremonies, and staff parties are included in the school's normal schedule and reflect the principal's beliefs about what is important. Unplanned cultural reinforcement might include a principal's comments during a faculty meeting, conversations with parents, the selection of the type of discipline given to students for inappropriate behavior, attendance at afterschool activities, and the choice of outfit to wear during a school pep assembly or spirit day. These types of activities convey to the staff and community what the principal believes is important, and they typically occur throughout the workweek for the principal. All that he or she does is regarded as setting and reinforcing the norms for the school; thus, the principal and sometimes close family members are on stage at school and in public. He or she is the leader and conveys what is expected and important.

Adaptation Activities

Adaptation activities are defined as the school's ability to accurately understand and accommodate the external environment. The school's success at offering programs consistent with its community's norms and expectations is related to its success in sustaining community support. Schools and school districts lose support and respect if they lose touch with their community. Schools must constantly adapt to deal effectively with environmental pressures and must employ sensitive monitoring mechanisms that provide reliable and timely information on the external environment.

The principal must build a cohesive staff that understands and effectively communicates with the community—a staff that adjusts its programs to match the needs of the children, parents, and the larger community. Principals often read the community by joining social and business groups where they interact with community members and unobtrusively discern their wishes. Through active membership in organizations, principals can understand and interpret the community more effectively and alter the school's programs and activities to align with community wishes. Other typical activities initiated by the principal and designed to anticipate community wishes are community surveys, school newsletters, open houses, curriculum nights, parent-teacher conferences, and parent advisory groups.

A second part of this adaptation function is to engage in multiple public relations efforts to persuade the public to support the programs, teachers, and goals of the school. Schools must convince the public of the need to support the local school with tax dollars and volunteer help and must especially emphasize the overall concept of the importance of education to children. Newsletters directed to the community and public displays of the school's activities such as band concerts, art displays, and athletic events play major roles in building community support for schools. The principal's role is to stage these activities as information for parents and demonstrations of the school's excellence.

Adaptation is also defined in terms of the ability of schools to keep up with the changing technology. This means that the staff actively experiments with new instructional methods and constantly surveys available resources for new curricular material. Planned and meaningful staff development activities that focus on keeping the staff current are signs of a school ready to take advantage of potential opportunities.

Goal Attainment

Goal attainment is defined as the ability of the school to define objectives, mobilize resources, and achieve desired ends. Goal attainment is widely recognized as an important measure of effectiveness. The billions of dollars spent annually on standardized achievement tests and continuing emphasis on No Child Left Behind are evidence of this recognition. Typically, goal attainment is defined by productivity, resource acquisition, efficiency, and quantity and quality standards. In addition to processes that might lead to goal attainment, such as establishment of quality control or resource allocation systems, actual outcomes typically defined in student terms are also important dimensions of school effectiveness. The most common is academic achievement, however, student affective outcomes such as student self-concept also play critical roles. For example, Brookover, Beadie, Flood, Schweitzer, and Wisenbaker (1979) found that student measures such as academic norms, academic futility, future expectations, present expectations, and teacher expectations seem to be intertwined with overall school climate and to account for a significant amount of variance in student academic achievement.

Increased pressure from state departments of education, superintendents, and many community members to increase student academic performance has forced principals to take a more active role in the instructional process. Now expected to be the instructional leader, principals must engage in many activities: guiding the selection of effective curricular content, diagnosing individual and group student academic needs, assigning students to teachers and programs that will increase their chances of academic success, selecting teaching materials and methods that will help increase test scores, and motivating students to do well on the tests. In many ways principals are the head coach and motivator within the school. This calls for the principal to have genuine expertise in the psychology of teaching and learning and to be a teacher of teachers, not simply the building manager.

Integration

Integration is defined as the ability of the school to organize, coordinate, and unify the various school tasks necessary for achievement. Integration is the extent to which the component subsystems or people trust others' competence and work together in a coordinated fashion. In this sense, integration as it applies to schools typically refers to a pattern of organizational and interpersonal mechanisms that serve to link the various human subcomponents of the school. When integration is loose or trust and respect are absent, the result is often that the staff and students are exposed to repetition (because the staff doesn't believe the material was adequately taught in the previous courses or the principal generates an excessive number of rules to ensure compliance), significant gaps or overlaps in the curriculum (because few people are aware of what is taught at the other levels), and a general absence of a developmental sequence that capitalizes on prior learning. Other indirect measures of integration are the extent of cohesion-conflict among and between different school groups. As conflict arises, coordination of the educational program and social development suffers and inefficiency happens.

The principal's role is to ensure that all the entities within the school function together in a desirable direction.

Thus, principals may spend weeks coordinating the curriculum between the math and science department or between the second- and third-grade teachers to ensure students experience a meaningful and coordinated program of study. They might also spend considerable time sequencing a program for an individual special education student to make sure that when the student is mainstreamed, instruction is not interrupted or out of step with previous learning. Scheduling various activities within the building is a common principal activity that helps maintain integration within the school and smooth functioning of the building. Successful integration also involves the delivery of noninstructional services for children such as lunch programs, bus transportation, safety programs, and a host of mundane services such as heat, light, computers, textbook services, and lawn and building maintenance.

Examples of typical behaviors in which a principal might engage in each of the four clusters can be observed in Table 4.1. For example, a principal's attendance at a

Table 4.1   Examples of Specific Tasks Within Four Generic School Organizational Processes

Specific Task	Adaptation	Integration	Maintenance	Goal Attainment
Planning	Establishing communication links to the external environment; organizing new ideas and suggestions received from the outside; generating alternative implementation strategies	Identifying and establishing key coordination points and linkages; pinpointing areas where coordination within the organization is inadequate; establishing change strategies	Establishing strategies to build common school culture	Identifying student outcomes objectives consistent with school and district goals
Decision Making	Focused on establishing priorities for the use of new procedures and methods of implementation	Focused on improving internal efficiency and communications between schools' subunits	Focused on involving individuals as a means of gaining commitment and developing a common culture	Focused on identifying and promoting practices that result in student learning
Reorganizing	Realign roles and responsibilities to implement and sustain new procedures	Realign roles and responsibilities to facilitate cooperation, smoothness of work flow, and minimization of overlap	Realign roles and responsibilities to reduce school and individual cultural conflicts; harmonize individual roles and expectations with those of the organization if possible	Realign roles and responsibilities within the school to maximize student achievement
Evaluating	Examination of the extent to which the school's programs and clients' expectations are consistent; measurement of the extent of implementation	Examination of the extent of work duplication, work flow, and efficiency of the school	Examination of the extent to which employees believe in school-sanctioned customs and values	Examination of student outcomes
Approaching conflict	Client preferences and improvement of practice are the driving forces	Conflict between work subunits is bad because it leads to inefficiency; typically dealt with by structural or rule changes	Conflict over values is divisive because it results in loss of school focus; dealt with by indoctrination and removal of employees not sharing the majority's values and beliefs	Conflict over goals is divisive; thus, schools must take steps to reduce variance from specific outcome goals through removal, reassignment, retraining, and recruitment

(*Continued*)

Table 4.1 (Continued)

Specific Task	Adaptation	Integration	Maintenance	Goal Attainment
Goal setting	Focused on establishing feedback links to clients and implementation of new practice based on that feedback	Focused on increasing internal efficiency	Focused on building and maintaining a common culture and belief system	Focused on careful articulation of student outcome goals, instructional methods, materials, and procedures
Communication	Increasing the flow of information between the school and external agencies and interest groups	Increasing the flow within the school to reduce redundancy	Increasing the opportunity to share common experiences and demonstrate system values thus building a sense of unity	Increasing the opportunity to convey information about intended student outcomes and desirable teaching processes
Meeting	Opportunity to increase feedback and gather new ideas from external constituents and knowledge bases	Opportunity to internally exchange information to facilitate smoothness of work flow among units	Opportunity to demonstrate common behavioral expectations, reinforce desired values, and promote unity in a group setting	Opportunity to develop curricular programs and common instructional strategies to attain specific goals
Motivating	Adaptation of new ideas and methods to increase effectiveness and satisfy clients	Maximize efficiency within school and district	Promote school cohesion and direction	Attain student outcome goals

convention where the techniques of cooperative learning are being demonstrated would fall into the cluster of behaviors that would affect the adaptation category. Working with a curriculum committee to help define school goals and select tests to measure the accomplishment of these goals would fall under the goal attainment cluster.

What Principals Should Do: The ISLLC Standards

In the mid-1990s the Council of Chief State School Officers formed the Council's Interstate School Leaders Licensure Consortium (ISLLC) as part of a partnership with the National Policy Board for Educational Administration. Together with other major leadership organizations throughout the nation, they developed and published a set of six model standards (see Table 4.2) reflecting the group's consensus on what principals should know and understand; what they should be able to do; and what they should believe and value (Council of Chief State School Officers [CCSSO], 1996). These standards became widely adopted in state principal licensure programs and have become the generally accepted norms around which many educational administration preparation programs have been formed.

Subsequently, the Mid-continent Research for Education and Learning (McREL) added to this list based on a review of the existing literature they conducted (Mid-continent Research for Education and Learning, 2004). The expanded list is termed "Balanced Leadership Frame-

work" and currently is the field's best representation of what principals should do, believe, think, and know. Obviously, the original ISLLC standards and the reformulated list represent current thinking and are not the ultimate answer to what constitutes effective leadership. Moreover, conforming to all or most of the expectations contained in either list will not guarantee success as a principal. As illustrated below, the important thing is to know which behaviors are important in a given situation to achieve the desired goal and then successfully execute those particular sets of behaviors.

Research About Principals' Leadership

Society is always searching for the perfect leader: one who will overcome challenges, lead the people to prosperity, serve as the community's moral or spiritual guide, and generally help them achieve their dreams. Such individuals sometimes emerge and accomplish remarkable things; however, most have emerged unpredictably and effectively served for only short durations. In the past century, there has been an attempt to scientifically identify these prospective leaders and systematically groom them for leadership roles. These identification efforts are often classified into four phases: the search for personal characteristics of great leaders, the search for effective leadership styles or clusters of behaviors, the search for effective leadership behaviors in particular contexts, and lastly, more contemporary views of leadership based on examining the desired outcomes and the context within which this leadership

Table 4.2   ISLLC and McREL's Balanced Standards

ISLLC—The principal is an educational leader who promotes the success of all students by

- Facilitating the development, articulation, implementation, and stewardship of a vision of learning that is shared and supported by the school community

- Advocating, nurturing, and sustaining a school culture and instructional program conducive to student learning and staff professional growth

- Ensuring management of the organization, operations, and resources for a safe, efficient, and effective learning environment

- Collaborating with families and community members, responding to diverse community interests and needs, and mobilizing community resources

- Acting with integrity, fairness, and in an ethical manner

- Understanding, responding to, and influencing the larger political, social, economic, legal, and cultural context

McREL's Balanced Leadership Reformulations—The principal

- Recognizes and celebrates school accomplishments and acknowledges failures

- Is willing to and actively challenges the status quo

- Establishes strong lines of communication with teachers and among stakeholders

- Recognizes and rewards individual accomplishments

- Fosters shared beliefs and a sense of community and cooperation

- Is directly involved in the design and implementation of curriculum, instruction, and assessment practices

- Protects teachers from issues and influences that would detract from their teaching time or focus

- Adapts his or her leadership behavior to the needs of the current situation and is comfortable with dissent

- Establishes clear goals and keeps those goals in the forefront of the school's attention

- Communicates and operates from strong ideals and beliefs about schooling

- Involves teachers in the design and implementation of important decisions and policies

- Ensures that the faculty and staff are aware of the most current theories and practices and makes the discussion of these a regular aspect of the school's culture

- Is knowledgeable about current curriculum, instruction, and assessment practices

- Monitors the effectiveness of school practices and their impact on student learning

- Inspires and leads new and challenging innovations

- Establishes a set of standard operating principles and procedures

- Is an advocate or spokesperson for the school to all stakeholders

- Demonstrates an awareness of the personal aspects of teachers and staff

- Provides teachers with the materials and professional development necessary for the successful execution of their jobs

- Is aware of the details and undercurrents in the running of the school and uses this information to address current and potential problems

- Has quality contact and interactions with teachers and students

might occur. (See Immegart [1988] for an extended discussion of this topic.)

Personal Characteristics of Great Leaders

Early studies of leadership were characterized by a search for personal qualities that separated superior from average leaders. They tended to focus on such factors as intelligence, dominance, self-confidence, energy level, educational background, philosophical orientation, sex, age, and so forth. This psychological approach to leadership was based on the assumption that individual behavior is determined in part by each unique personality structure. That is, what a person is may be as significant a determinant of leadership behavior as what one is expected to do. One theme in this approach is the "great person" view which holds that leaders are born and not made, that nature is more important than nurture, and that instinct is more important than training. While these early studies laid the foundation for subsequent work, they were of limited value. After 50 years of research, about all that could be concluded from these studies is that effective leaders tended to be taller than the general population, generally White, male, possessing dominant personalities, self-confident, with high energy levels and above average intelligence. Boyan (1988) concluded that the exploration of the association of personal variables with administrator behavior must be assessed as disappointing and to date has contributed little that enlightens present understanding or directs further study of administrative behavior. Results from these early studies have, however, promulgated more complex views of leadership that spawned a series of studies on leadership styles.

Behavioral Styles of Effective Principals

If personality variables were poor predictors of principal effectiveness, researchers reasoned that perhaps, if they examined clusters of behaviors or principal leadership styles, more productive results would be discovered. Thus, between 1950 and 1980 major research initiatives were launched to examine a wide variety of styles ranging from those more precisely defined (consideration, aggressive, directive, initiating structure) to those with great appeal in the popular press (heroes, princes, supermen, democratic, autocratic). The overall goal of these studies was to find the most effective leadership style. In these studies, style generally referred to a disposition for action where a set pattern of behaviors would be exhibited by the leader in a specific situation. Typical examples described by Immegart (1988) are the nominal idealized categories such as the characterization of leaders as heroes, princes, supermen, tyrants, nerds; topological categorization exemplified by terms such as participatory, employee-centered, humanistic, idealistic; and the dichotomous or continuous style categorizations typified by the popular concepts of initiating structure versus consideration, nomothetic versus idiographic leadership, and democratic versus autocratic control. However the style was conceived, the overall goal of this set of studies was similar to previous ones on leadership traits—to discover the optimum set of behaviors that was the most effective.

Similar to the trait tradition of inquiry, the leader behavioral style research tradition has, for the most part, been abandoned. As Immegart (1988, p. 262) pointed out, the research paradigm has generated much conflicting evidence and "it has become apparent that most effective or successful leaders demonstrate style variability: that is, they score high on both or all style dimensions employed in studies." Methodological shortcomings of these studies include an overreliance on reputed or reported data rather than actually observing in schools what principals did; relying on subjective information from subordinates of the

principal who might not be in a good position to actually know what the principal does; frequent use of convenience samples; and endless repetition of studies of the same type.

While results of these studies yielded important findings about the relationship of certain principal behaviors to teacher satisfaction and task accomplishment (primarily measured through the Leader Behavior Description Questionnaire [LBDQ] developed at Ohio State), the results seemed to be dependent on the desired outcome and context. For example, if the principal wanted to increase staff morale, a consideration style of leadership was most effective. If the goal was to increase test scores, then more initiating structure behavior seemed to work best. Results from these studies of style clearly indicated that most effective or successful principals could demonstrate a wide repertoire of styles and appropriately select the style that matched the task at hand. A secondary finding was the revelation of the importance of the congruence between the leadership style, the expectations of the group, and the nature of the task. The match between what was expected by the staff in terms of leadership style, what was executed by the principal, and what was needed to address the problem often determined the satisfaction level of the staff and the degree to which the goal was met. As Immegart (1988) concluded, the implications of these results from principal style research are twofold: first, effective leaders need to exhibit a repertoire of styles; and second, the optimal style is related to situation, context, and task. In summary, no leadership style is preferable or more effective in all situations.

Contingency Studies

Current investigation in educational leadership has shifted to situational studies that consider many variables and their possible interacting influence. These approaches focus on characteristics of the leader and the situation. They describe and attempt to measure characteristics which can provide the leader with useful behavioral guidelines based on various combinations of personal and situational contingencies. Contingency theories not only highlight the interactive complexity of leadership phenomena, but also provide potential leaders with useful concepts for assessing various situations and for demonstrating leadership behaviors that are situationally appropriate.

Contingency studies have provided guidance about leadership in general and have demonstrated the importance of simultaneously examining the interaction of context, leadership style, and outcome definition when drawing conclusions about what leadership is appropriate for a given situation. These studies show promise but are still plagued with methodological problems. Among these issues is an endless litany of small sample sizes, a focus on a handful of variables—often excluding extremely important variables—and a general limitation in their ability to link multiple variables together in meaningful ways. Clearly, they represent a step forward but still offer only limited guidance for principals in their daily leadership activities.

Contemporary Views of Leadership

Historically, principal effectiveness research progressed from an examination of a small number of variables (height, educational background, personality variables) to multiple systems of style variables (autocratic, considerate, forceful), to the study of how these variables interact in given situations with different outcome variables. Current research emphasis extends this trend by simultaneously examining multiple systems of variables and their interactive effect on each other and the outcome. Figure 4.1 illustrates this complex view of leadership around which contemporary studies are focused.

Decision Context

Decision context is defined as the environment in which the principal's action must be taken:

- Transformational—where the focus is to get the staff to work toward the greater good
- Moral—where the focus is on making sound judgments based on some moral principle
- Managerial—where the focus is on making the most rational decision for the school
- Participative—where participation of the staff is most important
- Outcomes—the end result of the leader's actions
- Political—the focus is on gaining power and influence
- Symbolic—the focus is on setting examples and presenting images

- Structural—the focus is on attaining goals (typically test results)
- Humanistic—the focus is serving the needs of the staff, parents, and students

Obviously, not all the variables suggested above would be considered in each study; rather, most researchers select sets of variables from one or more domains for investigation. For example, a researcher could examine how various principal personality traits (confidence, directive, conscientiousness, openness) influence specific belief systems (autocratic vs. participatory) that influence a principal's perceived leadership style, which ultimately influences the extent to which the principal is effective in gaining political power within the school. Examples would include Bacharach and Mundell's (1993) examination of how various groups come to agreement over the political values underlying school practices, Blase's (1993) examination of the politics of school groups and how they use their influence to affect the daily behavior of the principal, and Snyder and Ebmeier's (1992) study concerning how parents influence the principal's behavior and consequently the overall climate of the school. Heck and Hallinger (1999) provided a comprehensive review of this literature.

This complex view of leadership promises more definitive findings but also contains problems. The first and most difficult is the lengthy number of potential variables to be examined at any given time. Selecting the most important ones and accurately measuring their presence is time-consuming and expensive. The more variables included in any study, the larger the sample size, the more instruments must be employed to collect the data, and the more complex the analysis. Given limited time and resources, well-designed studies of needed complexity have been few in number and have declined in recent years.

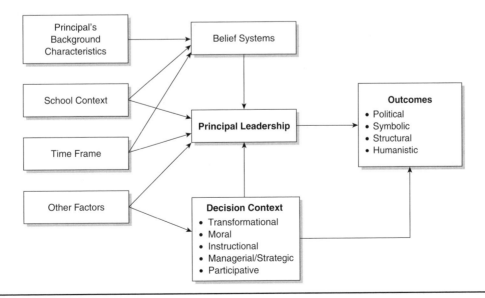

Figure 4.1   Contemporary Conceptions of Principal Leadership

Advice for Principals From the Research

As one can deduce from the discussion above, the last 100 years of educational research do not offer principals much specific advice about how to effectively lead organizations due to the complexity of leadership itself and the relatively brief period during which research has been conducted. Current research offers principals some guidance for understanding how organizations function, thereby indicating what actions might be appropriate in given circumstances. For example, if the problem faced by the principal calls for quick action, then current research would call for a more directive leadership style. In contrast, if the problem is poorly defined or the solution not apparent, then a more collaborative leadership style is preferable. By understanding the crux of the problem (transformational, moral, instructional, strategic, participative) and the intended outcomes (political, symbolic, humanistic, structural), a more rational sample of possible principal actions can be selected. The current research can help the principal frame the problem more effectively which should lead to better solutions and actions. Fortunately, some emerging literature in the field of educational leadership offers advice and examples of how this analysis might take place and how it can benefit the principal's leadership (see Bolman & Deal [2002] and Johnson [1996] for examples).

How Teachers Become Principals

Career Paths

Nationally, there are about twice the number of certified administrators as available administrative positions. However, almost half of these administrative certificate holders are not actively seeking positions for a number of reasons. Many find contentment as classroom teachers, others are unwilling to relocate to areas where jobs are more plentiful, some are not interested in assuming the time demands and stress associated with being a principal, and still others never had any intent to become administrators when they obtained their administrative credentials. They did so mainly to advance on the teachers' salary scale. Thus, overall the need for *quality* new principals is relatively high across the nation and many school districts lament that they are having great difficulty finding good candidates for building leadership roles. This is especially true for urban districts and schools located some distance from major metropolitan areas. In contrast, competition for available principalships in wealthier suburban districts is keen.

The majority of principals began their educational careers as classroom teachers. Some principals enter the office from paths that took them through the classroom, curriculum, or subject matter supervisory roles in central offices, and then to the principal's office. Others may have moved from the classroom to the assistant principal's role, then to the principal's office. Smaller numbers of principals began their careers as school psychologists or speech pathologists. Fewer still have become principals through alternative routes to licensure from non-education roles.

If you are an aspiring teacher who's thinking about becoming a principal, go to the Web site of the state department of education in any state in which you are interested and read the requirements for principal's licensure or certification. Incorporate those requirements into your planning for your ongoing professional preparation, degree work, and licensure preparation. You might also want to check with the state department of education to see if supply and demand employment studies have been conducted in the state of interest. These studies will give you good information about the availability of principalship positions in the state, the locations of these vacancies, and starting salaries.

Educational Expectations

In order for an aspirant to pursue a license to qualify for employment as a principal, it is not unusual for the state in which the principal's license is sought to include language in the licensure requirements stating that the aspirant will have successfully completed a teacher preparation program at an accredited institution and will have had varying periods of successful experience as teachers (typically 3 years).

There's a statistical concept known as degrees of freedom that may help clarify your thinking about career alternatives and educational expectations. This concept says that every choice one makes reduces opportunities—degrees of freedom—to make other choices. You should begin to consider carefully that teachers may decide to become counselors, school psychologists, subject matter supervisors, principals, or other kinds of administrators. Once you've decided, you either close the door on becoming something else or make other options more time-consuming and expensive to pursue.

If you decide to become a principal, you'll need to obtain a license that prepares you and provides the required credential for the role. A majority of aspiring principals choose preparation programs on the bases of proximity, cost, and perceived convenience. To gain an understanding of the work and expense involved in obtaining your principal's license, check the Web sites of education agencies in any states in which you have an interest. Generally speaking, you'll find that a master's, specialist's, or doctoral degree in educational administration is required. If you earn a master's in curriculum, reading, or some related field, you may be able to complete a certification or licensing program in fewer hours than you would need to complete for a graduate degree. In most states, you will also need to complete the PRAXIS examination for principals and a field experience or internship.

Getting Needed Experience

A principal's primary obligation is to ensure that the school is safe (Marzano, 2003). It follows that any experience having potential to improve the principal's ability to establish and maintain a safe school would be beneficial. Teachers who complete an effective program of preparation for licensure as principals will study safety-related content and, more importantly, will complete a well-designed internship which addresses school emergency planning and drills, the location and operation of master controls for utilities, emergency codes and warning systems, and so on.

In addition, the aspiring principal should devote concentrated effort to the acquisition of knowledge and skill in how one effectively leads in the crucial matter of delivering clear, effective curricular content—a guaranteed and viable curriculum (Marzano, 2003). Contemporary principals need to be competent leaders of standards-based instruction based on clear, measurable standards, benchmarks, and indicators. This obligates the contemporary principal to be a proficient educational evaluator and assessor, one who can interpret and draw effective inferences for teaching from test data. Teachers can gain knowledge and skill relevant to evaluation and assessment by independent reading, participating in study groups or service opportunities, attending workshops, and taking classes on educational assessment and educational testing and measurement. Applied knowledge and skill can be acquired by participating as an active member of your school's school improvement team, your district's assessment team, and volunteering for assessment-related tasks at the state level.

Aspiring principals also should become involved in activities that provide experience working with parents and the larger school community. These might include working with your school's parent teacher organization, helping plan back-to-school nights, and helping with the school newsletter. Being a productive volunteer can provide valuable experience and also provide exposure that boosts your stock when you're applying for administrative jobs. As you prepare to become a principal, you should create opportunities to be actively involved in professional development—both developing and delivering it. Also seek opportunities to practice teacher evaluation. Effective graduate programs will often include formal instruction and internship experiences that prepare you for the important task of teacher evaluation. Being a congenial and effective colleague is a valuable asset for the aspiring principal. The ability to promote, develop, and maintain collegiality is equally valuable.

Life as a Principal

Job Expectations

When thinking about principals' job expectations it will help to be mindful that there are two primary sources of "job expectations for the principal": first, the principal's own expectations, and second, the expectations others hold. When principals find themselves in job-threatening difficulty, it's often the case that they've placed themselves at serious odds with one or more angry parents or others. These kinds of situations invariably involve rancorous differences of opinion about job expectations. The principal, in someone's opinion, wasn't fair, was arbitrary, failed to use good judgment, treated someone insensitively, used inappropriate language, or another of an almost endless list of actual or perceived insults.

What should the principal do in this important arena of job expectations? Work hard. Work smart, be courteous, be helpful, be visible, be enthusiastic, be approachable, be kind, be competent! Be comfortable. Be yourself. As for what others expect, you'll serve yourself well if you take specific steps to inform yourself about that rather than speculating about it. As you work with individuals or groups, it's always helpful to work out mutually acceptable ways of achieving mutually held goals. Effective communication skills are indispensable to the principal's ability to establish and maintain effective working agreements on job expectations. As the new principal meets new colleagues and patrons, remember that they generally expect you to be cordial, natural, pleasant, and interested. When you meet with your parent teacher organization council for the first time, they might appreciate refreshments. They also might appreciate an approach that's more along the lines of "What do we hope to accomplish together this year?" rather than "Here's what I expect you to do for the school this year."

Included among the others who expect certain things from principals are their supervisors. The quality of relationship you establish and maintain with district-level supervisors will be decisive in determining their opinions of you and your work. The extent to which you and your supervisors hold positive professional and personal mutual regard will be a barometer of your professional success. It will also directly affect the understanding and appreciation your supervisors hold of your job expectations. Where significant disparities between the supervisor's and the principal's understanding of the principal's job expectations exist, dysfunctional relationships and troubled performance are almost sure to follow.

Demands on Personal Time

Classic studies of principals' work behavior by Martin and Willower (1981) and Kmetz and Willower (1982) yielded two findings that are especially telling about the nature of the work, one, there is a challenging quantity of it, and two, it comes at the principal in a virtually uninterrupted stream. A principal's work literally changes on a minute-by-minute basis. Accordingly, it requires effective organizational skills and tolerance for ambiguity. It is also often the case that what a principal had planned to do during a given period of time will be supplanted by unplanned events: traumatic injury of a student or staff member, or law enforcement officials appearing to question or take custody of students or staff members, for example. At other times the principal will need to inform students of a family member's unexpected death, become involved in parental disagreements over child custody, or attend emergency meetings of various kinds. In the face of all such events, the principal must reschedule and work around unexpected tasks. All of this requires principals to extend work days, weeks, and years.

Demands on principals' time increases with the level of the school. Elementary schools, with their relatively light schedule of afterschool or evening activities, exert the least taxing demands on their principals' personal time. Middle schools are more demanding, given their relatively heavier program of extracurricular activities. But high schools, with their extensive extracurricular activities, provide opportunities for principals to literally spend every night at school. While it may be possible for larger high schools' administrative teams to divide the workload, it is nevertheless still true that in many school communities, the job expectation is if it's a school activity, in town, out of town, weekend, or whenever—the principal's expected to be there. If you don't like high school kids, and don't like high school basketball and football, and don't like high school drama and debate and music, and don't like high school track and field, and soccer, and baseball, you shouldn't be a high school principal.

Becoming a school principal carries with it an expectation that you'll be at school until the work's done. If you have family or civic obligations that are unrelated to school, you will want to have realistic discussions with significant others about the probable increase in work-related demands on your personal time. These discussions are especially essential for professionals with young families. There is a good probability that school events will sometimes conflict with special family events. It's important that your family understand and support your career aspirations, disruptions and all. How you go about establishing these understandings is equally important. Civil, sensitive conversations will serve better than unilateral announcements.

Impact on Family Life

If you have a family, you respect, value, and love them and avoid doing things that adversely affect that relationship. Included in the list of things to avoid would be making career decisions without fully, fairly, and authentically including family in honest evaluation of the probable costs and benefits of career choices for the family. If you have a family with very young children, your youthful enthusiasm about becoming a principal may literally sweep your spouse into less than fully considered support for your decision, only to have him or her wake up one or more years later, asking What on earth did I do?

If you are that young parent of young children you may not fully appreciate the family stress that is almost certain to result when you feel obligated to attend the school performance, game, or concert and miss your child's or spouse's birthday or your anniversary. Or perhaps you're a more mature principal who's been offered the opportunity to head a bigger, more prominent school in a bigger, more prominent community at a significantly higher rate of compensation. But there are two problems: one, your daughter's a junior at your current school and she just loves it and wouldn't dream of graduating from any other school, and two, your spouse is a successful professional in your present community. Does the prospect of this "big deal job" you've been offered really offer enough to offset the uprooting of a daughter's dream of graduating with her class and your spouse's sacrificial surrender of a treasured professional position? These are professional and personal issues principals deal with on a relatively frequent basis.

Web Sites

Profiles of School Leaders

At the Ontario Institute for the Study of Education you will find a comprehensive, navigable document that will allow you to gain helpful insights about your levels of development in selected areas of principal responsibility (http://leo.oise.utoronto.ca/~vsvede/).

General Information About Education and Principals

The Educational Resource Information Center (ERIC) is a government-sponsored repository of articles, conference reports, and other research about all aspects of education (www.eric.edu.gov). A second source of information is the weekly newspaper *Education Week*, which can be viewed on the Web (www.edweek.org). The Web site has search capabilities and also includes job postings in educational administration. Finally, the Education Commission of the States, a consortium of state departments of education, also posts a Web site (www.ecs.org) that will give you access to hundreds of reports, surveys, statistical facts, and position papers on a variety of issues in education. This site will allow you to connect to all the individual state departments of education.

Principal Professional Organizations

Principals typically belong to either the National Association of Secondary Principals (www.nassp.org) or the National Association of Elementary School Principals (www.naesp.org) and their state affiliates. Sometimes principals will also belong to the American Association of School Administrators (www.aasa.org), although that organization is primarily directed toward superintendents. Any of these sites provide a wealth of information about conferences, careers of principals, job openings, publications, policy, and legislation of importance to principals.

Journals

Published journals that might help expand the information in this chapter generally fall into two categories. Trade journals constitute the first type and tend to focus on pragmatic problems principals face every day. They are less scholarly but helpful to practitioners (*Educational Leadership, Phi Delta Kappan, NASSP Bulletin*). In contrast *Educational Administration Quarterly, School Leadership,* and *Educational Evaluation and Policy Analysis* are very theoretical, contain articles more abstract in nature with less direct application, and are mostly intended for educational researchers. All of these journals have Web sites and post many of their articles online.

References and Further Readings

Bacharach, S., & Mundell, B. (1993). Organizational politics in schools: Micro, macro, and logics of action. *Educational Administration Quarterly, 29*(4), 423–452.

Blase, J. (1993). The micropolitics of effective school-based leadership: Teachers perspectives. *Educational Administration Quarterly, 29*(2), 142–163.

Bolman, L. G., & Deal, T. E. (2002). R*eframing the path to school leadership.* Thousand Oaks, CA: Corwin Press.

Boyan, N. (1988). Describing and explaining administrative behavior. In N. Boyan (Ed.), *Handbook of research on educational administration* (p. 82). New York: Longman.

Brookover, W., Beadie, C., Flood, P., Schweitzer, J., & Wisenbaker, J. (1979). *School social systems and student achievement: Schools can make a difference.* New York: Praeger.

Callahan, R.E. (1962). *Education and the cult of efficiency.* University of Chicago Press: Chicago.

Council of Chief State School Officers. (1996). *Interstate school leaders licensure consortium: Standards for school leaders.* Washington, DC: Author.

Heck, R., & Hallinger, P. (1999). Next generation methods for the study of leadership and school improvement. In J. Murphy & K. S. Louis (Eds.), *Handbook of Research on Educational Administration* (2nd ed., pp. 141–162). San Francisco: Jossey-Bass.

Hoy, W. K. & Miskel, C. G. (2005). *Educational administration: Theory, research, and practice* (7th ed.). New York: McGraw-Hill.

Immegart, G. (1988). Leadership and leader behavior. In N. Boyan (Ed.), *Handbook of research on educational administration* (pp. 259–278). New York: Longman.

Johnson, S. (1996). *Leading to change: The challenge of the new superintendency.* San Francisco: Jossey-Bass.

Kmetz, J., & Willower, D. (1982). Elementary school prinicipals' work behavior. *Educational Administration Quarterly, 18*(4), 62–78.

Martin, J., & Willower, D. (1981). The managerial behavior of high school principals. *Educational Administration Quarterly, 17*(1), 69–90.

Marzano, R. J. (2003). *What works in schools: Translating research into action.* Alexandria, VA: Association of Supervision and Curriculum Development.

Mid-continent Research for Education and Learning. (2004). *The leadership we need: Using research to strengthen the use of standards for administrator preparation and licensure programs.* Aurora, CO: Author.

Parsons, T. (1960). *Structure and process in modern society.* Glencoe, IL: Free Press.

Sergiovanni, T. J. (2005). *The principalship: A reflective practice perspective* (5th ed.). Needham Heights, MD: Allyn & Bacon.

Sergiovanni, T. J., & Starrat, R. J. (2007). *Supervision: A redefinition* (8th ed.). Boston: McGraw-Hill.

Simon, H. A. (1997). *Administrative behavior* (4th ed.). New York: The Free Press.

Snyder, J., & Ebmeier, H. (1992). Empirical linkages among principal behaviors and intermediate outcomes: Implications for principal evaluation. *Peabody Journal of Education, 68*(1), 75–107.

5

Superintendents

Paul Kelleher

Trinity University

The role of the superintendent is dynamic—shaped and reshaped by social, cultural, political, and economic forces.[1] It has evolved since its advent in the early 19th century from clerks for powerful boards to professional educational leaders like Horace Mann in the late 19th century, to corporate CEOs in the era of scientific management of schools in the first half of the 20th century.

Profound social, political, and economic changes occurred in the last decades of the 20th century, brought about by events such as the Supreme Court decision outlawing segregation in schools, the Vietnam War and Watergate, globalization, and the perception that poor schools hurt America's global competitiveness. These changes have resulted in a number of educational reforms: the standards and accountability movement and the No Child Left Behind (NCLB) mandates, teacher empowerment, parent involvement in decision making, site-based management, and school choice. These reforms have further transformed the role of the superintendent, requiring renewed emphasis on skills of instructional leadership, communication, political strategy, and collaboration. These changes have also led to calls to reconceive the superintendency with a focus on "valued ends of school organizations—student learning, democratic community, and social justice" (J. Murphy, 2002a, p. xi).

The next section outlines different stages in the development of the superintendent's role. New stages did not replace earlier responsibilities but added layers to them, making the position increasingly more complex.

History and Evolution of the Superintendent's Role

Clerk to the Board of Education: 1820–1850

Consistent with constitutional authority that assumed state and local rather than federal control of education, local school boards in cities and towns established and led the first school districts in the United States. They appointed the first superintendents to be their clerks, functionaries who carried out their directives on a day-to-day basis. The early colonists had an "anti-executive bias" (Brunner, Grogan, & Björk, 2002, p. 212) that severely proscribed the authority of the first superintendents. Local citizen boards intended to maintain lay control of schooling and "were reluctant to appoint superintendents to direct the schools" (p. 214).

Professional Educator: 1850–1900

Superintendents remained relatively weak. As boards focused their lay expertise on managing growing and evolving school districts, however, superintendents became more responsible for the instructional program (Brunner et al., 2002, p. 216). As teacher-scholars, superintendents identified themselves as educational professionals and as teachers.

Citing political corruption and partisan politics, the national superintendents' organization advocated a reduced role for boards and an expanded role for superintendents.

Superintendents explicitly committed themselves to a democratic mission—achieving the equity in opportunity for all children that Horace Mann envisioned and providing the universal schooling that Thomas Jefferson espoused to ensure an educated citizenry for the democracy (Brunner et al., 2002, p. 215).

Efficient Manager: 1900–1950

In the late 19th century, business leaders, concerned that the United States was not economically competitive, criticized public schools, which were struggling to deal with waves of immigrant children and the transitions from a rural, agrarian society to an urban, industrial society. These business leaders claimed that public schools were inefficient and ineffective. They wanted schools to run more like businesses (Cuban, 2004, p. 159).

At the turn of the century and well into the first half of the 20th century, superintendents embraced faith in the efficiency benefits of scientific management. The self-image of superintendents changed from that of a scholar to that of a businessman (Callahan, 1962). In this political climate, a factory model of schooling prevailed—"large classes, rigid schedules, and uniform approaches to instruction" (Johnson, 1996, p. 271)—with its emphasis on providing suitable workers for industrial America and its values of efficiency, competition, and standardization.

Embracing the role of manager also enabled superintendents to consolidate power. Hierarchical organizations characterized by top-down control became the norm in public schools. This bureaucratic structure ensured superintendents' authority over operational areas and helped to define a corporate model of governance that limited the school board's role to broad policy concerns (Björk, Glass, & Brunner, 2005, p. 26).

In this era of scientific management, the social justice concerns expressed by superintendents in the second stage were a distant memory. Cubberly, for example, believed that the influx of immigrants was serving "to dilute tremendously our national stock and to corrupt our civic life" (Tyack & Hansot, 1982, p. 127). He advocated separation of the races in education. Valuing diversity was clearly not a priority during this stage (Brunner et al., 2002, p. 220).

Communicator and Politician: 1950–Present

In the second half of the 20th century, school systems became far different. Major social, economic, and political events transformed our society. Student demographic diversity exploded; their personal and social needs increased; the federal mandates for special education and English Language Learning to meet their diverse needs proliferated. Students were no longer, if they ever were, "raw materials ready to be processed in an education factory" (Johnson, 1996, p. 272). District staffs expanded and became more complex and specialized. They were less easily controlled by superintendents.

After World War II, the sorting and selecting mission of factory schools became increasingly untenable. Clarity and consensus about the purposes of schooling no longer existed. Boards of education became far more diverse and far less accepting of the superintendents' authority. The increasing ethnic, racial, and linguistic diversity among parents and students also increased the difficulty of any ready consensus emerging among competing factions about what educational goals to adopt or what educational practices to follow (Johnson, 1996, p. 154). The dilemma between equity (the belief in equal education for all children) and excellence (the need for all children to reach high standards) caused conflict in public debate. Superintendents had to exercise political skills—finding allies, building coalitions—to be successful.

The publication of *A Nation at Risk* in 1983 began the most sustained period of school reform in our history. The standards and accountability movement of the last 20 years has permeated schools more than any earlier reforms. As anxiety has grown about America's ability to compete in a global economy, school reform has become a national priority, and a steady drumbeat of media criticism of the performance of public schools has increased public skepticism. People no longer accept the underlying assumption of professionalism that school people have special knowledge and skills not possessed by the general public (Owen, 1998, p. 4).

Instead of working in an environment that expects and accepts unilaterally exercised authority, superintendents now function in a school world in which power is divided among the various participants in the schooling enterprise. Blumberg (1985) stated that, beginning in the mid-1960s, we have seen "diminished power of the superintendent. . . . If there ever was such a thing as the 'Imperial Superintendent,' . . . the concept is no longer in vogue" (pp. 60–61). Superintendents can no longer issue orders. They must persuade and cajole.

What Is the Superintendent's Job?

With the daily press of their direct responsibilities for students and teachers, principals sometimes wonder about the superintendent, who has no such direct responsibilities, "What does he (or less frequently she) do all day?" The work of superintendents is often not visible to others. They spend much of their time in meetings with individuals and small groups, often behind closed doors. They also spend much time out of the district, at regional and state meetings.

Today's superintendent fills a number of essential roles that substantially affect the effectiveness of schools in meeting the needs of children. The superintendent may

- shape and articulate vision and values as "moral steward" of the system (J. Murphy, 2002b, p. 75);

- develop and manage the system's financial, physical, personnel, and political resources as chief operational officer;
- be the public face of the school system to its constituents and stakeholders as chief advocate and publicist;
- be the system's lightning rod and the first target of blame;
- buffer the system from the external environment, including the board of education;
- be the gatekeeper who distinguishes a harmful intrusion (e.g., micromanagement of instruction) from a helpful one (e.g., adoption of a research-based instructional model);
- manage the system's relations with external organizations, including the state education department, unions, suppliers, PTAs, community groups, and business partners;
- develop and manage all the system's human resources, including both instructional and non-instructional staff;
- plan and implement professional development programs for the various workforces;
- allocate resources to schools and programs;
- help the board initiate systemwide policies and programs—curricular, co- and extracurricular, or operational—and ensure their coherence and coordination (Smylie, 2006, p. 7).

Who Superintendents Are Today

We know curiously little about superintendents. In reporting the dearth of demographic information, Hodgkinson and Montenegro (1999) called them the "invisible CEOs" and decried the irony that so little attention is paid to a group in public education that is so important to the quality of schools (p. 5).

One group that has regularly surveyed superintendents since the 1920s is the American Association of School Administrators (AASA). The 2007 AASA Mid-Decade Study found that superintendents are aging, with an average age of 54.5, the oldest median age in any study this century (American Association of School Administrators [AASA], 2007, p. 19). Increasing numbers of superintendents appear to be entering the superintendency later in their careers. As a result, the average number of years served in the superintendency will likely decline since "most state retirement systems 'silently' discourage employment past 60" (p. 16).

Trend data from the AASA studies over 30 years indicates that between 1970 and 2000, the average tenure of superintendents in a specific position did not change significantly, ranging from 5.7 to 7 years (Björk, Keedy, & Gurley, 2003, as cited in Björk et al., 2005). The average tenure reported in the latest study is 5.6 years.

Urban superintendents, however, often have markedly different demographic characteristics. Political battles among contentious board members and other local politi-cians often catch urban superintendents in the crossfire. The latest data available from the Council of Great City Schools (2006) indicate that the average tenure for a superintendent in their sample (59 of 65 member districts reporting) is now 3.1 years, up from 2.8 years in 2003.

Why does the length of a superintendent's tenure in a district matter? Experts have long held that deep, institutional change in how school systems work takes significant time—a matter of years not of months. Moreover, leadership instability leads to changes in district direction that disrupt ongoing improvement momentum and effort and distract everyone from focusing on instruction to analyzing political shifts. Waters and Marzano (2006) reported that leadership stability in the superintendency has an impact on student learning. Two studies they reviewed show a statistically significant correlation between the length of superintendent tenure and improved student achievement.

The AASA study noted that most superintendents continue to be White and male, but the number of female superintendents has grown markedly from 6.6% in 1992 to 13.2% in 2000 and to 21.7% in 2007 (AASA, 2007, p. 17). Despite this recent increase, women remain significantly underrepresented in the superintendency in contrast to their numbers in the teaching and school administration workforces. Sixty-five percent of teachers and 43% of principals are women (AASA, 2007, p. 30). Björk (1999, p. 3) observed that according to U.S. Department of Labor statistics, the public schools' superintendency is the most male-dominated executive position in the United States. Despite long-term understanding of the problem, by some estimates men are 20 times as likely as women to advance from teaching to the superintendency (Skrla, 1999, p. 3).

When a woman does advance to the superintendency, she frequently finds herself in a classic double bind:

> Everything she does to enhance her assertiveness risks undercutting her femininity, in the eyes of others. And everything she does to fit the expectations of how a woman should talk risks undercutting the impression of competence that she makes. (Skrla, 1998, p. 8)

This no-win situation appears to exist despite evidence that, especially in today's collaborative superintendency with its emphasis on interpersonal relationships, women may be more successful than men (Skrla, 1999, p. 3).

During the 1990s, the number of minority superintendents increased from 3.9% to 5.1% (AASA study, 2000, p. 15). Many of the superintendents of color serve in urban districts. The latest data from the 2006 Council of Great City Schools survey indicate that 54% of respondents were people of color, a decline from 63% in 1997. The current statistics "leave the nation far behind in attempting to more closely reflect in public school leadership the gender and racial make-up of its students" (Hodgkinson & Montenegro, 1999, p. 19).

Overall, despite dramatic changes in the superintendent's role, the demographic profile of those serving in it has not changed. The overwhelming majority of superintendents are White men over 50 years of age. Despite the increasing diversity of school districts, minorities and women are seriously underrepresented, except in urban districts where the majority of superintendents are men of color.

How Superintendents See Their Jobs

In the last two decades, the national spotlight on the shortcomings of public schools has eroded public confidence and increased demands for demonstrable improvement. At the same time, the superintendent's job responsibilities have increased and become more complex. NCLB requirements have increased workload as well as the pressure on superintendents to prove that they can improve student learning. Smylie (2006) pointed out that with these changes comes "increased potential for role ambiguity, conflict, fragmentation, stress, increased risk of failure, diminished sense of reward" (p. 7). In the 2007 AASA study, the majority (59%) of superintendents felt NCLB has had a "negative impact" (p. xvii).

Despite these pressures, superintendents continue to be both confident and optimistic about their abilities. Public Agenda's Reality Check 2006 reported that superintendents have a "positive, almost buoyant outlook" (p. 1). They think their school systems are not just good but excellent. In fact, 93% think that the education children are receiving today is better than what they received when they were in school. The 2007 AASA study reported that nearly 90% of superintendents are satisfied or very satisfied with their jobs.

Superintendents in minority, lower income school districts have significantly less positive perspectives. They are much more likely than superintendents in mainly White, higher income schools to perceive a serious dropout problem (67% to 36%) and to feel that "too many students get passed through the system without learning (44% to 25%)" (AASA, 2007, p. 12).

Fuller, Campbell, Celio, Immerwahr, and Winger (2003) also found that urban superintendents have a pessimistic perspective. Responses from 100 of the nation's largest urban and ex-urban superintendents reveal that they think their jobs are "undoable." The conditions of these superintendencies (e.g., board instability, patronage politics, lack of authority over crucial hiring decisions) "set them up for failure" (Fuller et al., 2003).

Despite the overall positive feelings, superintendents express strong frustration with red tape and the increasing constraints that new laws and regulations impose on school governance. In the 2006 Public Agenda survey, 64% of superintendents agreed that "markedly reducing the number of mandates and the bureaucracy and paperwork associated with them" (p. 21) would make them more effective leaders.

A primary responsibility of superintendents is to plan and manage school district budgets, and funding issues constitute their major headache. Public Agenda (2006) reports that the "vast majority believe schools need more money" (p. 3). In 2005 and 2006, AASA brought together state superintendents of the year for discussion. "The lack of resources in an era of high stakes testing quickly took center stage" (AASA, 2005, p. 3). Superintendents complained that NCLB is underfunded and does not provide sufficient money to enable the long-term change the law envisions.

A key relationship for all superintendents is with the school board. Perceptions of the state of these relationships today appear mixed. Nearly 70% of superintendents complain about board interference in their work. Almost two thirds agree that boards too often seek to hire superintendents whom they can control (Public Agenda, 2001, p. 9). On the other hand, the AASA (2007) study reports that 93% of superintendents feel their working relationship with the school board is good or excellent (p. xv).

Despite overall satisfaction, the stress levels expressed by superintendents have increased markedly. In the 2007 AASA study, 44.3% reported considerable or very great stress, the highest stress levels reported in any AASA study (p. xvi). Public Agenda (2001) reported that an overwhelming majority of superintendents surveyed (over 80%) feel that "managing harsh political criticism and political heat" (p. 26) is an everyday job activity. A similar majority believe that their positions have forced them to make serious compromises in their personal and family lives.

Discussions among superintendents confirm that "day-to-day challenges can erode a superintendent's spirit" (AASA, 2005, p. 3). Kelleher and Van Der Bogert (2006) describe typical stories of superintendents who feel "exhausted and 'burned out'" with "little hope of positive change" and who are "looking forward eagerly to an early retirement" (p. 11).

NCLB has certainly increased stress, in part because the NCLB results often contradict those of state and local accountability systems. Superintendents have to explain to stakeholders and constituents the "mixed and confusing messages" caused by discrepancies between schools highly rated by state systems but in need of improvement under NCLB (AASA, 2006, p. 8).

Blumberg's (1985) study found that superintendents also felt quite positive. In general, "they liked what they were doing, felt challenged, had fun, and often were simply quite excited by their personal and professional prospects" (p. 137). Yet, Blumberg also commented that "the people who hold this office seem to be becoming increasingly aware of the emotional costs involved" (p. 155). He describeed several sources of their growing distress: "the slowness of the decision-making process; boredom; loneliness; feelings of inadequacy; concern over compromises of ethics; and feelings of personal stress" (p. 138).

Blumberg described one unique stressor for superintendents in America—the perception in their communities that they are "public property" (1985, p. 156). The community expects that they will be accessible and available on any day at any time; community members feel they can intrude on the superintendent's personal and family life; and they feel that, as the custodian of the community's educational values for its children, the superintendent's personal conduct should be above reproach (Blumberg, 1985, p. 156).

Overall, superintendents' emotional perceptions of their jobs seem as complex as the jobs themselves—ranging from the buoyant optimism expressed to Public Agenda surveyors to the despair shared at times with some researchers in more confidential settings. The explanation for this variance may be that superintendents develop a reflexive ability to put on a positive public face. The variance may also reflect the situational roller coaster that defines the work itself. In the midst of trying to figure a way out of a crisis, it is common to feel and express more negative feelings than when one has gotten back on top of things. And superintendents regularly engage in crisis management.

Leadership Challenges

Recent educational reforms have created new leadership challenges for superintendents. Historically the superintendent enacted three roles—educator, manager, politician—which received different emphases in different eras. Today, the complexity of leadership challenges require that superintendents enact the three roles simultaneously, moving between them as needed.

Effect of NCLB on Instructional Leadership

Today, NCLB, the most powerful intrusion of federal power into public schools in our history, has had a major effect on how superintendents enact their roles, especially regarding instructional leadership. In the 1980s, at the start of the accountability movement, Blumberg (1985) found that superintendents focused less on instructional leadership and more on managerial and political dimensions. Today, the emphasis has shifted to providing greater leadership for change.

Superintendents describe themselves as having a "laser-like focus" on student outcomes (AASA, 2005, p. 12). The responsibility for ensuring the academic proficiency of all students, and especially for narrowing the achievement gap, has pushed superintendents to emphasize the strategies of data-driven instructional decision making, such as creating organizational processes to review performance data regularly, disaggregating student achievement data, and sharing it publicly.

The impetus of NCLB for more muscular instructional leadership has also led to a renewed emphasis on the superintendent's role as applied social scientist. The law requires use of scientifically based research. Superintendents, or their close advisors, must know how to evaluate what works and what does not when choosing instructional practices.

Superintendents today must "create coherence" in curriculum and instruction (Petersen & Barnett, 2005, p. 126). They, or their close advisors, must have an expertise in curriculum—its scope, sequence, and alignment—in order to lead the organization to change and accomplish ambitious instructional goals. They also must have the ability to motivate, focus, and support teachers and principals in continual conversations about issues of teaching and learning (Petersen & Barnett, 2005, p. 122).

Teacher of Teachers

Instructional leadership requires superintendents to become "teachers of teachers." Johnson (1996) found that this "teaching mission" is critically important to a superintendent's success (p. 275). Through their roles as teachers, superintendents convinced others to lead with them, to participate in shaping a vision for change, to take principled stands about important issues, to accept responsibility for defining and solving problems, and to engage colleagues in finding better approaches to schooling (Johnson, 1996, p. 278).

Teaching teachers affects student learning. In a meta-analysis of 27 studies conducted between 1970 and 2005, Waters and Marzano (2006) found a statistically significant correlation between superintendent instructional leadership behaviors and student achievement. They identified several leadership activities including setting non-negotiable district goals and achievement targets by a consensus that includes the board of education and other constituent representatives; mandating districtwide, research-based instructional strategies, continual monitoring of progress by classroom "walkthroughs" and other review activities; and establishing and funding districtwide professional development aligned with the instructional program.

Waters and Marzano also found a paradoxical correlation between the level of site-based autonomy and student achievement. How can both district control and building autonomy be important factors? Effective superintendents allow school sites "defined autonomy" (Waters & Marzano, 2006, p. 13)—that is, the freedom to make instructional decisions within the framework established by the goals and the mandated instructional program.

Authoritative but Collaborative Leadership

Can a superintendent lead by charisma that inspires and, along with the positional authority of the role, compels people to change? Many people, frustrated by complexity and confusion, ask these questions out of a yearning for the heroic leader who can come into a district, clean up, and lead the district forward through the sheer force of his (usually in this image) personality. Johnson described heroic leaders as those who "clarify problems, create order, inspire confidence, and make things right" (Johnson, 1996, p. 7). She suggested that this image of leadership is unrealistic for several reasons including the limitations on the positional power of today's superintendent and that heroic leadership does not inspire in others the sustained commitment to reform necessary for successful change.

Elmore (2000) also pointed out that there are only a few "larger than life" leaders in any society and that "Few visionary leaders have had any effect on the dominant institutional patterns of American education" (p. 2). He suggested that another reason people in school yearn for heroic leaders stems from the belief that the core of teaching and learning is ineffable—that it is magical, mystical, and artistic—and not reducible to rational formulation, organization, or management. They believe that administrators protect teacher-artists from external scrutiny and control; that leadership should be loosely coupled to the technical core of teaching and learning; and that leaders only influence the school organization by personality characteristics, not by competence in organizational and management skills (p. 8).

Effective district leadership that brings about instructional change balances authoritative or appropriately directive (but not authoritarian or oppressively controlling) and collaborative approaches. The "defined autonomy" of schools that Waters and Marzano (2006) described is an example. Schools retain control of instructional decision making but within a clear, non-negotiable framework of goals defined by the district. This balanced approach is both top-down (articulating core values, establishing accountability structures) and bottom-up (including all constituents meaningfully and developing leadership in others). In this process, leadership is less hierarchical. The superintendent's role shifts from the top of the organizational structure to the hub of a complex network of interpersonal relationships.

Collaborative leadership that improves instruction also develops leadership throughout the organization. Elmore (2000) argued that this "distribution" of leadership is the only way to accomplish the complex work of large-scale instructional improvement (p. 15). Johnson also depicted this more collaborative style that develops leadership capacity: "The emerging conception of leadership is one of reciprocal influence, through which individuals holding different roles collaborate to improve education" (Johnson, 1996, p. 13).

Skepticism About Educational Change

Overcoming deep-seated skepticism about the possibilities for educational change is another leadership challenge. Superintendents expect to bring about change. Few enter the job planning to maintain the status quo. Bringing about change, nevertheless, can be a daunting challenge. In most districts, many veteran teachers set down roots and stay for 25 or more years. As we have seen, superintendent tenure

is much shorter—6 to 7 years at best. Johnson (1996) described how teachers and administrators are inured to each new cycle of change with the advent of a new superintendent because of decades of school reform activity characterized by finger-pointing, failed promises, and lack of follow-through. Superintendent turnover makes staff especially skeptical and mistrustful of yet another initiative. Staff cynics cite the metaphor of the revolving door of administrative change to justify their inaction.

Leading Through Managing

Another leadership challenge is integrating leadership and management. The literature about running organizations often distinguishes between the two. The domain of management is the "mundane work of making a bureaucracy work" (March, 1978, as quoted in Johnson, 1996, p. 219). The domain of leadership is the purposeful work of fundamentally changing what the organization does. Although there is validity to this distinction, it does not capture the more complex interrelationship between effective management and leadership. Johnson argued that the separation of leadership and management is a social construct that is misleading and inaccurate. Successful superintendents do both simultaneously. "In no district did we find evidence of effective leadership without effective management" (Johnson, 1996, p. 239). In fact, they manage in order to lead.

Henry Mintzberg, who has researched and written about leadership and management for over 30 years, also sees a more complex relationship. He rejects the idea that "leadership is something bigger and more important" than management. "Management without leadership is sterile; leadership without management is disconnected and encourages hubris" (J. T. Murphy, 2006, pp. 527–528).

Another way that leadership theorists have made the distinction between leadership and management functions is through the contrast of *transactional* and *transformational* leadership. *Transactional* leadership maintains the status quo. The leader meets the needs of followers, and they give the leader the support necessary to continue. Organizational equilibrium remains undisturbed. *Transformational* leadership produces change by developing commitment to shared values and capacity to translate those values into action. Organizational equilibrium shifts. Educational change requires transformational rather than traditional transactional leadership.

But Johnson (1996) found a more complex relationship between the two. Superintendents have to first meet the transactional expectations of constituents before transformational leadership is possible. The expectations for new superintendents are distinctly transactional at first. Teachers and principals feel that if the superintendent responds to their needs—for budget support, facilities maintenance, and other basics—then they might be willing to comply with the superintendent's initiatives. Although meeting basic needs at this transactional level is necessary, it is not, Johnson found, sufficient to produce a more transformational, more reciprocal relationship, in which mutual commitment to change can occur. Superintendents have first to prove their mettle as managers (p. 131).

Hardwired Political Tensions

Politics is "an enduring characteristic of public schooling. . . . It is not inherently corrupt" (Björk & Gurley, 2005, p. 168). Often we think of politics as unsavory activity. We characterize as "political" any actions that appear underhanded, manipulative, or in pursuit of selfish ends. But political skills in building support for policies and programs, in fashioning compromises, and in resolving differences constructively—practiced ethically—are crucial tools for superintendents. "Thinking politically means identifying and engaging the key constituencies whose behaviors affect the education of children" (Heifitz, 2006, p. 512). A key leadership challenge is to be effective in this dimension of the superintendent's role: politician.

In an open, diverse society, community conflict inevitably occurs as groups vie for influence, power, and resources. Arguably, the possibilities for conflict have increased in recent years as community power structures and the local boards they elect have become more pluralistic and less dominated by a powerful elite. Superintendents today have to be able to read and navigate increasingly complex political landscapes.

Political savvy is especially important in the superintendent's relationship with the board of education. Board-superintendent teamwork is consistent with the new emphasis on collaborative leadership. Arguing that authority for moving any school district forward has multiple sources in the system and the community, today's superintendents talk less about themselves as "superintendents"—individuals in whom authority to run the system is vested—and more about the "superintendency"—the network they have built of staff, board, and even community members who participate with them in system governance. Kelleher and Van Der Bogert (2006) described explicit efforts, some more successful than others, by superintendents they studied to build such board-superintendent teams.

The realities of shared governance are considerably messier and more complex, however, than slogans about the value of shared leadership suggest. Among themselves, superintendents often complain most about board actions. One reason for their frustration is that boards and superintendents have different roles, specifically defined in state law and, generally, in district policy. Among the responsibilities that set superintendents apart from the board is managing the relationship between the board and school organization, an area fraught with possibilities for conflict. Board members want access to teachers and administrators in order to fulfill their oversight responsibilities. Superintendents want to be sure that board access does not lead to micromanagement. Amid these role conflicts, board-superintendent trust is always tenuous.

Board-superintendent tension is hardwired into the relationship and it is not a new phenomenon, although it may have been exacerbated by the social upheaval of the late 20th century. As described earlier, the superintendent's role has evolved through political conflicts with boards of education over the power that superintendents would have to run schools.

Elmore (2000) agreed about the cultural and historical roots of today's board-superintendent tension. Citing Madison's *Federalist Papers,* he reminds us that "institutions of government exist to play the interests of competing factions against each other, so as to prevent the tyranny of one faction over all others" (p. 18). Competing factions, jockeying for more power, are "hardwired into the culture and institutional structure" (p. 18).

Employee unions, especially the teachers' unions, are the other group with whom political tension is hardwired. In the starkest terms, the relationship with the union is a struggle for power and authority over who is going to make educational decisions. In the history of collective bargaining in schools, negotiated contracts have steadily expanded beyond salary, benefits, and basic working conditions and encroached on issues of curriculum, pedagogy, and organization.

This struggle for power necessarily makes the relationship adversarial. But the superintendent cannot afford to treat union leaders as enemies. In the politics of the school system, he or she will sooner or later need their support or at least their acquiescence. Johnson (2006) found that it is essential for superintendents to establish firm, fair, and respectful relationships with union leaders (p. 185).

Blumberg's (1985) study revealed that maintaining such a sound and positive relationship with the teacher's union is complex because the board is watching and judging the superintendent's performance with the union. Inherently, board members are jealous of their management prerogatives, and, as Blumberg pointed out, they may, as laymen, be suspicious of an unholy alliance developing between their professional administrator and the professional educators in the union (p. 98). As the man in the middle between the board and the union, the superintendent must balance these conflicting interests.

The accountability movement has weakened the political power of teacher unions in Washington and state capitals. This loss may positively affect superintendents in their work with unions. Traditionally, at the national and state levels, the two major teacher unions—the American Federation of Teachers (AFT) and the National Education Association (NEA)—had substantial influence on policy makers, especially liberal democrats who were historically sympathetic to the needs and interests of the organized labor movement. The ascendance of conservatives to political power in Washington has coincided with a loss of influence and power for labor unions in general.

NCLB and the focus of policy makers on issues of teacher quality and school improvement has further weakened support for the primary agenda of teachers' unions—improving salary and working conditions of the rank and file. Although the law arguably has had more effect on the daily work of teachers than any other federal law ever, the law has "few, if any, fingerprints of the two national teachers' unions on its mandates" (Honawar, 2007).

Teachers' union leaders are responding to this changed context. Johnson surveyed 30 local union leaders in six states and found a recognition that this new political reality demands new responses (Johnson, 2007, as cited in Honawar, 2007). Old style, adversarial relationships have given way to more collaborative efforts to work alongside superintendents and other administrators. According to Johnson, local union leaders "see the importance of framing arguments for improved salaries and working conditions within the context of improved schools and building a better teaching force" (Johnson, 2007, as cited in Honawar, 2007).

Superintendents today often describe themselves in no-win positions where any significant decision they make will alienate and upset someone or some group. At the AASA Forum in 2005, Paul Houston, a former superintendent, said of his own experience, "I had to get a thicker skin. People who didn't even know me were always saying bad things about me" (AASA, 2005, p. 8). A factor that often contributes to their no-win position is that, unlike elected politicians, superintendents do not have partisan coalitions on whom to rely for support in times of trouble. And, unlike politicians who cannot be easily removed from office until the next election, superintendents serve at the pleasure of the school board and can be removed at any time.

In addition to managing micropolitics—contention, conflicts, and their resolution within the school system—the superintendent must also be skillfully involved in the macropolitical worlds of state and our nation's capitals since state and federal policies determine so much of what occurs inside the schoolhouse. These responsibilities require that superintendents and their representatives be well known to policy makers and well informed about policy development so that they can influence it appropriately. "Politics and policy making are closely linked in that the objective of the former is to accomplish the latter" (Björk & Gurley, 2005, p. 171).

In summary, politics and conflict are embedded in the role of superintendent. To be effective, a superintendent must respond to the unique political context of the district and establish viable working relationships with all political players, especially the board and the unions. Superintendents must build coalitions among the various actors who have power in school decision making, negotiate effective compromises, and force and trade concessions when necessary.

Balance Between Control and Autonomy

Another leadership challenge for superintendents today is managing an organizational paradox—that is, positively affirming the culture and climate of the organization and yet bringing about changes to both. They must walk a fine line between promoting change and the discomfort it can create and yet respecting the climate and culture of the organization (Owen, 1998, p. 6).

To be effective in managing this paradox, superintendents must find the appropriate balance between controlling decisions far from the classroom and allowing teachers and principals to make decisions closer to the point of instruction.

NCLB has heightened the tension in this dilemma. Superintendents face an increased need for coordination of curriculum and instruction across grades and levels in the interest of improved student learning and the clear benefit of the empowerment of individuals and school sites in the interest of building their capacity to make more effective decisions about student learning. Waters and Marzano (2006) found that superintendents successful at improving student learning both centrally control the "ends" and grant "defined autonomy" for school sites to control the "means." Most of the superintendents in Johnson's study acknowledged the tensions involved in this dilemma by "two seemingly different directions"—both greater site-based autonomy and greater public accountability (1996, p. 246).

Elmore (2000), too, described the balancing act that superintendents must master between the control necessary for ensuring systemwide improvement and the autonomy that teachers and principals need to be able to achieve improvement. He advocated distributing leadership throughout the organization. In this model, district leadership can provide guidance and direction by clarifying the "glue of a common task or goal-instructional leadership" (p. 15) and by strengthening the culture—the commitment to a common set of values and beliefs. Superintendent leadership initiatives in these two areas will help ensure the necessary coordination and standardization for improvement to be consistent across the system.

Leader as Learner

One last leadership challenge, perhaps the most demanding for the character and personality of a superintendent, is learning and growth. NCLB and related policies have committed the nation's schools to bring all students to high levels of achievement. Reaching that goal requires fundamental and far-reaching changes in how schools operate. Heifitz (2006) described this ambitious goal as an adaptive challenge—one that requires new thinking and understanding, a break with how schools operated in the past, as well as new norms and new work practices. Unlike technical challenges that have known solutions that can be found in a manual or a set of written procedures, adaptive challenges have no known or proven solutions. The new, adaptive solutions must be created and take into account idiosyncratic variables of context and people (Heifitz, 2006, p. 512).

Conflict is inevitably a part of responding to adaptive challenges. Uncertainty, confusion, and anxiety characterize the searching for answers outside of existing paradigms and conflicting with current values and norms. Under these circumstances, superintendents truly become lightning rods drawing the resistance and opposition from those threatened by adaptive change. Under attack, a normal, reflexive human response is to become defensive. Under attack, however, superintendents must develop reflective responses in which they learn not take criticism and attack personally. To be effective in building support for adaptive responses, they must, instead, recognize personal attack too as a normal and reflexive response toward a person in power in any context demanding adaptive response. They must be able to acknowledge the criticism, listen to it, and respond to it constructively (Heifitz, 2006, p. 512). In counseling superintendents not to be defensive, Paul Houston says, "It's really about being humble enough to know that maybe someone else has a better idea" (AASA, 2005, p. 7).

Adaptive challenges require that superintendents be comfortable not knowing answers. They must understand that they will be effective when they "lead with questions rather than answers" (Heifitz, 2006, p. 512). Kallick (2006) described the "habits of mind" of the best superintendents she has known: listening, flexibility, and openness to learning (pp. 226–229). Jentz (2006, pp. 230–238) talked of the need for leaders to accept and even "embrace the confusion" they will frequently feel when confronting organizational problems and to employ it as a resource for mobilizing energy for inquiry in themselves and others. Better decisions will result. Jentz also argued that that the learning and change necessary for leading successful adaptive response is first of all about oneself. Put simply, superintendents must discover the discrepancies between what they think they do and how they actually behave and learn to compensate for them.

Conclusion

All successful 21st-century superintendents must integrate high performance in all three dimensions of the role—educational leader, politician, and manager—that have evolved over time. High performance for superintendents today, though, is not just about mastering the "means" of effectiveness—strategies, skills, and processes; it is also about putting those tools of effective leadership and management to "valued ends" (J. Murphy, 2002a, p. xi).

A superintendent must focus on purposes—not only on what leadership is but what leadership is for (Furman, 2003, as cited in Fusarelli & Fusarelli, 2005, p. 198). Leading thinkers about school administrators (e.g.,

Murphy and Sergiovanni) have described this purposeful leadership. One of a superintendent's broad purposes should be moral—creating shared commitments among all school community members to values like social justice and equity and ensuring that school practices, activities, and decisions reflect those moral and ethical commitments. A second purpose is educational—developing and maintaining a deep knowledge of teaching and learning, keeping a focus on the goal of improving teaching and learning, and providing the direction and support that faculty and students need to be successful. A third purpose is community-building. Superintendents must help create learning communities for staff and students. But they should be social activists as well as applied social scientists (Fusarelli & Fusarelli, 2005), engaging the broader community in interpreting and committing to values that should guide education in a democracy. In the role of community builder, superintendents must be skilled in crossing the cultural divides that characterize our diverse society and in enabling others to cross them.

In these purposeful roles, effective 21st-century superintendents cannot be detached authority figures at the top of the bureaucratic hierarchy. They cannot afford to be distant from the publics that make up their constituencies. Nor can they envelop themselves in a cloak of professional authority. In the complex and turbulent environment in which today's schools exist, they must be out there at the hub of the organization and at the center of local coalitions and networks—listening hard, explaining clearly and persuasively, responding quickly, and building alliances. In all three dimensions of their work—as instructional leaders, operations managers, and politicians—they must be expert communicators and political strategists.

The successful school system itself must be a flexible organization in which leadership recognizes the necessary interdependence of the whole organization with its surrounding government, social agencies, parents, and business groups, as well as its internal interdependence. In such a fluid and dynamic school world, leadership authority will not just reside in the positional leaders, such as the superintendent, but will be distributed throughout the organization. In this less hierarchical, more informal organizational structure, collaboration in the interest of creative problem solving will be prized and rewarded. These dynamic relationships will unleash energy that strengthens commitment and purpose and ultimately produces sustained improvement of instruction (Johnson, 1996, p. 275).

Note

1. This chapter is drawn, in part, from Kelleher & Van Der Bogert, (2006). It is also drawn, in part, from Chapter 10 of Sergiovanni, Kelleher, McCarthy, & Wirt (2004).

References and Further Readings

American Association of School Administrators. (2000). *The 2000 study of the American school superintendency.* Arlington, VA: Author.

American Association of School Administrators. (2005). *Leadership for change: National superintendent of the year forum.* Arlington, VA: Author.

American Association of School Administrators. (2006). *Leadership for change: National superintendent of the year forum.* Arlington, VA: Author.

American Association of School Administrators. (2007). *The state of the American school superintendency: A mid-decade study.* Arlington, VA: Author.

Björk, L. (1999). Collaborative research on the superintendency. *AERA Research on the Superintendency SIG Bulletin, 2*(1), 1–4.

Björk, L., Glass, T., & Brunner, C. (2005). Characteristics of American school superintendents. In L. Björk & T. Kowalski (Eds.), *The contemporary superintendent.* (pp. 19–43). Thousand Oaks, CA: Corwin Press.

Björk, L., & Gurley, D. (2005). Superintendent as educational statesmen and political strategist. In L. Björk & T. Kowalski (Eds.), *The contemporary superintendent.* (pp. 163–186). Thousand Oaks, CA: Corwin Press.

Björk, L., Keedy, J., & Gurley, D. (2003). Career patterns of American superintendents. *Journal of School Leadership, 13*(4), 406–427.

Blumberg, A. (1985). *The school superintendent: Living with conflict.* New York: Teachers College Press.

Brunner, C., Grogan, M., & Björk, L. (2002). Shifts in the discourse defining the superintendency: Historical and current foundations of the position. In J. Murphy (Ed.), *The educational leadership challenge: Redefining leadership for the 21st century.* (NSSE 101st Yearbook, pp. 211–238). Chicago: National Society for the Study of Education.

Callahan, R. (1962). *Education and the cult of efficiency.* Chicago: The University of Chicago Press.

Council of Great City Schools. (2006). *Urban school superintendents. Characteristics, tenure, and salary: Fifth survey and report.* Washington, DC: Author.

Cuban, L. (2004). *The blackboard and the bottom line.* Cambridge, MA: Harvard University Press.

Elmore, R. (2000). *Building a new structure for school leadership.* Washington, DC: The Albert Shanker Institute.

Fuller, H., Campbell, C., Celio, M. B., Immerwahr, J. H., and Winger, A. (2003). *An impossible job? The view from the urban superintendent's chair.* Seattle, WA: Center on Reinventing Public Education.

Fusarelli, B., & Fusarelli, L. (2005). Reconceptualizing the superintendency: Superintendents as applied social scientists and social activists. In L. Björk & T. Kowalski (Eds.), *The contemporary superintendent.* (pp. 187–206). Thousand Oaks, CA: Corwin Press.

Goldring, E., & Greenfield, W. (2002). Understanding the evolving concept of leadership in education: Roles, expectations, and dilemmas. In J. Murphy (Ed.), *The educational leadership challenge: Redefining leadership for the 21st century.* (NSSE 101st Yearbook, pp. 1–19). Chicago: National Society for the Study of Education.

Heifitz, R. (2006). Educational leadership: Beyond a focus on instruction. *Phi Delta Kappan 87*(7), 512.

Hodgkinson, H., & Montenegro, X. (1999). *The U.S. school superintendent: The invisible CEO.* Washington, DC: The Institute for Educational Leadership.

Honawar, V. (2007). AFT no longer a major player in reform agenda. *Education Week* [online]. Retrieved January 31, 2007, from http://edweek.org/ew/articles/2007/01/31/21aft.h26.html

Jentz, B. (2006). Making our own minds the object of our learning: Three reasons to seek self-knowledge. In P. Kelleher & R. Van Der Bogert (Eds.), *Voices for democracy: Struggles and celebrations of transformational leaders.* (NSSE 105th Yearbook, pp. 230–238). Chicago: National Society for the Study of Education.

Johnson, S. (1996). *Leading to change: The challenge of the new superintendency.* San Francisco: Jossey-Bass.

Kallick, B. (2006). Constructivist superintendents. In P. Kelleher & R. Van Der Bogert (Eds.), *Voices for democracy: Struggles and celebrations of transformational leaders.* (NSSE 105th Yearbook, pp. 226–229). Chicago: National Society for the Study of Education.

Kelleher, P., & Van Der Bogert, R. (2006). The landscape of the superintendency: From despair to hope. In P. Kelleher & R. Van Der Bogert (Eds.), *Voices for democracy: Struggles and celebrations of transformational leaders.* (NSSE 105th Yearbook, pp. 10–28). Chicago: National Society for the Study of Education.

Murphy, J. (Ed.). (2002a). Editor's preface. *The educational leadership challenge: Redefining leadership for the 21st century.* (NSSE 101st Yearbook, pp. xi–xii). Chicago: National Society for the Study of Education.

Murphy, J. (2002b). Reculturing the profession of educational leadership: New blueprints. In J. Murphy (Ed.), *The educational leadership challenge: Redefining leadership for the 21st century.* (NSSE 101st Yearbook, pp. 65–82). Chicago: National Society for the Study of Education.

Murphy, J. T. (2006). An interview with Henry Mintzberg. *Phi Delta Kappan, 87*(7), 527–528.

Owen, J. (1998). *The roles of the superintendent in creating a community climate for educational improvement.* Paper presented at the Annual Conference of the American Educational Research Association, San Diego, CA.

Petersen, G. J., & Barnett, B. G. (2005). The superintendent as instructional leader: Current practice, future conceptualizations and implications for preparation. In L. G. Björk & T. J. Kowalski (Eds.). *The contemporary superintendent: Preparation, practice and development* (pp. 107–136). Thousand Oaks, CA. Corwin Press.

Public Agenda. (2001). *Trying to stay ahead of the game.* New York: Author.

Public Agenda. (2006). *Reality check 2006: The insiders: How principals and superintendents see public education today* (Issue No. 4). New York: Author.

Rank, M. R. (2004). *One nation underprivileged: Why American poverty affects us all.* New York: Oxford University Press.

Sergiovanni, T. J. (1989). Value-driven schools: The amoeba theory. In H. J. Walberg & J. J. Lane (Eds.), *Organizing for learning: Toward the 21st century* (pp. 31–40). Reston, VA: National Association of Secondary School Principals.

Sergiovanni, T. J., Kelleher, P., McCarthy, M., & Wirt, F. M. (2004). *Educational governance and administration* (5th ed.). Boston: Pearson.

Skrla, L. (1998). *The social construction of gender in the super-intendency.* Paper presented at the Annual Conference of the American Educational Research Association, San Diego, CA.

Skrla, L. (1999). *Femininity/masculinity: Hegemonic normalizations in the public school superintendency.* Paper presented at the Annual Conference of the American Educational Research Association, Montreal, Quebec, Canada.

Smylie, M. (2006, April). *Research on superintendents and the superintendency: Comments on voices for democracy: Struggles and celebrations of transformational leaders. 105th Yearbook of the National Society for the Study of Education, 2006.* Paper presented at the meeting of the American Educational Research Association, San Francisco.

Tyack, D., & Hansot, E. (1982). *Managers of virtue: Public school leadership in America.* New York: Basic Books.

Waters, J. T., & Marzano, R. (2006). *School district leadership that works: The effect of superintendent leadership on student achievement.* Working paper. Denver, CO: McREL.

6

Counselors

SHERI BAUMAN AND HUGH CRETHAR

University of Arizona

Shool counselors contribute to the academic mission of schools by delivering comprehensive developmental counseling and guidance programs to enhance the academic, career, and personal development of all students. In this chapter, we briefly describe school counselors historically. We then clarify the current vision of school counseling and discuss the obstacles that school counselors face when they seek to implement this model. We discuss the school counselor as a person and review what is known about job satisfaction, job stability, and job prospects in this profession. We review the theoretical underpinnings of school counseling as a profession and review the methods and approaches used in practice. Since at least 1964, school counselors in the United States have been employed in elementary schools; counselors in secondary schools were common for decades before that. School counselors deliver developmentally appropriate guidance curriculum in classroom settings. They teach skills necessary for academic, career, and personal success and present lessons on topics that enhance school safety and climate. In many states and school districts, counselors have a sequential curriculum for all grade levels that includes a set of competencies or standards that students are expected to meet at each grade level. Specific objectives for reaching those standards and methods for assessing student progress are also included. School counselors also work with students individually and in small groups to help students make informed choices (e.g., courses, programs, schools, postsecondary options related

to academic needs) and provide counseling to assist students with challenges that interfere with their ability to focus on academics. School counselors also consult with teachers, administrators, and parents to collect, analyze, and present data to demonstrate how they have had an effect on student progress.

Professional school counselors are represented by the American School Counselor Association (ASCA), a national organization originally chartered in 1953 as a division of the American Guidance and Personnel Association (AGPA), now known as the American Counseling Association (ACA). At the time of the foundation of ASCA, school counselors were commonly referred to as guidance counselors and it was assumed that they focused primarily on administrative tasks such as maintenance of student records. ASCA is now the largest division of ACA, with a membership of over 22,000 school counselors. ASCA has always played a key role in advocating for school counselors as central to the mission of K–12 education. School counselors have moved beyond a narrow focus on vocational guidance to a focus on high academic achievement for all students. The membership of ASCA has been instrumental in the development of professional standards, ethical guidelines, and training standards for school counselors nationwide. School counselors are thus responsible for functioning within the bounds of the Ethical Standards for School Counselors (American School Counselor Association [ASCA], 2004a) as well as the ACA Code of Ethics (American Counseling Association

[ACA], 2005). In an effort to clarify the roles and responsibilities of the modern school counselor, ASCA developed the National Standards for School Counseling Programs (Campbell & Dahir, 1997) as well as the ASCA National Model (ASCA, 2005).

The field of school counseling originated with the work of Jesse B. Davis, who implemented moral and vocational guidance activities in the early 1900s. However, Frank Parsons is most commonly credited as the "father of guidance." His work (and that of his followers) served as part of the Progressive Movement in the United States; it focused on offering developmental services to children to provide vocational guidance and to enhance self-understanding and growth. The vocational guidance movement was intended to better prepare students for the workplace and to help children who had dropped out of school. The work of school-based counselors eventually broadened to also include personal, social, and educational concerns. Between 1930 and 1970, the field of school counseling took on mental health and personal adjustment foci and grew significantly in representation in schools due to federal acts such as the National Defense Education Act of 1958. In the 1970s, school counseling began to emphasize developmental guidance programs, inspired by the work of C. Gilbert Wrenn, that acknowledged emerging developmental theories.

Initially, school counselors were perceived to be providing services only to certain groups of students: those having personal adjustment problems and those who were college bound. Wrenn (1962) advocated that school counselors should focus on the developmental needs of all students rather than only on the needs of those who are at risk or college bound. His influence began the movement of the field of school counseling to developmental counseling.

Since the early 1990s, the focus of school counseling has been on the development and promotion of comprehensive school counseling programs. This movement rests on the philosophy of Norm Gyspers and his associates, who first developed the Comprehensive Guidance Program Model (CGPM) in the 1970s (Gyspers & Hendersen, 2000; Gyspers & Moore, 1974). The developmental approach differs from the traditional model of school counseling in significant ways. Table 6.1 contrasts the two perspectives.

The overarching goals of comprehensive school counseling programs are to serve all students through the promotion of normal development and to address the challenges that arise in the lives of students through reme-

Table 6.1   Comparison of Traditional and Developmental School Counseling Programs

Traditional	Developmental
Crisis Counseling	Prevention & Crisis Counseling
Career Information Services	Career Development & Planning
Programming/Scheduling	Program Design & Management
Reactive	Proactive
Clerical/Task-Oriented	Goal/Objective-Oriented
Record Keepers	Use of Data to Effect Change
Unplanned Activities	Planned Daily Activities
Loosely Defined Role and Responsibility	Focused Mission and Role Identification
Unstructured	Accountable
Ancillary Support Personnel	Integral Members of Educational Team
Individual Students' Concerns	Whole School and System Concerns/Issues
Service Provider, 1 to 1 and Small Groups	Leader, Planner, Program Developer
Work in Isolation or With Other Counselors	Teaming and Collaboration With All Educators in School to Resolve Issues
	Involving the Whole School, Family, and Community
Involvement Primarily With Students	Involvement With Students, Parents, Education Professionals, Community, Community Agencies
Dependence on Use of System's Resources for Helping Students and Families	Brokers of Services for Parents and Students From Community Resources/Agencies as Well as School System's Resources
Post-Secondary Planners With Interested Students	Champions for Creating Pathways for All Students to Achieve High Aspirations
Clinical Model Focused on Student Deficits	Counseling Model, Building on Student Strengths

diation and prevention. Within this framework, effective school counseling is largely measured by increases in the academic achievement of students. The ASCA National Model describes four components of the school counselor's role: guidance curriculum, individual planning, responsive services, and system support. In response to the CGPM as well as the school reform movement of the late 1990s and early 2000s, the American School Counselor Association (ASCA) developed the ASCA National Model (ASCA, 2005). The four themes of the ASCA National Model are (1) leadership, (2) advocacy, (3) collaboration, and (4) systemic change. These themes overlap as school counselors who work within this model serve as leaders engaged in promoting systemic change through advocacy and collaboration. The ASCA National Model is relatively new and thus has not been fully implemented throughout the nation.

Although CGPM and the ASCA National Model represent clear advances in conceptualizing an organizational structure for school counseling programs, these approaches have some deficiencies. The prescriptive nature of these models creates three basic problems: (1) the programs in these models are not linked to a set of identified needs, but instead are based on a preconceived set of competencies; (2) recommended interventions are not linked to expected outcomes; and (3) the evaluation of outcomes is not clearly linked to the development and improvement of interventions (Brown & Trusty, 2005). Furthermore, some assumptions and recommendations in the ASCA National Model are based more on theory and clinical lore than on research. As these concerns are addressed, it is likely that the structure and approach of the ASCA National Model will continue to evolve.

Another concern is that the expectations of administrators may not coincide with the role of the school counselor described in the model. Quasi-administrative tasks and sundry clerical chores have historically been assigned to counselors by their administrators. Individual counselors need to advocate for a program and role that aligns with current thinking about the best way for counselors to enhance student success. This will require reassignments of tasks and changes in the ways that counselors spend their time.

Because school counselors have teaching responsibilities for the guidance curriculum, states have, in the past, required that they have some experience as a classroom teacher as a condition for certification. The limited research on this question has produced evidence that school counselors with and without teaching experience are equally effective. Although only three states currently require teaching experience for school counselor certification, there remains the perception that school counselors need teaching experience to be effective, and some individual schools and districts maintain this requirement. This position maintains that schools are an educational, rather than a clinical, setting and that all personnel need to have an appreciation for the context and culture of schools. Just as school administrators typically begin their careers in the classroom, some believe that is also necessary for school counselors. Particularly in their role as consultants to teachers, it is argued that a teaching background enhances counselors' credibility. This same line of reasoning, however, could be used to say that being a parent enhances a school counselor's (or teacher's or principal's) credibility with parents; it has never been suggested that parenthood be a requirement to be an educator. We maintain that school counselors' training and expertise, and the quality of their contributions, are sufficient to overcome these biases. Dixon Rayle (2006) found no difference in perceived job stress and the sense that they mattered to others between school counselors who had been teachers and those who had not, and also reported greater job satisfaction in school counselors who had not been teachers.

Interestingly, school counselors are trained in master's degree programs that have the same core requirements as those for counselors in mental health and counseling settings. The differences in training commonly are the addition of a few school counseling–specific courses and the practicum and internship experiences, which are in the K–12 school setting. The core requirements for master's degrees in counseling are: Human Growth and Development, Counseling Theories, Individual Counseling, Group Counseling, Social and Cultural Foundations, Testing/Appraisal, Program Evaluation, and Career Development. These requirements are established by the Council for Counseling and Related Educational Programs (CACREP), which grants approval to graduate training programs. Most programs, even if they are not CACREP approved, follow the basic requirements that CACREP has established.

The Person and the Job

School counselors are interested in helping others. They are understanding, compassionate, good listeners, and they are sensitive to others' feelings and needs. To be successful, school counselors need to be adaptable and flexible to deal with a variety of situations and people. They must be good at collaborating and have a high tolerance for stress. They need to have excellent communication skills, and they should be resourceful in gathering information and solving problems. Although some school counselors are former teachers, often those to whom students are drawn to discuss personal concerns, others made career changes because of a desire to improve the lives of children and a conviction that schools are places to reach many children.

Although national data are not available, research reporting demographics of school counselors consistently finds the vast majority of current school counselors are Caucasian females. Also, in many studies, the largest age group is 50 and above.

While the work setting is the same for all school personnel, counselors often have longer days or school years.

The need to meet with parents (who may be unable to miss work for meetings during school hours) and others, and to accomplish other record-keeping or data-collection tasks while being available to students and staff during regular school hours, may mean arriving early or leaving later than classroom teachers. Duties for registration of new students often begin before teachers report for duty in the fall and extend beyond the end of the school year. Counselors are generally paid for the extended-year period, but districts and states vary in whether they compensate counselors on the teachers' salary scale or a separate scale.

Data from 2004 indicated that the median annual salary for elementary and secondary school counselors was $51,160, which was the highest among counselors across settings (Ruhl, n.d.). In 2003–04, there were 60,800 employed in elementary schools and 40,600 working in secondary schools. Almost a third of elementary counselors were part-time, compared to only 6% of secondary counselors (National Center for Education Statistics, 2007). Elementary counselors had an average caseload of 372 students, while secondary counselors worked with an average of 321 students. Elementary counselors are generally the only counselor in the school (and many work part-time in several schools), while secondary counselors are generally part of a counseling department. School counselors in high-poverty schools had somewhat larger average caseloads (380) than those in low-poverty schools (346).

Several studies have examined job satisfaction and stability among school counselors. One source (Ruhl, n.d.) reported that 60% of new school counselors leave the field within two years. DeMato and Curcio (2004) surveyed members of the Virginia School Counselor Association who worked in elementary schools; they were interested in changes in job satisfaction after a state requirement mandating elementary school counselors was dropped, and mandated high-stakes testing was implemented. Previous surveys (1988 and 1995) had found that 93.4% and 96.3% of elementary school counselors were satisfied with their jobs, respectively. DeMato and Curcio reported that 91% of elementary school counselors surveyed were satisfied or very satisfied with their jobs. As in the previous studies, the only source of job satisfaction that was rated in the "dissatisfied" range was compensation. Baggerly and Osborn (2006) surveyed elementary and secondary school counselors in Florida and reported that 85% of their sample was satisfied or very satisfied with their jobs. However, 13% of participants were undecided about whether they would continue in the career, and 11% were planning to quit or retire. On average, the counselors in this sample perceived increased job stress in the previous two years, with middle and high school counselors reporting a greater increase in stress than elementary counselors.

The only national survey of job satisfaction among school counselors found that elementary-level counselors were most satisfied with their jobs and experienced the least degree of job-related stress of all levels (Dixon Rayle, 2006). High school counselors were the least satisfied with their jobs, had the highest levels of job-related stress, and had the lowest levels of perceived mattering to others. Middle school counselors reported the highest levels of perceived mattering. They reported that they mattered most to students and least to teachers with whom they worked, while elementary counselors perceived they mattered most to the parent group.

The U.S. Department of Labor (2006) projects that employment for school counselors will grow at least as much as the national average through 2014. Factors that bode well for the future are increasing numbers of states mandating elementary school counselors and increased responsibilities of school counselors. Budgetary constraints, however, are likely to work against job growth, unless grants and subsidies provide increased support for school counseling positions. Rural and inner-city schools are likely to see the greatest job growth for school counselors.

Theory

Today's school counselor works to deliver a comprehensive developmental school counseling program. These programs are defined as (a) comprehensive in scope, (b) preventive in design, and (c) developmental in nature (ASCA, 2005). In theory, programs that are comprehensive in scope focus on the needs of all students, K–12, with an emphasis on students' academic success and successful development. School counseling programs are preventive in design in that they teach students the skills and provide them learning opportunities that empower them with the ability to learn. School counselors deliver programs of preventive education that provide academic, career, and personal/social development experiences. Comprehensive developmental school counseling programs are designed to meet the needs of students throughout all developmental stages. Services are sequentially planned in order to meet the needs of children and adolescents as they progress through the developmental pathways.

The philosophy of developmental counseling provides the basic assumptions on which the field is based. These assumptions are as follows:

- Students normally develop in ways similar to those of others their same age.
- Despite these similarities, each student's needs are based on a unique combination of individual, cultural, and contextual variables.
- If students are offered a curriculum that is both developmental and preventive in nature, they will be able to develop life skills that enhance their ability to communicate effectively, resolve conflicts, make good decisions, act responsibly, and live fulfilling lives.
- The school counselor has the responsibility for the design and implementation of the developmental school counseling program.

- A coordinated approach to school counseling ensures that (a) the skills and training of the counselor are used to optimum advantage, (b) the invaluable work of social workers, nurses, and psychologists interface effectively with the counseling program, (c) the classroom teacher's important role in guidance is strengthened, and (d) parents, caregivers, and other community resources are kept informed and urged to participate more actively in the education of children.
- School counselors take a systems perspective on helping students. They are involved in shaping school climate, implementing preventive programs, and advocating for the needs of all students.
- School counselors are most effective when they respond to students' needs with individual, group, and classroom guidance approaches based on the assumption that as individuals grow, they encounter developmental challenges that, if met, enable them to act in ways that best serve them and society responsibly and positively.
- The counseling program and its components need to be systematically and regularly evaluated for effectiveness. Changes to the program and services rendered should be made regularly in response to these evaluations.

School counselors commonly divide their work into three domains of focus: career, academic, and personal/ social development. Career development focuses on the acquisition of skills, attitudes, and knowledge that prepare students to transition from school to work and from job to job across the lifespan. Counselors provide services to help students understand and respond well to the intersection of their personal qualities, training, and education with their career choices. School counselors focus on the academic development of all students and focus on providing services that maximize students' ability and desire to learn, helping them make connections between their academic development and their personal and career development, and ultimately make informed decisions regarding their futures. Finally, it is important for counselors to address students' personal and social development.

Methods Used by School Counselors

Individual Counseling

School counselors provide many services to students and are trained to use various methods and approaches to support the development of students. One of the methods they use is individual counseling, or one-on-one meetings with students. Sometimes such meetings focus on academics, such as reviewing the student's progress toward graduation, reviewing scores on standardized tests, making decisions about courses to take, and sorting out post–high school options. School counselors also provide individual counseling focused on personal or social concerns. Students are referred to school counselors (or refer themselves)

when personal concerns interfere with their ability to focus on academics. School counselors have training in basic counseling skills just as do mental health counselors, and they are well-trained to work with individual students who need support. School counselors exhibit the core conditions identified by Carl Rogers (1957), which are believed to create the climate necessary for counseling to be helpful: empathic understanding, congruence/genuineness, and unconditional positive regard.

School counselors also learn basic counseling theories, skills, and techniques. Some rely on a particular counseling theory to guide their practice, while others may integrate techniques from a number of theoretical perspectives. Counseling theories that are particularly suited to the school setting include Brief Solution-Focused Counseling (BSFC), Reality Therapy (now known as Choice Theory), Rational Emotive Behavioral Therapy (REBT), and other Cognitive Behavioral Theories. In the school setting, however, where the focus is on academics and the national average school counselor-to-student ratio is 479:1 (with 229:1 at the high school level and 882:1 at the elementary level), school counselors are unable to provide long-term ongoing counseling to individuals. In some urban settings, this ratio can swell to over 1,000 high school students to one counselor. These ratios include schools with no counselors in the calculations; many elementary schools do not have school counselors on staff. In many schools, counselors will meet with an individual student a limited number of times (often established by district policy) and refer those who need more intensive services to providers in the community. School counselors do not turn away students in need, but help manage the urgent situation while assisting them in obtaining long-term professional help.

When students with behavioral problems are referred to the school counselor, the counselor does not function as a disciplinarian. Rather, the counselor will help the students with personal issues that may be causing the inappropriate behaviors. If the problems cannot be resolved in a few meetings, the school counselor may refer the student for outside services or to the child study team in the school to consider other strategies for helping the child behave more appropriately.

Group Counseling

Group counseling is another method used by school counselors. Working with a small (3–10) group of students who share common concerns is not only a more efficient use of counselor time, but may be more effective. Groups provide the opportunity for members to learn from each other and to practice skills with peers. Yalom and Leszcz (2005) described a set of curative or therapeutic factors that explain the effectiveness of groups. Those that are most applicable to school groups are listed in Table 6.2.

Groups are appropriate at all school levels, but the length and format must be adjusted to fit capabilities and needs of participants. At the elementary level, groups will

Table 6.2   Therapeutic Factors in Groups

Therapeutic Factors	Explanation
Instillation of Hope	When students see others who have successfully managed the problem, they are more hopeful that they too can overcome their challenges.
Universality	Getting to know other students with similar challenges helps students realize they are not alone. This is a very powerful factor.
Altruism	Students benefit from helping others. They feel valued and useful. This may increase self-esteem.
Development of Socializing Techniques	The group provides an opportunity to learn and practice social and interpersonal skills.
Imitative Behavior	Members may learn new behaviors by observing and modeling other members.
Catharsis	Students may express feelings and emotions they have been unable to express in other situations and often feel relieved and cared for by the group.
Direct Advice	Other members may have suggestions for handling challenges.
Interpersonal Learning	Group members receive feedback from others and may realize how they affect others. Some members may take the opportunity to use the feedback and experiment in the group with new ways of relating to others.

typically have fewer members (3–5) and meet for shorter periods (20–30 minutes), sometimes more than once per week. Middle school groups can be effective with up to 8 members, and meetings of 45–50 minutes, usually coinciding with class periods, are the usual schedule. Middle school groups may have weekly meetings for 6–8 weeks. Groups in high schools may have up to 12 members, and they may meet weekly for a semester or longer, depending on the needs of the group and availability of time.

With the emphasis on academic achievement, teachers and administrators may be reluctant to release students from classes to attend groups. Counselors need to respond to this challenge in several ways by educating the stakeholders in the ways in which personal issues interfere with learning, by collecting and analyzing data that demonstrate the positive outcomes of the groups, and by using creative scheduling strategies to protect students' time in class (meeting during lunch or before or after school) although these arrangements may not be ideal. Other counselors arrange a rotating schedule for groups so that students do not often miss the same class or activity.

Groups in schools are usually either psychoeducational groups or counseling groups. Psychoeducational groups, or guidance groups, have the goal of imparting needed information to generally well-functioning individuals. The small group format allows information to be presented, discussed, and often practiced using a variety of skill-building exercises. These groups are usually structured around a particular focus, such as stress management, body image, divorce, substance abuse prevention, and so forth. Some schools offer groups for students whose parents are in the military or for students who have an incarcerated parent. Students who are invited to participate in guidance groups are usually considered at risk for devel-

oping problems, and the group is designed to prevent problems from developing. Psychoeducational groups are geared toward prevention.

Counseling groups help students who are experiencing problems and focus on providing support, feedback, and problem solving. Some of the topics mentioned for guidance groups may also be the focus of counseling groups, but there is less focus on providing information and more emphasis on providing emotional support and addressing problems that are occurring as a result of these situations. Most school counseling groups assist students to recognize and use their strengths and resources. Some counseling groups have little structure, allowing students to bring up issues that concern them in the moment. These groups are used more often with older students. Other groups incorporate a focus on changing self-defeating behaviors, helping members apply such changes outside the group, and improving interpersonal skills. School counselors help group members develop norms for behavior in the group, which always include confidentiality and respect for others. Counseling groups may be offered to students who have experienced a loss, who have a difficult family situation, who have been victimized in school, or who have had substance abuse problems. Parental permission is generally required when students participate in groups at school.

Classroom Guidance

Classroom guidance lessons are planned and delivered by school counselors in the classroom setting. Here the counselor serves all students, not merely those in crisis. The lessons are focused on teaching related to the personal/social, academic, and career domains. Counselors are educated about human development, and they consider needs of students at different stages of development when designing lessons. School counselors develop guidance curricula that are based on sound developmental and educational principles. Often counselors have a regular schedule of classroom visits and presentations that are designed to teach useful skills and behaviors. Experts recommend that guidance curricula be aligned with academic areas and include identified goals, objectives, specific competencies, and standards by which students' achievement of the competencies can be measured.

Elementary and middle school counselors spend much of their time doing classroom guidance lessons (35%–40%); whereas high school counselors spend less (20%). Topics vary with age. Elementary lessons may teach students about friendship, conflict, making choices, etc. At middle and high school, the focus shifts to more academic issues, such as selecting courses, test anxiety, effective interpersonal communication, etc. Typically, classroom teachers remain in the classroom and are then able to reinforce the lessons presented by the counselor.

The guidance curriculum may include prevention programs that focus on issues that interfere with student learning and with leading productive lives. Many schools are concerned about school violence and bullying and substance abuse, and the counselor is often the most prepared and best-informed person to coordinate school efforts to prevent such problems. Presenting classroom lessons enhances the visibility and credibility of the counselor. Thus, students who have needs are more likely to approach the counselor. Through frequent classroom participation, counselors also have an opportunity to observe students and note those that may need other services (individual or group counseling) without waiting for the student to seek out the counselor.

Consultation

Consulting means the counselor works with someone other than the student in order to help the student. The person with whom the counselor consults might be a classroom teacher, an administrator, a caregiver, or a member of an outside agency that is working with the student. The goal of the consultation is to help the student. The school counselor uses his or her expertise and communication skills to provide help and information that will allow others to better serve the student.

The school counselor may gather information about the student to get a more complete picture of the student's needs. If a student is referred to the counselor because of classroom behavior problems, the counselor may consult with teachers and parents in addition to meeting with and observing the student. The counselor may also work with teachers to implement different strategies that might change the student's behavior. At an IEP, 504, or child study team meeting, the counselor consults with team members and offers suggestions. The school counselor is an advocate for the student, ensuring that the student's interests are represented and that the outcomes are appropriate for the situation and the child. The counselor can also serve as a consultant to the entire school, and often does so when engaging in activities or plans to improve school climate or implementing new programs.

Outreach

School counselors might request outside agencies to assist the school in projects, such as arranging for guests at school career fairs or soliciting shadowing experiences for students interested in a particular career. Outreach also involves identifying outside programs, agencies, and opportunities for students. There may be special programs, summer opportunities, or correspondence and online courses about which the counselor gathers and disseminates information.

Family outreach is particularly important. Various strategies are used to engage families (open house events, career days, and parent-teacher conferences). While popular, these activities typically reach only some families, so school counselors use other strategies to communicate with families. Welcome letters sent to students when the year begins introduce school counselors and emphasize their interest in forming partnerships with families. Packets, flyers, and other materials about the school counselor are provided with the letter. Some counselors distribute calendars on which important counseling-related events are noted and use newsletters to advertise activities and make announcements.

School counselors establish relationships with key community resources that reflect and represent the cultural diversity of the school. Both formal and informal community resources may be needed, and maintaining ongoing relationships with "cultural brokers" who can assist with translation and serve as a liaison to diverse communities facilitates the process.

School counselors are in an excellent position to change negative perceptions that some parents and caregivers hold of the school by making home visits or telephone calls to families when problems are not the focus. This conveys the message that the counselor is interested in the positive accomplishments of students, not just negative behaviors. Such activities are particularly useful when parents' or caregivers' jobs, transportation and child care concerns, and other obstacles make it difficult for them to come to school. School counselors in schools where parent participation has historically been low may incorporate innovative elements to bring them to the school. Providing meals, holding raffles for goods and services, and providing child care at events are often successful at increasing participation. These strategies involve outreach to community partners, who may donate food or services for these occasions.

In many communities regular meetings of all human service agencies are held, and school counselors attending these meetings can establish personal networks with other professionals. This creates a pool of resources to call upon when needs arise and provides an opportunity for school counselors to educate other agencies about students.

Crisis Response

A *crisis*—as defined by school counselors—is an unpredictable event outside the normal school experience that creates extreme stress and disrupts the normal functioning of many students and staff in the school. The event might occur outside the school, but if it affects the school, a crisis response is needed. Typically, school counselors are members of a crisis response team and often serve on district-level crisis response teams. Because of their knowledge of students and staff, school counselors are in a unique position to provide crisis response services and to advise administrators. Teachers often need support during and after a crisis, and counselors can provide teachers with accurate information and even prepare written instructions or scripts for communicating information to students. Counselors may conduct classroom discussions related to the crisis and provide support and referrals to teachers who are personally affected. Counselors use their knowledge of students to identify those most likely to need additional or emergency mental health services (typically those closest physically to an incident or emotionally to a deceased student or staff). They then make appropriate referrals and expedite those for students at high risk. They also often contact families to make them aware of the crisis and the need for close attention to their child. For many students, support groups and brief individual counseling with the school counselor will be sufficient. Counselors also monitor affected persons over the long term because a crisis has both immediate and long-term consequences that vary among exposed individuals.

School counselors strive to build trusting relationships with parents and guardians. These relationships position the counselor as the person that caregivers will best respond to when they need to be informed of a crisis. School counselors also ensure that the school's response is culturally appropriate and sensitive. For example, when there is a death of a student or staff member, school counselors demonstrate cultural awareness by responding to students and their families in a culturally sensitive manner. They may call upon outside agencies (or counselors from other schools) for assistance in a large-scale crisis. Having well-established relationships with those agencies and personnel expedites that process.

Using Data

School counselors frequently use data and have responsibilities for coordinating the administration of standardized tests. They are skilled at helping students and parents understand and interpret test results so that they can use them effectively. They are able to assist teachers and administrators in using assessment results appropriately.

School counselors also use specialized tests that help students make informal decisions. Aptitude tests (such as the Armed Forces Vocational Aptitude Battery) and tests required by colleges (Scholastic Aptitude Test and the American College Test) are examples of such tests. School counselors may also administer career interest inventories to assist students in planning future courses and career paths, and sometimes they use other inventories to enhance students' awareness of different personality styles (e.g., the True Colors system).

School counselors, and all other education professionals, must demonstrate that they contribute to student achievement. The American School Counselor Association (2005) asserts: "Professional school counselors use data to show the impact of the school counseling program on school improvement and student achievement." The recent emphasis on accountability has elevated the importance of this function.

While school counselors have often collected self-reports and personal feedback from students, parents, and teachers about services they have received, such data are less useful than measures with adequate psychometric properties (meaning they have demonstrated reliability and validity). When implementing programs, counselors might collect pretest and posttest data to find out whether the students have learned the material or made anticipated changes as a result of the program. Ideally, they use control or comparison groups to ensure that the observed changes are the result of the new program and not simply the result of something else.

School counselors collect, summarize, and present data to various stakeholders. They are careful to ensure their data collection procedures and analyses are clear and accurate, since important decisions are often made based upon such data.

Application

Imagine that a school suspects that bullying at school is interfering with students' ability to focus on academics. The school counselor provides skills to assist the school in reducing the incidence of bullying.

School counselors gather accurate information about the prevalence of bullying and the situations and locations where it occurs. Using this information, school counselors reach out to others in the school community, including parents, caregivers, and students, to form a committee to oversee efforts to improve it. Counselors consult with colleagues and the professional literature to obtain current information about existing programs, and the committee selects the program most beneficial for their needs. Once a program is selected, school counselors often train the school staff in how to use the program. School counselors help the school create or enhance a positive school climate, and they include curricular components of the program in the guidance curriculum. Despite hard work, it is unlikely that the problem will be eradicated immediately. School counselors therefore intervene with individuals affected by bullying, providing support and assertiveness skills training to victims, empathy training and anger management skills to bullies, and help-seeking skills to bystanders. Counselors engage caregivers, who need information about the program, and provide suggestions for responding at home and notification when children are involved in bullying incidents at school. In the event of a crisis related to bullying, as has unfortunately occurred in recent years, school counselors commonly implement crisis response protocol.

Future Directions

Although the ASCA National Model is widely disseminated among school counselors, there is not universal agreement that this is the best approach. Some critics argue that the model currently is not flexible enough to adapt to individual schools, whose needs vary by setting (urban, suburban, rural), availability of resources, and local philosophies of education. Others contend that administrators are reluctant to free school counselors from quasi-administrative and clerical tasks. Comprehensive developmental programs will not be implemented if administrative support is lacking, despite state adoptions. Further, the model has been criticized for insufficient emphasis on cultural diversity and for ignoring the mental health functions school counselors can provide. Who will provide mental health services and programs for at-risk youth if the school counselor is providing more broad-based services to all students? Dixon Rayle (2006) in a national sample of school counselors at all levels found that those who had implemented comprehensive competency-based programs believed they mattered more to others at work and had significantly greater job satisfaction than those who were not using comprehensive programs. School counselors and administrators need to work together to decide whether the comprehensive developmental program is an appropriate model for all schools, and if so, how local needs and diversity can be addressed within the model.

School counselors are likely to be encouraged to take a larger role in special education programs (ASCA, 2004b). In addition to helping to identify students who may be eligible for these services, school counselors are increasingly involved in helping teachers accommodate students who receive special education services and in efforts to smooth the school-to-work transition for these students. They will continue to play an essential part in supporting and advocating for these students, and they will be engaged in assessing the needs of these students and providing services as needed. Finally, school counselors' guidance curricula will assist all students by promoting respect for diversity.

As educators increase attention to critical transition points (elementary to middle school, middle school to high school, and high school to postsecondary school or work),

school counselors will be taking on more responsibilities for planning and implementing effective programs to help students make these adjustments. The most critical need in the future of school counseling is for outcome research on school counseling services that uses rigorous scientific methods. Soft data, such as testimonials about a program, will no longer be sufficient to justify programs. School counselors and counselor educators need to collaborate to produce and disseminate the kind of research that satisfies the demands for accountability in education.

Conclusion

We have reviewed the evolution of the school counseling profession from its origins in the vocational guidance movement at the turn of the 20th century to its current emphasis on comprehensive developmental programs for all students. We noted that school counselors are no longer isolated from the activities of the school, but now occupy central leadership roles. Although school counselors once focused on college-bound students and student in crisis, contemporary school counselors provide a range of services, including the delivery of a classroom guidance curriculum that is sequential and competency based.

The profession of school counseling is anchored in philosophical propositions that provide a coherent rationale for school counseling services. School counselors believe that the developmental process is universal, although the unfolding of developmental events varies among students. They see children and schools from a systems perspective; that is, they recognize that individuals do not exist in a vacuum, but affect and are affected by others and their environment. Modern school counselors have a strengths-based, rather than a deficit-focused, perspective on student needs and development.

Most school counselors are satisfied with their jobs, but job-related stress has increased in recent years. Job prospects for school counselors are at least average, and compensation is higher than that of other counseling specialties. We described the many strategies and approaches used by school counselors in their work and gave an example of how their many roles often intersect in addressing school bullying. In this chapter, we argued that school counselors are leaders in schools; they are strong advocates for students, concerned about school climate and working to create a positive and inclusive atmosphere in which all students flourish. They work collaboratively with others in the school and in the community to enhance student success. We clarified that school counselors need to collect and disseminate data that demonstrate their effect on the educational outcomes of students.

We discussed two controversial issues in the field: the development and implementation of the ASCA National Model and the question of the need for teaching experience for school counselors. These issues are likely to continue to be important in the future.

References and Further Readings

American Counseling Association. (2005). *ACA code of ethics and standards of practice.* Alexandria, VA: Author.

American School Counselor Association. (2004a). *Ethical standards for school counselors.* Retrieved August 2, 2007, from http://www.schoolcounselor.org/files/ethical%20 standards.pdf

American School Counselor Association. (2004b). *Position statement: Special-needs students.* Retrieved April 10, 2008, from http://www.schoolcounselor.org/content.asp?contentid=218

American School Counselor Association. (2005). *The ASCA national model: A framework for school counseling programs.* Alexandria, VA: Author.

Baggerly, J., & Osborn, D. (2006). School counselors' career satisfaction and commitment: Correlates and predictors. *Professional School Counseling, 9,* 197–205.

Brown, D., & Trusty, J. (2005). *Designing and leading comprehensive school counseling programs: Promoting student competence and meeting student needs.* Belmont, CA: Thomson Brooks/Cole.

Campbell, C. A., & Dahir, C. A. (1997). *The national standards for school counseling programs.* Alexandria, VA: American School Counselor Association.

Coleman, H., & Yeh, C. (Eds.). (2008). *Handbook of school counseling.* Mahwah, NJ: Lawrence Erlbaum Associates.

DeMato, D. S., & Curcio, C. C. (2004). Job satisfaction of elementary school counselors: A new look. *Professional School Counseling, 7,* 236–245.

Dixon Rayle, A. (2006). Do school counselors matter? Mattering as a moderator between job stress and job satisfaction. *Professional School Counseling, 9,* 206–215.

Erford, B. T. (2003). *Transforming the school counseling profession.* Upper Saddle River, NJ: Merrill Prentice Hall.

Gyspers, N. C., & Henderson, P. (2000). *Developing and managing your school guidance program* (3rd ed.). Alexandria, VA: American Counseling Association.

Gyspers, N. C., & Moore, E. J. (1974). *Career guidance, counseling, and placement: Elements of an illustrative program guide (a life career development perspective).* Columbia, MO: University of Missouri.

Herr, E. L. (2001). The impact of national policies, economics, and school reform on comprehensive guidance programs. *Professional School Counseling, 4,* 236–245.

National Center for Education Statistics. (2007). *The condition of education.* Retrieved July 31, 2007, from http://nces.ed.gov/ programs/coe/2007/section4/table.asp?tableID=727

National Center for Transforming School Counseling at The Education Trust. Retrieved April 10, 2008, from http:// www2.edtrust.org/EdTrust/Transforming+School+ Counseling/main.x

Rogers, C. R. (1957). The necessary and sufficient conditions of therapeutic personality change. *Journal of Consulting Psychology, 21,* 95–103.

Ruhl, C. (n.d.). *Becoming a school counselor.* Retrieved July 31, 2007, from http://www.education.org/articles/becoming-a-school-counselor.html

Schmidt, J. (2002). *Counseling in schools: Essential services and comprehensive programs* (4th ed.). Boston: Allyn & Bacon.

Sciarra, D. T. (2004). *School counseling: Foundations and contemporary issues.* Belmont, CA: Thomson Brooks/Cole.

Thompson, R. A. (2001). *School counseling: Best practices for working in the school* (2nd ed.). Philadelphia: Brunner-Routledge.

United States Department of Labor. (2006). *Occupational Outlook Handbook.* Retrieved April 10, 2008, from http://www .bls.gov/oco/ocos067.htm#outlook

Wehrly, B. (1981). Developmental counseling in United States schools: Historical background and recent trends. *International Journal for the Advancement of Counselling, 4*(1), 51–58.

Wrenn, C. G. (1962). *The counselor in a changing world.* Washington, DC: American Personnel and Guidance Association.

Yalom, I., & Leszcz, M. (2005). *Theory and practice of group psychotherapy.* New York: Basic Books.

Zytowski, D. G. (2001). Frank Parsons and the progressive movement. *The Career Development Quarterly, 50,* 57–65.

7

SCHOOL PSYCHOLOGISTS

THOMAS OAKLAND

University of Florida

Education is served by many professions, including specializations in education (e.g., regular and special education teachers, administrators, school counselors), occupational therapy, psychology, physical therapy, and social work. Each has different preparation and a different mission. The quality of services students receive is enhanced when the various professions work in concert to meet the needs of individual students, and groups of students, as well as those of the institutions in which they work.

Strong professional services rest on a strong and relevant base of empirical knowledge guided by legal and ethical standards. Professionals (i.e., those certified or licensed to provide services) are expected to have acquired this knowledge and know how and when to apply it when serving others.

The profession of psychology has a number of clinical subspecializations. The most common include clinical, counseling, and school psychology. By tradition, clinical psychologists typically treat persons with severe disorders. Although they may see children, they usually work with adults who either can afford private services or are receiving treatment or counseling through social service programs. Counseling psychologists typically work with persons experiencing common, albeit perplexing, life changes (e.g., marriage, divorce, a birth or death, job changes). Although they too may work with children, they also work most often with adults.

In contrast, school psychologists typically work with students who display behavior, learning, or social-emotional problems within the context of schools. Their work may include direct services to students or indirect services to them by consulting with their teachers and parents. School psychologists typically work in public schools that serve students from all racial and ethnic backgrounds and family income levels. Thus, they too serve this population. Children who display psychological problems are more likely to receive services from a clinician prepared as a school psychologist than as a clinical or counseling psychologist.

Although most school psychologists in the United States work in schools, those in some countries have their offices in the general community, not in schools, and provide a wide range of publicly supported services to children, not only to students. The decision that school psychologists in the United States should practice in schools has had a decisive effect on the nature of their services, professional preparation, and regulations.

School psychology traces its roots to child development, clinical psychology, and special education. School psychology typically acquires its scholarship and practice base from psychology and its permission to practice from education. School psychologists commonly work with students in special education rather than regular education. School psychology services are most prevalent when their services are consistent with current theory and research, relevant to education, sanctioned through law, and affordable.

This chapter discusses the status of school psychology. It draws heavily on prior publications, including Oakland

(2000) and Jimerson, Oakland, & Farrell (2007). Persons are encouraged to read Fagan & Wise (2007) for a more comprehensive discussion of school psychology. This chapter begins by discussing the social contexts that led to the development of psychology, including school psychology, first as a discipline and then a profession. The history of school psychology, as well as its current status, including its professional associations; a definition of school psychology; prevailing philosophies guiding preparation and practice; services provided by school psychologists; the demographic characteristics of school psychologists; and professional licensure are discussed next. This chapter concludes with a discussion of federal legislation, other professional standards and guidelines, and journal resources together with issues currently affecting school psychology.

Social Contexts and the Development of Psychology

Two important and interrelated events occurred in Western Europe and the United States during the latter half of the 19th century: significant social changes due to the industrial revolution and the laying of the scientific foundation for the discipline of psychology.

Throughout most of recorded history, lifestyles generally were characterized by personalized, rural, family-centered environments dependent on agriculture and small family-run businesses. Members of the immediate and extended family generally took care of one another's needs as best they could.

Children were raised to follow in their parents' footsteps, boys to assume responsibility for the farm or small business, and girls to marry, raise children, and assume other important domestic duties. Children were expected to work at an early age. Education generally was restricted to teaching basic reading and number facts, typically within the home. Families required the services of very few professionals, including physicians, as family members and close friends assumed responsibility for their common and special needs. Life generally was geared to the passage of seasons, not hours, and thus generally was stable.

During the 1800s, however, many lifestyles changed. People were thrust into depersonalized, urban, industrially centered environments. Life changes associated with these conditions were exacerbated when families migrated to a new country. Boys were less able to follow in their fathers' vocational footsteps. Child labor laws restricted their work, thus creating time for, and in some locations requiring, at least an elementary education. Both boys and girls were educated. Education began to replace lineage and physical endurance as important pathways to personal success and social stability. Life became geared to the passage of hours and thus was less stable.

In school settings, behavioral problems exhibited by children that were or may have been overlooked in homes often became evident. Some children displayed remarkably high levels of cognitive ability. Others learned slowly, some had sensory or physical problems, still others attended school irregularly, were unruly, or displayed other qualities that differed from their peers or standards acceptable to teachers. Teachers needed assistance to help address these students' educational needs.

With increasing urbanization, other problems emerged that may have been overlooked or simply were not evident in smaller and more personalized settings, or, if identified, were attended to by families and friends. For example, more children were orphaned, were brought before the law for repeated misdemeanors or even felonies, ran away from home, or exhibited other emotional, mental, or social problems that warranted public attention. New public and private agencies and institutions were established to care for their needs, including juvenile courts, alms houses, settlement homes, and state-run institutions for those with visual and auditory impairments, mental retardation, and social-emotional disturbances.

Professionals with expertise in the social sciences were needed to assist agency personnel in accurately assessing children's needs, diagnosing their problems, and suggesting primary, secondary, and tertiary prevention methods to address their needs and those of society. The professions of psychology and social work emerged, in part, from these conditions.

Need for a Discipline of Psychology

Since their origin, people are likely to have had an abiding interest in human behavior, including why people do what they do, ways to enhance performance and avoid problems, and how to understand themselves and others. The discipline of psychology (i.e., its knowledge base) had to be created before the profession of psychology could be formed. The discipline of psychology has been influenced by two important and different sources: philosophy and science (principally biology and physics).

Some historians consider the writings of Plato, Socrates, and other eminent philosophers to be the foundation and guiding light for psychology. Additionally, Hippocrates established the first ethical code, albeit for physicians, and speculated on the psychological origins of behavior. For example, in 350 BC, he described four humors or temperaments associated with bodily fluids thought to control or at least influence behavior. Later, another Greek, Galan, extended Hippocrates' work by describing four pathological temperaments (i.e., choleric, melancholic, phlegmatic, and sanguine).

Centuries later, the empirical foundation for the emerging science of psychology was established through the work of Wundt in Germany, Galton in England, and Binet in France, along with others. For example, in 1879, Wundt established the first psychology laboratory in Leipsig, Germany, to study reaction time to physical properties, infused principally by theory and research from physics. At about the same time, Galton established a laboratory in London to examine prevailing personal qualities. His work was highly influenced by his cousin, Charles Darwin, who published the highly acclaimed *The Origin of Species* in 1859, a book that outlined an organic theory of evolution. Thus, Galton's interests centered more on biology. He was one of the first to discuss the biological base of behavior, especially its familial links.

In the early 1900s, Binet, together with his colleague Simon, recognized the importance of developing tests to better understand individual differences that could affect children's development, including their academic success. They were asked by the Minister of Public Education in Paris to develop tests that could help differentiate children who were likely and unlikely to benefit from regular public school instruction, thereby identifying a group of students who needed special education services. Their 1911 test of intelligence was translated into various languages and became used in many countries, including the United States.

The first widespread use of tests occurred in China more than 3,000 years ago. Measures of problem-solving skills, visual spatial perception, divergent thinking, creativity, and other qualities that reflect important talents and behaviors were used somewhat commonly. Later, under the Sui dynasty (581–618 AD), a civil service examination system was initiated consisting of three parts: regular examinations stressing classical cultural knowledge, a committee examination before the emperor stressing planning and administrative features, and a third examination on martial arts. Forms of this assessment system continued in China until 1905. The British East India Company and much later, in 1884, the U.S. civil service examination system modeled China's successful efforts to use tests of psychological abilities to identify needed talent. The first widespread modern application of technology from psychology in Western civilization occurred during World War I when verbal and nonverbal intelligence tests were used to screen recruits. Importantly for school psychology, beginning in the early 1900s, school administrators also recognized the value of measures of intelligence and other personal qualities, thus providing a pathway for psychologists to gain employment in schools through their exclusive use of such tests.

Nevertheless, the growth of professional specialties in psychology first required the growth of the discipline of psychology. This growth occurred during the first half of the 20th century. At first, courses in psychology often were offered either in departments of philosophy or education. Later, separate departments of psychology along with psychological laboratories were established. These later resources were needed to educate doctoral students in scientific psychology and to provide them with resources needed to engage in research and other forms of scholarship. The formation of professional associations and the creation of scholarly journals also helped develop an infrastructure needed for the science of psychology to flourish.

The discipline of psychology grew slowly and somewhat steadily during the first half of the 20th century.

The entry of the United States in World War II signaled important changes for psychologists: their engagement in another war effort and later the provision of their clinical services to returning veterans. The federal government looked to the discipline of psychology for methods to assist in identifying the recruit's personal qualities and to assign them to various important positions (e.g., sonar specialists, pilots, officers). Many professors received research support to address important war-related issues. The result of these efforts during the early to mid-1940s convinced government officials and much of the public that the discipline of psychology had matured sufficiently to warrant professional status.

A Growing National Need for Clinical Services

Many of the 17 million service personnel returning from World War II displayed physical and psychological (e.g., post-traumatic stress) difficulties that required continued care in Veterans Administration (VA) hospitals. These hospitals required the services of skilled clinical psychologists to address the veterans' needs. But given the newness of the discipline of psychology, few universities offered clinical training programs. Thus, because of an insufficient number of psychologists to provide needed clinical services, the federal government provided funds to psychology departments to create graduate programs in clinical psychology and to fund graduate students to specialize in clinical psychology who later were required to work in VA hospitals.

Early History of School Psychology

In 1986, Lightner Witmer established the first psychology clinic at the University of Pennsylvania. This event generally is seen as marking the origin of school psychology. Witmer envisioned the preparation of pedagogical or psychological experts to work with children who did not benefit from ordinary educational methods. He later embodied this vision by serving as a school psychologist.

School psychology and other applied areas of psychology grew slowly during the next 60 years. Psychology departments, dominated by experimental scientists, generally were not interested in applied psychology. Before 1920, there were an estimated 100 to 150 self-proclaimed school psychologists in the United States, few of whom were qualified psychologists. In 1950, only ten universities offered specific programs to prepare school psychologists.

The emergence of clinical psychology following World War II signaled the later emergence of school psychology. The public recognized the value of providing psychological services to children and youth, especially within the context of schools. The rise of special education services, first to students with physical disorders (e.g., those with mental retardation, visual impairment, or auditory impairment) and later to students with psychological disorders (e.g., learning, emotional, or social disabilities), also led to an increase in the need for school psychological services and thus increases in the preparation and employment of school psychologists. Again the federal government provided some financial support to create graduate programs in school psychology.

Current Status of School Psychology

Professional Associations

The strength of a profession is directly linked to the strength of its professional associations. Two strong national professional associations serve school psychology: the American Psychological Association (APA; www.apa.org), principally its Division of School Psychology, and the National Association of School Psychologists (NASP; www.naspweb.org). The APA has approximately 170,000 members, about 2,500 of whom are members of its Division of School Psychology. The NASP has approximately 25,000 members. In addition, most states have established professional associations. Other national organizations working on behalf of school psychology include the Council of Directors of School Psychology Programs, National Association of State Consultants in School Psychology, Society for the Study of School Psychology, and Trainers of School Psychology.

School psychologists report belonging to a variety of different professional organizations. Approximately 72% belong to the National Association of School Psychologists, 74% to state school psychological associations, 32% to the National Education Association, 31% to local teacher unions, 20% to the American Psychological Association, 13% to the American Psychological Association's Division of School Psychology, 9% to the American Federation of Teachers, and 8% to the Council for Exceptional Children.

A Definition of School Psychology

Both national associations have approved definitions of school psychology. The definitions display considerable consistency. The APA's definition follows:

> School psychology is a general practice and health service provider specialty of professional psychology that is concerned with the science and practice of psychology with children, youth, and families; learners of all ages; and the schooling process. The basic education and training of school psychologists prepares them to provide a range of psychological assessment, intervention, prevention, health promotion, and program development and evaluation services with a special focus on the developmental process of children and youth within the context of schools, families, and other systems.

School psychologists are prepared to intervene at the individual and systems level, and develop, implement, and evaluate preventive programs. (Council of Directors of School Psychology Programs, 1998)

Prevailing Philosophy Guiding Preparation and Practice

Current professional research literature as well as legal and ethical codes establish standards for practice. Furthermore, a prevailing view—particularly among advocates of doctoral-level school psychology—emphasizes the importance of a scientist-practitioner model for professional preparation and practice. This model advocates the belief that applications of psychology, including school psychology, should be supported empirically and theoretically and derived from a body of literature held in high esteem. This scientist-practitioner model emphasizes the importance of reciprocal relationships between scholarship and practice within psychology; each contributes to the other. Thus, doctoral-level school psychologists are expected to contribute to science and to base their practices on it.

Programs designed to prepare school psychologists at the master's or special degree levels recognize that their graduates are unlikely to become engaged in and to contribute through research. Instead, their students are prepared to be good consumers of professional literature. Thus, emphasis is placed on ways to acquire and evaluate relevant information, not to contribute to the science of psychology.

Preparation of School Psychologists

Approximately 8,500 students are enrolled in the more than 200 school psychology programs. Approximately 1,900 students graduate yearly with one of three degrees: master's, specialist, or doctorate.

Among these programs, about one third offer graduate preparation at the master's level (e.g., typically two years of coursework), one third at the specialist level (e.g., typically two years of coursework and one year of internship), and one third at the doctoral level (e.g., typically four or more years of coursework, a dissertation, and one year of internship). Programs that offer doctoral preparation also may offer specialist-level preparation.

There are no national qualifications for admission into school psychology programs. Each program specifies its own admission criteria. Applicants generally must obtain at least an average score on the internationally administered Graduate Record Examination (GRE). Because all school psychology programs are at the graduate level, all students have completed an undergraduate degree (e.g., bachelor of arts, bachelor of science). While previous degrees in psychology and education make candidates more competitive for admission, such degrees are not required. Successful applicants often have experience working with children and some have been teachers; however, a teaching credential is not required to become a school psychologist.

Efforts to prepare school psychologists have been influenced heavily by accreditation standards promulgated by the National Association of School Psychologists and the American Psychological Association. Quality school psychology programs adhere to these standards. Programs offering only specialist degrees tend to be consistent with National Association of School Psychologists standards, and those offering only doctoral-level degrees often are consistent with the American Psychological Association standards. The National Association of School Psychologists standards are summarized in the following section.

Standards for Academic and Professional Preparation

Training standards delineated by the National Association of School Psychologists (2000c) have affected the curriculum and structure of most school psychology programs that offer a specialist degree and many that offer a doctoral degree. These training standards address the program's structure, domains of school psychology training and practice, field experience and internships, performance-based program assessment, and program support and resources. The National Association of School Psychologists standards " . . . serve to guide the design of school psychology graduate education by providing a basis for program evaluation and a foundation for the recognition of programs that meet national quality standards through the National Association of School Psychologists program approval process" (National Association of School Psychologists, 2000c, p. 7).

The academic and professional preparation of school psychologists typically emphasizes the following eleven areas: (1) data-based decision making and accountability; (2) consultation and collaboration; (3) effective instruction and development of cognitive skills; (4) socialization and development of life skills; (5) student diversity in development and learning; (6) school and systems organization, policy development, and climate; (7) prevention, crisis intervention, and mental health; (8) home-school-community collaboration; (9) research and program evaluation; (10) school psychology practice and development; and (11) information technology.

By incorporating these training standards, programs emphasize the core academic knowledge in a number of areas:

- psychology (e.g., development, learning and cognition, educational, personality, social, experimental, biological, statistics, and research design)
- assessment services (e.g., intellectual, academic, adaptive, emotional, and social assessment)
- intervention services (e.g., behavioral, affective, educational, and social-systems)

- focus on children and youth (e.g., within the context of classrooms, schools, families, communities, and other systems)
- interpersonal skills (e.g., establishing trust and rapport, listening and communication skills, respect for the views and expertise of others, recognition of the assets and limitations of other professionals, and a mature understanding of issues and effective methods to address them)
- professional decision-making skills (e.g., considers important qualities that characterize the child and the contexts within which the child is being raised, is informed by research, and is motivated by problem-solving orientations that consider the viability of alternative courses of action)
- knowledge of statistical methods and research design (e.g., often prepared within one of two models: as a good consumer of research and other forms of scholarship or as a scientist-practitioner)
- knowledge of legal and ethical basis for services (e.g., laws, administrative rulings, and other regulations as well as ethical codes governing practice).

Services Provided by School Psychologists

The specialty of school psychology provides professional services within six broad delivery systems.

School psychologists typically are seen as the experts in individual assessment. Thus, they frequently conduct individual psychoeducational evaluations with students referred for possible special education services (e.g., those with suspected behavioral, emotional, learning, mental, and social problems that affect their school performance) as well as those who may qualify for gifted classes. School psychologists use tests and other assessment methods, including record reviews and classroom observations, to evaluate a student's cognitive ability (i.e., intelligence and achievement); adaptive behavior; and affective, emotional, linguistic, and social characteristics.

Indirect services are provided to students by working with parents or guardians, teachers, principals, and other educators who have more direct and ongoing contact with students. Indirect services may involve participation in child study teams, inservice programs, consultation, and collaboration.

Direct services are used to promote a student's academic, behavioral, emotional, and social development through tutoring, teaching, or counseling. These services may be performed individually or in a group.

Research and evaluation services are intended to assist a school, school district, and the profession to make decisions on empirically validated results and thus to develop a body of literature on which to base practices.

Supervision and administration services enable school psychologists to administer pupil personnel and psychological services. In this capacity, they are responsible for conceptualizing and promoting a comprehensive plan for these services, hiring and supervising personnel, promoting their development, and coordinating these services with other psychological and social services provided in the community.

Prevention services are designed either to prevent the occurrence of problems or to minimize their deleterious effect should they occur. Prevention programs often focus on drug and alcohol abuse, suicide, dropouts, school violence, and pregnancies. Prevention programs may occur at one of three levels: primary prevention (e.g., before problems surface), secondary prevention (e.g., when problems surface and are dealt with immediately in an effort to minimize their effect and prevent the occurrence of other problems), and tertiary prevention (e.g., when problems are persistent and require continued professional service, often to help support the maintenance of a person or system).

Settings in Which School Psychologists Work

School psychologists work in numerous settings, including public and private schools, special schools, centers, and private practice. Seventy-eight percent are employed in public school settings. Among them, most work within the context of special education. Some work in university settings (7%) and private practice (5%). Smaller numbers work in mental health clinics, hospitals and other medical settings, and in research centers. Thus, school psychologists enjoy many employment opportunities. Moreover, employment opportunities are very strong nationally (Fagan & Wise, 2007).

The quantity and nature of services often differ for preschool, elementary, and secondary students. Nationally, school psychologists devote about 5% of their time to preschool, 60% to elementary, 20% to middle school, and 15% to senior high students. School psychologists who work mainly in special education typically devote about 32% of their time to students with learning disabilities, 22% to those with behavioral and emotional problems, 14% to those with mental retardation, and 16% to the general school population. School psychologists also devote smaller percentages of time to students who are talented and gifted (4%) and to those exhibiting acuity (3%), physical (2%), and speech (2%) disorders.

When asked how they actually spend their time and how they preferred to spend their time, school psychologists indicated they actually spend about 54% but would prefer to spend 40% of their time in assessment activities, they spend 23% but would prefer to spend 30% of their time in interventions (e.g., counseling, program development), they spend 18% but would prefer to spend 23% on consultation, and they spend 1% but would prefer to spend 4% on research.

Demographic Characteristics of School Psychologists

Approximately 3,300 school psychologists work in the United States. They are found in all 50 states and are most numerous in states with large populations and in the Northeast, Midwest, and West (e.g., California, Illinois, Ohio, New Jersey, New York). As is true of other countries, proportionately more school psychologists are found in urban and suburban areas than in rural areas. Their average age is 45 and on average they have 13 years' experience as a school psychologist. Ninety-three percent are White; approximately 2% are Black, 3% are Hispanic, and 72% are female. The ratio between school psychologists and students is estimated to be approximately 1:1,680 nationally. Between one fourth and one third of school psychology positions in the United States meet the ratio of 1 school psychologist for every 1,000 students as recommended by NASP (Fagan & Wise, 2007).

Salaries of School Psychologists

Salaries vary somewhat between states and are influenced by one's years of experience and level of licensure. School psychologists working in elementary and secondary schools average about $55,000 per year. Those with 10 through 14 years of experience earn approximately $75,000, and those with 20 through 24 years of experience earn approximately $85,000. On average, school psychologists in the United States with doctoral degrees earn about $90,000 and those with master's degrees average $62,000.

Professional Preparation and Licensure

A number of countries have established national licensure provisions in which a license to practice psychology may be granted to persons with a bachelor's degree in psychology. In contrast, within the United States, each state establishes standards for certifying or licensing school psychologists and licensing psychologists. The standards for school psychologists and other psychologists differ. In addition, state departments of education generally regulate the practice of school psychology within schools. State psychology boards typically regulate the independent (i.e., out of school) practice of psychology, including school psychology. Thus, there are considerable differences in the licensure standards from state to state. All certification and licensing laws require graduate degrees.

The Practice of School Psychology Within Schools

A few states only require school psychologists to be certified (e.g., to have a degree from a school psychology program). Most states require school psychologists to be licensed. Licensure typically requires a candidate to have a degree from a school psychology program and to pass one or more tests that assess the candidate's knowledge of education and psychology, including its laws and ethics. Some state licensure laws require at least a master's degree while others require a specialist degree. No state requires school psychologists to meet licensure requirements as a psychologist. A national certification process allows school psychologists to become certified and licensed in more than one state.

The Independent Practice of School Psychology

All states allow psychologists to engage in private practice. Most states also allow school psychologists to engage in private practice. Those with a doctoral degree (e.g., doctor of philosophy, doctor of education, or doctor of psychology) generally are allowed to offer a wider range of services than those with a master's or specialist degree. Approximately one third of school psychologists have a doctoral degree and are licensed as a psychologist. A license to practice psychology generally qualifies one also to practice as a school psychologist.

Federal Legislation

As noted earlier, strong professional services rest on a strong and relevant base of empirical knowledge guided by legal and ethical standards. School psychology practice is influenced heavily by federal legislation that becomes established in policies promulgated by state education agencies and carried out by local education agencies (Oakland & Gallegos, 2005). These include the 1964 Civil Rights Act, the Individuals with Disabilities Education Act, Section 504 of the Rehabilitation Act of 1973, the Family Education Rights and Privacy Act of 1974, and the No Child Left Behind Act of 2001.

For example, in 1975, the U.S. Congress passed Public Law 94–142 (Education of All Handicapped Children Act), subsequently codified as the Individuals with Disabilities Education Act. This initial and later legislation requires school districts that receive federal funds to develop and implement policies that ensure a free, appropriate public education to all children with disabilities. Amendments to this act (e.g., Public Law 105–17 and Public Law 108–446) have provided further guidelines regarding the education of children with disabilities. The Individuals with Disabilities Education Act of 2004 is the most recent legislation governing special education. In addition, Public Law 107–110, the No Child Left Behind Act (2002)—a regular education initiative—emphasizes a school's accountability for promoting achievement, local control and flexibility, expanded parental choice, and use of effective research-based instruction.

Such legislation has important implications for the preparation and practices of school psychologists. Both the Individuals with Disabilities Education Act of 2004 and the No Child Left Behind legislation underscore the importance of implementing instructional strategies supported by empirical evidence. Moreover, the Individuals with Disabilities Education Act of 2004 allows schools to discontinue use of a discrepancy formula to identify students with learning disabilities and to refer students for possible learning disabilities only after they do not show progress following intensive services. Given the recency of this legislation, its full effect on school psychology practices will not be known for years.

Other Professional Standards and Guidelines

All professions are expected to establish uniform and recognized standards (qualities that should be adhered to) and guidelines (qualities that one should consider adhering to) applicable to professional, scientific, educational, and ethical issues. Various standards that exemplify the profession's values and principles and that serve the needs of service providers, clients, educators, the society, and legal bodies have been developed. Those developed by the APA include *Ethical Principles in the Conduct of Research with Human Subjects* (American Psychological Association [APA], 1973), *Standards for Educational and Psychological Testing* (American Educational Research Association, American Psychological Association, & the National Council on Educational Research, 1999), and *Ethical Principles and Code of Conduct of Psychologists* (APA, 2002). Guidelines prepared by them include *Psychology as a Profession* (APA, 1968), *Guidelines for Conditions of Employment of Psychologists* (APA, 1972), and *Guidelines and Principles for Accreditation of Training Programs in Professional Psychology* (APA, 1996). In addition, the APA's Division of School Psychology has addressed various issues by developing the following position papers: *Guidelines to Work Conditions for School Psychologists; Test Protocols in Relation to Sole Possession Records; School Personnel Qualified to Provide Psychological Services to Pupils/Students, School Staffs, and Parents; School Psychology Internship;* and *State Legislative Mandates for School Psychological Services Encouraged.*

The National Association of School Psychologists also has established standards, including *Principles for Professional Ethics* (National Association of School Psychologists [NASP], 2000a). Its position papers include *School psychology: A blueprint for training and practice II* (Ysseldyke et al., 1997), and *Guidelines for the Provision of School Psychology Services* (NASP, 2000b).

Professional Journals and Newsletters

Five national professional journals are intended to advance the knowledge and practice base of school psychology: *Journal of School Psychology, School Psychology Quarterly, Psychology in the Schools, School Psychology Review,* and *Journal of Applied School Psychology.* Several school psychology journals that also are received by many school psychologists include *The California School Psychologist, School Psychology International,* and the *Canadian Journal of School Psychology.* Newsletters from the NASP (i.e., *the Communiqué*), the APA's Division of School Psychology (i.e., *The School Psychologist*), and various state associations also contribute to the dissemination of information among school psychologists. Numerous textbooks also discuss school psychology.

Issues Affecting School Psychology

Whether school psychology should affiliate more with psychology or education remains a vexing issue. Some view school psychology as a specialty within the profession of psychology whose research base is derived largely from the discipline of psychology. Others view school psychology as a profession separate and independent from psychology and more clearly allied with education. Those who work in schools frequently identify closely with their colleagues in education; however, most of the scholarship and technology used in their work comes from psychology.

Furthermore, legal and financial issues that often transcend both psychology and education increasingly govern practices. Thus, whether school psychology is more aligned with psychology or education is somewhat irrelevant because legal and financial issues affect all psychologists who practice in education. For example, federal legislation (e.g., the Individuals with Disabilities Education Act) delineates regulations to which states must adhere in order to receive federal funds. These regulations include numerous guidelines regarding Individualized Education Plans, appropriate means of determining whether students may have access to special education services, the education of children with disabilities, and evidence that students are receiving support (e.g., school psychology) services.

School psychology, like other professional specialties, exists to serve the public. Thus, changes in our society, especially in education, warrant corresponding changes in the ways school psychologists are prepared and serve. Issues that affect education have a particularly noticeable effect on school psychology. Public education is struggling with various issues: an increase in children from low-income homes (who historically have achieved at below average levels and thus display higher levels of educational failure), an influx of students who are not fluent in English, increased incidence of behavior and social problems, increased incidence of students in some disability categories (e.g., attention deficits, autism), teachers who often are not well prepared to provide the various services expected of them, and the placement of students with severe levels of disorders in regular education classrooms. These issues affect the work of school psychologists.

Federal legislation and resulting state and local school district policy increasingly affect the nature of school services, including psychological services. Practitioners increasingly feel they have become the handmaidens of public (i.e., federal) policy, resulting in diminished professional judgment and limitations in their services (e.g., they have become largely restricted to those associated with assessment).

Large numbers of able students are entering school psychology programs at a time of diminished faculty resources. Those faculty who helped establish the specialty of school psychology have or soon will retire. Too few doctoral students are becoming professors and instead are electing to enter school or private practice. The manner in which these and other issues are resolved will discernibly affect school psychology.

References and Further Readings

American Educational Research Association, American Psychological Association, & the National Council on Educational Research. (1999). *Standards for educational and psychological testing.* Washington, DC: Authors.

American Psychological Association. (1968). *Psychology as a profession.* Washington, DC: Author.

American Psychological Association. (1972). *Guidelines for conditions of employment of psychologists.* Washington, DC: Author.

American Psychological Association. (1973). *Ethical principles in the conduct of research with human subjects.* Washington, DC: Author.

American Psychological Association. (1996). *Guidelines and principles for accreditation of training programs in professional psychology.* Washington, DC: Author.

American Psychological Association. (2002). Ethical principles of psychologists and code of conduct. *American Psychologist, 57,* 1060–1073.

Council of Directors of School Psychology Programs. (1998). *Newsletter of the Council of Directors of School Psychology Programs, 17*(1), 8.

Fagan, T. K., & Wise, P. S. (2007). *School psychology: Past, present and future* (3rd ed.). Bethesda, MD: National Association of School Psychologists.

Jimerson, S., Oakland, T., & Farrell, P. (2007). *The handbook of international school psychology.* Thousand Oaks, CA: Sage.

National Association of School Psychologists. (2000a). *Principles for professional ethics.* Bethesda, MD: Author.

National Association of School Psychologists. (2000b). *Guidelines for the provision of school psychology services.* Bethesda, MD: Author.

National Association of School Psychologists. (2000c). *Standards for training and field placement programs in school psychology.* Bethesda, MD: Author.

National Association of School Psychologists. (2000d). *Standards for the credentialing of school psychologists.* Bethesda, MD: Author.

Oakland, T. (2000). School psychology. In C. Reynolds & E. Fletcher-Janzen (Eds.), *Encyclopedia of special education* (2nd ed., pp. 1597–1599). New York: John Wiley & Sons.

Oakland, T., & Gallegos, E. (2005). Legal issues associated with the education of children from multicultural settings. In C. Frisby & C. Reynolds (Eds.), *Comprehensive handbook of multicultural school psychology* (pp. 1048–1078). New York: John Wiley & Sons.

Ysseldyke, J., Dawson, P., Lehr, C., Reschly, D., Reynolds, M., & Telzrow, C. (1997). *School psychology: A blueprint for training and practice II.* Bethesda, MD: National Association of School Psychologists.

PART III

LEARNERS

DEVELOPMENTAL CONTEXT

8

DEVELOPMENT

PreK–2

CHRISTINE MASSEY

University of Pennsylvania

KIMBERLY BRENNEMAN

Rutgers University

In this chapter we survey theories and research related to children's development from the preschool years through age 7. We focus particularly on young children as *learners* and consider both what they bring to learning in various domains as well as what kinds of environments and experiences can support their learning, development, and successful transition to formal schooling. Research in recent decades has revealed significant areas of competence in preschoolers. Despite fragile performance in some respects, their learning accomplishments are quite remarkable, though not completely understood. Traditional, broad stage theories of development, which emphasized deficits in preschool thinking and characterized it as concrete and limited, have given way to new theories that propose a rich variety of learning mechanisms implicating innate learning endowments as well as subtle and intricate interactions with the social and physical world. Although debate continues as to whether early learning mechanisms are specific to particular domains or more general, recent progress in the field has come from detailed studies of learning in particular areas rather than attempts to pursue grand integrative theories. These studies attempt to understand and specify (1) starting points in learning and development, (2) what in the environment does (or does not) support learning, (3) mechanisms by which what the child brings to learning interacts with what is available in the environment, and (4) how to characterize in precise ways the learning that is being accomplished. Child development researchers now span disciplines (e.g.,

psychology, anthropology, linguistics, education, neuroscience, and even computer science) and employ multiple methods. Educators are increasingly approaching preschool as the foundation of formal education rather than a form of day care, and policy makers and legislators are investing more in early education, often with the goal of improving equity and long-term outcomes for vulnerable populations.

Major Theoretical Approaches

Questions about the sources of development are often framed as nature versus nurture. Theorists debate the role of innate predispositions (nature) in developmental change. They also question the ways that the environment in which children develop influences how they develop (nurture). Psychologists also debate the shape of change. Is development best described as continuous or discontinuous? Those who favor continuity argue that basic thinking and reasoning skills do not change dramatically over the life span. Development is described as adding capacities and knowledge, not as replacing old modes of thought with new ones. Other theorists describe development as discontinuous and stage-like, with radically different modes of thinking emerging at various points in development. The ways these questions are answered influence debate about the purpose and form of educational experiences that young children should encounter. (For a detailed overview of major developmental theories and further references, see Miller, 2002.)

Piagetian Theory

Jean Piaget's developmental theory is one of the most influential in psychology. In contrast to behaviorism, which describes the learner as passive and developmental change as a response to environmental change, Piaget described an active learner who constructs knowledge. Like behaviorists, Piaget did not grant babies many innate abilities, but he did describe simple mental structures with which infants act on the environment and begin to build knowledge. For him, development results from an inter-action between the cognitive structures of the child's current maturational level and the environment as the child attempts to adapt to the environment. *Adaptation* occurs as the learner *assimilates* new information into existing knowledge structures and when mental structures change to *accommodate* new information that does not fit into them. Through adaptation, the learner attempts to maintain *equilibrium* or a balance between current cognitive structures and input from the environment. Development generally proceeds through small, local changes; however, Piaget posits that at certain points in human development, imbalance throughout the learning system becomes too great, requiring a radical restructuring of knowledge to a more adapted form. These across-the-board changes result in a new developmental stage, characterized by a new mode of thought. Piaget's description of discontinuous development includes four universal, invariant stages. The second of these, the preoperational stage, occurs from about age 2 until 6 or 7, making it most relevant to our discussion.

For Piaget, preoperational thought is symbolic but not yet abstract. The preoperational thinker uses words to describe the world and to communicate, but is unable to reason in complex ways. One hallmark of the preschool mind is the inability to hold multiple ideas about the same object or event. A famous example of this deficit involves the conservation of volume across a physical change. When water is poured from a short, wide container into a tall, thin one, preschoolers state that there is now more water. Piaget interpreted this result as evidence that children can only think about one aspect of the situation—the height of the container—and cannot coordinate this information with the corresponding change in the container's width. A related phenomenon is egocentrism, in which the young child does not separate his or her own perspective or knowledge from that of others. Other proposed deficits include separating causes from effects, confusing characteristics of animate and inanimate objects, misunderstanding class inclusion (e.g., that an object is both a rose and a flower), and failing to reason arithmetically.

Given Piaget's commitment to invariant, maturation-based stages of development, education is not viewed as a means to accelerate movement through the stages nor to ameliorate cognitive immaturities. Instead, the goal of education is to support the learner's intellectual independence and autonomy. Teachers of young children can support this aim by providing an environment in which children are given concrete materials to explore, are encouraged to be curious and ask questions, and are instilled with confidence in themselves as capable learners.

Vygotskian Theory

Like Piaget, Lev Vygotsky viewed the child as an active participant in knowledge construction. Vygotsky, however, described development as a necessarily social phenomenon. Learning is critically dependent on interactions with thinkers who are more cognitively advanced than the child. Knowledge construction depends on teachers, parents, and peers who *scaffold* a child's thinking and introduce *socio-cultural tools* such as language, systems of literacy, procedures, and supporting technologies. Scaffolding is a process by which the mature thinker, through discussion, supports and guides the learner's attempts to move forward on a developmental pathway. Vygotsky described a *zone of proximal development,* which is the distance between the child's independent level of thinking and the level he or she can achieve when supported by a sensitive partner. The mature thinker provides input and support early in an inter-action. As the child internalizes a skill, the partner withdraws the scaffold. The notion of a learner's developmental level is somewhat elastic in Vygotsky's view and depends on the supports available. Language is central to Vygotskian theory. The talk between learners and learning partners becomes self-speech as the child internalizes advanced forms of thinking.

Vygotskian theory has different implications for early education than Piagetian theory. Although both describe the learner as perception-bound and incapable of abstract thinking, for Piaget these cognitive immaturities will be resolved by the maturing child acting on the environment. For Vygotsky, movement to mature levels of thought requires that the child interact with the environment and, critically, the people in it. Teaching, then, involves assessing each learner's zone of proximal development and providing experiences that are a bit more advanced than the child can handle independently. Development occurs as cognitive challenges are met and new ones are presented.

Reconsideration of Stage Theories of Development

In the 1970s and 1980s, a number of psychologists challenged traditional views of young learners. These researchers believed that if children were actively constructing knowledge as Piaget suggested, then it was unlikely that drastic and sweeping cognitive changes occurred. Instead, they believed that simpler but authentic forms of abstract thought could be found early in development. They suspected that Piaget's methodology masked competence that could be revealed using different research procedures (e.g., Gelman & Baillargeon, 1983). By and large, research has borne out this prediction. Although Piaget's findings almost always replicate when his procedures are used, the developmental literature now includes many reports of preschoolers' competence in understanding causality, animacy, simple arithmetic, conservation, perspective-taking, and so forth, when these are probed using different methodology.

Piaget's and Vygotsky's description of a learner who constructs knowledge through interaction with the environment is still generally held to be true; however, current research does not support a description of cognitive development as a series of general restructurings. In what follows, we describe approaches to cognitive development that, while theoretical in nature, more precisely describe mechanisms of learning, supporting environments for learning, and what is actually being learned. The goal for many researchers has become to not just assess cognitive capabilities of the average learner at a given age but to study the *processes* of knowledge acquisition as they occur.

Information Processing Approaches

Information processing theorists describe human thought by comparing it to computing. Development involves changes in hardware (brain maturation) and software (thinking strategies or cognitive processes). The young learner is granted basic thinking skills that become more elaborate, flexible, and faster with age and experience. Microgenetic methods, in which problem-solving strategy use is observed over repeated trials during a period of rapid change, have proven useful for illuminating cognitive change in individual learners of different ages across a variety of problem types, including scientific reasoning, arithmetic computation, social problem solving, and others (Chen & Siegler, 2000). By focusing on learning as it occurs, rather than just assessing the knowledge that results from learning, microgenetic methods reveal that learning paths are not characterized by abrupt change from less mature strategies to more mature ones. Instead, change is gradual. Robert Siegler (1996) likens the process to "overlapping waves" in which multiple strategies that are applicable to a problem coexist and compete with one another. How often a learner uses any one strategy will rise as others fall, creating something like overlapping waves. As the brain matures and problem-solving experience accrues, new strategies develop and the learner becomes better able to map strategies onto relevant problems. Development also involves increasing the speed, accuracy, and flexibility with which appropriate strategies are employed. Environmental influences are explored by varying the input learners receive as they solve problems (e.g., different verbal prompts from a teacher or different formats for math problems). Microgenetic work illustrates that for an individual learner knowledge acquisition is gradual and somewhat bumpy, and illuminates the variability in learning paths of different children.

Domain Specific Approaches

The retreat from the hypothesis that development proceeds through a series of universal, general stages has prompted researchers to investigate young children's learning and development in particular knowledge domains. This research reveals considerable variety both in the kinds of learning that young children are capable of and in the theoretical explanations for how they do it. The following sections survey areas of theory and research in early childhood by considering patterns of learning and development in four domains: spoken (or signed) language, literacy, number concepts, and "theory of mind."

Language Acquisition

Researchers who study the acquisition of spoken or signed language portray children's learning in a remarkably different light from the concrete, perception-bound thinker of Piaget or Vygotsky. Both theorists characterized young children's language and concepts as fundamentally different from, and less sophisticated and abstract than, those of adolescents and adults. Contemporary researchers, however, emphasize how quickly and accurately children acquire their native language. (See Fisher & Gleitman, 2002, for an overview and for specific references.) Indeed, children outstrip adult learners with respect to certain aspects of language, such as phonology (the spoken sounds of a language) and subtle points of grammar (also known as syntax). This is evident in immigrant families, in which children and adults begin second language learning simultaneously. As Johnson and Newport have shown, the adult learners—even after many years of using the new language daily—will almost certainly speak with accents and make subtle grammar and usage errors. The younger the children were when they started learning the new language, the better their language will be. Indeed, children who are younger than about 7 years old when they start second language learning usually become indistinguishable from native speakers. Young children's superiority as language learners has been interpreted as evidence for a critical period for achieving native levels of language competence.

How do children accomplish this learning? Clearly, languages must be learned—children learn the language, accent, and local usage features of the surrounding linguistic community. Yet, it is also the case that children (at least those without particular impairments) do not require deliberate tutoring or instruction to acquire spoken language. Though it is common in many cultures (and especially middle-class American homes) to make intentional efforts to cultivate children's language, young children in a broad range of social and cultural environments, including ones in which relatively little language is addressed directly to them, will nevertheless become competent speakers in relatively few years. That is, children are good at *learning* language without being *taught* it.

In fact, adults' language knowledge is often not consciously available to them and so cannot be used to teach. Studies of children's acquisition of various aspects of grammar in different languages indicate that learning does not seem to rely heavily on being corrected for grammatical errors. Indeed, children either make surprisingly few mistakes—that is, when a new construction comes into their spoken language, it is often correct—or they persist in making errors for a time despite adult corrections (as when preschoolers systematically overgeneralize regular verb patterns to irregular verbs, producing such constructions as "bringed" or "goed").

Theorists posit a variety of learning mechanisms for human children's unique language learning abilities. An important area of debate concerns whether language learning depends on innate knowledge or learning mechanisms specific to language or whether it involves more general mechanisms. Following the influential work of Noam Chomsky, many theorists have pursued the idea that children possess some innate knowledge of grammatical structures that are universal to all human languages. In this view, although languages vary in many ways, they also share common organizational principles and structures. Because the child is born with knowledge of these universal aspects of grammar, the learning task is more like selecting which particular variations from a highly constrained set are present in their community's language than constructing a grammatical system from scratch.

Recently, researchers have emphasized another ability that children bring to language learning: the ability to interpret the referential and communicative intentions of speakers, using such cues as eye gaze and emotional expression. Whereas older, associative accounts of word learning claimed that a child learned words by hearing an adult utter the word while the child contemplated the named object, recent theories suggest that children are likely to shift attention to what they think the *adult* is focusing on or intending when they hear the new word spoken. For example, 2-year-old children distinguish between a speaker's intentional and accidental actions, using the former but not the latter to interpret what the speaker is referring to. Young children are also good at eliciting *joint attention* from adults and prompting linguistic input, such as when a toddler points at an airplane and says something like, "Dat?"

Gleitman and her colleagues Landau and Naigles have proposed another information source used by children to map meanings to the utterances they hear. They argue that once a child acquires some basic knowledge of language, he or she can use it to "bootstrap" new understandings using structural cues in the sentences themselves. For example, consider the sentences "Big Bird is daxing Cookie Monster" versus "Big Bird and Cookie Monster are daxing." In the first sentence, Big Bird is the subject of the verb and Cookie Monster is the object, indicating that Big Bird is doing something to Cookie Monster (e.g., feeding). In the second sentence, Big Bird and Cookie Monster are both subjects of the verb, indicating that they are engaging in the same action together or equally (e.g., dancing). Children as young as 2 years old use these kinds of grammatical cues to infer new word meanings. As children's command of language grows, they potentially make increasing use of this kind of syntactic bootstrapping.

Of course, no one expects that young children have *explicit* knowledge of subjects and objects or transitive and intransitive verbs—though their ability to produce and comprehend various utterances indicates that they are processing these elements. Both the learning processes and the child's resulting knowledge of language are assumed to be implicit. In general, as successful as their language learning is, children's metalinguistic abilities—that is, their abilities to reflect on and articulate their knowledge of language—tend to be weak. As with adults, the rapid processing children do as they engage in speech dialogue is largely unconscious and possibly inaccessible (a point which pertains to the next topic: learning to read).

Learning to Read

In contrast to children's natural, universal, and robust facility in learning to produce and comprehend spoken language, learning to read fluently generally requires deliberate teaching and sustained practice. Children who are not taught to read typically will not learn on their own. Many children who are deliberately taught nevertheless do not achieve fluency.

While fluent reading involves orchestrating many skills, the foundation of reading is the insight that written symbols represent sounds in speech. Written English, like most writing systems, is based on an *alphabetic* principle by which symbols stand for phonemes (the individual sounds that make up words). Other written systems may be *ideographic* (such as traditional Chinese characters that directly represent meanings) or *syllabic* (in which written symbols correspond to syllables composed of several phonemes). Alphabetic systems are efficient, in that many fewer symbols are needed to represent the spoken language. But the cognitive mapping between symbol and speech sound is also more abstract, which poses problems for some learners.

Although children in the late preschool and early school years have generally mastered phonology for the purposes of speaking and listening, it may be hard for them to access phonemes directly and consciously. Phonemes are abstract entities, embedded in the speech stream. In natural speech, breaks between the phonemes in a word are not discernible—they blend into each other. It is impossible to pronounce most phonemes individually—you must combine them with other sounds to articulate them—but the same individual phoneme is pronounced slightly differently in different contexts. In English the mapping between phonemes and letters is particularly messy—the same letter can map to several phonemes and the same sound can map to multiple letters. Although babies are excellent at extracting the phonemes of new languages that they hear (an ability that seems to peak by 8 months of age!), isolating phonemes in a *consciously* accessible form, as one must learn to read with an alphabetic system, is a very different matter. There are significant individual differences in children's ability to do this.

Becoming a competent reader requires quite a bit more than understanding the basic principle of symbol-sound mapping. One set of skills involves learning to recognize and discriminate the written symbols (letters), understanding the conventions of print (e.g., spaces between words, periods at the end of sentences), and mapping the actual correspondences between individual letters, or clusters, and sounds (e.g., "th"). These skills allow the reader to *decode* text—literally, to go from printed symbols to the corresponding spoken words—in what is sometimes described as a bottom-up process. But reading texts with good comprehension also involves top-down processes, such as inferring the author's intentions, filling in information that is assumed but not stated, and recognizing the conventions of different genres (e.g., newspaper, package label, various styles of fiction, etc.). With sufficient practice, many readers automatize the decoding processes, allowing them to execute them quickly and with relatively little load on working memory. This frees memory and attention for processing the text's meaning. In contrast, readers for whom decoding individual words remains laborious may have a difficult time extracting meaning from text. By the time they finish decoding one word, they have forgotten what came before, making it difficult to connect words into phrases and sentences. For students who struggle to decode text, reading becomes a difficult and even embarrassing chore, and it can be challenging to maintain their investment and motivation in the learning process.

Though the research literature on reading makes clear that expert readers fluently deploy and coordinate both bottom-up and top-down processes, questions about how to teach these component skills and their coordination, while preserving reading as a meaningful and enjoyable experience, have been controversial in reading education. Indeed, polarized forms of phonics approaches (emphasizing decoding skills as the entry point into reading) versus whole language approaches (embedding reading and writing for meaning in ongoing classroom activities) led to a particularly contentious period known as the Reading Wars in curricular and pedagogical debates about teaching reading. Recently, many schools have adopted balanced literacy programs, recognizing that learning to read involves gaining a comprehensive suite of skills.

There is also greater recognition of the considerable variation among children in where the learning difficulties lie and what approaches are most helpful. Emphasizing one aspect of reading to the exclusion of others tends to leave educators with a limited and less flexible tool kit for helping all children learn to read.

Recent research also identifies better ways to assess and address reading differences and disabilities among learners. Numerous studies provide evidence that reading disability is associated with impairments in phonological processing, including the ability to access individual speech sounds and to work with them in flexible ways, such as creating words that rhyme (McCandliss & Wolmetz, 2004). Some impairments may appear very early in development; recent work suggests that differences in how infants process speech sounds can predict differences in reading abilities years later. Carefully designed and controlled intervention studies provide encouraging evidence about teaching materials and strategies that can lead to significant improvements for children who struggle to learn to read. In particular, interventions that focus on explicit training in phonological awareness and alphabetic decoding skills can lead to major improvements for children with mild to severe reading impairments.

Number, Counting, and Arithmetic

Representing and reasoning with numerical quantities is not just a school subject—it's a basic capacity of human thought. Human infants in the first 6 months of life show some ability to process precise quantities and to compare events involving adding or subtracting items for very small set sizes (up to three). Infants also show an increasing ability to discriminate among larger sets of different sizes, but seem not to do so in precise ways. For example, 6-month-olds discriminate between sets of 8 versus 16 dots but not 8 versus 12 dots. Interestingly, it seems to take several years before children can make precise discriminations among sets larger than a few items (e.g., four versus five). This suggests that the mechanism infants use to track the numerosity of small set sizes could differ from those used by older children.

During the preschool years, children represent and act on quantities in ways that are clearly mathematical. Preschoolers almost universally count. Most 3-year-olds, for instance, can count sets of objects up to about ten, and their behavior, tested in a variety of experiments, indicates that they are not simply engaging in rote recitations of the count list or blind imitations of counting behavior. Rochel Gelman and C. R. Gallistel (1978) have identified five *counting principles* that characterize preschool children's counting abilities:

1. *One-one correspondence*: Counting involves pairing the objects to be counted with numerical tags (usually count words) so that each object receives one and only one tag.

2. *Stable order*: The tags used for counting should always be used in the same order.

3. *Cardinality*: The last number tag used in the count corresponds to the total number of objects in the set.

4. *Order irrelevance*: Although the tags must have a stable order, it doesn't matter in what order you count the objects, as long as each one is counted once and only once.

5. *Abstraction*: Counting can be applied to any set of discrete objects or events—people, hand claps, jumps, telephone rings, and so forth.

Evidence that preschoolers' counting follows these principles comes from experiments in which children are asked to judge a puppet's counting. Preschoolers will, for instance, declare that the puppet is wrong if he counts the same item twice or skips an item. But they will accept a correct count from the puppet, even if it differs from the way they would do it themselves—for example, by skipping around rather than counting down the row in order—as long as the other counting principles are not violated. Despite these skills, children's own counting performances show a lot of situational and individual variability. Performance demands in counting are fairly high. The child must keep track of which items have been counted and which have not, where he or she is in the tag list, and so forth.

There is some controversy as to whether (1) counting principles are innate or available very early in development and provide the structure that facilitates children's learning ("principles first" view); (2) experience watching and imitating conventional counting leads to the abstraction of some or all of the principles; or (3) the developmental process involves an interweaving among some form of early or innate knowledge, experience, and the progressive abstraction of counting principles. Regardless of one's position on the sources of competence, however, number knowledge is a particularly clear example of an area in which new (post-Piagetian) methods have led to a reassessment of young children's capabilities. Most children arrive at school with an understanding of counting and using counting to solve simple mathematical problems, as well as magnitudes and ordering for small numbers (National Research Council [NRC], 2001a); however, there are also systematic differences in young children's mathematical abilities that arise from variations in their early experiences.

Recent years have brought growing concern in U.S. education about persistent achievement differences among socioeconomic groups. Identifying and closing these achievement gaps has become an urgent priority at national, state, and local levels. In mathematics, students from lower socioeconomic groups and from families with lower levels of parental education show significant gaps in their mathematical skills when they enter kindergarten. Griffin, Case, and Siegler (1994), for example, found delays in poor inner-city children's ability to identify which of two single-digit numbers was larger, to judge which of two single-digit numbers is closer to a third single-digit number, and to solve simple addition problems if they were presented ver-

bally rather than with physical objects. They hypothesized that these children might lack a conceptual structure, which they termed the "mental number line," and they developed a curriculum for kindergarteners that involves games and number-line activities that target the development of various components of this conceptual structure. An intervention study demonstrated learning improvements that were maintained through the end of first grade.

Preschool children can participate in and learn from a variety of number-based activities and experiences. Indeed, traditional advice to delay mathematical activities until children reach a more advanced developmental stage (particularly Piaget's concrete operations) has basically been turned on its head. Findings such as Griffin, Case, and Siegler's indicate that an enriched mathematical environment is advantageous to young children and may help address persistent equity issues in mathematics education. But it is equally important to base decisions about number activities in preschool on what is known about the development of number concepts and skills in young children, rather than indiscriminately pushing down an academic curriculum from grade school. (See Flavell, Miller, & Miller, 2001, for additional discussion and references related to young children's number knowledge as well as the following section on "theory of mind.")

Theory of Mind

Number research provides compelling examples that preschoolers are more competent than traditionally thought. Similar evidence comes from research into children's "theory of mind." Researchers who study theory of mind, or naïve psychology, investigate understanding that people, unlike other physical objects in the world, have mental states such as beliefs and desires and that these have causal power. That is, people's beliefs and desires cause them to act in certain ways. Further, people can have false beliefs that lead them to behave in ways that do not accord with objective reality. (For example, if I believe that it is raining I will carry an umbrella regardless of whether it really is raining outside.) Recall Piaget's description of the young child as able to reason only about concrete objects and as unable to hold contradictory representations in mind simultaneously. Clearly, that sort of thinker would be unlikely to reason about and reflect on ideas, thoughts, and beliefs, let alone to separate his or her own knowledge and beliefs from those of others. Reflecting on others' desires and beliefs would be especially difficult when these conflict with the mental states of the child himself or herself.

Evidence for very early attention to the knowledge states of self and others was described in the language development section. A toddler who elicits a parent's attention while pointing at an object or who shifts attention to the object being regarded by the speaking adult could be showing at least implicit awareness that he or she does not know some piece of information and that another person could know. Empathy researchers find that toddlers will comfort others in distress by patting them or bringing a favorite toy. One could interpret this behavior as evidence of awareness, on some level, of others' feelings and as an effort to change them. Very young children also seem to act on the perceived desires of others. Eighteen-month-olds will offer food to another person based on the person's earlier display of joy over that food (and disgust with another). More importantly, they do so even when the person's preferences differ from their own.

By age 3, children's language includes mental terms such as think and know, and children begin to talk explicitly about various aspects of mental life. Children this age distinguish objectively real objects from imagined ones, for example, being able to tell which dog (real or imagined) could be petted and seen by others. They are able to explicitly describe their own and others' knowledge state under certain circumstances. Most 3-year-olds who were asked whether they knew what was shown on a hidden picture accurately said yes if they had seen the picture and no if they had not. By age 4, children can go a step further to describe the causes of that knowledge or lack thereof. That is, they can say that they know what's on the picture because they saw it or that they do not know because they did not see the picture. Although some 3-year-olds (on some tasks) can reason about beliefs and their implications for behavior, fuller understanding is found among 4-year-olds.

Researchers use *false belief tasks* to explore understanding of the links between informational access, belief, and behavior. Although details vary across studies, one popular version is as follows: An experimenter shows a 3- or 4-year-old a familiar crayon box and asks what's inside. The child reasonably answers, "Crayons." When the box is opened, though, it has pennies inside. The experimenter closes the box and asks the child the key false belief question—what will another person (who hasn't seen inside) say is in the box? Results show that most 4-year-olds can overcome their own knowledge of reality (pennies) to accurately predict the false beliefs (crayons) of others.

The literature on theory of mind capabilities suggests that assessing another's desires develops before the ability to identify beliefs and that, not surprisingly, children can assess true beliefs earlier than false beliefs. Further, the studies described above suggest that children act on implicit knowledge about mental states before they can explicitly describe those understandings. Preschool children are clearly coming to understand their own minds and those of other people. They can use this information to predict and make sense of the behavior of others. These skills have interesting implications for social and cognitive aspects of school learning.

Theory of mind capacities affect a child's intrapersonal and interpersonal skills, which in turn affect school success. At the intrapersonal level, a child who can reflect on his or her own knowledge and identify gaps in it has taken the first step toward filling those gaps. This child can seek information from a teacher, a peer, or by other means. Children who cannot consistently evaluate their own knowledge are less able to take charge of their learning in this way. In the late preschool and early elementary years, children also begin to spontaneously use strategies to enhance their memories. Children who can reflect on the workings of their own minds are positioned to participate fully in learning by employing strategies to find out what is not yet known, such as asking questions when confused and using mnemonic devices to remember new information or aid recall. Although some theory of mind abilities emerge in the preschool years without direct intervention, classroom practices that explicitly encourage children to reflect on their own knowledge—what they already know, what they need to find out, how they might find out—support their development as effective learners and problem solvers (NRC, 2001b).

Theory of mind skills are also critical for participating fully in classroom discourse. Imagine how strange it could seem that a teacher, an adult authority, would ask a child, "What's 2 + 2?" or "What day is it?" In normal discourse, one asks questions to get information one does not know, but in a school situation, adults ask questions with a different motivation. They know that 2 + 2 = 4, and they know what day it is. They ask the questions to assess the child's knowledge. A learner who can entertain hypotheses about the different motivations of others will adapt easily to this interaction style. (Having experience at home or in preschool with this sort of interaction will also help.) Theory of mind skills also underpin modes of thought related to science and argument. A child who believes (as very young preschoolers seem to) that simply perceiving an object leads to complete knowledge of it will not understand that others could have different interpretations of the same observations or evidence. Clearly, this idea must change for learners to engage in activities such as hypothesis testing in science, debate, argumentation, and persuasive writing.

Beyond the ability to undertake styles of discourse critical to mature thinking and school learning, a child who is sensitive to the needs and desires of others is likely to engage in positive social interactions in the classroom. Theory of mind skills underlie children's ability to understand the viewpoints of others, to cooperate with them, and to resolve emotional and intellectual arguments. These skills in turn affect the quality of interactions with the peers and adults with whom children learn. The clear message coming from the developmental literature is that cognitive, motivational, and socioemotional development are interdependent, critical contributors to readiness for learning in school.

Effective Learning Environments for Young Children

The idea that socioemotional and cognitive development are intertwined and interdependent dovetails with ideas about the best ways to care for and educate young children. Whereas child care and education were traditionally thought of as separate, current thinking holds that the two are mutually dependent. The child who feels secure, loved, and emotionally supported is in a better position to explore the world and to interact positively with teachers in learning situations. With larger numbers of young children in school and day care settings, parents, educators, and researchers alike are recognizing the need for, and beginning to demand, quality educational experiences for young children. This demand likely arises from the accruing evidence that children are more capable learners than traditional theories and educational practice reflect. Also, we now know that quality learning experiences in the PreK years can yield positive effects for later school learning.

Assessments of long-term programs designed to prepare underprivileged children for school (such as Head Start) provide information about the characteristics of quality educational settings and positive outcomes that can be achieved in such settings. Child outcome results vary according to the specifics of the program, but comprehensive reviews of the findings suggest that, while IQ gains are not maintained, positive effects include fewer special education placements, reduced grade retention, reduced criminal behavior, and long-term achievement gains on standardized tests. Programs with positive outcomes tended to share certain characteristics including coherently organized curricula that support the development of school-relevant knowledge and thinking skills; qualified teaching and supervisory staff; low staff-to-student ratios; small class sizes; and strong, supportive relationships between families and schools. Barnett, Hustedt, Hawkinson, and Robin, 2006 evaluated the new wave of publicly funded state preschool programs using benchmarks that reflect similar features.

As the research reviewed in this chapter indicates, designing supportive learning environments for young children is not a simple, obvious matter. On the one hand, despite great variety in cultural practices in child rearing, many aspects of development seem to proceed normally and reliably in naturally occurring environments that have not been specifically designed with children's development in mind. On the other hand, some aspects of development clearly benefit from an enriched set of learning opportunities, and potentially troublesome developmental gaps among individual children or between groups of children from different backgrounds can be ameliorated by early interventions. (See publications from the National Research Council, 2000 and 2001b, for a detailed discussion and references related to early learning environments and development.)

Translating developmental research into the design of learning environments is no easy task. Often, complex findings are oversimplified and distorted. Weak or inadequate attempts at applying research may fail to yield desired results and can cause educators and policy makers to distrust research in general. One area for caution, for example,

is the recent explosion of attention to early brain development, which has led to a number of dubious attempts to exploit the public's interest. Toy manufacturers, computer game developers, and curriculum publishers have marketed "educational" products that are purported to enhance young children's brain development. In fact, it is premature to attempt to apply developmental neuroscience findings to designing products or experiences for young children. Most neuroscience data comes from animal studies. Although new brain imaging techniques are enabling innovative research with humans, many of these techniques are not suitable for use with young children, and there is relatively little developmental data available, especially for normally developing children. We are on more secure ground with well-established findings that children thrive in social environments in which they can interact frequently and spontaneously with adults and peers, where there are opportunities for language-rich discussions, where they are respected and encouraged as learners, and where toys and other materials allow them to explore freely.

Conclusion

This is an exciting time in the study of early childhood. There is an expansive and unprecedented sense of the richness and intricacy of the phenomena of learning and development during this period. The field is also witnessing a generative period theoretically, with a multiplicity of viewpoints, methodological approaches, and proposed mechanisms being actively pursued. While this multiplicity may be frustrating to someone seeking a simple, clear answer to the question of how young children develop, it is stimulating to those willing to accept the complexity of development during this amazing time of life. Particularly exciting are the prospects for collaboration among child development researchers, educators, and policy makers to create rich supporting environments and study their effects on young children's learning and development.

References and Further Readings

Barnett, W. S., Hustedt, J. T., Hawkinson, L. E., & Robin, K. B. (2006). *The state of preschool 2006*. New Brunswick, NJ: National Institute for Early Education Research. Retrieved from http://nieer.org/yearbook

Chen, Z., & Siegler, R. S. (2000). Across the great divide: Bridging the gap between understanding of toddlers' and older children's thinking. *Monographs of the Society for Research in Child Development, 65*, 1–96.

Fisher, C., & Gleitman, L. R. (2002). Language acquisition. In H. F. Pashler (Series Ed.) & C. R. Gallistel (Volume Ed.), *Stevens' handbook of experimental psychology, vol 1: Learning and motivation*, (3rd ed., pp. 445–496). New York: Wiley.

Flavell, J. H., Miller, P. H., & Miller, S. A. (2001). *Cognitive development* (4th ed.). Englewood Cliffs, NJ: Prentice Hall.

Gelman, R., & Baillargeon, R. (1983). A review of some Piagetian concepts. In J. H. Flavell & E. Markman (Eds.), *Handbook of child psychology (4th ed.). Vol. 3: Cognitive development* (pp. 167–230). New York: Wiley.

Gelman, R., & Gallistel, C. R. (1978). *The child's understanding of number.* Cambridge, MA: Harvard University Press.

Griffin, S. A., Case, R., & Siegler, R. S. (1994). Rightstart: Providing the central conceptual prerequisites for first formal learning of arithmetic to students at risk for school failure. In K. McGilly (Ed.), *Classroom lessons: Integrating cognitive theory and classroom practice* (pp. 25–49). Cambridge, MA: MIT Press.

Johnson, J., & Newport, E. (1989). Critical period effects in second-language learning: The influence of maturational state on the acquisition of English as a second language. *Cognitive Psychology, 21,* 60–99.

Landau, B., & Gleitman, L. R. (1985). *Language and experience.* Cambridge, MA: Harvard University Press.

McCandliss, B. D., & Wolmetz, M. (2004). Developmental psychobiology of reading disability. In B. J. Casey (Ed.), *Developmental Psychobiology, Vol. 23* (pp. 69–110). Washington, DC: American Psychiatric Publishing.

Miller, P. (2002). *Theories of developmental psychology* (4th ed.). New York: Worth.

Naigles, L. (1990). Children use syntax to learn verb meanings. *Journal of Child Language, 17,* 357–374.

National Research Council. (2001a). *Adding it up: Helping children learn mathematics.* J. Kilpatrick, J. Swafford, & B. Findell (Eds.), Mathematics Learning Study Committee, Center for Education, Division of Behavioral and Social Sciences and Education. Washington, DC: National Academies Press.

National Research Council. (2001b). *Eager to learn: Educating our preschoolers.* Committee on Early Childhood Pedagogy. B. T. Bowman, M. S. Donovan, & M. S. Burns (Eds.). Commission on Behavioral and Social Sciences and Education. Washington, DC: National Academies Press.

National Research Council & Institute of Medicine. (2000). *From neurons to neighborhoods: The science of early childhood development.* Committee on Integrating the Science of Early Childhood Development. J. P. Shonkoff & D. Phillips (Eds.). Board on Children, Youth, and Families, Commission on Behavioral and Social Sciences and Education. Washington, DC: National Academies Press.

Siegler, R. S. (1996). *Emerging minds: The process of change in children's thinking.* New York: Oxford University Press.

9

DEVELOPMENT

3–5

HEATHER A. DAVIS

The Ohio State University

My third grade teacher told my mother there was a lot going on in my mind. How did she guess?
—John Philo Dixon, *The Spatial Child*

Understanding children's thinking, including their decision making in social situations, is a hard task for teachers. A keen understanding of developmental theory can help teachers interact with and meet the needs of their students more effectively. Unfortunately, developmental research is often discussed out of context. One challenge in applying findings from developmental psychology to classrooms is figuring out how to translate a construct in a way that changes or clarifies how teachers instruct and interact with students (Davis, 2004). The purpose of this chapter is to assist readers in identifying common themes in the cognitive and socioemotional characteristics of third- through fifth-grade students and to identify guidelines for modifying classroom instruction and interactions to be developmentally appropriate.

The Challenges of Being a Preadolescent

One task of developmental psychologists is to identify what defines each developmental period. Biologically, the period from 8 to 11 years old tends to be defined by what it is sandwiched between. Preadolescents are, in part, defined by their lack of experience with the biological changes associated with puberty. The "pre" implies they are still somewhat childlike, and yet it is during this period that preadolescents experience a dramatic change in their thinking.

A consistent finding among scholars is that the period from 8 to 11 years old is defined by children's attempts to

understand themselves in the wake of copious performance feedback. Erik Erikson identified tasks, what he termed developmental crises, which are characterized by contexts and tasks children and adults face throughout their life span. For Erikson, the period when children enter and transition through primary school is defined by their attempts to understand what it means to be industrious, to successfully accomplish the tasks allotted by teachers and peers. Sroufe, Egeland, Carlson, and Collins echo Erikson's call dubbing the period of middle childhood "the era of competence" (2005, p. 148). Children who experience success with tasks transition into adolescence feeling valuable and productive, while children who struggle and fail move into adolescence feeling inferior to those around them.

Robert Havighurst (1971) took a much broader approach to describing developmental tasks, identifying a broader set of interpersonal and social tasks. In this vein, Hughes (1999) argues that in addition to the need for industry, preadolescent children are striving to satisfy their needs to belong and to have order in their worlds. This still seems to be too narrow a characterization to encompass the wealth of findings. What persists from across early childhood to and through preadolescence in the literature is the child's pursuit of greater and greater control over their "self," what scholars like Ryan, Connell, and Deci call self-determination, coupled with their limited skills in regulating their behaviors. In order to truly feel self-determined, students must feel competent, autonomous, and connected in their classroom environment (Ryan, Connell, & Deci, 1985). From this perspective, I identified four critical tasks that reflect the preadolescent child's attempt to feel competent, autonomous, and connected throughout third through fifth grade:

- *Managing Symbols—Making Sense of the World:* How do I make sense of more and more information and what should I do with information that conflicts with what I feel, what I believe, or what I know?
- *Merging Conceptions of Effort and Ability:* How do I make sense of not knowing and of making mistakes? What does it mean to try hard and succeed or fail?
- *Understanding Classroom Relationships:* Who matters in this class and where do I stand compared to the other students in this class?
- *Regulating Academic Behaviors and Emotions:* What does it mean to set goals, to create a plan of action, and to be responsible for the result? How do I resolve conflicts when I disagree with a teacher or someone in my class?

The following sections flesh out each theme, highlighting changes in children's thinking and the ways in which qualitative differences in how preadolescents view the world shape the nature of their intellectual and social interactions. Sroufe et al. argue that understanding where children are developmentally involves understanding "the totality of the person's history" (2005, p. 150). This includes the history of how the child has adapted to changes in his or her environment and the constraints of the current context. Preadolescents come to school with a wealth of prior knowledge. In addition to informal learning, children have acquired foundational subject matter knowledge from their formal experiences in PreK–2 classrooms. Children also bring with them emerging conceptions of friendship and social roles, rules and fairness, status and conflict. By third grade, some children will have already experienced problems with teachers, classmates, and academic subject matter. These past failures and successes create pathways for future failures and future successes—but not in an inevitable way. Thus it is the task of third- through fifth-grade teachers to discover each child's emerging schooling history and think in terms of what developmental trajectory students are following and how to maximize their opportunities for growth.

What developmental changes allow for children to see their world in a more dynamic way? Table 9.1 summarizes

Table 9.1   Developmental Challenges Facing Third- to Fifth-Grade Students and Their Teachers

	Cognitive Processing Milestones	*Acquiring New Cognitive Tools*	*Internalizing Language and Culture*
Managing Symbols: Making Sense of the World	Increased capacity to concentrate, hold, process, and store new knowledge. More practiced skills become automatic. Actively making connections between new experiences and prior knowledge. Knowledge becoming more structured as children organize what they know around salient principles. Increasing knowledge and practice with strategies to learn, but limited in ability to monitor implementation and success of strategies.	Students with prior experience bring intuitive understandings with many symbols. Intuitive understandings may resist change. Able to identify sequences and to classify symbols into different categories and subcategories. Struggle to identify fundamental, defining principles.	Increasing focus on comprehension. Children are able to understand the meaning of words from basic definitions. Can appreciate that one word can have multiple meaning. Learning to relate the meaning of individual words to each other to abstract broader meaning. Flexible understanding of language enables word humor and to "play" with language. Able to understand grammatical structures associated with telling stories.
Merging Conceptions of Effort and Ability	Able to draw cause-and-effect inferences. Increasing awareness and attention to how one's performance compares with others in the class. Increasingly more likely to attribute their successes and failures on tasks to stability ability than to effort.	Children view themselves as active agents, able to create knowledge. Increasing sense of self as possessing stable internal qualities. Begin to differentiate, organize, and coordinate multiple representations of themselves across variety of capacities.	Internalizing language of classroom praise: What does it mean to be smart, get it right, to work/try harder, or try again? Focus in games-with-rules is to understand social constructions of "winning" / "losing" and what it means to play on a "team." Children driven by desire to understand what it means to be and to feel industrious. Will engage in behaviors that protect them from feeling inferior.

(Continued)

Table 9.1   (Continued)

	Cognitive Processing Milestones	*Acquiring New Cognitive Tools*	*Internalizing Language and Culture*
Understanding Classroom Relationships	Children can begin to reason about what is right and wrong, and make some moral evaluations. Sensitive to and seeking to understand mores and norms. Increasing awareness of their own and others' psychological mental states. Recognize emotions can be blended and multiple.	Seeking to understand social hierarchies, social categories, and the relative importance of social events. Able to understand complementary roles, reciprocity, and mutual respect. Play characterized by rule-oriented games. Increasingly able to understand another's perspective. Use skills to anticipate, cooperate, and manipulate others.	Understanding social concepts, like rules and roles, begin to guide behavior. Struggle to understand what it means to be similar, be in a group, and to conform. Increasing communication skills enable peers to negotiate what they want. Have internalized the "arguing process" and the exent to which argumentation leads to resolution. Increasing mastery of conversational skills including advanced questioning skills, shifting the focus of conversations, and infering the intent of unclear or inconsistent comments.
Regulating Behavior and Emotion	Children able to selectively attend, set goals, make plans, and adapt strategies. Increasingly able to reflect on behavior, thoughts, and strategies. Increasing ability to inhibit primary, and often inappropriate, mental and behavioral responses and to delay gratification.	Developing understanding of will, autonomy, and obligation. To be autonomous is to be self-regulated. Morality is relative, people can agree to change the rules when they want to. Shift from analogical reasoning, that is using what you know about one problem to solve another, to scientific-based reasoning, where children make evidence-based arguments.	Increasingly able to read nonverbal language from adults and peers, to identify masked emotions, to mask their own emotions, and to express blended emotions. Acquiring sociolinguistic behaviors such as learning to be silent, make eye contact and personal space, interact with adults, respond to questions, and interrupt in appropriate ways. Increasingly able to understand temporal, spatial, and comparative terms.

the major developmental changes that occur during this period, organized in each row by the four defining tasks. It is important to understand that within the field of developmental psychology there are several traditions, each having a lens (i.e., perspective) that controls which aspects of change are viewed as underlying the unique way 8- to 11-year-old children think about their worlds. The first column lists changes 8- to 11-year-old children evidence in the way they process information from a Cognitive Science perspective. From this perspective, they are able to manage a more dynamic world because of changes in the amount of information they can manipulate mentally, their efficiency with connecting new information to things they have already learned, and their growing repertoire of problem-solving strategies. Qualitative differences in preadolescent thinking from younger children reflect changes in their capacity to manage more and more information in their intellectual and social worlds. The second column lists the different kinds of cognitive tools preadolescent children acquire from a Piagetian perspective. Jean Piaget outlined a theory of cognitive development and qualitative differences in children's thinking that not only reflects

their ability to process more information, but also reflects meaningful changes in the way they understand and organize information. Piaget described how children acquired each of these cognitive tools in a predictable sequence so as to ultimately support their understanding of the world and support their ability later on, as adults, to think in complex ways. Preadolescents are defined by their struggle to acquire what Piaget called conservation tools, or basic principles that enable us to hold the world together and view it as predictable. The third column lists changes in 8 to 11 year old children's language acquisition from a Sociocultural perspective. Lev Vygotsky outlined a theory of cognitive development that argued language—a defining tool of one's culture—plays a crucial role in shaping thinking. Language serves as a gatekeeper to full participation in a community. It is not merely that children are able to communicate better, but that the greater their literacy, the more flexible their thinking becomes. In Table 9.1, language is broadly defined to include elements of more implicit semiotics (i.e., cultural symbols) and nonverbal language communication skills. Throughout preadolescence, children learn about the multiplicity of symbols and learn that words, expressions, postures, and actions can have multiple meanings that can vary across their family, peer, school, and larger cultures.

Managing Symbols: Making Sense of the World

By third grade, children have acquired a wide repertoire of symbols, or mental representations. The term *symbol* refers to the mental images we hold of object, actions, and relationships. By preadolescence, children have become so adept at acquiring symbols that when they encounter a new word or a new experience they can use the context surrounding the word to glean the name and meaning of the new symbol. Preadolescents are focused on comprehension. They are able to understand the meaning of words from basic definitions and can appreciate that one word may have multiple meanings. Their flexible understanding of language enables them to participate in word humor and to play with language. Their increased understanding of grammatical structures can spur them toward telling stories and writing letters.

Physically, their increased gross and fine motor skills allow them to adeptly manipulate and explore their world, and their increased capacity to concentrate, hold, process, and store new knowledge allows them to retain many experiences. They are actively making connections between new experiences and prior knowledge. Practiced skills become automatic, freeing up space for more attention to new things to learn.

But the seminal marker of this period is that children's thinking becomes more sophisticatedly patterned. The acquisition of new knowledge compels them to find ways to organize what they know around salient principles. As toddlers and young children, the principles children chose to organize their understandings tended to be superficial—guided by look, size, or conduct. In cases where they had limited experience, their classifications might have been crude, grouping things together in a way that would not make sense to an older child or adult. But as children transition to and through preadolescence they begin to encounter failure with some of their intuitive conceptions (Ben-Ze'ev & Star, 2001). When teachers talk about children holding misconceptions in science or social studies, they are usually describing incidents of children having classified something inappropriately. But the term *intuitive conception* is used more broadly to describe the prior knowledge structures children use when trying to understand something new. From this perspective, children's attempts to understand new events using old understandings, even when children have accurately organized their knowledge, represent a type of intuitive approach to understanding. These intuitive understandings can, essentially, interfere with new learning. Thus, the central challenges for teachers of preadolescents are to (1) assess children's intuitive understandings, (2) consider how their own

understanding of the event differs, and (3) create opportunities for children to reorganize the symbols they have acquired around adult principles.

Organizing symbols according to basic principles that enable us to hold the world together and view it as predictable is a life-long task; each time adults encounter new phenomena they make sense of it by identifying the underlying principles that define the event. In this way, preadolescent thinking begins to approach adult thinking. Piaget called the principles that define events and allow humans to view the world as predictable *conservation skills*. Conservation skills include:

- *Identity:* Understanding that phenomena or events have properties that define them and make them unique. Changing these properties, not conserving them, essentially changes the phenomena or event.
- *Reversibility:* Understanding that phenomena or events have superficial properties that can be changed and changed back. Disrupting them does not change the phenomena or event.
- *Seriation:* Understanding that phenomena or events have sequences that define them that must be conserved, or held constant. For example, when employing a mnemonic for the order of operations algorithm for solving complex math equations (PEMDAS, i.e., Parentheses, Exponents, Multiplication, Division, Addition, Subtraction), which sequences must be held constant?
- *Classification:* Understanding that phenomena or events can be classified, sometimes into multiple categories. Understanding which classifications work and, in some cases, whether there are superordinate and subordinate categories (i.e., within continents there are cities embedded in countries).
- *Amount and Volume:* Understanding that phenomena or events can have multiple dimensions that define them. For example, when studying planets, children learn that multiple dimensions need to be held constant in order for a plant to sustain life.

Teachers of preadolescents need to identify when children are not employing these conservation skills to understand assigned academic tasks. To do this teachers need to break down, or deconstruct, their curricula and anticipate where children will get stuck. Children who do not organize their thoughts around conservation tools are said to evidence preoperational thought because they have not yet acquired the cognitive tools to understand dynamic events. Children who organize their understandings around conservation tools are said to evidence concrete-operational thought. An additional challenge for teachers of preadolescents is that children may not acquire these cognitive tools at the same pace in each content area. Piaget applied the term *décalage* to children's tendency to exhibit characteristics of more than one developmental period simultaneously. For example, while a child might evidence concrete thinking in language arts, enabling him or her to write stories that have correct grammatical structure, he or she may struggle in math to solve problems with multiple, sequenced steps. The more experience children have had with an event, the more likely their thinking is to be organized and complex.

The Case of Teaching Fractions

Nowhere can the dilemmas of intuitive understandings interfering with new learning be seen more clearly than in the case of learning fractions. In mathematics instruction, learning fractions is a focal task for children in Grades 3 through 5. Children enter third grade with a solid understanding of addition and subtraction of whole numbers and the ability to quickly recall addition and subtraction facts. Moreover, earlier teachers will have introduced concepts of decimals, place value, base 10, and multiplication. When learning about fractions, many of children's intuitive conceptions about whole numbers interfere with their ability to fully understand part-to-whole relationships. Figure 9.1 demonstrates how whole number progression can interfere with understanding sequence in fractions.

When learning about whole numbers, children acquire an accurate understanding sequence that as the number gets larger the amount or size increases. This intuitive conception is disrupted when they learn fractions. When numbers appear in the denominator, the sequential relationship is reversed: as the number in the denominator gets larger, the amount or size of the fraction gets smaller. Until children understand that fractions have unique properties (identity) that must be held constant with a distinct sequential relationship, they will struggle when learning fractions.

Acquiring conservation skills is ultimately needed to truly understand fractions. Children must understand that fractions can change in appearance but still remain the same fractional amount. For example, oranges and grapefruits are not the same size; however, one-half of an orange is the same fractional amount as one-half of a grapefruit. Moreover, children need to understand that fractional quantities are distinct from each other—that in terms of the fractional quantity, one-half of an orange is more than one-fourth of a grapefruit. Without understanding identity (whole-to-part relationships hold constant) and reversi-

bility (superficial features like size and shape change), children may be deceived by the relative size of pieces of fruit. Teachers need to create activities that trouble children's intuitive notions of quantity, ultimately pushing them to question, If fractions are not about absolute size, then what are factions?

As children's learning of fractions becomes more complex, so does their classification scheme. Intuitive notions of base 10 and multiplication, which allow children to easily classify groups of numbers into mutually exclusive categories of 10s, 100s, 1,000s, or multiples of 3s, 4s, and 5s, and so forth, interfere with the complex classification system needed for fractions. In that fractions can be transformed to appear with common denominators, children must learn that each fraction has a root quantity (i.e., the lowest common denominator) and can, when transformed, also belong to any number of other groups. In other words one-half can be represented as two-fourths, three-sixths, or four-eighths and in doing so can belong to the fourths, sixths, and eighths families. But, in not sharing the same root quantity, it does not belong to other families: thirds, fifths, sevenths. Even more confusing is how to transfer these principles of multiple classifications and multiple representations of fractional quantities to understand how whole numbers can be represented in alternate ways (see Figure 9.2). To fully understand fractions, children must come to think about math in radically different, more flexible ways.

The power of Piaget's theory is that during this period children are struggling to acquire conservation skills in all subject areas. The challenges of writing a story someone else can understand are to carefully select words that have unique meaning (Identity), to transform them into past or future tense when necessary (Reversibility), to sequence them in a predictable way (i.e., sentence structure), and to organize their presentation in a way that describes characters, involves a plot, and finds resolution (Classification). Understanding the history of a people involves identifying critical events that held meaning for people of that region; understanding how the unfolding of events shaped the way

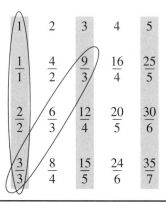

Figure 9.2 The Challenge of Understanding Fractions in Terms of Multiple Representations and Multiple Classifications

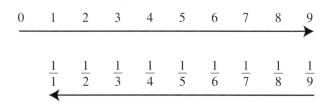

Figure 9.1 The Challenge of Understanding Fractions in Terms of Their "Reverse" Sequence

people thought about themselves and their country; being able to organize a series of events together to understand the worldview of a cohort of peoples; being able to look across peoples and classify different types of events that, when they happen, affect peoples' lives in similar ways. Errors children make when they mismatch definitions, mislabel the order in a series, or misapply an algorithm can reveal to teachers the ways in which they view the phenomena in a qualitatively different way from their students. Preadolescents need activities that reveal underlying principles so that they may reorganize their existing symbols in more sophisticated ways.

Merging Conceptions of Effort and Ability

Ten-year-old children have been preparing their entire lives for the competence they show now. Their reasoning skills are supported by years of wrestling with cognitive problems in their real and fantasy worlds. (Sroufe et al., 2005, p. 172)

In trying to feel competent, preadolescents must understand their failures and successes. By the time they enter third grade, children view themselves as active agents and able to create knowledge. They can draw cause-and-effect inferences between actions and outcomes, and they are developing an increasing awareness of how their performance compares with peers. "As the individual becomes increasingly aware of her or his uniqueness, so she or he becomes increasingly aware of other's appraisals and expectations" (Durkin, 1995, p. 300). At the same time, the literature on preadolescents' sense of self also indicates they have an increasing sense of their self as possessing some stable internal qualities. They are beginning to differentiate, organize, and coordinate multiple representations of themselves across settings and capacities. It is during the period of preadolescence that children's conceptions of effort (i.e., what it means to work hard) and ability (what it means to be smart) begin to merge. They are more likely to attribute success and failure on tasks to something stable about their ability rather than to their efforts. In observing their work and comparing it to other children in their class, preadolescent children may notice they don't have to work hard to get the right answer, that sometimes they work hard and still get the wrong answer, or that sometimes they don't work as fast as peers. Many begin to make connections that working hard indicates that they are not smart. Even their play becomes a venue for trying to meet their competence needs. Hughes (1999) notes that play during preadolescence tends to focus on games with rules as a way to understand social constructions of winning, losing, and what it means to be on a team. Dweck (1999) argues that this is a dangerous time. Her research suggests that children who believe ability is fixed and has little to do with effort can develop a maladaptive pattern of motivation toward school, avoiding challenging tasks and engaging only when success on a task is guaranteed.

As Erikson described, preadolescent children are driven by desire to understand what it means to be and to feel industrious. They will engage in behaviors that protect them from feeling inferior. What can teachers do to help preadolescent children feel competent in the classroom and avoid confirming, maybe even challenge, their notion of ability as stable and fixed? Hughes' (1999) research suggests that teachers need to think about the nature of classroom activities and their students' engagement in play. He notes the difference in convergent and divergent forms of play. "The experience of working with puzzles and other toys that suggest a single correct way to play with them may teach children there are correct answers and encourage them to seek them out. Playing with open-ended materials, on the other hand, may tell a child that numerous approaches can be taken to any problem and the possibilities for the use of one's creative imagination are limitless" (Hughes, 1999, p. 187). Likewise, teachers can design activities that are convergent (suggesting the existence of a single correct answer) and divergent (suggesting either the existence of multiple correct solutions or multiple routes to a single solution). Children's success or failure on a task could be attributed to unstable and controllable factors such as the strategies they selected or the way they framed the problem.

Likewise, Dweck (1999) urges teachers to watch how they praise student success. She cautions against using global praise such as "good job" or solely praising the outcomes of student work. Students can attribute this type of praise as commenting on their abilities. Instead, she suggests, "We can rave about their effort, their concentration, the effectiveness of their study strategies, the interesting ideas they came up with, the way they followed through. We can ask them questions that show an intelligent appreciation of their work and what they put into it" (Dweck, 1999, p. 8). This can be challenging for both teachers and students because strategic learning itself is still developing. Bjorklund (2005) reminds us that increasingly complex tasks and instruction bring with them the challenge for preadolescents to learn new, more complex strategies (i.e., multistep, organizing, elaborating). These new strategies may cost mental effort to implement. Preadolescents can easily become frustrated when they struggle to master complex tasks with complex strategies and do not find immediate success. Students need to see their time as an investment in learning how to learn.

Learning From Functional Failures

What is consistent across the literature, however, is that protecting students from failure on academic tasks is also not the answer to helping them feel competent. "Giving students easy tasks and praising their success tells the students that you think they are dumb. It's not hard to see why. . . . Wouldn't you feel that the person thought you weren't capable of more and was trying to make you feel

Table 9.2   Characteristics of Adaptive Learners

	Responses of Adaptive Learners		
Source of Frustration	Change Something About the Task	Change Something About Themselves	Change Something About the Situation
When students perceive the demands are excessive (i.e., difficult or unfamiliar tasks)	Students can adapt to the stress of a difficult task by simplifying or streamlining the task. This might include relating material to something familiar or breaking it into its parts.	Students can adapt to the stress of a difficult task by changing they way they see, understand, or perform the task. This might include reconsidering the purpose of the task, envisioning positive results, or practicing the necessary skills.	Students can adapt to the stress of a difficult task by changing their surroundings. This might include seeking assistance from their teacher or peers or asking if they can do an alternate task.
When students perceive the demands are insufficient (i.e., tasks that are boring or where there is too much support)	Students can adapt to the stress of a boring task by attempting to increase the challenge or interest level of the task. This might include speeding up the pace or adding embellishments to the task.	Students can adapt to the stress of a boring task by changing they way they see, understand, or complete the task. This might include reconsidering or changing the focus of the task or co-opting two tasks into one.	Students can adapt to the stress of a boring task by changing their surroundings. This might include asking to complete an easy task alone, teaching another student about the task, or inviting complexity by working with peers.

NOTE: Table adapted from Rohrkemper & Corno (1988, p. 307).

good about your limited ability?" (Dweck, 1999, p. 4). In their study of adaptive learning (see Table 9.2), Rohrkemper (now known as McCaslin) and Corno describe the ways in which student success on easy tasks can backfire. They define adaptive learning as, "Students who strive, seek goals, that involve mental risks, and can learn from their mistakes" (Rohrkemper & Corno, 1988, p. 299).

How can students learn to persist in the face of failure and critique if they are always protected from it?

> Uninformative success, or success that occurs without increased understanding, does not further learning any more than does mindless failure. . . . Meaningful learning has much to do with false starts, thwarted tries, and frustrated attempts. Shielding students from this also shields them from learning not only the content under consideration, but also the processes of learning, achieving, and what we call adaptive learning. (Rohrkemper & Corno, 1998, p. 303)

This challenges teachers to really confront how they conceptualize error or failure and respond to it in their own learning and teaching. Is failure something they fear and avoid? If so, why? Do they seek to make sense of their own limits, their own struggles in order to grow as problem solvers? And, if so, in what ways do they model this for their students? Choosing to teach in a way that supports adaptive learning is tough for both the students and the teacher because it inevitably means students must face the emotional consequences connected to failure: stress, anger, frustration, as well as their concerns over their own competence. "We do not suggest that stress in and of itself is positive, but that learning to cope with and modify stressful situations is an important outcome of education" (Rohrkemper & Corno, 1988, p. 296). In this vein, Rohrkemper and Corno argue that teachers must learn to "titrate" the stress associated with failure on tasks. This involves monitoring the frequency, timing, placement, magnitude, and aggregation of social and academic failures students in their class are experiencing. Likewise, Goldstein (1999) emphasizes that teaching for adaptive learning involves striving for students to understand that their teacher designs classroom activities from a position of caring: caring about the content, caring about learning, caring about individual students' understanding. Because teachers care about the way students see themselves as problem solvers, they give students tough problems to work through and help them find creative solutions. Because they care about students' ability to meet failure head-on, and to persist through to a solution, they give students tasks that are challenging and in which they may not be immediately successful. This is what sociocultural scholars call seeking intersubjectivity—teachers helping students to understand their motives and striving to understand the perspective and motives of their students.

Understanding Classroom Relationships

From their initial entrance in school, children seek to understand classroom social relationships (Davis, 2003). The developmental literature is clear: Students who feel like they belong in their classroom, who have supportive relationships with peers and teachers, do better in school. They evidence more adaptive forms of motivation, including a willingness to be socially responsible and to seek help, and they are more engaged in learning tasks. This trend sustains throughout children's K–12 schooling and beyond to college. But teachers face different challenges in cultivating a sense of belonging in their classroom at each phase. In general, preadolescents' relationships to teachers are a type of hybrid of the parent relationship, as are peer relationships of siblings (Sroufe et al., 2005). Children who have experienced conflict or alienation in their parent and sibling relationships carry these burdens with them as they enter school and struggle to connect with their teachers and peers. Early positive relationships with teachers and peers at school, however, can have a compensatory effect. Likewise, initial conflict or alienation with teachers and peers at school can cause children with supportive parent and sibling relationships at home to be wary of school and teachers. Thus, third- through fifth-grade teachers must be sensitive at the start of the school year to the cues children send about wanting or avoiding relationships. Moreover, teachers must be cautious about attributing early conflicts to relationships children have outside of school. Additionally, the developmental literature suggests that children are interpreting all of their interactions within the classroom with a specific lens: Who matters in this class and where do I stand?

Socialization Through Peer Groups

Hughes (1999) notes that friendships and play in the classroom serve an important social function. They allow children to stretch themselves cognitively, to learn the value of roles, and to use role-play as a way to understand their own intentions and actions in what Selman (1980) called "self-reflective role-taking." But social interaction and play appear to take an interesting turn during preadolescence. The rise in friendships is coupled with a startling rise in bullying and victimization that appears to peak around the fifth grade. Aggression also takes on a different character. Whereas toddlers and young children may engage in instrumental aggression in which they strike out physically to get something they want, preadolescents tend to engage in hostile aggression. While it may be more overt and physical in boys and more exclusionary and relational in girls, the intent is the same: The goal is to hurt another person in order to get what you want. Cognitively, preadolescents are increasingly able to understand another's perspective and can these skills to anticipate, cooperate with, and manipulate others. More disturbing are findings from Pellegrini, Bartini, and Brooks (1999) that suggest teachers may not be accurate in distinguishing acts of aggression from rough-and-tumble play (particularly in boys).

Where does this rise in aggression originate? It may, in part, reflect preadolescents' desire to understand their social standing in the classroom. Researchers studying social dominance argue children and adults differ in their orientations toward being dominant and that it is during

preadolescence that children begin exploring issues of dominance inside and outside the classroom (Pellegrini et al., 1999).

Developing an inclusive classroom culture requires teachers to be savvy to the ways in which children are exploring issues of dominance and to offer alternative conceptions of dominance. This includes identifying the ways in which children subjugate each other: by excluding each other from play and work groups, through sarcasm or fault-finding commentary on each other's work, and by silencing perspectives other than their own. Teachers need to help preadolescent children use their confidence, authority, and influence to lead their peers in inclusive ways. Specifically, they need to help students learn about what it means to be a leader, including the characteristics of good leaders, and to understand that their choices about how to treat a peer in the classroom fundamentally reflect moral decisions.

The Classroom as a Microcosm of Society: Norms and Stereotypes

The relationship between values and education has always been a checkered one. Despite the claims in each generation that society is experiencing, to some extent, moral decline, there is rarely any agreement about whether teachers should express their values in the classroom or should their classrooms essentially be value-free. Reforms toward character education are frequently criticized for being biased in the values they address. Yet, teachers serve as models in their classrooms. Their every interaction, every decision is judged by students to reflect what they care about. Do their classroom practices reflect that they care about the inclusion, growth, and achievement of all students in the class, or just some? If we align ourselves with a progressive view of values in the classroom—one that favors developing children's moral decision making—the debate about values in education becomes absurd. From this perspective, teachers have the responsibility to create safe opportunities for their students to engage in moral decision making. These opportunities enable students to think about what it means to be in different kinds of relationships, to be responsible, to set boundaries, to evaluate laws and moral imperatives, to participate as a citizen, and to make tough adult decisions that may or may not have a clear answer.

The period of preadolescence is characterized by an important shift in children's moral thinking. Kohlberg described children's thinking as conventional, guided by their understandings of good and bad, law and order. Wadsworth (2004) notes that throughout elementary school, children are acquiring information about social norms, or what is considered right and wrong in society, from their interactions in the classroom. He also notes that children's sense of will and autonomy—what they want to do—may be distinct from what they know they should do based on those social norms. It is during pread-olescence that children begin to reason about what is right and wrong and make some moral evaluations. They are sensitive and seek to understand classroom mores and norms as well as the social hierarchies and social catego-ries that result. In her seminal book, *Why Are All the Black Kids Sitting Together in the Cafeteria?*, Beverly Tatum (1997) describes how young children begin notic-ing and questioning social differences early. She argues that by preadolescence many children may have already learned it is not appropriate to talk about race, class, gen-der, or other social differences. Yet, it is during preadoles-cence that children become aware that these differences matter in society, that they result in social stratifications. They may have internalized stereotypes about people who are different from themselves, and they may approach peers who are different in ways that perpetuate the exist-ing status quo.

What can teachers do to cultivate a culture in their classroom where all students belong regardless of race, sex, gender, religion, or sexual orientation? Teachers need to capitalize on preadolescents' increasing awareness of their own and others' psychological states. Teachers can take advantage of students' ability to understand comple-mentary roles, reciprocity, and mutual respect. As they struggle to understand what it means to be similar, be in a group, and to conform, preadolescents need to be encour-aged to assume the perspective of another and to trouble the accuracy of social stereotypes and the validity of social norms that subjugate one group of people to the service of another.

Regulating Academic Behaviors and Emotions

Earlier I argued that to overlook preadolescents' need for autonomy would be to overlook one of the challenges and accomplishments of the period. Zimmerman (2002) argues the period of adolescence is defined by children's ability to achieve self-regulation. While it would be inappropri-ate for a third-, fourth-, or fifth-grade teacher to assume preadolescents could regulate their own behavior, it is important to recognize preadolescent children have the potential to engage in some self-regulatory behavior with the support of an adult. It is during this period that chil-dren should be asked to assume some responsibility for regulating behaviors that were largely externally regulated by parents or teachers in the past. Research suggests that, cognitively, preadolescent children are able to selectively attend, set goals, make plans, and adapt their strategies. They are increasingly able to understand temporal, spa-tial, and comparative terms. And they are increasingly able to reflect on their behavior, thoughts, and strategies with support. Most third-grade children are able to inhibit primary, and often inappropriate, mental and behavioral responses in order to delay gratification. In part, the

potential to engage in self-regulated behaviors reflects cognitive changes in their problem-solving abilities. Dur-ing preadolescence, children shift from analogical reasoning (i.e., using what they know about one problem to solve another) to scientific reasoning (i.e., making evidence-based arguments). It is this emerging ability to engage in more future-oriented, data-driven, multistep thinking that allows children to participate in goal setting and strategy selection, and to monitor their own progress, reflecting on successes and failures. Teachers only need to create opportunities for children to engage in such activi-ties. It is during this period that teachers can work with children to develop an adaptive understanding of what it means to be autonomous: specifically, that being autono-mous means being self-regulated. Children may not always succeed in setting appropriate goals, selecting the best strategy, or identifying the sources of success and failure; however, teachers can use these types of inter-actions as opportunities to facilitate self-regulatory behavior during adolescence.

Self-regulation not only entails managing one's own behavior, but also regulating one's emotional responses. It is during preadolescence that children become increas-ingly able to read nonverbal messages, to identify masked emotions, to mask their own emotions, and to express blended emotions. They are acquiring sociolinguistic behaviors such as learning to be silent, making eye contact and respecting personal space, interacting with adults, responding to questions, and interrupting in appropriate ways. Finally, throughout preadolescence, children are internalizing appropriate emotional norms such as when it is appropriate to be angry and show anger.

The challenge for teachers is that many self-regulatory behaviors are learned implicitly. Thus, some children may enter third grade able to engage in rudimentary self- and emotion-regulatory behaviors while others may not. That children have not acquired some skills to regulate their emotions by the time they enter third grade is okay; how-ever, it is the task of teachers during this period to help children to develop some skills before moving on to mid-dle school. Perhaps this period can best be characterized as a period of "co-regulation" (Hickey & McCaslin, 2001) in which teachers support and assist preadolescent children in engaging in self-regulatory behaviors.

How can teachers participate in co-regulating students' behavior? Zimmerman (2002) describes four stages in the development of children's self-regulatory behaviors. In the first stage, children observe adults modeling self-regulatory behaviors. In other words, teachers must make their own regulation visible to their students. Teachers might do this by sharing with students the goals they set for the unit, by sharing with them how they planned the unit and the strategies they selected, and by participating with students in reflecting on the successes and failures of meeting the unit's goals. In the second stage, children emulate the self-regulatory behaviors they have observed. It is during this phase that children need to be given more opportunities to participate in setting goals, choosing strategies, and evaluating outcomes. During the fourth stage these behaviors fall under self-control, and it is during the final stage that children are truly able to self-regulate their behavior and emotions in class.

What Does This Mean for Teachers Wanting to Enact Developmentally Appropriate Practice?

What Norms Can I Anticipate?

Fundamentally, developmental psychology can be used to help teachers think about their classroom, plan activities, and reflect on their successes and failures given what we know about the normative, or typical, characteristics of preadolescent children. This chapter describes the ways in which 8- to 11-year-old children tend to approach academic tasks differently from adults. When evaluating unit goals or lesson plans, these findings ask teachers to consider: What does it mean to make activities concrete, or hands-on, from a Piagetian perspective? Teaching in a developmentally appropriate way means teachers of preadolescents need to consider the extent to which the activities they design reveal underlying principles that define the phenomena or event. Teachers need to consider what representations (i.e., language or symbols) students need to have in order to be successful with the activity. They need to think about the ways in which preadolescents' intuitive theories, particularly theories that emerge from preceding academic units, interfere with their understanding of new concepts. They need to identify which elements of the phenomena or event must be conserved in order to truly understand its uniqueness. This might include defining sequences and salient ways of classifying as well as revealing to students the superficial characteristics that may deceive them.

Teachers also need to be aware of preadolescents' tendency toward social comparison and the ways in which their comparisons can go awry. In making social comparisons, preadolescents may come to the conclusion that their ability is a fixed entity and that they are either smart or stupid compared to their peers. They also may strive to be on top by making choices that subjugate their peers. Teachers seeking to meet preadolescents' needs for belonging need to identify ways to integrate discussions of leadership, altruism, and social responsibility. They need to challenge stereotypes that not only exist within domains (e.g., "Girls can't do math.") but also in the larger social arena (e.g., "Poor kids fail."). This might include establishing classroom norms that everyone can succeed, that members of the class are responsible for success, and that part of the teacher's role is to identify when students are engaging in thinking or behavior that presupposed they or another member of the class cannot be successful.

What Are the Potentials and Limits of Children's Thinking?

There is inherently a limit to only looking at normative, or typical, development. That is, of course, teachers may overlook children who exceed or are slower to achieve developmental indicators in one or more areas.

> Unfortunately having a toolbox full of tools designed to reach only 68% of our target population (the average or "typical" students) would not be viewed as a proud accomplishment. The magnitude of our task, then, is defined by our goal to reach and support the growth of all our students. (Davis, 2004, p. 255)

Thus, teachers working with preadolescent populations need to be sensitive to some children's struggles to see underlying principles no matter how many times they are presented with them and in how many different ways teachers strive to reveal them—and that is okay. Some children will be slower on the developmental curve and may not develop these skills until they reach adolescence. Teachers need to monitor the motivation, the strategy use, and the effort of these children and to reassure them (and their parents) when all other patterns appear adaptive that learning will happen. Some children merely need more opportunities to explore phenomena than teachers are able to provide in class (or in a single academic year). Learning to be creative and to tease out when developmental shifts undermine achievement is important for teachers. Telling children who are not ready to learn that they should work harder may be construed as saying that they are not smart. Not so. Developmental shifts have little to do with effort and ability. We cannot, nor can the child or the child's parents, make children develop before they are ready. Likewise, teachers of preadolescents need to have a fluid understanding of the characteristics of adolescent thinking because some of their students, particularly those in fifth grade, may already evidence the abilities to engage in abstract thinking. As noted earlier, in the absence of challenge, these children may come to attribute their uninformative successes in the classroom in terms of their fixed ability and may, in turn, establish motivation patterns that do not serve them well as they transition to middle school and beyond.

What Does It Mean for Teachers to Preserve Childhood for Their Students?

Fundamentally, the task of all primary teachers is to preserve childhood for their students. All developmental psychologists agree that thinking at each stage of development serves a purpose. When children struggle and fail, it is our natural inclination, as adults, to protect them from those failures, to find quick fixes that help them to succeed; however, scholars across the fields of developmental psychology and education agree that teachers of preadolescents need to monitor the frequency of uninformative success and the value of functional failure. "When students in our classes struggle to understand, it may be important to step back from our own agenda and validate the child's perspective" (Davis, 2004, p. 256). Teachers need to be particularly sensitive to creating learning environments where preadolescent children can fail in a safe, meaningful way. This entails creating classrooms where children can make mistakes on academic tasks and learn from them, can explore the stereotypes they hold and ask the tough questions about the way society works, and can learn to assume responsibility for pursuing their own goals even if that means failing the first time.

References and Further Readings

Ben-Ze'ev, T., & Star, J. (2001). Intuitive mathematics: Theoretical and educational implications. In B. Torff & R. J. Sternberg (Eds.), *Understanding and teaching the intuitive mind: Student and teacher learning* (pp. 29–56). Mahwah, NJ: Lawrence Erlbaum Associates.

Bjorklund, D. F. (2005). *Children's thinking: Cognitive and individual differences* (4th ed.). Belmont, CA: Wadsworth.

Corno, L., & Snow, R. (1985). Adapting teaching to individual differences among learners. In M. C. Wittrock (Ed.), *Third handbook of research on teaching* (pp. 605–629). New York: Macmillan.

Davis, H. A. (2003). Conceptualizing the role of student-teacher relationships on children's social and cognitive development. *Educational Psychologist, 38*, 207–234.

Davis, H. A. (2004). One cognitive-developmentalist speaks as an educator. *Theory Into Practice: Special Issue on Developmental Psychology Implications for Teaching, 43*, 253–259.

Dixon, J. P. (2000). The spatial child. In D. N. Sattler, G. P. Kramer, V. Shabatay, & D. A. Bernstein (Eds.), *Child development in context: Voices and perspectives* (pp. 81–84). Boston: Houghton Mifflin.

Durkin, K. (1995). *Developmental social psychology: From infancy to old age.* Oxford, UK: Blackwell.

Dweck, C. (1999). Caution—praise can be dangerous. *American Educator, 23*, 4–9.

Goldstein, L. S. (1999). The relational zone: The role of caring relationships in the co-construction of mind. *American Educational Research Journal, 36*, 647–673.

Havighurst, R. J. (1971) *Developmental tasks and education* (3rd ed.). New York: Longman.

Hickey, D. T., & McCaslin, M. (2001). A comparative, sociocultural analysis of context and motivation. In S. Jarvela & S. Volet (Eds.), *Motivation in learning contexts: Theoretical advances and methodological implications* (pp. 33–55). Oxford, UK: Pergamon & EARLI.

Hughes, F. P. (1999). *Children, play and development* (3rd ed.). Boston: Allyn & Bacon.

Pellegrini, A. D., Bartini, M., & Brooks, F. (1999). School bullies, victims, and aggressive victims: Factors relating to group affiliation and victimization in early adolescence. *Journal of Educational Psychology, 91*, 216–224.

Rohrkemper, M., & Corno, L. (1988). Success and failure on classroom tasks: Adaptive learning and classroom teaching. *Elementary School Journal, 88*, 296–312.

Ryan, R. M., Connell, J. P., & Deci, E. L. (1985). A motivational analysis of self-determination and self-regulation in education. In C. Ames & R. Ames (Eds.), *Review of research on motivation in education, Volume 2: The classroom milieu* (pp. 13–51). Orlando, FL: Academic Press.

Selman, R. L. (1980). *The growth of interpersonal understanding.* San Diego, CA: Academic Press.

Sroufe, L. A., Egeland, B., Carlson, E. A., & Collins, W. A. (2005). *The development of the person: The Minnesota study of risk and adaptation from birth to adulthood.* New York: The Guilford Press.

Tatum, B. D. (1997). *Why are all the Black kids sitting together in the cafeteria? And other conversations about race.* New York: Basic Books.

Wadsworth, B. J. (2004). *Piaget's theory of cognitive and affective development* (5th ed.). Boston: Pearson.

Zimmerman, B. J. (2002). Achieving self-regulation: The trial and triumph of adolescence. In F. Pajares & T. Urdan (Eds.), *Academic motivation of adolescents* (Vol. 2, pp. 1–27). Greenwich, CT: Information Age Publishing.

10

DEVELOPMENT

6–8

STACEY S. HORN, KAREN L. DRILL, MARCY J. HOCHBERG, JUSTIN HEINZE, AND TONY FRANK
University of Illinois at Chicago

During the middle school years (Grades 6 to 8), young people go through many significant and rapid developmental transitions (Lerner et al., 1996). Although the most notable and visible transition during this developmental period is puberty and the related biological changes that occur, early adolescence is a time of significant cognitive and social transitions as well. Scholars have suggested that, aside from early childhood, there is no other developmental period in which individuals undergo so many changes so rapidly (Lerner et al., 1996). These developmental transitions both affect and are affected by the social contexts in which early adolescents engage. Additionally, the interaction of these developmental transitions and the contexts in which early adolescents are engaged lead to several critical issues, such as identity and sexuality development, issues of peer harassment, and mental and emotional health. These issues have significant implications for teachers and for the teaching and learning process.

In this chapter, we first briefly review the major transitions that occur during this developmental period. Then, we discuss the implications these transitions have for the three primary social contexts (families, peer groups, and school) in which early adolescents are engaged. Finally, we discuss some of the critical developmental issues that arise during early adolescence as a result of these transitions and the implications for teachers.

Developmental Transitions in Middle School

Physical Transitions

Puberty

Puberty is a significant developmental transition that is marked by hormonal changes, neural development, skeletal and muscular growth, and significant changes in adolescents' height and weight, and the development of primary and secondary sex characteristics. The process of physical maturation is complex, varied, and cannot be defined by key events or stage attainment (e.g., beginning menstruation or the appearance of pubic and body hair); but rather, it should be viewed as a developmental transition that begins before birth (Archibald, Graber, & Brooks-Gunn, 2003).

In the mother's womb, the fetus is exposed to hormones that serve an organizing function related to later pubertal development. The introduction of these hormones during fetal development ultimately determines sex differentiation of the baby. Beginning around middle childhood (usually around age 6 for females, 8 for males), sex hormone levels begin to rise, serving as an activating mechanism—a process termed *adrenarche* (Archibald et al., 2003). The adrenal gland and the hypothalamus-pituitary-gonadal axis regulate the production and distribution of important hormones including androgens and estrogens. The circulating levels of hormones throughout puberty trigger physical changes in the body and are associated with emotional dispositions and, in some cases, behavior.

Throughout pubertal development, the release of growth hormones results in dramatic skeletal and muscular development. The beginning of puberty is often accompanied by a growth spurt—typically beginning with the hands, feet, and head, followed later by the legs and arms, and finally growth of the trunk (Steinberg, 2008).

Males and females share many aspects of developmental change, but physical development differs between boys and girls. Males generally experience greater muscular development due to higher levels of testosterone, while females tend to see an increase in body fat. The timing also tends to be different: Peak growth velocity occurs around age 12 for females and two years later for males (Susman & Rogol, 2004). Concomitant weight gain occurs about the same time as height change in males, but is usually delayed 6 months in females. During this rapid growth period, males may notice a broadening of the shoulders; females can expect a widening of the hips and cervix. In males, the enlargement of muscles in the larynx, typically around age 14, causes the voice to crack resulting in an adult voice generally by age 15.

Primary and secondary sex characteristics also develop during adolescence. Menarche (first menstruation) and spermarche (production of sperm) usually occur several years after the onset of puberty (between ages 10 to 16 for females, 12 to 14 for males; Steinberg, 2008). Males experience enlargement and smoothing of the testicles, as well as lengthening of the penis, while females experience the growth of the labia and clitoris. Secondary sex characteristics—those not directly concerned with reproduction—also develop in adolescence. Breast development (budding) in females begins around age 8 and continues through ages 14 to 15 (Steinberg, 2008). The growth of body hair, occurring in both males and females on the arms, legs, face, and pubic region accompanies breast or penis and testicular development in relatively predictable patterns.

Timing and Tempo of Puberty

Although all adolescents who are healthy and properly nourished go through the developmental transitions associated with puberty, the timing and tempo of the physical developments that accompany this transition vary between individuals. Each can be affected by biology and the environment in which the adolescent is reared. Although the timing of puberty has not often been associated with either positive or negative biological effects, early or late puberty can have important psychological and social consequences. Early pubertal development is associated with increased social pressure and adult role expectations for both sexes, but seems to be more acutely felt by early developing girls (Dorn, Susman, & Ponirakis, 2003). Research on early maturation in males is mixed, with some studies reporting

higher levels of popularity and self-image (Mustanski, Viken, Kaprio, Pulkkinen, & Rose, 2004) and others suggesting a tendency to engage in high-risk behaviors (Dorn et al., 2003). Early maturing females are at a greater risk for depression, early and unsafe sexual behavior and substance use, eating disorders, and poor body image (Dorn et al., 2003).

Body Size and Image

Because pubertal maturation is associated with rapid body growth, adolescents are often conscious of the way their changing bodies look and feel. Perceived pubertal timing, or how adolescents feel about their own development, can be an indicator of psychological adjustment (Alsaker & Flammer, 2006). As females begin to gain weight compared to their prepubescent peers, they sometimes become dissatisfied with their body and appearance, which can lead to disordered eating and weight issues.

Cognitive Transitions

Significant cognitive changes happen during this period due to physiological changes in the brain as well in young adolescents' reasoning, perspective-taking, and the ways they understand their world. The brain continues to mature and develop throughout adolescence. Three primary changes occur in the brain during adolescence. First, there is thickening of the myelin sheath—a fatty layer that protects the neurons—which helps increase the efficiency of the transmissions being carried between neurons. Second, a process of synaptic pruning begins, whereby the brain pares down and eliminates unused connections between neurons (Steinberg, 2008). The preadolescent brain is not an efficient processor. At the onset of puberty, synaptic pruning refines and strengthens the pathways of connections frequently used while eliminating connections that are not developed. The third major change takes place in the prefrontal cortex, the part of the brain that deals with thinking ahead, anticipating risks and rewards, planning, and regulating impulses and desires. During early adolescence, the prefrontal cortex becomes denser through a thickening of the gray matter and, as a result, individuals become better able to execute the functions described above.

These physiological changes increase efficiency and allow for improvements in how young adolescents process information. Myelination speeds up the synaptic transmissions, so that information travels faster through neural networks (Blume & Zembar, 2007). The refining of the synaptic pathways frees up working memory by increasing automatization, the process whereby something becomes so familiar that you do not have to monitor it.

Physiological and cognitive changes create a foundation for development in the young adolescent's thinking. Notably, thinking in adolescence is different than thinking in childhood in five major areas. Adolescents are better able to think about hypothetical possibilities, to think abstractly, and to think multidimensionally. Additionally, adolescents become better at metacognition and also move toward thinking more relatively, rather than just in absolutes (Keating, 2004).

Many changes in adolescent thinking are related to developmental changes in cognition proposed by Piaget (1972). Piaget posited that during early adolescence, individuals move from concrete operational thinking to formal operational thinking. One of the key elements of formal operational thinking is the ability to think about hypothetical concepts. This provides an enhanced ability to generate and evaluate various possibilities, to consider multiple dimensions in assessing a situation, and to continue developing propositional logic (Piaget, 1972). With formal operations, adolescents expand upon deductive reasoning and use inductive reasoning—inferring what might be likely or possible from a body of evidence. The broadening of abstract thinking allows for an appreciation of multiple meanings and nuances that increases adolescents' understanding of sarcasm, metaphor, and satire.

These changes have implications for how early adolescents understand their own thought processes. As their metacognitive abilities develop, adolescents display greater self-reflection and introspection. Some features of this self-consciousness particular to adolescence have been called "adolescent egocentrism" (Elkind, 1967). One manifestation of this has been termed the *imaginary audience*. This refers to the phenomenon in which the individual adolescent imagines that others are intensely interested and focused on his or her characteristics and behavior. The second feature of adolescent egocentrism takes the form of a *personal fable,* or the adolescent's belief that his or her experiences, feelings, and reactions are unique and have never been experienced by anyone before. This personal fable may help adolescents develop self-esteem by affirming what makes them distinct individuals, but it also contributes to a sense of invincibility in the face of risk or danger.

Social Cognitive Transitions

Along with the physiological and cognitive changes taking place, significant shifts also occur in how young adolescents think about themselves and their world including meaningful changes in how adolescents understand and reason about moral, social, and personal issues (Nucci, 2001; Turiel, 1983).

Turiel (1983) has posited that there are distinct domains of social knowledge that individuals use to understand their social worlds and to make decisions: the moral, the social-conventional, and the personal domains. The moral domain is focused on issues of harm, fairness, and equality; the social-conventional domain involves knowledge related to norms, rules, and conventions that serve to structure social interactions; and the personal domain is concerned with those areas that we believe are up to us as individuals and, therefore, outside the realm of societal

regulation (Nucci, 2001). Turiel (1983) argued that these domains develop independently of each other and are constructed from different types of social experiences and interactions. Understanding how reasoning develops differently across these domains can help parents and educators interact more effectively with adolescents.

Although even very young children recognize that hitting someone is wrong, children's notions of fairness and equality—moral domain issues—change over time. Young children believe in a concept of fairness in which everything must be equal. As the ability of young adolescents to consider others' perspectives and positions increases (that is, the ability to put themselves in another's shoes), they begin to understand that equity must be considered as well (Turiel, 1983).

Individuals' understanding about social conventions also develops throughout childhood and adolescence. Development within the social-conventional domain becomes increasingly complex as young people begin to understand both the necessity of conventions in promoting social interaction and the arbitrariness of the form conventions take within different contexts or cultures—for example, the recognition that dress codes in schools serve to decrease social comparison and conflict and the recognition that different schools may have different dress codes. Young children view conventions as rules established by authority figures that must be followed. As young people move into adolescence, they begin to recognize that conventions are contextually based, inconsistently adhered to, and sometimes subject to disagreement. Lacking the cognitive capacity to fully appreciate the role such norms serve in structuring social interactions, young adolescents often dismiss or resist conventions because they are viewed simply as the dictates of authority (Turiel, 1983). Early adolescents often test established conventions by questioning dress codes or other school policies. Research has indicated that helping young people grapple with the purpose of social conventions may assist them in coming to appreciate why rules, norms, and conventions exist (Nucci, 2001).

Early adolescence is also a time of changes in adolescents' beliefs about what they should be able to decide for themselves—beliefs within the personal domain—such as one's hairstyle, the privacy of one's diary, and other elements of personal expression (Nucci, 2001). During this period, adolescents begin to explore who they are as separate from their families and begin to develop a distinct identity and increased autonomy. This increased autonomy leads to an expansion of the number and types of decisions adolescents feel should be under their legitimate control.

Contexts of Development

Family

One notable social transition in early adolescence is the shift from reliance on parents and other adults to increased reliance on peers. Clearly, young people do not completely reject their parents (Smetana, 2004), but during this developmental period they begin to question who they are as separate from their families and others and begin to explore their own identities. These transitions have significant implications for early adolescents' relationships with their parents.

The most significant disruption to the family system happens around puberty (Laursen, Coy, & Collins, 1996; Smetana, 2004). During this time, early adolescents begin to expand the boundaries of the personal domain and the issues they consider to be under their control, and they begin to question the rules of parents and other authority figures. Even though research suggests that young people remain emotionally close to and dependent on their parents for many types of social and emotional support, parent-child conflict peaks during this developmental period and emotional closeness declines slightly. This increase in parent-child conflict is directly related to early adolescents' bids for autonomy and their testing of personal boundaries (Smetana, 2004).

Parents and early adolescents do not engage in conflict over everything. In fact, research suggests that parents and adolescents typically have similar beliefs and attitudes about core values and that conflict between parents and adolescents typically revolves around mundane issues such as cleaning one's room, doing chores, and dress (Smetana, 2004). Smetana (2004) suggests that the increase in conflict during early adolescence results from parents and adolescents ascribing different meanings to issues, specifically regarding who controls the issue.

During early adolescence families begin the process of shifting from predominantly asymmetrical relationships, in which parents have more power, to symmetrical power relationships, in which parents and adolescents are partners in decision making. As young people expand the domain of issues they believe are under their personal jurisdiction and control, parents continue to see many of these issues as under their control or as affecting the larger social order or family system. Thus, they believe they have legitimate authority to regulate adolescents' behavior regarding these activities (Smetana, 2004). This type of conflict is particularly frequent during early adolescence when families try to establish "where to draw the line between parental control and authority and adolescents' autonomy over the self" (Smetana, 2004). As the family system adjusts to the increasing capacities and independence of the adolescent, and parents begin to recognize their child's needs for autonomy and control over their own lives, this type of conflict declines.

The quality of the relationship between parents and children before this developmental period has a significant effect on how families will adjust and on the developmental outcomes for adolescents. When parents exercise a developmentally appropriate degree of restrictiveness and affordance of autonomy, and display high degrees or warmth, nurturance, and support, early adolescents tend to regulate their own emotions and behaviors well, engage in advanced decision-making processes, and resist negative peer influence (Smetana, 2004). When parents are overcontrolling, conflict tends to be more frequent and of higher intensity. Overcontrol often leads to negative psychological outcomes for adolescents, such as increased delinquency, depression, substance use or abuse, and eating disorders (Hasebe, Nucci, & Nucci, 2004). Negative developmental outcomes also occur when parents do not exercise enough control over adolescents (e.g., providing too much autonomy), even though conflict tends to be less pronounced in these families.

Individual, family, or contextual factors that cause stress during this developmental period or exacerbate the mismatch between parents' and adolescents' expectations can affect parent-adolescent relationships and conflicts, as well as related individual outcomes for adolescents. The pattern, developmental timing, and intensity of parent-adolescent conflict in immigrant families may differ given the cultural contexts in which these parents were raised as compared to those of their children (Greenberger & Chen, 1996). Further, for families that are under extreme levels of stress (e.g., facing parental divorce or loss of job), parents may not realize that early adolescents' bids for autonomy and rejection of parental authority are normative and necessary; thus, they may have fewer resources to deal adequately with these issues (Steinberg, 2008).

Peers

As young people move away from complete dependence on their families, the peer group becomes increasingly important. During middle school, peer relationships become a primary social context in which young people try to make sense of their social worlds. As children transition into early adolescence, peer relationships become more complex and change in function and structure. Early adolescents' peer relationships include dyads (friendships) and small groups (cliques). Reputation and status-based groups of adolescents or peer crowds also emerge. Further, the functions of peers and peer relationships also change.

Friendships become less about proximity and engaging in shared activities and more about shared values, interests, trust, and reciprocal disclosure. Within high-quality friendships—which involve reciprocated affection and disclosure—loyalty, self-disclosure, and trust become salient features. Friendships continue to be marked by higher levels of prosocial and positive behaviors, emotional reciprocity, and intensity, but also continued levels of conflict (Rubin, Bukowski, & Parker, 2006). In particular, early adolescent friendships involve high levels of jealousy and possessiveness as young people struggle to construct an understanding of how to balance individual needs and desires within their social relationships (Rubin et al., 2006).

Additionally, in early adolescence, social groups become more significant and social cliques form (Brown,

2004). Cliques tend to be primarily same-sex and, in many cases, same-race and are highly cohesive and exclusive. In early adolescence peer cliques provide social and emotional support and provide many adolescents with a sense of belonging to a group separate from their families. These groups provide early adolescents with a set of relationships through which to gain important social information and feedback regarding their emerging identities.

With the onset of puberty, adolescents spend more time interacting with opposite-gender peers in mixed-gender social groups or cliques (Brown, 2004). These mixed-gender cliques function as a way for heterosexually attracted early adolescents to begin exploring their emergent sexuality and to engage in heterosocial behavior in relatively safe and supportive environments. This group-level heterosocial activity serves as a precursor to dyadic dating behavior and serves to socialize adolescents in heterosexual identities and behaviors, as well as gender roles and norms (Horn, 2004).

As a result of the importance that belonging to a group has for early adolescents, peer interactions become focused on regulating membership within particular social groups, often through bullying, victimization, and social aggression such as gossiping. Because of developmental gains in social cognition, social comparison becomes more prevalent and status hierarchies emerge (Parker & Gottman, 1989), with peer cliques being stratified into low- and high-status groups. This early stratification is often accompanied by emergent forms of peer crowds, such as "populars" and "nerds," that take on more importance as adolescents move into high school and continue to explore their identities.

Peer conformity and influence increases throughout early adolescence and tends to peak late in middle school or early in high school. While many people think peer influence has only negative effects on young people, research suggests that for most adolescents, the peer group is a source of influence toward positive and prosocial behaviors and values and that peer relationships lead to positive and adaptive development for young people. It is through interacting with peers that young people learn about issues of fairness, trust, and reciprocity and learn how to take someone else's perspective (Selman, 2003). Additionally, peer relationships and groups provide essential contexts in which adolescents begin to develop identities separate from their families, and thus they provide important feedback to adolescents as they try on and test out different expressions of identity.

School

Young adolescents spend most of their time at school. The school environment can have an important developmental effect on early adolescents, and the challenge for schools is to create an environment where young people can succeed. For many American adolescents, Grades 6, 7, and 8 are associated with the transition from primary school to middle or high school. At a time when students are experiencing pubertal changes and the formation of different aspects of their identity, they must also contend with the new academic challenges and responsibilities that secondary school entails. For many young people, the convergence of these developmental and contextual transitions leads to a decrease in self-esteem, school engagement, motivation, or achievement, and increased risk for mental-health problems, such as depression.

The adolescent's response to the new school climate, and the standards and expectations learned from their interactions with new teachers, can have a significant effect on future performance. It is the responsibility of the school, then, to create a context that both supports and motivates maturing students in developmentally appropriate ways—what Eccles (2004) terms stage-environment fit. An optimal stage-environment fit synchronizes school changes with the developmental changes students are already experiencing. Consider, as an example, students' perceptions of adult support. As students move to the middle-school environment, they often seek to gain the approval of non-parental adults (Eccles, 2004). Accordingly, students who feel their teachers are supportive and engaged in their learning show higher levels of achievement and lower levels of delinquency (Eccles, 2004). Teachers' values, beliefs (or biases), and expectations play an important role in the development of student-teacher relationships and can affect motivation, acclimation, and persistence.

School climate extends beyond the classroom. Schools that value academic achievement and empower their students' learning can positively affect not only student motivation, but also that of parents and teachers (Eccles, 2004). In early adolescence, when students have a heightened sense of how they appear to others, those school climates that endorse competition and social comparison are more likely to lead to nonadaptive learning strategies for students (Roeser & Lau, 2003). When a positive environment is combined with supportive teaching, students are better able to develop a positive student identity, demonstrate increased intrinsic motivation and academic interest, cultivate pride in accomplishments, and develop positive social relationships (Roeser & Lau, 2003).

It is necessary, then, to eliminate as many discrepancies as possible between the individual's developmental stage needs and the new environment. An introduction of multiple classes and teachers usually occurs when students move into the middle grades. It is important for them to feel they have an element of control over decisions and choices that occur in this new learning environment (Roeser & Lau, 2003). Positive feedback from teachers can have an important effect on students' emotional well-being, which in turn motivates them to learn (Roeser & Lau, 2003). When possible, teachers should also encourage parental involvement in the learning process. When parents participate in a young adolescent's education, there are more parent-child interactions at home, better attitudes about learning (on the part of both parent and child), and achievement gains for the child (Epstein & Dauber, 1991).

Critical Issues in Middle School Development

In this section, we focus on three critical issues related to the developmental and contextual transitions discussed above, which take on increased importance during early adolescence and have implications for the health and well-being of young people: identity and self-esteem, sexuality, and peer harassment.

Identity and Self-Esteem

To reiterate, early adolescents undergo various biological, cognitive, and social changes—each of which intersects to affect identity development during this critical period. Erikson (1968) highlighted adolescence as a critical period for the formation of identity. Critical to attaining a cohesive or achieved identity is the process of exploring the available options within a particular identity domain (e.g., religion or vocation) and then committing oneself to a particular course of action within that domain (Marcia, 1980). According to Marcia, individuals can be described as being in one of four identity statuses depending on whether or not they have engaged in these two processes (exploration and commitment):

1. *Identity diffusion:* incoherent, disjointed sense of self; adolescent has neither explored nor committed to an identity
2. *Identity foreclosure:* commitment to a role or series of roles without engaging in exploration; typically in response to external pressure from important social others
3. *Moratorium:* active search for identity but no clear commitment
4. *Identity achievement:* commitments to identity roles based on active exploration of options

Most young people enter early adolescence in a state of identity diffusion; they have not yet begun the process of exploring identity options or committing themselves to particular identities. Because early adolescents are less likely to engage in formal operational thinking, they are also less apt to generate and compare alternative identities, a critical component of the exploration phase (moratorium). Some early adolescents settle upon an identity (e.g., future career) as a result of parental or social influence or control without exploring the range of options available to them, characteristic of the identity foreclosure status. According to Archer and Waterman (1983), identity foreclosure in early adolescence could "set the stage for a severe emotional or identity crisis later in life" (p. 207).

So during adolescence and early adolescence in particular, young people should be afforded opportunities and time to try on and test out different types of identities (Marcia, 1980). Through this process, young people discover ways of being that make sense to them and commit to certain expressions of identity over others. By early adulthood, most individuals have developed an achieved identity based on identity commitments in a number of domains. Critical to this process is the way in which adolescents construct an understanding of themselves in differing and multiple roles and relationships.

Due to their advancing cognitive abilities, adolescents' understanding of who they are becomes multifaceted. Thus, another key developmental task of adolescence is differentiating aspects of the self that emerge in different roles and relationships, and subsequently integrating these multiple selves into a cohesive self-narrative (Harter, 1998). Because of their ability to think multidimensionally, adolescents perceive themselves differently depending on the context they are in (e.g., good-natured when with friends, moody when with parents). This differentiating of the self can lead to extreme cognitive conflict as young people try to construct a sense of the "real me" from the varied and sometimes conflicting "me's" that exist in different contexts. This sense of conflict is particularly apparent during the transition from early to middle adolescence when young people recognize the contradictions (good-natured in one context but moody in another) within their self-system, but do not yet have the cognitive maturity to recognize that particular contexts may elicit certain types of self-descriptors. They may not have the capacity to reconcile these conflicting descriptions of the self into a cohesive self-narrative (Harter, 1998). As they mature cognitively, adolescents begin to construct an integrated sense of self through coordinating differing aspects of self into higher-order abstractions (e.g., emotionally adaptable).

In summary, early adolescence is a time when self and identity become highly significant to adolescents as they explore who they are as separate from their families. Educational contexts should provide early adolescents with multiple outlets and activities in which to explore their emergent identities and should support them in making sense of the multiple and differentiated selves that manifest during this process. Contexts that do not provide a match with adolescents' developing selves can decrease adolescents' self-esteem.

Effect of Transitions on Self-Esteem

During adolescence, the self-system may be disrupted and threatened cognitively and biologically. Physical changes affect how one perceives oneself and also raise questions about whether one develops normatively. Early adolescents have a heightened awareness of how they are perceived by others, and they are especially aware of gender norms regarding physical appearance (Horn, 2004). Researchers have found that early adolescents compare themselves to cultural and social standards of beauty and often find themselves falling short, leading to decreased self-esteem (Friedman & Brownell, 1995). Notably, girls have a steeper drop in self-esteem than boys given that their biological changes move them further away from the cultural ideal (i.e., increase in body fat, weight gain) and are particularly prominent in early maturing girls (Alsaker & Flammer, 2006). In early adolescence, students experience many social shifts that affect their identity, including their relationships with peers, parents, and school staff. One change, as described earlier, occurs during the shift from elementary schools and self-contained classrooms into departmentalized middle schools where adolescents become part of a larger, more anonymous social system. This changed school structure may increase comparisons with peers regarding skills, abilities, and behaviors and has been directly linked to an increase in anxiety immediately after the transition from elementary to middle school.

Harter's research on adolescent development has focused specifically on how self-esteem and self-concept vary depending on context and how adolescents construct a self (Harter, 1998). Adolescents' sense of self is affected by others' evaluation and recognition (Harter, 1998). Therefore, adolescents may be part of a feedback loop in which evaluations by others affect their sense of self, and the self that they project outward influences the way others perceive them (Harter, 1998). Some research has suggested that psychosocial problems may occur when there is a discrepancy between one's actual self and identity and others' expectations.

Sexuality

Exploring one's sexuality, sexual feelings, and desires is a normative developmental process for early adolescents who are approaching or have achieved puberty. This means coming to understand who one is romantically and sexually attracted to, what those attractions and desires mean, and whether and how to act on those attractions. For most students, these attractions will be toward opposite-sex peers (heterosexually oriented). For some adolescents, these attractions will be toward same-sex peers (homosexually oriented) or based on something other than gender (bisexually oriented). For students whose attractions are not heterosexually oriented, early adolescence can be a particularly difficult developmental period. Some may choose to come out to themselves or important others. Still others will continue to explore and understand these attractions by themselves, while some may suppress or deny these attractions and take on heterosexually oriented behaviors and relationships.

Regardless of one's (emerging) sexual identity, early adolescence is often a time of sexual experimentation and exploration. Some experimentation is normative for young people and is part of a longer, gradual socialization process into what it means to be a mature and healthy sexual adult (Brooks-Gunn & Paikoff, 1993). For many,

however, experimentation can lead to engaging in behaviors before one is ready cognitively or socially and to negative experiences and potentially long-term negative developmental consequences (Halpern, Joyner, Udry, & Suchindran, 2000).

The progression of sexual activity and behavior begins in early adolescence with the advent of sexual fantasy and masturbation (Steinberg, 2008). For many young people, partner behavior and activity also begins in middle school and progresses from things such as holding hands, kissing, and necking to behaviors involving touching breasts and genitals through clothes and under clothes. While some young people move from these activities to oral and vaginal-penile intercourse during middle school, the average age of first vaginal-penile intercourse in the United States is around 15 or 16 years of age. This varies by gender, race, and ethnicity, with girls and Asian American students experiencing later sexual debut than boys and individuals from other ethnic groups, respectively. About 33% of students have had heterosexual intercourse by the age of 15 and about 6% have engaged in this activity by the time they are 13 (Centers for Disease Control and Prevention, 2006).

Involvement with sexual intercourse during middle school has serious implications for young people, and it is often associated with a negative developmental profile that includes drug and alcohol use, less religious involvement, more deviance, and less school engagement (Brooks-Gunn & Paikoff, 1993). Sex before age 15 is associated with developmentally inappropriate autonomy. Research suggests that the younger adolescents are when they first engage in sexual intercourse, the more likely they are to have unprotected sex, exposing themselves to the risks of pregnancy, STDs, and HIV/AIDS (Kaestle, Halpern, Miller, & Ford, 2005). Conversely, research provides no evidence of negative developmental effects for adolescents who delay sex until after age 16 (Savin-Williams & Diamond, 2004).

Families and schools play a major role in socializing young people toward healthy sexual development. For most students, many of these changes happen during the middle school years. Schools that are developmentally in step with their students will help them to make sense of these biological changes and the emerging sexual desires that go along with them.

Peer groups also play a major role in adolescents' sexual socialization. Adolescents often use their peer relationships to make sense of their developing bodies and minds and their emerging understandings of their sexuality (Horn, 2004). Not only do adolescents discuss these changes with their friends, but they also use the larger peer-group structure to understand these changes. Unfortunately, this often takes the form of peer exclusion and harassment.

Peer Exclusion and Harassment

Early adolescence is a time when young people begin to question who they are and to explore their identities. One way they do this is through their peer groups. Thus, issues of group belonging, social comparison, and group conformity become highly salient. All of these things can lead to increased levels and different forms of peer harassment.

Being harassed by one's peers is a common experience for middle school students. Surveys of peer harassment in middle school suggest that nearly 50% of students report experiencing some kind of harassment during the school year (Juvonen, Nishina, & Graham, 2000) or within a two- to four-week time frame (Nishina, Juvonen, & Witkow, 2005). Between 40% and 70% of middle school students report witnessing peer harassment in their schools (Nishina, et al., 2005).

In addition to the frequency of peer harassment during the middle school years, changes in how early adolescents evaluate and reason about issues of peer exclusion and harassment also occur (Killen, Margie, & Sinno, 2005). This is largely due to social-cognitive development during this period. Research suggests that all individuals draw upon and coordinate different types of knowledge (e.g., fairness, group norms, personal prerogative) to make decisions. How this knowledge gets coordinated and applied to issues of peer-group inclusion or exclusion changes with development. Like younger children, many adolescents view exclusion based solely on one's social-group membership in a particular race, gender, or peer group as wrong from a moral viewpoint (i.e., unfair or hurtful). Adolescents are more likely than children, however, to evaluate excluding someone from a peer or friendship group as acceptable (Killen et al., 2005). Adolescents are more likely to justify peer-group exclusion as acceptable by making appeals to such things as group identity or norms, group functioning, or personal choice (Killen et al., 2005). This suggests that as children get older they have an increased knowledge of the conventional features of groups that are legitimately necessary for the organization and maintenance of groups, as well as an expanded understanding of issues that are inherently personal and legitimately up to the individual to decide (Nucci, 2001). Adolescents' developing understandings of social systems—and their expanded sense of the personal domain—are related to how they understand and make decisions about their peer relationships.

These social-cognitive changes, as well as the biological changes related to puberty, lead to shifts in the type and nature of peer harassment during early adolescence. Generally, there is a shift in peer harassment from direct and physical to indirect and social (Craig, Peplar, Connolly, & Henderson, 2001). This includes things like social exclusion, ostracism, and gossip. Research suggests, however, that verbal teasing and taunting is the most common type of peer harassment experienced by early adolescents during the middle school years (Nishina et al., 2005). Further, there is an increase in peer harassment that is sexual in nature (Craig et al., 2001), likely related to the biological transitions occurring at this time. Early adolescents use social and sexual harassment to sanction others who do not adhere to peer norms. Thus, harassment is often targeted toward students identified as or perceived to be gay or lesbian. Anti-gay language is commonly used by students in teasing or harassing their peers, even if they are not identified as gay, lesbian, or bisexual. There are also increases in harassment based on normative assumptions about gender and gender roles.

The costs of peer harassment are high. Experiencing peer harassment leads to many negative and often long-term consequences for both individuals who are the victims of harassment and the perpetrators. Victims of peer harassment report higher levels of social withdrawal, loneliness, and depression than their nonvictimized peers. They are also more likely to have negative attitudes toward school, lower levels of school engagement, and lower self-esteem (Juvonen, et al., 2000). Nearly 60% of boys who researchers classified as bullies in Grades 6 to 9 were convicted of at least one crime by the age of 24; 40% of them had three or more convictions by age 24.

Peer harassment also can have negative consequences for the entire school community because it contributes to a hostile school climate and leads to decreases in school engagement and performance for all students. In extreme circumstances, unchecked peer harassment has also contributed to more serious forms of school violence in which students who were victimized took retribution on the school community with guns and other weapons.

Conclusion

Early adolescence is a time of numerous and varied developmental changes. During this developmental period adolescents are undergoing physical, cognitive, and social changes that greatly affect how they view themselves, their relationships, and the broader world. Because of the many changes and the rate at which developmental change occurs during this period, it is critical that early adolescents have adequate and appropriate support and guidance to navigate these changes. Middle schools are uniquely positioned to provide this support and guidance. Schools that are developmentally in step with the needs, capacities, and normative changes of early adolescence can have a tremendously positive effect on how young people navigate this challenging development period.

References and Further Readings

Alsaker, F. D., & Flammer, A. (2006). Pubertal maturation. In S. Jackson & L. Goossens (Eds.), *Handbook of adolescent development* (pp. 30–50). New York: Psychology Press.

Anderman, E. M., & Maehr, M. L. (1994). Motivation and schooling in the middle grades. *Review of Educational Research, 64*, 287–309.

Archer, S. L., & Waterman, A. S. (1983). Identity in early adolescence: A developmental perspective. *Journal of Early Adolescence, 3*, 203–214.

Archibald, A. B., Graber, J. A., & Brooks-Gunn, J. (2003). Pubertal processes and physiological growth in adolescence. In G. R. Adams & M. D. Berzonsky (Eds.), *Blackwell handbook of adolescence* (pp. 24–47). Malden, MA: Blackwell.

Blume, L. B., & Zembar, M. J. (2007). *Middle childhood to middle adolescence: Development from ages 8 to 18.* Upper Saddle River, NJ: Pearson.

Brooks-Gunn, J., & Paikoff, R. (1993). Sex is a gamble, kissing is a game: Adolescent sexuality and health promotion. In S. Millstein, A. Petersen, & E. Nightingale (Eds.), *Promoting the health of adolescents: New directions for the twenty-first century* (pp. 180–208). New York: Oxford University Press.

Brown, B. B. (2004). Adolescents' relationships with peers. In R. Lerner & L. Steinberg (Eds.), *Handbook of adolescent psychology* (pp. 363–394). New York: Wiley.

Centers for Disease Control and Prevention. (2006). Youth behavior surveillance—United States, 2005. *Morbidity and Mortality Weekly Report, 55*(SS-5), 1–108.

Craig, W. M., Peplar, D., Connolly, J., & Henderson, K. (2001). Developmental context of peer harassment in early adolescence: The role of puberty and the peer group. In J. Juvonen & S. Graham (Eds.), *Peer harassment in school: The plight of the vulnerable and victimized* (pp. 242–262). New York: Guilford Press.

Dorn, L. D., Susman, E. J., & Ponirakis, A. (2003). Pubertal timing and adolescent adjustment and behavior: Conclusions vary by rater. *Journal of Youth and Adolescence, 32*(3), 157–167.

Eccles, J. (2004). Schools, academic motivation, and stage-environment fit. In R. Lerner & L. Steinberg (Eds.), *Handbook of adolescent psychology* (pp. 125–152). New York: Wiley.

Elkind, D. (1967). Egocentrism in adolescence. *Child Development, 38,* 1025–1034.

Epstein, J. L., & Dauber, S. L. (1991). School programs and teacher practices of parent involvement in inner-city elementary and middle schools. *The Elementary School Journal, 91,* 289–305.

Erikson, E. (1968). *Identity, youth, and crisis.* New York: Norton.

Friedman, M. A., & Brownell, K. D. (1995). Psychological correlates of obesity: Moving to the next research generation. *Psychological Bulletin, 1,* 3–20.

Greenberger, E., & Chen, C. (1996). Perceived family relationships and depressed mood in early and late adolescence: A comparison of European and Asian Americans. *Developmental Psychology, 32,* 707–716.

Halpern, C., Joyner, K., Udry, J., & Suchindran, C. (2000). Smart teens don't have sex (or kiss much either). *Journal of Adolescent Health, 26,* 213–225.

Harter, S. (1998). The development of self-representations. In W. Damon & N. Eisenberg (Eds.), *Handbook of child psychology: Social, emotional, and personality development* (Vol. 3, pp. 553–617). Chichester, UK: Wiley.

Hasebe, Y., Nucci, L. P., & Nucci, M. S. (2004). Parental control of the personal domain and adolescents' symptoms of psychopathology: A cross-national study in the United States and Japan. *Child Development, 75*(3), 815–828.

Horn, S. S. (2004). Adolescents' peer interactions: Conflict and coordination among personal expression, social norms, and moral reasoning. In L. Nucci (Ed.), *Conflict, contradiction, and contrarian elements in moral development and education.* Mahwah, NJ: Lawrence Erlbaum Associates.

Juvonen, J., Nishina, A., & Graham, S. (2000). Peer harassment, psychological adjustment, and school functioning in early adolescence. *Journal of Educational Psychology, 92,* 349–359.

Kaestle, C. E., Halpern, C. T., Miller, W. C., & Ford, C. A. (2005). Young age at first sexual intercourse and sexually transmitted infections in adolescents and young adults. *American Journal of Epidemiology, 161,* 774–780.

Keating, D. K. (2004). Cognitive and brain development. In R. Lerner & L. Steinberg (Eds.), *Handbook of adolescent psychology* (pp. 45–84). New York: Wiley.

Killen, M., Margie, N. G., & Sinno, S. (2005). Morality in the context of intergroup relationships. In M. Killen & J. Smetana (Eds.), *Handbook for moral development* (pp. 155–183). Hillsdale, NJ: Lawrence Erlbaum Associates.

Laursen, B., Coy, K., & Collins, W. A. (1996). Reconsidering changes in parent-child conflict across adolescence: A meta-analysis. *Child Development, 69,* 817–832.

Lerner, R. M., Lerner, J. V., vonEye, A., Ostrom, C. W., Nitz, K., Talwar-Soni, R., et al. (1996). Continuity and discontinuity across the transition of early adolescence: A developmental contextual perspective. In J. Graber, J. Brooks-Gunn, & A. Peterson (Eds.), *Transitions through adolescence: Interpersonal domains and context* (pp. 3–22). Mahwah, NJ: Lawrence Erlbaum Associates.

Marcia, J. (1980). Identity in adolescence. In J. Adelson (Ed.), *Handbook of adolescent psychology* (pp. 159–187). New York: Wiley.

Mustanski, B. S., Viken, R. J., Kaprio, J., Pulkkinen, L., & Rose, R. J. (2004). Genetic and environmental influences on pubertal development: Longitudinal data from Finnish twins at ages 11 and 14. *Developmental Psychology, 40*(6), 1188–1198.

Nishina, A., Juvonen, J., & Witkow, M. R. (2005). Sticks and stones may break my bones, but names will make me feel sick: The psychosocial, somatic, and scholastic consequences of peer harassment. *Journal of Clinical Child and Adolescent Psychology, 34,* 37–48.

Nucci, L. P. (2001). *Education in the moral domain.* Cambridge, UK: Cambridge University Press.

Parker, J. G., & Gottman, J. M. (1989). Social and emotional development in a relational context: Friendship interactions from early childhood to adolescence. In T. J. Berndt & G. W. Ladd (Eds.), *Peer relations in child development* (pp. 95–131). New York: Wiley.

Piaget, J. (1972). Intellectual evolution from adolescence to adulthood. *Human Development, 15,* 1–12.

Roeser, R. W., & Lau, S. (2003). On academic identity formation in middle school settings during early adolescence. In T. M. Brinthaupt & R. P. Liplka (Eds.), *Understanding early adolescent self and identity: Application and interventions* (pp. 91–132). Albany: SUNY Press.

Rubin, K. H., Bukowski, W., & Parker, J. G. (2006). Peer interactions, relationships, and groups. In W. Damon (Series Ed.) & N. Eisenberg (Volume Ed.), *Handbook of child psychology, Vol. 3: Social, emotional, and personality development* (6th ed., pp. 619–700). New York: Wiley.

Savin-Williams, R., & Diamond, L. M. (2004). Sex. In R. Lerner & L. Steinberg (Eds.), *Handbook of adolescent psychology* (pp. 189–232). New York: Wiley.

Selman, R. (2003). *The promotion of social awareness: Powerful lessons from the partnership of developmental theory and classroom practice.* New York: Russell Sage.

Smetana, J. G. (2004). Adolescent-parent conflict: Resistance and subversion as developmental process. In L. Nucci (Ed.), *Conflict, contradiction, and contrarian elements in moral development and education* (pp. 69–91). Mahwah, NJ: Lawrence Erlbaum Associates.

Steinberg, L. (2008). *Adolescence* (8th ed.). Boston: McGraw-Hill.

Susman, E., & Rogol, A. (2004). Puberty and psychological development. In R. Lerner & L. Steinberg (Eds.), *Handbook of adolescent psychology* (2nd ed., pp. 15–44). Hoboken, NJ: John Wiley & Sons.

Turiel, E. (1983). *The development of social knowledge: Morality and convention.* Cambridge, UK: Cambridge University Press.

11

DEVELOPMENT

9–12

BECKY WAI-LING PACKARD AND MAUREEN E. BABINEAU

Mount Holyoke College

The high school years, Grades 9 to 12, are complex and interesting with regard to students' development and learning. The age range is vast during high school, spanning the teenage years, or what is called *adolescence.* Ninth graders are transitioning from early adolescence to middle adolescence, and graduating seniors have transitioned to late adolescence. This age group is challenging for educators because young people change in so many different ways. Broadly speaking, adolescence brings biological, physical, cognitive, and social changes. These changes have implications for the educational lives of students and for educators who work with teens in and out of schools. An awareness of these changes and the kinds of challenges they bring can improve our ability to provide the opportunities that can make a difference in teens' lives.

It was not until the turn of the century that psychology and education began to focus on adolescent behavior. Since then, the study of adolescence has taken many forms. G. Stanley Hall (1904), an early psychologist, viewed adolescence as a time of stress and turbulence characterized by mood shifts and difficulties. Although he acknowledged that the environment plays a bigger role in adolescence than it does in childhood, he emphasized biological factors; it is well-known that adolescents change physically with the onset of puberty. In contrast, the history of adolescent development was also shaped by Margaret Mead (1928) who believed that one's development was in large part influenced by culture. Mead's groundbreaking, highly controversial research took her to Samoa, where she illustrated that stress and turbulence were not universal hallmarks of adolescence, but more likely a by-product of United States culture.

The age-old nature versus nurture debate still underlies many of the perspectives in development as relevant to education. For years, intelligence tests were regarded as indicators of intellectual potential and natural smarts. In recent years, even higher stakes are associated with standardized testing (see Part IX: Assessment, this volume). Now this research is coupled with a broader understanding that these tests have bias, favoring the perspectives of particular students, and the recognition that environmental factors including testing conditions also influence student performance. The sharp nature versus nurture, or biological versus environmental, debate is no longer a real debate because biological and environmental factors are recognized as contributors in development and in the educational lives of high school students.

Background: A Closer Look at Home, School, and Community Factors

In recent decades, research has intensified with regard to contextual perspectives. This means that our understanding of development is more complex than it once was, and our understanding of development is also more rich and nuanced. It is no longer a matter of looking at a student's intelligence test or past achievement. One must also consider the intersection of many factors including family, peers, afterschool activities, school context, and even larger economic changes that may influence the resources for learning in a school or within a neighborhood. To do this is to take an ecological view of development.

Urie Bronfenbrenner (1979) was a major pioneer of the ecological perspective, which involves looking at the entire social ecology of students including their economic resources; their social position within the larger world; their family's network, job, or neighborhood; and also the more direct influences of the contexts of home, school, and community. This ecological perspective provides at least two useful viewpoints. First, educators need to be mindful of the macrolevel, including the variety of larger political, social, and economic factors that indirectly influence young people, and how these factors may trickle down to influence students in their home and school lives. For example, major changes in federal policies or a slowdown in economic growth may lead businesses to close. Parents may lose their jobs and struggle to provide for their families. This stress may trickle down into the home, and the students may be forced to increase their own work hours, leaving no time for homework. An awareness of these issues can help educators to better understand students because one can appreciate how complex individual behavior actually is. It may be less about a parent choosing to be involved or a student deciding to invest in academics. Choices may not be so clear-cut when basic survival is salient.

This perspective also reminds educators that there are important immediate and direct influences or contexts for development outside of the home. In today's busy world, young people participate in many contexts including extracurricular activities, sports, and clubs. Further, some students also are actively involved in their communities through religious affiliations or structured youth programs. Many high school students are involved in paid employment or volunteer experiences that provide insights into the world of work and community service. Taking an ecological perspective can be especially hopeful, then, because if there is a lack of support within the home context, there may be support in another context. Learning more about students' out-of-school lives in conjunction with school can be critical in viewing the entire student. Next, we highlight some of the key findings relevant to the immediate contexts in which students participate.

Parents as the First Teachers

Parents are important people from whom adolescents continue to draw encouragement and security as they move from childhood into adulthood. Parents are most helpful when they support their children in a developmentally appropriate manner, which means that they allow the adolescent space to develop as an individual separate from the family while maintaining a strong sense of belonging within the family. Even though teens are striving for some separation, most teens want to know their parents are available and interested in their growth. Providing scaffolding can be important, because it is crucial for adolescents to gain problem-solving tools on their own but they need some assistance to do so. When parents act as a sounding board, encouraging their teens to make low-risk decisions on their own and talk through possible consequences of actions, they are providing scaffolding. In this way, teens have support, but they also gradually increase the autonomy and responsibility for their actions. In fact, research indicates that when parents collaborate in decision making with appropriate support, rather than dictating the outcomes or engaging in a completely hands-off manner, their teens report higher feelings of self-competence. Even though parenting styles differ across cultures, encouraging young people to make their own decisions while offering appropriate gradients of help is generally positive.

Parents also act as teachers in how they choose to spend family time. Young people tend to take interest in activities that their parents introduce to them or provide resources to facilitate. For example, when parents talk about particular interests (e.g., medical discoveries, literature) or take family trips to particular destinations (e.g., museums, hiking trails), they are likely to inspire interest. It is difficult for a young person to become interested in something to which there has been no exposure. Parents also provide a context in which adolescents view their abilities by how they discuss them. Parents may communicate to their children that they have natural ability or that they lack it. Research suggests that parents may be more likely to explain to daughters that their poor performance in math is due to a lack of ability (e.g., you are just not good at this) whereas they may be more likely to say to their sons that it is due to a lack of effort (e.g., you just did not try the right strategies). During adolescence, however, teens do not spend the majority of their time in the home. They have interactions with peers, teachers, and others who also provide an interpretive lens for their interests and abilities.

Peer Groups as Mirrors

In school and out, wanting to belong to a peer group is a key motivator of teens. Peers can provide a mirror to adolescents as they consider what kind of person they want to become. In other words, they spend time with those whom they hope will reflect the image they want to convey. Indeed, striving for a sense of group identity can sometimes override any individual sense of identity.

Peer groups can take the form of organized cliques or social categories. For example, research by Eckert (1989) documented the existence of known cliques including "jocks" and "burnouts." In her study, group membership was associated with participation in particular activities. Jocks participated in school-sanctioned activities whereas burnouts completely avoided these activities. Peer group membership influenced students' friendships, activities, relationships with teachers, and long-term academic outcomes. One important finding was that social class was associated with peer group membership; lower-income neighborhood teens tended to become "burnouts" and higher-income neighborhood teens tended to become "jocks." In addition, it has been found that during transitions between middle school and high school, teens can change their peer group membership in much the same way that they originally enter a peer group: through the activities in which they participate. By engaging in new and different activities, especially high-status activities such as sports or nonacademic clubs, adolescents can change their peer group membership (see also Chapter 60, "Students as Social Beings," Volume II).

Teachers as Socializers

Students spend much of their day with teachers. Teachers provide an important lens on the world and, more importantly, on how young people see their academic potential and themselves more generally. Typically, having positive relationships with teachers—even one teacher—has been associated with positive benefits for students, including persistence in school. Teachers can facilitate or act as a gatekeeper for opportunities by recognizing talent and encouraging students.

It has been consistently proven that teachers can have a profoundly positive or negative lasting influence on students. This can differ from student to student and teacher to teacher; however, by and large, when students form a strong sense of their ability and interest in a subject, students can remember the teacher that sparked that interest and even the kinds of activities that they did in class together or what the teacher said or did to make an impact. Likewise, students know when a teacher does not believe in them and their capabilities. As early as the first grade, students know if a teacher thinks that they are smart or not. This can be communicated through differential treatment, including praise or attention. During high school, students are actively trying on various interests and, as a result, a teacher's interest in them or validation of their capabilities can influence their academic pathways to the degree that they would be more inclined to continue with the study of a subject or less likely, as the case may be.

Communities as Alternative Spaces

Although community influences, including religious and youth organizations, have always played a role in development, it was not until the 1990s that research and funding for initiatives in this area were so concentrated. Teens who participate in community organizations can pursue projects that have personal meaning and often forge relationships with supportive adults who believe in them. Participation can range from joining an afterschool computer club, to attending an intensive summer enrichment program, to being involved in a community service project at a local hospital. Furthermore, young people can discover new talents and capabilities within out-of-school contexts because they are not constrained by school curriculum requirements. Numerous programs have shown how they foster creativity and success in young people who may not have otherwise found success before.

Perhaps the most well-known community-based project is Big Brothers Big Sisters. Young people, typically from single-parent or low-income families, are matched to a responsible adult for a year-long mentoring relationship. The research on this project has found that if matches are not sustained for the full year, the effect of participation on the young person is likely more negative than positive. This program emphasizing long-term mentoring has inspired the development of many similar programs targeting high school students. In addition, the program is one of the first to engage in a systematic large-scale evaluation that both illustrated its effectiveness and provided cautions with regard to successful implementation. Mentor selection and training are very important. When constructed and implemented effectively, mentoring relationships can be life-changing for teens, especially those for whom the home or school presents difficulties.

Major Concepts in Adolescent Development

Identity and Efficacy

Identity development is a central task that teens engage in during high school. This is the process of figuring out answers to the questions, who am I? and what do I want to become? Many agree with Erikson (1968) that adolescents struggle with identity, trying on different identities and striving to develop a sense of the future. In the United States, trying on a career identity is often a central feature of this complicated process. It is debatable whether young people actually get much support within schools, or elsewhere, to figure out the answers to these questions. Nevertheless, young people set off to explore their options in courses and in extracurricular activities, and they are influenced by the media. Exploration is critical; decision making without adequate exploration is referred to as premature foreclosure, a state in which students are influenced by what others tell them rather than their own experience. In schools, engaging in long-term projects or community service ventures helps young people to feel that they are productive, contributing members of society while also providing contexts to explore possible identities.

Harter, Bresnick, Bouchey, and Whitesell (1997) identified many spheres for developing perceptions of capabilities including academic, athletic, social, and emotional. Thus, it is not so much the actual capability as it is a perception of capability (motivation experts call this self-efficacy). It is important to approach identity development holistically. By being aware of capabilities across multiple domains, educators can encourage their students to try to draw upon their feelings of capability in one domain when aiming to grow in another.

Researchers who study future-oriented identity, including Markus and Nurius (1986), who use a possible selves perspective, have argued that multiple future selves influence students' motivation. What one hopes to become in the future, even though unformed, is a strong motivator of the kinds of activities that one engages in or aims to avoid. Students have both hoped-for selves and feared selves, and these selves vary in number and intensity; the few most important and vivid will be powerful. As mentioned, these future images are important when thinking about motivation because they guide students into action. If adolescents imagine themselves as future college students or as certain kinds of professionals, they are more likely to engage in academic coursework. In contrast, if they do not have future images that require academics, then they may be less likely to invest in such schoolwork. Thus, it is important early on to introduce students to many future possibilities and to encourage them to see themselves in many different ways. This is not to suggest that students should be pressured to go to college or to choose an occupation early. It just means that trying on possibilities can impel students to commit valuable energies that can leave many rather than few options open in the future.

Given the multitude of selves in operation, conflict among future selves can arise. For example, a student's desire to become a doctor may conflict with a desire to raise a large family, or a desire to be popular among friends may conflict with a desire to spend a lot of time training for a sport. It is not that someone cannot have multiple compatible future selves; instead, within the student's mind, it may be difficult to contemplate how to work toward one self without jeopardizing another. In addition, it has been found that students who struggle with academics may decide not to invest in that part of themselves, and instead dedicate their investment in another domain, such as the arts, athletics, or even delinquent activities. Some have called the turning away from academics an oppositional school identity. This has been studied within ethnic minority youth with an emphasis on African American youth who may see academics as a middle-class White enterprise in which they cannot successfully participate (see Fordham & Ogbu, 1986). Shifting energies from one domain to another is sometimes referred to as compartmentalization of selves, and it can serve as a protective mechanism for students so they feel that they are not necessarily failing in an area, but instead are choosing not to invest in that area.

Another important aspect of identity development is having a plan for achievement. It is not enough for students to declare a goal for the future (e.g., I want to be a scientist). Students must also have a plan for how to get from point A to point B. This goal-directed plan is typically referred to as a self-regulatory plan. The student organizes activity in a strategic manner in order to create the conditions to meet goals. The development of self-regulatory plans is an important area for educators to help young

people (for further elaboration see Part IV: Motivation and Classroom Management, this volume).

Self-Esteem, Voice, and Well-Being

During adolescence, individuals can begin to think more abstractly and idealistically. As mentioned, young people are striving to figure out who they really are and may try to distinguish real or true selves from ideal or inauthentic selves. One's perception that they are true to themselves can have positive implications for overall well-being. At the core of one's self is a sense of self-esteem, or how much one likes or feels good about oneself, and is linked closely to one's sense of self-worth, or the sense that one is a worthy, deserving person. Self-esteem is believed to be an aspect of a person that is developed, grown, and strengthened. In recent years, more attention has been paid to concerns about inflated self-esteem because it has been associated with juvenile delinquency. There are also concerns about trying to artificially inflate self-esteem by handing out tokens to make students feel good about themselves void of any deed (e.g., everybody wins an award no matter what). It is believed by some that improving self-esteem is not necessarily an important goal and that improving self-efficacy is more important.

Boys at this age typically have higher self-esteem than girls. Girls, in contrast, may take a downward turn in self-esteem. Pipher (1994) was in fact perplexed over the number of girls with plummeting self-esteem in her clinical practice. She argued that several factors contributed to the loss of one's true self, including the pressure that girls have to hide their true opinions for fear of losing relationships. It is not surprising then that the notion of voice has been described as related to maintaining a strong sense of self-esteem. Some argue that girls lose their voice when they hide their true opinions, and in doing so, they lose contact with their true selves. It is unclear whether a threat to voice or self-esteem is pervasive across all girls, only girls, or for any adolescent regardless of gender. Some argue that these issues are more likely to face middle-class White girls because of cultural norms and pressures for girls to be "nice" and not to speak their minds, whereas others who study urban teen girls of color, for example, have found an opposite tendency: adolescent girls are socialized to speak out on issues (Way, 1995). In addition, some argue that self-esteem struggles may affect both male and female students, but in different ways, with boys more likely to act out and girls more likely to be depressed (Nolen-Hoeksema & Girgus, 1994).

These constructs are important for educators for many reasons. First, young people bring how they feel about themselves into the classroom and to afterschool programs. A teacher may be puzzled if a student appears reluctant to challenge viewpoints in class or to voice an opinion. Students may fear retribution from classmates or fear losing their friends if they engage in class. Thus, it is important for students to gain experience challenging authority constructively, including the use of debates and long-term projects that encourage the use of contrasting viewpoints. Out of school, numerous successful initiatives include adventure camps and theatre programs that encourage teens to take healthy risks and reinforce self-esteem.

Some students with low self-esteem also struggle with depression, and there are more frequent reports of teen depression in recent years. Students may find it difficult to concentrate in class if they are struggling with their own feelings of self-liking or with depression. Changes in medications can exacerbate school difficulties. Thus, one cannot assume that a student is uninterested or unmotivated; lack of engagement may signal a deeper problem.

Resilience and Persistence

Resilience, defined as one's ability to persist in the face of difficulties and endure despite adverse circumstances, is an important outcome for the positive development of adolescents. Even though certain risk factors and adversities are faced by many young people, it is the ability to withstand these that is imperative. Resilience can be fostered and developed by promoting protective factors which can buffer young people when they encounter negative circumstances. In high school, individuals' beliefs and capabilities are very malleable, which may contribute to the ability to enhance resilience.

Within the individual, enhanced social ability, developed skills (e.g., sports, dance, art), positive self-worth, strong problem-solving self-efficacy, intellectual ability, and spirituality have all been identified as key protective factors that can be promoted by school systems, families, and communities. When adolescents develop a close relationship with a parental figure, they are more likely to exhibit increased resilience. A parental figure can help young people to hold high expectations for their development and to find effective coping strategies when they face roadblocks; by modeling these strategies and encouraging their use, adults can teach adolescents to internalize them. If parents provide support at home for homework, for example, they can help their teens to persist when difficulties arise. This can take the form of encouraging them to write down questions to ask at school the next day or brainstorming other strategies.

Beyond parents, we know that close caring relationships with other adults such as a mentor at a community program, a coach, or a teacher can also foster resilience. Having at least one valued adult who cares and believes in the teen's capability can go a long way to communicate that he or she is not alone. While it is the case that having socioeconomic advantages also contributes to resilience, this is often due to having increased resources. Thus, it is possible to overcome adversity and accomplish goals by making use of available social resources at school and in the community.

All risk factors are not created equal. Indeed, one area of high risk that seems to be especially impenetrable to resiliency outcomes is exposure to violence. When students, particularly males, are exposed to high levels of violence, they are at a high risk of academic failure in reading and math, and resilience interventions may be especially necessary. Certainly, individual and environmental differences contribute to developmental outcomes, but it is important to pay attention to the type of challenges facing young people in order to develop appropriate interventions.

Learned helplessness is a response that develops when an individual no longer sees a connection between his or her efforts and the outcomes. Simply put, when one has learned helplessness in a domain, it means that the person lacks a perception of control and is inclined to give up. To combat these feelings, teens can be reminded of previous success and control. It can also help when students have a mastery goal, or a goal to improve capacity or understanding, and when students have positive self-efficacy. By providing exposure to positive role models who demonstrate the capability to persist in the face of difficulty, and possible strategies that can be used to problem solve, students may be more likely to persist.

Topics of Interest and Debate

Living in a (High-Tech) Culture of Performance

In today's schools, there is immense pressure to perform. Standardized testing receives acute attention, and even real estate is marketed in conjunction with school district averages. Grades are also so important because more students are going to college, and so college acceptances are more competitive. High school students contend with performance pressure and fears that they may not have the grades to make it into elite colleges. Especially in highly competitive school districts, it can be challenging for a student to stand out from peers without excelling above and beyond in many domains. School districts stand to lose resources and control of schools if they do not perform at particular levels, leading many teachers to feel constrained in the curricular opportunities they are able to present their students. While the main purpose of school has tended to be academic in nature, in recent years, this has become more stringent in many districts where the focus is on raising test scores. In struggling school districts where test scores are tied to diplomas, school dropout is rampant.

Pressure to achieve creates other problems. Cheating has become a pervasive problem among high school students. Often, cheating starts in middle school, where academic expectations begin to accelerate, and then follows students into high school and college, where performance is directly linked to gaining access to top career opportunities or graduate programs. Furthermore, living in a high-tech world makes cheating easier, because Web sites that catalog tests and term papers are only a click away, and the resources are still new enough that there is not a clear understanding of how to give proper credit to online resources.

What is beginning to emerge in research on academic integrity is a sense among young people that cheating is normal and therefore acceptable. The behavior is becoming so culturally normalized that some educators are frustrated that many students no longer see it as a big deal. Many educators and school boards will agree that parents do not always support the school's efforts to tame cheating; sometimes parents support a child they know is being less than honest because they too are aware of the high stakes associated with performance. There is a need for parents and teachers to be educated in the proper use of online resources.

Furthermore, pertaining to the issue of academic integrity, there is a concern that the larger moral thread in society is unraveling and we are seeing the repercussions of this in today's teens. In other words, academic dishonesty may be a symptom of a larger problem. In response, many schools are implementing character or moral education programs that teach young people that they are capable of leading healthy, positive lives if they make thoughtful choices. One major resource for character education programming in K–12 schools is the Character Education Partnership, a nonprofit organization. Principles emphasized include trying to make the world a better place and doing the right thing even if it is not the easiest or most personally gratifying option. These programs are controversial because they may appear to resemble religious doctrine rather than educational guidance.

The diagnosis of learning disabilities is another issue related to high pressure to perform academically. There is greater sensitivity to the needs of students now more than ever before, leading to a greater diagnosis of a wider range of learning disabilities. But there may also be a greater frequency of diagnosing learning disabilities among low-performing students in high-income communities that want to maintain their high averages because students with learning disabilities have their standardized test scores calculated separately. Research on learning disabilities suggests that young people vary in how they react to the diagnosis: some feel generally incapable because they incorporate the diagnosis into their entire identity while others find productive coping strategies to achieve great success. This is an area of debate as well and will need further monitoring with regard to how to individualize education but continue to support students in a highly politicized climate.

When Does Enrichment Become Overload?

There is a growing concern among educators about the number and intensity of students' extracurricular activities. Many teens, especially middle- and upper-middle-class teens, are scheduled with lessons and activities without much downtime. On the one hand, it is recognized that enrichment activities are important for the development of students. Another perspective on this overscheduling of teens, however, is that too much of a good thing can be detrimental and lead to overload.

The first potentially negative outcome is that adolescents are losing valuable sleep. Sleep deprivation is an area of concern for adolescents. Research suggests that teens need at least 9 hours of sleep per night to be at their best. During adolescence, the biological clock for sleep, or one's circadian timing, shifts during puberty. This shift often leaves adolescents wanting to stay up later and wanting to sleep longer in the morning. The lives of adolescents, at least during the school year, do not support these sleep requirements. Many teens' lives are rather full with school, homework, a job, and extracurricular activities.

Some school systems, in an effort to support developmental sleep needs, have actually changed their school schedules by starting classes later in the morning. Adolescent experts contend that high school students are sleeping in the classroom because they are not sleeping at night. This lack of sleep affects students' ability to think and to perform at their best in school. Aspects of out-of-school life, including sleep, certainly can influence a student's in-school life and performance.

Is participation in team sports a positive pastime or are teens getting burnt out by too much? Evidence suggests that there are many positive outcomes from participation in team sports such as constructive peer relationships, decreased risk of drug use, increased self-confidence, and enhanced cooperation skills. For some, however, participation in team sports can bring about stress and sadness to the point where one leaves sports altogether. Today, sports teams are typically organized differently than they were in years past when everyone at every level was encouraged and supported by adults to play. In today's fast-paced world, the level of competition, travel, expense, and parental involvement and ties to higher education (e.g., the possibility of a college scholarship), can change a once enjoyable pastime into an area of high stress for some teens.

Adult interference in sports is one major concern. Although parental involvement is usually viewed as positive, recently there has been a trend for parents to become overinvolved in micromanaging their child's sports participation and thus interfering with the positive outcomes of sports participation. Similar to the academic realm, this may stem from parents feeling the pressures associated with their child's performance. Statistically speaking, across the nation only a small percentage of high school students will receive an athletic scholarship to college and even fewer become professional athletes. Still, the pressure from many parents to achieve one of these coveted spots persists. Continuing athletic activity for all students, for enjoyment and healthy competition, is and should be a priority for high schools.

Drug Use and Abuse

Communities and schools alike have dealt with the issue of substance use and abuse in schools for decades.

Many intervention and educational strategies have been implemented to inform students, limit the use of substances, and offer counsel to those who may already have a problem. To that end, schools provide education and support to both teens and families. Although there is not extensive research on what the best intervention practices are, we do know that strategies used with younger children are not effective for high school students. Because of developmental differences, prevention and informational programs used in the earlier grades have shown to be ineffective in reducing substance abuse for teens. Promising interventions in high schools include implementing peer mentoring and peer-facilitated groups. Currently, approximately one third of public schools offer some kind of substance abuse programming. The Phoenix House, a nonprofit organization, provides nationally recognized prevention and treatment programs. The American Council of Drug Education can also provide updated information about educational prevention programming.

Traditional schools are challenged when aiming to implement programming. Teachers often do not have the qualifications to present and offer discussion of the prevention materials, and students in high school are less likely to talk openly with their academic instructors about substance use or abuse. This can present a real difficulty for a teen who is trying to get clean or stay sober while also trying to get an education in an environment where substance use is a part of daily life among peers. Indeed, the rate of relapse is high among teens. One intervention approach that offers hope, specifically to students who have been identified as having a substance abuse problem and are committed to staying clean, is enrolling in a designated recovery high school. At a recovery high school, recovering students gain a peer group that is supportive and staff that are trained in relapse prevention and in helping to manage stress. Currently, there are about 20 recovery high schools across the United States.

Educators would like to believe that students can go to school and get an education without fear of relapsing, but unfortunately the problem is only growing with the normalization of drug use in general among teens. More teens are prescribed prescription drugs, whether for attention-deficit/hyperactivity disorder, depression, or other diagnoses. Generally speaking, prescription drugs are making their rounds within schools, and there may be a lack of understanding with regard to their potential dangers.

Future Directions

There are several topics that were not explored in this chapter but require attention from educators as they emerge and develop. First, there needs to be greater awareness of cross-cultural and, more specifically, global relationships for teens in the United States. Young people are more aware of global conflict and the potential for terrorism since 9/11. Researchers too have paid attention to these changes, especially as they influence particular groups of young people such as Muslim American youth who may find their identities as Americans and as positive young people under threat. Certainly, a greater emphasis on the role of civic engagement and global awareness in the education of high school students is worth examining.

The overscheduled, high-tech lives of young people bring a continued focus on stress, depression, and also violence. Violence in schools has filled the headlines; it is unclear that young people, or adults for that matter, know how to manage interpersonal conflict or depression in productive ways. Educating and supporting the whole adolescent, including emotional and physical well-being, will be a focus in the coming years. We expect continued growth of alternative schools, such as the recovery high school, that attend to the individualized needs of young people in today's world.

Along those same lines, we anticipate a greater focus on the connections between schools, families, businesses, and other community resources. With greater support, families with fewer resources are able to more fully participate in the education of their teens. For example, adult literacy programs for parents who speak English as a second language are in great demand, with waiting lists often very long. Several innovative partnership programs have been developed around the country, in which area businesses have provided much needed human and economic support for area schools. Since identity development is such a salient task in adolescence, business partnerships also provide great venues in which young people can explore their career options and meet various professionals. A closer look at the potential of these programs and their influence on the development and achievement of high school students will be needed in the coming years.

Conclusion

The high school years present challenges for educators especially in today's high-tech and high-demand world. Young people may be changing in so many different ways depending on whether they are emerging from childhood or entering adulthood. Biological, cognitive, and physical changes all take place, and the academic and future potentials of young people are influenced by many social factors. Using an ecological perspective, we can appreciate the influences of parents, peers, and teachers, as well as community, economic, and political factors.

Young people strive to develop their identities and capacities in many different domains through academic and extracurricular activities. Maintaining strong self-esteem and voice despite peer pressures and desires to maintain relationships can be challenging. It is important for high school students to learn ways to cope with adverse circumstances. Involvement in mentoring programs, or other opportunities where young people can gain valuable life skills, can help them to buffer even very difficult barriers.

Several topics are salient in discussions concerning the learning and development of today's high school students. There is a serious culture of performance in schools, especially surrounding performance on standardized tests and admissions to colleges. Cheating has become more prevalent. Some of this may be due to our living in a high-tech culture with online resources and a lack of knowledge of how to properly credit or use them. Parental pressure has also gained much attention. Increased stress from an overload of enrichment activities can cause sleep deprivation and influence academic struggles. Furthermore, substance abuse is a serious and pervasive problem facing many teens, leading to the development of prevention and treatment programs in addition to alternative schools. Future directions, including a greater focus on global awareness, school violence, and community-business partnership programs can help to further support high school students. Ultimately, it is the education and development of the whole adolescent, with recognition of the circumstances facing an adolescent and resources afforded to his or her family and community that can help us to be truly successful educators in the 21st century.

References and Further Readings

Arnett, J. J. (1999). Adolescent storm and stress, reconsidered. *American Psychologist, 54*(5), 317–326.

Bronfenbrenner, U. (1979). *The ecology of human development.* Cambridge, MA: Harvard University Press.

Carskadon, M. A. (Ed.). (2002). *Adolescent sleep patterns: Biological, social, and psychological influences.* New York: Cambridge University Press.

Cooper, H., Valentine, J. C., Nye, B., & Lindsay, J. J. (1999). Relationships between five after-school activities and academic achievement. *Journal of Educational Psychology, 91*(2), 369–378.

Eckert, P. (1989). *Jocks and burnouts: Social identity in the high school.* New York: Teachers College Press.

Erikson, E. H. (1968). *Identity: Youth and crisis.* Oxford, UK: Norton & Co.

Evans, E. D., & Craig, D. (1990). Teacher and student perceptions of academic cheating in middle and senior high schools. *Journal of Educational Research, 84*(1), 44–52.

Fordham, S., & Ogbu, J. U. (1986). Black students' school success: Coping with the burden of "acting White." *The Urban Review, 18,* 176–206.

Gilman, R., Meyers, J., & Perez, L. (2004). Structured extracurricular activities among adolescents: Findings and implications for school psychologists. *Psychology in the Schools. Special Issue: Positive Psychology and Wellness in Children, 41*(1), 31–41.

Hall, G. S. (1904). *Adolescence.* New York: Appleton.

Harter, S., Bresnick, S., Bouchey, H., & Whitesell, N. R. (1997). The development of multiple role-related selves in adolescence. *Development and Psychopathology, 9,* 835–854.

Markus, H., & Nurius, P. (1986). Possible selves. *American Psychologist, 41*(9), 954–969.

Mead, M. (1928). *Coming of age in Samoa.* New York: Morrow.

Morrissey, K. M., & Werner-Wilson, R. J. (2005). The relationship between out-of-school activities and positive youth development: An investigation of the influences of communities and family. *Adolescence, 40*(157), 67–85.

Nettles, S. M., Mucherah, W., & Jones, D. S. (2000). Understanding resilience: The role of social resources. *Journal of Education for Students Placed at Risk, 5*(1), 47–60.

Nolen-Hoeksema, S., & Girgus, J. S. (1994). The emergence of gender differences in depression during adolescence. *Psychological Bulletin, 115,* 424–443.

Pedersen, S., & Seidman, E. (2004). Team sports achievement and self-esteem development among urban adolescent girls. *Psychology of Women Quarterly, 28*(4), 412–422.

Pipher, M. (1994). *Reviving Ophelia: Saving the selves of adolescent girls.* New York: Ballantine.

Richards, M. H., Larson, R., Miller, B. V., Luo, Z., Sims, B., Parrella, D. P., et al. (2004). Risky and protective contexts and exposure to violence in urban African American young adolescents. *Journal of Clinical Child and Adolescent Psychology, 33*(1), 138–148.

Taggar, S. V. (2006). Headscarves in the headlines! What does this mean for educators? *Multicultural Perspectives, 8*(3), 3–10.

Way, N. (1995). "Can't you hear the strength and course that I have?" Listening to urban adolescent girls speak out about their relationships with peer and parents. *The Psychology of Women Quarterly, 19*(1), 107–128.

PART IV

MOTIVATION AND
CLASSROOM MANAGEMENT

12

Cognitive Approaches to Motivation in Education

Jessica J. Summers

University of Arizona

Often, educators who learn that research on the study of student motivation exists ask, "How can I motivate my students?" This then presents researchers with the difficult task of explaining that studies about student motivation are derived from complex theories that are deductive in nature, and that this literature is meant to be descriptive rather than prescriptive. Hearing this response, the educator usually has an excellent follow-up question: Why does the research exist if it is not meant to help educators? Typically, only researchers read studies about student motivation and the educators are left without access to this information if they are not familiar with the theories, methodologies, and purposes for conducting the research. The purpose of this chapter is to make some of those theories and findings accessible and to summarize the meaning of this research in real educational contexts.

Before discussing the relevance and application of expectancy-value theory, attribution theory, and achievement goal theory, one must first know why these three theories in particular are important to educators. Research has focused on two major aspects of motivation beliefs: control/competence and value. Control beliefs are the students' perceptions about the likelihood of accomplishing desired outcomes under certain conditions; competence beliefs are the student's perceptions about his or her capability to accomplish certain tasks (Schunk & Zimmerman, 2006). Value beliefs are the reasons why an individual would want to become or stay engaged in an academic task (Anderman & Wolters, 2006). Expectancy-value theory is a very comprehensive motivational theory in that it incor-

porates aspects of both competence and value, while attribution theory and achievement goal theory focus mostly on control or competence. All three theories have an important place in interpreting why students are or are not motivated, and they complement each other by offering suggestions for improving motivation and achievement in both research and practical contexts.

This chapter begins with a brief review of each theory and relevant research in the motivation literature, including ways in which they are similar and different, followed by a summary of how these findings might apply in classroom settings. Other important motivation theories that are reviewed in this text, but are not covered in this chapter, are affect, interest, and social cognitive theories. Because this chapter was written with intent to briefly summarize an entire history of motivation research, readers may want to refer to more comprehensive texts for detailed information such as the *Handbook of Educational Psychology* (e.g., Anderman & Wolters, 2006; Schunk & Zimmerman, 2006) or *Motivation in Education: Theory, Research, and Applications* (Schunk, Pintrich, & Meece, 2008).

Theories and Research

Can I Learn and Why Do I Learn?
Principles of Expectancy-Value Theory

To reiterate, expectancy-value theory is a comprehensive motivational theory, and although all three motivational theories incorporate some aspect of competence or control, only expectancy-value theory focuses explicitly on the role of value. Some would argue that because Weiner was a student of Atkinson, the originator of expectancy-value attribution theory contain aspects of value as well as expectancy. Weiner, however, uses Atkinson's definition of value in his own attributional model, which is more like affect than values defined in modern expectancy-value theory. Because the theory is cognitive in nature, most of the research has capitalized on the beliefs that students have and how these beliefs affect their academic behavior. Less research has been done on other aspects of the theory, such as investigating the student's social world where these beliefs come from, or exploring the student's cognitive processes (e.g., students' perceptions of the social environment or interpretations and attributions of past events) that are necessary for developing these beliefs. Therefore, this summary focuses on aspects of the theory that have empirical support for classroom application. The two main beliefs that are studied most often are students' *expectations for success,* or whether they believe they can accomplish an academic task, and students' *valuing of the academic task,* or their reasons for choosing to do the task (Schunk et al., 2008).

Expectations for task-specific success are closely tied to students' perceptions of competence, and research has shown that both expectancy for success and competence beliefs correlate with grades, effort, and persistence (Wigfield, 1994; Wigfield & Eccles, 1992). There are four kinds of values that students might have about a task: utility value, attainment value, intrinsic value, and cost beliefs (Wigfield & Eccles, 1992). Utility value is the usefulness of the task for individuals in terms of their future goals. Attainment value is the importance of doing well on a task. For example, boys might believe that it's important do to well in math and science because of gender-related expectations. Therefore, they may have high attainment goals for math- and science-related activities because these subjects are central to one's sense of self as a boy (Wigfield & Eccles, 1992). Intrinsic value is the enjoyment one experiences while engaged in a task. For example, some students really enjoy participating in game-like tasks at school because games tend to make learning fun and meaningful (Bergin, 1999). The final and fourth value associated with expectancy-value theory is cost. Cost beliefs are perceived negative aspects of engaging in the task, and they may cause someone to choose a less desirable task over something more desirable. For example, a student who does homework rather than going over to a friend's house to play video games has probably acknowledged that completing a homework assignment is associated with less cost (e.g., giving up a social opportunity) than not doing homework. Many students, however, choose not to do their homework because something else (e.g., playing video games) has outweighed the value of completing the assignment. At times, students' negative affect state prevents them from engaging in academic tasks, particularly if they believe they will probably not succeed at the task (Wigfield & Eccles, 1992).

Some of the most prominent expectancy-value research has concerned changes among children's perceptions of expectancy and value beliefs at different developmental stages as well as proposed differences between gender and ethnic groups. Remember that competence is closely related to expectancies for success. Children tend to report a significant drop in their self-perceptions of competence and valuing of academic tasks, but are more accurate in reporting their competence and values in junior high and high school than in elementary school (Eccles, 1983; Eccles, Wigfield, & Schiefele, 1998). While some argue that these changes are primarily developmental, either because young children can't process all the information necessary to understand their true ability levels relative to others (Blumenfeld, Pintrich, Meece, & Wessels, 1982) or because young children are naturally optimistic about their own abilities (Assor & Connell, 1992) and values (Wigfield & Eccles, 1992), others argue that the educational environment (e.g., grades, teacher feedback) plays a bigger role in developmental changes over time.

How do gender and ethnic groups differ with regard to expectancy and value beliefs? Research suggests that boys generally have higher perceptions of ability and tend to value tasks in mathematics and sports, while girls have higher perceptions of ability and tend to value tasks in reading, English, and social activities (Eccles, 1983; Eccles et al., 1998; Wigfield & Eccles, 1992). Interestingly, although there is no available evidence that African American students have lower perceptions of ability relative to Caucasian students, African American students' perceptions of ability are less likely to predict grades than Caucasian students (Graham, 1994). Additionally, African American, Hispanic American, and European girls tend to nominate high-achieving girls as people they admire and respect compared to African American and Hispanic American boys, who nominate low-achieving boys as people they admire and respect (Graham, Taylor, & Hudley, 1998). Little is known about why or how these different gender and ethnic groups are motivated. It is up to both scholars and educators to fill in these gaps with both theoretical and application-based research to help serve different kinds of students in the classroom.

One aspect of the expectancy-value model that has not been investigated is cognitive processes. Wigfield and Eccles (1992), however, have defined students' cognitive processes in part by interpretations and attributions for past events. Attribution theory, as developed by Weiner (1985, 1986), explains how students interpret their performance by looking for reasons that can explain success or particularly failure on academic tasks. Therefore, the main questions answered by expectancy-value theory are, Can I learn? and Why do I learn?, and the main question answered by attribution theory is, Why did I fail?

Why Did I Fail? Principles of Attribution Theory

Attribution theory is related to expectancy-value theory in that students' perceived causes of outcomes (particularly failure, since students are less likely to look for reasons why they were successful) can influence their expectancies for future success. Historically, there have been three motivational dimensions of attribution beliefs that have been examined in education research: (1) the locus dimension, or whether the cause is internal or external to the student; (2) the stability dimension, or how stable the cause is over time; and (3) the controllability dimension, or how controllable a cause is. Although the locus dimension (internal versus external) and controllability dimension (controllable versus uncontrollable) are most related to affective reactions after failure (such as sadness, guilt, or shame), it is the stability dimension of attribution theory that is most linked with expectations for success. When students receive poor grades or negative feedback for their performance, they immediately look for reasons why they did so poorly. Those reasons may contribute to increased or decreased amounts of effort and persistence on future assignments. According to attribution theory, the most adaptive reasons for failure are things that the student can control, are internal, and are unstable. The least adaptive reasons for failure are things that the student cannot control, are external, and are stable. For example, if a student attributes his or her failure to low ability, this is a stable characteristic that may cause less effort or persistence on future assignments. In contrast, if a task is difficult but the student expects future tasks to be less difficult (an unstable characteristic), he or she may try harder and exert more effort on the next related task. It should be mentioned that attributions are sometimes made in instances of success, especially when the success was unexpected, and stability may have the opposite effect on future effort and persistence when searching for causes of success. For example, a student who attributes success to ability (stable) will persist on future tasks, whereas a student who attributes success to how easy the task is (unstable) may not persist on future tasks.

Besides environmental antecedents of attributions such as task difficulty, teacher grades, and task consistency, there are personal factors that also lead to attributions for success and failure. For example, students know that certain events are only causal under certain circumstances, which means causality must follow certain rules if attributions are to occur. Students' attributions are perceived, and they are sometimes incorrect or inappropriate ways of looking at causes for failure and success. Finally, one's own personal history of success or failure has a very strong influence over attributional decisions on current and future tasks. Therefore, some students choose attributions that are adaptive, while others choose attributions that are maladaptive because of these personal factors. The good news is that attributions can be changed to be more adaptive if the student receives feedback on how they can make those changes.

Like expectancy-value theory, attribution theory research has also focused on developmental, gender, and ethnic differences in school-aged children. Unlike expectancy-value theory, however, there has also been research on intervention strategies that can help change students' attributions to be more adaptive, known as attributional retraining. According to Nicholls (1990), very young children (aged 3 to 5 years) do not differentiate ability and effort, ability and difficulty, or ability and luck, whereas older children (aged 9 to 10 years) are able to at least partially differentiate ability from effort, difficulty, and luck. It wouldn't make much sense for an early childhood educator to try and explain attributional differences to students, but by late elementary school and early middle school, teachers can help their students achieve by influencing their beliefs through attributional retraining. In studies that have used attributional retraining techniques, students were given verbal praise for their ability as opposed to their effort when students were *successful* (Schunk, 1983, 1984), but were given verbal praise for their effort as opposed to their ability when students had *failed* (Dweck, 1975). Teachers can use attributional retraining techniques to help students have more adaptive attributions in both success and failure situations. The research on gender and ethnic differences in students' attribution patterns is less clear than expectancy-value theory (Eccles, 1983; Eccles et al., 1998; Graham, 1994), but more research is needed to find out if there are indeed any differences and why students are different on these dimensions.

How Can I Get What I Want? Principles of Achievement Goal Theory

Goal orientations are the reasons for engaging in achievement behaviors (Pintrich, 2003). Therefore, goal orientation theory explains the cognitive processes students go through when making decisions about how to reach a desired objective. Dweck's theory of intelligence explains the type of goal orientation that students adopt (Schunk et al., 2008). Specifically, students with an entity theory of intelligence, who believe that ability is stable, will most likely adopt a *performance goal* when engaged in a task; performance goals are defined as demonstrating competence, striving to be the best, or seeking recognition for achievement (Dweck & Leggett, 1988). On the contrary, students with an incremental theory of intelligence, who believe that ability is unstable, will most likely adopt a *mastery goal* when engaged in a task; mastery goals are defined as focusing on learning, developing new skills, or trying something challenging (Dweck & Leggett, 1988). For example, if after receiving negative feedback, it is important for a student to learn the material presented in the next assignment and he or she has an incremental view of intelligence, then his or her goal is associated with *mastering* the task at hand. Thus, the mastery-oriented student will strive for improvement to learn the material better for the next assignment. But if it is important for the student to get a better grade or do better than peers and he or she has an entity view of intelligence, then this goal is associated with *performing* well on the task. Thus, the performance-oriented student will strive for a higher grade relative to others for the next assignment.

Additional research has indicated that there may be different types of mastery and performance goals, which may be characterized as either approach or avoid (Elliot & Harackiewicz, 1996), and that students may have multiple goals operating simultaneously to reach their objective (Barron & Harackiewicz, 2001; Pintrich, 2000). Performance-approach goals can be differentiated from performance-avoid goals in the following way: if a student wishes to best others and look good in comparison to peers by earning a high grade on the next assignment, then the student has performance-approach goals. In contrast, if a student wishes to avoid failure and looking incompetent in front of others by earning a high grade, then this student has a performance-avoid goal. Research has shown performance-avoid goals are associated with lower levels of engagement and achievement (Elliot & Harackiewicz, 1996; Midgley & Urdan, 1992). The research on performance-approach goals is less clear; some say it is adaptive for earning higher grades (Skaalvik, 1997; Wolters, 2004) while others say it reduces the likelihood of help-seeking (Ryan, Hicks, & Midgley, 1997). Some have argued that students can also have mastery-approach and mastery-avoid goals (Elliot, 1999). For example, a student who wishes to really learn and understand has a mastery-approach focus, but a student who wishes to avoid misunderstanding or complete the task perfectly has a mastery-avoid focus. Optimally, educators would prefer that students have a mastery-approach goal orientation, since educational objectives often focus on what students learn. Those who believe that students can have multiple achievement goals that act simultaneously have found that certain combinations of mastery- and performance-approach goals are more adaptive than others, since educational expectations demand that in addition to learning, students also perform well by achieving good grades in order to be successful (Midgley, Kaplan, & Middleton, 2001; Pintrich, 2000), particularly in middle school and high school where grades and competition are emphasized.

In recent research on achievement goal theory, more attention has been paid to the role of classroom goal structures, or the kinds of goals that teachers have for their students in the classroom. Teachers with a performance-oriented approach to instruction create an external goal structure, emphasizing high test scores, competitive practices, and social comparison of ability. These criteria for success tend to be consistent with the tenets of the No Child Left Behind Act and can lead to more performance-oriented classroom goal structures (Ciani, Summers, & Easter, in press). Teachers with a mastery-oriented approach to instruction focus more on individual development and learning, such as affording students the opportunity to demonstrate new abilities, providing motivational support for learning, and helping students to understand complex topics (Turner

et al., 2002). Research suggests that the more performance-oriented students believe their teachers to be, the more performance-oriented the students tend to be themselves. On the other hand, the more mastery-oriented teachers are perceived to be, the more students report themselves as being mastery-oriented (Wolters, 2004). For the most part, a mastery classroom goal structure is associated with positive student outcomes, whereas a performance classroom goal structure is associated with negative or inconsistent outcomes (Turner et al., 2002; Wolters, 2004). According to this research, it is in the best interest of teachers to structure their classrooms using a mastery-goal format. But additional research indicates that students had higher achievement and were more likely to seek help in classes that combined performance and mastery elements in the form of traditional seatwork and group learning tasks (Linnenbrink, 2005).

Theoretical Comparisons

Expectancy-value theory posits attribution as a cognitive process that is crucial to the formation of competence and expectancies. According to Weiner (2000), some of the causal properties of attribution theory map into expectancy beliefs. In particular, Weiner claims that if a cause is stable, then the same outcome will be anticipated again following a success or failure. On the contrary, failure due to unstable factors will not be an indicator of future failure. Therefore, the expectations for success and failure are determined by causal antecedents of one's attributional beliefs, and it is typically more adaptive for students to adapt unstable attributions following failure than stable attributions.

Like attribution theory, goal orientation theory is also related to expectancy-value theory. Specifically, goals, like expectancy for success and value for tasks, can explain why students engage in cognitive tasks (Eccles & Wigfield, 2002). Although "goals" appear in the contemporary expectancy-value model as a predictor of students' task values and expectancy beliefs (Wigfield & Eccles, 1992), it refers in this context to what students strive for (e.g., "I want to become a doctor") as opposed to mastery and performance goals. Wigfield (1994) suggests that these different types of goals can be integrated theoretically by assuming that goals in the form of broader life plans predict expectancies and values, with expectancies and values determining more specific goals in specific achievement situations. For example, a student who wants to become a doctor should have high expectancy for success in biology classes if he or she wants to be successful and have concurrent values associated with courses that have high utility for becoming a doctor. These expectations and values may lead to a combination of mastery (i.e., learning the material) and performance goals (i.e., doing well relative to others) in courses that are relevant to becoming a doctor. Empirically, research indicates that mastery goals are related to greater valuing of academic material (Wolters, Yu, & Pintrich, 1996), and performance goals are related to declines in valuing of academic material (Anderman et al., 2001). Therefore, it is in a teacher's best interest to help students either become more mastery-oriented by using strategies that enhance a mastery classroom goal structure or value the material students are learning by making tasks more meaningful and interesting.

Although attributions and achievement goals are both popular theories of motivation in the education literature, little recent research has tied them together explicitly (see Ames & Archer, 1988; Dweck & Leggett, 1988; Elliott & Dweck, 1988; Nicholls, 1984; Nicholls, Patashnick, & Nolen, 1985, for earlier examples). But there are theoretical links between why a student believes that he or she fails a task and how the student gets what he or she wants from the task (which is how achievement goals are defined here). Recall that Dweck's model of goal orientation (Dweck & Leggett, 1988) relates to students' beliefs about intelligence: someone who has an entity theory of intelligence believes intelligence is fixed, and someone who has an incremental theory of intelligence believes intelligence is malleable. It is possible that if a student experiences failure, the attributions may depend on the students' view of intelligence (a personal factor): a student with an entity view would likely have maladaptive attributions, since fixed intelligence cannot be controlled and is stable, whereas a student with an incremental view may have adaptive attributions since malleable intelligence can be controlled and is unstable.

Applications of Theory in Classroom Settings

Case Example

The best way to depict the differences and similarities between expectancy-value theory, attribution theory, and goal orientation theory is an example. Thinking about why children engage in a homework assignment can be examined from multiple dimensions of motivation. Their choice to engage in the homework task initially is usually associated with the value that a student has for homework; in this case it may be utility value. If students believe that they will be successful on their assignment, they will be more likely to exert effort while they are doing homework if they have a high expectation for success (students' choices for academic activities are determined by their values, and performance on the activity is determined by their expectations for success). Consider what happens when a student receives a graded homework assignment after submitting it the day before and does not get the grade expected (perhaps the student expected an "A" but earned a "D" on the assignment). According to attribution theory, the student immediately looks for reasons for doing so poorly, and those reasons may contribute to increased or decreased amounts of effort and persistence on future homework assignments. In this scenario, the most adaptive reasons for failure are things that the student can control, are internal, and are unstable. After earning the undesired "D" for homework, a student might think about how to do better on the next homework assignment. A student with an incremental view of intelligence, who also feels it is important to learn the material presented in the next assignment, will have goals associated with *mastering* the task. On the other hand, a student with an entity view of intelligence, who wants to get a better grade or do better than peers, will have a goal associated with *performing* well on the task at hand. The process of student motivation in this example is represented in Figure 12.1, along with other possible associations between beliefs that have been mentioned previously in this review. This figure is not meant to show causal relationships nor is it a suggested empirical model of how students' beliefs should be considered. It is merely a schematic diagram of this particular example.

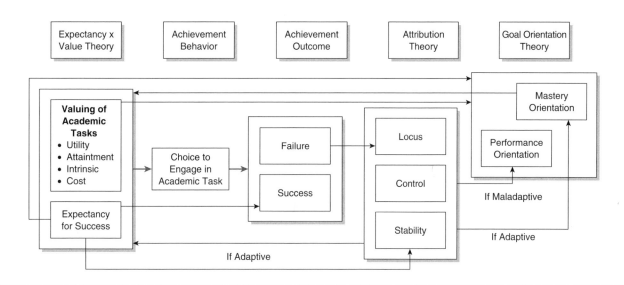

Figure 12.1   Schematic Diagram of Motivation Relationships in Homework Example

What Can Teachers Do to Enhance Student Motivation?

Most of the research in cognitive approaches to motivation has been mostly correlational in nature and, therefore, is designed to describe current classroom contexts rather than attempt to introduce new motivational strategies in classrooms and examine them experimentally (Urdan & Turner, 2005). Thus, most of the recommendations that researchers make to teachers is based on very general aspects of what they observe in typical classrooms, and they cannot make prescriptive recommendations that claim "this is what works for students." The recommendations in this section are therefore based on empirical evidence in a very limited sense, and one must assume that what works for some students may not work for all students.

There are many considerations teachers must make before implementing new motivational strategies in the classroom, such as developmental appropriateness of the strategy, prior student achievement, and curriculum goals. As most educators know, the academic expectations placed on junior high and high school students differ from what elementary school children face. Older students are faced with a more structured, competitive environment than younger students, which can cause overall perceptions of abilities and values to change. So what can educators do for students who have low perceptions of ability or decreased value for academic tasks as they progress through the academic system? Some suggestions from Schunk et al. (2008) and Urdan and Turner (2005) include the following: (a) let students know that beliefs about competence can be controlled or changed; (b) decrease the amount of relative ability information that is made public to students; (c) offer reasons for schoolwork than include the importance or utility value of the task; (d) model value in the content of the lesson; (e) activate personal interest through opportunities for choice; and (f) praise students for their accomplishments. We can think about how these suggestions might apply to help motivate students to do their homework: The teacher should make sure that grades on assignments will not be publicly available, offer good reasons (based on importance and utility) for doing the assignment, and perhaps give students some amount of choice either between assignments or within the same assignment. As most educators know, however, students will often find a way to compare themselves to others if it is important to their sense of self-concept and they have strong attainment value for the task (Summers, Schallert, & Ritter, 2003). Teachers must weigh both classroom factors and students' personal factors when assessing students' valuing of academic tasks.

According to Urdan & Turner (2005), there is not much research that explicitly connects teacher behaviors and student motivation in the classroom. The general recommendation for teachers based on the research is to assess students' attributions for success and failure before and after tasks, and to encourage students via attributional retraining to change any attributions that may diminish their sense of control (Schunk et al., 2008). In the homework example, teachers may want to assess the student's attributions and offer feedback that is appropriate, accurate, and focused on the unstable, changeable causes for failure that might increase the student's sense of control over the task.

Some intervention studies have been conducted in the goals research in which teachers who implemented mastery goal strategies in their classrooms saw either no change in their students' motivation (Ames, 1990) or a slight decrease in performance-approach goals (Anderman, Maehr, & Midgley, 1999), but nonmastery goal classrooms reported a significant decline in motivation. In general, teachers are advised to make student evaluation private, to emphasize understanding and challenge, and to use cooperative learning strategies (Midgley & Urdan, 1992). One of the specific recommendations made by Schunk et al. (2008) to help increase students' mastery goal orientation in classrooms is to use heterogeneous cooperative groups to foster peer interaction, because cooperative learning is often associated with increased mastery goals among individual students (see the following for examples: Abrami, Chambers, D'Apollonia, Farrell, & DeSimone, 1992; Battistich, Solomon, & Delucchi, 1993; Nichols & Miller, 1994; Sharan & Shaulov, 1990). The ways in which teachers use collaborative or cooperative learning can vary, and the benefits of group work are specific to the conditions of group-related tasks. For example, Summers (2006) found that students in groups who collectively valued the academic goals of group work were likely to adopt individual motivational strategies associated with performance-avoidance goals over time, despite the fact that increased levels of mastery were expected. Perhaps this was because classroom practices associated with social learning and collaboration may make students more conscious of others' evaluations, thus leading them to adopt motivational goals of self-protection, or because students in this study were asked to change groups on a regular basis. In any case, cooperative and collaborative learning are excellent strategies to help foster positive academic outcomes as long as they are incorporated correctly and with little chance of social comparison occurring. In our homework example, teachers might ask students to do their homework separately but collaborate on tasks that are based on knowledge acquired from the homework assignment to foster learning, accountability, and peer support.

In addition to group work, other ways in which teachers can foster mastery motivation are suggested by the acronym TARGET, which stands for Task, Authority, Recognition, Grouping, Evaluation, and Time (Epstein, 1989). The recommendations based on the TARGET literature are as follows (Ames, 1990): (1) allow task variation, help students see the relevance of tasks, and keep tasks at a challenging level; (2) offer students the opportunity to take leadership roles in their own learning; (3) recognize and offer specific feedback on student effort, progress, and accomplishments; (4) use small-group work to help students assume more responsibility for learning; (5) keep evaluation practices private to avoid social comparison and focus on individual improvement; and (6) adjust the time required for completing work depending on the nature of the task.

Conclusion

This chapter provided an overview of three motivational theories—expectancy-value theory, attribution theory, and achievement goal theory—and provided suggestions for classroom application based on the research on these theories. Like most of the literature on student motivation, these suggestions were in no way meant to be prescriptive. Researchers are at a disadvantage in that they do not experience classrooms the way that educators do, but they do understand that there are very complex dynamics at work in classrooms on a day-to-day basis that cannot be parsimoniously applied to one single theory or application. Therefore, it us up to educators to decide how this information applies to any particular student or situation now that the information has been "translated" into a more accessible format. Similarly, teachers can assist researchers by helping them understand more about what works and what doesn't work based on practical field experience. For example, in recent research on teachers' motivational practices in classrooms, Turner and Christensen (2007) documented a process by which they were able to introduce fundamental concepts and implementation strategies from motivation theory to a group of math teachers in a very collaborative way. Researchers and teachers met on a monthly basis to discuss issues and answer questions such as, Where does motivation come from? What hampers students' motivation in mathematics? What are some obstacles to making changes to current instructional practice? Teachers then tried these suggestions in their classrooms and reported back to the researchers and other teachers about what worked and what did not. Results indicated that the teachers who were able to successfully change their beliefs about motivation and learning were more likely to change instruction to foster student motivation (Turner & Urdan, 2007). Future research could make similar use of intervention methodology by partnering researchers and teachers to inform motivation practices in holistic and meaningful ways.

References and Further Readings

Abrami, P. C., Chambers, B., D'Apollonia, S., Farrell, M., & DeSimone, S. (1992). Group outcome: The relationship between group learning outcome, attributional style, academic achievement, and self-concept. *Contemporary Educational Psychology, 17,* 201–210.

Ames, C., & Archer, J. (1988). Achievement goals in the classroom: Students' learning strategies and motivation processes. *Journal of Educational Psychology, 80,* 260–267.

Ames, C. A. (1990, April). *The relationship of achievement goals to student motivation in classroom settings.* Paper presented at the annual meeting of the American Educational Research Association, Boston.

Anderman, E. M., Eccles, J. S., Yoon, K. S., Roeser, R. W., Wigfield, A., & Blumenfeld, P. (2001). Learning to value math and reading: Individual difference and classroom effects. *Contemporary Educational Psychology, 26,* 76–95.

Anderman, E. M., Maehr, M. L., & Midgley, C. (1999). Declining motivation after the transition to middle school: Schools can make a difference. *Journal of Research and Development in Education, 32,* 131–147.

Anderman, E. M., & Wolters, C. A. (2006). Goals, values, and affect: Influences on student motivation. In P. A. Alexander & P. H. Winne (Eds.), *Handbook of Educational Psychology* (2nd ed.). Mahwah, NJ: Lawrence Erlbaum Associates.

Assor, A., & Connell, J. P. (1992). The validity of students' self-reports as measures of performance affecting self-appraisals. In D. H. Schunk & J. L. Meece (Eds.), *Student perceptions in the classroom* (pp. 25–47). Hillsdale, NJ: Lawrence Erlbaum Associates.

Barron, K., & Harackiewicz, J. (2001). Achievement goals and optimal motivation: Testing multiple goal models. *Journal of Personality and Social Psychology, 80,* 706–722.

Battistich, V., Solomon, D., & Delucchi, K. (1993). Interaction processes and student outcomes in cooperative learning groups. *The Elementary School Journal, 94,* 19–32.

Bergin, D. (1999). Influences on classroom interest. *Educational Psychologist, 34,* 87–98.

Blumenfeld, P. C., Pintrich, P. R., Meece, J., & Wessels, K. (1982). The formation and role of self-perceptions of ability in the elementary classroom. *Elementary School Journal, 82,* 401–420.

Ciani, K. D., Summers, J. J., & Easter, M. A. (in press). A "top-down" analysis of high school teacher motivation. *Contemporary Educational Psychology.*

Dweck, C. S. (1975). The role of expectations and attributions in the alleviation of learned helplessness. *Journal of Personality and Social Psychology, 31,* 674–685.

Dweck, C. S., & Elliott, W. S. (1983). Motivational processes affecting learning. *American Psychologist, 41,* 1040–1048.

Dweck, C. S., & Leggett, E. L. (1988). A social-cognitive approach to motivation and personality. *Psychological Review, 95,* 256–273.

Eccles, J. S. (1983). Expectancies, values and academic behaviors. In J. T. Spence (Ed.), *Achievement and achievement motives* (pp. 75–146). San Francisco: Freeman.

Eccles, J. S., & Wigfield, A. (2002). Motivational beliefs, values, and goals. *Annual Review of Psychology, 53,* 109–132.

Eccles, J. S., Wigfield, A., & Schiefele, U. (1998). Motivation to succeed. In W. Damon (Series Ed.) & N. Eisenberg (Vol. Ed.), *Handbook of child psychology: Vol. 3. Social emotional and personality development* (5th ed., pp. 1017–1095). New York: Wiley.

Elliot, A. J. (1999). Approach and avoidance motivation and achievement goals. *Educational Psychologist, 34,* 169–189.

Elliot, A. J., & Harackiewicz, J. M. (1996). Approach and avoidance achievement goals and intrinsic motivation: A mediational analysis. *Journal of Personality and Social Psychology, 70,* 461–475.

Elliott, E. S., & Dweck, C. S. (1988). Goals: An approach to motivation and achievement. *Journal of Personality and Social Psychology, 54,* 5–12.

Epstein, J. (1989). Family structures and student motivation: A developmental perspective. In C. Ames & R. Ames (Eds.), *Research on motivation in education* (Vol. 3, pp. 259–295). San Diego, CA: Academic Press.

Graham, S. (1994). Motivation in African Americans. *Review of Educational Research, 64,* 55–117.

Graham, S., Taylor, A. Z., & Hudley, C. (1998). Exploring achievement values among ethnic minority early adolescence. *Journal of Educational Psychology, 78,* 4–13.

Linnenbrink, E. A. (2005). The dilemma of performance-approach goals: The use of multiple goal contexts to promote students' motivation and learning. *Journal of Educational Psychology, 97,* 197–213.

Midgley, C., Kaplan, A., & Middleton, M. (2001). Performance-approach goals: Good for what, for whom, under what circumstances, and at what cost? *Journal of Educational Psychology, 93,* 77–86.

Midgley, C., & Urdan, T. (1992). The transition to middle school: Making it a good experience for all students. *Middle School Journal, 24,* 5–14.

Nichols, J. D., & Miller, R. B. (1994). Cooperative learning and student motivation. *Contemporary Educational Psychology, 19,* 167–178.

Nicholls, J. G. (1984). Achievement motivation: Conceptions of ability, subjective experience, task choice, and performance. *Psychological Review, 91,* 328–346.

Nicholls, J. G. (1990). What is ability and why are we mindful of it? A developmental perspective. In R. Sternberg & J. Kolligian (Eds.), *Competence considered* (pp. 11–40). New Haven, CT: Yale University Press.

Nicholls, J. G., Patashnick, M., & Nolen, S. B. (1985). Adolescents' theories of education. *Journal of Educational Psychology, 77,* 683–692.

Pintrich, P. R. (2000). Multiple goals, multiple pathways: The role of goal orientation in learning and achievement. *Journal of Educational Psychology, 92,* 544–555.

Pintrich, P. R. (2003). A motivational science perspective on the role of student motivation in learning and teaching contexts. *Journal of Educational Psychology, 95,* 667–686.

Ryan, A. M., Hicks, L., & Midgley, C. (1997). Should I ask for help? The role of motivation and attitude in adolescents' help-seeking in math class. *Journal of Early Adolescence, 17,* 152–171.

Schunk, D. H. (1983). Ability versus effort attributional feedback: Differential effects on self-efficacy and achievement. *Journal of Educational Psychology, 75,* 848–856.

Schunk, D. H. (1984). Sequential attributional feedback and children's achievement behaviors. *Journal of Educational Psychology, 76,* 1159–1169.

Schunk, D. H., Pintrich, P. R., & Meece, J. L. (2008). *Motivation in education: Theory, research, and applications* (3rd ed.). Upper Saddle River, NJ: Pearson Education.

Schunk, D. H., & Zimmerman, B. J. (2006). Competence and control beliefs: Distinguishing the means and the ends. In P. A. Alexander & P. H. Winne (Eds.), *Handbook of Educational Psychology* (2nd ed.). Mahwah, NJ: Lawrence Erlbaum Associates.

Sharan, S., & Shaulov, A. (1990). Cooperative learning, motivation to learn, and academic achievement. In S. Sharan (Ed.), *Cooperative learning: Theory and research* (pp. 173–202). New York: Praeger.

Skaalvik, E. M. (1997). Self-enhancing and self-defeating ego orientation: Relations with task and avoidance orientation, achievement, self-perceptions, and anxiety. *Journal of Educational Psychology, 89,* 71–81.

Summers, J. J. (2006). Effects of collaborative learning on individual goal orientations from a socioconstructivist perspective. [Special issue]. *Elementary School Journal: The Interpersonal Contexts of Motivation and Learning, 106,* 273–290.

Summers, J. J., Schallert, D. L., & Ritter, P. M. (2003). The role of social comparison in students' perceptions of ability: An enriched view of academic motivation in middle school students. *Contemporary Educational Psychology, 28,* 510–523.

Turner, J. C., & Christensen, A. (2007, August). *"They just aren't motivated:" The development and change of teachers' motivational practices in the classroom.* Paper presented at the Biennial Meeting of the European Association for Research on Learning and Instruction, Budapest, Hungary.

Turner, J. C., Midgley, C., Meyer, D. K., Gheen, M., Anderman, E. A., Kang, Y., et al. (2002). The classroom environment and students' reports of avoidance strategies in mathematics: A multimethod study. *Journal of Educational Psychology, 94,* 88–106.

Turner, J. C., & Urdan, T. (2007, November). *Development and change of teacher beliefs and practices in mathematics.* Paper presented at the Biennial Meeting of the Southwest Consortium for Innovative Psychology in Education, Phoenix, AZ.

Urdan, T., & Turner, J. C. (2005). Competence motivation in the classroom. In A. J. Elliot & C. S. Dweck (Eds.), *Handbook of Competence and Motivation* (pp. 297–317). New York: Guilford.

Weiner, B. (1985). An attributional theory of achievement motivation and emotion. *Psychological Review, 92,* 548–573.

Weiner, B. (1986). *An attributional theory of motivation and emotion.* New York: Springer-Verlag.

Weiner, B. (2000). Intrapersonal and interpersonal theories of motivation from an attributional perspective. *Educational Psychology Review, 12,* 1–14.

Wigfield, A. (1994). Expectancy-value theory of achievement motivation: A developmental perspective. *Educational Psychology Review, 6,* 49–78.

Wigfield, A., & Eccles, J. S. (1992). The development of achievement task values: A theoretical analysis. *Developmental Review, 12,* 265–310.

Wolters, C. A. (2004). Advancing achievement goal theory: Using goal structures and goal orientations to predict students' motivation, cognition, and achievement. *Journal of Educational Psychology, 96,* 236–250.

Wolters, C. A., Yu, S., L., & Pintrich, P. R. (1996). The relation between goal orientation and students' motivational beliefs and self-regulated learning. *Learning and Individual Differences, 8,* 211–238.

13

PERCEIVED CONTROL, COPING, AND ENGAGEMENT

ELLEN SKINNER AND TERESA GREENE

Portland State University

Perceived control is one of the most robust predictors of student resilience and academic success all across the elementary, middle, and high school years. Children and adolescents who are confident and optimistic are more likely to select challenging tasks; set high and concrete goals; initiate and maintain constructive engagement; deal productively with obstacles and setbacks; maintain access to their highest quality problem solving, concentration, and focus even under stress; seek help as needed; rebound from failure; and eventually develop more adaptive strategies of self-regulated learning. Cumulatively, through this approach to schooling (sometimes referred to as a mastery or action orientation), students actually learn more and so develop higher levels of objective competence. In contrast, children and adolescents who doubt their own efficacy are more likely to show a helplessness (or state) orientation in which they set diffuse goals, prefer easy tasks, remain passive, become anxious and distracted, ruminate, give up, or try to escape from difficult encounters, avoid help, and lose access to their own best hypothesis testing and strategizing skills. Eventually, this pattern hinders learning enough that students' actual competencies begin to fall behind those of their age mates.

Mastery and helplessness have been the subject of multiple major theories and hundreds of experimental and naturalistic studies over the last 50 years. Starting with work on locus of control and continuing with formulations focusing on attributions, learned helplessness, self-efficacy,

and naïve theories of intelligence, the area of perceived control has been the site of some of the richest and most careful theorizing and empirical examination to date about the nature and functioning of children's motivation, self-regulation, engagement, coping, and development (Elliot & Dweck, 2005; Stipek, 2002; Wigfield, Eccles, Schiefele, Roeser, & Davis-Kean, 2006).

The sheer volume of work as well as the territoriality of some of its proponents makes it difficult to construct a coherent picture of how and why perceived control has such pervasive effects on academic functioning. The goal of this chapter is to present a developmental framework that allows for an integrated conceptualization of the facets and functioning of perceived control, with special emphasis on how they are shaped by teachers, curricula, classroom contexts, and development. Because the empirical success of control constructs tends to crowd out additional players, this chapter also includes a description of how perceived control interacts with other important resources for motivation and coping.

What Is the Nature of Control?

One explanation for why the effects of control are so evident across the entire life span is that it reflects a fundamental human psychological need. The basic idea is that all humans (and other higher mammals) come with the inborn desire to be effective in their interactions with the social and physical context (White, 1959). Referred to as the need for competence, effectance, or mastery, this organismic perspective posits that all people are intrinsically motivated to produce effects, to make things happen (Elliot & Dweck, 2005; Elliot, McGregor, & Thrash, 2002; Harter, 1978; Koestner & McClelland, 1990). The underlying function of effectance motivation is to provide energy and direction for figuring out how the world works, and in so doing to fuel the development of a range of actual competencies effective in creating desired and preventing undesired outcomes. Such motivation is a source of curiosity and interest and of energy for the extended trials and errors and subsequent practice needed to discover and hone effective actions. The evolutionary value of this kind of motivation is obvious: Any species that dedicates time and energy to learning how to be effective will eventually develop a rich action repertoire, as well as knowledge about opportunities and constraints in the environment. In times of trouble, this competence is the key to both surviving and thriving.

Schools are supposed to be one of the chief vehicles for fostering effectance motivation. Unfortunately, however, research demonstrates that schools do not generally fulfill students' need for competence; children's perceived competence, feelings of control, and academic motivation decline steadily throughout elementary, middle, and high school (Stipek, Recchia, & McClintic, 1992; Wigfield et al., 2006). The good news for educators is that, from an organismic perspective, effectance motivation cannot really be lost. Underlying even the most alienated student is a potential wellspring of motivation. Nevertheless, a detailed understanding of the entire competence system is needed if parents and teachers are to succeed in nourishing children's perceived control with all its resultant benefits.

What Are the Key Constructs of Control?

The more one reads about perceived control, the easier it is to become confused about the cluster of control-related terms. Some researchers conclude that they are all pretty much the same, whereas other researchers argue that a single construct can be identified that is best. But a thoughtful analysis suggests that, although many concepts can be differentiated, the role of each must be carefully considered in order to create a comprehensive picture of the entire system involved (Skinner, 1996). The notions of competence and effectance motivation can provide a useful framework for organizing the functions of different control constructs.

According to these metatheories, the basic building blocks of competence start with experiences of control. Also referred to as *generative transmission,* these are experiences of exerting personal force that is effective in producing intended outcomes. Experiences of control can be distinguished from *objective control conditions,* or the actual action-outcome contingencies that exist in the context (Seligman, 1975). For example, the more difficult a task, or the more outcomes are based on luck, chance, or

other uncontrollable factors (like skin color or gender), the lower the objective control conditions. Experiences of control can also be distinguished from *subjective* or *perceived control,* or people's interpretations of their control experiences. People can maintain high expectations of control in the face of low objective conditions and a history of failure, just as they can interpret hard-won success on difficult tasks as due to luck or other factors outside their control.

Conceptualizations of Control

There are at least five main theories of perceived control: value-expectancy models, locus of control, causal attributions, learned helplessness, and self-efficacy (see Heckhausen, 1991; Stipek, 2002; or Wigfield et al., 2006, for more details); a developmental model integrating these constructs has also been proposed. We briefly describe each theory before specifying its place in the competence system. As part of value-expectancy models, *expectancies of success,* or outcome expectancies, are people's estimations of the probability that they can produce desired outcomes (Atkinson, 1964; Wigfield & Eccles, 2000). *Locus of control,* originally also part of value-expectancy models, has come to refer to generalized expectations that desired outcomes are contingent on internal factors (such as one's own behavior or relatively permanent characteristics) versus external factors (like luck, chance, fate, or powerful others; Lefcourt, 1992; Rotter, 1966).

Theories of *causal attribution* depict the process by which people ascribe their successes and failures to a variety of causes (such as effort, ability, task difficulty, or luck) that differ on their underlying dimensions (internality, stability, intentionality, and controllability; Weiner, 1986, 2005). Theories of *learned helplessness* originally focused on how experiences of objective noncontingency create a syndrome of negative effects when they are generalized to contingent environments (Seligman, 1975). Later, theories of explanatory style posited that attributing experiences of noncontingency to internal, stable, and global causes produces these deficits (Abramson, Seligman, & Teasdale, 1978; Peterson, Maier, & Seligman, 1993). At about the same time, theories of *self-efficacy* were proposed that originally distinguished beliefs about whether responses were effective in producing outcomes (referred to as response-outcome expectancies and compared to locus of control and helplessness) from efficacy expectations or "the conviction that one can successfully execute the behavior required to produce the outcome" (Bandura, 1977, p. 193). In subsequent formulations, this theory has come to focus almost exclusively on self-efficacy (which also implies response-outcome contingencies) and its effects (Bandura, 1997).

As depicted in Figure 13.1, a developmental conceptualization designed to integrate these theories distinguishes three kinds of beliefs: (1) *perceived control,* or generalized expectancies that the self can produce desired and prevent undesired outcomes (similar to expectancies of success); (2) *strategy beliefs,* or generalized expectancies about the

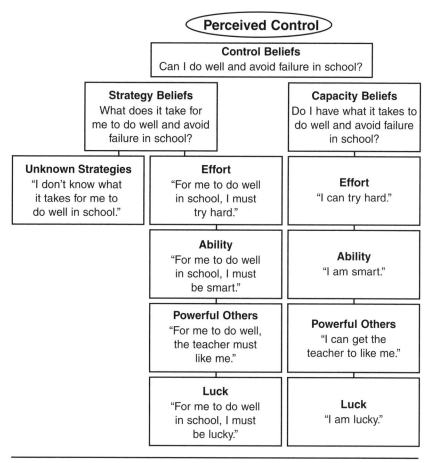

Figure 13.1   An Integrative Developmental Conceptualization of Perceived Control

effectiveness of certain causes (such as effort, ability, powerful others, luck, and unknown) in producing desired and preventing undesired outcomes (similar to locus of control, causal attributions, explanatory style, or response-outcome expectancies); and (3) *capacity beliefs,* or generalized expectancies about the extent to which the self possesses or has access to potentially effective causes (similar to self-efficacy or perceived ability; Connell, 1985; Skinner, 1995, 1996). Unknown strategy beliefs, or a child's conviction that he or she has no idea how to do well in school, are some of the most pernicious and maladaptive beliefs children can hold, and developmentally, they are some of the earliest predictors of academic helplessness (Connell, 1985; Skinner, Zimmer-Gembeck, & Connell, 1998).

Regulatory and Interpretative Functions of Control

In shaping control experiences, perceived control has two main functions: (1) when preparing to take on an activity, expectations of control have a *regulatory* function in that they shape how people approach and engage in the task; and (2) following an action-outcome episode, they have an *interpretative* function, in that they help translate the meaning of the experience for future control. The beliefs that regulate

action are generalized expectations of control (the sense that "I can do it"); this connection is supported by findings that perceived control, expectancies of success, and self-efficacy are strong proximal predictors of motivation and performance (see Wigfield et al., 2006). In contrast, following performance outcomes, the beliefs used to interpret the meaning of action-outcome episodes are ones that focus on the likely causes and one's own role in producing the success or failure; this connection is supported by findings that causal attributions, explanatory style, and strategy and capacity beliefs are important predictors of emotional and motivational reactions to success and failure experiences (see Peterson et al., 1993; Weiner, 1986, 2005).

The link *between* interpretative and regulatory beliefs is especially interesting. One of the most important things about how people explain their successes and failures are the implications these interpretations have for subsequent expectancies of control. So for example, the belief that failure was caused by a stable internal cause (such as ability) not only creates short-term emotional and motivational deficits (like embarrassment, discouragement, and exhaustion), but also contributes to long-term expectations that future outcomes are not likely to be under one's control. This pathway, from causal attributions to performance expectations, is a key mechanism: All theories that focus on interpretative beliefs (i.e., causal attributions, learned helplessness, locus of control) agree that it is the pathway through which such beliefs have their effects on subsequent effort and performance.

Profiles of Control

An integrative developmental perspective suggests that all the kinds of beliefs considered in major theories of perceived control play a role in action sequences. As a result, the most powerful predictor of a child's motivation and performance will be the child's *profile* of control beliefs. Optimal profiles of beliefs include high control, high effort strategy, and high capacity beliefs combined with low reliance on all the uncontrollable strategies (ability, powerful others, luck, and unknown). In contrast, maladaptive profiles of beliefs incorporate low control, low effectiveness of effort, and low capacity beliefs combined with high dependence on all the uncontrollable strategies. Scores created to reflect these profiles are strong predictors of engagement, achievement, and eventually, retention or dropout, all the way from elementary to high school (e.g., Connell, Spencer, & Aber, 1994; Connell, Halpern-Felsher, Clifford, Crichlow, & Usinger, 1995; Skinner et al., 1998).

What Are the Consequences of Control for Academic Resilience and Success?

Because an enormous body of research has demonstrated the effects of perceived control across most domains, and especially in times of stress and difficulty, investigators have attempted to uncover the mechanisms of its widespread beneficial effects. Many decades of study have revealed pathways that are more various, pervasive, and subtle than researchers first imagined. For example, in keeping with the assumption that control reflects an organismic need, research has demonstrated that the effects of prolonged exposure to noncontingency or loss of control are physiological, affecting the integrated neurological and biological systems involved in stress reactivity, immune functioning, emotion, attention, learning, and brain development (Gunnar & Quevedo, 2007).

Consequences are also psychological, shaping concurrent motivation, volition, emotion, and cognition, as well as future-oriented states such as optimism and hope (Kuhl, 1984). The consequences of control can be clearly observed on the plane of action, in engagement, self-regulation, and coping (Skinner, 1995). Through their effects on students' choices about which activities to pursue (e.g., elective classes), control beliefs also play a decisive role in determining the learning opportunities available to adolescents (Wigfield et al., 2006). By contributing to how youth engage in planning and preventative action, perceived control can even have an effect on the likelihood that they will encounter future stressful events. Moreover, the effects of control are also relational—social partners respond differently to a child with a mastery orientation compared to a helplessness orientation. In fact, perceived control seems to confer advantages during all phases of an action episode, including planning, strategizing, action implementation, and utilization of feedback.

Two of the most important pathways through which control shapes children's academic progress are by affecting the quality of their engagement and by influencing how they cope with setbacks (Skinner, 1995; see Table 13.1). In

Table 13.1   Consequences of Perceived Control for Academic Functioning and Resilience

High Perceived Control Mastery Orientation	Low Perceived Control Helplessness Orientation
Engagement in Academic Activities	*Disaffection in Academic Activities*
Approach work with enthusiasm and vigor	Procrastinate
Set high and concrete goals	Avoid challenge
Enjoy challenges	Diffuse goals
Focus and concentrate on task	Lose track of intentions
Follow through on intentions	Easily distracted
Break tasks into manageable sequential parts	Self-derogatory thoughts
Employ a variety of alternative strategies	Feel anxious
Maintain access to all cognitive resources	Lose access to cognitive resources
Perform close to the ceiling of one's capacity	Remain passive
Use "failure" as information about how to improve performance	Do just enough to get by
Actually learn more	Quit as soon as possible
	Actually learn less
Adaptive Coping with Obstacles and Setbacks	*Maladaptive Coping with Obstacles and Setbacks*
Less distress	More distress
Fewer involuntary stress reactions (such as panic or avoidance)	More involuntary stress reactions
More determination and persistence	Truncated efforts
More flexible and creative problem solving	Rumination, excuses
Better use of self-regulatory strategies	More rigid problem solving
Seek help when needed	Less use of self-regulatory strategies
More planning and proactive coping	Avoid help
More preemptive action like study and practice	Conceal problems
	Avoid challenge
	Give up quickly

fact, as demonstrated by research on learned helplessness, the most marked differences between the performances of mastery-oriented versus helplessness-oriented children can be seen following exposure to failure (Dweck, 1999; Seligman, 1975). Think aloud protocols, in which children reveal their thought processes when they encounter obstacles (e.g., Diener & Dweck, 1978), show that children with a helplessness orientation soon devolve into worry, doubts about their capacities, and irrelevant digressions. These thought processes sap their energy and interfere with access to cognitive competencies (like problem solving or hypothesis testing) which they were able to utilize. In contrast, mastery-oriented students do not seem to be involved with self-congratulatory reflections. Instead, their entire motivational and cognitive resources are focused on problem solving: what to do next, what might work, what they have learned so far. This allows them to derive maximum information from their task interactions, even figuring out sooner if the problem is too hard for them or unsolvable altogether.

How Can Control Shape Academic Development?

The experience of control is dynamic, creating action episodes or cycles in which perceived control both shapes a student's approach to school and is shaped by that student's history of successes and failures with academic tasks (see Figure 13.2). These cycles are self-verifying or amplifying—children initially "rich" in perceived control, through the way they engage in learning activities and cope with challenges, become "richer" over time, whereas children who doubt their competence, through the ways they deal with academic tasks, actually forfeit opportunities for control and so verify their initially low expectations (Schmitz & Skinner, 1993). Cumulatively, these different approaches also have an effect on social partners—teachers respond with more involvement and autonomy support to students who are more actively engaged in the classroom, whereas teachers increasingly withdraw their support or become more coercive with students who are more disaffected (Skinner & Belmont, 1993). Actively engaged students are also more likely to hang out with actively engaged peers at school, which likewise supports the development of their own motivation (Kindermann, 2007).

Although not yet documented completely, these cycles of engagement seem to be critical building blocks for student resilience and academic development. Some theorists argue that a history of constructive engagement with academic tasks in school, with its resultant experiences of mastery, success, and learning, is the gateway to key developmental milestones in later childhood, including the development of self-regulated learning, ownership of

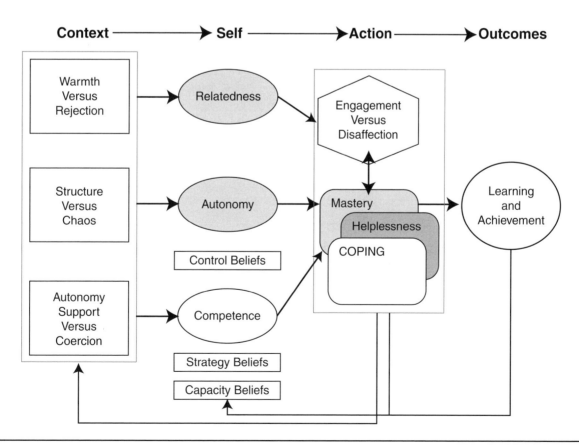

Figure 13.2 A Process Model of the Functioning of Perceived Control

one's own academic progress, internalizing the value of schooling, and eventually fostering the construction of an identity that includes high achievement. These resources are needed to support children through the normatively difficult transitions to middle and high school (Eccles, 2004). That not all students achieve these milestones may be one reason why children who are struggling academically lose the most ground during school transitions (Wigfield et al., 2006).

How Do Developments Challenge Control Experiences and Expectancies?

The overwhelming majority of studies on perceived control focus on individual differences. However, parallel to this work, a narrow band of research continues to explore developmental changes in perceived competence, expectancies of success, and other facets of perceived control as well as age-graded shifts in the cognitive, emotional, behavioral, and motivational processes likely to underlie them (for reviews, see Elliot et al., 2002; Flammer, 1995; Heckhausen, 1991; Skinner, 1995; Stipek, 2002; Weisz, 1986; Wigfield & Eccles, 2002). Some of the most interesting studies investigate age changes in how children deal with challenges and failures (Dweck, 1999, 2002). This developmental research reveals normative changes in the processing of causal information; in the accuracy of children's performance estimates; in their emotional and behavioral reactions to success and failure; in the information they use to evaluate their own competence; in their conceptions of potential causes such as effort, task difficulty, luck, chance, and ability; and in the very nature of the self.

Reviewers of this work are left with an apparent paradox: How is it possible that the effects of perceived control are invariant across development—from infancy through old age—if at the same time, almost all aspects of perceiving control and processing control relevant information show regular and marked age-graded changes? One way of resolving this puzzle is to posit that effectance motivation and feelings of efficacy are sources of energy and joy throughout the life span while at the same time, the kinds of interactions that children need to experience control, and especially the ways they process success and failure, do change systematically with age (Dweck, 2002; Elliot et al., 2002; Skinner, 1995). The challenge for parents, educators, and schools more generally is to help bring children and adolescents through a series of normative developments, which for the most part represent improvements in adaptive functioning, while creating or maintaining a competence system that is vibrant and resilient.

Transition to Performance Evaluation

In the early elementary grades, children have high and optimistic expectations for their success in school, which are unrelated to their actual performances (e.g., Stipek et al., 1992). Teachers want students to try hard and to be well-behaved, and children understand these values. Slowly over the first years of school, however, children begin to comprehend that the point of school is not effort, but performance outcomes, and their normative perceived competence declines and comes to reflect teachers' evaluations as expressed by grades. Children continue to endorse the effectiveness of effort in producing good outcomes, but they start to differentiate effort from other potential causes (such as task difficulty, chance, and luck). Repeated failure begins to undermine children's beliefs that they understand how to do well in school, and unknown strategy beliefs become a major predictor of student disaffection from learning in the classroom (e.g., Connell, 1985). In other words, more accurate performance evaluations (a cognitive gain) come at the expense of decreases in optimism about future performances and a vulnerability to losing confidence that one knows how to produce success and prevent failure in school.

Social Comparison

From middle to late elementary school, children become more interested in using the performance of their peers as a yardstick against which to measure their own success. This capacity reflects a cognitive gain in that the representation and integration of information about others' performances on similar tasks allow a child to distinguish task difficulty (when everyone performs poorly) as a source of performance outcomes. Better estimations of task difficulty, however, come with a potential downside. If one is performing poorly on tasks (e.g., homework or tests) on which everyone else is doing well, this can be interpreted one of two ways: either one needs to apply more effort or one might as well give up. For children who are regularly performing below their peers, social comparisons are discouraging and can undermine engagement. In other words, developing the capacity to use information about the performance of others to calibrate estimations of task difficulty (a cognitive gain) brings with it the potential vulnerability of denigrating one's own performance and potential.

Differentiation of Ability From Effort

In the late elementary school or early middle school grades (between the ages of 10 and 12), children come to understand the cognitively complex notion of ability. As an inferential concept, ability is an invisible capacity that can only be inferred from a pattern of performance outcomes: success on normatively hard tasks with little effort. To make such inferences, children must be able to understand inverse compensatory relations among causes, specifically, that with outcomes held constant, effort and ability are inversely related to each other (Miller, 1985; Nicholls, 1984). This means that smart children do not need to try as hard and that for the same outcome (e.g., the same grade), children who exerted less effort are more able. With this cognitive advance comes the vulnerability described as "the double-edged sword of effort" (Covington & Omelich, 1979). Students know that effort is valued by teachers, but high exertion that ends in failure can imply low ability. At this point, the facets of perceived control that best predict engagement (and that are best predicted by performance) change from those centered on the capacity to exert effort to those focused on one's own level of ability. In other words, the development of more complex causal schema introduces a potential vulnerability to failure.

The Complexity of Developmental Advances

Early in research on the development of learned helplessness, investigators assumed that young children, because they did not have the cognitive skills to infer ability, were immune to the effects of failure, and that once they acquired mature conceptions of ability, all children would be more likely to become helpless. Subsequent research has revealed that both of these conclusions were premature. For younger children, in keeping with research showing that even infants and higher mammals show helplessness, it has been demonstrated that there is no age at which children are free from the effects of repeated failure. Instead, the experiences that trigger helplessness and the concepts used to generalize its effects are different for younger children. In early elementary school, the more concrete the tasks and the more directly observable the outcomes, the more children are affected by repeated failure (e.g., Boggiano, Barrett, & Kellam, 1993). Moreover, although young children cannot make complex inferences about the relations of patterns of outcomes to conceptions of ability, they can and do form views of their traits (e.g., goodness and badness) as fixed and immutable (Dweck, 1999). These are the experiences and belief systems that make young children more vulnerable to helplessness.

For older children and young adolescents, the picture is equally complex. It turns out that when children acquire the capacity to make inferences about inverse compensatory relations among causes, they will apply these schema to effort and ability only in cultures (such as the United States) in which adults hold conceptions of ability as a fixed entity that can be diagnosed from level of performance (Nicholls, 1984; Rosenholtz & Simpson, 1984). Moreover, these mature conceptions must be transmitted to children, for example, by parents who respond to children's failures by doubting their capacities (Burhans & Dweck, 1995) and through experiences in classrooms where the climate is organized around evaluating and ranking students' ability (i.e., a performance orientation). Most insidiously, these messages must be internalized by children, so that they are convinced that their own ability is a fixed immutable entity that can be assessed and demonstrated by every performance (Dweck, 1999). In other words, developmental advances open up windows of opportunity that can be used to promote or undermine

children's sense of control, depending on the messages that cultures and contexts (as embodied by parents and teachers) communicate about the nature of ability, competence, or "personal force" (Dweck, 1999).

What Are Other Important Sources of Academic Motivation and Resilience?

Researchers can afford the luxury of focusing exclusively on control constructs in predicting learning and achievement. Practitioners, on the other hand, because they always deal with a whole child in an actual context, must attend to the many other contributors to engagement and coping. If teachers and principals focus too narrowly on a sense of competence and control, they may miss other opportunities to promote students' academic development. And, even worse, the very techniques and interventions that teachers employ to support perceptions of control sometimes have unintended negative consequences for other motivational processes (Deci & Ryan, 2000).

At least two other fundamental psychological needs have been identified that shape motivation across the life span (Connell & Wellborn, 1991; Deci & Ryan, 1985). The first is the need for relatedness or belongingness, as conceptualized and studied by attachment theories (Bowlby, 1969/1973). In terms of academics, this would be reflected in children's desire and interest in forming close and secure connections to their teachers, peers, and the school itself, and in the corresponding internal working models of whether children feel welcome in school or feel that their teachers and peers value and care about them. The second need is for autonomy, as conceptualized and studied by self-determination theory (Deci & Ryan, 1985, 2000). In terms of academics, this refers to children's interest and desire to authentically express their genuine preferences and actions, and the corresponding self-regulatory styles about the extent to which their participation in school activities (like homework) is motivated by external or introjected factors (such as fear of punishment or guilt) as compared to identified reasons (such as personal importance) or intrinsic reasons (like fun; Ryan & Connell, 1989). For specific practices to be effective in fostering a sense of control, they must be realized in a climate of pedagogical caring that supports autonomy.

What Promotes or Undermines a Sense of Control?

By the time they start school, children have already had a history of experiences with whether adults are available and sensitive to their needs. Their first interactions with teachers build on those experiences. Children who are unsure of their caregivers are slower to trust and like their teachers, and so are also less likely to initiate interactions, request help, or turn to their teachers for aid and comfort.

Hence, an important first step in promoting motivation is build a caring, trusting relationship between teacher and student. Although it is easy to assume that such close relationships are more important for young children, it turns out they are also critical for adolescents' motivation in school; if anything, close relationships with teachers become *more* important in middle and high school, partly because the overall quality of student-teacher relationships is declining (Eccles, 2004; Wigfield et al., 2006).

Experiencing control requires that children be actively engaged in learning tasks, and so curricular and classroom practices that promote engagement are good for the development of control. One of the most important contributors is the nature of the academic work itself. The more that academic activities are interesting, challenging, fun, and relevant to students' real lives, the more children will want to participate in them and the more effort they will exert in working on them. Theories of intrinsic motivation, flow, and interest highlight the deadening effects of activities like work sheets and drill when contrasted with real-world, project-based learning, such as constructing museum exhibits, building robots, planting gardens, or writing musicals. Throughout these activities, the theme of choice can be emphasized, since it allows children to tailor activities to their own interests (Deci & Ryan, 2000).

Structure Versus Chaos

Critical to the development of control is *structure*. At its most general, structure refers to the provision of information about routes toward producing desired and preventing undesired outcomes, as well as provision of support for following those pathways (Connell & Wellborn, 1991; Skinner, 1995). The opposite of structure is *chaos,* and it refers to contexts in which expectations are low and conditions are noncontigent, arbitrary, confusing, unpredictable, or objectively uncontrollable. It is useful to break the larger construct of structure into multiple practices (see Table 13.2), but the general principle is that any feature of relationships, curricula, or classroom climate will promote control to the extent it shows children and adolescents how to exert effort that is effective in producing outcomes that matter to them.

Focus on Process

Good teaching is critical to a sense of control (Stipek, 2002). The best teaching shows children *how* to do something of value—how to solve a problem, write a persuasive essay, calculate the volume of a swimming pool, decipher the meaning of Shakespeare. Teaching children how things work, how to learn, how to figure things out, how to evaluate different hypotheses and strategies, how to consult other sources for ideas and information—these practices help children master material. At the same time, they also teach children the value of industriousness and how to learn for themselves—how to deploy effort so that it can be

Table 13.2 Classroom Practices That Promote a Sense of Control

1. Create a climate of warmth and caring.
2. Support autonomy and self-determination.
3. Find and create interesting, relevant, fun, and challenging academic activities.
4. Teach strategies by focusing on the processes of learning.
5. Provide clear process feedback.
6. Monitor individual progress and improvement.
7. Treat mistakes as friends.
8. Encourage revision and repair.
9. Initiate adaptive help.
10. Provide opportunities for practice and study.
11. Model enthusiasm, strategizing, hypothesis testing, and resilience.
12. Expect improvement in students' performance.

effective in achieving desired aims. In many ways, these practices are the direct teaching of adaptive strategies of self-regulation. The experiences they create for children are at the core of a sense of control.

When adults lead children to focus on the processes of learning, they highlight the importance of effort, strategies, and alternative routes to desired outcomes, the value of challenging tasks as opportunities for learning, and the long-term payoff of steady practice and hard work (Dweck, 1999). Teachers can provide praise and feedback, but it is most beneficial to a sense of control if these focus on how children take on challenges, apply themselves, and persevere. It is especially important to help children reflect on and experience their own individual improvement over time. It is difficult to monitor each child's pattern of progress and to provide an analysis of how it was accomplished, but the value of these practices is lasting in terms of their effects on student engagement and perceived control.

Mistakes Are Our Friends

One of the most critical facets of control is how children interpret their mistakes. Are they failures, indicating low ability and no chance of success, or are they information, acting as guideposts about more effective routes to desired outcomes? Teachers often see graded performances as an end in themselves. But the message that learning ends with an evaluation is a damaging one for a sense of control. Instead, if mistakes (including low performances) can be seen as next steps and as targets for future development, then students are focused on the feedback provided by grades and teacher comments. Opportunities to revise and repair, to restudy and retake, may seem unfair to students who did well the first time. But they communicate to all students that the goals in the classroom are not to scrape out a barely passing grade, but instead to actually learn things of lasting value—so if you did not get them the first time, get back to work and learn them!

It is important for teachers to directly model the processes that reflect and bolster a sense of control. Teachers, through their own approach to teaching, can show that challenge is good, confusion is normal when attempting difficult projects, easy tasks are not very much fun, it is okay not to know everything, and much can be learned by analyzing mistakes. Talking aloud while solving problems or thinking through alternative approaches can reveal to students the processes that go into learning. They can also directly demonstrate the adaptiveness of seeking information and help (e.g., turning to the encyclopedia or to group problem solving).

De-Emphasize Evaluating Ability and Pleasing the Teacher

It is easy to commend students for a high performance or to praise their talents and abilities. These practices, however, no matter how well intended, have a negative effect on a sense of control (Dweck, 1999). They draw children's attention to their abilities and outcomes, and imply that the measure of success for adults is the grade itself and that ability is the decisive factor in producing it. Although many adults actually believe this, the implications for a child's engagement are not positive. Such practices can lead children to focus on academic tasks as measures of ability and opportunities to demonstrate their prowess. If these are students' primary goals, they tend to prefer tasks that are easy (to guarantee success) or impossible (to deflect attributions away from ability), to give up quickly if high outcomes are not easily forthcoming (since high effort threatens ability), or to produce high outcomes by any means necessary (including cheating; Dweck, 1999).

Power assertion and coercive practices also undermine the development of competence and control (as well as autonomy and relatedness; Deci & Ryan, 1985). If rules are arbitrary or unevenly enforced, children quickly learn that pleasing the teacher is the only route to success. Students may submit or they may rebel, but they are likely to lose focus on the genuine pathways to learning. It is important to highlight that many practices adults do not deem coercive, such as competition, rewards for high performance, honor roll, and praise for success, nevertheless are experienced as undermining autonomy and intrinsic motivation by students, especially as they get older (Deci & Ryan, 2000). It is also worth noting that clear structure, that is, reasonable, clear, and appropriate practices and rules that are fairly enforced, does not necessarily undermine autonomy. The key issue seems to be students' *experiences* of teacher practices—for example, whether students perceive feedback as an attempt to control their behavior or as helpful information (Ryan, 1982).

Conclusion

A sense of competence and control are powerful allies during the hard work of learning and in dealing with challenges and setbacks. This is true for teachers as well as for students. When teachers hold high expectations for students and are convinced that they can become more competent through striving and practice, students' experience the power of effort and begin to really understand the processes of learning. These experiences promote a sense of control that, in turn, supports constructive engagement and adaptive self-regulation. These form cycles, both within student learning and between teachers and students, that verify and elaborate mutual feelings of efficacy and a deeper understanding of how to accomplish important tasks. Cumulatively, over the course of a student's academic career, these pay off in a sense of pride and ownership in one's own learning and in the development of actual competence, which are sources of lasting satisfaction to students and teachers alike.

References and Further Readings

Abramson, L. Y., Seligman, M. E. P., & Teasdale, J. D. (1978). Learned helplessness in humans. *Journal of Abnormal Psychology, 87,* 49–74.

Atkinson, J. W. (1964). *An introduction to motivation.* Princeton, NJ: Van Nostrand.

Bandura, A. (1977). Self-efficacy: Toward a unifying theory of behavioral change. *Psychological Review, 84,* 191–215.

Bandura, A. (1997). *Self-efficacy: The exercise of control.* New York: W. H. Freeman.

Boggiano, A. K., Barrett, M., & Kellam, T. (1993). Competing theoretical analyses of helplessness: A social-developmental analysis. *Journal of Experimental Child Psychology, 55,* 194–207.

Bowlby, J. (1973). *Attachment and loss. Vols. 1 and 2.* New York: Basic Books. (Original work published 1969)

Burhans, K. K., & Dweck, C. S. (1995). Helplessness in early childhood: The role of contingent worth. *Child Development, 66,* 1719–1738.

Connell, J. P. (1985). A new multidimensional measure of children's perceptions of control. *Child Development, 56,* 1018–1041.

Connell, J. P., Halpern-Felsher, B. L., Clifford, E., Crichlow, W., & Usinger, P. (1995). Hanging in there: Behavioral, psychological, and contextual factors affecting whether African American adolescents stay in school. *Journal of Adolescent Research, 10*, 41–63.

Connell, J. P., Spencer, M. B., & Aber, J. L. (1994). Educational risk and resilience in African-American youth: Context, self, action, and outcomes in school. *Child Development, 65,* 493–506.

Connell, J. P., & Wellborn, J. G. (1991). Competence, autonomy and relatedness: A motivational analysis of self-system processes. In M. R. Gunnar & L. A. Sroufe (Eds.), *Minnesota symposium on child psychology* (Vol. 23, pp. 43–77). Chicago: University of Chicago Press.

Covington, M. V., & Omelich, C. L. (1979). Effort: The double-edged sword in school achievement. *Journal of Educational Psychology, 71,* 169–182.

Deci, E. L., & Ryan, R. M. (1985). *Intrinsic motivation and self-determination in human behavior.* New York: Plenum Press.

Deci, E. L., & Ryan, R. M. (2000). The "what" and "why" of goal pursuits: Human needs and the self-determination of behavior. *Psychological Inquiry, 11,* 227–268.

Diener, C. I., & Dweck, C. S. (1978). An analysis of learned helplessness: Continuous changes in performance, strategy, and achievement cognitions following failure. *Journal of Personality and Social Psychology, 36,* 451–462.

Dweck, C. S. (1999). *Self-theories: Their role in motivation, personality, and development.* Philadelphia: Psychology Press.

Dweck, C. S. (2002). The development of ability conceptions. In A. Wigfield & J. S. Eccles (Eds.), *Development of achievement motivation* (pp. 57–88). San Diego: Academic Press.

Eccles, J. S. (2004). Schools, academic motivation, and stage-environment fit. In R. M. Lerner & L. Steinberg (Eds.), *Handbook of adolescent psychology* (pp. 125–153). New York: Wiley.

Elliot, A. J., & Dweck, C. S. (Eds.). (2005). *Handbook of competence and motivation.* New York: Guilford.

Elliot, A. J., McGregor, H. A., & Thrash, T. M. (2002). The need for competence. In E. L. Deci & R. M. Ryan (Eds.), *Handbook of self-determination theory research* (pp. 361–387). Rochester, NY: University of Rochester Press.

Flammer, A. (1995). Developmental analysis of control beliefs. In A. Bandura (Ed.), *Self-efficacy in changing societies* (pp. 69–113). New York: Cambridge University Press.

Gunnar, M. R., & Quevedo, K. (2007). The neurobiology of stress and development. *Annual Review of Psychology, 58,* 145–173.

Harter, S. (1978). Effectance motivation reconsidered: Towards a developmental model. *Human Development, 21,* 34–64.

Heckhausen, H. (1991). *Motivation and action.* Berlin: Springer-Verlag.

Kindermann, T. A. (2007). Effects of naturally-existing peer groups on changes in academic engagement in a cohort of sixth graders. *Child Development, 78,* 1186–1203.

Koestner, R., & McClelland, D. C. (1990). Perspectives on competence motivation. In L. A. Pervin (Ed.), *Handbook of personality: Theory and research* (pp. 527–548). New York: Guilford Press.

Kuhl, J. (1984). Volitional aspects of achievement motivation and learned helplessness: Toward a comprehensive theory of action control. In B. A. Maher & W. A. Maher (Eds.), *Progress in experimental personality research* (pp. 99–171). New York: Academic Press.

Lefcourt, H. M. (1976). *Locus of control: Current trends in theory and research.* New Jersey: Lawrence Erlbaum Associates.

Lefcourt, H. M. (1992). Durability and impact of the locus of control construct. *Psychological Bulletin, 112*(3), 411–414.

Miller, A. (1985). A developmental study of the cognitive basis of performance impairment after failure. *Journal of Personality and Social Psychology, 49,* 529–538.

Nicholls, J. G. (1984). Achievement motivation: Conceptions of ability, subjective experience, task choice, and performance. *Psychological Review, 91,* 328–346.

Peterson, C., Maier, S. F., & Seligman, M. E. P. (1993). *Learned helplessness: A theory for the age of personal control.* New York: Oxford University Press.

Rosenholtz, S. J., & Simpson, C. (1984). The formation of ability conceptions: Developmental trend or social construction? *Review of Educational Research, 54,* 31–63.

Rotter, B. (1966). Generalized expectancies for internal versus external control of reinforcement. *Psychological Monographs, 80* (Whole No. 609).

Ryan, R. M. (1982). Control and information in the intrapersonal sphere: An extension of cognitive evaluation theory. *Journal of Personality and Social Psychology, 43,* 450–461.

Ryan, R. M., & Connell, J. P. (1989). Perceived locus of causality and internalization: Examining reasons for acting in two domains. *Journal of Personality and Social Psychology, 57,* 749–761.

Schmitz, B., & Skinner, E. (1993). Perceived control, effort, and academic performance: Interindividual, intraindividual, and multivariate time-series analyses. *Journal of Personality and Social Psychology, 64*(6), 1010–1028.

Seligman, M. E. P. (1975). *Helplessness: On depression, development, and death.* San Francisco: Freeman.

Skinner, E. A. (1995). *Perceived control, motivation, and coping.* Thousand Oaks, CA: Sage.

Skinner, E. A. (1996). A guide to constructs of control. *Journal of Personality and Social Psychology, 71,* 549–570.

Skinner, E. A., & Belmont, M. J. (1993). Motivation in the classroom: Reciprocal effects of teacher behavior and student engagement across the school year. *Journal of Educational Psychology, 85,* 571–581.

Skinner, E. A., Zimmer-Gembeck, M. J., & Connell, J. P. (1998). Individual differences and the development of perceived control. *Monographs of the Society for Research in Child Development 6*(2–3, Serial No. 254).

Stipek, D. J. (2002). *Motivation to learn: From theory to practice* (4th ed.). Boston: Allyn & Bacon.

Stipek, D. J., Recchia, S., & McClintic, S. M. (1992). Self-evaluation in young children. *Monographs of the Society for Research in Child Development, 57*(2, Serial No. 226).

Weiner, B. (1986). *An attributional theory of motivation and emotion.* New York: Springer.

Weiner, B. (2005). Motivation from an attributional perspective and the social psychology of perceived competence. In A. J. Elliot & C. S. Dweck (Eds.), *Handbook of competence and motivation* (pp. 73–84). New York: Guilford.

Weisz, J. R. (1986). Understanding the developing understanding of control. In M. Perlmutter (Ed.), *Minnesota Symposium on Child Psychology: Vol. 18. Social cognition* (pp. 219–278). Hillsdale, NJ: Lawrence Erlbaum Associates.

White, R. W. (1959). Motivation reconsidered: The concept of competence. *Psychological Review, 66,* 297–333.

Wigfield, A., & Eccles, J. S. (2000). Expectancy-value theory of motivation. *Contemporary Educational Psychology, 25,* 68–81.

Wigfield, A., & Eccles, J. S. (2002). *Development of achievement motivation.* San Diego: Academic Press.

Wigfield, A., Eccles, J. S., Schiefele, U., Roeser, R., & Davis-Kean, P. (2006). Development of achievement motivation. In W. Damon (Series Ed.) & N. Eisenberg (Vol. Ed.), *Handbook of child psychology (6th Ed., Vol. 3). Social, emotional, and personality development* (pp. 933–1002). New York: Wiley.

14

Proactive Classroom Management

Carolyn M. Evertson and Inge R. Poole

Vanderbilt University

The phrase *proactive classroom management* may at first seem like a contradiction in terms. A common conception of classroom management is that it is synonymous with discipline and behavior control. The term is associated with strategies for controlling students' behavior, responding to disruptions, reacting to misbehavior, meting out appropriate rewards and punishments, and generally keeping the noise down. In contrast to this conception, we argue in this chapter that the term *classroom management* be broadened beyond student behavior control to include "the actions teachers take to create an environment that supports and facilitates both academic and social-emotional learning" (Evertson & Weinstein, 2006, p. 4).

Everything the teacher does has implications for the classroom, from creating the setting, decorating the room, and arranging the chairs; to speaking to children and handling their responses; to putting routines in place, then executing, modifying, and reinstituting them; to developing and communicating rules so that they are understood by students. Consistent with the definition we propose is the idea that enacting such a classroom requires forethought, planning, and advance consideration of the integrated systems that will support students' social, emotional, and cognitive learning. Effective classrooms are developed through proactive classroom management.

On the surface, smoothly running, academically focused classrooms may have the look of management in absentia or no management at all (Randolph & Evertson, 1995).

What appears to be a seamless flow of interactions among teacher, students, and content is actually thousands of small decisions that direct the events unfolding and contribute to an overall climate. They are carefully orchestrated at a complex level so that meaningful learning can occur. Most of the decisions about how a classroom will function are made implicitly or explicitly before students arrive. It is the nature of these decisions that shape the classroom culture.

Because management actions communicate information about the norms, expectations, routines, knowledge, and participation valued in the classroom, the teacher's first task is to determine what messages about knowledge and participation students will need to understand. Conceptions of learning that emphasize students' active construction of knowledge, including how to regulate their own behavior and interact socially with others, do not fit with conceptions of management as merely behavioral control, compliance, and obedience (McCaslin & Good, 1992). Learning-centered classrooms are much more complex than traditional classrooms in terms of long- and short-term goals enacted, variety and flexibility of activities offered, and opportunities for multiple roles for students and teachers provided.

In this chapter, we describe the unique characteristics of classrooms that make proactive planning necessary, including the time before students' arrival, once students have arrived, and once misbehavior occurs. We also cite research supporting teacher action toward developing smoothly running classrooms. Simultaneously, we address the distinct needs of creating learning-centered classrooms. Finally, we discuss continuing issues and debates about classroom management.

Unique Characteristics of Classrooms

To provide a loose analogy, classrooms share several characteristics with formal meetings. For example, both are gatherings of people with a leader and some form of agenda. Regardless of the topic of the meeting or the content of the classroom, there are expectations about the purpose, the content, the time frame, the leadership, and who can participate and in what ways. It is easy to identify if these gatherings are well or poorly run. What may not be as easy to discern, however, is what makes them so. To consider what is meant by *well-run classrooms,* we first describe some of the unique characteristics of classrooms that distinguish them from formal or informal meetings and other types of human gatherings.

Classrooms are distinct from meetings in a variety of ways and vary on many dimensions; yet, there are identifiable core characteristics across these variations. In general, classrooms typically involve:

- one teacher leading instruction for 20 to 40 students of varying backgrounds;
- a designated period of instructional time each weekday;
- a physical space including equipment, furniture, and materials in which to coordinate all instruction and interactions;
- dynamic settings in which actions and events change rapidly;
- a designated purpose (e.g., specified content area[s] to cover); and
- accountability for demonstrating evidence of student learning.

As dynamic systems, classrooms adjust to reflect the developing community of their members. Classrooms also adapt to the pressures and vulnerabilities of a group of individuals learning new information and skills. As purposeful entities, classrooms focus instruction on information or skill in specific areas. School districts and governmental agencies may legislate the academic content to be covered in schools, but specific classroom tasks offer the opportunities for students to engage with this content in ways that make it meaningful and accessible. As accountable units, classrooms connect students and judgments, teachers and evaluations. While we might prefer to minimize this accountability, the overwhelming majority of classrooms provide evaluative statements about a student's performance to the student or parents. Most districts maintain student records across years of schooling, and all public schools in the United States fall under current accountability legislation (i.e., the No Child Left Behind Act).

Proactive Classroom Management

Kounin's (1970) landmark study on group management concluded that how teachers prevented problems from occurring differentiated more versus less effective managers. The preparatory work that a teacher completes enhances the likelihood that students will know what to expect. This forethought occurs in three areas: proactive actions teachers take before the students' arrival, proactive interactions teachers plan once students arrive, and proactive reactions teachers prepare for when students misbehave. All of these actions integrate into a system of proactive classroom management to minimize disruption, distraction, and interference with students' academic and social-emotional learning.

Actions Before Students' Arrival

Unfortunately, it is a rare teacher education program that provides preservice teachers with observation or student teaching time at the start of the school year. This lack of access can communicate that a teacher's job begins when students arrive. But before students walk in the door, there are a number of actions a teacher takes to prepare the physical, social, and instructional space.

Teachers must ask, What are the goals I want to set for myself and my students? This question focuses attention on explicitly acknowledging the philosophy that will drive a teacher's approach to teaching, stating the desired results, and framing the subsequent decisions he or she will make. Goals might include teaching all first-grade students to read, focusing chemistry students' attention on safety in the science lab, and modeling the social behavior desired from middle-schoolers. Then teachers need to ask, How do I construct the physical space to support these goals? What rules will frame the social interactions? What overarching curriculum will guide my daily instructional decisions?

Physical Space

Proactive planning of the physical space includes both the layout of furniture and the design of accesses and pathways. The arrangement of a classroom provides clues to students of the types of interactions expected. When rows of chairs face a podium, participants are cued to an expectation that one individual will do most of the talking; whereas chairs set in a circle communicates that all participants are expected to speak. A typical classroom contains a teacher's desk, student desks and chairs, some type of presentation equipment (e.g., overhead projector on a cart), and storage (e.g., bookshelves, cabinets). Some of these items will be movable, while others may not.

When deciding how to arrange the movable furniture, a major consideration is determining what types of instruction will occur. If it is to be a more traditional classroom wherein the teacher will lead whole-group lessons, the teacher may arrange the furniture in rows that face a dry erase board or presentation screen. If the teacher anticipates teaching small groups of students, he or she may place sets of desks together. With each arrangement possibility, the teacher needs to consider where the instruction will be presented, how to keep an eye on each student, and how the selected arrangement will look to each student. If the presentation is going to be from a single location, the teacher can stand at that place and test whether or not he or she could see students seated in all of the chairs. If the presentation is in multiple locations, the teacher should note if all students can be seen from each location as well as the transition between. To imagine the students' perspective, a teacher can sit in each of the chairs. From the students' point of view, the teacher and any presentation materials should be easily visible.[1]

In learning-centered classrooms, teachers do not determine physical arrangements primarily to provide personally assigned individual space. Rather, the spatial environment is designed to facilitate collaboration. Some teachers in learning-centered classrooms plan the arrangement of their rooms in advance; others set up the room arrangement after negotiations with their students. Lambert (1995) concluded that seating flexibility—as opposed to a perpetually fixed seating arrangement—is a necessary prerequisite for an interactive classroom.

Some researchers (David, 1979) have found that students consistently listed adequate personal space and having private places as concerns. The emphasis on collaboration in learning-centered classrooms should not be misinterpreted to mean that students never work alone. Not all students learn in the same way. Classrooms that nurture a social environment can also attend to students as individuals. Teachers can plan for students to have greater choice about when and where they might need personal space. Teachers also need flexibility to confer either with groups or privately with individual students.

Appropriate room arrangements that support the curriculum will often shift across grade levels, and these tend to become more formalized with increasing grade levels. Therefore, teachers at higher grade levels who are establishing learning-centered environments may be especially aware of the shift from prevailing norms as they arrange seating to support more face-to-face interaction. If room arrangements change, students must be socialized to working in these different configurations.

Just as important as the arrangement of furniture is the design of empty space. The aisles between furniture are the pathways students use to move through the classroom. Placement of these aisles can anticipate students' needs to move in and out of their chairs to access classroom materials, to work in small groups, and to enter and exit the classroom (e.g., end of class, fire drill). Careful forethought about the aisles helps avoid congestion at key areas in the classroom such as a door, wastebasket, pencil sharpener, bookshelves, or materials cabinets. Preparation of a place for students' personal belongings prevents the build-up of clutter in passageways and keeps students safe. Aisles are also a teacher's pathways through the classroom. Aisles should allow a teacher to interact with each individual student and to retrieve needed instructional materials.

Furthermore, the design of the physical space in a classroom either supports or constrains interferences to students' attention. Windows, doors, class pets, restrooms, wastebaskets, and pencil sharpeners are all examples of potential distractions to the students seated nearby. As students pass through the aisles or congregate at an area, their peers may find the commotion too inviting to ignore. Effective classroom arrangements reduce distractions, encouraging the students' focus to be on the instruction at hand.

Social Space

The social space of a classroom comprises the exchanges between teacher and students and among students. Before students' arrival, a teacher can plan the basic structure of this space by considering what norms should be established and what expectations endorsed.[2] Norms are the familiar ways of interacting in a particular setting that develop across interactions. For example, the norm for riding on an elevator is that a passenger enters, selects a floor button, faces the door, provides room for fellow passengers to enter or leave as needed, and exits when the selected floor is reached. Expectations are the desired behaviors in a given situation. Elevator passengers have the expectation that departing passengers will be allowed to leave before embarking passengers enter.

When a teacher proactively plans for the norms and expectations that he or she wants established in the classroom, the teacher considers the types of interactions he or she hopes students will have and the ways they will behave. For example, the teacher may set a goal for students to listen during instruction to maximize the available instructional time. In this case, the teacher may want a norm established for students to give their full attention when he or she begins to speak at the start of class by preparing themselves and their space for instruction when they enter. To establish this norm, the teacher may write a rule that states, "Be in your seat and ready for class when the bell rings." The teacher will also need to design the associated procedures for entering the classroom quietly, placing completed homework in the designated bin, being seated, placing texts and notebooks on desks, and beginning the displayed task before the bell's ring.

Teachers of learning-centered classrooms must provide students the following knowledge:

- how and when to move from group to group
- what the appropriate noise and voice levels are for group interactions
- how, when, and from whom to get help with academic content
- how, when, and from whom to get help with procedural content

- how, when, and where to obtain needed materials (Evertson & Randolph, 1999)

Teachers typically plan to have a manageable set of general rules (e.g., five to eight), or written expectations, posted in the classroom. A multitude of procedures, or patterns for completing classroom tasks, are designed to support these written rules. Advance planning of rules and procedures can help establish group norms that support, as opposed to inhibit, student learning.

Instructional Space

The instructional space of a classroom consists of all of the student learning goals associated with the class and may be guided by district, state, or federal mandates, as well as the textbook. The learning goals should contain both the deep ideas of a subject (e.g., history holds the bias of those who recorded it) as well as the skills and abilities necessary to attain these deep ideas (e.g., locating a primary document, identifying its author[s], considering it within its historical context, and determining its potential bias). Before students' arrival in the classroom, a teacher can organize the instructional space by planning the overarching curriculum. For a beginning teacher, this may simply be getting familiar with the assigned text(s) for the class or the subject area standards, for example the National Science Standards (National Research Council [NRC], 1996).

A teacher's classroom management system communicates the teacher's beliefs about content and the learning process. It also circumscribes the kinds of instruction that will take place in a particular classroom. Room arrangements, rules, and routines that all point to the teacher create a different learning environment than one in which these elements point to the students or turn students toward each other. Content will be approached and understood differently in each of these settings. Furthermore, intellectually demanding academic work and activities in which students create products or encounter novel problems require complex management decisions.

The actions that a teacher takes before students' arrival prepares the physical, social, and instructional space to ensure that appropriate goals are set and can be accomplished. Ignoring preparation before students' arrival invites unnecessary complexity to teaching. A lack of action sets up the process of teaching much like building a plane while piloting it in the air, literally flying by the seat of your pants. Effective teachers practice proactive classroom management before students' arrival. In addition, teachers must also plan for interactions once students arrive.

Interactions Once Students Arrive

Once students arrive in the classroom, the teacher's prior planning is merged with a developing knowledge of indi-vidual students and the class as a whole. The first few weeks of interactions are critical in establishing norms and expectations for the year. The getting started period offers special opportunities to set a positive tone for success. In a series of studies (Emmer, Evertson & Anderson, 1980; Evertson, 1985, 1989; Evertson & Emmer 1982; Evertson, Emmer, Sanford, & Clements, 1983), researchers documented the importance of the first day of school for establishing these expectations. In fact, teachers who take time at the beginning of the year to teach units with lower content demands and higher emphasis on procedures are more likely to have classrooms that function effectively and that truly facilitate student learning in the long run (Emmer et al., 1980). Students in elementary and secondary classrooms who receive explicit information and signals early in the school year become socialized and settled in more quickly.

Relational Interactions

Trust is a key component of an effective classroom. Yet this implicit understanding between students and teacher cannot be demanded nor does it automatically emerge as a factor of sharing a classroom. Teachers establish trust by being dependable and by establishing a dependable environment. The relational interactions within a classroom foster dependability when a teacher puts into practice the norms and expectations planned for the social space of the class. These norms and expectations are typically outlined through class rules and procedures.

A teacher who opens the school year by providing instruction in class rules and procedures increases the percentage of students who have access to and engage in academic instruction across the year (Emmer et al., 1980). This instruction includes posting the rules, discussing what these rules look like in action (which can include student role-play), and identifying the consequences of breaking the rules (see the section Reactions Once Misbehavior Occurs below). Additionally, this instruction comprises classroom procedures. Teaching these procedures includes explaining the desired behavior and its rationale, demonstrating the behavior, helping students practice the behavior, providing positive consequences[3] to students for meeting the expectation, and providing instructive feedback when students are not meeting the expectation in full.

For example, the procedures for debate in a civics class include the time limits of 5 minutes to explain an argument, 3 minutes to counter the argument, and 2 minutes for rebuttal. The civics teacher identifies these limits, demonstrates the timer signaling the end of a student's turn, and then helps the class practice using the designated limits. When students effectively complete their arguments within the allotted time, the teacher compliments their performance. If students do not finish by the signal, the teacher stops their turn and reminds them of the procedure. The practice continues until the procedure is habituated. A maintenance reminder of the procedure may be required on occasion.

In learning-centered classrooms, teachers establish norms of participation by creating activities that allow students to practice participating in discussion and then recognizing student behaviors both publicly and privately that support the norm. Making public what is meant by a successful assignment—defined not by mere completion, but by having garnered information from others and contributed to others' collective knowledge—helps students understand how participation in the classroom manifests itself in academic work.

Participation in a learning-centered classroom is also defined in other ways. Norms such as students calling on each other and contributing to the discussion without teacher direction, and students looking at the person who is speaking rather than the teacher, might be part of the shared norms for classroom participation. Students' and teachers' roles become less clearly delineated. For example, students may take responsibility for teaching each other and even for instructing the teacher during class discussions. As in the classroom described by Randolph and Evertson (1995), the teacher's roles and tasks were sometimes delegated to students, the students' roles taken on by the teacher, and both shared in the negotiation of meaning.

Thus, teachers alone do not establish and support classroom norms; students also play a vital role. For example, students communicate norms for participation when a new student arrives to join an already formed research team. Instead of waiting for directions to be given by the teacher, the students in the group immediately engage the newcomer and describe his or her possible new role. Contrast this experience to a student's entering during a more teacher-directed lesson, in which the student might have joined by sitting quietly, listening to the teacher, and working independently until the teacher had time to explain classroom procedures. One means teachers have for observing students following the designated rules and procedures is monitoring.

Monitoring is moving through the room, with either the teacher's eyes or person, to supervise the students' academic and social behavior. As a teacher monitors the class, he or she looks for evidence of engagement and may reward this if it supports continued on-task behavior. The teacher also looks for disengagement and redirects the student to the desired behavior (see the section Reactions Once Misbehavior Occurs below). When a teacher moves through the room to monitor, it is easier to apply positive consequences to an individual student's actions and respond to individual acts of misbehavior. Monitoring also provides a teacher with information regarding a student's academic performance.

Instructional Interactions

Once students arrive in the classroom, a teacher enacts daily instructional plans that lead students toward estab-lished goals. These daily plans are sequenced to connect students' previous learning with the present content. Each step of instruction builds upon previous steps. For example, a Spanish teacher first has students practice repeating the basic conversational phrases for "Hello. My name is _____," and "It is nice to meet you." Next, the teacher asks students to say the phrases in context by introducing themselves to peers. Several lessons later the students may be using the phrases to present a brief role-play of meeting their future college roommate for the first time.

As a teacher establishes relationships with students, he or she becomes more aware of students' individual learning needs and interests. This information helps the teacher to plan more effective lessons. For example, when a middle school math teacher learns that a struggling student is a baseball fan, the teacher can plan a lesson on averages to work with actual baseball statistics. Providing the student this personal connection to the lesson may keep the student's interest long enough to learn the math content.

Across instruction, teachers use proactive classroom management to keep the interactions going smoothly. Teachers can assess if students are following the flow of instruction by checking student understanding. This check can occur as verbal questions and answers during instruction, seatwork, written summaries, homework, labs, quizzes, tests, or other forms of assessment. By checking to make sure students understand the content presented, a teacher can supplement instruction as needed to avert potential frustration and possible subsequent misbehavior. Teachers can also assist students with understanding their own learning process by providing instructional feedback. For example, if homework demonstrates a misunderstanding of subject-verb agreement, a written comment to see the teacher for a minilesson can provide timely and informative feedback.

Teachers provide additional guidance to meet instructional goals when they model the academic behavior they are seeking. Providing work samples, demonstrating lab exercises, and displaying class examples as they are generated are all ways teachers can model their expectations. Furthermore, teachers guide students to integrate multiple instructional goals when they proactively manage the transitions within their classrooms. These transitions occur between activities in a lesson, from lesson to lesson, and from one class to the next. At the beginning of a lesson, a teacher helps students shift into it by reviewing the previous lesson(s), indicating where the present lesson will go, and designating which materials the students need. Between segments of a lesson, a teacher identifies what has been covered, demonstrates how it applies to the next activity, and instructs students how to get themselves or their materials ready for the activity. At the close of a lesson, a teacher reviews with the class what has been covered, how it connects with the broader instructional goals set for that class, and prepares students for future instruction.

Proactive classroom management includes forethought concerning the many and varied interactions that take place once students arrive in a classroom. A teacher's anticipation of the relationships with and instruction of a class of students helps ensure a safe and smoothly run learning environment. Failing to anticipate these interactions promotes confusion for students much like airplane passengers would experience if airports did not provide directional signage, airlines did not use gates or schedules, and tickets did not correspond to a specific flight. Yet even when airports, airlines, and tickets all are coordinated toward pairing each passenger with the appropriate manifest on the correct plane at the specified gate at the right time, there are still people who miss the plane. Other passengers will introduce difficulties once the plane is in the air or even after the plane has landed. Similarly, a teacher's carefully planned actions and interactions will not prevent all possible glitches in a classroom. Therefore, proactive classroom management includes anticipating suitable reactions to student misbehavior.

Reactions Once Misbehavior Occurs

Despite the best laid plans, student misbehavior will occur. Reactions to this misbehavior require careful planning to ensure a teacher's responses are productive.

Anticipating Responses to Student Misbehavior

The interventions teachers prepare allow them to match the significance of a consequence to the seriousness of the infraction. For example, a teacher would want one consequence for students who forget to write their name on a physics assignment, but an entirely different response for students who are blatantly disrespectful to a substitute teacher. Interventions can also take into account students' intent. For instance, the consequence for bumping into a peer at recess varies from that administered for intentionally pushing the peer.

Two major categories of consequences, corrective and negative, are directly tied to interventions. Corrective consequences involve reteaching a desired behavior. If, for example, the procedure for lining up in a fourth-grade classroom is for students to stand, push in their chairs, and form a silent, single file line at the door, but the class is noisy and haphazard about following this procedure, a corrective consequence is for the teacher to have students return to their seats, review the procedure, and then try again. Negative consequences involve applying an undesired response to counter a student's misbehavior. If a student misuses access to a computer by visiting inappropriate Web sites, a negative consequence is for the student to lose the privilege of using the computer without direct supervision.

In classrooms where norms for behaviors are negotiated and sanctioned by both the teacher and students, students play a role in ensuring adherence to social norms and handling conflict. Some conflicts may arise as a natural outcome of the creation of an environment that fosters the exchange of ideas and are a normal part of classroom life (Putnam & Burke, 1992). For example, a classroom debate over a controversial topic will naturally foster strong differences of opinion among students. Other conflicts may occur as students encounter problems in learning to regulate their behavior and work responsibly with peers. According to Dewey (1938), in a collaborative community, control is part of the shared responsibility. Teaching students to resolve conflict is one way to share control.

Responsibility for managing conflict rests with all members of the classroom community. Teachers cannot assume that students already know how to resolve problems or how to help peers. Therefore, one task for the teacher is to create opportunities for students to learn how to manage conflict when it occurs. A classroom discussion about problems, such as playing during center time or not taking turns, is an opportunity for students to devise class strategies to address the problem. Peers often have a powerful effect on others' behaviors.

Managing conflict also has implications for the teacher who decides to use personal influence unobtrusively as a sanctioning technique instead of public "desists" (Bossert, 1979). Relying on personal rapport to influence behavior, some teachers privately hold needed conversations with students. The above examples illustrate three strategies teachers can prepare for learning-centered classrooms to handle conflict: (1) teaching students how to participate in handling the conflict, (2) leading discussions among students to resolve conflict, and (3) holding private discussions with individual students.

The range of interventions a teacher prepares includes such mild responses as moving closer to the student, making eye contact or giving a knowing glance, using a corrective consequence, or even ignoring the behavior if it self-corrects. These mild responses apply to situations such as making eye contact with two students whispering during a silent reading time, gesturing for a student to be seated who stands to go to the trash can during a test, asking a student to remeasure the mass of an item after she zeroes the scale, or ignoring a student who accidentally knocks a book off a peer's desk and picks it back up.

Mild responses are appropriate only for minor misbehaviors or accidental misdeeds. Students interpret applying a more serious consequence for a minor offense as an attack. This perceived confrontation may lead to student defensiveness or a counterattack. For example, sending a student to in-school suspension for not having a title page on his book report (as opposed to asking the student to supply one or marking off the designated number of points) could lead to a verbal outburst or the student's refusal to complete other assigned tasks. If occurring publicly, other students may sense a break of trust and join in the resistance. Research on student perspectives on classroom management (Hoy & Weinstein, 2006) indicates that students suggest the types of strategies employed need to be fair and reasonable. Students consider public reprimands, harsh sanctions, and negative group sanctions for individual misbehavior as unacceptable means for handling conflict and other disciplinary problems.

Moderate interventions can entail using a more involved corrective consequence, confiscating a distracting item, relocating the student within the room, or removing a student privilege. When an initial mild intervention does not result in stopping the misbehavior, or if a student's misbehavior disturbs his or her own or peers' learning opportunities, a moderate intervention is necessary. In the example given earlier, if the students continue to whisper during silent reading time despite connecting with the teacher visually, the next step could be to quietly indicate the students are to move away from one another. For another example, if a student's handheld media player is distracting from learning opportunities, a teacher may indicate for the student to put the player on the teacher's desk and pick it up after class.

Serious interventions often involve removal of the student from the class. These and other issues are discussed further in Chapter 15. Serious interventions require documentation from the teacher, either of a significant incident or of a pattern of repeated misbehavior. The offending student may also be required to complete a description of or reflect in writing on the misdeed as a part of this documentation. Applying serious consequences also typically involves the school administration. An example of a serious infraction is discovering a junior high student defacing school property with a can of spray paint. The serious intervention would follow school, district, and legal stipulations, but might include a set time of in-school suspension and assistance in cleaning the damage. Documentation could include a police report of the vandalism, photographs of the graffiti, and a written statement from the student acknowledging his misdeed. Using a milder response for a serious infraction makes a teacher look timid and ineffective. Classmates can interpret this as an invitation to push the limits.

Reacting Consistently

With interventions, a teacher demonstrates dependability through the consistent application of consequences. In a high school English class, if a teacher docks late essays five points per day, students come to accept this penalty when applied consistently. But these same students will quickly complain, and may even push the established boundaries, if they sense the teacher offers an unfair extension only to some students. Consistency shows students a teacher's word is reliable and without favoritism.

One student who acts out, or the loose confederation of students who push the limits, serve the role of checking the boundaries within a classroom. They test the credibility of stated expectations, and because these actions are public, this provides information to the entire class. The more

students push the limit, the greater their need for information, and the greater the indication that they do not understand the real limits. Consistency both validates what a teacher says and supports the connections the teacher makes with students.

Inconsistencies prompt students to rethink what is expected and test to see if this new interpretation is true. Unpredictability shakes the foundation of what students know. In really chaotic classrooms this earthquake is repeated, sometimes on an interactional basis. Consistency is not easy. In fact, it can be tiring. Yet, initial efforts reassure students that what they have come to believe is reliable and these consistent reactions provide stability. As a result of feeling protected, students even will offer tolerance to the teacher they trust.

While the vast majority of reactions to student misbehavior will fall within the above discussion of interventions and their consistent application, we want to acknowledge that humor can also play a role. To be effective and to maintain the class's established trust, this humor must be kind rather than sarcastic and inclusive rather than alienating. For example, some middle school students continue to sit on a table at the back of the class after the teacher explains the expectation for them to sit in chairs during their break. The teacher consistently applies the consequence of having the offending students return to their assigned seats, effectively limiting the students' freedom during the break. As an alternative, the teacher could state humorously to students seated on the table, "I put the food I eat for lunch on that table," to prompt their moving to chairs.[4]

Anticipation of suitable responses to student misbehavior is an important component of proactive classroom management. Teachers who can prepare productive reactions and apply them consistently shift situations from probable disruption to potential instruction. Conversely, a teacher's reactive approach to student misbehavior could be akin to flight attendants ignoring warning signs (e.g., smoke) or waiting to provide emergency procedures until after the pilot indicates trouble. Instead, attendants begin each flight highlighting the safety features of an aircraft to ensure that during difficulty order, rather than chaos, and procedure, rather than panic, frame passengers' reactions. Simultaneously, the flight attendants identify consequences for prohibited behavior (e.g., federal fine for tampering with a smoke detector) and consistently apply these as needed. When teachers plan their reactions to student misbehavior and consistently apply them, students know what to expect. Students' resulting sense of security helps structure the class for joint success, even in an emergency.

Issues and Debates Within Classroom Management

No area of research is free of debate. Rather, it is the gentle tension of continued questioning in an area of study that keeps the research fresh, focused, and pertinent. Issues and debates are a frequent component of research on classroom management. As referenced early in the chapter, one key debate concerning this area of research focuses on the vocabulary itself. Differing from our use in this chapter, some see *classroom management* as distinct from instruction. The term *classroom management* to some is synonymous with "discipline," "punishment," or "control." And while some see *discipline* as the implementation of negative consequences or tight teacher control, others view this word as indicating the self-discipline we have as a goal for students to ultimately achieve. Without sufficient explanation or example, the mention of any one of these terms can bring about an unanticipated response when the listener's semantics clash.

One issue that has compounded the successful use of classroom management research has been the focus of educational research in general on the individual student or single interaction. This microperspective does not take into account the macrocontext of the classroom within which the individual lives or the single interaction occurs. Although this research perspective is important to enlarge our understanding of teaching and learning, its predominance has biased the educational research base in ways that sometimes leads to decisions being made out of context. A sea change of attitudes and perspectives across the educational research community is needed to continue progress in recognizing the value classroom management research has across settings and situations.

An additional issue in the past has been the absence of any primary, comprehensive compendium for reporting research in classroom management. Before 2006, published research on classroom management was scattered throughout professional journals and texts. This absence of a central source allowed gaps in the research to develop and widen in areas such as classroom management within urban settings. The resolution of this issue began with the publication of the *Handbook of Classroom Management: Research, Practice, and Contemporary Issues* (Evertson & Weinstein, 2006).

Conclusion

When we see a classroom in which the children are disruptive and the instruction fractured, the evaluation could be reached that the teacher's classroom management is bad. This judgment, however, glosses over some important components, blanketing the problems with an overloaded phrase rather than understanding that literally thousands of small decisions are adding up to this total picture. Is there trust within the relationships between teacher and students? Does the teacher have rules and procedures in place? Are they consistently reinforced? Do students know the goals they are working toward? Are expectations stated clearly?

Unless the observer has seen a number of classrooms with which to compare this one that is struggling, it is dif-ficult to identify the cracks in the system. Similarly, it takes a practiced eye to look at a setting and identify the areas in which the teacher and students have come to agreement and are working together toward the end goals. Invisibility is the hallmark of an effective classroom management system. It is difficult to identify what steps were taken to enact the effectively running classroom and nearly impossible to understand the previous agreements among the members that make the class run smoothly.

The intent of this chapter has been to hone the reader's eye, to make the invisible visible, accessible, and possible to enact. Therefore, we first used a loose comparison of meetings with classrooms to prompt a discussion of the unique characteristics of classrooms. Next, we defined classroom management as "the actions teachers take to create an environment that supports and facilitates both academic and social-emotional learning" (Evertson & Weinstein, 2006, p. 4). We argued for three areas of action for proactive classroom management. Actions taken before students' arrival prepare the physical, social, and instructional space students soon enter. Preparation for interactions with students once they arrive considers the emerging relationships with and instruction of a class of students. Anticipating reactions to students' misbehavior prepares consistent productive, instructional responses to emerging difficulties. Finally, we suggested points of debate for further study and application of the research on classroom management.

Notes

1. The Classroom Organization and Management Program (COMP: Creating Conditions for Learning), Peabody College, Vanderbilt University, uses the abbreviation VAD to draw attention to maximizing *visibility* and *accessibility,* while minimizing *distractibility* in a classroom's physical arrangement (Module 1, 7th edition, 2007). Visit http://www.comp.org for more information on this classroom management program.
2. Norms and expectations, as well as other pertinent topics, can be further explored at the IRIS Center for Faculty Enhancement Web site (http://iris.peabody.vanderbilt.edu).
3. Positive consequences apply desired responses to encourage continued appropriate behavior. Praise, prizes, and high-fives are examples of positive consequences.
4. We thank Stephen Thompson, Assistant Professor of Elementary Education, University of South Carolina, for this example.

References and Further Readings

Bossert, S. (1979). *Tasks and social relationships in the classroom: A study of instructional organization and its consequences.* New York: Cambridge University Press.

David, T. G. (1979). *Students' and teachers' reactions to classroom environments.* Unpublished doctoral dissertation, Department of Education, University of Chicago, IL.

Dewey, J. (1938). *Experience and education.* New York: Macmillan.

Emmer, E. T., Evertson, C. M., & Anderson, L. M. (1980). Effective classroom management at the beginning of the school year. *The Elementary School Journal, 80,* 219–231.

Emmer, E. T., Evertson, C. M., & Worsham, M. E. (2007). *Classroom management for elementary teachers* (7th ed.). Boston: Allyn & Bacon.

Evertson, C. M. (1985). Training teachers in classroom management: An experiment in secondary classrooms. *Journal of Educational Research, 79,* 51–58.

Evertson, C. M. (1989). Improving elementary classroom management: A school-based training program for beginning the year. *Journal of Educational Research, 83*(2), 82–90.

Evertson, C. M. (2007). *Classroom organization and management program (COMP): Creating conditions for learning* (7th ed.). Nashville, TN: Vanderbilt University.

Evertson, C. M., & Emmer, E. T. (1982). Effective management at the beginning of the school year in junior high classes. *Journal of Educational Psychology, 74,* 485–498.

Evertson, C. M., Emmer, E. T., Sanford, J. P., & Clements, B. S. (1983). Improving classroom management: An experiment in elementary classrooms. *The Elementary School Journal, 84*(2), 173–188.

Evertson, C. M., Emmer, E. T., & Worsham, M. E. (2007). *Classroom management for elementary teachers* (7th ed.). New York: Allyn & Bacon.

Evertson, C. M., & Randolph, C. H. (1999). Perspectives on classroom management in learning-centered classrooms. In H. Waxman and H. Walberg (Eds.), *New directions for teaching practice and research* (pp. 249–268). Berkeley, CA: McCutchan.

Evertson, C. M., & Weinstein, C. S. (2006). Classroom management as a field of inquiry. In C. M. Evertson and C. S. Weinstein (Eds.), *Handbook of classroom management: Research, practice, and contemporary issues* (pp. 3–15). Mahwah, NJ: Lawrence Erlbaum Associates.

Hoy, A. W., & Weinstein, C. S. (2006). Students' and teachers' knowledge and beliefs about classroom management. In C. Evertson & C. Weinstein (Eds.), *Handbook of classroom management: Research, practice, and contemporary issues.* Mahwah, NJ: Lawrence Erlbaum Associates.

The IRIS Center for Faculty Enhancement home page. Retrieved May 15, 2007, from http://iris.peabody.vanderbilt.edu

Kounin, J. S. (1970). *Discipline and group management in classrooms.* New York: Holt, Rinehart & Winston.

Lambert, N. M. (1995). Seating arrangements. In L. W. Anderson (Ed.), *International encyclopedia of teaching and teacher education* (pp. 196–200). Cambridge, UK: Cambridge University Press.

McCaslin, M., & Good, T. L. (1992). Compliant cognition: The misalliance of management and instructional goals in current school reform. *Educational Researcher 21*(3), 4–17.

National Research Council. (1996). *National Science Education Standards.* Washington, DC: National Academies Press.

Putnam, J., & Burke, J. B. (1992). *Organizing and managing classroom learning communities.* New York: McGraw-Hill.

Randolph, C. H., & Evertson, C. M. (1995). Managing for learning: Rules, roles, and relationships in a writing class. *Journal of Classroom Interaction, 30*(2), 17–25.

U.S. Department of Education. (2002). *No Child Left Behind: A desktop reference.* Retrieved May 15, 2007, from http://www.ed.gov/admins/lead/account/nclbreference/index.html

15

RESPONSIVE CLASSROOM MANAGEMENT

EDMUND T. EMMER

University of Texas

LAURA M. STOUGH

Texas A&M University

Teachers in classrooms since time immemorial have dealt with students whose behavior runs counter to their attempts to maintain an orderly environment for learning. Doyle (1978) cites notes from a teacher in 1865 regarding his management of misbehaving students:

> Had a notion to flog Perry about his insolence and his geography lesson but let him off with a lecture and a promise. I had hoped to manage my school without using timber but I am now about to conclude that it cannot be done. The wild spirit of these boys will not be tamed by promises and lectures.

Teachers and education have moved well beyond such primitive means of responding to perceived problems of students, particularly by emphasizing preventive methods. Nevertheless, since preventive strategies are not likely to eliminate problems entirely, teachers still need ways of responding to them when they do occur. It is also the case that problems can range from minor to severe, and from infrequent to commonplace. Many of the behavior problems that teachers encounter are short-lived and have no long-term consequences. But other problems threaten the climate for learning, which potentially may affect many students.

This chapter's focus is on those teacher decisions and actions that are in response to student behaviors that interfere with classroom order. We espouse Doyle's (1986) view of classroom management as being those activities and strategies that teachers use to establish and maintain order. In using the adjective *responsive* we are differentiating such teacher decisions and actions from those that are primarily proactive and prevent disruptions to classroom order. Naturally we'd prefer to always use proactive strategies, reflecting the adage, "An ounce of prevention is worth a pound of cure." But prevention doesn't always work, and we're not always clever enough to anticipate all the contingencies likely to be presented to us by students.

This chapter is concerned with strategies that are responsive to behavioral problems, as distinguished from responding to curricular or learning issues. Even though the latter types of problems may have effects on the overall behavioral climate and on students' willingness to cooperate, such issues are beyond our scope. When learning problems are the primary source of a student's behavioral difficulties, however, then responsive classroom management must also incorporate appropriate accommodations to the student's learning needs.

Here are some situations that highlight the range of managerial issues and concerns facing the classroom teacher. Put yourself in the place of the teacher and consider your goal and the best approach to handling the situation.

- After a few months of teaching her fifth-grade class, Ms. Johnson feels that she is losing her ability to maintain order. Whenever she attempts to start a new activity, it takes her several minutes to obtain her students' attention and get them ready to receive instruction. Constant talking by students and their movement around the room interrupt her lessons. Attempts to correct individual students go for naught while other students laugh and talk.

- Although Mr. Kim has generally good rapport with his middle school students and they respond positively to his instruction, two boys in the class often ignore him when he asks them to cease some off-task behavior. Then, when Mr. Kim follows the request with a more pointed redirection, the boys pointedly react with some hostility or derision. When an event escalates, it often leads to threats or a raised voice from Mr. Kim followed by continuing opposition from the boys.

- Mrs. Lopez is a member of her high school's teacher advisory committee. Because student tardiness to classes has become a nagging problem this year, several teachers on the advisory committee ask her to join them in recommending to the principal that tardiness be added to the school's zero tolerance code of conduct so that students are suspended after three unexcused absences over a semester. Mrs. Lopez is bothered by the high incidence of tardiness in her school, but she wonders whether suspending such students is the most appropriate strategy.

Why Do Teachers Find Classroom Management Difficult?

Classroom management is a primary area of concern for both experienced and new teachers. One explanation for this apprehension is that classroom interactions are unpredictable, and complex and happen quickly. Teachers have limited time to reflect on an appropriate course of action when misbehaviors occur, but at the same time must carry out consequences in full view of the students. Most teachers tend to avoid confrontation with their students (Ennis, 1996) and may find responding to problem behaviors in such a public forum uncomfortable. The cognitive demands of teaching, even when things go smoothly, are significant. Classroom researchers have noted that teachers make many decisions on the fly throughout the day, and it has been estimated that during classroom instruction teachers make a decision every two minutes (Clark & Peterson, 1986). Thus, teaching should be viewed as a complex skill that requires significant cognitive focus and energy. Behavioral challenges change the flow of classroom instruction, divert student attention, and slow the pace of instruction. Responding to problem behaviors can tax even the most experienced teacher's abilities.

Most teachers receive limited instruction in classroom management as part of their preservice training, and even a university-based program may not require coursework in classroom management. Similarly, while teachers usually attend workshops about particular types of behavioral interventions that are required by their district or state, these workshops do not seem to be sufficient—even experienced teachers identify classroom management as an area in which they would like still more training. Teachers who have not had sufficient training in how to assess and respond to behavioral challenges will be less effective in responding when they do occur.

Another feature of classroom life that affects classroom management is the expectation for students to gain mastery of a set curriculum, which requires them to engage in a predetermined series of classroom activities. Teachers are expected to oversee this process and, in the United States, are increasingly held accountable for the academic achievement of their students. Some researchers (e.g., Gathercoal & Nimmo, 2002; McCaslin & Good, 1992) suggest that these societal expectations for teachers may set up a dynamic of conflict and power between teacher and students. Certainly the aim of schooling is for students to learn, but when teacher-student confrontations occur in an environment where high-stakes accountability is in force, it may compound the stress teachers feel when behavior disrupts the learning process. Teachers who believe that they do not have enough time to carry out their many responsibilities may be particularly intolerant of behaviors that take away time from instruction.

The increasing linguistic and ethnic diversity of students in U.S. classrooms has also increased the diversity of skills that teachers need when responding to problem behaviors. Teachers with limited training in classroom management may not have mastered the breadth of strategies needed to teach a diverse group of students. Additionally, children with behavioral problems who have been traditionally placed in special education classrooms are increasingly being included in general education classrooms. Most teachers are unprepared for the significant behavioral challenges exhibited by these students. To address this problem, some districts use coteaching or collaborative teaching models in which special educators deliver instruction alongside general educators. Many studies have found that administrative support for coteaching is essential for its success and that teachers generally report that they benefit from participating in coteaching (Scruggs, Mastropieri, & McDuffie, 2007). In many cases, however, students who exhibit challenging behaviors are accompanied by teaching assistants to the general education classroom so that the assistant can intervene when these problem behaviors are exhibited in the general education classroom. Although some teaching assistants may do a fine job of interceding or even temporarily removing a student who acts out, problem behaviors can interrupt the flow of classroom instruction as well as serve as a negative model for other students.

In summary, teachers find classroom management difficult because it *is* a difficult skill. During their preparation for teaching, only limited attention is given to acquiring expertise in this demanding skill area. Classrooms contain a greater diversity of students, while at the same time teachers are expected to prepare their students in a high-stakes accountability environment.

Teacher Thinking About Classroom Management

How teachers think about classroom management affects their own instructional behavior, relations with students, and management of activities. Researchers have made a useful distinction between preactive and interactive thought and decisions—in other words, thinking that occurs before instruction, such as planning, versus thinking that occurs during face-to-face interaction with students, such as intervening with problem behaviors (Clark & Peterson, 1986; Shavelson & Stern, 1981). Since this chapter's focus is on responsive management, our concern is more with interactive thinking, although we acknowledge that preactive teacher thought can also be responsive in nature. For example, a teacher might spend time planning before class how to deal with a chronic problem or how to gain the cooperation of a class whose behavior has deteriorated. Clark and Peterson (1986) cited numerous studies showing that interactive teacher thinking and decision making are sensitive to departures from business as usual. That is, teachers monitor students during an activity and, as long as things go as planned, the teacher has no reason to alter course. An analogous situation is when driving on a familiar road, as long as nothing unusual takes place you do not alter your driving behavior and the trip is smooth. But when a dog darts into the roadway or a heavy rain occurs, you slow down, turn off the radio, and sit straighter in your seat. Similarly, when the flow of normal classroom activity is interrupted, then the teacher is on alert and will intervene if an acceptable strategy is easily implemented. The determination of how and when to intervene is dependent on a variety of factors. First, of course, is whether the teacher knows of an appropriate intervention, but the teacher must consider other factors.

Jackson (1968) identified enduring features of classroom life that he summarized as "crowds, praise, and power." He meant to call attention to how teachers must often deal with students—usually in a large group of 20 to 30. Classrooms are also places where students are evaluated frequently, so they receive positive or negative feedback about their performance and behavior. Finally, teachers have more power than students. The teacher's status is conferred by the formal institutional process. Teachers' power, however, is not absolute; it depends on their ability to secure the cooperation of their students.

Doyle (1986, 2006) added to Jackson's perspective. He noted that classrooms have unique characteristics that shape the behavior and thinking of teachers and students. These include multidimensionality, simultaneity, immediacy, unpredictability, publicness, and history. In other words, the teacher is faced with a complex setting in which several things are occurring at any given time that may (or may not) require attention.

Classroom characteristics have important effects on teacher thinking. The crowded conditions in which instruction takes place means that delays and interruptions are an inevitable part of life with which teachers and students must learn to cope. The exigencies of dealing with classroom life produce a degree of unpredictability for the teacher; lessons won't always go as planned and students can't be counted on to react as expected.

How do teachers adjust to the unpredictability of classroom life? Fenwick (1998) observed and interviewed junior high school teachers in order to learn about their thoughts and reasons for their classroom behaviors. Three themes emerged. First, teachers were focused on managing space, people, and objects. Second, teachers were concerned with managing student energy and engagement, in order to maintain the flow of activities during lessons. Finally, teachers managed their own identity and behavior.

The teachers in Fenwick's study were all experienced. Beginning teachers, even though they have spent thousands of hours as students in classrooms, are especially vulnerable to behavior management problems. Why? Perhaps because when they enter the classroom, new teachers have not fully developed the experienced teacher's more complex skill of managing space, energy, and self, nor are they able to draw from experience to discriminate what are feasible interventions from unworkable strategies. The immediacy, unpredictability, and crowdedness of classroom life require a management plan that organizes student and teacher behavior into routines that make day-to-day classroom life manageable.

Classroom Interventions

The phrase *responsive classroom management* implies that the teacher takes action in response to a classroom event. Responsiveness requires the teacher to monitor classroom activity and to be attentive to changes that occur in the classroom. As the literature on teacher thinking and decision making makes clear, teachers notice when there is an interruption to the flow of an activity or when student behavior disturbs classroom order. What different kinds of events disrupt the classroom routine?

One way to organize such events is by classifying their intensity and source (Emmer, Evertson, & Worsham, 2006). Minor problems are behaviors that are contrary to classroom rules or procedures, but that are only occasional and are not widespread. Examples include excessive side-talk during an activity, wandering around the room, interfering with other students who are trying to complete an assignment, or not working on an assigned task. Escalating or spreading problems are any minor problems that continue for more than a short time or involve more than one or a few students. Major problems disrupt a classroom activity for a significant time or prevent it from taking place, violate a significant school rule, or interfere with the teacher or other students' work. We don't include serious problems, such as fighting, suicide attempts, and weapons violations that typically occur outside of the classroom in our discussion of responsive classroom management. Of course these serious behaviors have effects on students, and teachers do take some action when these behaviors involve one of their students, but these events usually occur outside of the classroom. Such serious problems are usually managed by policies contained in a school district's discipline plan or are subsumed within a school's crisis management plan and responded to by the school district's crisis management team (Damiani, 2006).

Momentary inattention, occasional sidetalking, or daydreaming are not considered problems that require an intervention, because such behaviors are transitory and don't interfere with other students or with ongoing instruction. Moreover, when teachers do choose to respond to such behaviors they run the risk of slowing down activities, and they make too much of what is really a trivial behavior by calling attention to it.

We distinguish different types of problem events or behaviors because the teacher's response is dependent on the behavior's intensity or severity. Minor problems can usually be settled with interventions that are limited with respect to teacher time and energy. As problems become more intense and widespread, simple interventions are often not very effective, and the teacher's response requires more planning and energy; such interventions may also require the cooperation of others and alteration of classroom activities. From the standpoint of efficient use of teacher energy, as well as the need to preserve teacher and student time for instruction, it is preferable to limit interventions. But more involved interventions may be needed to counter a serious problem.

How teachers respond to problem behaviors can be determined by asking teachers what they do to deal with inappropriate behaviors or by observing teachers when students misbehave. Self-report allows us to get the teachers' view, but may be biased in a variety of ways. Observation provides a direct way to determine strategies, but it has limitations too. Observers aren't always in place to see what the teacher responds to (or misses), and it may be difficult to observe relatively rare but serious problems.

Research by Kounin (1970) analyzed videotaped lessons to identify teacher behaviors that were significant predictors of increased student on-task behaviors and that reduced student disruption. After several attempts to study characteristics of desist statements, Kounin identified "withitness," overlapping, and movement management as important teacher management behaviors. Withitness refers to the teacher's ability to detect inappropriate behavior and to signal awareness of it to students; overlapping is the ability to deal with more than one event at the same time; movement management refers to teacher skill in maintaining the momentum of whole class, teacher-led activities. Overlapping and movement management are proactive teacher skills; they prevent problems by keeping activities moving. Withitness, however, is both proactive and responsive as it prevents escalation by addressing minor problems early, before they can spread or become major.

The importance of withitness was corroborated in research by Emmer, Evertson, and Anderson (1980) and Evertson and Emmer (1982). These researchers observed both elementary and junior high school classrooms and obtained information about withitness by noting the degree to which teachers monitored students and stopped inappropriate behavior promptly. Teachers who exhibited these characteristics over multiple observations had classes whose students were more on task and were less disruptive, compared to teachers who were not very good at monitoring students or at stopping inappropriate behaviors promptly. Another study (Johnston, 1995), in middle school physical education classes, found that desists that were accurate and prompt (i.e., withit) were successful in returning students to the task 80% of the time as compared to 45% for desists that targeted the wrong students or were late.

The value of withitness is apparent. Teachers who are good observers of students detect problems early when these behaviors can be dealt with by simpler interventions. If a teacher is late in noting a problem, there is more potential for several students to become involved, and then an intervention is more apt to require greater time and attention. Moreover, if other students observe another student getting away with it, the teacher must then deal with this apparent inconsistency.

When a problem is chronic or major, other interventions may be needed. A national random sample of elementary and secondary school teachers was asked to describe the strategies that they used to manage the student who behaved the most inappropriately during the previous year (Ringer, Doerr, Hollenshead, & Wills, 1993). The categories used to classify the teachers' strategies included a reinforcement technique (e.g., positive reinforcement, praise, response cost, ignoring), an established behavior plan (e.g., Assertive Discipline or a self-developed plan), punishment (e.g., time-out, detention), proximity, conferences, or instructional techniques (e.g., peer tutoring, group instruction). The teachers' preferences are shown in Table 15.1.

Overall, elementary teachers used more interventions, though all teachers had a preference for conferences and proximity. Elementary teachers also made extensive use of behavior plans, and over half the sample used reinforcement, punishment, and instructional strategies. For middle and high school teachers, the next most endorsed intervention was instruction; the other three strategies were used only by small percentages of the samples. The more extensive use of interventions by elementary teachers could be the result of using a wider variety of factors, but surely one factor is the greater amount of contact time that elementary teachers have with the targeted student compared to the time spent with students in the secondary setting.

Why do teachers at all levels state a preference for using conferences and proximity to deal with major problems? Perhaps it is because proximity is an intervention that can

Table 15.1   Behavioral Techniques Chosen by Teachers (N = 228)

Variable	Reinforcement	Behavior Plan	Punishment	Proximity	Conference	Instruction
Type of School						
Elementary	59	70	57	73	87	56
Middle	16	12	19	80	86	52
High School	23	16	22	65	85	36

SOURCE: Adapted from Ringer, M., Doerr, P., Hollenshead, J., & Wills, G. (1993). Behavior problems in the schools: A national survey of interventions used by classroom teachers. *Psychology in the Schools, 30,* 168–175.

NOTE: Table shows the percentage of teachers who chose the technique; teachers could identify more than one strategy.

be used during instruction without interfering with the flow of the activity. It allows the teacher to be "withit" while maintaining the focus on the academic task more so than other, more intrusive interventions. Conferences may also have been highly endorsed because the problems addressed were not readily amenable to solution, and also because conferencing allows the problem behavior to be managed without an audience.

Nelson and Roberts (2000) provide insight into the difficulty of intervening in a classroom setting. Researchers observed 99 target students identified as disruptive in six schools (Grades 1 through 8) and compared them to 278 additional students who were identified as typical. The target students were observed until 20 episodes of inappropriate behavior had been observed by the researchers. Teacher reactions to the target students during the episodes were also noted. Each typical student was observed long enough to note at least three episodes of inappropriate behavior.

The most common teacher reaction to inappropriate behaviors of typical students was to redirect the student's behavior; this strategy was used 83% of the time. The second most preferred strategy was to reprimand (also referred to as issuing a desist) to the student (16% of the time). After the teacher used one of these strategies, the typical students stopped behaving inappropriately 93% of the time. Thus, simple interventions worked very well most of the time.

The situation was very different for the target students. Teachers used redirection 56% of the time and reprimands (desists) 37% of the time. But the target (disruptive) students stopped their inappropriate behavior only 24% of the time following the first teacher intervention. Certainly the target students were much less responsive to these initial teacher interventions than were the typical students. Furthermore, in 76% of these interactions the teacher was required to then deal a second time with the target student who had already ignored or negatively responded to the first intervention. One can imagine how a second interaction between student and teacher raised the stakes for both parties. Most teachers chose to continue to attempt to stop the inappropriate behavior. Only 7% of the time did a

teacher use the strategy of ignoring the inappropriate behavior after the first desist. During these second interactions a variety of strategies was observed: more commands or redirection, reprimands or desists, ultimatums, response cost (a penalty), dismissal from the classroom, or approval. Unfortunately, none of these strategies was particularly effective and inappropriate behaviors usually continued. In fact, Nelson and Roberts found that it took an average of four to five interventions before the target student's misbehavior stopped, which means that in some cases six, seven, or more interventions were needed to stop the behavior!

When a teacher intervenes four or more times with a student, the regular academic activity in the classroom has been interrupted significantly, to the detriment of the instructional program and student learning. Inappropriate behaviors have been modeled, so there is some likelihood of contagion to other students. There is also considerable potential for the target student to be labeled as a troublemaker and suffer (or enjoy!) the consequences of negative teacher and peer expectations. Finally, the teacher is likely to experience stress.

Problems caused by teacher intervention–student resistance cycles such as these lead to the judicious recommendation that teachers use techniques that avoid such escalation. A common example of an intervention that mitigates escalation is some form of time-out. Time-out is more fully referred to as time-out from positive reinforcement, wherein the student is removed from a classroom and thus from a potentially reinforcing environment. Nelson developed a strategy that requires the student to move to another teacher's classroom for some "think time" before returning to the class. Such a move interrupted the teacher intervention–student resistance cycle and allowed for both parties to take a break from the conflict. Other intervention strategies that can short-circuit the escalating cycle of action-reaction include a five-step intervention process (Jones & Jones, 2004) that allows the student to choose to exercise self-control in early steps, but that requires the student to leave the instructional area to develop a plan for change if these early steps don't succeed. Problem-solving approaches are commonly used to address escalating or major behavior problems that involve individual students. The setting for problem solving is usually a conference between the teacher and the student, away from the effects of a public audience. The teacher needs good communication skills to establish a basis for considering alternatives to the inappropriate behavior and to encourage the student to consider available choices. Problem solving often culminates in a written contract.

In addition to the relatively simple and easy to use in-class interventions (e.g., proximity control, eye contact, redirection, desist) and the more involved and time-consuming problem-solving strategies are other interventions that require varying amounts of teacher time and effort. These strategies include withholding a privilege or desired activity, assessing a penalty, assigning detention, or using a school-based consequence. These interventions can be effective, at least in the short run, at stopping the inappropriate behavior, but they have the disadvantage of focusing attention on the inappropriate behavior, and they do not, by themselves, help instruct students in what is appropriate behavior. Consequently, whenever an intervention to stop inappropriate behavior is used, teachers must consider whether students understand what behaviors are desirable and whether their classroom management system teaches positive behaviors to students. Although teaching students desirable behaviors is usually considered a proactive strategy, it can also be part of responsive classroom management. When teachers find that they are frequently using interventions to deal with inappropriate behavior, they should assess their expectations for student behavior, perhaps in consultation with another teacher, and reconsider the routines that they are using to manage the activity. This reflective process may lead to some new procedures that can be taught to students, along with a different teaching approach. Responsive classroom management is not simply reacting to and dealing with problem behaviors; it can involve establishing a positive classroom climate that responds to students' needs, thereby decreasing motivation for inappropriate behaviors and increasing student engagement (see Chapter 14).

Another set of interventions that are effective in reducing inappropriate behavior has been developed by behavior management specialists, special educators, and school psychologists who work in schools with teachers. Such interventions come from a long tradition of research in applied behavior analysis that emphasizes demonstrating the efficacy of behavior management programs by direct observation of target behaviors. Stage and Quiroz (1997) examined classroom-based research on such intervention strategies to determine the degree of effectiveness across multiple studies. The strongest effects were found for differential reinforcement of alternate behaviors, self-management strategies, and group contingency programs. Differential reinforcement uses rewards for students when they engage in desirable behaviors such as hand raising or work involvement that are functionally incompatible with problem behaviors such as interrupting and off-task

behavior. Self-management programs provide training for students to record and evaluate their own behavior. The teacher gives feedback so that the students learn to do this correctly and receive rewards when their behaviors improve. Self-management procedures emphasize student self-monitoring and learning responsibility for their own actions. Group contingency programs provide rewards for the entire class (e.g., a pizza party, activity time) when desirable behavior is exhibited and some goal or performance level is reached. A popular type of group contingency program is one that uses token reinforcers. Token reinforcers are objects that may be exchanged for something of value to a student. The token thus has symbolic as well as tangible value for the student. Systems in which students earn tokens and then can exchange them for objects or activities they desire are called token economies. In a simple token economy system, teachers award points or use marks on the board for good behavior; then the class is given extra recess time or free time once they have earned a predetermined number of points or marks. In more complex systems, teachers may design point cards or award small items, such as paper tickets or poker chips, which the student holds until a designated reward time when the teacher accepts these items in exchange for an item out of a selection of rewards. Token economies can be used to deliver positive reinforcement as we have described or can be used to reduce a behavior when the token is removed in response to undesired behaviors. Such systems are referred to as response cost token economies. The advantage of response cost token economies is that they enable the teacher to quickly respond to an undesired behavior with minimal fuss. A potential problem with response cost systems is with student bankruptcy wherein the student loses so many tokens that they can no longer receive a negative consequence through losing more tokens. The shrewd teacher will either design a token economy in which students can always earn tokens or one in which it is impossible for students to become bankrupt. Group contingency programs have the advantage of teaching desirable behavior and using peer pressure positively. Limitations include the time and effort required along with the potential for negative effects of using extrinsic rewards (for a discussion, see Cameron, 2001). For more extensive treatment of applied behavior interventions, the reader should consult additional sources, such as Alberto and Troutman (2006).

Schoolwide Responsive Strategies

Schoolwide models for conceptualizing academic and behavioral interventions have received increasing attention over the last decade. Schoolwide models extend beyond the immediate classroom but also usually include classroom-based responsive strategies that teachers can implement in response to problem behaviors. In particular, three-tiered models have been designed with the goal to prevent behavioral problems and to provide a plan for responsive strategies that teachers and schools can use when more complex or serious behaviors occur (e.g., Lewis, Sugai, & Colvin, 1998; Walker et al. 1996). Three-tiered models of schoolwide discipline divide behavioral interventions into three levels: primary, secondary, and tertiary. In these models, approximately 70%–85% of a school population is seen as being responsive to primary interventions, 10%–20% to secondary interventions, and tertiary interventions are required by only 5%–7% of the population.

In three-tiered models, primary interventions are provided to all students in a school and focus on strategies that prevent behavioral problems from occurring. Primary interventions may include providing reinforcement to students who comply with classroom expectations (e.g., being on time for class). Secondary interventions are used when preventive strategies designed for the primary level do not have an effect. Secondary interventions include more intensive behavioral interventions or simple individualized interventions such as social-skills instruction or increased family involvement. For example, if a teacher continues to have difficulty with some children not being on time for class, he or she may choose to call the parents and ask for support in encouraging these children to arrive on time.

Tertiary interventions are designed for individual children who have demonstrated severe and stable behavioral problems and who have not responded to other interventions. Tertiary interventions should involve a functional assessment, in which the goal of the problem behavior is analyzed and the context for the problem is considered. Functional assessments examine the targeted problem behavior across several school contexts, for example, the classroom in which the behavior is most troublesome, in other classrooms, and in the lunchroom to see if the behavior occurs consistently across all school contexts. Similarly, the behavior can be examined across multiple tasks or subjects (e.g., during reading and social studies). The objective of a functional assessment is to analyze how different school contexts might be serving as antecedents to problem behavior. Once the functional assessment is completed, the teacher should be able to see clear patterns, such as when and where and with whom the problem behaviors typically occur.

Tertiary interventions are usually provided to students identified as having a behavioral disorder and who have not responded to a secondary intervention. For instance, a teacher may respond to a student who engages in verbal conflicts with other students during class by using the secondary intervention strategies of telling them to stop and then separating them from the rest of the class. If these verbal conflicts continue or escalate, despite the teacher's consistent use of these strategies, a tertiary intervention may be needed. Tertiary interventions often include some form of a pull out program. Thus, should the behavior become unmanageable in the general education classroom, the student can be removed from the classroom and served in an alternate setting with a teacher or other school personnel who are prepared to address the behavior. While tertiary intervention may take place in an alternate setting, the ultimate focus is on returning the student to the general education setting as soon as the student is under behavioral control.

Positive behavioral support (PBS) is another behavioral change model that has been particularly influential in the field of special education. PBS refers to a systematic approach to preventing or reducing challenging behaviors by examining the context in which they occur and emphasizing the application of reinforcement in order to change behavior. Interventions are chosen to strengthen the antecedent-desired behavior relationship and to limit the use of punishment or response cost interventions. PBS also focuses on the social and contextual variables in the classroom or school setting that may be reinforcing the undesirable behavior. PBS has been used as part of schoolwide discipline programs, as well as part of individual interventions designed for students receiving special education services.

Teachers in schools that use schoolwide models are expected to follow school guidelines when problems become more intense or chronic in nature. The advantage of effective schoolwide systems is that expectations for behavior and selected interventions are consistent across classrooms and across teachers. These models require considerable training, commitment from administrators, and fidelity of implementation in order to be effective on a schoolwide level.

Responsive Classroom Management and Special Education Students

Students whose behavioral problems are chronic and intensive are usually referred for special education services. Special education students who have behavioral problems usually have a Behavioral Intervention Plan (sometimes known as a BIP) that is part of their Individualized Education Plan, which is required for all students receiving special education services. The BIP is designed after a functional assessment is completed on the student's behavior to identify factors that precede their acting-out behaviors, the settings for the behavior, as well as the types of reinforcement most likely to result in positive behavioral change. The BIP can be helpful to teachers because it documents past interventions, identifies reinforcers preferred by the students, and outlines a behavioral intervention for teachers to use. Another advantage is that it encourages teachers and administrators to consider alternatives. A disadvantage is that these plans are typically only discussed and formalized once a year when the Individualized Education Plan is developed.

For over three decades, students with chronic behavioral problems received educational services primarily in special education classrooms. Today, many students receiving special education services spend the majority of their school days in general education classrooms. The Individuals with Disabilities Education Act (IDEA) requires that students with disabilities, including those with behavioral disorders, be educated in the general education classroom with their nondisabled peers to the fullest extent possible. Even a student with a documented behavioral disorder cannot be excluded from the general education setting solely on the basis of the disability (Individuals with Disabilities Education Act [IDEA], 2004). In addition, while placement in another classroom may provide a lower teacher-student ratio and the opportunity for more intensive behavioral interventions, these placements may negatively affect student achievement. Studies of the effects of inclusion report more positive achievement outcomes for students with disabilities who are placed in inclusive settings (Soodak & McCarthy, 2006). Few studies exist, however, that suggest how inclusive classrooms are best managed to ensure these outcomes. Even less research exists on how classroom management practices used in general education classrooms may be similar to or different from those found to be the most effective in special education classrooms. Although the field of special education does have a tradition of examining the effects of interventions, they are typically designed for individual students rather than for whole-class use. What teachers need are techniques that have been used and proven effective in inclusive classrooms where students are receiving instruction in larger groups.

Students with intense, chronic behavioral problems who are not successful in the inclusive classroom may receive special education services in a separate classroom setting. These classrooms are staffed with special education teachers whose expertise is designing individualized behavioral interventions. Although there are not particular responsive strategies that are special education strategies, it is typical that special education teachers use interventions that are more individualized and that require more teacher time to implement than those used in the general education classroom. An example is how most special education teachers implement token economy systems. First, instead of applying the system to the classroom as a whole, the special education teacher designs a token system for a particular student, including reinforcers chosen to be particularly to his or her liking. Second, the timing for token distribution and how the behavior is to be reinforced is carefully considered. For example, a teacher may set a goal for a student who has difficulty staying on task to remain seated for 20 minutes. The student is then given a token for every 2 minutes spent on task. The system uses response cost as a way to provide the student additional feedback about behavior: When the student is not on task during a 2-minute period a token is removed. The number of tokens needed for a reinforcer is predetermined: Only when the student has 10 tokens may they be traded for the reward. Finally, the reinforcement comes close on the heels of success: No matter when the student ends up with 10 tokens, that is when he or she receives a reward. Obviously, this level of attention to the behavior of one student requires close monitoring and implementation, and so it is commonly used only if there is a low teacher-student ratio.

Some Final Words About Classroom Environment

Public school populations in the United States are becoming increasingly diverse, so teachers need to have a similarly diverse array of strategies in order to manage 21st-century classrooms. What may have worked well with predominately Anglo students in rural Michigan may not yield the same results with Hispanic students in an urban Texas district. What caused high-achieving students in an East Coast school to pay attention might be ineffective when used with students with behavioral disorders in East Los Angeles. What always flavors these interactions is the socioeconomic and cultural milieu in which they take place, and even more importantly, the emotional relationship between a class of students and their teacher. Some research (Weinstein, Curran, & Tomlinson-Clarke, 2003) reminds us that building and maintaining a positive relationship between teacher and students enhances what occurs in that classroom. Responsive classroom management occurs most successfully when teachers care not only about the effectiveness of their strategies and student behavior but also about the quality of their relationships with students.

References and Further Readings

Alberto, P. A., & Troutman, A. C. (2006). *Applied behavior analysis for teachers* (7th ed.). Upper Saddle River, NJ: Pearson.

Cameron, J. (2001). Negative effects of reward on intrinsic motivation—A limited phenomenon: Comment on Deci, Koestner, and Ryan. *Review of Educational Research, 71,* 29–42.

Clark, C., & Peterson, P. (1986). Teachers' thought processes. In M. C. Wittrock (Ed.), *Handbook of research on teaching* (3rd ed., pp. 255–296). New York: Macmillan.

Damiani, V. B. (2006). *Crisis prevention and intervention in the classroom: What teachers should know.* Lanham, MD: Rowman & Littlefield.

Doyle, W. (1978). Are students behaving worse than they used to behave? *Journal of Research and Development in Education, 11,* 13–16.

Doyle, W. (1986). Classroom organization and management. In M. C. Wittrock (Ed.), *Handbook of research on teaching* (3rd ed., pp. 392–431). New York: Macmillan.

Doyle, W. (2006). Ecological approaches to classroom management. In C. M. Evertson & C. S. Weinstein (Eds.), *Handbook of classroom management: Research, practice, and contemporary issues* (pp. 97–126). Mahwah, NJ: Lawrence Erlbaum Associates.

Emmer, E. T., Evertson, C. M., & Anderson, L. A. (1980). Effective classroom management at the beginning of the school year. *Elementary School Journal, 80,* 219–231.

Emmer, E. T., Evertson, C. M., & Worsham, M. A. (2006). *Classroom management for secondary teachers* (7th ed.). Boston: Allyn & Bacon.

Ennis, C. D. (1996). When avoiding confrontation leads to avoiding content: Disruptive students' impact on curriculum. *Journal of Curriculum and Supervision, 11,* 145–162.

Evertson, C. M., & Emmer, E. T. (1982). Effective management at the beginning of the year in junior high school classes. *Journal of Educational Psychology, 74,* 485–498.

Fenwick, D. T. (1998). Managing space, energy, and self: Junior high teachers' experiences of classroom management. *Teaching and Teacher Education, 14,* 619–631.

Gathercoal, P., & Nimmo, V. (2002, April). *Judicious discipline: 5 years later.* Paper presented at the Annual Meeting of the American Educational Research Association, New Orleans, LA.

Individuals with Disabilities Education Act Amendments of 2004, Pub. I. No. 105–17, 20 U.S.C. 1400 *et seq.* (2004).

Jackson, P. (1968). *Life in classrooms.* New York: Holt, Rinehart & Winston.

Johnston, B. D. (1995). "Withitness": Real or fictional? *The Physical Educator, 52,* 22–28.

Jones, V., & Jones, L. (2004). *Comprehensive classroom management: Creating communities of support and solving problems* (7th ed.). Boston: Allyn & Bacon.

Kounin, J. (1970). *Discipline and group management in classrooms.* New York: Holt, Rinehart & Winston.

Lewis, T. J., Newcomer, L. L., Trussell, R., & Richter, M. (2006). Schoolwide positive behavior support: Building systems to develop and maintain appropriate social behavior. In C. M. Evertson & C. S. Weinstein (Eds.), *Handbook of classroom management: Research, practice, and contemporary issues* (pp. 833–854). Mahwah, NJ: Lawrence Erlbaum Associates.

Lewis, T. J., Sugai, G., & Colvin, G. (1998). Reducing problem behavior through a schoolwide system of effective behav-

ioral support: Investigation of a schoolwide social skills training program and contextual intervention. *School Psychology Review, 27,* 446–459.

McCaslin, M., & Good, T. L. (1992). Compliant cognition: The misalliance of management and instructional goals in current school reform. *Educational Researcher, 21*(3), 4–17.

Nelson, J. R., & Roberts, M. L. (2000). Ongoing reciprocal teacher-student interactions involving disruptive behaviors in general education classrooms. *Journal of Emotional and Behavioral Disorders, 4,* 147–161.

Ringer, M., Doerr, P., Hollenshead, J., & Wills, G. (1993). Behavior problems in the schools: A national survey of interventions used by classroom teachers. *Psychology in the Schools, 30,* 168–175.

Scruggs, T. E., Mastropieri, M. A., & McDuffie, K. A. (2007). Co-teaching in inclusive classrooms: A metasynthesis of qualitative research. *Exceptional Children, 73*(4), 392–416.

Shavelson, R., & Stern, P. (1981). Research on teachers' pedagogical thoughts, judgments, decisions, and behavior. *Review of Educational Research, 51,* 455–498.

Soodak, L., & McCarthy, M. R. (2006). Classroom management in inclusive settings. In C. Evertson & C. Weinstein (Eds.), *Handbook of classroom management: Research, practice, and contemporary issues* (pp. 461–489). Mahwah, NJ: Lawrence Erlbaum Associates.

Stage, S. A., & Quiroz, D. R. (1997). A meta-analysis of interventions to decrease disruptive classroom behavior in public education settings. *School Psychology Review, 26,* 333–368.

Walker, H. M., Horner, R., Sugai, G., Bullis, M., Sprague, J., Bricker, D., et al. (1996). Integrated approaches to preventing antisocial behavior patterns among school-age children and youth. *Journal of Emotional and Behavioral Disorders, 4,* 193–256.

Weinstein, C., Curran, M., & Tomlinson-Clarke, S. (2003). Culturally responsive classroom management: Awareness into action. *Theory into Practice, 42*(4), 269–276.

16

ZERO TOLERANCE

A Reconsideration of Practice and Policy

H. JEROME FREIBERG AND AUGUSTINA REYES

University of Houston

The issues of school safety, discipline, and order have been an overriding concern for educators and citizens in America since the late 1800s. In 1908, Arthur Perry, the principal of School #85 in Brooklyn, New York, made this observation:

> "Discipline" in a school is a natural, to-be-expected, and ever-present problem. The discipline of a school may, and should, under ordinary conditions, improve from year to year; but as the work of the school means continuous process of admitting to the school register hundreds of pupils in their infancy and discharging them in their youth, just so will the problem of discipline be a continuous one. (Perry, 1908, p. 243)

Modern times see a continuation of public and educator concerns for safe and orderly learning environments (Rogers & Freiberg, 1994). Since the late 1960s, public opinion polls have been conducted by the Gallup Organization and reported by *Phi Delta Kappan*. These polls show that in 1971 discipline ranked third in leading school concerns. In 1982, a lack of discipline ranked first in public concerns. In 1992, it ranked third behind school finance and drugs, and for 1994 and 1998, "lack of discipline" in schools was joined by "fighting/violence/gangs" as the number one concern of the public (Elam, Rose, & Gallup, 1994). The Gallup Poll trend, as measured by public attitudes and concerns about public schools, continues to the present time, with student behavior and the lack of student discipline ranking first or second in the poll as the "biggest problem that public schools face" and there seems to be little hope that these concerns will change soon.

The National Institute of Education's [NIE] (1978) report to Congress, "Violent Schools—Safe Schools: The Safe School Study Report to Congress," reported that public fears concerning lack of discipline and violence in schools are well founded. In the Freiberg, Stein, and Parker (1995) study of a middle school located just beyond the city limits, 388 of 1,283 students—nearly one-third of the total school—were referred to the office for discipline in 1 month (October). Total frequency of discipline referrals for both one-time and repeated actions totaled 894 referrals for the same month. Some school environments foster an ethos of inappropriate behavior, which over time may escalate, leading to a highly unsafe teaching and learning environment. Additionally, little learning can take place in an environment in which students are removed from the classroom while their peers wait for order to be restored (Freiberg & Lapointe, 2006; Opuni, 1998, 2006; Opuni & Ochoa, 2002). Student behaviors that disrupt the learning environment have a rippling effect, influencing the disruptive individual, his or her classmates, the school, and subsequently near and far communities. Classroom disruptions steal valuable teaching and learning time (Freiberg, 1999; Freiberg & Lapointe, 2006; Opuni & Ochoa, 2002). School climate and student achievement are casualties of these disruptions, resulting in time off task, conflicts, and ineffective instructional management. A pattern of disruptions also engulfs school administration in noninstructional activities with hundreds or even thousands of hours spent in responding to disciplinary referrals to the office.

Sustained student misbehavior often inhibits instructional approaches that foster interactive teaching methods (Brophy, 1999; Cohen, 1986/1994). Teachers are reluctant to use manipulative tools in math for fear that they will become missiles rather than learning tools (Freiberg, Connell, & Lorentz, 2001). Disruptive behaviors may be symptomatic of other classroom, school, and societal problems that influence teachers and students. Brantlinger (1993) found family income levels of students resulted in differential treatment by teachers and administrators when students from higher- and lower-income families broke classroom and school rules. Moreover, Kounin (1970) demonstrated the relationship between teacher's management and instructional actions and student behaviors. Classroom management policies were also found to interfere with school reform initiatives. McCaslin and Good (1992) determined that educational reform efforts are stifled by "classroom management policies that encourage, if not demand, simple obedience" (p. 4). Wang, Haertel, and Walberg (1993) further highlight the implications of classroom management in the broader picture of school reform and student learning. Their meta-analysis of learning factors identified classroom management as being first in a list of five alterable variables that influence school learning. Discipline policies and practices have a significant influence on the learning outcomes of students. Weade and Evertson (1988) and Evertson and Weade (1989) found similar connections between classroom management and student achievement. A recent study of 14 elementary schools reported similar results (Freiberg, Huzinec, & Borders, 2007).

Defining Zero Tolerance

Zero tolerance is a theory grounded in policy, emerging from criminal law theory (Reyes, 2006). It attempts to eliminate discretionary decision making by individual formal authority figures, including school principals. The individual in authority is compelled to enforce the predetermined punishment without regard to circumstances. Theoretically, zero tolerance emerged as a policy tool used in criminal law and the military. During the Reagan Administration in the 1980s it was adopted by the federal government in the war against drugs (Reyes, 2006). While military drug experts saw reduced drug usage, the military did not declare a victory for zero tolerance or its ability to deter drugs in the military (Crawley, 2002). The use of zero tolerance policies does not indicate that sexual harassment, discrimination, domestic violence, and drug problems in the military will be eliminated, only that they may be decreased (Reyes, 2006).

In a study by the National Center for Education Statistics [NCES] (1998) zero tolerance was defined as "a school or district policy that mandates predetermined con-

sequences or punishments for specific offenses" (p. 33). NCES (1998) reported that 94% of the sample school districts surveyed used zero tolerance policies for serious student offenses, including violence, firearms, weapons other than firearms, and the use of alcohol and tobacco. Nationally 80% of schools use zero tolerance policies (Reyes, 2006).

Zero Tolerance in School Policies

Although zero tolerance policies were not declared a complete victory in the U.S. military, they became the model policies for K–12 public education (Reyes, 2006). High-profile school shootings and youth drug use in schools became the impetus for zero tolerance school discipline policies. In 1974, a small-town honor student opened fire in his high school, killing three and wounding nine in a well-planned attack (Reyes, 2006). Several other cases were sensationally reported throughout the nation. Many of the student killings have occurred in rural or suburban communities. In 1999, the shooting in Columbine, Colorado, only increased and justified the use of zero tolerance policies in school discipline (Vossekuil, Fein, & Reddy, 2002).

Although school shootings have occurred regularly in inner-city schools, the movement of violence to the "safety" of suburban and rural schools stunned the nation. National politicians responded to school shootings with zero tolerance school policies for guns, knives, and other weapons. The Gun-Free Schools Act (PL 103–227) was enacted in 1994 and mandated that schools expel students for a minimum of 1 year for bringing a gun to school. The federal law was tied to federal funding for public schools through the Elementary and Secondary Education Act (ESEA) of 1965. The ESEA required that federal funding be withheld from school districts that did not enforce the Gun-Free Schools Act. School district policies were contingent on state legislative policies. While the federal law provides a provision to modify expulsion based on extraordinary or mitigating circumstances, states adopted more prescriptive policies that could lead to expulsions (Reyes, 2006). Although the original intent of the 1994 Gun-Free Schools Act remains a priority for all American schools, some have criticized the expansion of zero tolerance policies to all school infractions as an elaborate legal ploy to exclude less desirable students (Reyes, 2001).

School shootings set the context for zero tolerance policies, but the overall need for safe school learning environments framed the context (Reyes, 2006). Evidence from the aftermath of Columbine and successful campus crime prevention efforts show that school climate and good relationships with students are the best crime prevention tools (Vossekuil et al., 2002). The Columbine catastrophe was the impetus for a report by the U.S. Secret Service entitled *The Final Report and Findings of the Safe School Initiative: Implications for the Prevention of Social Attacks in the United States* (Vossekuil et al., 2002). The authors examined 37 incidents of targeted school violence that spanned from 1974 to 2000, involving 41 attackers, and they concluded that other students within the school knew about the pending assault (Vossekuil et al., 2002). In 81% of the attacks, the attacker informed at least one other person that he was thinking about or planning a school attack. In 59% of attacks, more than one person had information about the attack before it took place. These individuals could have prevented the tragedy, but did not report it to authorities. The report further indicates that many of the shooters felt bullied, persecuted, threatened, attacked, or injured by others in school (71%), often being the daily target of others. The video interviews conducted by the Secret Service of the shooters, now in prison, show this level of helplessness and the lack of alternatives. Shooters turned to killing others to end their pain. Vossekuil et al. explain that 93% of shooters planned the school attack in advance, with 61% of attackers listing "revenge" as a motive. The findings of the study and examples like Twenty-Nine Palms, California; Fort Collins, Colorado; and Elmira, New York, suggest that crime prevention comes in investments in adult-to-student communication and relationships using resource personnel, counselors, staff development, and student management (Reyes, 2006; Vossekuil et al., 2002).

Zero Tolerance: The Texas Example

Like many other states, Texas created the Safe Schools Act to comply with a federal mandate. In 1995, the 74th Texas Legislature enacted the Safe Schools Act, Chapter 37, Law and Order of the Texas Education Code. The new discipline code included a section on the student code of conduct; a section on guns, knives, and other weapons; and a section on drugs. The Texas Safe Schools Act did not use the phrase *zero tolerance,* but it did emulate many of the zero tolerance policy requirements, including: (1) a nondiscretional enforcement policy, (2) the highly prescriptive, non-negotiable requirements of zero tolerance policy, and (3) the official removal of all of those in authority, including teachers and administrators, from the student discipline decision-making process. The school's responsibility for discipline became one of complying and enforcing the state law. The policy mandated that school districts' boards of trustees "shall . . . adopt a student code of conduct" (§37.001). The law used the language of "shall (be removed)" for required student removal from the regular classroom and the language of "may (be removed)" when the law specifies administrator flexibility (Reyes, 2006).

Throughout the United States, the role of school administrators is crucial to the administration of zero tolerance policies. The principal or other appropriate administrator, usually an assistant principal, must be responsible for all student removals from the regular instructional class. This does not mean that the administrator has discretion on what to do; it merely means that the administrator provides the official sanction.

The Texas policy for student behavior provides five options for mandatory and discretionary removals out of the regular classroom. The options include: 1) removal to a disciplinary alternative education programs (DAEP), 2) expulsions, 3) out-of-school suspension, 4) in-school suspension, and for urban areas, 5) the Juvenile Justice Alternative Education Program [JJAEP]. (Reyes, 2006)

Officially, the 1994 Gun-Free Schools Act provided the impetus for mandatory student expulsions and suspensions. It conditioned federal aid to the schools upon the state's adoption of policies to remove students who bring weapons to school (Reyes, 2006). The federal policy required that students be removed from school for 1 year. It also mandated that state policy report these students to law enforcement authorities.

Effect of Zero Tolerance

In practice, the policy of Subchapter G, Safe Schools, Chapter 37, Discipline: Law and Order disproportionately affected urban, African American, Hispanic, low-income, at-risk, and male student populations (Reyes, 2006). The 2000–01 Texas Public Education Information Management System (PEIMS) summary data for the state discipline program shows that of the 1,675,746 discipline actions recorded, approximately 95% were for "discretionary reasons" (Reyes, 2006, p. 15). While the intent of the federal policy was to remove guns, drugs, knives, and other weapons, the Texas policy resulted in only 5% of all removals for the intended mandatory removal reasons. A total of 798,666 students were removed from the regular instruction classroom at an average of 2.1 times per student. Zero tolerance policies served to criminalize the behavior of 20% of the state public school enrollment, targeting a disproportionate number of minority students (Reyes, 2006, p. 15).

African American and Hispanic students are removed from the regular classroom at rates that are disproportionately higher than their representation in the state enrollment data. In 2000–01, African Americans made up 14.4%, or 586,712, of the Texas K–12 enrollment (approximately 51% of these were male); however, they represented 22% of the Disciplinary Alternative Education Program (DAEP), 19% of the expulsions, 32% of the more severe out-of-school suspensions, 23% of the less severe in-school suspensions, and 26% of the Texas Juvenile Justice Alternative Education Program (JJAEP; Reyes, 2006, p. 17). In each removal category, 70% to 80% of the removals were African American males (Reyes, 2007). Latinos in 2000–01 made up 40%, or 1,650,560, of the K–12 enrollment in Texas (approximately 51% were male); however, they made up 47% of the expulsions, 43% of the out-of-school suspensions, and 45% of the JJAEP (Reyes, 2006). In each category, Latino males made up 70% to 80% of the removals (Reyes, 2006). An analysis of more current data for 2003–04 shows similar results. For example, in 2003–04 African Americans made up 14.2%, or 616,050, of the state K–12 enrollment (approximately 51% were male); however, they represented 23% of the DAEP, 24% of the expulsions, 34% of the more severe out-of-school suspensions, 24% of the less severe in-school suspensions, and 26% of the JJAEP, with African American males representing approximately 70% to 80% of the removals (Reyes, 2006, 2007).

Violence prevention in schools is a national, rather than a geographic-specific, concern. The U.S. government's national Centers for Disease Control (CDC; 2006) in Atlanta, known for its work in stopping health-related epidemics, sees school violence as a national epidemic issue.

The Perceived Need for Expanded Zero Tolerance Policies

Public concern regarding lack of school discipline helped set the conditions for expanding the use of zero tolerance policies to include lesser disciplinary infractions. While the emotions of murder in the schoolhouse, often repeated by the print and visual media, flamed the growing push for newer, tougher, zero tolerance school policies in state houses across the United States, the national school violence data does not seem to support the rush to implement new school violence policies. The former U.S. Surgeon General, David Satcher, stated that the 2000s have seen a substantial decline in overall violence by youth (Satcher, 2001). Additionally, the CDC's National Youth Risk Behavior Survey reports that school violence has significantly decreased overall from the 1990s (CDC, 2006).

But when we disaggregate the data spanning from 1993 to 2005, we see a mixed picture. The CDC's National Youth Risk Behavior Surveillance Survey, given in 1993 and again in 2005, indicates declines in a few areas with regard to school violence but increases in others (CDC, 2006). The greatest declines are seen in male students' responses to *"carried a weapon into a school at least once in past 30 days."* In 1993, 17.2% of male students answered affirmatively to this question, and in 2005, only 10.2% did. This may be due in part to the increased use of metal detectors in some secondary schools during the 1990s and the Gun-Free Schools Act of 1994 (discussed above, put into practice after the 1993 survey), mandating a 1-year expulsion for bringing firearms to school. Robert Skiba, the director of the Center for Evaluation and Educational Policy at the University of Indiana, in an education policy brief entitled "Zero Tolerance: The Assumptions and the Facts," (2004) concluded that the zero tolerance mandates from the Gun–Free Schools Act were the primary cause in the reduction of guns brought to school, but these mandates had little effect in other areas of school violence. The CDC's Youth Risk Behavior Surveillance Survey (2006) shows that survey respondents felt there were fewer guns brought into school in 2005 than in 1993. But there was an increase in affirmative student responses

to *"were threatened or injured with a weapon"* (Q1) and *"missed school due to safety concerns"* (Q3) from 1993 to 2005. Additionally, female students indicated in three of the five surveyed violence indicators (Q1, Q3, and Q5) that there were increases in school violence, as viewed by female students. Different age groups of students also present different profiles. Using the same CDC data (2006), it becomes apparent that ninth graders are, in general, the most prone to violence in school, even during overall declining periods of national school violence; they have higher percentages of violent behavior than tenth, eleventh, or twelfth graders.

Despite student safety concerns, schools continue to be safer places than either homes or communities (Kaufman et al., 1998) even though the overall threshold of youth violence remains very high. Schools are reflections of the larger society. The United States has the greatest proportion of prison inmates per 100,000 people and one of the highest gun murder rates in the world (3.42 per 100,000 people). England, however, has the lowest gun murder rate in the world (0.04 per 100,000 people)—100 times lower than the United States—according to the Geneva-based Small Arms Survey for 2004 (Graduate Institute of International Studies, 2004).

Making Examples of Some to Deter Others

According to the zero tolerance theory, the goal of a zero tolerance policy is not to rehabilitate an individual, but to deter future infractions by others; consequently, zero tolerance discipline policies may negatively affect the educational potential of those students punished by zero tolerance. Educational consequences of zero tolerance include: (1) being absent from school, (2) falling behind academically, (3) having failing grades, (4) losing contact with one's teacher, (5) losing contact with peers, (6) dropping out of school, and (7) moving down the school-to-prison pipeline (Civil Rights Project, 2000; Reyes, 2006).

The Texas law criminalizes student behavior. Several sections of the law have criminal consequences, including Class A, Class B, Class C, and Class D infractions. Table 16.1 provides a picture of how school policies criminalize often minor infractions. Carrying weapons to school or injuring a peer are very serious violations, but under the Texas law, lesser infractions such as returning to school after dismissal, parking violations, and making noise in class can carry equally severe consequences and affect a youngster for life. The law requires that students be charged, be entered into a national criminal database, pay for court costs, be sentenced, and complete their sentences. Some judges have complained that students are still juveniles, who have the right to expunge their criminal records, yet many low-income students and their families do not have the level of sophistication or the resources to return to the same jurisdiction to expunge their records (Reyes, 2006).

Table 16.1   Texas Education Code Criminal Activities for Student Behavior

Texas Education Code Section	*Activity*	*Offense*
Section 37.102 (c)	Operation and parking violations or vehicles on school property.	Class C misdemeanor
Section 37.107	Trespass on school grounds by unauthorized person. (Includes students who are dismissed at 1:00 p.m. and return to school before 3:30 p.m.)	Class C misdemeanor
Section 37.121	Fraternities, sororities, secret societies, and gangs.	Class C misdemeanor
Section 37.122	Possession of intoxicants on public school grounds.	Class C misdemeanor
Section 37.123	Obstructing or restraining the passage of a person at an exit or entrance by threats of force…without the authorization of the school district.	Class B misdemeanor
Section 37.124	Disruption of classes includes "emitting noise of an intensity that prevents or hinders classroom instruction and enticing or attempting to entice a student away from a class or other school activity that the student is required to attend . . . preventing or attempting to prevent a student from attending a class or other school activity that the student is required to attend; . . . entering a classroom without the consent of either the principal or the teacher, and through either acts of misconduct or the use of loud or profane language, disrupting class. . . ."	Class C misdemeanor
Section 37.126	Disruption of transportation.	Class C misdemeanor
Section 37.152	Personal Hazing Offense: commits . . . solicits . . . reckless permits . . . has firsthand knowledge . . .	Class B misdemeanor
	any offense . . .that does not cause serious bodily injury . . .	Class B misdemeanor
	does cause serious bodily injury . . .	Class A misdemeanor
	causes death of another	State jail felony
Section 25.093	Parents contributing to nonattendance.	Class C misdemeanor (with deferred disposition under Article 45.051, Code of Criminal Procedure)
Section 25.094	Failure to attend school 10 days or more in same school year or three or more days or parts of days within a four-week period.	Class C misdemeanor

SOURCE: Reyes, A. H. (2007). *Where Have All the Young Men Gone?* Symposium at the American Educational Research Association, Chicago, IL.

Avoiding the Jailhouse Connection

According to a study by the Harvard Civil Rights Project, school suspensions and expulsions lead to educational opportunities lost including dropping out of school, but more discouragingly, these exclusions create the school-to-prison pipeline (Civil Rights Project, 2000). According to the study, students who drop out of school and students who are suspended are more likely to also go to prison; students who are suspended are 30% more likely to enter the school-to-prison pipeline (Civil Rights Project, 2000). Gottfredson, Gottfredson, and Hybl (1993) also report that students who misbehave in school are at a higher risk of dropping out of school, abusing substances, and engaging in other delinquent behaviors. Later in life, they have greater problems adjusting to marital and occupational transitions. Texas Appleseed (2007), in collaboration with Advocacy, Inc. and the Texas Public Policy Foundation, produced a brief that reported statewide statistics on the school-to-prison pipeline. Using 2006 data, they found students who are sent to Discipline Alternative Education Placement (DAEP) centers due to inappropriate school behavior have five times the dropout rate of mainstream placements. The report also found that students who drop out are more likely to enter the juvenile justice system and then prison, with 80% of Texas prison inmates being school dropouts (Texas Appleseed, 2007). A pattern of disruptions weighs upon school administrators with thousands of hours spent in responding to disciplinary referrals sent to the office. Unfortunately, most parents are unaware of the potential for their sons or daughters to become part of the criminal justice system as a result of their behavior in classrooms, schools, or school surroundings.

Alternative Approaches to Zero Tolerance

The applications of zero tolerance behavior policies are not consistent across schools or districts, which results in inconsistent consequences for similar infractions. This seems to have a greater negative effect on minority students and those from impoverished economic backgrounds. The Secret Service report (Vossekuil et al., 2002) and subsequent comprehensive studies (Freiberg & Lapointe, 2006) find that hostile peers, uncaring adults, bullied students, and the lack of one person to provide hope for developing adolescents are a formula for further disasters. The killing of students by students is the extreme exception; however, many students dread coming to school, as the answers to the 2005 CDC survey questions "*were threatened or injured with a weapon*" and "*missed school due to safety concerns*" indicate. Both items saw a significant increase in affirmative responses from 1993 to 2005 for male and female respondents. To avoid these negative perceptions, a community's focus on prevention, caring, cooperation, organization, and community can be the key to deterring school violence (Freiberg, 1999). Perhaps acts of violence, dread for school, and threats to student safety may be lessened through caring school communities and nurturing families that work together to promote prosocial behavior and school effectiveness.

Educate Families About Violence

Parents are the first teachers. Recruiting parents' participation in violence prevention must reflect changes in the family, including working parents, caregivers, or single-family homes. Rather than one program or activity that engages parents, multiple approaches are needed that build upon parental interests such as miniworkshops that address individual and family needs, including "How to help your child succeed in school," "Managing a very tight budget," or "Where to find free holiday and weekend family activities." Additionally, parents' skills and education will help to deter their child's participation in media-derived violence. Letting parents know that viewing violence on television is potentially harmful to their child, and may cause violent behavior, should be a first step in violence prevention.

The level of simulated murders and other severe acts of violence in the media are taking their toll. The average elementary-aged child has seen 8,000 murders on television (Straton, 1995), and the growing dominance of video games causes a child or adolescent to be a direct participant in violence. A longitudinal study (Huesmann, Moise-Titus, Podolski, & Eron, 2003) of the effects of violent media on boys and girls showed that a high amount of childhood television-violence viewing correlates significantly with adult aggression 15 years into adulthood. Children that watched the most violent television programs were more likely to demonstrate violent behaviors as adults, including spousal abuse and criminal offenses (Huesmann, Moise-Titus, Podolski, & Eron, 2003). With this knowledge, parents can make better informed decisions while raising their child. Parent

involvement and education are a critical component in deterring school violence.

Begin With the Classroom

The centralized and mandated efforts of zero tolerance policies have shown they vary greatly from school to school and district to district. Improving school safety begins in the classroom. Much of the discussion about safe schools has looked at creating a protective barrier around the school. Yet the interconnectedness between classroom management, instruction, and learning within school has been a missing factor in discussions about safe, caring, and healthy learning environments. The press for self-motivated, active, and independent learners who need to flourish in a technological age is incongruent with learning under rigid school and classroom management practices that emphasize obedience, compliance, and limited participation. This incongruence creates its own levels of pressure and interpersonal conflict between teachers and learners. Changes in curriculum and instruction need to be aligned to instructional management approaches. Alterable variables, such as classroom management, that are classroom based need to be considered in the effort to reform and transform schools. Building systems that are peripheral to improving classroom interaction patterns will seriously limit improvement efforts.

Build School Connectedness

McNeely, Nonnemaker, and Blum (2002) report, "When adolescents feel cared for by people at their school and feel like a part of their school, they are less likely to use substances, engage in violence, or initiate sexual activity at an early age" (p. 138). School social development programs need to foster this feeling of caring and connectedness. Students who feel connected to school in this way also report higher levels of emotional well-being (Resnick et al., 1997). Resnick et al. identified school connectedness as the only school-related variable that was protective for every health risk outcome among adolescents. Programs that promote school connectedness should be sought out and implemented to diminish school violence. McNeely et al. (2002) report, "A classroom management program [Consistency Management and Cooperative Discipline, Freiberg, 1999] that increased school connectedness and promoted self-discipline found that after one year, 30%–100% fewer students were sent to the principal's office for acting out in class, fighting, or assault" (p. 138).

Alterable variables that are classroom-based require more extensive teacher training, both at the teacher preparation level and at the district professional development level. Comprehensive schoolwide discipline, management, and climate programs will reduce the levels and instances of inappropriate student behavior (Freiberg & Lapointe, 2006), resulting in fewer school dropouts (White-Cornelius, 2007). Students who enter the current discipline and juvenile justice systems as a result of minor nonviolent behaviors pay a very high social, emotional, and academic price for their actions that can carry forward for a lifetime.

Refocus Teacher Preparation

The last 20 years have seen a dramatic change in teacher education curriculum and the time it takes to prepare and certify a teacher for the classroom. In the past, certification was a 2-year process and was the exclusive domain of teacher colleges and universities. Now, by taking a narrow curriculum and passing a written exit examination, almost any person may achieve certification through any one of multiple paths from private for-profit companies to school districts and regional centers in just a year or less. One for-profit company will certify a teacher in 1 year by taking mostly Internet, and some face-to-face, classes during the evenings and weekends for as little as $4,000. In the past, knowledge about child and adolescent development, classroom management, learning environments, and content methods were a significant part of a quality teaching preparation.

Under the current system there is little time for learning how to create a safe, caring, and productive learning environment, despite the research that shows such environments have improved both mathematics and reading achievement (Freiberg et al., 2007; White-Cornelius, 2007). With a growing teaching force that is less prepared to draw upon an extensive repertoire of professional knowledge, there is greater reliance on a one-size-fits-all discipline approach. Rigid rules and absolutism have replaced pedagogical common sense based on extensive knowledge of children and youth. It has become evident that teachers for the new millennium need a broader approach, one that enables them to facilitate a continuum of teaching and management approaches.

Teachers need a comprehensive methodology to create classroom and school management systems that reflect greater independence and self-discipline in student learning and behavior. Preparing current and future teachers with the philosophical and pedagogical knowledge and skills needed to prevent minor student infractions from escalating is an important starting point in building student connectedness. When we rely on absolutism and rigid rules, without a comprehensive management approach, too often students become tourists in the classroom rather than active citizens in the teaching and learning process (Freiberg, 1996).

Provide Just-In-Time Professional Development

Efforts to sustain success and reduce violence in schools may require extended support, including staff development beyond what most school districts have provided in the past. Just-in-time staff development synchronizes professional development with teachers' need for knowledge and skills when they need it the most. Staff development in classroom management and student discipline, which is usually presented in August before school begins, should be moved to the time of the year (February, March, and April) when teachers have a high need for new management approaches, enabling teachers the time to assimilate and plan for the effective implementation of new ideas and programs for the fall. Before school workshops would then be refresher sessions that build on previous faculty development activities. Obtaining feedback from others about your teaching is another important key to successful professional development implementation, but obtaining feedback about oneself, with time to reflect, elevates the significance.

Feedback on teaching requires data, and it's this data that can help build a context for the issues and decisions teachers and administrators face daily. Research-driven school profiles, that use a range of data and instruments, should be part of each school's decision-making process. The findings should be for internal use, allowing schools to improve from within. Teams of people from a cross-section of the community should be involved with the school staff to support them in improving teaching and learning, based on the internal findings. Data regarding student discipline referrals, in-school and out-of-school suspensions, and alternative approaches to discipline and management should be a regular part of administrator and faculty or staff meetings. Providing professional development that is built around school data, when teachers and administrators have the opportunity to actually use it, will enhance the teaching and learning environment and provide a proactive and preventive model for educators.

Conclusion

Student behavior continues to be a growing concern for those involved in the education of youth, as well as the broader public. The persistently high levels of violence and the need for safe and caring places to learn is becoming a greater challenge for teachers in all geographic locations. Zero tolerance district policies should focus on their original intent—to eliminate guns and other weapons in schools. We must reduce or eliminate the criminalization of other, far less serious student misbehaviors. The drift away from the original policy has created a third tier of schooling (the second tier being special education) through alternative programs like DEAP, which have shown little long-term success and may become a pipeline to dropping out and later to prison. In order to make the transition from a zero-tolerance-for-everything policy to a rational policy that will keep our children and youth safe, we need to (1) work with families and caregivers to reduce the exposure of children to media violence; (2) build school connectedness to reduce bullying and student isolation and to bring students from being tourists in their schools to becoming citizens; (3) focus on the classroom as the place where change will occur first; (4) use school discipline and climate data to inform teaching and learning practice; (5) refocus on the original intent of zero tolerance policies to keep guns and other weapons out of school; and (6) expand prevention programs that complement the development of student self-discipline within a caring and supportive learning environment.

To begin this process, we must:

- provide a teacher preparation curriculum, regardless of the source, that emphasizes the core elements of teaching and learning that quick certification programs may have missed;
- encourage school districts to offer thematic professional development that enables all adults in the school to work as a team to improve the lives of the children and youth of our nation;
- build regional data centers or work with local colleges and universities that will assist small- to medium-sized school districts in collection, interpretation, and dissemination of discipline and climate data for use by educators and parents in districts and schools;
- create school- and district-level task forces that will semiannually review the results and effect of the zero tolerance and other school district discipline policies and report the findings with recommendations for changes and improvements;
- create statewide review groups to distribute information on the best discipline management programs and systems found nationally and internationally.

There are several issues raised by zero tolerance policies that extend beyond just student behavior and on the learning environment, the family, and the media. Promoting school connectedness, refocusing on teacher preparation and how adults and youth see each other will provide a paradigm shift toward the future. The 21st-century learner needs flexibility, independence, and self-discipline; however, we are anchored to an 18th-century discipline paradigm that we must change.

Acknowledgment

The authors wish to thank Ms. Stacey Lamb, a doctoral student in the Department of Curriculum and Instruction at the University of Houston and previously a fifth-grade teacher in the Spring Branch Independent School District in Houston, Texas, for her research assistance and feedback on this chapter.

References and Further Readings

Brantlinger, E. (1993). Adolescent's interpretation of social class influences on schooling. *Journal of Classroom Interaction, 28*(1), 1–12.

Brophy, J. (1999). Perspectives of classroom management: Yesterday, today, and tomorrow. In H. J. Freiberg (Ed.), *Beyond Behaviorism* (pp. 44–55). Needham Heights, MA: Allyn & Bacon.

Centers for Disease Control (CDC), National Center for Chronic Disease Prevention and Health Promotion. (2005). *Healthy youth! Youth online: Comprehensive results, 2005* [Data file]. Retrieved May 19, 2008, from http://apps.nccd.cdc.gov/yrbss/

Centers for Disease Control and Prevention. (2006, June 9). Youth risk behavior surveillance—United States, 2005. *Morbidity and Mortality Weekly Report, 55*, No. SS-5. Retrieved July 17, 2007, from http://www.cdc.gov/mmwr/PDF/SS/SS5505.pdf

Civil Rights Project (Harvard University). (2000). *Opportunities suspended: The devastating consequences of zero tolerance and school discipline policies.* Report from a National Summit on Zero Tolerance [Proceedings]. Cambridge, MA: Civil Rights Project.

Cohen, E. (1994). *Designing group work: Strategies for the heterogeneous classroom.* New York: Teachers College Press. (Original work published 1986)

Crawley, J. W. (2002, July 29). Military sees drug use rise despite tests and warnings. *San Diego Union-Tribune*, p. A1.

Crime Control Act of 1990. Public Law 101-647 Title I of 42 U.S.C. 46, §3750.

Elam, S., Rose, L., & Gallup, A. (1994). Phi Delta Kappa's 26th Annual Gallup/PDK Poll of the public's attitude towards public schools. *Phi Delta Kappan, 76*(1), 41–56.

Elementary and Secondary Education Act of 1965. 20 U.S.C. 6301 et seq. (PL 89-10).

Evertson, C. M., & Weade, G. (1989). Classroom management and student achievement: Stability and variability in two junior high English classrooms. *Elementary School Journal, 89*(3), 379–393.

Freiberg, H. J. (1994). Understanding resilience: Implications for inner-city schools and their near and far communities. In M. C. Wang & E. W. Gordon (Eds.), *Educational resilience in inner-city America: Challenges and prospects* (pp. 151–165). Hillsdale, NJ: Lawrence Erlbaum Associates.

Freiberg, H. J. (1996). From tourists to citizens in the classroom. *Educational Leadership, 54*(1), 32–36.

Freiberg, H. J. (Ed.). (1999). *Beyond behaviorism: Changing the classroom management paradigm.* Needham Heights, MA: Allyn & Bacon.

Freiberg, H. J., Connell, M. L., & Lorentz, J. (2001). The effects of Consistency Management on student mathematics achievement in seven Chapter I elementary schools. *Journal of Education for Students Placed At Risk, 6*(3), 249–270.

Freiberg, H. J., Huzinec, C. A., & Borders, K. (2007, April). *Classroom management and student achievement: A study of fourteen inner-city elementary schools.* Paper presented at the 2007 American Educational Research Association conference, Chicago, IL.

Freiberg, H. J., & Lapointe, J. M. (2006). Research-based programs for preventing and solving discipline problems. In C. M. Evertson & C. S. Weinstein (Eds.), *Handbook of classroom management: Research, practice, and contemporary issues* (pp. 735–786). Mahwah, NJ: Lawrence Erlbaum Associates.

Freiberg, H. J., Stein, T. A., & Parker, G. (1995). An examination of discipline referrals in an urban middle school. *Education & Urban Society, 27*(4), 421–440.

Gottfredson, D., Gottfredson, G. D., & Hybl, L. G. (1993). Managing adolescent behavior: A multiyear, multischool study. *American Educational Research Journal, 30*(1), 179–215.

Graduate Institute of International Studies. (2004). *Small Arms Survey, 2004: Rights at risk.* Geneva, Switzerland: Oxford University Press. Retrieved August 27, 2007, from http://www.smallarmssurvey.org/files/sas/publications/yearb2004.html

Gun-Free Schools Act of 1994. 20 U.S.C. 8921 (PL 103-882).

Huesmann, L. R., Moise-Titus, J., Podolski, C., & Eron, L. D. (2003). Longitudinal relations between children's exposure to TV violence and their aggressive and violent behavior in young adulthood: 1977–1992. *Developmental Psychology, 39*(1), 201–221.

Kaufman, P., Xianglei, C., Choy, S. P., Chandler, K. A., Chapman, C. D., Rand, M. R., et al. (1998). *Indicators of school crime and safety, 1998* (NCES 98–251, NCJ 172845). Washington, DC: U.S. Department of Education, U.S. Department of Justice.

Kounin, J. S. (1970). *Discipline and group management in classrooms.* New York: Holt, Rinehart & Winston.

McCaslin, M., & Good, T. (1992). Compliant cognition: The misalliance of management and instructional goals in current school reform. *Educational Researcher, 40*(3), 4–17.

McNeely, C. A., Nonnemaker, J. M., & Blum, R. W. (2002). Promoting school connectedness: Evidence from the National Longitudinal Study of Adolescent Health. *Journal of School Health, 72*(4), 138–146.

National Center for Education Statistics. (1998). *Violence and discipline problems in U.S. public schools: 1996–1997* (98–030). Washington, DC: U.S. Department of Education.

National Institute of Education. (1978). *Violent schools—Safe schools. The safe school study report to Congress* (Vol. 1). Washington, DC: Superintendent of Documents, the U.S. Government Printing Office.

Opuni, K. A. (1998). *Project Grad evaluation report.* Houston, TX: Center for Research on School Reform, University of St. Thomas.

Opuni, K. A. (2006). *The effectiveness of the Consistency Management & Cooperative Discipline (CMCD) model as a student empowerment and achievement enhancer: The experiences of two inner-city school systems.* Houston, TX: Center for Research on School Reform, University of St. Thomas.

Opuni, K. A., & Ochoa, M. A. (2002). *Project GRAD-Houston: 2001–2002 Program Evaluation Report.* Houston, TX: Center for Research on School Reform, University of St. Thomas.

Perry, A. (1908). *The management of a city school.* New York: Macmillan.

Resnick, M. D., Bearman, P. S., Blum, R. W., Bauman, K. E., Harris, K. M., Jones, J., et al. (1997). Protecting adolescents from harm: Findings from the National Longitudinal Study on Adolescent Health. *Journal of the American Medical Association, 278*, 823–832.

Reyes, A. H. (2001). Alternative education: The criminalization of student behavior. *Fordham University School of Law Urban Law Journal, 29*(2), 539–559.

Reyes, A. H. (2006). *Discipline, achievement, and race: Is zero tolerance the answer?* Lanham, MD: Rowman & Littlefield.

Reyes, A. H. (2007, April). *Where have all the young men gone?* A paper presented at Symposium at the American Education Research Association, Chicago, IL.

Rogers, C., & Freiberg, H. J. (1994). *Freedom to learn* (3rd ed.). Columbus, OH: Prentice Hall.

Rose, L. C., & Gallup, A. M. (2002, September; 2003, September; 2004, September; 2005, September; 2006, September). 34th–38th Annual Phi Delta Kappa/Gallup Polls of the public's attitude towards the public schools. *Phi Delta Kappan.* Retrieved August 13, 2007, from http://www.pdkintl.org/kappan/kpollpdf.htm

Satcher, D. (2001, January). *Youth violence: A report of the surgeon general.* Washington, DC: U.S. Department of Health and Human Services. Retrieved July 17, 2007, from http://www.surgeongeneral.gov/library/youthviolence/youvioreport.htm

Sharon, S. (1993). *Handbook on cooperative learning methods.* Westport, CT: Greenwood.

Skiba, R. (2004). *Zero tolerance: The assumptions and the facts* (Education Policy Briefs 2, No. 1). Bloomington: Indiana University, Center for Evaluation & Educational Policy.

Straton, J. (1995). *How students have changed: A call to action for our children's future.* Alexandria, VA: American Association of School Administrators.

Texas Appleseed. (2007). *Keeping schools safe while reducing dropouts.* Retrieved September 12, 2007, from http://www.texasappleseed.net/projects_school-to-prison.shtml

Texas Education Code Annotated. §37.002 (b)(1)- §37.152. Vernon Supp *Law and Order.* Vernon Supp. (2006).

Vossekuil, B., Fein, R. A., & Reddy, M. (2002). The final report and findings of the Safe School Initiative: Implications for the prevention of social attacks in the United States. Washington, DC: United States Secret Service and United States Department of Education.

Wang, M. C., Haertel, G. D., & Walberg, H. J. (1993). Toward a knowledge base for school learning. *Review of Educational Research, 63,* 249–294.

Weade, G., & Evertson, C. M. (1988). The construction of lessons in effective and less effective classrooms. *Teaching and Teacher Education, 4*(3), 1–18.

White-Cornelius, J. (2007). Learner-centered teacher-student relationships are effective: A meta-analysis. *Review of Educational Research, 77*(1), 113–143.

PART V

LEARNING

17

BEHAVIORAL

TIMOTHY J. LANDRUM
University of Virginia

KIMBERLY A. McDUFFIE
Clemson University

A behavioral view of teaching and learning is based on the fundamental idea that behavior is controlled by its consequences. Put simply, behaviors that are followed by consequences that are perceived as pleasant or desirable tend to occur more frequently. Conversely, behaviors that are followed by unpleasant or undesirable consequences tend to occur less frequently. There are at least five common behavioral operations based on this general principle, and each is described briefly in this chapter. These include positive reinforcement, negative reinforcement, extinction, response cost punishment, and punishment using aversives. Note that the last of these—the application of aversives—is highly controversial, and in educational contexts the use of aversives has been all but abolished.

Behavioral theory is seen at work in education most obviously in the management of classroom behavior, but its theories and operations can be used to teach, enhance, and maintain a number of specific social and academic behaviors as well. Subsequent sections of this chapter include (a) a brief overview of behavioral theory, (b) a description of the basic behavioral operations that form the foundation of educational practice from a behavioral perspective, (c) several examples of how these operations might be observed in or applied to classroom practice, and (d) discussion of the practical limitations of a behavioral view, including common criticisms of a behavioral approach to teaching.

Behavioral Theory

Behavioral theory was well established in the first half of the 20th century in experimental and clinical settings as researchers examined a number of behavioral operations that could be used to modify and shape the behavior of animals and later humans. John B. Watson is often credited with introducing the foundational concepts of behaviorism in the early 1900s. Watson also emphasized a more objective focus in psychology, which contradicted much of the prevailing thought of his time. Instead of focusing on thoughts, feelings, or unobservable introspections, Watson believed that psychology would benefit tremendously by taking a more objective view of observable behavior. Beginning in the 1930s, the most prominent behavioral scholar was B. F. Skinner, whose work was important in his description and elaboration of the fundamentals of *operant conditioning*. Operant conditioning encompasses several principles which form the basis for the behavioral techniques that have become hallmarks of behaviorism as applied to teaching and learning in classrooms. The most important among these may be reinforcement, punishment, and extinction. Briefly, reinforcement refers to an increase in the frequency of responding, punishment refers to a decrease in the frequency of responding, and extinction refers to a decrease in the frequency of a previously reinforced response. A fuller definition of these principles and applied examples of each are provided in subsequent sections of this chapter.

The layperson most often envisions early behavioral theorists and researchers teaching white rats or pigeons to press a bar or touch a button to receive a reward; indeed, it is true that much of the early work in behavioral theory focused on animals in laboratory settings. In the latter half of the 20th century behavioral theory was applied in earnest to education. In the 1960s, tremendous growth occurred in the application of behavioral theory to classroom learning and behavior problems, and an emphasis on research in applied (i.e., real) settings became increasingly common. The systematic application of behavioral theory to clinical problems marked the development of *applied behavior analysis*—a method for the study of behavior and analysis of the variables that cause or set the stage for behavior to occur (i.e., antecedents), as well as the variables that determine whether a behavior is likely to increase or diminish in occurrence (i.e., consequences). This type of analysis of behavior, a careful and systematic look at sequences of antecedent-behavior-consequence (frequently referred to as A–B–C analysis), has become a hallmark of teachers' efforts to analyze and solve classroom behavior problems, and also provides the foundation for more formal applications of functional analysis, or functional behavior analysis (FBA). In fact, in the 1997 amendments to the Individuals with Disabilities Education Act (IDEA), specific language was included requiring educators to conduct an FBA for students with disabilities exhibiting severe behavior problems. The rich literature that has accrued in the area of applied behavior analysis in the last half of the 20th century has provided educators a substantial research base from which to draw when addressing learning and behavioral problems in classrooms. The next section delineates the most commonly used and useful behavioral procedures this literature has made available to educators.

Methods: Basic Behavioral Operations

The five basic behavioral operations that are most readily applied to teaching and learning include (a) positive reinforcement, (b) negative reinforcement, (c) extinction, (d) response cost punishment, and (e) punishment involving the application of aversives.

Positive Reinforcement

The concept of reinforcement is often misunderstood, and the need to distinguish between positive reinforcement and negative reinforcement may add to this confusion. Consider first the term *reinforcement* itself. It is important to note that the term reinforcement describes an *effect*, namely that a behavior is strengthened or made more likely to occur by the consequences that follow it. Thus, if a teacher or parent implements some form of consequence after the occurrence of a behavior, and the behavior is observed to be more likely to occur as a result, then reinforcement is said to have occurred. Conversely, consequences that are implemented following behavior that do not affect the likelihood of behavior occurring again—regardless of the intent of the person providing the consequence—cannot be said to result in reinforcement. In practice, teachers make a common semantic error when they say that they tried "reinforcement," but it didn't work or that they have given students some type of "reinforcement," but that the students' behavior did not improve. Again, a particular consequence is said to be a reinforcer when and only when its contingent use results in increased rates or likelihood of behavior occurring.

The notion of contingency is a critical element of the definition of reinforcement, but this may easily escape the notice of teachers in day-to-day classroom practice. To use behavioral theory to influence behavior, consequences that follow a behavior cannot occur at random or only some of the time. Consequences must occur contingently. In order to conclude that a particular consequence has an effect on a specific behavior, the effect of that consequence must be assessed when it is applied *when and only when* the behavior in question occurs. Suppose a teacher has trouble with students who show up late for class. The teacher decides to give points to students when they are on time to class. Points can be exchanged later for computer time, and the teacher believes that this consequence might increase the rate at which students come to class on time. If the teacher only awards these points on some of the occasions that students are on time, or worse, awards points occasionally when students show up late, the contingency requirement is violated. There would be no basis upon which to draw any conclusion at all in this case about the effectiveness of points for computer time as a reinforcer for coming to class on time.

Note in the preceding example that if the teacher had been able to implement this consequence contingently, always giving points to students who were on time and never awarding points to students who were late, a conclusion could be drawn about the effect of this consequence. If arrival to class on time improved, even for some students, it could be concluded that points for computer time indeed served as a reinforcer for on-time arrival for these students. If the arrival of other students was not influenced, it would further be concluded that computer time was not a reinforcer for these particular students' on-time arrival. This latter notion, that some consequences are reinforcing for certain behaviors in some students but not necessarily in others, presents a challenge to teachers to continually monitor the effect of all of their behavior management strategies on all students.

Given that the term *reinforcement* refers only to the effect that is observed when a behavior is made more likely to occur, a further distinction must be drawn between positive reinforcement and negative reinforcement. It may be easiest to grasp the distinction between the two by associating the term *positive* with adding and the term *negative* with subtracting, or taking away. *Positive reinforcement,* then, is the effect that occurs when a behavior is strengthened because something is added to a situation by a teacher, parent, or other caregiver. (In fact, consequences need not be added by a person; some consequences are said to be naturally occurring, such as the classic example of a child touching a hot stove.) Note that what is added to the situation can take many forms. A social gesture or positive words (e.g., praise, a smile, a pat on the back), an activity or privilege (e.g., extra recess, time to play a computer game, choice of where to eat lunch), or a tangible object (e.g., food, toys, or stickers) can have a reinforcing effect on behavior.

Behavioral theory posits that behavior is maintained by consequences; it does not matter whether those consequences are planned or delivered intentionally. It is for this reason that the A–B–C analysis described earlier may be quite valuable for teachers. Consider the following example: A student disrupts class by asking irrelevant questions or making off-task comments (e.g., What time is lunch? or This class is boring.). A teacher would be wise to analyze what happens when this behavior occurs to help determine what consequences are maintaining this behavior, or making it more likely to occur. For example, do other students laugh? Does the teacher come over and give the child individual attention? In such cases, the student's disruptive behavior may be reinforced, even though this is clearly not what the teacher wanted or intended to happen.

Negative Reinforcement

If positive reinforcement refers to the effect of a behavior being strengthened when something is added, it is easy to understand that negative reinforcement refers to a behavior being strengthened when something is taken away. The logic here is that with positive reinforcement, what is added when a behavior occurs must be something desirable, at least for that particular student. With negative reinforcement, what is taken away must be perceived as unpleasant or undesirable by the student if its removal is to have the effect of strengthening a behavior. Two examples are common in schools. Suppose a teacher promises students that if they work hard and complete an entire assignment before the class period ends, they will not be given a homework assignment for that evening. If students increase their work behavior and effort during class in order to complete the assignment, and thus avoid the homework assignment, then negative reinforcement has occurred. That is, their work behavior in class increased because of the removal of a consequence they wished to avoid. Consider a situation in which students who earn A's for each grading period during the academic year are exempted from taking a final exam for a given course. If in fact particular students' effort, work behavior, accuracy, or productivity increased during the year, we could say that these behaviors were negatively reinforced. In practice, teachers may seldom plan and use negative reinforcement

intentionally; one reason for this is that some sort of negative or undesirable consequence must be in place for them to remove. Unfortunately, negative reinforcement may be at work in a much more common way that can reciprocally influence the behavior of both teachers and students. This is known as the negative reinforcement trap.

The Negative Reinforcement Trap

In the early 1980s, Gerald Patterson described the negative reinforcement trap in terms of coercion that often occurs within families (e.g., Patterson, 1982). He described a process in which a child might be directed by a parent to complete a task or chore, such as cleaning the bedroom. Finding the request and the prospect of cleaning the room unpleasant, the child resists, complains, and whines, which results in the parent repeating the request, perhaps with greater emotion and increasing threats of punishment. A negative cycle of nagging and whining often follows, with each participant escalating the negative behavior they are displaying toward the other. What Patterson described as the negative reinforcement trap, however, occurs when a parent gives in. If a parent, understandably stressed by the child's whining and complaining and possibly facing a multitude of other family and work responsibilities as well, finally relents and stops demanding that the child clean the bedroom, the whining and complaining predictably stop as well. But what has happened according to behavioral theory is that the behavior of both parties—the negative behavior—may have been negatively reinforced, and thus may be more likely to occur in the future, perpetuating this negative cycle. The child obviously found the parent's demands, nagging, and the prospect of cleaning the room unpleasant; the child wished to avoid these. By whining and complaining, the child accomplished this goal. The whining was negatively reinforced because an unpleasant consequence (cleaning the room, the parent's nagging) was removed. We would predict based on this exchange that the child will whine and complain again the next time the parent makes this same request.

The danger of the negative reinforcement trap, however, lies in what happens to the parent. The parent's clear goal was to have the child clean the bedroom, but this goal was waylaid by the child's complaining and whining. Assuming the parent found the whining aversive and wished to avoid it, we might conclude that the parent's relenting (ceasing the demanding and nagging) was also negatively reinforced. Thus we would predict that this behavior too will be more likely to occur in the future. It is precisely because each participant's behavior was negatively reinforced that Patterson termed such interchanges *negative reinforcement traps.*

Consider a classroom example of the negative reinforcement trap. If a student disrupts a math class persistently and with increasing intensity, a teacher may be taxed to the point that he or she considers removal of the student from the room the only option. Perhaps the student is sent to the hallway, to another teacher's room, or to the office (in theory to complete class work independently). This interchange carries the hallmark characteristics of a negative reinforcement trap. The teacher found the student's disruptions aversive, and sending the student out of the room removed that aversive. The teacher may now be more likely to remove students from the room in the future when they are disruptive. It seems highly likely that the student found math class (or perhaps just this particular topic, assignment, or teacher) less than enjoyable (i.e., aversive) and wished to avoid it. The disruptive behavior was negatively reinforced when the demands of math class were essentially taken away. It is now predictable that this student will disrupt class again in the future when he or she finds it aversive, and more important, the teacher will be more likely to remove the student from the classroom. As with the parenting example, both parties got what they wanted in the short term, but the ultimate goals (cleaning the bedroom and participating appropriately in math class) were not accomplished. The interchange is a trap because both parties' behavior was negatively reinforced.

Extinction

If reinforcing consequences have come to maintain the occurrence of a particular behavior, it is also predictable that if those consequences cease or are taken away, the behavior will decrease. The cessation of behavior when the consequences supporting it are withdrawn is called *extinction*. In classrooms, extinction is important in at least two ways. The first is in the application of extinction by planned ignoring. Students often engage in disruptive or off-task behavior because it garners the attention of others. Suppose a child calls out answers, makes inappropriate comments, or asks irrelevant questions during a lesson or activity that requires hand raising before responding. If the teacher attends to these off-task responses, even in a seemingly neutral or negative way (e.g., "We're not talking about lunch now" or "Please don't call out answers before you raise your hand"), it is possible that this attention is reinforcing, causing the behavior to re-occur. In this case, the teacher may choose to ignore the off-task comments, instead focusing on students who are raising their hands or otherwise responding appropriately. According to behavioral theory, the disruptive student's off-task comments will decrease when the attention that was supporting them is no longer provided.

There are two important caveats for the teacher considering the use of extinction in this way. The first is to be aware of an *extinction burst,* a predictable but temporary increase in the behavior that is being ignored. The extinction burst is quite understandable; if a student is acting out in order to get attention from peers or teachers, and suddenly they ignore the student's acting out, a logical response would be to act out more, or more loudly, to try to get the attention he or she is used to receiving. While such an increase is predictable, so too is the cessation that

occurs as long as the attention or other reinforcer that was originally supporting the behavior is not reintroduced. The second caveat is to be certain that it is teacher attention that is supporting or maintaining the behavior in the first place. If a student is acting inappropriately because it garners the laughter or attention of classmates, there is no reason for a teacher to try ignoring such behavior.

The desirable behavior students display, and which teachers hope will continue to occur, is also subject to extinction if positive consequences are withdrawn. If students have learned that assignment completion or appropriate playground, hallway, or bus behavior, for example, results in some form of reinforcement, they may well discontinue this positive behavior if positive consequences that originally supported these behaviors are withdrawn. Thus a behavioral theorist might argue that even students who seem to display positive behavior without obvious or overt systems of reinforcement in place probably still need at least intermittent reinforcement in some form so that their positive behavior is recognized and does not diminish.

In addition to the reinforcements that typify most of behavioral theory as it is applied to education, there are procedures designed to decrease behavior. *Punishment* refers to the effect of a behavior becoming less likely to occur as a result of some contingency. There are two broad types of punishment: response cost punishment and punishment involving the application of aversives.

Response Cost Punishment

Many educators, and particularly special educators, favor a strong emphasis on positive procedures to increase appropriate behavior. A part of the theory underlying an all-positive emphasis is that as appropriate behavior is taught and reinforced, there are fewer opportunities for students to engage in inappropriate or negative behavior. Many times the strategy used by teachers is to teach incompatible behaviors to replace negative behavior. To eliminate students' out-of-seat behavior, teachers can simply reinforce in-seat behavior. To reduce talking out in class, they can reinforce students for listening quietly to the teacher or others. But research suggests that positive-only procedures may fall short of dealing effectively with all negative behavior. Response cost punishment offers one alternative procedure for responding to negative behavior in a way that will reduce it. Put simply, response cost punishment is the removal of some portion of an earned reinforcer contingent upon the occurrence of an undesirable behavior. Suppose that students earn points during the day for turning in their homework, completing class assignments, displaying appropriate behavior in the classroom, and the like. They accumulate points throughout the day that can be exchanged at a later time for some social, tangible, or activity reward. To use response cost, a teacher takes away an earned point or points when misbehavior occurs. The negative response (misbehavior) thus costs the students some measure of reinforcement. The major benefit of a response cost system is that a student who misbehaves at one point during the day, but otherwise has had a productive, positive day, will still earn most of the available reinforcement. Response cost systems work especially well within management systems that use points or tokens. Students earn points for a variety of prosocial or positive academic behaviors they might engage in, but they also lose points for negative or disruptive behavior. In this system it is particularly important that students clearly understand the rules and consequences, knowing exactly what behaviors and responses earn them points as well as those that cause them to lose points. It is also critical that students have ample opportunities to earn reinforcement before losing any for misbehavior, as well as opportunities to essentially earn back reinforcers they have lost.

Punishment Involving the Application of Aversives

As mentioned previously, the use of aversives is highly controversial and has been all but abolished in most educational settings. The theory underlying aversives is the opposite of positive reinforcement. The contingent application of an aversive stimulus—one that causes physical or emotional pain or discomfort—will result in a decrease in the likelihood of occurrence of behavior. Aversives can range from harsh physical punishments, like spanking or hitting, to milder aversives that cause emotional rather than physical discomfort, such as scolding or verbal reprimands. There are three dangers of harsh aversives: (a) the use of aversives provides a model of aggressive, negative behavior for students; (b) applying aversives does not teach students positive behavior (i.e., it does not show students what to do, focusing instead only on what not to do); and (c) aversives may teach students to avoid the person applying the punishment rather than to stop engaging in the behavior.

In contrast to harsh aversives, there is some evidence that milder aversives can be effective in reducing misbehavior, especially when combined with other positive procedures designed to teach and reinforce appropriate behavior. "Soft reprimands," as described by O'Leary, Kaufman, Kass, and Drabman (1970), can be especially effective. According to the work of O'Leary et al., and more recently Walker, Ramsey, and Gresham (2004), an effective reprimand simply tells a student that a particular behavior is unacceptable, explains why it is unacceptable, and tells the student what to do instead. Moreover, appropriate reprimands are not delivered in public and are delivered calmly and quickly.

Applications of Basic Behavioral Operations

Examples of the most common behavioral procedures typically applied or observed in classrooms are teacher praise, the use of token systems, and the combination of reinforcement approaches with extinction, known as differential

reinforcement. Because the notion of contingency is important to all of these procedures, it is reiterated here.

Many behavioral procedures are named using the term *contingency* or *contingent*. For example, in the literature on teacher praise, the term *contingent teacher attention* is often used. Teachers and others concerned with managing behavior must be carefully attuned to the extent to which any consequences that occur are truly contingent upon the occurrence of a targeted behavior. The term *contingent* means simply that the consequence occurs when and only when the behavior in question occurs. Suppose a teacher wishes to know whether providing stickers to students will improve their rates of on-task behavior. To assess this, the teacher must provide stickers to students when and only when they are on task; if stickers are provided when students are not on task or to some students who are on task and some who are not on task, the teacher will never know for sure what effect stickers have on students' on-task behavior.

Teacher Praise

Teacher praise, or contingent teacher attention, is among the most researched interventions teachers can use to enhance the social and academic behavior of students. Strain, Lambert, Kerr, Stagg, and Lenkner (1983) observed that "literally hundreds of classroom based studies have shown that teachers' delivery of social reinforcement can result in improved academic performance . . . rule following and good school deportment . . . cognitive and linguistic performance . . . and increased social responsiveness" (p. 243). The idea behind teacher praise is simple: it is positive reinforcement that uses social attention from the teacher as the reinforcer.

There are several elements associated with the effective use of teacher praise. First, praise must be contingent, occurring when and only when the desired behavior occurs. Second, praise must occur in close temporal proximity to the behavior. Telling a child today that his or her behavior on the playground yesterday was very good may have little direct effect on playground behavior. Finally, praise must be motivational; the words and tone must convey to the student that his or her work, effort, or behavior was of high quality (e.g., "Nice work!" or "Great job!") or was greatly appreciated (e.g., "Thanks so much for doing that!"). But these motivational statements alone are not effective unless coupled with more information about how or why the work or effort was of high quality. For example, if a student has crafted a particularly well-written paragraph, a simple "nice job!" is unlikely to produce much effect. It would be more effective to add specific information such as "your paragraph has as great topic sentence and several very specific supporting details."

Token Systems

Reinforcement may take many forms, including social gestures, activities or privileges, or tangible objects.

Because delivering some of these in the context of classrooms and teaching is not always feasible (e.g., using food reinforcers for individual responses during an academic lesson), token or point systems have been developed to very effectively provide the same reinforcing effect. With token systems, some marker (perhaps a physical token or chip, maybe a checkmark or star on a chart) is used to represent the actual reinforcer that will be delivered later. The token provides immediate feedback to the student that he or she has just displayed the desired behavior. The rules and rewards associated with token or point systems are explained to students in advance so that they know specifically how to earn points and what points may be exchanged for later. Such systems can be tailored easily to the needs and characteristics of individual classrooms and students. Where needs are greatest, for example with younger children or with those who display high rates of negative or disruptive behavior, a more frequent exchange of points for more powerful reinforcers may be necessary. This might involve the opportunity to exchange points as frequently as the end of each class period; perhaps a student earns some tangible reward or minutes of a preferred activity at the end of class if he or she has completed work satisfactorily and exhibited an acceptable level of appropriate behavior. With older students or those whose learning or behavioral difficulties are not as great, the exchange of points may be less frequent. For these students the exchange of points for desired items or preferred activities might occur only at the end of a school day or even at the end of the week.

Differential Reinforcement

Although the utility of both reinforcement and extinction for helping students improve their behavior has been well established, it is perhaps the combination of the two that occurs most frequently in classrooms and produces the greatest benefit. Indeed, it would be unusual to observe a classroom situation in which one is used exclusive of the other. The teacher who decides to use extinction by ignoring a student's off-task comments during a lesson, for example, will surely attend positively to those students who are paying attention and responding appropriately. This strategy, sometimes called praise-and-ignore, applies to individual students as well as to groups. The individual student is praised when he or she is on task, or behaving or responding appropriately, and ignored when behavior is off task. The teacher applying this strategy to a larger group in the classroom likewise looks for students who are on task, complying with requests, or participating appropriately in a lesson or activity, and praises those students for their efforts. At the same time, students who are disruptive or otherwise noncompliant are ignored, at least temporarily. In such cases, it is important for the teacher to provide positive attention as soon as a previously off-task student begins attending or participating appropriately.

Limitations and Criticisms of a Behavioral View

Despite a rich empirical basis, a behavioral view of teaching and learning has been subject to significant criticism. Three of the most common criticisms are that behavioral procedures (a) are akin to bribery or coercion for good behavior; (b) might improve behavior or responding temporarily in the presence of programmed reinforcers, but these effects do not generalize; and (c) undermine students' intrinsic motivation.

Bribery and Coercion

Concerns about bribery and coercion suggest that students may be coerced into behaving in ways that they might not otherwise choose, and it is indeed possible that behavioral procedures could be used in unethical ways. The notions of coercion and bribery, however, are typically applied to situations in which individuals are induced to commit immoral or unethical acts. The foundations of applied behavior analysis and most textbooks on the topic provide a clear emphasis on the ethical use of such procedures. Ethical use of applied behavior analysis requires that behavioral procedures be used to improve students' positive behavior and reduce or eliminate negative behaviors in ways that increase students' independence or enhance their dignity. This includes changing behavior in ways that help students achieve academic and school success, as well as prepare students for work or other postschool environments. A second element of this principle is that parents or guardians, as well as students themselves, must be key participants in establishing behavioral goals.

Failure to Generalize

When teachers or parents use behavioral procedures effectively, the desired effects of an intervention are often seen readily in the context in which the intervention is implemented. But the ultimate goal of any behavioral intervention is to engender lasting change in behavior that occurs at other times, in other places, and in other, different contexts. For example, teachers hope that the behaviors their students learn in their classroom will generalize to other classrooms. In fact, the criticism that behavioral procedures often fail to produce generalized responding has proven valid to some extent. In a landmark paper published in 1977, Stokes and Baer reviewed some 270 behavior intervention studies and found that approximately 120 of these contributed to what they called an emerging "technology of generalization" (p. 350). Unfortunately, at that time the largest number of studies reviewed fell into a category Stokes and Baer called "train and hope" (1977, p. 351). In other words, in most studies researchers did not program for generalization at all.

Researchers have since focused increasingly on ways to actively program for generalization, and a number of the strategies originally described by Stokes and Baer have proven successful in this regard. For example, programming common stimuli introduces elements of the original intervention or intervention setting into other environments to encourage students to display similar behavior in those environments. Introduction to natural maintaining contingencies relies on the idea that there are naturally occurring reinforcers that will help maintain behavior if students are exposed to them. For example, a teacher may teach antisocial students how to initiate positive interactions with other students on the playground by using modeling, direct instruction, and role-playing activities in the classroom. If the teacher then arranges for students to practice initiating positive interactions on the playground, and as a result of practicing these new skills, the antisocial students are invited to join in games or activities by other students, the newly taught behaviors may come to be supported by naturally occurring outcomes.

Extrinsic Rewards and Intrinsic Motivation

A criticism of the traditional behavioral view that was popularized by Alfie Kohn in the 1990s suggested that students' intrinsic motivation is undermined by the introduction of artificial, extrinsic rewards. Indeed, Kohn and few others have essentially called for an end to the use of praise and other forms of reinforcement (e.g., Kohn, 1993). Other scholars questioned Kohn's ideas and offered reviews of the behavioral literature, which lent significant support to the idea that rewarding consequences are an essential part of effective classroom and behavior management, particularly for students experiencing significant behavioral challenges (e.g., Cameron & Pierce, 1994). Given the hundreds of studies that have shown positive effects of behavioral procedures on the social and academic behavior of students of all ages and ability levels, it would seem unwise for teachers not to make use of such tools.

Conclusion

The behavioral approach to teaching and learning is based on decades of research documenting the positive effects of consequences on improving students' academic and social behavior. A number of specific behavioral operations are based on the fundamental idea that behavior is controlled by its consequences. These include positive reinforcement, negative reinforcement, extinction, response cost punishment, and punishment involving the application of aversives. Examples of these operations can be seen in classroom applications of such things as teacher praise, token reinforcement systems, and differential reinforcement. Critics of the behavioral view posit that behaviors learned in one setting do not generalize to other times and places and that extrinsic rewards somehow undermine students' intrinsic motivation. Although generalization continues to be a concern and researchers are increasingly addressing generalization in the context of intervention research, the overwhelming body of literature on basic behavioral procedures supports this approach as a research-based set of teaching and management tools that teachers should be familiar and proficient with if they are to provide students with the best opportunity to experience social and academic success.

References and Further Readings

Alber, S. R., & Heward, W. L. (1997). Recruit it or lose it! Training students to recruit positive teacher attention. *Intervention in School and Clinic, 32,* 275–282.

Alberto, P., & Troutman, A. (2006). *Applied behavior analysis for teachers* (7th ed.). Upper Saddle River, NJ: Prentice Hall.

Brophy, J. (1981). Teacher praise: A functional analysis. *Review of Educational Research, 51,* 5–32.

Cameron, J., & Pierce, W. D. (1994). Reinforcement, reward, and intrinsic motivation: A meta-analysis. *Review of Educational Research, 64,* 363–423.

Hall, R. V., Lund, D., & Jackson, D. (1968). Effects of teacher attention on study behavior. *Journal of Applied Behavior Analysis, 1,* 1–12.

Kohn, A. (1993). *Punished by rewards.* Boston: Houghton Mifflin.

Maag, J. W. (2001). Rewarded by punishment: Reflections on the disuse of positive reinforcement in schools. *Exceptional Children, 67,* 173–186.

O'Leary, K. D., Kaufman, K. F., Kass, R. E., & Drabman, R. S. (1970). The effects of loud and soft reprimands on the behavior of disruptive students. *Exceptional Children, 37,* 145–155.

Patterson, G. R. (1982). *Coercive family process.* Eugene, OR: Castalia Publishing Company.

Stokes, T. F., & Baer, D. M. (1977). An implicit technology of generalization. *Journal of Applied Behavior Analysis, 10,* 349–367.

Strain, P. S., Lambert, D. L., Kerr, M. M., Stagg, V., & Lenkner, D. A. (1983). Naturalistic assessment of children's compliance to teachers' requests and consequences for compliance. *Journal of Applied Behavior Analysis, 16,* 243–249.

Walker, H. M., Ramsey, E., & Gresham, F. M. (2004). *Antisocial behavior in schools: Strategies and best practices* (2nd ed.). Pacific Grove, CA: Brooks/Cole.

18

Information Processing

Richard E. Mayer

University of California, Santa Barbara

The primary goal of education is to help people learn. More specifically, the goal is to help people learn in ways that will allow them to use what they have learned in new situations—a process that can be called *problem-solving transfer* (Mayer & Wittrock, 2006). To accomplish this goal, it is useful for educators to have a clear understanding of how the human mind works.

This chapter explores the information processing view of learning, which currently offers the most comprehensive, best supported, and most widely accepted theory of how people learn (Bransford, Brown, & Cocking, 1999; Bruning, Schraw, Norby, & Ronning, 2004; Mayer, 2008). In this chapter, I summarize the main tenets of information processing theory; compare information processing theory with other views of learning; summarize the implications of information processing theory for learning, instructing, and assessing; summarize contributions of the information processing view in education including psychologies of subject matter, cognitive process instruction, and instructional design; and explore future directions for theories of learning in 21st-century education.

Theory

Humans are processors of information. This simple statement summarizes the essence of information processing theory. According to the information processing view of how the human mind works, people take in information from the outside world through their eyes and ears, construct an internal mental representation, apply cognitive processes that mentally manipulate the representation, and use their representations to plan and carry out actions. As you can see, two key elements in information processing theory are cognitive representations and cognitive processes. Information from the outside world is transformed in the learner's cognitive system by cognitive representations; cognitive processes then perform mental computations, or the systematic manipulation of the learner's knowledge.

In short, the "information" part of information processing refers to the learner's cognitive representations and the "processing" part of information processing refers to the learner's cognitive processes. Human information processing involves building, manipulating, and using cognitive representations. According to the information processing view, learning involves cognitive processing aimed at building cognitive representations.

Research in cognitive science offers three important principles that should be part of any educationally relevant theory of how people learn (Mayer, 2001, 2005a):

1. *Dual channels*: People have separate channels for processing verbal material and pictorial material (Paivio, 1986).
2. *Limited capacity*: Within each channel people are able to attend to only a few pieces of information at any one time (Baddeley, 1999; Sweller, 1999).
3. *Active processing*: Meaningful learning occurs when people engage in appropriate cognitive processing during

learning, including attending to relevant incoming material, mentally organizing the material into a coherent cognitive structure, and integrating the material with relevant existing knowledge (Mayer, 2001; Wittrock, 1989).

Information Processing Model of Learning

Figure 18.1 presents a framework for describing the human information processing system based on the principles described above (Mayer, 2001). Information from the outside world—such as a textbook lesson or a teacher-led classroom demonstration—enters the learner's cognitive system through the eyes and ears and is represented briefly in sensory memory. If the learner pays attention, some of the material is transferred to working memory for further processing (as indicated by the selecting words and selecting images arrows in Figure 18.1). Next, the learner may engage in deeper cognitive processing of the material in working memory, such as mentally organizing the material (as indicated by the organizing words and organizing images arrows) and integrating it with relevant prior knowledge from long-term memory (as indicated by the integrating arrow), and the resulting learning outcome can be stored in long-term memory.

Three Kinds of Memory Stores

As you can see, this information processing framework has three main memory stores: sensory memory, working memory, and long-term memory. Sensory memory is an unlimited but temporary store for holding incoming sensory information in which visual images and sounds last for a fraction of a second. Sensory information that impinges on the eyes is temporarily held as a fleeting visual image in visual sensory memory, and sensory information that

impinges on the ears is temporarily held as a fleeting sound in auditory sensory memory. Working memory is a limited-capacity store in which a few pieces of incoming and retrieved material can be held and processed. Aspects of the visual images that are attended to are held in working memory as pictorial images and, when mentally organized by the learner, can be converted into a coherent pictorial representation (i.e., a pictorial model). Aspects of the auditory sounds that are attended to are held in working memory as sounds and, when mentally organized by the learner, can be converted into a coherent verbal representation (i.e., a verbal model). Further processing occurs in working memory as connections are built between the verbal and visual models with relevant knowledge retrieved from long-term memory. Thus, working memory is the venue for knowledge construction, but the amount of knowledge that can be held and the amount of processing that can take place at any one time is subject to capacity limitations. Long-term memory has unlimited capacity and is the storehouse for knowledge that has been constructed in working memory.

Three Kinds of Cognitive Processes During Learning

As you also see in Figure 18.1, this framework has three main kinds of cognitive processes: selecting, organizing, and integrating. By attending to aspects of material in sensory memory, the learner can transfer it to working memory for further processing. In Figure 18.1, selecting is indicated by the arrows from sensory memory to working memory. By mentally organizing the material in working memory, the learner can construct a coherent cognitive structure. Organizing is indicated by the arrows within working memory. By retrieving relevant prior knowledge and connecting it logically with incoming material in working memory, the learner can construct a meaningful

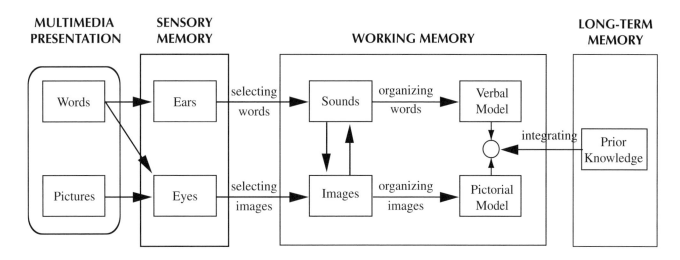

Figure 18.1 Human Information Processing System

learning outcome. Integrating is indicated by the arrow from long-term memory to working memory. In addition, the learner can make connections between corresponding aspects of the verbal and pictorial models as indicated by the arrow between them.

Active cognitive processing for meaningful learning requires that the learner engage in all three kinds of cognitive processing during learning—selecting relevant information, organizing it into coherent cognitive representations, and integrating it with other representations and knowledge from long-term memory. Finally, the arrow from working memory to long-term memory signifies a fourth kind of cognitive process—encoding the newly constructed knowledge in long-term memory.

Three Kinds of Cognitive Load

In the information processing model in Figure 18.1, each of the two channels in working memory is limited in capacity. Sweller (1999, 2005) and Mayer (2001, 2005a; Mayer & Moreno, 2003) identified three different kinds of cognitive load in working memory: extraneous cognitive processing (or extraneous cognitive load), essential cognitive processing (or intrinsic cognitive load), and generative cognitive processing (or germane cognitive load). Extraneous cognitive processing does not support the instructional goal and is caused by ineffective presentation format. For example, if a text lesson contains a lot of extraneous information and pictures, learners may focus mainly on that information instead of the key information. Similarly, in a group learning situation students may spend their time discussing topics that have nothing to do with the instructional task. An important instructional goal is to minimize extraneous processing, such as by eliminating extraneous material from the lesson.

Essential cognitive processing is needed to mentally represent the presented material (i.e., the process of selecting in Figure 18.1) and is caused by the complexity of the material to be learned. For example, a topic such as how lightning storms develop is complex because there are many interacting elements such as the effects of differences in air temperature and differences in electrical charge. An important instructional goal is to manage essential processing, such as by providing pretraining in the names and characteristics of the key elements or presenting the material in segments.

Generative cognitive processing is deeper cognitive processing (i.e., the processes of organizing and integrating in Figure 18.1) and is primed by the learner's motivation to understand the material. An important instructional goal is to foster generative processing, such as asking learners to explain a lesson to themselves.

Overall, learners have a limited capacity for processing information in working memory, so instruction should be designed to minimize extraneous cognitive processing, manage essential processing, and foster generative processing.

Five Kinds of Knowledge

According to the information processing view, learning involves knowledge construction. An important contribution of the information processing view is the analysis of several qualitatively different kinds of knowledge:

1. *Facts*: descriptions of things or events, such as "Earth is the third planet from the sun."
2. *Concepts*: principles or models (such as having the concept of place value for written numbers) and categories or schemas (such as knowing what a dog is)
3. *Procedures*: step-by-step processes, such as knowing how to carry out the long-division procedure for 425 divided by 17
4. *Strategies*: general methods, such as knowing how to summarize a paragraph
5. *Beliefs*: thoughts about one's cognitive processing, such as believing "I am good at learning about how the mind works."

Learners possess all five kinds of knowledge in long-term memory, and proficiency in most complex tasks requires being able to coordinate among them (Anderson et al., 2001; Mayer, 2008). Metastrategies are strategies for how to manage and coordinate all the types of knowledge, and they are an important aspect of the knowledge of successful learners (McCormick, 2003).

Competing Views of Learning

Over the course of the past 100 years, researchers in psychology and education have posited four major metaphors of learning: response strengthening, information acquisition, knowledge construction, and social construction.

Learning as Response Strengthening

Learning as response strengthening—a popular view in the first half of the 20th century—conceptualizes learning as strengthening and weakening of associations. According to this view, the learner is a recipient of rewards and punishments and the teacher is a dispenser of rewards and punishments; a common instructional method is drill and practice. What is the relation of this view to the information processing view? In its traditional behaviorist form, the response strengthening view holds that rewards automatically strengthen associations and punishments automatically weaken them. In contrast, research in the information processing tradition has shown that it is not rewards and punishments per se that cause learning but rather it is the learner's interpretation of the rewards and punishments (Lepper & Greene, 1978). In short, according to the information processing view, learners apply cognitive processing to the information in their environment including the rewards and punishments they receive.

Learning as Information Acquisition

Learning as information acquisition—a popular view in the mid-20th century—conceptualizes learning as adding information to long-term memory. According to this view, the learner is a recipient of information and the teacher is a dispenser of information; a common instructional method is lecturing or assigning readings. This is an early version of information processing theory in which information is seen as a commodity than can be transferred from one person's memory to another person's memory. In contrast, a more recent version—reflected in the knowledge construction metaphor—focuses on knowledge (which consists of cognitive representations in the learner's memory system) rather than information (which consists of symbols that exist in objective reality for all to see) and focuses on the constructive processes (such as selecting, organizing, and integrating) rather than acquisition processes (such as simply adding information to memory). In short, many of the criticisms of the information processing view are attacks on the learning as information acquisition view, whereas the current version of the information processing view is reflected in the learning as knowledge construction metaphor.

Learning as Knowledge Construction

Learning as knowledge construction—a popular view since the last third of the 20th century—conceptualizes learning as building coherent cognitive structures. According to this view, the learner is an active sense maker and the teacher is a cognitive guide; an exemplary instructional method is asking learners to engage in self-explanation as they read or providing worked examples along with problems to solve. This view best epitomizes the information processing view of human cognition.

To better understand the distinction between learning as information acquisition and learning as knowledge construction, consider a lesson in which the teacher asks the class to view a 5-minute narrated video on how lightning storms develop. Which view of learning is this lesson most consistent with? It certainly is consistent with the information acquisition view because the instruction presents information for the learner to acquire. It would be consistent with the knowledge construction view only if the instructor also helps to guide the learner's cognitive processing of the material—that is, if the instruction encourages the learner to select relevant information (such as focusing on key steps in the process), mentally organize it (such as building a causal chain of the key steps in the process), and relate it with prior knowledge (such as remembering knowledge related to each step, including why hot air rises). When the learners are inexperienced they may need some guidance in how to make sense of the material. This can be done by providing pretraining in the key terms (*positively charged particle* and *negatively charged particle, freezing level,* etc.), by highlighting key steps, by reminding students of their prior knowledge concerning temperature differences and differences in electrical charge, by breaking the lesson into segments that can be paced by the learner, by asking learners to explain each segment to themselves, and many other techniques that help learners process the material more deeply. Overall, the learning as information acquisition view is consistent with instruction that simply presents information to be learned, whereas the learning as knowledge construction view requires both presenting information and making sure the learner processes it appropriately.

Learning as Social Construction

Learning as social construction—an emerging view in the latter part of the 20th century—conceptualizes learning as a sociocultural event that occurs within groups as members work together to accomplish some authentic task. An exemplary instructional method is working together as a group on a significant academic project.

How does the learning as social construction metaphor compare with the information processing view? The answer depends on whether one takes a cognitive or radical approach. According to the cognitive version of social constructivism, people build cognitive representations when they work together on a task. This view is consistent with the basic tenets of the information processing view because individual learners are applying cognitive processes and building cognitive representations. According to a radical version of social constructivism, learning does not occur within learners and teaching does not emanate from teachers but rather is a sociocultural construction produced by a group and stored as a cultural product of the group (Phillips & Burbules, 2000). This view of social constructivism is not consistent with the information processing view, nor does it offer testable hypotheses needed to qualify as a scientific theory.

Implications

The information processing view has implications for learning, instructing, and assessing.

Implications for Learning

What is learning? Learning is a long-lasting change in the learner's knowledge as a result of the learner's experience. This definition has three components:

1. Learning is long lasting, so fleeting changes such as mood changes do not count as learning.
2. Learning is a change in knowledge, so changes in knowledge must be inferred from changes in behavior.
3. Learning is a result of experience, so changes due to fatigue, injury, or drugs do not count as learning.

One of the most contentious aspects of this definition concerns the second element in the definition—namely, what is learned. According to the behaviorist view of learning, which dominated psychology and education in the first half of 20th century, what is learned is a change in behavior. According to the cognitive (or information processing) view of learning, which became dominant in the 1960s, what is learned is a change in knowledge. Knowledge is an internal, cognitive representation that is not directly observable, so it can only be inferred by changes in behavior. Thus, the information processing view focuses on changes in the learner's behavior as a way of determining changes in the learner's knowledge. A major implication of the information processing view is to modify the definition of learning so that what is learned is a change in knowledge rather than a change in behavior. The information processing view puts the construction of knowledge—or cognitive representations—at the center of learning.

Implications for Instructing

What is instruction? According to the classic view, instruction is concerned with presenting material to learners. In contrast, according to the information processing view, instruction is activity by the teacher intended to guide the learner's cognitive processing during learning. The information processing model summarized in Figure 18.1 contains three kinds of cognitive processes during learning: selecting relevant information for further processing, organizing the selected information into coherent representations, and integrating the information with appropriate knowledge from long-term memory. Meaningful learning—the construction of a meaningful learning outcome—requires that the learner engage in all three kinds of cognitive processes. Rote learning—the construction of rote learning outcomes—requires that the learner engage in selecting relevant knowledge but does not require the deeper processing of organizing and integrating. Finally, no learning occurs when the learner does not engage in any of the three kinds of cognitive processes.

A major challenge of instructional design is to present material and encourage appropriate cognitive processing in a way that does not overload the learner's information processing system. As you can see, a major implication of the information processing view is that the goal of instruction is more than simply presenting material; in addition, instructors must also guide the way that learners process the material. The information processing view changes the focus of instruction from presenting information to guiding the learner's processing of the presented information. The information processing view puts cognitive processing—such as selecting, organizing, and integrating—at the center of learning.

Implications for Assessing

What is assessment? According to the classic view, the goal of assessment is to measure performance, such as how many arithmetic problems a learner can solve in a given period of time. The classic view of assessment is concerned mainly with determining how much is learned. In contrast, the goal of assessment in the information processing view is to measure knowledge, including the degree to which the learning outcome is meaningful or rote. The information processing view is concerned mainly with what is learned, that is, "knowing what students know" (Pelligrino, Chudowsky, & Glaser, 2001).

The information processing view has useful implications for how to assess what is learned. The two most common ways of assessing learning outcomes are *retention tests*—such as asking the learner to recall or recognize what was presented—and *transfer tests*—such as asking the learner to use the material to solve a new problem. No learning is indicated by poor performance on both retention and transfer. Rote learning is indicated by good performance on retention and poor performance on transfer. Meaningful learning is indicated by good performance on both retention and transfer. Thus, according to the information processing view, the quality of learning outcomes can be inferred by examining the pattern of performance on a series of dependent measures, including retention and transfer tests. Other techniques for probing knowledge use coding systems based on interviews and observations. Techniques for assessing one of the five kinds of knowledge (i.e., facts, concepts, procedures, strategies, or beliefs) may not be appropriate for assessing other kinds. Thus, a major implication of the information processing view is to assess what is learned rather than how much is learned.

Major Contributions in Educational Psychology

One way to judge the value of the information processing view is to examine whether it has generated useful research. In this section, I describe three examples of how the information processing approach has provided useful contributions to research in educational psychology: psychologies of subject matter, cognitive process instruction, and multimedia instructional design.

Psychologies of Subject Matter

Psychologies of subject matter represent a shift from studying learning in general to studying how learning works within specific subject areas. For example, instead of asking, How do people learn? researchers studying psychologies of subject matter ask, How do people learn to read, to write, to comprehend text, to solve math problems, or to think scientifically? (Mayer, 2004).

In order to help people learn to carry out basic academic tasks—such as reading a sentence, comprehending a paragraph, writing an essay, solving a word problem, or conducting a scientific experiment—the first step is to specify the cognitive processes involved in the tasks. Based on an information processing view, progress can be made by asking, What are the cognitive processes required for an academic task? and What do you need to know in order to accomplish an academic task? For example, in order to solve a math story problem, students need to be able to engage in four cognitive processes:

1. *Problem translation*: converting each sentence of the problem into an internal mental representation by using factual knowledge (e.g., knowing how many cents are in a dollar) and linguistic knowledge (e.g., knowing that adding "s" turns a word into a plural)
2. *Problem integration*: organizing the information into a coherent statement of the problem—called a situation model—by using conceptual knowledge (e.g., knowing place value) and schematic knowledge (e.g., knowing problem types)
3. *Solution planning and monitoring*: devising a plan for solving the problem by using strategic knowledge (e.g., knowing how to break a solution plan into parts)
4. *Solution execution*: carrying out the plan to arrive at an answer by using procedural knowledge (e.g., knowing how to add, subtract, multiply, and divide numbers)

Research on expertise (Bransford et al., 1999; Mayer, 2008) shows that experts—or proficient performers—know something different than novices. For example, successful mathematical problem solvers are able to represent the problem using concrete objects, and when less successful students are given instruction in how to represent problems in this way their problem-solving performance improves (Lewis, 1989; Low & Over, 1989). An important contribution of the information processing approach is the pinpointing of specific knowledge needed for proficiency on academic tasks (Kilpatrick, Swafford, & Findell, 2001). Overall, psychologies of subject matter represent one of educational psychology's success stories in the late 20th century.

Cognitive Process Instruction

Cognitive process instruction involves providing focused instruction on cognitive processes needed for success on academic tasks. For example, if the goal is to improve reading comprehension, then students may need explicit instruction in how to engage in a process of self-explanation in which they try to explain discrepancies they find in the text as they read. Students who are taught how to engage in self-explanations show large improvements in their reading comprehension (Roy & Chi, 2005). Pressley and Woloshyn (1995) and Pressley and Harris (2006) have shown how cognitive process instruction can be applied across the curriculum. Thus, an important contribution of the information processing approach is the focus on teaching specific cognitive processes required for success in school. Cognitive process instruction has

been another one of educational psychology's success stories in the late 20th century.

Multimedia Instructional Design

Advances in instructional design principles represent a third example of the contributions of the information processing view. In particular, the information processing view has contributed to the creation of a new generation of principles for how to design instructional messages (such as textbook and online lessons). In taking an information processing approach, the focus is on helping learners engage in appropriate cognitive processing of the presented material, while being sensitive to characteristics of the human information processing system.

For example, some basic principles for how to design multimedia instructional messages (i.e., lessons containing words and pictures) are coherence, spatial contiguity, modality, and redundancy (Mayer, 2001; Mayer & Moreno, 2003). People learn better when extraneous material is excluded from a lesson. The coherence principle is based on the idea that working memory capacity is limited, so when a learner is processing extraneous material, the learner may not be able to process relevant material.

People also learn better when corresponding printed words and pictures are placed near rather than far from each other on the page or screen. The spatial contiguity principle is based on the idea that working memory is limited, so when the learner uses processing capacity to scan between words at the bottom of the screen and the appropriate portion of the graphic, the learner may have inadequate remaining capacity for deep processing of the target material.

The modality principal holds that people learn better from graphics and concurrent narration than from graphics and concurrent on-screen text. When learners must attend to both graphics and printed words they must split their visual attention (in visual sensory memory) because the eyes can only look at one location at a time. When words are presented in spoken form, they enter the information processing system through the ears (and auditory sensory memory), thus off-loading some of the processing from the visual channel.

Another principal of multimedia instructional design is the redundancy principle. People learn better from graphics and concurrent narration than from graphics, concurrent narration, and concurrent on-screen text. Adding on-screen text creates the same split-attention problem described for the modality principle and invites extraneous processing in which learners waste limited processing capacity on trying to reconcile the two verbal streams.

As you can see, these principles and many others (Mayer, 2005b) are based on an information processing view. The information processing view has contributed to yet another of educational psychology's success stories—the development of theory-based instructional design principles that work when tested empirically (O'Neil, 2005).

Conclusion

The information processing view of learning holds that people construct cognitive representations by applying cognitive processes. The learner's construction of knowledge corresponds to the "information" side of information processing, whereas the learner's application of cognitive processes corresponds to the "processing" side of information processing. According to the information processing view, the main goal of education is to foster changes in the learner's knowledge. This goal is accomplished by devising instruction that helps guide the learner's cognitive processing during learning.

The information processing view has fundamental implications for 21st-century education. In the 21st century, the task of educators is not just to present information or to provide learning environments for students. In addition, a major challenge of educators is to guide how students process information during learning. To meet this challenge, educators would benefit from an understanding of how the human information processing system works.

References and Further Readings

Anderson, L. W., Krathwohl, D. R., Airasian, P. W., Cruikshank, K. A., Mayer, R. E., Pintrich, P. R., et al. (2001). *A taxonomy for learning, teaching, and assessing: A revision of Bloom's taxonomy of educational objectives*. New York: Longman.

Baddeley, A. D. (1999). *Human memory*. Boston: Allyn & Bacon.

Bransford, J. D., Brown, A. L., & Cocking, R. R. (1999). *How people learn*. Washington, DC: National Academies Press.

Bruning, R. H., Schraw, G. J., Norby, M. M., & Ronning, R. R. (2004). *Cognitive psychology and instruction* (4th ed.). Upper Saddle River, NJ: Prentice Hall.

Kilpatrick, J., Swafford, J., & Findell, S. (Eds.). (2001). *Adding it up: Helping children learn mathematics*. Washington, DC: National Academies Press.

Lepper, M. R., & Greene, D. (1978). *The hidden costs of reward*. Mahwah, NJ: Lawrence Erlbaum Associates.

Lewis, A. B. (1989). Training students to represent arithmetic word problems. *Journal of Educational Psychology, 79*, 521–531.

Low, R., & Over, R. (1989). Detection of missing and irrelevant information within algebraic story problems. *Journal of Educational Psychology, 79*, 296–305.

Mayer, R. E. (2001). *Multimedia learning*. New York: Cambridge University Press.

Mayer, R. E. (2004). Teaching of subject matter. In S. T. Fiske, D. L. Schacter, & C. Zahn-Waxler (Eds.), *Annual Review of Psychology* (Vol. 55, pp. 715–744). Palo Alto, CA: Annual Reviews.

Mayer, R. E. (2005a). Cognitive theory of multimedia learning. In R. E. Mayer (Ed.), *The Cambridge handbook of multimedia learning* (pp. 31–48). New York: Cambridge University Press.

Mayer, R. E. (Ed.). (2005b). *The Cambridge handbook of multimedia learning*. New York: Cambridge University Press.

Mayer, R. E. (2008). *Learning and instruction* (2nd ed.). Upper Saddle River, NJ: Prentice Hall.

Mayer, R. E., & Moreno, R. (2003). Nine ways to reduce cognitive load in multimedia learning. *Educational Psychologist, 38*, 43–52.

Mayer, R. E., & Wittrock, M. C. (2006). Problem solving. In P. A. Alexander & P. H. Winne (Eds.), *Handbook of educational psychology* (2nd ed., pp. 287–303). Mahwah, NJ: Lawrence Erlbaum Associates.

McCormick, C. B. (2003). Metacognition and learning. In W. M. Reynolds & G. E. Miller (Eds.), *Handbook of psychology: Volume 7, Educational psychology* (pp. 79–102). New York: Wiley.

O'Neil, H. F. (Ed.). (2005). *What works in distance learning: Guidelines*. Greenwich, CT: Information Age Publishing.

Paivio, A. (1986). *Mental representations: A dual coding approach*. Oxford, UK: Oxford University Press.

Pellegrino, J. W., Chudowsky, N., & Glaser, R. (Eds.). (2001). *Knowing what students know*. Washington, DC: National Academies Press.

Phillips, D. C., & Burbules, N. C. (2000). *Postpositivism and educational research*. Lanham, MD: Rowman & Littlefield.

Pressley, M., & Harris, K. R. (2006). Cognitive strategies instruction: From basic research to classroom instruction. In P. A. Alexander & P. H. Winne (Eds.), *Handbook of educational psychology* (pp. 265–286). Mahwah, NJ: Lawrence Erlbaum Associates.

Pressley, M., & Woloshyn, V. (1995). *Cognitive process instruction that really improves children's academic performance*. Cambridge, MA: Brookline Books.

Roy, M., & Chi, M. T. H. (2005). The self-explanation effect in multimedia learning. In R. E. Mayer (Ed.), *The Cambridge handbook of multimedia learning* (pp. 271–286). New York: Cambridge University Press.

Sweller, J. (1999). *Instructional design in technical areas*. Camberwell, Australia: ACER Press.

Sweller, J. (2005). Implications of cognitive load theory for multimedia learning. In R. E. Mayer (Ed.), *The Cambridge handbook of multimedia learning* (pp. 19–30). New York: Cambridge University Press.

Wittrock, M. C. (1989). Cognitive processes of comprehension. *Educational Psychologist, 24*, 345–376.

19

SELF-REGULATED LEARNING

ALLYSON FIONA HADWIN

University of Victoria

Early psychological theorizing about learning was grounded in behaviorism. Behaviorism posited that human behavior is shaped and controlled externally through stimuli and reinforcers. In contrast, contemporary perspectives recognize that people are not just shaped by environmental input, but also play a role in controlling their own learning and outcomes. This ability to control and shape outcomes is often called human agency. In his social learning theory, Albert Bandura suggested that agency, or the capacity to intentionally plan for, control, and reflect upon our actions, is what makes us human. Understanding the processes by which learners set goals, plan for, execute, and reflectively refine and adapt learning is a primary focus of self-regulated learning theory. In recent years, self-regulated learning has been recognized both nationally and internationally as an important construct in education. It has attracted the attention of researchers and educators alike. As a result, a variety of theories and models have emerged to describe the role of self-regulated learning in academic success.

Defining Self-Regulated Learning

Self-regulated learning is the deliberate planning, monitoring, and regulating of cognitive, behavioral, and affective or motivational processes toward completion of an academic task. During this process students are guided by environmental or contextual features of the task and by their own personal beliefs and goals. Self-regulated learners are intentional learners who choose targets or goals and make plans for their learning. These learners are strategic in adopting and adapting a range of tools and strategies to improve learning. They check their progress and intervene when things are not going as planned. One way to think about self-regulated learning is to think of conducting experiments about your own learning. You identify a problem, make hypotheses, and set goals. To achieve those goals, you make plans and set procedures in action. As you are working, you collect informal data about how things are going. By tracking what is happening to your initial goals and hypotheses, you draw conclusions about your progress. Based on your conclusion you may make changes to your initial plans and procedures or revise previously set hypotheses. Thus, when things do not go as planned, you begin another cycle of experimentation. When this recursive process is applied to learning, we call it self-regulated learning.

Zimmerman (1989, 2000) describes self-regulated learners as those who are motivationally, cognitively, and behaviorally active in their own learning. These learners persist when faced with difficulties or challenges and experiment or test different strategies in order to optimize learning outcomes. Self-regulated learning is also conceptualized as a lifelong process, meaning SRL develops and improves over time and across tasks. Perhaps more important, research shows that students can learn to become self-regulated; productive self-regulation is learned and refined under supportive instructional conditions.

Models of SRL share some central features including (a) agency and goals, (b) metacognition, (c) motivation, (d) adaptation or regulation, and (e) feedback.

Agency, Goals, and Self-Regulated Learning

Human beings are by their very nature agentic. This means learning does not merely happen to students. Instead, learners have the capacity to take control of their learning by intentionally planning and controlling learning processes and products. The agentic nature of learning implies that all learners set goals for themselves; they have ideas about what they are trying to do or to achieve. Those goals may or may not be in line with the goals others set for them; nevertheless, personal goals guide decision making and learning activities.

Goals exist at multiple levels, meaning students may have life goals (I want to be an engineer), course goals (I want to learn as much as I can in this course), and task goals (I want to understand this chapter), each of which shapes learning engagement. We often talk about goals that are far from the specifics of the task (e.g., life goals and course goals) as distal goals and goals that are specific to the current task (e.g., I want to understand this chapter) as proximal goals. Learners also hold multiple goals. For example, a learner may have goals about affect (I want to lower my anxiety while studying), goals about performance (I want to get all the questions correct), and goals about cognition (I want to remember this theory).

Finally, goals may be about processes or outcomes. Process goals outline the ways in which a student can attain a desired eventual target. They provide criterion for properly executing components or steps in a task. When students engage in a rather complex task, they may be aided by breaking the task into smaller steps and setting these steps as "goals in process." For example, in writing a research paper for a course, students can set small goals, such as deciding a topic, conducting a literature search for two hours a day, and organizing the literature, and use these goals as their criterion for proper execution of their essay writing. These goals are most effective in early stages of the mastery process.

Outcome goals are the student's desired eventual goals. They provide criterion for examining performance. For example, a student may have an outcome goal to produce a 500-word essay. Outcome goals may be more useful later in the mastery process because they also provide an indirect measure of process attainment.

Overall, goals provide important criteria or standards upon which self-regulating learners can monitor or self-check their performance and progress during, and after, learning. Without goals, there would be nothing to self-monitor, and without self-monitoring, students would be unable to regulate, adapt, or adopt strategies to realign their learning. When we talk about agentic or intentional learning, we always assume intent translates into some sort of goal, and goals in turn drive self-regulated learning.

Metacognition, Self-Monitoring, and Self-Regulated Learning

Metacognition is a common contemporary term in the field of educational psychology. At its most simple level, it is knowledge about cognition (metacognitive knowledge) and regulation of cognition (metacognitive control or regulation). Flavell (1979) was among a group of researchers to introduce the notion that metacognition and metacognitive monitoring play important roles in learning and the development of learning strategies.

Metacognitive knowledge refers to what learners know and believe about themselves, the task, and strategies for completing the task. The belief that "I am not very good at this type of task" is an example of metacognitive knowledge. Metacognitive knowledge is essentially information in memory that may or may not be activated consciously or unconsciously. Furthermore, it may or may not be accurate. Nevertheless, it is widely accepted that metacognitive knowledge plays a central role in self-regulated learning by influencing goals and plans, strategies, and motivational engagement in tasks.

Metacognitive monitoring refers to self-checking thought processes and existing knowledge in order to make evaluations about how well you are doing when measured against a desired set of standards. Many researchers describe metacognitive monitoring as the hub of self-regulated learning. Monitoring in self-regulated learning is more than just cognitive monitoring. It involves a sophisticated checking system, in which learners compare where they are with where they should be (or would like to be) with respect to different kinds of goals. Thus, self-regulated learners monitor progress with respect to goals and standards associated with cognition, motivation, behavior, and affect.

Metacognitive control refers to exercising human agency to adapt or change (a) cognitive conditions, such as beliefs and self-knowledge; (b) task conditions, such as number of available resources; (c) thinking and engagement, such as moving from memorizing to translating ideas; and (d) standards, such as the acceptable level of mastery for this task. Metacognitive control is believed to be exercised as a result of information generated through metacognitive monitoring. Metacognitive control is exercised when monitoring uncovers a discrepancy between desired and actual state whether it be with respect to behavior, motivation, or cognition. Exercising metacognitive control is the act of adapting or regulating specific aspects of learning.

Motivation, Self-Efficacy, and Self-Regulated Learning

Although there is some debate about how motivation weaves into self-regulatory processes, there is fairly consistent agreement that motivation plays an important role in self-regulated learning. Motivation is a complex construct. It includes outcome expectations, judgments of efficacy, attributions, and incentives or values.

There are at least three ways motivation weaves into self-regulated learning. First, motivational knowledge and beliefs inform self-regulated learning by influencing the kinds of goals that are set, strategies that are chosen, and even persistence in a given task. For example, if a student feels anxious about a writing assignment, that anxiety might influence the kinds of goals the student sets for successfully completing the task. A student with high anxiety might lower goal expectations for performance and weight a goal to reduce anxiety as a parallel and equally weighted goal. Second, self-regulatory engagement in learning produces new motivational knowledge and beliefs that shape future engagement in both the current and future tasks. When a strategy for managing time during a writing activity is unsuccessful, a student may revise personal beliefs about how successful she or he can be in this writing activity or generate an anxiety response about finishing the writing task at all.

Finally, students can self-regulate motivational states during learning. For example, when a student experiences initial anxiety about a writing task, she or he may search memory for strategies that might help alleviate anxiety (such as positive self-talk). In this example, the student's perceptions of affect were not in line with his or her standards for the acceptable level of anxiety in a given task. As a result, she or he evaluated that there was a problem and experienced the drive or motivation to change the level of anxiety.

Self-efficacy is a motivational construct that is frequently discussed and researched in the field of self-regulated learning. Bandura (1977) first introduced the importance of self-efficacy in learning. Self-efficacy is one's beliefs about one's capabilities to successfully perform a specific task to a specific level of competence. For example, a student with high self-efficacy for writing believes that he or she is able to produce a high-quality essay. Self-efficacy beliefs influence choice of task, performance, persistence, and level of effort or engagement. Consistent with other forms of motivation described above, self-efficacy beliefs (a) can influence the ways students engage in a task (e.g., engaging minimal effort in choosing and adapting effective strategies); (b) can emerge as a product or outcome of self-regulatory engagement in a task (e.g., generating a low-efficacy judgment for future writing tasks after encountering planning challenges that were not successfully overcome); and (c) can be regulated by the learner (e.g., engaging positive self-talk about what can be successfully accomplished).

Feedback and Self-Regulated Learning

Feedback is an essential component of self-regulated learning. Feedback can be self-generated in the form of self-evaluations or generated by others. The product of self-monitoring during task engagement is internal feed-

back. As students monitor their progress against a set of motivational, behavioral, or cognitive standards, they generate feedback about how they are doing with respect to those standards and evaluations of what is or is not working. Furthermore, when self-regulating students judge that things are not going well, or in more sophisticated terms that a discrepancy exists between current and desired performance, they may seek out additional external feedback. External feedback may include comments from friends, comparisons with peers, or remarks from the teacher.

Feedback provides information students can use to revise, add to, or replace knowledge about strategies, tasks, beliefs, self, and metacognition. In this way, it is a necessary component of the self-regulatory cycle. Feedback can help students more accurately attune their understandings of a task, revise and reshape goals, evaluate the effectiveness of strategies, and revise knowledge of themselves as learners. While self-monitoring generates internal feedback for the learner, it may be best complimented with other forms of external feedback that help learners better attune their self-monitoring activities and the goals and standards upon which they base self-evaluations.

Models of Self-Regulated Learning

Although self-regulated learning was introduced well over 20 years ago, research has increased exponentially since Zimmerman and Schunk's book (2001). Because many models of self-regulated learning exist, only a sampling is presented below.

Zimmerman's Sociocognitive Model

Zimmerman (1989, 2000) built upon Bandura's (2001) sociocognitive model to propose a triadic model of self-regulated learning that is well recognized in the field of educational psychology and beyond. Zimmerman's model of self-regulated learning posits three basic forms of self-regulation: environmental, behavioral, and personal (covert) self-regulation. Environmental self-regulation is students' regulation of their social and physical surroundings. For example, a student studying for an exam may turn off the television (physical) or approach a peer or teacher for help (social). Behavioral self-regulation refers to students' control over their overt activities. For instance, a student may keep a written record of the number of hours he or she has studied each week. Personal (covert) self-regulation pertains to the regulation of cognitive beliefs and affective states; for instance, a student may set a self-evaluative standard to increase his or her motivation. These three influences interact reciprocally in a feedback loop (also called triadic feedback loop). As such, students must be sensitive to variations in their environmental, behavioral, and cognitive states in order to be optimally self-regulating. Furthermore, Zimmerman identified three important characteristics in self-regulated learning: self-observation (monitoring one's activities), self-judgment (self-evaluation of one's performance), and self-reactions (reactions to performance outcomes).

Winne and Hadwin's Recursive Model

Winne and Hadwin (1998) proposed a model of self-regulated learning as studying. This model depicts self-regulated learning as unfolding over four flexibly sequenced and recursive phases of learning. In the first phase (Task Understanding), students construct a representation of a presenting academic task. This representation draws on task, context, self, and motivational knowledge to produce a personalized profile of the task at hand. This task profile is influenced by motivational conditions (e.g., I am not very good at this type of task), task conditions (e.g., I don't have much time to complete this), cognitive conditions (e.g., knowledge about this topic or concept area), and metacognitive conditions (e.g., knowledge about tactics and strategies that I can draw upon when I get stuck). The task perception generated by a learner is personalized; this means it represents his or her understanding of the task and may not match the interpretation that was intended by the teacher or instructional designer.

After constructing a personalized interpretation of the task, goals are set and plans for engaging in the task are initiated (Phase 2). Goal setting and planning affords opportunities for students to distinguish between what they think they are supposed to do (task perceptions) and what they want to actually set out to do or achieve. Goal setting involves constructing a profile of standards for what you want to achieve and choosing methods to achieve those goals.

The third phase puts that plan into action. Sometimes this phase involves testing different plans and strategies or balancing between multiple competing goals. For example, students might balance the goals of researching a paper thoroughly with the goal of finding enough time to practice for an upcoming soccer tournament.

Ideally, in a fourth phase students adapt or regulate their studying processes. Adaptation might be backward reaching, such as going back to review the task and update task understanding. For example, when students notice that they seem to be doing something different than the rest of the class, they often go back to consult the initial instructions or task description. Adaptation may also be forward reaching, such as changing beliefs or perceptions about ability to successfully complete this kind of task in the future. This model of self-regulated learning is recursive, meaning that monitoring during any phase might trigger adaptation in previous or subsequent phases.

Pintrich's Model of Self-Regulated Learning

Pintrich (2000) presented a framework that describes self-regulated learning as unfolding across four weakly sequenced phases with four intersecting areas for self-regulated learning. The four phases include (1) forethought, planning, and activation; (2) monitoring; (3) control; and (4) reaction and reflection. These phases are proposed to reflect a time-ordered sequence through which learners progress when working on a task, but the model does not propose that in practice phases must occur linearly or hierarchically. An important contribution of this model of SRL is that it attempts to tease apart how these phases evolve and are instantiated across four different facets or areas of self-regulation including cognition, motivation and affect, behavior, and context. In this way, it is acknowledged that learners plan for, monitor, control (often by applying strategies), and evaluate aspects of their learning extending well beyond just cognitive engagement. Cognitive strategies that students select and evaluate help them to learn and think, motivation strategies help them to manage motivation and affect, behavior strategies help them to increase and decrease effort, and contextual strategies help them to renegotiate tasks, change, or leave the context. Controlling and regulating strategy use for specific goals across these areas constitute the complex task of self-regulating learning.

Boekaerts' Model of Adaptable Learning

Boekaerts (2006) proposed a holistic model of self-regulated learning that attempts to account for the interaction between interrelated processes in SRL, including metacognitive control, motivation control, emotion control, and action control. This model of SRL proposes that individuals hold two main priorities that influence their behavior regulation: (a) expanding personal resources by developing and improving knowledge and skills (mastery) and (b) protecting or maintaining available resources to prevent loss, damage, and distortions (coping). Self-regulated learning from this perspective appraises and coordinates three sources of information in a dynamic internal working model: task and context information; cognitive and metacognitive knowledge and skills information; and self-system goals, knowledge, and beliefs.

In this model appraisal is unique to every learning task and situation, and serves a central role in directing goal-setting and goal-striving activities. An assumption in this model is that positive appraisals lead students to invest energy in increasing competence (a mastery mode) by adopting learning strategies. Negative appraisals lead students to prevent loss of resources and protect their ego (a coping mode) by adopting coping strategies. From this perspective, successful self-regulation sets goals, applies control to deal with success and failure, and balances goals related to mastery with those related to coping in order to optimize learning outcomes while preserving a sense of self.

Contrasting Models of Self-Regulated Learning

Each of these models of self-regulated learning attempts to grapple with the roles of intention and control in human learning. Each model acknowledges that learning unfolds in cycles that include (a) preparation or taking stock of the current situation in terms of the task, knowledge, and motivation, and making decisions about desired directions, goals, or states; (b) action or adoption of strategies for regulating or enacting change; and (c) reflection or appraisal that perpetuates evolution and change in current and future learning. That is to say, self-regulated learning across each of these models is concerned with the deliberate planning, monitoring, and regulating of cognitive, behavioral, and affective or motivational processes toward completion of an academic task.

Applying Self-Regulated Learning to the Classroom

Designing Classroom Tasks and Contexts

Not all classroom tasks and contexts are equal in guiding or promoting strategic self-regulated learning. Perry (e.g., 1998) has conducted numerous research studies to explore the types of tasks and contexts that support self-regulated learning. Perry's work demonstrates that even very young children can learn to self-regulate given the right instructional context. Six recommendations provide a framework for supporting SRL in the classroom.

Design Complex Tasks

In order to self-regulate learning, students need to be confronted with complex tasks that evolve over time. Although teachers may be reluctant to assign challenging and ambiguous tasks for fear of overwhelming young students, research has demonstrated that students are motivated by tasks that pose achievable challenges. This is consistent with Vygotsky's notion that optimal development occurs in a zone of proximal development; tasks should be set at a level between what a person can accomplish working alone and what can be accomplished with support or guidance from others.

Choice

One reason challenging tasks are optimal for promoting self-regulated learning is that they provide opportunities for students to make choices and engage in decision making about their learning. Choices might concern the nature of the task itself, such as choosing to work alone or with a partner, or choosing what items to include in a learning portfolio.

Control Over Challenge

Self-regulated learning is also supported when students are given choices to control the level of challenge of a task. When students have opportunities to control challenge, they learn to choose and set suitable goals based on their understanding of the domain, self, task, and context. For example, an occasion to work with peers gives students the opportunity to reduce the level of challenge by seeking help from a peer. Also, students have opportunities to control challenge when they can choose among tasks of differing levels of difficulty or when they have access to additional help resources as needed.

Self-Evaluation

To self-regulate learning, students need to be encouraged to monitor and evaluate their own progress rather than relying solely on external evaluation. Self-evaluation is important because it requires students to revisit task perceptions and articulate goals and standards they are using to evaluate themselves. In addition to helping students regulate their learning, self-evaluation provides a window into student task understanding and goal setting that may lead to instructional opportunities that help students better attune their understanding and implementation of tasks, strategies, and goals. Self-evaluation might be as simple as answering the questions, How am I doing? How do I know? Or it may be as complex as reflecting on the usefulness of a new learning strategy for promoting key thinking processes associated with understanding and remembering (selecting, monitoring, assembling, rehearsing, translating). Self-evaluation that encourages students to reflect on personal progress has potential to improve future learning because seeing mistakes as opportunities supports students to embrace a cycle of self-regulated learning.

Instrumental Support From Teachers

Instrumental support is the act of guiding students as they encounter difficulties by providing just-in-time instruction and scaffolding. In contrast to direct instruction, instrumental support is strategically timed to help students develop the necessary knowledge and skills as they encounter challenges. Furthermore, it is temporary support provided with the ultimate goal of helping students successfully complete tasks on their own. Teachers provide instrumental support when they engage students in discussions about tasks, use open-ended and thought-provoking questions, and cue students to think about aspects of their own self-regulatory activity. Instrumental support helps students to think about and generate accurate perceptions of tasks, identify and articulate learning goals to guide their progress, consider their own strengths and weaknesses with respect to tasks, and strategically adopt and revise strategies. Instrumental support is also important for helping control the challenge of a task.

Support From Peers

Much like instrumental support from teachers, peer support can help students control the level of challenge associated with a task and provide opportunities for self-evaluation and self-reflection. Peer support is important for self-regulated learning because peers model strategies and metacognitive thinking for one another.

Promoting Effective Task Interpretation

Developing accurate and complete understandings of assigned tasks is essential for successful performance and constitutes an important component of self-regulated learning. But academic tasks are often difficult to understand because they are layered with explicit and implicit information (often not well described), deeply embedded with disciplinary thinking and presentation genres, and use language that can have many meanings. Butler and Cartier (2004) have proposed research-based guidelines for instructors to promote effective task interpretation. Not surprisingly, these guidelines complement recommendations presented in the section above on designing classroom tasks and contexts.

Selection of Learning Activities

Accurate interpretation by students is built on thoughtful design and reflection by teachers. When teachers design a learning activity, they might consider the following: (a) their goals for student learning and how those goals relate to the task, (b) what specific tasks are required and which are desired, and (c) what is communicated about the nature of academic work and thinking through descriptions of tasks. For example, when creating an engineering design project, teachers might consider if the description of the design task conveys a commitment to helping students develop specific competencies related to grappling with ill-defined and authentic engineering problems.

Structure of Instruction

It is also important to be explicit about more than the task criteria or procedures themselves. Students need instruction that supports developing accurate perceptions of the kind of thinking that is encouraged and valued; strategy knowledge that should develop or be demonstrated; and the kind of metacognitive knowledge, monitoring, and evaluation that should be engaged during task completion.

Evaluation Processes

Evaluation and feedback provide important information to students about the nature of the task and strongly influence student interpretations of tasks. In order to help students interpret tasks, evaluation criteria should be aligned with task purposes. When students are encouraged to engage in self- and peer-evaluation activities, they are forced to grapple with the specifics of the task and to clarify task interpretations. When students are asked to generate grading rubrics, they must also clarify and make public their task interpretations. When students are asked to translate or interpret feedback that they receive about an academic task or assignment, they are invited to monitor and evaluate task interpretations. These types of activities assign instructional time and value to the act of task interpretation and afford opportunities for students to successfully self-regulate their learning processes by starting with goals and standards that are in line with the instructors.

Strategy Instruction and Interventions to Enhance Self-Regulation

While some debate exists in the literature about the need for direct strategy instruction, there is consensus students need to develop strategy knowledge to self-regulate learning.

Self-Regulated Strategy Development Approach (SRSD)

SRSD is an instructional approach for supporting self-regulated strategy development (cf. Harris, Graham, & Mason, 2003). Although the implementation and evaluation of SRSD has focused primarily on writing instruction and students with learning disabilities, SRSD has been successfully implemented in other domain areas such as reading and mathematics. Extensive research about SRSD has demonstrated its effectiveness. Teachers can easily apply the instructional approach in large class instruction and small group tutoring, and students trained using the SRSD approach improve the quality of their writing, knowledge about writing, approaches to writing, and self-efficacy about writing tasks.

SRSD has three main goals: (a) developing strategy knowledge, (b) supporting students to monitor and regulate strategy use, and (c) promoting self-efficacy and positive beliefs. As students engage in flexibly sequenced SRSD stages, they are continually encouraged to use strategies in other contexts, monitor and reflect upon successes and failures in using strategies, and revise and modify strategies accordingly.

SRSD consists of six main stages that frame strategy instruction. Stages may be ordered differently, combined and modified to suit particular students and contexts. Stage 1 (develop and activate background knowledge) focuses on developing the knowledge and skills necessary to use strategies and self-regulated learning procedures. In writing, students might be reminded of story-planning strategies they have used before or a planning strategy for getting started with writing. In stage 2 (discuss it) the teacher and students discuss strategies to be learned including steps or procedures in implementing the strategies; ways of remembering the strategy, such as a mnemonic; and how, when, and why to use the strategy. In stage 3 (model it) a teacher or peer models the strategy. Emphasis is placed on sharing the kind of metacognitive thinking that accompanies strategy use such as self-talk about the strategy process, monitoring, and evaluation. Students and teachers discuss the modeling process as well as the kind of self-talk that accompanied each step or action. In stage 4 (memorize it) students commit the strategy to memory. They may do this by developing mnemonics and external memory aids. Stage 5 (support it) and stage 6 (independent performance) represent a transition from using the strategy with some external prompting and guidance to implementing the strategy independently.

Strategic Content Learning Approach (SCL)

Butler (1998) posited that in order for students to learn to monitor and regulate strategy use, they need opportunities to develop and individualize their own learning strategies. As a result, the strategic content learning approach (SCL) introduces students to a framework for strategically approaching and engaging in new tasks. It reserves explicit strategy instruction for occasions when students are not able to activate, draw upon, or revise strategies they already hold in their own repertoire. In SCL, structured and explicit instruction target the self-regulatory process rather than strategies themselves. Students are encouraged to construct knowledge and strategies with the goal of promoting strategy transfer. Discussion provides a means for sharing ideas and constructing transactional understandings about learning. Although SCL was originally extensively implemented in one-to-one tutoring sessions, it was later successfully implemented in larger group contexts.

The instructional approach for SCL follows a sequence of four steps. In step 1 (the task analysis stage), students are encouraged to analyze a task by exploring and articulating task demands, criteria, and parameters. Since many students have misconceptions about academic tasks, this step is a critical component of the SCL approach. Step 2 (strategy selection, adaptation, or invention) encourages students to make decisions about learning strategies they might use based upon the task performance criteria identified in stage 1. SCL recognizes that students often have a repertoire of strategies to choose from. Even when they do not, they are often able to use their knowledge about the task and domain to invent their own strategies. As a result, the SCL tutor encourages the student to brainstorm and occasionally provides suggestions or ideas to consider. Rather than being directed to adopt a strategy, students are empowered to make decisions about their own strategies. Students are encouraged to articulate or record these strategies as sequences of activities so that they have a reference point for monitoring strategy use. In step 3 students monitor strategy use. They are prompted to articulate what is working, what is not working, and reasons for success or challenges using the strategies. Finally, in step 4 students

are supported to evaluate the effectiveness of the strategies they have used and to make necessary revisions in those strategies for future use. In this way, students begin to construct a library of their own strategies that have been individualized and self-tested.

The SCL approach to strategy instruction is designed to help students think through their own learning tasks, make decisions about those tasks and the strategies they use, and develop skills and habits associated with reflecting upon and revising strategies.

Self-Regulation Empowerment Program (SREP)

Cleary and Zimmerman (2004) developed and tested the self-regulation empowerment program (SREP), designed to help students become more self-sufficient and independent in their learning. In addition to advocating a preliminary diagnostic component to identify motivational and strategic weaknesses, the program focuses on a three-step process for modifying or improving motivational and strategic weaknesses. The empowerment step (step 1) strives to help students gain perceptions of control of their learning. Specifically, it guides students to make connections between their strategy use and success or failure outcomes. This step uses methods and tools for self-recording and monitoring specific aspects of progress, including sources of errors and success. The study/learning strategy step (step 2) supports students to increase their repertoire of strategies. Strategies are supported by modeling, coaching, and guided practice such as that described in the next section. The final step (step 3) guides students to make use of the cyclical feedback loop in self-regulated learning. Students are taught to engage in forethought (e.g., set goals, articulate plans), record performance, evaluate goal attainment, and self-reflect about how strategies helped or hindered and ways to adapt or improve the effectiveness of strategies.

Sociocognitive Modeling and Self-Regulatory Competence

Sociocognitive modeling is the process of observing more capable others as they pattern thoughts, beliefs, and strategies associated with self-regulated learning (Schunk, 1987). Students can learn to regulate their own learning when they have opportunities to observe a proficient model, participate in guided practice, and receive instrumental feedback about their learning. Modeling is most effective when it is matched to a student's level of self-regulatory competence.

First, students are introduced to the instructions and provided with a modeled demonstration. This is followed by students engaging in a hands-on activity that is supported through guided practice. During guided practice, the model provides corrective feedback and self-regulatory training. Through self-regulatory training students are supported to verbalize goals, plans, and strategies. Modeling sessions wrap up with independent practice during which students self-reflect by verbalizing self-monitoring, beliefs, and self-evaluations.

Under the right conditions, modeling can lead to the acquisition of knowledge and strategies as well as increased self-efficacy for successfully completing tasks. Coping models who demonstrate skills and strategies for coping with stressful or challenging conditions are most effective when students have encountered failure. In contrast, mastery models who demonstrate strategies for correctly working through tasks, may be more effective under other conditions. Models are effective when observers perceive them as competent, regardless of model age, and when learners are exposed to multiple peer models. Children are more influenced by models they perceive as similar in ability to themselves.

Contemporary Issues and Future Directions

Social Aspects of Self-Regulated Learning

Historically, self-regulated learning was considered to primarily involve individual cognitive, metacognitive, motivational, and behavioral processes (Zimmerman 1989, 2000). Social context or environment was a factor influencing those individual processes. Over the last 20 years, however, increasing emphasis has been placed on understanding the role of social and contextual influences on self-regulated learning. As a result, new models and languages for describing social aspects of self-regulated learning have emerged. Although debate continues about these perspectives, awareness of these factors is important for understanding the current state of the field. Three main terms frame discussions about social aspects of self-regulated learning: self-regulated learning, co-regulated learning, and socially shared regulation of learning.

Self-regulated learning is the process of becoming a strategic learner by actively monitoring and regulating metacognitive, motivational, and behavioral aspects of one's own learning. The focus of research is the individual learner with environment as an influence (Schunk & Zimmerman, 1997). Social context is examined separately or manipulated as an independent variable. Research on the individual aspects of self-regulated learning has relied heavily on self-reports, think aloud protocols, interviews, and various performance measures.

Co-regulated learning is the transitional process in a learner's acquisition of self-regulated learning, during which experts and learners share a common problem-solving plane and self-regulation is gradually appropriated by the individual learner through interactions (e.g., McCaslin & Hickey, 2001). Research on co-regulated learning focuses on aspects of interaction, speech, and discourse with an emphasis on scaffolding and interdependence. Data primarily consist of interaction and discussion records. Research about co-regulated learning strives to examine the ways social practices support individuals to appropriate self-regulatory knowledge and processes. Social support in the form of scaffolding tends to take on some of the self-regulatory processes or burdens, rather than merely instructing or prompting students to engage in those processes.

Socially shared regulation of learning refers to the processes by which multiple others regulate their collective activity. From this perspective, goals and standards are co-constructed, and the desired product is socially shared cognition. Similar to co-regulated learning, interaction and discussion records are primary sources of data in the study of shared regulation. Unlike research about co-regulation, however, research about shared regulation tends to examine contributions, roles, the evolution of ideas, and the ways groups collectively set goals, monitor, evaluate, and regulate their shared social space. Examining socially shared regulation requires a shift toward new forms of instructional tools, data collection, and data analysis that acknowledge individuals as part of social entities and shared tasks.

To date, research exploring and comparing self-, co-, and socially shared-regulation of learning have not been conducted. Targets for future research include developing analytical techniques for examining shared regulation in social task spaces and experimenting with research designs and methodologies that allow transitions from the individual to the different ways in which self and social inform the regulation of learning.

Technology and Self-Regulated Learning

Current research on self-regulated learning explores ways technologies (particularly computer-based learning environments) can be used to support and research self-regulated learning. Research and discussion about computers as tools for supporting self-regulated learning include: (a) scaffolding self-regulated learning and metacognition in computer-based learning environments, (b) researching the design and features of pedagogical agents in supporting self-regulation, and (c) creating Web-based environments and tools that foster strategy use and self-regulation. In creating and researching instructional innovations for self-regulated learning, these new technologies afford opportunities to collect new types of data about self-regulated learning unfolding over time and across context. Software such as *gStudy* (Winne, Hadwin, Nesbit, Kumar, & Beaudoin, 2005) can be used to collect logfile traces of student engagement with the software. Data of this type have not been harnessed in the study of self-regulated learning but have been used in fields such as computer and information science to conduct usability testing.

New technologies afford opportunities to design and compare instructional programs, interventions, and environments as well as collect new kinds of data about students' learning and strategy use.

Acknowledgment

I would like to thank Mika Oshige and Mariel Miller for their thoughtful feedback and careful editing on earlier drafts of this chapter.

References and Further Readings

Azevedo, R. (2005). Computer environments as metacognitive tools for enhancing learning [Special Issue]. *Educational Psychologist, 40,* 193–276.

Azevedo, R., & Hadwin, A. F. (2005). Scaffolding self-regulated learning and metacognition: Implications for the design of computer-based scaffolds [Special Issue]. *Instructional Science, 33,* 367–565.

Bandura, A. (1977). Self-efficacy: Toward a unifying theory of behavioral change. *Psychological Review, 84,* 191–215.

Bandura, A. (2001). Social cognitive theory: An agentic perspective. *Annual Review of Psychology, 52,* 1–26.

Boekaerts, M. (2006). Self-regulation and effort investment. In E. Sigel & K. A. Renninger (Vol. Eds.), *Handbook of Child Psychology, Vol. 4, Child Psychology in Practice* (pp. 345–377). Hoboken, NJ: John Wiley & Sons.

Boekaerts, M., Pintrich, P. R., & Zeidner, M. (2000). *Handbook of self-regulation.* San Diego, CA: Academic Press.

Butler, D. L. (1998). The Strategic Content Learning approach to promoting self-regulated learning. In B. J. Zimmerman & D. Schunk (Eds.), *Developing self-regulated learning: From teaching to self-reflective practice* (pp. 160–183). New York: Guilford.

Butler, D. L., & Cartier, S. C. (2004). Promoting effective task interpretation as an important work habit: A key to successful teaching and learning. *Teacher's College Record, 106,* 1729–1758.

Butler, D. L., & Winne, P. H. (1995). Feedback and self-regulated learning: A theoretical synthesis. *Review of Educational Research, 65,* 245–281.

Cleary, T. J., & Zimmerman, B. J. (2004). Self-regulation empowerment program: A school-based program to enhance self-regulated and self-motivated cycles of student learning. *Psychology in the Schools, 41,* 537–550.

Flavell, J. H. (1979). Metacognition and cognitive monitoring: A new era of cognitive developmental inquiry. *American Psychologist, 34,* 906–911.

Harris, K. R., Graham, S., & Mason, L. H. (2003). Self-regulated strategy development in the classroom: Part of a balanced approach to writing instruction for students with disabilities. *Focus on Exceptional Children, 35,* 1–16.

McCaslin, M., & Hickey, D. T. (2001). Self-regulated learning and achievement: A Vygotskian view. In B. J. Zimmerman & D. H. Schunk (Eds.), *Self-regulated learning and academic achievement: Theoretical perspectives* (2nd ed., pp. 227–252). Mahwah, NJ: Lawrence Erlbaum Associates.

Perry, N. E. (1998). Young children's self-regulated learning and contexts that support it. *Journal of Educational Psychology, 90,* 715–729.

Pintrich, P. R. (2000). The role of goal orientation in self-regulated learning. In M. Boekaerts, P. Pintrich, & M. Zeidner (Eds.), *Handbook of self-regulation* (pp. 452–502). Orlando, FL: Academic Press.

Puustinen, M., & Pulkkinen, L. (2001). Models of self-regulated learning. *Scandinavian Journal of Educational Research, 45,* 269–286.

Schunk, D. H. (1987). Peer models and children's behavioural change. *Review of Educational Research, 57,* 149–174.

Schunk, D. H., & Zimmerman, B. J. (1997). Social origins of self-regulatory competence. *Educational Psychologist, 32,* 195–208.

Schunk, D. H., & Zimmerman, B. J. (1998). *Self-regulated learning: From teaching to self-reflective practice.* New York: Guilford.

Winne, P. H., & Hadwin, A. F. (1998). Studying as self-regulated learning. In D. J. Hacker, J. Dunlosky, & A. C. Graesser (Eds.), *Metacognition in educational theory and practice* (pp. 277–304). Mahwah, NJ: Lawrence Erlbaum Associates.

Winne, P. H., Hadwin, A. F., Nesbit, J. C., Kumar, V., & Beaudoin, L. (2005). *gSTUDY: A toolkit for developing computer-supported tutorials and researching learning strategies and instruction* (Version 2.0) [Computer Program]. Burnaby, BC, Canada: Simon Fraser University.

Zimmerman, B. J. (1989). A social cognitive view of self-regulated academic learning. *Journal of Educational Psychology, 81,* 329–339.

Zimmerman, B. J. (2000). Attaining self-regulation: A social cognitive perspective. In M. Boekaerts, P. R. Pintrich, & M. Zeidner (Eds.), *Handbook of self-regulation* (pp. 13–39). San Diego, CA: Academic Press.

Zimmerman, B. J., & Schunk, D. H. (2001). *Self-regulated learning and academic achievement* (2nd ed.). Mahwah, NJ: Lawrence Erlbaum Associates.

20

PIAGET AND VYGOTSKY

Theory and Practice in Early Education

RHETA DEVRIES

University of Northern Iowa

Jean William Fritz Piaget (1896–1980) and Lev Semyonovich Vygotsky (1896–1934) are two giants in psychology and education whose theories of mental development are highly influential. Each pursued research and sought to explain mental development in a way that was more satisfactory than the nondevelopmental associationist or subjectivist theories that held sway earlier. Here, the reader will find highlights of personal histories, a discussion of theoretical similarities and differences, and a comparison of how these theories are currently reflected in American educational practices.

Personal Histories

The personal histories of Vygotsky and Piaget provide clues to the sources of their ideas—the contexts in which *their* minds developed. Although contemporaries, Piaget and Vygotsky never met. They did, however, read and comment on each other's early work. It is obvious that Piaget's long life of 84 years gave him the opportunity to develop his research and theory much further than could Vygotsky in his short life span that was tragically ended by tuberculosis at the age of 37. Followers of Vygotsky agree that what we have are actually fragments of an unfinished work.

Vygotsky

Vygotsky was born in 1896 to educated parents. His father was a bank official, a socially active citizen who initiated the founding of an excellent public library where young Lev read voraciously. Vygotsky grew up as the Russian Empire was breaking down. He was not sent to school but was tutored by a student who had returned from Siberia where he was sent for revolutionary activities. Later Vygotsky entered a private classical school where he was well-liked and started a school debating society, taking a leadership role in discussions of problems of literature, history, art, and philosophy.

At the age of 17, Vygotsky had a gold medal for academic achievement but nevertheless had to fight for entry into the Imperial University of Moscow because czarist rules allotted only 3% of student places to Jews. Vygotsky studied law at this university but also studied at the unofficial people's university, Shanyavsky University, which was not regulated by the government and had complete autonomy in academic affairs. Privately funded Shanyavsky was open to women as well as men and to all, regardless of nationality, religion, or political views. Here Vygotsky could hear liberal, democratically minded scientists who enjoyed the opportunity to lecture without censorship. This account of Vygotsky's story is based largely on Michail Yaroshevsky's (1989) biography.

Vygotsky's interests were primarily in literature, theatre, and art, especially philosophical analysis of art and art criticism. According to Yaroshevsky, Vygotsky's biographer, constant reading of Shakespeare's *Hamlet* during his university years was the means for confronting existential concerns and gaining insights into his inner self. Poetry (particularly Pushkin's tragic poems) and Shakespeare's

Hamlet appealed to his psychological interest in the individual and his fate. In 1917, the year of a revolution that shook Russia, Vygotsky received his law degree.

The following years were turbulent: Germany incorporated Gomel in its territory, his brother contracted tuberculosis, Vygotsky undertook a dangerous trip with his mother and brother to the Crimea to obtain treatment for his brother, and they became stranded in Kiev for months by the civil war. By the time they returned, Gomel was peaceful and Soviet power was restored. At this point, Vygotsky consciously began work to contribute to the building of a new culture. He taught literature at the first "labour school" established after the occupation. Later, he taught history of the arts, psychology, and philosophy and also gave lectures to various groups.

One of Vygotsky's main activities during his 5 years in Gomel was teaching pedagogical psychology at several educational institutions. He created a psychological laboratory at Gomel Teacher's College for the evaluation of children. As he worked to establish a new school and new culture, he began to view the teacher's role from the perspective of creating the conditions for changing the child's psyche.

While he was in Gomel, Vygotsky wrote a manuscript on understanding language in which he wrote that thought is impossible without the word but is not identical to it. This led him to studies of the relationship between the nonobservable act of thought and the word as a phenomenon of culture that is observable.

Vygotsky's studies in psychology led to a significant change in his thinking. In Russia experimental research was showing that behavior could be modified by external stimuli. This evidence of control over physiological responses by external stimuli led Soviet scholars to the principle of socially conditioned consciousness and behavior. In the early 1930s, Vygotsky developed a new model of the development of all "higher functions" that he expressed as "stimuli—the cultural sign as a psychological tool (leading to) the behavioral reaction" (in Yaroshevsky, 1989, p. 241).

Upon hearing Vygotsky make an outstanding presentation at an important national conference on psychology, the director of the Psychological Institute in Moscow offered Vygotsky a position. Vygotsky and his wife Roza moved to Moscow where they had a daughter. Vygotsky began working at the People's Commissariat for Public Education with blind and deaf children. Rejecting the old views of "abnormal" children, Vygotsky talked about positive characteristics of such children. He talked about the compensations children made for their deficiencies as "tools" and developed a theory of the mechanisms by which such individuals organize their minds.

At the same time, Vygotsky was studying how school-age children use speech and language to form mental tools that he posited as leading to the development of thought. He is best known for his research and theory concerning the development of and relationship between thought and speech. Vygotsky's theory is referred to as a sociocultural, cultural-historical, or social-historical theory. His idea was that learning (of language and other cultural tools) leads to development, in contrast to Piaget's notion that development makes learning possible.

Vygotsky was influenced by Charles Darwin's evolutionary theory and Ivan Pavlov's research showing that physiological and behavioral characteristics could be changed as a result of environmental challenges. Pavlov's demonstration of conditioned reflexes (for example, that a dog's natural salivation in the presence of food could be modified to become salivation at the sound of a bell) and his stimulus-response theory had a profound impact on Vygotsky's work, but Vygotsky modified this theory by inserting an "inner space" between the stimulus and the response. The influence of Marxian theory that humans are inherently social can be seen in Vygotsky's particular concern with showing the influence of culture and history of culture on phylogenetic and ontogenetic development.

Vygotsky is reported to have authored 120 publications, of which many are now available in English. *The Collected Works of L.S. Vygotsky* consists of six volumes. Vygotsky's work was suppressed during part of the 1930s in Russia but circulated underground and was continued by his colleagues and students. Further elaboration of Vygotsky's theory is presented in the course of comparing his theory with that of Piaget, in a later section.

Piaget

Piaget was born in Switzerland where his father was a professor of medieval literature. He was the oldest of three, having two sisters. In his autobiography, Piaget (1976) notes that his father had a scrupulous and critical mind and that his father taught him the value of systematic work. He said his mother was very intelligent, energetic, and good hearted, but that her rather neurotic temperament made family life difficult. He felt that a direct consequence of this situation was his early neglect of play for serious work—not so much to imitate his father as "to take refuge in a world that was personal but not imaginary" (p. 2). He always detested any flight from reality, an attitude he attributed to his mother's instability. For a while early in his career his interest in psychology was focused on problems of psychoanalysis and pathology, but in his lifework he preferred the study of normal cases and intellectual functioning to that of the "mischievous unconscious" (p. 2). This account of Piaget's work is based on his (Piaget, 1976) autobiography and Ducret's (1990) biography.

Piaget received all his schooling in Neuchâtel. From the age of 7 to 10 years, he was interested in birds, fossils, and seashells. According to Jean-Jacques Ducret (1990), Piaget's biographer, young Jean developed the habit of writing at a young age, perhaps because of observing his father work. Piaget (1976) recounts that at the age of 10 or 11 years, he sent a one-page article on albino sparrows he had seen in a public park to *The Journal of Natural History of Neuchâtel*. It was published, and his career was launched! At that point young Piaget wrote to the director of the Museum of Natural History, asking permission to study its collections of birds, fossils, and shells after museum hours. Director Godet invited the enthusiastic child to help him organize and label collections of shells. In exchange, Godet each week gave Piaget rare specimens for his own collection and offered advice on the shells and fossils Piaget gathered on long walks in Swiss romande and in Brittany (on summer vacations near his maternal grandmother). Most important, Godet inspired Piaget's lifelong interest and research on mollusks. When Mr. Godet died in 1911, Piaget at the age of 15 was knowledgeable enough to publish a series of articles on his own about mollusks. He recounted amusing experiences as a result of his publications. For example, colleagues he did not know wanted to see him, but as he was just a schoolboy, Piaget said he did not dare meet them. He was even offered the position of conservator of the mollusk collection at the Museum of Natural History in Geneva. Piaget responded that he still had 2 years of secondary school and could therefore not accept! In his autobiography, Piaget commented that these experiences were very important in his scientific formation and allowed him to catch a glimpse of what science represents before a series of religious and philosophical crises in adolescence absorbed all his time. Briefly, these crises related to the 6 weeks of Christian instruction insisted upon by his mother, a book on religious agnosticism philosophy discovered in his father's library, and his godfather's (Samuel Cornut, a Swiss scholar) recounting of Bergson's philosophy on long walks in the countryside. Piaget (1976) related that he experienced an emotional shock when he heard about Bergson's idea of the identification of God with life itself. Piaget was ecstatic because this allowed him to see in biology the explanation of everything and of the mind itself. The problem of knowledge suddenly presented an entirely new perspective and became a fascinating subject. Then he read Bergson and was disappointed because he felt that Bergson's ingenious argument unraveled at the end without any experimental evidence to support the philosophical ideas.

During this period in secondary school Piaget decided to devote his life to the biological explanation of knowledge. In fact, he realized this goal with his research-based theory of intelligence and knowledge. In 1936 he published *Origins of Intelligence in the Child* that described microanalytically how intelligence evolves from origins in organic reflexes of the baby at birth, and in 1937 he used the same data to discuss the evolution of knowledge of various aspects of reality such as space, time, causality, and so on. Thirty years later Piaget (1967) again addressed the issue of a biologically based theory of knowledge. Piaget's interest in biology continued throughout his life, and he conducted many experiments with mollusks. Piaget found clues to human adaptation in his research on mollusks' and sedum's adaptations to various environments.

Ducret (1990) notes that even though Piaget's narrow interests in biology gave way to epistemological and psychological research, the heart of this work never ceased to rest on the notion of biological organization and its laws.

By the time Piaget received his baccalaureate from secondary school in 1915, his health was affected by work on his mollusk studies; reading everything he could find and filling many notebooks on philosophy, sociology, and psychology; and preparing for his baccalaureate examinations. He was sent to recover in the mountains. There he filled his free time by writing a philosophical novel in which he expressed ideas that exactly prefigured the theory he would work out through later scientific research.

Piaget formally entered the University of Neuchâtel while in the mountains, and shortly after returning he received his license in natural sciences, then his doctorate in 1918, also in natural sciences, with a dissertation on the mollusks of Valais.

After his doctorate, Piaget became a traveling scholar. He spent a year in two psychological laboratories in Zurich and in Bleuler's psychiatric clinic, and two years in Paris, studying abnormal psychology, logic, and philosophy of science at the Sorbonne (University of Paris). Brunschvieg's historico-critical method and his appeal to psychology for explanations had a great influence on Piaget's thinking. When Piaget undertook a job in Paris that involved interviewing schoolchildren, he had his first encounter with their unique reasoning.

Piaget moved to Geneva in 1921 to become Head of Research at the Jean-Jacques Rousseau Institute and to teach a course on child psychology in the Faculty of Sciences at the University of Geneva. Piaget married Valentine Châtenay in 1923 with whom he had three children, two girls and a boy. He spent 4 years continuing his research in Geneva and teaching courses on psychology, philosophy of sciences, and sociology in Neuchâtel. In 1929 he became professor of the History of Scientific Thought in the Faculty of Sciences at the University of Geneva. The same year he became Director of the International Bureau of Education (located next door to the Rousseau Institute), a position he held until 1939. In 1932 Piaget became co-director, with Bovet and Claparède, of the Institute. He taught experimental psychology and sociology in Lausanne, and from 1939 to 1952 he was Chair of Sociology at the University of Geneva. He was appointed at the Sorbonne in 1952 where he gave a course on *Intelligence and Affectivity*, which was published in 1980.

Piaget remained in Geneva for most of his life. From 1907, the date of his first publication, he published 80 books that were translated into many languages and disseminated all over the world. It is fortunate for many that Piaget had "to write in order to think" as he noted in his autobiography (1976). He worked until the age of 84 to bring research evidence to the problem of how knowledge develops. He invented the field of genetic epistemology, a new branch of philosophy requiring scientific evidence for its assertions.

Piaget focused on the integration of biological, cognitive, and social aspects of mind. He studied how children adapt intellectually and morally to social and object worlds, recognizing that adaptation to the object world (referring to phenomena related to physics and chemistry) is the same in all social contexts. In all social environments babies' encounters with animate and inanimate objects and their own bodies pose problems that motivate efforts toward understanding. Like Vygotsky, Piaget said that children's environments may differ in social and physical characteristics that portend well or less well for their learning and development.

Comparison of Piaget and Vygotsky on Some Theoretical Points

Similarities listed here are similarities only up to a point. Scratching beneath the surface of similar ideas of Vygotsky and Piaget often reveals differences.

Development Is Characterized by Qualitative Changes

Changes in quality of thought refer to its nature or structure, not its quantity. Both Vygotsky and Piaget saw development as characterized by qualitative changes. Both rejected nondevelopmental theories then current such as Gestalt and associationist psychology. Both fought against an idea of quantitative change—accumulation of bits of information. Despite this similarity in their forward thinking, Vygotsky and Piaget focused on different aspects of development.

Vygotsky's theory focused on qualitative changes in a child's cultural development. He and his colleagues utilized phylogenetic and ontogenetic data to identify "genetic roots of thinking and speech" (Vygotsky, 1934/1987). Vygotsky also examined cultural and social-historical influences on qualitative changes in development of humans. For example, he compared the thought of primitive humans with that of children and found similarities such as belief in magic. Vygotsky (1930/1993) wrote about an "evolution of *forms of behavior*" (p. 37) through stages. He drew a phylogenetic picture of qualitative development of ways of gaining control over the environment—from the ape's tools to the use of psychological signs in primitive humans to higher mental functions in modern humans. The first stage is instinctual—innate behaviors just after birth such as moving hands and legs, crying, sucking the breast, and swallowing milk. None of these behaviors is learned but are "useful adaptations to the environment" (Vygotsky, 1930/1993, p. 41). The second stage consists of conditional reflexes as a result of training or learning, and the third is the intellect that results from blocking of instinctual or conditional reflexes.

Piaget's account of qualitative stages begins with a microanalytic study of how infants from birth adapt to the world of objects in space and time. Unlike Vygotsky, he saw this period not of mere instincts but of innate reflexes that babies differentiate and organize into systems of mental relationships. Piaget saw a broad qualitative change at about 2 years of age with beginning symbolic development, not just language but also gesture and especially imitation and pretense. Piaget found a qualitative change in 4-year-olds who can make a line of eight tokens in correspondence to an existing line of eight yet nevertheless believe that when one line is lengthened, the longer row has more tokens. Piaget called this the stage of preoperational reasoning. By 7 or 8 years, at the stage of concrete operations, most children understand that number is independent of length or space occupied. The stage of formal operations occurs in adolescence for those able to think about hypotheses and make scientific deductions. Piaget's new genetic epistemology, which sought to explain stage changes, was rooted in biology. He sought scientific evidence to answer philosophical questions—the fundamental, overarching question being how new knowledge develops.

Social Factors Play an Important Role in Development

The most important similarity has usually been considered a great difference between these theorists. Many otherwise educated professionals say they need Piaget for intellectual development and Vygotsky for social development. But Piaget and Vygotsky are equally insistent on the important role of social factors in child development.

As noted by Moll and Whitmore (1993), Vygotsky "viewed thinking not as a characteristic of the child only, but of the child-in-social-activities with others" (p. 19). With regard to social factors, Vygotsky was concerned with cultural influences on development. He studied how children learn cultural tools in school.

Piaget is often misunderstood as viewing the child as a lonely scientist apart from the social context (for example, Bruner, 1985). This misconception may have arisen because Piaget did, in fact, tell a story recounted to him by a mathematician friend who as a child one day was fascinated by the fact that when he counted stones arranged in many different ways, he always counted 10. Piaget used this as an example of a child discovering the principle of order, one aspect of understanding number. But this little story certainly neither implies that all children experience such a conscious precocious moment nor represents the whole of Piaget's thought on how children come to acquire knowledge.

The misunderstanding of Piaget's position on the role of social factors in development derives from an incomplete reading of Piaget's work. When some people hear only of his effort to understand the origins of intelligence and knowledge in his own three children (Piaget, 1936/1950; 1937/1952), they conclude that his theory was based on only three children! Piaget's research with many collaborators included thousands of children. Some get an incorrect impression from knowing that his research utilized a research methodology of interviewing individual children to learn how they thought in domains such as substance, space, time, chance, and so forth. In fact, Piaget's early research focused on the role of social factors in development (in a number of articles and three books: in 1923, *Language and Thought of the Child;* in 1924, *Judgment and Reasoning of the Child;* and in 1932, *The Moral Judgment of the Child*). In virtually all of his publications on how knowledge or intelligence develops, Piaget referred at some point to the role of social factors in child development; he clearly recognized the importance of social factors.

In assessing the role of social factors in Piaget's theory, it is important to distinguish between his statements as an epistemologist and his statements as a psychologist. The main goal of his research was epistemological—to explain how knowledge develops, not how the individual child develops. When Piaget spoke as an epistemologist, he focused on general and universal—not individual—changes in knowledge or intelligence. When Piaget did talk about individual child development, he always talked about social factors. For example, Piaget (1964) discussed four factors in development, one of which is social transmission—although he believed this factor to be insufficient to account for the acquisition of knowledge. In addition to the books mentioned above, Piaget also talked about social factors in individual child development in his two books on education in 1949 and 1965.

Piaget (1932/1965) distinguished between heteronomous morality that is based on obedience to authority and autonomous morality that is based on self-constructed, personal convictions about what is right and good. These two types of morality correspond to two types of adult-child relationships.

A heteronomous relationship is coercive and supports a morality based on obedience to authority. When governed continually by the values, beliefs, and ideas of others, the child practices a submission that can lead to mindless conformity in both moral and intellectual spheres. Piaget argued that coercion socializes only the surface of behavior and actually reinforces the child's tendency to rely on purely external regulation.

Piaget contrasts the heteronomous adult-child relationship with a second type that is characterized by mutual respect and cooperation. The adult returns the child's respect by giving him or her the possibility to regulate behavior voluntarily. In so doing, the adult helps the child to construct a mind capable of thinking independently and creatively and to develop moral feelings of reciprocity. Obviously, children and adults are not equals. But when the adult is able to respect the child as a person with a right to exercise his or her will, one can speak about a certain psychological equality in the relationship. These ideas lead Piagetian constructivist educators to the view that teachers should minimize the exercise of *unnecessary* authority to

the extent practical. This philosophy is in contrast with the view of Vygotskians that ideal adult-child relationships are unequal.

The Function of Thought Is to Adapt to the World

Both theorists expressed this idea, but they differed in their conceptions of the "world" to which the child is adapting, how thought functions, and the nature of adaptation.

Vygotsky focused on the social-cultural world to which the child must adapt. He viewed thought as functioning with language and saw the nature of individual adaptation as an interpersonal process through acculturation that results eventually in thinking. Perhaps his best-known quote is that "every function in the child's cultural development appears twice: first, on the social level and, later, on the individual level. . . . All the higher functions originate as actual relations between human individuals" (Vygotsky, 1935/1978, p. 57).

Piaget saw the world to which the child must adapt as both social and physical. He viewed thought as functioning through a fundamental process of the mind's assimilating (mentally acting to recognize an aspect of experience already known or constructed) and accommodating (mentally acting by modifying content and structure of thought as a result of a contradiction to expectation in an aspect of experience) and saw the nature of adaptation as this process of assimilating and accommodating. In a posthumous work, Piaget (Piaget & Garcia, 1987/1991) understood meaning to be the essence of assimilating and accommodating.

Egocentrism Is a Characteristic of Children

Both Piaget and Vygotsky described the same phenomenon of egocentric speech in young children. This type of speech is not adapted to a listener but is for the child himself or herself. That is, it does not take account of another's perspective; it is not socialized speech. Piaget's 1923 book *Language and Thought of the Child* was widely read and translated. Vygotsky wrote an introduction to the Russian translation of this book that is critical of Piaget's early work. Vygotsky's criticism comprises a chapter in his 1934 book *Thought and Language,* later more accurately translated as *Thinking and Speech,* which appeared in a volume of collected works in 1987. Piaget responded to Vygotsky's criticisms in an introduction to the 1962 English translation of Vygotsky's 1934 book. The idea of egocentrism is the only point on which each commented on the other's work. Piaget wrote that Vygotsky misunderstood his point that egocentric speech is only one form of egocentric thought.

It is important to note that Piaget agreed with many of Vygotsky's criticisms (although he admitted he would not have been in so much agreement in 1934). Piaget clarified that he meant by "egocentrism" (better termed "centrism") an unconscious cognitive and emotional centering on one's own point of view—an inability to "decenter" or shift perspective. For him, egocentric speech was just one manifestation of an inability to decenter that Piaget's later research showed to be expressed in every domain of thought he studied. In all domains, according to Piaget, an individual must decenter in order to progress cognitively, morally, socially, and emotionally—intrapsychically and interpersonally. Piaget saw the mental operations necessary for logical thought as the same mental operations necessary for mental cooperation in interpersonal relationships.

This view is a very different interpretation of the facts of egocentric speech from that of Vygotsky who saw egocentric speech as the point of departure for inner speech. According to Yaroshevsky (1989), Vygotsky argued that *"the meaning of the word is the primary unit of consciousness"* (p. 297). This meaning comes from the culture and all its history of social relations and is meant to convey the idea that the individual's inner world is rooted in "something external, social, cultural, and historical" (p. 297).

Progress in Thought Occurs When an Individual Encounters a Difficulty or Obstacle

Briefly, for Piaget, the source of progress is disequilibrium (when an individual consciously realizes that what he or she thought is contradicted by experience). Only when disequilibrium occurs can the individual begin to figure out a more adequate understanding through a process of equilibration. Equilibration includes moments of uncertainty or disequilibrium, an intellectual as well as emotional experience. The emotional aspect may be feelings of puzzlement, frustration, surprise, and so forth. The discomfort of disequilibrium is the impetus for seeking solutions. The result of trying out an erroneous idea informs the child's next effort. Such error-informed experimentation describes an equilibration process. The child attains equilibrium when she or he constructs a more adequate network of mental relationships that enable the child to anticipate and avoid potential problems in trying to do something. Sometimes a child responds to a contradiction to an expectation by not accepting the result and repeating the same action over and over again. In this case, the child does not make new mental relationships until he or she decides to try something new. Sometimes an equilibration (making a new relationship) occurs so quickly that disequilibrium is hardly noticeable.

Reflexes Play an Important Role in Development

For Piaget (1936/1952) the origin of intelligence is in the biological reflexes of the infant at birth. The baby's first sucking is not precise, but as the infant tries to suck many objects, he or she adapts the sucking to the shape. As the baby finds hunger satisfied or not satisfied with sucking different objects, he or she begins to differentiate these and make the first mental relationships—between objects that satisfy hunger and those that do not.

Vygotsky also attributed an important role to reflexes. He was influenced by his Russian forebear, Ivan Pavlov, whose theory of conditional reflexes was very important to psychologists during the 1920s. Vygotsky used this theory but postulated complex psychological processes (of which speech was of principal importance) between stimulus and response that really contradicted Pavlov's mechanical theory without being politically incorrect in the environment of Soviet psychology's emphasis on physiological psychology.

The Relationship Between Learning and Development

Briefly, for Vygotsky, learning leads development, and, for Piaget, development leads learning.

Early Education Based on the Theories of Vygotsky and Piaget

The National Association for the Education of Young Children in its position statement (Bredekamp & Copple, 1997) says that principles of developmentally appropriate practice "are based on several prominent theories that view intellectual development from a constructivist, interactive perspective" (p. 13). From their citations, it is clear that the work of both Piaget and Vygotsky currently influence thought about early education. Convergences in educational thought and practice of Piagetians and Vygotskians testify to the growing consensus in the field about what constitutes high-quality early education.

Convergences in Educational Influences of Piaget and Vygotsky

It may be clarifying to consider eight convergences in educational practices of Piagetian constructivists and some Vygotskian educators.

1. *Children are active.* A number of Vygotskian educators do not take up the behaviorist aspects of Vygotsky's theory, but agree with Piagetians that the child is active in the construction of knowledge.
2. *Rote learning should be avoided.* Agreement also exists among Piagetians and some Vygotskians that rote learning is not consistent with their theories of learning.
3. *The whole language approach to literacy is advocated.* Followers of both Piaget and Vygotsky claim that the whole language approach to teaching literacy reflects their theories of educational practice.
4. *Collaboration of children in classroom activities is advocated.* Followers of both Piaget and Vygotsky also agree on the importance of children's collaboration.
5. *Establishing community in the classroom is important.* Vygotskians such as Moll and Whitmore (1993) talk about the connection of individuals in collective, interrelated

zones. Piagetians such as DeVries and Zan (1994) talk about the importance of a "feeling of community" in a classroom. While these conceptions may not be precisely the same, they provide a basis for considering children's co-constructions.

6. *Curriculum should be based on children's interests.* Both Piagetians and Vygotskians consider the element of interest essential to activities in a model program (Berk & Winsler, 1995; Bodrova & Leong, 2007; DeVries & Zan, 1994; Moll & Whitmore, 1993). These pairs of curriculum developers recommend that teachers consult children about what they want to study and view children's interests as crucial to successful individual construction of knowledge. They concur that the curriculum is an emergent process.

7. *External rewards should not be used with children.* DeVries and Zan (1994) and Berk and Winsler (1995) agree on this point, but Bodrova and Leong (2007) do not agree.

8. *Pretend play is an important part of the curriculum.* Followers of both Vygotsky and Piaget advocate organizing a center in the classroom to promote pretend play.

Constructivist Early Education

Constructivist education takes its name from Piaget's research showing that children actively create—construct—new knowledge from their experiences that goes beyond what they already know. The following main ideas from Piaget's research and theory are relevant to education:

- Children construct knowledge.
- Interest is necessary for the constructive process to begin and continue.
- Experimentation with physical phenomena is essential to the constructive process.
- Cooperation characterizes the interpersonal atmosphere in which the constructive process thrives.

A challenge for constructivist teachers is to identify content that intrigues children and arouses in them a need and desire to figure something out. Cooperation, according to Piaget, refers to the type of social context necessary for optimal development of intelligence or knowledge, and of emotional, social, and moral aspects of personality. By "cooperation," Piaget did not mean submissive compliance. For Piaget, cooperation is an essential characteristic of active education that respects the ways in which children think and the ways they transform their thinking by making new mental relationships. Mutual respect creates the basic dynamic in which individuals want and try to cooperate—that is, to operate in terms of one another's desires and ideas.

Each classroom and school has a sociomoral atmosphere. This is made up of the entire network of interpersonal relationships among children and between adults and children. In this atmosphere, children feel safe, securely attached to the teacher, and free to be mentally active. According to DeVries and Zan (1994), the first principle of constructivist education is that the teacher must establish a cooperative sociomoral atmosphere in which mutual respect is continually practiced.

A constructivist teacher tries to help children put aside their usual view of adults by relating to children as a companion or guide. Constructivist teachers express respect for children in a variety of ways: (a) having class meetings to discuss and evaluate how their classroom is and how they want it to be, (b) allowing children to make selected decisions about classroom procedures and curriculum, (c) encouraging children to discuss and make rules they feel are necessary to prevent or solve problems, (d) conducting social and moral discussions about interpersonal problems in children's literature and problems arising in the classroom, and (e) engaging children in conflict resolution with the goal of children learning to take account of another's point of view and resolve their own conflicts. These activities are defined and discussed in *Moral Classrooms, Moral Children* (DeVries & Zan, 1994).

Cooperating with children means that the constructivist teacher refrains from unnecessarily controlling children. Many people misunderstand this principle as permissiveness—that is, allowing children to do anything. The constructivist teacher is not permissive. Sometimes, of course, external control is necessary. When the teacher has to exercise external control, its negative effects can be minimized by empathizing with the child's feelings, explaining why the child must comply, and being firm but not mean. The goal of the constructivist teacher is to minimize external control to the extent possible and practical and to promote the child's internal control. In other words, teachers help children help themselves.

The constructivist classroom context embodies the characteristics of respect mentioned above. Teachers respect children's interests by giving children choices during activity time among such activities as pretend play, reading books, painting, listening to and acting out stories, playing musical instruments, and water, sand, and block building or woodworking. Constructivist activities added to this traditional curriculum in early education include physical knowledge activities (Kamii & DeVries, 1978/1993; DeVries, Zan, Hildebrandt, Edmiaston, & Sales, 2002) and group games (Kamii & DeVries, 1980; DeVries, et al., 2002). In physical knowledge activities, children engage with physical phenomena involving movement (physics) or changes (chemistry) in objects. They also engage in group games that require cooperation, even for competitive games. In all these activities, teachers plan, intervene, and evaluate in terms of mental relationships children have the possibility to make. For example, in a physical knowledge activity involving making marble pathways with lengths of wood having a groove down the middle, children can make the mental relationship between height of support (a block or box) and speed of marble or distance marble travels off the end of an incline. In a game of tag, children have the possibility to make the reciprocal relationship between chaser and one who is chased—between the intention to tag and the intention to avoid being tagged. All children's activities are thus evaluated in terms of what mental relationships children are making, including those that are social, emotional, and moral as well as intellectual.

Vygotskian Early Education

Vygotskian educators draw particularly on the idea of the zone of proximal development (ZPD), seeking to identify teaching that uses the competence of the adult or more capable peer as the guide for a child's participation in an activity. As noted above, this idea does not specify how to intervene in the ZPD. Fostering higher mental functions is an educational goal. Vygotskian educators differ widely in the teaching they present as models. Some examples of these models are given below.

Kamehameha Elementary Education Program (KEEP)

The Kamehameha Elementary School is the only school that has actually been based on Vygotsky's theory. In their book *Rousing Minds to Life: Teaching, Learning, and Schooling in Social Context,* Tharpe and Gallimore (1988) describe the development from 1970 to 1983 in Hawaii of an elementary school program based on "neo-Vygotskianism" (p. 6). They comment that "in no works known to us does he [Vygotsky] provide any useful treatment of instructional practice or in any way attempt a differentiated description of schooling processes" (p. 106). Therefore in trying to work toward a unified theory that includes a new discipline and science of schooling, they turned to present-day Vygotskians and to their own classroom experimentation for practical guidance. In writing about teaching in the ZPD, Tharpe and Gallimore (1988) list six means of assisting children's performance: (1) modeling, (2) contingency management of rewards and punishments, (3) providing feedback about accuracy of performance, (4) instructing on matters of deportment and assigning tasks, (5) questioning that requires a reply in language, and (6) cognitive structuring that organizes, evaluates, and groups and sequences perceptions, memory, and actions (p. 177). Like many other Vygotskians, Tharpe and Gallimore refer to the assistance of performance through scaffolding in which the child's role is simplified by means of "graduated assistance from the adult/expert" (p. 33). In this approach, rewards (including praise) and punishment are seen as props that strengthen learning through the ZPD. The importance of reinforcement to this approach is reflected by newly hired teachers spending "16 weeks learning to use praise effectively" (p. 193). This is in contrast to the constructivist view that praise should not be used to manipulate or control children; genuine appreciation, of course, is another matter, and constructivist teachers do sometimes praise children to express appreciation.

Tharpe and Gallimore (1988) note that in the kindergarten year, one of the teacher's responsibilities in the first few days of school is to teach children "the rules and the rest of the social system that make up the classroom and school" (p. 167). This contrasts with the constructivist approach in which children make classroom rules on the basis of the needs they experience for class members to regulate themselves by rules mutually agreed upon (DeVries & Zan, 1994).

Reciprocal Teaching

Palincsar, Brown, and Campione (1993) emphasize the importance of structured dialogues that provide guided practice toward the goal of understanding written texts. They give four concrete strategies for getting children to understand text:

1. asking questions about text;
2. summarizing to get consensus;
3. clarifying to restore meaning upon misunderstanding; and
4. predicting about an upcoming event.

They describe the teacher's scaffolding role in terms of cued elicitations, paraphrasing children's contributions, choral responses, framing children's responses, selective use of praise, and silence (Palincsar et al., 1993, p. 54).

Classifying Grocery Items

Rogoff and Gardner (1984) give an example of adult guidance of cognitive development in the ZPD with an activity involving classification of grocery items on shelves in a mock kitchen. A mother instructs her 7-year-old daughter in the organization of grocery items on shelves. Then she tries to get the child to take greater responsibility in remembering where the items go. The mother tells the child to put the margarine with the bread, gives hints by looking toward or pushing items in the direction of their correct placement, corrects the child's errors by giving the correct answer, and tells the child to think.

MOTHER, *picking out margarine and handing it to child*: This goes on bread.

(*Child studies item.*)

MOTHER: Where do you put that? (*Touches margarine, practically pushing it in the correct direction as a hint.*)

CHILD: Ah. (*Makes unintelligible comment, then places margarine appropriately and returns to Mother.*)

(*Mother picks out can of pineapple, hands it to child, and smiles expectantly at child, hinting with her eyes moving pointedly toward the correct shelf.*). . . .

MOTHER, *picking out ketchup and holding it toward child*: What is this?

CHILD: Ketchup. (*Moves to place it on incorrect shelf.*)

MOTHER: No.

(*Child pauses in midstep, waiting for more information.*)

MOTHER, *providing no cue*: Where does it go? Think.

(*Child backs up to center of room and appears to think.*)

MOTHER: Okay. (*Looks at appropriate shelf, capitulating in giving a cue.*)

(*Child makes no move.*)

MOTHER, *pointing at correct shelf*: It goes over here with the pickles and the olives.

(*Points at pickles and at olives, making her cue quite explicit.*) Okay?

(*Child nods and places item on correct shelf.*)

(Rogoff & Gardner, 1984)

For Rogoff and Gardner, this interaction illustrates how the mother tries to get the child to be more independently active and how the child seeks information needed for correct placement. In this situation, it is not possible for the child to figure out the correct placement because the organization on the shelves is arbitrary. It also contradicts in some ways the child's experience at home (for example, at home the margarine goes in the refrigerator, not by the bread on a shelf). This example is in contrast to a similar situation in constructivist classrooms in which the teacher asks children to put away materials at cleanup time. The particular placement of groups of toys is also arbitrary; however, the constructivist teacher emphasizes the sociomoral reason for correct cleanup organization. That is, if things are not put away in an organized fashion, people will not be able to find what they need. Thus children have the possibility to make a moral relationship between their actions of cleaning up and the well-being of the group.

Conclusion

Education based on Piaget's theory has been more fully detailed than education based on Vygotsky's theory. More consensus exists among Piagetian constructivist educators than among Vygotskian educators. Vygotskians and Piagetians are currently critical of the other's theoretical perspective. This derives principally from myths each group believes about the other group:

1. Piaget focused solely on individual intellectual development and did not recognize the important role of social factors.
2. Vygotsky focused solely on the role of culture and society in development and did not recognize the individual constructivist process.

Vygotskian educators have specialized in intellectual classroom goals, especially with regard to literacy. Piaget-

ian educators offer a broader view that can be seen as partially consistent with Vygotsky's theory, incorporating affective and moral as well as intellectual goals in the conception of developmental aims. Advocates of both Piaget and Vygotsky continue to develop the practical implications of these theories. It remains to be seen the extent to which they work toward convergence or divergence.

References and Further Readings

Berk, L., & Winsler, A. (1995). *Scaffolding children's learning: Vygotsky and early childhood education.* Washington, DC: National Association for the Education of Young Children.

Bodrova, E., & Leong, D. (2007). *Tools of the mind: The Vygotskian approach to early childhood education* (2nd ed.). Upper Saddle River, NJ: Pearson.

Bredekamp, S., & Copple, C. (1997). *Developmentally appropriate practices in early childhood programs.* Washington, DC: National Association for the Education of Young Children.

Bruner, J. (1985). Vygotsky: A historical and conceptual perspective. In J. Wertsch (Ed.), *Culture, communication, and cognition: Vygotskian perspectives* (pp. 21–34). Cambridge, UK: Cambridge University Press.

DeVries, R. (1997). Piaget's social theory. *Educational Researcher, 26*(2), 4–17.

DeVries, R. (2004). Why the child's construction of relationships is fundamentally important to constructivist teachers. *Prospects, XXXIV*(4), 411–424.

DeVries, R., & Edmiaston, R. (1999 [incorrectly printed as 1998]). Misconceptions about constructivist education. *The Constructivist, 13*(1), 12–19.

DeVries, R., & Zan, B. (1994). *Moral classrooms, moral children: Creating a constructivist atmosphere in early education.* New York: Teachers College Press.

DeVries, R., & Zan, B. (1995). Creating a constructivist classroom atmosphere. *Young Children, 51*(1), 4–13.

DeVries, R., Zan, B., Hildebrandt, C., Edmiaston, R., & Sales, C. (2002). *Developing constructivist early childhood curriculum: Practical principles and activities.* New York: Teachers College Press.

Ducret, J. (1990). *Jean Piaget: Biographie en parcours intellectual.* Neuchâtel et Paris: Delachaux et Niestlè.

Kamii, C., & DeVries, R. (1980). *Group games in early education: Implications of Piaget's theory.* Washington, DC: National Association for the Education of Young Children.

Kamii, C., & DeVries, R. (1993). *Physical knowledge in preschool education: Implications of Piaget's theory.* New York: Teachers College Press. (Original work published 1978)

Moll, L. (Ed.). (1990). *Vygotsky and education.* Cambridge, UK: Cambridge University Press.

Moll, L., & Whitmore, K. (1993). Vygotsky in classroom practice: Moving from individual transmission to social transaction. In E. Forman, N. Minick, & C. Stone (Eds.), *Contexts for learning: Sociocultural dynamics in children's development* (pp. 19–42). New York: Oxford University Press.

Palincsar, A. S., Brown, A. L., & Campione, J. C. (1993). First grade dialogues for knowledge acquisition and use. In E. Forman, N. Minick, & C. Stone (Eds.), *Contexts for learning: Sociocultural dynamics in children's development* (pp. 43–57). New York: Oxford University.

Piaget, J. (1950). *The origins of intelligence in children.* New York: International Universities Press. (Original work published 1936)

Piaget, J. (1952). Jean Piaget. In E. Boring (Ed.), *A history of psychology in autobiography* (Vol. 4, pp. 237–256). Worcester, MA: Clark University Press.

Piaget, J. (1952). *The construction of reality in the child.* New York: Basic Books. (Original work published 1937)

Piaget, J. (1962). *Language and thought of the child.* New York: Meridian Books. (Original work published 1923)

Piaget, J. (1962). *Commentary on Vygotsky's criticisms of Language and Thought of the Child and Judgment and Reasoning in the Child.* Cambridge, MA: MIT.

Piaget, J. (1964). *Judgment and reasoning in the child.* Totowa, NJ: Littlefield, Adams. (Original work published 1924)

Piaget, J. (1964). Learning and development. In C. Lavatelli & F. Stendler (Eds.), *Readings in child behavior and development.* New York: Harcourt Brace Jovanovich.

Piaget, J. (1965). *The moral judgment of the child.* London: Free Press. (Original work published 1932)

Piaget, J. (1967). *Biology and knowledge: Essay on the relations between organic regulations and cognitive processes.* Chicago: University of Chicago.

Piaget, J. (1970). Piaget's theory. In P. Mussen (Ed.), *Carmichaels' manual of child psychology* (3rd ed., Vol. I, pp. 703–732). New York: Wiley.

Piaget, J. (1976). Autobiographie. In G. Busino (Ed.), *Les sciences sociales avec et après Jean Piaget* (pp. 1–43). Geneva: Librairie Droz.

Piaget, J. (1980). *Intelligence and affectivity: Their relationship during child development.* Palo Alto, CA: Annual Reviews.

Piaget, J. (1985). *The equilibration of cognitive structures: The central problem of intellectual development.* Chicago: University of Chicago Press. (Original work published 1975)

Piaget, J., & Garcia, R. (1991). *Toward a logic of meanings.* Hillsdale, NJ: Lawrence Erlbaum Associates. (Original work published 1987)

Rogoff, B., & Gardner, W. (1984). Adult guidance of cognitive development. In B. Rogoff & J. Lave (Eds.), *Everyday cognition: Its development in social context* (pp. 95–116). Cambridge, MA: Harvard University Press.

Tharpe, R., & Gallimore, R. (1988). *Rousing minds to life: Teaching, learning, and schooling in social context.* Cambridge, UK: Cambridge University Press.

Tryphon, A., & Voneche, J. (1996). *Piaget—Vygotsky: The social genesis of thought.* East Sussex, UK: Erlbaum (UK) Taylor & Francis Ltd.

Van der Veer, R., & Valsiner, J. (1991). *Understanding Vygotsky: A quest for synthesis.* Oxford, UK: Blackwell.

Vygotsky, L. (1978). *Mind in society: The development of higher psychological processes.* Cambridge, MA: Harvard University Press. (Original work published 1935)

Vygotsky, L. (1981). The genesis of higher mental functions. In J. Wertsch (Ed.), *The concept of activity in Soviet psychology.* Armonk, NY: Sharpe. (Original work published 1930)

Vygotsky, L. (1987). Thinking and speech. In R. Rieber & A. Carton (Eds.), *The collected works of L.S. Vygotsky: Volume 1, Problems of general psychology.* New York: Plenum. (Original work published 1934)

Vygotsky, L. (1987). Problems of general psychology. In R. Rieber & A. Carton, A. (Eds.), *The collected works of L.S. Vygotsky: Volume 1, Problems of general psychology.* New York: Plenum.

Vygotsky, L. (1997). History of the development of higher mental functions. In J. Glick, R. Rieber, & M. Hall (Eds.), *The collected works of L.S. Vygotsky: Volume 4.* New York: Plenum.

Vygotsky, L. (1999). Scientific legacy: Cognition and language. In R. Rieber & M. Hall (Eds.), *The collected works of L.S. Vygotsky: Volume 6.* New York: Plenum.

Vygotsky, L., & Luria, A. (1993). Studies on the history of behavior: Ape, primitive, and child. V. Golod & J. Knox (Eds.). Hillsdale, NJ: Lawrence Erlbaum Associates. (Original work published 1930)

Yaroshevsky, M. (1989). *Lev Vygotsky.* Moscow: Progress Publishers.

21

MASTERY LEARNING

THOMAS R. GUSKEY

Georgetown College

Over the last four decades, few programs have been implemented as broadly or evaluated as thoroughly as those associated with mastery learning. Programs based on mastery learning operate today in nations throughout the world and at every level of education. When compared to students in traditionally taught classes, students in mastery learning classes consistently have been shown to learn better, reach higher levels of achievement, and develop greater confidence in their ability to learn and in themselves as learners (Anderson, 1994; Guskey & Pigott, 1988; C. C. Kulik, Kulik, & Bangert-Drowns, 1990).

This chapter describes how mastery learning originated and the essential elements involved in its implementation. It discusses the improvements in student learning that typically result from the use of mastery learning and how this strategy provides practical solutions to a variety of pressing instructional problems. Finally it explains the common misinterpretations of mastery learning and summarizes the results of research on its effects.

John B. Carroll's Model for School Learning

Although the basic tenets of mastery learning can be traced to such early educators as Comenius, Pestalozzi, and Herbart, a major influence on the development of modern versions was a 1963 article by Harvard University professor John B. Carroll entitled, "A Model for School Learning." In this article, Carroll challenged long-held notions about student aptitude. He pointed out that student aptitude traditionally had been viewed as the level to which a child could learn a particular subject. Children with high aptitude would be able to learn the most complex aspects of that subject, while those with low aptitude would be able to learn only the most basic elements. When aptitude is viewed in this way, children are seen as either good learners (high aptitude) or poor learners (low aptitude) with regard to the subject.

Carroll argued, however, that student aptitude more accurately reflects an index of learning rate. That is, all children have the potential to learn quite well but differ primarily in terms of the time they require to do so. Some children are able to learn a subject very quickly while others may take much longer. When aptitude is viewed as an index of learning rate, children are seen not simply as good and poor learners but rather as fast and slow learners.

Carroll then proposed a model for school learning based on this alternative view of aptitude. He believed that if each child were allowed the time needed to learn a subject to some criterion level, and if the child spent that time appropriately, then the child probably would attain the specified level of achievement. But if not enough time were allowed or if the child did not spend the time required, then the child would learn much less. The degree of learning attained by a child, therefore, can be expressed by the following simple equation:

$$\text{Degree of learning } f = \left(\frac{\text{time spent}}{\text{time needed}} \right)$$

In other words, degree of learning is a function of the time a child actually spends on learning relative to the time he or she needs to spend. If the time spent were equal to time needed, the learning would be complete and the equation would equal 1. If the time spent were less than the time needed, however, the learning would be incomplete by that proportion.

Carroll further identified the factors that he believed influenced the time spent and the time needed. He argued that both of these elements were affected by characteristics of the learner and by characteristics of the instruction. Specifically, he believed that the time spent was determined by a child's perseverance and the opportunity to learn. Perseverance is simply the amount of time a child is willing to spend actively engaged in learning. Opportunity to learn is the classroom time allotted to the learning. Time spent is determined by the child's persistence at a learning task and the amount of learning time provided. Time needed, on the other hand, Carroll believed was determined by the child's learning rate for that subject, the quality of the instruction, and the child's ability to understand the instruction, specifically represented by the following equation:

$$\text{Degree of learning } f = \left(\frac{\dfrac{\text{perseverance}}{\text{opportunity to learn}}}{\dfrac{\text{learning rate}}{\dfrac{\text{quality of instruction}}{\text{ability to undertand the instruction}}}} \right)$$

Again, a child's learning rate is a measure of the time required by the child to learn the concepts or skills under ideal instructional conditions. If the quality of the instruction were high, then the child would readily understand it and would probably need little time to learn. If the quality of the instruction were not as high, however, then the child would have greater difficulty understanding and would require much more time to learn. The quality of the instruction and the child's ability to understand the instruction interact to determine how much time is needed for the child to learn the concepts or skills.

Carroll's article made a significant contribution to learning theory. It set forth new guidelines for research into the concept of aptitude and identified specific factors that influence learning in school settings. His ideas about learning rate also prompted the development of numerous individualized instruction programs that allowed students to progress through a series of learning units at their own, self-determined pace. Two of the best known of these continuous progress programs were Individually Prescribed Instruction (IPI), developed at the University of Pittsburgh (Glaser, 1966), and Individually Guided Education (IGE), developed at the University of Wisconsin (Klausmeier, Rossmiller, & Saily, 1977). Carroll himself, however, did not address the problem of how to provide sufficient time or how to improve instructional quality. These issues were left unresolved.

Benjamin S. Bloom's Learning for Mastery

During the 1960s, Benjamin S. Bloom and his students at the University of Chicago were deeply involved in research on individual differences and ways to improve the teaching and learning process. Bloom was impressed by the optimism of Carroll's perspective on learners and particularly by the idea that students differ in terms of the time required for learning rather than their ability to learn. If aptitude were indeed predictive of the time a child would require to learn, Bloom believed it should be possible to set the degree of learning expected of each child at some mastery performance level. Then by attending to the instructional variables under teachers' control—the opportunity to learn and the quality of the instruction—teachers should be able to ensure that every child attains that specified level. Bloom believed that if sufficient time and appropriate instruction were provided virtually all students could learn.

To determine how this might be practically achieved, Bloom first considered how teaching and learning take place in typical group-based classroom settings. He observed that most teachers begin by dividing the concepts and skills that they want students to learn into smaller learning units. These units are usually sequentially ordered and often correspond to the chapters in the textbook used. Teachers then teach the unit concepts to all students in the same way, provide all students with the same amount of time to learn, and evaluate students' learning at the end with some form of test or assessment. The few students for whom the instructional methods and time were ideal learn excellently and perform well on the unit assessment. The largest number of students, for whom the methods and time were only moderately appropriate, learn less well. And students for whom the instruction and time were inappropriate due to differences in their backgrounds or learning styles learn very little and perform poorly on the unit assessment. Little variation in the teaching resulted in great variation in student learning. Under these conditions the pattern of student achievement was similar to the normal curve distribution shown in Figure 21.1.

To attain better results and reduce this variation in student achievement, Bloom reasoned that we would have to

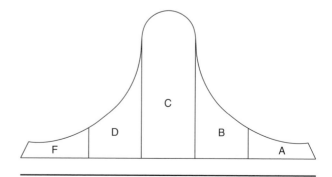

Figure 21.1   Distribution of Achievement in Traditional Classrooms

increase variation in the teaching. That is, because students vary in their learning styles and aptitudes, teachers must diversify and differentiate instruction to better meet students' individual learning needs. The challenge was to find practical ways to do this within the constraints of group-based classrooms so that all students could learn well.

In searching for such a strategy, Bloom drew primarily from two sources of evidence. First, he considered the ideal teaching and learning situation in which an excellent tutor is paired with each student. He was particularly influenced by the work of early pioneers in individualized instruction, especially Washburne (1922) and his Winnetka Plan, and Morrison (1926) and his University of Chicago Laboratory School experiments. In examining this evidence, Bloom tried to determine what crucial elements in one-on-one tutoring and individualized instruction could be transferred to group-based classroom settings.

Second, Bloom looked at studies of the learning strategies of academically successful students, especially the work of Dollard and Miller (1950). From this research he tried to identify the activities of high-achieving students in group-based classrooms that distinguish them from their less successful classmates.

Bloom saw value in teachers' traditional practice of organizing the concepts and skills they want students to learn into learning units. He also thought it important for teachers to assess student learning at the end of each unit. But the classroom assessments most teachers used seemed to do little more than show for whom their initial instruction was or was not appropriate.

Bloom believed that a far better approach would be for teachers to use their classroom assessments as learning tools, and then to follow those assessments with a feedback and corrective procedure. Instead of using assessments only as evaluation devices that mark the end of each unit, Bloom recommended using them as part of the instructional process to diagnose individual learning difficulties (feedback) and to prescribe remediation procedures (correctives).

This is precisely what takes place when an excellent tutor works with an individual student. If the student makes an error, the tutor first points out the error (feedback) and then follows up with further explanation and clarification (correctives) to ensure the student's understanding. Similarly, academically successful students typically follow up the mistakes they make on quizzes and assessments. They ask the teacher about the items they missed, look up the answer in the textbook or other resources, or rework the problem or task so that they do not repeat those errors.

With this in mind, Bloom outlined an instructional strategy to make use of this feedback and corrective procedure, labeling it "Learning for Mastery" (Bloom, 1968) and later shortening it to simply "Mastery Learning" (Bloom, 1971a). To use this strategy, teachers first organize the concepts and skills they want students to learn into learning units that typically involve about a week or two of instructional time. Following initial instruction on the unit, teachers administer a brief quiz or assessment based on the unit's learning goals. Instead of signifying the end of the unit, however, this assessment's purpose is to give students information, or feedback, about their learning. To emphasize this new purpose, Bloom suggested calling it a *formative assessment*, meaning "to inform or provide information." A formative assessment identifies for students precisely what they have learned well to that point and what they need to learn better (Bloom, Hastings, & Madaus, 1971).

Paired with each formative assessment are specific corrective activities for students to use in correcting their learning difficulties. Most teachers match these correctives to each item or set of prompts within the assessment so that students need to work on only those concepts or skills not yet mastered. In other words, the correctives are individualized. Correctives may point out additional sources of information on a particular concept, such as page numbers in the textbook or workbook where the concept is discussed. They may identify alternative learning resources such as different textbooks, learning kits, alternative materials, CDs, videos, or Web-based instructional lessons. Or they may simply suggest sources of additional practice, such as study guides, computer exercises, independent or guided practice activities, or collaborative group activities.

With the feedback and corrective information gained from the formative assessment, each student has a detailed prescription of what more needs to be done to master the concepts or skills from the unit. This just-in-time correction prevents minor learning difficulties from accumulating and becoming major learning problems. It also gives teachers a practical means to vary and differentiate their instruction in order to better meet students' individual learning needs. As a result, many more students learn well, master the important learning goals in each unit, and gain the necessary prerequisites for success in subsequent units.

When students complete their corrective activities after a class period or two, Bloom recommended they take a second formative assessment. This second, parallel assessment covers the same concepts and skills as the first, but is composed of slightly different problems or questions and serves two important purposes. First, it verifies whether the correctives were successful in helping students overcome their individual learning difficulties. Second, it offers students a second chance at success and, hence, has powerful motivational value.

Some students, of course, will perform well on the first assessment, demonstrating that they have mastered the unit concepts and skills. The teacher's initial instruction was highly appropriate for these students, and they have no need for corrective work. To ensure continued learning progress for these students, Bloom recommended that teachers provide them with special enrichment or extension activities to broaden their learning experiences. Enrichment activities are often self-selected by students and might involve special projects or reports, academic

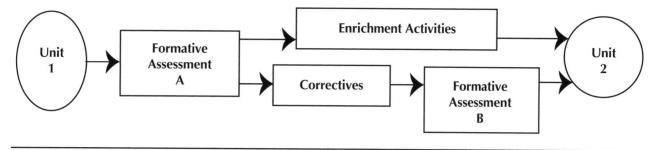

Figure 21.2   The Mastery Learning Instructional Process

games, or a variety of complex, problem-solving tasks. Figure 21.2 illustrates this instructional sequence.

Bloom believed all students could receive a more appropriate quality of instruction through this process than is possible under more traditional approaches to teaching. As a result, nearly all students might be expected to learn well and truly master the unit concepts or learning goals (Bloom, 1976). This, in turn, would drastically reduce the variation in students' achievement levels, eliminate achievement gaps, and yield a distribution of achievement more like that shown in Figure 21.3.

In describing mastery learning, Bloom emphasized that reducing variation in students' achievement does not imply making all students the same. Even under these more favorable learning conditions, some students undoubtedly will learn more than others, especially those involved in enrichment activities. But Bloom believed the variation among students in how well they learn specific concepts or master a set of articulated learning goals could eventually reach a "vanishing point" if teachers recognized relevant, individual differences among students and then altered instruction to better meet their diverse learning needs (Bloom, 1971b). In other words, *all* students could learn well the knowledge and skills prescribed in the curriculum. As a result, gaps in the achievement of different groups of students would be closed.

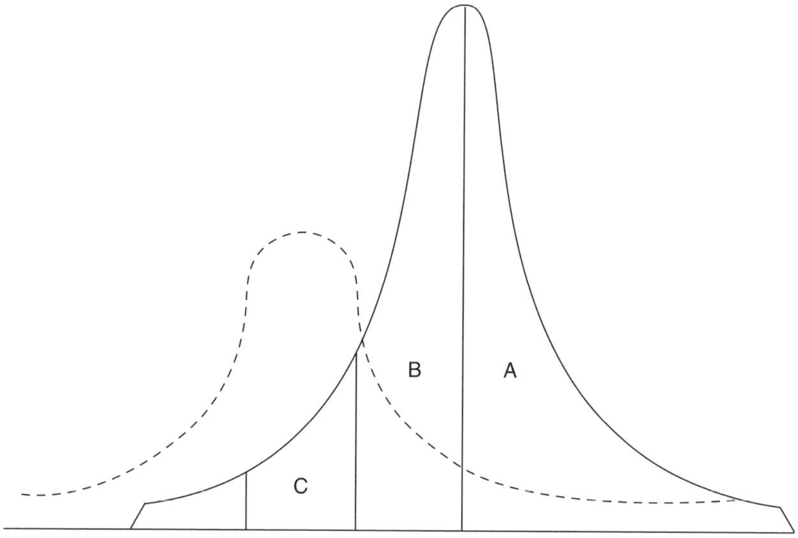

The Essential Elements of Mastery Learning

After Benjamin Bloom described his ideas, several of his students took up the task of clarifying mastery learning instructional strategies (e.g., Block, Efthim, & Burns, 1989), and numerous programs based on mastery learning principles sprung up in schools throughout the United States and around the world (see Postlethwaite & Haggarty, 1998; Reezigt & Weide, 1990; Wu, 1994; Yildiran, 2006). Although differing from setting to setting, those programs true to Bloom's ideas include two essential elements: the feedback, corrective, and enrichment process, and (2) instructional alignment (Guskey, 1997a).

Feedback, Correctives, and Enrichment

Teachers who use mastery learning provide students with frequent and specific feedback on their learning progress through regular, formative classroom assessments. This feedback is both diagnostic and prescriptive. It reinforces precisely what students were expected to learn, identifies what they learned well, and describes what needs to be learned better. The National Council of Teachers of Mathematics (NCTM) emphasizes this same element in its latest iteration of the standards for school mathematics. To overcome inequities in mathematics instruction, NCTM stresses the use of assessments that support learning and provide useful information to both teachers and students (National Council of Teachers of Mathematics [NCTM], 2000).

Feedback alone, however, does little to help students improve their learning. Significant improvement requires that feedback be paired with correctives: activities that offer guidance and direction to students on

Figure 21.3   Distribution of Achievement in Mastery Learning Classrooms

how to remedy their learning problems. Because of students' individual differences, no single method of instruction works best for all. To help every student learn well, therefore, teachers must differentiate their instruction, both in their initial teaching and especially through the corrective activities (Bloom, 1976). In other words, teachers must *increase* variation in their teaching to *decrease* variation in results.

To be effective, correctives must be qualitatively different from the initial teaching. They must provide students who need it with an alternative approach and additional time to learn. The best correctives present concepts differently and involve students in learning differently than did the initial instruction. They incorporate different learning styles, learning modalities, or types of intelligence. Although developing effective correctives can prove challenging, many schools find that providing teachers with time to work collaboratively—sharing ideas, materials, and expertise—greatly facilitates the process (Guskey, 2001).

Most applications of mastery learning also include enrichment or extension activities for students who master the unit concepts from the initial instruction. As described earlier, enrichment activities offer students exciting opportunities to broaden and expand their learning. They reward students for their learning success and challenge them to go further. Many teachers draw from activities developed for gifted and talented students when planning enrichment activities, both to simplify implementation tasks and to guarantee these students a high-quality learning experience.

Teachers implement the feedback, corrective, and enrichment process in a variety of ways. Many use short, paper-and-pencil quizzes as formative assessments to give students feedback on their learning progress. But formative assessments also can take the form of essays, compositions, projects, reports, performance tasks, skill demonstrations, oral presentations, or any device used to gain evidence on students' learning progress. In essence, teachers adapt the format of their formative assessments to match their instructional goals.

After administering a formative assessment, some teachers divide the class into separate corrective and enrichment groups. While the teacher directs corrective activities, guaranteeing that all students who need the extra time and assistance take part, the other students work on self-selected, independent enrichment activities. Other teachers pair with colleagues and use a team-teaching approach. While one teacher oversees corrective activities, the other monitors enrichments. Still other teachers use cooperative learning activities in which students work together in teams to ensure all reach the mastery level. Since students have their own personal scores on the formative assessment, individual accountability is ensured. Offering the entire team special recognition or credit if all members attain mastery on the second formative assessment encourages group responsibility.

Feedback, corrective, and enrichment procedures are crucial to mastery learning, for it is through these procedures that mastery learning differentiates and individualizes instruction. In every learning unit, students who need extended time and opportunity to remedy learning problems receive these through the correctives. Students who learn quickly and find the initial instruction highly appropriate have opportunities to extend their learning through enrichment. As a result, all students experience more favorable learning conditions and more appropriate, higher quality instruction (Bloom, 1977).

Instructional Alignment

While feedback, correctives, and enrichment are important, they alone do not constitute mastery learning. Bloom stressed that to be truly effective they must be combined with the second essential element of mastery learning: instructional alignment. Reducing variation in student learning and closing achievement gaps requires clarity and consistency among all instructional components (Bloom, 1971a).

Bloom believed three major components composed the teaching and learning process. To begin there must be specific ideas about what students are expected to learn and be able to do—that is, learning goals or standards. Next comes instruction that ideally results in proficient learners—students who have learned well and whose proficiency can be assessed through some form of assessment or evaluation. Mastery learning adds a feedback and corrective component, allowing teachers to determine for whom their initial instruction was appropriate and for whom an alternative approach may be needed.

Although essentially neutral with regard to what is taught, how it is taught, and how learning is assessed or evaluated, mastery learning requires consistency or alignment among these instructional components, as shown in Figure 21.4. For example, if students are expected to learn higher-level skills such as those involved in making applications, solving complex problems, or developing thoughtful analyses, mastery learning stipulates that instructional activities must be planned to give students opportunities to practice and actively engage in those skills. It also requires that students be given specific feedback on how well they have learned those skills, coupled with directions on how to correct any learning errors. Finally, procedures for assessing or evaluating students' learning should reflect those higher-level skills as well.

To ensure alignment among instructional components, teachers must make a number of crucial decisions. First, they need to decide what concepts or skills are most important for students to learn and most central to students' understanding. Teachers must determine, for example, if they want students to learn only basic skills or if they want students to develop higher-level skills and more complex cognitive processes. Second, teachers need to decide what evidence best reflects students' mastery of those basic or

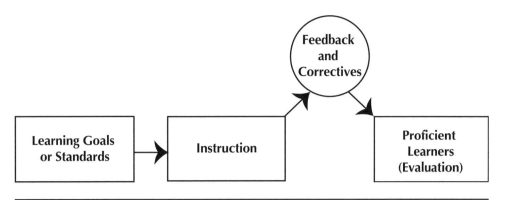

Figure 21.4   Major Components in the Teaching and Learning Process

higher-level skills. Critics sometimes challenge teachers' abilities to make these crucial decisions. But, in essence, teachers at all levels already make these decisions in conducting regular classroom activities. Every time they administer an assessment, grade a paper, or evaluate students' learning, teachers communicate to students what is most important to learn. Using mastery learning simply compels teachers to make these decisions more thoughtfully, intentionally, and purposefully.

Misinterpretations of Mastery Learning

Shortly after Bloom presented his ideas on mastery learning, people began to misinterpret them. Some early attempts to apply mastery learning, for example, were based on narrow and inaccurate understandings of Bloom's theory. These efforts focused only on low-level cognitive skills, attempted to break down learning into small segments, and insisted that students master each segment before being permitted to move on. Teachers were regarded in these programs as little more than managers of materials and record-keepers of student progress. Unfortunately, similar misinterpretations of mastery learning persist.

Nowhere in Bloom's writing, however, can this kind of narrowness and rigidity be found. In fact, Bloom emphasized quite the opposite. He considered thoughtful and reflective teachers vital to the successful implementation of mastery learning and continually stressed flexibility in its application. In his earliest description of the process, Bloom wrote:

> There are many alternative strategies for mastery learning. Each strategy must find some way of dealing with individual differences in learners through some means of relating the instruction to the needs and characteristics of the learners. . . . The nongraded school is one attempt to provide an organizational structure that permits and encourages mastery learning. (1968, pp. 7–8)

Bloom further emphasized his belief that instruction in mastery learning classrooms should focus on higher-level learning goals, not simply basic skills. He noted:

> I find great emphasis on problem solving, applications of principles, analytical skills, and creativity. Such higher mental processes are emphasized because this type of learning enables the individual to relate his or her learning to the many problems he or she encounters in day-to-day living. These abilities are stressed because they are retained and utilized long after the individual has forgotten the detailed specifics of the subject matter taught in the schools. These abilities are regarded as one set of essential characteristics needed to continue learning and to cope with a rapidly changing world. (Bloom, 1978, p. 576)

Modern research studies have shown mastery learning to be particularly effective when applied to instruction focusing on higher-level learning goals such as problem solving, drawing inferences, deductive reasoning, and creative expression (Arredondo & Block, 1990; Kozlovsky, 1990; Mevarech, 1981). When well implemented, the process helps teachers improve student learning and close achievement gaps in a broad range of learning goals from basic skills to highly complex cognitive processes.

Another misinterpretation comes from educators who believe that the constraint of limited class time will inhibit efforts to implement mastery learning (Guskey, 1997a). They assume that the introduction of feedback, corrective, and enrichment procedures will reduce the amount of material teachers will be able to cover. Teachers fear they will have to sacrifice coverage for the sake of mastery. Minor alterations in instructional pacing typically resolve this concern.

Early mastery learning units usually do require more time. Teachers who allot class time for students to complete corrective activities often find themselves behind other teachers who teach in more traditional ways after the first two or three units. But once students become familiar with the process, mastery learning teachers generally pick up the pace. Because students in mastery learning classes spend a larger portion of their time actively engaged in learning, they make more rapid progress than students in traditionally taught classes (Fitzpatrick, 1985). As students catch on to the process, they also do better on first formative assessments. With fewer students involved in correctives and less corrective work needed, teachers reduce the class time allocated to corrective activities. And because mastery learning students learn well the concepts and skills from early units, they are better prepared for later, more advanced units. Instruction in later units can therefore be more rapid and include fewer review activities. Most teachers discover that with slight adjustments in the pacing of their instruction—slightly more time spent in early units but less time in later ones—they can cover just as much material using mastery learning, and in some cases more, as they were able to using more traditional approaches to instruction (Block, 1983).

Research Results and Implications

Teachers who implement mastery learning generally find that it requires only modest changes in their instructional procedures. Excellent teachers use many aspects of mastery learning in their classes already, and others discover that the process blends well with their current teaching strategies. This makes mastery learning particularly attractive to teachers at all levels, especially considering the difficulties associated with new approaches that require major changes in teaching procedures.

Despite the modest nature of these changes, however, extensive research evidence shows that the use of mastery learning can have exceptionally positive effects on student learning (Block et al., 1989; Guskey & Pigott, 1988). Evidence gathered in Asia (Wu, 1994), Australia (Chan, 1981), Europe (Langeheine, 1992; Mevarech, 1981; Reezigt & Weide, 1990), and the United States (Walberg, 1990) shows the careful and systematic application of these elements can lead to significant improvements in student learning outcomes. Some researchers even suggest that the superiority of Japanese students in international comparisons of achievement in mathematics operations and problem solving may be due largely to the widespread use of instructional practices similar to mastery learning in Japan (Nakajima, 2006; Waddington, 1995).

Long-term investigations have yielded similarly impressive results. A study by Whiting, Van Burgh, and Render (1995), representing 18 years of data gathered from over 7,000 high school students, showed mastery learning to have remarkably positive influence on students' test scores and grade point averages as well as their attitudes toward school and learning. Another field experiment conducted in elementary and middle school classrooms showed that the implementation of mastery learning led to significantly positive increases in students' academic achievement and their self-confidence (Anderson et al., 1992). Even more impressive, a comprehensive, meta-analysis review of the research on mastery learning by C. C. Kulik et al. (1990) concluded:

> We recently reviewed meta-analyses in nearly 40 different areas of educational research (J. Kulik & Kulik, 1989). Few educational treatments of any sort were consistently associated with achievement effects as large as those produced by mastery learning. . . . In evaluation after evaluation, mastery programs have produced impressive gains. (C. C. Kulik et al., 1990, p. 292)

Research evidence also shows that the positive effects of mastery learning are not limited to cognitive or achievement outcomes. The process also yields improvements in students' confidence in learning situations, school attendance rates, involvement in class sessions, attitudes toward learning, and a variety of other affective measures (Block et al., 1989; Guskey & Pigott, 1988; Whiting & Render, 1987). This multidimensional impact has been referred to as the "multiplier effect" of mastery learning and makes it one of the most cost-effective means of educational improvement.

It should be noted that one review of the research on mastery learning, contrary to all previous reviews, indicated that the process had essentially no effect on student achievement (Slavin, 1987). This finding surprised not only scholars familiar with the vast research literature on mastery learning showing it to yield very positive results, but also large numbers of practitioners who had experienced its positive effects firsthand. A close inspection of this review shows, however, that it was conducted using techniques of questionable validity (Hiebert, 1987), employed capricious selection criteria (J. A. Kulik, Kulik, & Bangert-Drowns, 1990), reported results in a biased manner (Bloom, 1987; Walberg, 1988), and drew conclusions not substantiated by the evidence presented (Guskey, 1987, 1988). Two much more extensive and methodologically sound reviews published since (Guskey & Pigott, 1988; C. C. Kulik et al., 1990) have verified mastery learning's consistently positive effect on a broad range of student learning outcomes and, in one case (i.e., J. A. Kulik et al., 1990), showed clearly the distorted nature of this earlier report.

Conclusion

Researchers today generally recognize the value of the essential elements of mastery learning and their importance in effective teaching at any level of education. As a result, fewer studies are being conducted on the mastery learning process per se. Instead, researchers are looking for ways to enhance results further, adding additional elements to the mastery learning process that positively contribute to student learning in hopes of attaining even more impressive gains (Bloom, 1984). Work on the integration of mastery learning with other innovative strategies appears especially promising (Guskey, 1997b).

In his later writing Bloom, too, described exciting work on other ideas designed to attain results even more positive than those typically achieved with mastery learning (Bloom, 1984). These ideas stemmed from the work of two of Bloom's doctoral students, Anania (1981) and Burke (1983), who compared student learning under three different instructional conditions. The first was conventional instruction in which students were taught in group-based classes that included about 30 students and in which periodic assessments were given mainly for the purposes of grading. The second was mastery learning, in which students again were taught in group-based classes of about 30 students but were administered regular formative assessments for feedback, followed by individualized corrective instruction and parallel second assessments to determine the extent to which they mastered specific learning goals. The third was tutoring, where a good tutor was paired with each student. Students under tutoring were also administered regular formative assessments, along with corrective procedures and parallel second assessments, although the need for corrective work under tutoring was usually quite small.

The differences in students' final achievement under these three conditions were striking. Using the standard deviation (sigma) of the control (conventional) class as the measure of difference, Bloom's students discovered that:

> The average student under tutoring was about two standard deviations above the average of the control class (the average tutored student was above 98% of the students in the control class). The average student under mastery learning was about one standard deviation above the average of the control class (the average mastery learning student was above 84% of the students in the control class). . . . Thus under the best learning conditions we can devise (tutoring), the average student is 2 sigma above the average control student taught under conventional group methods of instruction. (Bloom, 1984, p. 4)

Bloom referred to this as the "2 Sigma Problem":

> The tutoring process demonstrates that *most* students do have the potential to reach this high level of learning. I believe an important task of research and instruction is to seek ways of accomplishing this under more practical and realistic conditions than the one-to-one tutoring, which is too costly for most societies to bear on a large scale. This is the "2 Sigma" problem. Can researchers and teachers devise teaching-learning conditions that will enable the majority of students under *group instruction* to attain levels of achievement that can at present be reached only under tutoring conditions? (Bloom, 1984, pp. 4–5)

Bloom believed that attaining this high level of achievement would probably require more than just improvements in the quality of group instruction. Researchers and teachers might also need to find ways of improving students' learning processes, the curriculum and instructional materials, the home environmental support of students' school learning, and providing a focus on higher-level thinking skills. Nevertheless, Bloom remained convinced that careful attention to the elements of mastery learning would allow educators at all levels to make great strides in their efforts to reduce the variation in student achievement, close achievement gaps, and help all children to learn excellently.

References and Further Readings

Anania, J. (1981). *The effects of quality of instruction on the cognitive and affective learning of students.* Unpublished doctoral dissertation, University of Chicago.

Anderson, S., Barrett, C., Huston, M., Lay, L., Myr, G., Sexton, D., et al. (1992). *A mastery learning experiment* (Technical Report). Yale, MI: Yale Public Schools.

Anderson, S. A. (1994). *Synthesis of research on mastery learning.* (ERIC Document Reproduction Service No. ED 382 567).

Arredondo, D., & Block, J. (1990). Recognizing the connections between thinking skills and mastery learning. *Educational Leadership, 47*(5), 4–10.

Block, J. H. (1983). Learning rates and mastery learning. *Outcomes, 2*(3), 18–23.

Block, J. H., Efthim, H. E., & Burns, R. B. (1989). *Building effective mastery learning schools.* New York: Longman.

Bloom, B. S. (1968). Learning for mastery. *Evaluation Comment, 1*(2), 1–12.

Bloom, B. S. (1971a). Mastery learning. In J. H. Block (Ed.), *Mastery learning: Theory and practice* (pp. 47–63). New York: Holt, Rinehart & Winston.

Bloom, B. S. (1971b). *Individual differences in school achievement: A vanishing point?* Bloomington, IN: Phi Delta Kappan International.

Bloom, B. S. (1976). *Human characteristics and school learning.* New York: McGraw-Hill.

Bloom, B. S. (1977). Favorable learning conditions for all. *Teacher, 95*(3), 22–28.

Bloom, B. S. (1978). New views of the learner: Implications for instruction and curriculum. *Educational Leadership, 35*(7), 563–576.

Bloom, B. S. (1984). The 2 sigma problem: The search for methods of group instruction as effective as one-to-one tutoring. *Educational Researcher, 13*(6), 4–16.

Bloom, B. S. (1987). A response to Slavin's mastery learning reconsidered. *Review of Educational Research, 57*(4), 507–508.

Bloom, B. S. (1988). Helping all children learn in elementary school and beyond. *Principal, 67*(4), 12–17.

Bloom, B. S., Hastings, J. T., & Madaus, G. (1971). *Handbook on formative and summative evaluation of student learning.* New York: McGraw-Hill.

Burke, A. J. (1983). *Students' potential for learning contrasted under tutorial and group approaches to instruction.* Unpublished doctoral dissertation, University of Chicago.

Carroll, J. B. (1963). A model for school learning. *Teachers College Record, 64,* 723–733.

Chan, K. S. (1981). *The interaction of aptitude with mastery versus non-mastery instruction: Effects on reading comprehension of grade three students.* Unpublished doctoral dissertation, University of Western Australia.

Dollard, J., & Miller, N. E. (1950). *Personality and psychotherapy.* New York: McGraw-Hill.

Fitzpatrick, K. A. (1985, April). *Group-based mastery learning: A Robin Hood approach to instruction?* Paper presented at the annual meeting of the American Educational Research Association, Chicago.

Glaser, R. (1966). *The program for individually prescribed instruction.* Pittsburgh, PA: University of Pittsburgh.

Guskey, T. R. (1987). Rethinking mastery learning reconsidered. *Review of Educational Research, 57*(2), 225–229.

Guskey, T. R. (1988). Response to Slavin: Who defines best? *Educational Leadership, 46*(2), 26–27.

Guskey, T. R. (1997a). *Implementing mastery learning* (2nd ed.). Belmont, CA: Wadsworth.

Guskey, T. R. (1997b). Putting it all together: Integrating educational innovations. In S. J. Caldwell (Ed.), *Professional*

Development in Learning-Centered Schools (pp. 130–149). Oxford, OH: National Staff Development Council.

Guskey, T. R. (2001). Mastery learning. In N. J. Smelser & P. B. Baltes (Eds.), *International Encyclopedia of Social and Behavioral Sciences* (pp. 9372–9377). Oxford, UK: Elsevier Science Ltd.

Guskey, T. R., & Pigott, T. D. (1988). Research on group-based mastery learning programs: A meta-analysis. *Journal of Educational Research, 81,* 197–216.

Hiebert, E. H. (1987). The context of instruction and student learning: An examination of Slavin's assumptions. *Review of Educational Research, 57,* 337–340.

Klausmeier, H. J., Rossmiller, R. A., & Saily, M. (1977). *Individually guided elementary education: Concepts and practices.* New York: Academic Press.

Kozlovsky, J. D. (1990). Integrating thinking skills and mastery learning in Baltimore County. *Educational Leadership, 47*(5), 6.

Kulik, C. C., Kulik, J. A., & Bangert-Drowns, R. L. (1990). Effectiveness of mastery learning programs: A meta-analysis. *Review of Educational Research, 60,* 265–299.

Kulik, J. A., & Kulik, C. C. (1989). Meta-analysis in education. *International Journal of Educational Research, 13*(2), 221–340.

Kulik, J. A., Kulik, C. C., & Bangert-Drowns, R. L. (1990). Is there better evidence on mastery learning? A response to Slavin. *Review of Educational Research, 60,* 303–307.

Langeheine, R. (1992, April). *State mastery learning: Dynamic models for longitudinal data.* Paper presented at the annual meeting of the American Educational Research Association, San Francisco.

Levine, D. U. (1985). *Improving student achievement through mastery learning programs.* San Francisco: Jossey-Bass.

Mevarech, Z. R. (1981, April). *Attaining mastery on higher cognitive achievement.* Paper presented at the annual meeting of the American Educational Research Association, Los Angeles.

Morrison, H. C. (1926). *The practice of teaching in the secondary school.* Chicago: University of Chicago Press.

Nakajima, A. (2006). A powerful influence on Japanese education. In T. R. Guskey (Ed.), *Benjamin S. Bloom: Portraits of an educator* (pp. 109–111). Lanham, MD: Rowman & Littlefield Education.

National Council of Teachers of Mathematics. (2000). *Principles and standards for school mathematics.* Reston, VA: Author. Retrieved April 30, 2007, from http://standards.nctm.org/document/index.htm

Postlethwaite, K., & Haggarty, L. (1998). Towards effective and transferable learning in secondary school: The development of an approach based on mastery learning. *British Educational Research Journal, 24*(3), 333–353.

Reezigt, B. J., & Weide, M. G. (1990, April). *The effects of group-based mastery learning on language and arithmetic achievement and attitudes in primary education in the Netherlands.* Paper presented at the annual meeting of the American Educational Research Association, Boston.

Slavin, R. E. (1987). Mastery learning reconsidered. *Review of Educational Research, 57*(2), 175–213.

Waddington, T. (1995, April). *Why mastery matters.* Paper presented at the annual meeting of the American Educational Research Association, San Francisco.

Walberg, H. J. (1988). Response to Slavin: What's the best evidence? *Educational Leadership, 46*(2), 28.

Walberg, H. J. (1990). Productive teaching and instruction: Assessing the knowledge base. *Phi Delta Kappan, 71,* 470–478.

Washburne, C. W. (1922). Educational measurements as a key to individualizing instruction and promotions. *Journal of Educational Research, 5*(1), 195–206.

Whiting, B., & Render, G. F. (1987). Cognitive and affective outcomes of mastery learning: A review of sixteen semesters. *The Clearing House, 60*(6), 276–280.

Whiting, B., Van Burgh, J. W., & Render, G. F. (1995). *Mastery learning in the classroom.* Paper presented at the annual meeting of the American Educational Research Association, San Francisco.

Wu, W. Y. (1994, April). *Mastery learning in Hong Kong: Challenges and prospects.* Paper presented at the annual meeting of the American Educational Research Association, New Orleans, LA.

Yildiran, G. (2006). *Multicultural applications of mastery learning.* Istanbul, Turkey: Faculty of Education, Bogazici University.

22

LEARNING IN SMALL GROUPS

NOREEN M. WEBB

University of California, Los Angeles

It is hard to exaggerate the interest in small-group learning in today's schools. Recognizing that students can learn by working with and helping each other, school districts, state departments of education, national research organizations, and curriculum specialists recommend, and even mandate, the use of peer-based learning. Teachers can choose from many commercially available guides and programs designed to help them plan, implement, and manage small-group learning. Whole schools have even been organized around students cooperating with each other as the primary mode of instruction. Undergirding these activities is a large body of research that shows the positive effects of small-group methods on student achievement, especially compared to other forms of instruction that involve less interaction between students (e.g., Slavin, 1995).

In spite of the potential for small-group work to foster student learning, most researchers agree that simply placing students in small groups does not guarantee that learning will occur. Rather, the extent to which students benefit from working with other students depends on the group dynamics and the nature of students' participation in group work. This chapter explores how group work is thought to benefit student learning and the many ways in which teachers might orchestrate small-group work to achieve those benefits. It does not catalog differences among small-group approaches, which often have such labels as cooperative learning, collaborative learning, peer tutoring, and peer-based or peer-directed learning, but considers all small-group contexts in which students are encouraged, expected, or required to work with each other to improve student learning.

Mechanisms for Learning From Peers

Piagetian Perspective

The view that cognitive conflict leads to higher levels of reasoning and learning derives principally from the work of Piaget (1932) and his followers. Cognitive conflict arises when a learner perceives a contradiction between her or his existing understanding and what the learner hears or sees in the course of interacting with others. This contradiction and its disequilibrating effect lead the learner to reexamine and question his or her own ideas and beliefs, to seek additional information in order to reconcile the conflicting viewpoints, and to try new ideas. Piaget suggested that exchanges with peers are more likely than exchanges with adults to promote children's cognitive development because children are likely to cooperate as equals, to speak at a level that other students understand, to challenge each other, and to share each other's point of view.

Numerous studies have examined the cognitive development of pairs of children working on conservation tasks that ask them to discuss whether some characteristics of objects (e.g., the volume of liquid) remain the same when others (e.g., the width or height of the container) change (De Lisi & Golbeck, 1999). When children who have not yet learned the principle of conservation are paired with children who have mastered it, the former often gain conservation knowledge whereas the latter rarely regress to giving incorrect responses. Students with and students without a knowledge of conservation have been shown to behave in different ways, with conservers asserting and justifying their answers, as well as producing counter-arguments, and non-conservers restating their original responses without any elaboration. Even non-conservers working together progress when they hold conflicting, but still incorrect, ideas, but not when they hold the same incorrect conception.

Vygotskian Perspective

Vygotsky (1978) posited that the benefits of collaboration occur when a more expert person helps a less expert person. With the help of a more skilled person, a process of negotiation and transformation enables the less competent person to carry out a task that the student could not perform without assistance, a process sometimes called scaffolding or guided participation. Through practice and internalization, new skills and knowledge become part of the student's individual repertoire (Tudge, 1990).

In peer-directed settings, students can often provide effective scaffolding and support due to their understanding of each other's misunderstandings and their ability to explain concepts in familiar terms (Noddings, 1985). Students may be especially able to provide each other assistance that is at the right level, rather than assistance that is beyond their teammates' understanding or assistance that is not necessary.

Effective scaffolding requires several conditions. Help provided must be relevant to the less proficient student's need for help, and it must be timely, correct, comprehensible, and at the level of help needed. Further, students receiving help must have the opportunity to use explanations to solve the problem or carry out the tasks and must use that opportunity for practice by attempting to apply the explanations received to the problem at hand (Vedder, 1985). Students must both have and take advantage of the opportunity to apply the information contained in the explanation. Empirical studies of the relationship between these behaviors and achievement support the power of the latter conditions. Receiving explanations has sometimes been found to be more strongly related to achievement than is receiving less elaborated responses, such as the answer to a problem without suggestions about how to solve it, or receiving no help at all; however, a stronger predictor of learning outcomes is whether students use the help they receive to solve problems on their own without assistance (Webb & Palincsar, 1996). This relationship is consistent with the Vygotskian notion that the process of learning is more than simply the transfer of knowledge from expert to novice. This perspective holds that the active participation of the learner is critical; the more competent partner helps the less competent partner not only by informing, correcting, and explaining, but also by forcing the latter partner to explain (Tudge, 1990).

Co-Construction of Knowledge

Students can also learn by co-constructing knowledge with their peers. Hatano (1993) showed how students can contribute different pieces of information or build upon others' explanations to jointly create a complete idea or solution. Researchers have documented how students can collaboratively build knowledge and problem-solving strategies that no group member has at the start by acknowledging, clarifying, correcting, adding to, building upon, and connecting each other's ideas and suggestions (e.g., Hogan, Nastasi, & Pressley, 2000). Such interactions help children co-construct and internalize strategies and concepts in many areas including identifying chemicals in chemical reactions, understanding of place value, learning principles of transformational geometry, learning how to multiply whole numbers, and so forth.

Co-construction requires a high degree of coordination among group members. Barron (2003) noted that highly coordinated groups acknowledge each other's ideas, repeat others' suggestions, and elaborate on others' proposals. Speakers' turns are tightly connected, with group members paying close attention to and responding to what other members do and say, giving space for others' contributions, and monitoring how the unfolding contributions relate to the problem-solving goal. Proposals are directly linked to the prior conversation and are acknowledged and discussed, not rejected or ignored. Interaction in such groups is marked by a high degree of joint attention and respect. According to Barron, highly coordinated groups simultaneously and successfully negotiate a dual-problem space consisting of a content space and a relational space.

Cognitive Elaboration Perspective

From a cognitive elaboration perspective, interacting with others may encourage students to engage in cognitive restructuring, by which they restructure their own knowledge and understanding. This occurs when students elaborate on their thinking during conversations with others. Specifically, explaining the material to others may promote learning by encouraging students to rehearse information, reorganize and clarify material, recognize their own misconceptions, fill gaps in their own understanding, strengthen connections between new information and previously learned information, internalize and acquire new strategies and knowledge, and develop new perspectives and understanding (Bargh & Schul, 1980). In the process of formulating an explanation, students may think about the salient features of the problem and generate self-explanations that help them to internalize principles, construct specific inference rules for solving the problem, and repair imperfect mental models (Chi, 2000). This process may help them develop a better awareness of what they do and do not understand. In addition, tailoring explanations to the difficulties of other students may push helpers to construct more elaborate conceptualizations than they would otherwise. Giving non-elaborated help (such as the answer to a problem without any accompanying explanation of how to solve it), on the other hand, is expected to have fewer benefits because it may involve less cognitive restructuring by the helper.

Research documents the strong relationship between giving explanations and achievement in small groups (Webb & Palincsar, 1996). Research on peer tutoring also demonstrates the effectiveness of giving explanations, with tutors who give more elaborate explanations (e.g., describing the relationship between the current problem and real-life examples; showing connections between ideas in the material being discussed) learning more than tutors who give less elaborate explanations (King, 1999).

The cognitive elaboration perspective is not necessarily independent of the Piagetian and Vygotskian perspectives, or of the co-construction model, but, instead, may be an integral part of them. In Piaget's model of sociocognitive conflict and learning, confronting others' contradictory ideas may involve explaining and justifying one's own position, with the potentially positive effects on learning described above. Similarly, the foregoing description of scaffolding in the Vygotskian perspective has already highlighted the active role that the less competent student plays. Specifically, explaining one's own thinking and understanding constitutes part of the process through which the less capable person constructs his or her knowledge. And during co-construction, students may justify their own ideas and elaborate on others' ideas, with new knowledge and understanding resulting.

Motivational Perspective

According to the motivational theory of Deutsch (1949), when groups work toward a common goal, students will praise, encourage, and support each other's contributions, resulting in more effort, a greater liking of the task and of other students. In a cooperative goal structure, group members can attain their own personal goals only if the group is successful. One way to create such a group goal is through the use of rewards or incentives. In Slavin's (1995) Student Teams Achievement Divisions (STAD), for example, teams work in a peer tutoring format to master information presented to the whole class and then take quizzes to assess individual achievement. Teams are rewarded based on the improvement of individuals in the team, thus holding both groups and individuals accountable. By making the team's success dependent on the individual learning of all members of the team, these group rewards ensure individual accountability and a feeling of personal responsibility for what happens in the group. This

motivates students to work hard toward the group goal, to encourage others to do the same, and to help each other in order to ensure the group's success. These processes increase the chance of a favorable group outcome and consequently a reward for each group member.

The use of group rewards is not without controversy. Lepper (1983) posited that extrinsic rewards can undermine intrinsic motivation and interest in the classroom, and that students may begin to pay more attention to obtaining the reward than learning the material. Students may invest the least effort necessary to obtain rewards or may choose to perform less challenging tasks. Students may help each other only as the means to an external reward rather than valuing helping each other and learning for their own sakes. When groups fail to obtain the reward, students may feel dissatisfied with themselves or others or may blame low performers for the group's failure.

Features of cooperative methods such as Slavin's STAD are intended to prevent these debilitating processes. To limit the focus on the reward, the incentive (e.g., a team certificate or mention in a classroom newsletter) is not designed to be highly desirable or to have high stakes. To ensure student effort, task difficulty is tailored to the capabilities of individual team members and no one is assigned overly difficult tasks. Finally, to reduce pressure on less capable group members, rewards are based on individuals' improvements in scores, not on their absolute performance. Cooperative learning methods that use both group rewards and individual accountability generally produce greater achievement than cooperative learning methods that include only one or neither of these components (Slavin, 1996).

Social Cohesion Perspective

Deutsch (1949) also described how students may be motivated to help each other because they care about the group and its members. To develop a sense of group identification and concern for others, a number of cooperative learning methods include team building and the development of social skills in order to build group cohesion instead of (or sometimes in addition to) using group rewards; this approach is the foundation of Johnson and Johnson's (1994) Learning Together. Team-building activities help team members to get to know each other and to experience success as a team. Social skills training focuses on interpersonal skills such as active listening, stating ideas freely, and accepting responsibility for one's behaviors, as well as small-group skills such as taking turns, sharing tasks, making decisions democratically, trying to understand others' perspectives, and clarifying differences (Gillies, 2004). Developing and using these skills helps group members to trust, accept, and support each other, to communicate accurately and effectively, and to resolve conflicts constructively.

Feedback on how well the group is functioning also helps to build cohesion. Discussing their group's interaction and how they might improve it (sometimes called group processing) helps groups to function more effectively. Having students share their thoughts and feelings about their own and their teammates' participation also helps groups to identify, understand, and solve general communication problems (disruptive or bullying behavior), provides positive reinforcement for student collaboration, and helps students to maintain good working relationships (Johnson & Johnson, 1994).

Debilitating Processes

Groups do not always function in ways that are optimal for learning. Researchers have documented a number of detrimental processes.

Unequal Participation

Individuals don't always have equal opportunities to participate in groups. Some members are much more active and influential than others. Personality characteristics may explain some effects such as extroverted, outgoing, and energetic members doing most of the talking. Status characteristics may also determine relative influence in the group (Cohen & Lotan, 1995). High-status students, especially those with high academic standing or peer status characteristics (perceived attractiveness or popularity), tend to be more active and influential than low-status individuals, while low-status individuals tend to be less assertive and more anxious, talk less, and give fewer suggestions and less information than high-status individuals. Social characteristics, such as gender or race, may also operate as status characteristics in heterogeneous small groups; boys and White students may be more active than girls and students of color.

Even artificially created status differences (such as classifying students' competence on the basis of fictitious test scores; Dembo & McAuliffe, 1987) can create imbalances in individual participation and influence.

Whereas some students may be shut out of interaction, other students may choose not to participate. Students may engage in social loafing, or diffusion of responsibility, which arises when one or more group members sit back and let others do the work, possibly because they believe that their efforts can't or won't be identified or are dispensable (Salomon & Globerson, 1989). This free-rider effect may turn into a sucker effect when the group members who complete all of the work discover that they had been taken for a free ride and start to contribute less to the group work in order to avoid being a sucker.

Students who choose not to be involved or who are excluded from group interaction will not experience the benefits of active participation described in the previous sections of this chapter. And the students who do participate will not benefit from the knowledge and perspectives of the passive students, and may even lead the group off track by pursuing the wrong task or suggesting incorrect solutions that are not challenged.

The goal of promoting the participation of all group members was the foundation of one of the earliest cooperative learning methods, jigsaw (Aronson, Blaney, Stephin, Sikes, & Snapp, 1978), which was designed to bring together students from different cultural backgrounds. In the jigsaw classroom, students are assigned responsibility for mastering a portion of the material, they meet to discuss that material with other students assigned the same topic, and then they return to their heterogeneous groups to teach their topic to the other members of their groups. Another early cooperative learning approach that also built in participation by all students is group investigation (Sharan & Hertz-Lazarowitz, 1980), in which students carry out research on their piece of a group project and then come together as a team to integrate their findings and plan a class presentation.

Failure to Seek and Obtain Effective Help

Another set of debilitating processes concerns the failure of students to seek help when they need it and to obtain effective help when they seek it. Students who do not seek help may never correct their misconceptions. Students may fail to seek help for many reasons (Nelson-Le Gall, 1992). Students may lack the metacognitive skills necessary to monitor their own comprehension and so may not realize that they don't understand the material or can't perform the task without assistance, or they may watch their teammates solve a problem or accomplish a task and assume that they can do it too.

Even if students are aware that they need help, they may decide not to seek it for fear of being judged incompetent and undesirable as a workmate, or they may not want to feel indebted to those giving the help (Newman, 1998). Or students may believe that help seeking is undesirable (as a result of classroom norms that call for students to remain quiet and work alone, or sex-typed norms that view help seeking as more appropriate for females than males) or they may have received antagonistic or unsatisfactory responses to previous help-seeking attempts. Students may also believe that no one in the group has the competence or resources to help, or that they themselves lack the competence to benefit from help provided.

When students seek help, they may select helpers who are nice or kind, or who have high status, rather than those who have task-relevant skills (Nelson-Le Gall, 1992). Students may not have effective strategies for eliciting help. In particular, the kinds of questions students ask often have important consequences for the kinds of responses they receive. Requests for help that are explicit, precise, direct, and targeted to a specific aspect of the problem or task are more likely to elicit explanations than unfocused questions or general statements of confusion. Asking precise questions makes it easier for other group members to identify the student's misconceptions or areas of confusion and to formulate effective help. General questions, in contrast, may signal a lack of ability, a lack of effort, or both. Students who appear to be loafing are typically less likely to receive help than those who appear to be working hard.

Even if group members are willing to help, they may not have the skills to provide effective explanations. Help-givers may have misconceptions themselves, may not be able to translate their thinking into appropriate or understandable language, may not provide enough detail or detail relevant to the help-seeker's particular difficulty or level of understanding, or may not be able to identify the help-seeker's problem.

Finally, whether a student obtains help may depend on the group's composition and the student's relative position within that group. For example, in groups that are heterogeneous in terms of student proficiency, middle-ability students may be left out of a teacher-learner relationship that develops between high-ability and low-ability members of the group; whereas the same middle-ability students may participate more actively in homogeneous groups, especially with regard to receiving answers to their questions (Webb & Palincsar, 1996).

Too Little or Too Much Cognitive Conflict

Although students can learn by resolving discrepancies in ideas, too little or too much conflict can be detrimental (Bearison, Magzamen, & Filardo, 1986). Infrequent conflict may reflect suppression of disagreements, or pseudocon-sensus or pseudoagreement, in which students minimize disagreements or pretend they don't exist. In these cases, incorrect ideas may go unchallenged. Too much conflict, on the other hand, may prevent group members from seeking new information to resolve their disagreements. If they spend all of their time arguing (especially if their aim is to win the argument regardless if they are right or wrong), they may never develop new insights.

Lack of Coordination

Group functioning and individual learning may also suffer from a lack of coordination of group members' efforts and participation (Barron, 2003). Group progress may be inhibited by low levels of attention to and uptake of members' suggestions, even when those suggestions are correct and potentially productive. In incoherent conversations, students advocate and repeat their own positions and ideas, ignore others' suggestions, reject others' proposals without elaboration or justification, and interrupt others or talk over them. Such lack of coordination and joint attention may undermine all of the processes through which individuals can gain by collaborating with others, including resolving conflicts, co-constructing knowledge and understanding, participating in scaffolding, giving and receiving help, and engaging in cognitive elaboration.

Other Negative Socioemotional Processes

Other negative socioemotional processes, such as rudeness, hostility, and unresponsiveness, can also impede group members' participation, cause groups to reject correct ideas, and prevent groups from solving problems correctly (Chiu & Khoo, 2003). Such processes can also suppress help seeking, especially when students are insulted when they seek help, receive sarcastic responses, or have their requests rejected or ignored. Students who carry out negative behavior may have their requests for help rejected. Even students who are knowledgeable may withhold information or refuse to provide help when insulted or taunted by others.

Approaches to Promoting Beneficial Group Processes

Researchers have designed a great variety of collaborative learning methods in order to promote beneficial group processes and inhibit detrimental group dynamics. Many, if not most, small-group approaches incorporate one or more of the components described here.

Preparing Students for Collaborative Work

Altering Expectations and Status Relationships

To promote equal participation among students in heterogeneous (especially multiracial) groups, Cohen and Lotan (1995) developed methods of minimizing status effects by altering high-status students' expectations about low-status students' competence. In expectation training, low-status students receive special training on both academic and nonacademic tasks, and then teach high-status students how to do the tasks. All students then work on unrelated activities in their heterogeneous groups. The important feature of this training program is changing high-status students' perceptions about low-status students' competence. Increasing the competence of low-status students without also manipulating the high-status students' expectations of the low-status students' performance (as it is when the low-status students teach the high-status students) is not sufficient to change the usual pattern of high-status students' dominating group interactions. A less time-intensive approach is the multi-ability intervention, which raises students' awareness of the multiple skills necessary to do the task. The teacher discusses with students the multiple abilities needed to solve complex problems (e.g., visual thinking, intuitive thinking, and reasoning), and when groups work on these tasks the teacher comments on particular contributions of low-status students and identifies the importance and value of their contributions.

All of these programs have shown success in reducing the relationship between status (based on language background, race, socioeconomic status, or academic ability, for example) and behavior in small groups. The more frequently teachers talk about the multiple abilities needed for a task (and emphasize that no one has all of the abilities) and comment on the value of low-status students' contributions, the greater the participation rate of low-status students and the smaller the gap between high-status and low-status students' participation rates.

Instruction in Explaining and Group Reasoning Skills

Many studies have incorporated instruction in academic helping and explaining behaviors (e.g., Gillies, 2004). Students are taught help-seeking and help-giving skills, such as asking clear and precise questions, giving explanations instead of answers, justifying their views, checking for understanding, checking others' answers, challenging others, and giving specific feedback on how teammates solve the problem. Compared to untrained groups, trained groups exhibit more explaining and often higher achievement.

Structuring Group Interaction

Some small-group approaches structure group interaction in specific ways or implement activities to guide groups' cooperation. Features of these methods include requiring groups to carry out certain strategies or activities, assigning students certain roles to play, or both.

Reciprocal Teaching

In teacher scaffolded instruction, referred to as reciprocal teaching, teachers help students carry out certain strategies designed to improve comprehension of text: generating questions about the text they have read, clarifying what they don't understand, summarizing the text, and generating predictions (Palincsar & Brown, 1984). Teachers initially take the leadership by explaining the strategies and modeling their use in making sense of the text. Then teachers ask students to demonstrate the strategies, but give them considerable support. For example, in order to help a student generate questions to ask groupmates, the teacher might probe what information the student gleaned from the text and help the student phrase a specific question using that information. The teacher gradually assumes the less active role of coach, giving students feedback and encouraging them. Students then carry out the text comprehension strategies in their small groups. With this method, students show considerable gains in reading comprehension and sometimes greater progress than with other cooperative learning approaches or in instruction without peer interaction.

Explanation Prompts

Some peer learning approaches give students specific prompts to encourage them to give elaborated explanations. Students may be prompted to describe what happens in science experiments, to find patterns in their results, to explain why results occur, to justify answers or opinions, or to connect real-world experiences to classroom learning. Such explanation prompts have successfully produced conceptually advanced explaining as well as more complete and deeper understanding of the material.

Guided Reciprocal Questioning

In guided reciprocal questioning, students ask each other high-level questions about the material. These questions are intended to help students monitor their own and each other's comprehension and to encourage students to describe and elaborate on their thinking. Students may be given "how" and "why" question stems to guide their discussions of text, for example, Why is . . . important? How are . . . and . . . similar (King, 1992, p. 113)? Or students may be given questions to help them co-construct and explain strategies for solving problems, such as What is the problem? What do we know about the problem so far? What information is given to us? and What is our plan (King, 1999, p. 101)? Groups' use of these high-level questions increases the frequency of elaborated explaining and produces greater learning than individuals using such questions outside of a collaborative context or engaging in group discussions without such question prompts.

Structured Controversy

In order to promote the benefits that arise when students try to resolve conflicting ideas, Johnson and Johnson (1995) built controversy into the group's task by subdividing groups into teams and requiring the teams to master material on different sides of an issue (e.g., should there be more or fewer regulations governing hazardous waste disposal). Then groups presented their views to the other team and synthesized the two positions. Compared to groups required to seek concurrence by working cooperatively and compromising, groups required to discuss opposing ideas often carried out more high-level discussion of the material and less description of the facts and information; they also attained higher achievement.

Cognitive Role Specialization

To facilitate high-level discourse and learning in groups, a number of approaches give students specific roles to play (usually alternated or rotated) in which they carry out specific cognitive activities. Students may be assigned such roles as recaller (also called learning leader or summarizer) and listener (also called active listener, learning listener, or listener/facilitator) that can be incorporated into scripts for groups to follow. The recaller summarizes the material and the listener is responsible for detecting errors, identifying omissions, and seeking clarification. Students then work together to elaborate on the material; they change roles for the next part of the task. Scripted cooperation usually produces greater student achievement than unstructured cooperation, as a result of students' explicit use of elaboration (O'Donnell, 1999). These scripts may be even more productive when students teach each other different material than when students have studied the same material; students may be less likely to worry about how others will evaluate their summaries, and may be less likely to make inferences about what others are saying and more likely to ask them to clarify their summaries.

In reciprocal peer tutoring, students receive training in how to model strategies such as summarizing text and in how to give explanations, corrections, and feedback about other students' work. They then alternate tutor and tutee roles during pair work. Some approaches pair more skilled and less skilled learners, whereas others pair students randomly or pair those with similar proficiency. Special attention is often paid to promoting high-level discourse during paired discussions, such as training tutors to give highly elaborated conceptual rather than algorithmic explanations to their partners (e.g., using real-life examples, discussing why an answer does or does not make sense; Fuchs et al., 1997). Reflecting the importance of the activity of the help-receiver, some peer tutoring models guide the tutor in helping the tutee to give high-level explanations (King, 1999). The tutor asks questions designed to encourage the tutee to provide explanations of the material, asks further questions to push the tutee to elaborate upon or justify their explanations as well as to correct incomplete or incorrect explanations, and asks questions to push tutees to make connections among ideas and to link new material to their prior knowledge. Observations of tutor-tutee discussions show that these strategies for increasing the level of pair discourse are usually highly successful with corresponding positive effects on achievement.

Manipulating the Group-Work Task

To maximize the participation of all group members, Cohen (1994) recommended that groups be given complex tasks or open-ended problems without clear-cut answers or procedures that cannot be completed very well by a single individual and that require the combined expertise of everyone in the group. Such tasks encourage groups to recognize the multiple skills and perspectives needed to complete the task and to value the different contributions that each student makes. Tasks or problems that can be completed by one student with the requisite skills, on the other hand, are more likely to limit the participation of students without those skills.

The Teacher's Role

Developing Classroom Goal Structures and Norms

The teacher can play an important role by working with students to mutually construct norms for how students should engage with each other during group work. The teacher can monitor and intervene in small-group dialogues in order to remind students about their obligations (e.g., to make sure that everyone participates, to describe their interpretations of problems and solutions, to share their thinking and solution methods with others, to justify their own answers, and to challenge each other's solutions) and to make specific suggestions for how students should behave in particular circumstances (e.g., stop another student and ask for help, be sure that everyone understands each other's problem-solving strategies; Yackel, Cobb, & Wood, 1991). The teacher can discuss with the whole class expected small-group behaviors and can use specific, as well as hypothetical, situations to initiate discussions with the class about students' responsibilities in collaborative work and to show examples of genuine dialogue between students.

Modeling Desired Discourse

Teachers also communicate their expectations for students' behavior through their own behavior. Two recent studies showed how students' behavior mirrored the very different styles of teacher interaction with those students. In one study in which teachers received little specific instruction in how to engage with students around the instructional material, the teachers tended to give unlabeled calculations, procedures, or answers instead of labeled explanations; they often instructed using a recitation approach in which they assumed the primary responsibility for solving the problem, having students only provide answers to discrete steps, and they rarely encouraged students to verbalize their thinking or to ask questions (Webb, Nemer, & Ing, 2006). In their cooperative groups, students adopting the role of help-giver showed behavior very similar to that of their teachers: doing most of the work, providing mostly low-level help, and infrequently monitoring other students' level of understanding. Students needing help did not use effective help-seeking skills nor did they often persist in seeking help, which reflected the expectations communicated by the teacher about the learner as a fairly passive recipient of the teacher's transmitted knowledge. In another study, the teachers were trained to use specific skills to challenge students' thinking and to scaffold their learning (e.g., asking questions that probed or attempted to clarify student thinking, challenging discrepancies in students' ideas, offering suggestions tentatively instead of directing students to follow certain procedures or strategies; Gillies, 2004). In these small groups, the students mirrored their teachers' behaviors (e.g., attempting to relate new information to ideas previously discussed).

Conclusion

The past several decades have produced a great deal of research investigating how and when students learn in small groups, as well as how small-group work might be orchestrated to produce desired learning outcomes. Moving considerably beyond characterizations of early research as "black box" in nature (Bossert, 1988–1989), research in this area has uncovered much information about the mediational processes that promote as well as inhibit learning in small groups.

Despite considerable progress in the field, however, there are a number of topics that need more attention. First, not enough is known about the role of student characteristics (e.g., ability, gender, cultural or racial background, personality) in group functioning to make recommendations to teachers about how to compose small groups. This issue is further complicated because the same student may behave and have quite different experiences in different groups; there is still debate about which characteristic(s) are most salient to groups when group members differ on multiple characteristics simultaneously. Second, although working in groups has positive effects on interpersonal attitudes and liking of the task (Solomon, Watson, Schaps, Battistich, & Solomon, 1990), little is known about whether the processes that promote these outcomes are consonant with those that promote learning. Third is the possible incompatibility of different goals of group work, such as individual learning versus group productivity. For example, depending on the nature of the task, processes that benefit individual students' learning may impede group productivity, such as when producing a high-quality group product is best and most efficiently accomplished when only the most skilled students contribute (Webb, 1995). How to balance these competing aims needs further study. Fourth, with the explosion of interest in online communication comes the natural question of whether collaborating with others in a remote environment functions similarly to the face-to-face group dynamics considered in this chapter. There is much interest in computer-mediated communication (Lou, Abrami, & d'Apollonia, 2001), but researchers have only recently begun to systematically study the issues of learning within this context.

Finally, there is a pressing need for more research on how to help teachers implement small-group learning in ways that fit their own classroom needs (O'Donnell & O'Kelly, 1994). Given the relentless demands on teachers and their time, a major challenge is how to enable teachers to create classroom learning environments that encourage beneficial small-group work, to prepare their students to interact collaboratively, to create small-group structures and tasks that are most appropriate for their own classrooms, to monitor and evaluate groups' progress, and to facilitate students' interaction with each other in ways that benefit all of their students.

References and Further Readings

Aronson, E., Blaney, N., Stephin, C., Sikes, J., & Snapp, M. (1978). *The jigsaw classroom.* Beverly Hills, CA: Sage.

Bargh, J. A., & Schul, Y. (1980). On the cognitive benefit of teaching. *Journal of Educational Psychology, 72,* 593–604.

Barron, B. (2003). When smart groups fail. *The Journal of the Learning Sciences, 12,* 307–359.

Bearison, D. J., Magzamen, S., & Filardo E. K. (1986). Socioconflict and cognitive growth in young children. *Merrill-Palmer Quarterly, 32,* 51–72.

Bossert, S. T. (1988–1989). Cooperative activities in the classroom. *Review of Research in Education, 15,* 225–252.

Chi, M. T. H. (2000). Self-explaining expository texts: The dual processes of generating inferences and repairing mental models. In R. Glaser (Ed.), *Advances in instructional psychology: Educational design and cognitive science* (pp. 161–238). Hillsdale, NJ: Lawrence Erlbaum Associates.

Chiu, M. M., & Khoo, L. (2003). Rudeness and status effects during group problem solving: Do they bias evaluations and reduce the likelihood of correct solutions? *Journal of Educational Psychology, 95,* 506–523.

Cohen, E., & Lotan, R. (1995). Producing equal-status interaction in the heterogeneous classroom. *American Educational Research Journal, 32,* 99–120.

Cohen, E. G. (1994). Restructuring the classroom: Conditions for productive small groups. *Review of Educational Research, 64,* 1–35.

De Lisi, R., & Golbeck, S. L. (1999). Implications of Piagetian theory for peer learning. In A. M. O'Donnell & A. King (Eds.), *Cognitive perspectives on peer learning* (pp. 3–38). Hillsdale, NJ: Lawrence Erlbaum Associates.

Dembo, M. H., & McAuliffe, T. J. (1987). Effects of perceived ability and grade status on social interaction and influence in cooperative groups. *Journal of Educational Psychology, 79,* 415–423.

Deutsch, M. (1949). An experimental study of the effects of cooperation and competition upon group process. *Human Relations, 2,* 199–231.

Fuchs, L. S., Fuchs, D., Hamlett, C. L., Phillips, N. B., Karns, K., & Dutka, S. (1997). Enhancing students' helping behavior during peer-mediated instruction with conceptual mathematical explanations. *Elementary School Journal, 97,* 223–249.

Gillies, R. (2004). The effects of communication training on teachers' and students' verbal behaviours during cooperative learning. *International Journal of Educational Research, 41,* 257–279.

Hatano, G. (1993). Time to merge Vygotskian and constructivist conceptions of knowledge acquisition. In E. A. Forman, N. Minick, & C. A. Stone (Eds.), *Contexts for learning: Sociocultural dynamics in children's development* (pp. 153–166). New York: Oxford University Press.

Hogan, K., Nastasi, B. K., & Pressley, M. (2000). Discourse patterns and collaborative scientific reasoning in peer and teacher-guided discussions. *Cognition and Instruction, 17,* 379–432.

Johnson, D. W., & Johnson, R. T. (1994). *Learning together and alone: Cooperative, competitive, and individualistic learning* (4th ed.). Boston: Allyn & Bacon.

Johnson, D. W., & Johnson, R. T. (1995). *Creative controversy: Intellectual challenge in the classroom.* Edina, MN: Interaction Book Company.

King, A. (1992). Facilitating elaborative learning through guided student-generated questioning. *Educational Psychologist, 27,* 111–126.

King, A. (1999). Discourse patterns for mediating peer learning. In A. M. O'Donnell & A. King (Eds.), *Cognitive perspectives on peer learning* (pp. 87–116). Hillsdale, NJ: Lawrence Erlbaum Associates.

Lepper, M. R. (1983). Extrinsic reward and intrinsic motivation. In J. M. Levine, & M. C. Wang (Eds.), *Teacher and student perceptions: Implications for learning* (pp. 281–318). Hillsdale, NJ: Lawrence Erlbaum Associates.

Lou, Y., Abrami, P., & d'Apollonia, S. (2001). Small group and individual learning with technology: A meta-analysis. *Review of Educational Research, 71,* 449–521.

Nelson-Le Gall, S. (1992). Children's instrumental help-seeking: Its role in the social acquisition and construction of knowledge. In R. Hertz-Lazarowitz & N. Miller (Eds.), *Interaction in cooperative groups: The theoretical anatomy of group learning* (pp. 49–68). New York: Cambridge University Press.

Newman, R. S. (1998). Students' help seeking during problem solving: Influences of personal and contextual achievement goals. *Journal of Educational Psychology, 90,* 644–658.

Noddings, N. (1985). Small groups as a setting for research on mathematical problem solving. In E. A. Silver (Ed.), *Teaching and learning mathematical problem solving* (pp. 345–359). Hillsdale, NJ: Lawrence Erlbaum Associates.

O'Donnell, A. M. (1999). Structuring dyadic interaction through scripted cooperation. In A. M. O'Donnell & A. King (Eds.), *Cognitive perspectives on peer learning* (pp. 179–196). Hillsdale, NJ: Lawrence Erlbaum Associates.

O'Donnell, A. M., & O'Kelly, J. (1994). Learning from peers: Beyond the rhetoric of positive results. *Educational Psychology Review, 6,* 321–349.

Palincsar, A. S., & Brown, A. L. (1984). Reciprocal teaching of comprehension fostering and monitoring activities. *Cognition and Instruction, 1,* 117–175.

Piaget, J. (1932). *The language and thought of the child* (2nd ed.). London: Routledge & Kegan Paul.

Salomon, G., & Globerson, T. (1989). When teams do not function the way they ought to. *International Journal of Educational Research, 13,* 89–99.

Sharan, S., & Hertz-Lazarowitz, R. (1980). A group-investigation method of cooperative learning in the classroom. In S. Sharan, P. Hare, C. D. Webb, and R. Hertz-Lazarowitz (Eds.), *Cooperation in education* (pp. 14–46). Provo, UT: Brigham Young University Press.

Slavin, R. (1996). Research on cooperative learning and achievement: What we know, what we need to know. *Contemporary Educational Psychology, 21,* 43–69.

Slavin, R. E. (1995). *Cooperative learning* (2nd ed.). Boston: Allyn & Bacon.

Solomon, D., Watson, M., Schaps, E., Battistich, V., & Solomon, J. (1990). Cooperative learning as part of a comprehensive classroom program designed to promote prosocial development. In S. Sharan (Ed.), *Cooperative learning: Theory and research* (pp. 231–260). New York: Praeger.

Tudge, J. R. H. (1990). Vygotsky: The zone of proximal development and peer collaboration: Implications for classroom practice. In L. Moll (Ed.), *Vygotsky and education: Instructional implications and applications of sociohistorical psychology.* New York: Columbia University Press.

Vedder, P. (1985). *Cooperative learning: A study on processes and effects of cooperation between primary school children.* Westerhaven Groningen, Netherlands: Rijkuniversiteit Groningen.

Vygotsky, L. S. (1978). *Mind in society: The development of higher psychological processes* (M. Cole, V. John-Steiner, S. Scribner, & E. Souberman, Eds. and trans.). Cambridge, MA: Harvard University Press.

Webb, N. M. (1995). Group collaboration in assessment: Multiple objectives, processes, and outcomes. *Educational Evaluation and Policy Analysis, 17,* 239–261.

Webb, N. M., Nemer, K. M., & Ing, M. (2006). Small-group reflections: Parallels between teacher discourse and student behavior in peer-directed groups. *Journal of the Learning Sciences, 15,* 63–119.

Webb, N. M., & Palincsar, A. S. (1996). Group processes in the classroom. In D. Berliner & R. Calfee (Eds.), *Handbook of educational psychology* (pp. 841–873). New York: Macmillan.

Yackel, E., Cobb, P., & Wood, T. (1991). Small-group interactions as a source of learning opportunities in second-grade mathematics. *Journal for Research in Mathematics Education, 22,* 390–408.

23

CONCEPTUAL LEARNING

ROGERS HALL

Vanderbilt University

JAMES G. GREENO

University of Pittsburgh, Visiting Professor
Stanford University, Professor Emeritus

Educators generally want students to understand the concepts and principles of the domains they study, rather than only acquiring routine, low-level knowledge and procedural skill. Although much research has focused on individuals learning rules or definitions for classifying stimuli (classically, e.g., Bruner, Goodnow, & Austin, 1956, and Shepard, Hovland, & Jenkins, 1961; for a more recent review, see Murphy, 2002), we consider conceptual learning and understanding more generally, taking a view developed initially by Wittgenstein (1953/2001), as participation in the activities of communities of practice.

In general terms, learning by an individual in a community involves progress from peripheral to full participation (Lave & Wenger, 1991). An important part of full participation is knowing the concepts a group uses in coordinating activities, deciding on goals and plans, evaluating and explaining actions, instructing newcomers, and communicating with each other. Communities of practice share conceptual systems that constitute figured social worlds (Holland, Lachicotte, Skinner, & Cain, 1998) or discourses (Gee, 1996), which are socially and culturally constructed realms of activity and interpretation in which the meaning and significance of actions are interpreted and evaluated. Newcomers are limited in their ability to participate in discourse partly because they do not fully share in the understandings that more experienced participants have of the meanings and significance of concepts. Learners in the community increase their understanding of this aspect of the group's common ground (Clark, 1996). Learners

develop identities as full participants in the community as they come to share and appropriate patterns of interaction and interpretation afforded by the community's practices.

Research on conceptual understanding in communities of practice has led to the idea that representational infrastructure in some disciplinary practice supports conceptual understanding by providing a material and social environment for understanding and purposeful activity. Representational infrastructure is an aspect of practice that is itself something to be learned, and in many cases, this infrastructure develops further through learning activity. Any social or cultural activity, including technical or scientific activities that are the focus of much formal instruction, depends upon shared representational resources—classification systems, devices that support decision making and memory, and use conventions—for doing and communicating about that activity. Bowker & Star (1999) studied how large-scale classification systems in medicine have changed with the introduction of new information technologies, with consequences both for medical practitioners and their clients. In routine use, representational infrastructure can be invisible, even though people learn by participating in activities supported by that infrastructure. But representational infrastructure is not always a stable background for processes of learning. When that infrastructure breaks down, when new forms of technology are introduced (or required), or when people set out to improve how they work together, there are processes of learning that change both participants in and the infrastructure for social or cultural practices.

Most activities in classrooms are intended to foster students' learning information, skills, and understandings that constitute knowledge in established academic disciplines. Students show that they have become proficient in the domain by participating successfully in discourse activities—often by performing well on tests, but also by providing other evidence such as conducting projects, carrying out analyses, making presentations, and writing reports in which concepts, information, and procedures of the discipline are used and discussed.

In nonschool settings, learning is often instrumental for some other specific purpose in the community. The most immediate goal of much school learning is to prepare students to show what they have learned rather than to participate in some other activity. As a result, students' understanding and use of the concepts they learn in school are often limited to the narrow set of activities in which they learned and displayed their ability to perform school tasks.

Learning and Developing Concepts Out of School

Several research studies have provided important information about conceptual learning and development in practices other than school learning. We present examples that illustrate three general principles. First, learning concepts is critical for progressing from peripheral to full participation. Second, concepts and their meanings develop and evolve in settings of practice and are maintained in practices because they are useful in conducting the community's activities. The local history of discourse involving the development and use of a concept in a community is an important part of the concept's meaning in that community. Third, concepts can migrate from one community to another, and significant tailoring of a concept's meaning can occur as a community adapts the concept to its practices.

Concepts Are Learned Through Participation in Practices

Participating successfully in a social practice requires understanding the meanings of concepts at multiple levels. Many concepts are in the contents of the community's activity, referring to categories of material and products of the community's work, to properties of situations, or to methods or procedures that are performed, including discourse activities such as conducting analyses and writing reports. Some concepts are central for organizing and understanding the community's practices and can refer to fundamental aspects of character and identity. For example, in scientific practice concepts of evidence and explanation are crucial, as are aspects of identity such as being a careful and accurate experimenter and a truthful reporter of empirical results.

A case involving fundamental conceptual understanding and identity was contributed by Cain (1991; discussed by Lave & Wenger, 1991, and Holland et al., 1998). In this case conceptual learning was central in newcomers' learning, that is, in their transition from peripheral to full participation in the community. The community was Alcoholics Anonymous (AA), in which becoming a full participant involves a fundamental change in conceptual understanding of the person's identity. Individuals who join and stay in AA come to understand alcoholism as an illness and to develop an identity of being an alcoholic person. Like other alcoholics, they are incapable of controlling their consumption of alcohol unless they completely avoid taking even one drink. To achieve this they become nondrinking alcoholics, practicing sobriety.

Cain (1991) found that to support members in the practice of sobriety, AA had a powerful representational infrastructure that included telling of personal stories and recognizing the durations of abstinence from drinking. Attaining the identity of a sober alcoholic requires adopting two fundamental beliefs: (1) alcoholism is an incurable disease, and (2) control of one's drinking requires turning over one's will and life to a Higher Power. The personal story is well established in AA practice, and new members experience its components when they converse with seasoned or senior members and when they attend meetings. The stories include a progression in which the teller identifies herself or himself as having had problems while drinking, but they believed that drinking did not cause the problems. At some point the individual hit bottom and then turned to AA and became a different person, a nondrinking alcoholic. The elements of the story afford new members, who identify with experiences of formerly drinking alcoholics, the prospect of achieving a similar transformation. Learning to participate fully in AA includes becoming adept at telling one's story about previous drunkenness and one's conversion to sobriety, thereby providing a model for newer members. Cain documented ways in which newcomers' participation in meetings and interaction with senior members of AA resulted in changes in newcomers' telling of their life stories that corresponded to learning this key aspect of AA's representational infrastructure. The representational infrastructure of AA also included collecting tokens (poker chips) as public acknowledgement of individual members' persistence in sobriety.

In the large body of literature on cognitive development, many studies have focused on conceptual growth (e.g., Murphy, 2002, Chapter 10). Interpretations of the findings of these studies generally hold that children develop mental structures that correspond to sophisticated understanding in domains such as classification, conservation of material, and number. But another interpretation is that conceptual growth is progress in participating in the discourse of a community of practice within a culture. Of course, conceptual growth involves more than advancing purely linguistic aspects of discourse; discourse practices also include representational infrastructure, such as ways of organizing information, attending to significant aspects of situations, and making inferences based on relations between concepts that correspond to regularities in the material and social world. The important point, we believe, is that children's development of understanding in general conceptual domains occurs in the social and cultural environment that they inhabit and occurs as children grow in capabilities for communicating with other people. We expect that general conceptual growth in early childhood depends on rich representational infrastructures that are available, in unfortunately very different degrees, to young children. In conversational interaction, children experience things to have conversations about: toys to be described and animated in narrative play; books to be read, elaborated, explained, and related to their experience; games to be played with older peers and adults; learning environments such as museums, zoos, and parks; photographs of their families, friends, and themselves; video entertainments; and materials and guidance for learning to draw and write (Bransford et al., 2005; Rogoff, Paradise, Mejía Arauz, Correa-Chavez, & Angelillo, 2003).

Concepts Evolve in the Activities of Communities

Communities maintain practices that include stable meanings of the concepts that they use. At the same time, communities change aspects of their practices by introducing new concepts and changing the meanings of concepts. This can happen as a community adapts to changes in societal conditions in which it operates, or through efforts to improve the effectiveness of its activities. The main goal of some communities is the improvement of conceptual understanding or innovations in technology that necessarily change the meanings of concepts.

Nersessian, Kurz-Milcke, Newstetter, & Davies, (2003) studied activity in a bioengineering laboratory, where the primary goal was development of artificial blood vessels that could be implanted in humans to repair circulatory functioning. To accomplish this, the laboratory activity system would need to develop a device that was beyond current scientific understanding, and such a device would involve concepts they did not yet possess. Nersessian et al. referred to this laboratory, and others they studied, as evolving distributed cognitive systems. They were distributed in the sense that cognitive activity was a joint product of the several human participants interacting with each other and with the material systems that they developed in their research. They were evolving in the sense that artifacts and the bioengineering researchers' understandings were continually changing through their activity.

Viewed as part of this distributed cognitive system, concepts functioned in the laboratory to organize activities, goals, and evaluations of progress. The lab's representational infrastructure, including meanings of concepts, was embedded in patterns of interaction of persons, material, apparatus, and measuring instruments. These were continuously changing as devices were modified and

new versions were designed and constructed. Newcomers to the lab, often undergraduate assistants, understood devices more superficially than experienced researchers, focusing more on difficulties of making them work (which all lab members experienced). Experienced researchers understood the functional uses of a device and knew some of the history in which the design of a device evolved as the nature of its behavior in simulating biological material became better known. The experienced researchers also were positioned with what Pickering (1995) called conceptual agency. They designed devices and formulated experiments to test their capabilities; whether the devices then behaved successfully was determined by the devices and materials used in the tests, which Pickering called material agency. This relation was understood well, for example, by a researcher, some months after joining the lab, who saw "a device as an *in vitro* site for 'putting a thought [his thought] into the bench top and seeing whether it works or not'"(Nersessian et al., 2003, p. 862).

Engeström (2001) studied a case involving two communities of practice in health care, medical professionals in a primary pediatric care facility and specialists in a hospital to which the primary care professionals referred children for treatment by specialists. In interviews with providers and parents of these children, Engeström found that there were problems in coordinating the treatment children received. When a child was referred to a specialist, that physician might refer the child to another specialist, and multiple diagnoses and treatments could proceed without the knowledge of the primary care department. This was not optimal care, and it was inconsistent with the primary care department's responsibility.

Engeström organized and studied an intervention in which members of the two professional communities designed a practice that addressed the problem. Their new practice was a result of conceptualizing the problem in a way that differed from their previous (disparate) understandings and included a concept of coordinated care that they generated in their discussions. In Engeström's theoretical analysis, problems can arise in a practice because of contradictions in its underlying assumptions. Here, assumptions about efficiency in treatment contradicted assumptions about maintaining coordination of patients' care. Engeström brought members of the two professional communities together to discuss the problem and showed them videos of parents voicing their distress regarding their children's care. The result was a design for a new practice; the amended representational infrastructure included constructing treatment plans for children that would provide information for both groups of practitioners to better understand conditions of medical care.

Concepts Migrate Between Communities, Adapting to Practices

Concepts and the representational infrastructure through which they are learned and used change over time, both within the activities of a work group and through the identification and resolution of conflicts between work groups within an organization. Concepts also migrate across work groups—with consequences for their local practices—through active processes of borrowing and adapting representational infrastructure. Hall and colleagues (Hall, Wieckert, & Wright, 2008; Hall, Wright, & Wieckert, 2007) have studied processes of learning, teaching, and generalizing statistical concepts when statisticians advise clients across different research domains (e.g., the community ecology of social insects, the epidemiology of infectious disease). Consultations between research clients and statisticians involve purposeful efforts to displace some aspect of the client's existing infrastructure for representation and modeling with another way of working. Thus, consultations are a disruption in the client's project timeline, and within the consultation different ways of assembling the client's future work are created and compared.

In a consultation between a biostatistician and entomologists (Hall et al., 2007), the clients were attempting to borrow uses of cluster analysis (CA) from published literature in order to identify new termite species. A senior research client proposed using CA to *confirm* insect groups they had already observed; however, the consulting biostatistician pointed out that CA finds clusters regardless of their meaning, so could not be trusted in this epistemic role. Instead, another senior researcher proposed that they use CA to *discover* insect groups, which could later be confirmed using independent field and laboratory data. This seemingly simple, narrative repair in how CA should be used in the client's work avoided a logical error and, once adopted in the group's work practices and described in journal articles, was borrowed by other research groups to become a standard method for identifying insect group structures. As a critical part of this larger migration of concepts, consultations involved basic discursive processes of narrative assembly that ordered objects in the client's work, people on the project as human labor and spokespersons for objects, and statistical techniques or concepts.

In a second discourse practice common in consultations, statisticians told parables that offered clients alternative subject positions in stories about statistical inference and data modeling. These stories had highly evaluative outcomes, depending on which position a client took. In the case of entomologists seeking to borrow CA from previously published studies, the statistician compared their situation to using blood type shown on a California driver's license. The lead entomologist initially responded from the position of a harried Type O blood donor (i.e., dealing with constant requests to give blood), but later realized that in the statistician's completed parable, he would grant licenses on the basis of blood type (i.e., blood type is a real structure, but it has nothing to do with obtaining a driving license; similarly, CA might discover structures that had little relevance for insect classification).

A third, recurring discourse practice found in Hall et al.'s comparative analysis was the use of analogy to borrow and modify statistical methods or approaches to modeling that appeared in prior publications, sometimes out of field for research clients. Findings here are similar to Dunbar's (1995) studies of scientific research groups, but in Hall et al.'s cases, consulting statisticians worked as brokers (Star & Griesemer, 1989; Tuomi-Grohn, Engeström, & Young, 2003; Wenger, 1998) to map and evaluate analogies that were brought into consultations by research clients. In a case where research epidemiologists were seeking to estimate the number of young children hospitalized with influenza (Hall et al., 2008), the lead researcher borrowed a capture-recapture estimate from prior publications in epidemiology, but made an overly narrow assumption about matching hospital days for two screening procedures. The consulting statistician advised that matching days were not required, yet the client was not convinced, posing an extreme case in which a 1-day screen would be incorrectly (he thought) combined with a 7-day screen. After further discussion and illustrative calculations, the statistician was able to convince the client to use all screening days, and the resulting, published estimate of children with influenza was more robust. In the same consultation, the statistician convinced epidemiologists at a national public health agency that screens with quite different coverage could be combined, as long as there were no dependencies among them. As a result, new studies and a national influenza monitoring program for adults were undertaken, using the client's extreme negative case (1 versus 7 screening days) as a feature of the new health surveillance system.

These case studies of learning and developing concepts out of school show that conceptual systems are implemented as representational infrastructures that support the activities, learning, and communication of participants from multiple generations within a work group. But these cases also show how concepts and supporting infrastructure evolve in and across the activities of communities, either through processes of experimentation and incremental refinement or through interventions specifically designed to identify and work through contradictions within an organization's mission. In still other cases, concepts are borrowed and adapted across work groups or organizations, sometimes with the help of brokers whose professional activities span different disciplinary contexts and work groups. Thus, in the cases of statistical consultation studied by Hall and colleagues, conceptual development in activity systems appeared to advance along two dimensions at once. Work practices—including what needs to be learned by newcomers, what counts as a finding or argument, and how to communicate about these things—changed to accommodate borrowed conceptual structures within the local history of a work group. But at the same time, for brokers like the consulting statisticians, local problems and adaptations required for borrowing conceptual systems provided rich material for the extension of existing concepts or the discovery of new concepts that might prove useful across the different purposes and local work settings of particular clients. In this sense (see also Engeström, 2007), disrupting representational infrastructure to work more effectively in the future involves both aspects of horizontal (within local work groups) and vertical (across groups) conceptual development.

Several structural features of concept learning and development in these out-of-school case studies bear further discussion. The temporal duration of conceptual change in these cases is diverse, ranging from days or weeks in interactions between a small number of people (e.g., the consultation over use of capture-recapture methods to count cases of child influenza), to multiple years and interactions between members of larger work groups (e.g., the refinement of artificial vascular tissue media or adopting cluster analysis as a method to discover structure in field entomology). Processes at different levels of analysis and different timescales contribute to conceptual change in these cases, and these processes appear to involve aspects of human agency and interaction that have typically been attributed to individual mental processes operating at smaller scales in time, place, and participation. In summary, the components of representational infrastructure are more diverse and productive for activity than a narrow view of notational systems and their proper use might suggest. This diversity includes forms of narrative description that compare the consequences of alternative ways of using the concept (e.g., using cluster analysis to confirm versus discover candidate structures) or tries to borrow and adapt concepts that expand the meaning of the concept within and across work groups (e.g., adapting prior use of a statistical concept to cover a new situation or developing new statistical methods that cover multiple, particular consultations).

Learning Concepts of Disciplines in School

In school, students learn concepts and methods that have been developed in intellectual disciplines and that are considered generally valuable for educated members of society. Teachers, textbooks, and other resources represent disciplinary communities. The goal is to have students learn to participate in practices that are valued in society, including practices that are preparatory for further disciplinary learning. If concepts are aspects of activity, we must question the kinds of activities in which students typically learn concepts in school. These activities should include opportunities for pursuing generality with conceptual agency if school learning is to have value beyond its specific learning context.

Concepts Are Learned Through Participation in Practices

Curricula can be designed so that concepts are learned in activities where they function and can thereby be understood as resources for practice. Jurow (2004) studied middle school students participating in project-based activities designed to teach them about the mathematics of population modeling (Greeno & MMAP, 1998; Stenning, Greeno, Hall, Sommerfeld, & Wiebe, 2002). Jurow observed that representational systems for modeling—like tables or graphs of fish population growth—operate by conventions that have already been designed to record and summarize multiple, concrete instances. Thus, in conventional use, these systems provide powerful resources for generalizing (Latour, 1990). For example, looking at a graph of population values over time, a skilled reader sees an ordered progression of values and can make inferences about intervening events, trends, and what might happen to the population in the future. But students must learn these conventional uses in order to use representational systems to generalize about population dynamics. In the cases studied by Jurow, several representational systems (i.e., tables, graphs, and constraint networks coordinated in a computer interface) provided means for asking and answering functional questions about population models that spanned multiple contexts (e.g., How large must a student-designed tank be to accommodate a growing population of fish? Then later, how many fish could live within the carrying capacity of a larger stream reach?). In Jurow's study, these "what if" questions, either embedded in the curriculum or asked by the teacher, prompted students to engage in two basic discursive processes: linking one context with another (e.g., current and future fish populations, in different habitats) and conjecturing about what might happen in alternative models (e.g., a predator/prey model of interacting fish populations, with and without human intervention). Both processes involved conversations in which representations were treated as models of population growth, and students took up positions either as makers or users of alternative models. As interactive environments for learning, episodes of linking and conjecturing structured students' participation (Erickson, 2004) in increasingly sophisticated ways of using representations as models.

In this sense, linking and conjecturing provided opportunities for students to learn about the representational infrastructure of modeling. Jurow also found that what students counted as adequate participation varied across contexts of assessment. For example, some students stopped with the first answer they felt would earn credit on daily work sheets, while others anticipated giving explanations in later classroom discussion and thus continued to seek alternative or more convincing population models. Different expectations about assessment produced tensions within student groups regarding what was to be learned, and these tensions influenced how students engaged with instructional activities. In another study of project-based learning, Engle (2006) specifically asked what might lead to transfer of causal explanations in classroom activities designed to support inquiry learning (Brown & Campione, 1994). A group of students studying why some whale species are endangered spent several weeks constructing a multicausal explanation, in which relatively low birth rates (whales give birth every few years) combined with intense pressure from human hunting would decrease the whale population to the point of endangerment. Through a careful retrospective analysis of group activities, Engle demonstrated that although the content of this explanation was made available to group members, their learning was substantially enabled by their teacher's efforts to establish links across contexts in which such an explanation would be useful or relevant. Specifically, the teacher framed student activities as extending across instructional contexts, alerting students to how a causal explanation might be relevant across time (e.g., linking past instructional activity with current and future activity) and how their participation in inquiry might span wider social contexts (e.g., students were framed as authors of causal explanations that would be relevant in whole class discussions). In this way, the teacher's framing regularly broadened the participation structure of students' learning, and by Engle's argument, encouraged them to use their explanations in ways that were generative outside the original context of learning. This provides a situational explanation for transfer of learning that combines aspects of content (e.g., texts describing endangered species) and the interactional contexts in which that content is engaged by students (e.g., linking current and past inquiry to conversations anticipated in the future).

Concepts Evolve in the Activities of Communities

The second general principle that we consider is that concepts and their meanings evolve in the activities of groups and communities. Our situational account emphasizes that meanings and uses of concepts have important aspects that are local, including the histories of their local development and use. The nonschool examples of this principle that we discussed (Nersessian et al.'s 2003 study of a bioengineering laboratory and Engeström's 2001 study of two groups involved in medical care) illustrate the principle of local evolution and inclusion of local history in meanings of concepts in professional communities.

When this principle of conceptual learning is recognized in school, the learning communities of classrooms function as constructors of concepts and their meanings, including representational infrastructures that embody and support conceptual understanding. Students are positioned in these activities with conceptual agency in Pickering's (1995) sense. This can support students' development of disciplinary identities in which they are entitled and capable of questioning, criticizing, and adapting resources of the discipline, rather than only being able to use these resources mechanically.

The Algebra Project (Moses & Cobb, 2001) exemplifies this principle of classroom constructivism. Students engage in an activity together, such as taking a trip or learning a game, and their shared experience is then used to ground the development of mathematical concepts and methods.

Moses & Cobb design learning activities in which classroom communities develop mathematical concepts and representations in discourse that they characterize, following Quine (1981), as a regimented version of ordinary language. The concepts and representational infrastructure that classroom communities construct have meaning and significance in their practice, including a history in which the students have significant agency and authorship.

Godfrey and O'Connor (1995) studied the development of a representational practice in an Algebra Project classroom taught by Godfrey. The mathematical concept involved was difference between two quantities or numbers, which has both a magnitude and a direction. The class, led by the teacher but with significant content initiated by students, developed symbols that referred to both these properties for representing differences between the heights of individuals. One symbol illustrated the students' role in authorship of representational infrastructure particularly well. One of the students proposed that the magnitude of a difference could be represented by a unit he called the handspan, meaning the distance between the tips of the fingers and the base of the palm. Other members of the class raised questions, including a difficulty because this use of the term *handspan* would conflict with its ordinary meaning of the distance between the ends of the thumb and smallest finger when the hand is spread. The class determined that this was a significant issue and settled on the term *vertical handspan*. In developing this representation, students discussed significant issues in the design of symbols, and thus had opportunities to learn important aspects of the concept of numbers that have signs as well as magnitudes, with their history of these considerations integral in their local version of the concept.

Engle and Conant (2002) analyzed an extended episode of learning in two fifth-grade classes organized according to principles of the Fostering Communities of Learners project (Brown & Campione, 1994). The classes conducted investigations of endangered species, with different student groups studying different species. Part of the class' representational infrastructure was a poster that was constructed midway through the unit to display what each group had found by that time. In the groups studying whales there was a controversy over whether it was appropriate to include orcas in their report, because on a field trip they had heard a staff person say that, although most people think killer whales are whales, they are really dolphins. They discussed this for 27 minutes, debating the significance of physical features in taxonomic classification, the authority of sources, and the linguistic convention that the animals are called killer *whales*. This discussion became an integral part of the group's conceptual understanding, as indicated clearly during a report the group gave to a newly arrived student teacher, who was told that they had "a big ol' argument" about the proper classification of orcas. Engle and Conant analyzed interactions in the class and hypothesized that the students' productive disciplinary engagement and the conceptual learning that they accomplished were enabled and supported by practices that encouraged problematizing disciplinary issues that students had authority to resolve. Students were accountable for supporting their positions with evidence and had access to resources that informed their development of positions on issues.

The local history of conceptual discourse shapes a group's understanding and meaning of a concept. It also provides the group with resources that can benefit their learning. Schwartz and Martin (2004) studied ninth-grade students participating in a discussion of how to construct a numerical indicator of variability in samples produced by different baseball pitching machines. The samples differed both in average accuracy and variability. Following this activity, the students were given instruction in a standard index of variability, the average absolute deviation from the mean. The students who had previous experience with constructing an index learned more successfully than other students who had not had that experience. This is further evidence that conceptual learning in a community occurs more readily when the representational infrastructure through which the concept is understood is part of inquiry activities of the community rather than just being presented as something to learn.

Concepts Migrate Between Communities, Adapting to Practices

Teaching a concept in school always involves migration of the concept across a boundary—actually, across several boundaries. Except for the occasional visits of practicing members of a discipline to classes, the route of a concept from a community of disciplinary scholars into classrooms includes adoption in communities of curriculum writers, teacher educators, and teachers, all of whom must adapt the function and meaning of the concept for use in their various practices. In a different set of practices, the teacher and students of a classroom community adopt some version of the concept in learning and displaying their knowledge.

For each of these adaptations, there is concern that the adapted version of the concept be consistent with some important aspects of the concept's meaning in the disciplinary community. There are disputes about which aspects of meaning should be preserved. Preserving correctness in recitation of facts and definitions and in performance of routine procedures is sometimes taken as sufficient for purposes of general education. But many educators and members of disciplinary professions advocate more ambitious educational aims, ones that involve understanding and the ability to use concepts and methods of the disciplines that students study. Some efforts, usually focused on curricula, have worked to improve the accuracy of students' understanding of concepts and principles. Alternatively, there also are efforts to change curricula and classroom practices so that students will have opportunities to learn how to understand and reason with concepts in ways that are consistent with patterns of understanding and reasoning that are characteristic in disciplines (Brown, Collins, & Duguid, 1989). These efforts are aimed toward students developing valuable habits of mind of the kinds that have evolved in disciplinary practice, including ways that members of the disciplinary community formulate problems and questions, organize information, formulate and evaluate arguments, and assemble and evaluate evidence.

Regardless of which aspects of understanding and skill are important for students to learn, an important question is, What kinds of learning environments and activities allow students to develop the kinds of understanding and skill that are valued? The view that conceptual understanding is embedded in social practice emphasizes that different learning practices in classrooms provide opportunities for conceptual learning that reflect different aspects of understanding.

Boaler (1993/2002) studied mathematics teaching and learning in two secondary schools in England. Although the schools were virtually identical demographically, they taught in strikingly different ways over a period of 3 years. In one of the schools, students learned mathematics in a traditional practice where teachers described and explained a procedure and students did problem sets as seatwork and homework. In the other school, students learned mathematics by carrying out investigations, each of which typically lasted about 3 weeks. Teachers presented concepts and procedures when these could be used to understand and make progress on students' projects.

Boaler's (1993/2002) findings showed that adaptation of mathematical concepts to these different teaching practices resulted in striking differences in what students learned. In the school using mathematical investigations, students learned to appropriate mathematical concepts and methods in their projects and to apply them to generate information relevant to their own questions. In contrast, students participating in more traditional pedagogy learned to recognize cues for which procedure to use and how to perform procedures correctly. These students later understood mathematics to be about a collection of procedures one needed to perform correctly. Students participating in classroom investigations, in contrast, understood mathematics to be a collection of tools for use in solving problems and making sense of situations. Boaler concluded that students in these schools also developed different mathematical identities, with those from investigations classrooms displaying higher levels of conceptual agency in the mathematics they were learning (i.e., Pickering's 1995 distinction between conceptual and material agency).

Conclusion

We have taken the general view, initially developed by Wittgenstein (1953/2001), that concepts are resources of social practice, and meanings are the ways that concepts function in activities of communities. We have considered three principles of conceptual learning that are implications of this general view and discussed research studies in which these principles are exemplified. First, concepts are learned by individuals through their participation in the practices of a community, and conceptual learning is an integral part of learning in which individuals progress from peripheral to full participation. Second, conceptual learning occurs in communities; concepts change as communities progress in their understanding and in developing practices and technologies that are increasingly effective. Third, conceptual learning occurs as concepts migrate across boundaries between communities, with adaptation of the concepts' meanings to make them functional in the community that receives them.

This view of concepts as resources for communication, understanding, and reasoning in social practice contrasts with the understanding of concepts that has shaped most educational practice. In the prevailing view, learning concepts is assumed to be acquisition of knowledge structures, represented as schemata that contain (a) patterns of features that define and characterize examples of the concept and (b) procedures in which values of variables in the concept's definition can be inferred or used to infer values of other variables that are related to the concept. Use of the concept involves recognizing the pattern of features that characterizes the concept, instantiating the variables in the schema with features of the situation, and carrying out procedures to infer values of other variables.

In this prevailing view of conceptual learning and understanding, much attention is given to the issue of transfer. Students may show evidence that they have learned a concept by giving correct answers about its meaning, identifying examples correctly, or performing inferential procedures correctly in a test. But when asked questions or given problems that differ from those used in instruction in some way, they often do not succeed. The problem, according to the mainstream view, is that they failed to transfer knowledge they had acquired to the novel situation. Perhaps the knowledge they acquired lacked the generality that it should have had, or perhaps they did not acquire needed procedures for instantiating their general schema in the kind of situation that was presented in the transfer test.

In the situational view that we take in this article, knowing a concept is not considered an abstraction from practice; instead, all conceptual understanding is assumed to be embedded in social practices. At the same time, social practices and individuals' participation differ in ways that encourage or discourage generality of knowing. Knowledge of a concept is not assumed to be inherently general or specific. Instead, in activities that potentially could be informed by a concept, communities' or an individual's practices vary in their extent of affording use of that concept (or concepts) in a broad range of settings. Generative use of any knowledge is

always a constructive act, which often requires creativity and sometimes moral courage.

Learning practices that are often used to teach concepts in school focus on the use of concepts primarily in taking tests. Although test items can be constructed to provide different informational contexts from those present during learning, testing unavoidably provides only a very limited kind of activity in which to apply one's understanding of a concept. Therefore, if we agree that conceptual understanding is knowing how to participate in activities that are informed by the meaning of a concept, testing provides a poor representation of the kinds of activities that most people would want to have students learn to participate in successfully. And school instruction that emphasizes successful test taking as the main goal of learning fosters a narrow form of understanding. Understandably, students do not expect that what they learn in school to be relevant to other activities.

We propose that to make school instruction for conceptual understanding more effective, curriculum design, teaching, and teacher preparation and development should attend to a range of activities and practices in which students could be prepared to use the concepts they are learning, and to the kinds of activities and ways of being positioned in learning through which conceptual understanding in practice can be fostered. This is not a recommendation to avoid explicit discussion of concepts and their meanings, or to necessarily depend on students' processes of discovery to reach correct versions of disciplinary concepts. It is a recommendation to teach concepts that are inherently generative—that is, that contain the basis for their generality as a characteristic of their internal content—in ways that are more likely to succeed.

Consistent with research we have reviewed, two important factors contribute to students' learning concepts that then become generative resources in their activity. One is that the activity in which concepts are learned uses them generatively, rather than only as information to be remembered or as procedures to be executed. The other is that students are positioned in learning activity with conceptual agency, that is, with agency to appropriate, adapt, question, and modify conceptual meanings in the discipline. Students need to learn with conceptual agency in settings where the representational infrastructure supports more than narrow test performance.

At the same time, this research reveals why changing the leading activities of school learning to support generative use of concepts and conceptual agency in students' participation is fundamentally challenging. Whether in the project-based teaching studied by Jurow (2004) or in the cycles of inquiry studied by Engle (2006), engaging tasks need to be organized in ways that build functional relevance for mathematics or science, and students' generative use of concepts needs to be made visible and available for conversation and refinement in culminating or benchmark activities. Designing instruction so concepts are learned through participation in activities that use them as resources also requires building participation structures in classrooms so students have significant conceptual agency. In short, the representational infrastructures used in classrooms need to be fundamentally reconstructed. Departing from the "grammar of schooling," as Tyack and Tobin (1994) characterized it, incurs a heavy cost. Just as cultural expectations about language use can lack congruence (Erickson, 2004; Ladson-Billings, 1995), expectations about the representational infrastructure of schooling can lack coherence and place barriers in the way of students' learning. While overcoming these barriers can be difficult, we hope that the challenges of changing practices, including representational infrastructures, do not deter designers and other educational professionals from accomplishing the changes that research shows are needed for students to succeed in meaningful conceptual learning in their school activities.

Acknowledgment

The authors wish to acknowledge the Spencer Foundation for support in writing this chapter. This took the form of a grant to Greeno (Grant Number 200300029) and partial support to Hall for a fellowship year (2007–08) at the Center for Advanced Study in the Behavioral Sciences.

References and Further Readings

Boaler, J. (2002). *Experiencing school mathematics: Traditional and reform approaches to teaching and their impact on student learning* (revised and expanded edition). Mahwah, NJ: Lawrence Erlbaum Associates. (Originally published in 1993)

Bowker, G. C., & Star, S. L. (1999). *Sorting things out: Classification and its consequences.* Cambridge, MA: MIT Press.

Bransford, J., Vye, N., Stevens, R., Kuhl, P., Schwartz, D., Bell, P., et al. (2005). Learning theories and education: Toward a decade of synergy. In P. Alexander & P. Winne (Eds.), *Handbook of Educational Psychology* (2nd ed.), pp. 209–244. Mahwah, NJ: Lawrence Erlbaum Associates.

Brown, A. L., & Campione, J. C. (1994). Guided discovery in a community of learners. In K. McGilly (Ed.), *Classroom lessons: Integrating cognitive theory and classroom practice* (pp. 229–270). Cambridge, MA: MIT Press/Bradford.

Brown, J. S., Collins, A., & Duguid, P. (1989). Situated cognition and the culture of learning. *Educational Researcher, 41,* 32–42.

Bruner, J. S., Goodnow, J. J., & Austin, G. A. (1956). *A study of thinking.* New York: Wiley.

Cain, C. (1991). Personal stories: Identity acquisition and self-understanding in Alcoholics Anonymous. *Ethos, 19,* 210–253.

Clark, H. H. (1996). *Using language.* Cambridge, UK: Cambridge University Press.

Dunbar, K. (1995). How scientists really reason: Scientific reasoning in real-world laboratories. In R. J. Sternberg & J. E. Davidson (Eds.), *The nature of insight* (pp. 365–395). Cambridge, MA: MIT Press/Bradford.

Engeström, Y. (2001). Expansive learning at work: Toward an activity theoretical reconceptualization. *Journal of Education and Work, 14,* 133–156.

Engeström, Y. (2007). Enriching the theory of expansive learning: Lessons from journeys towards coconfiguration. *Mind, Culture, and Activity 14*(1–2), 23–39.

Engle, R. A. (2006). Framing interactions to foster generative learning: A situative explanation of transfer in a Community of Learners classroom. *Journal of the Learning Sciences, 15*(4), 451–498.

Engle, R. A., & Conant, F. R. (2002). Guiding principles for fostering productive disciplinary engagement: Explaining an emergent argument in a community of learners classroom. *Cognition and Instruction, 20,* 399–483.

Erickson, F. (2004). *Talk and social theory: Ecologies of speaking and listening in everyday life.* Malden, MA: Polity Press.

Gee, J. P. (1996). *Social linguistics and literacies: Ideology in discourses* (2nd ed.). London: Falmer Press.

Godfrey, L., & O'Connor, M. C. (1995). The vertical hand span: Non-standard units, expressions, and symbols in the classroom. *Journal of Mathematical Behavior 14*(3), 327–345.

Greeno, J. G., & Middle School Mathematics through Applications Project Group (1998). The situativity of knowing, learning, and research. *American Psychologist, 53*(1), 5–26.

Hall, R., Wieckert, K., & Wright, K. (2008). How does cognition get distributed? Case studies of making concepts general in technical and scientific work. In M. Banich & D. Caccamise (Eds.), *Generalization of knowledge: Multidisciplinary perspectives.* New York: Psychology Press.

Hall, R., Wright, K., & Wieckert, K. (2007). Interactive and historical processes of distributing statistical concepts through work organization. *Mind, Culture, and Activity, 14*(1&2), 103–127.

Holland, D., Lachicotte, W., Jr., Skinner, D., & Cain, C. (1998). *Identity and agency in cultural worlds.* Cambridge, MA: Harvard University Press.

Jurow, A. S. (2004). Generalizing in interaction: Middle school mathematics students making mathematical generalizations in a population modeling project. *Mind, Culture, and Activity, 11*(4), 279–300.

Ladson-Billings, G. (1995). Toward a theory of culturally relevant pedagogy. *American Educational Research Journal, 32*(3), 465–491.

Latour, B. (1990). Drawing things together. In M. Lynch & S. Woolgar (Eds.), *Representation in scientific practice* (pp. 19–68). Cambridge, MA: MIT Press

Lave, J., & Wenger, E. (1991). *Situated learning: Legitimate peripheral participation.* Cambridge, MA: Cambridge University Press.

Moses, R. P., & Cobb, C. E., Jr. (2001). *Radical equations: Math literacy and civil rights.* Boston: Beacon Press.

Murphy, G. L. (2002). *The big book of concepts.* Cambridge MA: MIT Press/Bradford.

Nersessian, N. J., Kurz-Milcke, E., Newstetter, W. C., & Davies, J. (2003). Research laboratories as evolving distributed cognitive systems. In R. Alterman & D. Kirsh (Eds.) *Proceedings of the Twenty-Fifth Annual Conference of the Cognitive Science Society* (pp. 857–862). Mahwah, NJ: Lawrence Erlbaum Associates.

Pickering, A. (1995). *The mangle of practice.* Chicago: University of Chicago Press.

Quine, W. V. (1981). Success and limits of mathematization. In *Theories and things* (pp. 148–155). Cambridge, MA: Harvard University Press/Belknap.

Rogoff, B., Paradise, R., Mejía Arauz, R., Correa-Chavez, M., & Angelillo, C. (2003). Firsthand learning by intent participation. *Annual Review of Psychology, 54,* 175–203.

Schwartz, D., & Martin, T. (2004). Inventing to prepare for future learning: The hidden efficiency of encouraging original student production in statistics instruction. *Cognition and Instruction, 22,* 129–184.

Shepard, T. N., Hovland, C. I., & Jenkins, H. M. (1961). Learning and memorization of classifications. *Psychological Monographs: General and Applied, 75* (13, whole no. 517)

Star, S. L., & Griesemer, J. R. (1989). Institutional ecology, "translations" and boundary objects: Amateurs and professionals in Berkeley's Museum of Vertebrate Zoology 1907–39. *Social Studies of Science, 19,* 387–420.

Stenning, K., Greeno, J. G., Hall, R., Sommerfeld, M., & Wiebe, M. (2002). Coordinating mathematical with biological multiplication: Conceptual learning as the development of heterogeneous reasoning systems. In M. Baker, P. Brna, K. Stenning, & A. Tiberghien (Eds.), *The role of communication in learning to model* (pp. 3–48). Mahwah NJ: Lawrence Erlbaum Associates.

Tuomi-Grohn, T., Engeström, Y., & Young, M. (2003). From transfer to boundary-crossing between school and work as a tool for developing vocational education: An introduction. In T. Tuomi-Grohn & Y. Engeström (Eds.), *Between school and work: New perspectives on transfer and boundary-crossing* (pp. 1–18). Amsterdam: Earli.

Tyack, D., & Tobin, W. (1994). The "grammar" of schooling: Why has it been so hard to change? *American Educational Research Journal, 31*(3), 453–479.

Wenger, E. (1998). *Communities of practice: Learning, meaning and identity.* Cambridge, UK: Cambridge University Press.

Wittgenstein, L. (2001). *Philosophical investigations: The German text* (with a revised English translation, 3rd ed.) G. E. M. Anscombe (Trans.). London: Blackwell. (Original published 1953)

PART VI

BUILDING LEARNING ENVIRONMENTS

24

DESIGNING LEARNING ENVIRONMENTS

CHRISTOPHER J. HARRIS AND RONALD W. MARX

University of Arizona

PHYLLIS C. BLUMENFELD

University of Michigan

Current perspectives on learning in classrooms make clear that students learn best when they are engaged in their learning and helped to develop rich conceptual understanding. These views on learning, often referred to as constructivist perspectives, propose that students actively and socially construct their knowledge. A challenge facing educators is how to create classrooms that support this learning.

Increasingly, educators have recognized the need to reconfigure classrooms as environments that encompass the complex individual and social processes necessary to promote understanding. For a learning environment to succeed, teachers need to change their traditional role of information delivery to effective scaffolding that supports students in integrating and applying ideas. In this type of learning environment, students also have new roles. They need to be more invested and responsible in their learning as they engage in authentic tasks, collaborate with classmates, and use technology for research and problem solving.

A number of K–12 programs have been developed that help teachers and students create ambitious learning environments. Examples include environments for elementary science and mathematics such as Rochel Gelman's *Preschool Pathways to Science,* Douglas Clements' *Building Blocks* mathematics environment for early elementary students, and Nancy Songer's *BioKIDS* science environment for upper elementary classrooms. Secondary environments include *Cognitive Tutors,* a computer-based mathematics learning environment developed by researchers at Carnegie Mellon University; John Mergendoller and colleagues' *Problem-Based Economics;* and *Project-Based Science,* developed by researchers at the University of Michigan. These environments for learning are carefully designed, theoretically framed, research-based programs that support all facets of the learning context. They represent ambitious pedagogy and strive for ambitious outcomes. Many include technology, such as computers or Web-based communication tools, either as a primary focus or as an important component. These environments for learning are changing the face of education.

In this chapter, we examine how learning environments are engineered to support ambitious teaching and learning. We begin by considering the role of learning theory in the design of learning environments. We then examine the methods used to create and study environments. Next, we introduce features of learning environments and describe selected learning environments according to these features to illustrate how similar features are instantiated differently across environments. We close by discussing challenges and future directions in the design of environments for learning.

Learning Theory and Learning Environments

In contrast to previous views that emphasized learning as a process of transferring information from teachers or texts to learners, new views emphasize that learners are active constructors of knowledge. Accordingly, learning occurs through a constructive process in which students modify and refine what they know as they explore and try to make sense of the world around them. Students possess prior knowledge that they use to interpret learning experiences and construct new knowledge.

There are various formulations of constructivism and they explain different aspects of learning. Under this broad constructivist umbrella are two major perspectives on human learning. The first is cognitive in nature and focuses on individual thinking and learning. The second is social in nature and focuses on social interaction and the role of interactions within social contexts. Both perspectives are central in informing the design of new environments.

Cognitive Perspective

The cognitive perspective emphasizes the role of the individual in learning and is concerned with how complex information is handled mentally by learners, including how learners remember information, relate new information to prior knowledge to build schemas or knowledge networks that organize ideas, and develop understanding. Research on cognition suggests that prior knowledge and its organization plays a considerable role in learning and performance. For example, cognitive research provides insight into the skills and knowledge that underlie expert and novice performance. This research indicates that experts and novices differ in the amount and organization of knowledge and in their ability to apply knowledge to solve problems, comprehend text, and respond to situations. Simply put, experts and novices differ in their cognitive resources, especially strategies for learning and performing tasks. Experts from all disciplines draw from a richly structured information base and are more likely to recognize meaningful patterns of information when problem solving. Experts know their disciplines thoroughly and their understanding of subject matter allows them to see patterns, identify relevant information, and notice inconsistencies or discrepancies that are not apparent to novices.

Research on how people learn and acquire expertise in various disciplines has given rise to notions about how to help students learn specific subject area content. Most students are novices in the content areas of reading, writing, mathematics, science, and social studies. They think differently from adult experts and draw from an information base that is often comprised of informal ideas that they have acquired through their everyday experiences. When working on mathematics problems, for instance, students will often apply thinking and reasoning strategies that are qualitatively different from what mathematics educators expect. This is because students draw from a limited set of cognitive resources to make sense of school mathematics. They are unfamiliar with the practices of mathematicians and the strategies that expert mathematicians use to solve problems and generate knowledge.

Many new environments for learning are designed to help students develop competence in content areas. Informed by studies on how novices think and what misconceptions they have, these environments strive to move students toward sophisticated ways of understanding that are characteristic of experts. Some of these environments provide tutoring and guidance in the use of strategies and thinking processes typical of experts. An example of this type of environment is Jack Mostow and colleagues' computer-based reading environment, *Literacy Innovation that Speech Technology ENables (LISTEN)*. LISTEN uses intelligent instructional software that provides specific hierarchical tasks and assistance to help elementary school students develop reading competence. In LISTEN, reading is guided and supported in one-on-one interactions between the individual student and computer. The computer acts as an expert tutor. It displays stories and uses speech recognition software to listen to children read aloud. Students wear headsets with microphones attached as they read aloud stories matched to their estimated reading levels. LISTEN software assigns stories to students based on their individual performance, monitors students' reading, and provides feedback and hints. The software is based upon a careful analysis of reading skills and modeled after expert reading teachers.

Cognitive theory informs how to help students accomplish tasks and engage in specific thinking processes. The cognitive perspective has its roots in the work of Swiss psychologist Jean Piaget who focused on the mental structures underlying knowledge; he studied how children advance from novice to expert ways of thinking by constructing increasingly sophisticated knowledge. The body of research on human cognition has provided critical insight into how students think and reason about how the world works, how experts acquire their expertise, and the cognitive demands of thinking and problem solving in a range of situations and domains.

Social Perspective

The social perspective is concerned with how learning is shaped by participation in activity and interactions within social contexts. This view draws from the work of Russian psychologist Lev Vygotsky who argued that all learning originates in, and is a product of, the settings in which learners navigate. This means that knowledge is contextualized, and learners build knowledge and deepen their understanding through observations and interactions with the physical world as well as discourse and participation in activities with others. In this sense, learning is regarded as inherently social and the setting for learning—consisting of materials, activities, learners, and social interactions among learners and teachers—shapes the knowledge that is produced.

Vygotsky's ideas are prominent in the work of designers of learning environments. One of his most influential ideas is that meaningful learning occurs when learners are engaged in rich social activity in which they communicate, collaborate, and form a learning community. In a classroom learning community, teachers and students engage collectively in learning that produces shared understandings. Such a community consists of people collaborating on problems or projects, relying on one another for assistance when needed, and sharing, discussing, and debating ideas. Based on just such a notion of community, Ann Brown and Joseph Campione developed *Fostering Communities of Learners (FCL),* an environment for grades one through eight that fosters learning by developing group knowledge about a topic. In FCL, students and teacher select a topic of interest and then break into research groups that focus on relevant aspects of the topic. Research groups pursue different but related questions and then explain their work to the other groups. Collectively, the groups then synthesize the information to form a comprehensive understanding of the topic. To showcase their new understandings, students produce group reports, poster displays, and presentations or demonstrations. A feature of FCL is the jigsaw group, a learning group that contains a member representing each initial research group. In this new group, each jigsaw member is responsible for teaching their research information to everyone else. Thus, each member represents a piece of the puzzle that provides important and different knowledge for understanding the topic.

An important idea that has emerged from the work on the role of community in learning is the notion of communities of practice. Introduced by Jean Lave and Etienne Wenger (1991), a community of practice describes a situation in which robust knowledge and understandings are socially constructed though talk, activity, and interaction in an authentic, real-world context. In classrooms, this means having students communicate and engage in activities that reflect the discipline under study. For instance, establishing a community of scientific practice requires that learners participate in activities similar to that of scientists. This entails engaging in scientific inquiry much like scientists do, but in ways that are appropriate and meaningful for students. Such an approach actively involves students in scientific practices such as conducting investigations, making observations, gathering and analyzing data, and reporting findings. A benefit of situating science learning in an authentic context is that it provides a meaningful and motivating backdrop for introducing students to the conventional language, practices, tools, and values of the scientific community.

Another influential idea from Vygotsky is the critical importance of supporting learners to accomplish tasks that they otherwise cannot accomplish on their own. Vygotsky coined the phrase *zone of proximal development* to represent the capacity that learners have to perform tasks with the help of others that they would not be able to perform on their own. Helping learners advance by moving through a zone of proximal development requires support. Theorists refer to this specialized support as *scaffolding.* Instructional scaffolding is the support provided to a learner or groups of learners by a more knowledgeable person, such as a teacher, to help advance learning. In recent years, the notion of scaffolding has been expanded to include learning technologies, such as computer software, that help learners participate in activities that are just beyond their abilities. Scaffolding can help structure a learning task, guide learners through a task, and support thinking, planning, and performance. In a classroom community of practice, scaffolding is essential for aiding learners in developing disciplinary skills and knowledge.

An example of an environment that incorporates extensive scaffolding in a community of practice is *Guided Inquiry supporting Multiple Literacies (GIsML),* developed by Anne Marie Palincsar and Shirley Magnusson. GIsML is a science environment for elementary classrooms that promotes student learning through guided inquiry. The term *guided* refers to the teacher's role in scaffolding the development of students' science knowledge and reasoning as they proceed through cycles of inquiry. In GIsML, students work in pairs or small groups to conduct hands-on investigations in which they collect and analyze data and then report findings to the class. The role of the teacher is to support student thinking through key issues of investigation, such as specific questions to drive the investigation and the design of methods. When it is time to report findings, the teacher assists and guides students in making claims and supporting those claims with evidence (Palincsar & Magnusson, 2001). This process engages students in using the tools, language, and ways of reasoning that are characteristic of scientific inquiry.

From the social perspective, learning depends on the experience and knowledge of students, the knowledge and skills of the teacher, the design of tasks, the tools that are available, and the community that is developed. Furthermore, these factors are interdependent; a change in one will influence the effect of others on learning. Environments developed along social perspective lines include tasks that are typical of those used in the disciplines, instructional scaffolding by more knowledgeable others, tool use that supports learning, and development of learning communities that engage students in practices representative of the subject under study.

Relevance of Theory for Creating Environments

Theory serves as a blueprint that helps designers envision the instructional landscape for building environments. By starting with theory, designers are able to anticipate how to support and organize learning. This anticipatory thinking is important for articulating the how and why of instruction. The *how* is what teachers and students will do during instruction or, more broadly, how the environment will work to promote learning. When designers start with a theoretical framework, they can envision the kinds of classroom activities and interactions necessary to motivate and sustain learning. The *why* provides explanatory power or insight into why designed instructional activities and interactions are productive for learning. Theory explains why particular instructional experiences, when structured and enacted in particular ways, are more or less likely to result in learning. For example, social constructivist theory provides direct guidance for how to support students as they engage in inquiry through techniques that scaffold thinking, planning, and performance in the inquiry process. Scaffolding is important because it guides learners through a task, reducing confusion and increasing the likelihood that students will attend to the important ideas.

Learning environments based on constructivist theories often incorporate components of both cognitive and social views. Increasingly, designers recognize that both aspects need to be addressed when developing learning environments. The *Cognitive Tutors* environment developed by John Anderson and colleagues at Carnegie Mellon University is a computer-based learning environment for secondary school mathematics classrooms. Cognitive Tutors is based on a cognitive theory of learning and performance that describes how individual learners acquire and learn to use mathematical knowledge. Cognitive Tutors software provides tutoring by presenting problem-solving situations to students individually, monitoring students' solution steps, and providing feedback. The environment is centrally focused on individual cognition, but the designers also attend to the social context in which Cognitive Tutors is used. They consider how individual tutor use can be integrated with classroom instruction and collaborative problem-solving experiences. By joining cognitive and social perspectives, they are able to make *Cognitive Tutors* comprehensive and usable for teachers and students.

Designing and Studying Learning Environments

To engineer learning environments, designers need to have a deep understanding about the reality of classrooms and schools. They need expertise in how people learn and the conditions that give rise to learning. They also need to understand academic standards and disciplinary content, the types of tasks and instructional materials that can help students attain learning goals, the role of the teacher in orchestrating instruction, and how to assess learning. Many learning environments feature technology as a tool for learning. To effectively design for learning with technology, designers need to grasp the benefits and challenges of using technologies in classrooms. Finally, designers need to work well with others because the building of learning environments is often too complex for any one designer.

Designers typically work in interdisciplinary teams, with members drawn from education, psychology, computer science, and cognitive sciences. These professionals are centrally concerned with how people learn and how to configure environments to optimally support learning. Many are part of an emerging interdisciplinary field known as the learning sciences, which is comprised of researchers who study teaching and learning in a variety of settings, including school classrooms. The goal of the learning sciences is to better understand the cognitive and social processes that promote learning and to use this knowledge to create learning environments that help teachers teach more effectively and students learn more deeply. A hallmark of the learning sciences is collaboration among researchers with diverse professional backgrounds and ways of thinking to envision and design the schools and classrooms of the future.

Design teams often include disciplinary specialists from mathematics, the sciences, or the social sciences as well as teachers who can help designers think through how materials can be enacted and sustained in real-world classrooms. Because all aspects of an environment are designed, bringing together experts with a range of skills and perspectives is essential. A team working on the design of a middle school mathematics learning environment, for instance, might include an educational psychologist who understands how children think and reason mathematically and the kinds of instructional practices that can best support mathematics learning, a mathematician familiar with the mathematics content and standards, a literacy specialist who can guide the development of text materials for math learning, an expert on educational technology who can design computer tools to support learning, and a mathematics teacher who can provide insight into how teachers might best be supported in enacting the environment. Another key person is a mathematics education researcher who can study how the newly designed environment is enacted by teachers and students in classrooms and the effect of the environment on math learning.

The Design Cycle

The designing and building of learning environments is an iterative process that proceeds through cycles of design, implementation, and evaluation. The first step in the cycle, design, is the process of going from a set of ideas derived from theory to a usable, workable, instructional road map for enacting the environment. For example, designers of the learning environment *Project-Based Science (PBS)* draw from social constructivist theory to inform the design of the environment. The key social constructivist ideas include active construction, situated learning, and social interaction, among others. These theoretical ideas serve as design principles that provide insight into the kinds of classroom activities necessary to support learning. The first principle, active construction, emphasizes the importance of having students actively construct their knowledge by participating in real-world science activities. The second principle, situated learning, suggests that students need to work in an authentic context that mirrors practices in the scientific community. This means providing a context in which students can use and explore scientific practices and apply scientific ideas so they can more readily see the relevance of their participation in activities. Social interaction, the third principle, addresses the need for students to work with one another to conduct investigations and to discuss their ideas and findings. Collaboration helps students build shared understandings of scientific ideas and the nature of science as they engage in discourse with their classmates and teacher. These principles define clearly specified activities within the PBS environment. Design principles are pathways from theory to practice; they are starting points for envisioning how a learning environment might come together.

Early in the design cycle, designers face uncertainty because the initial design of an environment is really only a tentative plan. Instructional sequences and activities are sketched; instructional materials such as a teaching guide and student workbooks are drafted; and technology tools, if integral to the environment, are initially developed. At this point, the hard work is just beginning as designers then move their design work to the complex classroom setting.

In implementation, the second step, the newly designed environment is enacted in a small number of classrooms. Implementation is where teachers and students bring an environment to life and often times, this is where tensions between the intended and enacted environment emerge. The intended environment is the ideal environment envisioned by designers; the enacted environment is what the environment actually looks like and how it works in the hands and minds of teachers and students in everyday classrooms. Implementation is a moment of truth for designers as they get a first glimpse into the practical realities of trying to create an effective environment for learning. Perhaps not surprisingly, issues often arise in early implementation efforts. This is where the third step, evaluation, comes into play.

Evaluation involves the careful study of the implementation. This is a critical step. By studying how an environment is enacted, designers get comprehensive accounts of what works in practice and what does not. This information is used for revising features that do not work as anticipated. For example, in early implementations of PBS, designers found that students were unaccustomed to working in groups and discussing ideas. Students were not used to learning from their own inquiries and had difficulty engaging in productive discussions with one another and the teacher. These issues required PBS designers to rethink how students could be more effectively supported in collaborative inquiry. PBS designers added teacher supports to the instructional materials that included a range of teaching strategies for fostering scientific inquiry and examples of questions and prompts to support discourse. Scaffolds from teachers, peers, and technology were incorporated to guide students through learning activities. Once these and other modifications were made, the PBS environment was implemented and studied again, using data collected from the implementation to inform the next round of design and implementation. After several cycles of design, implementation, and evaluation, the result was a research-based innovation that had been extensively field-tested for usability and effect on student learning and motivation.

The approach to designing environments described here is often referred to as *design-based research*. Design-based research can be traced back to the work of Ann Brown who was one of the first education researchers to promote the idea of designing, enacting, and studying innovations such as learning environments within everyday school settings. According to Brown, researchers can gain important insights about the conditions of learning by bringing theory into practical educational contexts (Brown, 1992). Design-based research enables designers to test whether their theoretical assumptions are usable in the real world. As designers follow a design-based research cycle, they generate knowledge that applies to classroom practice and leads to stronger connections between theory and practice. This work also contributes to a richer understanding of the guiding learning theories. Well done design-based research, then, is likely to yield theoretical and practical insights necessary to advance knowledge by informing theory, design principles, or practice recommendations.

Scaling Learning Environments

Once learning environments have been field-tested in a small number of settings, the challenge is to test their usability in a wide variety of circumstances. To *scale up* means to take a learning environment that is successful in a few settings and expand the implementation beyond those classrooms and teachers who participated in the design-based research cycle. This involves modifying a learning environment for widespread use with many teachers and students throughout a district, or across districts in a state, or in multiple schools and districts around the country.

When designers prepare to go to scale, their focus shifts from considering an environment's implementation within one or several classrooms to implementation in the larger context of schools and school systems. This kind of design work is substantially different and requires designers to attend to professional development for teachers, consider school and district resources for implementation, redesign technology to work within the existing infrastructure of schools, and modify materials and activities for effective use by a wide range of teachers and students. A central goal is to modify the environment so that it is usable and sustainable given school realities, yet provides opportunities and supports for teachers and students to enact innovative and ambitious instruction. To achieve this goal, designers supply teachers with highly specified and developed materials that are critical for ensuring success. Highly specified and developed materials provide teachers with a model of how to enact an environment as well as resources and strategies to promote learning. Educational researchers Deborah Ball and David Cohen coined the term *specified and developed* to emphasize that materials should specify a clear theoretical stance, learning goals, intended teaching practices, and guidelines for enactment (Ball & Cohen, 1996). Furthermore, materials should include resources for teachers and students to use, such as student workbooks and readers, assessments, teacher manuals, and professional development materials that provide examples of ways to enact an environment.

Scaling up also entails modifying environments so that they align with important learning goals found in district, state, and national standards. This is another essential way that designers make their environments usable and sustainable for schools and districts. School administrators and teachers are unlikely to adopt an innovative environment if it does not emphasize content and instructional practice recommendations made in state and national standards documents. Additionally, designers are increasingly finding that they need to show that their environments improve learning as measured by high-stakes tests. For this reason, many discipline-based learning environments emphasize recommendations made in state and national standards documents and include assessments that are aligned with important learning goals.

Features of Environments for Learning

Building a comprehensive learning environment requires that designers attend to the major features of the learning setting. Features are basic aspects of learning environments that influence student learning and performance. Major features include goals, tasks, instructional materials, social organization, teacher, technology, and assessment.

Goals

The goals of learning environments can be academic, social, metacognitive, or developmental. A learning environment might encompass all four types of goals or only one or two. Academic goals focus on disciplinary content and often include learning about disciplinary practices and norms. Goals can also be social, such as the interpersonal goal of learning to work cooperatively, the motivational goal of improving attitudes and promoting interest, and the communicative goal of learning the discourse modes of different disciplines. A third type of goal, metacognitive, promotes a disposition for thinking and reasoning. These are mental habits such as persistence and posing questions that support self-directed or self-regulated learning. Developmental goals tend to focus on moving students forward in terms of knowledge and expertise.

Tasks

Tasks are specific activities that students perform to learn academic content and skills. Learning environments usually emphasize authentic tasks that reflect the work of experts and require students to use their knowledge and skills in real-world situations. Authenticity in a social studies learning environment, for instance, might mean engaging students in tasks that are similar to what histori-

ans do in ways that are appropriate and meaningful for students. This might entail students researching an historical topic of interest and then presenting information in a historically correct manner, using terms and making arguments and explanations as historians would.

Instructional Materials

Learning environments often provide materials to support and guide enactment. Teachers have a unique position in enactment because their use of materials shapes the potential of the environment for enhancing student learning. Increasingly, designers recognize teachers' important role and develop materials that are designed to be educative for teachers. The materials provide targeted assistance to teachers to support their learning so that they, in turn, can better support student learning. Environments that provide educative materials might include a comprehensive guide for enactment with rationales for activities; background on content; guidance in how to use materials and technology with students; examples of questions and prompts to support discourse; and teaching strategies for fostering inquiry, scaffolding student learning, or for building communities of practice. When materials are not extensively developed and teachers play a central role in enacting the learning environment, teachers need to have considerable expertise to meet the goals set by designers.

Social Organization

Many learning environments require that students actively engage in learning, communicate their ideas, and learn from one another. These environments promote a social context that allows students to feel comfortable asking questions, seeking help, and responding to questions. Students collaborate and communicate around authentic tasks and investigations, and they participate in a community of practice that mirrors the discipline under study. Some learning environments are linked to communities that extend beyond the classroom. They might support community participation by encouraging students to present findings to audiences in the community, such as local interest groups and students in other classes. Students' community reach might be further extended to other schools and communities by publishing on the Internet. Technology-based learning environments, for instance, often connect students with other students across school sites to collect, share, and interpret data.

Teacher

The success of any learning environment depends on the teacher, even though the role of the teacher can vary considerably across environments. In some learning environments, teachers play a central role. Their instructional efforts to scaffold student learning, orchestrate group problem solving and investigation, facilitate discussions, and assess understanding are critical. In others, the teacher's position in enacting the learning environment is less central to helping students meet goals. This is the case for computer-based tutoring environments where the technology provides a high level of guidance and is the major influence on student learning. A challenge for teachers in enacting any type of environment is ensuring that the way the environment is enacted matches the theoretical stance of the environment. This requires that teachers have a firm understanding of the learning theory and goals underlying an environment.

Technology

Learning environments use technologies for many purposes. Students in many innovative learning environments are actively involved in using technology tools, such as Internet search engines for research, e-mail or instant messaging for communicating with peers and experts, and visualization or simulation software to create and study models. Some designers place technology at the core of their learning environments and provide custom-designed software tools to support students' knowledge building and knowledge integration. Some of these environments are designed to foster collaborative inquiry. Other computer-based environments are designed for individual work. Still other learning environments may use technologies although they are not central to the enactment of the environment. Increasingly, teachers need technology expertise because they are primarily responsible for troubleshooting and using technology tools to leverage learning.

Assessment

Most learning environments include or recommend several types of assessments to evaluate students' learning. Individual and group portfolios, student reports and presentations, and traditional tests are characteristic of many environments. In some, students design and build artifacts that showcase their learning. Assessments in discipline-based learning environments typically target content knowledge, reasoning skills, and students' understanding of the nature of the discipline. Some environments might also assess students' motivation, including interest, feelings of efficacy, and goals for learning.

Summary

Although many learning environments share most, if not all, of the features described above, they differ in the emphasis they place on particular features and how they instantiate them. For instance, technology is the core in some environments; in others it is secondary or not present at all. Another difference is that content might be addressed through problem-based tasks representative of a particular discipline in some environments, and project-based tasks may be used in others. Learning environments also encompass different types of social organization and differ in their overarching goals. Features of any particular environment are presumed to work together to foster learning in an educational setting. This is because the goals and instantiations of each feature of a learning environment derive from the same underlying theoretical ideas about learning.

Examples of Environments for Learning

This section presents summaries of two learning environments designed to support ambitious teaching and learning. Each environment has a strong theoretical foundation: one environment is grounded in the social perspective, the other in the cognitive perspective. Each offers a different way of bringing theory into design and practice. Brief descriptions are included of goals, the types of tasks and instructional materials used to reach the goals, social organization of the environments, the role of the teacher, the use of technology, and how learning is assessed.

Project-Based Science

In a Project-Based Science (PBS) learning environment, middle school students engage in real-world investigations in ways that are similar to how scientists conduct inquiry. Developed by Joseph Krajcik, Ronald Marx, Phyllis Blumenfeld, Elliot Soloway, and others at the University of Michigan, PBS promotes instruction and learning through carefully designed and developed inquiry projects. Projects are framed around a driving question that guides instruction and serves to organize students' investigations. Driving questions are crafted to encompass science content and to connect with students' interests and curiosities about the world. For instance, students learn about microbiology and infectious diseases by engaging in inquiry tasks framed around the question, How can good friends make me sick? In this project, students explore how a communicable disease spreads through a community. A central goal of the PBS environment is to have students engage in extended inquiry to understand science content and practices that are outlined in state and national standards. Another important goal is to contribute to students' attitudes toward science.

The theoretical foundation of PBS draws from a social constructivist perspective that emphasizes active, situated, and collaborative learning. In PBS classrooms, students are provided with a meaningful context in which to explore the driving question over a sustained period of time. For example, the driving question, Why do I need to wear a helmet when I ride my bike? situates the science topic of force and motion in an issue that is likely to be of interest to students. As students become involved in the project, they collaborate with peers and with their teacher to ask and explore smaller questions that contribute to understanding the driving question. They conduct investigations, weigh evidence, write explanations, and discuss and present findings. As they pursue answers to the driving question, they participate in situated activities that help them learn scientific content and practices relevant and necessary to construct a meaningful response.

Students in PBS classrooms produce artifacts, or products, that showcase their learning. For example, students create models that represent scientific phenomena, develop concept maps that illustrate their understanding of complex ideas, and prepare presentations and reports that explain their findings and the evidence for those findings. Teachers often use students' artifacts for assessment purposes in combination with traditional tests. Additionally, surveys are used to explore students' perceptions of the learning environment and its influence on attitudes toward science and motivation to learn science.

PBS uses technology tools and resources such as Web-based databases, model-building software, handheld technologies, and the Internet for interactive inquiry. Computers and other technologies extend students' thinking by providing access to information and opportunities to communicate, explore phenomena, and build scientifically accurate models that represent phenomena.

Teachers play a central role in PBS classrooms by orchestrating instruction so that students develop the important skills and stance necessary for engaging in inquiry. They provide instructional scaffolds that help students engage in productive discussions with one another and their teacher, plan and carry out investigations, analyze data, and present findings. Highly specified and developed teacher materials that help create and sustain a PBS environment include detailed lesson descriptions and supports that clearly identify learning goals; examples of students' likely ideas; questions and tasks for guiding and monitoring student understanding; instructional strategies to support students as they engage in inquiry; and key ideas that teachers can emphasize in helping students make sense of their inquiry experiences.

Cognitive Tutors

Technology is the centerpiece of the Cognitive Tutors learning environment developed by John Anderson, Albert Corbett, Kenneth Koedinger, and others at Carnegie Mellon University. Cognitive Tutors is a computer-based environment for high school mathematics classrooms that uses intelligent instructional software to teach students such topics as algebra, geometry, and integrated math. Cognitive Tutors software provides one-to-one tutoring by presenting problem-solving situations to students individually and monitoring and guiding students as they work through the tasks. The central goal of the environment is to raise mathematics achievement by developing students' math problem-solving abilities and deepening their math knowledge.

Cognitive Tutors is based on a cognitive theory of learning and performance that proposes students learn best by doing rather than watching or listening. The software presents real-world problem-solving situations that require students to apply math knowledge and practice specific math skills. For instance, the algebra tutor emphasizes algebraic reasoning through such problems as comparing car rental options, engineering a highway, and organizing to make and sell T-shirts. As students engage in the problem-solving tasks, they also become adept at using and interpreting mathematical representations such as tables, graphs, and symbolic expressions.

Cognitive Tutors software monitors students' problem-solving performance by following students as they work through a task and providing feedback. Each Cognitive Tutor employs a cognitive model that represents the skills and strategies required to complete each task. When a student makes an error, the tutor initially displays an error message and provides on-demand hints; multiple hints are available for each step of a problem to ensure that the correct path to a solution is followed. An error message serves as a prompt that allows a student to correct errors without assistance. Multiple hints allow the student to succeed with minimum assistance. The tutor provides tailored practice on math skills until students reach mastery performance levels. Once a student reaches mastery on a particular math skill, the tutor stops presenting new problems for that skill.

The Cognitive Tutors environment integrates individual tutor use with classroom instruction that includes collaborative problem-solving activities and class discussions. The teacher facilitates classroom instruction and circulates and assists students as they interact with the tutor. The teacher needs to have subject matter knowledge, be familiar with tutor software (including how to troubleshoot technical issues), and be comfortable facilitating collaborative problem solving.

Instructional materials that help teachers enact the environment accompany the software. The materials include a problem-based textbook for students and a teacher's guide that consists of assignments, assessments, teaching suggestions, and classroom management techniques. The purpose of the textbook and classroom activities is to extend the development of concepts emphasized in the software.

Assessment is an integral part of the Cognitive Tutors environment. Cognitive Tutors software includes step-by-step assessments of students' mathematical skills and provides a skill report to identify math skill levels and progress for each student. Assessments provided in the teacher's materials include exams, quizzes, and rubrics for grading class presentations. Teachers are also encouraged to create and share their own assessments in an online teacher community.

Challenges and Future Directions

Designing an environment for learning requires significant time, effort, and resources. A design-based research team will typically work for three or more years to develop, modify, and refine a learning environment. Designers work closely with teachers in classrooms to observe how an enactment unfolds and to study how the environment enhances learning. The iterative approach enables a design team to modify their environment in a real-world setting, carefully observe as teachers introduce the refinements, and then make further adjustments as needed. In fact, designers may follow teachers' classes over several years to gain insight and guidance into optimally supported learning.

This approach requires long-term partnerships between educational researchers, school administrators, and teachers. It requires that schools change their culture and routines to support innovative practice and that designers find creative ways to help teachers reconfigure their classrooms as environments for ambitious learning. It is clear that contemporary learning environments represent a considerable departure from the type of classroom experience with which most teachers, students, administrators, and parents are familiar. Learning environments, then, pose special challenges that require considerable knowledge, skill, and foresight to address.

Future Directions

The present work on learning environments marks efforts to design the schools of the future. These first generation environments provide a glimpse of the potential of this work for transforming classrooms. Students in these environments have been introduced to new ways of learning. They solve meaningful problems, collaborate with others, use cutting-edge technology, and create artifacts that showcase their learning. They gain important knowledge and skills, appreciation for disciplinary practices, and new dispositions for learning. For designers, these environments provide a rich context for interdisciplinary research. As this work continues, we will gain a better understanding of how instructional interactions shape learning and how effective environments can be designed.

A necessary next step is to design environments for a wider range of school contexts. This is important for scaling up. Schools are becoming more linguistically and culturally diverse every year, and carefully designed environments that support students from different backgrounds is essential. Similarly, designers need to examine how learning environments can be created or adapted for inclusiveness of special needs learners. There is evidence that learning environments can help address diversity because they offer a variety of instructional techniques, activities, technology tools, and different ways for students to participate.

Conclusion

New knowledge about how people learn has enriched understanding of how to create successful conditions for learning. Learning environments represent an expanded view of teaching and learning that encompasses the social context and recognizes the complexity of instruction. Over the next decade, new learning environments will emerge that may prove critical for preparing students for the 21st century. This chapter examined the building of learning environments in schools and classrooms. It is important to note that many others are being designed for informal learning settings such as museums, science centers, and afterschool programs.

Learning environments represent ambitious pedagogy and strive for ambitious outcomes. The designers of these environments are committed to transforming schools and classrooms into dynamic places where teachers teach more effectively and students learn more deeply. Design-based research is a new approach that strengthens the bridge between learning theory and educational practice and advances our understanding of both. Design work is challenging and complex, requiring collaborations among educational researchers, teachers, disciplinary experts, school leaders, and others. The work is vital for improving schools to meet the needs of our rapidly changing knowledge-based and technological society. The schools of the future are on the horizon, and the interdisciplinary efforts of designers promise to create innovative environments that will serve as a foundation for the next generation of schools.

References and Further Readings

Ball, D. L., & Cohen, D. K. (1996). Reform by the book: What is—or might be—the role of curriculum materials in teacher learning and instructional reform? *Educational Researcher, 25*(9), 6–8.

Blumenfeld, P., Marx, R. W., & Harris, C. J. (2006). Learning environments. In W. Damon, R. M. Lerner, K. A. Renninger, & I. E. Sigel (Eds.) *Handbook of child psychology, 6th edition, volume 4: Child psychology in practice* (pp. 297–342). Hoboken, NJ: Wiley.

Bransford, J. D., Brown, A. L., & Cocking, R. R. (Eds.). (2000). *How people learn: Brain, mind, experience, and school* (Expanded Ed.). Washington, DC: National Academies Press.

Brown, A. L. (1992). Design experiments: Theoretical and methodological challenges in creating complex interventions in classroom settings. *Journal of the Learning Sciences, 2*, 141–178.

Brown, A. L., & Campione, J. C. (1994). Guided discovery in a community of learners. In K. McGilly (Ed.), *Classroom lessons: Integrating cognitive theory and classroom practice* (pp. 229–270). Cambridge, MA: MIT Press.

Corbett, A. T., Koedinger, K. R., & Hadley, W. S. (2001). Cognitive Tutors: From the research classroom to all classrooms. In P. Goodman (Ed.), *Technology enhanced learning: Opportunities for change* (pp. 235–263). Mahwah, NJ: Lawrence Erlbaum Associates.

Davis, E. A., & Krajcik, J. S. (2005). Designing educative curriculum materials to promote teacher learning. *Educational Researcher, 34*(3), 3–14.

Design-Based Research Collective. (2003). Design-based research: An emerging paradigm for educational inquiry. *Educational Researcher, 32*(1), 5–8.

Gelman, R., & Brenneman, K. (2004). Science learning pathways for young children. *Early Childhood Research Quarterly, 19,* 150–158.

Krajcik, J., & Blumenfeld, P. (2006). Project-based learning. In R. K. Saywer (Ed.), *Cambridge handbook of the learning sciences* (pp. 317–334). New York: Cambridge University Press.

Lave, J., & Wenger, E. (1991). *Situated learning: Legitimate peripheral participation.* New York: Cambridge University Press.

Maxwell, N., Bellisimo, Y., & Mergendoller, J. (2001). Problem-based learning: Modifying the medical school model for teaching high school economics. *Social Studies, 92,* 73–78.

Palincsar, A. S., & Magnusson, S. J. (2001). The interplay of first-hand and second-hand investigations to model and support the development of scientific knowledge and reasoning. In S. Carver & D. Klahr (Eds.), *Cognition and instruction: Twenty-five years of progress* (pp. 151–193). Mahwah, NJ: Lawrence Erlbaum Associates.

Sarama, J., & Clements, D. H. (2004). Building blocks for early childhood mathematics. *Early Childhood Research Quarterly, 19,* 181–189.

Saywer, R. K. (Ed.). (2006). *Cambridge handbook of the learning sciences.* New York: Cambridge University Press.

Singer, J., Marx, R. W., Krajcik, J., & Chambers, J. C. (2000). Constructing extended inquiry projects: Curriculum materials for science education reform. *Educational Psychologist, 35*(3), 165–178.

Songer, N. B. (2006). BioKIDS: An animated conversation on the development of curricular activity structures for inquiry science. In R. K. Sawyer (Ed.), *Cambridge handbook of the learning sciences* (pp. 355–369). New York: Cambridge University Press.

Vygotsky, L. S. (1978). *Mind in society: The development of higher psychological processes.* Cambridge, MA: Harvard University Press.

25

SYSTEMATIC INSTRUCTION

BARAK ROSENSHINE

University of Illinois at Urbana-Champaign

The research on effective teaching conducted since 1974 has revealed a pattern that is particularly useful for teaching explicit skills or a body of content. This pattern, which might be called systematic instruction (Katz, 1994), is a systematic method of teaching new material, a method that includes presenting material in small steps, pausing to check for student understanding, and requiring active and successful participation from all students.

Although this pattern came primarily from research in reading and mathematics instruction in elementary and junior high schools, the results are applicable to any systematic or "well-structured" (Simon, 1973) area of knowledge. These results are relevant for teaching mathematical procedures and computations, reading decoding, science facts and concepts, social studies facts and concepts, map skills, grammatical concepts and rules, and foreign language vocabulary and grammar.

This pattern has also been used with modifications to teach students complex cognitive skills such as essay writing, reading comprehension, and problem solving in mathematics. In these cases, students are provided with scaffolds and other techniques that support the student and reduce the difficulty of the task (Rosenshine & Meister, 1992).

The research on teaching has found that when effective teachers teach well-defined concepts and skills, they:

- begin a lesson with a short review of previous, prerequisite learning;

- present new material in small steps, and allow student practice after each step;
- provide considerable active practice for all students;
- ask many questions, check for student understanding, and obtain responses from all students;
- guide students during initial practice;
- provide systematic feedback and corrections;
- continue practice until students are independent and confident.

The major components of systematic instruction include teaching in small steps and allowing student practice after each step, guiding students during initial practice, and providing all students with a high level of successful practice. Each of these instructional procedures will be described more fully later.

School-Based Origins

These results come from research in classrooms that was designed to identify the instructional procedures used by the most successful teachers. In this research the investigators first gave pretests and posttests to a number of classrooms, usually 20 to 30 classrooms, and usually in reading or mathematics. After making appropriate adjustments for the initial ability of the students, the investigators identified those teachers whose classes made the highest achievement gain in the subject being studied and those teachers whose classes made the least gain.

The observers then sat in these classrooms, observing and recording the frequency with which teachers used various instructional behaviors. The observers usually recorded the number and type of questions, the quality of the student answers, and the responses of a teacher to students' answers. Many investigators also recorded how much time was spent in activities such as review, presentation, guided practice, and supervising seatwork. Some investigators recorded how the teachers prepared students for seatwork and homework. Other observers recorded the frequency and type of praise, and the frequency, type, and context of criticism. The overall attention level of the class and sometimes of individual students was also recorded. This information was then used to describe how the most successful teachers were different from their less successful colleagues.

Initially, the studies were correlational. The correlational studies were followed by experimental studies in which the investigators developed a manual for teaching based, in part, on findings from the correlational studies. One group of teachers received the manual and was taught to use these behaviors in their teaching and the control teachers were asked to continue their regular teaching. These studies have shown that the teachers who received the manual performed many of the instructional procedures that were suggested. For example, they asked students more questions and spent more time presenting new material. The investigators also found that students of the teachers in the experimental classes obtained higher achievement scores than did students of the control group.

The results from the experimental studies supported the findings of the earlier correlational studies. By and large, these experimental studies showed that the teachers in the experimental groups used more of the new behaviors they were taught to use, and the posttest scores of their classrooms—adjusted by regression for their initial scores—were significantly higher than scores in classrooms taught by the control teachers. The results of both sets of studies are incorporated in this chapter.

Correlational studies of this type, studies in which the investigators identified the instructional procedures that were used by the most successful teachers were conducted as early as 1948 (Barr, 1948). Subsequent studies by Flanders (1970) and by Medley and Mitzel (1959, 1963) initiated over a decade of research on teacher-effects research. The best known of the later studies were those by Stallings and Kaskowitz (1974) who studied Follow-Through classrooms, Good and Grouws (1977, 1979) who studied teachers of fourth-grade mathematics, and Brophy and Evertson (1976) who studied the teaching of first-grade reading.

Rosenshine (1971) summarized the earliest studies. The correlational studies and the experimental studies in this tradition are described in detail by Brophy and Good (1986), and the experimental studies in this tradition were described by Gage and Needles (1989).

Systematic Instruction, Direct Instruction, and Similar Terms

Gage (1978) referred to these studies as research on "teacher effectiveness." Medley and Mitzel (1963) referred to the same research as "process-product research" because of the emphasis on conducting correlations in these studies. Brophy and Good (1986) used the title "teacher effects." McDonald and Elias (1976) looked at a pattern of the results in one of their studies and wrote that the successful teachers used a pattern that they called "direct instruction," a term which Rosenshine (1976) began to use extensively. Unfortunately, the term *direct instruction* is confusing today because it is now used to refer to both the specific findings of the teacher effects research and also to any teacher-led instruction. There is no way to avoid this problem because many educators who use the term *direct instruction* are not aware of the many meanings this term has. Others have used the term *explicit teaching* to refer to the same pattern. Katz (1994) introduced the term *systematic instruction* to describe the findings of the teacher effects research and uses that term for the explicit sequence of instruction and the emphasis upon providing guided practice. Systematic instruction is a more descriptive term than direct instruction and is less ambiguous.

Information Processing Research

The research on human cognitive architecture—on how information is acquired, stored, and retrieved—has major implications for teaching (Kirschner, Sweller, & Clark, 2006; Mayer, Information Processing, Chapter 18; Kirschner & van Merriënboer, Ten Steps to Complex Learning: A New Approach to Instruction and Instructional Design, Chapter 26.). Although the major work on human cognitive architecture occurred after the teacher-effects research had ended, this research on information processing fits the findings on classroom instruction quite well and adds to our understanding of the findings from the teacher-effects research.

The Limitations of Our Working Memory

Current information processing theories suggest that there are limits to the amount of information we can process effectively. We are limited-capacity processors. We can only handle a few pieces of new information (about seven) in our working memory at one time. When we are presented with too much new information our working memory becomes swamped, a condition that is called cognitive overload. When overloaded, we become confused and we do not process the new material (Tobias, 1982).

Thus, teachers need to be cautious in the amount of new or difficult material they present at any one time.

The Need for Student Processing

New material needs to be processed before being transferred from our working memory to our long-term memory where it is stored and used. Unless we elaborate on, review, and rehearse the new material there is a good chance that it will not be retained. Thus, teachers need to provide active practice for all students. Such practice is facilitated if the teacher guides and encourages student processing by asking questions, requiring students to summarize main points, having students tutor each other, and supervising students as they practice new steps in a skill.

The level of processing of new material is also important. Requiring students to review, compare and contrast, summarize, and draw conclusions results in a higher level of processing and better retention and application than asking students to simply repeat the material. As Brown and Campione (1986) put it: "Understanding is more likely to occur when a student is required to explain, elaborate, or defend his or her position to others; the burden of explanation is often the push needed to make him or her evaluate, integrate, and elaborate knowledge in new ways" (p. 1066).

The Importance of a Well-Connected Cognitive Network

It is currently thought that the information in our long-term memory is stored in interconnected networks called knowledge structures. The size of these structures, the number of connections between pieces of knowledge, the strength of the connections, and the organization and richness of the relationships are all important for processing information and solving problems. It is easier to assimilate new information and easier to use prior knowledge for problem solving when one has more connections and interconnections, stronger ties between the connections, and a better organized knowledge structure. When the knowledge structure on a particular topic is large and well-connected, new information is more readily acquired and prior knowledge is more readily available for use. Education is a process of developing, enlarging, expanding, and refining students' knowledge structures.

A major difference between an expert and a novice is that the expert's knowledge structure has a larger number of knowledge items, the expert has more connections between the items, the links between the connections are stronger, and the structure is better organized. A novice, on the other hand, is unable to see these patterns and often ignores them.

Chase and Chi (1980), who have studied how expertise is acquired, wrote:

> The most obvious answer is practice, thousands of hours of practice . . . For the most part, practice is by far the best pre-

dictor of performance. Practice can produce two kinds of knowledge . . . a storage of patterns and a set of strategies or procedures that can act on the patterns. (p. 12).

Experts See Patterns

When novices look at a chess board, they tend to see individual pieces. But when experts look at chessboards, they see the patterns that the pieces form. When chess players are shown the pieces in a chess game and asked to memorize them, the expert chess players are able to memorize the positions of up to 32 pieces despite the limitations in the size of our working memories. The experts overcome these limitations because they have grouped these pieces into five or six patterns. As proof, it was shown that when expert chess players are shown chess pieces placed randomly on a chess board, they are only able to recall the placement of five or six pieces—just like ordinary people.

This difference between seeing individual pieces and seeing patterns characterizes the differences between experts and novices in a wide number of fields. Novices see individual bits of information, whereas experts, through practice and study, have grouped information into patterns. When novice teachers look at classrooms they tend to see individual activities, whereas expert teachers group the activities they see into patterns.

The advantage of organizing knowledge into patterns is that a pattern only occupies a few bits in our limited working memory. Thus, having larger and better connected patterns frees up space in our working memory. This available space can be used for reflecting on new information and for problem solving. This development of well-connected patterns (also called unitization and chunking) and the concomitant freeing of space in the working memory is one of the hallmarks of an expert in a field.

Dancers initially see one move and then another, and eventually they merge the steps into phrases and then into longer sequences. After learning the steps and the phrases and after extensive practice, the dance becomes a chunk, becomes one seamless movement. As the dance becomes automatic, less space is required in the working memory and the dancers are able use the available space to focus on the moment-to-moment nuances of the performance. Education, then, is the development of well-connected and elaborate knowledge structures. These structures allow for easier retrieval of old material, permit more information to be carried in a single chunk, and facilitate the understanding and integration of new information.

The Development of Automaticity

When words, concepts, and intellectual skills are highly practiced—are overlearned—they can be recalled automatically from a person's long-term memory. Automaticity means without conscious thought and without taking up any of the limited space in our working memory. When prior learning is automatic, space is left free in our working memory that can be used for comprehension and higher-level thinking.

Fluent decoding is an example of automaticity. A skilled reader reads without having to sound out words. This skill is the result of extensive practice. When reading is automatic, then more space is available in the working memory and that space can be used for comprehension.

Educational Implications

The research on human cognitive architecture suggests that it is important for the teacher to provide "instructional support" when teaching students new material (see Tobias, 1982). Such support occurs when the teacher (1) breaks material into small steps to reduce possible confusion; (2) structures the learning by giving an overview or an outline; (3) gives the learner active practice in each step to move the new learning into long-term memory; and (4) provides for additional practice and overlearning so that the learners can use the new material or skills effortlessly.

As we shall see, the most effective teachers in the teacher-effects research applied the research on human cognitive architecture extremely well, and there is a close fit between the results of the research on human information processing and the instructional practices of the most effective teachers.

Six Teaching Functions

I have divided the results from the empirical research on teacher effects into six teaching functions: review, presentation of new material, guided practice, feedback and corrections, independent practice, and weekly and monthly reviews. These results are summarized in Table 25.1. Similar functions have also been developed by Good and Grouws (1979) and Russell and Hunter (1981).

Gage (1978) has noted that these general principles represent "the scientific basis for the art of teaching." Yet a good deal of art is needed to translate this material into specific lessons. Teachers have to make decisions on the amount of material that will be presented at one time, the way in which it will be presented, how guided practice will be conducted, how specific errors made by specific students will be corrected, the pace and length of the lesson, and how they will work with different students. A great deal of thought, creativity, and flexibility is also needed to apply the results of the research to specific instances of teaching lessons on long division, on the Constitution, on grammar, and on reading comprehension.

All teachers use some of these functions some of the time. These findings, after all, came from the study of observed classroom instruction. But the differences between the effective and ineffective teachers were in how they used these functions. Effective teachers applied these instructional procedures consistently and systematically, and ineffective teachers used each function less effectively.

Table 25.1   Teaching Functions

1. Review

   Review homework

   Review relevant previous learning

   Review prerequisite skills and knowledge for the lesson

2. Presentation of new material

   State lesson goals or provide outline

   Teach in small steps

   Model procedures

   Provide concrete positive and negative examples

   Check for student understanding

   Avoid digressions

3. Guide student practice

   High frequency of questions or guided practice

   All students respond and receive feedback

   High success rate

   Continue practice until students are fluid

4. Provide corrections and feedback

   Give process feedback when answers are correct but hesitant

   Give sustaining feedback

   Reteach material when necessary

5. Independent practice

   Students receive help during initial steps or overview

   Practice continues until students are automatic (where relevant)

   Teacher provides active supervision (where possible)

6. Weekly and monthly reviews

SOURCE: Rosenshine, B. (1987). Explicit teaching. In D. Berliner & B. Rosenshine (Eds.), *Talks to teachers* (pp. 75–92). New York: Random House.

Daily Review

Effective teachers in these studies began their lessons with a 5- to 8-minute review which included a short review of previously covered material, correction of homework, and review of prior knowledge that was relevant to the day's lesson. These reviews ensure that students have a firm grasp of the prerequisite skills for the day's lesson. The teachers' activities can include reviewing the concepts and skills necessary to do the homework; having students correct each other's papers; asking about points at which the students had difficulty or made errors; and reviewing or providing additional practice on facts and skills that need overlearning. Daily review could also include a short test on items similar to the homework assignment.

One example of effective daily review is in a successful reading program (American Federation of Teachers, 1998). In this program 5 minutes are spent in daily review of sight words—words from prior stories and words from forthcoming stories in the reader. The teacher presents the word lists and the students say the words in unison and, when necessary, they reread the lists until the reading is fluent. The students read at the rate of a word a second, which makes it possible for a class to review 150 sight words in less than 4 minutes.

Daily review was also part of a successful experiment in elementary school mathematics (Good & Grouws, 1979). In this study, teachers in the control group, who had said that they review every day, actually reviewed on only 50% of the days they were observed. The teachers in the more successful experimental group, who had received training in daily review, conducted review and checked homework 80% of the days they were observed.

The importance of practicing daily review can be justified both by the empirical research on teaching and by the research on human cognitive architecture. As Chase and Chi (1980) noted, the development of expertise requires practice, "thousands of hours of practice." Daily review is practice. Practicing previous learning can serve to strengthen the connections in our knowledge structures and can thus help us to recall that material effortlessly and automatically.

Presenting New Material

The daily review is followed by the presentation of new material. Effective teachers spent more time presenting new material and guiding student practice than did the ineffective teachers (Evertson, Anderson, Anderson, & Brophy, 1980; Good & Grouws, 1979). Evertson, Anderson et al., (1980) found that the most effective mathematics teachers spend about 23 minutes per day in lecture, demonstration, and discussion in contrast to 11 minutes spent by the least effective teachers. The effective teachers used this extra time to provide additional explanations, give many examples, check for student understanding, and reteach material when necessary. Their objective was to provide sufficient instruction so that the students could do the independent practice—the time they spent working on their own—with minimal difficulty. In contrast, Evertson, Anderson et al. (1980) and Good and Grouws (1979) found that ineffective teachers spent less time presenting new material. These teachers gave shorter presentations and explanations and then asked the students to practice independently before they were competent enough to do so. Under these conditions, students made more errors during independent practice.

At the start of the presentation, effective teachers first focused the students' attention on what they were to learn and do. Then, they proceeded to teach new material "in small steps" (Brophy & Good, 1986) and only taught one point at a time. These teachers gave short presentations,

provided many examples, and followed this material with guided practice. As noted earlier, presenting too much new material at one time may confuse students because their short-term memory is unable to process it. Dorothy DeLay, an esteemed violin teacher whose students included Itzhak Perlman, Nadja Salerno-Sonnenberg, and Gil Shaham, made this same point when she recommended to violin teachers that they should first analyze the problem and then simplify the task into steps so that the student can succeed and not be overwhelmed by its difficulties.

Smith and Land (1981) found that it is also important for the teacher to avoid ambiguous phrases, such as "sort of" and "a few," or phrases that may easily be misinterpreted, such as "as you can see" and "it is obvious that." These phrases are vague and may confuse a student who is learning new material. Digressions can also cause problems, because the extraneous information is too much for students to process, resulting in confusion.

Effective teachers also stopped to check for student understanding. They asked questions about the material. They asked students to summarize the presentation to that point or to repeat directions or procedures. Sometimes they asked students whether they agreed or disagreed with other students' answers. This checking has two purposes: it causes the students to elaborate upon the material they learned and augment connections in their long-term-memory, and it also tells the teacher whether parts of the material need to be retaught.

At the end of their presentation the ineffective teachers simply asked, Are there any questions? When no students asked questions, these teachers assumed that the material had been learned. Another error is to ask a few questions, call on volunteers to hear their (usually correct) answers, and then assume that the class understands and has learned from the volunteers.

The following suggestions for effective presentation have emerged from the experimental and correlational classroom literature:

- Provide outlines
- Organize material so that one point can be mastered before the next point is introduced
- Checking for understanding during the presentation
- Avoid digressions

Guiding Student Practice

After the presentation, the teacher conducts guided, supervised practice. The major purposes of guided practice are to (1) supervise students' initial practice on a skill so that the students don't internalize errors, (3) check for understanding (Hunter, 1982) of the material, and (3) provide the active practice and elaboration that are necessary to move new learning into long-term memory.

As noted, the research on information processing has revealed that we have to spend a lot of time processing the new material to learn it. We need to spend time rephrasing, rehearsing, and summarizing the new material so that we can readily retrieve it from our long-term memory when applying it to new situations.

Teacher questions and student discussion are a major way of providing this practice. By asking questions, a teacher directs and guides the necessary processing and elaboration that are needed to process and store the new information in long-term memory. Questions also allow a teacher to check for understanding (Hunter, 1982), that is, to determine how well the material has been learned and whether there is a need for additional instruction.

A number of correlational studies (e.g., Stallings & Kaskowitz, 1974) have shown that effective teachers asked more questions than ineffective teachers. These correlational studies were followed by experimental studies (Anderson, Evertson, & Brophy, 1979; Good & Grouws, 1979) in which teachers were taught to use a high frequency of questioning during guided practice. In both experimental studies, the students of teachers in the experimental groups achieved higher scores on the posttest than did students of teachers in the control groups.

Two types of questions are usually asked during guided practice: questions that call for specific answers and process questions, or questions that ask the students to explain the process they used to answer the question. In a correlational study of junior-high-school mathematics instruction (Evertson, Anderson et al., 1980), the most effective teachers asked an average of 24 questions during the 50-minute period, whereas the least effective teachers asked only 8.6 questions. The most effective teachers asked 6 process questions during each observed period, whereas the least effective teachers asked only 1.3 questions.

Teaching in Small Steps

Sometimes the presentation of new material and guided practice are combined so that a teacher only presents a small amount of new material and then follows this presentation with guided practice. This pattern of short presentations and guided practice has been called "teaching in small steps" (Brophy & Good, 1986). One might expect that with younger, slower students, or when the material is new or different, that these shorter segments of presentation and guided practice would be most effective.

Variations in Guided Practice

Teachers have developed a number of ways to guide student practice. When learning procedures that have a number of steps, such as two-digit multiplication, students need sufficient practice on the first step before going to the next. Guided practice could consist of going over the skills in small steps with teacher supervision. Some students practice at the board, while others work at their seats. When the teacher feels they are ready, the students proceed to the next step. If they are not ready, then the teacher provides additional practice.

When teaching an elaborate skill, such as using a computer package, or solving a geometry problem, or writing an essay, a teacher might first ask students to restate the steps that were taught so that he or she can resolve any confusion before students begin independent practice. Then the teacher could supervise students as they begin to practice, guiding them through each procedure until they can perform each step without errors.

Increasing Student Participation

Imaginative teachers can increase the amount of active student participation by involving all students in answering questions instead of simply having individual students answer the teacher. Examples of procedures for increasing student participation include having each student

- tell the answer to a neighbor;
- write the answer and an explanation on a sheet of paper;
- summarize the main idea in one or two sentences, writing the sum (mary on a piece of paper and sharing this with a neighbor, or repeat the procedures to a neighbor.

Other procedures, such as the following, allow teachers to monitor the entire class:

- Have each student write the answer on a slate that he or she then holds up
- Ask students to raise their hands if they know the answer
- Allow one student to answer and have the other students signal whether they agree or disagree

Some teachers use choral responses to provide sufficient practice when teaching new vocabulary or lists of items; or when teaching students to identify parts of things, such as parts of a plant, book, or dictionary; or to discriminate among related concepts, such as metaphor, simile, and personification or adverbs and adjectives. Choral responses can make the practice seem more like a game. To be effective, however, all students need to start together, on a signal. When students do not start together, only the fastest students answer and the others do not receive adequate practice.

Of course, all teachers use guided practice; however, the most effective teachers spend more time in guided practice, more time asking questions, more time checking for understanding, more time correcting errors, and more time having students solve problems with teacher guidance.

High Percentage of Correct Answers

Effective teachers have a high success rate (Fisher et al., 1978). In a study of fourth-grade mathematics, Good and Grouws (1979) found that 82% of the answers were correct in the classrooms of the most successful teachers, whereas the least successful teachers had a success rate of 73%. The optimal success rate appears to be about 75 to

80% during guided practice, suggesting that effective teachers combine both success and sufficient challenge. The most effective teachers obtained this success level by teaching in small steps, that is, by using the combination of short presentations and supervised student practice and by providing sufficient practice on each part before proceeding to the next. In other words, if the success rate is slow when the teacher begins the guided practice, the teacher continues with practice and explanations until the success rate is high.

Provide Feedback and Correctives

During any recitation or demonstration, how should a teacher respond to a student's answer? Researchers who observed and coded classroom instruction recorded the frequency and type of teacher questions, the correctness of the student responses, and teacher responses to students' answers. These studies showed that when a student was correct and confident, it was most appropriate for a teacher to then ask another question, or give a short statement of praise (such as "Very good") and thus continue the momentum of the practice.

But when a student was correct but hesitant, many of the successful teachers also provided process feedback. Process feedback (Good & Grouws, 1979) is the teacher saying, "Yes, that's right, because . . ." and then explaining the process one goes through to arrive at the correct answer. By providing an additional explanation or repetition of the process in this manner, the teacher provides that student, and likely others, with the additional learning needed to instill understanding and confidence.

When students made an error, the effective teachers helped them by simplifying the question, providing hints, or reteaching the material. But the ineffective teachers often supplied the correct answer and then moved on to the next student. Whether one uses hints or reteaching or reteaching outside the lesson, the important point is that unless the errors are corrected, misconceptions and problems will remain.

Many of these strategies also apply to older students. In a review of effective college teaching, Kulik and Kulik (1979) found that instruction is more effective when (a) students receive immediate feedback on their examinations, and (b) students have to do additional study and take another test when their quiz scores do not reach a set criterion. Both points seem relevant to this discussion: students learn better when the feedback is as immediate as possible, and errors should be corrected before they become habitual.

Conduct Independent Practice

Independent practice provides students with the additional review and elaboration that they need to become fluent in a skill. This need for fluency and independence applies to many of the procedures that are taught in school: dividing decimals, reading a map, conjugating a regular verb in a foreign language, completing and balancing a chemical equation, operating equipment, and applying safety procedures. This need for fluency also applies to facts, concepts, and discriminations that must be used in subsequent learning.

A good deal of substantial practice is usually needed in order to attain fluency in a skill. When students become fluent—when they can perform rapidly, successfully, and automatically (Bloom, 1986) and no longer have to think through each step—they can then devote their full attention to comprehension and application.

Independent practice should involve the same material as the guided practice. If the guided practice dealt with identifying types of sentences, then the independent practice should also focus on identifying types of sentences. It would be inappropriate to follow instruction in types of sentences with an independent practice assignment that asked students to write a paragraph using two compound and two complex sentences, because students have not been prepared for this activity.

Managing Independent Practice

Sometimes it may be appropriate for a teacher to practice some of the homework problems with the entire class before students take the work home or engage in independent practice. Fisher et al. (1978) found that teachers who spent more time in guided practice had students who were more engaged during seatwork. This finding suggests the importance of adequately preparing students before seatwork. Fisher et al. (1978) also found that classrooms where the teacher had to stop at students' desks and give a great deal of explanation during seatwork were also classrooms where the error rates on the students' papers were the highest. Having to stop and provide explanations during seatwork suggests that the initial explanation and guided practice were not sufficient.

Fisher at al. (1978) also found that students are more engaged during seatwork when the teacher circulates around the room and monitors and supervises their work; however, the optimal time for these contacts averaged 30 seconds or less. The need for longer contacts, as noted, was a sign that the guided practice had not been sufficient.

In summary, students are more engaged during independent practice when the teacher circulates and when there has been sufficient explanation and preparation before the independent practice begins.

Weekly and Monthly Review

Some of the successful programs in elementary schools provided for frequent review. In the successful experimental study that Good and Grouws (1979) conducted, teachers in the experimental group were asked to review the previous week's work every Monday and the previous month's work every fourth Monday. These reviews and tests were intended to provide the additional practice needed to develop skilled, successful performers who can apply their knowledge and skills to new areas. Kulik and Kulik (1979) found that, even at the college level, classes that had weekly quizzes scored better on final exams than did classes that had only one or two quizzes per term.

The need and value of frequent review fits the findings on human cognitive architecture. Review can serve to reinstate and elaborate prior learning; review can also strengthen and extend connections within and between cognitive structures. Review, then, can help students develop patterns and unify their knowledge, and review can enhance the development of automaticity in the area of study.

Modifications for Difficult Material

When the material is difficult and possibly confusing, or when it involves a complicated series of steps, then it is more effective to break the instruction into smaller steps and have a series of sequences of instruction, guided practice, and independent practice during a single period. Thus the teacher (1) provides an explanation, (2) checks for understanding, (3) leads the students through guided practice, and (4) supervises independent practice for the first step and then repeats the procedure for each subsequent step. This procedure is particularly effective for difficult material or slower students.

I have seen a math class in which the teacher led practice after each step in a sequence and continued practice until she was convinced the students had mastered each step. At that time, I visited a class in the next room where this small-step procedure was not being practiced, and I was impressed with how confident the students in the first class looked and how bedraggled many of the students in the second room looked.

Modifications for Different Learners

The time spent in these six functions should also be modified to suit different learners (see Table 25.2). When students are faster or older, or when the material is less difficult, then less time needs to be spent in review and more time can be spent on new material (although teachers often overestimate how much new material can be learned at a given time). Similarly, in such cases there is less need for guided practice and less need for independent practice in class. More of the independent practice can be done as homework because the students do not need as much help. But even in these situations, it is more efficient to return to small-step instruction when the material becomes difficult.

When learners are younger and slower, or when the material is difficult for all students, then more time ought to be spent in review, less time in presentation of new material, and more time in both guided and independent practice. During independent practice, there should be more supervision and a greater emphasis on all students becoming quick

Table 25.2 Modifications to Suit Different Students

Slower Students	Faster Students
More review	Less review
Less presentation	More presentation
More guided practice	Less guided practice
More independent practice	Less independent practice

Modification for Difficult Material

Presentation

Guided practice

Supervised independent practice

and accurate. When material is particularly difficult, some teachers (Evertson, 1982) use a series of cycles of short presentation, guided practice, and independent practice.

Conclusion

Current research on human cognitive architecture and the research on teacher effects have shown that it is most effective to teach in a systematic manner, providing instructional support for students at each stage of learning. The effective teacher begins with a review of prerequisite skills, relating the current material to past learning, and then teaches the new material in small steps. He or she uses short presentations and follows each presentation with questions. After the presentation, the teacher guides students as they practice the new skill and continues this guidance until all students have been checked and received feedback. Guided practice is followed by independent practice, which is continued until students can perform the new skill independently and fluently.

Instruction in new material begins with full teacher control. The teacher diminishes control through the lesson so that at the end students are working independently; but the progression is done in a systematic and supportive manner. This progression moves from teacher modeling, through guided practice using prompts and cues, to independent and fluent performance by the students. But at each step there is a need to monitor student learning, guide student practice, and provide additional support when students need it.

References and Further Readings

American Federation of Teachers. (1998). *Building on the best, learning from What Works: Seven promising reading and*

English language arts programs. American Federation of Teachers, Washington, DC.

Anderson, L., Evertson, C., & Brophy, J. (1979). An experimental study of effective teaching in first grade reading groups. *The Elementary School Journal, 79,* 193–222.

Barr, A. S. (1948). The measurement and prediction of teaching efficiency: A summary of the investigations. *Journal of Experimental Education, 16,* 203–283.

Bloom, B. S. (1986, February). Automaticity. *Educational Leadership, 56,* 70–77.

Brophy, J., & Evertson, C. (1976). *Learning from teaching: A developmental perspective.* Boston: Allyn & Bacon.

Brophy, J. E., & Good, T. L. (1986). Teacher behavior and student achievement. In M. C. Wittrock (Ed.), *Handbook of research on teaching* (3rd ed., pp. 328–375). New York: Macmillan.

Brown, A. L., & Campione, J. C. (1986). Psychological theory and the study of learning disabilities. *American Psychologist, 41,* 1059–1068.

Chase, W., & Chi, M. (1980) Cognitive skill: Implications for spatial skill in large-scale environments. In J. Harvey (Ed.), *Cognition, social behavior, and the environment.* Hillsdale, NJ: Lawrence Erlbaum Associates.

Evertson, C. E. (1982). Differences in instructional activities in higher- and lower-achieving junior high English and math classes. *Elementary School Journal, 4,* 329–350.

Evertson, C. E., Anderson, C., Anderson, L., & Brophy, J. (1980). Relationship between classroom behaviors and student outcomes in junior high mathematics and English classes. *American Educational Research Journal, 17,* 43–60.

Evertson, C. E., Emmer, E. T., & Brophy, J. E. (1980). Predictors of effective teaching in junior high mathematics classrooms. *Journal of Research in Mathematics Education, 11,* 167–178.

Fisher, C. W., Filby, N. M., Marliave, R., Cohen, L. S., Dishaw, M. M., Moore, J. E., et al. (1978). *Teaching behaviors, academic learning time, and student achievement: Final report of Phase III-B, Beginning Teacher Evaluation Study.* San Francisco: Far West Educational Laboratory for Educational Research and Development.

Flanders, N. A. (1970). *Analyzing teacher behavior.* Reading, MA: Addison-Wesley.

Gage, N. L. (1978). *The scientific basis of the art of teaching.* New York: Teachers College Press.

Gage, N. L., & Needles, M. C. (l989). Process-product research on teaching: A review of criticisms. *The Elementary School Journal, 89,* 253–300.

Good, T. L., & Grouws, D. A. (1977). Teaching effects: A process-product study in fourth grade mathematics classrooms. *Journal of Teacher Education, 28,* 40–54.

Good, T. L., & Grouws, D. A. (1979). The Missouri mathematics effectiveness project. *Journal of Educational Psychology, 71,* 143–155.

Hunter, M. (1982). *Mastery teaching.* El Segundo, CA: TIP Publications.

Katz, L. G. (1994). *The project approach.* Champaign, IL: ERIC Digest, ERIC Clearinghouse on Elementary and Early Childhood Education. (ERIC Document No. ED368509)

Kirschner, P. A., Sweller, J., & Clark, R. E. (2006). Why minimal guidance during instruction does not work: An analysis of the failure of constructivist, discovery, problem-based, experiential, and inquiry based teaching. *Educational Psychologist, 41,* 75–86.

Kulik, J. A., & Kulik, C. C. (1979). College teaching. In P. L. Peterson & H. J. Walberg (Eds.), *Research on teaching: Concepts, findings, and implications.* Berkeley, CA: McCutchan.

McDonald, F., & Elias, P. (1976). *The effects of teaching performance on pupil learning, Vol. I: Beginning teacher evaluation study, Phase 2.* Princeton, NJ: Educational Testing Service.

Medley, D. M., & Mitzel, H. E. (1959). Some behavioral correlates of teacher effectiveness. *Journal of Educational Psychology, 50,* 239–246.

Medley, D. M., & Mitzel, H. E. (1963). Measuring classroom behavior by systematic observation. In N. L. Gage (Ed.), *Handbook of Research on Teaching.* Chicago: Rand-McNally.

Rosenshine, B. (1971). Teaching Behaviors and Student Achievement. Slough, England: National Federation for Eucational Research.

Rosenshine, B. (1976). Classroom instruction. In N. L. Gage (Ed.), *The psychology of teaching methods* (75th NSSE Yearbook). Chicago: University of Chicago Press.

Rosenshine, B., & Meister, C. (1992, April). The use of scaffolds for teaching higher-level cognitive strategies. *Educational Leadership, 49*(7), 26–33.

Russell, D., & Hunter, M. (1981). Planning for effective instruction: Lesson design. In *Increasing your teaching effectiveness.* Palo Alto, CA: The Learning Institute.

Simon, H. A. (1973). The structure of ill structured problems. *Artificial Intelligence, 4,* 181–201.

Smith, L., & Land, M. (1981). Low-inference verbal behaviors related to teacher clarity. *Journal of Classroom Interaction, 17,* 37–42.

Stallings, J. A., & Kaskowitz, D. (1974). *Follow-through classroom observation.* Menlo Park, CA: SRI International.

Tobias, S. (1982). When do instructional methods make a difference? *Educational Researcher, 11,* 4–10.

26

TEN STEPS TO COMPLEX LEARNING

A New Approach to Instruction and Instructional Design

PAUL KIRSCHNER
Utrecht University

JEROEN J. G. VAN MERRIËNBOER
Open University of the Netherlands

The subject of this chapter, ten steps to complex learning (van Merriënboer & Kirschner, 2007), was recently published as a practical and modified version of the four-component instructional design (4C-ID) model originally posited by van Merriënboer in 1997. These ten steps are mainly prescriptive and aim to provide a practicable version of the 4C-ID model for teachers, domain experts involved in educational or training design, and less experienced instructional designers. The model described here will typically be used to develop educational or training programs, which can have a duration ranging from several weeks to several years, aimed at the acquisition of complex cognitive skills (in this chapter referred to as complex learning).

Complex Learning

Complex learning is the integration of knowledge, skills and attitudes; coordinating qualitatively different constituent skills; and often transferring what was learned in school or training to daily life and work. There are many examples of theoretical design models that have been developed to promote complex learning: cognitive apprenticeship (Collins, Brown, & Newman, 1989), 4-Mat (McCarthy, 1996), instructional episodes (Andre, 1997), collaborative problem solving (Nelson, 1999), constructivism and constructivist learning environments (Jonassen, 1999), learning by doing (Schank, Berman, & MacPerson, 1999), multiple approaches to understanding (Gardner, 1999), star legacy Schwartz, Lin, Brophy, & Bransford, 1999), as well as the subject of this contribution, the Four-Component Instructional Design model (van Merriënboer, 1997; van Merriënboer, Clark, & de Croock, 2002). These approaches all focus on authentic learning tasks as the driving force for teaching and learning because such tasks are instrumental in helping learners to integrate knowledge, skills, and attitudes (often referred to as competences), stimulate the coordination of skills constituent to solving problems or carrying out tasks, and facilitate the transfer of what has been learned to new and often unique tasks and problem situations (Merrill, 2002b; van Merriënboer, 2007; van Merriënboer & Kirschner, 2001).

Though the first two goals are essential for education and training and should not be underestimated, the fundamental problem facing instructional designers is education and training's apparent inability to achieve the third goal, the transfer of learning. Instructional design (ID) theory needs to support the design and development of programs that will help students acquire and transfer professional competencies or complex cognitive skills to an increasingly varied set of real-world contexts and settings. *The Ten Steps to Complex Learning* approach to ID (van Merriënboer & Kirschner, 2007) claims that a new ID approach is needed to reach this goal. In the next section, this holistic design approach is presented.

Holistic Design

Holistic design is the opposite of atomistic design where complex contents and tasks are usually reduced to their simplest or smallest elements. This reduction is such that contents and tasks are continually reduced to a level where they can easily be transferred to learners through a combination of presentation (i.e., expository teaching) and practice. This approach works very well if there are few interactions between those elements, but often fails when the elements are closely interrelated because here the whole is much more than the sum of its separate parts. Holistic design approaches to learning deal with complexity without losing sight of the separate elements and the interconnections between them. Using such an approach solves three common problems in education, namely, compartmentalization, fragmentation, and the transfer paradox.

Compartmentalization

ID models usually focus on one particular domain of learning (i.e., cognitive, affective, psychomotor) and within that domain between models for declarative learning that emphasize instructional methods for constructing conceptual knowledge and models for procedural learning that emphasize methods for acquiring procedural skills. This *compartmentalization*—the separation of a whole into distinct parts or categories—has had negative effects in vocational and professional education.

Any good practitioner has highly developed cognitive and technical skills, a deep knowledge of the work domain, a good attitude toward that work, and keeps all of this up-to-date. In other words, these different aspects of professional competencies cannot be compartmentalized into atomistic domains of learning. To counter this compartmentalization, holistic design integrates declarative, procedural, and affective learning to facilitate the development of an integrated knowledge base that increases the chance of transfer.

Fragmentation

Most, if not all, ID models are guilty of *fragmentation*—the act or process of breaking something down into small, incomplete, or isolated parts—as their basis (see Ragan & Smith, 1996; van Merriënboer & van Dijk, 1998). Typically they begin by analyzing a chosen learning domain. They then divide it into distinct learning or performance objectives (e.g., recalling a fact, applying a procedure, understanding a concept), and then they select different instructional methods for reaching each of the separate objectives (e.g., rote learning, skills labs, problem solving). For complex skills, each objective corresponds with one subskill or constituent skill, and their sequencing results in part-task sequences. The learner is taught only one or a very limited number of constituent skills at the same time, and new constituent skills are gradually added until—at the end of the instruction—the learner practices the whole complex skill.

The problem here is that most complex skills are characterized by numerous interactions between the different aspects of task performance with very high demands on their coordination. Learning and instruction that is based upon such fragmentation of complex tasks into sets of distinct elements without taking their interactions and required coordination into account fails because learners ultimately cannot integrate and coordinate the separate elements in transfer situations (Clark & Estes, 1999; Perkins & Grotzer, 1997; Spector & Anderson, 2000; Wightman & Lintern, 1985). To remedy this, holistic design focuses on highly integrated sets of objectives and their coordinated attainment in real-life performance.

The Transfer Paradox

Instructional designers often either strive for or are required to achieve efficiency. To this end they usually select methods that will minimize the (1) number of practice items required, (2) time spent on task, and (3) learners' investment of effort to achieve the learning objectives. Typical here is the situation in which students must learn to diagnose different types of technical errors (e.g., e1, e2, e3). If a minimum of three practice items is needed to learn to diagnose each error, the designer will often choose to first train students to diagnose e1, then e2, and finally e3, leading to the following learning sequence: e1, e1, e1, e2, e2, e2, e3, e3, e3.

Although this sequencing will probably be very efficient, it yields *low transfer* of learning because it encourages learners to construct highly specific knowledge for diagnosing each distinct error, only allowing them to perform in the way specified in the objectives. If a designer aims at transfer, and with the objective to train students to diagnose as many errors as possible, then it would be better to train students to diagnose the three errors in a random order leading, for example, to a different sequence such as e3, e2, e2, e1, e3, e3, e1, e2, e1.

This sequence will probably be less efficient for reaching the isolated objectives, because it will probably increase the needed time-on-task or investment of learner effort and might even require more than three practice items to reach the same level of performance for each separate objective as the first sequence. In the long run, however, it will help learners achieve a *higher transfer of learning* because it encourages them to construct general and abstract knowledge rather than knowledge only related to each concrete, specific error and will thus allow learners to better diagnose new, not yet encountered, errors. This is the transfer paradox (van Merriënboer & de Croock, 1997), where methods that work best for reaching isolated, specific objectives are not best for reaching integrated objectives and transfer of learning. Holistic design takes this into account, ensuring that students confronted with new problems not only have acquired specific knowledge to perform the familiar aspects of a task, but also have acquired the necessary general or abstract knowledge to deal with the unfamiliar aspects of those tasks.

Four Components and Ten Steps

The Ten Steps (van Merriënboer & Kirschner, 2007) is a prescriptive approach to the *Four-Component Instructional Design model* (4C-ID; van Merriënboer, 1997) that is practicable for teachers, domain experts involved in ID, and instructional designers. It will typically be used for developing substantial learning or training programs ranging in length from several weeks to several years or that entail a substantial part of a curriculum for the development of competencies or complex skills. Its basic assumption is that *blueprints for complex learning* can always be described by *four basic components*: learning tasks, supportive information, procedural information, and part-task practice (see Table 26.1).

The term *learning task* is used here generically to include case studies, projects, problems, and so forth. They are *authentic whole-task experiences* based on real-life tasks that aim at the integration of skills, knowledge, and attitudes. The whole set of learning tasks exhibits a high variability, is organized in easy-to-difficult task classes, and has diminishing learner support throughout each task class.

Supportive information helps students learn to perform nonroutine aspects of learning tasks, which often involve problem solving and reasoning. It explains how a domain is organized and how problems in that domain are (or should be) approached. It is specified per task class and is always available to learners. It provides a bridge between what learners already know and what they need to know to work on the learning tasks.

Procedural information allows students to learn to perform *routine aspects* of learning tasks that are always performed in the same way. It specifies exactly how to perform the routine aspects of the task and is best presented just in time—precisely when learners need it. It quickly fades as learners gain more expertise.

Finally, *part-task practice* pertains to additional practice of routine aspects so that learners can develop a very high level of *automaticity*. Part-task practice typically provides huge amounts of repetition and only starts after the routine aspect has been introduced in the context of a whole, meaningful learning task.

Each of the four components corresponds with a specific design step (see Table 26.1). In this way, the design of learning tasks corresponds with step 1, the design of supportive information with step 4, the design of procedural information with step 7, and the design of part-task practice with step 10. The other six steps are supplementary and are performed when necessary. Step 2, for example, organizes the learning tasks in easy-to-difficult categories to ensure that students work on tasks that begin simple and smoothly increase in difficulty, and step 3 specifies the standards for acceptable performance of the task which is necessary to assess performance and provide feedback. Steps 5 and 6 may be necessary for in-depth analysis of the supportive information needed for learning to carry out nonroutine aspects of learning tasks. Finally, steps 8 and 9 may be necessary for in-depth analysis of the procedural information needed for performing routine aspects of learning tasks.

Designing With the Four Blueprint Components

Figure 26.1 shows how the four blueprint components (also see the left hand column of Table 26.1) are interrelated to each other.

Learning Tasks

Learners work on tasks that help them develop an integrated knowledge base through a process of *inductive learning*, inducing knowledge from concrete experiences. As a result, each learning task should offer whole-task practice, confronting the learner with all or almost all of the constituent skills important for performing the task, including their associated knowledge and attitudes. In this whole-task approach, learners develop a holistic vision of the task that is gradually embellished during training. A sequence of learning tasks provides the

Table 26.1 The Four Blueprint Components of 4C-ID and the Ten Steps to Complex Learning

Blueprint Components of 4C-ID	Ten Steps to Complex Learning
Learning Tasks	1. Design Learning Tasks
	2. Sequence Task Classes
	3. Set Performance Objectives
Supportive Information	4. Design Supportive Information
	5. Analyze Cognitive Strategies
	6. Analyze Mental Models
Procedural Information	7. Design Procedural Information
	8. Analyze Cognitive Rules
	9. Analyze Prerequisite Knowledge
Part-Task Practice	10. Design Part-Task Practice

SOURCE: Van Merrienboer, J. J. G., & Kirschner, P. A. (2007). *Ten steps to complex learning.* Mahwah, NJ: Lawrence Erlbaum Associates.

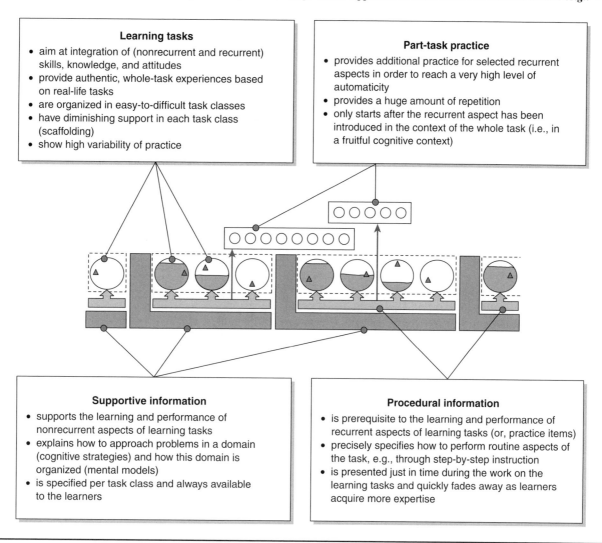

Learning tasks
- aim at integration of (nonrecurrent and recurrent) skills, knowledge, and attitudes
- provide authentic, whole-task experiences based on real-life tasks
- are organized in easy-to-difficult task classes
- have diminishing support in each task class (scaffolding)
- show high variability of practice

Part-task practice
- provides additional practice for selected recurrent aspects in order to reach a very high level of automaticity
- provides a huge amount of repetition
- only starts after the recurrent aspect has been introduced in the context of the whole task (i.e., in a fruitful cognitive context)

Supportive information
- supports the learning and performance of nonrecurrent aspects of learning tasks
- explains how to approach problems in a domain (cognitive strategies) and how this domain is organized (mental models)
- is specified per task class and always available to the learners

Procedural information
- is prerequisite to the learning and performance of recurrent aspects of learning tasks (or, practice items)
- precisely specifies how to perform routine aspects of the task, e.g., through step-by-step instruction
- is presented just in time during the work on the learning tasks and quickly fades away as learners acquire more expertise

Figure 26.1   A Schematic Training Blueprint for Complex Learning

backbone of a training program for complex learning. Schematically:

always provides the backbone of a training program for complex learning. Schematically, it looks like this:

Variability

In line with the earlier discussed transfer paradox, it is important that the chosen learning tasks differ from each other on all dimensions that also differ in the real world, so that learners can abstract more general information from the details of each single task. There is strong evidence that such variability of practice is important for achieving *transfer of learning*—both for relatively simple tasks (e.g., Paas & van Merriënboer, 1994; Quilici & Mayer, 1996) and highly complex real-life tasks (e.g., Schilling, Vidal, Ployhart, & Marangoni, 2003; van Merriënboer, Kester, & Paas, 2006). A sequence of different learning tasks thus

Task Classes

It is not possible to use very difficult learning tasks with high demands on coordination right from the start of a training program, so learners start work on relatively easy whole-learning tasks and progress toward more difficult ones (van Merriënboer, Kirschner, & Kester, 2003). Categories of learning tasks, each representing a version of the task with the same particular difficulty, are called *task classes*. All tasks within a particular task class are equivalent in that the tasks can be performed based on the same body of general knowledge. A more difficult task class requires more knowledge or more embellished knowledge for effective performance than the preceding, easier task classes. In the training blueprint, the tasks are organized in an ordered sequence of task classes (i.e., the dotted boxes) representing easy-to-difficult versions of the whole task:

Support and Guidance

When learners start work on a new, more difficult task class, it is essential that they receive support and guidance for coordinating the different aspects of their performance. Support—actually *task support*—focuses on providing learners with assistance with the products involved in the training, namely the givens, the goals, and the solutions that get them from the givens to the goals (i.e., it is product oriented). Guidance—actually *solution-process guidance*—focuses on providing learners with assistance with the processes inherent to successfully solving the learning tasks (i.e., it is process oriented).

This support and guidance diminishes in a process of *scaffolding* as learners acquire more expertise. The continuum of learning tasks with high support to learning tasks without support is exemplified by the continuum of support techniques ranging from fully-reasoned case studies through partially worked out examples using the completion strategy (van Merriënboer, 1990; van Merriënboer & de Croock, 2002) to conventional tasks (for a complete description see van Merriënboer & Kirschner, 2007). In a training blueprint, each task class starts with one or more learning tasks with a high level of support and guidance (indicated by the grey in the circles), continues with learning tasks with a lower level of support and guidance, and ends with conventional tasks without any support and guidance as indicated by the filling of the circles:

Recurrent and Nonrecurrent Constituent Skills

Not all *constituent skills* are the same. Some are controlled, schema-based processes performed in a variable way from problem situation to problem situation. Others, lower in the skill hierarchy, may be rule-based processes performed in a highly consistent way from problem situation to problem situation. These constituent skills involve the same use of the same knowledge in a new problem situation. It might even be argued that these skills do not rely on knowledge at all, because this knowledge is fully embedded in the rules and conscious control is not required because the rules have become fully automated.

Constituent skills are classified as *nonrecurrent* if they are performed as schema-based processes after the train-ing; nonrecurrent skills apply to the problem solving and reasoning aspects of behavior. Constituent skills are classified as *recurrent* if they are performed as rule-based processes after the training; recurrent skills apply to the routine aspects of behavior. The classification of skills as nonrecurrent or recurrent is important in the Ten Steps (van Merriënboer & Kirschner, 2007) because instructional methods for the effective and efficient acquisition of them are very different.

Supportive Versus Procedural Information

Supportive information is important for nonrecurrent constituent skills and explains to the learners how a learning domain is organized and how to approach problems in that domain. Its function is to facilitate *schema construction* such that learners can deeply process the new information, in particular by connecting it to already existing schemas in memory via *elaboration*. Because supportive information is relevant to all learning tasks within the same task class, it is typically presented before learners start to work on a new task class and kept available for them during their work on this task class. This is indicated in the L-shaped shaded areas in the schematic training blueprint:

Procedural information is important for constituent skills that are recurrent; procedural information specifies for learners how to perform the routine aspects of learning tasks, preferably in the form of direct, step-by-step instruction. This facilitates rule automation, making the information available during task performance so that it can be easily embedded in cognitive rules via *knowledge compilation*. Because procedural information is relevant to the routine aspects of learning tasks, it is best presented to learners exactly when they first need it to perform a task (i.e., just in time), after which it quickly *fades* for subsequent learning tasks. In the schematic training blueprint, the procedural information (black beam) is linked to the separate learning tasks:

Part-Task Practice

Learning tasks provide whole-task practice to prevent compartmentalization and fragmentation. There are, however, situations where it may be necessary to include part-task practice in the training, usually when a very high level of automaticity is required for particular

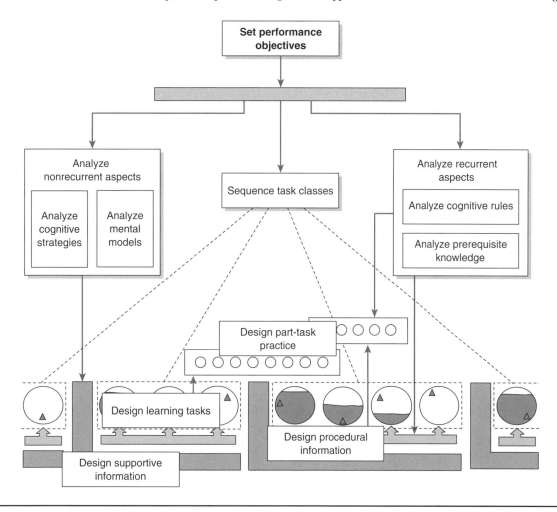

Figure 26.2   The Ten Activities (grey boxes) in Designing for Complex Learning

recurrent aspects of a task. In this case, the series of learning tasks may not provide enough repetition to reach that level. For those aspects classified as to-be-automated recurrent constituent skills, additional part-task practice may be provided—such as when children drill the multiplication tables or when musicians practice specific musical scales.

This part-task practice facilitates rule automation via a process called *strengthening*, in which cognitive rules accumulate strength each time they are successfully applied. Part-task practice for a particular recurrent aspect of a task can begin only after it has been introduced in a meaningful whole-learning task. In this way, learners start their practice in a fruitful cognitive context. In the schematic training blueprint, part-task practice is indicated by series of small circles (i.e., practice items):

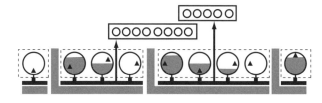

Ten Steps

Figure 26.2 presents the whole design process for complex learning. The grey boxes show the ten activities that are carried out when properly designing training blueprints for complex learning. These activities are typically employed by a designer to produce effective, efficient, and appealing educational programs. This section explains the different elements in the figure from the bottom up.

The lower part of the figure is identical to what was just discussed. For each task class, learning tasks are designed to provide learners with variable whole-task practice at a particular difficulty level until they reach the *prespecified standards* for this level, whereupon they continue to the next, more complex or difficult task class. The design of supportive information pertains to all information that may help learners carry out the nonrecurrent problem solving and reasoning aspects of the learning tasks within a particular task class. The design of procedural information pertains to all information that exactly specifies how to carry out the recurrent, routine aspects of the learning tasks. And finally, the design of part-task practice may be necessary for selected recurrent aspects that need to be developed to a very high level of automaticity.

The middle part of the figure contains five activities. The central activity—*sequence task classes*—describes an easy-to-difficult progression of categories of tasks that learners may work on. It organizes the tasks in such a way that learning is optimized. The least difficult task class is at the entry level of the learners and the final, most complex or difficult task class is at the final attainment level defined by the performance objectives for the whole training program.

The analyses of *cognitive strategies* and *mental models* are necessary for learners to achieve the nonrecurrent aspects of carrying out the task. The analysis of cognitive strategies answers the question, How do proficient task performers systematically approach problems in the task domain? The analysis of mental models answers the question, How is the domain organized? The resulting systematic approaches to problem solving and domain models are used as a basis for the design of supportive information for a particular task class.

The analyses of *cognitive rules* and *prerequisite knowledge* are necessary for learners to achieve the recurrent aspects of carrying out the task. The analysis of cognitive rules identifies the condition-action pairs that enable experts to perform routine aspects of tasks without effort (IF condition, THEN action). The analysis of prerequisite knowledge identifies what learners need to know to correctly apply those condition-action pairs. Together, the results of these analyses provide the basis for the design of procedural information. In addition, identified condition-action pairs help to specify practice items for part-task practice.

The upper part of the figure contains only one activity, *setting performance objectives*. Because complex learning deals with highly integrated sets of learning objectives, the focus is on the decomposition of a complex skill into a hierarchy describing all aspects or constituent skills relevant to performing real-life tasks. In other words, the specification of performance objectives and standards for acceptable performance for each of the constituent skills, and a classification of the skills within these objectives is either nonrecurrent or recurrent.

As indicated by the arrows, some activities provide preliminary input for other activities. This suggests that the best order for performing the activities would be to start with setting performance objectives, then to continue with sequencing task classes and analyzing nonrecurrent and recurrent aspects, and to end with designing the four blueprint components. Indeed, the ten activities have previously been described in this analytical order (e.g., van Merriënboer & de Croock, 2002). But in real-life design projects, each activity affects and is affected by all other activities. This leaves it an open question as to which order for using the ten activities is most fruitful.

A Dynamic Model

The model presented takes a *system dynamics* view of instruction, emphasizing the *interdependence* of the elements constituting an instructional system and recognizing the dynamic nature of this interdependence, which makes the system an irreducible whole. Such a systems approach is both systematic and systemic. It is *systematic* because the input-process-output paradigm where the outputs of particular elements of the system serve as inputs to other elements, and the outputs of particular design activities serve as inputs for other activities is inherent to it. For example, the output of an analysis is the input for the design of supportive information in the blueprint. At the same time, it is actually also *systemic* because the performance or function of each element directly or indirectly affects or is affected by one or more of the other elements—thereby making the design process highly dynamic and nonlinear. For example, this same analysis of nonrecurrent aspects of a skill can also affect the choice and sequencing of task classes.

The Pebble-in-the-Pond: From Activities to Steps

M. David Merrill (2002a) proposed a *pebble-in-the-pond* approach for instructional design that is fully consistent with the Ten Steps. It is a content-centered modification of traditional instructional design in which the contents-to-be-learned, and not the abstract learning objectives, are specified first. The approach consists of a series of expanding activities initiated by first casting a pebble in the pond; that is, designing one or more learning tasks of the type that learners will be taught to accomplish by the instruction. This simple little pebble initiates further ripples in the design pond. This prescriptive model is workable and useful for teachers and other practitioners in the field of instructional design.

A Backbone of Learning Tasks: Steps 1, 2, and 3

The first three steps aim at the development of a series of learning tasks that serve as the backbone for the educational blueprint:

Step 1: Design Learning Tasks
Step 2: Sequence Task Classes
Step 3: Set Performance Objectives

The first step, the pebble so to speak, is to specify one or more typical learning tasks that represent the whole complex skill that the learner will be able to perform following the instruction. Such a task has in the past been referred to as an *epitome*, the most overarching, fundamental task that represents the skill (Reigeluth, 1987; Reigeluth & Rodgers, 1980; Reigeluth & Stein, 1983). In this way, it becomes clear from the beginning, and at a very concrete level, what the training program aims to achieve. Normally, providing only a few learning tasks to learners will not be enough to help them develop the complex skills necessary to perform the whole task. Therefore, another unique characteristic of the pebble-in-the-pond approach is—after casting the first whole learning task pebble into the pond—to specify a progression of such tasks of increasing difficulty such that if learners were able to do all of the tasks identified, they would have mastered the knowledge, skills, and attitudes that are to be taught. This ripple in the design pond, or step 2, involves the assignment and sequencing of learning tasks to task classes with different levels of difficulty. Tasks in the easiest class are at the learners' entry level, whereas tasks in the most difficult task class are at the training program's exit level. To give learners the necessary feedback on the quality of their performance and to decide when learners may proceed from one task class to the next, it is necessary to state the standards that need to be achieved for acceptable performance. This next ripple in the design pond, or step 3, consists of the specification of performance objectives that, among other things, articulate the standards that learners must reach to carry out the tasks in an acceptable fashion. In this way, the pebble-in-the-pond approach avoids the common design problem that the objectives that are determined early in the process are abandoned or revised later in the process to correspond more closely to the content that has finally been developed.

Component Knowledge, Skills, and Attitudes: Steps 4 to 10

Further ripples identify the knowledge, skills, and attitudes necessary to perform each learning task in the progression of tasks. This results in the remaining blueprint components, which are subsequently connected to the backbone of learning tasks. A distinction is made here between supportive information, procedural information, and part-task practice. The steps followed for designing and developing supportive information are as follows:

Step 4: Design Supportive Information
Step 5: Analyze Cognitive Strategies
Step 6: Analyze Mental Models

Units of supportive information that help learners perform the nonrecurrent aspects of the learning tasks related to problem solving and reasoning are connected to task classes, and more complex task classes typically require more detailed or more embellished supportive information than easier task classes. If useful instructional materials are already available, step 4 may be limited to reorganizing existing instructional materials and assigning them to task classes. Steps 5 and 6 may then be neglected. But if instructional materials need to be designed and developed from scratch, it may be helpful to perform step 5, where the cognitive strategies that proficient task-performers use

to solve problems in the domain are analyzed, or step 6, where the mental models that describe how the domain is organized are analyzed. The results of the analyses in steps 5 and 6 provide the basis for designing supportive information. Analogous to the design and development of supportive information, steps 7, 8, and 9 are for designing and developing procedural information:

Step 7: Design Procedural Information
Step 8: Analyze Cognitive Rules
Step 9: Analyze Prerequisite Knowledge

Procedural information for performing recurrent aspects of learning tasks specifies exactly how to perform these aspects (and is thus procedural) and is preferably presented precisely when learners need it during their work on the learning tasks (i.e., just in time). For subsequent learning tasks, this procedural information quickly fades, often replaced by new specific information for carrying out new procedures. If useful instructional materials such as job aids, quick reference guides, or even Electronic Performance Support Systems (EPSSs; van Merriënboer & Kester, 2005) are available, step 7 may be limited to updating those materials and linking them to the appropriate learning tasks. Steps 8 and 9 may then be neglected. But if the procedural information needs to be designed from scratch, it may be helpful to perform step 8, where the cognitive rules specifying the condition-action pairs that drive routine behaviors are analyzed, and step 9, where the knowledge that is prerequisite to a correct use of cognitive rules is analyzed. The results of the analyses in steps 8 and 9 then provide the basis for the design of procedural information. Finally, depending on the nature of the task and the knowledge and skills needed to carry it out, it may be necessary to perform the tenth and final step:

Step 10: Design Part-Task Practice

Under particular circumstances, additional practice is necessary for selected recurrent aspects of a complex skill in order to develop a very high level of automaticity. This, for example, may be the case for recurrent constituent skills that cause danger to life and limb, loss of expensive or hard to replace materials, or damage to equipment if not carried out properly and quickly. If part-task practice needs to be designed, the analysis results of step 8 (i.e., the condition-action pairs) provide useful input. For a detailed description of the Ten Steps see van Merriënboer and Kirschner (2007).

Ten Steps Within an Instructional Systems Design Context

The Ten Steps will often be applied in the context of *Instructional Systems Design* (ISD). ISD models have a broad scope and typically divide the instructional design process into five phases: (a) analysis, (b) design, (c) development, (d) implementation, and (e) summative evaluation. In this so-called ADDIE model, formative evaluation is conducted during all of the phases. The Ten Steps is narrower in scope and focus on the first two phases of the instructional design process, namely, task and content analysis and design. In particular, the Ten Steps concentrates on the analysis of a to-be-trained complex skill or professional competency in an integrated process of task and content analysis and the conversion of the results of this analysis into a training blueprint that is ready for development and implementation. The Ten Steps is best applied in combination with an ISD model to support activities not treated in the Ten Steps, such as needs assessment and needs analysis, development of instructional materials, implementation and delivery of materials, and summative evaluation of the implemented training program.

References and Further Readings

Andre, T. (1997). Selected micro-instructional methods to facilitate knowledge construction: Implications for instructional design. In R. D. Tennyson, F. Schott, N. Seel, & S. Dijkstra (Eds.), *Instructional design—International perspectives: Theory, research, and models* (Vol. 1, pp. 243–267). Mahwah, NJ: Lawrence Erlbaum Associates.

Clark, R. E., & Estes, F. (1999). The development of authentic educational technologies. *Educational Technology, 39*(2), 5–16.

Collins, A., Brown, J. S., & Newman, S. E. (1989). Cognitive apprenticeship: Teaching the craft of reading, writing and mathematics. In L. B. Resnick (Ed.), *Knowing, learning, and instruction: Essays in honor of Robert Glaser* (pp. 453–493). Hillsdale, NJ: Lawrence Erlbaum Associates.

Gardner, H. (1999). Multiple approaches to understanding. In C. M. Reigeluth (Ed.), *Instructional design theories and models: A new paradigm of instructional theory* (Vol. II, pp. 69–89). Mahwah, NJ: Lawrence Erlbaum Associates.

Jonassen, D. H. (1999). Designing constructivist learning environments. In C. M. Reigeluth (Ed.), *Instructional design theories and models: A new paradigm of instructional theory* (Vol. II, pp. 215–239). Mahwah, NJ: Lawrence Erlbaum Associates.

Kirschner, P. A., Carr, C. S., van Merriënboer, J., & Sloep, P. (2002). How expert designers design. *Performance Improvement Quarterly, 15*(4), 86–104.

Kirschner, P. A., Sweller, J., & Clark, R. E. (2006). Why minimal guidance during instruction does not work: An analysis of the failure of constructivist, discovery, problem-based, experiential, and inquiry-based teaching. *Educational Psychologist, 46*(2), 75–86.

McCarthy, B. (1996). *About learning.* Barrington, IL: Excell Inc.

Merrill, M. D. (2002a). A pebble-in-the-pond model for instructional design. *Performance Improvement, 41*(7), 39–44.

Merrill, M. D. (2002b). First principles of instructional design. *Educational Technology Research and Development, 50,* 43–59.

Merrill, P. (1980). Analysis of a procedural task. *NSPI Journal, 17*(2), 11–26.

Nelson, L. M. (1999). Collaborative problem solving. In C. M. Reigeluth (Ed.), *Instructional design theories and models: A new paradigm of instructional theory* (Vol. II, pp. 241–267). Mahwah, NJ: Lawrence Erlbaum Associates.

Paas, F., & van Merriënboer, J. J. G. (1994). Variability of worked examples and transfer of geometrical problem solving skills: A cognitive-load approach. *Journal of Educational Psychology, 86,* 122–133.

Perkins, D. N., & Grotzer, T. A. (1997). Teaching intelligence. *American Psychologist, 52,* 1125–1133.

Quilici, J. L., & Mayer, R. E. (1996). The role of examples in how students learn to categorize statistics word problems. *Journal of Educational Psychology, 88,* 144–161.

Ragan, T. J., & Smith, P. L. (1996). Conditions theory and models for designing instruction. In D. Jonassen (Ed.), *Handbook of research on educational communications and technology* (2nd ed., pp. 623–650). Mahwah, NJ: Lawrence Erlbaum Associates.

Reigeluth, C. M. (Ed.). (1987). *Instructional theories in action: Lessons illustrating selected theories and models.* Hillsdale, NJ: Lawrence Erlbaum Associates.

Reigeluth, C. M., & Rodgers, C. A. (1980). The elaboration theory of instruction: A model for structuring instruction. *Instructional Science, 9,* 125–219.

Reigeluth, C. M., & Stein, F. S. (1983). The elaboration theory of instruction. In C. M. Reigeluth (Ed.), *Instructional design theories and models: An overview of their current status* (pp. 335–381). Hillsdale, NJ: Lawrence Erlbaum Associates.

Schank, R. C., Berman, T. R., & MacPerson, K. A. (1999). Learning by doing. In C. M. Reigeluth (Ed.), *Instructional design theories and models: A new paradigm of instructional theory* (Vol. II, pp. 161–181). Mahwah, NJ: Lawrence Erlbaum Associates.

Schilling, M. A., Vidal, P., Ployhart, R. E., & Marangoni, A. (2003). Learning by doing something else: Variation, relatedness, and the learning curve. *Management Science, 49,* 39–56.

Schwartz, D., Lin, X., Brophy, S., & Bransford, J. D. (1999). Toward the development of flexible adaptive instructional designs. In C. M. Reigeluth (Ed.), *Instructional design theories and models: A new paradigm of instructional theory* (Vol. II, pp. 183–213). Mahwah, NJ: Lawrence Erlbaum Associates.

Spector, J. M., & Anderson, T. M. (Eds.). (2000). *Holistic and integrated perspectives on learning, technology, and instruction: Understanding complexity.* Mahwah, NJ: Lawrence Erlbaum Associates.

Sweller, J., Kirschner, P. A., & Clark, R. E. (2007). Why minimal guidance during instruction does not work: A reply to commentaries. *Educational Psychologist, 47*(1), 115–121.

van Merriënboer, J. J. G. (1990). Strategies for programming instruction in high school: Program completion vs. program generation. *Journal of Educational Computing Research, 6,* 265–285.

van Merriënboer, J. J. G. (1997). *Training complex cognitive skills: A four-component instructional design model for technical training.* Englewood Cliffs, NJ: Educational Technology Publications.

van Merriënboer, J. J. G. (2000). The end of software training? *Journal of Computer Assisted Learning, 16,* 366–375.

van Merriënboer, J. J. G. (2007). Alternate models of instructional design: Holistic design approaches and complex learning. In R. A. Reiser & J. Dempsey (Eds.), *Trends and issues in instructional design and technology* (2nd ed., pp. 72–81). Upper Saddle River, NJ: Merrill/Prentice Hall.

van Merriënboer, J. J. G., Clark, R. E., & de Croock, M. B. M. (2002). Blueprints for complex learning: The 4C/ID-model. *Educational Technology Research and Development, 50*(2), 39–64.

van Merriënboer, J. J. G., & de Croock, M. B. M. (1997). Strategies for computer-based programming instruction: Program completion vs. program generation. *Journal of Educational Computing Research, 8,* 365–394.

van Merriënboer, J. J. G., & de Croock, M. B. M. (2002). Performance-based ISD: 10 steps to complex learning. *Performance Improvement, 41*(7), 33–38.

van Merriënboer, J. J. G., & Kester, L. (2005). The four-component instructional design model: Multimedia principles in environments for complex learning. In R. E. Mayer (Ed.), *The Cambridge handbook of multimedia learning* (pp. 71–93). New York: Cambridge University Press.

van Merriënboer, J. J. G., Kester, L., & Paas, F. (2006). Teaching complex rather than simple tasks: Balancing intrinsic and germane load to enhance transfer of learning. *Applied Cognitive Psychology, 20,* 343–352.

van Merriënboer, J. J. G., & Kirschner, P. A. (2001). Three worlds of instructional design: State of the art and future directions. *Instructional Science, 29,* 429–441.

van Merriënboer, J. J. G., & Kirschner, P. A. (2007). *Ten steps to complex learning.* New York: Taylor & Francis.

van Merriënboer, J. J. G., Kirschner, P. A., & Kester, L. (2003). Taking the load of a learner's mind: Instructional design for complex learning. *Educational Psychologist, 38*(1), 5–13.

van Merriënboer, J. J. G., & Sweller, J. (2005). Cognitive load theory and complex learning: Recent developments and future directions. *Educational Psychology Review, 17,* 147–177.

van Merriënboer, J. J. G., & van Dijk, E. M. A. G. (1998). Use and misuse of taxonomies of learning: Dealing with integrated educational goals in the design of computer science curricula. In F. Mulder & T. van Weert (Eds.), *Informatics in Higher Education* (pp. 179–189). London: Chapman and Hall.

Wightman, D. C., & Lintern, G. (1985). Part-task training for tracking and manual control. *Human Factors, 27,* 267–284.

27

TEACHER EXPECTATIONS

CHRISTINE RUBIE-DAVIES

The University of Auckland

All teachers have expectations for students, as they should. Teacher expectations are notions teachers hold about students' long- and short-term performance—beliefs teachers hold about what students are capable of achieving on a daily and long-term basis. They are important because teachers base planning and instruction on expectations for student achievement, behavior, and success. Hence teacher expectations can have both direct and indirect effects on student performance.

Various types of teacher expectation effects have been identified, but the most commonly acknowledged are self-fulfilling prophecy and sustaining expectation effects. Self-fulfilling prophecy effects were originally identified by Merton (1948). When applied to education they are originally false expectations of a student that lead to a teacher acting toward a student in particular ways so the student eventually fulfills the teachers' originally erroneous expectations. For example, a teacher interacted with Peter before he was assigned to her class. Based on these casual interactions, the teacher decides Peter is able. When he arrives in her class she ignores portfolio information indicating he is average. Instead she plans challenging learning experiences for Peter, actively encourages his success, provides clear learning feedback, and assigns him good grades. By year's end Peter is performing at levels the teacher expected.

Sustaining expectation effects, originally identified by Cooper and Good (1983), are probably more common in education but are also more difficult to identify because sustaining expectation effects do not change student performance levels. Indeed the teacher can frustrate the potential for change (Good, 1987). In this scenario a teacher carefully reads portfolio information related to Charlotte before the child enters his class. The information indicates Charlotte is average, so the teacher plans work for her at an appropriate level despite noticing Charlotte appears to complete tasks easily and quickly. Not wanting to pressure her, the teacher ignores these observations and continues to plan average-level work. Thus Charlotte's average performance is maintained despite possibilities of greater achievement given the opportunity.

Researchers agree teacher expectations and teacher expectation effects exist, but disagree about the strength and significance of these effects. For example, Brophy (1983) reported teacher expectation effects are mostly quite small, whereas Blatchford, Burke, Farquhar, Plewis, and Tizard (1989) described quite large effects. This may be because opportunity to learn is often considered a mediating variable for teacher expectation effects. In the British classrooms Blatchford et al. studied, students had fairly individualized programs that offered more variable opportunities to learn than in American classrooms where there is more whole-class teaching. It could be argued that if expectation effects are cumulative, however large or small, over time they may result in large effects, at least for some students. On the other hand, most teacher expectations are accurate and learning opportunities for students appropriate; this may explain why expectation effects are sometimes

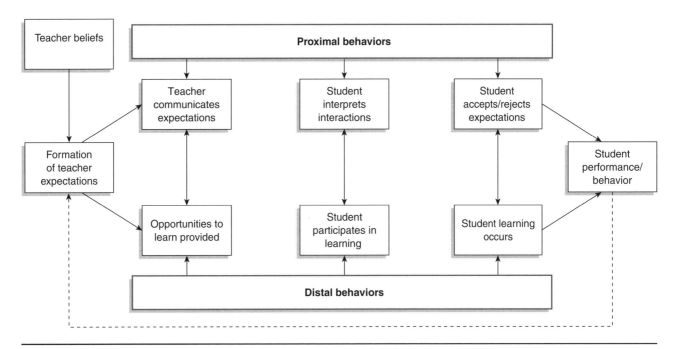

Figure 27.1   The Role of Proximal and Distal Behaviors in the Communication of Teacher Expectations

regarded as being less consequential for student learning (Jussim, Eccles, & Madon, 1996). But where expectations are inaccurate, especially where they are well below student potential, there can be profound effects on student achievement, particularly when compounding factors are considered.

Expectations are evidenced through both proximal and distal interactions of the teacher with students. In this chapter proximal interactions are deemed to be direct interactions teachers have with students, including both verbal and nonverbal messages teachers provide. Distal interactions are interactions over which students mostly have little control. They include teacher's planning and subsequent learning opportunities for the student, and the classroom instructional and socioemotional environments. Figure 27.1 illustrates the mediation of teacher expectation effects and shows the importance of proximal and distal teacher interactions for student outcomes.

Teachers form expectations based on information they have about prior student performance. For example, Mrs. Bailey is a teacher. Her expectations will interact with her pedagogical and implicit beliefs about Michael, her student, and about how best to implement teaching to support his learning. She will then plan learning experiences for Michael. The upper section of the model indicates the role of the teacher's proximal behaviors in communicating teacher expectations. Mrs. Bailey communicates her expectations for Michael's learning through verbal interactions, behavior toward him, and nonverbal messages. Michael interprets his teacher's interactions and behaviors as illustrating her high or low expectations for him. He can choose to accept his teacher's expectations as accurate and com-

plete his learning experiences accordingly. Alternatively, if he perceives his teacher's expectations as low he may put in additional effort to demonstrate his capabilities, hoping to change Mrs. Bailey's expectations. At this level the student does have some control over whether or not he accepts the teacher's expectations.

The lower section of the model relates to the role of the teacher's distal behaviors in communicating teacher expectations. On this side of the model, Mrs. Bailey plans learning opportunities for Michael based on her expectations for his achievement. She provides him with learning experiences she decides will help him to make progress in his learning. Michael participates in these activities, and his active engagement results in learning at the level planned and delivered. On this side of the model, however, Michael has little input. The opportunities for learning are decided by his teacher, and depending on the appropriateness and challenge of the learning activities, Michael can make average, advanced, or slow progress.

The teacher expectation model has solid lines between most aspects and a dotted line from student to teacher. The dotted line shows the influence of the student's performance and behavior on the teacher and plays a lesser role than the teachers' expectations for the student. It could be argued the relationship between student performance and teacher expectations is reciprocal. Indeed some students will influence teachers more than others, but research by Kuklinski and Weinstein (2001) suggests overall the influence is greater from the teacher to the student than the opposite. These researchers further suggest that younger students (below Grade 5) are more vulnerable to teachers' expectations than older students such that teachers may have self-fulfilling prophecy effects on younger students and sustaining expectation effects on older students (Grades 5 and above).

A Brief Background of Teacher Expectation Research

Teacher expectation research began with the seminal work of Robert Rosenthal. He had previously conducted experiments with laboratory assistants who trained rats to go through a maze. Rosenthal (1963) told some assistants their rats were maze-bright and would learn quickly while others were told their rats were maze-dull. Rosenthal showed when assistants believed their rats were smart they did indeed learn more quickly than rats whose assistants had been told were slow. Rosenthal reasoned that when assistants held particular expectations about their rats, they interacted with the rats in ways which meant the rats learned to go through the maze in congruence with the assistants' expectations. It seemed logical to apply this reasoning to teachers and students.

In the now famous Pygmalion experiment (Rosenthal & Jacobson, 1968), Rosenthal told teachers in one elementary school that some students had been identified as ones who would bloom during that year. When students were tested at the end of the year, Rosenthal found indeed the bloomers had made larger improvements than others. Rosenthal argued teachers must have interacted differently with the randomly identified bloomers and these interactions led the students to advance beyond what was previously anticipated. Although this research was both hailed and severely criticized at the time, it became the founding study for a very fruitful area of psychological research.

Rosenthal's contention that teachers interacted differently with students for whom they held high or low expectations led other researchers to attempt to identify differential teacher behaviors. In a classic early study, Brophy and Good (1970) conducted observations in four first-grade classrooms to isolate teacher behaviors that differed when interacting with high- or low-expectation students. This study formed the basis for a later review of several studies in which Brophy (1983) identified 17 teacher behaviors that varied depending on whether teachers were interacting with high- or low-expectation students. His review showed that teachers demanded less of low-expectation students. Brophy's review also demonstrated that teachers criticized low-expectation students for failure more often than other students and yet praised low-expectation students less frequently for success. Cooper and Good (1983) focused on direct verbal interactions between teachers and students. They reported that teachers interacted more often with high-expectation students in public and low-expectation students in private. This differential interaction was explained by teachers as an endeavor to preserve student self-esteem; high-expectation students were questioned more in public because they were more likely to respond correctly, whereas low-expectation students were questioned in private because they were less likely to feel embarrassed if their answers were incorrect.

The Unintended Curriculum

Students, however, are aware of teachers' differential interactions and consequently infer whether their teacher considers them smart or not. From these interactions students may learn lessons that were not intended. Students gain the impression some are considered better than others. Such messages are conveyed not only through direct verbal teacher-student interactions but also nonverbally through smiling, nodding, leaning toward or away from students, sighing, or rolling eyes. Weinstein (2002) showed that students can clearly articulate teacher behaviors that inform them of their classroom status. Sadly, all too many children could recall critical incidents where a student was publicly humiliated or insulted by their teacher.

Students can identify specific teacher and instructional practices that reveal information about their teacher's expectations. They report that teachers praise and reward high achievers and criticize and punish low achievers. They talk about teachers more frequently calling on high achievers than low achievers. Students also describe teachers making comments like, "You are so smart!" when high-expectation students are successful and teachers merely praising effort when low-expectation students accomplish something. Another practice students relate is differences in assigned work; only certain students are given remedial work and the teacher spends more time helping them. Although students recognize teachers should give such students additional support, they are aware other students are allowed far more independence; such teacher practices provide students with notions about their place in class. Some teachers publicly displayed charts indicating student achievement levels in particular curriculum areas (sometimes trying to disguise these by using group names). But more worrisome is that many students report teachers who frequently point out able and less able students in class by announcing test results publicly or informing students if they work hard they could reach the top group (and the converse).

Some students are particularly vulnerable to teachers' expectations. These include students from minority groups, lower socioeconomic groups, and girls in math and science. Such students are more likely to accept teachers' low expectations for their achievement, adhere to stereotypes for their groups, and reduce self-expectations. In turn they may achieve at levels lower than their potential might suggest.

Mechanisms of the Unintended Curriculum

So far this chapter has explored some proximal behaviors of teachers that communicate expectations to students.

It seems likely some teachers will have greater expectation effects than others, and so this section will concentrate on differential teacher factors that could contribute to expectation effects. The following section will explore some distal behaviors and teacher characteristics that contribute to the expression of teacher expectations. Specifically, this section will describe the importance of opportunity to learn, teacher efficacy, and teacher beliefs as distal means by which teachers' expectations can influence students.

Arguably the most significant distal factor in communicating teacher expectations is opportunity to learn. Students learn when and what they are given the opportunity to learn. Students who are given challenging learning experiences are more likely to achieve at higher levels than students of similar ability who are given low-level, repetitive activities. Students are mostly assigned work by teachers that they complete, and these learning experiences contribute to what is learned. Student achievement is influenced largely by the learning opportunities students receive.

Grade assignment is coupled with task allocation. Teachers tend to reward the academically rich. They believe students who achieve at high levels work harder than students who do not. Jussim and Eccles (1992) showed that teachers do not accurately judge the amount of effort students expend in completing homework. They found low-ability students often spent more time on homework than high-ability students but were not rewarded by their teachers. Yet this perception of high achievers expending greater effort is pervasive and can lead to teachers allocating grades to students above what they deserve. This bias is evident particularly where student work is borderline. If a teacher has high expectations for a student, a higher grade is likely to be allocated to that student's work, whereas if the teachers' expectations for a student are low, then there is greater probability a lower grade will be assigned.

In addition, teachers tend to accept work from low-expectation students they would not accept from high-expectation students. Whereas high-expectation students performing below expectation may be encouraged to improve their efforts, low achievers working below capability may not.

Cognitive engagement also influences what students learn. Tasks that are exciting and interesting for students are more likely to result in cognitive engagement and improved progress than mundane activities, yet researchers (Gamoran, 1992) report low-expectation students are more often given structured, repetitive activities than high achievers. It is important that such students are challenged by and enthused about learning if they are to cognitively engage in tasks. Such students should be given more opportunities to learn, not less. Similarly, researchers (Zohar, Degani, & Vaaknin, 2001) have shown higher order questioning is often reserved for the academically able. If low-expectation students are not given opportunities to think at higher levels, or time to process and extend thinking, lower levels of cognitive processing is a possible

outcome. Again, student opportunity to learn may be constrained.

Teacher factors can provide a mechanism for the unintended curriculum. One such factor is a teacher's self-efficacy for teaching. Teaching efficacy is the belief teachers hold about their ability to teach. Ross (1998) showed that teachers high in self-efficacy for teaching have positive beliefs about their ability to make a difference to student learning and their expectations are likely to be higher. Such teachers set challenging learning goals for students rather than adhering strictly to the curriculum. They are more likely to use a wide range of teaching strategies (such as small-group learning and individualized programs) and to implement creative and experimental techniques to assist learning.

Conversely, teachers with low teaching efficacy may feel less competent in their ability to make a difference to student learning and are less able to improve the skills of low-expectation students. Less confident in their teaching ability, low-efficacy teachers are more likely to structure lessons at a whole-class level rather than teaching students in small groups (which is more difficult but more effective). Such teachers can exacerbate the differences between low- and high-ability students as they spend less productive time with them.

Teacher beliefs about learning and teaching also play a role in teacher expectations and the unintended curriculum. Often, teacher beliefs are implicit but can affect teacher planning and therefore student learning. For example, when teachers are influenced by societal stereotypes related to ethnicity or social class it affects their instructional practices. Beliefs may include the attitude that White students are superior to African American students or that students from low socioeconomic areas lack discipline and appropriate academic support for schooling. Such beliefs may lead teachers to carefully structure the instructional environment so that students are controlled. When this happens students are likely to be given fewer intellectually stimulating tasks, less autonomy, and diminished opportunities to work in collaborative groupings with peers. A rigid, nonstimulating environment may reduce students' opportunities to learn.

Student Characteristics

Ethnicity and social class are student characteristics that can influence teachers' expectations for students and translate to differing instructional environments. Teachers may pay attention to particular student attributes and form expectations according to stereotypes and beliefs held about students with those attributes. The influence of ethnicity and social class will be more fully discussed later. Other student characteristics investigated in relation to teacher expectations include diagnostic labels, gender, physical attractiveness, personality and social skills, language style, teacher/student background, names, and other siblings. The influence of each of these student characteristics on teachers' expectations will be discussed briefly.

Diagnostic labels can have a powerful influence on teachers' expectations. In one experiment (Stinnett, Crawford, Gillespie, Cruce, & Langford, 2001), researchers provided 144 preservice teachers with a written description of an elementary school child. The description was held constant but labels included in the description varied. The preservice teachers were told that the child had no label, had attention-deficit/hyperactivity disorder (ADHD), was in special education, or was on Ritalin (used to medicate children with ADHD). Where the child had no label but was said to be on Ritalin, he was judged to have greater attentional difficulties than if he was in special education. When the child was said to have ADHD and to be in special education, he was described as having more difficulties than when the child had no label. The authors of this experiment suggested the label evoked negative judgments in teachers and low expectations for student behavior.

It is generally acknowledged gender can influence teachers' expectations. The available evidence suggests teachers have lower expectations for girls than boys in science and mathematics, particularly at upper secondary school and college levels. Low expectations can negatively influence girls' choices in furthering their education in advanced science and math as well as in pursuing careers in these areas. In an experimental study (Page & Rosenthal, 1990), teachers were asked to design and teach a math lesson for students who were White, Asian, male, and female. They found when students were male, and particularly if they were Asian, teachers taught the lesson at a faster pace and included more concepts than when students were White and female. Consequently, Asian and male students learned more by the end of the lesson. The opposite scenario occurred for reading where White females were at a small advantage. This study suggested stereotypes can have an effect on teachers' beliefs and expectations, in turn affecting instructional practice.

Teachers have higher expectations for students regarded as attractive than for the physically less appealing; however, this biasing of expectations is moderated once teachers become familiar with their students. In other words, teachers favor attractive students when shown photos before meeting their students but once interacting daily, attractiveness becomes less meaningful in affecting teachers' expectations (Dusek & Joseph, 1985).

Not surprisingly, teachers have higher expectations for students with engaging personalities and high levels of social skills. Such students are likeable, and this may influence teachers' expectations. Moreover, engaging students tend to be compliant and demonstrate appropriate classroom behavior, which may contribute to their teachers' positive assessments and expectations.

A teacher may have lower expectations of a student whose language style differs from the teacher's. Similarly, incongruent student and teacher backgrounds may result in low expectations for learning. Moreover, teachers tend to have lower expectations for students who do not speak English as their first language. Considering increasing numbers of students who have dissimilar backgrounds to their teachers and alternative languages and language patterns, larger proportions of students may be disadvantaged by teachers' low expectations than previously believed. Minority groups are more likely taught by teachers who are White and middle class than by teachers from their own cultural and social background.

Small effects on teachers' expectations have been found for student names, although this influence is more likely when students have an experienced rather than inexperienced teacher (Dusek & Joseph, 1985). When a teacher has had a particularly difficult student whose name was, for example, Jeremy, expectations for another student named Jeremy may be low. The resulting interactions with the teacher can influence student behavior and achievement, which in turn may confirm the teacher's beliefs about how "Jeremys" might behave.

Previous experience with an older sibling can affect a teacher's expectations (Dusek & Joseph, 1985). For example, if an older sibling is particularly able the teacher may expect a younger sibling to perform comparably. This may not be borne out. As with names and attractiveness, the teacher is likely to adjust expectations in line with performance once the younger sibling and his or her achievement levels become more obvious.

Ethnicity and Social Class

Much teacher expectation research has concentrated on the salience of student ethnicity and social class for teachers' expectations. Researchers generally agree social class affects teachers' expectations; teachers have higher expectations for middle-class students than they do for students from low socioeconomic areas. Researchers are divided over whether ethnicity plays a more or less relevant role in teachers' expectations. This section will explore a small sample of studies that have investigated the effect of ethnicity and social class on teachers' expectations.

Wigfield and colleagues (Wigfield, Galper, Denton, & Seefeldt, 1999) investigated beliefs of first-grade teachers about former Head Start and non-Head Start children's motivation, academic performance, social skills, and future educational prospects. The researchers found differences in teachers' attitudes toward students in line with ethnicity rather than Head Start status. They found teachers rated White students higher than African American students on ability (although there were no differences), on ease in making friends, on teachers' enjoyment in working with them, and on teachers' expectations for students' grades the following year. This study showed that teachers had low expectations and beliefs about students who were African American.

Recently, McKown and Weinstein (2008) showed that in particular classrooms, teachers' expectations for European American and Asian American students were much higher (between .75 and 1.00 standard deviations higher) than for African American and Latino students with similar achievement. This disparity was evident in classes where teachers differentiated in several discriminatory ways between treatment and interaction with high- and low-expectation students. The large differences in expectations and teacher expectancy effects evident for teachers considered high-differentiating were not found in classes where high- and low-expectation students were treated similarly.

In New Zealand there has been much debate about the low achievement of Maori and Pacific Island students. Several intervention programs have attempted to alter the achievement of these groups, but little change has been documented. Rubie-Davies, Hattie, and Hamilton (2006) investigated teachers' expectations in reading of European, Asian, Maori, and Pacific Island elementary school students (the four largest ethnic groups in New Zealand). The researchers found teachers' expectations for the achievement of all students other than Maori were well above student achievement. The beginning of year achievement of Maori was similar to European and Asian students' attainment (and all were well above Pacific Island students). By year's end, however, Maori students had made much less progress than other groups and achieved significantly below their Asian and European counterparts. An interesting aspect of this study was that teachers' expectations for Pacific Island students were high and were not for Maori. Both groups are mostly found in lower socioeconomic groups. The researchers suggested teachers may have higher expectations for Pacific Island students because teachers perceive more home support for Pacific Island students and greater parental interest in education.

The instructional practices of teachers in low socioeconomic areas differ from those of teachers in middle-class areas. Researchers (Solomon, Battistich, & Hom, 1996, April) reported teachers working in low socioeconomic areas believed students' behavior was poor and so kept tight control of them. Student autonomy was reduced, and students were engaged in structured whole-class activities with little opportunity for interaction with peers. Hence students received less engaging and challenging forms of education that could have enhanced their performance. Ennis (1998) poignantly revealed teacher attitudes and expectations of inner-city high school students through interviews with teachers and students. Many teachers expressed harsh, unconstructive views about students and pessimistic attitudes toward their futures. But when students (classified as disruptive and disengaged) were interviewed they articulated extreme disenchantment from allegedly inferior teaching and expressed a desire for quality teaching from more caring teachers. Successful teachers in inner-city high schools emphasized the importance of developing trusting, caring relationships with students. They recognized a need to build bridges, have high expectations for students, offer lots of genuine positive attention, and give students second chances while increasing student responsibility for learning.

Class Level Expectations

It would seem some inner-city teachers believe students are disruptive and lack interest in schooling while other inner-city teachers believe they can motivate students to succeed. Differing expectations of students possibly result in teachers practicing differently, and hence the lived experiences of students in discrete classrooms can be quite dissimilar. The differing expectations of individual teachers may be thought of as class level expectations since teachers tend to have such expectations for all students in their classes. Although much has been written about teacher expectations for individual students, there has been little focus on class level expectations in the literature. This is despite calls from Brophy (1985) two decades ago signaling class level expectations may well have greater importance for student achievement than individual teacher-student expectations. Indeed a meta-analysis (a synthesis of research findings) of 136 expectation studies (Harris & Rosenthal, 1985) showed that class level teacher behaviors, such as creating a warm socioemotional climate and developing a friendly classroom environment, had greater effects on students than individual teacher-student interactions, such as wait time and smiling more at high-expectation students, which had been the focus of research.

Several years ago Babad, Inbar, and Rosenthal (1982) identified teachers they classified as high- and low-bias. High-bias teachers could be readily influenced by biasing information. When given false information about some students, teachers responded and planned using the false information rather than using their observations of student performance. Conversely, low-bias teachers were not readily swayed, and they interacted with students according to observable achievement. Different teachers and their responses resulted in differing outcomes for students.

In extensive research over several years, Weinstein (2002) identified teachers she called high- and low-differentiating. High-differentiating teachers discriminated in several ways between high- and low-expectation students, constantly reinforcing ability differences. In contrast, low-differentiating teachers made differences in expectations and ability much less obvious. For example, high-differentiating teachers made frequent reference to students being in or aiming for the top group, whereas this discrimination was uncommon among low-differentiating teachers. Brattesani, Weinstein, and Marshall (1984) showed that for low-differentiating teachers, expectations explained around 3% of the variance in student end-of-year achievement, whereas for high-differentiating teachers this variance was 14%—a marked difference. This divergence may offer an explanation for variations in the magnitude of teacher expectation effects found by researchers. Teacher propensities differ and expectation effects can also differ.

Rubie-Davies (2007) identified high- and low-expectation teachers as those whose expectations for their classes were well above or well below students' achievement.

Students of high-expectation teachers made very large improvements in reading ($d = 1.01$), and those of low-expectation teachers made only very small gains ($d = .05$). Additionally, student self-perceptions changed in the expected direction over one year (Rubie-Davies, 2006), that is, self-perceptions of students with high-expectation teachers increased and those of students with low-expectation teachers declined dramatically. Substantial differences were found in the pedagogical beliefs and instructional practices of the respective teachers (Rubie-Davies, 2005, 2007). Beliefs and practices of high- and low-expectation teachers and high- and low-differentiating teachers appear to be similar. Those that seem to make a difference for student learning are highlighted below.

Expecting Student Success

Weinstein (2002) described the facilitative practices of low-differentiating teachers and the directive practices of their counterparts. The identified practices aligned closely with those of high- and low-expectation teachers described by Rubie-Davies (2005, 2006, 2007). The differences appear to lie largely in the following areas: grouping, materials and activities, the evaluation system, the motivational system, and classroom relationships. These will be discussed in the following sections. Where the findings were similar for both high-expectation and low-differentiating teachers, only high-expectation teachers will be referred to with comparable reference to low-expectation teachers when there are similarities with teachers who are high-differentiating.

Grouping

Many teachers group students for instruction in some curriculum areas, particularly those showing linear development of skills such as reading and math. Ability groups can, however, provide students with clues about expected capabilities, especially where students are seated in ability groups or where teachers make frequent reference to the relative standing of such groups. High-expectation teachers offset this differentiation by instructing students in ability groups but not seating students in these groups. Moreover, reading activities were completed in mixed ability groupings. Sometimes groupings were socially based, sometimes students chose activities and worked with varying peers depending on the activity; at other times students worked on whole-class or mixed ability group activities assigned by the teacher.

Materials and Activities

The classroom tasks students are assigned, ways they are paced, and how they are monitored can provide students with information about ability. When curriculum material is sequential, students readily decide their place-ment in class, and when instructional activities are highly differentiated such differences become salient. In low-expectation classrooms, teachers tend to closely monitor low-ability students whereas high-ability students are often allowed to complete work independently. Arguably, differences in assignment of curriculum and monitoring of students may be effective teacher practices. Students, however, readily interpret such differences as conveying meaning about teachers' expectations. Effects can be minimized by ensuring students work in a variety of groupings and engage in similar challenging and interesting learning activities. Comparable tasks may have divergent processes for achieving learning, and individual learning can be enhanced through participation in exciting tasks that encourage high level thinking in all students.

The Evaluation System

The evaluation system can deliver powerful messages about teachers' expectations. High-differentiating teachers believe intelligence is fixed and are far more likely to provide students with direct feedback about ability than low-differentiating teachers. Practices include achievement charts in the classroom, asking students to raise their hands if they answered test questions correctly, or frequent references to top and bottom groups (even with disguised group names). Belief in fixed ability translates into expectations about student achievement that can affect teachers' conceptions about their influence on student learning. If teachers believe ability is fixed, they are less likely to believe they can have much effect on student learning. Conversely, teachers who believe ability is malleable tend to take responsibility when students do not learn a concept and try creative approaches to teaching. High-expectation teachers understand achievement of all students will improve with appropriate help and feedback from the teacher and peers. Success is attributed to effort and failure to task difficulty (Weinstein, 2002).

The Motivational System

Teachers can create an extrinsic or intrinsic motivational system. Low-expectation teachers stress performance goals with emphasis on competition. Students achieve status through gaining individual points, stickers, and public teacher recognition. In contrast, high-expectation teachers foster task mastery goals with emphasis on setting individual goals and monitoring progress. These teachers consider student interests in planning learning experiences that are interesting and fun for students, which fosters intrinsic motivation. High-expectation teachers provide students with choices of learning activities and peers groups, which may further stimulated student motivation. If points and stars are allocated by low-differentiating teachers at a group level, students are encouraged to support and help each other. Hence cooperation rather than competition is promoted.

Classroom Relationships

The ways high- and low-expectation teachers structure grouping, materials and activities, and the evaluation and motivational systems affect the instructional environment students engage in. Differences in the instructional environment appear to parallel differences in the socioemotional environment. In regard to high- and low-expectation teachers, these apply particularly to student-teacher relationships, teacher responses to students, and peer relationships.

It is recognized that some students perceive the affective environment of any classroom differently from others. But some core variations in teacher behaviors may create similar rather than dissimilar socioemotional environments for most students. For example, high-expectation teachers maintained student dignity, praised students for their efforts, and respected students, who in turn respected their teachers. In contrast, low-expectation teachers at times criticized low-achieving students, used put downs, and called them names when their achievements were not viewed favorably. Furthermore, high-expectation teachers used largely positive preventive management techniques, appropriate praise, and encouraging statements. Low-expectation teachers were inclined to use negative reactive classroom management and inappropriate praise.

This section has explored teacher expectations and beliefs at the class level. The implicit beliefs that high- and low-expectation teachers hold about grouping, appropriate activities for more and less able students, and how students are evaluated and motivated translate into differing instructional and socioemotional environments for students. It is possibly these class environments that account for differing effects of teacher expectations on student academic and social outcomes.

Future Directions

Teacher expectations and their effects have been studied for around 40 years. A large body of findings supports the notion that teacher expectations are important for student learning. Expectations may have greater salience for some students than others, particularly in classrooms where teachers differentiate markedly in treatment and support of high- and low-ability students. It is common to hear calls for teachers to have high expectations for all students, yet there is a paucity of research into the phenomenon of class level expectations. This is an obvious direction for future research.

Expectation studies undertaken at the whole-class level indicate possible relationships between teachers' expectations, implicit beliefs, and instructional practices that emanate from pedagogical conceptions. These notions and practices contribute to instructional and socioemotional environments in which students learn and perhaps speak to the quantity and quality of what is learned. Because this is a further neglected area in teacher expectation research,

future studies could more clearly establish relationships between teachers' expectations, beliefs, and practices. The unraveling of such associations could serve to inform teacher professional development and teacher education programs.

Concerns about effects of teacher expectations relate to issues about equality for all students. All students are entitled to quality schooling. Questions about teachers' expectations and implicit beliefs are questions about fairness and social justice. Answers to these questions can lead to enhanced educational outcomes for all students.

Conclusion

Teacher expectation research began in the 1960s and has burgeoned ever since. This is partially because of a universal acceptance of the existence of teacher expectations and consequent attempts to discover their significance for student outcomes. Researchers have investigated specific teacher behaviors that provide salient clues to students about teachers' expectations. Both self-fulfilling prophecy effects (where originally false conceptions are ultimately confirmed) and sustaining expectation effects (where teachers do not adjust teaching in line with student performance) have been documented in some classrooms.

Students can identify proximal teacher behaviors (verbal and nonverbal) that provide them with information about teachers' expectations for achievement. These include nodding, smiling, and praising high-expectation students more than low achievers. But there are distal teacher behaviors that may have greater effects on student learning. These include teacher efficacy, pedagogical beliefs, and opportunity to learn. Arguably, opportunity to learn has most effect on student learning since students will learn what they are given the opportunity to learn. They are likely to learn more in classrooms where learning experiences are challenging and exciting and where higher order thinking skills are fostered.

Some student characteristics appear to influence teacher expectations more than others. Those that have greater effects are ethnicity, social class, gender, and diagnostic labels, but other characteristics that can have effects are student attractiveness, language style, student background, personality and social skills, names, and other siblings. This chapter has discussed in depth the effects of social class and ethnicity on expectancy and argued that teacher expectations tend to be lower for students from low socioeconomic areas and some ethnic minorities.

It appears some teachers have greater effects on students than others when expectations are at the whole-class rather than the individual level, because they affect all students. There may be relationships between teacher expectations and implicit beliefs that translate into differences in instructional and socioemotional classroom environments. Teachers with high expectations for all students have differing beliefs about grouping, materials and learning activities, evaluation and monitoring systems, student autonomy, and types of relationships they foster with students and their peers.

The investigation of class level teacher expectations is an appropriate direction for future research offering opportunities to evaluate the equality of education. Arguments about differences in teachers' expectations and differential practices with some students are debates about fairness of treatment and provision of equal opportunities to learn for all students.

References and Further Readings

Babad, E., Inbar, J., & Rosenthal, R. (1982). Pygmalion, Galatea and the Golem: Investigations of biased and unbiased teachers. *Journal of Educational Psychology, 74,* 459–474.

Blatchford, P., Burke, J., Farquhar, C., Plewis, I., & Tizard, B. (1989). Teacher expectations in infant school: Associations with attainment and progress, curriculum coverage and classroom interaction. *British Journal of Educational Psychology, 59,* 19–30.

Brattesani, K. A., Weinstein, R. S., & Marshall, H. H. (1984). Student perceptions of differential teacher treatment as moderators of teacher expectation effects. *Journal of Educational Psychology, 76,* 236–247.

Brophy, J. E. (1983). Research on the self-fulfilling prophecy and teacher expectations. *Journal of Educational Psychology, 75*(5), 631–661.

Brophy, J. E. (1985). Teacher-student interaction. In J. B. Dusek (Ed.), *Teacher expectancies* (pp. 303–328). Hillsdale, NJ: Lawrence Erlbaum Associates.

Brophy, J. E., & Good, T. L. (1970). Teachers' communication of differential expectations for children's classroom performance: Some behavioral data. *Journal of Educational Psychology, 61,* 365–374.

Cooper, H., & Good, T. (1983). *Pygmalion grows up: Studies in the expectation communication process.* New York: Longman.

Dusek, J. B., & Joseph, G. (1985). The bases of teacher expectancies. In J. B. Dusek (Ed.), *Teacher expectancies* (pp. 229–250). Hillsdale, NJ: Lawrence Erlbaum Associates.

Ennis, C. D. (1998). Shared expectations: Creating a joint vision for urban schools. In J. Brophy (Ed.), *Advances in Research on Teaching. Expectations in the Classroom* (Vol. 7, pp. 151–182). Greenwich, CT: JAI Press.

Gamoran, A. (1992). Is ability grouping equitable? *Educational Leadership, 50*(2), 11–17.

Good, T. L. (1987). Teacher expectations. In D. C. Berliner & B. V. Rosenshine (Eds.), *Talks to Teachers* (pp. 159–200). New York: Random House.

Harris, M. J., & Rosenthal, R. (1985). Mediation of interpersonal expectancy effects: 31 meta-analyses. *Psychological Bulletin, 97*(3), 363–386.

Jussim, L., & Eccles, J. S. (1992). Teacher expectations II: Construction and reflection of student achievement. *Journal of Personality and Social Psychology, 63*(6), 947–961.

Jussim, L., Eccles, J. S., & Madon, S. (1996). Social perception, social stereotypes, and teacher expectations: Accuracy and the quest for the powerful self–fulfilling prophecy. In M. P. Zanna (Ed.), *Advances in Experimental Social Psychology* (Vol. 28, pp. 281–388). San Diego: Academic Press.

Kuklinski, M. R., & Weinstein, R. S. (2001). Classroom and developmental differences in a path model of teacher expectancy effects. *Child Development, 72,* 1554–1578.

McKown, C., & Weinstein, R. S. (2008). Teacher expectations, classroom context and the achievement gap. *Journal of School Psychology, 46,* 235–261.

Merton, R. K. (1948). The self-fulfilling prophecy. *The Antioch Review, 8,* 193–210.

Page, S., & Rosenthal, R. (1990). Sex and expectations of teachers and sex and race of students as determinants of teaching behavior and student performance. *Journal of School Psychology, 28,* 119–131.

Rosenthal, R. (1963). The effect of experimenter bias on the performance of the albino rat. *Behavioral Science, 8,* 183–189.

Rosenthal, R., & Jacobson, L. (1968). *Pygmalion in the classroom: Teacher expectation and pupils' intellectual development.* New York: Holt, Rinehart & Winston.

Ross, J. A. (1998). The antecedents and consequences of teacher efficacy. In J. Brophy (Ed.), *Advances in Research on Teaching. Expectations in the Classroom* (Vol. 7, pp. 49–74). Greenwich, CT: JAI Press.

Rubie-Davies, C. M. (2005, December). *Exploring class level teacher expectations and pedagogical beliefs.* Paper presented at the New Zealand Association for Research in Education Annual Conference, Dunedin, New Zealand.

Rubie-Davies, C. M. (2006). Teacher expectations and student self-perceptions: Exploring relationships. *Psychology in the Schools, 43,* 537–552.

Rubie-Davies, C. M. (2007). Classroom interactions: Exploring the practices of high and low expectation teachers. *British Journal of Educational Psychology, 77,* 289–306.

Rubie-Davies, C. M., Hattie, J., & Hamilton, R. (2006). Expecting the best for students: Teacher expectations and academic outcomes. *British Journal of Educational Psychology, 76,* 429–444.

Solomon, D., Battistich, V., & Hom, A. (1996, April). *Teacher beliefs and practices in schools serving communities that differ in socioeconomic level.* Paper presented at the American Educational Research Association annual meeting, New York.

Stinnett, T. A., Crawford, S. A., Gillespie, M. D., Cruce, M. K., & Langford, C. A. (2001). Factors affecting treatment acceptability for psychostimulant medication versus psychoeducational intervention. *Psychology in the Schools, 38*(6), 585–591.

Weinstein, R. S. (2002). *Reaching higher: The power of expectations in schooling.* Cambridge, MA: Harvard University Press.

Wigfield, A., Galper, A., Denton, K., & Seefeldt, C. (1999). Teachers' beliefs about former Head Start and non-Head Start first-grade children's motivation, performance, and future educational prospects. *Journal of Educational Psychology, 91*(1), 98–104.

Zohar, A., Degani, A., & Vaaknin, E. (2001). Teachers' beliefs about low-achieving students and higher order thinking. *Teaching and Teacher Education, 17,* 469–485.

PART VII

SOCIAL CONTEXT

28

History of Schooling

Dionne Danns

Indiana University Bloomington

Christopher M. Span

University of Illinois at Urbana-Champaign

Schooling in the United States has a long and sordid history. Those who have studied the specifics of its development recognize that schooling is arguably the most important advancement in the nation. Every generation of American citizens has relied on schools to teach children essential lessons and knowledge that will aid them in their future economic, social, and civic responsibilities. How schools became the primary vehicle for inculcating and teaching students these lessons is the focus of this essay. It offers a brief overview, from the colonial era to the near present, of some of the most important developments in the history of schooling in the United States and illustrates how time, space, personalities, and expectations determined its evolution. As we will demonstrate, schools did not benefit everyone equally. Some children, whether because of their race, gender, religion, societal status, or some other extraneous factor, were systematically denied or hindered from receiving a quality education. As such, the legacy of schooling in the United States should not be seen as a linear collective history that everyone, regardless of their background, experienced. Rather, for nearly 400 years schools were the ultimate laboratory for testing and retesting issues of access, equity, affordability, utility, and democracy itself.

Colonial Era (1607–1776)

During the colonial era, schooling was not seen as a priority for the masses or a necessary expenditure for most colonies. Notwithstanding, schooling for all at the public's expense took root very early in some, particularly in the New England area. The most noteworthy developments occurred in Massachusetts. The colony had a system of schools for its children within 30 years of its establishment. The colony was founded in 1620 with the arrival of Pilgrims from England, and major advances in education occurred after Puritans arrived in 1634. Within 2 years, colonists founded the Boston Latin Grammar School, which to date is recognized as the first secondary school in the United States, and by 1647, colonial Massachusetts instituted statutes that called for the development of a system of schools for all at the public's expense.

Early settlers in Massachusetts did not come to obtain quick riches or venture upon new lands. They left England primarily to avoid religious and social persecution. The early settlers in Massachusetts came as intact nuclear families, many were educated and were educators, and most came with the intent of establishing a new permanent community in the colony. Schooling was a foremost consideration in this new community. In 1635, Boston town officials saw it necessary to hire a teacher for its children. The towns of Ipswich and Charleston also started schools that year. In 1638, Cambridge set aside three acres of land for school purposes, and in 1639, Dorchester, Newbury, and Salem all established schools. Within the first decade of settlement, according to historians Urban and Wagoner (2004), "seven of the twenty-two towns in Massachusetts had taken some public action on behalf of schooling" (p. 41).

Religion and schooling went hand-in-hand in Massachusetts. This is apparent in the first school law of the colony. The Old Deluder Satan Law (1647) called for the establishment of an elementary school for every 50 families in the colony and for a grammar school to be established in every large town. Similar developments happened elsewhere in the New England region. In 1642, for example, colonial Connecticut ordered that schools be established for the benefit of its children in its two most populated towns, New Haven and Hartford. These schools would be supported from funds drawn from the "common stock of the town" (Urban & Wagoner, 2000, p. 42.) The same was true in Rhode Island and New Hampshire. In fact, by the beginning of the 18th century, both Rhode Island and New Hampshire passed school statutes ensuring that all children within the colonies received a free education.

By far the greatest educational advancement to occur in this region was the establishment of institutions of higher education. In 1636, Harvard was founded in Cambridge, Massachusetts. In 1707, Yale was founded in New Haven, Connecticut. In 1746, Princeton was founded as the College of New Jersey in Elizabeth, New Jersey. It relocated to Princeton and renamed itself in 1756. In New Hampshire, Dartmouth was founded in 1763, and in Providence, Rhode Island, Brown University was founded in 1765. These institutions of higher education were founded primarily as theological seminaries to train future clergymen for public service in their respective locales. The rise of these universities highlighted not only the advocacy for education, but also the religious tensions and sectarian rivalries among early colonists and how they used schooling to advance their ideals. Harvard was founded by Puritans; Yale was established out of disillusionment with Harvard's growing tolerance for religious flexibility; Princeton was founded because of the religious rigidness of Yale; Dartmouth was founded out of enthusiasm stirred by the religious revivals of the Great Awakening; and Brown was founded by Baptists. Despite their sectarian differences each of these early institutions of higher education had commonalities; the most noteworthy being that they all expected to preserve their ways of life by using schools to teach and train future generations of children in their ideals.

In the southern colonies—North Carolina, South Carolina, and Georgia—schooling at the public's expense would not develop until after the Civil War. The primary reason for this underdevelopment was slavery. In an effort to keep African Americans enslaved or free illiterate, Whites in the South invariably undermined their own educational advancement. To slaveholders, a literate slave was dangerous and this contention became even more ensconced in the decades following the American Revolution. Nearly every American colony, and later state, prohibited or stridently restricted teaching free and enslaved African Americans in the South to read or write. South Carolina was the first. As early as 1740, the colony enacted a law that prohibited any person from teaching a slave how to read or write. Thirty years later, colonial Georgia followed South Carolina's precedent and enacted similar code that forbade the teaching of slaves. The laws against teaching enslaved African Americans to read and write following the American Revolution grew out of a variety of fears and concerns, the most straightforward concerned the use of literacy as a means to obtain freedom (such as the forging of passes for escape). During the antebellum era, other southern states developed their own laws that prevented African Americans—enslaved or free—from learning. These combined efforts to keep African Americans illiterate in the South concomitantly kept Whites from establishing a viable school system for even its educable youth until after the Civil War and slavery's demise.

American Revolution (1776–1800)

During and after the American Revolution, the call for schooling took on greater meaning. Its most outspoken advocate was Virginia native and author of the Declaration of Independence, Thomas Jefferson. Three times between 1779 and 1818, Jefferson proposed before the Virginia legislature a plan calling for the establishment of schools at the public's expense. Each time Jefferson's plan was soundly rejected. In 1779, Jefferson published *A Bill for the More General Diffusion of Knowledge*. In it he outlined a detailed plan for the establishment of schools in Virginia. Jefferson calculated how many schools should be established in the state, who should teach in these schools, what children would learn, and how schools would be funded through local and state taxation. Jefferson called for nothing less than a three-tiered plan for universal education for all free children in Virginia. The first tier, elementary schools, guaranteed every free child in the state received 3 years of schooling at the public's expense. These schools would teach children reading, writing, arithmetic, geography, and history. The second tier, grammar schools, was designed for young boys to continue their learning. In these schools students would learn advanced mathematics, physical sciences, languages, world and American history, and philosophy. The smartest male student of each district elementary school would be afforded a scholarship to attend grammar school and thereafter the university, if he could not afford to continue his education. Through these schools and merit-based scholarships, Jefferson assumed he would find young, bright minds that ordinarily would never be given an opportunity to advance beyond a common status. By way of his educational plan, Jefferson firmly believed a few "geniuses" would "be raked from the rubbish"; the rubbish being the average poor yeoman farmer in Virginia.

Notwithstanding, Jefferson was not the only advocate for the development of schools during the revolutionary era. While Jefferson concentrated his energies on Virginia, others, such as Benjamin Rush and Noah Webster, articulated their own ideas of the role schools should play in their respective states and the new republic. In 1786, Rush, a professor of chemistry and medicine at the University of Pennsylvania, wrote a plan calling for the establishment of public schools in Pennsylvania. In this plan Rush outlined his vision of a new republic that would use schools as a vehicle to promote sound moral values, patriotism, nationalism, and a homogeneous people in thought and action. Although Rush's plan concentrated on Pennsylvania, his proposal by extension spoke to the educational needs of all citizens in the new nation. Rush believed every child should learn what it means to be a patriotic citizen with sound moral values, and schools could be the catalyst to teach children these important lessons.

Noah Webster, author of the *American Spelling Book* and *American Dictionary of the English Language*, was very much in agreement with Jefferson and Rush that the direction of the nation's future depended heavily on the amount and type of education its citizenry received. He believed schools should inculcate in youth messages of unity, nationalism, and morality. Children of the young republic should learn American history, even an American language, to best foster a strong sense of nationalism and an identity that was distinct from England and other European countries. Webster devoted most of his time and energies to design and provide the texts necessary to achieve this aim.

Common School Movement (1820–1860)

Between 1820 and 1860, schooling slowly began to flourish in the United States. By 1860, of the 34 states in the Union, every state (as part of their admission into the Union) had adopted school law that required public schooling at the state's expense for its educable youth, and nearly half had effectively implemented a viable school system. Schooling occurred from Massachusetts to California, and the school development to occur in this time span has been labeled by historians as the Common School Movement. "Common schools" was the ideological slogan used by school reformers in this era to describe a particular type of schooling experience. The schools were to be free, universal, centralized, and offer a common curriculum and quality schooling experience to students regardless of their background. No single person should serve as the representative or spokesperson for an era or movement, but arguably the most charismatic personality of this era was Horace Mann.

Mann, aptly named by many educational historians as the "Father of the Common School Movement," was the first secretary of education for Massachusetts and he served this post from 1837 to 1848. The job was no easy task. Although schooling early in Massachusetts's history was highly valued, Mann faced a society that had relegated schooling a nonimportant public matter. As such, the statewide school system he inherited as secretary of education

was in utter disarray. Schools were underfunded, facilities were in wretched condition, teachers were poorly trained and underpaid, there was very little uniformity, and public interest or resources to rectify these problems barely existed. Nonetheless, during his tenure, Mann addressed many of the problems plaguing public schools in Massachusetts. Within a decade, he instituted a series of schooling initiatives to improve educational facilities, and standardized the curriculum and teacher training; he borrowed and implemented key educational reforms from abroad to advance public schooling in Massachusetts; he made schooling compulsory for 6 months out of the year; and his rhetoric and actions redirected the mindset of many state citizens who, before Mann, saw public education as a burden rather than an asset to society.

Much of Mann's success came from his deep-seated belief in the transformative power of education. Mann believed every child, whether rich or poor, male or female, immigrant or native born, Protestant or Catholic, should be entitled to a quality education. In school, students would learn more than the rudiments of knowledge. They would learn sound morals, time management and social efficiency skills, and the meaning and utility of integral concepts such as freedom, democracy, and citizenship. In Mann's mind, education was the birthright of every child born in the nation; it was a panacea to many societal problems, such as crime, illiteracy, and poverty, and if given the proper resources and support, education could serve as the great equalizer of society. It could alleviate poverty, ease religious tensions, produce social harmony, and give immigrants and native born persons a common heritage—even make them a common people.

Despite the fact that countless educational reformers throughout the nation adopted many of the measures Mann proposed and implemented in Massachusetts, not every one agreed with Horace Mann. "Universal" standards or a "common experience" did not necessarily include children who were deemed inferior, different, or strange, such as Black children or Irish Catholics (Urban & Wagoner, 2004). In 1849, one year after Mann resigned from his post as secretary of education, African American Benjamin F. Roberts sued the city of Boston on behalf of his 5-year-old daughter Sarah, accusing the city of perpetuating a system of unequal segregated schools. Sarah Roberts had to walk past five White elementary schools to attend the Smith School, a dilapidated educational facility designated for the city's Black children. Roberts argued the Smith School was vastly inferior to the five White schools his daughter had to walk past and requested his daughter be allowed to attend one of them to accommodate her educational needs. His request coincided with a new city ordinance that mandated all Boston children attend a school nearest to their residence. The *Roberts* (1849) case went before the Massachusetts Supreme Court, and it was the first legal suit against school segregation in the country. Roberts's lawyers, abolitionist Charles Sumner and Boston's first Black attorney, Robert Morris, argued that all persons were equal before Massachusetts's law and that race-based distinctions were not permissible in the state. They further argued that racial segregation characterized all African Americans as inferior and that a segregated Black school could not equal a segregated White school because of the stigma associated with segregation.

The Massachusetts Supreme Court was not persuaded by the argument, however, and ruled that schooling segregated by race was not a violation of Massachusetts law as long as schools were equally provided for. Despite the court ruling, Benjamin Roberts was not dismayed. He continued to agitate on behalf of his daughter and, in 1855, Massachusetts legislature passed a law prohibiting race-based school assignments.

Religion revealed similar tensions. In New York City, Bishop John Hughes of the Roman Catholic Church, vehemently opposed the common school model of education. Hughes was Irish Catholic and felt that the city's efforts to establish a common educational experience for all New York City children denigrated both Irish people and Catholicism. In his mind, the common schools of New York were asking Irish children to give up too much of themselves—their culture and religion—in the name of education. Common schools were inculcating Irish Catholic children in the common culture, religion, experiences, and expectations of White Anglo-Saxon Protestants. To Hughes this was unacceptable. In 1840, when city school officials refused to adhere to the request brought forth by Hughes and other concerned Irish Catholics, Hughes petitioned school officials to reallocate a portion of the city's common school fund for their own personal use. What emerged from these protests and reallocated funds was the creation of a completely alternative school model: Catholic schools.

Beginnings of the Modern School System (1860–1900)

Before the 20th century, the greatest advancements in the history of schools occurred between 1860 and 1900. It was during this time period that schools became more permanent, uniformed, inclusive, and universal. The modern school and university that students today recognize and attend originated during this time period. The schools arose amid a nation at war and during a time of recovery and retrenchment. The Civil War (1861–65) was fought, slavery was upended as a consequence of the war, and the nation amended the Constitution to include a population previously held in bondage. In 1862, in the midst of war, Congress passed the Morrill Act. Under the act, each state would receive 30,000 acres of federal land to use for educational purposes. Every state was expected to use a portion of the lands for the establishment of an agricultural and technical college for the educational benefit of its citizenry. The act, named after House Representative Justin Smith Morrill of Vermont, ushered in a new commitment

on the part of the federal government to aid educational reformers in their efforts to advance education throughout the nation. As new states joined the Union west of the Mississippi, so too did schools and institutions of higher education because of the Morrill Act.

Still, not every region equally benefited from the Morrill Act. Because they had seceded from the Union, most southern states could not take advantage of Morrill until their readmission to the Union following the war. These states seceded from the Union in April 1861 in an attempt to preserve the states' right to maintain and perpetuate slavery. Slavery not only limited the region's access to obtaining federal lands and monies for the creation of additional institutions of higher education, it also crippled the South's development of a viable school system. As the East, Midwest, and West were all establishing schools for its general population, the South had only paid homage to the idea. Only North Carolina had taken serious strides to develop a statewide system of schools before the Civil War. Notwithstanding, after the Civil War every southern state amended its constitution to include provisions that promoted the establishment of a comprehensive school system at the state's expense.

The irony of this development was that former slaves led the call for universal education in the region. Freed people's universal demand for education invariably served as the catalyst for bringing public schooling to the South. The demand was so great that every southern state revamped its constitution to include provisions for public schools. The African American delegates in attendance at these constitutional conventions were the leading advocates. Their relentless efforts secured public schooling for not only African American children, but for all children—regardless of race, gender, class, or previous condition of servitude. Consequently, African Americans in this era attended school in greater numbers than ever before. From 1870 to 1885, their attendance rates were equal to, if not greater than, Whites. And by 1900, the illiteracy rate among African Americans under the age of 40 was virtually nonexistent. By 1885, however, school gains for African Americans came virtually to a halt. White southerners who opposed Black advancement and the changes that befell the South following the Civil War had regained nearly complete control over the region. Legalized segregation became commonplace and schools for Whites in the South progressed at the expense of schools designated for "colored" children. African Americans had emerged from slavery with a belief that schools would educate them for citizenship, but the schools afforded to them after 1885 primarily educated them for domestic, industrial, and agricultural servitude.

Despite the dual system of schooling that developed in the South, schooling elsewhere in the nation became an ingrained and favored institution. School reformers throughout the nation continued to revamp schools to become more accessible, centralized, uniformed, bureaucratic, and functional to the needs of society. They established the length of school days and terms, and they passed compulsory school laws that required children to begin school at a certain age and attend school until at least the age of 14. Schools were no longer simply institutions of learning; they were now the pathways to greater social and economic mobility. The more schooling one had, the greater the chances of obtaining the kind of work and lifestyle one desired. Children were now going to school to learn how to live and work in the American social order, rather than going to school to become a more knowledgeable citizen. The expertise and credentials that students attained in schools were quickly becoming valuable commodities for access, opportunities, and resources in adulthood.

Some institutions, however, benefited more from this trend than others. For instance, high schools and colleges, particularly in urban areas, became critical institutions to advance these expectations. Although most children never attended a high school or a college in the 19th century (historians best estimate that only 5% of all children— regardless of background—between the ages of 12 and 17 were enrolled in a high school in the year 1900), both of these institutions would nonetheless become the primary vehicles for promoting these societal expectations and teaching children these practical and life adjustment skills for the greater part of the 20th century.

The Progressive Era (1900–1940)

It is hard to understand the history and evolution of schools in the first half of the 20th century without an understanding of the dynamic and ever-changing political economy of the United States during this time period. At the dawn of the 20th century, America was a nation engrossed in the Industrial Revolution, attending to increased unionization, immigration, and urbanization. With common schools firmly, though unevenly, in place in both the North and the South, progressive reformers at the turn of the 20th century focused their attention on how to Americanize the new wave of southern and eastern Europeans that were entering the nation. By 1920, there were more Americans in cities than in rural areas and many of those city residents were foreign-born or children of foreign-born parents. Diverse groups of progressive reformers decided to restructure schools to scientifically sort students, efficiently organize school administration, and make the curriculum more relevant to the interest of students and the needs of society.

American urbanization came as a result of the shifting national and world economies and as the number of agricultural workers decreased and the number of manufacturing workers increased. The year 1920 not only marked the shift in the nation from rural to urban, but it also marked the shift from predominantly agricultural work to manufacturing work. The United States had become one of the leading mass producers in the world as work moved from complex skilled tasks to deskilled tasks in the age of mass production. With the deskilling of work, there were also

decreased wages and decreased power on the part of workers to decide the future of their work conditions and environment. Agricultural mechanization led to the migration of farm workers to cities in search of work. Accordingly, factories increased both in number and size.

These changes led to greater extremes between the wealthy and the poor as unregulated industries meant unimagined wealth for a handful of American businessmen. Historians have aptly named these businessmen robber barons; they included men such as famed industrialists John D. Rockefeller and Andrew Carnegie. While they individually amassed great wealth, their workers struggled to live a life above poverty because of the low wages and benefits they were afforded. This led to increased unionization as workers collaborated to ensure fair wages and benefits. Unionization also led to hundreds of strikes as workers protested for better wages, benefits, and work environments.

Immigration fueled these economic and social developments. Immigrants' nations of origin shifted from northern and western European countries such as England, Ireland, France, and Germany to southern, eastern, and central European countries; Asian countries such as China, the Philippines, and Japan; and Latin American countries such as Mexico and Puerto Rico. Between 1906 and 1910, 4.5 million new immigrants arrived in the United States from Europe, and 78% of those came from Italy, Greece, Russia, Hungary, Poland, Lithuania, Czechoslovakia, and Bulgaria. Nearly half were Jews who fled persecution from Russia. These new immigrants brought with them their desires to obtain opportunities and citizenship as well as very distinct cultures, appearances, and languages that Americans would use to deny them access to resources, opportunities, and even citizenship.

During this era, schools once again were called upon to address the drastic changes befalling American society. State officials, the business community, and concerned citizens looked to educational reformers to identify ways that schools could ease growing strife, train students to work and live in an industrial economy, and to educate and Americanize immigrant children. Tensions grew as educators quickly recognized that the traditional models of education that proved to be effective in the 19th century could no longer address the changes occurring in society or the increasing demands for all children to be schooled. Both the curriculum and efficiency of schools came under fire. The everyday citizen criticized the traditional classical curriculum for its failure to motivate students. Industrialists were firmly convinced the curriculum was irrelevant and could not meet the needs of the modern industrial age. City officials complained about high dropout rates, rising illiteracy, and increasing incidents of juvenile delinquency among urban youth. And some educators themselves believed that school management practices were wasteful and inefficient.

Enter the progressive educator; an educator that sought to use schools to address many of the societal problems hindering progress in society. Progressive educational reformers formed two distinct groups: administrative progressives and pedagogical progressives. Administrative progressives were concerned with running schools efficiently. They were not necessarily concerned with using schools as a way to change society. Their main concern was a cost-effective school system with efficient and organized school management. At the time, schools were run by ward politicians who were often corrupt and who squandered school funds. Administrative progressives also dealt with curriculum in terms of social efficiency. They wanted to find the best methods to sort students based on their skills and abilities. They created curriculum differentiation with different tracks for students based on the academic goals of students. Students who were college bound took different classes from those who were going to be common laborers. To justify the sorting of students, intelligence tests were used to determine where students would be placed and their future value to society. The use of these tests began during World War I when army officers were tested with Alpha and Beta tests. Test results determined whether a solider would be in the infantry on the frontlines of war or a commissioned officer who would command soldiers. The rest of the exams were given to schools, and a series of other exams were created and dispersed to schools. Many exams were unreliable—meaning the test did not necessary measure intelligence in any meaningful way—and were culturally biased because they tested not only the student's aptitude, but also his or her awareness and understanding of the cultural experiences of dominant society. Nonetheless, these standardized tests often determined the curriculum track of a student.

This era also led to increased bureaucracy in schools. For example, school subject departments were created with department heads. There was hierarchy for school cooks, janitors, and administrators. The superintendent's staff had people to deal with finance, curriculum, and day-to-day operations. Each area had its own hierarchy, which led to further bureaucracy.

The administrative progressives laid the foundation for what we have come to see as normal for schools: tracking, bureaucracy, testing, and elected school boards. They also succeeded in consolidating numerous local school districts into larger city and county districts. They did succeed in incorporating large numbers of immigrants into the American mainstream. But their work did not go without criticism. Historian David Tyack (1974) made the following criticisms about the administrative progressives:

1. Increased bureaucratization led to more concerns about positions and regulation of rules than a child's educational development. In other words, expanding bureaucracies made it increasingly difficult to respond to the needs of students.
2. The concern about taking politics out of school led to a realignment of power from ward politicians to experts.

3. Efficiency was thought to lead to equal opportunity; however, schools have been systematically ineffective in dealing with children of the poor.
4. The system was created to be good for all, but has not always been best for the pluralistic American society.
5. Because the system is believed to be so efficient, those who are ill-served by it typically receive blame when they are unable to succeed as a result of it.

The pedagogical progressives are the other group of educational progressives; they were interested in changing the instructional practices in schools. Although they had differences in their philosophies and practices, they commonly believed that the traditional classical curriculum needed to be replaced with a varied curriculum to meet the needs of students. They also believed that learning should be more activity based and less rote memorization. Finally, they believed that school content and aims should reflect the social conditions because schools should aid in the solving of social problems.

Among the best known and least understood of pedagogical progressives was John Dewey. Dewey believed that education was an interaction between the child and the curriculum as well as the school and society. He did not want to do away with subjects, but thought that there were better ways for subjects to be taught. For example, students at the Chicago University Lab School he started would take field trips to museums and historical sites to learn history and went to parks and forests to study biology. They used the larger world around them to learn about the subjects they were studying. Dewey also saw schools as essential to the progression of democracy. In his mind, schools should teach democratic values such as tolerance and respect for the rights of others. He saw schools as a miniature model of society and believed in developing individuals to their fullest capabilities; if this was done, they would be able to benefit and contribute to society.

As did the administrative progressives, pedagogical progressives also had their critics. Some argued that educational endeavors such as Dewey's were harder to convey to poor children and were really just a fad for elites. The methods tended to work best for children from affluent families because of their social and cultural capital. Others felt that the methods were not proper ways to teach reading and computation skills. Still others believed that learning history on field trips meant that students would not learn important dates and names of the past. For the most part, Dewey's methods were not properly applied even though he and others influenced generations of educators.

High schools also changed during the progressive era. The National Education Association (NEA) had committees study the structure of schools to create a more uniformed curriculum. One committee, named the Committee of Ten, was led by Harvard University President Charles Elliot. The committee decided on little variation in the curriculum. All students would take English, history, math, science, and foreign language. Those destined for college would study classical or modern languages and take advanced science and math courses. Many thought the committee's recommendations were inappropriate for the changing economy. A second committee known as the Kingsley Commission, formally Cardinal Principles of Secondary Education, created a differentiated curriculum based on various academic tracks for students. Homeroom, physical education, health, and citizenship classes would bring together students from the college bound, vocational, and general tracks.

Secondary education became more necessary as technological changes led to increased white-collar positions. It was believed that more educated workers would lead to more production and efficiency, thereby expanding the economy. In 1890, girls outnumbered boys in high schools 2 to 1 and performed better on tests. Because of concern that girls would enter male dominated fields, a differentiated curriculum, with courses such as home economics and clerical studies, was established for girls. The goal was to steer girls into only certain arenas of the public sphere.

Schooling for African Americans, Asian Americans, and Latinos (specifically Mexican Americans) was largely segregated throughout the country. As African Americans migrated by the hundreds of thousands to northern urban areas during the great migration from World War I to the Great Depression, many were segregated into separate neighborhoods, and subsequently segregated schools, because of discriminatory practices and restrictive covenants on the part of realtors. As Latinos and Asians immigrated to the United States, separate schools and neighborhoods were also created for them in the Southwest and West. All of these groups used protest and the courts to challenge and upend segregated schooling for their children before World War II. In spite of successful court cases, the majority of African Americans, Mexican Americans, and Asian Americans remained segregated either by law (de jure) or in practice (de facto) well into the late 20th century.

During the 19th century, national policy for Native American schooling focused on deculturalization, the attempt to strip Native Americans of their culture and replace it with a more "civilized" and Christianized culture. Off-reservation boarding schools were the preferred place to teach Native American children. In the early 20th century this type of schooling was viewed as cruel and unsuccessful because it largely failed to change the culture of Native American children or to create a place for them in mainstream society. The Merriam Report (1928), formally known as "The Problem of Indian Administration," criticized the failed government policies of the past. It suggested that the type of schooling experience Native American children needed was one that directly related to and incorporated their own culture and families. As such, it was recommended that all children be schooled on reservations rather than away from them. Later in the century, government policies focused on self-determination for American Indian education.

By World War II, more students were attending and completing high schools, colleges, and universities; the structure of schools looked much the way it does today; and segregation along racial, and in some cases class, lines was firmly in place throughout the nation. The postwar era would be the time of the Cold War and internal attempts to create equalization in schooling as well as the larger American society.

Schools During the Postwar Era (1945–Present)

During the post-World War II (WWII) era, the federal government became increasingly involved in public schools. The federal government had some involvement in schools before WWII; however, its role expanded after the war. After the Soviets launched Sputnik during the Cold War, Congress passed the National Defense Education Act in 1958. Many felt the United States educational system needed to be more focused on science and math to win the Cold War. The act gave categorical funding to math, science, and foreign languages. The money was allocated in grants for curriculum development.

The 1954 *Brown v. Board of Education of Topeka, Kansas* Supreme Court decision declared segregation inherently unequal, and *Brown II* (1955) decreed that "all deliberate speed" should be used to upend segregation in the nation's schools. The *Brown* decision was one of many Supreme Court decisions that affected school desegregation throughout the country. Part of the argument was that school segregation was a violation of the 14th Amendment, which guaranteed every citizen equal protection and consideration under the law. This same argument was made in *Mendez v. Westminister* (1946) in Orange County, California. In *Mendez*, the court ruled that the school district purposely segregated Mexican American children based on their Latinized appearance and gerrymandered school boundaries. The court also acknowledged that there were no statutes that permitted their segregation and that the 14th Amendment and the Treaty of Guadalupe Hidalgo (1848) guaranteed equal rights to Mexican Americans. The NAACP also joined this suit, submitting a brief in support of Mexican Americans. The landmark *Brown* decision, however, had a national effect on segregated education, although many now debate its true effect.

In spite of these cases, many states were extremely slow to desegregate their schools. Title VI of the 1964 Civil Rights Act—passed during the civil rights movement—allowed the federal government to withhold federal funds from school districts and their programs if they segregated or discriminated against children because of their race, color, or national origin. The threat to withhold funds along with other Supreme Court decisions led to desegregation throughout the nation, but more successfully in southern states. Desegregation was highly controversial because it pitted governors against presidents, Black and

Brown against White, and neighborhood against neighborhood. Busing was one of the desegregation remedies approved by the Supreme Court, because in many northern areas segregated neighborhoods led to segregated schools. But busing, like other remedies for desegregation, resulted in protest, with people blocking school doors, assaults on students who participated in desegregation attempts, and financial burden on school districts. As many Americans became fed up with civil rights and busing, the Emergency School Assistance Act was passed in 1972. It provided funds to reward districts for voluntary desegregation. Funds could not be used to pay for court ordered activities and regular educational programming. The act was a clear opposition to busing.

Segregation and discrimination were not the only issues affecting schools during this era. During the 1960s, considerable attention was given to the effect of poverty on the progress of society. Countless academic studies illustrated that poverty was a systemic problem in the country. President Lyndon B. Johnson launched the War on Poverty campaign in an attempt to combat the issue. Numerous acts were passed. The Economic Opportunity Act (1964) provided programs such as Upward Bound, Head Start, Job Corps, and work study for college students. In 1965, the Elementary and Secondary Education Act (ESEA) was passed; it provided funds to aid underresourced schools or build new schools. Title I provided compensatory funding for basic education of poor children through pullout programs. Separate Title I personnel were included. The Bilingual Education Act (1968) was an extension of the ESEA; it provided funds to encourage local school districts to use approaches incorporating native-language instruction. *Lau v. Nichols* (1974) reinforced the Bilingual Education Act. In *Lau*, non-English speaking Chinese students sued officials of the San Francisco Unified School District because they felt officials used their limited proficiency in English to deny them equal educational opportunities. The Supreme Court ruled that the civil rights of these non-English speaking Chinese children were violated and that schools had to put forth a better effort to accommodate the linguistic educational needs of students with limited English proficiency.

Title IX was passed in 1972, and it provided gender equality in sports and higher education. This act led to greater access to higher education, professional schools, career education, employment, and math and science education; it also addressed sexual harassment and the treatment of pregnant and parenting teens. Before Title IX, medical and law schools had quotas on the number of women they would accept. In 1972, women received just 9% of medical degrees, and in 1971, just 7% of law degrees. By 1994, however, 38% of all medical degree and 43% of all law degree recipients were women. Another act passed by the federal government was the Education of All Handicapped Children Act of 1975. This act provided handicapped children with public education to meet their special needs. It gave access to public schools for students with disabilities.

Many of the acts enacted and court cases won were steps taken to correct past inequalities and to bring the nation closer to its promise of equality. But as the century neared its close, movements for civil rights, women's rights, Black and Brown Power, and Native American and Asian American rights waned. Many of the acts were in place to lead to more equitable education for all students. The last quarter of the century saw a backlash against these laws and court cases as White students now had to compete with everyone for what seemed like limited access to privileges White men with means had for centuries. Beginning with *University of California Regents v. Bakke* (1978), in which the Supreme Court ruled 5-4 that the University of California, Davis School of Medicine could not establish racial quotas in admissions, the courts began to chip away at affirmative action. *Bakke* implied that public education should operate as if colorblind. Other court cases continued to chip away at affirmative action and the *Brown v. Board* decision. The nation's schools have resegregated and continue to be unequal.

The end of the century also led to efforts to create more school choice with charter schools, homeschooling, vouchers, and high-stakes testing. Some argue that these moves are meant to lead to a more privatized form of schooling, which could spell the end of the public school system as we have come to know it. Others argue that choice would improve the education for all as public schools would have to work harder to compete for students. Charter schools are one of the attempts at more school choice. These schools are a part of the public school system; a local agency applies for a charter at the public's expense. They are allowed to bypass local and state bureaucracy in their decision making. Another form of school choice, homeschooling, has become more popular as parents who reject the common morality of schooling want to educate their children in their own religion or traditions. States have varying regulations of these schools. Another school choice option is vouchers. Vouchers allow the public funding for a child to attend a private school of their choice. Vouchers are particularly controversial because funding could be used for private religious schools, possibly blurring the separation of church and state. The No Child Left Behind Act of 2001 (also part of the ESEA) allows parents to transfer their children from low-performing schools to better schools within the district if there are seats available. This allows a limited choice to parents. The schools are determined to be low-performing if the students have not met the adequate yearly progress on the high-stakes test. These various choice options are currently available to only a limited number of students.

The turn of the 21st century saw new immigration challenges as the Immigration Act of 1965 led to yet another shift in immigration. Latinos, Asians, West Indians, Africans, and other groups migrated in mass to this nation. Complaints from native-born people sound similar to the complaints at the turn of the 20th century. As cities declined and suburbs expanded, cities sought redevelopment and gentrification. Changes in the economy from manufacturing industries to service and technological industries, from national to global, has led to new challenges for schools and the American society. Schools are now more segregated than they were at the time of the *Brown* decision, and the Supreme Court has recently ruled against voluntary desegregation plans in Seattle, Washington, and Louisville, Kentucky, that allowed the use of race to ensure resegregation would not occur. While many things have changed in schools and the larger American society, many things also seem to remain the same.

References and Further Readings

Donato, R. (1997). *The other struggle for equal schools: Mexican Americans during the civil rights era.* Albany: State University of New York Press.

Fraser, J. W. (2001). *The school in the United States: A documentary history.* New York: McGraw-Hill.

Kaestle, C. F., & Smith, M. S. (1982). The federal role in elementary and secondary education, 1940–1980. *Harvard Educational Review, 52,* 384–408.

Kliebard, H. M. (2004). *The struggle for the American curriculum, 1893–1958* (3rd ed.). New York: Routledge Falmer.

Norton, M. B., Katzman, D. M., Escott, P. D., Chudacoff, H. P., Paterson, T. G., & Tuttle, W. M. Jr. (1994). *A people and a nations: A history of the United States, Volume II: Since 1865* (4th ed.). Boston: Houghton Mifflin.

Rury, J. L. (2004). *Education and social change: Themes in the history of American schooling* (2nd ed.). Mahwah, NJ: Lawrence Erlbaum Associates.

Spring, J. (2004). *American education* (11th ed.). Boston: McGraw-Hill.

Tyack, D. B. (1974). *The one best system: A history of American urban education.* Cambridge, MA: Harvard University Press.

Urban, W. J., & Wagoner, J. L., Jr. (2000). *American education: A history* (2nd ed.). Boston: McGraw-Hill.

Urban, W. J., & Wagoner, J. L., Jr. (2004). *American education: A history* (3rd ed.). Boston: McGraw-Hill.

29

URBAN EDUCATION

DOROTHY SHIPPS

City University of New York

This chapter describes how urban education is different from suburban or rural schooling in the students served, its organizational and environmental complexity, and governance. The second part explains criticisms directed at urban education and recent reform efforts. The chapter concludes with suggestions for thinking differently about the dilemmas of urban education.

What Is Urban Education?

Urban education is schooling provided to residents who live in cities: dense settlements at the center of economically and socially interdependent regions. In 2004, about 6% of the 14,076 school districts in the United States were urban school systems, but they contained 26% of the nation's schools and educated more than 14 million, or 30%, of all students (National Center for Education Statistics [NCES], 2007). Urban education differs from suburban or rural education in two ways. High proportions of students labeled poor or minority attend schools in urban districts. Urban education is organized on a large scale in a complex environment and consequently has a distinctive governing structure. These characteristics have been apparent for more than a century.

Concentrations of Students

Urban schools educate many immigrant students. Since the late 19th century, immigrant families and their first-

and second-generation offspring have constituted a large portion of the minority population of urban schools. They typically speak a language other than English at home and were raised in small towns and villages in poor countries across the globe. Urban schools are expected to socialize them into the pace and intensity of city life, and prepare them for the modern workplace and for citizenship in the American form of democracy.

During a period that coincides with the reorganization of urban school systems into what we recognize today—1890 to 1920—city schools educated the children of nearly 11 million southern, central, and eastern Europeans who arrived before 1924. This massive migration constituted about 17% of the nation's total population in 1890. Most of these new immigrants worked in low-skill, low-wage industrial jobs, partly because they arrived with an average of 4 to 6 years of schooling at a time when native born Americans averaged 8 to 10 years (Perlmann, 2005).

Children of the new immigrants were several times more likely to record low IQ scores, be held back a grade, and drop out of high school than children of native born Americans. But the second and third generations, numbering 11 to 12 million by 1970, no longer were so stigmatized and had the same likelihood of graduating high school as native-born Americans (Perlmann, 2005). Large education gaps between the new immigrants and other native-born Americans of European origin were erased. Intermarriage helped blur cultural expectations. The Great Depression and subsequent loss of union jobs encouraged the second and third generation to stay in school. And laws in 1924 imposed strict quotas on immigrants, lowering the significance of being the children (or grandchildren) of foreigners. Even as they were being assimilated, Latinos became a new minority of immigrants.

Although Mexicans have been a small proportion of the population since the nation was founded, they now constitute 60% of a wave of Latino immigrants that has expanded the U.S. population by about 8 million since 1970. High birth rates make Mexican Americans the largest single minority group among those born between 1996 and 2000. Like earlier immigrants, they are concentrated in low-skill, low-wage jobs and, in 2004, 47% of their children attended urban schools. Second and third generation Mexican Americans, however, are not closing the education gap as fast as the Europeans before them. As recently as 2005, 25% to 28% of Mexican American children did not graduate from high school. Consequently, their economic prospects are lower than their immigrant parents' (NCES, 2007; Perlmann, 2005). Slow educational progress is partly explained by the continuing low level of schooling among new immigrants, rising wage inequality that draws school-age youth into work, and the undocumented status of many Mexicans, which discourages contact with government employees, but also the intense segregation of Latinos in public schools.

Many urban school systems also have high proportions of Black students, which began with the Great Migration of emancipated cotton pickers and sharecroppers who were recruited for industrial jobs in Northern cities during World War I. Most Blacks are not voluntary immigrants, but rather the descendents of slaves, a fact that distinguishes their social, economic, and political experience from other Americans. If war-created labor shortages drew them north, Black parents also wanted to raise their children without the burdens of segregation or the strain of being at the bottom of the Southern social hierarchy (Sanjek, 1996). Instead, they found de facto segregation in Northern cities confining them in congested slums where the schools were substandard.

Poverty and debilitative drug epidemics helped to shape a worrisome syndrome of social risks for Black youth that included, by 2000, high rates of unemployment (21%), incarceration (13%), and unwed teenage motherhood (7%; Perlmann, 2005, p. 84–88). Also affecting Black youth are the lower academic expectations that mostly White, middle-class, female teachers have for Black students, lower funding in schools where they predominate, and the misunderstandings between teachers and students that stem from cultural differences. Tracking Black students' performance over time shows that their high school graduation rates increased in the 1970s, and college enrollment rates grew over the 1990s. Yet gaps between the average test scores of Black students and those of non-Latino Whites on national tests have remained essentially unchanged since 1992. Such achievement gaps are evidence of lingering inequalities in urban education where nearly half of all Black students attend school (NCES, 2007).

Large numbers of low-income families also send their children to urban schools. In 2004, for example, 47% of children attending city schools were living in poverty or near it, including 57% of the nation's poorest children (NCES, 2007). High proportions of low-income families reflect another historical pattern; extreme poverty plagued many immigrant families in the early years of the 20th century. Since 2004, concentrated poverty has been growing again in cities. Children from low-income families are, on average, less healthy than children in wealthier families because they have less nutritionally balanced diets; uneven access to preventative health care; live in congested, polluted neighborhoods; and often have unstable housing. Lead poisoning, which increases aggressive behavior and learning difficulties while lowering intelligence test scores, is one such poverty-related health problem disproportionately affecting city children.

Learning is, therefore, a challenging activity for low-income children, requiring unusual commitments from parents and teachers. But parents living in poverty also read less to their children and engage them in adult conversations less often than their middle-class counterparts (Rothstein, 2004). And urban schools serving poor families are less likely to have highly qualified, experienced teachers than suburban or rural schools (NCES, 2007). Nor do they have the school psychologists, nurses, social workers, speech therapists, and library aides of suburban or rural schools.

These student characteristics make up one pattern that distinguishes urban schools from others. Nearly half of all urban students live in poverty and most of them are immigrants or Blacks. Urban students also score lowest on all national tests (NCES, 2007), and the odds are so stacked against them that schools with predominantly low-income, minority students only have a 1 in 300 chance of getting good test scores (Harris, 2006). The question this pattern raises about urban education is, Why do race, class, and status matter so much in urban education?

Urban Education Size, Organization, and Governance

Urban education is large-scale schooling. In 2004, 64 of the largest 100 school systems in the United States encompassed cities of at least 50,000. The smallest of these big city school systems had 46,600 students, 98 schools, and over 3,100 teachers, while the largest, New York City, had 1.25 million students, 1,225 schools, and over 70,000 teachers. In contrast, the typical school district had fewer than 2,500 students and little more than five schools (Dalton, Sable, & Hoffman, 2006). This too is a longstanding pattern in education: urban districts have historically been the largest in the nation.

At the end of the 19th century, urban school systems began sorting and ranking employees and students and adopted the technology of time and product measurement to pursue efficiency. These changes were explicitly modeled after the corporation, widely believed at the time to be the most efficient form of social organization. For example, the "platoon system" in Gary, Indiana, educated large numbers of diverse students by keeping every classroom and outdoor space in continuous use ("100% efficiency") and educating children based on "a process of scientific measurement leading to a prediction as to one's future role in life" (Kliebard, 1987, p. 99). Today's urban school systems inherited the value of efficiency and bureaucracies as a means to achieve it. They still have more specialized positions and more subunits than smaller systems, and they continue to perfect the methods of measurement to determine educational productivity. The corporate model remains an organizational template; in the biggest cities, top school bureaucrats are paid like corporate executives, some much more than the highest paid state governor.

Some research suggests that large, bureaucratic districts are educational innovators because their expert employees interpret new laws, develop guidelines for change, and solicit program funding. But these same systems often are unresponsive to parents, requiring specialized knowledge to accomplish basic tasks like enrolling a child or locating a particular district official. This is a particular problem for low-income, Black, and immigrant families, who often lack the social capital needed: shared understandings of how the system works, trust of system leaders, and the ability to work in concert without the need of an incentive payment or coercion (Clarke, Hero, Sidney, Fraga, & Erlichson, 2006; Orr, 1999).

Urban education's complexity—the interrelatedness of the school system, other city agencies, and private groups with one another—means that educational decisions often have unintended and unforeseen consequences, and policies enacted elsewhere affect what the schools can do. For example, lax enforcement of environmental standards by health departments increases the challenges of teaching students exposed to toxins such as lead. Similarly, housing authorities that fail to provide enough safe and stable housing for low-income families encourage frequent moves and make it harder for children to maintain academic progress. Further, the culture of second chances in many urban school systems can conflict with law enforcement's no excuses approach to disruptive youth. Social agencies may also expect urban schools to be one-stop service centers for their low-income and immigrant clients (Fong, 2004).

Such complex interactions between urban schools and social service providers began at the turn of the 19th century when both institutions were being formed. Women's groups and settlement house workers saw that the children of immigrants were unsupervised during long stretches of the day and judged them vulnerable to radical ideas and gangs. To dissuade children from such temptations, they created, paid for, and operated kindergartens, playgrounds, afterschool activities, and vacation schools—all of which were eventually absorbed into the educational system or other city agencies. Worries about unsupervised youth also lead to mandatory education laws that made American city

schools the only ones in the world to offer free secondary education to everyone by 1900. Massive school building programs designed to inspire high-minded thinking and reverence for learning, "far superior to the European school" of the era, involved urban education in neighborhood development (Teaford, 1984, p. 263–265). Contemporary neighborhood and religious organizations follow in their predecessor's footsteps, providing ancillary services, seeking curricular changes, and demanding high-quality facilities for their students (Warren, 2001).

Urban school systems are woven into the economic fabric of the city. This began when the American Industrial Revolution benefited from what has been called "the great leap forward in power, speed, energy, and adaptability" (Warner, quoted in Abu-Lughod, 1999, p. 116), creating huge assembly line factories and revolutionizing work. The same period drew millions of European immigrants whom industrial leaders assumed would be laborers. Vocational programs and schools were envisioned to give these youngsters the technical skills and workplace discipline needed for the industrial workplace. Shops and scientific and homemaking laboratories replaced desks and slates in many classrooms. Today, many urban children attend similar programs in high schools dedicated to preparing them for a vocation instead of managerial or professional work.

City schools are also important consumers. They contract with a large variety of businesses for services and supplies. School systems have long depended on educational firms for textbooks and tests, but in the last two decades the variety of core educational services being purchased from private vendors has increased dramatically in urban school systems. Preschool, afterschool, and special education services, business audits, performance assessments, and the management of groups of schools are all recent examples.

Foundations, guiding the decisions of wealthy patrons for a fee, and business associations, investing in product and market development, seek social change and an economic edge by influencing how schools are run and what they teach. Both have influence and use it to gain the attention of policy makers. Between them, they have recently catalyzed substantial change in urban school organization, structure, and curricula (Shipps, 2006).

State and federal officials choose to locate experimental programs in urban schools where students are performing least well, citizens have complaints, large-scale adoption permits study their effects, and the results receive media attention. For example, charter schools—publicly funded schools governed by an outside organization under contract with the state that are permitted to ignore some rules to innovate—constituted only 4% of all schools in 2005, but more than half of them were located in cities. States also punish urban schools. Journalists report on urban education as part of the city political beat, sometimes finding sufficient evidence of financial corruption or professional malfeasance to justify state takeover or fiscal receivership.

Not only is urban education embedded in the local economy and politics through a range of interagency relationships, economically-oriented programs, private contracts, well-heeled reformers, and highly publicized state and federal demands, city schools are also influenced by unions through direct action campaigns and collective bargaining. City teachers were the first to unionize, a process that began in 1895 in Chicago (Murphy, 1990). Since collective bargaining was achieved in New York City in 1962, urban teachers' unions have been more assertive than suburban or rural unions in easing workplace conditions for teachers, initiating peer review of teachers instead of (or in addition to) supervision by principals, demanding a say in school decisions, and most recently, negotiating to operate individual schools (McDonnell & Pascal, 1988).

Urban politicians also want a say in the future of the system. To ensure it, they sometimes agree to alter who makes decisions. In the early decades of the 20th century, mayors supported laws that replaced school trustees, each representing one of the city's immigrant neighborhoods, with a much smaller, elected school board. Centralizing decision-making authority was one way to make school board service attractive to the city's elite, whose advice (and financial contributions) were important to city hall (Tyack & Hansot, 1982). A few cities went further, insisting that the mayor handpick those who would run the schools (Shipps, 2006). Today, the boundaries between city government and school decision making remain blurred. Cities have contentious educational politics partly because local politicians believe their performance ratings and re-election prospects are tied to the school system's reputation.

These organizational and governance characteristics comprise a second pattern that distinguishes urban education: large size helps ensure that educational bureaucrats are skilled, but also adds rules and regulations that make routine tasks difficult. The number and variety of outsiders influencing educational processes and outcomes, and the often competing interests among them, makes city school systems most complex. Combined, these attributes raise a second question: Have size and competing interests made urban education ungovernable?

When urban education's bureaucratic and complex governance is combined with high proportions of low-income, Black, and immigrant students, the result is a two-tiered school politics. White, middle-class natives can influence urban education in ways that the majority of families served cannot. For example, Blacks living in well-established urban communities who seek educational improvements may call upon abundant social capital, which they use to influence policy makers. But if the improvements require support from other groups with which these Blacks have no history of cooperation and few common networks or interests, then intergroup social capital is required. In its absence, changes may occur but not benefit Black children (Orr, 1999). In multi-ethnic cities where different immigrant communities live in isolated enclaves and misunderstand one another, competition among them limits each to second-tier gains. One community or another might benefit from an affirmative action program, but their leaders do not determine which problems are attended to or how policy is formed (Clarke et al., 2006). Thus, a third question arises: How can the politics of urban education be harnessed to overcome the obstacles of race, class, and social standing?

Criticism and Reform of Urban Education

Urban education is often criticized and frequently reformed. It is faulted for lingering gaps between the school completion and performance gaps between low-income, Black, and immigrant children and non-Hispanic Whites. Urban schools are criticized for being too bureaucratic, inefficient, and costly. And city politics may overly influence educational decision making.

Closing Performance Gaps

Some critics argue that attendance and achievement gaps were closed within three generations for southern, central, and eastern Europeans in the early 20th century, proving that continuing low performance by urban immigrants and Blacks is an avoidable disgrace. If allowed to continue, they argue, cities will become permanently divided between middle-class Whites who live well because they have earned college degrees and those with a high school education or less who are confined to dense, badly maintained neighborhoods with inadequate services. This critique of urban education argues for equalizing the educational opportunities among different communities so the two-class city does not become American's future, and fundamentally is a call for educational equity (Rothstein, 2004).

Desegregation

In *Brown v. Board of Education*, the 1954 U.S. Supreme Court declared state-mandated school segregation unconstitutional because it deprives minority children of an equal education. After two decades of massive public resistance and civil rights demonstrations, the court extended its rulings to encompass northern cities in 1973, and allowed test scores and performance gaps to be used as evidence of discrimination in 1977. The resulting urban education desegregation plans involved busing (mostly Black) children from one school to another, redrawing school district boundaries, permitting intra- and interdistrict student transfers, and providing schools with extra services and programs. By the 1990s, few White children remained in city systems. The high costs of mandated services and the continuation of tracking (sorting) students within schools led to new court rulings that released urban school districts from court-ordered desegregation efforts if they had made a "good faith" effort at compliance (Tatel, 1992–1993, p. 63). Urban schools were rapidly resegregated. Low-income students returning to their neighborhood schools lost access to the middle-class social capital that affects college-going, job prospects, and housing options.

Effective Schools

The effective schools approach to urban education's performance gaps had a different impetus. A 1966 federally commissioned study, known as the Coleman Report, concluded that the resources of schools did not influence student learning as much as students' socioeconomic and family characteristics (Coleman et al., 1966). But some educators were unwilling to accept the problems this created for urban education. They had studied a few poorly resourced urban schools with large numbers of low-income, Black, and Latino students that nevertheless produced respectable test scores. Most had strong principals with high expectations for student success and teachers who valued teamwork; these schools had disciplined classrooms and orderly halls, and they emphasized basic skills and regularly monitored student progress (Purkey & Smith, 1983). This approach encouraged whole school reform rather than programs designed for disadvantaged children. Although the strategy proved successful in a few schools, it was difficult to transfer or sustain, thereby failing to make a difference on a scale necessary to improve urban education as a whole (Elmore, 1996).

Standards

With desegregation having been abandoned and the whole school reform approach too limited, another approach emerged. Deteriorating education standards were blamed for poor performance. The standards movement, initiated by the national report "A Nation at Risk" in 1983, won over some civil rights advocates, who embraced common standards, believing that different standards for different student groups simply justifies existing inequalities. Common standards have meant rigorous national standards, or failing that, the close monitoring of state standards to ensure their basic comparability. The No Child Left Behind Act (NCLB) of 2001 embodied these principles. It withheld federal antipoverty education funds from states (and consequently cities) that did not hold all children to the same high expectations, test their performance yearly in Grades 3 through 8, and publicly report the results. But NCLB did not specify which student services states were required to provide for struggling students and overtaxed school systems, and the largest proportion of schools failing to meet state performance standards were in cities. The law has been criticized for insufficient attention (and funding) to predominantly Black, Latino, and low-income schools (Rebell & Wolff, 2007) and for educational inflexibility in the face of diversity. Reauthorization was postponed in 2007 because Congress was uncertain whether the law should be scrapped, strengthened with new mandates, or better funded.

Fixing the System

Other critics focus on the organization of urban districts, arguing that they are too bureaucratic, held hostage by union contracts, or disorganized. These structural characteristics are the reason why, no matter how hard educators try to close performance gaps, little is accomplished. Those focusing on bureaucracy believe Black, Latino, and low-income families' educational needs are thwarted by school administrators who monopolize information and aspire to expand their sphere of influence (Peterson, 1985). Those who identify teachers' unions as the main problem facing urban education believe the unions curtail managerial decision making through collective bargaining, use member dues to lobby against change, and buy influence with lawmakers. Others focus on organizational complexity, which they believe is in need of intergovernmental coordination to lessen the effects of unintended negative consequences (Smith & O'Day, 1991).

Restructuring

Most critics of urban school bureaucracy look to current best practices in large corporations for the antidote. If school administrators' jobs were modeled after managers in the 19th-century corporation, then updating them in modern management techniques should alleviate problems. Restructuring—a term borrowed from the corporate sector—means focusing on the customer, identifying the core business, holding everyone accountable for outcome targets, and devolving decisions about how to meet targets to unit managers. Some envision business as the ultimate customers since they employ school graduates. Focusing on core services encourages outsourcing—contracting with firms or consultants to provide noncore services for a fee. They want teachers and students held accountable for performance targets and view school principals as the key decision-making managers. But restructuring is not a silver bullet. Not everyone agrees that the business of education is workforce preparation (Cuban & Shipps, 2000). Some see too much self-interest by business leaders who stand to benefit from contracts that are weakly enforced. Others argue that restructuring allows business leaders to abandon their own responsibility for poor economic conditions by blaming educators (Cuban, 2005).

Systemic Reform

In the early 1990s, systemic reform, as it became known, aimed to align state and national laws with local instructional policies by coordinating state-mandated curriculum frameworks, student assessments, instructional materials, and teacher professional development opportunities (Fuhrman, 1993). Some advocates wanted to jump-start broad change by initially narrowing the focus to one set of laws or relationships; others would be added later when success was demonstrated in the first. Another group of advocates redefined the responsibilities of different governing authorities to keep them from conflicting and created new intergovernmental coordinating roles for policy makers. But systemic reform proved unwieldy. Implementation was presumed to follow if the laws and rules were aligned—a belief that proved unfounded, partly because relatively little thought was given to how nongovernmental actors would react (Cohen & Ball, 1990).

Privatization and Choice

Teachers' union critics want collective bargaining curtailed, but most believe this cannot be done without also injecting market discipline in the schools. If markets provided the ultimate standard, then parents would avoid schools with a poor reputation while seeking out good ones, thereby spurring more like them (Chubb & Moe, 1990). In one version, schools are funded with educational vouchers—tuition certificates that families cash in for either private school tuition or public school costs. Targeted voucher experiments became common in the mid-1990s through statewide options or urban programs for low-income, Black, and immigrant children. Yet vouchers have not become widespread, partly because they have the potential to "erase municipal boundaries, dissolve neighborhood ties, lower housing prices, and upset student enrollments" in suburban schools, but also because the student performance results are mixed (d'Entremont & Huerta, 2007, p. 40). Charter schools, first proposed by teachers' unions and other educators as a voucher alternative, are a more popular parental choice in urban school districts; such schools can pilot new approaches but do not challenge the traditional organization of urban education.

Changing Decision Makers

Some say that the wrong decision makers have been in charge; consequently, urban education policy is overly influenced by city politics, particularly by city elections. Mayoral machines, in which the mayor controls policy by offering tangible benefits to each constituency in exchange for their loyalty, depletes city resources without improving services. Today, the argument goes, urban education reflects the vestiges of machine politics because it employs the largest workforce in the city and has the biggest budget, making it an attractive place to employ political appointees, purchase goodwill from businesses and community-based organizations with sole-source contracts, and hide deficits (Mirel, 1993). Education decision making is centralized and distorted. Low-income, Black, and Latino students are being failed by urban schools because their parents' votes can be more easily

(and cheaply) purchased with jobs in the system (Rich, 1996). In this critique, poor school performance characterizes urban education because mayors are not focused on improving them.

Decentralization

Initially, decentralization was intended as an alternative to desegregation stalled in cities by White backlash against integration (or "White flight"). These early plans involved creating new administrative subunits between the central board (dominated by city elites) and the schools, which were mostly serving low-income Black and immigrant children. The new organizational units were meant to involve minority parents in decision making. Some community activists envisioned community control as a way to build the social capital of low-income Black and Latino communities. But the first wave of decentralization was soon criticized for its own neighborhood-level patronage and cronyism, and a lack of democratic participation (Ravitch, 1988). A second wave in the 1990s made parents decision makers in their own children's schools, where it was presumed they had the most at stake and would avoid unwise decisions (Bryk, Sebring, Kerbow, Rollow, & Easton, 1998). But these local school councils proved to be most effective in schools where the parents were already middle-class. Principals co-opted many parent councils, and councils themselves seemed to legitimize decisions that central officials had already made, while failing to equalize resources across the system (Malen, Ogawa, & Kranz, 1990).

Mayoral Control

Paradoxically, the latest effort to change the governance of urban schools is to formalize the informal power of the mayor. When made the head of the school system, the mayor's educational decisions are a matter of public record. Each voter's task is theoretically simplified; every vote cast is a referendum on the mayor's educational performance. This is said to be more democratic because more citizens vote for mayor than for school boards. Mayors can better coordinate city services and schooling than superintendents, it is argued, because mayors have longer tenure than the typical urban superintendent and are not beholden to an educational bureaucracy. Mayors may also call upon sources of funding not available to school boards for balancing school budgets and to avoid teachers' strikes. And some argue, mayors have incentive to do whatever is needed to post test score gains (Wong, Shen, Anagnostopolous, & Rutledge, 2007). But mayors in charge of the schools keep a tight lock on information and spin the education coverage to their advantage, often failing to release bad news. They avoid sharing authority; some even turn formerly public school board meetings into private advisory councils. With one person in charge, his or her talents become paramount. And voting for mayor is not a single-issue choice, so citizens may get the mayor they want for policing or property taxes, but not the education mayor they need (Henig & Rich, 2004).

Urban Education in the 21st Century

Urban education in the 21st century inherited most of its defining characteristics from a century ago. Those characteristics—a preponderance of immigrant, Black, and low-income students and a large bureaucratic organization in a complex and highly political environment—have become its defining problems. If the poor performance data on the urban education cited at the beginning of this chapter is adequate evidence, decades of reform have left these problems largely intact. This combination of sticky problems and slippery solutions suggests that we may need to take these defining characteristics as inevitable and routine, and reframe the problems instead.

We might reconceptualize race, class, and economic status differences as inevitable, even desirable, tackling instead the negative social consequences they have for children in urban schools. We might focus less on minority group behavior, performance, and distinctiveness using a standard measurement ruler, and more on how Whites, Blacks, Latinos, and other immigrants experience the categories that define them. The goal would be to give more responsibility for fixing the negative consequences of race, class, and ethnic differences to the most powerful without lowering expectations for anyone. As one researcher writes, "everybody [currently] blames the teachers, parents, and students . . . toiling in city schools . . . rather than the parents moving out to the suburbs, governors, or presidents" (Pollack, 2004, p. 51). Shifting the emphasis would mean distinguishing between the effects of racial and ethnic classifications on Blacks, Whites, and Latinos and how these terms are used as categories of personal identity. Since the students to whom the term minority refers are beginning to predominate in suburban school systems (NCES, 2007), this definitional characteristic of urban education may soon become a characteristic of American public education in general. Sooner rather than later, we may define urban education by its organizational and political characteristics more than its students' socioeconomic status.

Standards, systemic reform, and mayoral control all suggest ways that 21st century urban schooling can reconceptualize size, bureaucracy, and complexity too. Standards reveal the power of high expectations and goals to guide reform in a big system. Systemic reform acknowledges the importance of prioritizing some activities across the bureaucracy and between levels of government, so they do not work at cross-purposes. Mayoral control focuses on the leadership needed to sustain a coalition of action in the face of bureaucratic inertia, complex motives, and unintended consequences. All three implicitly acknowledge that politics is required to change urban education. Coalitions must be built and sustained, leadership identified, laws passed, and implementation monitored by citizens with a stake in the outcome. Acknowledging the political importance of urban education may help us get beyond comparisons of social and economic capital without denying their real consequences. The politics of building civic capacity, for example, involves cooperation across boundaries of race and class, economic status and neighborhood (Stone, Henig, Jones, & Pierannuzi, 2001). It focuses attention on coordinating the many local interconnected civic institutions that are needed to improve schooling, but also on the full and equal participation of low-income, Black, Latino, and other immigrant parents. It is simultaneously a grassroots process of community organizing and an elite effort to mobilize resources and clarify goals. Those looking for civic capacity in urban school reform have generally found it lacking so far, but it may be the one overlooked resource for improving urban education.

References and Further Readings

Abu-Lughod, J. L. (1999). *New York, Chicago, Los Angeles: America's global cities*. Minneapolis: University of Minnesota Press.

Bryk, A. S., Sebring, P. B., Kerbow, D., Rollow, S., & Easton, J. Q. (1998). *Charting Chicago school reform: Democratic localism as a lever for change*. Boulder, CO: Westview Press.

Chubb, J. E., & Moe, T. M. (1990). *Politics, markets and America's schools*. Washington, DC: The Brookings Institution.

Clarke, S. E., Hero, R. E., Sidney, M. S., Fraga, L. R., & Erlichson, B. A. (2006). *Multiethnic moments: The politics of urban education reform*. Philadelphia: Temple University Press.

Cohen, D. K., & Ball, D. L. (1990). Relations between policy and practice: A commentary. *Educational Evaluation and Policy Analysis, 12*(3), 249–256.

Coleman, J., Campbell, E., Hobson, C., MacPartland, J., Mood, A., Weinfield, A. F., et al. (1966). *Equality of educational opportunity* (Research Report). Washington, DC: U.S. Government Printing Office.

Cuban, L. (2005). *The blackboard and the bottom line: Why schools can't be businesses*. Cambridge, MA: Harvard University Press.

Cuban, L., & Shipps, D. (Eds.). (2000). *Reconstructing the common good: Coping with intractable dilemmas*. Stanford, CA: Stanford University Press.

Dalton, B., Sable, J., & Hoffman, L. (2006). *Characteristics of the 100 largest elementary and secondary school districts in the United States: 2003–04* (No. NCES 2006–329). Washington, DC: National Center for Educational Statistics, U.S. Department of Education.

d'Entremont, C., & Huerta, L. A. (2007). Irreconcilable differences? Education vouchers and the suburban response. *Urban Education, 21*(1), 40–72.

Elmore, R. F. (1996). Getting to scale with good educational practices. *Harvard Educational Review, 66*(1), 1–26.

Fong, A. (2004). *Empowered participation: Reinventing urban democracy*. Princeton, NJ: Princeton University Press.

Fuhrman, S. H. (Ed.). (1993). *Designing coherent education policy: Improving the system*. San Francisco: Jossey-Bass.

Harris, D. N. (2006). *Ending the blame game on educational inequity: A study of high-flying schools and NCLB.* Tempe, AZ: Education Policy Studies Laboratory, Arizona State University.

Henig, J., & Rich, W. (Eds.). (2004). *Mayors in the middle: The politics of governance and urban school reform.* Princeton, NJ: Princeton University Press.

Kliebard, H. (1987). *The struggle for the American curriculum, 1893–1958.* New York: Routledge & Kegan Paul.

Malen, B., Ogawa, R. T., & Kranz, J. (1990). What do we know about site-based management? In S. Clune & J. Witte (Eds.), *Choice and control in American education* (pp. 289–342). San Francisco: Falmer Press.

McDonnell, L. M., & Pascal, A. (1988). *Teacher unions and educational reform.* Santa Monica, CA: Center for Policy Research in Education, Rand Corp.

Mirel, J. (1993). *The rise and fall of an urban school system: Detroit, 1907–1981.* Ann Arbor: University of Michigan Press.

Murphy, M. (1990). *Blackboard unions: The AFT and the NEA, 1900–1980.* Ithaca, NY: Cornell University Press.

National Center for Education Statistics. (2007). *Status of education in rural America.* Retrieved October 27, 2007, from http://nces.ed.gov/pubsearch/pubsinfo.asp?pubid=2007040

Orr, M. (1999). *Black social capital: The politics of school reform in Baltimore, 1986–1998.* Lawrence: The University Press of Kansas.

Perlmann, J. (2005). *Italians then, Mexicans now: Immigrant origins and second-generation progress, 1890–2000.* New York: Russell Sage.

Peterson, P. E. (1985). *The politics of school reform 1870–1940.* Chicago: University of Chicago Press.

Pollack, M. (2004). Race wrestling: Struggling strategically with race in educational practice and research. *American Journal of Education, 111,* 25–67.

Purkey, S., & Smith, M. S. (1983). Effective schools: A review. *Elementary School Journal, 83*(4), 247–252.

Ravitch, D. (1988). *The great school wars* (Vol. 2). New York: Basic Books.

Rebell, M. A., & Wolff, J. R. (2007). *Reauthorizing NCLB: A summary of recommendations.* New York: Campaign for Fiscal Equity, Teachers College, Columbia University.

Rich, W. (1996). *Black mayors and school politics: The failure of reform in Detroit, Gary, and Newark.* New York: Garland.

Rothstein, R. (2004). *Class and schools.* New York: Teachers College Press.

Sanjek, R. (1996). The enduring inequalities of race. In S. Gregory & R. Sanjek (Eds.), *Race* (pp. 1–17). New Brunswick, NJ: Rutgers University Press.

Shipps, D. (2006). *School reform, corporate style: Chicago 1880–2000.* Lawrence: University Press of Kansas.

Smith, M. S., & O'Day, J. (1991). Systemic school reform. In S. Fuhrman & B. Malen (Eds.), *Politics of curriculum and testing* (pp. 233–267). Bristol, PA: Falmer.

Stone, C. N., Henig, J., Jones, B. F., & Pierannuzi, C. (2001). *Building civic capacity: The politics of reforming urban schools.* Lawrence: University Press of Kansas.

Tatel, D. S. (1992–1993). Desegregation versus school reform: Resolving the conflict. *Stanford Law and Policy Review, 4,* 61–72.

Teaford, J. C. (1984). *The unheralded triumph: City government in America, 1870–1900.* Baltimore: Johns Hopkins University Press.

Tyack, D. B., & Hansot, E. (1982). *Managers of virtue: Public school leadership in America 1920–1980.* New York: Basic Books.

Warren, M. R. (2001). *Dry bones rattling: Community building to revitalize American democracy.* Princeton, NJ: Princeton University Press.

Wong, K. K., Shen, F. X., Anagnostopolous, D., & Rutledge, S. (2007). *The education mayor: Improving America's schools.* Washington, DC: Georgetown University Press.

30

Economics and School-to-Work

Bridget N. O'Connor

New York University

Lisa S. Ponti

New York University and Ramapo College

At a time when K–12 education is focusing on meeting standards in reading, writing, and math, students are increasingly not meeting those standards. Perhaps one of the biggest obstacles is that many students do not see the relevance of Shakespeare's plays or Euclidian geometry to their lives. In this chapter, we suggest that one way to instill meaningfulness into learning is to present these young minds with authentic problems and learning opportunities that allow them to apply what they are learning in the academic core. We will focus on how courses in economics and experiences in school-to-work programs can support academic learning; we'll also explore the issues involved in creating rigorous, relevant learning experiences. We will address issues surrounding how education about, for, and through work can create an informed citizenry that both understands its economic system and can operate well within it.

Economics education is about ensuring that students are knowledgeable about the economic system, capable of functioning in a complex economic environment, and aware of the wide range of financial services that are available to them. School-to-work (STW) programs are all about exploring occupations and creating an awareness of the skills they would need to succeed—to develop those skills, to choose careers, and to discover the industry and higher education options that would help them achieve their goals. Successful economics and STW programs integrate academic and career oriented studies; emphasize learning in the context of specific, applied tasks; and in the case of

some STW initiatives, link student work or work-based activities, both paid and nonpaid, back to the classroom.

The questions that are raised here for curriculum developers and teachers are the same as for absolutely every other high school subject area: What should be taught? Who should teach it? How should it be taught? and How can other academic foundations best be integrated with what is being learned? Additionally, what are the roles of parents, the community, and society in general in responding to these questions? For economics and school-to-work to have both rigor and relevance, the participation of these key stakeholders is arguably more important than in other disciplines.

We've organized this chapter by first discussing the what, who, and how of economics education and STW separately. Then, we'll bring them back together in a discussion of how they can be integrated with academic foundations. Our conclusions are a call for educators in all disciplines to bring these content areas into their classrooms.

Economics

The value of economics education can be seen on two levels. First, a well-rounded person should be well versed about how the economic system and its financial services operate. Second, citizens need an understanding of economics if they are to make informed decisions about public policy issues. Although most would agree with these statements, economics education options vary from school system to school system.

What Should Be Taught as Economics Education?

So even though we all espouse that everyone should be economically literate, little agreement exists as to what that means. Some suggest that macroeconomics, the discipline that studies our economic system and includes concepts such as supply and demand, opportunity costs, marginal cost and benefit analysis, and market prices are vital to an informed citizenry. Armed with an understanding of how markets work, citizens are in a good position to vote on the basis of informed decisions. For example, in a Gallup poll, college seniors were asked whether or not they thought the U.S. government should prohibit oil companies from raising the prices of oil and gas in response to a supply shock in the Middle East (Walstad & Allgood, 1999). Fully 40% of those surveyed felt that the government should, in fact, prohibit oil companies from raising their prices as a response to decreased supply. This response reflects a poor grasp of some of the most basic tenets of economics, namely the allocation of scare resources, supply and demand, and open markets. Perhaps Alan Blinder, former Vice Chairman of the Board of Governors of the Federal Reserve System and current professor of economics at Princeton University, said it best: "I believe that a society that has a higher average level of economic literacy will produce better economic policies because the people will demand more of their legislators" (Blinder in Salemi, 1998, p. 36).

On the other hand, high school level economics can be viewed through the lens of personal finance, and enough cannot be said about the need for students to be savvy consumers, particularly knowledgeable about credit cards, mortgages, banking, insurance, and investing. Personal finance offerings, however, have mistakenly been offered as remedial substitutes for academic-level math and have often lacked depth in what is covered. In other words, these offerings tend to be considered applied and remedial, not academic and mainstream. With current curricular trends toward pure academics, school systems that offer economics or personal finance courses usually err in one direction or the other (either the course is too rigorous or it is too easy).

Several organizations have recognized the need for and are pushing an agenda of financial literacy for the country's youth. They include the National Endowment for Financial Education (NEFE), the Jump$tart Coalition for Personal Finance, the National Council for Economic Education (NCEE), and the Financial Literacy and Education Commission (FLEC). Additionally, the Policies Commission for Business and Economic Education (PCBEE) has been actively engaged in establishing the role of business education in financial education. Descriptions of these organizations, along with their Web site addresses, are included in the References and Further Readings section of this chapter.

NEFE says the financial literacy problem is pervasive, citing a report that nationwide, high school seniors from all socioeconomic groups scored an average of just over 50% on general financial knowledge, a below failing grade (National Endowment for Financial Education [NEFE], 2002). This lack of financial competence can have devastating effects later in life, as illustrated by the rising level of personal debt of individuals and the increasing rate of bankruptcy filings. NEFE pushes its agenda as a means to address the gap between haves and have-nots. They argue that low-income and otherwise disadvantaged students have an even greater need to manage their own finances than their better-off counterparts.

Additionally, more than 75% of college undergraduates have credit cards, with most of them holding multiple cards and carrying average debt balances of over $2,700. Between 1990 and 1999, there was over a 50% increase in the annual bankruptcy filings among adults aged 25 and younger. This problem is exacerbated by the escalating debt students take on to finance their college education. In fact, 42% of undergraduate students enrolled in the 2003–04 academic year had accumulated student loan debt and had borrowed an average of $11,600 during the course of their studies (Berkner, Wei, & Carroll, 2006).

Furthermore, many students are taking on private debt to supplement what they are able to borrow under federally funded programs and do not always understand the terms and conditions of these loans. As a result, they are unpleasantly surprised by rising interest rates that are not capped and loans that have no provisions for forgiveness of late payments. The 2007 financial aid office scandal could perhaps have been mitigated to a certain extent if these borrowers had been more adept at comparing loan options and not relied solely on the advice given to them by their college financial aid or outside loan officers. Armed with knowledge of banking principles, students can better ensure that college lending officers structure the best possible loan packages.

Economics education is also part of the standards march. In 1998, NCEE, in connection with its "Campaign for Economic Literacy," enumerated 20 different economics standards that students should master in economics by the time they graduate from high school. These standards, which can be adapted for suitability at numerous grade levels, include such concepts as the scarcity of resources, how these resources are allocated, how market economies operate, and gains from trade and specialization. These standards are grounded in economic theory, and each standard also has personal applicability.

One example is Standard 17, which addresses the issue of understanding the effects of government policies and actions. This standard dictates:

> Students will understand that the costs of government policies sometimes exceed the benefits. This may occur because

of incentives facing voters, government officials, and government employees, because of actions by special interest groups that can impose costs on the general public or because social goals other than economic efficiency are being pursued. (National Council on Economic Education [NCEE], 1998, p. 40)

An everyday example of government involvement that has costs as well as benefits that would be of interest to students is the enforcement of minimum wage laws; and another for students who live in certain urban areas of the United States, the concept of rent control.

Recently, the Jump$tart Coalition (2007) developed a more specific personal finance-related definition of financial literacy that includes having skills to manage one's financial resources for life. National standards have been established in personal finance also and encompass such broad goals. These standards require that students be able to locate, evaluate, and apply financial information to their own lives. To do this, they must know how to set financial goals and create a plan to achieve these goals. Part of this involves developing income-earning potential, as well as the ability to budget their money, understand and use financial services effectively, meet their financial obligations, and build and protect their wealth. (Jump$tart Coalition, 2007).

Who Should Teach Economics?

Typically, states include economics as part of a business education or social studies curriculum. According to a 2007 NCEE survey, 49 states and the District of Columbia included economics in their educational standards. Iowa, the only state without any standards on the subject, included economics as a subset of social studies and required that social studies be taught in Grades 1 through 12. Among the 49 states that included economics in their educational standards, 17 offered a stand-alone, required economics course (NCEE, 2007). Although the other states include economics in their educational standards, they do not provide for separate instruction in the subject. Perhaps content is covered as part of other courses, but no data confirm this.

Given the nature of the standards established and the focus on basic concepts, the curriculum should be taught by qualified instructors who have extensive coursework or even degrees in economics if they are to be expected to provide some depth to these complex topics. With regard to personal finance, the NCEE survey revealed that only 40 states had personal finance standards, and these were often included within the economics standards. At the time of the survey, nine states required a course with personal finance content be offered, and only seven states required that a student take a personal finance course (NCEE, 2007).

The Policies Commission for Business and Economic Education linked the National Business Education Association's *The National Standards for Business Education* with a 2001 policy statement that suggests every business educator should be competent to provide financial education as well as take the leadership in its development and teaching through partnerships and a K–12 interdisciplinary approach (Policies Commission for Business and Economic Education [PCBEE], 2001). Because most business teachers have taken economics as part of their required business core content, this group of educators is very likely to be competent to teach in this arena.

How Should Economics Be Taught?

A successful macroeconomics course would be taught as a separate course and cover several basic concepts. Keeping the list of basic concepts short allows for more in-depth instruction of each topic, and repeated applications enhance the students' understanding of the material and increase their ability to apply such concepts. Some examples of these topics are supply and demand, markets, scarcity, opportunity cost, and marginal costs and benefits.

The personal finance standards can be taught as a distinct offering, but they could also be handled through an integrated curriculum approach so that students can gain the skills they need without having to spend more time on yet another subject. For example, math courses could have personal finance skills integrated into the existing coursework to include skills such as calculating loan amortization and credit card interest. The New York Stock Exchange supports the Securities Industry Association's Stock Market Game™, which is geared toward students in Grades 4 through 12 and marketed to teachers in all disciplines. In this real-time simulation, students are given virtual cash, and in teams decide how to invest their funds. As part of the learning experience, students follow current events and apply math skills in calculating their earnings. Throughout this virtual simulation, they buy and sell stocks online, and learn firsthand how current events affect stock prices. The developers have also added a national essay contest in which students compete for prizes on essays geared to financial issues. In their National Strategy for Financial Literacy, the FLEC also promotes the use of an integrated curriculum in teaching personal finance as a creative way of giving students valuable life skills, as well as ensuring that support for financial education is not cut when budgets fall or curricula change.

Another experiential-based curriculum is NEFE's High School Financial Planning Program® (HSFPP), a highly interactive curriculum that includes a wide variety of learning modules employing Web resources and student-run assessments. As part of their learning portal, NEFE also includes training modules for teachers, parents, and the general public. In the 2003–04 academic year, impact evaluation was conducted on this program, which is provided to schools at no cost. Findings showed that young people who studied the curriculum for as little as 10 hours not only significantly increased their understanding of money management, but also improved their financial behavior in the ensuing months (NEFE, 2004).

School-to-Work

The concept of learning through experience has been around for decades and is the conceptual rationale for STW programs. John Dewey, in *Democracy and Education* (Dewey, 1916), pushed for "occupations as context for learning" as a means of instilling meaning in learning. Dewey advocated against the notion of vocational *or* academic tracking in schools; he suggested that everyone could benefit from learning through experiential learning. Dewey's thinking evolved around experience and reflection, and resulted in his espoused passion for participatory learning—that we all have common and shared interests—and was also related to his passion for democracy. This is a terrific book to pick up and read—and reread—frequently; Dewey's ideas are timeless with his emphasis on the importance of experience in learning and the resultant development of community and democracy.

While occupational or vocational education was prevalent in comprehensive high schools for decades, the 1994 School-to-Work Opportunities Act attempted to link occupational training with academic and life skills, a key notion of Dewey's work. Under this act, states could receive up to $10 million annually in federal grants to support learning experiences designed to encourage career exploration, to provide students with opportunities to experience what it means to work, to develop skills students could use in the world of work, and to help students come to appreciate the relevance of their academic preparation to their lives and future careers. Most important, STW programs were marketed as a way to motivate all students to want to learn and for students to develop higher order problem-solving and creativity skills that they could apply in their future postsecondary education or employer-sponsored learning and development programs. The term *school-to-work* thus became shorthand to describe the goals of a myriad of experiential, work-based learning programs, and its use as a unifying term has continued beyond the initial legislation.

What Should Be Taught in School-to-Work?

STW goals have been advertised as a means to instill meaningfulness in schoolwork and merge academic with vocational goals. These goals followed reports from the Secretary's Commission for Achieving Necessary Skills (SCANS, 1991), which produced competency listings for skills needed to succeed in the workplace. The resultant complementary report has been foundational for revising many high school curricula. But the size of a school, its access to resources, and its community may actually expand or limit choices. Large urban public schools may

have paid cooperative work programs and job placement services for part-time employment, but STW programs housed in rural schools are often challenged. Suburban schools may even have an advantage over urban and rural districts because they tend to have high degrees of parental involvement and at the same time, access to city resources, including potential internship sites and active professional organizations in the community (Theobald, 1996).

STW or work-based learning initiatives tend to fall under one of four major categories: (1) career awareness, (2) skill development, (3) work-like experiences [nonpaid], and (4) work experiences [paid]. These organizing categories are used here to frame this discussion; however, the list cannot be exhaustive because numerous other new, innovative approaches are continually being implemented.

Career Awareness

Formal initiatives that focus on career awareness make an effort to help students match their own interests and abilities to broad arenas of career possibilities. Career education programs usually include business careers, but may go way beyond. Sometimes schools are organized around careers related to broad specific disciplines such as English, science, or math; or they can be organized around professions such as law, medicine, teaching, or engineering; or around job clusters such as health, hospitality management, real estate, or publishing. Career fairs are schoolwide events whereby representatives of professional associations, industry groups, or the area Chamber of Commerce stage booths where visitors have an opportunity to discuss careers and learn about part-time job opportunities as well as employer-sponsored learning and development programs. Academic institutions participate in such events too, often using them as recruiting sessions.

Mentoring programs require the participation of members of the community and the support of parents. They are usually designed to bring together an experienced job holder and a student who is interested in the mentor's line of work for informal, one-on-one sessions that are part counseling and part career awareness. A good mentor can provide invaluable advice to someone who truly wants to learn more about how to succeed in a particular line of work or adjust to a school or new community. Big Brothers Big Sisters is an example of a community-based mentoring program. Like their community counterparts, school-based mentoring programs often have the additional value of supporting students at risk of dropping out of school because mentors can help students see the connection between what they are learning in school to what they will see in the workplace. No strict guidelines exist for what makes a mentoring program work, but key variables for success include the establishment and buy-in of expectations ahead of time, making and sustaining appropriate matches, and the creation of a feedback loop to the organizing entity to ensure oversight.

Skill Development

Career academies and schools with career majors bring real problem solving to academic classrooms in an effort to show relevance and applied skills. Sometimes job skills are presented as problem-based learning. As California is considered a bell weather state, skill development through career academies may be on the verge of making a big comeback; Governor Arnold Schwarzenegger, who trained as a salesman in an Austrian high school, was cited in a recent report in the *Sacramento Bee* that highlighted Arthur Benjamin Health Professions High School, where the entire curriculum is organized around health care. For example, "students in an algebra class who calculated proper doses of medicine for a child; in a Spanish class, they participated in a discussion of how herbal remedies are used; and in a biology class, they used microscopes to examine how bacteria grew in different mediums—water, alcohol, or hand sanitizer" (Rosenhall, 2007, p. A1).

Tech prep programs take a much different approach to skill development. Begun in the 1980s as a means to develop a much-needed workforce as well as to ensure that noncollege bound students were receiving an education equivalent to their college-bound counterparts, tech prep programs were a reform effort for traditional vocational education programs that had become dumping grounds for the academically challenged. The concept broke the division between high school and college. A 2 + 2 tech prep program provided a means for students to earn a 2-year professional degree as part of their high school experiences. Tech prep ensured that the high school curriculum was rigorous and relevant for all students. The School-to-Work Opportunities Act gave new wind to these initiatives, providing funding for schools to expand their reach to businesses and industries that could partner with learning and development programs, often resulting in job placement immediately after high school (National Tech Prep Network, 2007). Other modifications of the original tech prep model allow all students to earn college credit (not necessarily an associate's degree) while still in high school. In such cases, courses are usually taught by college instructors in subjects including English, accounting, and economics.

Work-Like Experiences

Work-like experiences differ from work experiences in that these are nonpaid jobs. For example, students may work in the school store or other school-based enterprises. Internships, in which students are given highly supervised jobs in an area they might want to explore for a career, are another approach. Usually, internships are not paid work experiences. In service learning, students perform relevant, sustained community service as part of a class assignment. Key to the success of work-like experiences is that they are, indeed, related to a student's career exploration and are tightly monitored by both someone at the school and at the organization in which the student is working.

It is important for us to expand on the service learning practice here because its popularity is on the rise. The National Service Learning Clearinghouse reported that 10 years ago, 25% of K–12 students participated in service learning programs, and that number continues to increase (National Service Learning Clearinghouse [NSLC], 2007). It is important to note that the NSLC definition of service learning includes words like "reflection, discovery, civic responsibility, and community" and that learning outcomes are both for the learner and the participating agency. Students participating in service learning are expected to work in a meaningful, planned, and structured service; to reflect on what that experience meant to them; and to understand that such contributions strengthen their community (NSLC, 2007). Outcomes for cooperating organizations include seeing problems and opportunities with new perspectives and often creative solutions.

It is also important to note what service learning is *not*. It is not one-time volunteering; many organized programs require up to 40 hours of volunteer time. It is not work for which there is no direct supervision or opportunities to apply problem-solving, creativity, or other higher order skills. It is not just logging hours for community service. For service learning to be effective it requires preparation, action, and reflection; these are the hallmarks of all work-based education efforts.

Work Experiences

Sometimes work is just work. When a student works for money during afterschool hours, these afterschool jobs instill work values and habits whether or not the student intends to continue in that line of work after further training or education. Sometimes schools can act as job placement centers, helping make the match between potential employers and members of their student body. On the other hand, paid cooperative education and apprenticeships are tightly coupled with career intentions and usually entail paid part- or full-time work. The student who works part-time may need special scheduling for academic classes. Those working full-time may need opportunities to take academic classes during off hours.

Who Should Lead School-to-Work Initiatives?

Experiences that fall under the school-to-work umbrella obviously are quite different from traditional classroom-based classes. It takes a diverse skill set to organize a career fair or mentorship program, run a job placement office, or supervise interns. Few teacher certification programs exist around competencies needed to perform these tasks. Leaders in STW often come through business education programs; the business content of this focus includes management, marketing, communications, and accounting. Additionally, many central school district offices provide teacher training and maintain databases of service learning opportunities.

How Should School-to-Work Be Taught?

To understand learning, we need to know what motivates students to learn. Indiana University's T. James Crawford said, "No teaching method works if the student doesn't" (Crawford, circa 1980). The motivation to learn can be honed in school with an ultimate goal of preparing students to learn how to learn, thus preparing them for lifelong learning. Those practices that engage the learner in problems, in practice "make learning more significant than teaching—and writing, design, and formatting skills as important as lecturing techniques" (Jarvis, 2001, p. 27). This understanding should completely change methods of instruction that rest on the class lecture method. Building on John Dewey's work, Etienne Wenger posited that learning is not just of personal ability, but positioning yourself within a community. We learn with and from members of our community. Communities, he said, become stale when all they do is bump up against each other (Wenger, 2003). Accepting this premise, STW leadership is all about implementing interventions with a view to what needs to be learned as well as how to help workplace supervisors mentor their charges.

So perhaps the most important success factor in building STW programs is designing appropriate initiatives and taking a detailed, hands-on, personal interest in their development, implementation, and evaluation. Programs that are simply arranged with little or no feedback to participants (everyone involved) do not succeed. "Teaching" in STW is really a curricular and extracurricular management exercise that requires detailing learning goals, creating nontraditional assessments, and developing and implementing a mechanism for continual feedback. Moreover, because of resistance to change in educational practices, the STW champion must also be well versed in public relations if he or she is to advance the STW agenda.

How Can Economics and School-to-Work Be Integrated With Other Academic Instruction?

Personal finance (and to some degree, economics) and STW have been touted as a means to motivate students, providing relevancy to an academic program of study—relevancy that may be exactly what students need to stay in school and find meaning in their academic classes. Although it is true that some of the values behind the development of such programs were for the noncollege bound, this is extremely limiting; the learning outcomes of these programs are the knowledge and skill sets that all citizens need to possess if they are to make informed decisions about how they will spend their working lives, how to be an informed citizen and voter, and how to use the financial services that are necessary components of economic life.

Macroeconomics is an academic discipline, and when offered, students can take economics as part of a college-prep program of study. This course, however, like all other high school courses, should include opportunities for the development of critical reading skills, writing skills, and applied mathematics. Financial literacy, by definition, requires that students "read the fine print"; use math to calculate interest rates; and write business correspondence. School-to-work, on the other hand, will only succeed if it is linked with opportunities for students to use their academic foundations in the pursuit of solving work-based problems or real problems in the workplace. Ensuring that this happens requires the involvement of parents, the community, and society in general to develop the best of programs, implement them soundly, and provide feedback loops to all stakeholders.

No good idea succeeds on its own merit, however, and making money available for program development is not enough, as evaluation of STW grants has demonstrated. Those programs that succeeded had the cooperation of everyone involved: administrators, principals, teachers, counselors, parents, students, the community, and potential employers. As with any educational innovation or reform effort, courses and programs must be linked to educational objectives and all stakeholders need to be on board.

These stakeholder groups have distinct challenges. Because class schedules may need to be rearranged to support off-site jobs, principals have additional tasks. Many teachers of pure academic subjects must often be convinced of the value of such programs, and they must also learn to find or create real-life, work-based problems whose solution requires the application of what they are teaching. Moreover, many teachers do not have the administrative skills needed to manage programs that exist outside the classroom, and this can be a challenge. Career counselors may not understand the value of work-based education for their college-bound advisees, and so they may need convincing of their value. Also, more counselors, teachers, and administrators may be needed to help young adults choose and find work placements because these tasks are time consuming and often daunting.

Of course, there are challenges for the students themselves who have busy curricular and extracurricular schedules, and they must see the value of such learning experiences, like an enhanced resume for prospective university admissions offices or employers. And for any STW program, the community and employers often need coaching on how best to partner with teachers and curriculum designers to design work-based initiatives and learn to run and evaluate effective work and internship experiences. Moreover, schools are often very reluctant (and sometimes unable) to let outside forces help them establish curricula and standards. Finally, one of the most important and often most vocal obstacle are parents who may resist STW initiatives that they mistakenly believe track their children into vocational or remedial education.

Facing Realities

Readers of this chapter who are planning careers—or are in careers—as teachers in high school settings are in a position to make a real difference in the lives of their students. Our goal here has been to describe rationales, opportunities, and obstacles facing these two related, vital curricular areas. Even if you are not an economics teacher or school-to-work coordinator, we hope you are challenged to find ways to bring the work-a-day world into your classes. The 1994 School-to-Work Opportunity Act was not renewed by Congress because, as we suggested earlier, no good idea succeeds on its own merit. Stakeholders simply put up too many obstacles, failing to give a chance to the values of the act, which were to create awareness, relevance, and an understanding of skill sets needed to succeed in not just jobs, but careers. Many school systems read "school-to-work" to exclude the role of colleges and universities in students' planning. This was not the intent of the act. It is surprising that while the most popular undergraduate major today is business, most school systems are not giving students the perspectives on what a career in economics, finance, accounting, management, or marketing would be.

High school social studies teachers can sometimes become certified to teach economics with little or no coursework, and economics is not everyone's favorite subject to teach. Teachers trained in business education are more apt to have this background, but they sometimes do not want to be considered for these roles. It is also surprising that although we know learning initiatives that require active learner participation are in the best position to succeed, many teachers are unable (perhaps because of union restrictions, administrative mandates, or academic background) or unwilling to take a chance on developing lessons or curricula that differ from the mainstream.

Moreover, despite evidence that many schools consider their financial literacy and work-based learning efforts to be quite successful, critics argue that such reforms are not working, citing low levels of learning or suggesting that companies are using internship and apprenticeship programs as recruitment and training departments. Moreover, as schools are continually forced to cut back or eliminate elective offerings, education for and about work are often the first to go. One reason is that it is unclear what makes one initiative successful and another not. Another is that stakeholders are sometimes unable (because of time and money constraints) to develop exemplary programs or may simply not be convinced of these offerings' potential value.

Thus, it may be managing this public relations effort that is the major challenge for schools as they attempt to implement work-based learning initiatives. Confusion and unrealized goals often result as schools experiment with new approaches to learning. Former U.S. Secretary of Education Richard Riley said we need to shift educational paradigms in this country. Work-based education offers a new framework of opportunities for stakeholders to work together to solve educational problems if they can develop a shared vision, which requires the time, effort, and fiscal resources of all involved. A stakeholder who champions the initiative is required in any endeavor.

The goal of education for and about democracy is to instill in our children an appreciation for how to live and work in an exceedingly complex economic environment. John Dewey remains right; experience is often the best teacher, and learning through well-planned activities that are followed up by reflection is a surefire way to ensure motivation for learning and the application of academic skills in real-world problems and practices. Our citizenry needs to know how to make informed decisions about financial products, about national policies, about career options, and how best to make those careers happen. An educated person can apply what is learned in an academic setting. Active learning methods, used in situations that have meaning, result in learner engagement and the development of higher order thinking and problem-solving skills. All of these outcomes are the promise of economics and STW educational offerings that meet so many professed goals.

When we consider that the average person works at least 30 years, helping young adults know the kinds and types of careers open to them—careers that they will find interesting, rewarding, and supportive of their desired lifestyles—ensures that work and career decisions are made for the right reasons. When we engage students fully in their academic lives, we provide the relevance needed for everyone, with even more dramatic results when such programs help ensure that students remain in school. The trick here is to help students make the academic-work-life connections themselves. School systems provide the backdrop for learning practices. It is when school curricula coincide with the learning needs and values of students and their families that learning best happens.

As we close this chapter, we suggest locations where you can find more information about the services and organizations cited here. A sincere hope is that we have challenged you to think outside the box, to consider that learning at all levels of education and life requires skills that are best learned through active problem solving and experimentation. Perhaps armed with a new understanding of the values behind the desirability of economics education, financial literacy, and experiential learning opportunities whereby students can apply what they are learning, you will be in a terrific position to create these learning opportunities yourself.

Web Sites

Financial Literacy and Education Commission (FLEC)
http://www.mymoney.gov
The U.S. Senate established the Financial Literacy and Education Commission (FLEC) to improve the financial literacy of persons in the United States. Its Web site is a

clearinghouse of information about federal financial literacy programs and features links to private sector efforts including financial literacy programs, materials, and campaigns.

Jump$tart Coalition for Personal Finance
http://www.jumpstart.org

The Jump$tart Coalition for Personal Finance is a coalition of not-for-profit organizations, quasi-governmental agencies, and for-profit corporations dedicated to improving the financial literacy of the country's youth. It maintains a clearinghouse of materials for financial education.

National Business Education Association (NBEA)
http://www.nbea.org

The National Business Education Association (NBEA) supports the practice of teaching business subjects from Grades K through 16. NBEA has developed standards for the teaching of business subjects, and its advocacy committee lobbies to further the study of business education. The organization's Web site includes the listing of the Policies Commission for Business and Economic Education (PCBEE) Policy Statements.

National Council for Economic Education (NCEE)
http://www.ncee.net

The National Council for Economic Education (NCEE) is a broad based network of state level organizations, as well as university level centers, that provides educational resources for educators who share the view that economics must be included in the curriculum. Its board of directors includes top officers of Fortune 500 companies, Federal Reserve Regional banks, and universities.

National Endowment for Economics Education (NEFE)
http://www.nefe.org

The National Endowment for Economics Education (NEFE) was founded in 1992 with a mission to develop educational programs in financial planning for professionals and expanded its efforts to include financial education for consumers. In 1997, the NEFE elected to move away from educating professionals and focus solely on the financial education of the nation's consumers.

Policies Commission for Business and Economic Education (PCBEE)
http://www.nbea.org/curriculum/pcbee.html

The Policies Commission for Business and Economic Education (PCBEE), founded in 1959, is a consortium of three business education organizations: Delta Pi Epsilon, the NBEA, and the Association for Career and Technical Education. PCBEE declares its role as defining business and economic education as well as pushing for the teaching of economics. As part of its work, the commission develops two policy statements each year that focus on current concerns and issues in the field.

The Stock Market Game
http://www.stockmarketgame.org

The Stock Market Game™ is created by the nonprofit Foundation for Investor Education. Its stock market simulation is offered in real time and with support from the New York Stock Exchange and the Nasdaq Stock Market.

References and Further Readings

Bailey, T. R., Hughes, K. L., & Moore, D. T. (2003). *Working Knowledge: Work-based Learning and Education Reform.* London: Taylor & Francis.

Berkner, L., Wei, C. C., & Carroll, C. D. (2006). 2003–04 National Postsecondary Student Aid Study (NPSAS:04): Undergraduate Financial Aid Estimates for 12 States: 2003–04. Retrieved May 20, 2007, from http://nces.ed.gov/pubs2006/2006158.pdf

Crawford, T. J. (circa 1980). Lecture presented at Indiana University, Bloomington, IN.

Dewey, J. (1916). *Democracy and education: An introduction to the philosophy of education.* New York: Macmillan.

Jarvis, P. (2001). *Universities and corporate universities.* London: Taylor & Francis.

Jump$tart Coalition. (2007). *National standards in K–12 personal finance education* (3rd ed.). Retrieved May 17, 2007, from http://www.jumpstart.org/guide.html

National Council on Economic Education. (1998). *Economics America—National standards.* Retrieved October 6, 2005, from http://www.ncee.net/ea/standards/standards.pdf

National Council on Economic Education. (2007). *Survey of the states: Economic and personal finance education in our nation's schools.* Retrieved June 18, 2007, from http://www.ncee.net/about/survey2007/NCEESurvey2007.pdf

National Endowment for Financial Education. (2002). *Financial literacy in America: Individual choices, national consequences.* Retrieved December 4, 2004, from http://www.nefe.org/pages/whitepaper2002symposium.html

National Endowment for Financial Education. (2004). *Teens respond well to financial education, study shows.* Retrieved May 17, 2007, from http://www.nefe.org/news/news111504.html

National Service Learning Clearinghouse. (2007). *Service-learning is. . . .* Retrieved May 22, 2007, from http://www.servicelearning.org/welcome_to_service-learning/service-learning_is/index.php

National Tech Prep Network. (2007). *The ABCs of tech prep.* Retrieved May 17, 2007, from http://www.cord.org/upload-edfiles/ABCs%20of%20Tech%20Prep.pdf

Policies Commission for Business and Economic Education. (2001). *This we believe about the role of business education in financial education.* (Policy statement 69, 2001.) Retrieved May 17, 2007, from http://nbea.org/curfpolicy.html

Rosenhall, L. (2007, Feb. 24). Students prepare for college and work. *The Sacramento Bee.* p. A1.

Salemi, M. (1998). How economists can improve economic education [Electronic version]. *The Region 12*(4), 34–37. Retrieved October 11, 2006, from http://proquest.umi.com/pqdweb?did=37703653&sid=1&Fmt=4&clientId=9269&RQT=309&VName=PQD

Secretary's Commission for Achieving Necessary Skills. (1991). *What work requires of schools.* Retrieved June 19, 2007, from http://wdr.doleta.gov/SCANS/

Theobald, P. (1996). *The new vocationalism in rural locales.* Paper presented at the Annual Meeting of the American Educational Studies Association, Montreal, Canada.

Walstad, W., & Allgood, S. (1999). What do college seniors know about economics? [Electronic version] *The American Economic Review 89*(2), 350–354. Retrieved October 28, 2005, from http://proquest.umi.com/pqdweb?did=41912812&sid=1&Fmt=2&clientId=9269&RQT=309&VName=PQD

Wenger, E. (2003). Keynote address at 2003 Practice-Oriented Education Conference, Boston, MA.

31

RURAL EDUCATION

PAUL THEOBALD AND JOHN SISKAR

Buffalo State College

Historically, schools in rural settings are unique educational institutions in both their purpose and their development. Rural schools have been interdependent with the surrounding community. Much of the curriculum and policies of rural schools were designed and adapted to meet the needs and beliefs of the community, and the existence and development of the community was predicated, to a large extent, on what happened in the schools. Even today, one can find many examples of rural schools that are the strongest unifying factor and main support for the communities they serve. In those settings schools help shape the formal and informal boundaries of communities and the identity of community members. This tight school-community connection, however, while lingering in some locales, eroded significantly during the 20th century.

Starting with the beginning of the progressive movement in the 1930s and 1940s, rural schools have been pushed to standardize their policies and practices, consolidate individual schools into larger districts, and institute a curriculum removed or irrelevant to the place or community where the school resides. Today, many organizations, including The Rural School and Community Trust, the National Rural Education Association, and the National Center on Rural Education, work hard to ensure that rural education is given serious consideration. Mainstream groups like the National Education Association and the Educational Commission of the States have interest groups focused on rural education issues. From a 21st-century vantage point, rural schools appear to be a small, almost insignificant part of the total public educational endeavor in this country. But while this may appear to be the case, the reality is that rural schools represent fully one-third of the nation's total and rural students represent fully 20% of all public school students nationwide. Further, the traditional role and characteristics of rural schools reflect an education that is constructivist, place-based, democratic, and respectful of others. These are educational notions that challenge the current emphasis on standards and accountability.

Characteristics That Make Rural Education Unique

There are many factors that combine to make rural education an inherently unique enterprise. There is what sociologists call high "community capital" because people tend to live in rural locales by choice, given the fact that crime rates tend to be low, the locale is beautiful, and there is a strong sense of community. Rural people believe in protecting and supporting children. They tend to support public education and community-based schools.

Schools are perceived as either the most important, or an important, public institution in rural communities. The rural school can be a place that supports services for poor families and children. It is a community center that has facilities for public meetings, voting, exercise, and recreation. It might be the only library in the area and a resource for economic development. The school is often the largest employer and a major supporter of local businesses. Good schools are seen as a way to create a quality local workforce.

Rural schools also have substantial challenges. Rural communities are losing population and the population that remains is aging. Younger people are leaving, especially the most talented, for better jobs elsewhere. All of this results in low and declining property values that in turn result in a decreased ability to adequately fund schools through property taxes.

Poverty is a real issue as well. Most poor counties in the United States, 244 of the 250 poorest, are rural. On average, more children live in poverty in rural areas than in urban areas. Rural communities often struggle to provide adequate housing, access to quality health care, ensure proper nutrition, and supply adequate child care. In general, the infrastructure of the social services is weak. Also, there tends to be less access to philanthropic support from foundations or private individuals.

The remoteness of rural settings attracts a certain group of people, but is not attractive to everyone. There is limited access to goods, entertainment, shopping, and services, and less access to telephone, computers, and the Internet. This not only creates extra challenges for the teacher, it also creates a problem for the school in terms of recruiting and retaining teachers.

One characteristic that surprises many people is the high minority population that is found in rural areas.

> In many rural areas, minority students comprise a greater percentage of a school's population than in urban areas. Often, rural schools have high percentages of Native American and African American students who have unique educational challenges and needs. The number of Hispanic students is also rising in many rural communities, creating a need for additional specialized programs and teachers. (Malhoit, 2005, p. 11)

Cultural Concepts of Rurality and the Development of the Public School

A factor central to understanding rural education is America's cultural conception of rurality, or of what it means to be rural. Stereotypes are commonplace. Rural locales are places where hicks reside, or hillbillies and other country bumpkins, or maybe just "dumb farmers" or "dumb fisherman." This cultural message is ceaselessly delivered by a large variety of electronic media: radio, television, movie theaters, and even various types of computer software. All Americans, but especially impressionable young children, are taught lessons about rural life via televisions shows like *The Beverly Hillbillies*, *The Simple Life*, *The Bob Newhart Show,* and many others; or via movies such as *Deliverance* or *For Richer or Poorer*.

Further, it is completely permissible, and in fact particularly in vogue today, to poke fun at rural residents through the use of what has come to be called "redneck humor." The comedian Jeff Foxworthy has built a career doing this, and many others have followed in his footsteps. Whereas it is culturally out of step for a White person to tell Black jokes at this point in our history, anyone—not just rural dwellers themselves—may tell redneck jokes with total approbation.

This cultural dynamic has not been well studied. In fact, there is virtually no scholarship that yields much insight into this issue. It may be that the cultural trend to denigrate or castigate rural residents as backward or behind the times is a residual phenomenon that dates back to the breakdown of feudalism itself during the 18th century. Feudal power was rural, held by aristocrats and a royal family residing in large rural estates. It was finally usurped by the emerging urban bourgeoisie who grew increasingly wealthy by tapping manufacturing opportunities during the Industrial Revolution. Wealthy, but powerless, they demanded a political voice and political reforms such as extending the franchise, equalizing representation, and separating church and state. The rural opponents of these reforms were "unwilling to change with the times," or "unwilling to pay the price of progress." The fiery English social critic William Cobbett claimed to have witnessed the development of the trend to denigrate rural dwellers during his own lifetime (1750–1835), contending that it was not only England's industrial moguls who began to look down their noses at rural dwellers, but all manner of urban shopkeepers, bookkeepers, craftsman, clerks, and the like.

Since the creation of the United States was in itself a rejection of feudalism, it was also in some measure a rejection of rural power. There should be no surprise that our cultural development has tended to nurture this perspective related to rural life and living. It was gradually turned into a kind of cultural common sense to assume that the future would inevitably be an urban future and that success was something that happened in urban places. When family or neighbors saw real promise in a young man or woman, it was commonplace to proclaim that he or she would go far, meaning, of course, that he or she would end up in a far off urban center as one of society's sophisticates.

Enter the Public School Endeavor: Schools Seen as the Way Out

Although the establishment of what were initially called common schools was originally based on the idea that citizens required an education to shoulder the burden of democracy, the end goal of public schooling gradually shifted (especially in the wake of social Darwinist perspectives related to intellectual wherewithal) toward providing the skills and dispositions needed to become successfully employed. In short, schools gradually became entities designed to prepare students for an eventual occupational destiny.

Enmeshed in a culture steadfastly predicting an urban future for itself, the public school enterprise, especially throughout the 20th century, began to perceive rurality as a condition from which one could escape. Affirming what they understood to be common sense, teachers began to think of themselves as the purveyors of opportunity, the vehicle for success in urban America, missionaries of a sort steadfastly committed to saving talented rural youth and sending them on to urban places.

An excellent study of this very dynamic is Michael Corbett's *Learning to Leave: The Irony of Schooling in a Coastal Community* (2007) even though the setting is rural Nova Scotia. Corbett documents how three generations of rural Nova Scotia students pitted school definitions of success against their desire to stay home and become an adult part of their community. His work and that of many others helps us understand larger cultural perspectives related to rural life and living. With this in mind, we shouldn't find it surprising that rural education appears to be a small part of the public education endeavor when in reality it is a sizable segment of that endeavor.

Some Useful History

For most of our history as a nation, the dominant school experience was rural—almost the opposite of what exists today. As a consequence, many educational policies and practices that are taken for granted were fought over for decades in the nation's rural schools. It is important to recall that America's founding generation, and several thereafter, rejected the idea of creating systems of free schools. It wasn't until 50 years after the country's founding, during the late 1830s, that states began to create free school systems. The drive to create free school systems was coincident with the drive for universal manhood suffrage, the emerging women's suffrage movement, the establishment of abolitionist societies, the call for city parks and green spaces, the establishment of the Sunday school concept, the drive for prison reform, and the reform of insane asylums. In short, the establishment of free school systems was coincident with a growing democratic impulse in the United States, an impulse famously documented by a French visitor, Alexis de Tocqueville, in his classic text *Democracy in America* (1836).

As a consequence, as the 19th century progressed, any obstacle to free schools for all was increasingly seen as undemocratic. In fact, by the time Nebraska became a territory under the terms of the 1854 Kansas-Nebraska Act, certain key school issues had surfaced as litmus tests of a state's commitment to democratic principles. Did a state make provisions for a totally free education? Or was it permissible for local school officials to charge tuition? Did the state direct local school authorities to provide free textbooks to all students? Or did they countenance the requirement that parents must provide required texts? Was the state careful that all children meant *all* and that persons of color were not excluded? Were women allowed to serve on school boards or to hold the office of county or state

superintendent? What about tenant farmers living and working within a given school district? Could they vote at school board meetings, or were they prohibited from voting as nontaxpayers? Did the state leave loopholes that would allow for egregious discrepancies in funding the state's common schools? What about private religious, or in the parlance of the late 19th century, sectarian, schools? Did the state permit the dispersal of school funds to such schools? Where did the state stand on the issue of compulsory education? Was it enough to provide a system of common schools, or was the state ready to ensure that every child in the state attended one?

From a modern vantage point it is difficult to appreciate what a challenge it was to develop a free school system. Any school expenses that could be paid through a tuition charge saved local taxpayers money. Charging tuition was especially popular if a district contained tenant families who were not taxpayers. What is more, tenant farmers were typically denied a voice at school meetings and were therefore unable to protest the use of tuition for school funding. Many states failed to end tuition as a part of common school funding long after common schools were established. For example, New York continued the practice until the late 1860s.

Eligible voters in all states since the Jacksonian suffrage reforms of the 1830s included White males over age 21. The 14th Amendment to the U.S. Constitution added Black males to the list of voters. In the matter of voting for school board officers or voting at school board meetings, however, the vote was reserved for freeholders, or to those eligible to pay property taxes in the district. Since all decisions surrounding the provision of schools were a direct expense to local taxpayers, it was assumed that they alone should make the necessary decisions. Generally, women were allowed to vote if they were widows or by other means became property owners, but this was by no means a given and there was considerable confusion over the issue. Consequently, extending the right of women to vote in school elections and at school meetings became a political issue and one of the litmus tests for gauging the measure of democracy within a given state. Iowa, Nebraska, and North Dakota were among the first to officially sanction the right of women to be qualified to voice their views in the affairs of the school. An 1881 Nebraska school law amended earlier language by inserting a mere three words concerning who was eligible to vote at school board meetings, "Every voter *and every woman* who has resided in the district forty days, and is over twenty-one years of age, and who owns real property in the district, shall be entitled to vote at any district meeting" (Annotated Statutes of the State of Nebraska, 1881, p. 820).

A similar litmus test was whether or not tenant farmers who merely rented land in the district ought to be allowed to exercise a voice in the affairs of the schools their children attended. Once again, Nebraska was among the leaders in establishing this democratic provision. Just 2 years after expressly granting women this right, the school law related to who could vote in school elections and at school meetings was again amended, this time reading, "Every person, male or female, who has resided in the district forty days and is twenty-one years old, and who owns real property in the district, or personal property that was assessed in his or her name at the last annual assessment; *or has children of school age residing in the district*, shall be entitled to vote at any district meeting" (Compiled Statutes of the State of Nebraska, 1881. Second Edition with Amendments 1882, 1883, and 1885, p. 549).

States in the trans-Mississippi west were also leaders in promoting the cause of free textbooks for all schoolchildren, an issue that became a part of the Farmers Alliance and Populist Party platforms during the late 1880s and early 1890s. Most states ignored the popular demand for this provision until well into the 20th century. But as early as 1877, the state superintendent of public instruction reported that 66 Nebraska school districts had voluntarily purchased textbooks for all students in their schools. By 1880, the number rose to 246; by 1886, 422. In 1891, Nebraska became one of the first states in the union to pass legislation requiring all districts to provide free textbooks. Six years later this act was tested through litigation to see if various sorts of school supplies must also be provided freely. The Nebraska Supreme Court ruled that "we do not think the term *text-books* should be given a technical meaning, but that it is comprehensive enough to and does include globes, maps, charts, pens, ink, paper, etc., and all other apparatus and appliances which are proper to be used in the schools in instructing the youth" (*Affholder v. McMullen*, 1897, p. 544).

It is fair to look at the 19th century as the time when many of the bugs were worked out of America's public education system—though several, especially those related to race, were left unresolved, to be tackled in the next century. Because the 19th century educational experience was overwhelmingly rural, the terms and conditions of free public schooling were largely worked out in the nation's rural schools. But as the 19th century turned over to the 20th, the heyday of rural education was about to end. In keeping with cultural developments identified earlier, rural schools were gradually regarded as subpar, not as good as schools in the city. In fact, by the end of the first decade of the 20th century, it is possible to find references to a new concept, one that ostensibly held the power to convert rural schools into city schools.

Rural Education and School Consolidation

As noted earlier, for the largest part of our history as a nation, rural schools dominated the educational landscape and represented the typical school experience for average Americans in all states. They remained so until 1918 when urban schools became the most typical school experience for Americans. By the 1980s, however, the primary educational experience had shifted again to sub-urban schools. In the process, rural schools fell to the point where they are now, the *least* common school experience in the nation, albeit still a significant portion of the overall total.

This dramatic turnabout reflects the widespread embrace of an educational policy known as school consolidation. Few would argue with the proposition that school consolidation—closing a small school or schools to make a bigger one elsewhere—has nearly always been economically motivated. This is not to say that it has nearly always been touted as a school finance measure—far from it. Throughout the middle decades of the 20th century it became fashionable to equate school consolidation with school improvement. The popular cultural maxim, bigger is better, was often used to sell the concept. The argument went like this: why support a handful of poorly supplied and poorly taught one-room elementary schools when one well-supplied and well-taught school would do?

Of course, the school improvement argument was augmented with the economic one: a consolidated school will cost less—residents may pay lower taxes if a school consolidation plan is allowed to take place. It should be noted that these arguments lacked much in the way of persuasive power until technological developments (most notably the internal combustion engine) made it possible for school children to get to and from school at distances well beyond what they could reasonably walk. When the utility of the automobile and school bus was made even more attractive by the lure of indoor plumbing, central heating, electric lights, and so forth, school consolidation became overwhelmingly popular. Well-educated sophisticates were convinced that rural school consolidation couldn't proceed fast enough. Colleges and schools of education all across the country were filled with professors who possessed unquestioning faith in consolidation as a policy option that would always and everywhere improve the education of youth and save taxpayers money. It has only been in recent years that the wisdom of this policy has received serious scholarly scrutiny.

In practical terms, school consolidation meant first that farm children, instead of walking to a neighborhood one-room school, boarded a bus and went to school in town. The next wave of consolidation meant that children in and around very small towns no longer walked or were bussed to the town's school, but were bussed to yet another larger town some distance away. The third wave of consolidation was primarily confined to high schools and involved closing consolidated schools and combining the secondary schools of four and five towns into one or two county high schools. A fourth wave has been identified as well, this one moving back over towns that maintained K–8 attendance centers and closing them down in the interest of implementing the middle school concept.

Each successive wave has simultaneously generated more vigorous local opposition and further stretched the plausibility of the standard rationale supporting consolidation, namely that it will improve the educational program for children while it saves taxpayer money. In fact, as late as 2007, it is impossible to point to any substantive research which suggests that school consolidation may do these things. The reason has to do with a mix of factors, some economic (e. g., matters of scale) and some tied to the nature of teaching and learning (e. g., the significance of teacher-student ratios).

It was hardly the cost and rarely even the quality question that concerned the parents and children affected by proposed consolidations. Opposition to school consolidation was rampant because rural Americans psychologically connected the school with the well-being of their community. Community allegiance and affection were affronted by the very suggestion of closing down the local school—a circumstance that resulted in court challenges in every state. Again, as late as 2007, the courts, invariably deciding cases on the basis of past judicial precedent, allowed state and local educational authorities free reign with respect to determining the number of school buildings a district will support and which students will attend them. In other words, with some exceptions—victories in lower courts that were thereafter lost upon appeal—the courts have continued to defend consolidation as a viable school policy, the lack of evidence to support it notwithstanding.

Some educational researchers have tried to use research on optimal school size to defend efforts at consolidation. The concept rests on the assumption that a certain number of students will maximize a school's revenue while keeping the student-teacher ratio fairly low, thus maximizing student achievement. This assumption has some merit, but is very easily confounded by contextual variables. What if it takes a 2-hour bus ride one way to reach the total number of students deemed desirable? Such a circumstance would almost certainly jeopardize the academic performance of the students forced to spend 4 hours a day on a bus in addition to a regular school day; just as it would skew economies of scale by increasing transportation costs. It turns out that research on optimal school size lends little support for rural school consolidation.

Each new governor and each new group of state legislators, when faced with the first budget-cutting exercise, almost immediately jumps to school consolidation as a cost-saving measure. It is an easy, convenient solution. It affects only rural dwellers from the smallest communities—a distinct minority among state voters. For their part, residents of small communities are left to their own devices for fighting back. They might create partnerships with similarly targeted communities and schools, but, by and large, the nation's colleges and universities have ignored the plight of the victims of school consolidation.

Without question, in terms of sheer numbers, more pitched battles between local schools and state departments of education have been waged over the issue of consolidation than any other school issue. These battles, however, have been nonviolent and civil when compared with the battles waged by majority populations fearing the inclusion of racial and ethnic minority children within their schools. Although we tend to think of this as an urban or suburban phenomenon, this was not always the case. In fact, two of the five cases decided under the umbrella of *Brown v. the Board of Education of Topeka, Kansas* were rural schools. In some places in Texas and California, school consolidation as a policy option was used as a way to segregate racial minorities in one school while preserving another as a White school.

School consolidation represents a wonderful example of the power of cultural assumptions. Because of the antirural bias in our culture, symbolized by the treatment afforded rural dwellers in the media, we have uncritically adopted consolidation as a reform measure with almost no evidence to support it. We can't say with any certainty at all that it will improve student achievement or save money—yet the concept continues to be promoted and practiced in the 21st century.

There is more than a small irony that at the same time school consolidation is being touted, the trend in larger districts is toward adopting a small school model. In some cases it means creating schools within schools to take advantage of the power of close relationships to affect learning. Research shows smaller schools work better. Small schools consistently display better student achievement, higher graduation rates, fewer discipline problems, fewer violent incidents, less vandalism and theft, reduced truancy, less substance abuse, and decreased gang participation. Small schools have higher rates of participation in extracurricular activities and, in general, students feel greater school connectedness with less alienation. Similarly, teacher morale is better and teachers exhibit more positive attitudes when teaching in a small school setting.

Small schools are more likely to adopt new, more effective instructional strategies, like flexible scheduling, cooperative learning, interdisciplinary learning, and to create learning environments that are active and experiential. There is ample research that these strategies help students, especially minority and disadvantaged students. Other strategies—looping, multiage, and heterogeneous classes—that urban and suburban schools are trying hard to implement represent the traditional organizational structure of rural schools.

Small classes, often a hallmark of small schools and certainly the norm in rural schools, also helps students. When class size is less than 20, students produce higher academic achievement. The greatest gain is among disadvantaged and minority students. All of this demonstrates that inputs into the educational system are crucial variables related to student learning. The current policy milieu has completely shifted the educational focus to outputs, that is, standards met and test scores achieved. The intentions behind this shift may be laudable, but we are beginning to understand that this focus comes with significant costs. This is especially the case with the push to consolidate rural schools.

The Unmeasured Costs of School Consolidation

As noted earlier, buying into some of our most baseless cultural assumptions, such as bigger is better, educational policy makers have come to view school consolidation as synonymous with school improvement. During the past seven or eight decades, for instance, the United States went from supporting some 140,000 school districts down to just 16,000. Consolidation has been a defining characteristic of education throughout the 20th century. In the arena of educational policy we have set in motion a kind of community-destroying force. What is only now becoming clear is that the disintegration of community comes at an enormous cost. In fact, it is becoming apparent that the health and well-being of democracy itself rests on our ability to maintain healthy communities.

The award-winning work of Harvard sociologist Robert Putnam unveiled this insight. During the early 1990s, he and several colleagues went to Italy to study the implementation of a new governmental structure, one that put a good deal of decision making into local communities. Putnam was especially interested in why the north of Italy responded by establishing a vital, growing economy, while southern Italy languished on the verge of economic depression. In a book called *Making Democracy Work* (1993), Putnam and his colleagues argued that it was an abundance of local associations in northern communities that made democracy work by giving citizens a political role to play.

Scholars from a variety of disciplines—communitarians, as they came to be known—had already begun making the theoretical connections between healthy communities and well-functioning democratic processes by the time Putnam published his study of Italian democracy. But Putnam's work gave the scholarly community a chance to see how the argument works in a real-life situation. On the heels of this contribution, Putnam almost immediately set to work establishing the connection between the simultaneous and reinforcing diminishment of community and democracy in the United States. The result was the publication in 2000 of *Bowling Alone: The Collapse and Revival of Community in America.*

Bowling Alone is the story of the collapse of American participation in local associations of the sort that feed democratic participation. Americans across every demographic, whether it is race, income, gender, religion, or age, are participating less and less in the affairs of their local communities. As a sense of community disappears, democracy languishes. Many Americans—almost half—don't bother to vote, and most wouldn't think of running for office. Volunteering for a community project and charitable giving has fallen to the lowest levels ever. In part, these things have occurred because of increased television viewing, time spent commuting to and from work, and access to a large variety of entertainment options; but another part of the explanation is that political, economic, and educational policy has been demonstrably unkind to

American communities. School consolidation looms large in this regard, but larger cultural assumptions about where success lies are to blame too. When schools send the message that rural youth must leave their communities to be successful, they are tearing at the fabric of American community—contributing in a significant way to the collapse of community Putnam so ably identified.

The result is that the United States has become a far less democratic country over the past three decades—falling to near the bottom of the top 25 democracies on nearly every measure of democracy (Dahl, 2002). Still, Putnam identified the nation's small towns and rural places as locales that retain a sense of community, places where you can still see vestiges of community participation of the sort that animated this country much earlier in our history. Many believe that the nation's best hope for a more democratic future lies in an educational system that places a high value on human community. This argument contends that the next generation—enculturated into an ethic of attending to the needs of one's community, rather than to one's own future occupational self-interest—will be better equipped to deal with the dire social and ecological circumstances that they will inevitably inherit.

Rural Education in the 21st Century

What does the future hold for rural education? If the current educational and social climate continues and education is only examined in terms of the content students need to learn, rural education will continue to falter. With the widespread adoption of learning standards, there has been a tacit and unquestioned acceptance of the proposition that the primary, if not exclusive, purpose of schools is to teach content. One has only to look at the No Child Left Behind Act to understand this proposition.

Throughout the history of education in the United States, however, there has been continual debate and shifting policy related to the role of schools. While today's policy makers have focused on answering the question, What subject matter do students need to master? others have suggested that reforms in education should more closely reflect global societal and developmental concerns. They want to examine other questions, such as: Should schools be helping individuals develop their own strengths and interests? Do schools have a responsibility to develop citizens who will be able to contribute to society, and if so, does that mean that schools should help create an effective workforce, a citizenry ready to participate in democracy, or simply a literate populace? Should schools contribute to a society that is healthy and physically fit? Do we teach a subject because it will help children to understand the world or because society needs more experts in a given field?

Those interested in the needs of tomorrow's workforce recognize the need for the next generation of workers to be proficient with creative thinking and problem solving, working as part of a team, teaching others, working with diversity, interpreting and communicating information, and using computers to process information. Multiculturalists want students to have a deep understanding and empathy for people and cultures different from their own. Communitarians want students to understand the role of place and community. Constructivists want students to think and critically process information. Social reconstructivists, those who feel the purpose of schools is to solve society's problems, want students to actively participate in and attempt to better society. Many of these educational groups have rallied for more interconnected, interdisciplinary learning experiences so that students can understand the relationships between what they learn in one class or subject and another.

For instance, communitarians emphasize the study of place. A particular place on earth can be a kind of curricular lens through which all traditional school subjects may be closely examined in an integrated way. The immediacy and relevance of place in the lives of students can be a huge catalyst to deep learning. The exploration of community is an active and experiential approach, in which students will work with each other and with adults in the community. The discovery that develops as students learn why the place looks and feels as it does yields a kind of intellectual satisfaction that cannot be matched even by the complete mastery of a disconnected textbook curriculum.

Underpinning various theoretical perspectives is an understanding that students need to be connected to and working within their own community and the wider world on real-life problems. Students need a curriculum that goes beyond teaching content in isolation. They need to develop an appreciation and predilection for being actively engaged in society. They need to practice democratic processes and learn how to work collaboratively with people who may see the world differently.

All of these are things that traditional rural education does well. A dramatic example that will help illustrate the point is the case of the small town of Howard, South Dakota (population 900). A business teacher at the high school created a rough plan for a community-oriented learning unit. After acquiring the support of his principal and a minigrant of $500 from a nearby university, he worked with his students to develop a plan to measure the community's cash flow—how much was earned there, where it was spent, and what it was spent for. The students conducted town meetings with local business owners, consulted with the county auditor, and engaged in long debates with all stakeholders over the wording on their surveys.

It was a courageous undertaking, and the students were never shy about proceeding. They unabashedly asked community members throughout Miner County to reveal the intimate details of their income and spending habits. When the surveys were collected, the students found themselves with a phenomenal 64% response rate and an enormous amount of data to analyze. Using sophisticated statistical procedures, the students sorted data by income level,

spending location, spending category, and other parameters. All takes on the data revealed much the same lesson: the people of Howard spent most of their income in the larger and more distant cities of Mitchell and Sioux Falls.

Student analyses of the data were reported in the local newspaper before the school year was out. The community response was overwhelming. When Howard citizens saw how much they were spending outside of the community, they changed their spending habits. They bought much more locally. Revenue from local sales tax began to skyrocket. The county auditor reported that by the end of the summer, annual sales tax projections had already been exceeded. Based on the average number of times a locally spent dollar will turn over within a community, the county auditor estimated that the students had engineered a $6 to $7 million infusion into the local economy.

Needless to say, the Howard business students learned a good deal about economics: spending, saving, and the relationship between economic vitality and community well-being. They experienced what it feels like to do something worthwhile and to earn the respect of the community in the process. The subject matter, the audience outside the classroom, the interaction with community members, and the constructive nature of the learning process all heightened the students' academic achievement. Since this pedagogical experiment, Howard has developed a national reputation for aggressively combating policy decisions that might adversely affect it. The town was the subject of a *Wall Street Journal* article during the spring of 2005 (Eig, 2005). It represents a shining example of what rural education might be in the 21st century.

References and Further Readings

Affholder v. McMullen, 51 Neb. 91, 70 N.W. 544 (1897).

Annotated Statutes of the State of Nebraska 1881. (1881). Nebraska State Historical Society, Lincoln, NE.

Bauch, P. (2001). School-community partnerships in rural schools: Leadership, renewal, and a sense of place. *Peabody Journal of Education, 76*(2), 204–221.

Beaulieu, L. J., & Gibbs, R. (Eds.). (2005). *The role of education: Promoting the economic & social vitality of rural America.* Mississippi State, MS: Southern Rural Development Center.

Bell, C., & Newby, H. (1971). *Community studies.* New York: Praeger.

Bickel, R, Smith, C., & Eagle, T. (2002). Poor, rural neighborhoods and early school achievement. *Journal of Poverty, 6*(3), 89–108.

Bushnell, M. (1999). Imagining rural life: Schooling as a sense of place. *Journal of Research in Rural Education, 15,* 80–89.

Castle, E. N. (1998). A conceptual framework for the study of rural places. *American Journal of Agricultural Economics, 80,* 621–631.

The Compiled Statutes of the State of Nebraska, 1881. (Omaha 1885). Second Edition with Amendments 1882, 1883, and 1885. 549, Nebraska State Historical Society, Lincoln, NE.

Corbett, M. (2007). *Learning to leave: The irony of schooling in a coastal community.* Black Point, NS: Fernwood.

Cubberley, E. (1922). *Rural life and education: A study of the rural-school problem as a phase of the rural-life problem.* Boston: Houghton Mifflin.

Dahl, R. A. (2002). *How democratic is the American constitution?* New Haven, CT: Yale University Press.

Dewees, S., & Velazquez, J. A. (2000). Community development in rural Texas: A case study of Balmorhea public schools. *Journal of the Community Development Society, 31,* 216–232.

DeYoung, A. J. (Ed.). (1991). *Rural education: Issues and practices.* New York: Garland.

DeYoung, A. J., & Howley, C. B. (1992). The political economy of rural school consolidation. *Peabody Journal of Education, 67,* 63–89.

DeYoung, A. J., Howley, C. B., & Theobald P. (1995). The cultural contradictions of middle schooling for rural community survival. *Journal of Research in Rural Education, 11*(1), 24–35.

Edmondson, J. (2001). *Prairie town: Redefining rural life in the age of globalization.* New York: Littlefield & Rowman.

Eig, J. (2005, March 25). In a bid to hang on, Miner County, SD, downsizes dreams. *Wall Street Journal,* p. C–1.

Falk, W. W. (2004). *Rooted in place: Family and belonging in a southern Black community.* New Brunswick, NJ: Rutgers University Press.

Fuller, W. E. (1982). *The old country school: The story of rural education in the Middle West.* Chicago: University of Chicago Press.

Galbraith, M. W. (Ed.). (1992). *Education in the rural American community.* Malabar, FL: Krieger.

Gibbs, R. (2000). The challenge ahead for rural schools. *FORUM for Applied Research and Public Policy, 15*(1), 82–87.

Lyson, T. A. (2002). What does a school mean to a community? Assessing the social and economic benefits of schools to rural villages in New York. *Journal of Research in Rural Education, 17*(3), 131–137.

Malhoit, G. C. (2005). *Providing rural students with a high quality education: The rural perspective on the concept of educational adequacy.* Arlington, VA: Rural School and Community Trust.

Merz, C., & Furman, G. C. (1997). *Community and schools: Promise and paradox.* New York: Teachers College Press.

Putnam, R. D. (2000). *Bowling alone: The collapse and revival of American community.* New York: Simon and Schuster.

Putnam, R. D., Leonardi, R., & Nanetti, R. Y. (1993). *Making democracy work: Civic traditions in modern Italy.* Princeton, NJ: Princeton University Press.

Reynolds, D. R. (1999). *There goes the neighborhood: Rural school consolidation at the grass roots in early Twentieth-Century Iowa.* Iowa City: University of Iowa Press.

Schafft, K. A., & Brown, D. L. (2003). Social capital, social networks and social power. *Social Epistemology, 17,* 329–342.

Singh, K., & Dika, S. (2003). The educational effects of rural adolescents' social networks. *Journal of Research in Rural Education, 18*(2), 114–128.

Theobald, P. (1995). *Call school: Rural education in the Midwest to 1918.* Carbondale, IL: Southern Illinois University Press.

Theobald, P. (1997). *Teaching the commons.* Boulder, CO: Westview Press.

Theobald, P., & Nachtigal, P. (1995). Culture, community, and the promise of rural education. *Phi Delta Kappan, 77,* 132–135.

Tocqueville, A. D. (2000). *Democracy in America* (H. C. Mansfield & D. Winthrop, Trans.). Chicago; London: University of Chicago Press. (Original work published 1836)

Tyack, D. B. (1972). The tribe and the common school: Community control in rural education. *American Quarterly 24,* 3–19.

Wotherspoon, T. (1998). Education, place, and the sustainability of rural communities in Saskatchewan. *Journal of Research in Rural Education, 14*(3), 131–141.

Zekeri, A. A., Wilkinson, K. P., & Humphrey, C. R. (1994). Past activeness, solidarity, and local development efforts. *Rural Sociology, 59*(2), 216–235.

32

SOCIOLOGY OF EDUCATION

LAWRENCE J. SAHA

Australian National University

The sociology of education is a core field within the discipline of sociology; however, it is also considered a part of the discipline of education. This dual existence is one of the unusual characteristics of the sociology of education, and some say that one source of tension is the difference between those who see the sociology of education as a pure science and those who see it as an applied field of study.

Within sociology, the sociology of education overlaps with many other subfields, such as social stratification, race and ethnicity, and religion. Because of the broad range of topics within the sociology of education, there is hardly a subfield in sociology in which it does not have something to contribute.

This pervasiveness of the sociology of education is reflected in the popularity and general state of the discipline. In the International Sociological Association, the Research Committee on the Sociology of Education is one of the largest in terms of membership. Similarly, in the American Sociological Association, the section on the sociology of education is one of the largest. This pattern is reflected in other national sociological associations such as Australia's. The sociology of education is also represented in various professional education associations, including the American Educational Research Association, where it is visible as a special interest group. It is common for the subject to be taught in one or both academic departments in universities.

The sociology of education is a rapidly growing discipline in many countries. Reviews of the subdiscipline in the English-speaking world have been reported for the United States, Britain, South Africa, and Australia, and in other countries such as Germany, Spain, the Netherlands, and India. The sociology of education is a growing and relevant subdiscipline in sociology in many countries, even where it was once out of political favor.

Despite this popularity, the sociology of education has sometimes struggled for recognition and prestige compared to some other sociological subdisciplines, and some suggest that this is because of its dual representation in both sociology and education. For example, in the United Kingdom, Young (2002) reports that during the 1980s and 1990s the sociology of education began to disappear from university curricula, especially in departments of education and teacher training. As Young observed:

> It was in part a product of the specific location of the sociology of education in the United Kingdom in university education departments and was reflected in the tension between the theoretical demands of the subdiscipline and the practical demands of relating theories and findings to the problems facing teachers in schools and classrooms. (Young, 2002, p. 564)

What then is the sociology of education, and why is it so distinctive and important within sociology, and why is it sometimes contested? In this chapter I examine the sociology of education, its origins, its defining characteristics, its dominant theories and methods, some of its internal divisions, and some of the issues that are important today.

What Is the Sociology of Education?

The sociology of education is the study of educational structures, processes, and practices from a sociological perspective. This means that the theories, methods, and the appropriate sociological questions are used to better understand the relationship between educational institutions and society, both at the micro and macro levels.

The sociology of education is dominated by tension between those who regard it as a science and those who see it as an applied and policy-related discipline, and the tension is between the empirical and the normative, which is between the study of education scientifically as it is and the study of it in terms of what it ought to be. In the early history of the sociology of education, this distinction was sometimes reflected in the name used to describe the discipline. Those who saw the discipline as an objective science used the label "sociology of education," and those who saw it in policy and reform terms used the label "educational sociology."

This distinction is more than academic: it is reflected in differences in how the sociology of education developed in universities in various countries, particularly the United States and the United Kingdom. Apart from being taught as another subfield in sociology departments, sociology of education was taught in departments of education for teacher training in the United States. Often it was called "Social Foundations of Education" or some similar title. In the United Kingdom, the sociology of education early became identified with political arithmetic and thrived in the use of surveys and statistical analyses to learn how education was related to occupational attainment and career mobility (Floud, Halsey, & Martin, 1957). Some have argued that the first use of the sociology of education more closely reflected a Durkheimian approach in which education was seen in functional terms in the maintenance of social order, whereas the second was more closely linked with the notion of social transformation as espoused by Karl Mannheim. To understand this distinction, one needs to start at the beginning and examine how education became intertwined in the early beginnings of sociology itself.

The Early History of the Sociology of Education

Modern sociology was born out of the Industrial Revolution and the increasing awareness of radical shifts in the social structure of society, in particular in Europe and England. But it was during this period that education as we know it was also expanding, so that in a way, industrialization and educational expansion went hand in hand. Education did enter into the writings of the early classical sociologists, although not always in well thought-out forms.

Classical Origins

Karl Marx (1818–1883) never fully developed or integrated education into his theory of capitalism and social class. But he and Fredrick Engels did refer to education frequently in their writings about the class struggle. They advocated education for all, but they were primarily concerned with the type of education that was given to the children of the working classes and how this education served the interests of the ruling class, the bourgeoisie, in maintaining their social dominance. Although Marx did not focus directly on education in his theory of society, his ideas have formed the base of what later would become known as neo-Marxist sociology of education. This perspective is very much related to forms of reproduction theory, in which education is thought to serve as a mechanism for reproducing the class structure of society, thereby reproducing the privileges of the dominant class.

Max Weber (1864–1920) is not normally regarded for his focus on education in his early sociological writings. Nevertheless, his theory of social structure and the interplay between social class, social status, and power did acknowledge the importance of the mechanisms through which one social group could maintain its position in society. Credentials that reflected the possession of knowledge were one way in which individuals could make a legitimate claim for membership in particular class, status, or power groups. It follows implicitly that education, as a mechanism for the development and transmission of knowledge, is an important social institution in this stratification process.

The notion of education as a source of knowledge and its manifestation in educational credentials was also important in Weber's notion of bureaucracy and the increasing rationality of society. Weber believed that European society was developing a new kind of organization as forms of societal authority changed from traditional structures (for example, a monarchy) to rational structures (an elected Parliament). He thought this shift permeated the economic facets of society and particularly society's productive sectors. Industry and manufacturing gradually shifted from domestic and cottage production to factory production, and this required a new form of organizational structure called "the bureaucracy," or a type of hierarchical authority structure based on rational and legal rules. For Weber, the bureaucracy represented "the purest type of legal authority," and the concept has since become the foundation for sociological studies of organizations in modern society.

Weber's ideas have had a major effect on studies of the social organization of schools, and within them, the roles of principal and teachers and the hierarchical relationships between them. The study of teachers as professionals and of workers owes much to Weberian sociology. The study of teacher burnout and teacher accountability in the present trend toward high-stakes standardized testing is ultimately rooted in Weberian principles of organizational sociology and the sociology of bureaucracy.

The third, and perhaps the most important, of the classical sociologists who influenced the development of the sociology of education was Emile Durkheim (1858–1917). Durkheim held the chair of sociology at the Sorbonne in Paris, where he taught future teachers. Over and above his sociological writings, Durkheim wrote three works directly related to education in which we find the foundation of modern sociology of education: *Education and Society* (1922), *Moral Education* (1925), and finally *The Evolution of Educational Thought: Lectures on the Formation and Development of Secondary Education in France* (1938). These works are primarily the lectures for three of the courses that Durkheim gave to students, but they were preserved and published and today form the basis of any Durkheimian study of education.

Durkheim was a functionalist, which means that he was interested in the role that various social institutions played in society and in particular how they contribute to the maintenance of social order. This idea was important to his interest in and understanding of education. Durkheim believed schools were the primary socialization agent for the production of future adults. This is reflected in his work on moral education, which places the development of consensus and solidarity in society in the hands of the school. Durkheim did not believe these functions of education came about without conflict. Indeed, in his work *The Evolution of Educational Thought*, Durkheim traces the constant conflict between the church and state in France over the control of education. He did not see this as a conflict between a particular religious or theological dogma and the state, but rather as a conflict between the sacred and the secular, which he regarded as "the germ of that great struggle" (Durkheim, 1938/1977, p. 26).

Durkheim described education as a contested social institution in society. On the one hand, education established and maintained social consensus and solidarity through its socializing function, but on the other hand, the self-interest of individuals and groups requires the state regulation of education. Durkheim insisted education was responsible for the production of the ideal adult, yet he also recognized that education was a profession for those who participated in it. Many issues and areas of research in contemporary sociology of education are embedded in a Durkheimian understanding of education: the role of merit in educational selection and attainments, the role of teachers in schools, and the study of government and private schools, to name but a few.

Other Classical Sociologists

Other early social scientists recognized the importance of education. Three worth noting are Herbert Spencer (1820–1903), Thorstein Veblen (1857–1929), and Karl Mannheim (1893–1947). Although these social scientists did not have the same effect on the development of the sociology of education as did Marx, Weber, and Durkheim, they nevertheless merit mention because of the specific insights that each had about education.

Herbert Spencer was a contemporary of Marx, Weber, and Durkheim, but is not normally considered one of sociology's founding fathers. As a British evolutionary sociologist, Spencer is best known for his work *First Principles* (1862), in which he put forward a social Darwinist view of society. Like Durkheim, he was one of the few early sociologists who wrote a separate work on education, *Education: Intellectual, Moral, and Physical* (1861). He believed that education should act like other social institutions for the beneficial evolution of society. His work and ideas, particularly those relating to laissez-faire government policies, are relevant to issues such as school choice, the drift in enrollments from government to private schools, and the relationship between the vocational and academic curricula (Peel, 1971).

Thorstein Veblen was an economist interested in the behavior of social classes in industrial society. He argued that education was a site where social class issues were resolved and that working class children received an education which prepared them for their place in society while the leisure class children were prepared for a life of leisure. In this respect, Veblen's ideas resembled those of later neo-Marxist thinkers concerning the function of education in a class society. Veblen was also interested in large business corporations, and he studied how American universities were increasingly coming under the influence of big business and were declining as institutions of liberal education and intellectual curiosity.

Karl Mannheim, an immigrant to England from Germany after the Nazis rose to power, is primarily known for his work in the sociology of knowledge. His ambition was to develop a sociological epistemology whereby the truth of a statement could be explained in terms of the social location of its author. Mannheim was also concerned with the use of sociology for changing and transforming society—to avoid the pitfalls of Nazism—and to create a society based on rationalism and planned thinking. For Mannheim, education was an essential part of this process: " . . . to educate the individual out of his dependence on mass emotion . . ." (Coser, 1977, p. 440). Mannheim believed that education could bring about an integrated society with a common morality—almost the same type of integrated society which Durkheim believed education could produce. Mannheim's lecture notes were posthumously published and became one of the first systematic books in the sociology of education (Mannheim & Stewart, 1969). His contribution to the sociology of education was more applied than theoretical. Because he related education to social planning and social reconstruction, Mannheim frequently referenced Dewey in the United States, whom he admired (Coser, 1977).

These three sociologists followed closely in the footsteps of Marx, Weber, and Durkheim and helped lay the groundwork of modern sociology of education during the classical period. Their legacy can be found in the wide diversity of theoretical approaches and empirical work undertaken by sociologists of education today.

Contemporary Theoretical Approaches

By the 1970s, the sociology of education was a mainstream subfield within sociology but also was a contested field, sometimes scorned by outsiders and also disputed from within. Many disagreements within the sociology of education were manifestations of disagreements within sociology itself—the struggle between those who saw sociology as a science and those who saw it more in interpretive terms. In 1963 in the United States, the journal *Educational Sociology* was taken over by the American Sociological Association, and to emphasize the scientific rather than normative character of the journal, its name was changed to *Sociology of Education.*

Turner and Mitchell (1997) note that there are contemporary theoretical paradigms in the sociology of education that are exact derivatives of the three classical theorists. The functionalist theoretical perspective (derived from Durkheim) was particularly popular during the 1960s and 1970s. It made macrolevel attempts to explain the function of education in the maintenance of social order. Talcott Parsons was a key functionalist who saw the school and its classrooms as reflections of the social system; he also described the university's role in the maintenance of social order. He and his colleague felt that universities carried out four functions, namely (1) undergraduate training, (2) research and graduate training, (3) professional schools, and (4) relations between universities and the broader society (Parsons & Platt, 1973).

The Marxist legacy in sociology of education today is reflected in a number of theories that focus on education as a site for class conflict. Although Marx said little about education, neo-Marxists such as Louis Althusser and Antonio Gramsci established the importance of education in their interpretation of the dynamics of modern capitalism and the class struggle. Althusser (1971) argued that the schools in capitalist societies help preserve the position of the dominant class by teaching the dominant ideology whereby children learn to know and accept their place in society so that there is no challenge to the class structure. In this respect, schools are part of the ideological state apparatus whereby the dominant class maintains its dominant position. Where the dominant class has other state apparatuses at its disposal, such as the police, the school represents a form of symbolic violence through which the dominant ideology is maintained and the relevant knowledge, skills, and material relations to production are learned.

Antonio Gramsci focused his attention on the difference in knowledge available to the dominant and subordinate classes, and argued that the subordinate classes should ensure that they obtain the same knowledge as the dominant class. Only then, he thought, will the working classes be in a position to improve their place in the class structure. In other words, the working class has to compete on the same footing as the capitalist class if the class structure is to be changed. The problem, as Gramsci saw it, is that schools are controlled by those who control the dominant ideology, and therefore the ideas of the ruling class become the ideas taught in school.

Neo-Marxist ideas about education have played an important part in the development of the sociology of education since the 1960s. Many writers with this perspective have proposed their own versions of how education is controlled by the elite and how it helps to maintain elite status. Some examples of these writers and their works are Carnoy's *Education as Cultural Imperialism* (1974), Apple's *Ideology and Curriculum* (1979), Giroux's *Ideology, Culture, and the Process of Schooling* (1981), and Bourdieu and Passeron's *Reproduction in Education, Society, and Culture* (1977). But the overdeterministic versions of reproduction theories were challenged by some who argued that through culture, some disadvantaged students actively resist the kind of knowledge that could provide them with opportunities of social mobility. Such was the finding of Willis (1977) in his study of working class students in an industrial British town.

Closely related to the neo-Marxist approaches are a range of approaches that can be termed *critical theory.* Beginning in Germany with the Frankfurt School, various writers developed a perspective that regarded technology and the bureaucracy of late capitalism as the dominating force in society in ways difficult to recognize. They typified social life under capitalism with concepts such as the totally administered society, one-dimensional man, and communicative competence. This perspective applies to education and other social institutions. Critical theorists strive to both study and emancipate society from capitalist oppression. They seek to unmask the intrusion of this form of capitalism over social life, and therefore emancipate individuals from their false beliefs. In education, critical theory is relevant to the critical study of the curriculum (and the hidden curriculum), educational administration, and teacher education.

Not all conflict-oriented theories are derived from Marxist origins. As noted earlier, Weber also saw education as a source of credentials or legitimacy for claims to status positions. Therefore, ownership or control over the credentializing process constitutes a struggle or conflict between different societal status groups. Weberian approaches to the study of education are less likely to focus on social class, the economy, and the class struggle. Weberians tend to focus on the culture and lifestyles of different status groups and on the competition over credentials. Several classic examples of a Weberian approach are Collins' *The Credential Society* (1979) and Archer's *Social Origins of Educational Systems* (1979).

Other Weberian-related approaches in the sociology of education concern research on the bureaucratic structure of education. This field of study is less easily classified as a type of conflict theory, but it represents a link with Weber's writing. Recent work on aspects of education leadership, teacher professionalism, teacher satisfaction, teacher burnout, teacher accountability, and teacher unions, insofar as the studies take into consideration the bureaucratic structure of schooling, has Weberian origins.

The legacy of Durkheim in modern sociology of education is best reflected in studies of how schools contribute to the socialization of the young and how education contributes to a range of life outcomes, especially occupational attainment and social mobility. Durkheimian sociology of education tends to be functionalist. Therefore, studies that tend to take a positivistic approach to the study of educational processes, in particular those based on empirical data and explicit or implicit causal assumptions, are linked with forms of Durkheimian functionalism. Although sociologists now recognize that Durkheim did not ignore the presence of conflict in educational processes (Saha, 2001), there are few studies that have analyzed educational processes from his conflict perspective.

Contemporary sociology of education owes much to the founding fathers of sociology. Even the contemporary theoretical approaches are embedded in the foundation theories of sociology. The influence of these early "classical" sociologists remains influential in the discipline today.

The Interactionist Perspective

The legacy of Marx, Weber, and Durkheim in the sociology of education focuses on macrolevel processes, even though the unit of analysis might be the individual. In other words, both the functionalist and conflict paradigms direct attention to the relationship between aspects of social structures and the individual or groups. But there has long been a strong microlevel tradition in the sociology of education that focuses on the patterns of interaction in educational processes. The most well-known of these perspectives is symbolic interaction theory, which focuses on how the actions and interactions between people are the result of the meanings that people attribute to objects and to other people's actions. In short, symbolic interactionists take the view that in symbolic interaction theory, everything from the self to the patterns of interaction between individuals is the result of social processes.

The roots of symbolic interactionism are complex. They embrace phenomenologist philosophers such as Schutz and Husserl, but also some elements of the late Durkheim and Mead (Turner & Mitchell, 1997). The term *symbolic interactionism* was first used by Blumer (1969). Symbolic interactionism has evolved into a number of related perspectives, in particular the dramaturgical perspective Goffman described in *The Presentation of Self in Everyday Life* (1959) and the ethnomethodological per-

spective, which Garfinkle developed in *Studies in Ethnomethodology* (1967). The first of these focused on how the individual managed the social self in the process of interaction with others. The latter focused on the methods and social competence individuals use to construct social reality. These theoretical perspectives have influenced the understanding of interaction patterns between individuals in schools, especially the interactions between teacher and student, and student and student.

Interactionist theory also was important in the development of role theory, a perspective which focuses on the definition and perceptions of relevant roles that individuals follow in their daily lives. In some cases, the roles are in society, the result of social consensus. In other cases, roles are constructed. Role theory continues to be an important theoretical perspective that informs much of the way that administrators, teachers, and students go about their everyday duties (Biddle, 1997). In spite of some problems in role theory, Biddle comments that " . . . it is clear that the role orientation continues to offer insights for educators and a challenge for those who seek to understand what it means to be a teacher in today's world" (p. 515).

Emerging Perspectives for the 21st Century

The sociology of education is a dynamic field. Theory and research methods are continually evolving, and new perspectives have emerged that have little connection to traditional approaches. Toward the end of the 20th century, many attempts were made to evaluate the state of the sociology of education. These attempts called for a break with the past paradigms primarily because of the perceived breaks in the nature of society itself.

Torres and Mitchell (1995) identified three departures from the past that future research in the sociology of education must take: (1) there must be a new epistemology that differs from positivism and empiricism; (2) the sociology of education must confront the dilemmas caused by the break between modernism and postmodernism, and structuralists and poststructuralists, and (3) the sociology of education must resolve the challenges posed by these new theoretical approaches for educational research. Torres and Mitchell argue that today's increasing unpredictabilities render the previous notions of a scientific sociology of education difficult to sustain. Their critique of the sociology of education is actually a critique of sociology and social science generally.

Torres and Mitchell argue that the scientific model of linear and causal explanations cannot be sustained currently where behavioral events are more discontinuous and discrete. Thus, traditional notions of objectivity can be expected to give way to subjective approaches, which take into account both the knower and the known in attempts to understand a social world that is more complex and global than previous paradigms have recognized. Torres and Mitchell advocate a new sociology of education that incorporates topics hitherto neglected or unrecognized and that focuses on creating an educational system that produces a more democratic society free of prejudices and injustices.

Dale (2001) agrees that theoretical perspectives in the sociology of education are not linear. He argues, however, that the emergence of new theoretical perspectives is due to what he calls "the selection principle," namely through the political and social contexts within which sociologists of education operate. The evolution of theories in the sub-discipline is not due to any kind of inner dynamic. The sociology of education, unlike other subdisciplines in sociology, is closely tied to the training of professionals (that is, teachers). So, for Dale, political orientations toward the education profession affect what sociologists of education think and do. Therefore, every time there is an education reform, there will be a comparable effect on the theoretical orientations of sociologists of education, at least those affiliated with teacher training faculties.

Similarly, Hallinan (2000) has argued that the sociology of education lacks adequate education-related sociological theory: "The heavy reliance of sociologists of education on general social theory and on ideas and models from other sociological subdisciplines to study schooling demonstrates the greatest weakness in the area" (p. 3). Hallinan contends that education-specific theories need to be developed if sociology of education is to progress beyond its present state of knowledge. Her own volume reflects the types of theoretical developments she has in mind, for example a social-psychological theory of the social context and social construction of schooling, a theory of the organizational context of schools, and a sociological theory of race and ethnicity that would be relevant to research on these issues in schools.

As the sociology of education enters the 21st century, there is no single paradigm or theory that dominates the subdiscipline. Some sociologists argue that a unique theory still needs to be developed, and others appear content with a plurality of general sociological theories. Various reasons for this lack of consensus have been put forward. Two explanations have merit. First, the subdiscipline includes both a normative (applied) dimension and an objective (scientific) dimension. Researchers within each group have their own perceived appropriate theoretical perspectives. Second, the social and cultural contexts within which sociologists of education work have an effect on both the relevant substantive issues and the appropriate methodologies. According to some, however, this diversity in the sociology of education is precisely what gives the field its vitality and promise.

Empirical Methods in the Sociology of Education

Sociologists of education tend to use the full array of methodological techniques, both quantitative and qualitative, in their studies of education. Sociologists of education also have contributed to the development of both research methodologies, which have made important general contributions to sociology.

LeCompte (1997) observed that the use of qualitative research methodologies within the functionalist tradition were very popular in the early to mid-20th century. These studies used participant observation to provide a holistic view of schools and their location in community systems, like Hollingshead's *Elmstown's Youth* (1947) or an interpretive perspective, such as *Making the Grade* (1968) by Becker, Geer, and Hughes. These types of qualitative studies have continued and have adopted newer theoretical and methodological approaches such as the postmodernist theories and interpretive and narrative methodologies (Denzin, 1997). But LeCompte claims that the rapid development of large-scale quantitative studies from the 1950s onward dominated research in the sociology of education virtually until the end of the century (LeCompte, 1997). She argues that in the 21st century a newer qualitative tradition influenced by critical theory has returned. There are many labels for these new qualitative methodologies, from critical ethnography, where the researcher critically connects data with both its source and subjects under study, to biographical and narrative approaches, where the focus is on the subjects' lived experience.

While advances were made in qualitative methods, equal—if not more dramatic—developments in quantitative approaches were also made. Rapid improvements in computer technology and sophisticated advancements in statistical techniques facilitated these developments. Hallinan (2000) claims that since the 1960s sociologists of education have borrowed from econometrics and other fields to develop linear models for studying educational processes, and she points to the Coleman Report (Coleman et al., 1966) as an important example of this development. From this approach, many different strands of statistical analysis emerged. Perhaps the most important of these is the Wisconsin Model by Sewell and his colleagues (Sewell & Hauser, 1980), which focused on the relationships between educational aspirations, grades, and occupational attainments. This model has been replicated around the world, in places such as Canada, Latin America, Europe, Asia, and the Middle East, with surprisingly similar results.

Hierarchical linear modeling (HLM), another recent development in statistical analysis, has revolutionized research in the sociology of education and in sociology generally. The study of students in schools has always presented challenges for researchers because students are members of classrooms, and classrooms are part of schools. One could go further and note that schools exist in neighborhoods which in turn are parts of cities. Clearly, at each of these levels there could be some influence on schools, classrooms, and individual students. Traditionally, researchers nested the variables at one level, then used aggregate level values for the other levels for each student. But the development of hierarchical linear models makes possible the analysis of each level separately and linked (Raudenbush & Bryk, 2002). Thus, the study of the multiple levels of analysis that affect individual student academic achievement becomes more powerful and precise.

Because of the unique nature of educational research, various statistical techniques have been developed that eventually were incorporated into the research repertoire in the general sociological community. Researchers in sociology of education have led the way in the advancement of analytic techniques that continue to uncover new levels of understanding of what goes on in schools (Saha & Keeves, 2003).

The increasing availability of large longitudinal data sets and large comparative data sets across countries has also advanced quantitative research methods in the sociology of education. Longitudinal data are of particular importance to the study of educational processes "within the black box of the school" (Schiller, 2002, p. 403). Longitudinal studies can be either trend studies, where the same population is followed over time, or panel studies, where individuals are followed over time. The latter is more commonly used in sociology of education research (Schiller, 2002). Longitudinal studies play an important role in understanding the multiple factors that contribute to educational outcomes. These studies of education have been conducted in many countries by individual researchers and increasingly under government sponsorship. For example, the advances made by the development of the Wisconsin Model were based on longitudinal data. Between 1972 and 1996, the United States National Center for Education Statistics (NCES) conducted five major government-funded longitudinal studies, spanning students from primary to tertiary education.

International organizations have increasingly supported standardized questionnaire studies of school-aged youth across countries. These large international data sets have become popular among researchers who are interested in one or several countries. Examples of these studies are those of the International Association for the Evaluation of Educational Achievement (IEA) and the Program for International Student Assessment (PISA). These data sets have not only made it possible to advance our knowledge in a comparative context, but also have been responsible for the development of methodological strategies for dealing with cross-national analyses.

Some Research Themes in the Sociology of Education

The sociology of education is characterized by a number of dominant research themes. Often these themes are driven by research interests and sometimes by practical necessities. There are many areas in which sociologists of education work, but only a select few will be discussed here: gender, race and ethnicity, and teacher accountability and burnout.

Gender

Gender has not always been on the research agenda for sociologists of education. Before 1970, studies of educational achievement and attainment were often based on male-only samples, both in the United States and the United Kingdom. Since then, because of the feminist movement and educational expansion, more attention has been given to the education of girls. The gender gap is a persistent research theme. Early studies focused on male dominance in academic achievement and in education attainment, a pattern found across virtually all countries for which data were available. But in many countries the gender gap has been closing. In some countries, for example Australia, girls have overtaken boys in retention and attainment, and also in achievement in some subjects. The reversal has been so dramatic that discussions now focus on the "boy problem." Researchers have put forth biological, structural, and socialization or child rearing explanations for these gender differences.

Race, Ethnicity, and Minority Group Status

Sociologists have traditionally placed strong focus on the effects of race and ethnicity on a wide range of social and economic outcomes. In the United States, sociologists are particularly interested in the educational attainments of African American and the Hispanic populations. But in general, similar attention has been given to all minority groups, especially since movements of populations across national boundaries have increased, both voluntarily and nonvoluntarily. The study of racial and ethnic minorities has included indigenous, migrant, and refugee populations. Sociologists of education in the United States, Britain, Canada, and Australia have been particularly active in this research. They have identified many factors that work to the disadvantage of minority groups. Ogbu (1992) argued that a strong core curriculum was one factor that affected the learning process of these minority groups. Cultures of various racial and ethnic groups hold differing expectations about education that may affect the ways these students encounter a school system. Research has also found that the attitudes and values of various minorities affect educational attainment and achievement, particularly where multiple attitudes conflict with each other or attitudes conflict with the goals of the school (Mikelson, 1990). This conflict can exist between the attitudes and values of the home and the school.

Teacher Accountability and Burnout

Sociological studies regarding the teacher fall into two categories: the teacher as a professional and the teacher as a worker. Studies of the teacher as professional have examined teacher recruitment, the decision to become a teacher, and the professional careers and life cycles of teachers. Willard Waller (1932) conducted perhaps the first classical sociological study of teachers and teaching. A more recent study, itself a classic, is Lortie's *Schoolteacher* (1975), which looked at teaching as an occupation.

Some researchers argue there is a division between teaching as a profession and as an occupation, and that the increasing structural constraints of accountability, salary issues, and prestige have eroded its professional nature. These pressures have produced stress and alienation, resulting in increased teacher burnout. Often considered a psychological phenomenon, burnout also has a sociological dimension that seriously impedes teacher performance and effectiveness (Dworkin, 1987).

How effective are teachers? To answer this question researchers have conducted research in classrooms and investigated topics like teaching styles, teacher interaction with students, and teacher expectations, all of which have an effect on student outcomes (Good & Brophy, 1997). How the expanding practice of high-stakes testing is changing the roles of teachers is another recent research topic. Valli and Buese (2007) found that the passing of the Education Act of 2001 (No Child Left Behind) has increased teacher workloads and accountability, deteriorated classroom pedagogy, lowered the quality of teacher-student interaction, and increased teacher stress.

Conclusion

The sociology of education, as a subdiscipline of both education and sociology, has contributed much to the understanding of educational processes. As a source of information and training for future teachers, and as a source of information for policy makers, it continues to draw attention to the social context of what goes on in schools. The tensions within the sociology of education will no doubt continue, but the subdiscipline as a whole is so eclectic and robust that this can only be a sign of its strength. In either case, the sociology of education uniquely focuses attention on the social context of educational structures and processes, and its contribution will continue to be invaluable for understanding and reforming educational systems, particularly as they change to accommodate new social needs and new technologies.

References and Further Readings

Althusser, L. (1971). Ideology and ideological state apparatuses. In L. Althusser (Ed.), *Lenin and philosophy and other essays*. London: New Left Books.

Apple, M. (1979). *Ideology and curriculum*. Boston: Routledge & Kegan Paul.

Archer, M. (1979). *Social origins of educational systems*. London: Sage.

Becker, H. S., Geer, B., & Hughes, E. C. (1968). *Making the grade: The academic side of college life*. Chicago: University of Chicago Press.

Biddle, B. J. (1997). Recent research on the role of the teacher. In B. J. Biddle, T. L. Good, & I. F. Goodson (Eds.), *International Handbook of Teachers and Teaching* (Vol. 1, pp. 499–520). Dordrecht, Netherlands: Kluwer Academic Publishers.

Blumer, H. (1969). *Symbolic interactionism—Perspective or method*. Englewood Cliffs, NJ: Prentice Hall.

Bourdieu, P., & Passeron, J. (1977). *Reproduction in education, society and culture*. London: Sage.

Carnoy, M. (1974). *Education as cultural imperialism*. New York: McKay.

Coleman, J. S., Campbell, E. Q., Hobson, C. J., McPartland, J., Wood, A. M., Weinfield, F. D., et al. (1966). *Equality of educational opportunity*. Washington, DC: United States Government Printing Office.

Collins, R. (1979). *The credential society: An historical sociology of education and stratification*. New York: Academic Press.

Coser, L. A. (1977). *Masters of sociological thought: Ideas in historical and social context*. New York: Harcourt Brace Jovanovich, Inc.

Dale, R. (2001). Shaping the sociology of education over half-a-century. In J. Demaine (Ed.), *Sociology of education today*. London: Palgrave.

Denzin, N. K. (1997). Biographical research methods. In L. J. Saha (Ed.), *International encyclopedia of the sociology of education* (pp. 282–288). Oxford, UK: Pergamon Press.

Durkheim, E. (1922). *Education and society* (S. D. Fox, Trans.). Glencoe, IL: The Free Press.

Durkheim, E. (1925). *Moral education. A study in the theory and application of the sociology of education* (E. K. Wilson & H. Schnurer, Trans.). New York: The Free Press.

Durkheim, E. (1977). *The evolution of educational thought: Lectures on the formation and development of secondary education in France*. London: Routledge & Kegan Paul. (Original work published 1938)

Dworkin, A. G. (1987). *Teacher burnout in the public schools: Structural cause and consequences for children*. Albany: State University of New York Press.

Floud, J., Halsey, A. H., & Martin, F. (1957). *Social class and educational opportunity*. London: Heinemann.

Garfinkle, H. (1967). *Studies in ethnomethodology*. Englewood Cliffs, NJ: Prentice Hall.

Giroux, H. A. (1981). *Ideology, culture and the process of schooling*. London: Falmer Press.

Goffman, I. (1959). *The presentation of self in everyday life*. New York: Doubleday.

Good, T. L., & Brophy, J. (1997). *Looking in classrooms* (7th ed.). New York: Harper & Row.

Hallinan, M. T. (2000). Introduction: Sociology of education at the threshold of the twenty-first century. In M. T. Hallinan (Ed.), *Handbook of the sociology of education* (pp. 1–12). New York: Kluwer Academic/Plenum Publishers.

Hollingshead, A. B. (1947). *Elmstown's youth*. New York: Wiley.

LeCompte, M. D. (1997). Trends in qualitative research methods. In L. J. Saha (Ed.), *International encyclopedia of the sociology of education* (pp. 246–262). Oxford, UK: Pergamon Press.

Levinson, D. L., & Sadovnik, A. R. (2002). Education and sociology: An introduction. In D. L. Levinson, P. W. Cookson, & A. R. Sadovnik (Eds.), *Education and sociology* (pp. 1–15). New York: Routledge Falmer.

Lortie, D. (1975). *Schoolteacher*. Chicago: University of Chicago Press.

Mannheim, K., & Stewart, W. A. C. (1969). *An introduction to the sociology of education*. London: Routledge & Kegan Paul.

Mikelson, R. A. (1990). The attitude-achievement paradox among Black adolescents. *Sociology of Education, 63*, 44–61.

Ogbu, J. U. (1992). Understanding cultural diversity and learning. *Educational Researcher, 21*(8), 5–14.

Parsons, T., & Platt, G. (1973). *The American university*. Cambridge, MA: Harvard University Press.

Peel, J. D. Y. (1971). *Herbert Spencer: The evolution of a sociologist*. London: Heinemann Educational.

Raudenbush, S. W., & Bryk, A. S. (2002). *Hierarchical linear models: Applications and data analysis methods* (2nd ed.). Thousand Oaks, CA: Sage.

Saha, L. J. (2001). Durkheim's sociology of education: A critical assessment. *Education and Society, 19*(2), 19–31.

Saha, L. J., & Keeves, J. P. (2003). Leading the way: The development of analytic techniques in the sociology of education. In C. A. Torres & A. Antikainen (Eds.), *The international handbook on the sociology of education* (pp. 160–179). Lanham, MD: Rowman & Littlefield.

Schiller, K. (2002). Longitudinal studies: An introduction: Opening the black box. In D. L. Levinson, P. W. Cookson, Jr., & A. R. Sadovnik (Eds.), *Education and sociology: An encyclopedia* (pp. 403–408). New York: Routledge Falmer.

Sewell, W. H., & Hauser, R. M. (Eds.). (1980). *The Wisconsin longitudinal study of social and psychological factors in aspirations and achievements* (Vol. 1). Greenwich, CT: JAI Press.

Spencer, H. (1862). *First principles*. London: John Childs and Son.

Spencer, H. (1949). *Education: Intellectual, moral and physical*. New York: Hurst. (Original work published 1861)

Torres, C. A., & Mitchell, T. R. (1995). Introduction. In C. A. Torres & T. R. Mitchell (Eds.), *Sociology of education: Emerging perspectives* (pp. 1–18). Albany, NY: State University of New York Press.

Turner, J. H., & Mitchell, D. E. (1997). Contemporary sociological theories of education. In L. J. Saha (Ed.), *International encyclopedia of the sociology of education* (pp. 21–42). Oxford, UK: Pergamon.

Valli, L., & Buese, D. (2007). The changing roles of teachers in an era of high-stakes accountability. *American Educational Research Journal, 44*(3), 519–558.

Waller, W. W. (1932). *The sociology of teaching*. New York: Russell & Russell.

Willis, P. (1977). *Learning to labour: How working class kids get working class jobs*. Aldershot, UK: Gower.

Young, M. (2002). Sociology of education as critical theory. In D. L. Levinson, P. W. Cookson, & A. R. Sadovnik (Eds.), *Education and sociology* (pp. 559–569). New York: Routledge Falmer.

33

MULTICULTURAL EDUCATION

LAURI JOHNSON

University of Buffalo

Multicultural education is an idea or concept, a process, and an educational reform movement that assumes America's diversity should be reflected in the staffing, curriculum, instructional practices, policies, and values of our educational institutions (Banks & Banks, 2006; Grant & Ladson-Billings, 1997). Although the United States has always been diverse, between 1923 and 1965 restrictive policies limited immigration, particularly from countries outside of Europe. In the last three decades U.S. society has become increasingly both multicultural and multilingual. The 1990s witnessed a rapid influx of immigrants from Asia and Latin America, and a recent survey conducted by the U.S. Census Bureau estimates there are 11 to 12 million new immigrants. More than 20% of children in the United States are either foreign-born or have a parent who was born abroad. Although more stringent security and immigration screening was instituted after 9/11, refugees from conflict-ridden countries like Somalia, Sudan, Bosnia, and Myanmar continue to enter the country in steady numbers. Instead of moving to traditional gateway cities like New York, Chicago, and Los Angeles, recent refugees are settling in midsized cities like Seattle, St. Paul, Atlanta, and Buffalo where the cost of living is more affordable.

At the dawn of the 21st century, U.S. schools are more linguistically, culturally, religiously, ethnically, and racially diverse than ever before (Prewitt, 2002). Students of color (i.e., Black and African American, Hispanic and Latino, Asian American, and Native American) make up 43% of the national public school population. In some states, like California, and in the 20 largest urban school districts across the country, students of color constitute an overwhelming majority of the school population. Nationwide, 18.4% of school-age youth speak a language other than English at home. In some urban school districts, over 100 different languages are spoken. This demographic imperative is an important reason for developing and implementing multicultural education and making U.S. schools more responsive to the needs and perspectives of students from diverse groups and their families.

Despite the changing face of America, however, students from diverse racial, ethnic, and linguistic backgrounds continue to experience unequal educational opportunities and often do not see the history, values, and cultural knowledge of their home communities represented in the school curriculum. The racial achievement gap between White students and African American and Latino students has remained stagnant. The average twelfth-grade low-income student of color reads at the same level as the average eighth-grade middle-class White student. According to the 2000 census, 88% of White students graduate from high school, but the rate for Hispanics is just 56%. There is a gender gap in many high schools as well. Girls continue to be underrepresented in advanced math, science, and technology courses, and their test scores in these subjects often fall behind boys as they progress through school.

In response to these inequities, scholars, educators, and parents have called for an education that is both multicultural and equitable, one that incorporates culturally responsive curriculum and instructional methods, equitable assessment practices, and organizational structures that promote interaction across racial and ethnic lines and facilitate academic achievement for all students (Nieto, 2003). Multiculturalists believe that "all students—regardless of their gender, social class, and their ethnic, racial, and cultural characteristics—should have an equal opportunity to learn in school" (Banks & Banks 2006, p. 3).

Historical Development

Although the genesis of multicultural education is often traced to the civil rights movement of the 1960s, recent historical studies indicate that efforts by educators, parents, and community organizations to develop culturally responsive schooling date back at least to the 1930s and 1940s. Known at the time as intercultural or intergroup education, several urban school districts enacted policies to promote racial and ethnic diversity in the wake of racial and ethnic conflicts in the years before, during, and immediately after World War II. Intercultural advocates in cities like New York, Pittsburgh, Chicago, and Detroit produced curriculum materials on Black history and race relations, designed professional development programs that provided urban teachers a forum in which to develop and present their own intercultural curriculum projects, and instituted college courses for preservice teachers to promote cultural pluralism and improve human relations (Johnson, 2007).

In some school districts, such as New York City and Pittsburgh, intercultural education was also linked with community activism by parents and grassroots organizations to hire more teachers of color and improve racial attitudes through public education campaigns that involved radio programs, films, art exhibits, and multicultural children's literature. Characterized as "educating for democracy," intercultural education advocates contrasted America's stated democratic ideals of freedom and equality of opportunity during the war years with the historical reality of ongoing prejudice and discrimination toward those racial and ethnic groups who were disenfranchised and marginalized by school systems (Johnson, 2002).

Diversity work in the schools was largely halted during the Cold War era, when intercultural courses were criticized as "subversive and un-American," and several teacher union leaders who promoted intercultural education as well as scholars who were frequent guest speakers at intercultural workshops were subject to "red baiting" (Johnson, 2002). In the 1960s, the rise of the civil rights movement in the South, followed by the Black power movement in cities like New York, Chicago, and Oakland revived the demand for a school curriculum that accurately reflected African American history, values, and contributions.

During the late 1960s, ethnic studies programs sprang up in colleges and universities, and courses such as Black Literature and Chicano History were instituted in selected high schools across the country. Community and parent activists from Los Angeles to Brooklyn demanded more control over the content of the curriculum, more Black and Hispanic teachers and administrators, and more diverse representation and decision-making powers on local school boards.

With the passage of Title IX in the early 1970s, gender equity issues were included under the multicultural umbrella. Advocates pressed for equal funding for girls' athletics, the formation of school district committees to analyze textbooks for gender bias, and the implementation of single-sex classrooms to increase girls' participation and achievement in advanced math and science courses. By the late 1980s, some school districts, such as New York City, also included sexual orientation in their multiculturalism policy. The New York City Office of Multicultural Education produced two *Children of the Rainbow* elementary curriculum guides, which encouraged teachers to recognize and support "all kinds of families," including same-sex unions. The inclusion of picture books like *Heather and Her Two Mommies* and *Daddy's Roommate* on the teacher's bibliography of one of the curriculum guides proved controversial, and the New York City multiculturalism policy was rescinded in 1995 after a protracted political battle (Johnson, 2003). Throughout the historical development of multicultural education, community responses to curriculum and policies designed to encourage and promote diversity have been influenced by the shifting political and social contexts of individual schools, districts, and the larger society. In recent years multiculturalists have developed and refined sophisticated models to explain how multicultural education might transform K–12 school systems.

Models and Approaches to Multicultural Education

Three of the most comprehensive and widely known models for multicultural education have been developed by theorists James A. Banks, Christine Sleeter, Carl Grant, and Sonia Nieto. Banks' conceptual model of multicultural education (Banks & Banks, 2006) includes five interrelated dimensions. Content integration is the extent to which teachers use examples and content from a variety of cultures and groups to illustrate key concepts in their subject area or discipline. Banks acknowledges that more opportunities may exist to incorporate ethnic and cultural content in some subject areas, such as social studies, language arts, and music, rather than others, such as science and math. The knowledge construction process examines how teachers help students understand and investigate the implicit cultural assumptions, perspectives, and biases within a discipline and how the knowledge created reflects the positionality and lived reality of those who construct it. For example, students might analyze the knowledge construction process in science by studying how racism has been perpetuated by genetic theories of intelligence, Darwinism, and eugenics. Prejudice reduction describes the characteristics of student's racial and ethnic attitudes and presents strategies that can be used to reduce prejudice and develop democratic attitudes. Equal status contact that is cooperative, sanctioned by authorities, and helps students become acquainted with each other as individuals develop positive intergroup attitudes. An equity pedagogy examines how teachers modify their teaching to facilitate the academic achievement of students from diverse racial, cultural, and social-class groups. This includes teaching styles that are consistent with a wide range of learning styles within various cultural and ethnic groups. An empowering school culture and social structure examines grouping and labeling practices, participation in extracurricular activities, disproportionality in achievement, and the interaction of the staff and students across ethnic and racial lines to create a school culture that empowers students from diverse racial, ethnic, and cultural groups. Many of the school-based programs that promote diversity would fall under the content integration dimension, although curriculum materials and videotapes produced by national organizations like Teaching Tolerance (sponsored by the Southern Poverty Law Center in Montgomery, Alabama) also incorporate prejudice reduction.

Grant and Sleeter's (2003) model, which was developed through a review of the literature and observations of teachers, identifies five different approaches that address human diversity in the schools:

1. Teaching the exceptional and culturally different aims to assimilate students of color into the cultural mainstream and existing social structure, equipping people of color with the knowledge and skills to succeed in schools and society.

2. A human relations approach helps students of different backgrounds appreciate each other's similarities and differences and improves intercultural relations.

3. Single group studies focus on the experiences, contributions, and concerns of distinct cultural, ethnic, gender, and social-class groups often left out of the curriculum, such as African Americans and women.

4. Multicultural education is a combination of the first three approaches that attempts to "change school practices to bring about greater cultural pluralism and equal opportunity in society at large" (Grant & Sleeter, 2003, p. 8).

5. Education that is multicultural and social reconstructionist addresses social inequities in society "to prepare students . . . to deal constructively with social problems and to take charge of their own futures" (Grant & Sleeter, 2003, p. 8).

This last approach deals with all forms of group oppression as a whole. Classroom approaches that are social reconstructionist might emphasize democratic decision making and social action at the classroom level and the dismantling of tracking and high-stakes testing at the school level.

Nieto (2004) defines multicultural education as "a process of comprehensive school reform . . . that challenges and rejects racism and other forms of discrimination in schools and society and accepts and affirms the pluralism (ethnic, racial, linguistic, religious, economic, and gender among others) that students, their communities, and teachers reflect" (p. 346). Nieto advocates for multicultural education that permeates the curriculum, instruction, and interactions among teachers, students, and families; confronts issues of power and privilege in society; and challenges how racism and other biases are reflected in the structures, policies, and practices of schools. Her definition includes seven basic characteristics of multicultural education:

1. It is antiracist.
2. It provides a basic education.
3. It is important for all students.
4. It is pervasive.
5. It establishes social justice in education.
6. It is a process.
7. It incorporates critical pedagogy.

In Nieto's model the characteristics of multicultural education are expressed at five different levels that exhibit increasing awareness and commitment by educators. At the first level, monocultural education, racism is unacknowledged and the educational program supports the status quo. At the next level, tolerance, ethnic and women's studies courses may be offered as isolated courses, and policies that challenge racism and discrimination are initiated. At the acceptance level, the curriculum is inclusive of the histories and perspectives of a broader range of people, and the role of schools in social change is acknowledged. At the fourth level, respect, curriculum is explicitly antiracist and honest, students take part in community activities that reflect their social concerns, and both students and teachers use critical dialogue to see and understand different perspectives. Nieto's fifth and highest level of multicultural education incorporates the affirmation, solidarity, and critique. At this level all students learn to speak a second language, everyone takes responsibility for challenging racism and discrimination, and the curriculum and instructional techniques are based on an understanding of social justice as central to education. Although multiculturalists have developed comprehensive theoretical models, Gay (2001) notes that a gap continues to exist between the theory and practice of multicultural education in U.S. schools.

From Theory to Practice

In practice, schools often adopt a contributions or heroes and holidays approach to multicultural education that adds some cultural content but fails to challenge the underlying mainstream cultural assumptions of the curriculum or address systematic societal inequities. For instance, high school English teachers might include a novel by Toni Morrison or Amy Tan on their reading lists, or middle school teachers might add a unit on the civil rights movement to their existing social studies curriculum. Elementary school teachers often incorporate multicultural picture books in their classroom library for independent reading. Conflict resolution programs are developed in school districts to reduce prejudice and improve human relations, particularly in response to ongoing incidents of racial or ethnic conflict.

As Nieto (2003) suggests, however, "multicultural education needs to be accompanied by a deep commitment to social justice and equal access to resources. Multicultural education needs, in short, to be about much more than ethnic tidbits and cultural sensitivity" (p. 8). The challenge in the 21st century is how to bridge the gap between the theory and practice of multicultural education to address the vast inequities that continue to exist in U.S. public schools. Teachers and administrators need professional development in designing multicultural curriculum and instructional strategies that will help them respond to different learning styles, worldviews, and the funds of knowledge that diverse groups of students bring to the schools. Multiculturalists advocate the implementation of pedagogy and leadership that is "culturally relevant" or "culturally responsive" (Gay, 2000).

Culturally Responsive Pedagogy

Ladson-Billings coined the term *culturally relevant pedagogy* in *The Dreamkeepers* (1994), her now classic study of eight exemplary teachers of African American students. This instructional approach arises from previous anthropological work that noted a cultural mismatch between students from culturally diverse backgrounds and their White middle-class teachers, particularly in language and verbal participation structures. As defined by Ladson-Billings (1995a; 1995b), culturally relevant pedagogy rests on three propositions: (a) students must experience academic success; (b) students must develop or maintain cultural competence; and (c) students must develop a critical consciousness through which they challenge the status quo of the social order. Building on Ladson-Billings' study, Cooper (2003) investigated the practices of effective White teachers of African American students who had been nominated by the Black administrators and parents in their predominately African American schools. She found that they adopted many of the practices of effective African American teachers, including being "warm demanders" who held high expectations for academic achievement and becoming second mothers or "othermothers" to the children in their classroom.

In their model of culturally responsive teaching, Villegas and Lucas (2002) describe culturally responsive teachers as those who (a) have a sociopolitical consciousness; (b) affirm views of students from diverse backgrounds; (c) are both responsible for and capable of bringing about educational change; (d) embrace constructivist views of teaching and learning; and (e) build on students' prior knowledge and beliefs while stretching them beyond the familiar (p. xiv). In sum, most approaches to culturally relevant or culturally responsive instruction described in the multicultural education literature use students' culture as a vehicle for learning, and also teach students how to develop a broader sociopolitical consciousness that enables them to "critique the cultural norms, values, mores, and institutions that produce and maintain social inequities" (Ladson-Billings, 1995b, p. 162).

Although much of the research on culturally responsive practices has been applied to classroom teaching, recent efforts have attempted to apply a culturally responsive framework to school leadership. These studies have identified culturally responsive principals as those who emphasize high expectations for student academic achievement, exhibit an ethic of care or "empowerment through care," and maintain a commitment and connection to the larger community (e.g., Johnson, 2006; Reitzig and Patterson, 1998; Scheurich, 1998). Riehl (2000) also identifies three tasks that determine whether administrators are prepared to respond to diversity and demonstrate multicultural leadership. Such administrators foster new definitions of diversity; promote inclusive instructional practices within schools by supporting, facilitating, or being a catalyst for change; and build connections between schools and communities.

Critiques of Multicultural Education

Multicultural education has not been without its critics on both the right and the left of the political spectrum. In the early 1990s, a barrage of critiques emerged. Multiculturalists were attacked by conservatives in the popular media who called them too radical, while critical scholars and theorists argued that multicultural education was not radical enough. According to Sleeter (1995), these attacks corresponded to efforts to make multicultural education part of the required curriculum at the state and university level. This criticism was particularly evident in the conservative response to the development of New York State's *Curriculum of Inclusion*. A state taskforce made up largely of academics recommended revisions of the social studies curriculum to acknowledge institutional racism in U.S. history, but the curriculum revision was scuttled after a public outcry in the popular media.

Conservative critics argue that multicultural education is divisive, lacks intellectual rigor, is not founded on sound theory, and does not address the real causes of underachievement by racial and ethnic minority groups. Sleeter (1995) notes that many of the conservative's criticisms ignore the research and theory that multicultural education builds on, particularly anthropological and sociological work on cultural dissonance and knowledge construction conducted by scholars of color and feminists and critical scholars. She concludes that conservative's criticisms of multicultural education arise from the unease White America feels about its own future and reflects the efforts of the mainstream to pin its fears and anxieties on the threat of diversity.

Radical left critiques of multicultural education have been written mainly by critical theorists for an audience of theorists. They fault multicultural education for embracing individual mobility rather than collective advancement and structural equality. They argue that multicultural curriculum suggests psychological solutions to political problems, and they criticize the tendency of multicultural proponents to overestimate the ability of schools to influence the social and economic futures of poor students and students of color.

Radical critics have also argued that multicultural education's focus on a commonsense definition of culture reifies the cultural characteristics, symbols, perspectives, and affiliations of individuals from particular racial and ethnic groups and fails to acknowledge multiple and hybrid identities that result when race, gender, and sexual orientation intersect. Radical critics argue that when multicultural education is framed around learning about other cultures and dispelling stereotypes, the larger issues of structural inequality are ignored. They conclude that multicultural education should develop a more explicit critique of White racism, capitalism, and patriarchy (Sleeter, 1995). In the 21st century, several multicultural theorists have responded to these criticisms, by the radical left in particular, by acknowledging the growing complexities of racial and cultural identity development and by developing a more explicit focus on critical theories that analyze how race and racism systematically structure inequalities in schools and society.

Future Trends

Racial, ethnic, cultural, and religious diversity in the United States is projected to increase and become more complex in the foreseeable future. Hispanics are now the largest ethnic minority group in America (14.5%) and are growing at an estimate of 1.7 million people a year. The Census Bureau predicts that 25% of the U.S. population will be Hispanic by 2050. This growing Latino population is no longer concentrated in Florida and the Southwest, but distributed throughout the United States in Northeastern states like Massachusetts, Midwestern cities like Chicago and Milwaukee, and Southern states like South Carolina.

The current student population of the New York City public schools provides a glimpse of the demographic complexity that urban school districts will exhibit in the future. In New York City high schools, 10% of the students have immigrated in the last 3 years, most from Latin American and Asian countries. The overwhelming major-

ity are students of color (85%), including Black (35%), Hispanic or Latino (36%), and Asian (14%). These general racial categories, however, fail to capture the ethnic diversity within each racial group. For instance, Black students may be African American; first- and second-generation immigrants from Haiti, Jamaica, Trinidad, and other Caribbean nations; or African. The Latino population includes Dominicans, Puerto Ricans, Colombians, Ecuadorians, and Mexican Americans (along with several other Hispanic groups). Asian students include first- and second-generation Chinese Americans who immigrated from Taiwan, Hong Kong, and Mainland China; Koreans; South Asians; and Vietnamese. Many students classified as White or other are also ethnically diverse, thanks to recent immigration from the former Soviet Union, Eastern European countries, and several Middle Eastern nations.

In addition, there are a growing number of mixed race students throughout the country who claim a bicultural or multicultural identity and challenge our current understanding of racial categories. The 2000 census instruction to mark one or more races created the possibility of 63 racial categories and began to reveal the recent growth of this population. For instance, in the Pacific West, 8.9% of children identify as mixed race, and in the Southwest 19.8% identify as Latino and White. In the 21st century, these changes challenge educators to rethink existing racial categories and racial identity development processes as the population of mixed race students is likely to increase.

Resegregation and Accountability Pressures

Despite the growing diversity of the school-age population, recent court decisions and policy trends will have an effect on the implementation of multicultural education in the 21st century. There has been an overwhelming trend in recent years toward school district resegregation, particularly in states in the Northeast and Midwest. In 2006, roughly three-in-ten Hispanic (29%) and Black (31%) students attended schools that were nearly all-minority. The most segregated group by race and income are Latino students. Intensely segregated schools for African Americans and Latinos have particularly negative consequences because these schools have high concentrations of poverty and are linked to unequal resources and educational outcomes (Orfield, Frankenberg, & Lee, 2003). Some legal advocates have shifted the focus away from desegregation cases at the federal level and concentrated their efforts on fiscal equity lawsuits at the state level. Their aim is to redistribute resources to poor urban schools to ensure that all students receive a "sound basic education" (Rebell, 2005).

Other equity advocates continue to press for desegregation of the schools, although the 2007 Supreme Court decision that struck down voluntary public school integration plans in Seattle, Washington, and Louisville, Kentucky, narrows the strategies that public schools can use to achieve or maintain racial diversity. The resegregation of

U.S. schools is of grave concern for all students because classroom diversity and informal interaction across racial and ethnic groups can positively influence all students' learning and civic outcomes and improve intergroup relations and mutual understanding. In the 21st century, multicultural education advocates will have to develop new strategies to ensure that the public schools retain diverse student populations and garner equal resources for all schools. Because current policy trends have reinforced the movement toward neighborhood schools, efforts may include working with community development specialists and urban planners to advocate for the development of multi-income housing to create more economically diverse city neighborhoods.

The growth of accountability mandates and standardized testing since the mid-1990s has also proven challenging to teachers and school leaders who are committed to implementing multicultural curriculum in their classrooms and schools. As Ladson-Billings (2004) notes, "the entire history of standardized testing has been one of exclusion and social ranking rather than diagnosis and school improvement" (p. 60). The passage of the No Child Left Behind Act (NCLB) in 2001 required a system of accountability from each state that received federal funding and expanded the system of high-stakes testing in school systems across the country. With pressures to perform well on state-mandated tests, poor urban school districts that serve predominately students of color have increasingly relied on prescribed and scripted curriculum materials to find a quick fix for unsatisfactory test scores. These intensified efforts to improve performance in math and reading tend to drive other subjects out of the curriculum. Time devoted to social studies, science experiments, art, theater productions, music, and physical education is reduced, and students from diverse backgrounds are exposed to inflexible curricula and teaching strategies that violate their home cultures and languages (Sleeter, 2005). The challenge for multiculturalists in the 21st century will be to make a convincing case for multicultural curriculum and assessment approaches that incorporate multiple perspectives, multiple frames of reference, and multiple funds of knowledge. If student assessment is to be more culturally responsive for diverse students, advocates of multicultural education must garner support from school district, state, and national education leaders and policy makers to alter the current high-stakes testing environment. This suggests, as Sleeter (1995) notes, "that the work to come is political in addition to being pedagogical" (p. 92).

New Theoretical Approaches

As multicultural education comes of age, scholars in the 21st century continue to develop new theoretical approaches to analyze inequities in schools and address America's diversity. Some theorists advocate a primary focus on race and racism through antiracist education (Kailin, 2002) or critical race theory (Ladson-Billings, 2004). Antiracists

define White racism as the crucial determinant of the life chances of children of color. The focus of antiracist education is on the relations of domination rather than on difference alone, as is common in conventional multicultural approaches (Kailin, 2002). Antiracist pedagogy aims to empower through critically analyzing existing power relations and knowledge paradigms. Antiracist approaches to teacher education have generally been more prevalent in England and Canada, while critical multiculturalists in the United States have focused on critical race theory as an oppositional approach to interpret how race has influenced America's educational policies, practices, and systems.

Critical race theory (CRT) developed in critical legal studies in the 1980s in response to the inability of traditional civil rights legislation to uncover racial inequity and legal injustice and to help inform strategies of resistance. It was introduced to the field of education by William Tate and Gloria Ladson-Billings (Ladson-Billings & Tate, 1995) and has been used by a variety of scholars to analyze educational practices and policies over the last 13 years. CRT is marked by a number of defining elements. The first element is that racism is a normal, not aberrant or rare, fact of daily life in U.S. society and that the assumptions of White superiority are so ingrained in political, legal, and educational structures that they are almost unrecognizable (Delgado, 1995). As Milner (2007) notes, "Critical race theorists attempt to expose racism and injustice in all its forms and facets; explain the implicit and explicit consequences of systematic, policy-related racism; and they work to disrupt and transform policies, laws, theories, and practices through the exposure of racism" (p. 39).

Second, CRT scholars often use storytelling, narrative, autobiography, and parable as a way to expose and challenge social constructions of race and make visible the distinctive experiences of people of color. Emphasis is placed on the use of voice and naming one's own reality to create counter narratives to the dominant mainstream narratives (Ladson-Billings & Tate, 1995). Through this approach knowledge is reconstructed and communities of color are empowered to name their reality. Delgado (1995) points out an important distinction between the viewpoints of Whites and people of color: Whites don't see it as their perspective, but the truth.

A third tenet of CRT is Bell's (1980) theory of interest convergence; that is, historically, the interest of Blacks in gaining racial equality have been accommodated only when they have converged with the interests of powerful Whites. In Bell's (1980) view, "Whites may agree in abstract that Blacks (and other people of color) are citizens and are entitled to constitutional protection, yet still believe that justice can be remedied effectively without altering the status of Whites" (p. 522).

Critical theories of race like antiracism and CRT acknowledge the pervasiveness of racism in society and privilege the stories and experiences of people of color who have been negatively affected by racism to illustrate how social institutions and practices reinforce White privilege. Educational theorists have applied the tenets of CRT to analyze a range of educational policies and practices, including the racial achievement gap (Taylor, 2006), the politics of education (Lopez, 2003), community organizing for school reform (Su, 2007), and literacy curriculum (Rogers & Mosley, 2006).

Other multiculturalists have developed an international focus that investigates approaches to diversity in global contexts. Recent books compare the similarities and differences between multicultural policies in the United States and Canada (e.g., Joshee & Johnson, 2007), approaches to race and racism in Britain and the United States (e. g. Ladson-Billings & Gillborn, 2004), and the intersection of multicultural education and citizenship issues (Banks, 2004). Banks' (2004) edited volume, *Diversity and Citizenship Education: Global Perspectives*, pushes the boundaries of multicultural education beyond the politics of recognition in particular nation-states to a global conversation about justice and equality in a transnational arena. Chapters by scholars from Canada, Britain, South Africa, Brazil, Israel, Palestine, Russia, Japan, India, and China discuss how diversity and citizenship issues play out in particular national contexts and discuss issues such as the conflict between domestic multicultural education and cosmopolitan multiculturalism (where diversity is viewed as good for business); ethnic identity development in monocultural versus multicultural societies; and the importance of all students developing cultural, national, and global identifications. As a follow up to this volume, an international group of scholars in multicultural education developed a checklist and bibliography for teachers about how to integrate effective multicultural citizenship principles and concepts in K–12 classrooms (Banks et al., 2005). This international focus promises to expand our conceptions of multicultural education in the future as we begin to understand and incorporate a broader set of equity concerns worldwide.

Conclusion

In conclusion, at the dawn of the 21st century, many of the concerns debated in diverse U.S. school districts 70 years ago remain on the multicultural agenda. Critical issues in the coming century will include the need for more teachers of color; increased parent and community engagement in curriculum decisions and decision making; culturally responsive curriculum that reflects the history, values, and cultural knowledge of students from diverse backgrounds; and teacher and leadership certification programs that aim to prepare all educators to teach and lead for diversity. With a current U.S. teaching force that is 87% White and middle-class, professional development for experienced teachers and preservice teacher education programs are challenged to develop new approaches that will create a diverse and culturally sensitive teaching force. Possible strategies include career ladders to help teaching assistants

from racially and culturally diverse communities obtain teacher certification, the recruitment of a more diverse pool of teacher candidates who are culturally responsive, and ongoing professional development for preservice and inservice teachers on diversity issues. This professional development must go beyond one-shot diversity workshops with little follow through and include more in-depth immersion programs that would enable White preservice teachers to work with experienced teachers of color and other community leaders on joint projects that might expose them to insider's knowledge about race and racism and how to reduce prejudice.

The ongoing challenge remains—how to make the promise of multicultural education real by bridging the gap between theory and practice to provide an education for all students that "promotes social structural equality, affirms societal diversity, achieves academic excellence for all students, and prepares students to become active members of a democratic society" (Grant & Ladson-Billings, 1997, p. 186). Students and parents in America's schools deserve nothing less.

References and Further Readings

Banks, J. A. (Ed.). (2004). *Diversity and citizenship education: Global perspectives.* San Francisco: Jossey-Bass.

Banks, J. A., & Banks, C. A. M. (Eds.). (2006). *Multicultural education: Issues and perspectives* (6th ed.). Boston: Allyn & Bacon.

Banks, J. A., Banks, C. A. M., Cortes, C. E., Hahn, C., Merryfield, M. M., Moodley, K. A., et al. (2005). *Democracy and diversity: Principles and concepts for educating citizens in a global world* [Online]. Retrieved September 15, 2007, from http://depts.washington.edu/centerme/home.htm

Bell, D. (1980). *Brown v. Board of Education* and the interest convergence dilemma. *Harvard Law Review, 93,* 518–533.

Cooper, P. (2003). Effective White teachers of Black children: Teaching within a community. *Journal of Teacher Education, 54,* 413–427.

Delgado, R. (Ed.). (1995). *Critical race theory: The cutting edge.* Philadelphia: Temple University Press.

Gay, G. (2000). *Culturally responsive teaching: Theory, research, and practice.* New York: Teachers College Press.

Gay, G. (2001). Curriculum theory and multicultural education. In J. A. Banks & C. A. M. Banks (Eds.), *Handbook of research on multicultural education* (pp. 25–42). San Francisco: Jossey-Bass.

Grant, C. A., & Ladson-Billings, G. (1997). *Dictionary of multicultural education.* Phoenix, AZ: Oryx Press.

Grant, C. A., & Sleeter, C. E. (2003). *Turning on learning: Five approaches for multicultural teaching plans for race, class, gender, and disability.* New York: John Wiley & Sons.

Johnson, L. (2002). Making democracy real: Teacher union and community activism to promote diversity in the New York City public schools, 1935–1950. *Urban Education, 37*(5), 566–588.

Johnson, L. (2003). Multicultural policy as social activism: Redefining who counts in multicultural education. *Race, Ethnicity, and Education, 6*(2), 107–121.

Johnson, L. (2006). Making her community a better place to live: Culturally responsive urban school leadership in historical perspective. *Leadership and Policy in Schools, 5*(1), 19–37.

Johnson, L. (2007). Diversity policies in American schools: A legacy of progressive school leadership and community activism. In R. Joshee & L. Johnson (Eds.), *Multicultural education policies in Canada and the United States* (pp. 28–41). Vancouver, Canada: University of British Columbia Press.

Joshee, R., & Johnson, L. (Eds.). (2007). *Multicultural education policies in Canada and the United States.* Vancouver, Canada: University of British Columbia Press.

Kailin, J. (2002). *Antiracist education: From theory to practice.* Lanham, MD: Rowman & Littlefield.

Ladson-Billings, G. (1994). *The dreamkeepers: Successful teachers of African American children.* San Francisco: Jossey-Bass.

Ladson-Billings, G. (1995a). Toward a theory of culturally relevant pedagogy. *American Educational Research Journal, 32*(3), 465–491.

Ladson-Billings, G. (1995b). But that's just good teaching! The case for culturally relevant pedagogy. *Theory Into Practice, 34*(3), 159–165.

Ladson-Billings, G. (2004). New directions in multicultural education: Complexities, boundaries, and critical race theory. In J. A. Banks & C. A. M. Banks, *Handbook of research in multicultural education* (2nd ed., pp. 50–65). San Francisco: Jossey-Bass.

Ladson-Billings, G., & Gillborn, D. (Eds.) (2004). *The Routledge Falmer reader on multicultural education: Critical perspectives on race, racism, and education.* London: Taylor & Francis.

Ladson-Billings, G., & Tate, W. F. (1995). Toward a critical race theory of education. *Teachers College Record, 97,* 47–68.

Lopez, G. (2003). The (racially neutral) politics of education: A critical race perspective. *Educational Administration Quarterly, 39*(1), 68–94.

Milner, H. R. (2007). Race, culture, and researcher positionality: Working through dangers, seen, unseen, and unforeseen. *Educational Researcher, 36*(7), 388–400.

Nieto, S. (2003). Profoundly multicultural questions. *Educational Leadership 60*(4), 6–10.

Nieto, S. (2004). *Affirming diversity: The sociopolitical context of multicultural education* (4th ed.). New York: Allyn & Bacon.

Orfield, G., Frankenberg, E. D., & Lee, C. (2003). The resurgence of school segregation. *Educational Leadership 60*(4), 16–20.

Prewitt, K. (2002). Demography, diversity, and democracy: The 2000 census story. *The Brookings Review, 20*(1), 6–9.

Rebell, M. (2005). Court-ordered reform of state school aid. In L. Johnson, M. Finn, & R. Lewis (Eds.), *Urban education with an attitude* (pp. 33–40). Albany: State University of New York Press.

Reitzug, U. C., & Patterson, J. (1998) "I'm not going to lose you!" Empowerment through caring in an urban principal's practice with students. *Urban Education, 33,* 150–181.

Riehl, C. (2000). The principal's role in creating inclusive schools for diverse learners: A review of normative, empirical, and critical literature on the practice of educational administration. *Review of Educational Research, 70*(1), 55–81.

Rogers, R., & Mosley, M. (2006). Racial literacy in a second grade classroom: Critical race theory, whiteness studies, and literacy research. *Reading Research Quarterly, 41*(4), 462–495.

Scheurich, J. (1998). Highly successful and loving, public elementary schools populated mainly by low SES children of color: Core beliefs and cultural characteristics. *Urban Education, 33*(4), 451–491.

Sleeter, C. E. (1995). An analysis of the critiques of multicultural education. In J. A. Banks & C. A. M. Banks (Eds.), *Handbook of research in multicultural education* (pp. 81–94). New York: Macmillan.

Sleeter, C. E. (2005). *Un-standardizing curriculum: Multicultural teaching in the standards-based classroom.* New York: Teachers College Press.

Su, C. (2007). Cracking the silent code: Critical race theory and education organizing. *Discourse: Studies in the Cultural Politics of Education, 28*(4), 531–548.

Taylor, E. (2006). A critical race analysis of the achievement gap in the United States: Politics, reality, and hope. *Leadership and Policy in Schools, 5,* 71–87.

Villegas, A. M., & Lucas, T. (2002). *Educating culturally responsive teachers: A coherent approach.* Albany: State University of New York Press.

PART VIII

CURRICULUM K–12

34

LANGUAGE ARTS

Reading and Literacy in the Early Years

YETTA M. GOODMAN

University of Arizona, Professor Emerita

W hen Albert Einstein was asked late in life about schooling, he responded, "Accumulation of material should not stifle the student's independence." And he also believed that "advantage will come from how well [schools] . . . stimulate imagination and creativity" (Isaacson, 2007, pp. 6–7). The history of literacy learning and teaching in the early years reflects a struggle to address Einstein's concerns.

Research and theories about young children's literacy development have been evolving for well over a century. Language, literacy, and early childhood scholars have discovered how young children come to know what language, including literacy, is and what it does as a result of a range of diverse and social literacy practices in their homes, communities, and schools. Exploration of the controversies concerning literacy learning and teaching in the early years is essential to teachers, teacher educators, and researchers.

The teaching and learning of language and language arts are pervasive especially in preschool, kindergarten, and primary grades. Reading, writing, speaking, listening, and viewing (the language arts) are central to every subject. Written and oral language are the tools humans use to think about and to actively explore their worlds. Language forms are based on the functions language serves in society. Language development is taken for granted by the lay public. Since everyone uses language continually, it is easy for people to believe that they know how language works, how it is learned, and therefore how it should be taught.

Thus, recommended changes to language arts teaching and learning are often controversial, and innovative literacy practices are at odds with honored status quo practices.

To understand and take part in discussions about the controversies, teachers need to develop knowledge and understandings about the social, political, and historical contexts of young children's literacy learning. As teachers appreciate the learning capabilities of young readers and writers and the influences of classroom contexts on learning, they build and expand on children's literacy development and help young children become aware of their own contributions to their development.

The Nature of Language and Literacy Development

Oral and written language are symbiotic systems that humans use to communicate. Human language represents people's thinking, knowledge, and emotions. Language is so necessary to human interaction that when people are deaf, they develop the language of signing. Although language and thinking are not the same, they are integrally intertwined and necessary to support each other (Vygotsky, 1978).

Both oral and written language are flexible and change over time to meet the needs of an ever-changing society. Some people bemoan changes in language, claiming that change damages the beauty and meaning of language.

Language change results in the dialects and language variations found within all communities and in the range of forms and functions of oral and written language. Text messaging and blogging are examples of the changing nature of written language at the present time. Young children often amaze adults with their abilities to use the newest language forms.

Language development is a "continuous process of learning how to mean through language" (Webster, 2004, p. viii). Humans from birth construct ways to use different language forms and functions as they interact with others to make sense of their world. As young children use language, they are learning language and learning about language (Webster, 2004).

Knowledge About Oral Language Development

Studies of children's oral language development clearly document how young children construct oral language and their abilities to use language within their cultural contexts. Children's language development has been studied in the authentic settings of homes and schools (Brown, Cazden, & Bellugi, 1969; Loban, 1967; Webster, 2004). Psychologists and linguists often conclude that young children are linguistic geniuses because of the ease with which they develop language to communicate. Research shows that as children learn the language of their family and community, they build control over the sounds, grammar, and meanings of their mother tongue usually by the age of 5.

Research illuminates these language inventions. Children show that they know women have higher pitched voices than men as they respond with coos and babbles in higher tones with females than with males during their first year. Five-year-olds use different language when they talk with younger siblings than they do with adults. English-speaking children in kindergarten demonstrate knowledge of grammatical relationships when they run to their teacher and say, "Bobby hit Mary." The teacher understands the problem immediately and does not question who is hitting whom, assuming that children know subject-object relationships. When young children say, "I runned home," they are overgeneralizing the regular form of verbs (the -ed form on past tense) because it is the most common. They overgeneralize by using the regular rules first and later develop control over the irregular forms (ran). Their thinking about language is not yet conventional. They are inventing the way language works, building on their language knowledge at the time. Over time, through many varied language experiences and opportunities, they evolve toward conventional uses of language.

Knowledge About Literacy Development

As teachers and researchers developed knowledge about the capability of young children to learn oral language, they began wondering about the kinds of contributions young children make to their literacy learning. Since the 1970s, researchers in psychology, linguistics, and education have provided an extensive body of knowledge about the variety of writing experiences in which very young children engage and have documented how these experiences influence children's construction of knowledge about reading and writing (Teale & Sulzby, 1986). These studies involve in-depth and longitudinal analyses of children's spontaneous writing and reading in various contexts, with different socioeconomic backgrounds and with families that spoke languages other than English, and provided insight into children's social and personal literacy histories (Clay, 1979; Martens, 1996; Reyes, 2006; Taylor & Dorsey-Gaines, 1988). Young children, for example, invent wordings, spellings, punctuation, and spacings, and there is research on such discoveries in a range of languages including Chinese and Japanese as well as English and Spanish (Goodman & Martens, 2007).

Literacy learning and development in young children is highly complex. Yet in the cultural context of the home, literacy learning develops easily. Young children know how to hold pencils, pens, and markers and write on paper, note cards, and even walls. They know that certain marks they make are related to writing and others represent drawings. They know that numbers and the letters of the alphabet or characters in Chinese serve different functions and that books open and pages are turned in specific ways. Some children come to kindergarten and first grade reading conventionally.

Literacy is the social and cultural uses of reading and writing. The terms *reading* and *writing* often identify school subjects, and there are frameworks for teaching each separately. Literacy, on the other hand, is a cultural phenomena—a human invention that responds to the needs of a society. Literacy develops as members of society respond to authentic uses of reading and writing to record events, stories, histories, and business transactions.

One way to think about the literacy histories of young children is to consider the multiple roads to literacy (Goodman, 1997). Many children develop literacy concepts when they are read to by family members; they may finish the sentences in stories as they read along. They read to dolls or to friends who are willing to sit still long enough. Other children read by themselves, examining illustrations, pointing to the print, responding to pictures, or listening and following along in books with taped recordings.

Writing is another road to literacy learning. Young children write thank you notes, captions to accompany their pictures, and stories or letters to send grandpa and grandma, signing their names and using punctuation such as *XXX* and *OOO* to represent kisses and hugs. Parents rarely teach these in any direct way. Nor is the focus on correct form. Rather, caretakers focus on the importance of children participating actively in the social literacy experiences of the family. Another road to literacy is revealed during children's play. They read cereal boxes as they play store or are preparing food in their play kitchens, they write prescriptions and in charts when they play doctor, and they write menus and take orders when they play restaurant.

Print environment on the streets and throughout the neighborhood provides another road to literacy where children learn that print labels stores and offices, gives directions, and controls traffic patterns. They ask questions about what signs mean, remind their parents that they need to drive SLOW, or ask to get ice cream when they pass a Dairy Queen. Many children are now engaged in technology that leads to literacy as they sit in their parents' laps reading from or writing on a computer screen. They know that pushing certain keys (On, Enter, Print) results in specific operations. No literacy histories are exactly the same, but in these varied environments, children come to know what literacy is and what it does. Children experience literacy in various contexts (homes, communities, and schools) on their roads to literacy, and their experiences are influenced by the quality and length of time of their opportunities for literacy use and the accessibility and availability of literacy resources.

For at least a century, researchers and teachers have formulated theories about the nature of literacy development (Clay, 1979). Emilia Ferriero, an Argentinian psychologist, has gained international attention for the ways in which she illuminates young children's literacy constructions. She posits that children around the age of 2 or 3 first learn to distinguish between drawing and writing; then they become aware that writing has specific relationships to oral language, but this relationship is first meaning based. Young children believe that what is written has characteristics that represent the object being written about. The word *cow*, for example, is longer than the word *fly*. The word *mother* or the mother's name has more letters than the child's name because she is bigger. Father's name, as one child said, "has as many as a thousand" (Ferriero & Teberosky, 1982).

Children expand on their personally constructed knowledge of language as they actively participate in social literacy events and come to believe that written language is related to oral language syllables. Around age 5 or 6, young children who live in countries with alphabetic languages (English, Spanish) become aware that there is a relationship between sounds and specific letters, based on the children's perceptions of the sounds. They represent their syllabic and alphabetic knowledge most clearly in their writing. In English, children invent spellings that use consonants to represent words such as *HBR*. They place three appropriate consonant letters to represent the three syllables of *hamburger.* In Spanish, on the other hand, children spell words like *mariposa* (butterfly) as *AIOA,* using vowels (Ferreiro & Teberosky, 1982).

Jeanne Chall (1967) used research to support beginning reading instruction that emphasizes codes in which the child relates letters and words to the sounds of the language they already know. Research on children's spelling also adds to theories about literacy development, with rich information documenting how young children develop concepts about the ways written language represents the sounds of language (Read, 1975). Because they base their spelling on their knowledge of their mother tongue, teachers need to be knowledgeable about dialect and language variations of young children. All members of a language community speak a dialect form of the language; no one group has the correct form (Wolfram, Adger, & Christian, 1999). This discussion about language variation needs to also be considered in relation to the growing number of schoolchildren whose mother tongue is other than English or who grow up in bilingual homes (Freeman & Freeman, 2006). Young readers and writers need to learn how *their* oral language relates to written English (K. Goodman, 1993). For example, Spanish-speaking children may write the word *letter* as *lera* because they know the flap sound in Spanish is represented by *r* as in *perro* (dog). The same sound in English is represented with *tt* or *d*. A first-grade child from Brooklyn wrote under his picture: *Mi cah is pakt in the stret* (My car is parked in the street), representing the way he hears the *r* in car and parked. His sentence also shows that he is using his knowledge of the names of the letters for *i* and *e* to spell *Mi* and *stret*.

Children's early reading needs to be analyzed in a similar way. Children's miscues often make sense because they are predicting and considering the context of the story. They may read*, Dad's gonna take me to the circus* for *Father is going to take me to the circus*. They are anticipating a familiar voice in this story rather than the formal language sometimes used in basal readers. Careful analyses of children's writing and reading shows they are problem solving as they represent what they believe is written (Owocki & Goodman, 2002). English spelling, grammar, and punctuation is quite regular, but the rules are complex, reflecting historical influences, dialect variations, and arbitrary decisions made by printers and publishers. It took thousands of years to develop a conventional writing system for English. Young children need time to develop conventions too.

Teachers need to understand that when children use invented forms in their writing or make miscues in their reading, they reveal their knowledge about phonics, grammar, and ways in which language makes sense. The teacher then helps children understand that their representations (invented written forms) show their knowledge. Children are not simply making random errors or being sloppy. With insights into children's inventions, teachers are able to support children's growth and consider the most effective ways to help young students develop writing conventions. The more children are immersed in reading and writing authentic materials, the more they see their language represented in print and grow in their use of language conventions.

Using literacy is not always pleasant. Filling out forms for a hospital or social services can cause families distress. Homework may interrupt family routines and cause emotional responses. The attitudes that accompany such experiences are also part of children's literacy histories. The cumulated knowledge, attitudes, and emotions that children develop on their multiple and diverse roads to literacy become each child's personal and social literacy history. Children bring these attitudes, emotions, and knowledge to school. The more teachers learn from their observations about children's literacy histories, the more teachers are able to expand on children's knowledge.

Teaching Language Arts to Young Children: Focus on Literacy

Teaching and learning are symbiotic constructs. They relate and influence each other, but teaching does not directly cause learning to happen. Children decide what to learn and construct their own concepts. To support children's literacy learning, teachers organize a classroom environment that considers how children learn as well as the development of the curriculum. The teacher helps children make connections between what they know about literacy, their social and cultural history of literacy, and what is taking place in the classroom. The teacher considers district, state, and federal guidelines or mandates, but knows that the most effective teaching facilitates children's learning. New teachers need to be patient as they develop the ability to orchestrate the thousands of classroom interactions that take place daily and result in learning.

Most of the controversies in teaching literacy to young children surround instructional practices and curriculum development. The models for teaching language arts are broadly based on two divergent views of learning: the behaviorist view and the constructivist view.

Educators and parents with a behaviorist view of learning argue that children need to know the letters and sounds of the alphabet before they are ready to learn to read and write. They insist that children must know oral English before they are introduced to reading and writing. In this view, preschool and kindergarten programs engage in readiness activities for children. There is a specific sequence for learning the prerequisite skills before children read. Children must master phonological awareness before knowing the ways in which sounds relate to letters. They are then taught the names of letters and use this knowledge to recognize words. In this word recognition or phonics model of teaching, young learners first are taught to read and later read to learn. The focus is on the transmission of knowledge from the teacher directly to the child.

Commercially published packages with booklets, work sheets, and tests in carefully controlled sequences become the reading program. Teachers are told in accompanying manuals how to teach the material, what to say, and what to expect the children to respond. The skills are related to behavioral objectives and suggest predetermined goals measured by tests. Children learn from the smallest unit of language (sounds and letters) to a whole word. Comprehension is not a focus of teaching until third grade. Writing instruction consists of copying and handwriting exercises with letters and words. For example, the No Child Left Behind Act mandates commercial programs based on readiness activities and continual testing of young children. Teachers follow scripted materials in response to administrative fiats.

Literacy researchers and educators with a constructivist view of learning argue that children must focus on making sense as they read and write from their earliest experiences. Comprehension and reading are synonymous and central to all learning experiences. Children are active learners who construct their own meanings and develop knowledge about phonics, grammar, and meaning simultaneously as a result of being immersed in authentic literacy experiences. Authentic experiences use materials that reflect how language is used in the real world. This view is based on in-depth observations of young children in homes and schools as they engage in reading and writing during play or as they learn about the important issues in their world with peers and adults (Whitmore, Martens, Goodman, & Owocki, 2004). Innovative teachers and schoolwide-developed literacy programs promote curriculum experiences based on constructivist principles.

There are also educators who believe in balanced literacy instruction. This focuses on teaching skills and readiness activities, but also includes meaning-making experiences. The learning experiences children have are not supported by a coherent philosophy about children's literacy learning, but are based on instructional experiences that draw from different learning theories.

These controversies and differences make clear the importance of teachers' need to articulate their own beliefs about literacy learning and the principles that inform the ways they teach reading and writing. Thousands of research studies have explored which theories and instructional programs are best suited for young children's literacy learning, but the controversy continues. Different research studies produce confounding results; however, there is ample evidence that the role of the teacher is the most important factor in student achievement (Darling-Hammond, 2000).

Knowledgeable teachers build on the rich diversity of children's cultures, backgrounds, and interests to organize a classroom program with spaces where individual or small groups of children are immersed in a variety of literacy experiences. Early in their careers, teachers may make greater use of commercially published reading and writing programs to help them plan instructional experiences for kids. With growing knowledge and experience, commercial materials become tools that professional teachers use selectively as they develop literacy programs to meet the needs of the young learners in their classrooms.

Language Across the Curriculum

Classrooms should be places where young children have lots of time to inquire—to wonder and talk about their world, to participate in a range of opportunities, to answer their questions and solve their problems. Teachers document children's conceptual and literacy development by listen seriously, taking notes, and adding their observations to children's folders to document their growth for purposes of evaluation (Owocki & Goodman, 2002). They interview children and involve children in discussions about their own literacy development. Teachers take photos of children engaged in various learning experiences and display them on the wall. With a child or small group, the teacher reviews the pictures and discusses the learning that has taken place. The children become involved in self-evaluation.

There are spaces in classes in preschool and primary classrooms where young children experiment with growing plants; examine the globe; read with teddy bears or dolls; listen to books and music; play house, restaurant, and dress up to dramatize stories and songs: and build structures with blocks. The language arts—speaking, listening, reading, writing, and viewing—are emphasized during these experiences as children learn concepts in a wide range of subjects while they actively engage in reading, writing, and talking. The language arts are not ends in themselves, but tools for using language actively to expand on developing concepts. Such use of language arts teaching and learning is known as integrating the language arts with content areas, or language across the curriculum.

An example of such an integrated theme took place in the 1950s in that public school in which I was teaching in Southern California. The pregnancy of a mother volunteering in a kindergarten classroom stimulated a child to ask about how the mom's stomach could keep stretching and not hurt. The children were encouraged to discuss their interest in human growth and development with their family. Pregnant animals were kept in cages in the classroom that the children observed and cared for. Doctors and nurses visited the classroom to answer questions, provide plastic models of human bodies, and share pamphlets and videos. The children recorded the food the animals ate, weight gain, and related information as the animals and the mother changed sizes. After its birth, the baby was brought to the classroom, and children shifted their attention to how they grew after they were born. It is easy to imagine the amount of conversation, reading, and writing that took place during these learning experiences.

Children's themes also include explorations about language. As children sing songs and recite poetry, they explore the sounds of language and how those sounds correspond to writing. The children in one first-grade classroom wondered why *boot* and *foot* had different medial sounds. The teacher suggested that the children kept track of the various *oo* patterns they found in their reading and writing. They recorded their discoveries on the board for a few weeks and then wrote a set of rules they learned from their research. Teachers set aside time in the classroom regularly for lessons that focus on the study of language. (Y. Goodman, 2003).

The Importance of Writing

Writing supports the development of reading and occurs simultaneously with reading. Literacy development researchers believe that young children learn most about phonics, spelling, grammar, and the organization of compositions by engaging daily in writing (Graves, 1983; Smith, 1994).

In preschools and at the beginning of the year in kindergartens, the teacher may cover a table with white butcher paper and place a coffee can filled with a variety of writing implements within easy reach of the children. The children experiment with written forms and drawings, and talk with each other about the differences between their drawing and writing. There is a city phone book and a pad for messages by the play telephone or recycled cell phones in the house corner. There is a pad for writing receipts in the wheel toy area as tricycles line up for gas. Learning spaces in the room are thoughtfully designed and labeled. Cupboards are marked for snacks, different kinds of paper, blocks, and other supplies, and there are cubbies labeled with children's names and photos. The teacher may have put up some signs before children arrived at the beginning of the year, but students do much of the labeling so they know the function that written language serves in the classroom.

Some kindergarten teachers start literacy activities on the first day of school by having a large sign-in board at the door with pens, pencils, and markers available. The teacher invites the children to sign their names and observes carefully to see how comfortable the children are with writing and the way they use writing implements. Such sign-in sheets become an evaluation tool over the course of the year as the teacher displays them and discusses children's writing development with parents and administrators.

Language experience is an instructional approach involving both reading and writing experiences (Lee & Allen, 1963). Young children talk about and write about their experiences, which they later share with classmates, family members, and school administrators. Early in the year, some teachers act as scribes taking dictation. The children attend as the teacher writes, and they help the teacher make decisions about wording, spelling, and other language conventions. During selected teaching moments, the teacher thinks aloud to show the children the decisions he or she makes while writing. Language experience has its roots in teachers helping children talk, write, and later read about their experiences on class trips, with science experiments, with visitors to the classroom, in response to the reading of a good book, or as the result of completing a theme study. In addition to whole-class writing experiences, children are encouraged to write personal language experiences in journals daily and to share their journals with others. These are sent home to involve parents in their children's development.

There are many ways innovative teachers involve children in authentic writing and reading experiences. Consider the following example of an authentic experience. The classroom, or even the whole school, has a post office with mailboxes for individual children, and time is planned for children to write to each other. This experience may have resulted from a thematic unit the teacher organized on the role of the postal service when some children asked questions about the mail carrier they saw in the school office. The teacher bought postcards for the children to write and address to themselves or their parents. When the cards were received at home, the children read them to their families and reported back to the class about their experiences. The discussion was recorded and became a historical document that the children wrote with their teacher and was posted in the classroom for future reference.

As soon as children dictate their stories and write their own, teachers involve children in bookmaking—another example of authentic writing experience. The books are shelved in the classroom or school library. Students are excited as they consider themselves authors like their favorites. Some teachers involve the students in publishing literary magazines or poetry anthologies. As the children move into second and third grade, they write their stories as drafts, read them aloud to the class, and receive ideas for revision as they sit in the author's chair. They rewrite and illustrate their stories to be bound and placed in the classroom library. They learn about the conventions of story development, spelling, punctuation, and grammar as they engage in book publishing. Research studies of children's writing document the importance of writing on the development of children's literacy (Burrows, 1984; Dyson, 2003; Graves, 1983).

Reading and Literature

Teachers knowledgeable about the importance of children's literature report that they read to their students more than once a day. There is general agreement that children who are read to at home have a leg up on reading achievement. It is ironic that in some schools reading to children is considered an extracurricular activity rather than central to the curriculum.

The classroom library should contain a minimum of 500 books written by professional authors for young children and include child-authored books as well. Teachers can obtain books for their libraries by having children join book clubs, suggesting that parents donate books to the classroom library in honor of their child's birthday, or by using their own money to purchase books. City or community libraries may lend teachers a supply of books for classroom use for a specified time period. School librarians often work with teachers to gather books that support classroom theme studies and visit the classroom for special read alouds. When children are involved in organizing and maintaining the classroom library, they develop a range of literacy abilities such as alphabetizing, categorizing, and becoming knowledgeable about the variety of fiction and informational books and other written materials available for pleasure and informational reading.

Literacy learning has benefitted from the rich publications of children's literature available online, in book stores, and in libraries for very young children. There are lists of informational books and material in all subject areas, easy books for beginning readers, biographies for younger readers, and boxed sets of children's favorite authors. There are online bibliographies of children's books arranged by themes, areas of interest, proficiency, and age level. The more knowledgeable teachers are about children's literature, the more they are able to connect what children want to learn with opportunities for reading. Vivian Paley, a renowned kindergarten teacher, writes how Leo Leonni became the focus of a literature study in her kindergarten classroom (Paley, 1998). The discussions and insights of young working-class children in Chicago demonstrate clearly that the literature and the context teachers create have immense effect on learning.

Children must have a range of experiences with materials other than trade books. Telephone books, brochures gathered from travel agencies, banks, zoos and public libraries, menus, and a range of different encyclopedias and dictionaries provide reading opportunities that support inquiry and other classroom studies. Computers are a growing resource for expanding children's literacy explorations. Newspaper publishers provide sets of papers to encourage interest in current news and encourage students to write their own newsletters. Teachers often encourage very young children to bring newspapers to class so they can share with peers information about good television shows, movies, and children's book reviews. Children learn to find weather reports and sections of the newspaper that have articles that answer their questions about local issues.

The literacy experiences discussed here show that young children are learning and developing literacy continuously in the classroom. These experiences can meet the standards or objectives established by state or district guidelines, especially when facilitated by a knowledgeable and experienced teacher. These experiences provide evidence of the power of language in children's literacy learning. Literacy is not empowering in and of itself. It is only empowering when it is nurtured in democratic settings where children are involved in choice and negotiation about their literacy experiences. Teachers who organize classrooms in these ways are courageous, willing to take the necessary risks to invite young children to bring their cultural backgrounds and language histories to the classroom to support equity and social justice (Edelsky, 2006).

Commercially Published Textbooks

There is an ongoing debate about the use of trade books (books written for young children by professional authors) and language arts textbooks (basal readers, and handwriting, spelling, and grammar books) written specifically for the purpose of direct instruction. Children's literature in the United States and throughout the world provides a rich array of materials for knowledgeable and experienced teachers to use as part of a language arts curriculum without relying on commercial materials. And these fiction and nonfiction books become exemplars for a range of writing opportunities.

But there are still states and local school districts that mandate textbooks, which often become the reading program. There is a place for published commercial materials to be used selectively by teachers. What is troubling is when teachers are expected to slavishly use these materials—an expectation that stifles teachers who know their students, understand language and curriculum, and have the knowledge to select resources that support students' literacy learning.

It has been common practice since the first part of the 20th century for states or school districts to mandate reading textbook series (basals) that often follow specific scope and sequences and include detailed directions for teachers and tests for children. The reason for using such materials and programs was the lack of quantity and quality of children's literature and the perceived inability of teachers to make decisions about how to teach reading. Some administrators still use the same rationale for demanding teachers follow the organization of textbooks, even though teachers have degrees and certification. State departments of education show that they value the use of textbooks or basals over trade books when money is allotted for textbook selection but not for trade books.

Basals and other instructional materials are useful when teachers are in control of their selection and their uses. There are good stories and helpful suggestions in commercially published programs that add to the teacher's reading program and save time in developing materials. But the teacher must control their use. Some teachers invite the students to be critical readers of their textbooks and to evaluate them with criteria such as whether they are culturally accurate, whether the characters are well represented, whether the information is historically and scientifically appropriate, and so forth.

Critics of public education often advocate for the use of basals and textbooks. Back-to-basics advocates often bemoan the demise of schools because of what they characterize as uninformed teachers and teacher educators. Rudolph Flesch's *Why Johnny Can't Read* (1955) and his sequel 30 years later supported the use of commercial materials because of their focus on phonics and sequenced learning When textbooks are mandated and followed by the teacher, lockstep drill in teaching often results. The tests and questions at the end of book sections often imply an ideology in which the only questions worth considering have a single right or wrong answer. Basal readers are critiqued in *Basal Readers: A Second Look* (Shannon & Goodman, 1994).

Final Thoughts

Throughout this exploration of early years literacy teaching and learning, the focus is on teachers who must be knowledgeable about language, language learning and teaching, and the relationship of such knowledge to the development of curriculum in the classroom. Throughout their careers, such teachers take advantage of professional reading, advanced degrees, professional development, and teacher study groups to build their expertise. Teachers would benefit from thoughtfully planned courses in applied linguistics that focus on language study—language development; how language is used in society; the forms of language; the thinking processes individuals use to speak, listen, read, and write: and the power and politics of language in socioeconomic issues in a democratic and global society (Y. Goodman, 2003).

Teachers learn a lot from kidwatching (Owocki & Goodman, 2002)—observing children carefully with their growing knowledge, discovering the best practices that supports literacy learning, and knowing how to analyze data they gather from children's literacy experiences to provide evidence of the concepts young children construct on their multiple roads to becoming literate.

Literacy programs for young children are enhanced when educators are involved in the new developments, concerns, and controversies that face the teaching and learning of literacy to young children. Schools, administrators, and teacher education programs should work with teachers to establish study groups that explore the development of curriculum with all its complexity. Such explorations are already the focus of professional language and literacy organizations that organize conferences, publish print and online journals and books, and provide a range of services to teachers including support for study groups. Through active participation in professional organizations, teachers sustain their own professional development as they stay current in their field and develop opportunities to write and present to their colleagues. Early years language arts teachers benefit from professional organizations such as the National Council of Teachers of English (NCTE; http://http://www.ncte.org), the International Reading Association (IRA; http://www.reading.org), and the National Association for the Education of Young Children (NAEYC; http://www.naeyc.org).

Understanding literacy learning and teaching in the early years is a serious and complex undertaking. There is always more to learn about how to develop a literacy pedagogy and curriculum that establishes classrooms where young children have safe places to develop literacy and learn the concepts of social justice necessary to be contributing members of a democratic society. Emilia Ferriero (2003) reminds teachers, publishers, and early literacy researchers that

> Literacy is neither a luxury nor an obligation: it is a right. A right of boys and girls who will become free men and women, citizens of a world in which linguistic and cultural differences will be considered a wealth and not a defect. Different languages and different systems of writing are part of our cultural patrimony. Cultural diversity is as important as biodiversity: if we destroy it, we will not be able to recreate it. (p. 35)

References and Further Readings

Brown, R., Cazden, C., & Bellugi, U. (1969). *The child's grammar from I to III*. Minneapolis: University of Minnesota Press.

Burrows, A. (1984). *They all want to write: Written English in the elementary school* (4th ed.). Urbana, IL: National Council of Teachers of English.

Chall, J. S. (1967). *Learning to read: The great debate* (1st ed.). New York: McGraw-Hill.

Clay, M. (1979). *What did I write?* Exeter, NH: Heinemann.

Darling-Hammond, L. (2000). How teacher education matters. *Journal of Teacher Education, 51*(3), 166–173.

Dyson, A. (2003). *The brothers and sisters learn to write: Popular literacies in childhood and school cultures*. New York: Teachers College Press.

Edelsky, C. (2006). *With literacy and justice for all: Rethinking the social in language and education*. Mahwah, NJ: Lawrence Erlbaum Associates.

Ferreiro, E. (2003). *Past and present forms of the verbs to read and write*. (M. Fried, Trans.). Toronto, Ontario, Canada: Groundwork Books/Douglas & McIntyre.

Ferreiro, E., & Teberosky, A. (1982). *Literacy before schooling*. Portsmouth, NH: Heinemann.

Flesch, R. (1955). *Why Johnny can't read and what you can do about it*. New York: John Wiley.

Freeman, D., & Freeman, Y. (2006). *Teaching reading and writing in Spanish and English in bilingual and dual language classrooms*. Portsmouth, NH: Heinemann.

Goodman, K. (1993). *Phonics phacts*. Ontario, Canada: Scholastic Canada Ltd.

Goodman, Y. (1997). Multiple roads to literacy. In D. Taylor (Ed.), *Many families, many literacies* (pp. 56–62). Portsmouth, NH: Heinemann.

Goodman, Y. (2003). *Valuing language study: Inquiry into language for elementary and middle schools*. Urbana, IL: National Council of Teachers of English.

Goodman, Y., & Martens, P. (2007). *Critical issues in early literacy: Research and pedagogy*. Mahwah, NJ: Lawrence Erlbaum Associates.

Graves, D. (1983). *Writing: Teachers and children at work*. Exeter, NH: Heinemann.

Isaacson, W. (2007). *Einstein: His life and universe*. New York: Simon & Schuster.

Lee, D. M., & Allen, R. V. (1963). *Learning to read through experience*. New York: Appleton-Century Crafts.

Loban, W. (1967). *The language of elementary school children*. Champaign, IL: National Council of Teachers of English.

Martens, P. (1996). *I already know how to read: A child's view of literacy*. Portsmouth, NH: Heinemann.

Owocki, G., & Goodman, Y. (2002). *Kidwatching: Documenting children's literacy development*. Portsmouth, NH: Heinemann.

Paley, V. G. (1998). *The girl with the brown crayon: How children use stories to shape their lives*. Cambridge, MA: Harvard University Press.

Read, C. (1975). *Children's categorization of speech sounds in English*. Urbana, IL: National Council of Teachers of English.

Reyes, I. (2006). Exploring connections between emergent biliteracy and bilingualism. *Journal of Early Childhood Literacy, 6*(3), 267–292.

Shannon, P., & Goodman, K. (1994). *Basal readers: A second look*. New York: Richard C. Owen.

Smith, F. (1994). *Writing and the writer*. Mahwah, NJ: Lawrence Erlbaum Associates.

Taylor, D., & Dorsey-Gaines, C. (1988). *Growing up literate: Learning for inner city families*. Portsmouth, NH: Heinemann.

Teale, W., & Sulzby, E. (Eds.). (1986). *Emergent literacy: Writing and reading*. Norwood, NJ: Ablex Publishing Corporation.

Vygotsky, L. (1978). *Mind in society: The development of higher psychological processes*. Cambridge, MA: Harvard University Press.

Webster, J. J. (Ed.). (2004). *The collected works of M.A.K. Halliday* (Vol. 5). London/New York: Continuum.

Whitmore, K., Martens, P., Goodman, Y., & Owocki, G. (2004). Critical lessons from the transactional perspective on early literacy research. *Journal of Early Childhood Literacy, 4*(3), 291–325.

Wolfram, W., Adger, C., & Christian, D. (1999). *Language variation in schools and the community*. Mahweh, NJ: Lawrence Erlbaum Associates.

35

LANGUAGE ARTS

Reading and Literacy in
Adolescence and Young Adulthood

JUDITH K. FRANZAK

New Mexico State University

Adolescent literacy learning is a major focus in early 21st century secondary schooling in the United States. Partly as an outgrowth of widely-publicized efforts to increase reading achievement in early grades, policy makers, researchers, and educational leaders are turning their attention to the specific needs of adolescent literacy learners. Adolescent reading achievement in particular is the current focus of considerable national attention, especially in regard to struggling readers. Both the International Reading Association (IRA) and the National Council of Teachers of English (NCTE) have issued statements and policy briefs calling attention to the need for effective literacy instruction for adolescents. The federal government recently announced the Striving Readers program intended to increase student achievement in middle and high schools not meeting state benchmarks and to further the knowledge base of instructional techniques most effective in promoting adolescent reading achievement. All of these activities point to the important role of adolescent literacy learning in the 21st-century curriculum.

Although reading and writing in subject area disciplines such as history and science is an important aspect of promoting student learning, English language arts education is the primary content area for supporting adolescent literacy growth. This chapter provides an overview of English language arts education for adolescents with a specific focus on reading and the study of literature. Writing instruction and the study of language are critical compo-

nents of adolescent literacy learning as well. The intent of this chapter is to provide an overview of reading and the study of literature in secondary language arts with the recognition that reading and literary study are strongly affiliated with writing and language study. The first section of the chapter provides background on the specific needs of adolescent literacy learners. The second section discusses the theoretical base of reading and literature instruction and provides an overview of different pedagogical models used in secondary language arts classrooms. The third section of the chapter discusses the types of texts students typically encounter in language arts education. The chapter concludes with a discussion of promising developments and potential concerns in English language arts education.

Recognizing the Needs of Adolescent Literacy Learners

Supporting the literacy growth of teenagers begins with the recognition that students in Grades 6 through 12 have different needs than either elementary school students or adults. When students transition from elementary to middle school, it is generally assumed that they have learned basic processes of reading and writing. In middle school, they encounter new literacy demands, including the expectation that they read and write in content area disciplines such as social studies, mathematics, and science.

Engagement

An essential element in fostering adolescent literacy development is the concept of engagement. When students are interested in what they read and write, and are able to monitor their understanding, they are actively engaged in literacy learning. Although it may seem obvious that students need to be engaged in their learning, what is apparent from research is that many adolescents are *not* engaged by the texts and activities they encounter in the English language arts classroom. Engagement involves more than entertaining lesson plans or popular texts; it develops from the internal motivation of the adolescent literacy learner, as well as the classroom context in which he or she learns. Engagement is a complex phenomenon that differs with each individual. Because of this great variation, it is helpful to conceptualize engagement as a cycle of four interrelated elements that shift as the literacy learning context shifts. The key elements of engagement are motivation, cognitive strategies, choice and control, and social dimensions.

Motivation in literacy learning, in part, comes from the student's belief that he or she can succeed at the task. Many adolescent readers do not believe they can read the texts they encounter in a way that satisfies teacher and testing expectations. These students often rely on verbal explanations of the text provided by teachers and peers. Sometimes these students have not acquired the reading skills necessary for proficient reading of secondary school materials. In other cases, these students may possess the skills but lack confidence in their ability to apply the skills and strategies to their reading. In either case, student motivation increases when students learn to use reading strategies within the context of each discipline area. The use of cognitive strategies is essential to engagement because it is through knowing how to apply specific reading strategies and writing skills that students develop a sense of self-efficacy and motivation. Educators can help students by not encouraging them to rely exclusively on the teacher or peers to find out if they understood the text; this will eventually increase students' awareness of their own efficacy as readers. Teachers wanting to strengthen their students' sense of self-efficacy will often find out what the students see as their strengths as readers and build on these over the course of a year. Choosing texts that have rich potential engagement from an adolescent perspective is another important way teachers support adolescent readers' confidence.

In addition to self-efficacy, students need to sense purpose in their literacy learning to be motivated. This means that they understand why they are reading and writing certain kinds of texts and what they can expect to gain from the texts. Purpose in reading ties directly to what the reader wants out of a given text; it does not come from a student's desire to finish the task or earn a good grade. Teachers cultivate students' sense of purpose by helping individual students find texts that are meaningful to them, engaging students in inquiry about the importance of particular texts, and selecting texts that connect directly to adolescent issues.

Choice and control refers to providing students with choices about their literacy learning. Numerous studies have revealed the important role choice plays in motivation for adolescent readers. A large-scale study of middle school readers conducted by Ivey and Broaddus (2001) indicated that choice and availability of desirable reading material were prime motivational factors influencing the students' reading. When providing adolescent readers with choice about what texts they will read, a teacher must recognize that when given the opportunity to select their own reading material, adolescents in a number of studies have indicated a preference for texts that exhibit features not necessarily found in classrooms—they choose books based on movies or television, specialty magazines, comics, and cartoons. Allowing for choice and control is not equated with turning over all instructional decisions to students. When teachers accommodate students' needs for choice and control in their own literacy learning, they must retain the responsibility for guiding individual students in their development as readers and writers. Teachers can use their professional knowledge about adolescent literacy to draw upon student opinions and create recommended reading lists. Teachers can also provide students with options for assessment, ranging from written responses to artistic interpretations of literary works, to using discussion as a means of evaluating student learning.

Because reading and writing are social practices and serve as a means of communication, involving adolescents in the social dimension of literacy learning is also an important aspect of engagement. This means that students who are engaged are reading, writing, and using language to interact with others. Teachers who foster engagement through the social dimension of literacy create a reading community in which students share the social dimension of reading through talk, writing, and creative interpretation.

Strategic Reading Development

Adolescent literacy learners need specific instruction in the development of reading strategies. It is generally assumed by educators that secondary-level students possess basic decoding and comprehension skills. Extending these skills to develop the reading comprehension habits necessary for negotiating a range of complex texts is one of the goals of adolescent literacy education. In recent years, the trend toward explicit instruction in strategic reading has gained momentum. The underlying assumption for this practice is that strong readers possess and use a number of unconscious strategies when they read. These strategies are part of their reading process before, during, and after reading and include habits like predicting what will occur next in the text, questioning the text, and connecting to background knowledge. Strong readers rely on these strategies all the time, but struggling readers may not be aware of these strategies or know how to apply them in a specific discipline.

Discipline-Specific Literacy Practices

An aphorism often used to describe a key difference between early and secondary literacy instruction is that in early literacy students learn to read and in adolescent literacy students read to learn. Implicit in this statement is the idea that secondary students are expected to read texts from core content area disciplines such as math, English, science, and social studies and apply the knowledge gained from their reading to their overall learning in the discipline. Adolescents are also expected to use literacy to deepen their understanding of a wide range of elective subjects such as art history, business, and vocational classes. Knowing how to read and write in subject-specific ways is not an automatic outcome of general literacy development, however. Each discipline has its own particular literacy practices, and often adolescents are not aware of this. It may never occur to them that proficient reading of a computer science textbook requires different strategies than proficient reading of a Robert Frost poem. Disciplinary literacy practices include approaches to reading, ways of thinking, and specific uses of writing. To teach adolescents these concepts, teachers must draw upon and build on students' background knowledge or schemata about the topics and help them recognize the specific features of texts within a discipline. For example, texts in language arts classes are often narrative; thus, one important comprehension skill is the ability to enter the story world of the text (Wilhelm, 1997). In science, on the other hand, texts are often expository in nature. To read these texts successfully, students must identify main ideas and understand cause and effect. These examples illustrate the kinds of literacy practices used in different disciplines. Because adolescents are generally required to take courses in a minimum of four core disciplines (English, math, social studies, and science) and elective courses (e.g., family and consumer science, art, business), it is important that they receive explicit instruction in the particular ways of reading and writing that are fundamental to each discipline.

Social Dimensions of Adolescent Literacy Learning

Reading is much more than mastery of technical skills or knowledge. It is a complex social activity that involves multiple levels of social meaning, including the reader's identity, the classroom context, the author's identity, and the role of the text in any given social group. The culturally situated nature of reading recognizes that both readers and authors are members of specific social communities that shape their perceptions, attitudes, knowledge, and beliefs. Adolescents need teacher, peer, and whole-class relationships that support their development as sophisticated readers and thinkers.

Effective adolescent literacy instruction is predicated on the belief that adolescents need multiple opportunities to interact with others in the construction and comprehension of reading. In classroom practice, this means adolescents are engaged in meaningful discussions in which their inquiry and input is valued. The social dimension of literacy learning is not limited to discussion, but often includes writing and other forms of communication. When exploring the social dimension of literacy, adolescents are ideally engaged in interaction that deepens their understanding of texts and helps them recognize the social, political, and historical content and purposes within texts. Adolescents learn literacy practices most effectively when they feel they are members of dynamic and caring learning communities.

Recognizing and Valuing Diversity

An aspect of the social dimension of adolescent literacy learning is the importance of recognizing and valuing diversity in the English language arts classroom. Race, gender, class, religion, sexual orientation, and other identity characteristics are inextricably linked to the social dimensions of literacy learning. Because of a persistent achievement gap between White and non-White adolescent readers, it is vital for educators to recognize and respond to the diverse experiences and needs of these adolescents. In a policy brief, the National Council of Teachers of English (NCTE; 2007) points out that "Monocultural approaches to teaching can cause or increase the achievement gap and adolescents' disengagement with literacy" (p. 5). Multicultural literacy instruction incorporates several features. First, such instruction treats all literary traditions as valuable, rejects the privileging of some literary traditions over others, and recognizes that taste and value are cultural constructs. Thus, multicultural literature does not merely include several ethnic texts, but treats all texts as products of specific cultural traditions. Because literacy conveys cultural meaning and power, effective multicultural literacy instruction engages students in inquiry about how texts are valued in different contexts. Supporting adolescent literacy growth means recognizing that one-size literacy does not fit all. Research points to differences between the types of texts male and female students seem to enjoy (Smith & Wilhelm, 2002). Effective instruction recognizes the cultural frameworks of students, teachers, authors, and social communities and seeks ways to challenge literacy practices that are oppressive.

Multitextuality in Adolescent Lives

One of the most significant developments in adolescent literacy instruction is the recognition that students have rich lives outside of the classroom context. Often their nonschool literacy experiences involve digital or nonprint-based forms of text. With the growing recognition that adolescents negotiate complex literacy experiences that span their social worlds in and out of school, educators have turned their attention to exploring the role of multi-textuality in adolescent lives. This perspective acknowledges adolescents' out-of-school or voluntary literacy learning as a resource for school-based learning. By valuing students' indigenous literacy practices, multitextuality in the classroom engages students in the reading and production of texts that reflect authentic 21st-century literacy skills. Because contemporary literacy skills require familiarity with a host of competing narrative sources such as the Internet, books, television, and film, it is it is important for teachers and students to distinguish the unique demands of specific modes of literacy.

Reading and Literature in Secondary English Language Arts

Given the array of the adolescent literacy learner's needs, many schools and professional organizations expect all secondary teachers to share the responsibility for teaching adolescents how to grow as readers and writers. This collective approach to fostering literacy growth is known as reading and writing in the content areas. Although educators have recently given significant attention to adolescent literacy and many content area teachers are aware of the need to integrate literacy in their practice, it is the English language arts classroom where adolescent literacy learning is the central focus of curriculum and instruction.

When students think of English class, they might generally think of reading literature, writing essays, and occasionally doing grammar exercises. Reduced to its most basic elements, this vision of secondary English represents what is referred to as the tripod model of English curriculum (Applebee, 1974). This curricular model is based upon three strands of inquiry: language, literature, and composition. The three strands are inherently related, and English teachers are encouraged to teach the three subjects in an integrated manner. Although this model of language arts has been historically widespread in the secondary English classroom, a broader and more complex model of English language arts is espoused by the major literacy professional organizations. The National Council of Teachers of English (NCTE) has a long history of continually reevaluating the discipline of English to more clearly define and structure the field to more accurately reflect real-world literacy practices (as opposed to strictly school-based literacy practices like the five-paragraph essay). In 1996, the NCTE and the International Reading Association (IRA) copublished *Standards for the English Language Arts.* This set of standards specifically articulated a broad vision of English studies, the aim of which is to provide students with "the opportunities and resources to develop the language skills they need to pursue life's

goals and to participate fully as informed, productive members of society" (National Council of Teachers of English [NCTE] & International Reading Association [IRA], 1996, p. 3). The standards emphasize the shifting literacy demands of society and articulate the need for students to be conversant in reading, interpreting, and composing a diverse range of texts including nonprint media. The NCTE/IRA standards deliberately broaden the scope of study in English from the traditional tripod model to include subjects like speech and drama, technology, and media literacy. The NCTE/IRA standards do not treat these subjects as distinct facets of language arts that should be added into an existing curriculum. Rather, the standards articulate and emphasize the interrelated nature of English language arts as processes that are used to both compose and interpret a range of texts. The standards advance a view of language arts as both content and process. The NCTE/IRA standards are not intended to be prescriptive curricula, but instead are meant to create a shared and purposeful vision of the complex work of literacy education.

The NCTE/IRA standards enjoy broad support and have been used as the basis for state and district level standards throughout the country. In language arts, standards-based education usually does not rely on a specific set of texts that students are to read. Rather, standards-based education focuses on the types of texts students read, as well as the processes students apply in comprehending, interpreting, and appreciating the texts. Because there is no national curriculum in the United States, there is variation in the specific texts secondary students study, the types of writing they learn, and the range and depth of language study they are exposed to in secondary English classes. Despite this variation, there are important general trends in secondary reading and literature study.

Teaching Reading and Teaching Literature

A tacit understanding underlying curriculum in secondary English language arts is that reading is integral to the study of literature. Yet, just as adolescents who possess decoding and comprehension skills do not automatically know how to read a historical thesis, they also do not automatically know how to read a Gary Paulsen novel or a Shakespearean sonnet. This points to the need for secondary English teachers to incorporate explicit reading strategies instruction into their teaching of literature. The need for reading strategies instruction in the English language arts classroom for adolescents may seem obvious, but it has not always been addressed in classroom practice. Reasons for this include secondary English teachers' self-identified lack of knowledge about how to teach reading strategies and their deep commitment to the tradition of teaching literature (Ericson, 2001). This trend may be changing; the increased attention to adolescent literacy has resulted in the burgeoning of professional development materials specifically aimed at helping the secondary language arts teacher incorporate reading instruction. This movement is in response to the recognition that adolescents need explicit instruction and practice in the development of reading strategies associated with different kinds of texts. Teachers use a range of models, both informal and commercially-produced, to strengthen adolescents' strategic reading skills. Across the models there is general consensus on the need for the following: developing metacognitive awareness of one's own reading process, identifying the main idea and summarizing the text, drawing upon background knowledge, actively questioning during reading, visualizing, making inferences, and synthesizing information from the text with prior knowledge to create new understandings.

Teaching reading strategies to students in Grades 6 through 12 is a means of helping them better read, interpret, and appreciate a wide range of texts. In addition to teaching students the "how" of reading, secondary English curriculum has a strong foundation in teaching about and through texts; this literature instruction is what many consider to be the heart of the English curriculum. Literature instruction in the secondary school is often comprised of four areas: the literary works themselves, background information, literary terminology, and cultural information (Purves & Pradl, 2003). One of the most enduring approaches to teaching literature in the secondary classroom is the use of new critical theory. New criticism, developed by English scholars in the 1920s through the 1960s, espouses the importance of close reading of the text. It rejects the consideration of sociohistorical information in the evaluation of text and emphasizes the formal elements of text structure. New criticism suggests that there is a single correct way to read a text; a pedagogical manifestation of this theory can be found in the questions and answer sections that accompany literary passages in secondary English textbooks. For example, students might be asked to identify the use of metaphor in a poem or to analyze how an author resolves the conflict in a novel. This approach to literature instruction was widely used in the late 20th century and continues to thrive in secondary classrooms today.

A competing approach to teaching literature is the use of reader-centered (as opposed to text-centered) pedagogy. Rejecting the idea that each text has only one correct interpretation, reader response theory posits that each reading is unique. Reader response theory, as articulated by Louise Rosenblatt (1978), advocates that reading is a transaction between the reader and the text. Each transaction is unique, affected by the reader's past experiences, the circumstances of the reading, and the sociocultural factors influencing both the reader and the author. It is a process-centered approach in which the reader is an active participant in constructing meaning from the text. In secondary language arts curriculum, reader response theory provides the basis of a pedagogy that emphasizes personal response to literature. In this model, teachers ask students to reflect on and build their own interpretations of the text.

This approach is widely recognized for its ability to motivate readers by valuing their experience and background knowledge. A benefit of reader response theory is that it values an individual reader's schema and interpretation, and rejects the notion that there is only one valid way to read a work.

But reader response pedagogy in the secondary language arts classroom is problematic. English educators have made several observations about reader response theory in the classroom. An especially prevalent concern is how to evaluate what counts as a valid interpretation. Because of the emphasis on individual response, it is possible that virtually any interpretation suggested by a student could be a legitimate reading of the text. The flexibility inherent in reader response is not a substitute for rigor. Rosenblatt and others have pointed out that a valid interpretation is one that does not disregard evidence presented in the text. Thus, the criteria for evaluating quality in interpretation must account for the reader's experiences and knowledge as well as the content of the text. Another concern is that reader response ignores the cultural and political dimensions of both the reader's and the author's context. Critics charge that in classrooms where personal response is promoted as the main way of interpreting text, it is possible, for example, for White students to read the works of an author of color and not attend to elements of racism presented in the text. As with the concern about what constitutes a valid interpretation, this critique of reader response theory focuses on how it is manifested in secondary classrooms, not with reader response as a theoretical model. Reader response theory as articulated by Rosenblatt and others acknowledges the importance of examining the reader's sociocultural context. Teachers can address this concern by asking students to explore how their personal response is shaped by their social context. Teachers can also extend the learning about and through the text to take into account the political and social dimensions of the context in which the text was originally produced as well as the context in which students are reading it.

Secondary English language arts instruction is heavily influenced by developments in scholarship and pedagogy at the university level. Both new criticism and reader response theory have roots in the academy. Thus, it is not surprising that an emerging trend in secondary English literature instruction is the inclusion of many postmodern literary theories. These critical approaches to reading and interpreting literature start with the assumption that there is no universal truth and that all experience is subjective. In this vein, reader response theory is a type of postmodern literary theory. As discussed above, reader response theory has been particularly embraced in secondary English education. Other literary theories that have made inroads in adolescent literacy learning include feminist, Marxist, psychoanalytic, and critical race theory. A number of professional books and journal articles advocate for and provide pedagogical models for teaching adolescents how to read literature through a critical lens. Despite professional discourse that suggests the value of teaching students critical literary theory, it is difficult to gauge the influence of these theories in classroom practice. Arthur Applebee's large-scale national study of the teaching of literature in secondary schools (1993) found that the most common approaches to teaching literature were new critical and reader response. Interestingly, even though these two models are based upon diametrically opposed assumptions (that there is one correct reading and that each reading is a unique transaction), Applebee found that teachers did not see an incompatibility between the two traditions. This suggests that teachers use and even adapt certain features of literary theory in their instruction rather than subscribing to literary theory as doctrine.

Three Approaches to Teaching Text

English language arts teachers use theoretical lenses as a way to read and analyze text. These lenses influence how teachers shape the meaning adolescent readers derive from texts. Another important aspect of adolescent language arts education is the pedagogical approach teachers adopt when structuring the literature learning environment. There are three basic approaches to teaching text found in the secondary classroom: whole-class reading, literature groups, and independent reading.

In whole-class reading, all students read the same book at the same time. Teachers often use this teaching strategy because they want to create a shared literary experience among their students, building an inclusive and supportive learning community in the process. Another reason teachers opt to teach the same book at the same time to a whole class is they want to use features of the text as anchor lessons that students can refer to throughout the course of their learning. For example, a teacher may use a poem to teach personification or a nonfiction text to teach students how to identify and articulate a main idea. In some cases, teachers may also use whole-class reading to meet curricular requirements that students read specific texts, although with the advent of standards-based curriculum, such practices may be based on tradition more than official curriculum. Instruction that complements whole-class reading may use minilessons (20 minutes or shorter) that enhance students' understanding of the text. Because some students may rely on the teacher or peers for comprehension, it is especially important that teachers work with all students to ensure they are reading and comprehending the text during whole-class instruction. It is common practice for English teachers to intersperse whole-class reading with writing, visual, and kinesthetic activities.

The use of literature circles or reading groups is another approach to teaching texts in secondary classrooms. Students are grouped either by the teacher or through self-selection and read a common text in a small group. There are many variations of group reading; for instance, students may read a variety of texts on one topic. Again, as with whole-class reading, students share a common literary experience, but in the case of literature circles, the shared experience is with a smaller group. Literature circles provide students with an opportunity for discussion in which reluctant discussants may participate more actively because of the smaller group size. Because teachers are not the facilitators of the discussions, literature circles open the possibility for engaged, student-centered, authentic discussion. Literature circles also meet adolescents' needs for choice and control by allowing a degree of student choice regarding text selection, reading schedule, and even assessments.

One challenge of using literature circles in the classroom is how to manage multiple groups reading different texts. Harvey Daniels (2002), who is widely recognized as the most influential promoter of literature circles in the language arts classroom, suggests a combination of management and assessment techniques. One frequently used method is to assign roles to each reader in the group. These roles represent a range of reading behaviors, such as visualizing, developing vocabulary, and analyzing character development. Assigned roles are not an essential element of literature circles; teachers may prefer to use other means of assessing students, such as recording their discussions or creating multilayered tasks for the group to complete.

The final approach to teaching text in the English language arts classroom is independent reading, in which students read texts on their own. Independent reading fosters adolescent reading development when it is incorporated as a consistent and extensive classroom practice. Independent reading helps readers build fluency, develop vocabulary, and experience a variety of text formats and features. Research shows that independent reading practice is most effective when students select their own material, which may include magazines, newspapers, series books, or graphic novels. Teachers who incorporate independent reading in their classrooms often allow for student choice while reserving the right to approve student selections. To do this well, teachers need to be knowledgeable about their students as individuals and about a wide range of texts so that they can make appropriate recommendations and informed decisions. Significant teacher knowledge and preparation is required to meaningfully incorporate independent reading in the language arts classroom. The teacher's responsibilities in independent reading include maintaining an atmosphere conducive to reading; providing ample reading time in class; implementing assessments that provide information about students' engagement and comprehension; conferring with students about their reading; teaching minilessons on reading strategies, text features, and authors; and modeling engaged reading by reading and sharing personal enthusiasm for books.

All three of these approaches—whole-class instruction, literature circles, and independent reading—have benefits and limitations in classroom practice. No one method meets the needs of all readers; therefore, teachers should adopt more than one approach in their literature instruction.

The Range of Texts Taught in the English Classroom

Students need exposure to a range of different literary traditions. This section explores the characteristics of literature that students typically encounter in the secondary language arts curriculum.

The Expanding Canon

Despite standards-based curricula that promote outcomes instead of content coverage, the teaching of English language arts has been characterized by remarkable consistency in the actual texts used in classroom instruction. In a national study of the book-length works taught in English, Applebee reported uniformity in the most frequently taught texts. Nine of the 10 most frequently taught texts were written by White males of European descent, Harper Lee's *To Kill a Mockingbird* being the exception. Overall, the five most frequently studied authors were Shakespeare, Steinbeck, Twain, Dickens, and Henry Miller. These texts and authors reflect what for many years was considered the canon of high school literature. Often equated with classic literature, the traditional canon has been criticized for its inaccessibility to contemporary adolescent readers and for its exclusion of literary traditions emerging outside a White, male, or Eurocentric perspective. For some time, what texts should constitute the canon has been the topic of heated debate in academic circles. The fortunate carryover of this discourse has been the reshaping of the secondary English canon to include a richer range of texts.

No large-scale study of a similar nature has been conducted since Applebee's 1993 study, yet numerous indicators point to a shifting curriculum that now includes more authors of color, female authors, young adult literature, nonfiction, and popular (i.e., not specifically literary) texts. This shift is evidenced by such things as the range of authors included in literature textbooks, articles published in professional journals, and professional development materials published by national organizations. For example, a Web-based video workshop produced by the Annenberg Foundation provides an in-depth look at how to teach multicultural literature in high school (http://www.learner.org/channel/workshops/hslit/). Authors whose work secondary students may encounter in the classroom include Amy Tan, Alice Walker, James Baldwin, Leslie Silko, Chinua Achebe, Sandra Cisneros, and Langston Hughes. The inclusion of more authors of color and female authors in the secondary classroom recognizes that literary tradition encompasses many diverse experiences. It also reflects the population in secondary schools, which exhibits tremendous diversity. Students need to be exposed to texts in which their traditions and identity are represented.

The use of young adult literature in the 21st-century language arts curriculum is also widespread. Young adult literature, also known as adolescent literature or teen fiction, is—as its name implies—written primarily for adolescent readers. Main characters in these books are often adolescents, and the plots and themes of the texts reflect issues that are especially relevant to adolescents' interests.

Young adult literature deals with contemporary issues or historical issues with contemporary relevance and considers diverse perspectives, including cultural, social, and gender. It spans many genres, including poetry, series books, novels, graphic novels, and nonfiction. Many scholars identify the 1960s as the period in which authors and publishers began to specifically target the teenage reader. Although not all English teachers are eager to embrace this literature, adolescent readers find it appealing enough that the publishing sector devoted to their interests has grown tremendously. Today's adolescent literature reflects a broad range of styles, interests, genres, and perspectives. Teachers express concern that adolescent literature is not of sufficient quality to merit classroom time when there are classic works that have withstood the test of time and that the issues presented in adolescent literature are too controversial for the classroom. The first of these arguments has been resolved with some degree of consensus more so than the latter. Although individual teachers may appreciate or disregard specific young adult texts, the English language arts community as a whole has articulated the importance of young adult literature in the curriculum. Which young adult texts should be taught in classrooms is, at times, a source of controversy. This is apparent in the number of young adult titles listed in the American Library Association's (ALA) lists of the most frequently challenged books. In 2005, for example, 7 of the top 10 most frequently challenged works were young adult literature.

Digital, Nonprint, and Popular Culture Texts

Twenty-first-century literacy is predicated on the ability to understand and use digital and nonprint texts. Effective teachers of adolescent literacy take into account how popular and nonprint texts construct multiple positions that viewers and readers inhabit. As discussed earlier, it is important for educators to build bridges between adolescents' nonschool literacy practices and school-based learning to increase students' motivation and provide them with meaningful opportunities to develop relevant literacy skills. A key way of doing this is through the study and use of digital and nonprint texts. The Internet is an essential component of contemporary literacy; with the exponential increase in the amount of user-created text available online, the World Wide Web presents an especially rich venue for teaching about and through digital texts. Such literacy activities go beyond completing a Webquest or using the Internet to find information for a research project. Critical exploration of digital literacies engages students in the evaluation and creation of such Web-based text formats as wikis, blogs, electronic mailing lists, podcasts, and Web sites. Extending inquiry to explore the relationship between texts is called multimodal literacy. The benefits of purposefully incorporating digital literacies and nontraditional texts in the classroom are significant. Not only does this increase the possibilities for student engagement, but research demonstrates that it also increases student achievement in traditional literacy skills like writing paragraphs and comprehending print-based text (Hobbs & Frost, 2003).

Popular culture texts also support adolescent literacy learning. These texts may be print-based, such as zines (self-published magazines that offer an alternative to mass market media) or graphic novels, or they may be nonprint media, such as film and television. Again, the most effective pedagogical practice encourages critical viewing and analysis of the text structure, content, and purpose.

Conclusion

At the beginning of the 21st century, there is much to consider when evaluating how to best support adolescents in developing the literacy skills that they will need to be knowledgeable and empowered members of a global society. What is clear is that shifting literacy demands will affect how literacy is taught in secondary schools. How this will look in 5 or 25 years is difficult to say, but it is likely that students will be engaged in reading and composing a greater variety of texts than were their counterparts in the late 20th century. In the not too distant past, secondary English language arts teachers were relatively immune from the effects of No Child Left Behind because the legislation and policy initiatives were directed at supporting early literacy learning. Now, however, the pressure to meet prescribed achievement goals is felt in every middle and high school in the United States. In some schools, this pressure results in the adoption of a commercial reading program that promises to raise achievement. Although such programs may indeed increase student achievement on specific assessments, they contribute little to the development of the wide-ranging, purposeful literacy habits that adolescents need. Adolescent literacy educators must negotiate the competing demands to prepare students for 21st-century literacy and success on mandated assessments. Currently, there is little congruence between the assessments and the complex realities of being a competent literacy user in contemporary society. National professional organizations like the NCTE and IRA are increasing their presence in the policy arena to influence how adolescent literacy learners' needs are met now and in the future. A positive outcome of the intensified attention to adolescent literacy is the potential that more research, professional development, and shared knowledge will contribute to supporting the literacy development of all adolescents.

References and Further Readings

Alvermann, D. E. (2001). *Effective literacy instruction for adolescents.* Executive summary and paper commissioned by the National Reading Conference. Chicago, IL: National Reading Conference.

Alvermann, D. E., Hinchman, K. A., Moore, D. W., Phelps, S. F., & Waff, D. R. (Eds.). (1998). *Reconceptualizing the literacies in adolescents' lives.* Mahwah, NJ: Lawrence Erlbaum Associates.

Applebee, A. N. (1974). *Tradition and reform in the teaching of English: A history.* Urbana, IL: National Council of Teachers of English.

Applebee, A. N. (1993). *Literature in the secondary school: Studies of curriculum and instruction in the United States* (No. 25). Urbana, IL: National Council of Teachers of English.

Appleman, D. (2000). *Critical encounters in high school English: Teaching literary theory to adolescents.* New York: Teachers College Press.

Beach, R. (1993). *A teacher's introduction to reader-response theories.* Urbana, IL: National Council of Teachers of English.

Beers, K., Probst, R. E., & Rief, L. (2007). *Adolescent literacy: Turning promise into practice.* Portsmouth, NH: Heinemann.

Biancarosa, G., & Snow, C. E. (2004.) *Reading next—A vision for action and research in middle and high school literacy: A report to Carnegie Corporation of New York.* Washington, DC: Alliance for Excellent Education.

Cherland, M. R. (1994). *Private practices: Girls reading fiction and constructing identity.* London: Taylor & Francis.

Daniels, H. (2002). *Literature circles: Voice and choice in book clubs and reading groups.* Portland, ME: Stenhouse

Ericson, B. O. (2001). *Teaching reading in high school English classes.* Urbana, IL: National Council of Teachers of English.

Gee, J. P. (2000). Teenagers in new times: A new literacy studies perspective. *Journal of Adolescent & Adult Literacy, 43,* 412–420.

Greenleaf, C. L., Schoenbach, R., Cziko, C., & Mueller, F. L. (2001). Apprenticing adolescent readers to academic literacy. *Harvard Educational Review, 71*(1), 79–129.

Hobbs, R., & Frost, R. (2003). Measuring the acquisition of media-literacy skills. *Reading Research Quarterly 38,* 330–356.

Hull, G., & Schultz, K. (Eds.). (2001). *School's out! Bridging out-of-school literacies with classroom practice.* New York: Teachers College Press.

Ivey, G., & Broaddus, K. (2001). "Just plain reading": A survey of what makes students want to read in middle school classrooms. *Reading Research Quarterly, 36*(4), 350–377.

Kist, W. (2004). *New literacies in action: Teaching and learning in multiple media.* New York: Teachers College Press.

Moje, E. B. (2000). *All the stories that we have: Adolescents' insights about literacy and learning in secondary schools.* Newark, DE: International Reading Association.

Moje, E. B. (2002). Re-framing adolescent literacy research for new times: Studying youth as a resource. *Reading Research and Instruction, 41,* 211–228.

Moore, D. W., Bean, T. W., Birdyshaw, D., & Rycik, J. A. (1999). *Adolescent literacy: A position statement for the Commission on Adolescent Literacy of the International Reading Association.* Newark, DE: International Reading Association.

National Council of Teachers of English. (2007). *Adolescent literacy: A policy research brief.* Retrieved September 17,

2007, from http://www.ncte.org/library/files/Publications/Newspaper/Chron0907ResearchBrief.pdf?source=gs

National Council of Teachers of English & International Reading Association. (1996). *Standards for the English language arts.* Retrieved September 17, 2007, from http://www.ncte.org/about/over/standards/110846.htm

Purves, A. C., & Pradl, G. M. (2003). The school subject literature. In J. Flood, D. Lapp, J. R. Squire & J. M. Jensen (Eds.), *Handbook of research on teaching the English language arts* (pp. 848–856). Mahwah, NJ: Lawrence Erlbaum Associates.

Rosenblatt, L. M. (1978). *The reader, the text, the poem: The transactional theory of the literary work.* Carbondale, IL: Southern Illinois Press.

Schoenbach, R., Greenleaf, C., Cziko, C., & Hurwitz, L. (1999). *Reading for understanding: A guide to improving reading in middle and high school classrooms.* San Francisco: Jossey-Bass.

Smith, M. W., & Wilhelm, J. D. (2002). *"Reading don't fix no Chevys": Literacy in the lives of young men.* Portsmouth, NH: Heinemann.

Sturtevant, E., Boyd, F., Brozo, W., Hinchman, K., Mooore, D., Alverman, D. (2006). *Principled practices for adolescent literacy: A framework for instruction and policy.* Mahwah, NJ: Lawrence Erlbaum Associates.

Tatum, A. W. (2000). Breaking down barriers that disenfranchise African American adolescent readers in low-level tracks. *Journal of Adolescent & Adult Literacy, 44,* 52–64.

Tovani, C. (2000). *I read it, but I don't get it: Comprehension strategies for adolescent readers.* Portland, ME: Stenhouse.

Wilhelm, J. D. (1997). *"You gotta be the book": Teaching engaged and reflective reading with adolescents.* Urbana, IL: National Council of Teachers of English.

36

WRITING

SARAH J. MCCARTHEY

University of Illinois at Urbana-Champaign

Theories about how writers compose texts frame current research and pedagogy. Informed by LeFevre's (1987) paradigms for writing, Applebee's (2000) models of writing development, and Ward's (1994) analysis of various dialogic pedagogies, this chapter uses four frames to characterize research and practice in writing: emergent, cognitive, social constructivist, and critical.

Emergent

The emergent frame has its roots in a diverse set of sources: (a) phenomenological philosophy, (b) Bruner's (1962) studies of cognition and creativity, (c) Chomsky's 91965) view of language acquisition, and (d) the Paris Review interviews (Plimpton, 1963). Phenomenology is based on the idea that reality is organized and experienced by the individual through language. Bruner's early work focused on the ways in which children's learning developed through manipulation, representation, and symbolism of the external world, and Chomsky theorized that children acquired language through a series of successive grammars. The *Paris Review* interviewed 20th-century poets, novelists, and essayists about their work, highlighting the creative and often challenging process of exploration and discovery. The common focus was the writer finding voice and perfecting the craft of writing.

Two major studies of writing instruction in the classroom, one conducted in Britain (Britton, Burgess, Martin, McLeod, & Rosen, 1975) and the other conducted in the United States (Applebee, 1981), found that writing assignments tended to be limited in scope and purpose and typical assignments were fill-in-the blank exercises or first-and-final draft reports written for the teacher. Britton et al. (1975) developed a model that suggests learning to write is a process of learning to use language in different ways, from everyday language to formalized language in new genres to inform, persuade, or entertain. Writing follows a developmental continuum in which younger students engage in more expressive writing and older students move toward transactional and literary writing.

Educators enacted Britton's ideas, emphasizing writing for multiple purposes and audiences other than the teacher. For example, freewriting could help students generate ideas, and teachers and students could discuss those ideas with instructors asking open-ended questions about texts and processes. Elbow (1981) argued for using writing groups in which readers pointed to effective features of the text, summarized the author's ideas, described what they experienced reading the text, and showed their understanding by suggesting metaphors for the text. Instructors in this model are experienced coaches with whom a student can consult.

Calkins (1983) documented the progress of a third grader for 2 years. She found that peer conferences, teachers talking about writing, and the use of model texts assisted the student in developing composing strategies and confidence. From this work, she recommended workshops that incorporated student choice of topics, writing for real audiences, developing revision strategies, and sharing work with peers. Conventions such as capitalization and punctuation were taught through minilessons and the context of students' own writing. Teachers organized the workshop into a predictable structure and provided modeling and support for students. As teaching strategies for writing workshops were refined, teachers across the United States implemented aspects of the workshop.

Some teachers continue to implement workshops despite the current focus on state testing. Effective writing workshops demonstrate a particular convention or genre, provide authentic writing opportunities, use appropriate models such as books and other students' writing, and are guided by the teacher. Yet, conferring with students, helping students revise their work, and assessing students' progress are ongoing challenges to teachers implementing workshops. Teachers who have implemented workshops for years continue to do so; however, many teachers, especially in low-income schools, feel pressured to use mandated, packaged curriculum. The National Writing Project has helped maintain and enhance workshop models through its nationwide network of sites for professional development that emphasizes teachers as leaders who engage in writing and conduct inquiry into their own practices.

Writing workshops fit well with a developmental perspective of language and literacy that derives from the work of Marie Clay (1975). By focusing on the patterns underlying different forms of writing, Clay found that children used invented spelling as they developed more conventional spelling. Writing begins early as preschoolers become increasingly purposeful in representing concepts in their environment. Through immersion in print-rich environments and interacting with knowledgeable language users, children learn the forms and functions of print and learn to link meaning and form.

Sulzby (1985) found that kindergarten children used different forms of writing for different tasks such as words, sentences, or stories; they used immature forms of writing (e.g., scribble) when attempting a more difficult task like writing a story. Sulzby identified developmental patterns including drawing, making letter-like units, using random letters, using invented spelling, and then writing conventional words. Teale and Martinez (1989) followed kindergartners who participated in an emergent literacy writing program. They found that connecting writing to authentic purposes, literature, and to each other fostered students' writing development. Casbergue and Plauché (2005) found that a kindergartener developed through different stages as she gained control of mechanical aspects of writing; at times, she appeared to regress as she alternated focusing on form and meaning. Tolchinsky (2006) argued that children's writing development does not move unidirectionally from smaller to larger units, but rather through four stages. In the initial stage, meaning of the pattern is determined by the place it appears. The child proceeds through a gradual process of selecting and combining forms until he or she arrives at the alphabetic principle. The knowledge acquired at one level both guides and constrains what can be learned at other levels.

Studies with older students also support the premise that children develop writing skills as they mature. Bissex (1980) followed her own child's development from ages 5 through 10 and found that he used a variety of forms including signs, notes, and stories for communicative purposes. Her son developed a range of writing strategies from invented spelling to conventional spellings through his literate environment and interactions with his parents. Langer (1986) explored children's knowledge of genre at ages 8, 11, and 14 and found that children developed more complex prose structures and more elaboration in their writing with age and experience. Practitioners who work within the emergent framework have found that young children use a variety of genres in their writing. Research conducted from the emergent perspective highlights the developmental nature of children's writing as they interact with print.

Cognitive

Proposing a model of writing derived from cognitive psychology, Hayes and Flower (1980) challenged previous assumptions about how writers composed text. They identified three major components: (a) the task environment; (b) cognitive processes involved in writing such as planning, translating, and revision; and (c) long-term memory including knowledge of topic, genre, and audience. Emig's (1971) seminal study on the writing processes of twelfth graders reinforced that writing is a tool for reasoning and learning rather than a means to demonstrate knowledge already acquired. These researchers initiated cognitive studies that (a) identified recursive aspects of composing such as planning, organizing, drafting, and revising; (b) focused on the differences between novices and expert writers; and (c) suggested processes vary according to the task, context, and students' backgrounds.

To understand the role of memory, problem solving, text production, and motivation, researchers have investigated factors in the writing process. For example, good writers coordinate multiple subprocesses more easily than poor writers. Problem solving, decision making, and inferencing influence writers' representations of texts. Writers draw from their understanding of tasks and knowledge of their audience to compose texts, which involves producing parts rather than whole sentences (Hayes, 2000). But students often have difficulties identifying problems in their own texts and avoid making major revisions. Torrance and Galbraith (2006) suggest that the writing process is a set of "delicately balanced . . . interrelated processes" (p. 73) that are being frantically coordinated rather than the relatively strategic and deliberate process that Hayes and Flower described.

Bereiter and Scardamalia (1987) delineated two different writing processes: knowledge telling and knowledge transforming. Knowledge telling enables students to write about what they know about a topic; it is often appropriate for the narrow demands of school tasks. Knowledge transforming goes beyond telling to develop new ideas and transform writers' understandings. In their research on fifth-grade, tenth-grade, and adult writers, Bereiter and Scardamalia found that novice and expert writers differed in their composing behaviors. Elementary writers tend to do little planning or goal setting, instead using a what-next strategy of writing from one sentence to the next. Knowledge telling may be an adaptive function for novice writers when they are constrained by working memory or the task. Yet effective instruction can help students learn components of the process to improve their writing over time.

The cognitive model has influenced several intervention programs that help students to become motivated and strategic writers. Hidi and Boscolo (2006) found that providing instruction on argumentative writing and using extensive collaborative writing activities with junior high school students improved self-efficacy and interest in writing. Follow-up studies have shown that interest, self-efficacy, and self-regulation are closely related—usually an interested writer is also self-regulated; mastery of cognitive and linguistic tools tends to improve motivation.

Cognitive Strategy Instruction in Writing (CSIW; Raphael & Hiebert, 1996) and Concept Oriented Reading Instruction (CORI; Guthrie et al., 1996) were designed to help elementary students improve their writing and to increase their awareness of composing processes. Research investigating the effects of such instruction has demonstrated positive effects on students' ability to synthesize information from multiple sources; identify various text structures; and use strategies to collect information, organize information, and write reports. Guthrie et al. found that the increased use of strategies was highly correlated with students' motivation. A meta-analysis of studies of groups (experimental and control) and single subjects determined that strategy instruction improves students' writing performance (Graham, 2006). This is noteworthy because the effects on student writing were not related to the type of student, grade-level placement, type of strategy instruction taught, or genre.

Research from the cognitive frame has also examined the role of genre. A study of students' texts in grades kindergarten through five indicated that even the youngest students were able to differentiate between stories and informational texts, and produce the requested genre by second grade. Direct teaching of story structure improves children's understanding of those genres, and explicit instruction in composing different types of texts results in students outperforming those who did not receive explicit instruction (Donovan & Smolkin, 2006). Research from the cognitive frame has produced important information about the subprocesses writers use when composing text, the role of motivation on learning to write, the effects of explicit strategy instruction, and the effect of understanding genre on students' writing.

Social Constructivist

Social constructivist theories assume that knowledge is the product of negotiation and consensus among members of a discourse community and that writing is a psychological tool that mediates thought (Vygotsky, 1978). LeFevre (1987) articulated the foundations of social constructivism for writing: (a) the writer is influenced by the social context; (b) writing norms and genres build on knowledge from the past; (c) writing may be enhanced by an imagined dialogue with another; (d) writers involve others as editors, collaborators, and devil's advocates; and (e) social context influences how texts are received, evaluated, and used.

Bruffee's (1984) work made the link between social constructivist theory and writing in college classrooms; he suggested that instructors take advantage of the social nature of writing by supporting students' engagement in dialogue about their own writing. Englert, Mariage, and Dunsmore (2006) have translated the tenets of sociocultural theory into pedagogical principles for guiding instruction for elementary students. These principles mandate that teachers of writing should (a) offer cognitive apprenticeships to help students acquire tools, discourses, and actions; (b) facilitate performance in advance of requiring students' independent performance; and (c) establish communities of practice for writing in their classrooms.

The effect of the social constructivist frame is apparent in studies of writing conferences, collaboration, the role of community and context, and issues of identity and positioning. In ideal teacher-student conferences, the teacher invites the student to set the agenda and gives the student critical feedback, while the student responds, asks questions, and describes his or her own work.

Research on writing conferences has found that instructors differ in their approaches; some teachers are prescriptive and others are collegial. Ideally, teachers should vary their style to accommodate differences in students—teachers may adopt a facilitative style for students who are readily able to self-assess but a more directive style for students who face more challenges (Beach & Friedrich, 2006). Teachers tend to be less directive with strong writers than weak writers, and they elicit opinions more frequently from strong writers. Students' diverse backgrounds affect teacher-student interactions and help structure the event (Patthey-Chavez & Ferris, 1997). Tensions and miscommunication resulting in misevaluations of students' performance and lost teaching opportunities can occur during conferences. Freedman (1987) found that successful teachers had a strong writing philosophy, guided students but did not take over their students' writing, and established classroom activities that allowed students to communicate their ideas. In collaborative conferences teachers and students actively negotiate topic and structure, whereas students simply accept teachers' ideas in less collaborative conferences. Additionally, conferences function differently at various points in the writing process (e.g., prewriting, drafting, and revision), and students obtain different benefits depending on the circumstances (Sperling, 1998). High school students tend to revise surface and stylistic features of their writing depending on the classroom context and focus of instruction (Yagelski, 1995). Engaging assignments that allow for alternative perspectives can foster in-depth revision. In elementary schools, researchers have found that students' text revisions reflect conversations during conferences and that the conferences have differential effects on students with different levels of experience as writers (Fitzgerald & Stamm, 1992). Effective teacher feedback needs to be specific, descriptive, nonjudgmental, and varied according to the student's developmental level, language skills, and ability to self-assess.

Researchers investigating classroom interactions during writing time noted that not all "writing process" classrooms were alike; contexts shape classroom activities and student learning (Lipson, Mosenthal, Daniels, & Woodside-Jiron, 2000). Context includes factors such as the history of classroom events, teachers' own histories, and institutional, disciplinary, and social contexts (Prior, 1998). Factors such as students' knowledge of books or the writing topic, perceptions of teacher expectations, and the particular task also influence students' writing.

Sperling and Woodlief (1997) compared the writing environments of two tenth-grade classrooms, one in a White, middle-class school and the other in an urban, multiethnic school. They found that the teachers and students created quite different kinds of communities as expressed through teachers' goals and assignments and students' values for writing. Gutierrez (1992) found that the quality of instruction and the specific classroom context affected elementary students' learning to write. Writing increases in complexity and richness when children respond to each other, to readings, and to the teacher's suggestions. Other researchers have found that the nature of the writing opportunities, the quality of the student-teacher interaction during writing time, and the ways in which peers respond to one another influence students' understanding of the tasks and their willingness to engage in the composing process (McCarthey, García, López-Velásquez, Lin, & Guo, 2004). Although collaborative peer groups provide support for writing and development of ideas, students need training in strategies for providing specific responses as well as group process skills.

Research from the social constructivist frame has also found that cultural contexts affect students' attitudes toward writing, their positioning of themselves in relation to the tasks, and the ways in which they construct their identities as writers. Students' participation in writing classrooms depends on their perceptions of themselves and others, their attitudes toward writing, and their per-

spectives about what is important in each setting. Abbott (2000) found that students' motivation to write was strongly influenced by social context and the teacher's willingness to allow them to pursue their own interests. Age of students, their purposes for writing, and the context for writing are important factors that influence students' attitudes and performance.

Students use writing for a variety of personal and social functions, including the exploration of new roles and social identities (Kamberelis & de la Luna, 2004). McCarthey (2002) found that elementary students constructed their identities as writers in accordance with the school curriculum as well as the teacher's, their parents, and their peers' views of them as literacy learners. A yearlong study of a primary classroom revealed that students interwove social, emotional, and intellectual dimensions of themselves as they struggled to become writers within a workshop setting (Bomer & Laman, 2004).

Practices such as collaborative writing also derive from social constructivist theories. Daiute (1989) found that young children enjoyed writing together and enhanced their skills when they were encouraged to play and invent on the computer. Schultz (1997) identified many types of collaboration including sharing texts, writing about the same topic, and writing a single text in a fifth- and sixth-grade classroom that encouraged students to work together. Working in pairs can help students become aware of their decisions and enhance sharing of information during text production.

Research from the social constructivist frame has focused on writing conferences, classroom context, identity, and collaboration. The studies suggest that teacher-student conferences and response groups are effective in supportive contexts with quality instruction. Contexts affect students' motivation and identities, and the quality of their writing.

Critical

Paolo Freire (1970) based his pedagogy on the idea that it was essential to replace traditional banking models of education with dialogic, liberatory ones. He theorized that humans are able to reflect on their lives and take action to transform their worlds, yet many people cannot develop their full potential because of their social positions. Those who are oppressed and illiterate are unable to think critically about their positions. Therefore, educators can help others transform their situations by creating democratic relations within the classroom and bringing students into critical dialogue with one another.

Educators at the college level were the first to apply Freirean pedagogy to their composition classes, having students write about their everyday experiences and engage in dialogues about themes from their essays. For example, Shor (1987) advocated for writing classes that provide opportunities for students to engage in critical analyses of texts; reflect upon their own experiences as members of racial, cultural, linguistic, and gender groups; and compose texts that effect changes within a community.

Fairbanks (1998) demonstrated the potential for secondary students to become connected to their social and political contexts through writing. Students conduct projects in which they generate themes from concerns of their own lives, write texts, turn their problems into questions, and develop a service project that addresses a real-world problem. DeSitgter (1998) involved Latino and Anglo at-risk high school students in a reading and writing project that drew upon family histories to form a democratic community. In work exploring youth-run centers for LBGTQ (lesbian, bisexual, gay, transgender, queer) youth, Blackburn (2002) documented the ways in which youth transformed their literacy practices to claim and perform identities at the same time they worked for social change. Henry's (1998) study of African Caribbean adolescents found that allowing girls space to talk and write about their lives resulted in students' beliefs that they were learning and becoming empowered. A group of Australian elementary teachers have engaged students in social critique of texts (Comber, 2001). Bomer and Bomer (2001) have involved elementary students in activities to identify problems within their communities, conduct research projects together, and write to specific audiences to raise awareness of community issues.

While several writing programs have been organized to engage students in using writing to become more reflective about their social circumstances, other research studies have used a critical frame to consider issues of race, social class, gender, and ethnicity. For example, the narratives of 27 Puerto Rican and Mexican students written while they were in eighth grade and then again as juniors in high school revealed that these students were highly critical of both their educational experiences and their own academic decisions (Quiroz, 2001). In their work establishing a democratic, first- and second-grade classroom with a multicultural language arts curriculum, Solsken, Willet, and Wilson-Keenan (2000) found that a Latina student interwove her home, school, and peer languages in her writing to serve a variety of social and personal agendas; however the educators acknowledged that deeply rooted barriers in schools and society prevented them from noticing the sophistication of her texts.

Bakhtin's (1981) theories, which focus on language as mediation and highlight the struggle among diverse voices as they interact, has influenced writing research. Knoeller (2004) used a Bakhtinian framework to show how high school students created complex narratives (oral and textual) in which they reconciled multiple, competing perspectives on race relations and other social topics. Dyson (2003) documented the ways in which students from a first-grade classroom represented their official (classroom) and unofficial (out-of-school) worlds in their writing through a Bakhtinian frame. By drawing extensively on popular culture such as sports, cartoons, raps, and other features of the media and through their interac-

tions with a small circle of friends, students developed complex texts that rearticulated their literate identities. McCarthey (1994) examined the ways in which elementary writers struggled to assimilate and resist the authoritative voice of the teacher in their own texts. Lensmire (2000) used a Bakhtinian lens to provide a critique of writing workshops in the elementary schools, specifically noting that the conception of voice was limited; he provided an alternative conception of voice that emphasizes the struggle in which a student does something new with existing resources.

Studies from a critical frame have focused on the tensions that arise from individuals as members of different racial, socioeconomic, and linguistic groups, and the differences in power relations resulting from an inequitable society. Researchers have examined the conflicts between teacher's expectations and students' own goals in writing, as well as clashes between students' unofficial and official worlds. These researchers suggest that the seeds of change exist within these critiques. Therefore, researchers who frame their work within a critical perspective see the potential for writing to serve as a tool for revealing tensions and inequities and for reducing those inequities within the larger society.

Conclusion

The four frames serve to organize the theories, research, and pedagogy that have emerged in the last 30 years about writing. Each model has theoretical strengths and weaknesses in its conceptions of the writer, the processes of composing text, and the instruction that best supports students' learning to write. No single frame for understanding writing can capture the complexity of the process nor completely inform us about the best methods of instruction to enhance the abilities, motivations, and products of writers. But together the frames provide different lenses for viewing the processes, the writer, the context, and the text. By continuing to conduct research about the composition of written text, we can generate new understandings of writing.

References and Further Readings

Abbott, J. A. (2000). "Blinking out" and "Having the touch": Two fifth grade boys talk about flow experiences in writing. *Written Communication, 17,* 53–92.

Applebee, A. (1981). *Writing in the secondary school: English and the content areas* (Research Monograph 21). Urbana, IL: National Council of Teachers of English.

Applebee, A. (2000). Alternative models of writing development. In R. Indrisano, & J. R. Squire (Eds.), *Perspectives on writing: Research, theory, and practice* (pp. 90–110). Newark, DE: International Reading Association.

Bakhtin, M. M. (1981). *The dialogic imagination.* Austin, TX: University of Texas Press.

Beach, R., & Friedrich, T. (2006). Response to writing. In C. A. MacArthur, S Grahah, & J. Fitzgerald (Eds.), *Handbook of writing research* (pp. 222–234). New York: Guilford.

Bereiter, C., & Scardamalia, M. (1987). *The psychology of written composition.* Mahwah, NJ: Lawrence Erlbaum Associates.

Bissex, G. L. (1980). *Gyns at wrk: A child learns to read and write.* Cambridge, MA: Harvard University Press.

Blackburn, M. V. (2002). Disrupting the (hetero)normative: Exploring literacy performances and identity work with queer youth. *Journal of Adolescent and Adult Literacy, 46* (4), 312–324.

Bomer, R., & Bomer, K. (2001). *For a better world: Reading and writing for social action.* Portsmouth, NH: Heinemann.

Bomer, R., & Laman, T. (2004). Positioning in a primary grade workshop: Joint action in the discursive production of writing subjects. *Research in the Teaching of English, 38,* 420–466.

Britton, J., Burgess, T., Martin, N., McLeod, A., & Rosen, H. (1975). *The development of writing abilities.* London: McMillan Education, Ltd.

Bruffee, K. A. (1984). Collaborative learning and the "Conversation of Mankind." *College English, 46,* 635–652.

Bruner, J. (1962). *On knowing: Essays from the left hand.* Cambridge, MA: Harvard University Press.

Calkins, L. M. (1983). *Lessons from a child.* Portsmouth, NH: Heinemann.

Casbergue, R. M., & Plauché, M. B. (2005). Emergent writing: Classroom practices that support young writers' development. In R. Indrisano, & J. R. Paratore (Eds.), *Learning to write: Writing to learn* (pp. 8–25). Newark, DE: International Reading Association.

Chomsky, N. (1965). *Aspects of the theory of syntax.* Cambridge, MA: MIT Press.

Clay, M. M. (1975). *What did I write?* Auckland, New Zealand: Heinemann.

Comber, B. (2001). Classroom explorations in critical literacy. In H. Fehring, & P. Green (Eds.), *Critical literacy* (pp. 90–102). Newark, DE: International Reading Association.

Daiute, C. (1989). Play as thought: Thinking strategies of young writers. *Harvard Educational Review, 59*(1), 1–23.

DeStigter, T. (1998). The Tesoros Literacy Project: An experiment in democratic communities. *Research in the Teaching of English, 32,* 10–42.

Donovan, C. A., & Smolkin, L. B. (2006). Children's understanding of genre and writing development. In C. A. MacArthur, S. Grahah, & J. Fitzgerald (Eds.), *Handbook of writing research* (pp. 131–143). New York: Guilford.

Dyson, A. (2003). *Brothers and sisters learn to write.* New York: Teachers College Press.

Elbow, P. (1981). *Writing with power.* Oxford, UK: Oxford University Press.

Emig, J. (1971). *The composing process of twelfth graders* (Research Monograph 13). Urbana, IL: National Council of Teachers of English.

Englert, C. S., Mariage, T., & Dunsmore, K. (2006). Tenets of sociocultural theory in writing instruction research. In C. A. MacArthur, S. Grahah, & J. Fitzgerald (Eds.), *Handbook of writing research* (pp. 208–221). New York: Guilford.

Fairbanks, C. (1998). Nourishing conversations: Urban adolescents, literacy, and democratic society. *Journal of Literacy Research, 30*(2), 187–203.

Fitzgerald, J., & Stamm, C. (1992). Variations in writing conference influence on revision: Two case studies. *Journal of Reading Behavior, 24,* 21–50.

Flower, L., Hayes, J. R., Schriver, K., Stratman, J., & Carey, L. (1986). Detecting, diagnosis, and the strategies of revision. *College Composition and Communication, 37,* 16–55.

Freedman, S. W. (1987). *Peer response groups in two ninth grade classrooms* (Tech. Report No. 12). Berkeley: University of California, Center for the Study of Writing.

Freire, P. (1970). *Pedagogy of the oppressed.* New York: Seabury.

Graham, S. (2006). Strategy instruction and the teaching of writing: A meta-analysis. In C. A. MacArthur, S. Grahah, & J. Fitzgerald (Eds.), *Handbook of writing research* (pp. 187–207). New York: Guilford.

Guthrie, J. T., Van Meter, P., McCann, A. D., Wigfield, A., Bennett, L., Poundstone, C. C., et al. (1996). Growth of literacy engagement: Changes in motivations and strategies during concept-oriented reading instruction. *Reading Research Quarterly, 31,* 306–332.

Gutierrez, K. (1992). A comparison of instructional contexts in writing: Process classrooms with Latino children. *Education and Urban Society, 24,* 244–252.

Hayes, J. (2000). A new framework for understanding cognition and affect in writing. In R. Indrisano & J. R. Squire (Eds.), *Perspectives on writing: Research, theory, and practice* (pp. 6–44). Newark, DE: International Reading Association.

Hayes, J., & Flower, L. (1980). Identifying the organization of writing processes. In L. Gregg & E. R. Steinberg (Eds.), *Cognitive processes in writing* (pp. 3–30). Hillsdale, NJ: Lawrence Erlbaum Associates.

Henry, A. (1998). Speaking up and speaking out: Examining voice in a reading/writing program with adolescent African Caribbean girls. *Journal of Literacy Research, 30* (2), 233–252.

Hidi, S., & Boscolo, P. (2006). Motivation and writing. In C. A. MacArthur, S. Grahah, & J. Fitzgerald (Eds.). *Handbook of writing research* (pp. 144–157). New York: Guilford.

Kamberelis, G., & de la Luna, L. (2004). Children's writing: How textual forms, contextual forces, and textual politics co-emerge. In C. Bazerman & P. Prior (Eds.), *What writing does and how it does it* (pp. 239–277). Mahwah, NJ: Lawrence Erlbaum Associates.

Knoeller, C. P. (2004). Narratives of rethinking: The inner dialogue of classroom discourse and student writing. In S. W. Freedman & A. F. Ball (Eds.), *Bakhtinian perspectives on language, literacy, and learning* (pp. 148–171). Cambridge, UK: Cambridge University Press.

Langer, J. (1986). *Children reading and writing: Structures and strategies.* Norwood, NJ: Ablex.

LeFevre, K. (1987). *Invention as a social act.* Carbondale: Southern Illinois University Press.

Lensmire, T. (2000). *Powerful writing, responsible teaching.* New York: Teachers College Press.

Lipson, M., Mosenthal, J., Daniels, P., & Woodside-Jiron, H. (2000). Process writing in the classrooms of eleven fifth-grade teachers with different orientations to teaching and learning. *Elementary School Journal, 101*(2), 209–232.

McCarthey, S. J. (1994). Authors, text, and talk: The internalization of dialogue from social interaction during writing. *Reading Research Quarterly, 29*(3), 201–231.

McCarthey, S. J. (2002). *Students' identities and literacy learning.* Newark, DE: International Reading Association and National Reading Conference.

McCarthey, S. J., García, G. E., López-Velásquez, A., Lin, S., & Guo, Y. (2004). Writing opportunities for English language learners. *Research in the Teaching of English, 38,* 351–394.

Patthey-Chavez, G. G., & Ferris, D. R. (1997). Writing conferences and the weaving of multi-voiced texts in college composition. *Research in the Teaching of English, 31,* 51–90.

Plimpton, G. (Ed.). (1963). *Writers at work: The Paris Review interviews.* (2nd series). New York: Viking Press.

Prior, P. (1998). Contextualizing teachers' responses to writing in the college classroom. In N. Nelson & R. C. Calfee (Eds.), *The reading-writing connection: Ninety-seventh yearbook of the National Society for the Study of Education* (pp. 153–177). Chicago: University of Chicago Press.

Quiroz, P. A. (2001). The silencing of Latino student "voice": Puerto Rican and Mexican narratives in eighth grade and high school. *Anthropology and Education Quarterly, 32*(3), 326–349.

Raphael, T. E., & Hiebert, E. H. (1996). *Creating an integrated approach to literacy instruction.* Fort Worth, TX: Harcourt Brace College.

Schultz, K. (1997). "Do you want to be in my story?": Collaborative writing in an urban elementary classroom. *Journal of Literacy Research, 29*(2), 253–287.

Shor, I. (1987). *Critical teaching and everyday life.* Chicago: University of Chicago Press.

Solsken, J., Willett, J., & Wilson-Keenan, J. (2000). Cultivating hybrid texts in multicultural classrooms: Promise and challenge. *Research in the Teaching of English, 35*(2), 179–212.

Sperling, M. (1998). Teachers as readers of students' writing. *The reading-writing connection: Ninety-seventh yearbook of the National Society for the Study of Education* (pp. 131–152). Chicago: University of Chicago Press.

Sperling, M., & Woodlief, L. (1997). Two classrooms, two writing communities: Urban and suburban tenth-graders learning to write. *Research in the Teaching of English, 31,* 205–240.

Sulzby, E. (1985). Kindergartners as writers and readers. In M. Farr (Ed.), *Advances in writing research, Vol. 1. Children's early writing development* (pp. 127–199) Norwood, NJ: Ablex.

Teale, W., & Martinez, M. (1989). Connecting writing: Fostering emergent literacy in kindergarten children. In J. M. Mason (Ed.), *Reading and writing connections* (pp. 177–198). Boston: Allyn & Bacon.

Tolchinsky, L. (2006). The emergence of writing. In C. A. MacArthur, S. Graham, & J. Fitzgerald (Eds.), *Handbook of writing research* (pp. 83–95). New York: Guilford.

Torrance, M., & Galbraith, D. (2006). The processing demands of writing. In C. A. MacArthur, S. Graham, & J. Fitzgerald (Eds.). *Handbook of writing research* (pp. 67–80). New York: Guilford.

Vygotsky, L. (1978). *Mind in society.* Cambridge, MA: Harvard University Press.

Ward, I. (1994). *Literacy, ideology, and dialogue: Towards a dialogic pedagogy.* Albany: State University of New York Press.

Yagelski, R. P. (1995). The role of classroom context in the revision strategies of student writers. *Research in the Teaching of English, 29,* 216–238.

37

THREE PILLARS OF A SOUND MATHEMATICS EDUCATION

Curriculum, Teaching, and Assessment

DOUGLAS A. GROUWS AND MELISSA D. MCNAUGHT

University of Missouri

D ifficult mathematics classes were once considered necessary to filter out untalented students to ensure that the country had the skilled scientists and engineers needed to promote the nation's economic progress in a context of rapid social change and technological advancement. But today a strong mathematics education is considered a necessity for *all* students to be successful in their personal lives and in the workplace (National Council of Teachers of Mathematics [NCTM], 2000). Now, mathematics courses must function as a "pump instead of a filter" (White, 1988), moving all students successfully through the system. When considering how to reach the goal of "mathematics for all," one must consider every facet of mathematics education. The field is deeply rooted in mathematics, but must also take into account findings from other disciplines such as psychology and sociology. Classrooms involve complex dynamic systems, and many factors that are often considered the purview of other disciplines play vital roles in the amount and nature of the student mathematics learning that occurs. Despite this complexity, three constructs are important in any mathematics classroom: curriculum, teaching, and assessment.

The mathematics curriculum determines what content students study, while teaching involves interactions that shape the quality and the depth of the mathematics learned. Assessment provides important feedback for structuring and moving the learning process forward. Thus, attaining significant mathematics achievement "for all" requires a coherent curriculum, knowledgeable teachers employing effective teaching practices, and the use of assessments that accurately measure what students learn. This chapter addresses curriculum, teaching, and assessment with the realization that the interplay among these factors and out-of-class factors such as socioeconomic status are as important as the factors themselves.

Curriculum

Curriculum can be interpreted in various ways. Generally curriculum refers to the content students are expected to learn. However, when individuals speak of curriculum, they may be referring to instructional materials, textbooks, state standards, grade-level expectations, or lesson plans. Regardless of how one defines curriculum, the reality is that all of these determine what mathematics students are given the opportunity to learn.

The mathematics content students have been expected to learn has varied over time in response to many factors. For example, in 1957, the Soviet Union launched the *Sputnik I* satellite forcing the United States to reconsider its perceived position as the leader in space technology. After *Sputnik's* launch and with a concern for national security, President Eisenhower formally introduced the Space Race and teachers soon found themselves expected to prepare a new generation of engineers, scientists, and technologists. Consequently, during the 1960s, new mathematics curricula were designed and produced for this purpose. The term *New Math* refers to these curricular programs and they initiated dramatic changes in what mathematics was taught and how it was taught.

Directed and influenced by academic mathematicians, the driving force underlying these curricula was the idea that certain concepts, structures, and reasoning processes provided a common foundation for the specific topics taught within mathematics. A central tenet was that concentrating on unifying concepts such as sets, relations, and functions would allow students to develop a deeper understanding of mathematics rather than a focus on disconnected procedures learned through rote training. Developers of *New Math* soon discovered that writing new textbook materials was not sufficient to promote their intended changes. Teachers needed training to be able to implement the new textbooks and administrators needed to communicate to their communities the rationale behind reforming the mathematics curriculum. The poor student performance that followed these curricular changes was blamed on the *New Math* and the criticism is just, at least in part, but the mathematicians who created it continued to blame the lack of proper curricular implementation by the teacher in the classroom as the true cause of its demise. Parents became concerned about their children's mathematical learning and looked to the media to help convey their plea to go "back to the basics."

With the public perception that New Math materials were not satisfactory, the 1970s began to emphasize the development of basic computational skills and efficient algebraic manipulation. These curricular materials abandoned the formal language and concepts associated with the New Math materials and returned to an emphasis on more familiar ideas of computation. The National Science Foundation funded several conferences with the intention of improving mathematics education. Emerging from these conferences were concerns expressed by mathematics educators that skills were being emphasized without regard to their application or to the process of problem solving. Arguments about what mathematics is "basic" were heated and frequent following these conferences. This dialogue eventually led the National Council of Teachers of Mathematics (NCTM) to issue their *Agenda for Action* (1980) report. This agenda redefined basic skills to encompass much more than computational fluency. NCTM recommended that problem solving become the focus of school mathematics in the 1980s.

In 1983, the U.S. Secretary of Education released *A Nation at Risk*, a report that in large part proclaimed the demise of public education. "Our society and its educational institutions seem to have lost sight of the basic purposes of schooling, and of the high expectations and disciplined effort needed to attain them" (National Commission on Excellence in Education, 1983, p. 7). This document called for reform efforts in which schools were to "demand the best effort and performance for all students, whether they [were] gifted or less able, affluent or disadvantaged, whether destined for college, the farm, or industry" (p. 24). Since then vast resources have been spent on mathematics reform "for all."

Subsequently, NCTM published its vision of what school mathematics should be under the title *Curriculum and Evaluation Standards for School Mathematics* (NCTM, 1989). This vision represented a consensus that "all students need to learn more, and often different, mathematics and that instruction in mathematics must be significantly revised" (p. 1). This document quickly gained acceptance and was later widely endorsed by legislators and professional organizations such as the American Mathematical Society (AMS) and the Mathematics Association of America (MAA). With these endorsements the NCTM's *Curriculum and Evaluation Standards* began to reach the classroom.

The *Curriculum and Evaluation Standards* challenged the fundamental beliefs that had been held by many mathematicians, mathematics educators, and the general public for a number of years. It outlined an active learning environment (as opposed to the long-established focus on the processes of memorization and practice) and a greater emphasis on developing meaning and building conceptual understanding. With each grade level band (K–4, 5–8, 9–12), the *Standards* recommended concepts and skills that should receive increased attention, for example, real-world problems and statistics, and those that should receive decreased attention, e.g., complex paper-and-pencil computation. The *Standards* contended that *all* students could succeed with higher-level mathematics, if engaged in an investigative environment emphasizing conceptual understanding and collaboration among peers.

The de-emphasis on computational skills in the *Standards* soon came under attack and was often inappropriately publicized as the elimination of such skills from the curriculum. With the driving force of the *Standards* being mathematics for all, conservative mathematicians and some mathematics educators feared that the mathematics curricula would become "dumbed-down" in order for more students to be successful. Nevertheless, the National Science Foundation (NSF) called for and funded proposals for the development of curricula that would align with the *Standards*. The fundamental differences in beliefs and the discussions about what and how mathematics should be taught is what is often referred to by the term *math wars* (see Schoenfeld, 2004).

The shift away from memorization and rote application of procedures required that new materials be developed to help teachers promote students' conceptual understanding of mathematics. Historically, mathematics textbooks in the United States have integrated mathematics content at each elementary school grade level, while at the high school level they have traditionally segregated content according to specific foci such as algebra, geometry, and precalculus. When, in 1990, the National Science Foundation (NSF) began to finance the development of new curricula to embody the new vision set forth by the *Standards* the new textbooks that were developed were dubbed "standards based" materials, because they were meant to embody the instructional recommendations outlined in the *Standards*. Written primarily by mathematics educators with strong mathematical backgrounds, these materials were quite different from previous textbooks. The situations and problems posed often involved multiple possible solutions and solution strategies. They did not focus on repeated practice on given problem solving methods on strings of similar problems. The teaching method embodied in these materials focused on small-group work with increased attention to the use of technology, as will be discussed later.

In elementary and middle schools, textbook lessons were set in real-world contexts and were more problem-based than previously published textbooks. There was less emphasis on practice with computational algorithms, and in some programs there was a tendency to move content to lower grade levels. At the high school level, the conventional single-subject textbooks were replaced by textbooks that integrated the study of geometry, algebra, statistics, and so on, at every grade level. Thus, the high school materials formed an integrated approach to learning mathematics by including content from each content strand in each grade level textbook. The idea was that this would promote forming connections across mathematical ideas and develop a more coherent view of mathematics in general. These curricular materials are now typically called "integrated" mathematics. For more information regarding these "standards-based" curricular materials, see http://www.comap.com/elementary/projects/arc (Grades K–4), http://showmecenter.missouri.edu (Grades 5–8), or http://www.ithaca.edu/compass (Grades 9–12).

As mathematical reform swept the nation, the label of "standards-based curriculum" became prevalent. Curriculum once referred to as traditional even began to claim the label *standards-based*, "[y]et there is a significant difference between texts that have retrofitted their traditional 'demonstration and practice' approaches in order to better align themselves with the NCTM *Standards*, and curricula that were designed from the outset to embody the mathematical approaches and pedagogical principles advanced by the *Standards*" (Goldsmith, Mark, & Kantrov, 1998, p. 10). Few publishers made significant changes to integrate mathematical topics in the way the *Standards* recommended (Taylor & Tarr, 2003) perhaps reflecting a marketing concern that major changes would not be well received.

Critics of the new materials emerged and are becoming increasingly vocal. They call the curricula developed during this reform movement as "the new *New Math*" or "fuzzy math" (Grouws & Cebulla, 2000). Arguments reminiscent of the 1960s *New Math* era have been reincarnated as parents have become concerned that the mathematics their students need to know, especially basic skills, might not be learned. The recommendation to reduce emphasis on memorizing and practicing procedures has often been misinterpreted to mean that learning procedures are not necessary.

In 2000, the *Standards* were updated, refined, and published under the title, *Principles and Standards for School Mathematics* (PSSM). The revision took account of recent research (Kilpatrick, Martin, & Schifter, 2003), current thinking about what is most important to include in school mathematics (e.g., more attention to data analysis and informal statistics), and changes in mathematics (e.g., a focus on representation). The document also addressed some criticisms of the earlier *Standards* document. PSSM placed a greater emphasis on the importance of algorithms and computational fluency than the previous document. Its publication has not stemmed the discussion of what mathematics should be studied and how it should be taught.

Influences on Curriculum

Many influences shape the school curriculum, and thus the mathematics that students have an opportunity to learn. These factors include textbooks, state and local learning expectations, and mandated assessments. Furthermore, the emphasis placed on specific mathematical topics is affected by individual teachers' mathematical knowledge, instructional beliefs, and priorities. In recent years, the federal No Child Left Behind legislation (NCLB, 2002) mandated that states assist schools in closing the achievement gaps that exist among different groups of students (e.g., racial groups) by adopting and specifying challenging academic content that would be used by all districts in the state. In response, states developed new specific objectives which have become known as the states' grade-level expectations (GLEs). These expectations describe in detail what mathematics students are expected to learn at each grade level. Publishers utilize these GLEs in making decisions regarding what mathematics content to include in their textbooks. Developing textbooks that align to multiple state documents is difficult, particularly because there is little consensus among the states regarding the grade placement of mathematical topics (see Reys, 2006).

Dissatisfaction with student performance on international tests and the implications of these results have prompted further discussion about curriculum issues and actions to communicate more clearly what is important mathematics to teach. One example is NCTM's *Curriculum Focal Points for Prekindergarten Through Grade 8 Mathematics: A Quest for Coherence* (2007). This document identifies three essential mathematical topics to be comprehensively taught at each grade level (K–8) and its intent was to bring more curricular coherence across the nation's classrooms. The document provides a beginning point for states and districts to design more focused curricular expectations to address the common criticism that mathematics curriculum in the United States is "a mile wide and an inch deep" (Schmidt, McKnight, & Raizen, 1997). Other organizations that have not been satisfied with NCTM's efforts have developed their own recommendations to address their perception of the educational shortcomings that have resulted in low performance on international comparisons. See for example, the mathematics standards published by: Achieve (http://www.achieve.org/node/479), American Statistical Association (http://www.amstat.org/education/gaise), and College Board (http://www.collegeboard.com/about/association/academic/standard.html).

Regardless of the standards in place, or the curriculum in use, curriculum alone is insufficient to determine student learning. Teaching also plays a major role in shaping students' learning opportunities. The emphasis teachers place on different learning goals and topics, the expectations for learning that they set, the time they allocate for particular topics, the kinds of tasks they pose, the kinds of questions they ask, the types of responses they accept, the nature of the discussions they lead—are all parts of teaching and heavily influence what students learn and how they learn it.

Teaching

Surprisingly, even as late as the 1970s, the case needed to be made that teachers do, in fact, make a difference in what students learn in the classroom. As research progressed, it became exceedingly clear that teachers do indeed make an important difference (see for example, Good, Biddle, & Brophy, 1975). Important to note, some teachers are particularly effective in promoting student learning year in and year out with different groups of students. Even more important, it has become clear that it is what teachers *do* when they teach that seems to be particularly important, as opposed to what teachers *are*. That is to say that variables such as teaching experience, degrees held, content courses taken, and so on are not as important as what teachers actually do in the classroom. In other words, teach*ing* is not the same as teach*ers*. The focus in this section is on teach*ing*—classroom interactions among teachers and students around content directed toward facilitating students' achievement of learning goals. Characteristics of teachers can certainly influence their teaching, but these characteristics *do not determine* their teaching.

Documenting what particular features of teaching directly influence student learning is different. Classrooms are a complex system where teaching is embedded in a system of many different interacting features, thus the effect of teaching on student learning cannot be measured independently of the system in which they operate. It is this system that affects student learning, not the individual features of a particular teacher or teaching method. Furthermore, the results of teaching are mediated by the student (e.g., their interpretation of instruction, their time on task, and their prior knowledge).

It seems reasonable to tailor teaching methods to what we know from research rather than from intuitive notions that might be true or false, or from scholars' armchair speculations. The key to success in indetifying useful research findings is to look for patterns across teaching studies that produce similar positive effects on student learning within a common teaching goal. Following Hiebert and Grouws (2007), attention is now given to particular patterns that emerge from such an analysis in two goal areas: teaching for skill efficiency and teaching for conceptual understanding.

Different kinds of teaching facilitate different kinds of learning based on what students have had the opportunity to learn. Interestingly, there is not a simple correspondence between one method of teaching and skill efficiency and between another method of teaching and conceptual understanding. The best way to express current knowledge in the field is to describe some features of teaching that facilitate skill efficiency and some features of teaching that facilitate conceptual understanding, and to indicate where these features intersect.

Teaching for Skill Efficiency

Skill efficiency is defined as the rapid, smooth, and accurate execution of mathematical procedures. Results from several studies indicate that effective teaching toward this goal is characterized by a rapid instructional pace and includes extensive teacher modeling of the procedures to be learned with many teacher-directed product-type questions (see Good, Grouws, & Ebmeier, 1983). The teaching also displays a smooth transition from teacher demonstration to substantial amounts of error-free practice by students. Noteworthy in this set of features is the central role played by the teacher in organizing, pacing, and presenting information to meet well-defined learning goals.

The features of teaching identified above facilitate students' skill efficiency but what effect these features have on conceptual understanding is less clear because they have not been thoroughly researched.

Teaching for Conceptual Understanding

Conceptual understanding can be defined as the construction of relationships among mathematical facts, procedures, and ideas (Brownell, 1935), and its positive effects on student learning have been well demonstrated in research programs as The Missouri Mathematics Project (Good, Grouws, & Ebmeier, 1983). Two features of instruction emerge from the literature as especially likely to help students develop conceptual understanding of the mathematics topic they are studying: (1) attending explicitly to concepts; and (2) encouraging students to wrestle with the important mathematical ideas in an intentional and conscious way.

Attending explicitly to concepts refers to treating mathematical connections among facts, procedures, and ideas clearly and meaningfully. This includes such things as discussing the mathematical meaning underlying procedures, asking questions about how different solution strategies are similar to and different from each other, considering the ways in which mathematical problems build on each other or are special (or general) cases of each other, attending to relationships among mathematical ideas, and reminding students about the main point of the lesson and how this point fits within the current sequence of lessons and ideas.

In many ways, the claim that students acquire conceptual understanding of mathematics when teaching attends explicitly to mathematical concepts is a restatement of the general observation that students learn best what they have an opportunity to learn. This claim has support from numerous research studies that span multiple contexts and designs (see Floden, 2002). Both teacher-centered and student-centered teaching methods that have explicitly attended to conceptual development have shown higher levels of students' conceptual understanding than similar methods that have not attended to conceptual development directly. The ways in which concepts are developed in classrooms can vary—from teachers actively directing classroom activity to teachers taking less active roles, from methods of teaching that highlight special tasks or materials to those that highlight special forms of classroom discourse to those that highlight student invention of solution strategies. The evidence does not justify a "best" method of instruction to facilitate conceptual understanding, but it does support a feature of instruction that might be part of many methods: explicit attention to conceptual development of the mathematics. Students receiving such instruction develop conceptual understanding to a greater extent than students receiving instruction with less conceptual focus.

A second aspect of teaching associated with increased conceptual understanding is allowing students to struggle with important mathematical ideas. The word *struggle* is used to mean that students work at making sense of the mathematics; to figure out something that is not immediately apparent. This does not mean posing overly difficult problems that result in high levels of student anxiety and frustration. Rather, struggle here refers to solving problems that are within reach and grappling with key mathematical ideas that are comprehendible but not yet well formed (Hiebert et al., 1996). Struggling is the antithesis of being presented information to be memorized or being asked to practice what has been demonstrated by numerous examples. When students struggle, they devote high levels of energy to make sense of a situation rather than turning immediately to a prescribed and rehearsed method they have recently seen demonstrated. The struggle leads students to construct interpretations that connect new ideas to what they already know and to reexamine and restructure what they have already learned. This, in turn, yields content and skills that are learned more deeply and can be applied more easily to novel situations.

Teaching With Technology

One aspect of teaching that is gaining a lot of attention as an aid to increasing conceptual understanding is the use of various kinds of technology during instruction. Technology is engrained in our society and historically has yielded important scientific, economic, and cultural advances. However, the issue of technology in mathematics education has been a divisive topic for over two decades. On the one hand, many scholars feel that teachers should help students use technology to expand their knowledge beyond the limits of their skills to explore concepts that would be beyond their reach without technology. Other educators resist the notion of using technology for fear that students will become overly reliant on it and may even become unable to perform basic computations. In the 1989 *Curriculum and Evaluation Standards*, the National Council of Teachers of Mathematics called for all students to have access to calculators and computers at every grade level in order to investigate and solve problems. Having access to a tool does not guarantee its proper use. "One needs to be careful not to give the impression that technology itself makes the difference in teaching and learning. It is, of course, not the technology that makes the difference but rather how it is used and by whom" (Heid, 2005, p. 348).

Classroom technology can go well beyond the use of calculators. For example, virtual manipulatives are becoming more commonly used in the elementary grades. A virtual manipulative is defined as "an interactive, Web-based visual representation of a dynamic object that presents opportunities for constructing mathematical knowledge" (Moyer, Bolyard, & Spikell, 2002, p. 373). These are often replicas of frequently used concrete manipulatives such as pattern blocks, base-ten blocks, geometric solids, or colored rods. The use of these virtual manipulatives seems to promote making connections among various representations of concepts. They create a bridge between concrete 3-D manipulatives and the 2-D visual representations of the objects and eventually to the building of symbolic notations of abstract mathematical ideas. The flexible nature of the virtual pictorial representations, as opposed to static pictures, allows students to engage in investigation and clarification of their own thinking through experimentation (Moyer, Niezgoda, & Stanley, 2005). Many virtual manipulatives programs and applets are available free on the Internet. For more information visit the Web site of the National Library of Virtual Manipulatives (http://nlvm.usu.edu/en/nav/vlibrary.html).

Research at higher grade levels has established how graphing calculators can be used as a tool for connecting mathematics to other disciplines (Garofalo, Bennett, & Mason, 1999). One skill, for example, that students need to develop in any discipline, and to a greater extent in real life, is the ability to interpret graphs and statistical data. The graphing calculator as part of class discussion around examples from economics, geography, and civics can be used for "simplifying data gathering [to allow] more time for analyzing and interpreting data" (Drier, Dawson, & Garofalo, 1999, p. 21). Students can graph data and use the information to discuss the effects of economy, climate, latitude, and energy resources on the data. Scales of axes can be changed easily to discuss visual bias and effective analysis. "These types of explorations help teachers prepare students to become logical thinkers who are able to apply mathematics in the real world" (Drier, Dawson, & Garofalo, 1999, p. 25). "These activities promote authentic learning in that students are manipulating, determining, interpreting, and analyzing information relevant to real-world situations" (Garofalo, Bennett, & Mason, 1999, p. 104). This process ultimately prepares students to draw inferences and make informed decisions. Other software programs such as TinkerPlots and Fathom have also been specifically designed for students to investigate and analyze statistical concepts (for more information, see http://www.keypress.com). Geometric software programs such as the Geometer's Sketchpad (see http://www.keypress.com) have been found to be useful in helping student develop a comprehension of many geometric ideas and in fostering an understanding of graphical representations of algebraic concepts.

Computer algebra system (CAS) has become a common term used to refer to "tools that perform symbolic manipulation as well as generate graphs and perform numerical calculations" (Heid, 2005, p. 348). CAS has greater educational potential than a graphing calculator because it can manipulate algebraic expressions and equations in their symbolic form. These symbolic manipulations include simplifying algebraic expressions, changing forms of expressions, differentiation, factorization, solving equations, taking limits, series expansion, series summation, and matrix operations. This powerful tool can facilitate student mathematical investigations and discoveries (Drijvers, 2003).

The advantages of CAS are in the rapid execution of complex algorithms that typically bog students down when trying to understand a difficult concept. With a CAS system doing the procedural work, students can concentrate on understanding the concepts being considered and thus make sense of the mathematics. This results in a greater emphasis being placed on interpreting the meaning of results and determining when to apply information. Furthermore, "students are able to access high-level mathematical processes previously inaccessible to them" (Heid, 2003, p. 36). The role of CAS as an organizer for procedural tasks that must precede certain conceptual developments allows students to advance their conceptual mathematics knowledge before mastering complicated procedures. This gives a special advantage to a student who struggles with procedures so that he or she can still understand concepts. The higher level of conceptual knowledge that is garnered helps make the procedures involved make more sense.

Unfortunately, without proper facilitation by the teacher, students may become overreliant on the technology and generate answers they are unable to interpret. Thus, technology might be treated as a timesaving device with little emphasis on how to evaluate nonsensical answers and ignoring "algebraic insight" which can be derived from the procedural mathematics.

Technology is not a panacea, it can never replace effective teaching. It can, however, be a tool at the disposal of every teacher and student. Its effective use depends on skilled guidance by technologically knowledgeable teachers. The union of skilled teachers and intellectually engaged students generate the power of technology. Teachers must be mindful of the appropriate time to introduce technology in the classroom. Knowing when to use a tool is often as important as knowing how to use it. There should always be a basic understanding of the tool before its regular use in order to enhance learning. Clements and Sarama (2005) noted, "Computer programs should help and empower children to learn and meet specific educational and developmental goals more effectively and powerfully than they could without the technology" (p. 64)

When structuring one's teaching based on research, one should first consider the learning goals for students. Research suggests different teaching strategies depending on whether one's goal is skills development or conceptual development. A contrast has been made between teaching that encourages conceptual understanding and teaching that focuses on skill efficiency. Although these are not contradictory goals, they would likely be emphasized to different degrees in different systems of teaching, and the teaching features associated with reaching each goal are different. But it is important to keep in mind that studies show skill learning is relatively high in classrooms where features of teaching associated with conceptual development are being implemented.

Assessment

Various types of mathematics assessments are employed at the classroom, state, national, and international levels. As districts struggle to meet the adequate yearly progress (AYP) required by the No Child Left Behind Act of 2001 (NCLB, 2002), the link between curriculum and assessment has come under increased scrutiny by teachers, administrators, researchers, and state education department personnel. Almost all states have established grade-level mathematics expectations (GLEs) that are linked to state assessments (Linn, Baker, & Betebenner, 2002) in an attempt to focus mathematics instruction and improve student test scores.

Post-NCLB, states are required to participate in the National Assessment of Educational Progress testing program in reading and mathematics every other year in order to provide comparisons across states. The National Assessment of Educational Progress (NAEP) is the only national representative assessment of what students know and can do in various subjects. Also referred to as the "Nation's Report Card," its purpose is to provide policy makers and the public with information regarding student achievement. The intent is to provide information on a representative sample across the United States. The federal government now uses NAEP results for assessing state achievement levels.

The content of the NAEP mathematics assessment is not tied to curriculum but rather to a mathematics framework that describes the important mathematical knowledge and skills that are to be assessed. This framework identifies five major content strands: (1) number sense, properties, and operations; (2) measurement; (3) geometry and spatial sense; (4) data analysis, statistics, and probability; and (5) algebra and functions. Along with these content areas, NAEP assesses students' overall ability to use mathematics in three ability levels: (1) conceptual understanding; (2) procedural knowledge; and (3) problem solving. The target populations include students at Grades 4 and 8 (and in some years Grade 12). Student achievement is summarized in four levels: (1) below basic, (2) basic, (3) proficient, and (4) advanced.

Examining NAEP results over time provides an opportunity to examine achievement trends. From 1990–00, NAEP results showed continual improvement in student mathematics scores at Grades 4 and 8, but the achievement gaps between White students and their Black, Hispanic, and American Indian peers were wide and did not improve at either grade level. The overall mathematics scores in 2003 increased significantly over those in 2000, and the size of the achievement gaps also decreased (Lubienski & Crockett, 2007). Despite the decrease in the achievement gap, severe disparities between racial groups in achievement remain. The 2003 data indicate the percentage of students reaching basic, proficient, and advanced levels increased (Kloosterman & Lester, 2007). Furthermore, students at Grades 4 and 8 scored higher than the international average on the Trends in International Mathematics and Science Study (TIMSS) test. There is, therefore, some basis for optimism about the direction of mathematics achievement in the United States.

The mathematical performance of students is a highly visible area of interest. A series of international studies in mathematics conducted by the International Association for the Evaluation of Educational Achievement (IEA) has prompted extensive discussion of student achievement. The First International Mathematics Study (FIMS) was conducted in the 1960s and the Second International Mathematics Study (SIMS) followed in the 1980s. TIMMS, now known as the Trends in International Mathematics and Science Study, currently administers an assessment in mathematics every four years and targets two student populations: ages 9–10 and ages 13–14.

The focus of the TIMSS studies is measuring the curricular knowledge that students have learned in their respective programs. Subject matter specialists from all countries participating in the study contribute to the test development. TIMSS is similar in content to the NAEP assessment and it addresses five main strands of mathematics: number, measurement, geometry, data, and algebra.

Internationally, the United States is not in the top tier of countries at any grade level, although fourth-grade students fare better in these comparisons than do eighth-grade students. In 2003, Grade 4 students performed significantly above the international average outperforming 13 of the other 24 participating countries. Grade 8 students

also exceeded the international averages outperforming 24 of the 44 other participating countries (Gonzales et al, 2004). In contrast to NAEP, TIMSS scores for U.S. students did not change significantly between 1995 and 2003 for fourth grade (Kloosterman & Walcott, 2007). For eighth grade there was an increase between 1995 and 1999 but no measurable differences between 1999 and 2003 (Gonzales et al., 2004).

International studies continue to receive attention with the latest information available coming from the Programme for International Student Assessment (PISA) studies of students at the school-leaving age. The purpose of PISA is different than that of NAEP and TIMSS. PISA is designed for measuring mathematical literacy, reading literacy, and science literacy in 15-year-old students, the school-leaving age in many countries. In the last PISA assessment in mathematics (2003), general mathematics literacy and problem solving were tested separately. U.S. students performed significantly below the international average on both. For more detailed information on U.S. student performance see http://www.pisa.oecd.org.

Conclusion

Curriculum, teaching, and assessment all play influential roles in the mathematics students learn in the classroom. Curriculum controls what content students have the opportunity to learn, and thus should act as a vehicle for focusing attention on the most important mathematical ideas to be taught. Care must be exercised to ensure that student opportunities to learn are not limited to trivial mathematics and that students are challenged to learn to the full extent of their ability. Teaching determines both the quality and depth of the mathematical knowledge students acquire. This, in turn, directly affects whether students are able to use their mathematical knowledge in productive ways in their personal lives and in the workplace. Finally, assessment done well at the classroom, state, and national levels provides data useful for decision making that can improve all aspects of students' mathematical education.

References and Further Readings

Brownell, W. A. (1935). Psychological considerations in the learning and teaching of arithmetic. In W. D. Reeve (Ed.), *The teaching of arithmetic: Tenth yearbook of the National Council of Teachers of Mathematics* (pp. 1–31). New York: Teachers College, Columbia University.

Clements, D., & Sarama, J. (2005). Young children and technology: What's appropriate? In W. J. Masalski & P. C. Elliot (Eds.), *Technology supported mathematics learning environments: Sixty-seventh yearbook* (pp. 51–74). Reston, VA: National Council of Teachers of Mathematics.

De Lange, J. (2007). Large-scale assessment and mathematics education. In F. K. Lester (Ed.), *Second handbook of research on mathematics teaching and learning* (pp. 1111–1142). Charlotte, NC: Information Age Publishing.

Dewey, J. (1910). *How we think*. Boston: Heath.

Drier, H., Dawson, K., & Garofalo, J. (1999). Not your typical math class. *Educational Leadership, 56*(5), 21–25.

Drijvers, P. (2003). Algebra on screen, on paper, and in the mind. In J. Fey, A. Cuoco, C. Kieran, L. McMullin, & R. Zbiek (Eds.), *Computer algebra systems in secondary school mathematics education* (pp. 241–267). Reston, VA: National Council of Teachers of Mathematics.

Floden, R. E. (2002). The measurement of opportunity to learn. In A. C. Porter & A. Gamoran (Eds.), *Methodological advances in cross-national surveys of educational achievement* (pp. 231–266). Washington, DC: National Academies Press.

Garofalo, J., Bennett, C., & Mason, C. (1999). Plotting and analyzing: Graphing calculators for social inquiry. *Social Education, 63*(2), 101–104.

Goldsmith, L., Mark, J., & Kantrov, I. (1998). *Choosing a standards-based mathematics curriculum*. Portsmouth, NH: Educational Development Center, Inc., K–12 Mathematics Curriculum Center.

Gonzales, P., Guzman, J. C., Partelow, L., Pahlke, E., Jocelyn, L., Kastberg, D., et al. (2004). *Highlights from the Trends in International Mathematics and Science Study (TIMSS) 2003* (NCES 2005-005). Washington, DC: U.S. Department of Education, National Center for Education Statistics.

Good, T. L., Biddle, B. J., & Brophy, J. E. (1975). *Teachers make a difference*. New York: Holt, Rinehart, and Winston.

Good, T. L., Grouws, D. A., & Ebmeier, H. (1983). *Active mathematics teaching*. New York: Longman Inc.

Grouws, D. A., & Cebulla, K. J. (2000). Elementary and middle school mathematics at the crossroads. In T. L. Good (Ed.), *American education: Yesterday, today, and tomorrow: Ninety-ninth yearbook of the national society for the study of education* (pp. 209–255). Chicago, IL: The University of Chicago Press.

Heid, M. K. (2003). Theories for thinking about the use of CAS in teaching and learning mathematics. In J. Fey, A., Cuoco, C. Kieran, L. McMullin, & R. Zbiek (Eds.), *Computer algebra systems in secondary school mathematics education* (pp. 33–52). Reston, VA: National Council of Teachers of Mathematics.

Heid, M. K. (2005). Technology in mathematics education: Tapping into visions of the future. In W. J. Masalski & P. C. Elliot (Eds.), *Technology supported mathematics learning environments: Sixty-seventh yearbook* (pp. 345–366). Reston, VA: National Council of Teachers of Mathematics.

Hiebert, J., Carpenter, T. P., Fennema, E., Fuson, K., Human, P., Marray, H., et al. (1996). Problem solving as a basis for reform in curriculum and instruction: The case of mathematics. *Educational Researcher, 25*(4), 12–21.

Hiebert, J., & Grouws, D. (2007). The effects of classroom mathematics teaching on students' learning. In F. K. Lester (Ed.), *Second handbook of research on mathematics teaching and learning* (pp. 371–404). Charlotte, NC: Information Age Publishing.

Kilpatrick, J., Martin, W. G., & Schifter, D. (Eds.). (2003). *A research companion to Principles and Standards for School Mathematics*. Reston, VA: National Council of Teachers of Mathematics.

Kloosterman, P., & Lester, F. K. (Eds.). (2007). *Results and interpretations of the 2003 mathematics assessment of the National Assessment of Educational Progress*. Reston, VA: National Council of Teachers of Mathematics.

Kloosterman, P., & Walcott, C. (2007). The 2003 NAEP mathematics assessment: Overall results. In P. Kloosterman & F. K. Lester (Eds.), *Results and interpretations of the 2003 mathematics assessment of the National Assessment of Educational Progress* (pp. 23–42). Reston, VA: National Council of Teachers of Mathematics.

Linn, R. L., Baker, E. L., & Betebenner, D. W. (2002). Accountability systems: Implications of requirements of the No Child Left Behind Act of 2001. *Educational Researcher, 31*, 3–16.

Lubienski, S., & Crocket, M. (2007). NAEP findings regarding race and ethnicity: Mathematics, achievement, student affect, and school-home experiences. In P. Kloosterman & F. K. Lester (Eds.), *Results and interpretations of the 2003 mathematics assessment of the National Assessment of Educational Progress* (pp. 227–260). Reston, VA: National Council of Teachers of Mathematics.

Masalski, W. J., & Elliott, P. C. (Ed.). (2005). *Technology-supported mathematics learning environments: Sixty-seventh yearbook of the National Council of Teachers of Mathematics*. Reston, VA: NCTM.

Moyer, P. S., Bolyard, J. J., & Spikell, M. A. (2002). What are virtual manipulatives? *Teaching Children Mathematics, 8*(6), 372–377.

Moyer, P., Niezgoda, D., & Stanley, J. (2005). Young children's use of virtual manipulatives and other forms of mathematical representations. In W. J. Masalski & P. C. Elliot (Eds.), *Technology supported mathematics learning environments: Sixty-seventh yearbook* (pp. 17–34). Reston, VA: National Council of Teachers of Mathematics.

National Commission on Excellence in Education. (1983). *A nation at risk: The imperative for educational reform*. Washington, DC: U.S. Government Printing Office.

National Council of Teachers of Mathematics. (1980). *An agenda for action*. Reston, VA: Author.

National Council of Teachers of Mathematics. (1989). *Curriculum and evaluation standards for school mathematics*. Reston, VA: Author.

National Council of Teachers of Mathematics. (2000). *Principles and standards for school mathematics*. Reston, VA: Author.

National Council of Teachers of Mathematics. (2007). *Curriculum focal points for prekindergarten through grade 8 mathematics: A quest for coherence*. Reston, VA: Author.

No Child Left Behind Act of 2001, Pub. L. No. 107–110, 115 Stat. 1425. (2002).

Reys, B. J. (Ed.). (2006). *The intended mathematics curriculum as represented in state-level curriculum standards: Consensus or confusion?* Charlotte, NC: Information Age Publishing.

Rohrkemper, M., & Corno, L. (1988). Success and failure on classroom tasks: Adaptive learning and classroom teaching. *The Elementary School Journal, 88*, 296–312.

Schmidt, W. H., McKnight, C. C., & Raizen, S. C. (1997). *A splintered vision: An investigation of U.S. science and mathematics education*. Dordrecht, The Netherlands: Kluwer Academic Publishers.

Schoenfeld, A. H. (2004). The math wars. *Educational Policy, 18*, 253–286.

Stein, M. K., Remillard, J., & Smith, M. S. (2007). How curriculum influences student learning. In F. K. Lester (Ed.), *Second handbook of research on mathematics teaching and learning* (pp. 319–369). Charlotte, NC: Information Age Publishing.

Taylor, P. M., & Tarr, J. E. (2003). Meeting state standards via integrated mathematics curricula. In S. A. McGraw (Ed.), *Integrated mathematics: Choices and challenges* (pp. 229–238) Reston, VA: National Council of Teachers of Mathematics.

White, R. M. (1988). Calculus of reality. In L. A. Steen (Ed.), *Calculus for a new century: A pump, not a filter* (pp. 6–9). Washington, DC: Mathematical Association of America.

38

SCIENCE

DAVID L. FORTUS

Weizmann Institute of Science–Israel and Michigan State University

S cience education deals with the learning and teaching of science knowledge, practices, habits of mind, discourse patterns, and their relation to natural and man-made environments. Because of the importance of science to nations' economic, environmental, and general well-being, much attention has been devoted to helping the public develop awareness and understanding of science and the role it plays in their lives and preparing the next generation of scientists. Science knowledge is typically one of the subjects assessed in large-scale national and international tests such as the National Assessment for Educational Progress (NAEP; Grigg, Lauko, & Brockway, 2006) and the Trends in International Math and Science Study (TIMSS; Martin, Mullis, Gonzalez, & Chrostowski, 2004), underscoring the importance that is attributed to it.

Broadly speaking, the goal of science education is the development of science literacy. There are two different perspectives on science literacy: as conceptual understanding and as participation in a community of practice. The following section presents these two perspectives.

Science Literacy

Science Literacy as Conceptual Understanding

In 1990, Project 2061 of the American Association for the Advancement of Science published *Science for All Americans* (1990), which presented the conceptual understanding perspective of science literacy and made the case why it was important that all people, not just scientists, become literate in science. Project 2061 defined science literacy as a thorough knowledge of the key concepts and principles in science; an understanding of the interdependency of mathematics, science, and technology; a recognition of the strengths and limitations of science; and the ability to use this knowledge for personal and social purposes. The same organization published *Benchmarks for Science Literacy* (AAAS, 1993), which specifies what students should know and be able to do at the end of certain grades to attain science literacy by the end of high school. The National Research Council published the *National Science Education Standards* (National Research Council, 1996), which specifies not only science content standards, but also science teaching standards, standards for the professional development of science teachers, and standards for assessment in science education. Many countries have followed a similar process in developing their own science education standards. In the United States, the education department of each state then developed their own standards that often, but not always, draw on the national standards and benchmarks. These standards then guide or dictate, depending on the state, which science curricula can be used at various grade levels. Since the standards of individual states often conflict with those of other states and do not prioritize the various science topics, it becomes very difficult to develop curriculum that can be used in multiple states without expanding the scope of textbooks to cover everything required by every state at every grade (Roseman & Koppal, in press). As a result, U.S. science curriculum has often been criticized for being a mile wide and an inch deep.

This conceptual understanding perspective treats science learning as a process of building on students' prior ideas about the natural world. These ideas are often at odds with each other, contradict accepted scientific ideas, and are not coherent in the way that scientific theories are expected to be consistent and parsimonious (Driver, Guesne, & Tiberghien, 1985). For example, students may think that if a body is not moving then there is no force acting on it, while at the same time recognizing that a body resting on a table is subjected to the force of gravity. Interestingly, students across countries and cultures hold many of the same ideas. Finally, these ideas also tend to be stable and difficult to change, even when students are confronted with evidence to the contrary, and thus greatly influence future learning. Since the 1980s, research has documented students' typical ideas on a wide range of scientific topics; Duit (2007) has compiled many of these studies.

Science is learned through a process of conceptual change by which prior ideas are modified, exchanged, or added to. Posner, Strike, Hewson, and Gertzog (1982) identified four rational conditions needed to bring about conceptual change: (1) dissatisfaction with existing ideas, (2) intelligibility, (3) plausibility, and (4) fruitfulness of new ideas. In addition to these rational conditions, there are also other cognitive, affective, and contextual factors that influence conceptual change (Pintrich, Marx, & Boyle, 1993).

According to this perspective of science literacy, the teacher's role is to engage students with phenomena that are incompatible with their prior ideas and to present new ideas that can explain these phenomena. This perspective has been critiqued for conceiving of scientific literacy as the property of an individual rather than of social activity, which is the focus taken by the next perspective.

Science Literacy as Participation in a Community of Practice

This perspective focuses primarily on how students learn from social interactions rather than from their interactions with the material world. It builds on the work of Vygotsky (1986), anthropologists, and linguists. It views science literacy as the "ways of knowing, doing, talking, reading, and writing [about the natural world], which are constructed and reproduced in social and cultural practice and interaction" (Gee, 1996, p. 470). It views scientists as members of communities of practice rather than individuals interacting rationally with nature, and it draws on analyses of the norms and discourse patterns of scientific communities rather than on conceptual understanding of individuals (Anderson, 2007). Although the sociocultural tradition has been around for many years, science educators began to adopt this perspective only in the 1990s.

This perspective builds on students' prior experiences in their home communities. Some of these communities use language and have norms that are very different from those used by scientists. In contrast to the conceptual understanding perspective, in which teachers need to help students bridge the conceptual gap between their prior ideas and scientific ideas, the role of the teacher from this perspective is to help students bridge the cultural gap separating their home-based communities and the scientific community. Science learning is viewed as a process of apprenticeship in which one learns to adopt scientific language and norms for the purpose of participating in a community engaged in science.

Proponents of this perspective argue that the U.S. *National Science Education Standards* (National Research Council, 1996) overly emphasize facts and concepts and assume that knowing these ideas will naturally lead to the ability to participate in scientific communities. This perspective has been critiqued for not generating reproducible prescriptions for teaching or methods for assessing outcomes.

Scientific Inquiry

To support the development of science literacy that builds on both perspectives, many science educators recommend engaging students in authentic scientific inquiry that draws on a variety of scientific practices. Scientific inquiry is the various ways in which scientists study the world, use evidence to develop models and construct explanations, and communicate their ideas to their peers. A large number of pedagogies have been developed with the aim of incorporating inquiry into school science. Many of these pedagogies have several common features (Blumenfeld, Marx, Patrick, Krajcik, & Soloway, 1997) that I will discuss here:

- They are structured around authentic tasks for prolonged periods of time.
- They place high importance on the incorporation of phenomena, whether they are experienced first-hand or vicariously.
- They integrate the leaning of science concepts with engagement in scientific practices and the discourse that accompanies these practices.
- They encourage the use of alternative and formative assessments.
- They make use of computer-based technology.
- They build upon student collaboration.
- They view the teacher as a facilitator and a learner along with the students rather than as a source of knowledge.

Authentic Tasks

Since all learning is situational, it must be constructed in contexts that are significant and authentic to the students for it to be meaningful and useful outside the walls of school. One of the main ways to achieve this is to use driving questions, which are the hallmark of project-based science (Krajcik, Czerniak, & Berger, 2003). A driving question is a rich, open-ended question that connects with students' interests and curiosities, such as, Can I believe what I see? or How can I use trash to power my stereo? A successful driving question needs to meet six criteria:

1. *Feasibility*—It must be feasible for students to design and perform investigations to answer the question.
2. *Worth*—It must deal with the science content and practices that are aligned with national or state standards.
3. *Contextualization*—It should be anchored in the lives of learners.
4. *Interest*—It should be interesting and exciting to learners.
5. *Ethics*—Investigating it should not harm living organisms or the environment.
6. *Sustainability*—It should be able to sustain students' interest for a prolonged time.

Driving questions need to be tied to anchoring events (CTGV, 1992) that provide students with common experiences that can be returned to throughout the unit. For example, the anchoring event that accompanies the driving question, Can I believe my eyes? consists of the following sequence: In a darkened room, a black poster is illuminated with red light generated by an overhead projector covered with a red filter. The following message becomes visible:

a I e i e e   y e e

The red filter is replaced with a green filter and the following message appears:

C n   b l v m   y s?

The green filter is removed and the poster is illuminated with white light, revealing the following message:

Can I believe my eyes?

Phenomena

Since science deals with the understanding of natural and man-made environments, it would seem obvious that phenomena drawn from these environments should play a central role in science education. Unfortunately, this has not always been the case, as review of many middle school physical science textbooks showed (Kesidou & Roseman, 2002). Phenomena can play a central role in introducing, clarifying, and evaluating ideas. Students can interact with phenomena directly or vicariously. A teacher can demonstrate a phenomenon as when holding a pinwheel over burning trash to make it spin. Students can observe a phenomenon without the teacher's mediation as in witnessing that air bubbles are released when water is heated. Phenomena can be investigated in controlled laboratory settings, such as when studying heliotropism, or in uncontrolled settings, as during a field trip. Often it is impossible to give students direct access to certain phenomena, either because they are too big, small, fast, slow, far, or too dangerous. For example, most students have seen the moon rise above earth's horizon, but how many have seen earth rise above the moon's horizon? In many of these cases it is possible to interact with these phenomena vicariously, by watching videoclips, computer simulations, looking at photos, or by reading descriptions of the phenomena.

The science laboratory has been the traditional place where students get to investigate phenomena. Without diminishing the importance of the laboratory, which is often the only environment in which certain phenomena can be investigated, it is important that the laboratory is not the only place where students interact with phenomena; otherwise students may view science as something that is relevant and important only in laboratories rather than something that can be relevant and meaningful in many parts of their lives.

Scientific Practices

Scientific practices represent the disciplinary norms of scientists as they construct, evaluate, reason, and communicate (Lehrer & Schauble, 2006). When adapted for learners, scientific practices characterize how students use scientific knowledge to make sense of and explain the world. Examples of scientific practices that have been introduced into K–12 science curriculum are designing investigations and controlled experiments; developing evidence-based explanations; and constructing, evaluating, revising, and using models to explain, predict, and communicate. Practices are important because they help develop both types of science literacy. First, engaging in scientific practices supports learners in developing and using conceptual understanding because they involve understanding that is more meaningful than just describing and recalling phenomena. Second, scientific practices define an important aspect of what it means to partake in the norms and discourse patterns of the scientific community (Duschl, Schweingruber, & Shouse, 2007).

Alternative and Formative Assessment

Unlike summative assessment, which comes after instruction to determine what students have learned, formative assessment provides feedback to teachers and students about their progress while they are learning. Formative assessments are often embedded into instruction so that the students may be unaware that their learning is being assessed. These assessments usually make use of nontraditional data sources, such as student artifacts that are developed in the course of instruction. Student-produced artifacts, such as models, written explanations, and presentations, help them learn concepts, apply information, and represent their knowledge, but also allow for ongoing and contextualized assessment of learning through "understanding performances" (Perkins, 1992). Embedded assessments can allow teachers to make real-time adjustments to instruction so that it best fits the needs of their students.

Computer-Based Technology

Computer-based technology use is another core element of many inquiry-based curricula (Linn, 1997). These technologies come in many forms, for example microcomputer based laboratories (MBLs), visualizations and simulations, and data analysis programs. MBLs, which are data collection probes connected to a computer through an interface, allow students to record data that may not have been available to them otherwise, thus extending their observational capacity. Visualizations and simulations provide students with visual images of phenomena that might have been otherwise inaccessible. Data analysis programs and other digital environments can help clarify the problem space and allow students to focus on the most salient aspects of the problem at hand. By slowing or speeding up time, magnifying or compressing distances, computers can allow students to notice and make sense of relationships that would have otherwise gone unnoticed.

Student Collaboration

According to Webb and Palincsar (1996), "collaboration is convergence—the construction of shared meaning for conversations, concepts, experiences." Student collaboration is essential for constructing the second kind of science literacy, which focuses on social norms and disciplinary discourse. Students' understanding of the nature of science develops as they collaborate and engage in scientific discourse with others (Blumenfeld et al., 1997). By collaborating, students can learn from others' knowledge, reflect on their own ideas, appropriate scientific norms, and reach sophisticated performance. Students can collaborate with members of the same classroom or with people located elsewhere by using the Internet.

The Teacher as Facilitator

In all inquiry-based curricula, the teacher is seen as a facilitator to student learning, a guide rather than an imparter of knowledge. Driver, Asoko, Leach, Mortimer, and Scott (1994) describe the teacher as a tour guide who mediates between the students' prior knowledge, home cultures and norms, and scientific ideas, practices, and discourse patterns. Collins, Brown, and Newman (1989) used the analogy of a cognitive apprenticeship to describe the relationship between the teacher and students. By breaking down complex tasks into simpler ones, modeling

scientific attitudes, and providing feedback, the teacher scaffolds the learning process.

Learning Progressions

As mentioned earlier, traditional science textbooks often cover many topics with little depth because they try to cover conflicting standards from multiple states. This can lead to shallow and disconnected knowledge. Learning progressions offer a remedy to this situation by providing descriptions of successively sophisticated ways of thinking about key scientific concepts and practices across multiple grades. They provide coherence across grades and better alignment between standards, curriculum, and assessments.

Learning progressions are not developmentally inevitable; they entail targeted instruction and curriculum. They present learning more as an ecological succession than a series of discrete and sequential steps. Learning progressions are based on what is known about student learning, but are conjectural and need to be empirically tested. They are anchored at one end by what is known of students' prior ideas and at the other end by societal expectations of what students' should know and be able to do at the end of high school (Duschl et al., 2007). The development of learning progressions is iterative and cycles between theoretical refinement and empirical testing.

Learning progressions can guide the design of instruction, the specification of learning performances, and the development of tasks that allow us to infer students' competence. The following sections will elaborate on some of the characteristics of learning progressions.

Core Ideas

Recognizing that national and state science standards list more topics than any student could be expected to learn in depth within the typical time allotted to science classes and that science understanding is organized around conceptual frameworks that have great explanatory power, such as laws of conservation, learning progressions identify those core science ideas and practices that serve as the backbones for these conceptual frameworks and promote their learning in depth, even at the expense of other ideas that are not so central. The following criteria determine whether an idea or practice is pivotal to scientific thinking:

1. Explanatory power within and across disciplines or scales: The core ideas help one understand a variety of different ideas within or between science disciplines.
2. Powerful way of thinking about the world: The core ideas and practices provide insight into the development of the field or have had key influence on the domain.
3. Accessibility: The representations of core ideas and practices must be comprehensible to learners through their

cognitive abilities (age-appropriateness) and experiences with phenomena.

4. Key to scientific discourse: The core ideas and practices must be central to students' understanding of and engagement with scientific discourse and culture.

5. Building blocks for future learning: The core ideas are vital for future development for other concepts and lay the foundation for continual learning.

6. Support informed decision making: The core ideas help the individual participate intellectually in making individual, social, and political decisions regarding science and technology.

While these criteria are strongly aligned with the definitions given earlier for science literacy, they go further and provide additional measures for evaluating the centrality of different ideas.

Age Appropriateness

Learning progressions recognize that even very young children are capable of sophisticated and abstract thinking, of generalizing and making inferences, and of designing and using experiments to test their ideas (Metz, 1995). Upon beginning school, young children already have a wide repertoire of experience with and knowledge about the natural world, which can serve as an excellent starting point and foundation for instruction (Driver et al., 1985). Children's knowledge does not develop linearly across grades. Sometimes it occurs naturally as the result of maturation and everyday experiences. Other times it requires guided instruction and intentional effort on the child's behalf. For some children, a certain instructional sequence will lead to significant growth; for others, a different sequence is needed. Learning progressions do not dictate what needs to be or can be learned at different ages; they suggest possible paths through a web of possible connections, some of which may be more efficient than others (Duschl et al., 2007).

Curricular Coherence and Integrated Knowledge

Science knowledge can be disconnected, composed of bits and pieces with little relation to each other, or integrated, a rich network that considers how different things are connected and related to each other. Integrated knowledge allows chunking of ideas, identification of organizing themes, and relatively easy incorporation of new ideas into the network (Bransford, Brown, Cocking, Donovan, & Pellegrino, 2000; Clark & Linn, 2003). Integrated knowledge is one of the hallmarks of content experts. For knowledge to become integrated, one has to engage in a deliberate process of connecting, organizing, and structuring ideas (Ericsson, Krampe, & Tesch-Römer, 1993).

Curriculum is one of the primary resources teachers have for guiding instruction (Ball & Cohen, 1992) and has significant influence on the nature of the science knowledge that students construct (Roth, Anderson, & Smith, 1987), whether it will be integrated or disconnected. For curriculum materials to support the construction of integrated knowledge, they must be coherent (Roseman & Linn, in press; Shwartz, Weizman, Fortus, & Krajcik, in press). Coherent curriculum materials have two main characteristics: (1) they present content in a connected way that focuses on core ideas, and (2) they guide instruction in ways that are pedagogically sound, such as providing a sense of purpose, building on students' prior ideas, providing students with multiple opportunities to externalize their ideas, and including embedded formative assessments (Kesidou & Roseman, 2002). Since learning progressions take into account how the various aspects of science expertise interact while emphasizing the core ideas, they have the potential to serve as guides in developing curriculum that can foster knowledge integration.

Science Teachers

Teachers are probably the single most important factor in determining the quality of science education. In addition to having mastery of content they teach, science teachers must also understand what it means to be scientifically literate, how students learn science, how to design and implement supportive learning environments, and how to adapt curriculum to best meet the needs of their students, among many things (Duschl et al., 2007). Teachers need to be life-long learners that can model scientific ways of thinking, communicating, and engaging with phenomena.

Science Content Knowledge

Science is not a monolithic field, but comprises different disciplines, each having its own characteristic discourse patterns, internal logic, investigative tools, and so forth. For example, inquiry in physics is much more mathematical than it is in biology. Inquiry in Earth science is less laboratory-based than chemistry. Some schools offer classes in interdisciplinary science or in environmental science, which require teachers to have broad content knowledge in multiple disciplines and to understand the relationships between the various disciplines. Not surprisingly, students' science achievement improves when they have teachers with higher content knowledge in the discipline they teach. Unfortunately, many science teachers teach outside of their field of expertise, and this can affect their ability to clarify and explicate content as well as orchestrate classroom activities, such as engaging students in discussions (Sanders, Borko, & Lockard, 1993). Many teachers have a limited conception of science literacy as knowledge of a collection of facts and may be unaware of the role of scientific practices. This may be due to narrow and limited undergraduate education that typically focuses on content mastery and in turn is influenced by minimal credential requirements in many states, especially at the K–8 level.

Knowledge of Students and Student Learning

The development of science literacy is not a simple goal. For teachers to be able to support and guide their students in this endeavor, they need to have in-depth knowledge of how people construct science understanding, how they come to adopt the norms and practices of the scientific community, how to engage students with phenomena that will lead to intellectual growth, how to assess students' progress, how to adapt curriculum to meet their students' needs, and how to foster student collaboration.

Every teacher has been a learner, so they often generalize from their personal learning experiences to their students. Since many learned through rote memory, they envision the learning of science as getting the students' attention, breaking down content knowledge into small chunks and transferring this knowledge to the students' minds, then hoping that it sticks where it lands (Strauss, 2001). This model of teaching and learning is in stark contrast with what research indicates is the way people actually learn science, which is by engaging in scientific practices in authentic situations over time.

Shulman (1987) distinguished between content knowledge, pedagogical knowledge that is domain-insensitive, and pedagogical knowledge that is particular to a domain, often called pedagogical content knowledge (PCK). PCK in science involves knowing how to make science knowledge and culture plausible, meaningful, and useful to nonexperts and recognizing the typical stumbling blocks that learners face in constructing this knowledge (Zembal-Saul, Starr, & Krajcik, 2002). Little is known about the relationship between PCK and student learning in science, but a few case studies and expert to novice comparisons seem to indicate that it is a central factor in influencing student learning (Duschl et al., 2007).

Teachers are consumers of published curricula but designers of enacted curricula. The general quality of much of the available science curriculum materials in unsatisfactory (Kesidou & Roseman, 2002). Until abundant high-quality science materials are available, teachers need to select, evaluate, and modify existing curriculum materials to effectively meet the needs of their students and the expectations of their districts. Even when high-quality materials are available, their use can be challenging. High-stakes testing and overload force teachers to be concerned about the time and risks involved in adopting new high-quality materials that may require them to change their teaching practices. Knowing how to adapt curriculum materials is another important skill science teachers need to develop, yet it is underemphasized in most teacher preparation programs (Davis, 2006).

One of the ways curriculum materials can assist teachers in adopting them, adapting them, and maximizing their effectiveness is by incorporating educative features (Davis & Krajcik, 2005), which are features that are intended to promote teacher learning as the teacher uses the materials to guide student learning. Such features could develop teachers' content knowledge, demonstrate how to make connections between units and disciplines, provide information about the typical student's prior conceptions, make the designers' rationale transparent, and provide guides to making productive adaptations. But educative curriculum materials alone cannot remedy issues related to teachers' content knowledge, pedagogical knowledge, and pedagogical content knowledge. For them to be effective, they need to be part of a comprehensive teacher education and teacher development program.

Teacher Pre- and InService Professional Development

In general, less is known about teacher professional development in science than in mathematics and literacy (Borko, 2004). There are general characteristics of teacher professional development programs that appear to have a positive influence regardless of the field on which they focus. Whether there are additional characteristics that are unique to successful professional development programs in science is less clear.

Teacher inservice professional development programs need to be grounded in teachers' practice and consider their local expectations, constraint, and resources. These programs are usually provided by external facilitators, such as curriculum publishers. A review by the American Educational Research Association (2005) indicated that such programs should focus on improving student learning of content in the context of the particular curricula being used, draw on student artifacts, inform the teachers of the various connections between the various components of the curriculum, local standards, and assessments, and be ongoing—that is, provide teachers with multiple recurring opportunities to reflect on their practice rather than being one-shot, short-term workshops.

In many ways, the good science teacher professional development programs have much in common with high-quality science curriculum: (a) they are structured around authentic tasks (instructional practice in the context of a particular curriculum) for prolonged periods of time, (b) they place high importance on the incorporation of phenomena (student learning), and (c) they build on student (teacher) collaboration.

Diversity

Large-scale standardized tests have revealed significant gaps in science achievement among students of different racial, cultural, and socioeconomic backgrounds. Racial, cultural, and economic factors influence students' prior knowledge of and beliefs about science. Some of the societal factors that can detrimentally affect students' attitudes toward science are the lack of a personal connection with someone they identify with who is in a science-related profession, the media's stereotypical portrayal of scientists, college programs and professions that exclude women and people of color, and contrasts between the culture of science and the home culture (Eisenhart, Finkel, & Marion, 1996).

Most preservice teachers have little cross-cultural experiences and believe that they need to be color-blind and treat all students identically, rather than acknowledging that students are different and ignoring these differences undermines the goal of science literacy for all. Teachers often feel inadequately prepared to deal with the diverse needs of their students, especially those who are not native speakers of the dominant language. The tendency toward color-blindness can be reinforced by accountability policies that seldom make mention of students' home language and culture, and thereby reinforce the view that minorities are expected to assimilate to the dominant language and culture.

Although there have been attempts to deal with this issue by developing science curriculum materials that are culturally relevant, attempt to avoid gender stereotyping, and acknowledge the special needs of some learners, these materials are usually useful only for the particular linguistic or cultural groups; this makes their development prohibitive. Another approach is to develop design principles that can steer the development of high-quality materials and guides for teachers on how to effectively adapt such materials so that they maintain their relevance for diverse students (Lee & Buxton, in press).

Many states are beginning to incorporate science into their high-stakes tests to meet the science accountability requirements of the No Child Left Behind Act (2002). This policy will undoubtedly lead to major changes in the way science is taught. It remains to be seen whether these changes will lead to the closing of the achievement gap.

Conclusion

Expertise in science education requires mastery of a broad range of knowledge and skills. Teaching science requires more than a deep understanding of general themes in education (such as student learning, teaching, and teacher education), developmental and educational psychology, technology, sociology and culture, and assessment; science teachers must also have a deep understanding of at least a single science discipline, the nature of science, its discourse patterns, practices, and investigative norms, and its relationship to technology and society at large. It is a dynamic and developing field, drawing on knowledge gained from other fields, integrating them, and often leading the way in indicating possible new ways to improve education in general.

References and Further Readings

American Association for the Advancement of Science. (1990). *Science for all Americans*. New York: Oxford University Press.

American Association for the Advancement of Science. (1993). *Benchmarks for science literacy*. New York: Oxford University Press.

American Educational Research Association. (2005). *Studying teacher education: The report of the AERA panel on research and teacher education*. Mahwah, NJ: Lawrence Erlbaum Associates.

Anderson, C. W. (2007). Perspectives on science learning. In S. K. Abell & N. G. Lederman (Eds.), *Handbook of research on science education* (pp. 3–30). Mahwah, NJ: Lawrence Erlbaum Associates.

Ball, D. L., & Cohen, D. K. (1992). Reform by the book: What is—or might be—the role of curriculum materials in teacher learning and instructional reform? *Educational Researcher, 25*(9), 6–8, 14.

Blumenfeld, P. C., Marx, R. W., Patrick, H., Krajcik, J. S., & Soloway, E. (1997). Teaching for understanding. In B. J. Biddle, T. L. Good & I. F. Goodson (Eds.), *International handbook of teachers and teaching* (pp. 819–878). Dordrecht, The Netherlands: Kluwer Academic.

Borko, H. (2004). Professional development and teacher learning: Mapping the terrain. *Educational Researcher, 33*(8), 3–15.

Bransford, J. D., Brown, A. L., Cocking, R. R., Donovan, M. S., & Pellegrino, J. W. (2000). *How people learn: Brain, mind, experience, and school*. Washington, DC: National Academies Press.

Clark, D., & Linn, M. C. (2003). Designing for knowledge integration: The impact of instructional time. *The Journal of the Learning Sciences, 12*(4), 451–494.

Collins, A., Brown, J. S., & Newman, S. E. (1989). Cognitive apprenticeship: Teaching the crafts of reading, writing, and mathematics. In L. B. Resnick (Ed.), *Knowing, learning, and instruction: Essays in honor of Robert Glaser* (pp. 453–494). Hillsdale, NJ: Lawrence Erlbaum Associates.

CTGV. (1992). The Jasper series as an example of anchored instruction: Theory, program description, and assessment data. *Educational Psychologist, 27*(3), 291–315.

Davis, E. A. (2006). Preservice elementary teachers' critique of instructional materials for science. *Science Education, 90*(2), 348–375.

Davis, E. A., & Krajcik, J. (2005). Designing educative curriculum materials to promote teacher learning. *Educational Researcher, 34*(3), 3–14.

Driver, R., Asoko, H., Leach, J., Mortimer, E., & Scott, P. (1994). Constructing scientific knowledge in the classroom. *Educational Researcher, 23*(7), 5–12.

Driver, R., Guesne, E., & Tiberghien, A. (1985). *Children's ideas in science*. Philadelphia: Open University Press.

Duit, R. (2007). Bibliography—STCSE: Students' and teachers' conceptions and science education. Retrieved September 10, 2007, from http://www.ipn.uni-kiel.de/aktuell/stcse/download_stcse.html

Duschl, R. A., Schweingruber, H. A., & Shouse, A. W. (2007). *Taking science to school: Learning and teaching science in grades K–8*. Washington, DC: National Academies Press.

Eisenhart, M., Finkel, E., & Marion, S. F. (1996). Creating the conditions for scientific literacy: A re-examination. *American Educational Research Journal, 33*, 261–295.

Ericsson, K. A., Krampe, R. T., & Tesch-Römer, C. (1993). The role of deliberate practice in the acquisition of expert performance. *Psychological Review, 100*(3), 363–406.

Gee, J. (1996). *Social linguistics and literacies: Ideology in discourse* (2nd ed.). London: Falmer Press.

Grigg, W. S., Lauko, M. A., & Brockway, D. M. (2006). *The Nation's Report Card: Science 2005.* Washington, DC: National Center for Education Statistics.

Kesidou, S., & Roseman, J. E. (2002). How well do middle school science programs measure up? Findings from Project 2061's curriculum review. *Journal of Research in Science Teaching, 39*(6), 522–549.

Krajcik, J. S., Czerniak, C., & Berger, C. (2003). *Teaching children science in elementary and middle school classrooms: A project-based approach.* New York: McGraw-Hill College.

Lee, O., & Buxton, C. (in press). Science curriculum and student diversity: A framework for equitable learning opportunities. *The Elementary School Journal.*

Lehrer, R., & Schauble, L. (2006). Scientific thinking and science literacy: Supporting development in learning in contexts. In W. Damon, R. M. Lerner, K. A. Renninger, & I. E. Sigel (Eds.), *Handbook of child psychology* (6th ed., Vol. 4, pp. 153–196). Hoboken, NJ: John Wiley & Sons.

Linn, M. C. (1997). The impact of technology on science instruction: Historical trends and current opportunities. In D. Tobin & B. J. Fraser (Eds.), *International handbook of science education* (pp. 265–293). Dordrecht, The Netherlands: Kluwer Academic.

Martin, M. O., Mullis, I. V. S., Gonzalez, E. J., & Chrostowski, S. J. (2004). *Findings from IEA's Trends in International Mathematics and Science Study at the fourth and eighth grades.* Chestnut Hill, MA: TIMSS & PIRLS International Study Center, Boston College.

Metz, K. E. (1995). Reassessment of developmental constraints on children's science instruction. *Review of Educational Research, 65,* 93–127.

National Research Council. (1996). *National science education standards.* Washington, DC: National Academies Press.

No Child Left Behind Act. Public Law No. 107-110, 115 Stat. 1425. (2002)

Perkins, D. (1992). *Smart schools: Better thinking and learning for every child.* New York: The Free Press.

Pintrich, P. R., Marx, R. W., & Boyle, R. (1993). Beyond cold conceptual change: The role of motivational beliefs and classroom contextual factors in the process of conceptual change. *Review of Educational Research, 63*(2), 167–199.

Posner, G. J., Strike, K. A., Hewson, P. W., & Gertzog, W. A. (1982). Accommodation of a scientific conception: Toward a theory of conceptual change. *Science Education, 66*(2), 211–227.

Roseman, J. E., & Koppal, M. (in press). Using national standards to improve K–8 science curriculum materials. *The Elementary School Journal.*

Roseman, J. E., & Linn, M. C. (in press). Characterizing coherence. In M. C. Linn, J. E. Roseman, & Y. Kali (Eds.), *Delineating and evaluating coherent instructional design for education.* New York: Teachers College Press.

Roth, K. J., Anderson, C. W., & Smith, E. L. (1987). Curriculum materials, teacher talk and student learning: Case studies in fifth grade science teaching. *Journal of Curriculum Studies, 19*(6), 527–548.

Sanders, L. R., Borko, H., & Lockard, J. D. (1993). Secondary science teachers' knowledge base when teaching science courses in and out of their area of certification. *Journal of Research in Science Teaching, 30*(7), 723–736.

Shulman, L. S. (1987). Knowledge and teaching: Foundations of the new reform. *Harvard Educational Review, 57*(1), 1–22.

Shwartz, Y., Weizman, A., Fortus, D., & Krajcik, J. (in press). The IQWST experience: Coherence as a design principle. *The Elementary School Journal.*

Strauss, S. (2001). Folk psychology, folk pedagogy and their relations to subject matter knowledge. In B. Torff & R. J. Sternberg (Eds.), *Understanding and teaching the intuitive mind* (pp. 217–242). Mahwah, NJ: Lawrence Erlbaum Associates.

Vygotsky, L. (1986). *Thought and language.* A. Kozulin (Trans.). Cambridge, MA: The MIT Press.

Webb, N. M., & Palincsar, A. S. (1996). Group processes in the classroom. In R. C. Calfee & D. C. Berliner (Eds.), *Handbook of educational psychology* (pp. 841–873). New York: Prentice Hall.

Zembal-Saul, C., Starr, M. L., & Krajcik, J. (2002). Constructing a framework for elementary science teaching using pedagogical content knowledge. In J. Gess-Newsome & N. G. Lederman (Eds.), *Examining pedagogical content knowledge* (Vol. 6, pp. 237–256). Amsterdam: Springer.

39

SOCIAL STUDIES

JOHN D. HOGE

University of Georgia

CHARLES E. JENKS

Augusta State University

LINDA A. MITCHELL

Jacksonville State University

Social studies education encompasses a diverse formal curriculum in addition to a powerful set of school-based learning experiences. The formal curriculum is composed of content taken predominately from the social sciences and certain humanities. But content from many other subjects can be a legitimate part of social studies as it might either serve as a tool supporting social thinking and learning (e.g., using mathematical concepts to illuminate housing prices) or become a target of social studies instruction (e.g., examining issues related to stem cells to better understand the nature of public policy debates).

The subjects that most educators group under the label of social sciences are geography, political science, economics, sociology, anthropology, and psychology. The humanities featured in social studies are history, philosophy, religion, and aspects of art history and literature. History, geography, economics, and political science, typically called the core four, usually get the lion's share of time and attention in the social studies curriculum at all levels of education. Research and writing by scholars in these disciplines provides the content that is taught to students at all grade levels.

The formal curriculum is the purposefully taught social studies lessons that students encounter in schools. National, state, and local curriculum guides often specify the learning goals students are expected to achieve from this officially endorsed, prescribed social studies instruction. Textbooks and other instructional resources are used to help students learn the formal curriculum. This curriculum is open to public review and it is often tested to provide evidence of students' learning. The intellectual foundation of the formal curriculum comes almost exclusively from the social sciences and the humanities.

Beyond the formal social studies curriculum is an informal, hidden, or natural curriculum. For example, elementary schools typically recognize popular holidays with a variety of decorations, events, and programs that help to set a seasonal tone and rhythm to the school year. In addition to this typical set of seasonal events, all schools also foster a civic culture through such things as their code of conduct, their various administrative interactions with students and their parents, and the provision of extracurricular activities and clubs. These phenomena arguably join with the formal social studies curriculum as agents of intentional sociocultural learning that are designed to prepare young people for their future roles as engaged, active citizens within our representative democracy.

General Historical Overview of Development in the United States

In the early colonial days of our nation, social studies as a distinct school subject did not exist. Before the establishment of public education, only the wealthy would have their children tutored or attend private schools to learn reading, writing, arithmetic, and religion. Because instruction about world religions is now considered part of social studies, it could be argued that this was the first appearance of social studies.

With the overthrow of British rule in 1776, opinion in our nation began to shift toward the provision of universal education for all children as a necessity for a self-governing nation. Benjamin Franklin, Thomas Jefferson, and Noah Webster, among others, argued for adding civic education—composed primarily of lessons on our history and government—to the common school curriculum. Of particular importance was Jefferson's belief that citizenship education was a necessity in a democracy.

Further public sentiment in favor of tax-supported common schools gained momentum in the early decades of the 1800s. Horace Mann, a Massachusetts legislator, did much to sway opinion in favor of this new and uniquely American approach to education. Concerning the common school, Ornstein and Levine (1989) state:

Through a common or a shared program of civic education, it was to cultivate a sense of American identity and loyalty. Its major social purpose was to integrate children of various social, economic, and ethnic backgrounds into the broad American community. . . . It was to educate the future citizens of a country with self-governing political institutions. (p. 170)

The common school curriculum grew and changed throughout the 1800s. By the last quarter of that century, history and government were taught in many urban elementary schools to prepare students for the demands of citizenship in a diverse immigrant-based and rapidly industrializing society. At the turn of the 20th century, only a little over 6% of teenage Americans graduated from high school (Bohan, 2005). This fact helps us understand the crucial importance of elementary social studies as most Americans' only significant opportunity to learn the history, geography, economics, and government content needed for democratic citizenship. The growth of sociology, anthropology, and psychology as legitimate academic disciplines in their own right during the late 1800s and early 1900s laid the foundation for a diversification of social studies education in American high schools.

Bohan (2005) traced the roots of social studies in the United States to the Committee of Eight, a group formed in 1905 that recommended a highly nationalistic approach to American history at every grade level, with an oral approach in the early grades where reading skills were still being formed and reliance on textbook-based instruction in the later elementary grades. The focus for Grades 1 and 2 was Native Americans and public holidays; for Grade 3, biographical study of heroes and American independence; for Grades 4 and 5, historical scenes and persons of American history and the growth and development of the American nation; for Grade 6, a study of the European origins of American citizens (Bohan, 2005, p. 288). Much of this same content can be found in contemporary elementary schools.

In the early 1900s, communities began to extend education beyond elementary school, forming junior and senior high schools that sought to expand and strengthen the history and government lessons students had learned in elementary education. Lybarger (1991) notes that the 1916 Committee on Social Studies of the National Education Association's Commission on the Reorganization of Secondary Education popularized the term *social studies*.

The National Council for the Social Studies (NCSS) in 1921 vowed to bring together teachers and others interested in citizenship education through social studies. In response to the turmoil in high school social studies, the American Historical Association published a 16-volume commission report that secured a role for history as a unifying subject at the core of the social studies curriculum.

In the late 1950s, a social studies curriculum revision movement that came to be known as the new social studies (NSS) attempted to move instruction away from traditional methods that focused on the mastery of content and skills deemed important to citizenship transmission and acculturation, to emerging concepts and theories of the social sciences and teaching practices that engaged students in issues-oriented inquiries. The NSS curriculum revision era spanned more than two decades but was only minimally successful in altering the predominate patterns of social studies teaching (Rice, 1992). Of course, this period of great turmoil and discord in America was associated with the rise of the baby boom generation, the sexual revolution, the civil rights movement, the stresses of the Cold War, and the disastrous Vietnam War. Toward the end of the 1960s, educators began reexamining the role of junior high schools, arguing, among other things, that the developmental needs of adolescents needed more attention and that instruction needed to be more child-centered and provided through closely knit instructional teams. The middle school movement was born, and the National Middle School Association was formed in 1973 to encourage a continuing focus on the unique needs of youth.

With the election of Ronald Reagan in 1980, a turn toward conservatism took place in America that had many consequences for public education, such as changes in the role of the U.S. Department of Education and the way federal funds were distributed to states. Subsequent developments such as the Republican take over of Congress in 1994, the development of voluntary national standards in virtually all subject areas, and a number of other school reforms driven by America 2000, the first of President Bush's signature school improvement plans, had a substantial effect on education in general and social studies in particular. Within social studies this meant a return to a dominant focus on history, geography, economics, and government/civics/political science; a retreat from issues-oriented inquiry instruction; and attempts to bolster the presence of Western cultures' humanities content in the curriculum.

Relationship to Other
Subjects and School Culture

Social studies has many interconnections with other school subjects. The English, language arts, and literature curriculums, for example, typically include cultural literacy and communication goals that match similar aims within social studies instruction. For example, various forms of literature such as biography are often read in social studies classes to provide a more engaging or more detailed account of real life events. Science properly includes a historical perspective on its content and similarly often includes a much needed focus on public policy debates that surround leading-edge developments in scientific research and technology such as cloning, AIDS, and stem cell use. Foreign language instruction routinely engages students in the study of other nations' cultures, since this focus is the driving force behind the proper meaning and use of any language. Sex and drug education, to be effective, must reasonably go beyond diagrams and charts to consider elements of peer pressure and popular culture that influence young people's behavior. Career education, another and more obvious form of social studies, is often tied to the economic education strand of the curriculum.

It is crucial to reemphasize the importance of the total school environment as a complex and multifaceted setting for the learning of important lessons about what it means to be an American. School sports were not mentioned in the previous section, but they, too, are a powerful component of school culture and hold incredibly strong potential for good and harm within the lives of students and their families. Perhaps this realization partially explains why social studies teachers are often sports coaches or otherwise actively involved in the extracurricular life of their schools.

Professional Organizations

The preeminent professional organization for the social studies, the National Council for the Social Studies (NCSS), was formed in 1921 and currently has 26,000 members. The NCSS produced the voluntary national standards for social studies instruction, *Expectations of Excellence* (1994), and voluntary national standards for the preparation of social studies teachers. It publishes three journals: *Social Education*, *Middle Level Learning,* and *Social Studies and the Young Learner*. The NCSS is the parent organization for many affiliated regional and state social studies councils in addition to professional groups such as the College and University Faculty Assembly (CUFA), which publishes the leading academic journal *Theory and Research in Social Education*; the Council of State Social Studies Specialists (CS4); and the National Social Studies Supervisors Association (NSSSA), whose members are school district level social studies curriculum supervisors.

Although the NCSS is the leading organization that promotes social studies, it is important to note that each of the core four discipline areas also has a professional organization that promotes instruction within that particular subject. For example, history has the National Council for History Education (NCHE), geography has the National Council for Geographic Education (NCGE), and economics has the National Council for Economic Education (NCEE). Political science, whose professional organization is the American Political Science Association (APSA), has a subgroup that is concerned with precollegiate education, but much of the effort to improve government and civics classes has come from organizations such as the Center for Civic Education (CCE), the Constitutional Rights Foundation (CRF), the Close Up Foundation, and a variety of others.

National and State Standards

Expectations of Excellence (National Council for the Social Studies [NCSS], 1994), the voluntary national standards for K–12 social studies instruction, specified 10 themes, representing the social science and humanities disciplines but also incorporating some additional content themes such as global connections, science, technology, and society. Content learning outcomes for each theme were specified for upper elementary, middle, and high school social studies learning. A comprehensive skills matrix was provided in addition to a vision statement on "powerful social studies learning" (NCSS, 1994). Although the NCSS standards served as a comprehensive guide to social studies instruction, they lacked the subject matter specificity needed to direct discipline-centered instruction, drive curriculum development, or guide test development. The core four disciplines all produced their own comprehensive voluntary national standards during the mid-1990s. These curriculum guides were much more detailed than the NCSS's 10 themes for excellence in social studies. The voluntary national history standards ran into a hailstorm of conservative criticism, and the geography standards received a mixed review from geography teachers. Education is, of course, a state function, so states vary a great deal in their standards for the different content areas of social studies such as history (Brown, 2003).

Testing, Accountability,
and No Child Left Behind

Testing and accountability take on several forms in social studies. Many high school social studies courses, for example, culminate with a required district or state level end-of-course test that determines whether students pass or must retake required courses. In addition, students at many grade levels often have to take standardized, commercial achievement tests such as the Iowa Test of Basic Skills, the California Achievement Test, the Metropolitan

Achievement Test, or the Stanford Achievement Test, all of which include assessments of social studies content learning. Teacher accountability may extend beyond scrutiny of test scores, to include ways of checking adherence to pacing guides that specify what must be taught at a particular time of the school year.

Social studies educators have understandably tended to be strong advocates of academic freedom and local control of the curriculum; however, the exclusion of social studies from testing under the No Child Left Behind Act (NCLB) has left many believing that the social studies are being seriously neglected in favor of subjects that will be tested. Many believe that students are graduating without the understanding they need to function as effective citizens. Consequently, the NCSS has passed an official resolution urging that social studies be included in states' NCLB testing programs.

Staffing and Instructional Leadership

Staffing and instructional leadership varies widely in elementary, middle, and high schools. High schools, of course, must staff the required history, economics, geography, government, or civics classes. Highly qualified teachers are hired to meet these instructional needs. Other things being equal, high school social studies departments tend to prefer teachers who can also coach a sport or be otherwise involved in the extended extracurricular life of the school. High school teachers often work at several grade levels and are assigned up to four daily classes. Middle school social studies teachers are typically assigned to multisubject instructional teams, and they may or may not teach more than one grade level during the day. Middle school administrators also look for highly qualified teachers to cover the number of required classes that they must offer. Like their high school counterparts, middle school social studies teachers' job prospects are strengthened if they are able to coach a sport or sponsor a club, have earned a graduate degree, or hold special education or English as a second language certification. Elementary schools typically have no formal leadership in social studies. Teachers may collaborate on grade-level specific planning for social studies instruction for a grading period or the entire school year. At all school levels teachers may also have some input into the social studies textbook adoption for their school.

Instructional leadership within school systems for social studies varies considerably. In many cases, school- and even district-level instructional support personnel may be overworked and forced to cover more than one content or subject area (e.g., English and social studies). Ideally, teachers should have some well-qualified person whom they can call upon for advice and resources. But this is rarely the case and, as a result, teachers turn most often to colleagues, professional associations' conferences, and the Internet for help and ideas to improve their social studies teaching.

Elementary Social Studies

Contemporary Practice

The widening horizons scope and sequence became the dominant approach to the elementary social studies curriculum during the 1950s, and remnants of this scope and sequence remain today in most school systems. Topics or themes are typically used to structure the elementary social studies curriculum. For example, a fifth-grade unit on a specific Native American culture in the early 1800s might integrate content from history, anthropology, and geography. Alternatively, a first-grade unit on contemporary families would integrate content of sociology, economics, psychology, and perhaps religion.

Occasionally, teachers in elementary schools will devote some specific instructional time to a single discipline, but such discipline-focused studies are the exception rather than the rule in most elementary classrooms. The predominant approach to teaching elementary social studies is an integrated disciplines approach, and this approach is likely to remain popular in the future (Haas & Laughlin, 2001).

Controversies, Difficulties, and Issues

Several clear results of efforts to change elementary social studies are apparent, particularly in altering the outdated expanding environments scope and sequence, and improving textbooks and other curriculum materials. Half a dozen alternative scope and sequence arrangements have been promoted, but no one proposal has assumed a dominant position and vestiges remain of the early curriculums. Improved textbooks now include significant content on women and minorities, and they assiduously resist stereotypes in these depictions. Material on other nations is routinely included in elementary social studies, and it is not unusual to find some content that focuses on issues such as poverty and pollution as these phenomena exist both abroad and in the United States. Newer textbooks also typically address some of the most troubling and dubious actions of our government such as the removal of the Cherokees from the lower Appalachians, the internment of Japanese Americans, and the dropping of atomic bombs on Hiroshima and Nagasaki during World War II.

In addition to the controversies over what should be taught, elementary social studies has suffered from widespread general neglect in the curriculum, largely as a result of increasing attention being given to reading and math (VanFossen, 2005). This attention to reading and math is, of course, driven largely by high-stakes testing that is now associated with NCLB. Efforts to achieve high test scores are most apparent in schools that service low socioeconomic status (SES) families. Since these financially challenged families typically cannot afford summer camps or vacation trips, and the home environment itself may lack good books, computers, and newspapers, low SES schools that neglect social studies are eliminating the only chance these children may have for gaining early and potentially significant insights into history, geography, economics, or government, politics, and citizenship. The research of Brophy and Alleman (2006; 2007) demonstrated young students' severely limited knowledge about cultural universals (e.g., food, clothing, shelter, transportation) that has resulted from this lack of social studies education and the consequent need to refocus the elementary social studies curriculum.

The professional preparation of most elementary teachers is also implicated in the weakness of social studies as a school subject. College students who prepare to become elementary teachers often have very limited exposure to the social sciences and humanities with the noted exception of history. It would be a rare exception to encounter a preservice teacher with significant coursework in political science, economics, or geography. Further, most elementary teacher preparation programs have two or three times the curriculum and methods coursework in reading, math, and language arts as they do in social studies, where the norm is one course, the maximum is two, and the minimum is often no significant coursework at all—the teaching of social studies being addressed only in a combined methods course that encompasses a host of topics such as lesson planning and classroom management. Thus many elementary teachers enter their classrooms without a clue as to what to do and certainly no love of the subjects that comprise elementary social studies.

Future Challenges

First, we must do a better job of preparing elementary teachers to teach this subject, and we must persuade administrators that they are making a grave error if they omit this subject from a young person's formal education. Second, we must adopt an intellectually defensible and politically palatable scope and sequence for elementary social studies that can inspire creative, child-centered teaching while addressing the real-world learning needs of the students we serve in our classrooms (Katz, 1999). Brophy and Alleman's (2006) proposal for an elementary social studies curriculum centered on cultural universals meets these goals and it could also provide a basis for improved testing practices. Third, once social studies is fully reestablished in the curriculum with meaningful daily instruction, we need to have an ongoing program of curriculum development assistance that is driven by a strong sense of professionalism and pride-of-purpose, recalling that each child we reach may play a crucial role in creating peace, spreading liberty, and promoting human dignity.

Middle School Social Studies

Contemporary Practice

Social studies in the middle grades builds on the integrated, thematic approach most often used in the elementary grades and prepares students for the discipline-focused courses of high school. Middle grade teachers combine national and state social studies standards into a curriculum that addresses a variety of age-specific needs and local school district requirements. Middle grade teachers routinely use a variety of instructional strategies to actively engage their students, often drawing from information on wise social studies practice that was developed largely for elementary and high school students. Requirements for high-stakes exams also influence social studies instruction in the middle grades, tying teachers more closely to local curriculum guides and state standards.

The middle grade social studies curriculum includes history, geography, government and civics, and economics. States determine the order in which social studies topics will be taught and how they will be combined into a cohesive curriculum. Thus, curriculums vary significantly among the states. For example, Georgia's middle grade social studies students take 2 years of world history and 1 year of Georgia history. By contrast, California's middle grade social studies students study United States history, followed by world history, and then a return to United States history. Social studies units are usually based on the standards for history but integrate other social science disciplines into the history instruction. National and state standards also include requirements for instruction in a variety of skills such as spatial thinking and map use, historical thinking and reasoning, analysis of historical artifacts, and other critical thinking skills.

Preparing students for high-stakes testing is an important consideration for middle grade teachers. Fear that their students will fail to perform adequately on these tests causes some teachers to plan instruction that covers a wide range of materials. When this approach to instruction is combined with practice in test-taking skills, some teachers have found that test scores do improve in the short term. But many educators doubt whether students receiving this type of instruction are gaining the in-depth knowledge and understanding that will enable them to succeed in more advanced courses in high school and college or be effective citizens.

Middle grade social studies teachers often find that the most effective instructional strategies are those that require students' active participation, especially if students complete tasks that are similar to the tasks adults would undertake with the same types of information. Middle grade students are engaged when activities require them to gather and synthesize information, work with others to use this information to solve or analyze a problem, and then present their work to others. This is especially true when students are working on a complicated problem for which there is no right or wrong answer and when their conclusions must be defended publicly. For example, groups might research a list of early North American explorers, determine which four they believe are the most important and therefore worthy of full coverage in a social studies textbook, and make a group presentation arguing for the four they chose.

Use of technology in social studies classes has become an important issue in education. The most common use of technology in the middle grades is for guided research and creative projects. Some teachers have organized effective collaborations between students in different cities, states, or nations using e-mail, discussion boards, and chat technologies. Technology also provides social studies teachers access to a wealth of digital resources for enriching their lessons and allows students to use resources they would have been unable to access in the past. Assignments that require students to state and defend opinions, write from specific historical perspectives, or other nontraditional assignments help prevent plagiarism and other problems teachers sometimes fear when using technology.

Controversies, Difficulties, and Issues

Although middle grade teachers typically rely on national, state, and local standards to determine what they will teach, controversial content often intrudes into what would otherwise seem to be safe topics. For example, when learning about the civil rights movement, middle grade students may fixate on the most violent and atrocious acts and use their expanding skills and awareness of contemporary acts of racism to raise questions that demand the teacher's attention. Many educators suggest that teachers should make dealing with such controversial topics a regular part of their instruction. They contend that consideration of controversy, when coupled with effective tools and strategies, can help create a classroom environment where students are able to understand the importance of social studies skills and knowledge. Some teachers, however, are not comfortable including controversial topics in the classroom. They may fear that middle grade students would be unable to adequately comprehend and consider complex topics. These fears, as well as concerns that parents, administration, or community members may disapprove, can result in teachers giving inadequate attention to complex topics, attempting to provide fact-based instruction for issues on which the facts are not agreed, or simply skipping topics that might be controversial.

Other social studies educators suggest that fact-based, direct instruction should be the primary instructional strategy in the middle grades (Rochester, 2003; Schug, 2003). Inadequate knowledge about the subject that they are teaching, lack of familiarity with effective strategies for teaching more complex lessons, and a belief that middle grade students should focus on facts and deal with concepts and other complex subjects only after they have a firm foundation in the basics are reasons some teachers adopt this strategy. Use of problem-based instruction and controversial issues involves passionate beliefs on both sides, and although the NCSS and many other organizations have taken a stand supporting active, student-centered instruction, the controversy remains strongest at the middle grade levels.

Future Challenges

Middle grade social studies faces several challenges. The focus on high-stakes testing means that teachers will continue to struggle with how best to prepare their students. Teachers are challenged to routinely use instructional strategies that actively engage students while ensuring that their students gain the knowledge needed to perform well on these tests. The ability to do this is vital if high-stakes exams are going to be a positive influence on social studies instruction instead of influencing teachers to limit their instructional strategies as well as the topics they teach.

The majority of research on social studies instruction is at either the elementary or high school level, leaving middle grade teachers to adapt strategies that were designed for younger or older students. More research needs to be done to produce a body of wise practice to guide middle grade social studies instruction.

High School Social Studies

Contemporary Practice

High school social studies is typically an amalgam of distinct history, government, geography, and economics courses with history receiving the lion's share of coursework. Larger and wealthier high schools are often able to provide electives in the other social sciences and humanities and might also offer one or two issues-focused courses that cut across several disciplines. Classes are often tracked, with college-bound students often receiving Advanced Placement (AP) coursework while other students are taught either a general course or one covering much of the same AP course content but paced more slowly and demanding less homework.

Over the past two decades there has been considerable effort to reinvigorate high school history, geography, economics, and government and civics courses. Each core discipline has developed finely articulated voluntary national standards, and each has also engaged in a variety of teacher training and public outreach efforts to help achieve instructional excellence and increased public awareness of the disciplines' importance. Social studies teachers have been greatly aided by advances in computer technology and the immense growth of the Internet, where it is estimated that almost 80% of all Web sites contain information that fits within the social sciences and humanities disciplines (Braun & Risinger, 1999). Dramatically improved access to local, state, national, and international news, news archives, and other research tools has greatly simplified the acquisition of information needed for the study of historical or contemporary events.

Technology has also dramatically improved access to digital facsimiles of primary source documents. Additionally, television programming (e.g., The History Channel) has no doubt greatly enhanced the aura of history as a school subject. Geography teaching has benefited similarly from advances in computer technologies, especially the proliferation of Geographic Information Systems (GIS) and GIS-like electronic atlases based on the pinpoint accuracy of Global Positioning Satellite (GPS) data and often enhanced with satellite imagery that can be overlaid on map-like images. These modern mapping systems allow for a wide array of geographic inquiry and research, ranging from mapping social data such as income, education, health, and religion to physical data such as rainfall, soil characteristics, vegetation, crops, and minerals. An obvious consequence of this is that high school geography teachers are now much more able to blend together a study of a geographic theme, such as the connections among places, with the simultaneous exploration of a specific place. Such technology use allows students to function at a much higher and more engaging level of geographic learning. Technology has also enhanced the teaching of economics, with a variety of powerful simulations and greatly improved, often instantaneous, access to economic data. Popular government and civics materials now make frequent use of hands-on simulations such as mock trials, simulated congressional hearings, and close-up encounters with government officials and agencies. Service learning has also been a prominent addition to economics and civics instruction (Wade, 2000).

Controversies, Difficulties, and Issues

A prominent and continuing problem of high school social studies is related to the original creation of social studies as an area of learning that ideally sought to provide students with issues-focused, interdisciplinary instruction that addressed real-world problems. Most of the discipline-specific promotion and development of the past 20 years has discouraged and displaced this type of learning for students. Note, too, that the social studies philosophy favored empowering teachers and students to determine some of the issues or problems that they were going to examine, whereas detailed curriculum standards and related high-stakes testing discourages such classroom decision making.

Related to what some call an ideologically conservative retrenchment to single-discipline social studies instruction, are the continuing reports of student boredom and disaffection engendered by overreliance on lectures, notetaking, textbook reading, and multiple-choice testing. Students seldom see connections among their largely separate courses, and they may be discouraged from asking questions that depart from some predetermined instructional sequence tied to high-stakes testing. Teachers may discourage small-group work because they fear having to reign in excessive amounts of socialization and the potential threat of conflicts and eventual loss of class control. These fears may be exacerbated in classrooms that have clashing subcultures whether these are based on ethnic heritage, socioeconomic status, religious differences, cliques, or gangs.

Another difficulty is that teachers must be certified in one of the core disciplines to be considered highly qualified. This has defeated the concept of a broad-field certified teacher who is best capable of creating issues-oriented cross-curricular understanding of content that arguably might help create a new generation of citizens better prepared to deal with the cultural complexities we now face.

Our increasingly diverse society creates the inescapable relevance of multicultural education to citizenship preparation as an issue of paramount importance. If social studies teachers are to be successful in any setting, their preparation must include multicultural education, both in theory and practice.

Future Challenges

Pragmatically, the biggest challenge facing high school social studies teachers may be how to get their students to pass mandatory tests that serve as gateways to graduation. Methods of instruction are doubtlessly tied to students' motivation to learn (VanSickle, 1990) and to their successful mastery of course content, so teachers are well advised to use different strategies to increase learning within their classrooms.

A second challenge is for teachers to effectively use technology as a part of their instruction. Staying up-to-date takes time, but effective use of a wide variety of software, Web sites, and related digital technologies is essential to success in today's classrooms. Putting students into creative leadership roles in the use of technology is one way to help ensure higher levels of learning and greater task engagement.

A third challenge is the increasing diversity in our society and the very real social need we have to help every individual achieve a life of personal satisfaction while respecting and contributing to their community and our wider society. End-of-course test scores may open doors, but they say little about this broader and more significant realm to which we must devote substantial effort. Attention to this challenge demands that high school social studies teachers view their work as extending beyond delivering high-value instruction in their individual classes to also include contributions to the extracurricular life of the school.

Perhaps most troubling is, however, the millions of high school graduates who are never reached by the instruction they are offered and, as a consequence, end their formal education experience lacking a fundamental grounding in our culture and may therefore be destined to fail as responsible citizens. Approximately 50% of all Americans will never extend their formal education beyond high school, except perhaps to job-specific or career-oriented training. This being the case, high school social studies is effectively our last chance to reach millions of future citizens, to attune their minds conscientiously to the good that can come from becoming economically independent and financially literate, to inspire them with the many incredible people and events that have formed our history, to give them a grasp of the great geographic wealth of our nation, or to inure them to the sometimes unpleasant roles they must play as citizens fit to govern our nation. If history is any guide to the future, we can expect that these vitally important Americans—and their college-educated counterparts—will encounter economic turmoil, environmental challenges, healthcare problems, difficult wars, political corruption, and corporate misconduct. These and many other personal and public problems will predictably challenge their lives, and they strongly call for significantly improved high school social studies.

Conclusion

Social studies has been an integral part of the school curriculum in America since colonial times. The curriculum first existed at the elementary level and later became an important component of high school learning as communities extended access to tax-supported public education and as the social sciences and humanities grew to maturity. Recent research has documented a decrease in time devoted to elementary social studies instruction, a result often attributed to the advent of high-stakes testing connected to NCLB (VanFossen, 2005; Leming, Ellington, & Schug, 2006). Middle and high school social studies instruction does not appear to have suffered a reduction of instructional time, but often has been forced to narrow the instructional focus so that it aligns more precisely with end-of-course achievement testing. These trends, the diminution of elementary social studies often sending students into middle schools with poor preparation in the subject, and the narrowing of middle and high school social studies to content that can easily be assessed with multiple-choice tests doubtlessly have potentially negative consequences for our society's future.

Social studies is a complex and important school subject that focuses the powerful insights of the social sciences and certain humanities on our individual and collective lives. The cultures we navigate and negotiate become more complex, not less. Trends toward open cultural conflict as well as other forms of social discord and disaffection may overrun our schools' meager capacities to provide meaningful social education that can build well-reasoned allegiance to our society that logically derives from empowering future citizens with important social studies knowledge and skills. The social studies education we offer must at all times eschew any form of indoctrination. Social studies must continue to teach the important content and skills that provide an essential cohesiveness for our society, but this content must not be offered without a serious examination of alternative viewpoints. Gaining multiple perspectives on history, having one's eyes opened to powerful forms of geography that allow us to critically examine our cultural landscape, gaining key economic insights into

the operation of our economy and attaining personal financial literacy, and becoming aware of how our local, state, and national governments respond to special interest group pressures are all examples of how social studies can be meaningfully related to our lives. It is doubtful that powerful social studies learning can ever be achieved in classrooms that fail to engage students' thinking or provide opportunities for students to apply what they have learned and take responsible actions based on their learning. After all, these are the qualities that a self-governing representative democracy needs most from its citizens.

References and Further Readings

Adler, S. (Ed.). (2004). *Critical issues in social studies teacher education.* Charlotte, NC: Information Age.

Akenson, J. E. (1987). Historical factors in the development of elementary social studies: Focus on the expanding environments. *Theory and Research in Social Education, 5,* 155–171.

Barr, R., Barth, J. L., & Shermis, S. S. (1978). *The nature of the social studies.* Palm Springs, CA: ETC.

Bohan, C. H. (2005). Digging trenches: Nationalism and the first national report on the elementary history curriculum. *Theory and Research in Social Education, 33,* 266–291.

Braun, J. A. Jr., & Risinger, C. F. (Eds.). (1999). *Surfing social studies.* Washington, DC: National Council for the Social Studies.

Brophy, J., & Alleman, J. (2006). A reconceptualized rationale for elementary social studies. *Theory and Research in Social Education, 34,* 428–454.

Brophy, J., & Alleman, J. (2007). *Powerful social studies for elementary students* (2nd ed.). Belmont, CA: Thomson/Wadsworth.

Brown, S. D. (2003). *History standards in the 50 states.* (ERIC Digest). Bloomington, IN: ERIC Clearinghouse for the Social Studies/Social Science Education. (ERIC Document Reproduction Service No. ED482209)

Davis, O. L., Jr. (Ed.). (1996). *NCSS in retrospect* (Bulletin No. 92). Washington, DC: National Council for the Social Studies.

Evans, R. W. (2004). *The social studies wars: What should we teach the children?* New York: Teachers College Press.

Hass, M. E., & Laughlin, M. A. (2001). A profile of elementary social studies teachers and their classrooms. *Social Education, 65,* 122–126.

Henry, N. B. (Ed.). (1957). Social studies in the elementary school. (Part II: The fifty-sixth yearbook). Chicago, IL: University of Chicago Press and National Society for the Study of Education.

Hertzberg, H. W. (1981). *Social studies reform 1880–1980.* Boulder, CO: SSEC.

Jenness, D. (1990). *Making sense of social studies.* New York: Macmillan.

Katz, L. G. (1999). *Curriculum disputes in early childhood education.* (ERIC Digest). Champaign, IL: ERIC Clearinghouse on Elementary and Early Childhood Education. (ERIC Document Reproduction Service No. ED436298)

Leming, J. S., Ellington, L., & Schug, M. (2006). The state of social studies: A national random survey of elementary and middle school social studies teachers. *Social Education, 70,* 322–327.

LeRiche, L. W. (1987). The expanding environments sequence in elementary social studies: The origins. *Theory and Research in Social Education, 5,* 137–155.

Lybarger, M. B. (1991). The historiography of social studies: Retrospect, circumspect, and prospect. In J. P. Shaver (Ed.), *Handbook of research on social studies teaching and learning* (pp. 3–15). New York: Macmillan.

Mehlinger, H. D. (1992). The national commission on social studies in the schools: An example of the politics of curriculum reform in the United States. *Social Education, 56,* 149–153.

National Council for the Social Studies. (1994). *Expectations of excellence: Curriculum standards for social studies* (Bulletin No. 89). Washington, DC: Author. (ERIC Document Reproduction Service No. ED378131)

Ornstein, A. C., & Levine, D. U. (1989). *Foundations of education* (4th ed.). Boston: Houghton Mifflin.

Parker, W. C. (2001). Educating democratic citizens: A broad view. *Theory into Practice, 40*(1), 6–13.

Rice, M. J. (1992). Reflections on the new social studies. *Social Studies, 83,* 224–231.

Rochester, J. M. (2003). The training of idiots. Civics education in America's schools. In J. Leming, L. Ellington, & K. Porter (Eds.), *Where did social studies go wrong?* (pp. 6–39). Washington, DC: Thomas B. Fordham Foundation.

Schneider, D. (1993). Teaching social studies: The standards movement. *Clearing House, 67*(1), 5–7.

Schug, M. C. (2003). Teacher-centered instruction: The Rodney Dangerfield of social studies. In J. Leming, L. Ellington & K. Porter (Eds.), *Where did social studies go wrong?* (pp. 94–110). Washington, DC: Thomas B. Fordham Foundation.

Stanley, W. B. (Ed.). (2001). *Critical issues in social studies research for the 21st century.* Greenwich, CT: Information Age.

VanFossen, P. J. (2005). "Reading and math take so much time . . .": An overview of social studies instruction in elementary classrooms in Indiana. *Theory and Research in Social Education, 33,* 376–403.

VanSickle, R. L. (1990). Personal relevance in social studies. *Social Education, 54,* 23–27.

Wade, R. C. (Ed.) (2000). *Building bridges: Connecting classroom and community through service-learning in social studies* (Bulletin No. 97). Washington, DC: National Council for the Social Studies.

Wronski, S. P., & Bragaw, D. H. (Eds.). (1986). *Social studies and social sciences: A fifty-year perspective* (Bulletin No. 78). Washington, DC: National Council for the Social Studies.

Yeager, E. A., & Davis, O. L (Eds.). (2005). *Wise social studies in an age of high-stakes testing: Essays on classroom practices and possibilities.* Charlotte, NC: Information Age.

40

ARTS

DeWayne A. Mason

Patriot High School

Michael B. Krapes

Rubidoux High School

The 19th and 20th centuries saw policy makers and practitioners give scant attention to K–12 arts education (Boyer, 1983; Efland, 1990). Horace Mann failed to add art to Massachusetts' curriculum (Efland, 1990), and the Committee of Fifteen's recommendation of 60 minutes of drawing per week for elementary schools in 1895 barely surpassed the absence of arts in the Committee of Ten's proposal for secondary schools in 1893 (Tanner & Tanner, 1990). Boyer's (1983) study of American secondary education a century later found the arts "shamefully neglected" and "rarely required" (p. 98). Unfortunately, art curricula have apparently regressed since the 2001 passage of the federal No Child Left Behind Act (NCLB); a Center on Education Policy report (2006) concludes that this legislation has led to a 22% reduction of instructional time for art and music.

In this chapter we present our definition of art curriculum and argue that art education should receive greater emphasis and balance during the 21st century. We provide a brief review of the history and major conceptualizations of arts education during the 19th and 20th centuries. We then provide rationale for including arts in K–12 schooling and discuss art standards and art assessment. Finally, drawing from our experiences as K–12 practitioners, we propose a realistic perspective for creating K–12 art education programs.

Definitions

Curriculum has been variously defined (Jackson, 1992), leading to conceptions that are narrow ("a fixed course of study"), broader ("all organized experiences that occur under the direction of a school"), and broader still ("all experiences, planned and unplanned, under the direction of a school"). Theorists have expanded these definitions to include such facets as the hidden curriculum, the written curriculum, and the learned curriculum. Because different definitions lead to different topics, we define the arts curriculum as "the planned course of K–12 student learning outcomes (e.g., knowledge, conceptual understanding, and critical thinking skills) in visual art, dance, music, and theater." For this chapter, we focus on the visual arts, expanding beyond planned student learning outcomes to explain how visual arts curriculum might be more strategically derived, vibrantly presented, and learned.

Historical Perspective

The late 19th century and the 20th century saw art education moving toward wider acceptance as part of the K–12 curriculum. Progress was slow and unstable, however, especially during times of financial or perceived educational crisis. Early advocates such as Lowell Mason,

Horace Mann, and von Rydingsvard were influential in moving the arts forward (Efland, 1990; Wolf, 1992). Mann sought to create schools where all students beyond the privileged could study drawing, music, and natural objects. Mason produced songbooks and popular articles related to music, and von Rydingsvard sold mass-produced art reproductions to schools along with manuals on how to use them to teach various virtues. Wolf (1992) notes that arts education was therefore accepted not as a field of study but rather as "a tool or an occasion for producing citizens, a way to smooth, to civilize, and to inculcate . . ." (p. 948).

School leaders also responded to the need to create more practical and attractive programs for youth. Grammar schools gave way to infant schools, academies, and public schools aimed at enrolling every adolescent—not just those few attending university. Growing demands for workers (Tanner & Tanner, 1990), recognition that the Latin grammar school was too antiquated for serving societal needs, and the ostensible interest in creating a common school that conserved cultural values led arts curriculum to be based more on their service to "virtue, religion, citizenship, and industry . . ." than as a field of study (Wolf, 1992, p. 948).

In contrast to Boyer's (1983) finding that art was a rare requirement, a larger survey by Lehman and Sinatra (1988) found that art and music were taught in 90% and 93% of the schools, respectively, and that 22 states by 1989 had art graduation requirements. An Education Commission of the States (2007) report found that 35 states now have an arts requirement and 23 states require at least a semester of art credit alone. Rose and Gallup (2006) found that public interest in broadening the curriculum is currently high, as 58% of those polled nationally and 63% of public school parents responded that a wide variety of courses should be favored over fewer but more basic courses—a substantial increase in both cases from 44% in 1979.

Conceptualizations of Art Education

Wolf (1992) identifies four major conceptualizations in the evolution of arts curriculum: (1) arts education for craftsmanship, (2) arts education for creativity and self-discovery, (3) arts education for developing symbols and thinking, and (4) arts education for apprenticeship. Wolf (1992, p. 947) explains that this conceptual evolution involves the arts as a distinct form of knowledge; a press for the arts to become part of a common curriculum for all learners; research showing there to be sequences of development typical of art learners; the importance of teaching and learning artistic knowledge and skills; and interest in connecting art education classrooms to practices found in studios, museums, performance halls, and universities.

Arts Education for Craftsmanship

Wolf (1992) explains that early art educators tended toward efficiency methods used in industry and priority

curriculum areas such as reading and mathematics. Early art textbooks were dominated by elements of design, routine exercises, and a skills-based sequence of activities. When Walter Smith became Massachusetts' art director, his program focused on "drawing skills useful to industry" and "practicing isolated elements of design [curves and designs present in fabric, ornaments, and wallpaper] repetitively until they achieved a machinelike dependability" (Wolf, 1992, p. 948). According to Wolf, this curriculum provided students drawing tools to become skilled workers and to enhance their social status above what might have been predicted, without much personal expression or creativity.

Arts Education for Creativity and Self-Discovery

As the 20th century began, arts education reflected such social interests as evolution theory, psychoanalysis, industrial reform, as well as new artistic directions such as romanticism, cubism, and the arts and crafts movement—forms linked to individual imagination, spontaneity, and expression. Arts education became "a safeguard against the routine, the regular, and the predictable, something like an occasion, or a medium, for the development of creativity" (Wolf, 1992, p. 949). Now students were seen as free-spirited artists, discoverers, and natural inventors of self-expression—not students to be taught to draw and copy. Cultural changes and progressive education, derived in part from child-centered practices, led art educators to argue that the arts played a unique role in the curriculum—contributing to personality development and the creativity needed to become effective citizens. During this time, art teachers evolved from mentors of drawing skills to facilitators who provided the studio, materials, and occasions for various projects.

Arts Education for Developing Symbols and Thinking

Uneven results from progressive education, cultural shifts from behaviorism and romanticism, reaction to Russia's *Sputnik* success, and research that documented major patterns of language acquisition and cognitive and moral development led the view of arts education to shift from creativity and individualistic expression to a view of the arts as "earned conceptual development" (Wolf, 1992). Wolf writes that researchers and educators asserted that students slowly constructed (not discovered) rule systems embedded in the arts of their culture and that, hence, the arts were not simply occasions for self-expression and discovery but more a matter of learning, deserving careful instruction.

Visual arts researchers (e.g., Lowenfeld & Brittain, 1975) provided strong descriptions of the developmental stages, leading to implications for art instruction. Indeed, an understanding of these stages and the provision of active and developmentally appropriate instruction and materials, as well as peer interactions aimed at cognitive growth, partially replaced the earlier conceptions of art education. Art education now became focused on listening and looking at art, rule-governed thought, and efforts to develop students' ability to read the language and history of the arts.

Arts Education for Apprenticeship

The final conceptualization of arts education grew largely from three major controversies about educational practice that developed between 1960 and 1990: (1) the role of explicit teaching and development; (2) difficulties related to canons of art and intellect; and (3) the role of thoughtfulness in artistry. Wolf (1992) explains that concerns now centered on what occurred naturally rather than on what educators specifically wanted students to know or be able to do—"What occurs 'naturally' is not necessarily the foundation for a curriculum. Development establishes only a footing—it cannot dictate matters of value" (p. 953).

A second critique stemmed from disagreements about what constituted intellect and art, and the role of art history, art criticism, and aesthetics. Traditional definitions of IQ and ways of knowing were challenged by scholars. The need for a multicultural perspective in art history was expressed as well as whether arts education should be "rooted chiefly in *knowing how* to make art, or whether it should expand to include *knowing about*" art (Wolf, 1992, p. 956). It was argued that art appreciation increases when we understand the context of the work.

Research and theory on critical thinking also influenced the new conception of arts education (Wolf, 1992, p. 955). The mind was reconceptualized from that of a memorizer to that of a planner, reflector, and thinker about thinking (metacognition). This led to interest in narrowing the gap between thinking in typical school settings and thinking that occurs in authentic artistic contexts. Numerous researchers pointed to problems associated with teaching content and basic skills devoid of applications, and some noted that typical public school art was marginal in qualitative depth.

These three discussions led to the viewpoint of student as apprentice. According to Wolf, efforts to link school arts with expert practice generated two widely different curriculums: (1) discipline-based art education (DBAE), and (2) ARTS PROPEL. The DBAE approach focuses on introducing students to four major areas of artistic knowledge—art making, art history, art criticism, and aesthetics—and aims to develop visual literacy, or the ability to derive meaning from works of art. Students who learn components of a DBAE curriculum will gain skills in identifying key visual characteristics of artworks such as historical connections, use of art elements and principles, and expressive properties. Dobbs (2004, p. 706) describes the DBAE student as one who is able to converse about artwork in terms of elements and principles, how they were

made, and what they mean in the historical and cultural context. This student would also be able to identify quality and intentionality in works of art and be able to conceive, design, and create such.

Teachers using PROPEL (designed by researchers at Harvard Project Zero and Educational Testing Service) engage students in doing the work of the art field with extensive portfolio development through sustained involvement (Wolf, 1992, p. 957). This approach allows latitude for highly imaginative and innovative works and deep understanding of the work. This final conceptualization argues for mentors capable of modeling the performance and metacognition of seasoned artists in the field, authentic work in the arts, and restructuring of many present art education practices such as longer class periods, virtual and actual museum tours, and in-depth critiques.

Purposes of Art Education

Some policy makers may believe art education is a frill and intellectually inferior, but quality programs incorporate numerous higher-cognitive skills, some of which are untouched by other academic disciplines. The development and application of these advanced cognitive skills make the arts especially valuable for 21st-century education. The lack of understanding about substantive purposes of art can be traced to three of education's intellects: Jean Piaget, Lev Vygotsky, and Benjamin Bloom. Piaget's (1963) description of the intellectual development process focused on science and mathematics, giving less importance to the arts. Piaget's theory relegated the arts (nonpropositional thinking) to lower-order cognition, and arts education has suffered from this assumption. Vygotsky's (1962) theory suggests that knowledge is learned through forms of social mediation. Vygotsky described how knowledge is internalized but not how individuals construct through imagination and intuition. Bloom's (1956) widely accepted taxonomy of instructional objectives has reified the cognitive, affective, and psychomotor domains. Consequently, the arts have traditionally been grouped with noncognitive domains and afforded lower intellectual status (Efland, 2002).

At the very least, art courses must attempt to include higher-order thinking skills as curriculum objectives and as the focus of assessment before claiming ownership and responsibility for them. These cognitive skills overlap and involve aspects of each other in various ways; therefore a hierarchical taxonomy is not suggested. Table 40.1 describes the higher-cognitive purposes of art education highlighted by scholars

Schwartz (2000) reinforces the value of critical thinking common to arts education by asserting its overarching political usefulness of promoting, supporting, and maintaining the aims of a democratic society. Engaging critically with works of art, students practice the ideal democratic skills of suspending judgment, deliberation, debate,

Table 40.1   Higher-Cognitive Purposes of Art Education

Percipience: An ability to experience works of art for the sake of their constitutive and revelatory values or a perceptive stance taken by a reflective observer (Smith, 2006). (Found in reflective art making as well as while analyzing and discussing works of art.)

Cognitive flexibility: An ability to function in a variety of domains (Efland, 2002) and use a range of strategies to acquire knowledge. (Used during critical thinking while making and viewing art.)

Critical thinking: A general term to describe higher-order cognitive functions such as application, analysis, synthesis, interpretation, inference, and evaluation. (Used while making and seeking meaning from art.)

Reflective intelligence: An ability to activate higher-order cognitive skills using personal experience (Perkins, 1994, cited in Efland, 2002, p. 767). (Used while making and interpreting artworks.)

Imagination and imaginative processes: An ability to use mental imagery, visual metaphors, symbolism, juxtaposition, suggestiveness, narrative structuring, categorization, and schematizing functions (Efland, 2002). (Used during the process of organizing or reorganizing images, symbols, and metaphors to construct meaning or knowledge while making or critiquing works of art.)

Symbolic competence: The ability to represent knowledge in nonlinguistic symbolic forms. (Used during the process of developing original and personal symbols in making art.)

New forms of representation: The ability to visually communicate an individual's unique experience (Eisner, 1982). (Used in art making focused on representing experience via original symbols and imagery.)

Construction of new knowledge: An ability to use symbolic competence, new forms of representation, and imaginative processes to construct new knowledge.

Creativity: The ability to combine the cognitive processes such as cognitive flexibility, imaginative processes, and critical thinking in service of problem solving, expression, perception, or the construction of knowledge. (Used in art making and art viewing.)

Problem solving: The ability to discover what must be done to achieve a goal not readily available. (Used in making and viewing artwork, it is the perceiving, analyzing, interpreting, and resolving of the puzzle posed by the complexity of a given media toward the expression of an idea, message, meaning, or solution.)

Intuition: The ability to access knowledge without obvious logical thought and inference. (Used in art making and art viewing.)

Aesthetic appreciation: The ability to perceive aesthetically such complex concepts as elements of art, principles of design, art history, and sociocultural context. (Used in art making and art viewing.)

decision making, and other values such as tolerating different points of view.

Standards

Standards (shorthand for the more complete phrase *academic content and performance standards*) are what students are generally expected to know or be able to do. Standards, therefore, are "statements about what is valued" (National Council of Teachers of Mathematics [NCTM], 1989, p. 2). Tucker and Codding (1998) emphasize that to be useful, standards need to be specific, realistic, expressed in a common framework across the disciplines, and linked to reliable assessments. Usually, standards are supplemented with benchmarks that clarify the specific content or skills to be mastered and how such might be taught and assessed (Tucker & Codding, 1998). Unfortunately, standards vary widely among states, disciplines, and professional organizations. Furthermore, many state standards are unclear about intended outcomes for students, and many states simply have a glut of standards that render them highly problematic to teachers. Numerous scholars have stressed the practical need to make hard choices about what knowledge and skills are most essential so that adequate time may be given to instruction for learning and mastery. Moreover, many practitioners and scholars, while applauding the high expectations and noble goal of a single, world-class set of curriculum standards, assert that one size rarely fits all in public schooling, especially in the highly heterogeneous culture of the United States.

The document *National Standards for Arts Education: What Every Young American Should Know and Be Able to Do in the Arts* was created in 1994 by the Consortium of National Arts Education Associations. These standards for dance, music, theater, and visual arts were endorsed by over 50 professional organizations and supported by over 25 others. Used as a model by many states as they crafted their state art standards, the *National Standards for Arts Education* includes 6 standards and 44 benchmarks or achievement standards: 15 at Grades K–4; 14 at Grades 5–8; and 15 at Grades 9–12. An additional 10 benchmarks for demonstrating advanced art achievement are drawn for Grades 9–12. The 6 common standards are (1) under—standing and applying media, techniques, and processes; (2) using knowledge of structures and functions; (3) choosing and evaluating a range of subject matter, symbols, and ideas; (4) understanding the visual arts in relation to history and cultures; (5) reflecting upon and assessing the characteristics and merits of their work and the work of others; and (6) making connections between visual arts and other disciplines.

Authors of the *National Standards for Arts Education* explain that standards can make a difference in program quality and accountability, ensuring that arts education is focused, disciplined, and able to assess program results. They argue that the standards are sequenced, comprehensive, and aimed at developing "the problem-solving and higher-order thinking skills necessary for success in life and work . . ." (Consortium of National Arts Education Associations, 1994, p. 6). They conclude that the standards may be influenced by various educational changes during the 21st century as school days and years are restructured and as the goal of education changes from educational progress by grade level to student mastery.

Art Assessment

Assessment is broadly defined as "the systematic investigation of the worth or merit of some object (program, project, materials)" (Joint Committee on Standards for Educational Evaluation, 1981, p. 12). Assessment informs our focus on agreed upon standards, clarifies what we need to reteach and whether our instruction needs improvement, and enables larger program evaluation and accountability by administrators and policy makers. Improving the use of valid and reliable assessments would contribute to the legitimacy of art well into the future. Traditionally, K–12 art education has relied upon authentic forms of assessment. Teachers subjectively evaluate projects and portfolios through informal means or performance-based rubrics. Art educators worry that standardized assessment will artificially quantify key aspects of art such as imagination and creativity (National Assessment Governing Board, 1994). They also worry that adding standardized measures, especially those of lower-level knowledge and skills, will shift the focus inordinately to these lesser aims. Interest in accountability and addressing concerns about the biases and far-ranging goals of traditional authentic assessments have led to steady advances in art assessment, but the lack of inclusion in high-stakes accountability efforts diminishes the importance of art for administrators, educators, and the public (Boughton, 2004).

Portfolio assessments, widely used in higher education for assessment and admission to art programs, are the major tools for measuring success in the College Board's AP Studio Art program (1980) and the International Baccalaureate's (IB) Art and Design program (Boughton, 2004). These programs are exemplars of large-scale portfolio assessment, creating objectivity by training portfolio reviewers in procedures, standard-setting rubrics, and scoring guides; however, reliability is only ensured by the pooling of separately scored sections of the portfolio (Myford & Sims-Gunzenhauser, 2004). The following

authentic forms of assessment are assumed to measure the higher-cognitive skills sought by most art curriculums: large-group critiques, reflective or interactive journals, small-group critiques, and student-pair critiques (Freedman, 2003). In nearly every case, for art assessments to rise to higher levels of validity and reliability, these typically informal assessments should gather written or oral records, however impractical. In response to a perceived need for such standardization, the National Assessment of Educational Progress (Myford & Sims-Gunzenhauser, 2004) created a large-scale standardized assessment of art making based on the 1997 Arts Education Framework. This assessment, a timed drop-in format with both multiple-choice and open-ended items, was designed to capture the complex nature of art making, interpreting, and critiquing as well as assessing specific content knowledge. This framework provides a meaningful model for how states might develop standardized art assessments.

Critics of standardized testing in art have traditionally provided strong opposing philosophical positions, fearing loss of student freedom and homogenizing effects (Boughton, 2004; Gardner, 1996). Ironically, standardized tests carry the additional risk of informing art educators about that which they may not want to know, thus increasing their responsibility for teaching and learning in areas for which they have less preference. It is certainly easier to maintain an imbalanced art education curriculum related to individual teacher interests or preferences; however, by not participating in a balanced assessment program, high-stakes testing, or both, art educators risk maintaining their subject at a marginalized level. Of course, the issue of art assessment is always linked to fundamental curriculum questions about the purposes of K–12 art education.

Assessments of higher levels of cognition are difficult to construct, time-consuming to use, lacking in reliability, and therefore uncommon. Many argue that if these skills are assessed, then art teachers will more frequently teach them and see their presence increase. Each of the following higher-level skills can be assessed authentically in formal and informal ways, even using objective and standardized approaches that are potentially more valid and reliable. For many skills teachers may simply borrow authentic assessment methods from other disciplines such as writing and literature. Oral discussions are the preferred form of demonstration, but in the interest of reliability, writing samples are recommended. With the exception of creativity and construction of new knowledge (because of their breadth and complexity), higher-cognitive skills such as those reviewed in Table 40.1 may be assessed with the following strategies: objective multiple-choice questions with stimuli prompts, student writing samples, critiquing works of art or visual culture, performance-based activities aimed at solving particular problems, and using metaphors and personal symbolism in art making.

If K–12 art educators are to demonstrate their subject's true academic value and claim the cognitive territory that they own, they must move toward using valid and reliable measurement. To do this, ambiguous constructs such as imagination, creativity, and expression must be unwrapped and operationally defined—thus becoming objects of curriculum and assessment. Developing objective and standardized measures for areas previously untouched in the arts is not as difficult or as dangerous as it may seem. Research in cognitive psychology may enable art educators to see ways in which their constructs may be more operationally defined and objectively measured. Although it is beyond the scope of this chapter to operationally define these constructs or to describe highly specific standardized assessment tools, we suggest using more objective approaches for assessing higher cognitive functioning in art. Whether the curriculum bias tends toward emphasizing traditional art making (Burton, 2001), imaginative cognition (Efland, 2004), competence in understanding visual culture (Freedman & Stuhr, 2004), or other purposes, these aims use similar cognitive functions. Therefore, assessment of the higher-level cognitive functions in art with increasing standardization and objective measures is complementary to each of these curricula.

A Practical Perspective

The intent of our viewpoints, knitted after much reading, reflection, and collegial interaction, is to propose a practical picture of art education during the 21st century—what we hope to become as art teachers and what we advocate for colleagues and policy makers who influence how art education evolves in states and local school districts. Under the common grade structures of K–5, 6–8, and 9–12, we present 7 reforms that are needed to improve art education during the 21st century: (1) an emphasis on art for all K–12 students; (2) an emphasis on mastery of art fundamentals; (3) an organizational structure for art teaching at each level; (4) a balanced curriculum; (5) an approach to assessing art education; (6) a district and collegial orientation to art program development and exhibition; and (7) a call for research on the role of art in promoting learning, individual expression, and a more tolerant and nurturing society.

Art for All K–12 Students

Surveys show that far too many students are not enrolled in art classes. The 1977 National Assessment of Progress in Education (NAPE) found that only half of a national sample of eighth graders had taken or were taking art (Burton, 2004). Moreover, this same NAPE survey showed there was "no significant difference in the accomplishments of youngsters who were currently studying art and those that were not," that "94% of pupils failed to demonstrate even moderate creative abilities," and that "instruction had a negligible effect on the overall outcomes" (Burton, 2004, p. 562; Persky, Sandene, & Askew, 1998). Given these data and the aforementioned purposes of art education, we recommend that all K–12 students learn the fundamentals of art through participation in a systematic, standards-based, and mastery-oriented art program. As Burton (2004) notes, "the NAPE results together with other formal empirical studies lend credence to the small effects of art instruction on children's lives" (p. 568). Art education will continue to be marginalized and student outcomes will continue to be paltry until we aim all students toward mastering art fundamentals.

Mastery of Art Fundamentals

Studies of effective schools and effective teachers have consistently found that high student achievement is correlated with "expectations regarding their abilities to master the curriculum" and teachers providing "opportunities for students to practice and apply [new content]. They monitor each student's progress and provide feedback and remedial instruction as needed, making sure the students achieve mastery" (Good & Brophy, 2000, pp. 377–378). In view of these important findings, consistently confirmed by our teaching and learning experiences, we recommend a strong orientation toward a limited curriculum that is consensually derived, taught in depth, objectively assessed, retaught when necessary, and mastered to a point that the knowledge, concepts, and skills may be used during applications, subsequent learning opportunities, and postsecondary real-world experiences. We are convinced that for progress in art learning and application to increase, mastery of art fundamentals must become central.

Improving the Organizational Structure

Art teaching occurs within an organizational structure that answers questions such as, Who teaches the art curriculum? Who gets the art curriculum? For how long do they get the art curriculum? and What materials, equipment, and real-world resources are available? Answers to these and other structural questions vary widely among and within states, districts, and schools. Indeed, while rare, there are likely some enlightened schools, districts, and states that presently exceed the following structural recommendations.

At the K–5 level we recommend that certified art teachers engage all elementary school students in the district art curriculum for no less than 500 minutes per year (e.g., once a week for 20 minutes, once a month for 60 minutes). Elementary teachers rarely have the in-depth training required for a quality art education program, and their professional development is aptly placed on the more valued areas of teaching reading, mathematics, science, and social studies. This modest commitment would enable elementary students to accrue 50 hours or more of focused art instruction and hence carry forward to their middle schools a solid foundation of knowledge, concepts, and skills in art making, art history, and art critique including aesthetics and visual culture. At a minimum, where constraints preclude the use of certified K–5 art teachers, certified secondary art teachers who are most familiar with the district program should provide their elementary colleagues professional development on the essential art standards and aligned assessments and lesson plans that would enable student mastery at each individual grade or primary (K–2) and intermediate (Grades 3–5) level.

At Grades 6–8 we recommend that a certified art specialist engage all students in the art curriculum each year during their middle school careers for at least 1,500 minutes per year (e.g., 6 weeks for 50 minutes a day, 12 weeks for 50 minutes per day). This structure is reasonable given that middle school philosophy encourages exploratory programs such as band, music, technology, foreign language, and speech or drama. Such a structure would enable middle school students to experience at least an additional 75 hours of art curriculum. At a minimum, recognizing that elective and semester course structures are entrenched in many schools, a required semester course on fundamentals of art during a student's middle school career would ensure the curriculum continuity necessary for curriculum mastery by high school graduation.

At the high school level we recommend that a certified art teacher engage all students in a full-year art fundamentals course. At a minimum, a semester course of art fundamentals would be preferable to current practices in most states. This course should encompass key knowledge, concepts, and skills related to art history, art criticism, and the making of art. Students enrolled in this art fundamentals course—likely a culminating experience for most students—should attain mastery of the identified fundamentals, setting up important prerequisite appreciation, knowledge, and understanding for success in future art courses and real-life application experiences. At all three structural levels, art teachers should be supported with adequate supplies, equipment, and resources.

A Balanced Curriculum

We see K–12 art education organized as a spiral curriculum and reconceptualized as three subdisciplines: art making, viewing (Smith, 2006), and connections. Each of these subdisciplines includes knowledge, concepts, and critical thinking skills (including application). Art making is focused on production. Viewing is focused on engagement with examining works of art, especially masterworks from art history. And connections are focused on the demonstrated relevance and utility of arts education in students' lives outside the classroom including careers and participation in visual culture (Freedman, 2003). For parsimony, practicality, and increased relevance and student engagement, we see the need for three subdisciplines, rather than four (DBAE) or five (California Department of Education, 2004).

Art making knowledge and understanding at K–5 would center on the language of art including art elements, art principles, and vocabulary related to basic tools, techniques, media, and processes. For critical thinking at K–5,

students would use various media in basic representational, metaphoric, and symbolic (Efland, 2002) approaches to perceptual, experiential, and expressive problem solving. At the 6–8 level, the curriculum should review and build upon this same knowledge and conceptual understanding with a greater emphasis on applications to projects as well as new tools, techniques, media, and processes. Projects should integrate art elements and principles (e.g., a line and shape project emphasizing rhythm and movement) along with new principles of design and advanced forms of cognition, representation, and suggestiveness such as metaphor and symbolism. Teachers should encourage critical thinking by using various media to solve perceptual, experiential, and expressive problems. At the 9–12 level, knowledge and understanding would again include the language of art along with a broadening of information about (a) basic historical styles and artists, (b) additional media and their related processes, (c) imaginative cognitive processes such as metaphor, symbolism, and other forms of representation, and (d) increasing student awareness of their own creative process and developing a personal philosophy of art. Critical thinking at this level should include an in-depth focus on suggestive, representational, metaphoric, and symbolic approaches to solving personal or commercial artistic problems. This may include students employing the same imaginative cognitive approaches and creative processes as those used by specific artists or styles in art history.

Viewing knowledge at the K–5 level would include the language and definition of art, media categories, artists, artistic styles, and the masterworks of art history. Concepts would include exposure to and developing a familiarity with art exemplars, artistic styles, functions of art, and how to look at art in a stepwise process—for example, description, analysis, characterization, and interpretation (Broudy, 1987; Smith, 2006). Critical thinking skills are facilitated while analyzing and interpreting works of art and using an inquiry-based method of associative questioning (Freedman, 2003). At Grades 6–8 teachers would extend students' knowledge and understanding of the definitions and language of art, media categories, artists, artistic styles, and masterworks, as well as add information about the chronology of art history. Conceptual outcomes would include a sense of historical continuity and learning about various artists' styles, approaches, and purposes. There should be continued emphasis on fully understanding the stepwise critiquing process for examining art history exemplars, student work, and visual culture. At the 9–12 level, viewing knowledge would further emphasize the language and vocabulary of art, the critique process, and the chronology and deeper contextual factors of art exemplars, styles, and artists. Critical thinking approaches at this level would include more group, partner, and self-critique using inquiry-based methods of associative questioning directed toward art exemplars and students' own and other's works for various purposes.

Connections at the K–5 level are created by presenting students knowledge and concepts about art careers and the presence of art in their everyday visual world. Critical thinking would include analyzing visual culture as well as using knowledge and concepts for creating products in other academic subjects and real-life applications. At Grades 6–8 teachers should focus on increasing students' knowledge of art careers and art in visual culture, including the influence of visual culture on identity and values. Critical thinking activities would center on analyzing artifacts of visual culture and more advanced applications of art to other areas of students' academic and personal lives. At the 9–12 level, students would develop knowledge and concepts related to additional careers in the arts, artifacts of visual culture, suggestiveness in visual culture, and imaginative cognitive processes. The concepts would include imaginative cognition and critique processes, including visual culture's influence on issues such as identity, values, and contemporary problems. Critical thinking would be used for inquiry, problem solving, examination of contemporary problems and issues, and evaluation of visual culture in other areas of students' academic and personal lives.

Assessing Art Education

We recommend that art assessment during the 21st century become aligned with essential standards—those fundamentals identified as most crucial to subsequent learning and applications in and out of school. Unlike typical current practice, whereby standards are nonexistent or unrealistic and objective assessment is seriously lacking, we advocate creating valid and reliable measures of all fundamental standards at each of the three levels. At Grades K–5, we recommend an annual assessment that provides educators information about whether students are mastering important art concepts and skills. At Grades 6–8 and 9–12, we recommend midcourse and end-of-course assessments that identify student progress and outcomes of art learning. Such assessments should include a broad range of item types, appropriate to the standard, including items that assess higher levels of cognition. Further, results of such assessments should become the object of in-depth analyses aimed at program and instructional improvements, using both cross-sectional and longitudinal data. While many districts have now identified essential standards and created assessments to measure curriculum priorities in reading, English, mathematics, science, and social studies, we think such curriculum and assessment work should be extended to art and other important areas (e.g., music, health, technology, public speaking).

A District and Collegial Orientation to Program Development

Vital to developing and implementing most of our recommendations is a process for creating quality, context-specific standards, assessments, and program and instructional improvements: a structure of district leadership and support for collegial interaction. More than three decades of research have shown that school and classroom improvements are linked to collaborative efforts aimed at curriculum development and implementation, monitoring of student progress, and improvement of instruction (e.g., Little, 1981; Rosenholtz, 1989). Our personal experiences (Mason, Mason, Mendez, Nelsen, & Orwig, 2005) with strong district leadership focused on teacher-led efforts to develop essential standards, standards-based assessments, and standards-based instructional improvements have demonstrated the power of integrating research-based theory with the craft knowledge of teachers.

We recommend that district leaders use rotating teams that ultimately involve all teachers to develop essential art standards and assessments of these standards. Such work not only provides staff development in curriculum and assessment construction but also creates ownership and commitment toward high-fidelity implementation. District and school leaders should build calendars that enable all teachers to work on annual curriculum and assessment refinements, guides for pacing instruction, and common lesson plans that have theoretical potential or demonstrated success in ensuring student mastery of essential knowledge, concepts, and skills. Work presently underway at our high schools, based on frameworks articulated by Reeves (2002, 2006) and others (e.g., Ainsworth, 2003; DuFour, Eaker, & DuFour, 2005) demonstrate that development of such essential standards, assessments aligned to these standards, and focused teaching and reteaching can lead to significant gains in student achievement across all curriculum areas.

A Call for Research on Art Teaching

Our review of the literature on art education, though far from extensive, noted too little research on how various curriculums, programs, or instructional strategies influence important outcome variables such as imagination, creativity, and problem solving. We also came across no research on the effectiveness of different assessment strategies for improving learning. Descriptive, correlational, and experimental studies would be instructive in the areas of using state standards, essential standards, standards-based assessments, mastery-oriented learning units, and teacher-led collegial exchange aimed at sharing craft knowledge to improve student learning of art concepts and skills. Given our interest in the role of authentic learning, situated cognition, and public art, research on programs based on these components would be informative. Research, however, should be comprehensive, measuring an array of dependent variables so as to identify whether focusing on particular curriculum areas leads to trade-offs in other areas. We believe a well-constructed curriculum that balances essential knowledge and concepts with deep applications and critical thinking skills related to identified art fundamentals would be mutually reinforcing and bring about high levels of learning overall. Finally, nearly five decades of process-product research in basic skill areas have provided educators many findings that can be used to improve instruction and student outcomes. We saw no evidence of this type of research in our review of the art education literature, likely because dependent measures in many areas of art education are at an undeveloped stage or shy of appropriate validity and reliability. As measurement tools become available, however, such research would be valuable.

Conclusion

Art education has historically received too little attention in the K–12 curriculum, and recent state and national initiatives under NCLB have only served to diminish this dismal picture. In this chapter we argue for a stronger emphasis on art education during the 21st century—an emphasis that includes stronger curriculum balance, mastery of identified art fundamentals, and use of more valid and reliable assessments to improve instruction and student learning. Art education develops many higher-order cognitive functions valuable for business, personal expression and appreciation, and promulgation of a thriving and nurturing democratic society. These important higher-cognitive functions are absent or rare priorities in other areas of the K–12 curriculum. Policy makers as well as educational leaders should understand the true cognitive value of the arts in order to establish art programs that contribute these positive effects to all U.S. students and future citizens. When curriculum reflecting higher-order cognitive skill development becomes the standard, education in the arts will be understood and valued for its full potential and possibility.

References and Further Readings

Ainsworth, L. (2003). *Power standards: Identifying the standards that matter the most.* Denver, CO: Advanced Learning Press.

Bloom, B. S. (Ed.). (1956). *Taxonomy of educational objectives: Cognitive domain.* New York: McCay.

Boughton, D. (2004). Assessing art learning in changing contexts. In E. W. Eisner & M. Day (Eds.), *Handbook of research and policy in art education* (pp. 585–605). Mahwah, NJ: Lawrence Erlbaum Associates.

Boyer, E. L. (1983). *High school: A report on secondary education in America.* New York: Harper & Row.

Broudy, H. (1987). *The role of imagery in learning.* (Occasional paper 1). Los Angeles: Getty Center for Education in the Arts.

Burton, D. (2001). How do we teach? Results of a national survey of instruction in secondary art education. *Studies in Art Education, 42*(2), 131–145.

Burton, J. M. (2004). The practice of teaching in K–12 schools. In E. W. Eisner & M. D. Day (Eds.), *Handbook of research and policy in art education* (pp. 553–575). Mahwah, NJ: Lawrence Erlbaum Associates.

California Department of Education. (2004). *California framework for the visual arts.* Sacramento, CA: Author.

Center on Educational Policy. (2006, March). *From the capital to the classroom: Year 4 of the No Child Left Behind Act.* Washington, DC. Author. Retrieved July 27, 2007, from www.cep-dc.org/nclb/Year4/NCLB-Year4Summary.pdf

The College Board. (1980). *Advanced placement course description: Art.* New York: Author.

Consortium of National Arts Education Associations. (1994). *National standards for arts education: What every young American should know and be able to do in the arts.* Reston, VA: Music Educators National Conference. Retrieved July 27, 2007, from http://artsedge.kennedy-center.org/teach/standards/contents.cfm

Dobbs, S. M. (2004). Discipline-based art education. In E. Eisner (Ed.), *Handbook of research and policy in art education* (pp. 701–724). Mahwah, NJ: Lawrence Erlbaum Associates.

DuFour, R., Eaker, R., & DuFour, R. (2005). *On common ground: The power of professional learning communities.* Bloomington, IN: National Education Service.

Education Commission of the States. (2007). *Standard high school graduation requirements (50-state).* Denver, CO: Author. Retrieved July 29, 2007, from http://mb2.ecs.org/reports/Report.aspx?id=735

Efland, A. (1990). *A history of art education: Intellectual and social currents in teaching the visual arts.* New York: Teachers College Press.

Efland, A. (2002). *Art and cognition: Integrating the visual arts in the curriculum.* New York: Teachers College Press.

Efland, A. (2004). Emerging visions of art education. In E. W. Eisner (Ed.), *Handbook of research and policy in art education* (pp. 691–700). Mahwah, NJ: Lawrence Erlbaum Associates.

Eisner, E. W. (1982). *Cognition and curriculum: A basis for deciding what to teach.* New York: Longman.

Freedman, K. (2003). *Teaching visual culture: Curriculum, aesthetics, and the social life art.* New York: Teachers College Press.

Freedman, K., & Stuhr, P. (2004). Curriculum change for the 21st century: Visual culture in art education. In E. W. Eisner & M. Day (Eds.), *Handbook of research and policy in art education* (pp. 815–828). Mahwah, NJ: Lawrence Erlbaum Associates.

Gardner, H. (1996). The assessment of student learning in the arts. In D. Boughton, E. W. Eisner, & J. Ligtvoet (Eds.), *Evaluating and assessing the visual arts in education: International perspectives* (pp. 131–155). New York: Teachers College Press.

Good, T. L., & Brophy, J. E. (2000). *Looking in classrooms* (8th ed.). New York: Longman.

Jackson, P. W. (1992). Conceptions of curriculum and curriculum specialists. In P. W. Jackson (Ed.), *Handbook of research on curriculum* (pp. 3–40). New York: Macmillan.

Joint Committee on Standards for Educational Evaluation. (1981). *Standards for evaluation of educational programs, projects, and materials.* New York: McGraw-Hill.

Lehman, P., & Sinatra, R. (1988). Assessing arts curricula in the schools: Their roles, content, and purpose. In J. McLaughlin (Ed.), *Toward a new era in arts education: The Interlochen Symposium.* New York: American Council on the Arts.

Little, J. (1981). *School success and staff development in urban desegregated schools: A summary of recently completed research.* Paper presented at the annual meeting of the American Educational Research Association, Los Angeles.

Lowenfeld, V., & Brittain, W. L. (1975). *Creative and mental growth* (6th ed.). New York: Macmillan.

Mason, B., Mason, D. A., Mendez, M., Nelsen, G., & Orwig, R. (2005). Effects of top-down and bottom-up elementary school standards reform in an underperforming California district. *Elementary School Journal, 105*(4), 353–376.

Myford, C. M., & Sims-Gunzenhauser, A. (2004). The evolution of large-scale assessment programs in the visual arts. In E. W. Eisner & M. Day (Eds.), *Handbook of research and policy in art education* (pp. 637–666). Mahwah, NJ: Lawrence Erlbaum Associates.

National Assessment Governing Board. (1994). *Arts education assessment framework, 1997.* Washington, DC: Author.

National Council of Teachers of Mathematics. (1989). *Curriculum and evaluation standards for school mathematics.* Reston, VA: Author.

Persky, H. R., Sandene, B. A., & Askew, J. M. (1998). The NAEP 1997 arts report card: Eighth-grade findings from the National Assessment of Educational Progress (Report No. 1999–486). Washington, DC: National Center for Educational Statistics, U.S. Department of Education. Retrieved July 29, 2007, from http//nces.ed.gov/nationsreportcard/arts/

Piaget, J. (1963). *The origins of intelligence in children.* M. Cook (Trans.). New York: Norton. (Original work published 1952)

Reeves, D. B. (2002). *The leader's guide to standards: A blueprint for educational equity and excellence.* San Francisco: Jossey-Bass.

Reeves, D. B. (2006). *The learning leader: How to focus school improvement for better results.* Alexandria, VA: Association for Supervision and Curriculum Development.

Rose, L. C., & Gallup, A. M. (2006). The 38th annual Phi Delta Kappa/Gallup Poll of the public's attitudes toward the public schools. *Phi Delta Kappan, 88*(1), 41–56.

Rosenholtz, S. (1989). *Teachers' workplace: The social organization of schools.* New York: Longman.

Schwartz, D. T. (2000). *Art, education, and the democratic commitment: A defense of state support for the arts.* Boston: Kluwer.

Smith, R. A. (2006). *Culture and the arts in education: Critical essays on shaping human experience.* New York: Teachers College Press.

Tanner, D., & Tanner, L. (1990). *History of the school curriculum.* New York: Macmillan.

Tucker, M. S., & Codding, J. B. (1998). *Standards for our schools: How to set them, measure them, and reach them.* San Francisco: Jossey-Bass.

Vygotsky, L. (1962). *Thought and language.* Cambridge, MA: MIT Press.

Wolf, D. P. (1992). Becoming knowledge: The evolution of art education curriculum. In P. W. Jackson (Ed.), *Handbook of research on curriculum* (pp. 945–963). New York: Macmillan.

41

WELLNESS

Health, Nutrition, and Physical Education

ALESHA L. KIENTZLER

Re-Create Strategies

The goal of creating and maintaining wellness among adults has gained popularity recently; however this popularity has come at a time when physical education is disappearing from our schools and obesity, even in toddlers, is on the rise—two factors that do not indicate improvements, nor a focus, on the well-being of American citizens. Here I examine methods for creating a culture of wellness in schools and life. The first section defines wellness and its related components—internal and external sources. The second section examines the history of wellness and youth, with attention to changes in health beliefs over the past 50 years. The third section discusses why physical wellness is a critical priority in the 21st century, followed by an examination of modern physical education curricula. The last two sections present a model for reviving physical education through progressive wellness education design and discuss policy implications for successful long-term implementation.

What Is Wellness?

To be well is not the same as being healthy. The latter implies that one is free of disease and infirmity and has the ability to respond to the changing environment on both a cellular and social level. Health is generally based on physiological variables, such as blood pressure, muscular strength, flexibility, and cardiovascular conditioning, all of which work together to keep the body in balance. Main-

taining a high level of health is important, but it is just one component of being well. Although the term *wellness* exists on a continuum from a state of disease to optimal living, it is generally understood as an active process of becoming aware of and making choices toward a more successful existence. It involves self-responsibility, the desire to maintain balance, and the ability to resource energy required for appropriate tasks. Wellness is not a place where one arrives but rather a constantly evolving state of positive well-being. Ultimately, to be well implies functioning at a level oriented toward maximizing the potential of which an individual is capable—a state often associated with life satisfaction.

Although conceptions of wellness vary, the differences are slight. Wellness can be best understood as a multidimensional model that includes both internal and external sources of influence. Internal sources are connected to the individual and include social, emotional, intellectual, psychological, physical, and spiritual dimensions. External sources are connected to the environment and include things like government, family, school, career, culture, as well air and water. Internal sources can be understood as a circular and interactive model (often called the wellness wheel), in which no dimension is of greater importance than another. Thus, the internal dimensions share properties of being independent and interdependent in nature; that is, movement in each dimension has an effect on other dimensions, while also being affected by all other dimensions. These dimensions are not presented in hierarchical order, but rather as independent, equally important entities (see Figure 41.1).

Each dimension connected to an internal source falls within an individual's internal locus of control (i.e., one can affect and ultimately control each dimension with proper skill development and effort), and is largely influenced by one's perception (Adams, Bezner, & Stienhardt, 1997). People with a consistently high level of wellness often possess a high level of persistence and optimism. In contrast, the external sources (e.g., family, school, culture) are connected to an external locus of control (i.e., expectancy of control is outside of oneself, largely affected by fate or powerful people).

Dimensions of Wellness: Internal Sources

Six major dimensions compose internal sources of well-being: (1) social, (2) emotional, (3) intellectual, (4) psychological, (5) physical, and (6) spiritual. Social wellness refers to an individual perceiving support from key people in his or her life (e.g., family and friends) during difficult times, as well as the belief that he or she is able to provide support to others. More specifically, the dynamic between one's health and social wellness is determined by one's perception of social support, quality of support, gaining support from a person of choice (e.g., the need for a family member versus a friend, or a friend versus a family member), and developing reciprocal support systems. Broadly, social wellness generates the desire to contribute to the common welfare of one's community by encouraging a healthy living environment and initiating joint communication; inspiring harmonious relationships within one's family, friends, community, colleagues, and the world.

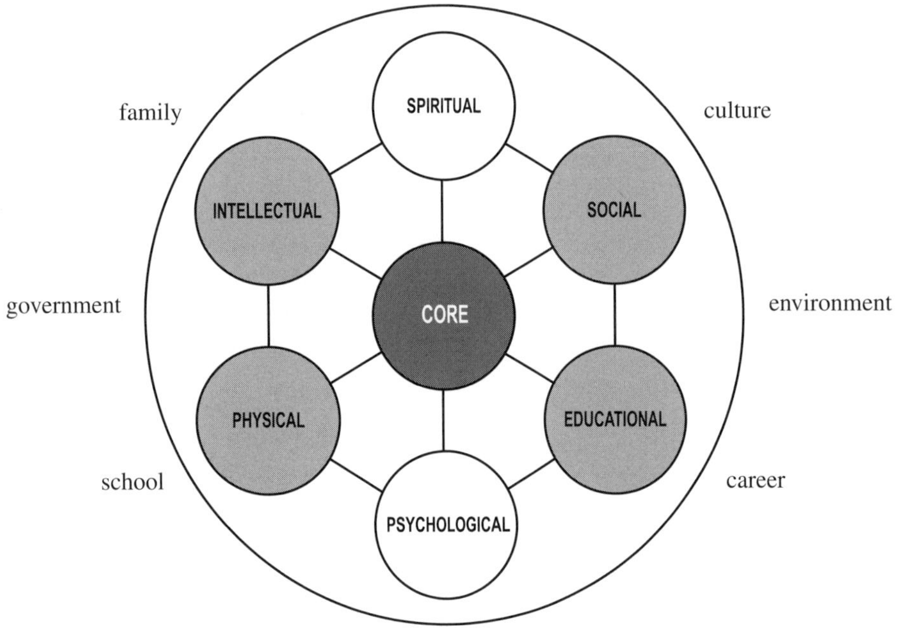

Emotional wellness highlights the importance of having awareness and acceptance of one's feelings. It includes the ability to understand one's limitations, deal effectively with stress, and maintain a sense of optimism during difficult times. To say that one is emotionally well implies that one has a positive internal image of one's self (i.e., self-identity and self-esteem), and in turn, is willing to take on challenges and risks, seeing conflict as an opportunity for growth. Although each dimension of wellness is interdependent, emotional wellness is positively associated with physical self-esteem and physical activity (Adams, Bezner, & Stienhardt, 1995) and negatively associated with issues of body dissatisfaction and disordered eating (Adams, Bezner, & Stienhardt, 1997).

Despite apparent interchangeability, intellectual and psychological wellness carry distinct meanings. Intellectual wellness refers to actively embracing opportunities for creative and stimulating thinking and learning. It encourages people to move beyond a feeling of self-satisfaction toward activities that will expand one's knowledge and potential. An intellectually well person exhibits curiosity about life (e.g., reading books, magazines, and newspapers; engaging in cultural activities), and has the desire to share his or her knowledge with others. Psychological wellness, on the other hand, is connected to the filter through which one sees the world. It is the perception that life will always work out in a positive manner—regardless of the situation at hand. Psychological wellness, also referred to as optimism, is often associated with hardiness and increases in self-esteem and general well-being. The Chinese proverb, "where the mind goes, the body follows," expresses this dimension of wellness most accurately; people who are psychologically well are the least likely to become ill, even when operating under high levels of stress (Sergerstrom & Miller, 2004).

Physical wellness provides almost immediate benefits that trickle into the psychological dimension of wellness; one develops a more vigorous and dynamic body and feels terrific, which can lead to the psychological benefits of increased self-esteem, self-control, and a sense of direction. Although maintenance and prevention concerning physical health is important, true physical wellness facilitates a proactive approach to health in which one strives for constant improvement in cardiovascular endurance, flexibility, and muscular strength through regular physical activity. This can be achieved through anything from sports (school, club, or recreational) and personal

Figure 41.1   The Wellness Wheel

fitness activities (e.g., aerobics, weight training, rollerblading, hiking), to general physical activity (e.g., yard work, leisure walking, pick up sports activities with friends). Being physically well also includes making healthy food choices on a regular basis—a behavior sometimes difficult to accomplish with nutrition recommendations changing on a regular basis. For example, "My Pyramid Plan," provided through the USDA (United States Department of Agriculture), is gaining national recognition as the standard for dietary guidelines, but does not incorporate headline news, such as the new recommendation to eat sustainable versus wild fish. Thus, making healthy food choices on a regular basis requires one to be aware of new information and be capable of discerning how to translate that information into action.

Spiritual wellness involves seeking meaning and purpose in life. It emphasizes the importance of having appreciation for the beauty of nature, the universe, and ultimately, something outside of one's self. When one is on the path of nurturing one's spiritual nature, questions such as, Who am I? and What is the meaning of my life? will emerge to guide one closer to a personal value system. The process of enhancing one's spiritual well-being can come in many forms, such as religion, meditation, nature walks, and quietude. Spiritual wellness becomes clear when one's actions become consistent with one's beliefs and values—both of which inform one's purpose in life. As with all dimensions of wellness, a strong association exists between spiritual wellness and positive health outcomes.

The Core of Wellness

The path of wellness is a deliberate process anchored by an individual's core, or true self. The core, located in the center of the wellness wheel (see Figure 41.1), is associated with one's spiritual wellness because it is one's personal ethics, values, spirit, or true self. It affects and is affected by each dimension of the wellness wheel, for the betterment or detriment of one's existence. Optimal human existence involves embracing and nurturing each dimension of wellness in a balanced fashion to maintain a healthy core. A common misconception, however, is that one must strive for balance as a starting point to greater wellness. As a result of this encompassing and largely conceptual goal, many people often become disenchanted and give up altogether. In contrast, it is important to find an entry point in one domain (e.g., emotional) with which you have a connection (e.g., "I would like to decrease my anger") and gradually move your attention to the other domains over time. This approach will allow for small wins and eventually yield a lifestyle of increased awareness, personal growth, and balanced living.

Dimensions of Wellness: External Sources

Life optimization involves a commitment to the path of wellness from the inside out, while understanding the effects coming from the outside in (i.e., dimensions connected to external sources of well-being). The challenge arises in gaining clarity around the degree to which an individual can influence external sources. For example, an individual might be thrown out of balance by frustration with a decision made by his or her state government concerning an issue important to the individual. The first question for the individual to consider is, Did I have the opportunity to vote on the issue? If the answer is no, then the individual should understand that his or her ability to affect the decision is slight. If the answer is yes, then the next question is, Did I actually vote? If the answer is no, then the case is closed. The individual had the opportunity to make an impact on his or her external world, but did not take the action. If the individual did vote, then he or she will need to understand that voting is probably the final extent of his or her influence. Worrying about the issue is wasted energy because it is, in this case, based on a false sense of control—the very thing that can cause the individual to be in a state of disease. The same approach can be applied to any situation existing outside of an individual's immediate control (e.g., a traffic jam, delayed airline flight, job layoff). Thus, learning how to identify and control the controllables (Janssen, 1996) is central to one's overall well-being.

When an individual operates from the inside out, he or she will have greater ease in identifying the elements over which he or she has control or can affect and will focus on these elements only. For example, when an individual is physically active on a regular basis, he or she tends to have healthier psychological and emotional wellness, and greater energy for creative and intellectual endeavors. The attention and increased awareness within each domain allows the individual to integrate thoughts and greater understanding around his or her purpose in life. As a result, the individual may determine that his or her purpose is connected to making an impact, even if partial, on external sources affecting his or her well-being, such as the air and water in his or her community. The individual may develop a coalition to educate local citizens about methods for keeping the water and air safe and clean, in turn enhancing his or her social well-being.

Wellness and Youth: A Brief History

In 50 years, Americans' conceptions of health and wellness have moved from fatalistic beliefs about the pre-eminence of biological explanations for illness to recognition of the key role of personal health decisions and behavior to prevent disease. Despite the positive shift in knowledge, concerns about the health of children and adolescents continue to make national headlines. Increases in stress, obesity, and type II diabetes, in conjunction with decreases in physical activity and proper nutrition, have created a need for immediate health interventions for children and adolescents.

Similar concerns about youth were expressed as long as 100 years ago. In 1898, Duckworth expressed disgust at the number of people who claim they do not have time for exercise. He asserted, "They gradually lose zest for what is so needful, so imperatively needful, if they are to maintain vigorous minds in vigorous bodies" (Duckworth, 1898, p. 5). An investigation of the Detroit public schools in 1914 "proved conclusively that the play of boys and girls has been on the decline. . . . Modern conditions have made people of all ages inactive. Under such conditions chronic disease is rapidly on the increase" (Pearl & Brown, 1927).

In 1898, people were pointing to advances in civilization, the high usage of omnibuses and tramcars, and the frequent attendance among young people at picture shows, as well as other nonactive forms of entertainment as reasons for declining health. The dangers of a sedentary lifestyle have prevailed. In 1979, the United States Public Health Service (USPHS) reported that over half of the deaths in the United States were caused by lifestyle and self-destructive behavior. Although this information has been available for over 25 years, it has influenced individual's attributional beliefs about others' behavior more than it has changed individual's own behavior. More specifically, the USPHS report highlighted the fact that children and adolescents are endangered primarily by their own behavior, thus asserting that prioritization of health promotion and prevention strategies is needed in order to improve their health and well-being. Today, physical inactivity among children and adults is still of primary concern. Too many hours watching television and sitting at a computer, along with the disappearance of physical education and increase in long workweeks, are just a few of the modern conditions that promote habitual inactivity.

Physical Wellness: A 21st-Century Priority

Despite increasing knowledge about the effect of all domains of wellness on one's overall health, Americans continue to focus solely on ways to improve physical wellness. Thus, most policy and programming efforts focus on this single dimension of wellness. Knowing what we know about the power of all aspects of wellness working together, it is no surprise that these policies and programs are not positively affecting physical well-being. Obesity, type II diabetes, heart disease, and arthritis are on the rise—all of which are now being diagnosed in children and adolescents. Further, the 21st-century approach of combating obesity among children and adults creates greater difficulty in gaining positive momentum due to simple semantics. The current approach tends to place people in a negative and defensive mode, with fear of failure at the forefront, rather than employing a prohealth and wellness approach to prompt positive action and the desire to be proactive. As a result, physical wellness continues to be a concern and will remain so until innovative programs and positive educational approaches are funded, implemented, and assessed, especially around the topic of obesity.

Obesity: Gaining Popularity

Obesity has reached epidemic proportions globally, with more than 1 billion adults overweight—at least 300 million of them clinically obese—and is a major contributor to the global burden of chronic disease and disability. Often coexisting in developing countries with under-nutrition, obesity is a complex condition, with serious social and psychological dimensions, affecting virtually all ages and socioeconomic groups. (World Health Organization, 2007)

Although obesity is a global epidemic, it has also increased dramatically among Americans from 1987 to 2000. Nearly 59 million adults are obese, the percentage of children who are overweight has more than doubled, and the percentage of adolescents tripled, since 1980. This is a disturbing increase. Obese children and adolescents who do not change their habits will remain overweight and obese in adulthood, resulting in increased risk for chronic diseases. Currently, chronic diseases are the leading cause of death among Americans and among the most costly health problems, but they are also among the most preventable. Adopting healthy behaviors such as eating nutritious foods, being physically active, and avoiding tobacco use can prevent or control the devastating effects of these diseases (National Center for Chronic Disease Prevention and Health Promotion, 2004a). Lack of attention to weight, diet, and physical activity has serious economic costs as well. In 1997, the cost for diabetes was estimated to be $98 billion (Mokdad et al., 2001). The annual cost of obesity in the United States is about $117 billion (National Center for Chronic Disease Prevention and Health Promotion, 2004b).

Many are attempting to make a change in their health status. In 2000, 38.5% of U.S. adults were trying to lose weight and 35.9% were trying to maintain weight. Of these adults, 72.9% reported changing diet and 59.5% reported increased physical activity. Unfortunately, few Americans who were trying to use diet and exercise to lose or maintain weight were following appropriate guidelines, such as eating 5 servings of fruits and vegetables daily or meeting recommended levels of activity (i.e., 30 minutes of moderate activity—activity that keeps you breathing lightly to somewhat hard—5 times a week; Mokdad et al., 2001). In contrast, most reported weight loss attempts have been underscored by quick fix approaches that include prescription drugs (e.g., Alli, Lipovarin) and fad diets (e. g., Nutri-Slim, Atkins, South Beach), and exclude exercise. Numerous public health organizations (e.g., World Health Organization, American Medical Association, American Public Health Association, and so forth) have launched programs to educate communities about ways to combat the obesity epidemic in their own city, but few to date have successfully demonstrated positive long-term effects. In 2001 the National Institutes of Health (NIH) launched the largest NIH-funded effort on weight loss and the first study to examine long-term effects of weight loss and exercise in type 2 diabetes. Participants, who will be followed for up to 11.5 years, are expected to follow the NIH-Lifestyle Program, which includes intensive diet and exercise guidelines designed to help participants lose at least 7% to 10% of their initial weight in the first year of the study. But until the results are reported and additional studies are conducted, the jury is still out regarding dependent measures responsible for lasting changes affecting weight loss. Thus, the obesity epidemic continues to spread worldwide.

Physical Activity and Youth

Many youth do not engage in regular exercise. According to the President's Council on Physical Fitness and Sports report, *Physical Activity and Sport in the Lives of Girls* (Kane & Larkin, 1997), about 50% of youth fail to participate in regular physical activity. Particularly disturbing is that 14% of youth are totally inactive; and young females (aged 12 to 21) are twice as likely to be inactive as young males. Those who are physically active tend to do better in school, are less likely to drop out, are less depressed, have improved ability to regulate emotions, and higher self-esteem than youth who are not physically active. Studies have also shown that exercise can have powerful academic and maturational benefits for youth (*President's Council on Physical Fitness and Sports Research Digest*, 1998); and for females, exercise positively addresses body image and related concerns (Kane & Larkin, 1997). Regular exercise and other wellness practices are not only instrumental in preventing or minimizing the effect of various illnesses, but also in maximizing creativity and optimism in one's life.

Disappearance of Modern Physical Education Curricula

Once, physical education courses were a regular part of American education at all levels. Since 1950, there has been a gradual erosion of frequency and quality of physical education programs. Physical education programs disappeared from schools largely because of societal pressure to respond to various crises. For example, the *Sputnik* crisis in 1957 was met by challenging American students to become better in math and science. The apparent success of the Japanese economy in the 1980s was met with repeated cross-national comparisons of student achievement and increasing demands that our students do better in math and science. Today's students are being asked to achieve new standards and higher goals (Nichols & Berliner, 2007). Policy makers and business influences have successfully focused the American curriculum narrowly on subject matter outcomes. Time for academic learning is considered so important that in some schools principals have cancelled recess so students can spend more time preparing for tests.

Too often, students are represented solely by their academic achievements versus being understood more broadly as social beings (McCaslin, 1996). It is lamentable that physical education programs have essentially become squeezed out of public school curriculum priorities. Yet it is also important to recognize that the golden age of physical education never existed in terms of how such programs affected students' decisions about wellness over a lifetime.

Current reductions in physical education programs run contrary to the goals of the U.S. Department of Health and Human Service's *Healthy People 2010* initiative. This report is a collection of nearly 300 national health promotion and disease prevention goals to be achieved by the year 2010. One main area of the initiative is the relationship between quality school physical education and healthy students. Three of the health objectives focused on school-based physical education are

- Objective 22.8 Increase the proportion of the nation's public and private schools that require daily physical education.
- Objective 22.9 Increase the proportion of adolescents who participate in daily physical activity.
- Objective 22.10 Increase the proportion of adolescents who spend at least 50% of school physical education class time being physically active.

The objectives will likely not be achieved, however. Nationwide, the percentage of students who attended a daily physical education class has dropped from 42% in 1991 to 28% in 2003 (Centers for Disease Control and Prevention, 2004). Only 8% of elementary schools, 6.4% of middle school and junior high schools, and 5.8% of senior high schools provide daily physical education or its equivalent (i.e., 150 minutes per week for elementary schools; 225 minutes per week for middle schools, junior high schools, and senior high schools) for the entire school year for students in all grades in the school (Burgeson, Wechsler, Brener, Young, & Spain, 2001). Even when students are participating in physical education, the benefits are in question (e.g., What percent of class time are students actually participating in consistent physical activity? Are students learning about bats, balls, and bases or, rather, how to make fitness a lifetime activity?). Further, 80% of states and 83% of all school districts excuse students from required participation in physical education for various reasons (Allensworth, Lawson, Nicholson, & Wyche, 1997, p. 85). Even if 100% of students participated in physical education, schools would still fall short of providing adequate time allocated for physical activity. This is especially disconcerting given the following recommendation of the American Heart Association:

All children age 2 and older participate in at least 30 minutes of enjoyable, moderate-intensity activities *every* day [italics added for emphasis]. They should also perform at least 30 minutes of vigorous [breathing somewhat hard to hard] physical activities at least 3–4 days each week to achieve and maintain a good level of cardiorespiratory (heart and lung) fitness. (American Heart Association, 2007)

Reviving Physical Education With Wellness Education: Program Overview

Partial features of wellness models are prevalent in schools. Stress management and life-skills components are generally found within wellness programs. Components often exist independently and in afterschool programs, in the absence of a comprehensive wellness curriculum. Typically schools will adopt only one of these wellness strategies, if any. For example, stress management programs have only been operating as an ad hoc option of the school curricula. Some of the skills being taught (e.g., biofeedback, diaphragmatic breathing, muscle relaxation training, and imagery and visualization exercises), however, could have a greater effect if integrated into existing school curricula.

While many would agree that stress management education is beneficial, many also agree that allocating time in the school curriculum for stress management class is challenging. Yet, a few life-skills programs have received space within the curriculum structure (see Gilbert & Orlick, 1996). The root of life-skills programs lies in mental training techniques used by successful athletes. These include, but are not limited to, goal setting, relaxation and energizing techniques, imagery training for performance enhancement and personal development, concentration and attention control strategies, how to effectively cope with stressors, learning to highlight positive experiences, and how to reach peak performance. Maintaining a positive perspective in life, effectively coping with stress, and learning to relax have all been correlated with successful performance. Thus, proponents of teaching mental training to children and adolescents feel the benefits will enhance their quality of life and provide them with increased clarity surrounding their life purpose.

To reiterate, wellness education incorporates stress management and some components of life-skills, and also includes a greater emphasis on physical activity, nutrition, spirituality, and self-care. Businesses, organizations, churches, and community groups are beginning to develop programs to educate youth about the importance of being well and incorporating physical activity and healthy food choices in hopes of eliciting positive behavioral change. But programs are still falling short and educational reform efforts are generally replete with inadequate conceptualization, implementation, and poor results.

Future Direction in Wellness Programming: A Co-Regulated Experience

Taking responsibility for one's health and well-being is a key element that distinguishes wellness programs. Peter Vidmar (1991), an Olympic athlete and member of the President's Council on Physical Fitness and Sports, is among the very few who highlight the need for youth to develop lifelong healthy habits in order to create long-term commitments to physical activity. Lifetime commitment to physical activity is a continuing challenge for youth: as age increases participation decreases. Although some policy makers, administrators, and teachers call for greater adherence to physical exercise among youth, most programs have failed to make a difference. The element largely neglected in physical education programs, the National Standards for Physical Education, and related research is the integration of mental training with physical training, or mind-and-body education. "There is an alarming apathy toward sustained physical well-being among the general population, and a corresponding ignorance of the mental relationship to the body," (Hickman, Murphy, & Spino, 1977). Unfortunately, very few elementary or secondary school physical education programs include mental skills and strategies (i.e., psychological wellness) to promote long-term commitment to participation and overall wellness.

In order to facilitate a lifelong commitment to wellness, programs need to include elements of self-regulation— understanding how an individual coordinates relatively long-term patterns of goal-directed behavior—to enable individuals to successfully regulate the whole self. Given the combination of internal and external sources affecting overall wellness, successful wellness programs must also include an understanding about individuals' needs within the context of their environment. As schools begin to renew their approach to physical education, special attention must be given to developing programs that contain authoritative knowledge and provide for challenging but manageable activities, while also helping students to maintain their involvement over time through co-regulation (McCaslin & Good, 1996).

The Co-Regulated Experience

Students do not learn alone. Students and their teachers, peers, parents, counselors, and the school context mutually exert a powerful influence on learning. Although the ultimate goal of education is often to create student self-regulation (see McCaslin & Good, 1998), it is preceded by a healthy student-teacher relationship, or co-regulation. McCaslin and Good (1996) present a model of co-regulation in which "teachers, through their relationships with students and the opportunities they provide them, support and 'scaffold' adaptive student learning" (p. 2). Specifically, the model embraces three domains of learning—motivation, enactment, and evaluation. Motivation, referred to as reality contact, is centered around knowledge of one's self and one's goals. It affords the questions, Where am I now? Where do I want to go (choice)? How hard will I have to work? and What are my motives (intrinsic, extrinsic, or both)? Enactment is concerned with protecting the self once the directional choice has been made (goal selected). Thus, elements of control enter the enactment domain and include "control over the self and control over the persons (e.g., teachers, peers) and physical resources of the classroom" (McCaslin & Good, 1996, p. 9). Once a choice has been made in the motivational stage, enactment ensures follow through and goals are reached. Evaluation is the third phase of the co-regulated learning model. This provides the opportunity for evaluating one's self after completing a task (reaching a goal) or during the task (if the opportunity exists). "Opportunity for evaluation includes tasks that consist of sub-goals or other markers of understandings-in-part or incomplete learning. Opportunity also includes time, because evaluation takes time" (McCaslin & Good, 1996, p. 14). The evaluative process can be carefully facilitated by the teacher (or the counselor or parent) to educate the student how to self-evaluate without comparison to other students and focus on a realistic appraisal about progress.

Development of a program founded on co-regulation strategies will become central to the successful revival of physical education in the 21st century. Teachers, administrators, and parents are already beginning to discuss how they can create a new model of physical education. This new model will require the immersion of teachers, counselors, parents, and peers within the school context to aid in individual student motivation and enactment in striving to enhance one's well-being. As viewed by McCaslin and Good (1996):

> Constellation of context, self, and other in students' setting, pursuit, and coordination of their goals, then, is what we mean by student motivation. We do not consider motivation a personal variable, one that resides only in the student. Nor do we look solely to the environment. In our conception, motivation is a shared, co-regulated variable which emerges through the integration of the student with the personal and task resources within the context of the classroom. Students clearly bring more than their physical selves to this formulation. (p. 9)

The co-regulation strategies presented by McCaslin and Good lend support for seeing students as social, emotional, spiritual, and intellectual beings existing within a physical self. The aim will be to tap into each of these elements through greater awareness of the physical self and to stimulate growth toward self-regulation in all areas.

Wellness Programming and Co-Regulation in Action

Kientzler (2004) pioneered a new model of physical education through the development, implementation, and assessment of a wellness curriculum designed for high school freshmen. Founded on the model of co-regulation, the curriculum, titled *Reach Your Peak: Maximizing Potential Through Physical Wellness©*, places emphasis on education about one's physical wellness (i.e., overall fitness and health), yet provides comprehensive experiential opportunities (e.g., biofeedback training, African drumming, weekend hikes, meditation, journal writing, field trips to grocery stores and health resorts) for students to gain understanding about the independent and interdependent nature of all domains of one's wellness. According to Nichols & Good (2004), "Comprehensive programs have considerably stronger potential to reduce harmful habits and to lay a foundation for happy living [a key component of the *Reach Your Peak* program] than programs that view youth in terms of their separate identities (smokers, cheaters, overweight student, etc.)" (p. 162). Curriculum implementation took place 4 days per week—75 minutes, 3 days per week and 120 minutes, 1 day per week—for a total of 15 weeks. Thus, importance was placed on the value of this curriculum from the start by allocating the same amount of time as that provided to math, science, and language arts instruction within the high school where it was implemented.

One major curriculum goal of the *Reach Your Peak* program was to elicit positive behavioral changes and increased cognitive awareness of one's physical self through coursework on how to take responsibility for one's well-being. Coursework emphasized co-regulated learning. That is, teachers, counselors, parents, and peers were integrated to support each participant in his or her pursuit toward a greater personal well-being. The comprehensive nature of the curriculum recognizes that students are social beings who need a co-regulated (McCaslin & Good, 1996) environment (i.e., social support) to develop personal responsibility for their health and wellness, and to find activities enjoyable and meaningful. The *Reach Your Peak* program is one attempt to provide a supportive environment through which adolescents find their motivation to be well, to move from a mindset of prevention and maintenance concerning their health toward a proactive and future-oriented presence of mind—one in which they are inspired to reach their fullest potential (see Kientzler, 2004 for program details).

Reach Your Peak was successful on many levels. Implemented as a quasi-experimental research design with nonequivalent groups (treatment and comparison), the program was assessed via pre- and posttest responses across numerous measures (e.g., Perceived Wellness Survey, Self-Description Questionnaire, Physical Self-Description Questionnaire, Nutrition Knowledge Assessment, multiple physiological variables, among others). Results indicated significant differences at posttest between the treatment (i.e., students enrolled in *Reach Your Peak*) and comparison groups in important ways. For example, the treatment group demonstrated a significant increase in physical activity levels, cardiorespiratory fitness (VO_2), and a significant decrease in blood pressure, ambient heart rate, body fat, and LDL cholesterol (the latter of which requires a lower score to be healthy). The comparison group reported a significant decrease in physical activity and demonstrated a significant increase in body fat and LDL cholesterol, while their cardiorespiratory fitness remained constant. Additionally, the students in the treatment group demonstrated a significant increase in attendance across all classes in both the fall and spring semesters, and the comparison group's attendance decreased. Significant increases in confidence pertaining to sport competence (i.e., knowing what to do, how to do it, and the perception that others believe they know what to do and how to do it) were demonstrated by the treatment group, but the comparison group lost confidence.

Positive transformations in and between each dimension of wellness were also reported by students enrolled in *Reach Your Peak* through journal writing, individual meetings with the teacher, group discussions, assignments, and the final exam. All students made connections between each dimension of their well-being and many other areas of their lives. Students understood the connection between their mind and body. "Improving my physical wellness has given me the confidence to attack other obstacles I have in life," reported one male student. Students made connections between their physical wellness and their social well-being. "If you focus on keeping yourself healthy and well, it will affect all areas of your life. If you eat healthy and exercise, you will feel better and therefore make your mind feel better. When you're happy, you'll make new friends and your social life will be boosted," stated one female student. Awareness of emotions and positive methods of dealing with them are crucial to healthy adolescent development. A female student realized an increased feeling of well-being through expressing herself, "I have changed because I now see that we control our emotions with what we think and how we act. An emotionally strong person isn't just someone who never cries, but it is someone who was given an emotional obsticle [sic] and they know how to deal with it." And even connections between physical and spiritual wellness were reported, as one male shared, "I have found the importance of having something/ someone as a spiritual significance. I also felt how to connect with the spiritual aspect of my life while doing physical activity." When asked to share three things they would take with them from the course (during the final week), student responses were balanced across wellness dimensions and included a broad spectrum of positive lessons. The top responses on behalf of females included increased confidence, knowing how to work out, relaxation techniques, nutrition habits, and mental training techniques. For males, responses included nutrition habits, positive thinking, knowing how to work out, improved relationships, and physical fitness.

Policy Implications

Results from the *Reach Your Peak* program assessment are important; significant changes in fitness and wellness among youth over a 15-week period are powerful. But these changes were witnessed at one level—a single class at a single high school. Results from the study have the potential to contribute to multiple schools, and multiple school districts, as well as inform policy makers, parents, and young people themselves. Unfortunately, insights about how to make exercise more attractive to students have come at a time when there is little structural support for providing students with state-of-the-art information about health, fitness, and nutrition. As noted earlier, traditional physical education has disappeared from many American schools; and the many benefits of wellness education programs are still not fully recognized by decision makers in education. Allocating time to include wellness in education is inadequate.

The challenge wellness education has faced in gaining enough credibility to be granted a full-time spot within national curriculum standards is rooted in history. In the 1914 issue of the *American Physical Education Review* (APER), C. F. Weege argued that physical training not only promotes the development of students' physical, mental, and moral capacities, but also "furnishes situations in the gymnasium that put the tools of mind to a trial and the pupil, by mastering these situations, sharpens his mind and becomes more deliberate, more persevering, and gains more-self-control" (pp. 513–514). Fifteen years later, the 1929 issue of APER discussed the need for society to realize that leisure time and physical play are a necessity for health and promoting a well-balanced life, for they have many physical and mental benefits (Richards, 1929). It appears that educators have been trying to gain credibility for a holistic approach to education for some time.

The valuation of wellness education—teaching youth how to reach their optimal human potential—has made progress since the early 1900s, but it has not been accepted nationwide. The need for greater involvement by the national government cannot be underestimated in achieving further acceptance. If all government efforts to improve the health and well-being of our nation's youth were directed in a more holistic manner (wellness programming) and mandated as part of national curriculum standards, perhaps the health of America's youth would change.

Colleges and universities could also play a role in promoting wellness education in elementary and secondary schools. If higher education institutions required a specific number of wellness curriculum credits, just as in mathematics, science, and language, perhaps elementary and secondary schools would develop comprehensive wellness courses to prepare students to meet the requirements. Students would learn to value their health and wellness simply by the message that colleges and universities value it by requiring credits for acceptance. Presently, lack of value is conveyed to students via the "null curriculum"; that is, what is not being taught is not important (Eisner, 1992).

It will take time to expose all U.S. citizens to quality wellness programs. Given the opportunity, youth reared in healthier school environments will become the leaders of our country in business, schools, communities, and government. They in turn will promote change within institutions and communities toward a greater respect for prioritizing wellness and the desire to maximize one's potential.

References and Further Readings

Adams, T., Bezner, J., & Steinhardt, M. (1995). Principle-centeredness: A values clarification approach to wellness. *Measurement and Evaluation in Counseling and Development, 28*(3), 139–147.

Adams, T., Bezner, J., & Steinhardt, M. (1997). The conceptualization and measurement of perceived wellness: Integrating balance across and within dimensions. *American Journal of Health Promotion, 11*(3), 208–218.

Allensworth, D., Lawson, E., Nicholson, L., & Wyche, J. (Eds.). (1997). *Schools and health: Our nation's investment.* Washington, DC: National Academies Press.

American Heart Association. (2007*). Exercise (physical activity) and children.* Retrieved July 31, 2007, from http://www.americanheart.org/presenter.jhtml?identifier=4596

Burgeson, C. R., Wechsler, H., Brener, N. D., Young, J. C., & Spain, C. G. (2001). Physical education and activity: Results from the School Health Policies and Programs Study, 2000. *Journal of School Health, 71*(7), 279–293.

Centers for Disease Control and Prevention. (2004). Participation in high school physical education—United States, 1991–2003. *Morbidity and Mortality Weekly Report, 53*(36), 844–847.

Duckworth, S. D. (1898). On the value of athletic exercise as a counter agent to the sedentary pursuits of urban population. *Mind and Body, 5*(49), 4–7.

Eisner, E. W. (1992). Curriculum ideologies. In P. Jackson (Ed.), *Handbook of research on curriculum.* New York: Macmillan.

Gilbert, J. N., & Orlick, T. (1996). Evaluation of a life-skills program with grade two children. *Elementary School Guidance and Counseling, 31*, 139–151.

Hickman, J. L., Murphy, M., & Spino, M. (1977). Psychophysical transformations through meditation and sport. *Simulation and Games, 8*(1), 49–60.

Humphrey, J. H. (1993). *Stress management for elementary schools.* Chicago: Charles C. Thomas.

Jackson, S. A., & Csikszentmihalyi, M. (1999). *Flow in sports: The keys to optimal experiences and performances.* Champaign, IL: Human Kinetics.

Janssen, J. J. (1996). *The mental makings of champions: How to win the mental game.* Tucson, AZ: Winning the Mental Game.

Kane, M., & Larkin, D. S. (1997). *President's Council on Physical Fitness: Report on physical activity and sport in the lives of girls.* Minneapolis: University of Minnesota, Center for Research on Girls and Women in Sport.

Kientzler, A. L. (1999). 5th and 7th grade girls' decisions about participation in physical activity. *Elementary School Journal, 99*(5), 391–414.

Kientzler, A. L. (2004). *Maximizing potential through physical wellness: An empirical study with high school freshman students.* Unpublished doctoral dissertation, University of Arizona.

McCaslin, M. (1996). The problem of problem representation: The summit's conception of student. Section 2: Framing the problem. *Educational Researcher, 25*(8), 13–15.

McCaslin, M., & Good, T. L. (1996). *Listening in classrooms.* New York: HarperCollins.

McCaslin, M., & Good, T. L. (1998). Moving beyond management as sheer compliance: Helping students to develop goal coordination strategies. *Educational Horizons, 76*(4), 169–176.

Mokdad, A. H., Bowman, B., Ford, E., Vinicor, F., Marks, J. S., & Koplan, J. P. (2001). The continuing epidemics of obesity and diabetes in the United States. *Journal of the American Medical Association, 286*(10), 1195–1197.

National Center for Chronic Disease Prevention and Health Promotion. (2004a). *Components of physical fitness.* Retrieved March 6, 2004, from http://www.cdc.gov/nccdphp/

National Center for Chronic Disease Prevention and Health Promotion. (2004b). *Improving nutrition and increasing physical activity.* Retrieved March 6, 2004, from http://www.cdc.gov/nccdphp/bb_nutrition/index.htm

Nichols, S. L., & Berliner, D. C. (2007). *Collateral damage: How high stakes testing corrupts America's schools.* Cambridge, MA: Harvard Education Press.

Nichols, S. L., & Good, T. L. (2004). *America's teenagers—myths and realities: Media images, schooling, and the social costs of careless indifference.* Mahwah, NJ: Lawrence Erlbaum Associates.

Orlick, T. (1998). *Embracing your potential: Steps to self-discovery, balance, and success in sports, work, and life.* Champaign, IL: Human Kinetics.

Pearl, N. H., & Brown, H. E. (1927). *Health by stunts.* New York: Macmillan.

President's Council on Physical Fitness and Sports Research Digest. (1998). *Physical activity for young people.* Retrieved September 9, 1998, from http://www.fitness.gov/digest_sep1998.htm

Richards, E. L. (1929). Mental aspects of play. *American Physical Education Review, 34*, 98–100.

Sergerstrom, S. C., & Miller, G. E. (2004). Psychological stress and the human immune system: A meta-analytic study of 30 years of inquiry. *Psychological Bulletin, 130*(4), 601–630.

Shillingford, J. P., & Mackin, A. S. (1991). Enhancing self-esteem through wellness programs. *The Elementary School Journal, 91*(5), 457–466.

United States Department of Health and Human Services. (2000). *Healthy People 2010* (2nd ed.). *Understanding and improving health and objectives for improving health* (2 vols.). Washington, DC: United States Government Printing Office.

United States Public Health Service (1979). *Smoking and health: A report of the surgeon general* (DHEW Publication No. [PHS] 79-50066). Washington, DC: United States Government Printing Office.

Vidmar, P. (1991). The role of the federal government in promoting health through the schools: Report from the president's council on physical fitness and sports. *Journal of School Health, 62*(4), 129–130.

Weege, C. F. (1914). Deliberation, reflection, determination, perseverance, and self-control as ends of physical training. *American Physical Education Review, 19*(107), 512–519.

World Health Organization. (2007). *Global strategy on diet, physical activity, and health: Obesity and overweight.* Retrieved, September 25, 2007, from http://www.who.int/dietphysicalactivity/publications/facts/obesity/en/

42

EARLY CHILDHOOD EDUCATION

Curriculum and Programs

FRANCES O'CONNELL RUST

Erikson Institute

> I have seen the world of the child grow smaller and smaller. . . . from a world in which children
> could learn as they grew in it, to a world so far beyond the grasp of children, that only the school can
> present it to them in terms which they can understand, can prepare them with knowledge of
> it so that they can take their places in it with confidence when the time comes.
> —Caroline Pratt, *I Learn From Children*, pp. xv–xvi

With this brief reminiscence, Caroline Pratt (1867–1954) begins her life story. She was 81 at the time and was revered then as she is now as one of the preeminent figures in early childhood education. Pratt's life's work was to shape a place for children and a way of working with them that would enable both the joy of discovery and ability to make sense of the world that were hers as a child while also preparing young children to "take their places" in the world as adults.

The educational dilemmas that she confronted then—purpose, curriculum, and method—are the very dilemmas that confront educators today. In the area of early childhood education, that is, education focused on children between the ages of birth and 8 years (as defined by the National Association for the Education of Young Children [NAEYC]), these issues are particularly acute because an increasing number of young children both here and around the world—30.3% of all children under 3 (United States Census Bureau, 2003) and nearly 50% of all 3- and 4-year-olds (National Center for Educational Statistics, 2000)—are participating in some form of care and education provided by individuals other than their parents. Hence, the issue of how as a society we choose to shape the environments in which our youngest members learn and grow assumes critical importance.

This chapter focuses on the curriculum and practice of early childhood—a contested territory. Throughout the 20th century, discussions of early childhood have been driven by debates between those who hold that work with young chil-dren before school age should be seen as child care and those who see it as education. Furthermore, there have been deep divisions among educators, policy makers, and the general public about whether educational services—kinder-garten, preschool, 4-year-old programs, child care—should be provided universally to all young children. Various dis-cussions of curriculum, of how children learn, of race and class, and of practice and professional preparation figure in these debates. And throughout is the question of the mode and extent of government involvement.

Curriculum

Traditional use of the term *curriculum* in education as a course of instruction suggests its Latin derivation, "a race, a race course, and a racing chariot." Jackson (1992) notes, "At the heart of the word's educational usage . . . lies the idea of an organizational structure imposed by authorities for the purpose of bringing order to the conduct of school-ing" (p. 5). This understanding of curriculum is quite different from how it is used in early childhood. First, there are no states in the United States, and only a few countries in the world, where there currently exists any universal and systematic policy and concomitant curricular vision for early childhood education. Second, the period from birth to age 8 is one in which there is so much change in a child's ways of knowing and interacting with the world, that it is almost impossible to impose a cohesive system or structure that addresses the wide range from infancy to primary school. Where such systems do exist, as in New Zealand (see Adema, 2006; Meade & Podmore, 2002), there has been a concerted effort to inform early childhood practice with the rich history of early childhood education, current research on learning and the role of culture and community in learning, and commitment to human rights and particularly the rights of the child (see UNICEF, 2002).

Foundations of Early Childhood Education

Williams (1992) and others trace the modern history of early childhood education and its acknowledgement of children being different from adults to the work of Jean-Jacques Rousseau (1712–88). Before that time, as Philippe Aries (1962) demonstrates in his discussion of the ways in which young children have been depicted historically in arts and letters, young children were viewed as miniature adults; infants and toddlers as babies.

Williams (1992) writes that Rousseau's work brought two important new dimensions to perceptions of children that have been fundamental to modern understandings of young children and their world and are foundational principles of most early childhood curricula. First was Rousseau's ability to see the young child as different from adults and "moving through a succession of stages, each of which had its own internal order and coherence" (Williams, 1992, p. 2). The second was his "insistence that children learned not through the abstractions of the written word, but through direct interaction with the environment" (Williams, 1992, p. 2).

Rousseau's theories were further articulated by Johann Pestalozzi (1746–27) and later by Fredrich Froebel (1782–52), both of whom argued for a child-centered, naturalistic education for young children. Pestalozzi developed a curriculum that placed importance on the guidance of parents and, according to Williams (1992), stressed manual dexterity "as a survival skill in the newly emerging industrial revolution" (p. 3). Froebel, writes Bruce (1987), "saw the mother as the first educator in the child's life—a revolutionary view at the time when only men were seen as capable of teaching children" (p. 29). For Froebel, the child must be seen as a whole. No one aspect of the child's development is more important than another. Williams (1992) holds that "Froebel is generally considered the founder of early childhood education not only because he was the first to design a curriculum specifically for young children . . . but because he introduced play as a major medium for instruction" (p. 5). But Williams also notes:

Froebel's notion of 'play' was substantially different from modern conceptions. He saw play as a teacher-directed process, largely imitative in nature and revolving around predetermined content. But he also understood play to be a form of 'corrective self-activity,' expressing children's emerging capabilities and reflecting their particular way of learning. (p. 5)

Maria Montessori (1869–52) seems a direct intellectual descendent of both Pestalozzi and Froebel. Her attention to children's small motor and sensory development, her invention of mathematical, sensory, and practical-life materials, her understanding of the need for a prepared environment scaled to a child's needs, and her articulation of a coherent method and approach hearken to Pestalozzi's emphasis on manual dexterity in children's work, as well as the importance of adults as guides in children's lives, and to Froebel's attention to the spiritual and intellectual life of the child.

New (1992) suggests that "both Froebel's and Montessori's methodologies represented a compromise between a child-centered approach and one that emphasized knowledge transmission, and their suggestions for projects that integrated the various subjects areas were often highly structured" (p. 288). For her, "the (20th) century's best and earliest advocate for an integrated early childhood curriculum was surely John Dewey" (p. 288). Dewey (1902/1990) saw wholeness to learning and to the focus of learning:

Abandon the notion of subject-matter as something fixed and ready-made in itself, outside the child's experience as also something hard and fast; see it as something fluent, embryonic, vital; and we realize that the child and the curriculum are simply two limits which define a single process. Just as two points define a straight line, so the present standpoint of the child and the facts and truths of studies define instruction. It is continuous reconstruction, moving from the child's present experience into that represented by organized bodies of truth that we call studies. (p. 189)

Dewey emphasized experience, support, and guidance from wise others, interaction with peers, and relevance (both development, as appropriate to the child's physical skill and ways of knowing, and cognitive, as appropriate to the child's interests and context).

Dewey's (1902/1990) vision of education and of how children learn has become core to whatever coherently American vision of early childhood education there is. Williams (1992) writes of Dewey and his followers:

While not rejecting the picture of children as innately creative beings, the progressive followers of John Dewey reached backward in time to reclaim some of Pestalozzi's understanding of learning through direct experience with the natural world, and forward into the new century to envision children as builders of a new social order—a democratic society. Progressive educators found the highly defined and teacher-directed Froebelian curriculum to be too removed from the challenges and problems of daily living. Instead, they suggested, a curriculum for young children should be designed to meet the circumstances children faced as members of a group living in a modern world. (p. 5)

Simultaneous with and following Dewey and Montessori, are Susan Isaacs and Margaret MacMillan in Britain and Pattie Smith Hill, Caroline Pratt, and Lucy Sprague Mitchell in the United States, all whose work many list as essential to current understandings of early childhood practice. "While these early childhood advocates each had a distinct point of view," writes Williams, "they all emphasized the centrality of process, and play as an expression of process in the growth, development, and education of young children" (1992, p. 7); and, in their work, they were inventors and shapers of the child-centered early childhood curricula for children that has become the hallmark of early childhood practice for school-age children the world over.

Psychology and Early Childhood Education

These pioneering thinkers did not address birth to age 3, the period of infancy and toddlerhood. Until the latter part of the 20th century, most educators gave little thought to very young children because their capacity for knowing, learning, and communicating was largely unexplored. True, there was a budding movement that focused on what Williams (1992) describes as "the child development perspective" (p. 7):

> The American Child Study Movement, under the leadership of G. Stanley Hall (1844–1924) was starting to influence early childhood practice. Observations of children's behavior in a variety of contexts began yielding powerful data that, in turn, were causing curriculum makers to rethink what were appropriate learning experiences for young children. . . . The complexity of the 'whole child' was beginning to reveal itself and to require increasingly sensitive applications of integrated approaches to teaching and learning.

But it was not until the work of Jean Piaget (1896–1980) and Lev Vygotsky (1896–1934) became available in English in the mid-1960s and early 1970s through the intervention of Jerome Bruner that the attention of psychologists and educators turned to the youngest children; and it was only then that scientists began to understand what many mothers and caregivers of young children already knew: the earliest years are times of amazing growth, of fantastic learning, and of extraordinary powers of thinking. Very young children, as Bransford, Brown, and Cocking (1999) have put it, "are very competent, active agents in their own conceptual development" (p. 68).

Jean Piaget

Piaget (1929/1975, 1952; Piaget & Inhelder, 1969) described children's cognitive growth as proceeding in four stages: sensorimotor, preoperational, concrete operational, and formal operational. The process from stage to stage is highly individual (Lee, 1992) and leads children's thinking from the general to the abstract as they construct their understandings of the world. Infants inhabit what Piaget describes as the sensorimotor stage of development. Here is when infants and toddlers learn about the world

through their senses: they watch carefully and can be surprised, they learn to bring objects to their mouths, they can distinguish voices and respond to sound, they know when they are uncomfortable. This is also the time when children develop physical skills: bringing their hands together, holding onto an object, turning over, getting up on hands and knees, crawling, walking, talking. Preschoolers enter what Piaget describes as the preoperational stage—now children interact with the world using language and physical movement to develop internal understandings of how the world works. Sometime between the ages of 7 and 9, children enter the period of concrete operations, and in their teens, they move into formal operations.

Children make their way through these various stages by engaging in reciprocal acts of assimilation and accommodation. With assimilation, children try to fit new knowledge into existing structures. With accommodation, they have to modify existing structures to make sense of new information or represent new skills (Piaget & Inhelder, 1969). Williams (1992) describes the ways in which children's play enables them to move in and out of these reciprocal activities:

> Play especially exercises the assimilation process, using action and frequently language as proving grounds for newly acquired ideas. As children proceed through the four periods of intellectual development . . ., play assumes a variety of forms; and within any one period, it can have multiple functions. Sensorimotor play, for example, generally revolves around practicing physical skills acquired through the use of the five senses. However, it can also be used as a medium for establishing social relationships. During the preoperational period, play might be used symbolically or constructively to solidify physical knowledge of one's surroundings, to practice problem solving in the adult world, or to create a microsociety in which to try out new capabilities or to refine social interactions. (p. 9)

For early childhood educators, Piaget's emphasis on children as knowing agents in their own learning and their ability to construct understandings of the world is critically important for shaping both environment and practice (New, 1992). Thus, the cradle and crib as well as the surround of early childhood centers and classrooms become important sources of information for children and, to go back to Montessori, these environments must be prepared thoughtfully and with understanding of how children learn.

Lev Vygotsky

Vygotsky's (1962, 1978) work offers a different and much broader conception of constructivism. Piaget's child operated alone in constructing an individualistic understanding of the world; Vygotsky has the child "collaborating with others in the co-construction of the higher structures of its own mind" (Lee, 1992, p. 206). Vygotsky suggests that children's learning is shaped and colored by their surroundings—by the people, the communities, the cultures into which children are born and within which they grow and learn. Learners' readiness for new ways of knowing can be facilitated in what Vygotsky termed *the zone of proximal development*—a cognitive bridge between what learners are able to do on their own and what they can do with help from a knowledgeable other. Both peers and teachers, parents, and other adults can act as the knowledgeable other.

As with Piaget, young children's play is a critical facet of their cognitive development but play in the Vygotskian frame is situated in the cultural ways of knowing and language or symbol systems available to children in their unique settings. Play functions as a major way by which young children integrate social, emotional, physical, and imaginative experience in a particular cultural surround. Thus, there are few hard and fast developmental milestones in Vygotskian theory. Rather, there is, as Cole, John-Steiner, Scribner, and E. Souberman so aptly named their translation of Vygotsky (1978), the notion that mind evolves *in* society.

What Vygotsky's theory offers is a broad and deep reassessment of ways in which learning takes place, and it suggests that the contexts of learning are multiple and complex. The work of both Piaget and Vygotsky make it clear that children, from the moment of birth, are primed for learning and that they actively pursue learning. Vygotsky's work makes it clear that all children, even infants, are deeply engaged in learning (Bransford, Brown, & Cocking, 1999).

Developmentally Appropriate Practice

The ring of scientific truth in the psychological research that grew out of Piaget's (1929/1975, 1952; Piaget & Inhelder, 1969) work and that of the child study movement presented difficulty for educators and policy makers. I say difficulty because, along with the stage theories of Erikson (1963) and Freud, this research, which appeared to so ably describe optimal learning environments and optimal learning treatments, seemed to completely overshadow the work of early childhood pioneers. Early childhood education became synonymous with theories of child development, and efforts to spur children's cognitive development took precedence in the field. As Williams (1992) noted, two schools of thought emerged from this perspective: one suggests that programs for young children (4- and 5-year-olds) should be framed around the traditional school subject areas and should engage children in "formal, academic skills such as reading and computation" (p. 12), and the other calls for a nuanced, child-centered approach for 4- and 5-year-old children. Seefeldt and Galper (1998) describe the split as between behaviorists and those who advocated a child-centered curriculum (p. 173).

Slowly and over time, resistance to stage theories and to an exclusive focus on cognitive development emerged most noticeably in the concept of developmentally appropriate practice (DAP; see Bredekamp, 1987), which is discussed in depth by Florez in Chapter 43. Essentially, DAP is an

attempt to create a balance for early childhood practitioners between adherence to strict timelines of development and the more fluid understandings of development that emerged from the work of Piaget and Vygotsky.

In the United States and around the world, the statement drew and has continued to draw both praise and criticism. Praise for the statement focuses on what it has enabled. It has given early childhood practice visibility and has put early childhood education in the limelight of education policy in this country and abroad. The criticism has come from those who question the "suitability of this approach for young children, for at-risk children, and for children from varying cultural backgrounds" (Huffman & Speer, 2000, p. 169). These critiques were foundational to the development of a new line of research and theory known as the reconceptualist perspective.

The Reconceptualist Perspective

In 1991, a special issue of the journal *Early Education and Development* edited by Swadener and Kessler launched a critique of DAP that zeroed in on the ways in which the editors claimed that "psychological and child development perspectives in the field" (p. 85) had come to dominate thinking and practice. It was Swadener and Kessler's (1991) contention that psychological and child development perspectives had "often served to narrow the parameters of inquiry within early childhood education to an almost exclusive analysis of children's development, and thus, eliminated other possible perspectives from which to view children and the early childhood curriculum" (p. 85). Although to many, DAP appears not to be a part of the psychological and child development perspectives that they attack, Swadener and Kessler hold that it is has a ring of homogeneity that suggests all children learn in the same ways and does not acknowledge family, community, and culture.

Situating the Reconceptualist Movement

The movement that Swadener and Kessler's (1991) work initiated owes much to Bronfenbrenner's (1979) theory of ecological environments, to Vygotsky's (1962, 1978) theory of the social construction of knowledge, and to Gardner's (1985) theory of multiple intelligences—interestingly, all psychologists who themselves pushed the field toward new ways of thinking.

Uri Bronfenbrenner

Bronfenbrenner (1979) described ecological environments using four propositions:

Proposition 1: A primary developmental context is one in which the child can observe and engage in ongoing patterns of progressively more complex activity jointly with or under the direct guidance of persons who possess knowledge and skill not yet acquired by the child and with whom the child has developed a positive emotional relationship. (p. 845)

Proposition 2: A secondary developmental context is one in which the child is given opportunity, resources, and encouragement to engage in the activities he or she has learned in primary developmental contexts, but now without the active involvement or direct guidance of another person possessing knowledge and skill beyond the levels acquired by the child. (p. 845)

Proposition 3: The developmental potential of a setting depends on the extent to which third parties present in the setting support or undermine the activities of those actually engaged in interaction with the child. (p. 847)

Proposition 4: The developmental potential of a child-rearing setting is increased as a function of the number of supportive links between that setting and other contexts involving the child or persons responsible for his or her care. Such interconnections may take the form of shared activities, two-way communication, and information provided in each setting. (p. 848)

Dramatically, Bronfenbrenner (1979) called into question the press for high IQ and achievement gains. "I argue," he wrote, "that such outcome-focused comparisons no longer represent a strategy of choice in research on human development. Specifically, they do little to increase our understanding of how ecological contexts affect the course of psychological growth" (Bronfenbrenner, 1979, p. 844). Bronfenbrenner (1979) situated children's healthy development to their relationships with significant others and their environments, and he pushed his argument toward the shaping of public policy of early childhood education:

If we were to examine systematically the actual contexts in which children in our society spend their waking hours, I predict that many of the settings would be found to fall substantially short of meeting either set of requirements [a reference to Propositions 1 and 2 above]. Specifically, in many places and for many hours, children probably do not have available to them valued adults who engage them in progressively more complex joint activities, nor is the situation likely to be one that provides resources and incentives for children to engage in complex activities previously learned. (p. 846)

The implications for child care and education are unmistakable: the two cannot be separated. Hence, neither can the preparation and continued support of early childhood practitioners or the fact of inadequate facilities for young children continue to be separated and ignored.

Howard Gardner

Like Bronfenbrenner (1979), Howard Gardner's (1985) theory of multiple intelligences helped to move the discussion of child development and education away from an achievement focus. Gardner posits seven intelligences: linguistic, logical-mathematical, spatial, bodily-kinesthetic, musical, interpersonal, and intrapersonal. These emerge with differing strengths in deep connection to the child's

environment. Gardner (1991) takes issue with Piaget's stage theory as too inflexible and too individualistic: " . . . people do learn, represent, and utilize knowledge in many different ways. . . . Such well documented differences among individuals complicate an examination of human learning and understanding" (p. 12).

It was with these antecedents and the cumulative evidence of classroom-based research that the critique of DAP was launched, thereby opening the field to new voices, new perspectives, and, most important, the opportunity to reexamine curriculum and practice in early childhood education.

Toward New Understandings of Early Childhood Education

As this review shows, there has been considerable debate in the field of early childhood education about several fundamental issues. Chief among these is whether care and education belong together as early childhood education. Policy with regard to this issue has in many countries, including the United States, tended to keep the two separate, designating care as the central activity of the home and education as the central activity of the school and, therefore, the state. In this country, in England (Smith, 1994), and in many western countries, efforts to implement all-day kindergarten, universal prekindergarten, and to support families needing child care have all been shaped by this debate. Thus, although early childhood education has increasingly been embraced around the world, public policy has generally focused on preschool-age (3 to 5 years old) children's experience of school to the exclusion of attention to the learning and development of younger children.

One major barrier to redefining the field to encompass birth to age 8 is the equation of services to the youngest children and their families as outreach to the children of the poor (Meade & Podmore, 2002). Countering this perspective, however, is a growing body of research cited by Kuamoo (2007); Bowman, Donovan, and Burns (2001); and Barnett (2005) regarding the critical importance of the care and educational experiences of the early years for children's later success in school. Another barrier has been what Swadener & Kessler (1991) and Fleer (2006) describe as a failure on the part of educators and policy makers to move the field beyond a conceptualization of development as "ages and stages" (Fleer, p. 131) to a reshaping of early childhood practice and curricula in ways that add and infuse both local knowledge and beliefs and cross-cultural developmental and educational research:

Through normalizing difference rather than recognizing only one cultural developmental trajectory, expectations in relation to development can be problematized immediately. Building institutional and cultural intersubjectivity gives teachers permission to move away from an evolutionary model of development and toward a revolutionary model, thus eliminating the perspective that any difference to normalized western development would be constituted as a 'disease' of normal child development. (Fleer, 2006, p. 138)

These views are enacted in two curricula: that of Reggio Emilia in Italy and that of the nation of New Zealand. Both bring care and education together and are completely in and of their cultural contexts.

Bringing Care and Education Together in Early Childhood

Debate persists about images of the young child, optimal methods, environments, and configurations to support children's learning. Three grand experiments demonstrate the possibilities inherent in flexible, context-sensitive, well-supported programs that bridge the birth to 8 continuum. These are Head Start with the later addition of Early Head Start in the United States; Reggio Emilia, an Italian municipality's post-World War II effort to ensure a solid beginning for all of its children; and New Zealand's recent move to a common early childhood curriculum for children from birth to age 8. Each of these see young children as different from adults, recognizes that children learn in different ways, and positions the family and community as essential partners and guides in the child's development. Each recognizes early childhood is a time of extraordinary physical, cognitive, and emotional growth—so much so that its effect is felt throughout the life span.

Head Start

Head Start was created in 1965 as part of Lyndon Johnson's war on poverty as a means of stopping the cycle of poverty. It provides comprehensive education, health, nutrition, and parent involvement services to low-income children and their families across the United States. Initially, the program focused on children ages 3 to 5. In 1994, the Administration on Children, Youth, and Families (ACYF), which currently administers all Head Start programs, initiated Early Head Start. The program was designed as a two-generation program to enhance children's development and health, strengthen family and community partnerships, and support the staff delivering new services to low-income families with pregnant women, infants, or toddlers. It was expanded in 1995 and 1996 and brought under the Head Start umbrella. Today, Early Head Start operates in 664 communities and serves approximately 55,000 children (Mathematica Policy Research, Inc., 2002).

Since its inception, Head Start itself has served more than 22 million preschool children in more than 1,600 sites in every state and nearly every county in the nation. Understandably with a program as large, complex, and long lived, evaluations of Head Start have been mixed with some researchers claiming early on that the academic benefits are quickly washed out (see Cicirelli, 1969), though numerous studies since have shown that the children for whom the program is intended do benefit academically. Furthermore, the program's positive effect on young children of poverty and their families—the intended focus of the program—is increasingly acknowledged (see Oden, Schweinhart, Weikart, Markus, & Xie, 1996). Additionally, researchers have found that greater opportunities for former Head Start students to lead productive lives accrue over time (see Schweinhart & Weikart, 1997).

Reggio Emilia

Reggio Emilia is a small town in Italy with a resident population of approximately 130,000 people. Just after World War II, the townspeople came together and decided on a plan to provide high-quality, full-time child care for all the children under 6 years old in the town. They set aside 12% of the town's budget for this purpose and began the renovation of buildings throughout the town as sites for children's centers. Subsequently, the child care model of Reggio Emilia has achieved worldwide attention from educators, psychologists, and policy makers in large part because of its attention to children's symbolic languages—drawing, sculpture, art, and writing—in the context of a project-oriented curriculum (see Edwards, Gandini, & Forman, 1993; Reggio Children, 2008), but also because of the extraordinary settings which are these early childhood centers.

Each classroom has two teachers who are often found working with small groups of children. The environment of each center is considered the third teacher, and this shows in a variety of ways throughout the city's 22 centers: each center emphasizes the children's work through documentation, the display of children's completed and ongoing projects in and around the classrooms. Time is considered "an ally, not an enemy" (New, 1992, p. 310). Children stay with their teachers for 3 years. Each day's schedule evolves in a fluid, holistic way that enables both small- and large-group activities, exercise, naps, and meals, as well as large amounts of free play that allow children to get deeply into their various projects.

The centers are beautifully furnished; they are light and airy, with child-sized furnishings throughout. Infant rooms are designed to enable young children's earliest efforts to interact with their world. For example, children who are learning to crawl can move from soft floor mattresses in what look like little Pullman compartments right onto the floor when they wake up. Children of all ages eat lunch together with their teachers family-style in small groups of varying ages in dining rooms that feel like home rather than like a school.

There is genuine commitment to these children's centers across the community and deep engagement by parents in their children's learning. They are acknowledged by teachers as equal partners in the children's education. As New (1992) notes, "there is an articulated belief in the ability of parents to participate in a variety of meaningful ways to children's early education. These beliefs combine to create an atmosphere of community and collaboration that characterizes adult relationships with one another as well as their efforts with the children" (p. 312).

The Early Childhood Curriculum of New Zealand

The Labor government of New Zealand moved in 2000 to bring the care and education of young children together under the ministry of education—with a commitment to necessary funding and to the improvement and training of all early childhood educators. According to Meade and Podmore (2002), the country had been primed for this decision by the intensive work of a state services commission work group who, drawing on research—particularly Bronfenbrenner's (1979) theory of the ecology of human development, Schweinhart and Weikart's (1985, 1997) research regarding Head Start and the High/Scope curriculum, and Lazar and Darlington's (1982) research suggesting that the care and education of young children cannot be separated—were instrumental in shaping an approach to early childhood education that was both in synchrony with research in the field and embracing of the complex cultures of the country.

Addressing the concerns of the diverse cultural groups in New Zealand, and particularly the country's indigenous Maori population, was critical in the shaping of the national early childhood curriculum and the provision of free early childhood education (birth to school entry) throughout the country to children.

Meade and Podmore (2002) write, "The title *Te Whaariki* translates from the Maori language as 'a woven mat for all to stand on'" (p. 23). Alvestad and Duncan (2006), write that the title "illustrates both the nature and content of the document—that of a woven mat—interweaving the strands, goals, aspirations, and the view of the child and the family/*Whānau[1]* for all the early childhood services in New Zealand" (p. 33). About the curriculum plan as a whole, they write, "There is no prescription on method, but a shared vision for outcomes for children in New Zealand" (p. 33).

Although it may be too soon to assess the effect of the new curriculum, Meade and Podmore (2002) write that implementation and assessment ("trialling") of the various strands of the curriculum has been ongoing "across a range of early childhood services including child care centers, kindergartens and play centres, and language immersion centres" (p. 23)—all as a means of bringing the parts of the curriculum together as a whole.

Toward the Future

Each of these programs has brought care and education together under one umbrella. Each provides a good example of ways in which policy and practice can come together and represents an act of will on the part of government. All of these emerged as a result of intensive research and collaboration and a consensus-built vision of a society's future.

Head Start moved gradually toward an embrace of children from birth to 3 years old and has remained true to its mission of serving the poorest children and their families to prepare children for school. Both Reggio Emilia and New Zealand break through the focus on poverty that has bound early childhood programs for so long. The New Zealand program of free early childhood for all goes further than any program anywhere and certainly than any state-funded program to embrace the powerful tug of culture.

Will the schism between those who focus on care and those who focus on education remain in early childhood education? Will the propensity to provide state-funded early childhood programs only to poor children persist? One hopes not, and there is good research to support that hope (see Bowman, Donovan, & Burns, 2001). Yet, there is much to be done to arrive at the point of implementing policies that bring care and education together as early childhood education.

Enmeshed in the continuing debate are political and economic issues (parental leave policies, family support, on-site child care, providing care and education for all who wish it); educational issues (who determines the content, mode, and effectiveness of early childhood education, professional preparation and support over time, optimal environments); and the issues that grow out of personal and societal belief systems. It will not be easy to answer these questions and to shape new ways of embracing early childhood education for all. The Head Start experiment makes clear that research over time is essential if we are to really understand the powerful effect of early childhood on the lives of adults and the future of societies. What is needed now is continuing research and a commitment of the research and policy communities to dialogue with families and communities to enact policies that will, in the long run, benefit both our youngest children and the societies in which they will take their places.

Note

1. *Whānau* is the Maori term to describe family. This term, however, includes a much wider understanding of family grouping than just the nuclear family and blood relations.

References and Further Readings

Adema, W. (2006). Towards coherent care and education support policies for New Zealand families. *Social Policy Journal of New Zealand, 28,* 46–76.

Alvestad, M., & Duncan, J. (2006). "The value is enormous—It's priceless I think!" New Zealand preschool teachers' understandings of the early childhood curriculum in New Zealand—A comparative perspective. *International Journal of Early Childhood, 38*(1), 31–45.

Aries, P. (1962). *Centuries of childhood* (R. Balkick, Trans.). New York: Knopf.

Barnett, S. (2005). *Hearing on early childhood education: Improvement through integration.* (Testimony to the House

Subcommittee on Education Reform, April 21, 2005). New Brunswick, NJ: National Institute for Early Education Research (NIEER). Available at http://nieer.org/resources/research/TwoWay.pdf

Bowman, B. T., Donovan, S., & Burns, S. (Eds.). (2001). *Eager to learn: Educating our preschoolers.* Report of the National Research Council, Committee on Early Childhood Pedagogy, Commission on Behavioral and Social Sciences and Education. Washington, DC: National Academies Press.

Bransford, J. D., Brown, A. L., & Cocking, R. R. (1999). Chapter 4: How children learn. *How people learn: Brain, mind, experience, and school* (p. 67–102). San Francisco, CA: Jossey-Bass.

Bredekamp, S. (Ed.). (1987). *Developmentally appropriate practice in early childhood programs serving children from birth through age 8 (expanded edition).* Washington, DC: National Association for the Education of Young Children.

Bronfenbrenner, U. (1979). Contexts of child rearing. Problems and prospects. *American Psychologist, 34*(10), 844–850.

Bruce, T. (1987). *Early childhood education.* London: Hodder and Stoughton.

Cicirelli, V. G. (1969). *The impact of Head Start: An evaluation of the effects of Head Start on children's cognitive and affective development. Vols. I–II.* Athens, OH: Westinghouse Learning Corporation, Ohio University.

Dewey, J. (1990). *The child and the curriculum* (P. Jackson, Ed.). Chicago: University of Chicago Press. (Original work published 1902)

Edwards, C., Gandini, L., & Forman, G. (Eds.). (1993). *The hundred languages of children: Education for all of the child in Reggio Emilia, Italy.* Norwood, NJ: Ablex.

Erikson, E. (1963). *Childhood and society.* New York: W. W. Norton. (Original work published 1950)

Fleer, M. (2006). A sociocultural perspective on early childhood education: Rethinking, reconceptualizing and reinventing. In M. Fleer, S. Edwards, M. Hammer, A. Kennedy, A. Ridgway, J. Robbins, & L. Surman (Eds.), *Early childhood learning communities: Sociocultural research in practice* (pp. 3–14). NSW, Australia: Pearson Education Australia.

Gardner, H. (1985). *Frames of mind: The theory of multiple intelligences.* New York: Basic Books.

Gardner, H. (1991). *The unschooled mind: How children think and how schools should teach.* New York: Basic Books.

Huffman, L. R., & Speer, P. W. (2000). Academic performance among at-risk children: The role of developmentally appropriate practices. *Early Childhood Research Quarterly, 15*(2), 167–184.

Jackson, P. W. (1992). Conceptions of curriculum specialists. In P. W. Jackson, Ed., *Handbook of research on curriculum,* pp. 3–40. New York: Macmillan.

Kuamoo, M. (2007). *Resources about early childhood education. A resource guide from the National Clearinghouse for English Language Acquisition.* Retrieved June 17, 2007, from http://www.ncela.gwu.edu/resabout/ecell/intro

Lazar, I., & Darlington, R. (1982). Lasting effects of early education: A report from the Consortium for Longitudinal Studies. *Monographs of the Society for Research in Child Development, (47)*2–3, 1–151.

Lee, P. C. (1992). Constructivist perspectives on children. In L. R. Williams & D. P. Fromberg, Eds., *Encyclopedia of early childhood education,* pp. 206–207. New York: Garland.

Mathematica Policy Research, Inc. (2002). *Making a difference in the lives of infants and toddlers and their families: The impacts of Early Head Start. Executive Summary.* Washington, DC: Administration on Children, Youth and Families. Department of Health and Human Services.

Meade, A., & Podmore, V. N. (2002). Early childhood education policy co-ordination under the auspices of the Department/Ministry of Education. *A case study of New Zealand.* UNESCO: Early Childhood and Family Series #1.

National Center for Educational Statistics. (2000). *America's kindergartners.* Washington, DC: U.S. Department of Education and Educational Research and Improvement (NCES-2000-070).

New, R. (1992). The integrated early childhood curriculum. In C. Seefeldt (Ed.), *The early childhood curriculum: A review of current research* (2nd ed., pp. 286–324). New York: Teachers College Press.

Oden, S., Schweinhart, L, Weikart, D., Markus, S., & Xie, Y. (1996). *Summary of the long term benefits of Head Start study.* Washington, DC: Head Start Third National Research Conference, June 20–23.

Piaget, J. (1952). *The origins of intelligence in children.* London: Routledge & Kegan Paul.

Piaget, J. (1975). *The child's conception of the world.* London: Routledge & Kegan Paul. (Original work published 1929)

Piaget, J., & Inhelder, B. (1969). *The psychology of the child.* London: Routledge & Kegan Paul.

Pratt, C. (1990). *I learn from children.* New York: Harper & Row. (Original work published 1948)

Reggio Children. (2008). *Reggio children—The one hundred languages of children.* Retrieved June 15, 2008, from http://zerosei.comune.re.it/inter/100exhibit.htm

Schweinhart, L. J., & Weikart, D. P. (1985). Evidence that good early childhood programs work. *Phi Delta Kappan, (66)*8, 545–551.

Schweinhart, L. J., & Weikart, D. P. (1997). The high/scope preschool curriculum comparison study through age 23. *Early Childhood Research Quarterly, 12*(2), 117–143.

Seefeldt, C., & Galper, A. (1998). *Continuing issues in early childhood education* (2nd ed.). Upper Saddle River, NJ: Merrill.

Smith, E. A. (1994). *Educating the under-fives.* London: Cassells.

Swadener, B. B., & Kessler, S. (1991). Introduction to the special issue. *Early Education and Development, 2*(2), 85–94.

UNICEF. (2002). *Convention on the right of the child.* Retrieved July 1, 2007, from http://www.unicef.org/crc/crc.htm

United States Census Bureau. (2003). P70–89. A Child's Day: 2000 (Selected indicators of child well-being). Table D1. Early child care experiences—characteristics of children and parents: 2000. *Survey of Income and Program Participation*, 1996 Panel, Wave 12. Retrieved July, 2007, from http://www.census.gov/population/socdemo/well-being/p70-89/00tabD01.pdf

Vygotsky, L. (1962). *Thought and language.* Cambridge, MA: MIT Press.

Vygotsky, L. (1978). *Mind in society. The development of higher psychological processes* (M. Cole, V. John-Steiner, S. Scribner, & E. Souberman, Eds.). Cambridge, MA: Harvard University Press.

Williams, L. R. (1992). Determining the curriculum. In C. Seefeldt, (Ed.), *The early childhood curriculum. A review of current research* (2nd ed., pp. 1–15). New York: Teachers College Press.

43

EARLY CHILDHOOD EDUCATION

The Developmentally Appropriate Practice Debate

IDA ROSE FLOREZ

University of Arizona

How should 5-year-olds spend their day? Should taxpayers fund preschool play time? Should 4-year-olds be expected to name the letters of the alphabet? Should they be expected to count to 10 or 20? These questions reflect debates about the purposes and goals of early childhood education. The most influential organization addressing these concerns is the National Association for the Education of Young Children (NAEYC), a professional association representing over 100,000 early childhood professionals. NAEYC's efforts have shaped how people think about the education of young children both in the United States and abroad (Raines & Johnston, 2003). The organization has influenced policy and practice by publishing position statements and research briefs designed to influence policy and legislation, by developing a gold-standard accreditation system for private and public child care centers and schools, and by providing professional development and literature for the early childhood community.

In 1987 NAEYC published its seminal position statement, *NAEYC Position Statement on Developmentally Appropriate Practices in Early Childhood Programs Serving Children From Birth Through Age 8* (Bredekamp, 1987). The statement was designed to guide administrators of early childhood centers seeking NAEYC accreditation and to clarify the concept of developmentally appropriate practice (DAP); but it did much more. According to Raines and Johnston (2003), the 1987 position statement:

> Irrevocably changed the thinking and discourse about practices in early childhood programs. Since its recent entry into the professional education lexicon, the term developmentally appropriate practices and the concept it represents have been adopted and used extensively by educators, policy makers, and businesses. Both the concept and the term have affected early childhood program practices; national, state, and local policies for curriculum and assessment; marketing of commercial early childhood materials and programs; and standards for early childhood educator preparation. (p. 85)

In 1997 the statement was revised and expanded, and it is currently undergoing a second revision.

NAEYC's advocacy has focused national attention on the need for quality early childhood education. Still, DAP is controversial. According to NAEYC, developmentally appropriate practice is an approach to early childhood education that employs "empirically based principles of child development and learning" (Bredekamp & Copple, 1997, p. 9). Such a proposition seems inarguable. How can anyone dispute that the education of young children should be based on scientifically derived knowledge? But the matter is not so simple. The universal acceptance of DAP has faced significant challenges (Dickinson, 2002). DAP casts early childhood education as a dichotomy in which practice is either developmentally appropriate or inappropriate. Many in the early childhood field object to this dichotomized way of thinking about educating children. DAP is also plagued by definitional, empirical, and theoretical difficulties. These difficulties result in misunderstandings about and misapplications of DAP (Raines & Johnston, 2003). Unfortunately, most people who work with young children are not well-trained (Karp, 2006), so early childhood practitioners often lack the expertise to adapt DAP. Finally, many in the early childhood field argue that DAP reflects Caucasian, middle- and upper-class values and object to labeling other cultures' ways of raising children as inappropriate (Delpit, 1988; Lubeck, 1998; O'Brien, 1996).

This chapter discusses these challenges and makes recommendations for reconceptualizing early childhood best practice. NAEYC has responded to previous critiques by revising the position statement, which it intends to do every 10 years. Although regular revision is helpful, it is unlikely that everyone in NAEYC's broad sphere of influence will simultaneously revise their beliefs and practices. Despite many helpful changes in the 1997 revision, many of the ideas found in the 1987 statement (such as an age-based definition of DAP) still affect thinking about early childhood education. Thoughtful analysis of DAP must consider how the concept has been articulated and used from its inception. Therefore, this analysis considers DAP as a conceptual whole: as it is represented in both the 1987 and 1997 statements (and their accompanying documents) and how it is generally used in early childhood research, practice, and policy. The framers of DAP recognize that educating young children is a messy, complex affair and welcome discussion about DAP (Bredekamp & Copple, 1997). This chapter hopes to contribute to the dialogue.

Dichotomies and Developmentally Appropriate Practice

Sorting ideas into categories is one of the earliest cognitive skills humans develop. Dichotomous categorizing (this *is* an animal; this *is not* an animal) is prerequisite to more elaborate and complex concept formation. Thus, when explaining a new concept, dichotomies are intuitively appealing. For this reason, DAP is outlined in a dichotomous framework (Bredekamp & Copple, 1997). According to Bredekamp and Copple, "People construct an understanding of a concept from considering both positive and negative examples. For this reason the chart [describing DAP] includes not only practices that we see as developmentally appropriate, but also practices we see as inappropriate or highly questionable for children of this age" (1997, p. 123).

As appealing as dichotomies are, there are compelling reasons to avoid them. First, evidence rarely supports dichotomous explanations of development (Gutierrez & Rogoff, 2003). For example, the DAP statements label preschool programs that focus on pre-academic skills inappropriate (Bredekamp & Copple, 1997). Yet, many preschoolers can successfully acquire such skills (Kessler, 1991). Second, dichotomies are merely prerequisites to more complex thinking. Since they artificially cast phenomena as either/or categories, they reduce complexity of thought. Such narrow thinking interferes with developing rich, evolving conceptions of young children's develop-

ment. For example, although it would be inappropriate to use stickers or candy to teach typically developing 3-year-olds to make eye contact when greeting friends, using such artificial reinforcers may be an appropriate intervention for a child with an autism spectrum disorder. But once the child has acquired the skill, continued use of reinforcers would be inappropriate. Thus, using artificial reinforcers is not categorically appropriate or inappropriate: It is simply a method that can be effective under certain circumstances. Meeting children's diverse needs requires flexible thinking. Recognizing this need, the authors of the 1997 statement argue to end dichotomous thinking about educating young children (Bredekamp & Copple, 1997). Still, dichotomous thinking is at the core of DAP. DAP represents one side of an either/or debate between two theoretical schools of thought: behaviorism and constructivism.

Behaviorism explains learning and development in terms of responses to environmental reinforcers and punishers and carefully manages the use of time (Skinner, 1984). Therefore behavioral methods carefully control environmental factors such as the delivery of reinforcers and the pace of instruction. From a behavioral perspective, adequate reinforcement plus sufficient time leads to increased learning. Behavioral methods were successfully used during World War II to rapidly train a victorious U.S. military. Shortly after the war, with the launch of the Russian satellite *Sputnik*, the United States began to fear that the Soviet Union was becoming the world's technological leader. This fear spawned reform movements designed to fix American public schools and reestablish the dominance of the United State's in the global economy. Demonstrated success during WWII solidified behavioral approaches as the methodology of choice for American's educational reform efforts.

After initial enthusiasm, the reform momentum of the 1960s and 1970s faded, but the idea that U.S. schools needed to be fixed did not (see Chapter 28, this volume, for a discussion of educational reform movements). Recent reform efforts have varied in their support for or opposition to behavioral classroom methods. Educational reform in the 1980s combined emerging cognitive theories such as information processing with behaviorism's emphasis on efficiency, promoting the idea that those in public schools—teachers, students, administrators—need to do more and need to achieve more. With demands to do more and achieve more, it logically followed from behavioral theory that children and teachers need more time. Schoolwork was sent home to be completed in the evening and on weekends, school days were lengthened, and so was the school year. But even with lengthened days and years there is never enough time to do everything one is expected to do in a public school classroom. With the length of the school day and year maximized, extending academic instruction to younger children logically follows. If there isn't enough time to teach reading in first grade, perhaps reading instruction should start in kindergarten. Similarly, if there isn't enough time to teach school routines and letter recognition in kindergarten (because the day is filled with learning to read and write), perhaps these skills should be taught in preschool. After all, note those who argue for more academic rigor, many 4- and 5-year-old children capably acquire these academic skills (Stipek, 2006).

In contrast to those who promote more academic rigor at early grade levels, many early childhood educators champion the benefits of an unhurried, unstructured early childhood experience. From their perspective, engaging preschool and kindergarten-age children in direct instruction of academic skills pushes children beyond their developmental level and can negatively affect long-term academic outcomes. The 1987 statement clarified NAEYC's position that behaviorally controlled learning environments are inappropriate for young children and promoted a very different theoretical orientation called constructivism. Constructivism is the theoretical belief that children are naturally curious and actively construct knowledge. Children act upon their environments rather than their environments acting upon them. Constructivism is a cognitive theory that conceptualizes learning as changes in mental representations and associations rather than changes in behavior. Jean Piaget, the best known constructivist theorist, is referenced frequently in the DAP statements. The 1987 statement uses Piaget's stages of cognitive development (Piaget, 1952) in its definition of DAP and articulates a Piagetian view of learning: "Knowledge is not something that is given to children as though they were empty vessels to be filled. Children acquire knowledge about the physical and social worlds in which they live through playful interaction with objects and people" (Bredekamp, 1987, p. 52). The 1997 statement also describes an overt constructivist position: "Children are active learners, drawing on direct physical and social experience as well as culturally transmitted knowledge to construct their own understandings of the world around them" (Bredekamp & Copple, 1997, p. 13).

Educational practices based on constructivist theory look very different than those based on behaviorism. Classrooms and curricula based on behavioral influences emphasize efficiency and thus require structured environments. Classroom space and time is well-defined with specific activities occurring in specific areas according to schedule. Constructivist classrooms are considerably more unstructured. Space is loosely arranged with children free to engage in a variety of activities in areas of their choosing. Though teachers establish routines for snacks, bathroom trips, story time, and indoor and outdoor play, activities are not governed by strict schedules. In theory, children's interests and preferences influence allocation of time and resources.

The teacher's role is also different in constructivist and behavioral classrooms. Constructivism emphasizes children as agents of their own learning. Adults serve as facilitators and provide environments enriched with opportunities for children to experiment with objects and satisfy their own curiosity. The 1987 statement says, "In developmentally appropriate programs, adults offer children the choice to participate in a small group or in a solitary activity [and] provide opportunities for child-initiated, child-directed practice of skills as a self-chosen activity" (Bredekamp, 1987, p. 7). Conversely, behaviorally organized classrooms are teacher-directed. The schedule, learning goals, and activities are chosen and monitored by the teacher. Children's choices are often limited to selecting from a range of predefined choices ("You may look at books in the reading nook or on the patio").

Curriculum also differs between constructivist and behavioral classrooms. Constructivists use emergent curriculum that allows children to use various materials and methods rather than copying teacher-made examples. Consistent with constructivism, NAEYC considers it inappropriate for adults to reject "children's alternative ways of doing things" and to place great importance on children reproducing something the teacher has constructed (such as a holiday art project) or imitating the teacher's way of performing a task (such as peeling or buttering bread or threading beads; Bredekamp & Copple, 1997, p. 127). Behaviorally-based programs use convergent curriculum that incorporates predefined learning activities with teacher-defined correct responses that are the same or similar for all the children. Such curricula are identified as inappropriate by NAEYC for all young children up to and including Grade 3.

Finally, classrooms based on constructivist and behavioral theory differ in the use of play versus academic work. Piaget (1952) emphasized children's need to engage in object play to develop cognitively. Thus constructivist preschool and kindergarten classrooms are designed to facilitate children's exploration and discovery. Indeed, play is viewed by many child advocates as "absolutely essential to advancing children's development" (Kagan & Lowenstein, 2004, p. 59). The 1987 statement describes play as "an essential component of developmentally appropriate practice" (Bredekamp, 1987, p. 3) and calls for a 1-hour minimum devoted to free play daily. Unlike constructivist-based programs, in a behavioral framework play is often viewed as an encroachment on academically engaged time. Play may be used as a break from more valued academic work, as an opportunity for physical development, as a reward for academic productivity, or as a way to help children enjoy school and thus reinforce achievement. But in a behavioral frame, play is not inherently valued as a mechanism of learning and development.

Unfortunately, framing early childhood best practice as a dichotomy between appropriate constructivist methods and inappropriate behavioral methods does not allow the field to develop rich, nuanced conceptions of how best to educate young children. Alternative ways of conceptualizing professional practice will be discussed later.

DAP and Cultural Compatibility

Another controversial DAP issue is the claim by critics that many practices identified as developmentally inappropriate are time-honored ways of raising children in many cultures. Some argue that DAP represents Caucasian, European American child-rearing practices rather than universal developmental principles. They note that many indigenous cultures, such as Native Hawaiian and Native American, raise children to be cooperating members of an extended family and close-knit community, rather than stressing independence and autonomy. In many cultures, it is unacceptable for young children to choose not to participate in a teacher-initiated activity. Similarly, the idea that classrooms should be "child-centered" with "child-directed" activities or that "adults [should] respond quickly and directly to children's needs, desires and messages" (Bredekamp, 1987, p. 9) does not align with the way many cultures raise children. In many cultures, it is expected that children respond quickly and directly to adults' messages.

The 1997 DAP revision emphasizes the need for culturally sensitive practice (Bredekamp & Copple, 1997, pp. 41–52); however, the revision did not address the concern that DAP's fundamental philosophy defining children's role in relationship to adults is not compatible with many families' cultural values and practices (Goldstein & Andrews, 2004; Gutierrez & Rogoff, 2003). Critics also question the application of developmental research findings to all children. Piaget studied exclusively northern Europeans, primarily his own children. Critics argue that one cannot assume that findings based on such a narrow population adequately describe all children.

DAP Definitional, Empirical, and Theoretical Difficulties

A final area of difficulty for DAP concerns definitional ambiguity, shaky empirical support, and a narrow theoretical focus.

Definitional Difficulties

Both terms used to define DAP, *developmentally* and *appropriate,* are ambiguous, leading to conundrums. For example, much of DAP recommendations are simply good teaching practices—for children of all ages. Referring to these practices as developmentally appropriate for young children implies that these practices are not necessarily appropriate for older students. The word *appropriate* poses its own dilemmas. What is appropriate to one may be inappropriate to another. There are ways around this ambiguity. Other professions do not define practice by the notion of appropriateness. There is no such thing as legally appropriate practice or medically appropriate practice. Rather, most professions embrace a best practice approach in which minimal standards and ideal guidelines are articulated. Adopting a best practice framework would reduce ambiguity and provide a way to identify differences in quality while reserving the label inappropriate for those practices

that are unambiguously unacceptable for all children (e.g., abuse and neglect).

Fuzzy definitions also affect recommendations for practice. For example, the 1987 statement says, "Children of all ages need uninterrupted periods of time to become involved, investigate, select, and persist at activities" (Bredekamp, 1987, p. 7), but the frequency and duration of "uninterrupted periods of time" is left undefined. Similarly, the 1997 revision identifies what is inappropriate for 6- to 8-year-olds: "Teachers lecture to the whole group and assign paper-and-pencil practice exercises or work sheets to be completed by children working silently and individually at their desks" (Bredekamp & Copple, 1997, p. 165). Does the statement mean such direct instruction, used daily in thousands of primary classrooms around the world, is categorically inappropriate? Oddly, the same page identifies direct instruction as developmentally appropriate. In another example, the 1987 statement encourages adults to "move quietly" in early childhood classrooms (Bredekamp, p. 9), and the 1997 statement lists as inappropriate a classroom in which the noise level is "stressful and impeding conversation and learning" (Bredekamp & Copple, p. 125). Yet, two pages later the 1997 statement says that it is inappropriate when "teachers make it a priority to maintain a quiet environment" (p. 127).

These contradictions result in real problems. For example, early childhood practitioners must wrestle with the controversy over phonics-based and whole language literacy instruction. Traditional instruction relies on basal readers and teacher-directed, behavioral methods. Whole language, a constructivist approach, is broadly defined as one in which children construct meaning from text; use functional, relevant language; read "real" literature (as opposed to basal readers); and work in cooperative groups. Use of intact pieces of literature (rather than excerpts or abridgements), students' selection of reading material, and integrated language arts instruction is attractive to many early childhood teachers (Jeynes & Little, 2000). According to a recent meta-analysis of early literacy studies, "the evidence suggests that low-SES [low-socioeconomic status] students in Grades K–3 benefit from basal instruction more than they do from whole language instruction. If the results of our synthesis accurately depict reality, using a whole language approach with low-SES children could widen the gap between advantaged and disadvantaged students" (Jeynes & Little, 2000, p. 31).

In a nod toward the growing evidence that many children, especially those from low-SES backgrounds, make more reading progress with basal instruction, the 1997 statement comments on the whole language versus phonics controversy by saying the two approaches are "quite compatible and most effective in combination" (Bredekamp & Copple, 1997, p. 23). As Table 43.1 illustrates, the same statement also identifies as appropriate practices consistent with a whole language approach and identifies as inappropriate practices commonly found in basal reader/phonics-based programs (Bredekamp & Copple, 1997, p. 172).

Table 43.1   NAEYC 1997 Developmentally Appropriate Versus Developmentally Inappropriate Reading Instruction

Appropriate	*Inappropriate*
Children have numerous opportunities to read or hear high-quality children's literature and nonfiction for pleasure and information; discuss readings; draw, dictate, and write about their experiences; plan and implement projects involving research at suitable levels of difficulty; jointly create with teachers lists of steps to follow in accomplishing a project; interview various people to obtain information for projects; make books; listen to recordings or view films of children's books; and use the school library and classroom reading areas regularly.	The focus of the reading program is the basal reader, used primarily in reading groups and with accompanying workbooks and work sheets. Even capable readers must complete the same work sheets and the basal reader, although they have skills and interests in reading far more advanced material. Less able readers are given very limited exposure to interesting text. Through groupings teachers use, they make it clear which children are in the lowest reading group.

Thus, even though the 1997 editors call for an end to either/or thinking, they later articulate a clear declaration aligning whole language with best practice and basal reading programs with poor-quality teaching (e.g., disregarding students' reading level and humiliating them). Missing from DAP is a discussion of how teachers might implement best practice strategies within a basal reading curriculum or how the two approaches might be combined.

Empirical Difficulties

There are two major weaknesses in the empirical support for DAP. First, many recommended strategies have no empirical basis. The 1997 statement claims 12 empirically derived principles which drive DAP recommendations. But more often than not, the guidelines make recommendations without providing empirical evidence, or, in many cases, merely provide a citation without making explicit links between research findings and the recommended strategy. As mentioned earlier, the 1987 statement says children of all ages "need uninterrupted periods of time to become involved, investigate, select, and persist at activities" without discussing how much time children need at various ages, how uninterrupted time benefits children's development, or how research from the cited references supports the recommendation.

Further, when discussing how to respond to child misbehavior, the 1987 statement says, "Adults facilitate the development of self-esteem by respecting, accepting, and comforting children, regardless of the child's behavior." The statement goes on to describe respectful ways practitioners can interact with young children with which many would agree; however, there is no empirical support offered for the idea that comforting children regardless of their behavior "facilitates the development of self-esteem." There *is* empirical evidence, however, that comfort or affection following misbehavior will likely increase misbehavior (Ormrod, 2008; Skinner, 1984).

The second weakness in the empirical support for DAP is inconsistent evidence linking DAP with improved educational outcomes. One challenge facing DAP is its claim that developmental research neatly translates into specific applications. But this is not the case. Most developmental research, especially the work of Piaget, occurred in controlled, laboratory settings that may not transfer to classrooms (Ormrod, 2008; Piaget, 1952). Contemporary clinical research also has limited direct applicability to educational settings. For example, despite the plethora of new information about brain development, relatively little is known about how young children actually learn (Neuman & Roskos, 2005). Thus, laboratory science is insufficient to inform effective classroom practice.

Findings from applied research on DAP are also insufficient. Studies in the 1990s seemed to support the effectiveness of DAP (Raines & Johnston, 2003). Researchers found a positive effect for cognition and emotional factors and that DAP was beneficial for all children regardless of race or socioeconomic backgrounds. Interestingly, research on social development—a primary focus for DAP classrooms—was inconclusive (Raines & Johnston, 2003). Recent research is not so favorable. For example, according to Van Horn, Karlin, Ramey, Aldridge, & Snyder (2005), DAP is related to better educational outcomes in some areas for some students, and other studies find little to no improvement in educational outcomes. Effects of developmentally appropriate versus developmentally inappropriate instruction vary by children's grade level, gender, SES background, and ethnicity. Van Horn et al. (2005) elaborate: "The research assessing the effectiveness of DAP is highly inconsistent. These studies suggest differential patterns of outcomes for developmentally inappropriate practices (DIP) and DAP programs across academic subjects, in particular, that *DIP may be more effective than DAP* [italics added] for teaching reading skills" (p. 336).

Theoretical Difficulties

Theory is the foundation of any scientifically informed field of practice: it frames what is known, determines which questions need to be asked, and informs inferences about best practice. Much of the controversy regarding DAP can be traced to a particular view of development (espoused by Piaget and many of his contemporaries) called stage theory. In developmental theory *stage* is specifically defined as "a hierarchical progression of growth spurts with periods of plateau in between." These growth spurts are marked by qualitative developmental change in which the quality (not merely the quantity) of a child's skill or ability is distinctly different than it was previously. The child is able to think more complexly. For example, Piaget demonstrated that preschool children are unable to conserve mass, volume, or number—that is, they have difficulty maintaining a correct understanding of how much there is of something if the appearance of it changes though the amount remains the same. If one shows a 4-year-old a 3-inch tall, 2-inch diameter cylinder of clay, and then, while the child is watching, smashes the clay into a 1-inch thick pancake with a 4-inch diameter, the child will almost always say the pancake has less clay than the cylinder. After about the age of 6, when posed with the same dilemma, children roll their eyes at the absurd question and indicate that of course the amount of clay remains the same. The understanding that the amount of clay remains the same, despite its appearance, requires the child to attend to and process two dimensions (height and width) simultaneously and to also mentally reverse the process (unsmash the clay). Piaget also demonstrated that preschoolers reason from an egocentric point of view—they do not take another person's perspective—and that adolescents reason abstractly whereas elementary age children do not.

In a strict stage theory, each stage starts and ends by attaining more complex forms of mental manipulation. In between these qualitative change bookends lies a developmental plateau—a period of time during which relatively little developmental growth occurs. According to stage theory, progression through stages occurs spontaneously according to genetically programmed timelines. It is believed that age-related development occurs with minimal variation regardless of environment. Thus, one expects certain skills and behaviors of a 3-year-old child and qualitatively different skills and behaviors of a 10-year-old. This belief in maturational unfolding also has implications for adult-child interactions. Because cognitive stages are thought to unfold without adult assistance, Piaget's stage theory describes limited roles for adults in young children's experiences. Piaget believed adult involvement in many aspects of children's activities such as play, actually interferes with children's development (Morrow & Schickedanz, 2006).

Recently, many have questioned the soundness of strict stage theory. Contemporary developmental research indicates developmental stages are not as closely related to age as previously thought (Bredekamp & Copple, 1997; Ormrod, 2008). For example, when conditions differ from Piaget's controlled experiments, many preschool children readily conserve mass, liquid, and number. Further, many preschool children demonstrate an understanding of other people's feelings, and elementary age children frequently demonstrate abstract thought. New brain research indicates children's brains produce new neurons and neural connec-

tions, reorganize and strengthen existing neural pathways, and de-clutter brain structures by pruning superfluous neurons (Sousa, 2006) even when there is no observable evidence of cognitive growth. Research also indicates these neurological processes are highly affected by children's experiences. Neurons that are not stimulated die off. Yet it may take weeks, if not longer, for neural connections to become organized and strengthened enough to support observable developmental change. Thus, periods of plateau during which development does not appear to advance is anything but stagnant. By waiting for observable readiness to emerge, as posited by stage theory, parents and educators may withhold development-promoting experiences. In deference to these empirical developments, the 1997 DAP statement notes that "there are serious limitations to the use of age-related data" (Bredekamp & Copple, p. 37). Still, the NAEYC list of empirically-based principles does not discuss the new empirical findings related to the limitations of stage-based decision making. Practitioners who do not carefully read the entire 185-page document may not discover this crucial shift in NAEYC's position.

Although stage theory can outline a rough idea about how young children develop, evidence does not support the use of developmental stages to frame what is appropriate to expect of typically developing children at different ages or to define rules of practice or standards for instruction.

Future Directions for Early Childhood Theory, Research, and Best Practice

To reiterate, educating young children is a complex and messy affair. Such an endeavor requires guiding theories that explain contradictory and multifaceted phenomena. One such theory was developed by Lev Vygotsky, a Russian educational psychologist (1897–1934). Vygotskian theory, also called sociocultural theory, has gained increasing popularity over the past three decades. Vygotskian theory agrees with the Piagetian belief that children construct knowledge from their environment rather than merely absorb it and that qualitative change is an important part of children's development.

In sharp contrast, however, Vygotsky believed learning could lead development, rather than developmental attainment being a prerequisite for learning. Translating Vygotskian notions into developmentally appropriate terminology: DAP (for any age) are practices in which adults (or more skilled learners) provide experiences and help that allow learners to perform tasks and skills they would not be able to perform independently. These experiences further children's development. Thus, sociocultural theory contrasts with the view that one must wait for development to unfold before teaching children more complex skills and that by merely providing an enriched physical environment children will spontaneously construct knowledge and acquire skill.

There are several other important ways in which socio-cultural theory differs from Piagetian theory that provide for richer, more complex conceptualizations of early childhood best practice. Piaget and Vygotsky's theories were developed from very different theoretical questions. Whereas Piaget was interested in how children construct knowledge, Vygotsky was frustrated with the dichotomies between psychological theories. Vygotsky sought to unify dichotomies. Indeed he praised an American behaviorist, Thorndike, for his empirically sound and educationally practical descriptions of psychological theory. In his preface to the Russian translation of an educational psychology text written by Thorndike, Vygotsky says, "The most important feature of Thorndike's book—its practical orientation . . . is evident from the structure of each sentence. It is wholly geared to practice, wholly created to meet the needs of the school" (Vygotsky, 1926/1997, p. 149). Yet Vygotsky also praised Piaget: "Psychology owes a great deal to Jean Piaget. It is not an exaggeration to say that he revolutionized the study of the child's speech and thought" (Vygotsky, 1934/1986). A Vygotskian orientation can help researchers and practitioners step back from the DAP debate and consider how seemingly opposing ideas can explain how young children develop and learn. For example, Vygotskian practitioners do not ask if play or academic work is appropriate or inappropriate for young children. Rather, they ask how adults can support children's play and academic work so that the activities promote learning and development (Bodrova & Leong, 2007; John-Steiner & Mahn, 1996).

Vygotsky's theory also relies on a different developmental metaphor than Piaget's stair-step maturation. For Vygotsky, development entails the passing on of cultural or cognitive tools. In the same way that physical tools help people master their physical environment, cognitive tools help people master their psychological or intellectual environment. Vygotsky believed that children developed by internalizing increasingly complex cognitive tools used by their culture. For example, contemporary cultures use traffic signs and rules to organize how vehicles and pedestrians travel. As children develop, adults help them learn these rules of the road so that they can get around safely. Similarly, young children learn counting (a cognitive tool) to master the quantitative aspects of their environment. They use this tool when they are told they may have two cookies or that three children may leave a kindergarten room to get a drink. As children develop, these tools facilitate their acquisition of even more complex tools (counting helps children later learn addition).

Vygotsky viewed development as adults turning over increasingly complex cognitive tools to young children through a process he called mediation. Mediation occurs within what Vygotsky called the zone of proximal development, or ZPD. The ZPD represents the developmental zone between what the child can do independently and the child's maximum performance when provided with adult or peer assistance. For example, a 4-year-old child may not be able to count 20 objects independently, but with an adult holding her hand and counting with her, the child begins to coordinate all the necessary cognitive and fine motor movements to one day count independently.

Vygotskian practitioners do not ask if it is appropriate to teach 4-year-olds early literacy skills. Instead, if the skill represents a necessary cognitive tool, they develop ways to mediate the required tool within the child's ZPD. Methods might include setting up print rich play areas (Morrow, 1991), engaging children in literacy events during dramatic play (Morrow & Schickedanz, 2006), helping children develop written plans that describe their play (Bodrova & Leong, 2007), and using direct instruction.

Because development is conceptualized as the mediation of culturally defined cognitive tools, culture is the central developmental consideration. Thus Vygotsky's theory is compatible with culturally diverse child-rearing practices. Sociocultural practitioners do not categorize child-directed activities as appropriate and adult-directed activities as inappropriate. Rather they recognize that children need the ability to initiate and regulate self-selected activity and the ability to follow adult directives. Neither is inappropriate.

Piaget's and Vygotsky's theories also differ regarding the role of adults in children's development. Piaget acknowledged the importance of social interactions, especially in regard to peer interactions in moral development. But he was much more concerned with children's interactions with objects. Stressing the motivating nature of children's curiosity, he encouraged the practice of letting young children freely explore environments enriched with interesting objects. With such exploration, cognitive development was assumed to spontaneously emerge. Thus, Piagetian practice promotes hands-off roles for parents and teachers in early learning experiences and especially in children's play (Morrow & Schickedanz, 2006).

Vygotsky, however, differentiated between those cognitive skills that emerge spontaneously and those that require mediation by more competent members of the culture. He demonstrated that lower mental functions, such as reflexes or automatically attending to the source of a startling sound, emerge spontaneously but that higher mental functions, such as deliberate or focused attention, language, and logical reasoning, do not emerge spontaneously—rather they are mediated by more competent individuals. Therefore, interactions between mentors and children are crucial to development. From a sociocultural perspective, teachers and parents should actively engage young children in joint activity during which adults mediate important cognitive tools. In a Vygotskian frame, adults have significant and active roles in sociodramatic play (play in which children take on and act out imaginary adult roles and themes).

Sociocultural theory provides a unifying way to think about the major controversies affecting early childhood education. The theory provides a helpful way to frame research and practice regarding play and academics. Lesley Mandel Morrow has studied the effects of adults engaging preschool children in literacy activities during sociodramatic play. She and her colleagues found that children engage in literacy activities more often when adults help guide their play than when children simply play in print rich environments (Morrow & Schickedanz, 2006).

In another example of how Vygotskian theory can help early childhood best practice move past the DAP debate, early childhood researchers Elena Bodrova and Deborah Leong (2001) developed tools for teachers to use to scaffold young children's acquisition of early literacy skills during sociodramatic play. In their program, teachers help kindergarten children develop play plans in which children describe their intended play activities. At first, children dictate plans to an adult who represents the child's ideas in simple drawings and words. Then children draw their own pictures and dictate verbal descriptions to an adult scribe. In the final stage, children illustrate and write their own plans. Using play plans scaffolds children's ability to mentally represent how they will play, to record those plans in print representations, and then to use those print representations to guide their play.

Bodrova and Leong (2001) compared urban kindergartens in their program with similar urban schools that used traditional methods. Children in the experimental schools demonstrated significantly stronger early literacy skills. Kindergarteners in the experimental program wrote more words, increased the complexity of their writing, and demonstrated more improvement in sound-symbol correspondence, better understanding of the concept of a sentence, better phonemic encoding of words, more consistent use of writing conventions, and more accurately spelled words. Their research and the work of other sociocultural researchers demonstrates the potential for sociocultural theory to resolve the theoretical and empirical difficulties faced by the early childhood field and yield a framework for reconceptualizing early childhood best practices.

Conclusion

In its advocacy for meaningful educational experiences for young children, NAEYC adopted a developmentally appropriate framework for identifying and describing early childhood best practice. NAEYC's developmentally appropriate practice position statement has drawn both criticism and praise, prompting NAEYC to revise the position statement and attempt to clarify misunderstandings. Still, greater definitional, theoretical, and empirical clarification of early childhood best practice is needed. The early childhood field needs definitions of best practice that support complex understanding of how children learn and develop. There is a growing consensus that for young children those things academic are intrinsically embedded in relationships, imagination, and creativity. When a child climbs into a teacher's lap to share a story or composes a make-believe shopping list, it is neither academic nor nonacademic. It is both, and more.

Recently, NAEYC leaders have moved the organization toward better definitions of early childhood best practice. Marilou Hyson, Associate Executive Director for Professional Development at NAEYC, recently highlighted changes in how NAEYC conceptualizes early childhood classrooms:

> Our understanding of the place of academic content in the early childhood classroom has changed [since the 1980s]. Without a nurturing, playful, responsive environment, an academic focus may diminish children's engagement and motivation. But a 'child-centered' environment that lacks intellectual challenges also falls short of what curious young learners deserve. (2003, p. 23)

Similarly, a 2003 NAEYC publication encourages "approaches that favor some type of systematic code instruction along with meaningful connected reading report children's superior progress" (Neuman, Copple, & Bredekamp, 2003, p. 12).

These changes are encouraging. Still, if new conceptualizations about teaching young children are to significantly influence early childhood practice, changes must also be made in theoretical reasoning and terminology. Critical analysis of developmental theory requires differentiating between Piaget and Vygotsky. Such a differentiation allows the use of Piagetian theory to describe general patterns of cognitive development. Adopting a sociocultural model would allow early childhood best practice to move beyond dichotomies and to embrace culture as the central consideration in teaching young children. Sociocultural theory holds great promise for helping educators and researchers redefine early childhood best practice. Still, caution must be exercised as the field moves forward. No theory can adequately describe all aspects of how best to stimulate children's growth. Wherever sociocultural theory fails to adequately inform early childhood practice, the theory must either be further developed, refined, or used in conjunction with other theories.

Moving past dichotomous thinking and embracing more complex theoretical models also requires a change in terminology. The language of a discipline defines the discipline (Vygotsky, 1926/1997). Attempting to define how young children should be taught through an appropriate versus inappropriate dichotomy fosters misunderstanding and inhibits rich, complex thinking. Adopting a best practice sociocultural model would allow the early childhood field to be shaped by a variety of valid and important perspectives.

References and Further Readings

Bergeron, B. S. (1990). What does the term whole language mean? Constructing a definition from the literature. *Journal of Reading Behavior, 22,* 301–329.

Bodrova, E., & Leong, D. L. (2001). Tools of the mind: A case study of implementing the Vygotskian approach in American early childhood and primary classrooms. (Innodata Monographs 7). International Bureau of Education, Geneva, Switzerland.

Bodrova, E., & Leong, D. L. (2007). *Tools of the mind: The Vygotskian approach to early childhood education.* Upper Saddle River, NJ: Merrill/Prentice Hall.

Bredekamp, S. (Ed.) (1987). *Developmentally appropriate practice in early childhood programs serving children from birth through age 8: Expanded edition.* Washington, DC: National Association for the Education of Young Children.

Bredekamp, S., & Copple, C. (Eds.). (1997). *Developmentally appropriate practice in early childhood programs: Revised edition.* Washington, DC: National Association for the Education of Young Children.

Delpit, L. D. (1988). The silenced dialogue: Power and pedagogy in educating other people's children. *Harvard Educational Review, 58,* 280–298.

Dickinson, D. K. (2002). Shifting images of developmentally appropriate practice as seen through different lenses. *Educational Researcher, 31*(1), 26–32.

Goldstein, L. S., & Andrews, L. (2004). Best practices in a Hawaiian kindergarten: Making a case for *Na honua mauli ola. hulili: Multidisciplinary research on Hawaiian wellbeing, 1,* 133–146.

Gutierrez, K. D., & Rogoff, B. (2003). Cultural ways of learning: Individual traits or repertoires of practice. *Educational Researcher, 32,* 19–25.

Hyson, M. (2003). Putting early academics in their place. *Educational Leadership, (60)*7, 20–23.

Jeynes, W. H., & Little, S. W. (2000). A meta-analysis of studies examining the effect of whole-language instruction on the literacy of low-SES students. *The Elementary School Journal, 101,* 21–33.

John-Steiner, V., & Mahn, H. (1996). Sociocultural approaches to learning and development: A Vygotskian framework. *Educational Psychologist, 31,* 191–206.

Kagan, S. L., & Lowenstein, A. E. (2004). School readiness and children's play: Contemporary oxymoron or compatible option? In E. F. Zigler, D. G. Singer, & S. J. Bishop-Josef (Eds.), *Children's play: The roots of reading* (pp. 59–76). Washington, DC: Zero to Three Press.

Karp, N. (2006). Designing models of professional development at the local, state, and national levels. In M. Zaslow & I. Martinez-Beck (Eds.), *Critical issues in early childhood professional development* (pp. 225–230). Baltimore: Brookes.

Kessler, S. A. (1991). Early childhood education as development: Critique of the metaphor. *Early Education and Development, 2,* 137–152.

Lubeck, S. (1998). Is DAP for everyone? A response. *Childhood Education, 74,* 299–302.

Morrow, L. M. (1991). Promoting literacy during play by designing early childhood classroom environments. *The Reading Teacher, 44,* 396–402.

Morrow, L. M., & Schickedanz, J. A. (2006). The relationships between sociodramatic play and literacy development. In D. K. Dickenson & S. B. Neuman (Eds.), *Handbook of early literacy research: Volume 2.* New York: Guilford Press.

Neuman, S. B., Copple, C., & Bredekamp, S. (2003) *Learning to read and write: Developmentally appropriate practices for young.* Washington, DC: National Association for the Education of Young Children.

Neuman, S. B., & Roskos, K. (2005). The state of state pre-kindergarten standards. *Early Childhood Research Quarterly, 20,* 125–145.

O'Brien, L. M. (1996). Turning my world upside down: How I learned to question developmentally appropriate practice. *Childhood Education, 73,* 100–103.

Ormrod, J. E. (2008). *Educational psychology: Developing learners* (6th ed.). Upper Saddle River, NJ: Pearson.

Piaget, J. (1952). *The origins of intelligence in children* (M. Cook, Trans.). New York: Holt.

Raines, S. C., & Johnston, J. M. (2003). Developmental appropriateness: New contexts and challenges. In J. P. Isenberg & M. R. Jalongo (Eds.), *Major trends and issues in early childhood education: Challenges, controversies and insights* (2nd ed.). New York: Teachers College Press.

Skinner, B. F. (1984). The shame of American education. *American Psychologist, 39,* 947–954.

Sousa, D. A. (2006). *How the brain learns* (3rd ed.). Thousand Oaks, CA: Corwin Press.

Stipek, D. (2006). No Child Left Behind comes to preschool. *The Elementary School Journal, 106,* 255–265.

Van Horn, M. L., Karlin, E. O., Ramey, S. L., Aldridge, J., & Snyder, S. W. (2005). Effects of developmentally appropriate practices on children's development: A review of research and discussion of methodological and analytic issues. *The Elementary School Journal, 105,* 325–351.

Vygotsky, L. (1986). *Thought and language* (A. Kozulin, Trans.). Boston: The MIT Press. (Original work published 1934)

Vygotsky, L. (1997). Preface to Thorndike. In R. W. Rieber & J. Wollock (Eds.), *The collected works of L. S. Vygotsky: Volume 3: Problems of the theory and history of psychology* (R. Van Der Veer, Trans.). New York: Plenum Press. (Original work published 1926)

Zigler, E. F., Singer, D. G., & Bishop-Josef, S. J. (2004). Introduction. In E. F. Zigler, D. G. Singer, & S. J. Bishop-Josef (Eds.), *Children's play: The roots of reading* (pp. 15–32). Washington, DC: Zero to Three Press.

44

SPECIAL EDUCATION

JAMES M. KAUFFMAN

University of Virginia, Professor Emeritus

Special education is intended for students who are exceptional—significantly different from the average. The difference may be either desirable or undesirable. Just how different from average and in what ways a student must be different to merit special education are perpetual controversies. Furthermore, a difference alone does not entitle a student to special education under current law: the difference must interfere to a significant extent with his or her education. Just what constitutes significant interference with education is a matter of judgment and therefore another perpetual issue. In spite of controversies, special education is now an integral part of public education about which every teacher should know (Kauffman & Hallahan, 2005; Huefner, 2006).

Most students receiving special education have disabilities. They are far below average in one or more of the following abilities, with related special education categories included in italics: thinking (cognition; *mental retardation*), academic learning (learning not consistent with intellectual ability; *specific learning disability*), recognizing and controlling emotions or behavior *(emotional disturbance)*, using speech in communication *(communication disorder)*, hearing *(deafness or impaired hearing)*, seeing *(blindness or impaired vision)*, moving or maintaining physical well-being *(physical disability or other health impairment)*. Special education categories also include *autism* (or *autism spectrum disorders*), *traumatic brain injury*, and *severe* or *multiple disabilities (e.g., deaf-blindness)*. These students have been or can be predicted to be unsuccessful in the general education curriculum with instruction by a regular classroom teacher (Kauffman & Hallahan, 2005).

Special education is also appropriate for students whose abilities are significantly above average—those with special gifts or talents. Gifted education receives comparatively little attention and has not been mandated by federal law as of 2007. It has been left to state and local education authorities (Hallahan, Kauffman, & Pullen, 2009).

A variety of words may be used to describe exceptionality, including *emotional or behavioral disorder* (rather than *emotional disturbance*), *autism* or *Asperger syndrome* (instead of *autism spectrum disorder*), *challenge* (rather than *disorder* or *disability*), or a more general term, such as *developmental disability*. The variety and change in labels makes special education difficult to study, but the key points are that students with disabilities have problems that significantly impede their school progress and gifted/talented students learn extraordinarily fast.

History

Special education was offered in mid-19th-century institutions for blind, deaf, and mentally retarded persons. By about the mid-20th century, special education for blind, deaf, physically disabled, mentally retarded, emotionally disturbed, communication-impaired, and gifted students was common in American public schools. Most special education in that era was provided in special classes and special schools.

In the later decades of the 20th century, special education categories of specific learning disability, autism, and traumatic brain injury were added. Other disabling conditions, such as attention deficit disorder (ADD, later called attention-deficit/hyperactivity disorder, or ADHD) were recognized in the 20th century but were not then accorded a specific category in special education law. Beginning in the 1970s, special education was mandated by federal law for all students with disabilities in the legally recognized categories. Those with problems not having a particular category (e.g., ADHD) were covered under the law only if they could be included under an existing category (e.g., specific learning disability or other health impairment in the case of ADHD; Hallahan et al., 2009).

Professional and Parent Organizations

Organizations of professionals and parents have played a major role in the development of special education. In the 1920s, the Council for Exceptional Children (CEC) was founded. It is an international organization, primarily composed of educators dedicated to advocacy of special education for disabled and gifted students. Most other professional organizations with concern for students with specific exceptionalities originated in the early to mid-20th century. Other parent organizations advocating services for children with particular exceptionalities, such as The Arc (originally the Association for Retarded Children), also date from the 20th century. Many advances in treatment and law would not have occurred at all or would have been delayed for a much longer time without the advocacy of parents (Hallahan et al., 2009).

Federal Special Education Law

Until 1975, special education for students with disabilities was left to state or local law. In 1975, the federal law now known as IDEA (in its 2004 version, the *Individuals with Disabilities Education Improvement Act,* IDEIA) mandated special education for all students judged to have disabilities. The law has been renamed and revised several times since 1975, with the most recent revision as of this writing being in 2004 and sometimes referred to as IDEA 2004 (Huefner, 2006; Yell, 2005).

The federal law was enacted primarily in response to the demands of parents of children with disabilities that the needs of their children be addressed by public education. IDEA requires not only appropriate education for all students with disabilities but related and supplementary services as well. Major provisions of the law from its inception until its 2004 version include a free appropriate public education (FAPE) in the least restrictive environment (LRE) chosen for each individual from a continuum of alternative placements (CAP) and delivered according to an Individualized Education Program (IEP). Related and supplementary services allow the student to receive FAPE and might include transportation, physical therapy, or other help.

Not all of the requirements of IDEA are mentioned here, only the central ones. Furthermore, IDEA is not the only law addressing disabilities and special education or the only federal law governing public education.

International Scope

The historical foundations of special education can be traced to Europe in the late 18th and early 19th centuries. Special education flourished in many European nations during the 20th century, and it also became a prominent part of American public schooling in the 20th century. By the late 20th century, special education had become a part of public education in all developed nations of the world. All of the major concepts and issues discussed here apply to all nations of the world in which special education is offered (Hallahan et al., 2009).

Major Concepts in Special Education

In the late 20th and early 21st centuries, approximately 1 in 10 students in U.S. public schools received special education. Before the federal law was passed, many students with disabilities received no education or were institutionalized. After federal law required schools to provide special education in 1975, the percentage of the school population receiving special education grew substantially and fewer children were sent to institutions. Understanding basic concepts about exceptionality and special education will help teachers avoid making inappropriate assumptions and referring students for special education who do not need it (Kauffman & Hallahan, 2005).

Inability Versus Disability

An inability is not always a disability, but a disability is always an inability. Inability simply means that a person cannot do something, but the reason may be due to a disability, age, or a lack of receiving effective instruction. A disability means that a person cannot do something that most people of the same age receiving similar instruction can do. Before identifying a student as having a disability, it is critically important to make sure that he or she has had sufficient opportunities to learn.

Disability Versus Handicap

A disability is something a person cannot do, although the circumstances (e.g., age, instruction, environment) would lead you to expect that the person should be able to do it. A handicap is a circumstance imposed on a person so that they cannot do what they could if the conditions are changed or the environment is altered. For example, lack of a ramp imposes a handicap on a person who uses a wheelchair. The person may have a disability in walking or climbing stairs but have a handicap when it comes to entering a building or classroom that has no access other than stairs. Appropriate adaptations remove a handicap for a person who can use a computer but cannot use it in the standard way because of a disability (e.g., cannot type using his or her fingers because of physical impairment). For these reasons, appropriate modifications and adaptations are mandated in school facilities, equipment, and programs.

High- and Low-Incidence, Mild and Severe, and Multiple Disabilities

Some disabilities occur more often than others. Disabilities that occur relatively frequently—high-incidence categories—include communication disorders, specific learning disability (SLD), mental retardation (MR), and emotional disturbance (ED).

Most disabilities are mild; relatively few are severe. Communication disorders, SLD, MR, or ED can be severe even though they are high-incidence disabilities. Significant impairment of hearing or vision is comparatively uncommon, so both are considered low-incidence disabilities. Total deafness or blindness is severe and low-incidence as well.

Disabilities may also occur in combination. For example, a student may have both mental retardation and emotional disturbance; brain injury and communication disorders in combination with emotional disturbance; physical disability, impaired vision, mental retardation, and communication disorders. Combinations of disabilities—multiple disabilities—make an individual's problems more difficult to address and may make the person's disability severe even though the separate disabilities are relatively mild. Deaf-blindness, which is by definition a multiple and severe disability, is extremely low-incidence. Some disabilities (brain injury and autism spectrum disorders, for example) are nearly always multiple (Stichter, Conroy, & Kauffman, 2008).

Nature and Degree of Difference

Both disabilities and giftedness are differences of degree in particular abilities. Exceptionalities are differences in abilities valued by a society. Differences in color of skin, hair, or eyes, for example, do not matter much to most people, although differences in ability to move, talk, read, and reason do matter a lot in our society for purposes of defining disability or giftedness. Not every difference from the typical defines a disability in our society—only differences judged to be significant do. Ability to reason, for example, may be considered a disability only if it is far below that of typical individuals the same age or a gift only if it is far above those the same age. Disabilities and giftedness are just matters of judgment that (a) the difference in question matters for purposes of defining exceptionality in education and (b) the difference is extreme enough to meet a stated criterion.

Disabilities and Abilities

A major concept in special education is that a person's disability does not preclude finding that the person has important abilities. For example, a child may have a severe physical disability but have average or even superior cognitive ability. Assuming that an individual who cannot move very much or very skillfully cannot think well is a mistake that special education is designed to avoid. Moreover, it is now well understood that some individuals are twice exceptional—that is, they have extraordinary gifts or talents combined with a disability, perhaps even severe and multiple disabilities. Special education is intended to focus on making the maximum use of the abilities a student has regardless of any disabilities that he or she might have.

Major Controversies

Special education is characterized by controversies generated by three realities: (1) special education now accounts for a substantial proportion of the school population and an even greater proportion of the education budget, (2) American society has been sensitized to abuse and neglect of people who have disabilities, and (3) American society is ambivalent about education for its gifted students. These critical realities must be considered in addressing any of the controversies discussed here; otherwise, any proposed solution will fail eventually, if not immediately. Both the monetary and the social costs and benefits of special education must be considered to garner public support (Hallahan et al., 2009; Kauffman & Hallahan, 2005).

Language

The language of special education can be very confusing. Not only is it characterized by many acronyms (e.g., LRE for least restrictive environment; SLD for specific learning disability; CEC for Council for Exceptional Children), but it often includes labels that are indistinguishable in practice (e.g., emotional disturbance, emotional and behavioral disorders, behavior disorders, behavioral challenges, and so on).

Specific labels generate a lot of controversy, in part because they are sometimes used inappropriately or abusively, as epithets rather than as helpful descriptors. Certain terminology is denounced by nearly everyone as both outmoded and derogatory (e.g., idiot, moron, imbecile, which were 19th-century terms used to designate various degrees of mental retardation). Other terms, such as *mental retardation,* are now said by some, but not most, people to be regressive and derogatory. The organization first known as the American Association on Mental Deficiency (AAMD) later changed its name to the American Association on Mental Retardation (AAMR) and then to the American Association on Intellectual and Developmental Disabilities (AAIDD). In general, attempts have been made to change words (labels) to signify the same phenomenon with terms considered less offensive. Thus, disabilities and disorders are sometimes called challenges under the assumption that *challenge* is a less stigmatizing term.

In essence, some argue that labels with negative connotations should be studiously avoided because they are stigmatizing. Others counter that the problem of stigma is not found in the word itself but in how people interpret the term (e.g., that *mental retardation* is stigmatizing only because of how people view what we call mental retardation, not because of the term itself). Changing the term, they argue, confuses people temporarily but does nothing to resolve the problem of stigma because people soon attach the same meanings to the new term as to the old one. Using a euphemism (a supposedly more pleasant term) to refer to undesirable characteristics fools people for a short time and results in a backlash of ridicule when people figure out what the euphemism refers to.

One controversy regarding language is whether we should use what is called person-first language. Advocates of person-first language consider it inappropriate to refer to an *emotionally disturbed child;* rather, they contend, one should use the construction *child with emotional disturbance.* The idea is that individuals are not their disabilities. Hence, it is wrong to refer to a *physically disabled young man* because the inference could be drawn that the disability defines the young man or sums up his existence. *Young man with a physical disability* is ostensibly better language because it signifies the young man first and indicates that he has a disability, not that he is a disability or that his disability defines him. Others argue that person-first language is not only cumbersome but calls special attention to a person's disability by its unusual construction. For example, we consider it perfectly acceptable to refer to a car salesman and do not urge people to use the construction *man who sells cars* instead, and we may call a woman in a bank a teller or a redhead without assuming that being labeled as such leads us to assume that such designations define everything about her. Yet, the circumlocutions required by person-first language have been widely adopted.

Another argument about language is that the differences we call disabilities should not be considered undesirable. Accordingly, some do not wish to use terminology such as *person with a disability* but only speak of a *person with differing abilities.* Although some embrace this point of view, others observe that if disabilities are not recognized as such and considered undesirable there will be lots of confusion about what disabilities are and little or no motivation to address the special needs of those who have them.

Some have argued for an end to all labeling because labels are stigmatizing. Others counter with the observation that labels cannot be avoided unless we stop talking about the phenomenon to which we refer. They note that a label is only the word we use to describe something, and we cannot give up labeling it without giving up communication about whatever that thing is. Although it is true that

we can change labels or stop saying words that are in common use, the alternative to common labels is to speak in code or use euphemisms.

Identification

Identification of disabilities and giftedness by test scores alone or by judgment alone (whether that of a teacher, a psychologist, a parent, or someone else) is highly suspect. Those who identify students for special education, whether due to disabilities or giftedness or both, are expected to use their judgment in addition to the results of tests and measures of the student's performance. By law, no single test score and no one person's judgment is to be the basis for identification. In the past, it was too easy to identify a student as needing special education, or to overlook those who needed it, without sufficient evidence. Both false identification and failure to identify exceptionality are rightly considered abusive of a student's right to appropriate education.

Still controversial are the particular tests, performances, and judgments that should be used in identification. Also at issue, even given the particular tests, performances, or judges, is the criterion or cutoff for identification. The controversy about identification thus involves both measurement and judgment.

All measurement contains error, regardless of the test or assessment procedure. That is, no measurement is perfect. Any test or other attempt to measure performance will result in errors, both those known as false positives (false identification in this case) and false negatives (errors in which the individual should have been identified but was not). Consequently, the most accurate measurement—the measurement tool and procedure producing the fewest errors—is important so that as few individuals are falsely identified and as few are overlooked as possible. But another issue is judging which is the worse error to make—falsely identifying a child who has no disability or failing to identify a child who does. With any given procedure, false negatives will increase as false positives decrease, and vice versa; there is a reciprocal relationship between one type of error and the other. Although accuracy is important, one must weigh the consequences of the proportion of errors—mistakes in identifying students in proportion to mistakes in not identifying students.

Because of the inherent difficulties in measuring the things that are used to define disability and giftedness, some educators have proposed giving up measurement altogether. Their argument is that measurement is a useless, unreliable, biased, demeaning, and wasteful exercise. Others counter that measurement is essential for accountability and that giving up on measurement means reliance on unspecified, subjective judgments alone.

The criterion for any exceptionality is arbitrary. That is, a particular level of difference is chosen as the threshold for defining disability or giftedness, and it can be changed. Arbitrary in this context does not mean fickle, random, or detached from objective criteria, but merely chosen from among possibilities—constructed willfully, not determined by nature. Although this kind of arbitrariness characterizes many important rules and laws in our society (for example, voting or driving age, income defining poverty or a tax bracket, or the score required to pass a state test), we recognize the importance of having a criterion or cutoff.

Because defining exceptionality, regardless of how exceptionality is measured or judged, is arbitrary in the sense that the criterion can be (and in some cases has been) changed, some educators have argued for abandonment of identification. Their argument is that we should simply recognize that all students are different, and that differences are not something about which we can make good yes/no judgments regarding exceptionality. They object to sorting students into categories. Others counter that we cannot provide special education for students without identifying those who should receive it and that this requires sorting those who do have from those who do not have exceptionalities.

Perhaps the most controversial aspect of identification in IDEA 2004 is the introduction of the notion of response to intervention (RTI) as a means of identifying learning disabilities. RTI requires that the general education teacher use instructional practices and other interventions that scientific evidence supports and monitor their student's response. If the student responds to practices that scientific evidence supports, then he or she is not identified as needing special education; only if the student does not respond is special education considered. RTI is proposed as an alternative to identification of specific learning disability by a discrepancy—the difference between a student's performances on intelligence and achievement tests (with those showing a marked discrepancy between estimated ability and achievement being identified as having a specific learning disability). Some see RTI as the solution to improper identification; others see it as only another, and inferior, way of assessing individuals and determining whether they need special education. Those who question RTI ask how much response how quickly to what intervention is enough to avoid identification of a specific learning disability.

Identity and Self-Concept

Much has been made of the feelings of inferiority, disgust, fear, and other negative feelings attached to having a disability or to having a family member who has a disability. Ruined identity is one of the reasons for trying to find language that is easier to accept. But the designation of disability, regardless of the language used to describe it, seems always to bring disappointment, pain, and anxiety. In response to such reactions and in attempts to improve self-concept, some have taken the position that a particular difference (e.g., deafness) is not really a disability. They might argue that loss of a difference considered disabling threatens a person's cultural identity.

Others have noted that the most radical advocacy of disability rights seems contrary to the notion that disability does not define identity. A person can be proud of his or her identity without attaching positive value to all of his or her characteristics. People need affiliation some of the time with others who share their particular interests, problems, or characteristics, and people with exceptionalities are not exempted. Such affiliation is not always based on positive characteristics (consider Alcoholics Anonymous, for example). Furthermore, disabilities are, by definition, characteristics that most people in our society see as disadvantages that should be removed if possible. Finally, the counterargument goes, the disadvantages we call disabilities are not matters that can be humanely redefined as characteristics that do not matter or do not cause disadvantage. True, disappointment, pain, and anxiety accompany the designation of disability, but the same is true of physical illness or addiction. The most humane response to any exceptionality is not denial or redefinition but recognition, acceptance, and effective treatment.

Placement

Perhaps the most contentious issue in special education of the late 20th and early 21st centuries is place—in which schools and classrooms exceptional students should be taught. Using acronyms common in special education, IDEA calls for FAPE in the LRE chosen from a CAP—federal law requires free appropriate public education in the least restrictive environment chosen from a continuum of alternative placements. But the federal law is open to interpretation, and therein lies the controversy. Some, who advocate full inclusion (education of exceptional students in regular schools and classes only), deem education appropriate only if it is delivered in the regular classroom and consider the regular classroom least restrictive in all cases (or the LRE idea as outmoded). They also replace the requirement of a continuum of alternative placements with the idea of a continuum of alternative services (meaning that widely differing, alternative services can all be delivered in the regular classroom). Full inclusion is sometimes tempered to mean that inclusion in the regular classroom to the greatest extent possible is the most important goal—more important than effective instruction. That is, full inclusion, even in its tempered version, suggests that the place of instruction is more important than the effectiveness of instruction or that instruction is most effective only if it is delivered in a regular classroom.

Those who question inclusion (whether full or not) as the priority of special education point out that IDEA requires the following: (a) placement decisions made on an individual basis, not a policy of automatic inclusion or exclusion of all students with disabilities; (b) placement decisions made after, not before, determination of instructional needs; (c) greater concern for instruction than for location; and (d) not only a continuum of services but a full continuum of placement options including hospital or homebound instruction, residential education, special day schools, self-contained classes, resource rooms, and instruction in regular classrooms with special assistance as needed. IDEA prohibits placing a student in a group based solely on his or her categorical label, placement decisions made before determination of instructional need, elimination of placement options, and placement made because it is already available in a school district.

The inclusion controversy continues in special education because the place and the nature of instruction involve conflicting notions of discrimination, rights, and fairness, as well as conflicting criteria for success and interpretations of law. The controversy will not be resolved without agreement about achieving the goals of equal rights and fairness for students with exceptionalities. (Crockett & Kauffman, 1999).

Disproportionality

Some categories of special education contain proportions of students whose gender or ethnic identities are markedly discrepant from their proportion in the general school-age population. The most controversial disproportionalities involve the overrepresentation of African American students in special education for those with emotional disturbance and mental retardation and their underrepresentation in special education for the gifted. Some suggest that African American students are more often identified as having certain disabilities and less often identified as gifted because of racial bias or prejudice.

Others observe that African American children more often experience disadvantages and deprivations that may account for these disproportionalities. Research evidence to support unequivocally either explanation of the disproportionalities is lacking. Nevertheless, sound arguments have been made that social justice in American life requires that the inequities in education and disproportionalities in special education be addressed effectively and without delay. Clearly, this is one controversy involving the possible abuse and neglect of students by education, whether general or special, and by other agencies as well.

Still another issue involving special education is perception of the negative aspects of identification as having a disability and the benefits to those who receive special education because their disability is recognized. Those who decry the disproportional identification of African American students for special education for students with disabilities emphasize the spoiled sense of self that accompanies such identification and downplay the benefits of special education. Those who see disproportional identification in less negative terms tend to emphasize the benefits of receiving special education.

Relationship to General Education

The relationship between general and special education is a long-standing controversy. The proper role of each in relation to the other has been hotly debated, and attempts to improve the education of all children, such as the No Child Left Behind Act (NCLB), have added to the contentiousness. The issue is complicated by the placement of some students in regular classrooms for some subjects under IDEA.

In the past, students receiving special education because they had disabilities often did not take state-mandated tests, so their progress could not be compared to that of other students. Under IDEA and NCLB, most students with disabilities now must take the same tests as their nondisabled peers. Proponents of this requirement argue that most students with disabilities should be expected to pass the same tests as nondisabled students—in fact, that they can and will pass the same tests if they are given appropriate instruction. Those who question this expectation point out that it is unreasonable and unfair, and that although students with disabilities should be expected to achieve all they can, the average for those with disabilities will always be lower than the average for those without disabilities, even if both groups receive the best possible instruction.

In the 1970s, it became popular to call for the integration of general and special education, such that the difference between them would become increasingly imperceptible. A common suggestion was that general and special education should not be separate systems but a single system that serves all students. Those who questioned the demand for a single, integrated system pointed out that special and general education are both part of public education and, therefore, already part of a single system. They argued that any effective subpart of a system must have its own identity, authority, budget, and personnel (e.g., just as teacher education must have these in a university, special education must have them in public schools; and just as a research and development unit in a business must have these, various subunits of the public schools, such as athletics or music, must have them).

Another decades-old line of argument is that special education should develop and give to general education those ways of working with exceptional children that have been found successful, such that special education will gradually become superfluous (i.e., work itself out of business). Still another is that general education should become so effective and supple that it meets the needs of all students without the necessity of identifying any for special education. Those questioning these ideas have pointed out that realities of measurement preclude the elimination of low achievement and that special education will always be necessary to serve the extremes, regardless of how good general education becomes.

A popular idea of the late 20th and early 21st centuries is that general and special education teachers should work together. That is, they should collaborate and consult with each other to discover what is best for the student or coteach classes in which some, but not all, students are identified as having exceptionalities. Although collaboration, consultation, and coteaching captured the imagination of many, research has not shown that these are better than instruction from a special education teacher alone in meeting the needs of exceptional children. Those who question the collaboration, consulting, and coteaching models point to the necessity of individualized, focused, intensive, persistent instruction that a trained special education teacher alone can provide. They argue that although special education teachers do need to help general education teachers accommodate a wider range of pupils, students with disabilities need the specialized instruction that only a special education teacher working alone can provide.

Cost

Special education costs more per student than general education—in fact, several times more. Thus, although special education may serve 10% of the school population, it may account for 25% of the budget. The disproportional cost of special education is a particularly hot issue for administrators and taxpayers.

The extra costs of special education are not difficult to explain. Perhaps the most obvious and greatest contributor to higher cost is the student-teacher ratio; special education teachers generally teach much smaller groups of students than do general education teachers. Furthermore, special education students often require special transportation and other related services and special materials or equipment.

Those who decry the high cost of special education are likely to argue that too many students are identified as needing it and that equity demands equal expenditures for all students. Those who attempt to justify the high cost of special education are likely to argue that only those students who actually need special education have been identified and that equal opportunity for these students demands higher expenditures. The argument becomes how much is too much and how little is too little to spend for special education.

Special education is funded by a combination of local, state, and federal monies. The federal contribution to the extra cost of special education has never come close to that mentioned in federal legislation. Consequently, the cost of special education has become a particularly controversial issue for state and local authorities.

What Makes Special Education Special

Some have argued that special education is not really special, that good teaching is good teaching regardless of the students. According to this reasoning, a good general education teacher individualizes for students and can provide, as part of a truly flexible general education, anything that a special educator can provide.

In response, others have noted that special education often has not been what it should be, that it is often provided by poorly prepared teachers, and that it shares the same dimensions of instruction used in general education.

They argue that what makes special education truly special is not placement but instruction. Specifically, special education is instruction that is more highly individualized and makes use of special methods that are not feasible in general education. (Cook & Schirmer, 2006; Kauffman & Hallahan, 2005).

Individualization

One point of view is that individualization is part of teaching. That is, all teachers are expected to be aware of what each individual student is doing and make accommodation for individual differences. To the extent that a teacher does not meet these expectations, he or she is professionally inadequate.

A competing point of view is that special education teachers focus on the individual; general education teachers necessarily focus on the group. In fact, some have pointed out that IDEA is about education for individuals, whereas NCLB is about education for groups. According to this view, special education teachers go well beyond what general education teachers can be expected to do in the way of individualizing goals, making instructional adaptations, and meeting students' individual needs.

One can make the case that special education is not special because it individualizes for students whereas general education does not, but because it involves *greater* individualization. As is true of many other distinctions in life (consider the very definition of disability), the difference is one of degree, not of kind. Therefore, the distinction between general and special education is the degree of individualization, not the total absence of individualization (general) versus individualization (special).

Dimensions of Instruction

Greater individualization of education is possible in special education because of its modulation of several dimensions of instruction. Again, general education involves the use of all of these dimensions of instruction, and special education becomes special because of the degree to which a teacher is able to alter them. All teachers, whether in general or special education, use the same basic instructional strategies, but this small reality belies the larger truth that the degree to which these strategies are used matters a great deal.

The dimensions of instruction that a special education teacher may alter include at least the following: pacing or rate, intensity, persistence, structure, reinforcement, pupil-teacher ratio, curriculum, and monitoring or assessment. Special educators, to a greater degree than general educators, may vary the speed with which tasks are presented or the rate at which students proceed in subject matter. They may also vary to a greater degree the intensity of instruction, for example its demandingness, the repetitions required, and the size of the steps in learning. To a greater degree, they are able to alter the structure of their classrooms, meaning such things as rules, expectations, and teacher control. They may also vary to a greater degree the consequences of performance (reward, for example), pupil-teacher ratio, and the curriculum (what is taught). Finally, the frequency and type of monitoring and assessment of progress may be more finely attuned to the individual in special education.

Curriculum and Methods

Some students with exceptionalities study the same curriculum as general students, and their teachers use the methods considered appropriate for students without exceptionalities. In fact, one of the more successful accommodations for gifted students is acceleration, merely moving them ahead of their age mates in school grade. Other students require highly specialized curriculum (e.g., Braille and orientation and mobility skills for blind students; sign language for deaf students; basic self-care skills such as toileting, grooming, cooking, and dressing for those with severe mental retardation).

With IDEA 2004 and NCLB has come the expectation that all (or nearly all) students will learn the same curriculum and be assessed by the same tests. Thus there has been considerable pressure to align special education with the general education curriculum. Some special educators have suggested that Individualized Education Programs (IEPs) for students with disabilities should not be aligned with the general education curriculum because students with disabilities often need to learn different things in different ways compared to their peers who do not have disabilities.

Sometimes the curriculum and methods of instruction have been inappropriate for exceptional students receiving special education, as has been the case for students in general education. At its best, or in its truest sense, special education ensures that students who are exceptional, whether they have disabilities or are gifted or both, receive the specialized instruction that is most suitable for them as individuals. What is studied and how it is taught are not the same for all students.

Future Directions

The direction that special education will take in future years is anyone's guess (Hallahan et al., 2009). One possible scenario is that special education will collapse entirely, becoming an invisible part of general education. In fact, special education seems likely to vanish if two arguments are taken seriously: (1) whatever schooling is right and good for one student is right and good for all, and (2) all students should be expected to meet the same standards. Another possibility is that special education will shrink, such that only those with the most severe disabilities will be eligible for it. This seems likely if authorities recognize that a few students have truly special needs but argue that

special education has become too large, serves too many children, is often provided to children who do not actually need it, and takes too large a proportion of the education budget. Still another possible direction is resurgence and acceptance of assertions that special education is a good idea and that only improved teacher preparation and specialized, effective instruction can make special education what it should be. This is likely to occur only if there is agreement that special education is primarily about instruction, not place; that special education teachers must have special instructional skills; that special education is worth the extra cost; and that success should be judged by what students achieve with versus without special education, not by whether the achievement of exceptional children approximates that of typical students.

The future of special education depends on two primary considerations: (a) judgments of economic feasibility, given the fiscal constraints faced by the nation, states, and localities; and (b) public conceptions of fairness and social justice. Special education has always been in part about money and in part about society's attitudes toward children, fairness, and opportunity. Fairness and the worth of education for exceptional children will always be issues.

Conclusion

Special education is designed for exceptional learners—those far above or far below typical students in particular knowledge or skills. Exceptional learners may have special gifts or talents or have one or more disabilities: mental retardation, specific learning disability, emotional disturbance, communication disorder, impaired hearing, impaired sight, physical disability or other health impairment, autism spectrum disorders, traumatic brain injury, or severe or multiple disabilities. Sometimes other labels are used for these categories. Attention-deficit/hyperactivity disorder (ADHD) is sometimes considered a learning disability or is included as other health impairment.

Special education became a part of American public education in large cities in the late 19th century. Parent and professional organizations date from the early 20th century. The federal Individuals with Disabilities Education Act (IDEA) dates from 1975 and requires free appropriate public education (FAPE) in the least restrictive environment (LRE) chosen from a continuum of alternative placements (CAP) and delivered according to an Individualized Education Program (IEP). Special education is international in scope.

Major concepts in special education include: (a) distinction between inability and disability; (b) difference between disability and handicap; (c) related services; (d) recognition of mild, severe, high-incidence, low-incidence, and multiple disabilities; (e) nature and degree of difference; and (f) both abilities and disabilities are important and individuals can be twice exceptional, that is, have disabilities and special gifts or talents at the same time.

Major controversies in special education include: (a) the language used to describe exceptionalities; (b) identification, identity, and self-concept of individuals with exceptionalities; (c) placement; (d) disproportional identification; (e) the relationship between general and special education; and (f) cost. Special education is made special by individualized instruction and alteration of one or more of the following to an extent not feasible in general education: pacing or rate, intensity, persistence, structure, reinforcement, pupil-teacher ratio, curriculum, and monitoring or assessment.

The future of special education is unknown and could take any one of several directions. Its future will depend on judgments of economic feasibility, given the fiscal constraints faced by the nation, states, and localities, as well as public perceptions of fairness and social justice.

References and Further Readings

Byrnes, M. (Ed.). (2002). *Taking sides: Clashing views on controversial issues in special education.* New York: McGraw-Hill.

Cook, B. G., & Schirmer, B. R. (Eds.). (2006). *What's special about special education? Examining the role of evidence-based practices.* Austin, TX: PRO-ED.

Coots, J. J., & Stout, K. (Eds.). (2007). *Critical reflections about students with special needs: Stories from the classroom.* Boston: Allyn & Bacon.

Crockett, J. B., Gerber, M. M., & Landrum, T. J. (Eds.). (2007). *Achieving the radical reform of special education.* Mahwah, NJ: Lawrence Erlbaum Associates.

Crockett, J. B., & Kauffman, J. M. (1999). *The least restrictive environment: Its origins and interpretations in special education.* Mahwah, NJ: Lawrence Erlbaum.

Hallahan, D. P., Kauffman, J. M., & Pullen, P. C. (2009). *Exceptional learners: Introduction to special education* (11th ed.). Boston: Allyn & Bacon.

Huefner, D. S. (2006). *Getting comfortable with special education law: A framework for working with children with disabilities* (2nd ed.). Norwood, MA: Christopher-Gordon.

Kauffman, J. M., & Hallahan, D. P. (2005). *Special education: What it is and why we need it.* Boston: Allyn & Bacon.

Kauffman, J. M., & Hallahan, D. P. (Eds.). (2005). *The illusion of full inclusion* (2nd ed.). Austin, TX: Pro-Ed.

Lloyd, J. W., Kameenui, E. J., & Chard, D. (Eds.). (1997). *Issues in educating children with disabilities.* Mahwah, NJ: Lawrence Erlbaum Associates.

Mazurek, K., & Winzer, M. A. (Eds.). (1994). *Comparative studies in special education.* Washington, DC: Gallaudet University Press.

Morris, R. J., & Mather, N. (Eds.). (2008). *Evidence-based interventions for students with learning and behavioral challenges.* Mahwah, NJ: Lawrence Erlbaum Associates.

Sorrells, A. M., Rieth, H. J., & Sindelar, P. T. (Eds.). (2004). *Critical issues in special education: Access, diversity, and accountability.* Boston: Allyn & Bacon.

Speece, D. L., & Keogh, B. K. (Eds.). (1996). *Research on classroom ecologies: Implications for inclusion of children with learning disabilities.* Mahwah, NJ: Lawrence Erlbaum Associates.

Stichter, J. P., Conroy, M. A., & Kauffman, J. M. (2008). *An introduction to students with high-incidence disabilities.* Upper Saddle River, NJ: Merrill-Prentice Hall.

Warnock, M. (2005). *Special educational needs: A new look.* (Impact No. 11). London: Philosophy of Education Society of Great Britain.

Yell, M. L. (2005). *The law and special education* (2nd ed.). Upper Saddle River, NJ: Prentice Hall.

Ysseldyke, J. E., Algozzine, B., & Thurlow, M. L. (2000). *Critical issues in special education* (3rd ed.). Boston: Houghton Mifflin.

45

TEXTBOOK REFORM

JERE BROPHY

Michigan State University

Textbooks are supposed to serve as valuable learning resources for students by succinctly synthesizing the gist of the curriculum and helping them to understand and apply it. But analyses conducted in recent decades indicate that most American textbooks are not fulfilling these functions effectively. Instead of presenting networks of connected content structured around powerful ideas, they tend to address too much breadth in not enough depth. This makes it difficult for students to construct meaningful and connected understandings that they can apply to their lives outside of school. Consequently, students tend to rely on rote memorizing of disconnected bits of content that will be difficult to access and apply in the future. This chapter will describe this problem in detail, explain how it developed, consider how it might be remedied, and suggest ways that teachers might cope with it in the meantime.

Introduction

Textbooks are intended to be key instructional resources for K–12 teachers and students. They are not designed to be the only instructional resource, and curriculum content should not be limited to what is included on their pages. Nor should they be used in ways that limit students' school learning experiences to reading textbooks, filling out work sheets composed of closed-ended or short-answer knowledge and comprehension questions, and then taking tests featuring similar questions. These approaches to instruction rightly have been criticized as boring and restricted to lower levels of cognitive processing. But they represent inappropriate use of textbooks, not problems inherent to textbooks themselves.

When used optimally, textbooks serve as key components in much more varied and powerful programs of curriculum and instruction. In these programs, the curriculum is broader than the content of the textbooks, and students are engaged in a variety of learning activities in addition to (and where appropriate, instead of) those included in the textbooks and any ancillary materials that accompany them. To the extent that its content and activities are closely aligned with the course or unit goals, a textbook will synthesize most of the important facts, concepts, principles, and skills that the teacher wants to develop. Textbook reading and related activities can be especially valuable for providing students with an initial base of common knowledge that will be developed during class discussions and application activities, and subsequent review of the highlights featured in a good textbook helps students to synthesize and retain what they have learned. By presenting the gist of a lesson or unit in a single source, good texts make it much easier for students to access and synthesize this material than it would be otherwise.

Textbooks vary in their usefulness as learning resources in particular instructional situations (i.e., in courses taught for selected purposes and goals, at specified grade levels, to particular students). The most valuable texts possess certain characteristics. First, their difficulty level is suited to the grade level and to the prior knowledge and other background characteristics of the students. Second, their content is valid, important, and well-aligned with state and district guidelines for the course. Third, and most relevant to the issues addressed in this chapter, they represent their content coherently and develop it in ways that support the learners' construction of corresponding understandings.

In summary, a good textbook is not merely a content reference but a learning resource: it helps students to develop connected understandings of the course's most important facts, concepts, principles, and skills. Unfortunately, research on American textbooks suggests that they have not been fulfilling their potential as learning resources and that the problem has been worsening in recent decades.

Problems With American Textbooks

Analyses of K–12 textbook series have produced different conclusions at different times. Authors comparing developments from the 1950s through the 1970s noted improvements such as more and better graphics; better historical coverage of minorities, women, and everyday life; more accurate and better conceptualized content; inclusion of primary source material and tabular and graphic data along with narrative text; and suggestions for a broader range of learning activities. More recently, however, such celebrations of progress have been supplanted by a spate of highly critical analyses (Elliott & Woodward, 1990; Wiley, 1977).

Contemporary textbooks have been described as flashy in appearance but limited in value as learning resources for a number of reasons. They try to cover too much, so that they truncate, treat superficially, or confuse coverage of even important topics. The writing features dry sentences all about the same length, with few adjectives to enliven the text; few examples or vignettes to give roundness to ideas; and too many paragraphs that are unclear because the material is too compressed and elliptical. Contemporary textbooks lack contexts to make facts meaningful, and excessive space is allocated to pictures and graphics of limited usefulness. All of these and other structural features of texts affect students' ability to understand and remember the texts' content, especially its most important ideas.

Most texts do not make enough use of the following structural features that would make them more considerate to their readers and more useful as learning resources:

1. organization around key ideas embedded within chronological order, cause/effect, problem/solution, comparison/contrast, or other logical structures
2. signaling of sequences and subparts of the presentation
3. discourse consistency
4. cohesive elements that relate sentences or paragraphs to one another

5. explication (stating things directly rather than requiring readers to infer them; linking content to previously presented knowledge; orienting readers to central ideas or purposes; clarifying new ideas with examples or analogies; highlighting and defining new terms)
6. appropriate conceptual density (not introducing too many ideas too quickly; first introducing an idea, then clarifying it, then giving examples before going on to the next idea)
7. metadiscourse (talking directly to readers to convey the author's point of view or to direct them to do something such as answer a question)
8. instructional devices such as tables of contents, glossaries, indexes, graphic overviews, inserted questions, diagrams, summaries, review questions, and application problems, as well as spacing, indentation, boxes, and other formatting (Chambliss & Calfee, 1989; Dreher & Singer, 1989; McCabe, 1993)

The most recently published texts usually do contain many of these instructional devices and formatting features, but often without effective organization and explication of content. Consequently, they have the appealing look of pages in weekly news and entertainment magazines, but this does not make them effective learning resources (Graves et al., 1991; Tyson-Bernstein, 1988).

Beck and McKeown (1988) closely analyzed middle school history and geography textbooks and found three common problems. First, they found lack of evidence that clear content goals were used to guide text writing with an eye toward what students were supposed to learn. Consequently, texts read as chronicles of miscellaneous facts rather than as narratives built around key themes. Second, the textbooks made unrealistic assumptions about students' prior knowledge. Key elements needed to understand a sequence were merely alluded to rather than explained sufficiently. Third, there were inadequate explanations that failed to clarify causal connections between actions and events. These problems with the structural coherence of texts limit their value as learning resources for students, who often must struggle even to locate main ideas, let alone to emerge with a network of connected understandings. They also create motivation problems, because students' levels of interest and enjoyment of texts are associated closely with the texts' coherence and understandability (much more so than with inclusion of interesting details or a zesty, magazine style of writing; Beck & McKeown, 1988; Beck, McKeown, & Gromoll, 1989).

Brophy and Alleman's (1992/1993) investigations of elementary social studies textbook series revealed many of these same limitations, along with additional problems with the content and other problems with the learning activities suggested in the texts themselves or in the teachers' editions. The stated goals frequently did not appear to have been the primary considerations driving curriculum development. Few of the activities labeled critical thinking or application actually called for these cognitive processes. There was little attention to students' preexisting knowledge or misconceptions. Captions and questions accompanying photos or illustrations focused on irrelevant details instead of connecting them to key ideas, and suggested content development questions focused on locating miscellaneous facts rather than on structuring reflective discussion of the content. There was little use of data retrieval charts or other mechanisms for analyzing and synthesizing content in ways that promote understanding. Many of the suggested follow-up activities focused on trivial aspects of the content, did not promote progress toward significant social education goals, or were unnecessarily time-consuming or complicated. Likewise, many of the skills exercises and most of the activities ostensibly intended to promote integration across subjects lacked significant educational value. Test questions were mostly limited to factual recognition and retrieval items that required little if any critical thinking, development of arguments, sustained writing, or authentic applications.

Further review of learning activities revealed that many were mostly busywork: word searches, cutting and pasting, coloring, connecting dots, learning to recognize states from their outlines, or memorizing state capitols and state symbols. Others were built around peripheral definitions or facts that had little application potential, and some distorted content representation because they were built around exotic rather than typical examples. Skills curricula often were intrusively imposed on knowledge curricula in ways that used isolated bits of knowledge as bases for skills exercises; for example, students were asked to chart or graph unimportant information that was never used or to count how many states' names begin with the letter *C*. Many integration activities, in particular, were forced or pointless (alphabetize the state capitols; look up the geographical coordinates for Revolutionary War battle sites; Brophy, 1992; Brophy & Alleman, 1992/1993).

Science texts similarly have been described as overly lengthy (one first-year high school biology textbook exceeded 1,000 pages), crammed with far too much material, and yet lacking in both continuity and narrative perspective. A typical science text introduces more new vocabulary than a typical foreign language text. Examinations of science texts repeatedly have highlighted serious problems in clarity and coherence, even regarding the most important concepts and principles. Research on science learning has revealed that students have difficulty constructing clear understandings of certain key science concepts, and the main reason for this is that these concepts are not explained and illustrated clearly in the textbooks. Typically, the texts do not sufficiently take into account students' prior knowledge, provide representations that clarify abstract ideas effectively, or include examples and exercises that would enable students to apply and appreciate the validity of the ideas. The texts present a lot of miscellaneous information, but do not provide systematic support for learning connected networks of content structured around powerful ideas (Haury, 2000; Kesidou & Roseman, 2002; Stern & Roseman, 2004).

These problems extend to include even mathematics textbooks. School mathematics texts in the United States, compared to those in other countries, are notably bulkier. This is because they address many different topics in response to the multiple demands of state and district mathematics standards, not because they develop topics in more depth. Countries that are notably successful on internationally administered mathematics achievement tests tend to select a few critical topics for each grade and then develop these topics in sufficient depth to allow their students to master them. Then they go on to new topics the following year, again developing them in depth. In contrast, American textbooks tend to distribute topics over several years rather than treat them comprehensively in any single year. Consequently, much time each year is spent reviewing topics taught in previous years, but without pursuing the topics in sufficient depth to ensure lasting mastery.

Typically, little or no space in these textbooks is devoted to discussion of students' strategies or progressions in their thinking, and explanations of mathematical processes are frequently omitted. Instead, much of the space in the text is devoted to decorative artwork that has little connection to the mathematical content and sometimes is confusing or distracting to students. Often hurriedly produced in response to developing market conditions, these texts usually are rushed into print without sufficient pilot testing and without being assessed and certified for quality through a process set up by the federal government (no such process exists in the United States; Grouws & Cebulla, 2000; Hook, Bishop, & Hook, 2007; Kilpatrick, Swafford, & Findell, 2001).

International comparisons have repeatedly characterized American mathematics textbooks as overcrowded with topics, lacking in content emphasis, repetitious across years, and low in expectations for what students could accomplish (Schmidt, McKnight, Cogan, Jakwerth, & Houang, 1999). A study sponsored by the American Association for the Advancement of Science (AAAS) concluded that only 4 of 12 middle school mathematics textbooks could be rated as satisfactory, and these 4 had been produced through major projects supported by the National Science Foundation. None of the popular commercial textbooks achieved a satisfactory rating.

How the Problems Developed

Research has demonstrated repeatedly that most American teachers lean heavily on the textbook series to provide both content bases and suggested questions and activities to include in their teaching. Yet, evaluations of these textbooks typically lead to disparaging characterizations such as mile-wide but inch-deep, parade of facts, glorified encyclopedias, or trivial pursuit. How has this situation come to pass, and why hasn't something been done about it?

The root of the problem lies in that textbook publishers must respond to multiple and conflicting market pressures rather than to a single set of curriculum standards and guidelines. Unlike most other countries, the United States does not have a single national curriculum regulated by a national ministry of education. Our federal government does have a Department of Education that assumes responsibility for research and information dissemination, special education, and other functions, but decisions about curriculum and instruction are left to the states and districts.

As part of the culture wars that developed within American society in recent decades, political, ethnic, and religious action groups began lobbying states and districts, seeking changes in school policies. Typically, they called for changes in textbook adoption guidelines that would specify inclusion, exclusion, or officially sanctioned treatment of certain curricular topics. As a result, more and more states and districts shifted from relatively generic to increasingly specific guidelines for what is to be included in the curriculum. In U.S. history, for example, California wants detailed treatment of the Gold Rush, Texas wants detailed treatment of the Alamo, the former Confederate states want detailed treatment of the Civil War, including battles fought locally, and many states want versions of U.S. history that focus on the positive and minimize attention to the negative. Most new demands on publishers call for adding new topics without removing coverage of topics already addressed.

In their attempts to respond to all of these local demands while creating textbook series intended to be used across the country as a whole, the publishers gradually added more and more content to each textbook. In response to ever broader coverage, the textbooks became fatter and fatter. Then they became less coherent as well, as the depth of coverage of even the most important topics was reduced to accommodate still more breadth. Textbooks were saying less and less about more and more.

Coherence also suffered because some states and districts began using readability formulas or other ostensible measures of textbooks' difficulty levels to pressure publishers to make their textbooks easier for students to read (and presumably, to learn from). Readability formulas combine measures such as average commonality of words, average number of words per sentence, and average number of letters per word to yield estimates of the grade-level appropriateness of texts. As a result of inclusion of these types of difficulty-level specifications in state and district textbook adoption guidelines, shorter but vaguer words were substituted for longer but more specific ones, and longer sentences were chopped into shorter ones that omitted connection words (therefore, so that, because, etc.). These changes made it harder for students to follow explanations and note cause-effect linkages. The texts became easier to read in the sense that sentences were shorter and vocabulary was simpler, but they became harder to learn from because specific and integrated explanations gave way to vague and disconnected content.

Treatment of controversial topics became especially vague or incomplete because of regional or local objections to certain content. Some states forbade or placed tight restrictions on teaching about topics such as birth control, evolution, global warming, alternatives to capitalism, market economics, or American interventions in other countries. These restrictions often created serious coherence problems, especially in biology or life science texts written without reference to evolution (a major organizing concept in these disciplines).

Publishers were reluctant to violate restrictions imposed by even one or two states, because this could cost them a significant share of the market. This was especially true if the states were heavily populated and among the adoption states that only allow districts to spend state funds on textbooks that are included in their official adoption lists.

Tyson-Bernstein (1988) identified an additional pressure on publishers that contributed to the coherence problem: states' and districts' emphasis on adopting textbooks with a current-year publication date. This forces publishers to constantly rush new editions of their textbook series into print, without taking time for careful editing and field testing. The new editions have new covers, new front matter (emphasizing the latest buzz words), and new design features and illustrations that give them a different look. But they usually do not have new content or even correction of errors in the content of previous editions.

The publishers know that teachers and other members of textbook adoption committees rarely have much time to examine their books in detail, and that adoption decisions are often influenced primarily by the books' publication dates, their cosmetic features, and the claims made about them in their front matter or in advertising brochures. Some teachers seek curriculum packages that include ready-made lesson plans and labor-saving extras such as workbooks, test packs, reproducibles, posters, and resource books. Others favor series that they think will help prepare their students for state-imposed tests.

In summary, the emphasis on breadth over depth of coverage reflects the publishers' attempts to cover all of the topics and skills listed in state and district curriculum guides. Problems with clarity and coherence (not to mention zest and style) in the writing can be traced to the imposition of readability formulas, constant pressures for new editions, and avoidance or sanitized treatment of controversial topics. Local adoption decisions are often made hurriedly and superficially, so that cosmetic features (jazzy layouts, buzz words highlighted in large type in the front matter, colorful photos and illustrations) get undue attention at the expense of careful analysis of the significance and coherence of the content (Tyson-Bernstein, 1988).

Although these trends have been recognized for at least 20 years, Sewall (2005) noted that the problem continues to worsen. As a result of mergers and acquisitions in the publishing industry, most school districts now purchase textbooks from one of just four remaining large companies serving the elementary and secondary market. All of these companies feel compelled to respond to the market pressures described previously, so the content of their textbooks is similarly mile-wide but inch-deep, bland, and incoherent.

Having been told that today's students cannot or do not want to read text-heavy or information-loaded texts, the publishers have been transforming their textbooks into picture and activity books instead of clear, portable, simply designed, and text-centered primers. There are fewer words and more white space per page, and the text that remains is broken up with bright photographs and colorful formatting. Instead of producing coherent texts, publishers are focusing on staying within state and district guidelines and competing by making the texts visually attractive and offering enticements such as free samples, teacher consultants, study guides, workbooks, technology, Spanish-language versions, detailed teachers' editions, binders, answer keys, discounts, premiums, and other enticements (Sewall, 2005).

The textbook series are attractively packaged and presented to teachers in ways that suggest they are complete curricula that have been carefully developed by experts and revised to meet the needs of students at each grade level (and recently, to suggest that using them will enable students to meet state standards). But these series are not written by the kinds of experts that teachers envision.

A writing team composed of professors and teachers with special expertise or interest in the subject matter develops outlines for the materials and provides feedback about early drafts. Most of the actual writing, however, is done by employees of the publishing company or freelance writers who are not recognized experts in the field. Also, the textbook series are not painstakingly developed and revised through successive field testings. Usually there is no systematic classroom testing at all—just revisions in response to the comments of reviewers. The publishers are interested in feedback from teachers, but their concerns about content are driven primarily by the textbook adoption guidelines established by states.

Potential Solutions

The publishers appear to have lost sight of the major, long-term goals that reflect the aims and purposes of the K–12 school subjects. Fundamental change is unlikely unless they restore the basic notion of developing curricula as a means to accomplish major goals phrased in intended student outcomes—capabilities and dispositions to be developed in students and used in their lives outside of school, both now and in the future.

Ideally, a curriculum is goal oriented and all of its components are aligned accordingly. Everything in it, the content as well as the questions, activities, and evaluation devices, is included because it is expected to promote progress toward the major instructional goals. Content is selected for its potential for life application and is developed and applied accordingly. Skills are selected and used as tools for applying knowledge in ways that promote progress toward

the major goals. They are included in the curriculum in places where they are needed for this purpose and are developed and used in natural, authentic applications. Appreciations, values, attitudes, and behavioral dispositions also are developed in natural and authentic ways suited to the content being addressed in a unit. Questions and activities focus on developing understanding and appreciation of cause-and-effect relationships, and on encouraging critical thinking and thoughtful decision making about applications. Evaluation devices feature questions and assignments that call for communicating major understandings and for engaging in inquiry, problem solving, critical thinking, decision making, and other higher-order applications.

Textbooks could be key components in such a well-aligned curriculum, synthesizing its major aims, purposes, and goals and presenting its most important facts, concepts, principles, and skills. This ideal is unlikely to be approached, however, as long as the current system continues. Changing it would require mechanisms to move toward establishing a national curriculum. This idea is controversial, however, especially in the United States, where education traditionally has been considered a state and local function and federal intrusion is viewed with suspicion. Also, national curricula often introduce problems of their own, such as national chauvinism and ignoring or slighting the experiences of minorities. Yet, they do facilitate the preparation of more coherent textbooks. Ideally, the national curriculum would be developed through sustained efforts over many years. It might be limited to content that achieved consensus across a broad range of stakeholders. It also might be designed to require only 50% to 75% of the available teaching time, with the rest reserved for content identified in state and local guidelines. Pending such developments, the current problems with textbooks will continue.

Coping in the Meantime

In the meantime, teachers need to make their own personal curricula as coherent as possible, and to help their students stay aware of the instructional goals and regulate their learning efforts accordingly. To make good decisions about what to teach and how to teach it, teachers need to establish worthwhile goals and keep these goals in sight as they develop and implement unit plans. This can be difficult, because as curriculum guidelines get translated into separate strands and then become segmented by grade level and by units within grades and lessons with units, the goals that are meant to guide the entire process sometimes fade into the background, along with many of the originally recognized connections and intended life applications. For example, consider the following social studies goals:

- *Districtwide goal*: Prepare young people to become humane, rational, participating citizens in an increasingly interdependent world.

- *Program-area goal for social studies, K–12*: Enable students to appreciate that people living in different cultures are likely to hold many common values but also some different values that are rooted in experience and legitimate in terms of their own cultures.
- *Grade-level goal for social studies, Grade 1*: To understand and appreciate that the roles and values of family members may differ according to the structure of the family, its circumstances, and its cultural setting.
- *Unit-level goal for social studies, Grade 1*: To understand that families differ in size and composition.

This last (unit-level) goal is phrased in purely descriptive, knowledge-level language, and it is trite for a unit goal even at the first-grade level. It makes no reference to the concepts concerning cultures and roles that are referred to in the higher-level goals, nor to the related values and dispositions (multicultural appreciation and citizen participation). Unless the teacher has a coherent view of the purposes and nature of social education, or unless the manual does an unusually good job of keeping the teacher aware of how particular lessons fit within the big picture, the result is likely to be a version of social studies that is long on isolated practice of facts and skills but short on integration and application of social learning.

In this case, students might learn a few obvious generalities about families (they differ in size and composition, they grow and change, and their members work and play together), but not much about variations in family roles across time and culture, the reasons for these variations, or the lifestyle trade-offs that they offer. This will not do much to advance students' knowledge of the human condition, help them put the familiar into broader perspective, or even stimulate their thinking about family as a concept.

To avoid such problems, teachers will need to identify the capabilities and dispositions that they want to develop in their students throughout the year as a whole and in each instructional unit. Then they can examine instructional materials in light of these goals. It helps to begin by reading the student text (i.e., not the teacher's manual, which contains more guidance and information), noting places where additional structuring or input will be necessary to focus students' learning on important ideas. Teachers then should study the manual, assessing its suggested questions, activities, and evaluation devices to determine the degree to which they will help students accomplish primary instructional goals. They may need to augment the text with additional input (or replace it with something else if necessary), skip pointless questions and activities, and substitute other questions and activities.

In addition to taking these steps to clarify major goals in their own minds and present their students with more coherent instructional resources and activities, teachers can structure and scaffold their students' learning in ways that make it easier for them to keep the major goals in mind and regulate their learning strategies accordingly. In structuring material for students, teachers can establish a sense of purpose, connect with the students' prior knowledge (both by building on valid knowledge and addressing misconceptions), present representations of concepts and principles that students can understand, provide varied activities to practice and apply the learning, and guide students' interpretation of what has been learned.

For students who might be expected to have difficulty learning from even adapted materials, teachers might supplement their adaptation efforts with study guides that include questions and activities to help students recognize and note key points, as well as provide a structure for reflection. Teachers might also provide alternative reading materials or lead the students through the most difficult parts of texts, taking time to elaborate on big ideas and make sure that students understand them.

Other useful techniques include helping students to see how the textbook as a whole and its chapters and sections are organized, emphasizing the major organizing concepts, and providing glossaries or in other ways highlighting and making sure that students learn important new terms. Teaching and providing practice in basic text comprehension strategies (summarizing, predicting, clarifying, synthesizing) is helpful in all of the subjects, not just literacy.

Wills (2007) has described how some teachers coped with both textbook limitations and high-stakes testing pressures following mandated increases in the instructional time allocated to literacy and mathematics (the focus of the state's high-stakes testing program). The school's principal left it up to individual teachers to decide how they would accommodate this mandate. One teacher eliminated physical education, reasoning that her students had greater needs for rich science and social studies curricula. Most teachers, though, reduced the time allocated to science and social studies to less than half of what it had been before.

Teachers who had been teaching a barren curriculum simply persisted with this approach, except that now they required their students to read and answer questions about textbook chapters at home, so they could spend most class time going over the answers. Meanwhile, teachers who understood the value of thoughtful discourse scrambled to find ways to retain this emphasis while still addressing the full range of prescribed content.

The most successful teacher eliminated or reduced coverage of content she deemed less important so that her units still included discussions and other activities that asked students to analyze, interpret, or apply their learning to address challenging problems or issues. She made time for this by skipping certain chapters of the textbooks and eliminating the need to work through other chapters by providing her students with succinct summaries of key facts and main ideas. Although she expected her students to read relevant chapters for background and occasionally exposed them to videos or other input sources, her classroom discussions were focused on the material contained in her handouts, which briefly and clearly covered the important information she thought her students needed to know. Her solution was not completely satisfactory, but it did enable her to sustain a focus on big ideas and thoughtful classroom discourse.

New teachers usually are not yet ready to make these kinds of curricular decisions, so they may have to lean heavily on their textbook series at first; however, they can take steps to speed up their acquisition of the needed expertise. To begin, they might study their state and district guidelines for the subject(s) and grade level(s) they teach, with an eye toward identifying the content considered most important. Then, to get a broader perspective, they might consult two other sets of valuable resources: (1) teacher education textbooks in each subject (elementary, middle, or secondary level, as appropriate), and (2) Web sites sponsored by the major organizations concerned with K–12 teaching of each subject (National Council of Teachers of Mathematics, National Council for the Social Studies, and so on). Those textbooks and Web sites are especially good sources of information on each subject's purposes, goals, big ideas, and major skills and dispositions.

Finally, rather than struggle alone, it is helpful if new teachers take steps to find mentors and colleagues to help them. Experienced teachers who already have made curricular adaptations are especially valuable, preferably colleagues at the same school. It also is helpful to form professional discussion and problem solving groups with colleagues, meeting often enough to allow for sustained and coordinated efforts. In any case, it is important that new teachers take steps to make their curricula more goal-oriented and coherent, weaning themselves from overdependence on the textbook series as soon as possible.

References and Further Readings

Beck, I., & McKeown, M. (1988). Toward meaningful accounts in history texts for young learners. *Educational Researcher*, *17*(6), 31–39.

Beck, I., McKeown, M., & Gromoll, E. (1989). Learning from social studies texts. *Cognition and Instruction*, *6*, 99–158.

Brophy, J. (1992). The *de facto* national curriculum in elementary social studies: Critique of a representative example. *Journal of Curriculum Studies*, *24*, 401–447.

Brophy, J., & Alleman, J. (1992/1993). Elementary social studies textbooks. *Publishing Research Quarterly*, *8*, 12–22.

Chambliss, M., & Calfee, R. (1989). Designing science textbooks to enhance student understanding. *Educational Psychologist*, *24*, 307–322.

Dreher, M., & Singer, H. (1989). Friendly texts and text-friendly teachers. *Theory Into Practice*, *28*, 98–104.

Elliott, D., & Woodward, A. (Eds.). (1990). *Textbooks and schooling in the United States*. Chicago: University of Chicago Press.

Graves, M., Prenn, M., Earle, J., Thompson, M., Johnson, V., & Slater, W. (1991). Improving instructional text: Some lessons learned. *Reading Research Quarterly*, *26*, 111–121.

Grouws, D., & Cebulla, K. (2000). Elementary and middle school mathematics at the crossroads. In T. Good (Ed.), *American education: Yesterday, today, and tomorrow* (pp. 209–255). Chicago: University of Chicago Press.

Haury, D. (2000). *High school biology textbooks do not meet national standards* (ERIC Digest). Columbus, OH: ERIC Clearinghouse for Science, Mathematics, and Environmental Education. (ERIC Digest No. ED359048)

Hook, W., Bishop, W., & Hook, J. (2007). A quality math curriculum in support of effective teaching for elementary schools. *Educational Studies in Mathematics*, *65*, 125–148.

Kesidou, S., & Roseman, J. (2002). How well do middle school science programs measure up? Findings from Project 2061's curriculum review. *Journal of Research in Science Teaching*, *39*, 522–549.

Kilpatrick, J., Swafford, J., & Findell, B. (Eds.). (2001). *Adding it up: Helping children learn mathematics*. Washington, DC: National Academies Press.

McCabe, P. (1993). Considerateness of fifth-grade social studies texts. *Theory and Research in Social Education*, *21*, 128–142.

McKnight, C., & Schmidt, W. (1998). Facing facts in U.S. science and mathematics education: Where we stand and where we want to go. *Journal of Science Education and Technology*, *7*, 57–76.

Schmidt, W., McKnight, C., Cogan, L., Jakwerth, P., & Houang, R. (1999). *Facing the consequences: Using TIMSS for a closer look at mathematics and science education*. Dordrecht, Netherlands: Kluwer.

Sewall, G. (2005). Textbook publishing. *Phi Delta Kappan*, *86*, 498–502.

Stern, L., & Roseman, J. (2004). Can middle-school science textbooks help students learn important ideas? Findings from Project 2061's curriculum evaluation study: Life science. *Journal of Research in Science Teaching*, *41*, 538–568.

Tyson-Bernstein, H. (1988). *A conspiracy of good intentions: America's textbook fiasco*. Washington, DC: Council for Basic Education.

Wiley, K. (1977). *The status of pre-college science, mathematics, and social science education: 1955–1975* (Vol. 3). Washington, DC: National Science Foundation.

Wills, J. (2007). Putting the squeeze on social studies: Managing teaching dilemmas in subject areas excluded from state testing. *Teachers College Record*, *109*, p. 1980–2046.

Woodward, A. (1987). Textbooks: Less than meets the eye. *Journal of Curriculum Studies*, *19*, 511–526.

PART IX

ASSESSMENT

46

STANDARDIZED TESTS

AMY M. OLSON AND DARRELL SABERS

University of Arizona

W hat is a standardized test? People often think about #2 pencils, stuffy classrooms, and high-stakes tests when they think about standardized testing. We see in the media that standardized tests are a hallmark of the No Child Left Behind (2001) era. As such, much of the coverage of standardized tests involves accusations of bias or arguments that tests take time away from teaching. We refer the reader to Section XVI of Volume 2 (Federal, State, and Community Policies) for arguments for and against these views. Our purpose is to focus on the nature of standardized tests. We hope that in learning about standardized testing, readers can become critical consumers of testing-based statistics and arguments. For further insight into common misperceptions about tests and data interpretation, see Bracey (2006).

Defining Standardized

What does it actually mean for a test to be standardized? Cronbach (1960) argued that standardized tests were those in which the conditions and content were equal for all examinees. He defined a standardized test as "one in which the procedure, apparatus, and scoring have been fixed so that precisely the same test can be given at different times and places" (p. 22). Standardizing testing conditions and content is meant to increase the reliability of examinees' scores by reducing sources of error extraneous to the abilities or skills being measured. For example, if examinees

were given different directions for completing the test (e.g., to guess versus to leave a question blank when the correct answer is unknown), some differences in scores could be the result of directions rather than ability. Standardization attempts to reduce this possibility by holding as many factors as possible constant in testing.

Nearly 40 years later, the *Standards of Educational and Psychological Testing* (American Educational Research Association [AERA], American Psychological Association [APA], & National Council on Measurement in Education [NCME], 1999) reflects a shift away from focus on equal content, but a continued emphasis on equal conditions. Accordingly, standardization is a form of test administration designed to maintain "a constant testing environment" such that the test is conducted "according to detailed rules and specifications" (p. 182).

The testing community has also seen shifts in the level at which conditions are held equal. Sometimes it is necessary to provide accommodations to particular examinees. A new definition of standardization reflecting these changes exists today. What has remained constant across the changing definitions of standardization, however, is a focus on the purpose of standardization: to ensure fairness.

Placing Standardization on a Continuum

The strict definition of standardization proposed by Cronbach was never completely realized. Standardized test conditions suggest fixed administration procedures, but as Brennan (2006) argues, "It is particularly important to understand that psychometrics is silent with respect to which conditions of measurement, if any, should be fixed" (p. 9). Standardized administration conditions may or may not include time allotted, materials used (e.g., calculators, #2 pencils), and instructions given. To keep all such conditions equal would be unlikely in the real world. Most testing occurs in classrooms, where teachers likely respond to the different needs or questions of their students. Further, the early definition of standardization suggested that content, like conditions, should also be identical for all examinees. Equality of content may mean that the same items are given or it may mean that the same content domain is covered for all examinees. Test designers need to specify which conditions and content should be equal.

Thus the definition of standardization seems straightforward, but the application can be fairly complicated. Imagine a continuum of standardization with Cronbach's definition (identical content and conditions) at one end and variations in content or conditions at the other. Many standardized tests today fall closer to the second description.

Identifying Variations in Content

Content can vary when individually administered tests are adapted to the examinee. For example, early intelligence tests often used basals and ceilings. Basals and ceilings are generally used in tests meant to span a developmental age range or range of material or ability. The practice continues today in tests like Test of Early Mathematics Ability, 3rd edition (TEMA-III). A test administrator begins the test at the item expected to be appropriate for an examinee of a particular age or grade. A ceiling occurs at the lowest consecutive number of items (5 on the TEMA) the examinee answers incorrectly. The basal is the lowest consecutive number of items (again 5 on the TEMA) the examinee answers correctly. If a basal has not been determined by the time the examinee reaches a ceiling, the test administrator will move backwards through the test beginning at the entry point until a basal is established (or until the lowest item has been given). The examinee does not complete items below the basal or above the ceiling, and the total score reflects the assumption that he or she would have answered questions below the basal correctly and questions above the ceiling incorrectly.

Test designers incorporate basals and ceilings to shorten the length of the test and minimize examinees' frustration when asked to answer questions that are too difficult or boredom when asked to answer questions that are too easy. Additionally, items at either end of the difficulty spectrum do not provide useful information about an examinee's ability level. Consider the implications of the use of basals and ceilings for the definition of standardization. When basals and ceilings are used, there is no guarantee that examinees are given the same items. Even within a relatively small age range, there may be examinees who do not take all the same items. To the extent that content differs from item to item, content is not standardized.

Furthermore, the interpretation of examinees' total scores reflects assumptions about success or failure. Assumptions about student scores below basals and above ceilings are only as good as the sequence of test items. If the test is constructed to be used with basals and ceilings, the items must progress from easy to difficult. If items were calibrated on a representative sample, the test designers had the opportunity to put items in the necessary sequence—for that sample of students. Ordering items puts restrictions on the ability of test developers and content theorists to vary material (e.g., imagine a math test in which all addition problems were in the beginning so that students whose basals were higher than this level were not tested at all on addition). The correct sequence for one group may vary widely from another. Consider these issues: What if states or instructors teach material in a different order? What if the test has been translated? What if students from different socioeconomic or cultural backgrounds have differential exposure to particular content or themes? These questions point to the importance of understanding how similar the current sample of examinees is to the sample who took the items for sequencing, because the difficulty order of items may not be comparable across all groups.

Content may differ for individual examinees for other reasons. In computerized adaptive testing, groups of examinees can be given a test via computers, but the items they receive can be individually adapted so that examinees take a larger proportion of items with difficulties around their own ability levels. We distinguish computerized adaptive testing (CAT) from computer-based testing (CBT), a test given via a computer. CBT can be highly standardized because the test is administered the same way; all examinees are provided the same instructions and materials in every administration. Our interest lies in CATs, which attempt to estimate the examinee's ability more efficiently (with fewer items) than traditional tests. CAT developers create large item banks with items calibrated to span the ability range of the population to be tested. CATs use items ordered from easy to difficult on a scale, and examinees can be ordered from less proficient to more proficient on the same scale depending on their performance on the calibrated items. For item-level CATs, one can assume that an examinee who answers correctly is at least as proficient as the item was difficult. One can also assume that an examinee who answers incorrectly is not as proficient as the item was difficult. The computer adapts, responding with more difficult items when examinees answer correctly and easier items when examinees answer incorrectly. One benefit of this process is that it generally takes fewer items to establish an examinee's level of proficiency. Traditional tests must have a range of item difficulties that covers the ability range of the population for which the test is designed; examinees are given all of these items, even those well outside their ability range.

There are a number of consequences associated with CAT efficiency. One consequence is that each item is scored before the next one is given, and the examinee cannot return to previous items should a later item trigger information helpful in solving a previous item. Another consequence is that since items are presented based on difficulty and the examinee's performance, there is less control over content and order than test designers would normally have (Hendrickson, 2007). Examinees are not expected to be at the same level; the items needed to estimate their abilities are not expected to entirely overlap. Yet, designers of large-scale group tests still attempt to standardize content by creating item banks with items matched on content but varying in difficulty. Thus in CAT, as in the use of basals and ceilings, items taken by different examinees are not identical. Test developers must take steps to ensure that examinees have similar exposure to content. The more closely a test and curriculum are aligned, the more difficult it is for test developers to ensure similar content, which is why adaptive testing is more often seen with tests designed to measure general abilities or skills developed over an extended time.

Multistage adaptive tests are a response to perceived problems with item-level CATs. Like item-level CATs, multistage adaptive tests are more efficient than conventional tests because the items given are selected based on the examinee's performance. The difference is that multistage adaptive tests adapt less often, after groups of items called testlets. Examinees can review previous items within a testlet and the content coverage of testlets can be more easily balanced (Hendrickson, 2007).

Now consider the implications of individual adaptations for standardization. We will use an example relevant for college students, the Graduate Record Examination (GRE). Students pursuing graduate education are often required to take the GRE General Test, which is composed of three sections: Verbal, Quantitative, and Analytical Writing. The first CAT versions of the GRE were given in 1993 (Zwick, 2006). Examinees who are administered the test by computer take a CAT version of the Verbal and Quantitative sections. The Analytical Writing section is composed of two essays that may be computer administered, but are not computer graded. An examinee's score on the two CAT sections depends on performance on the items and also on whether all items were completed in the given time (http:// www.ets.org). The GRE is thus a speeded test and is standardized in terms of time allotted.

There are ways in which the GRE is not standardized. For example, examinees take the GRE on computer, but where computer facilities are not available, examinees complete a paper test. In 1999, the paper test was discontinued for students in the United States (Zwick, 2006), but paper formats are still used in some countries (http://www .ets.org). The format is therefore not standardized, but the test remains speeded regardless of format.

Items are not the same for all examinees because the computer version of the GRE is a CAT. Which questions an examinee receives depends on performance on previous items and on considerations of the test designers. As noted with basals and ceilings, test designers must attempt to take into account content coverage. It would not be fair for a person to receive a high score on the Quantitative section by completing only algebra problems while another person must successfully complete algebra, geometry, and interpretation from graphs to receive the same score. Test developers must ensure that content is similar for all examinees.

On the paper GRE, an examinee's raw score is the number of correct responses from the total number of items given. The paper raw scores and the CAT scores are converted to scaled scores via equating (http://www.ets.org), a process that takes into account the item difficulties to ensure that individuals of similar ability receive similar scores even if they took different items. (Equating technically produces what are known as tau-equivalent scores rather than equivalent scores, because CAT scores should be more reliable than paper scores.) Consider the implications of scoring: Imagine two high-performing students take the GRE. The first student takes the CAT version while the second student takes the paper test. Both perform well, but the consequences of missing an item for the second student are more severe than they are for the first student. Why would this be? The CAT responds to high performance by providing more difficult items. The second student's test cannot adapt. In other words, it is likely given their performance that the first student receives a more difficult test than the second student. Missing more difficult items is less costly for the first student because scoring reflects item difficulty. At first glance, it may not seem fair; it may even seem like the first student receives more chances to do well on the test. But consider this: If the second student misses items on a medium-difficulty test designed for the majority of examinees, chances are he or she would not have been given as many high-difficulty items on a CAT. The test is fair, because scoring takes into account the different items given.

Identifying Variations in Administration

With Cronbach's definition, standardization provides all examinees with identical opportunities to demonstrate their abilities on a test. We have already seen that standardization today no longer means identical items, but rather comparable content over different items. What about identical chance for success? One thing standardization does not (cannot) do is equalize the skills that examinees bring to exams. Typically, equalization is something that test designers do not wish to do. Examinees with more expertise or ability have a better chance of scoring well. Tests are designed to differentiate examinees for some purpose. If the purpose is to determine which examinees have particular knowledge or skills, it would not be helpful for all examinees to score the same; however, sometimes test users need to be concerned with imposing fairness on what examinees bring with them to a test. Legislation regarding testing has highlighted the importance of testing accommodations as a means to ensure fairness rather than equality of testing conditions.

In *Breimhorst v. Educational Testing Service* (2001), a student sued ETS after his score on the Graduate Management Admissions Test (GMAT) was flagged with an asterisk because he used an accommodation for extended time on the test. He argued that the flag, which ETS used to signify that his score may not be comparable to other scores due to the use of nonstandard conditions, caused graduate programs to interpret his performance differently than they would the performance of other examinees. The flag resulted in unfair bias in decision making. To deny the student accommodations would have been unfair. The Breimhorst settlement also indicated that identifying his score as different was unfair. Even though test conditions were not standardized, the score-based decisions should follow the same criteria as were used for other examinees. Presence of a flag reduced that possibility. The crux of the case was the content being tested. Unlike the GRE, the GMAT does not consider speed to be part of the content domain being measured. If the student took longer, but completed comparable content, the scores should be interpreted the same way.

A few cautionary statements should be made, however. First, if time is truly not meant to be considered part of the content domain being measured, then why set a time limit at all? The Breimhorst settlement is only valid if time really does not affect scores. If students who do not need accommodations would see improved performance with extended time, then time is part of the domain being measured and the issue of flagging must be revisited (or all students should be given as much time as they feel necessary to complete the exam). Unfortunately, research into the effects of accommodations is not regularly undertaken. Second, the individuals who set accommodations (e.g., the individuals responsible for crafting a student's Individualized Education Plan) may not be well-versed in the psychometric considerations associated with standardization. Thus, it would be beneficial for both measurement researchers and accommodations experts to work together to better understand the role of accommodations in standardized testing.

Clearly the language of standardization has shifted from equality to fairness. The shift is paralleled in the *Standards* (AERA, APA, NCME, 1999), with 12 standards directly related to fairness in testing. Of these, ". . . six standards refer to interpretation, reporting, or use of test scores; three to *differential measurement or prediction*; and three to equity or sensitivity" (Camilli, 2006, p. 226). Of particular interest for understanding the shift from equality to fairness in testing conditions is Standard 7.12, which states, "The testing or assessment process should be carried out so that examinees receive comparable and equitable treatment during all phases of the testing or assessment process" (AERA, APA, NCME, 1999, p. 84). The conditions of a test must be made fair for all examinees through providing accommodations (such as extended time or use of Braille) to the extent possible without infringing on the content domain being measured. Steps should be taken to account for variance extraneous to the purpose of the assessment in ways that are fair (even when these steps require conditions that are not equal).

The new definition of standardization reflects a preference for fairness over equality. Items examinees receive may not be identical, but to be fair, all examinees should be tested on similar content. Likewise, conditions may differ, but only in ways that result in fair assessment of the relevant abilities or skills that examinees bring to tests.

Interpreting Scores on Standardized Tests

Understanding Norm-Referenced and Standards-Based Approaches

Two approaches to making an examinee's performance meaningful are common: norm-referenced and standards-based comparisons. In the norm-referenced approach, the examinee's score represents an indication of how his or her performance compares to the performances of other examinees in one or more comparison groups of interest (called norm groups). Depending on the purpose of the assessment, test users may wish to compare examinees to a single group or to several groups. For interpreting performance on an intelligence test, the group of interest is a national sample of individuals of the same age as the examinee. For interpreting the score on an achievement test, one may want comparisons with several groups. One of those groups may be a national group, and other groups may be local students or students who have had similar preparation for that particular achievement area. Comparisons are made through the use of a reported score, often a percentile rank (PR) representing the percentage of individuals in the particular group whose scores are below the examinee's score. Mid-interval PRs, combining the percentage below with half of the percentage obtaining the same score as the examinee, are also common. On an intelligence test, the PR is usually transformed to an IQ, a standardized score scale with a mean of 100 and a standard deviation of 15.

With the standards-based approach, the student's score is compared with standards of performance that have been set before examination to indicate a subjective judgment of the quality of the performance. Rather than comparing a score with other individuals, this approach is based on comparing a score with desired levels of achievement established by a panel of experts and associated with verbal or numeric labels. Different panels of experts and different methods of standard setting result in different definitions of levels such as proficient or failing. For example, the set of levels used for the National Assessment of Educational Progress (NAEP) includes Basic, Proficient, and Advanced. Arizona has defined four levels to be used with their standards-based test: Falls Far Below the Standard, Approaches the Standard, Meets the Standard, and Exceeds the Standard. The levels and meanings used by states for their testing programs differ from each other and from the NAEP. The No Child Left Behind Act (NCLB) requires states to define a label indicating a student meets the state standard for proficiency.

The differences between norm-referenced and standards-based score interpretations should not be ignored, and many newspaper accounts of school performances are misunderstood because knowledge of these differences is lacking. For example, when comparing how well students achieved in one school district in Arizona, a newspaper informed readers that norm-referenced scores demonstrated that students were performing above national average in mathematics and below average in reading. When state standards-based levels of achievement were reported, the same newspaper informed readers that more students were meeting or exceeding standards in reading than in mathematics. As a result of these different interpretations, the judgment about which subject was more problematic for Arizona students depended on which account was cited. Such differences may result from different tests being used, but in this case it was due to using different approaches to reporting outcomes. The state's standards-based levels were not aligned with the national norm comparisons. The state levels for "Meets the Standard" in reading were set much lower than for mathematics (Sabers & Powers, 2005). That is, students performing about average in both reading and mathematics according to national norms were assigned the label "Approaches the Standard" in mathematics and "Meets the Standard" in reading according to the state's standards.

Selecting Norms:
National Sampling Projects and Test Users

The use of a national norm group is so common that some people have used the term *norm-referenced test* to refer to a standardized test where the results are reported as national percentile ranks. But it is not the test that is norm referenced; rather, it is the interpretation of the scores. It is important to note that it is difficult to obtain a sample that truly represents the national performance on any test. A large "anchor test study" (see Linn, 1975) comparing the norms for achievement tests demonstrated that there were substantial differences among the norms reported for some tests. Although each set of norms represented the results of a national sampling project, reported student achievement was different depending upon which groups were used for comparison. Baglin (1981) offered a possible explanation: self-selection bias, the result of schools accepting or declining an invitation to be part of the standardization group for a particular test, caused the samples to differ from each other and from a true national sample. For example, some schools appear more likely to participate in a norming study when the test

company is also the company they rely on for textbooks. In contrast, the personnel of other schools believe they are already doing too much testing and do not wish to participate in additional testing for test companies (or for NAEP).

There have been other attacks on national test norms as well. Cannell (1988) suggested that the reports on student performance given by school systems and states tended to be overly optimistic, and termed the phrase *Lake Wobegon effect* to describe the similarity to that mythical location in Garrison Keillor's stories where all of the students were above average. One explanation for how well students seemed to be performing when compared to national norms was that the national sample data included scores from unmotivated students who did not see a meaningful reason to participate. Examples of teachers telling students during standardization that this test won't really count perhaps did more than reduce student anxiety. In other words, the administration conditions and the subsequent performance of students when the test is being given for norming purposes simply may not be comparable to the administration conditions and student performance observed for the same test when there are high stakes for students, schools, and states. During norming, students may see the test as practice and therefore not make genuine attempts to do their best. Students may be more motivated to perform well when high stakes are involved. The extent to which this explanation is legitimate was never subjected to vigorous study, but these types of considerations should be a part of score interpretation.

If national norms are not really national, what is the proper approach to obtain better norm-referenced interpretations? User norms are a popular alternative, as these norms represent students who have similar reasons for taking the test. With user norms, motivated students who know they will be evaluated based on their performance produce the scores that are collected for the norm group. Tests reported with national samples of user norms include the GRE, ACT, and SAT. Another example of user norms is the local norm, or the sample consisting of the examinees in a local setting, such as when the comparison group consists of all students in a particular grade in an entire school district or state.

Comparing Examinees
Then and Now: Interpreting the GRE

The GRE is an excellent example of combining both approaches to reporting scores. The test is intended to be used by graduate programs, providing scores that can give additional information beyond undergraduate grade-point averages and other measures used in the selection of students for admission, fellowships, and scholarships. The test is taken by a subset of college students who intend to apply to graduate school; so comparing examinees to a national sample of college students would not be useful. Rather, the interpretation of scores is made more meaningful by comparison to user norms—the performances of other examinees who are also aspiring to graduate school admission.

A performance on the GRE General Test is given meaning by two different comparisons. The first comparison, for the Verbal and Quantitative sections, is with a score that ranges from 200 to 800 in 10-point intervals. This score has been used for half a century and is retained for purposes of continuity across decades. Originally, the score was described as centered on 500 with a standard deviation of 100 for each of the two sections of the test, but the current averages and standard deviations are different. The other section of the GRE has changed through the years and is currently called Analytical Writing, with scores reported on a standards-based scale ranging in half-point intervals from 0 to 6. The second comparison for all three sections is a PR describing the percentage of examinees over a recent 3-year period who scored lower than the specified score. The 3-year period provides a database of well over 1 million examinees and allows for a current comparison that is quite different from the reported score based on the original scaling group. Thus, one type of score allows for longitudinal comparisons across years while the other type is more useful for comparing the status of current applicants. One can see from the average scores that Verbal scores are now substantially lower and Quantitative scores much higher for current examinees than for the original test development sample. One can also see from the current PRs how each individual student compares with the other applicants for admission to a graduate program.

ETS (2006) provides information showing that the performance on the Verbal and Quantitative sections must be interpreted differently. Although originally the scores on these two sections were concordant, there is a great discrepancy in the performances based on the June 2002 to July 2005 sample (the most recent group). The top score (800) on Verbal surpasses over 99% of the users in the group, whereas the top score on Quantitative (800) surpasses only 94%. The average score on Verbal is 467; on Quantitative it is 591. Many people interpreting scores are misled by these shifts if they use the original 500 as their concept of average.

Most students take the GRE as a CAT, and the advantages of the computer version are easily seen with the GRE. As we noted, students are not expected to take items that do not make an important contribution to determining their score. But not every item presented to a student is scored as part of the test. New items may be included to calibrate scale values before being included in the regular item bank. The students taking the test do not know which set of items is experimental, and thus are motivated to provide realistic data on the item difficulty. With a large item bank, the content of the scored items is balanced so that the meaning of the scores does not differ greatly because of item selection. Thus GRE as a CAT appears very efficient for large samples of examinees, and the design allows

meaningful comparison of scores both longitudinally and with the current examinees.

Changing Populations: Recentering the SAT

Due to changing populations of examinees over decades, the SAT faced similar problems with the scale scores as those seen with the GRE. Originally, the mean of the SAT scores equaled 500 for Verbal and for Math, but by 1990 the average Verbal scores were about 50 points lower than the Math scores. Why would this be? The populations of students taking the SAT (and the GRE) changed. Educators have explained the curriculum differences that may have contributed to the change in test scores—students taking more mathematics courses and placing less emphasis on reading and vocabulary. Other population changes may result from schools encouraging students who are less similar to the original examinee populations to take the tests.

The decision was made to recenter the SAT to make the scale more meaningful for current examinees. Recentering resulted in the new score scale again having an average of 500 on each portion of the SAT (Dorans, 2002). Before the recentering, many individuals believed they were lower in Verbal than in Math ability (even if they performed near the average on both sections) because they misunderstood how the averages had changed over time. Dorans reports that recentering the SAT scores improved test users' interpretation of student performance, but shifts in the average scores on each section are already occurring. By 2006, the newly named SAT Reasoning Test scores averaged 518 for Math and 503 for Critical Reading (formerly Verbal). Recentering may be necessary again in the future. It may be important for the GRE to be recentered in the same way as the SAT, and test developers may wish to realign the GRE as well. Realignment would spread out the scores at the top of the scale; recall in 2006, 6% of students in the GRE Quantitative sample obtained the top score.

A disadvantage of recentering is that the longitudinal comparison of test scores is no longer evident with new scores. The SAT Reasoning Test can be used to compare score changes over the past decade and a half, but the longer-term comparisons were lost with the recentering. The test developer must weigh the advantages and disadvantages of every change. An advantage of having tests on different scales or having different averages for sections of the tests is that people might be more likely to consider each test as being different from others. When scores on different tests are comparable, the tests might be considered to be replacements for each other. For example, many people interpret an IQ as a measure of intelligence without considering what test was taken, a problem because different intelligence tests measure different traits. The sophisticated reader of test information must understand what a test measures as well as how scores are to be interpreted.

Understanding the Labels in Standards-Based Approaches

Given the difficulty of interpreting score performance based on norm comparisons, one might wonder whether it would be simpler to report standards-based information. But what does a label like proficient mean? The National Center for Educational Statistics (2007) has compared the performance of students across states by mapping state standards to the NAEP scale for reading and mathematics. The definition of proficient is established independently by each state, and the percentage of students being classified as proficient depends on that definition. The more challenging the level established by the state, the lower the percentage of students who will be identified as proficient. Typically, the degree of achievement necessary to reach the level of proficient is lower by the state definition than by the NAEP standard. In the 2005 sample for comparing Grade 8 reading scores, North Carolina had the lowest standard accompanied by an estimated 88% proficiency for their students. South Carolina had the highest standard accompanied by an estimated 30% proficiency. Because of the differing definitions, one cannot determine which state has the better readers.

Furthermore, a state can change the percentage of students at the proficient level drastically by altering the difficulty of the standards. In the 2003 Grade 8 mathematics comparison, Arizona had a very high standard associated with the "Meets the Standard" label (actually, one point above the NAEP "Proficient" cut score) that was accompanied by a disappointing 21% proficiency. In the 2005 comparison, Arizona had dropped their standard almost to the level of the NAEP cut score for "Basic," the lower category, and reported 61% proficiency. This change in the percentage of students reaching proficiency associated with changes in standards cannot be interpreted meaningfully; one cannot determine whether the students tested in 2005 performed better or worse than the students tested 2 years earlier. Naïve readers, however, may think the greater percentage of students reported as "Meets the Standard" indicates improvement in the state's educational system.

Combining Approaches: The GRE and ACT

The ambiguity of the label *proficient* across states, grades, and subjects demonstrates the need for more than just standards-based reporting. The GRE Analytical Writing section is a good example of the combination of approaches to allow meaningful test interpretation. With the standards-based approach, the GRE has provided score level descriptions to help the reader understand what each score means on this section of the general test. For example, for scores 4 and 3.5, the description is: "Provides competent analysis of complex ideas; develops and supports main points with relevant reasons and/or examples; is adequately organized; conveys meaning with reasonable clarity; demonstrates satisfactory control of sentence struc-

ture and language usage but may have some errors that affect clarity" (ETS, 2006, p. 23). In addition, each score level (in half-point increments) is associated with a percentile rank to give a norm-referenced interpretation based on a current sample of over 1 million examinees. For the October 1, 2002, to June 30, 2005, sample, 32% of the examinees scored lower than 4.0; 17% scored lower than 3.5. The use of both standards-based and norm-based score information in this example provides users with a much clearer understanding of what examinees' scores mean than would be possible with only one approach.

Another example of combining approaches to make score interpretation more meaningful is the use of benchmarks with the ACT. According to the 2006 *ACT High School Profile Report,* "A benchmark score is the minimum score needed on an ACT subject-area test to indicate a 50% chance of obtaining a B or higher or about a 75% chance of obtaining a C or higher in the corresponding credit-bearing college course" (p. 6). In 2006, the percent of ACT-tested students ready for college-level coursework by this criterion ranged from 69% in English composition to 27% in biology. Such information can help counselors assist students in making decisions about their preparation for college.

States may also choose to combine approaches in their state assessments. These dual purpose assessments embed items from a nationally-standardized test in a state-developed standards-based test to provide both national PRs and standards-based scores for interpretation. The advantage of this combination is that it allows schools to spend less time testing students than would be required to administer both a nationally normed and state standards-based test. However, fewer nationally-standardized items are given than standards-based items, the nationally-standardized items are not given in their intended context, and the validity of this combination has not been documented.

Understanding the Unit of Comparison

When reporting performance, one should compare groups to groups and individuals to individuals. A misuse of norms is often encountered in newspaper reports when the average performance of all students in a school is compared with a collection of individual scores. Because individual scores have much more variability than do group means, the result of comparing a school average with individual students is that all schools appear nearer to average than actual performances are. This issue is not related to the Lake Wobegon effect mentioned earlier, but is more a central tendency effect; the truly extreme-scoring schools (both those far above and far below the mean) are not identified as being as different from average as they really are.

Some tests are devised only for group interpretations. The NAEP does not report scores for individual students; however, NAEP data provide ample opportunity to compare subgroups. The NAEP sampling method allocates different samples of items to students within a school. By carefully selecting and recording demographic characteristics of each examinee, NAEP allows performance comparisons for racial/ethnic and gender groups on various subsets of items. If an adequate representative sample of schools within each state participated in the NAEP program, it would not be difficult to use the test as a national test for comparing states. These comparisons would be fairer to the states than comparisons made with the volunteer samples that take the ACT or SAT.

One needs to know a great deal about the tests and the samples before interpreting score differences, partly because the groups are not equally represented in these samples. For example, comparisons of gender groups with the ACT and SAT produce different results. In the 2006 ACT national sample, there were 646,688 females and only 517,563 males (3% of the students did not report gender). If the additional examinees are lower-scoring students, as is often the case, then the picture presented by the obtained scores is misleading. On the SAT, males score higher than females on both Critical Reading and Math, whereas on the ACT males score higher on Math, Science, and Total and females score higher on English and Reading. Females score higher on Writing on both tests. In general, different students take the ACT and the SAT. Differences in the populations and in the content of the two tests contribute to the score differences observed between males and females.

Conclusion

Issues of fairness in testing have resulted in a new definition of standardization. Content and administration do not need to be identical, but rather sufficiently comparable for all examinees. Fairness is also important in interpretation of test scores. Scores are interpreted with reference to comparison groups or predetermined standards for performance. Combining norm-referenced and standards-based approaches may lead to better understanding, but readers must understand what tests were designed to measure and how scores were intended to be interpreted. We believe simply gaining a better understanding of the ways of making performance meaningful would do much to aid individuals in accomplishing the primary goal of standardization: making fairer decisions based on test information.

References and Further Readings

ACT. (n.d.). *ACT high school profile report: The graduating class of 2006, national.* Retrieved July 16, 2007, from http://www.act.org/news/data/06/pdf/National2006.pdf

American Educational Research Association, American Psychological Association, & National Council on Measurement in Education. (1999). *Standards for educational and psychological testing.* Washington, DC: American Educational Research Association.

Baglin, R. F. (1981). Does "nationally" really mean nationally? *Journal of Educational Measurement, 18,* 97–107.

Bracey, G. W. (2006). *Reading educational research: How to avoid getting statistically snookered.* Portsmouth, NH: Heinemann.

Breimhorst v. Educational Testing Service, *Settlement Agreement,* Case No. 99-3387 (N.D. Cal. 2001).

Brennan, R. L. (2006). Perspectives on the evolution and future of educational measurement. In R. L. Brennan (Ed.), *Educational measurement* (4th ed., pp. 1–16). Westport, CT: Praeger.

Camilli, G. (2006). Test fairness. In R. L. Brennan (Ed.), *Educational measurement* (4th ed., pp. 221–256). Westport, CT: Praeger.

Cannell, J. J. (1988). Nationally normed elementary achievement testing in America's public schools: How all 50 states are above the national average. *Educational Measurement: Issues and Practice, 7,* 5–9.

Cronbach, L. J. (1960). *Essentials of psychological testing* (2nd ed.). New York: Harper & Row.

Dorans, N. J. (2002). Recentering and realigning the SAT score distributions: How and why. *Journal of Educational Measurement, 39,* 59–84.

Educational Testing Service. (2006). *GRE Graduate Record Examinations 2006–2007 guide to the use of scores.* Retrieved July 16, 2007, from http://www.ets.org/gre/edupubs.html

Hendrickson, A. (2007). An NCME instructional module on multistage testing. *Educational Measurement: Issues and Practice, 26,* 44–52.

Linn, R. L. (1975). Anchor test study: The long and the short of it. *Journal of Educational Measurement, 12,* 201–214.

National Center for Education Statistics. (2007). *Mapping 2005 state proficiency standards onto the NAEP scales* (NCES 2007-482). Washington, DC: Author.

No Child Left Behind Act of 2001. P. L. 107–110, (2002). Retrieved July 30, 2007, from http://www.ed.gov/policy/elsec/leg/esea02/index.html

Sabers, D., & Powers, S. (2005). The condition of assessment of student learning in Arizona: 2005. In D. R. Garcia & A. Molnar (Eds.), *The condition of pre-K–12 education in Arizona: 2005* (pp. 9.1–9.15). Retrieved August 7, 2007, from http://epsl.asu.edu/aepi/Report/EPSL-0509-116-AEPI.pdf

Zwick, R. (2006). Higher education admissions testing. In R. L. Brennan (Ed.), *Educational measurement* (4th ed., pp. 647–679). Westport, CT: Praeger.

47

TRADITIONAL TEACHER TESTS

CAROLINE R. H. WILEY

University of Arizona

All students experience various classroom assessments, ranging from pop quizzes to essays to traditional multiple-choice tests. Undoubtedly, there has been some time in your life when you questioned the fairness of a classroom test. Unfortunately, some teachers likely proceed with assessments and interpretations without giving student complaints legitimate credence and use that same assessment the following year. This does not describe all classroom testing experiences, but most of us can recall at least one experience where this scenario rings true.

Reasons for this situation include: (1) lack of sufficient training in constructing tests in teacher preparation programs, and (2) a mismatch between educational measurement theory and practice on the proper construction of teacher-made tests. Also, research is more focused on construction and interpretation of standardized tests, even though they have little direct application in classrooms—standardized test results are not received in a timely enough manner to directly affect instruction, making it difficult for teachers to apply standardized test results in their teaching.

Despite the insufficient focus on teacher-made tests in teacher education programs, it is important for teachers to have the knowledge and skills to construct and use traditional classroom tests. This chapter discusses the properties and importance of traditional teacher-made objective tests in classroom settings. The effects of increased employment of high-stakes standardized tests on the use of traditional classroom tests in a standards-based era also are discussed.

Need for Assessment

As Horace Mann is deemed the father of American education, so too is Ralph Tyler the father of curriculum and instruction. Tyler's book, *Basic Principles of Curriculum and Instruction* (1949), played a seminal role in reforming the then current state of instructional practices. Tyler called for a focus on educational objectives that were to be planned, taught, and evaluated. Until that point there were no real measures of accountability of learning in place. After Tyler, evaluation of objectives became a fundamental component to ensuring that desired student learning was being achieved. Subsequently, objectives became the basis of classroom assessment. Benjamin Bloom's, *Taxonomy of Educational Objectives* (1954) provided educators a way to classify learning and assessment tasks for years to come. Objectives are the key ingredients to making the planning, instructional, and evaluation of phases of instruction flow together.

Overview of Teacher-Made Tests

Standardized Versus Nonstandardized

There are two major categories of tests: standardized and nonstandardized. Standardized tests are administered and scored using fairly uniform standards. They can be used to make either norm-referenced (relative comparisons) or criterion-referenced (absolute comparisons) interpretations of student learning. Until the No Child Left Behind Act of 2001, many standardized tests were used to make norm-referenced interpretations of student learning. Currently, 45 states administer a criterion-referenced state standardized test (*Education Week*, 2007); however, to reiterate, test results are rarely returned in a timely manner, thus minimizing the potential instructional effect.

Nonstandardized tests, or teacher-made tests, are exactly that—tests constructed by individual teachers. There are no standardized procedures in construction, administration, or scoring. Most student assessment exists in the form of classroom-level tests. Historically, traditional teacher-made objective summative tests, or tests used at the completion of learning, composed typical testing practice.

Teacher-made tests can be used for either criterion- or norm-referencing; however, Black and William (1998a) reported that teachers tend to make norm-referenced (i.e., social comparative) interpretations. Criterion-referenced interpretations, however, are more appropriate: students can perform a certain skill regardless of how others perform.

Prevalence

Stiggins and Bridgeford (1985) found that the majority of teachers reportedly use teacher-made tests and that use increased with grade level: 69% of second-grade teachers versus 89% of eleventh-grade teachers. Most teachers (75%) reported having some concern about their own tests; higher grade level teachers were most concerned about improving them.

McMillan and Workman (1998) reported that many teachers assess basic facts, knowledge, and rules; use short-answer or objective test questions (Frary, Cross, & Weber, 1993); have difficulty with constructing higher-order thinking questions; and have low levels of competency regarding classroom assessment, specifically communicating results. McMillan (2001) found that secondary teachers reported using their own assessments (98%) more frequently than prepackaged assessments (80%). It is unclear whether these assessments were objective or performance-based. Although older studies indicate that formal tests occupy 5 to 15% of students' time, more recent figures are unavailable (Crooks, 1988).

Teacher Perspectives

Teachers perceive teacher-made tests as important. They view their use of traditional tests in high regard (Pigge & Marso, 1993) and put more weight on teacher-made tests (versus other assessment methods) when assigning final grades (Boothroyd, McMorris, & Pruzek, 1992). Despite the high frequency of reported use, teachers tend to be quite independent and somewhat reluctant to share ideas in developing and using their tests (Cizek, Fitzgerald, & Rachor, 1996).

Much research indicates that some teachers lack the sufficient competency in measurement and assessment necessary to justify how test results are currently used (Stiggins & Bridgeford, 1985; Boothroyd, McMorris, & Pruzek, 1992). This may be because preservice teachers perceive courses that focus on traditional teacher tests and measurement as less valuable than those that focus on alternative assessment methods (Taylor & Nolen, 1996).

Prepackaged Tests

Teachers now commonly use tests that are included in prepackaged programs or textbooks. Most comprehensive school reform programs, textbooks, and many curriculum programs now come with ready-made assessments.

Teachers are busy and some readily welcome prepackaged tests with open arms. They provide quick access to assessments and given what research has shown about teacher competency in test construction, it is understandable that teachers use these tests with too little concern. Prepackaged tests, however, are not a panacea for improving student learning. Prepackaged tests are developed for a general student under general learning circumstances. McMillan (2007) points out three key points regarding the use of published tests:

1. A textbook's or curriculum program's text does not ensure high quality. Similarly, many tests are accessible via organizational or peer collaboration Web sites. Teachers need to assess the quality of any test they encounter.
2. Tests of high quality do not necessarily measure the learning outcomes intended by a teacher. Not all textbooks align with teachers' learning objectives, especially under the No Child Left Behind Act. This is because local education agencies have had difficulty adopting textbooks that align with their state's standards.
3. The language and presentation of concepts on tests that publishers use may differ from that used by the teacher. Instruction and assessment must be aligned.

Nevertheless, teachers can modify prepackaged tests. It will take more effort and time than just using the commercial test, but the instructional gain may prove to be higher than just accepting the status quo. The advantage of a teacher-made test or modified commercial test over a prepackaged test is the ability to adapt to a local environment (e.g., different learning abilities, cultural backgrounds, and so forth) to ensure that test results are used appropriately.

Instructional Importance

Two commonly reported uses of teacher-made tests are for grading and reporting and for diagnosing learning difficulties (these topics will be discussed later). Tests serve other important functions such as allowing teachers to make accurate instructional decisions, determining student's prior knowledge, and determining the effectiveness of instruction.

Tests can be used both formatively and summatively to help assess student learning. It is common practice to use tests in a summative fashion—at the end of instruction as an assessment *of* learning, rather than during instruction as an assessment *for* learning. Black and William (1998b) contend that effective implementation of formative assessment can raise educational standards and is an important aspect of effective teaching because the teacher focuses on higher-order thinking and less on grades, administers many assessments, and provides high-quality feedback. It also allows for learning to occur on an individual level. Paper-pencil tests play an important role in formative assessment—they help teachers gauge learning and modify instruction.

Tests should focus on both higher and lower cognitions of learning—not just rote memorization—and be shared with colleagues. Often there is a disconnect between teachers' instructional intent and the assessments they choose to measure learning. When tests align with developing a deeper understanding, their utility becomes greater.

One way of ensuring that instruction aligns with assessment is to use a test blueprint (table of specifications). Just as an architect builds a building from a blueprint, a teacher can use a blueprint to build tests. Blueprints allow teachers to make sure that the learning objectives from a unit are assessed on the test at appropriate levels of cognition (see Figure 47.1). Typically, blueprints use Bloom's original

(Bloom, 1954) or revised taxonomy (Anderson & Krathwohl, 2001), but any cognitive taxonomy can be used. Recommendations for creating test blueprints can and ought to be modified to meet teachers' needs. Another valuable feature that can be added to blueprints is item types, which can help teachers gauge how much time the test will take.

Using Assessment Results

Part of using teacher-made tests to their fullest extent is using the results appropriately and efficiently. Simply returning test scores to students is not nearly enough to enhance learning. If anything, it creates higher anxiety for students because it puts more emphasis on the grade rather than on comprehension. If teachers construct high-quality tests, provide high-quality corrective feedback, and reassess, then students will experience positive assessment experiences.

Consider Situation 1.

Situation 1:

Anne received a 72 on a quiz on multiplication facts. The only feedback on the quiz was the grade and which items she got wrong. The teacher proceeded with the unit on converting percentages to simplified fractions. On the unit test, Anne received a 69.4, where again the feedback only indicated which items she got wrong. Since the teacher rounded

Grade 8: Arizona Geography Summative Test*	Knowledge	Comprehension	Synthesis	Matching Set (90 sec)	Muliple Choice-complex (90 sec)	Short Answer (45 sec)	Restricted Response (15 min)	T	%
1. State Facts									
1.1 Identify state capital.	1					1		1	6%
1.2 Recall current population.	1					1		1	6%
1.3 Recall date of state inauguration.	1					1		1	6%
1.4 Recall current state policymakers.	4			1(4 it.)				4	22%
2. Cities									
2.1 Locate major cities on a map.	5					5		5	28%
2.2 Hypothesize about population and industrial growth in Arizona.			1				1	1	6%
3. Topography/Climate									
3.1 Describe the differences in topography between northern and southern Arizona.		3				3		3	17%
3.2 Explain why there are topographic/climactic differences.		2				1	1	2	11%
Total	5	5	1	0	4	8	2	18	100%
Percentage	28%	28%	6%	0%	22%	44%	11%	100%	
Total Time				90 sec	360 sec	360 sec	30 min	45 min	

*This is a shortened example of an instructional unit, so objectives may not be comprehensive.
[1] Bloom's Original Taxonomy has 6 hierarchical levels. Knowledge is the lowest, Evaluation is the highest (Bloom, 1954).

Figure 47.1 Test Blueprint Example

Anne's score up to a 70, Anne was satisfied with her grade and the teacher moved on to the next unit.

The teacher in Situation 1 failed to provide Anne with proper corrective feedback and remedial action. The quiz only provided indication of performance and offered no direction for Anne to focus her learning. The teacher should have given Anne feedback about what specifically she got wrong on the test and some direction to the right answer. In addition, before the unit test, the teacher should have given Anne additional assessments (homework, work sheets, quizzes, oral questioning, etc.) to ensure that she clarified the problems she had with multiplication facts. Similar situations can interfere with students' motivation to learn and promote a focus on not failing rather than on achieving mastery (authentic and higher-level understanding).

Understanding that one score is just one measure of an entire domain of measurements to be taken and that the inferences drawn about student learning must be appropriate given the nature of the test are also important concepts for teachers to know.

Data Analysis and Tracking

Teachers do not need to be statisticians to do analyses on student achievement data. Many statistical tools are available through programs that are likely already available to them. Simple statistics (e.g., mean, median, mode, and range) provide great insight to the quality of instruction and learning, as do more advanced statistics (e.g., standard deviation and correlation). Tracking student, class, and even grade-level trends serves great instructional purposes for teachers.

Tracking longitudinal student trends on various concepts can assist teachers in seeing individual strengths, weaknesses, improvements, and so forth. When teachers have a better grasp on students' learning difficulties, they can provide precise remedial work. Data analysis of teacher-made test data can also help teachers over the years determine which concepts are difficult to teach. For these problematic areas, teachers can modify instruction and administer the same tests both before and after instruction to help ascertain mastery of learning.

Collaborating with colleagues and devising grade-level analysis procedures can also provide great insight regarding students' performance and can help create uniform interpretations within a school. Additionally, visual data analysis is an informal yet useful method for interpreting results. Teachers can construct simple charts and graphs to get a better grasp of student performance.

For example, Table 47.1 shows five math test scores for three students from the first quarter of school. Based on the means alone, which is a common practice, one would conclude that all three

Table 47.1   Student Math Test Scores

	John	Bill	Mike
Test 1	86	76	92
Test 2	82	80	88
Test 3	83	84	84
Test 4	85	88	80
Test 5	84	92	76
Mean	84	84	84
Range	4	16	16

students performed about the same; however, the range and trend of scores is very different. Figure 47.2 visually displays the longitudinal trend of scores. These results can help the teacher see that Bill made great improvement, Mike's performance declined, and John performed about the same on all five tests. If the teacher regularly looked at trends in student data, after Test 3, the teacher could have looked into why Mike's test scores have been decreasing and made appropriate instructional decisions.

Data analysis can also be used at the class level. Figure 47.3 displays a histogram (frequency count) of the Test 1 scores of a class (10 students). Using this graph the teacher can obtain a better estimate of how the class did as a whole. The mean was 84.8. When combined with Table 47.1, the teacher can see that John scored near the average on Test 1, Bill scored below average, and Mike scored above average. These norm-referenced comparisons should not drive instructional decisions, but they do provide additional insight to student performance. If the class mean was lower than 84, maybe 65 or 69, this would alert the teacher to inadequate instruction of content or a poorly constructed test, or perhaps the students did not study.

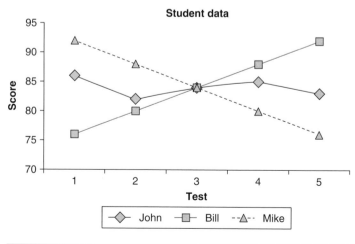

Figure 47.2   Student Math Trends

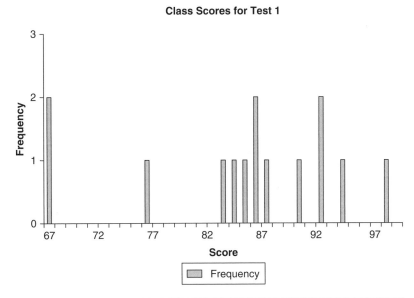

Figure 47.3   Histogram for Test 1

Measurement Theory Versus Classroom Application

Teachers must be concerned with reliability and validity of their assessments. There is, however, much debate regarding to what extent classroom tests should possess certain technical properties and the types of statistical computations teachers ought to perform. In almost any classroom assessment textbook there is some mention of reliability and validity of assessment of learning. Some textbooks are very detailed and offer exact calculations of various types of reliability and validity evidence (Nitko, 2004); some are focused less on the numerical properties and more on conceptual understanding (Popham, 2005).

The biggest obstacle preventing teachers' comprehension and application of reliability and validity is the mismatch between educational measurement theory and actual classroom processes. A strict focus on measurement theory tends to dehumanize and threaten the very essence of teacher-student relationships. It is difficult for teachers to think of student learning only in numerical terms, and there is no reason why they should. Teachers ought to be concerned about the effects of any assessment on student motivation and emotion. It is therefore beneficial to present the topics of reliability and validity in ways similar to how teachers ought to think—from a student's perspective.

Reliability

Reliability is how consistent or stable assessment results are, or that results from a given assessment will generalize to later conditions; scores will yield similar results across different time periods, different forms of a test, or both. Calculating reliability coefficients can be an arduous task that teachers may not benefit much from, have the statisti-

cal expertise to do, or most important, have the time to do.

Measurement Error

Rather than calculating coefficients, teachers ought to be aware of the importance of the concepts of reliability and how they can help improve assessment of student learning. When assessing students, consistency is important. Teachers want to be able to say confidently that student test scores are not a function of measurement error, or unpredictable error. Measurement error is the error associated with the act of measuring a certain attribute and is essentially the heart of reliability. A common example is a weight scale. Often, different weights are yielded on different scales and at different times. One may weigh more at night than in the morning; or weigh more on a cheap scale in the bathroom than on the expensive scale at the gym; or may get on the scale, get off, then get right back on and read two completely different measurements. Regardless, if off by 1 pound or 20, it is still an inconsistent measurement—some sort of error makes the observed weight not equal the true weight had there been no error. The problem is that there is error in all measurements—elimination of error is impossible. True measures of certain attributes can never be obtained; instead, estimates are the best measures that can be produced and we hope that the observed measurement is as close to the true as possible. Essentially, the goal is to reduce error as much as possible.

Practical Applications

This notion of error is very useful when assessing students. It is very common for educators, policy makers, parents, and students to take a single test score and make highly significant inferences based on that one score, not realizing that it is just one measure of student achievement. For example, consider the following situations.

Situation 2:
Johnny received an 83 on Mrs. Smith's geology test taken on Monday. Johnny takes the same test on Friday and receives a 95. Mrs. Smith is quite perplexed and after inquiry finds out that on Sunday night Johnny was ill and only slept for 2 hours.

OR

Situation 3:
Johnny received an 83 on Mrs. Smith's geology test taken on Monday. Johnny took the same test on Friday and received a 66. Come to find out Johnny really did not study

for the test on Monday and so guessed on the majority of the answers.

Often, teachers do not give the same test twice and so in Situation 2, Johnny's true geological performance would be underestimated and in Situation 3 it would be overestimated. Eliminate the Friday test and Johnny would undoubtedly have no complaints in Situation 3, but be very upset in Situation 2, and either way Mrs. Smith would be ignorant of Johnny's true performance.

Consider a different example.

Situation 4:

Mrs. Smith administered a geology test on Monday. Her daughter was ill all weekend long, so she did not have time until 1 a.m. Monday morning to construct the test. Consequently, the test was prone to error, confusing directions, and nonsensical items. The class average on the test was 72. Johnny was sick the first 3 days of the week, so missed the exam. Mrs. Smith allowed him to take a make-up on Friday and had ample time to construct a new test. Johnny scored a 92, and she concludes that his knowledge of geology is well above that of the class.

Situation 4 is exemplary of how test construction error can affect consistency of scores. It is very likely that the rest of the class would score higher had they taken the make-up test with Johnny. In this case, the error within the test itself gives Mrs. Smith less certainty that the results are indicative of students' true performance levels. This situation is also exemplary of how error can affect validity, which will be discussed in the following section. Think of a test as a scale—the score will vary depending on the conditions surrounding the measurement. The higher quality the scale, or test, used to take the measurement, the greater the likelihood that the observed measurement will be closer to the true measurement.

These sources of error contribute to the dependability of scores, thus influencing the inferences drawn about test performance, which is why educators would be remiss to not consider them. Although there are statistical ways to estimate reliability, often the assumptions of large sample size and large variation in scores are not met at the classroom level. After all, teachers ultimately do not want a wide range of scores; they desire all students to do well. Therefore, a conceptual approach is more appropriate.

Validity

Validity is the accuracy of the inferences and uses of test results. Where reliability is concerned with consistency and generalizability of results, validity is concerned with whether tests actually measure what they are purported to measure and whether the use of any test is appropriate. Similar to reliability coefficients, validity coefficients can also be calculated and are subject to the same concerns.

From a students' perspective, validity is about fairness. When students interpret a test as being an unfair measure of achievement, the validity of the interpretation of results is often undermined. Reconsider Situation 4. Because the test was so error-prone, it is erroneous for Mrs. Smith to conclude that Johnny performed well above the class. In this case, Mrs. Smith is drawing an invalid inference about students' geological achievement. Most of the students who took the test on Monday will perceive the test to be an unfair assessment of their true achievement; instead of measuring geological achievement, the test measures other irrelevant factors.

It is important to note that fairness is not the same across all students: what some students consider fair, may be considered unfair by others. For example, some students may have trouble concentrating in the middle of the day or after lunch. Some may be easily affected by outside disturbances, and some may simply not test well, but do possess content knowledge. All of these situations affect the validity of test results, but it is the teacher's responsibility to detect and adjust these difficulties as warranted. Teachers need to determine to what extent different perceptions of unfairness affect student assessment, and diagnose and treat the problems accordingly.

Systematic Error

As with reliability, it is easier to make the argument that teachers ought to be more concerned with logically applying the concept of validity and less concerned with the statistical application. Where reliability is concerned with unpredictable error, validity is concerned with systematic error, or predictable error. Systematic error affects the accuracy of the measure, not the consistency. Referring to the scale example, consider that one is using a very high-quality scale (Olympic quality), but calibrated the scale incorrectly (the zero point starts at the 2 pound mark). Every time a measurement is taken it will consistently be off by 2 pounds. In this case, the error is not unpredictable as in reliability; rather it is completely predictable—consistent but inaccurate measurements are taken. This is a key concept in understanding reliability and validity: reliability is a necessary but not sufficient condition for validity—something can be reliable without being valid, but to be valid, it must be reliable.

Practical Applications

Showing evidence of validity is not always as simple as a mere statistic. One type of evidence for validity is showing that one's content is both representative and relevant to stated learning goals. This is something that teachers need to do. Tests should include items that are representative and relevant to instruction, regarding both content and level of cognitive demand. For example, if the instructional unit covered spelling U.S. cities and the test included items that covered locating U.S. cities, it would invalidate the use of the assessment results, especially if there are high-stakes inferences drawn about student ability to spell U.S. cities. Similarly, given the same instructional unit, if the test included only one U.S. city to spell, that too would invalidate the use of results. The sample of test items was not large enough to make an appropriate inference about students' ability to spell U.S. cities.

A test blueprint, as noted, is a great tool for ensuring that tests are aligned with instruction, specifically for the longer summative unit or chapter tests. This visually allows the teacher to see what objectives are being measured, by how many and what types of items. A more informal method of checking for evidence of validity is to have colleagues familiar with the content review the test.

It is important that educators are able to assert confidently that students' performance on a test reflects the interpretations being made. Being cognizant of intended learning goals, test content, and test development and scoring procedures helps prevent invalid inferences from being drawn.

Standards for Proper Test Construction

The *Code of Professional Responsibility in Educational Measurement* (National Council on Measurement in Education [NCME], 1995) and the *Standards for Teacher Competence in Educational Assessment of Students* (STCEAS; American Federation of Teachers, National Council on Measurement in Education, & National Educa-

tion Association, 1990) are intended to provide educators support in the development of fair and high-quality tests. The main standards in the STCEAS are that teachers should be skilled in (1) choosing and developing appropriate assessments; (2) administering, scoring, and interpreting results from both published and teacher-made tests; (3) using assessment results when making instructional decisions; (4) developing valid grading procedures; (5) communicating assessment results to others; and (6) recognizing unethical and inappropriate uses of assessment results.

Types of Tests

There are two common forms of paper-pencil tests that teachers make: constructed response and selected response. Constructed response items include essay items and short-answer or fill-in-the-blank items (FIB). Selected response items include multiple-choice, matching, and true/false items. Teachers report using short-answer and multiple-choice tests with the most frequency (Frary, Cross, & Weber, 1993); however, in some subjects like language arts, essay questions are used more frequently. See Table 47.2 for strengths and limitations of various item formats.

Constructed Response

Essay tests are very common in subjects like language arts, literature, and social studies, where synthesis and organization of ideas or other higher-order thinking skills

Table 47.2   Item Format Characteristics

	Strengths	Limitations
Constructed response (CR)	Can get to HOTS*; relatively easier to construct than SR items	Subjective and time-consuming scoring; lengthy administration time, thus limited sampling of content; bluffing in students' responses
Essays	Can get to HOTS	Difficult to word so that all students interpret the question the same way; scores heavily influenced by writing ability
Short-answer/fill-in-the-blank	Good for computations and recall, when offering a selection of responses makes answer obvious	Difficult to elicit one correct response; cannot easily assess HOTS; often scoring rubrics are not used when they should
Selected response (SR)	Can ask many questions; fast and objective scoring	Difficult item construction; difficult to assess HOTS; blind guessing of students' responses
Multiple-choice	Can get to higher cognitive levels compared to other SR items	Difficult to construct plausible distractors, thus creating inadvertent cues
Matching	Good for measuring simple associations	Limited to lower cognitive levels; directions are often confusing or absent
True/false	When measuring cause and effect relationships can get to higher cognitive levels; can ask many questions	Difficult to construct so that statement is 100% true or 100% false; often confusing wording; little diagnostic assessment of learning available; most influenced by guessing

NOTE: *Higher-order thinking skills (HOTS).

(HOTS) are more important than lower levels of learning. Although short-answer and fill-in-the-blank questions are considered constructed response items, they are typically more objective than essays and require students to write a one- or two-worded response.

Selected Response

Multiple-choice (MC) items are the most common item format among classroom teachers. Matching items provide a fast and efficient way for measuring simple associations (e.g., books and their authors, people and their birthdays, and so forth). True/false items involve a binary categorization of any given statement and come in varying formats: right/wrong, correct/incorrect, fact/opinion, etc.

Combining Formats

It is quite common for teachers to include multiple item formats on a single test. So long as careful attention is given to test construction and layout, this allows teachers to assess learning in a variety of ways and at cognitive levels ranging from simple recall to synthesis and evaluation of concepts. When this is done, however, extended essays are often not used due to time constraints. Rather, restricted-response essays (usually one to two paragraphs) are used in conjunction with some combination of selected response item types.

Writing Quality Tests

As discussed earlier, being equipped with the knowledge and skills to construct high-quality tests is desired not only so that one can administer high-quality assessments, but also so that one can assess the quality and appropriateness of prepackaged tests. The previously discussed assessment standards provide general guidelines for proper assessment use, but the question of how to actually write quality tests still remains.

Guidelines

Situation 5:
Sue and Joe just took a Civil War test in Mr. Clark's class. They discuss how they think they did during lunch. By the time their conversation is over, they have summed up the following complaints:

- *Items 4 and 7 had two correct answers.*
- *Sue thought she could reuse the responses on the matching set and Joe thought he couldn't.*
- *Item 10 was offensive to Joe because his great-great-grandfather was a slave owner.*
- *Item 12 used a word that neither knew.*
- *Both figured out that the answer to item 5 was in item 8.*
- *Items 6 and 9 were never covered in class.*

Unfortunately, Situation 5 is a far too common occurrence in classroom testing. Poorly constructed tests, similar to that in Situation 5, affect students' motivation to achieve mastery, create unnecessary test anxiety, and make the scoring and interpreting of results significantly harder for the teacher. Fortunately, there are ways for teachers to eliminate such scenarios.

The key components to constructing good classroom tests are (1) content knowledge, (2) clear learning outcomes, (3) knowledge and awareness of students' developmental processes and of the cognitive processes invoked by tasks, and (4) an understanding of the properties of different item formats. Constructing classroom tests can be implemented in three major steps: (1) aligning test items to the learning objectives of the unit, (2) following recommended guidelines for test construction, and (3) evaluating the test after test administration. The following are recommended guidelines for general test construction. For specific guidelines regarding specific types of items see sources listed in the References and Further Readings section at the end of this chapter.

1. Aligning Test Items to Learning Objectives

Keeping instruction and assessment aligned are important for maximizing student learning. Test blueprints can greatly assist in ensuring that test items assess desired instructional content, include a representative sample of the content, and that the number of items on the test is appropriate given time allocations.

2. Following Recommended Guidelines for Test Construction

Depending on different item formats, recommended guidelines will change (see Kubiszyn & Borich, 2007; Nitko, 2004). There are, however, universal guidelines that can be applied across formats.

1. Provide clear directions.
2. Avoid ambiguous or trick questions.
3. Do not provide unintentional cues in either the item itself, or in other items on the test.
4. Avoid complex or unfamiliar vocabulary or syntax.
5. Use general rules of grammar in constructing items.
6. Check for bias or offensive language.
7. Check for appropriateness of content; do not assess trivial information.
8. Physically format the test appropriately.
   a. Arrange items of similar format together to minimize confusion to students and maximize time.
   b. Provide proper amount of space for students' responses.
   c. Be consistent when using blanks (FIB), vertically or horizontally displaying alternatives (MC, T/F).
   d. Avoid page breaking in the middle of an item.
10. Create the test with enough time to proofread, take the test yourself, and possibly have a colleague review the content.

3. Evaluating the Test After Test Administration

This third step is often omitted from teachers' routines, primarily due to lack of statistical expertise and lack of time. This step, however, is arguably the most underrated step in test construction for making valid inferences about student learning. If a test is poorly constructed, students will likely perform poorly. Their performance is then interpreted incorrectly, thus affecting instructional and motivational components of learning. Another effect of omitting this step is the future use of unrevised tests. Teachers often recycle tests over multiple years; if there are poor-quality items, they should be revised before readministering. Evaluating tests can also inform the quality of teacher instruction. Sometimes the test is well constructed, but the instruction of the concept may have been inadequate or even absent. Teachers can then make appropriate adjustments to the current test scores, or more optimally, reteach and retest.

Judgmental Review

Popham (2005) discusses two types of item improvement approaches that teachers can take: judgmental and statistical. Judgmental item improvement is more of an informal process that requires teachers to essentially review their tests on their own, with their students, and with colleagues. It is similar to the pretest review, only it takes place after test administration. Asking students what they thought of the test is an excellent method to gauge test quality; however, students are not the experts—teachers are. When using student review, teachers need to use their professional judgment and determine which comments are authentic and which are retaliatory or self-serving.

Statistical Review

Statistical item analysis involves computing the percentage of students who got an item correct (item difficulty); the difference between the percentages of higher scoring and lower scoring students who got the item correct (item discrimination); and with multiple-choice items, an analysis of which scoring students used each alternative. In measurement theory it is assumed that higher scoring students' scores can be trusted more than lower scoring students scores, therefore it is useful to compare the two groups (item discrimination). More students from the higher scoring group than the lower scoring group should get an item correct because they are said to have more knowledge, relatively speaking. In classroom tests, although it is ideal to have all students do well on a test, examining item discrimination can help find faulty test items. These three procedures can lead to the identification of improperly functioning items, thus leading to more accurate performance results and better future tests. Table 47.3 displays some likely scenarios resulting from an item analysis and how to use the results in conjunction with expert judgment.

Item analyses are rarely carried out in actual practice, despite their relative benefits. Opponents of classroom level item analyses assert that it assumes too much faith in the isolated results and argue that results are too unstable due to small sample sizes, lack of variation in scores, lack of expertise, and most important, lack of time. Despite

Table 47.3   Item Analysis Scenarios

Scenario	Possible Explanation Based on Professional Judgment	Possible Action
A. Less than 50% of the students got item wrong	1. Not taught well	1. Don't count item
	2. Not studied well	2. Count item
	3. Poorly constructed	3. Don't count item
B. 100% got item right	1. Too easy/trivial content	1. Don't count item
	2. Taught well/mastery achieved	2. Count item
	3. Studied well/mastery achieved	3. Count item
C. More lower scoring students (LSS) than higher scoring students (HSS) got item right	1. Another distractor was similar to the correct answer, but only the HSS had enough knowledge to pick it	1. Requires expert judgment
	2. The item contained ambiguous information that only the HSS had enough knowledge to pick up on	2. Requires expert judgment
	3. Error on the teacher's score key	3. Check score key and rescore
	4. The item is well-constructed and statistic is a function of small sample size	4. Count item
D. 100% in HSS got item right and 0% in LSS got item wrong	1. Unknown explanation	1. Requires expert judgment
E. Not all distractors were used by the LSS	1. Distractor is too implausible	1. Revise distractor for future use
	2. LSS had enough knowledge to know that distractor was wrong, but not enough to know the right answer	2. Keep distractor for future use

these criticisms, when given proper training, teachers ought to statistically evaluate their summative tests and use their expert judgment to draw inferences about test construction. Just because the numerical results signal a potential problem, it does not imply that there actually is a problem. But that judgment should have to be made rather than go completely unnoticed.

Item analyses do take a great deal of time if teachers are to do it by hand rather than through the use of a statistical program. There is, however, a statistical program written by Gordon Brooks available online that will compute an item analysis at http://oak.cats.ohiou.edu/~brooksg/tap .htm (Brooks & Johanson, 2003).

Scoring Tests

Properly prepared tests hold little value if they are not scored adequately. To enhance student learning, the scoring of tests and feedback of test performance should take place in a timely manner. Doing so allows any misconceptions in content to be readily addressed and fixed before moving on to new content.

With objective teacher-made tests, scoring is usually not a problem given their objective nature. Nevertheless, teachers are human and humans make mistakes. Two ways to catch an objective scoring mistake is in an item analysis or through student review of the test items.

Scoring subjective items is of more concern because reliability is at stake. The more subjective an item is, the more unreliable scoring becomes. Ways to increase scoring reliability are to construct clear scoring rubrics before test administration and modify as needed after administration, but before actual scoring, and adhere to the rubric. Often, teachers will spend the time to create a rubric and then not completely follow it, or worse—they won't create a rubric at all. Although depth of rubrics will vary based on item format, rubrics ought to be created for all constructed response items.

One way to account for scoring reliability is to calculate an interrater agreement coefficient, which involves two or more raters scoring the same items and calculating the proportion of time the raters gave the same score. More details on scoring tests, especially essay tests can be found in the sources listed in the References and Further Readings section.

Policy Implications

Effects of High-Stakes Testing

The advent of high-stakes testing may have clouded the general advantages of traditional teacher tests. Although standardized tests do not have a direct effect at the classroom level, they do have an indirect effect. Because of the high-stakes nature of many standardized tests, classroom level tests are evolving to mimic their format and content. Also, high-stakes standardized tests have such severe consequences that policy makers and the public have put traditional teacher tests on the back burner. Although there is some evidence that high-stakes tests improve general classroom assessment practices (better and more frequent formative assessment, focus on HOTS), there is also some evidence showing the negative effects (focus on rote learning, increased test preparation) of high-stakes testing (McMillan, 2005). There is, however, little evidence regarding the direct effect of high-stakes testing on the use of teacher-made tests.

One of the more controversial issues is teacher evaluations based on student performance on high-stakes tests. From a more pragmatic perspective it could be argued that if high-stakes tests assess students' achievement of state standards and teachers teach or assess those standards throughout the year using teacher-made tests, then students should do well on the state tests if they did well on teacher-made tests. Although that is a very tunnel-visioned perspective that creates much debate, the argument suggests that teachers' use of high-quality, teacher-made tests can have a positive effect on teacher evaluations.

Teacher Assigned Grades

Perhaps traditional teacher tests have received less attention in recent years because of the validity and reliability problems often associated with them. To reiterate, research has shown that teachers lack sufficient knowledge to construct and use test results in valid and reliable ways. Earlier research cited the reasons were due to ineffective training, but recently experts in the field have suggested motivational reasons, suggesting that teachers ignore the recommended measurement guidelines for fear of affecting students' motivational drive. Teachers have reported that effort and improvement matter, and as teachers it is difficult not to reward students for trying. Although this sounds laudable, it does distort the meaning of grades and teacher-made tests. Good quality tests take a considerable amount of time to construct; to award grades based on nonachievement factors essentially debases all of that time spent.

Teachers frequently report that teacher-made tests account for the majority of assigned grades. If the tests are poorly constructed or inappropriately interpreted, then the grades derived based on those tests are equally poor and inappropriate. The problems of grade inflation, different and unreliable grading scales both within and between schools, can be associated with the need for better accountability measures, thus the standards-based era.

There are reports that high school GPAs have increased, while student performance on standardized tests has not (Reports: Grades improving, 2007). This is not to suggest that teacher-made tests should model standardized tests, but merely to suggest that something is awry in content, instruction, or assessment. If, however, the increase in

GPA is due to better instruction, then there is either a possible mismatch between instructional content and standardized test content or the standardized tests are poorly constructed.

Many states offer college financial incentives to students who score high on the state standardized test. Because of low passing rates, however, many states are now devising alternatives for students to qualify for financial scholarships. For example, in some states, a C or better can overrule a passing score on the state test. If this is the case, then teacher-made tests ought to show evidence of both reliability and validity. Some argue that it is detrimental to have such high stakes attached to a single test score, but it is equally detrimental, if not more so, to have such high stakes attached to multiple invalid and unreliable test scores.

Future Directions

The role of teacher-made tests is very different from that of decades ago. Increasingly high-stakes policy implementations and impatient policy makers have shaped the way classroom assessment currently looks. Disconnects between measurement theorists and classroom practitioners has not faded. Teacher preparation programs continue to view classroom assessment as of secondary importance and focus more on alternative methods of assessment, rather than on applying traditional measurement aspects to a realistic classroom environment. While both play vital roles in student learning, both need equal attention in training. Current educators ought to be trained in common measurement techniques so that beginning teachers have a model to follow in their first years of teaching, and measurement theorists need to take into account the role of student-teacher relationships and realistic classroom environments when devising classroom assessment recommendations.

There is no question that teachers want their students to learn in the best ways possible. Various assessment mechanisms provide teachers the tools to help students learn. The difficulty is helping teachers understand how to use each tool efficiently and appropriately. If student learning is to be measured, teachers need to know how and when to use what tools and be able to make useful interpretations within their own context of maximizing time and student learning.

References and Further Readings

American Federation of Teachers, National Council on Measurement in Education, & National Education Association. (1990). *Standards for teacher competence in educational assessment of students.* Retrieved July 7, 2007, from http://www.unl.edu/buros/bimm/html/article3.html

Anderson, L. W., & Krathwohl, D. R. (2001). *A taxonomy for learning, teaching, and assessing: A revision of Bloom's original taxonomy of educational objectives.* New York: Longman.

Black, P., & William, D. (1998a). Assessment and classroom learning. *Assessment in Education: Principles, Policy, and Practice, 5*(1), 7–77.

Black, P., & William, D. (1998b). Inside the black box: Raising standards through classroom assessment. *Phi Delta Kappan Online, 80*(2), 139–144.

Bloom, B. S. (1954). *Taxonomy of educational objectives.* New York: Longman.

Boothroyd, R. A., McMorris, R. F., & Pruzek, R. M. (1992, April). *What do teachers know about measurement and how did they find out?* Paper presented at the annual meeting of the National Council on Measurement in Education, San Francisco, CA.

Brooks, G. P., & Johanson, G. A. (2003). TAP: Test Analysis Program. *Journal of Psychological Measurement, 27*(4), 303–305.

Cizek, G. J., Fitzgerald, S. M., & Rachor, R. E. (1996). Teachers' assessment practices: Preparation, isolation, and the kitchen sink. *Educational Assessment, 3*(2), 159–179.

Crooks, T. (1988). The impact of classroom evaluation practices on students. *Review of Educational Research, 58*(4), 438–481.

Education Week. (2007). *Quality counts 2007: From cradle to career.* Bethesda, MD: Author.

Frary, R. B., Cross, L. H., & Weber, L. J. (1993). Testing and grading practices and opinions of secondary teachers of academic subjects: Implications for instruction in measurement. *Educational Measurement: Issues and Practice, 12*(3), 23–30.

Kubiszyn, T., & Borich, G. (2007). *Educational testing and measurement: Classroom applications and practice* (8th ed.). Hoboken, NJ: Wiley.

McMillan, J. H. (2001). Secondary teachers' classroom assessment and grading practices. *Educational Measurement: Issues and Practice, 20*(1), 20–32.

McMillan, J. H. (2005). *The impact of high-stakes test results on teachers' instructional and classroom assessment practices.* (ERIC ID: ED490648)

McMillan, J. H. (2007). *Classroom assessment: Principles and practice for effective standards-based instruction* (4th ed.). Boston: Allyn & Bacon.

McMillan, J. H., Myran, S., & Workman, D. (2002). Elementary teachers' classroom assessment and grading practices. *The Journal of Educational Research, 95*(4), 203–213.

McMillan, J. H., & Workman, D. J. (1998). *Classroom assessment and grading practices: A review of the literature.* (ERIC ID: ED453263)

National Council on Measurement in Education. (1995). *Code of professional responsibilities in educational measurement.* Washington, DC: Author.

Nitko, A. J. (2004). *Education assessment of students* (4th ed.). Upper Saddle River, NJ: Merrill Prentice Hall.

Pigge, F. L., & Marso, R. N. (1993, October). *A summary of published research: Classroom teachers' and educators' attitudes toward and support of teacher-made tests.* Paper presented at the annual meeting of the Midwestern Educational Research Association, Chicago, IL.

Popham, W. J. (2005). *Classroom assessment: What teachers need to know* (4th ed.). Boston: Allyn & Bacon.

Reports: Grades improving despite weak test scores. (2007, February). *CNN.com.* Retrieved February 22, 2007, from

http://www.cnn.com/2007/EDUCATION/02/22/math
.reading.scores.ap/index.html?eref=rss_education

Stiggins, R. J., & Bridgeford, N. J. (1985). The ecology of classroom assessment. *Journal of Educational Measurement, 22*(4), 271–286.

Taylor, C. S., & Nolen, S. B. (1996). What does a psychometrician's classroom look like? Reframing assessment concepts in the concept of learning. *Education Policy Analysis Archives, 4*(17), 345–357.

Tyler, R. W. (1949). *Basic principles of curriculum and instruction.* Chicago: University of Chicago.

48

PORTFOLIO ASSESSMENT

SUSAN M. BROOKHART

Duquesne University

Portfolios have been around for a long time, showcasing the work of artists for example. In education, however, discontent with standardized tests and other traditional assessment measures led to experimentation with their use for assessing student achievement in school classrooms. Although this movement was brewing for a while, it took off in the mid-1980s. Shortly thereafter, experimentation with portfolios spread to large-scale assessment purposes tied to school reform efforts. This usage peaked in the early to mid-1990s, and then waned as the current accountability movement grew.

There are many definitions of portfolios. One that has become somewhat standard is the definition developed around 1990 by the Northwest Evaluation Association. A portfolio is a purposeful collection of student work (both purpose and clear criteria for quality work should be stated) that includes student involvement in its construction and student reflection on its contents (Arter & Spandel, 1992). This definition distinguished portfolios, as this chapter will use the term, from weekly folders or other collections of children's work that teachers or parents have always saved from refrigerator door displays and the like. Portfolio assessment requires intentional student reflection. That reflection should be at least implicit in the selection of work. Preferably, reflection should be explicit, with reflection tags, work logs, or essays included in the collection.

The underlying purpose of portfolios is to make meaning from evidence. The power of the method lies in the presence of student work for review. Assessment of the quality of student work is right there next to the evidence, making for a fuller, richer description than a score or grade noted in a spreadsheet. In addition, students are more involved in interpreting the evidence of their own progress in portfolio assessment than in testing, or even in teacher-graded performance assessment. Portfolio assessment can be very learner-centered.

Although various authors have developed many categories and labels, there are two general types of portfolios. A showcase or best work portfolio contains evidence of the level of student achievement of intended learning targets; that is, it illustrates what the student can do, not how he or she arrived at that point. A growth, learning, or process portfolio, as it is variously called, contains evidence about students' learning processes. The classic of this type is the writing portfolio that includes several drafts and comments for each piece or a collection of pieces that shows improvement over time, as subsequent pieces show more developed skills than early pieces.

In either case, the presence of the student work itself, and not just a grade or even narrative comments, is what makes the portfolio unique. For anyone, reviewing the evidence allows a deeper, multifaceted understanding of the achievement. Especially for younger children, whose reasoning is aided by concrete examples, being able to see progress or achievement goes further toward helping them understand it than reviewing a list of grades or scores alone. Portfolios are touted for encouraging this kind of review and developing the lifelong learning skills of self-regulation and self-evaluation.

At least two related underlying stances can be found in the literature written when portfolios became popular. Some authors were interested in their use because of an interest in authentic assessment. Authentic assessment in this sense means using assessment tasks that are more like real work than are traditional tests. Doing and reviewing one's own work, and reflecting on one's own learning, are things that educated people need to do in future schooling and in life. A second argument for portfolio use is related. Some authors wrote about the power of portfolios to harmonize curricular goals, instruction, and assessment (sometimes called assessments worth teaching to). The argument was knowing that portfolio assessment will be used will encourage a different type of teaching than knowing that a test will be used. In this argument, portfolios were a tool for school reform.

Portfolios do entail some intentional merging of assessment and instruction. Even if the portfolio's main stated purpose is assessment, class time is usually devoted to constructing the portfolios: selecting the pieces to include and reflecting upon what they mean. The ways in which this is accomplished vary widely, but in all cases require intentional review of learning goals, consideration of the criteria for quality work, and some sense of what has been learned and what still remains to be done. This is, of course, a description of learning as much as it is of assessment. At least, using class time to construct portfolios requires planning and intentional incorporation into lesson time. At most, teachers can use the act of constructing a portfolio as part of instruction itself.

The range of types of portfolios is broad. The two general categories—for showing best work or for showing growth and learning over time—play out in many ways. Portfolios began in the arts but have spread to other subjects, and there is now a sizeable portfolio literature in reading, mathematics, science, and other subjects.

Portfolios vary in time span according to their purpose. Some elementary schools, for example, experimented with portfolios that began in first grade, covered all or most subjects, and followed students through the years until their graduation from the school. Some districts experimented with portfolios that would travel with students from elementary to middle school or middle school to high school (in one subject or in several), in hopes of giving future teachers a more nuanced understanding of the students they received. Other portfolio projects are subject-specific, contained within one year and classroom. Still others are narrower in scope, tied to a particular unit or subset of curricular goals.

Finally, portfolios vary in the ways they are used. Portfolios that serve purely formative purposes may be evaluated with teacher-student or peer conferences. Most classroom portfolios in the United States, however, serve at least some summative function and are scored in some way. Usually portfolios are scored with rubrics that describe the level of quality on various predetermined criteria, either for the portfolio as a whole or piece-by-piece. Sometimes the criteria are developed jointly by the teacher and students.

In addition to their value for fostering individual learning habits, portfolios have value because of the interactions they can sustain. Again the operative piece here is the availability of the evidence (the student work) itself, which focuses student, teacher, and parent communication over evidence. As the student interacts with the work, the learning is reified; that is, it becomes a concrete thing that gives students, teachers, and parents something to talk about. Communication about student achievement using portfolios can occur informally among students or between students and teachers. Portfolios are also used formally as the basis for all kinds of conferences, student-student (e.g., peer editing), student-teacher (e.g., conferencing with individuals about their work during class), and parent-teacher or student-parent-teacher. Some schools or classes that make portfolios a major component of their work have portfolio celebrations—open-house-like events that are part class presentations and part social.

Portfolios raise several issues of ownership. Student involvement can range from minimal (or nonexistent, for those who are willing to call it a portfolio without student involvement) to all-encompassing. One ownership issue is who gets to say what goes in the portfolio. Teachers often require certain items or devise a framework within which students must work (specifying, for example, at least two of a certain kind of piece must be included but allowing the students to select which two). A second ownership issue is the question of whose work the portfolio represents. Unlike on-demand, closed-book tests, most classroom assignments scaffold student performance in some way. Materials are provided, directions are given, sometimes collaboration with other students is allowed or encouraged, and teacher assistance is available. Thus the picture of student achievement illustrated by some portfolios is a picture of what students can do within the structure of a particular classroom environment. Whether this is a good thing or a bad thing depends on the purpose for which the portfolio is to be used. A third ownership issue is who owns, and keeps, the portfolio—the student, the teacher, or the school.

Research has been done on the effects of classroom-based portfolios. Evidence about their effectiveness on achievement measured by more conventional tests is mixed. Evidence about the development of student self-regulation and self-assessment skills, and about dispositions among students who used portfolios is a little more consistent. Classroom-based portfolios used for formative purposes and integrated with instruction do tend to foster these qualities.

Thus far, the discussion has focused on classroom-based uses of portfolios. To reiterate, portfolios became popular in a time when large-scale accountability was a growing concern, but before the No Child Left Behind Act of 2001 that centralized accountability requirements.

During the 1990s, many felt that using portfolios as part of large-scale assessment would motivate a kind of school reform that would help students develop the complex knowledge and skills needed for 21st-century life and work. This led to some notable projects, many of which are no longer in place.

Research has largely concentrated on portfolios' reliability and validity for accountability reporting and decision making. The overall conclusion supported by studies of both classroom-based and large-scale uses of portfolios is that portfolios are better for classroom purposes than for large-scale purposes. They are better for formative assessment purposes than for summative purposes. And they are best when they are used intentionally as part of both instruction and assessment. These, of course, are generalizations. A few specific portfolio projects are exceptions. These general findings, however, are useful to teachers who are considering using portfolio assessment in their own teaching. Classroom formative uses of portfolios are very powerful tools for both instruction and assessment.

Brief History of the Movement

Calfee and Perfumo (1996) reported that the earliest reference to writing portfolios they could find in ERIC was a report by Sweet (1976), and the portfolio described was a one-page checklist. In the late 1970s and 1980s, portfolios were discovered and became so popular that they were used for all sorts of things, whether they were the most appropriate assessment for the purpose or not. Portfolios arose out of a search for assessments that would encourage lifelong learning skills and student responsibility. They arose during a time of school reform where one of the objectives was to encourage complex thinking and student ownership and agency regarding their work. Portfolio projects began to spring up in classrooms and schools, and writing portfolios were a special case, because of the natural fit between portfolios and the writing process. A growing emphasis on the writing process, instead of just the finished product, and the founding of the Bay Area Writing Project in 1972 and the National Writing Project in 1974, demonstrated the advantages of portfolio assessment.

Portfolios spread because of their potential to tap the higher-order thinking and problem solving that educators were realizing needed more attention in subjects besides writing. Portfolio projects became a popular vehicle for teacher collaboration in the same spirit of reform. Many of these small projects worked well and became a vehicle for communication among teachers and between teachers and students. Very quickly after portfolios began to develop a following as a productive classroom assessment method, educators began wondering if the benefits of portfolios would scale up to support school reform via their use in large-scale assessment.

In 1988 the state of Vermont began the development of a statewide portfolio assessment system. Vermont had not had a statewide assessment system and hoped that using portfolios for large-scale assessment would promote student's reflection skills and avoid some of the pressures that large-scale standardized testing programs can bring. Other states have experimented with portfolios in some form, most notably for writing assessment, but Vermont was the only state that based its state accountability reporting mostly on performance-based, nonstandardized tasks.

The Vermont portfolio assessment program yielded extensive evaluation and produced a lot of literature about portfolio scoring and use of portfolio scores for high-stakes purposes. A major finding was that portfolios did not meet the requirements of reliability of scoring sufficient for the reporting purposes Vermont intended. Different scorers did not agree sufficiently on the quality of portfolios scored with rubrics. Because of the low reliability, validity evidence was difficult to interpret (unreliable measures may have low correlations with other measures of interest simply because of unreliability), but in general, Vermont writing and mathematics portfolios were not related to other measures of writing and mathematics. In addition to its technical problems, the Vermont portfolio assessment program was expensive.

For all these reasons, Vermont no longer uses a portfolio assessment system. The state of Kentucky, however, also an early experimenter with state-level portfolio assessment, still uses a writing portfolio. The state's original interest in portfolios came as part of an educational reform movement. Like Vermont, Kentucky intended that more performance-based assessment systems would avoid some of the pressures of large-scale standardized testing (narrowing of the curriculum and overuse of work sheets in instruction).

During this reform era in the early and mid-1990s, Maryland and California also experimented with assessment reform. The California Assessment Program (CAP), a writing assessment program, influenced writing instruction and assessment, particularly in secondary schools, in the late 1980s. It was replaced with the California Learning Assessment System (CLAS) in 1990. Both of these programs featured open-ended, authentic tasks and included portfolios as part of their design. Political changes and public pressure ended these state-funded experiments with assessment reform in 1994. The attempt to go "beyond the bubble" (the expression used in California to mean going beyond standardized tests and their bubble-in answer sheets) had ended.

Thus, beginning in the late 1980s and peaking by the mid-1990s, portfolios were tried as part of large-scale state assessment but found unreliable in the classical sense. Standardization was one of the main issues. Making portfolio tasks more standardized tasks makes for more reliable scoring, but that misses some of the point of using a portfolio in the first place. Training a large enough pool of raters was another issue, and so was cost.

During this same period, several funded research and development projects experimented with the development of portfolios. Harvard's Project Zero was associated with the Arts PROPEL and APPLE Projects. Arts PROPEL was a joint project with the Educational Testing Service and the Pittsburgh Public Schools. It focused on student learning in three aspects of the arts: production, perception, and reflection. Portfolios became one (of two) ways to document the creative process. Arts PROPEL had somewhat more success with reliability of portfolio scoring than did the state of Vermont, but within this purpose of arts assessment. The APPLE (Assessment Projects and Portfolios for Learning) Project was a more straightforward investigation of what was required for the ongoing implementation of portfolios in schools, for evaluating both programs and individual students.

The New Standards Project was a joint research and development effort of the National Center on Education and the Economy and the Learning Research and Development Center at the University of Pittsburgh. The New Standards Project, true to its name, developed both a set of benchmarked performance standards for elementary, middle, and high school students and the means to assess them. This project is still running and has resulted in the publication of standards for student achievement and portfolio tasks and rubrics that are available for purchase.

How to Design a Classroom Portfolio Assessment

Portfolio assessments are quite varied; however, it is possible to describe the basic steps for creating a portfolio assessment system in a classroom. For both learning and best-works portfolios, the first thing to do is identify the purpose for the portfolio. That purpose should include the classroom learning targets and curriculum or state goals it will serve, whether the purpose will be formative (learning) or summative (best-works), and the audience (who will be the users of the portfolio system—who creates and who gets the information and for what uses). Possible purposes include, but are not limited to, the following:

- formative assessment—as a vehicle for student reflection and teacher feedback, for diagnosing student needs and planning next steps, for informing instructional planning;
- summative assessment—of student accomplishment of learning goals, including grading;
- program evaluation and/or accountability reporting;
- communication—as a vehicle for communicating with parents, or with future teachers.

At this point, one possible decision is that a portfolio is not the most appropriate assessment method for the purpose. If it is appropriate, continue with the following steps. Specify in greater detail exactly what achievement dimensions the portfolio will assess. This specification includes the content from the learning goals but also extends to the cognitive complexity, reflection and self-regulation skills, or dispositions or habits of mind desired as the focus of portfolio evidence. Because portfolios are a big undertaking and require significant investments of student time and effort, portfolios should assess important, central learning goals that require complex thinking and involve tasks that are meaningful to students. Portfolios are not a good way to assess routine knowledge or recall of facts.

When these foundational issues have been decided and written down, more practical planning for portfolios should follow. Plan the organization of the portfolio, defining for example how many and what types of entries will be needed to give evidence of student content knowledge and cognitive process for intended use of the information. Several pieces of completed writing in different genres would establish student achievement of writing standards, for summative evaluation and grading. Sets of drafts of individual papers at various stages throughout the writing process, at the beginning, middle, and end of the year, would be more useful for student reflection on how he or she was developing as a writer.

Plan who will decide what goes in the portfolio, the timing of those entries, when and how individual pieces will be evaluated, how the portfolio will fit into classroom routines, whether there will be conferences associated with portfolio use, who may see the contents of the portfolio, who owns the final contents, and so on.

Then plan the scoring or evaluating of the portfolio. For solely formative use, evaluation may be entirely by feedback and conferencing. For most uses, rubrics of some sort will be used. Identify or create rubrics that describe performance levels on attributes appropriate to the portfolio's purpose. For example, for a writing portfolio designed to furnish evidence of good use of the writing process, the quality of drafting and editing might be evaluated along with the quality of the finished pieces. For a writing portfolio designed to furnish evidence of finished-product writing quality, only qualities of the finished pieces might be evaluated. With or without rubrics, portfolios are also an excellent vehicle for teachers to give verbal feedback to students. Teachers can provide written feedback on the portfolio itself, or, especially for younger students, they can provide oral feedback using the portfolio as the focus of brief student conferences.

Holistic rubrics are used to evaluate the whole portfolio simultaneously. One rubric—one dimension with a set of quality level descriptions—is used. This type of scoring is quick to use and works well when the portfolio is used for summative purposes like a final grade. Analytic rubrics are used to evaluate the portfolio on several dimensions, each with a set of quality level descriptions. For example, a writing portfolio might have separate rubrics for content/ideas, organization, style/voice/word choice, and mechanics. Analytic rubrics take longer to use than holistic rubrics because several judgments must be made. But they are better for giving feedback to students because they identify areas of strength and weakness.

Classroom portfolio scoring will often be done by only the teacher. The dependability of scoring can be checked by having another person cross-check a few portfolios. When double-scoring is used, there are two approaches to dependability. One is independent scoring, then calculating the percent of agreement. Another is a consensus approach, sometimes called moderation, where any disagreements are discussed and resolved. Keeping in mind the question, Would another person agree with this score? helps focus scoring even if there is no double-scoring. Use clear rubrics, consistently applied, as if the scoring was going to be checked against someone else's.

The results of this planning process will be quite varied. Some portfolios have a cover sheet or entry log as the first entry that functions as a table of contents. Entry logs sometimes have space for other information; for example, the rationale for including the piece, the rubric score for the piece, or the date an entry was put in the portfolio. Teachers sometimes make up these sheets as a checklist, specifying two pieces of narrative writing and one piece of persuasive writing and so on, with space for the student to name the selections. Other portfolios are much less prescribed, with entries put in and removed over time as their usefulness expires. Such fluid portfolios are better suited to formative assessment.

Some portfolios are in sections; for example, literacy portfolios may have a reading section that contains a book log and a writing section that contains compositions. Some portfolios are rather unified, such as math portfolios with entries that demonstrate solution of a succession of different types of problems, each composed of paper-and-pencil work plus a reflection about the work's strengths and challenges. Other portfolios represent a variety of work, like a science portfolio that includes unit tests, lab reports, photographs and essays about projects, and reflections.

The reflection methods in portfolios also vary. Some portfolios have student reflections on each entry, either on a separate sheet or on an attached sticky note. Reflections may be required responses to teacher questions (e.g., Why did you select this piece? What does this piece show about your learning?) or may be free-form. Formatted reflections sometimes even include multiple-choice questions (e.g., How satisfied are you with your work on this piece? with a list of choices). Usually, the teacher decides what kinds of reflections are required. Other portfolios have overall reflections, done as an essay written after the work is collected and placed either at the front or the back of the portfolio.

Implementation Issues, Dilemmas, and Barriers

Portfolios have developed a loyal following, but they have also raised issues. As noted, scoring reliability is one of these issues. The most frequently reported difficulty is time. Implementing portfolios well takes both a lot of planning and classroom time. Save portfolio assessment for occasions when its advantages specifically match the assessment purpose, so the time is well spent and portfolios are worth the investment.

Another barrier some teachers have reported is that using portfolio assessment has implications for instruction, so instruction has to be changed. This is particularly problematic if the instructional changes; for example, giving students control of selection and evaluation of some or much of their work, go against the teacher's style of teaching or personal values. Self-reflection needs to be taught. Time needs to be arranged in classroom lessons for students to work on their portfolios. Resources and materials need to be arranged.

A final issue for portfolios is that they require teacher professional development. Many portfolio projects have a professional development component. There is a learning curve for teachers as they make portfolios part of their teaching repertoire. Teachers go through stages of development in their ability to use portfolio assessment skillfully. Experience is important for getting the most out of portfolios, for doing them well, and for not stumbling over the potential barriers.

Digital portfolios are attracting more and more attention. Electronic storage eliminates one of the barriers to portfolio implementation—storage space. Digital portfolios, however, share with other kinds of portfolios the purpose of driving content and plans for assessment. Clear learning goals are still central. Going digital doesn't change that. Entries in digital portfolios can be constructed with the same building blocks that construct any electronic files, depending on their nature: word processors, digital still or video cameras, spreadsheets, presentation software, and the like. These files can be simply stored in a folder on a computer or, more and more frequently, are stored in portfolio software that allows for organizing the artifacts, storing reflections, and recording scores or teacher comments electronically.

Currently, software developers are marketing products that handle electronic portfolios, or e-portfolios. Typically, these software products allow for storage of student work in the form of electronic files and for scoring with rubrics. Some of these programs are Web-based. Some allow the students to keep their electronic files, some retain ownership for the school, and some allow access only with a current subscription. Beware of e-portfolio systems that claim to solve portfolio problems beyond electronic storage and convenience. Setting purpose, ensuring that portfolios are actually used as intended, identifying and using appropriate rubrics (if scored), and so on, require human judgments that are the responsibility of the portfolio system users.

Is a Portfolio an Assessment?

Is a portfolio an assessment itself or something else? Some, most notably Stiggins (2005), originally considered portfolios to be a communication method and not an assessment per se. He saw a portfolio as a collection of individual assessment information whose purpose was to communicate information about student achievement to teachers, parents, and students themselves. Thus he classified portfolios as a communication tool in the same toolbox as grades, narrative reports, and conferences.

The history of portfolios shows that they have been used as an assessment method, and most educators now consider portfolios an assessment method in their own right. The failed experiments with using portfolios for large-scale assessment certainly considered them as a method in their own right—treating them like tests (for example, standardizing tasks and directions) and using their results like they would any other assessment results for accountability and reporting. The classroom uses to which portfolios have been put, whether formative or summative, have also treated portfolios as an assessment in their own right.

Because of their nature, however, portfolios retain that overlap of instruction and assessment. They contain real examples of student work that can be reviewed, rediscovered, and reinterpreted—and those actions constitute a powerful kind of instruction. Thus while the consensus is that portfolios are an assessment method, they are unusual in that their construction allows them to float between instruction and assessment more easily than any other kind of assessment. Any assessment use (for example going over classroom test results) has the potential to inform and even become part of instruction. But portfolios take to this naturally.

Another difference between portfolios and many other types of assessment is the way they lend themselves to multiple interpretations. Of course any assessment results do that to some extent. Because of their history and nature, portfolios easily invite multiple interpretations. The original uses of portfolios, for artists and others to display their work, were not scored, but rather interpreted anew by each viewer. An architect reviewing a portfolio of interior designs might be appraising the designer's ability to fit into one project or to work in one company. The same designer might show the same portfolio to a furniture manufacturer who reviews it to appraise the designer's ability to fit into an entirely different project or job.

As portfolios migrated into classrooms and were adapted for school use, the purpose of the portfolio became defined by classroom learning targets. However they are called (objectives, goals, targets), learning targets are the basis on which classroom instruction and assessment are planned and are the building blocks for the curriculum that the classroom work serves. Thus school portfolios, now defined as purposeful collections of work, usually serve the central purpose of providing evidence and explanations of achievement of a set of learning targets. Even so, because student work is multidimensional, there are lots of other things to see in it. A set of papers that show a student has read and understood

Hamlet, for example, might also show that the student has a good sense of humor, or can write particularly moving narrative prose, or makes a lot of punctuation errors, or any one of a number of things—large and small—that are not directly related to the stated purposes of the portfolio.

Studies have investigated the effects of portfolio use on instruction. There is some evidence that portfolios have an effect on instruction. Teachers often report that portfolios facilitate learning by encouraging students to look back at their work and see where they have been and how far they have progressed.

Studies have also investigated the effects of portfolio use on learning. There is some evidence that students who use portfolios regularly—in portfolio assessment systems that are well conceived and managed—increase their mastery goal orientation. That is, they learn the value of learning for its own sake. Of course, not every portfolio user becomes a self-regulated, self-evaluating, self-starter. But on average, portfolios can foster this kind of orientation over test-driven instruction and assessment.

Some studies have investigated whether students who regularly use portfolio assessment systems increase their achievement levels as measured by conventional standardized tests. These results have been mixed. It is not clear whether the reason for the mixed results is that portfolio use has no real effect on achievement or that standardized tests do not measure the kind of complex learning that portfolios develop.

The term *portfolio culture* has been used to describe a classroom environment in which, because of the use of portfolios, review and reflection about one's work come to be valued. In such an environment, it is safe for students to describe both strengths and weaknesses of a piece of work. Assessment is seen as a repetitive process, with ongoing revision not only allowed but valued. This contrasts with a classroom environment that values getting good scores for everything (sometimes called a testing culture). Seeing errors or less than perfect work as an opportunity for learning or information for improvement is important to a portfolio culture, and it is also important for developing honest self-evaluation and self-regulation skills. The term is not used as much in current literature as it was in the 1980s and early 1990s. The formative assessment literature has picked up this thread for discussion, so the concept is still around.

Portfolio Stories

Perhaps more than any other kind of assessment, portfolio assessment has collected stories that have fueled the argument for their use and inspired loyalty among teachers committed to their use. This is not surprising—it follows from the learner-centered nature of the method. Dramatic and heart-warming anecdotes illustrate the power of portfolios and show that when it works, it works well.

Hebert (2001) tells the story of Tim, a second grader trying to explain to first graders how the portfolios they are about to begin making will help them learn:

> He held out both pieces of writing—one in each fist—to the upturned faces of the first graders and simply said "*See?*" . . . his teacher asked Tim what he wanted the first graders to see. "Well," he said, "there are more words on this page. I use upper and lower case letters here." And as if just then realizing the difference between his first grade and second grade writing he simply added, thrusting one fist forward and then the other for emphasis, "This is words; but *this* is a story." (p. 2)

Richard is a middle school student in a study by Underwood (1998, p. 185), who had thrown a tantrum when his first trimester portfolio was graded B instead of the A he wanted. At the end of the year, he wrote in his portfolio reflection: ". . . .you can see how this portfolio project has helped me understand literature. I've also found out a lot of things about myself as a reader this trimester, and what I'm interested in. I learned that when I'm challenged I'll think of ways to understand things. . . ."

Lubell (in a chapter in Martin-Kniep, 1998, p. 78), quotes the final reflection of an academically successful high school student whose self-evaluation was a surprise to her:

> What boggles me is that I remember being somewhat pleased with my original baseline. It is only now that I can read over it and see the true mess that it really is. For one thing, the whole thing lacked direction. My initial opening sentence did little more than state that I had read a story and a poem. . . . My final essay had direction; . . . my analysis of the two given works was much more advanced, both in organization and in presentation of argument. . . .

Lubell goes on to illustrate how portfolios can be equally powerful with students with special needs. All types of learners can benefit from portfolio assessment if it is well implemented, and they all have stories.

Current Uses and Future Directions

Portfolios have proven themselves to be effective for formative assessment. They have not proven themselves to be efficient, effective methods for large-scale assessment. Thus currently, and arguably into the future, the role for portfolios is and will continue to be primarily classroom-based.

Another current development in education is an increased awareness of, research on, and interest in classroom formative assessment. Classroom formative assessment (assessment for the purpose of giving students and teachers information they need to support learning) is just entering a period of discovery in the 2000s in the way that portfolios began their period of discovery in the 1980s. Both formative assessment and portfolio assessment are difficult to do well. If done well, however, formative assessment is a hugely effective support for student achievement and, at the same time, support for student motivation.

These two will probably join together in the future. Portfolios will become recognized as a specific and particularly effective method of formative assessment for certain kinds of learning targets. Developmental learning targets (long-term skills and abilities like learning to write or problem solving, for example) are well served by an assessment method that allows students to review work over time, reflect on what is being learned and what still needs to be done, and plan strategies for improvement (self-regulation). Mastery learning targets (like learning specific facts and concepts or specific skills) are less well served by this kind of assessment. Given the research and wisdom of practice that has accumulated about portfolios, it seems reasonable to predict that they will be less "used for everything" and more known as a recommended method for the specific use of formative assessment of developmental learning targets.

Another current development yet to be explored to its full potential is the way in which portfolio assessment can support development of student self-regulation, skills at asking questions, evaluation, and making decisions about next steps. This was one of the original reasons that portfolios were touted (see Wolf, 1989, for example), and it remains one of their biggest assets. Research has begun to demonstrate that this happens, and teachers are generally aware of this. A future direction will probably be the development of a repertoire of portfolio practices to intentionally foster specific kinds of self-regulation skills, along the lines of recommendations for practice that already exist about how to construct portfolios for specific intended academic learning outcomes.

No section on future directions of portfolios would be complete without mentioning writing portfolios. Writing portfolios may be the most authentic assessment—without even trying—because they are very close to what real writers actually do. Real writers plan, draft, edit, and review, then edit and review some more, whether or not there is a requirement to put such things in a portfolio. Writing portfolios are thus here to stay; they are and will remain an excellent vehicle for both instruction and assessment in writing.

Finally, portfolio assessment is still used in some places for three kinds of high-stakes decisions: for state writing assessments, for state alternative assessments, and for a part of district high school graduation requirements. Some states (e.g., Kentucky) use portfolios for statewide writing assessment for all students. Most states use one of three types of assessments for special education students eligible to use alternative standards of achievement and alternatives to the state test for No Child Left Behind reporting: portfolio assessment, performance assessment, or comprehensive rating scales of achievement. And some school districts use a portfolio as part of high school graduation requirements, often in conjunction with a senior presentation or project, with a review of grades, or with standardized test scores.

Portfolios in Teacher Education

Although this chapter has been mostly about portfolios for K–12 education, it is worth noting that the use of portfolios in teacher education has somewhat paralleled the use of portfolios in K–12 education. Portfolios are used in three different ways in teacher education: learning portfolios, employment portfolios, and assessment portfolios. All are intended to show teachers' practical knowledge and their reflection on their own professional development. Learning portfolios are used within courses or programs for formative assessment. Employment portfolios are used to show samples of student teachers' work to prospective employers. Assessment portfolios are used as part of programs' outcomes assessment and may be a requirement for graduation.

Similar things have been discovered for teacher education portfolios as for K–12 portfolios. They are more useful for classroom-based (that is, course or sometimes program) assessment than for summative assessment (for example, as a requirement for graduation). Research has shown that student teachers use their portfolios in at least two different ways. Some engage in genuine reflection for self-development. Others simply treat the portfolio as they would any assignment that carries a grade, and complete the requirements.

There are many programs that use teacher education portfolios as a graduation requirement and may delay graduation until all required work—including the portfolio—is in, but in no case of which this author is aware has any candidate been denied a teaching degree solely on the basis of an unsatisfactory portfolio. Because of the reliability issues involved in portfolio scoring, that would not only be a bad idea, it would probably not stand up to a legal challenge. Nor should it. The research findings on teacher education portfolios say similar things to the findings for K–12 portfolios. The main effectiveness lies in the insights that the teacher education students get from keeping them, not the information the teacher education faculty gets from the scores.

Conclusion

Portfolios have a long history in some disciplines, like art, but their use as a classroom assessment method began in the 1980s and was coupled with school reform efforts. Portfolios had a brief trial in the large-scale assessment arena, but it is now pretty well established that they are best suited—indeed are powerful tools—for classroom formative assessment. In certain cases, they can also serve classroom summative assessment. Their main asset is that they require student involvement, they compel student self-reflection, and they encourage student self-regulation as learners. These qualities in turn both support student achievement of school learning goals and also cultivate the habits of lifelong learning.

References and Further Readings

Arter, J., & Spandel, V. (1992). Using portfolios of student work in instruction and assessment. *Educational Measurement: Issues and Practice, 11*(1), 36–44.

Calfee, R., & Perfumo, P. (Eds.). (1996). *Writing portfolios in the classroom: Policy and practice, promise, and peril.* Hillsdale, NJ: Lawrence Erlbaum Associates.

Gearhart, M., & Herman, J. L. (1998). Portfolio assessment: Whose work is it? Issues in the use of classroom assignments for accountability. *Educational Assessment, 5,* 41–55.

Hall, B. W., & Hewitt-Gervais, C. M. (2000). The application of student portfolios in primary-intermediate and self-contained-multiage team classroom environments: Implications for instruction, learning, and assessment. *Applied Measurement in Education, 13,* 209–228.

Hebert, E. A. (2001). *The power of portfolios: What children can teach us about learning and assessment.* San Francisco: Jossey-Bass.

Koretz, D., Broadfoot, P., & Wolf, A. (1998). Special issue: Portfolios and records of achievement. *Assessment in Education, 5*(3), 301–480.

Koretz, D., Stecher, B., Klein, S., & McCaffrey, D. (1994). The Vermont Portfolio Assessment Program: Findings and implications. *Educational Measurement: Issues and Practice, 13*(3), 3–16.

LeMahieu, P. G., Gitomer, D. H., & Eresh, J. T. (1995). Portfolios in large-scale assessment: Difficult but not impossible. *Educational Measurement: Issues and Practice, 14*(3), 11–28.

Mansvelder-Longayroux, D. D., Beijaard, D., Verloop, N., & Vermunt, J. D. (2007). Functions of the learning portfolio in student teachers' learning process. *Teachers College Record, 109,* 126–159.

Martin-Kniep, G. O. (1998). *Why am I doing this? Purposeful teaching through portfolio assessment.* Portsmouth, NH: Heinemann.

Niguidala, D. (2005). Documenting learning with digital portfolios. *Educational Leadership, 63*(3), 44–47.

Paulson, L., Paulson, P. R., & Meyer, C. A. (1991). What makes a portfolio a portfolio? *Educational Leadership, 48*(5), 60–63.

Stiggins, R. J. (2005). *Student-involved assessment FOR learning.* Upper Saddle River, NJ: Prentice Hall.

Sweet, J. (1976). The experience portfolio: An approach to student writing. *English Journal, 65,* 50.

Tierney, R. J., & Clark, C. (1998). Portfolios: Assumptions, tensions, and possibilities. *Reading Research Quarterly, 33,* 474–486.

Underwood, T. (1998). The consequences of portfolio assessment: A case study. *Educational Assessment, 5,* 147–194.

Wolf, D. P. (1989). Portfolio assessment: Sampling student work. *Educational Leadership, 46*(7), 35–39.

Wolfe, E. W., Chiu, C. W. T., & Reckase, M. D. (1999). Changes in secondary teachers' perceptions of barriers to portfolio assessment. *Assessing Writing, 6*(1), 85–105.

49

CURRICULUM-BASED ASSESSMENT

LYNN S. FUCHS AND DOUGLAS FUCHS

Vanderbilt University

Monitoring student progress is an important form of classroom assessment. Teachers use progress monitoring for two purposes. The first purpose is to determine whether a student's academic development within an academic year is proceeding well. Second, when a student is not progressing adequately, teachers use progress monitoring to design an individualized instructional program that promotes better academic growth. The form of progress monitoring with the strongest scientific evidentiary base is curriculum-based measurement. A large body of research shows that curriculum-based measurement produces accurate descriptions of student development in reading and math. Moreover, formal school-based experiments (where teachers are randomly assigned to plan instruction with and without curriculum-based measurement) demonstrate that when teachers use curriculum-based measurement to inform their instructional decision making, their students achieve better. Curriculum-based measurement is therefore relevant to discussions about education in the 21st century, when the focus on improving student outcomes dominates education reform. In this chapter, we briefly explain the conventional approach to progress monitoring, known as mastery measurement. Then, we introduce best practice in progress monitoring, in the form of curriculum-based measurement. We explain how curriculum-based measurement differs from mastery measurement and provide an overview of curriculum-based measurement. Then we describe curriculum-based measurement in reading and in math;

we explain guidelines for using curriculum-based measurement to make instructional decisions; we note how computer applications are designed to make curriculum-based measurement easier for teachers to use; and we explain how progress monitoring generally and curriculum-based measurement in particular are an important component in the education reform known as responsiveness to intervention. Finally, we discuss future directions and provide a summary of this chapter.

Mastery Measurement: The Conventional Approach to Progress Monitoring

Thirty years ago, the dominant approach to progress monitoring was mastery measurement. With mastery measurement, the teacher specifies a hierarchy of instructional objectives that constitute the annual curriculum. For each objective in the sequence, the teacher devises a test. The goal is to use this test to assess student mastery of the skill. When a student achieves mastery, the teacher simultaneously shifts instruction and assessment to the next skill in the hierarchy. In this way, learning is conceptualized as a series of short-term accomplishments that are believed to accumulate into broader competence. This form of progress monitoring is reflected in most basal reading and math programs. Also, years ago, it was popularized with the Wisconsin Instructional Design System (see http://www.wids.org) and Precision Teaching (e.g., http://www.celeration.org).

At about that same time, Stanley Deno at the University of Minnesota launched a systematic program of research on the technical features, logistical challenges, and instructional effectiveness of progress monitoring. The initial focus of that research program was mastery measurement, but several technical difficulties associated with mastery measurement quickly emerged. For example, to assess mastery of a specific skill, each item on a mastery measurement test addresses the same skill. Unfortunately, such testing is potentially misleading because many low achievers can, for example, read consonant-vowel-consonant words (like *cat*, *dog*, *fun*) if they know that all the words on the test conform to that same phonics pattern. Similarly, some low achievers can solve addition with regrouping problems if they know to regroup for all problems on the test. By contrast, when a text mixes words with different phonetic patterns or a test mixes math problems of different types (as occurs in the real world and on high-stakes tests), these same students no longer perform the mastered skill competently. This questions mastery measurement's assumption that mastery of a series of short-term accomplishments accumulates into broad-based competence. It also means that students who have mastered a lot of objectives during the school year may not be able to use their knowledge in flexible ways or score well on the state tests at the end of the year. So, mastery measurement can lull educators into a false sense that their students are making progress.

Best Practice in Progress Monitoring: Curriculum-Based Measurement

How Curriculum-Based Measurement Differs From Mastery Measurement

To address this and other important problems associated with mastery measurement, Deno (1985) conceptualized an alternative approach to progress monitoring now known as curriculum-based measurement. Each weekly curriculum-based measurement is an alternate form, representing the many skills and strategies that the teacher expects students to be competent with at the end of the year. In this way, curriculum-based measurement circumvents mastery measurement's technical difficulties because curriculum-based measurement requires students to simultaneously integrate, on every weekly test, the various skills required for competent year-end performance. As students learn the necessary components of the annual curriculum, their curriculum-based measurement score gradually increases. Also, because each weekly test is comparable in difficulty and conceptualization, the average increase per week in the curriculum-based measurement scores (called slope) can be used to quantify a student's rate of learning. Educators use slope to gauge a student's responsiveness to the instructional program and to signal the teacher if the student's instructional program is not working well and

needs to be modified. Curriculum-based measurement therefore differs from mastery measurement in two major ways (see Fuchs & Deno, 1991, for a discussion). First, curriculum-based measurement's focus is long-term so that testing methods and content remain constant, with equivalent weekly tests spanning the school year. Second, curriculum-based measurement is standardized so that the behaviors to be measured and the procedures for measuring those behaviors are prescribed, and those prescribed procedures have been documented to be accurate and meaningful (i.e., to be reliable and valid).

To illustrate how curriculum-based measurement is used, let's say that a teacher establishes a reading goal for year-end performance as competent second-grade performance. Then, relying on established methods, the teacher identifies enough passages of equivalent, second-grade difficulty to provide weekly assessments across the school year. Each week, the teacher (or aide) has the student read aloud from a different passage for 1 minute; the score is the number of words read correctly. Each simple, brief assessment produces an indicator of overall reading competence because it requires a multifaceted performance. This performance entails, for example, a reader's skill at automatically translating letters into coherent sound representations, unitizing those sound components into recognizable wholes and automatically accessing lexical representations, processing meaningful connections within and between sentences, relating text meaning to prior information, and making inferences to supply missing information. As competent readers translate text into spoken language, they coordinate these skills in a seemingly effortless manner (Fuchs, Fuchs, Hosp, & Jenkins, 2001).

Because the curriculum-based measurement passage-reading fluency task reflects this complex performance, it can be used to characterize overall reading expertise and to track its development in the primary grades. That is, it serves as an overall indicator of reading competence. Alternatively, curriculum-based measurement can be structured so that instead of assessing one behavior that serves as an overall indicator of academic competence, like passage-reading fluency, it systematically samples the various skills that constitute the annual curriculum. With curricular sampling, the weekly curriculum-based measurement test presents the student with items that represent the variety of skills the teacher will address over the course of the academic year.

With either approach, each progress-monitoring test collected across the school year is of equivalent difficulty. For that reason, the scores can be graphed and directly compared to each other. Moreover, a slope (i.e., average increase per week) can be calculated on the series of scores to quantify the rate of improvement. This strategy for characterizing growth is more sensitive to individual differences than those offered by other classroom assessments. In addition, curriculum-based measurement is sensitive to growth made under a variety of treatments. In a related way, teachers' instructional plans developed in response to curriculum-based measurement incorporate a wide range of instructional methods. For example, in reading, instructional plans developed in response to curriculum-based measurement incorporate decoding instruction, repeated readings, vocabulary instruction, story grammar exercises, and semantic-mapping activities. So, curriculum-based measurement is not tied to any particular instructional approach.

Perhaps most important, however, studies indicate that curriculum-based measurement progress monitoring enhances teachers' capacity to plan programs for and affect achievement among students with serious learning problems. The methods by which curriculum-based measurement informs instructional planning rely on the graphed scores. If a student's rate of improvement is judged to be inadequate, the teacher revises the instructional program. Research (see Fuchs & Fuchs, 1998, for summary) shows that with curriculum-based measurement decision rules, teachers design more varied instructional programs that are more responsive to individual needs, that incorporate more ambitious student goals, and that result in stronger end-of-year scores on standardized reading tests, including high-stakes state tests. In addition, when curriculum-based measurement is designed to systematically sample the skills embedded in the annual curriculum, performance on the individual skills represented on each assessment can be analyzed. This kind of skills analysis enhances the quality of instructional programming.

Curriculum-Based Measurement Measures in Reading

As already stated, curriculum-based measurement can take one of two forms. It can rely on a single behavior that functions as an overall indicator of competence in an academic area or it can systematically sample the annual curriculum. In reading, most well-researched curriculum-based measurement systems take the overall indicator approach.

Kindergarten

At kindergarten, the major alternatives for curriculum-based measurement reading measures are phoneme segmentation fluency, rapid letter-naming, and letter-sound fluency. With phoneme segmentation fluency, the examiner says a word and the student says the sounds that make up the word (i.e., the tester says, *cat*; the child says, /c/ /a/ /t/). The examiner provides as many test items within 1 minute as the rate of the child's response permits. With rapid letter-naming, the examiner presents a page of lowercase and uppercase letters randomly ordered; then the student says as many letter names as he or she can in 1 minute. With letter-sound fluency, the examiner also presents a page with lowercase and uppercase letters randomly ordered; this time, however, the student says sounds for 1 minute. Compared to phoneme segmentation fluency,

rapid letter-naming and letter-sound fluency are easier for teachers to learn to administer, and reliability tends to be stronger. On the other hand, compared to rapid letter-naming, phoneme segmentation fluency and letter-sound fluency are better targets for instruction because they relate more transparently to what children need to learn to read. For this reason, phoneme segmentation fluency and letter-sound fluency may guide the kindergarten teacher's instructional behavior more effectively, but such studies to confirm this have not been conducted.

First Grade

At first grade, two curriculum-based measurement reading measures have been studied. One approach involves combining nonsense word fluency and passage-reading fluency. Students begin the year on nonsense word fluency and move to the more difficult performance indicator, passage-reading fluency, in January. With nonsense word fluency, students are presented with a page of consonant-vowel-consonant pseudowords (like *bav* or *guj*) and have 1 minute to decode as many as they can. With passage-reading fluency, students are presented with first-grade text (each alternate form is a passage of roughly equivalent difficulty), and students read aloud for 1 minute. Alternatively, schools use a constant measure across all of first grade: word identification fluency, where students are presented with a page showing 50 high-frequency words (each alternate form samples words from a list of 100 words and presents the 50 in random order). Students read as many words as possible in 1 minute. The advantage of nonsense word fluency is that it maps onto beginning decoding instruction, potentially providing teachers with input for instructional planning. The downside of the nonsense word fluency/passage-reading fluency combination is that modeling student development over the course of first grade is not possible because the measure changes midyear. By contrast, word identification fluency can be used with strong reliability, validity, and instructional utility across the entire first-grade year. This also makes it possible to model the development of reading skill across the entire time frame. In addition, in a study that contrasted nonsense word fluency to word identification fluency (Fuchs, Fuchs, & Compton, 2004), the technical features of word identification fluency substantially exceeded those of nonsense word fluency.

Grades 2–6

At Grades 2 and 3, the curriculum-based measurement passage-reading fluency measure provides the strongest source of information on reading development. Each week one test is administered, with the student reading aloud from a different passage for 1 minute; the examiner counts the number of words read correctly within the 1-minute time frame. The accuracy (reliability), meaningfulness (validity), and instructional usefulness of this simple measure have been demonstrated repeatedly (see Fuchs & Fuchs, 1998, for summary). At Grades 4 through 6, however, as students move from learning to read to reading to learn, some studies suggest that the validity of the curriculum-based measurement passage-reading fluency task begins to decrease (Espin, 2006). This suggests that use of a different measure that more directly taps comprehension may be warranted beginning at Grade 4 or 5. One alternative for the higher grades, which is efficient for teachers to use on a regular basis, is curriculum-based measurement maze fluency. With maze fluency, students are presented with a passage from which every seventh word has been deleted and replaced with three word choices, only one of which makes sense in the blank. The student has 2 or 3 minutes to read and restore meaning to the passage by replacing blanks with words. The score is the number of correct replacements. Espin (2006) provided evidence that maze fluency demonstrates strong accuracy (reliability) and meaningfulness (validity) and models reading development well beginning at fourth grade and continuing through eighth grade.

Curriculum-Based
Measurement Measures in Math

Although most reading curriculum-based measurement systems rely on the overall indicator approach to model the development of competence, some math curriculum-based measurement systems rely on the overall indicator of competence whereas others rely on systematic sampling of the annual curriculum.

Kindergarten

At kindergarten, research has focused primarily on an overall indicator approach to curriculum-based measurement in math. The most promising measures are quantity discrimination (where students are presented with a page that shows pairs of numerals and have 1 minute to circle the larger quantity for each pair); number identification (where students are shown a page of numerals and have 1 minute to name the numbers); and missing number (where students are presented with strings of numerals, with the last numeral missing, and have 1 minute to fill in the missing numerals). Some forms of validity have been shown to be strong (e.g., Baker et al., 2002; Lembke & Foegen, 2006). Yet some work suggests that when these measures are used for progress monitoring, students may learn these specific tasks and reach the top score on the test within a month or two (Lembke & Foegen, 2006). To address this problem, Seethaler and Fuchs (2006) developed and are assessing a curriculum-sampling curriculum-based measurement approach at kindergarten, where a variety of computation and concepts or applications are systematically sampled on each alternate form. That study, which is under way, is assessing how well the curriculum-sampling curriculum-based measurement system, used at the beginning of kindergarten, forecasts students' development of math competence at the end of first grade. At the present time, it is unclear which curriculum-based measurement measure is sound for monitoring math progress at kindergarten.

Grades 1–6

Most progress-monitoring research in math at first grade parallels the work conducted at kindergarten using quantity discrimination, number identification, and missing number. As with kindergarten, although some forms of validity look strong, the threat of students reaching the top score on the test quickly looms larger at first grade than at kindergarten. Alternatively, a curriculum-sampling curriculum-based measurement approach at first grade has been shown to index progress effectively and to forecast the development of serious math difficulties at the end of second grade (Compton, Fuchs, & Fuchs, 2006; Fuchs et al., 2005). In a similar way, work at Grades 2 through 6 (Deno, Jiban, & Spanjers, 2006) demonstrates the validity of a curriculum-sampling curriculum-based measurement approach, and other research (see Fuchs & Fuchs, 1998) illustrates how teachers can use the curriculum-sampling curriculum-based measurement approach in math to design more effective instructional programs.

Guidelines for Using Curriculum-Based
Measurement to Make Instructional Decisions

Regardless of which approach to curriculum-based measurement is used (overall indicator versus curriculum sampling), decision rules help teachers employ curriculum-based measurement for two purposes: (1) to determine whether a student's academic development within an academic year is proceeding well, and (2) when a student is not progressing adequately, to design an individualized instructional program that promotes academic growth.

For determining whether a student's academic development within an academic year is proceeding well, the teacher periodically considers the student's rate of improvement (i.e., slope) against the rate of improvement demonstrated by other students in the class and by national norms for expected rate of improvement. Figure 49.1a is a sample curriculum-based measurement report for one class, as shown on page 455. This composite graph depicts the progress of students in the bottom 25% of the class, students in the middle 50% of the class, and students in the top 25% of the class. Under this class graph, students are identified as "students to watch" or "most improved" (within the past month). Then, based on their overall passage-reading fluency curriculum-based measurement score, students are sorted into groups requiring instruction on comprehension, fluency, or decoding (and if decoding, which type of phonetic pattern warrants attention). In Figure 49.1b (on page 456) each student's instruction designation is presented; In Figure 49.1c (on page 457) the

Class Summary
Teacher: Hoover
Report through 12/17

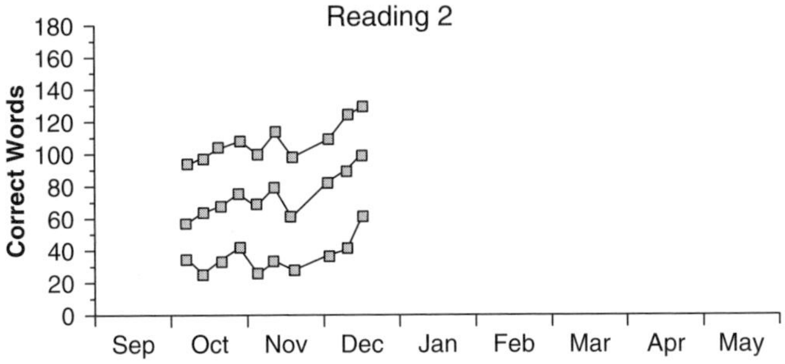

Students to Watch

Shane Moss
Yolanda Navarro
Maria Argueta
Teresa Rodriguez
Gregory Brown

Most Improved

Teresa Rodriguez
Tanasha Storey
Nicholas Norton
Ethan Hunter
Ashley Anderson

Comprehension

Alex Gray
Alicia Scott
Ashley Anderson
David Jackson
Donald Harrison

Activities

Ethan Hunter
Janice Andrews
Nathaniel Dunbar
Paul Minton
Victor Sandoval

Fluency Practice

Mica Netter
Nicholas Norton
Terrance Reeves

Phonics Instruction

MAT/Last	Time	Car	Beat	Happy
Gregory Brown	Gregory Brown	Yolanda Navarro	Shane Moss	
Maria Argueta	Maria Argueta			
Teresa Rodriguez	Shane Moss			
William Douglas	Teresa Rodriguez			
	William Douglas			
	Yolanda Navarro			

Public

Benjamine
 Everson
Tanasha Storey

Running

Figure 49.1a Sample Curriculum-Based Measurement Report

students' slopes of improvement are shown. Figure 49.1d (on page 457) is designed to bring to the teacher's attention those students who are noticeably behind their classroom peers in their current curriculum-based measurement score and their slope of improvement.

When a student is chronically identified as not making good progress (as shown in Figure 49.1d on page 457),

curriculum-based measurement is then used to design an individualized instructional program that promotes academic growth. This is usually done by the special educator or the reading or math specialist (see Fuchs & Fuchs, 1998, for summary of research). For helping practitioners plan effective instruction, decision rules are tied to the slope (i.e., rate of improvement) on the graphed scores in

Class Skills Profile
Teacher: Hoover
Report through 12/17

Name	Comprehension	Fluency	MAT/Last	Time	Car	Beat	Happy	Public	Running
Alex Gray	C								
Alicia Scoot	C								
Ashley Anderson	C								
Benjamine Everson			■	■	■	■	■	■	■
David Jackson	C								
Donald Harrison	C								
Ethan Hunter	C								
Gregory Brown			■	□	□	□	□	□	□
Janice Andrews	C								
Maria Argueta			□	□	□	□	■	□	□
Mica Netter		F							
Nathaniel Dunbar	C								
Nicholas Norton		F							
Paul Minton	C								
Shane Moss			■	■	■	■	■	■	■
Tanasha Storey			■	■	■	■	■	■	■
Teresa Rodriguez			□	□	□	□	□	□	□
Terrance Reeves		F							
Victor Sandoval	C								
William Douglas			■	□	■	■	■	■	■
Yolanda Navarro			■	□	□	□	□	□	□

□ Cold. Missing most of these words.
▨ Warm. Getting some of these worlds right.
■ Hot. Getting most of these words right.

MAT/Last: Closed syllable, short vowel, e.g., bed, top, hit, cat bump, mast, damp
Time: Final e, long vowel, e.g., cake, poke, same, woke, mine, rose, gate
Car: Vowel r-controlled, e.g., fur, nor, per, sir, her, tar
Beat: Two vowels together, e.g., soap, maid, lean, loaf, paid, meal
Happy: Divide between two like consonants, e.g., lesson, bubble, battle, giggle,
Public: Divide between unlike consonants, e.g., elbow, walrun, doctor, victim, admit
Running: Dividing between double consonants with suffix, e.g., batter, sipped, hitting, tanned bitten

Figure 49.1b   Sample Curriculum-Based Measurement Report

conjunction with the goal set for year-end performance. Once the year-end goal is set, it is placed onto the student's individual graph. A straight line connects the student's initial several scores with that goal. This line is called the goal line. This goal line is compared to the student's actual rate of improvement (i.e., a trend line representing the student's slope). When a student's trend line is flatter than the goal line, the teacher revises the instructional program in some important way in an attempt to effect better slope of improvement. After several weeks of implementing this instructional revision, the teacher analyzes the student's graph in the same way, comparing the goal line against the student's new trend line. If progress looks strong enough to realize the end-of-year goal, the program revision is considered successful (although data analysis continues to ensure strong improvement across the school year). If, however, progress looks inadequate to realize the end-of-year goal, then the teacher experiments with a different method for revising the instructional program. Research (see Fuchs & Fuchs, 1998) shows that this kind of data-based decision making used in conjunction with curriculum-based measurement produces more varied instructional programs, which are more responsive to individual needs, which result in more ambitious student

Class Scores

Teacher: Hoover

Report through 12/17

Name	Score	Growth
****Already on grade level		
Ethan Hunter	132	+4.86
Victor Sandoval	130	+2.36
Alicia Scoot	121	+4.51
Alex Gray	117	+3.92
Nathaniel Dunbar	106	+0.90
David Jackson	104	+1.56
Paul Minton	95	+1.59
Ashley Anderson	95	+2.38
Janice Andrews	93	+0.56
Donald Harrison	85	+2.44
Mica Netter	81	+0.89
Nicholas Norton	80	+3.44
**** On track for completing year on grade level		
Terrance Reeves	68	+2.57
Benjamine Everson	66	+1.23
Tanasha Storey	60	+3.50
****At risk for completing grade below grade level		
William Douglas	44	+1.50
Shane Moss	41	+2.12
Yolanda Navarro	30	+1.52
Maria Argueta	29	+0.38
Teresa Rodriguez	24	+2.36
Gregory Brown	8	+0.88

Figure 49.1c   Sample Curriculum-Based Measurement Report

Class Statistics

Teacher: Hoover

Report through 5/27

Score

Average score	84.5
Standard deviation	37.0
Discrepancy criterion	47.5

Slope

Average slope	+1.84
Standard deviation	1.11
Discrepancy criterion	+0.73

Students identified with dual discrepancy criterion

	Score	Slope
Gregory Brown		

Figure 49.1d   Sample Curriculum-Based Measurement Report

goals, and which produce stronger end-of-year scores on commercial, standardized achievement tests including high-stakes state tests.

Computer Applications

With curriculum-based measurement, teachers administer tests according to standardized procedures, graph the resulting scores, and apply prescribed rules to the graphed scores to optimize decision making. Conducting these progress-monitoring curriculum-based measurement activities requires some training and experience, which may involve attending workshops and implementing progress monitoring with the guidance of experienced colleagues. At the same time, we note that over the past 20 years, computer applications have become available. These programs are designed to ease the technical requirements for progress monitoring. Typically, teachers administer the tests and then enter the scores they collect. Then, the computer automatically graphs the scores and applies decision rules. This is illustrated in the computer-managed report shown in Figure 49.1. Some software programs are more sophisticated in that they also automatically collect the data and score the student's test, while the student interacts directly with the computer. If computers are routinely available, then a teacher may wish to consider technological options that reduce the amount of training and experience needed to implement curriculum-based measurement. (See http://www.studentprogress.org for a consumer report type of analysis of curriculum-based measurement products, some of which offer computer aids.)

Progress Monitoring and Curriculum-Based Measurement as Essential to Responsiveness to Intervention

What is Responsiveness to Intervention?

No instructional method, even those validated using randomized controlled studies, works for all students. For this reason, as schools implement validated interventions within general education, the effects of those interventions on children's academic performance must be assessed. That way, children who do not respond adequately can be identified promptly for more intensive intervention. For students who fail to respond to a second, more intensive level of programming, a third tier of instruction with greater individualization is implemented, and response continues to be assessed. This iterative process, with which interventions of increasing intensity and individualization are conducted and their effects are continually assessed, describes the education reform known as responsiveness to intervention.

Responsiveness to intervention is conducted within the context of a multi-tier prevention system. The first tier of a multi-tier prevention system is primary prevention where the intensity of instruction reflects general education practice, with or without the use of individual accommodations and adaptations that fit within the general education program and can be managed by the general education teacher. The second tier refers to secondary prevention, which incorporates a greater level of intensity than can ordinarily be accomplished within general education. That is, instruction is delivered in small groups (e.g., three to five students), typically by well-trained (although not necessary certified) tutors, using a prescriptive, research-based or validated intervention. Such a protocol is typically implemented for 10 to 20 weeks. Within some models, multiple doses of small-group, research-based tutoring is used to strengthen effects. If the Tier 2 protocol proves ineffective, then an even more intense level of instruction, the third tier or tertiary intervention, is conducted. This most intense level of instruction is individually formulated and involves individual or dyadic instruction. It often is conducted under the auspices of special education

resources, using special education certified teachers who are well versed in how to design individually tailored instruction. Within a responsiveness-to-intervention system, therefore, assessment plays three important roles: (a) identifying who should be targeted for attention; (b) quantifying responsiveness to intervention among those targeted for attention; and (c) tailoring individualized instructional programs for the most unresponsive subset of children. Curriculum-based measurement figures prominently for all three purposes.

Identifying Who Should Be Targeted for Attention

Within this scheme the first assessment function is identifying a subset of the school population that is suspected to be at risk for poor learning outcomes. These students become the focus of the responsiveness-to-intervention system. Typically, a brief measure is administrated to all students in a school or within targeted grade levels within a school. Then, a cut-off is applied that specifies what score on the test is associated with inadequate performance on a valued outcome measure, such as a high-stakes test. All students scoring below this cut-off are designated at risk for poor outcome.

This screening, which relies on a one-time test administration, is known as benchmark assessment. Technically, it is not a form of progress monitoring, which requires more frequent (typically, at least monthly) assessment. We do note, however, that prominent screening tools borrow curriculum-based measurement tools because the reliability and validity of curriculum-based measurement is strong and because the measures tend to be brief. We also note that benchmark assessment for the purpose of screening (i.e., designating risk) carries a significant danger of identifying false positives (i.e., designating students for tutoring within a multi-tier prevention system when, in fact, those students would go on to develop strong academic skills without tutoring). For example, in a recent first-grade responsiveness-to-intervention experiment (Fuchs, Compton, Fuchs, & Bryant, 2006), 50% of the control group, who had been designated at risk according to benchmark screening but who did not actually receive tutoring, spontaneously recovered by the end of the first semester of first grade. False positive errors are expensive for a responsiveness-to-intervention system because they require that costly resources be allocated to students who do not require them.

Because benchmark screening, especially at kindergarten and first grade, typically overidentifies students for Tier 2 tutoring, one-time screening should probably constitute only the first step in designating risk status. That is, we recommend that students who are first suspected to be at risk based on benchmark screening be followed with 5 to 8 weeks of progress monitoring while Tier 1 general education is implemented. The purpose of this short-term progress monitoring is to gauge response to Tier 1 general education and thereby confirm that the suspected risk, based on benchmark screening, more likely constitutes actual risk for reading or math failure. Such short-term progress monitoring greatly increases the precision of designating who requires a Tier 2 intervention and therefore avoids wasting costly Tier 2 services on students whose academic skills would develop nicely without that special intervention.

Quantifying Responsiveness to Intervention

Within a multi-tier prevention system, a second purpose for progress monitoring occurs at Tier 2, where tutoring is based on standard treatment protocols. With a standard treatment protocol, a validated or research-based approach to intervention is implemented in small groups. The assumption is that a vast majority of students should respond well to the validated or research-based tutoring. If a child responds poorly to instruction that benefits most students, then the responsiveness-to-intervention assessment process eliminates instructional quality as a viable explanation for poor academic growth and, instead, provides evidence of a disability. The purpose of progress monitoring at Tier 2 is to determine whether students do or do not respond to validated small-group tutoring; that is, to provide early intervention to students who benefit and to identify the subset of students who do not benefit for a more intensive level of instruction. The students who fare well (and respond) are returned to Tier 1, where progress monitoring is continued to assess whether any additional Tier 2 tutoring is required.

Tailoring Individualized Instructional Programs

When the Tier 2 progress-monitoring data indicate that the student has responded inadequately to Tier 2 tutoring, the student enters tertiary, or Tier 3, intervention. This is typically conducted with special education resources and personnel. At the tertiary or Tier 3 level, instruction differs from Tier 2 because it is (a) more intensive (usually involving longer sessions conducted in smaller groups, if not individually); and (b) individualized (rather than relying on a validated treatment protocol). At Tier 3, progress monitoring is essential for two purposes: (1) to inductively formulate instructional programs that are optimal for the individual student and (2) to determine when the student's response to Tier 3 instruction is adequate to warrant a return to Tier 1 primary prevention (general education, with or without accommodations or modifications) or to Tier 2 small-group tutoring with continued progress monitoring so that tertiary intervention can be re-initiated as needed.

Conclusion

An essential component of classroom assessment is systematic progress monitoring. Teachers use progress monitoring for two purposes. First, teachers use progress monitoring to determine whether a student's academic development within an academic year is proceeding well. Second, when a student is not progressing adequately, teachers use progress monitoring to design an individualized instructional program that promotes academic growth. The form of progress monitoring with the strongest scientific evidentiary base is curriculum-based measurement. A large body of research shows that curriculum-based measurement produces accurate descriptions of student development in reading and math. In addition, formal school-based experiments, where teachers are randomly assigned to plan instruction with and without curriculum-based measurement, demonstrate that when teachers use curriculum-based measurement to inform their instructional decision making, their students achieve better. Research on the use of curriculum-based measurement for the purpose of identifying students with learning disabilities represents a new avenue of scientific inquiry. In addition, research designed to expand curriculum-based measurement to other grade levels and content areas is under way.

References and Further Readings

Baker, S., Gersten, R., Flojo, J., Katz, R., Chard, D., & Clarke, B. (2002). *Preventing mathematics difficulties in young children: Focus on effective screening of early number sense delays* (Technical Report No. 0305). Eugene, OR: Pacific Institutes for Research.

Compton, D. L., Fuchs, D., Fuchs, L. S., & Bryant, J. D. (2006). Selecting at-risk readers in first grade for early intervention: A two-year longitudinal study of decision rules and procedures. *Journal of Educational Psychology, 98*, 394–409.

Compton, D. L., Fuchs, L. S., & Fuchs, D. (2006). *The course of reading and mathematics disability in first grade: Identifying latent class trajectories and early predictors.* Manuscript submitted for publication.

Deno, S. L. (1985). Curriculum-based measurement: The emerging alternative. *Exceptional Children, 52*, 219–232.

Deno, S. L., Jiban, C., & Spanjers, D. (2006, February). *Monitoring math progress: Grades 1–6.* Paper presented at the annual meeting of the Pacific Coast Research Conference, Coronado, CA.

Espin, C. (2006, February). *The technical features of reading measures.* Paper presented at the annual meeting of the Pacific Coast Research Conference, Coronado, CA.

Fuchs, D., Compton, D. L., Fuchs, L. S., & Bryant, J. D. (2006, February). *Prevention and identifying reading disability.* Paper presented at the annual meeting of the Pacific Coast Research Conference, Coronado, CA.

Fuchs, L. S., Compton, D. L., Fuchs, D., Paulsen, K., Bryant, J. D., & Hamlett, C. L. (2005). The prevention, identification, and cognitive determinants of math difficulty. *Journal of Educational Psychology, 97*, 493–513.

Fuchs, L. S., & Deno, S. L. (1991). Paradigmatic distinctions between instructionally relevant measurement models. *Exceptional Children, 57*, 488–501.

Fuchs, L. S., & Fuchs, D. (1998). Treatment validity: A unifying concept for reconceptualizing the identification of learning disabilities. *Learning Disabilities Research and Practice, 13*, 204–219.

Fuchs, L. S., Fuchs, D., & Compton, D. L. (2004). Monitoring early reading development in first grade: Word identification fluency versus nonsense word fluency. *Exceptional Children, 71*, 7–21.

Fuchs, L. S., Fuchs, D., Hosp, M., & Jenkins, J. R. (2001). Oral reading fluency as an indicator of reading competence: A theoretical, empirical, and historical analysis. *Scientific Studies of Reading, 5*, 239–256.

Lembke, E., & Foegen, A. (2006, February). *Monitoring student progress in early math.* Paper presented at the annual meeting of the Pacific Coast Research Conference, Coronado, CA.

Seethaler, P. M., & Fuchs, L. S. (2006). *Reliability, concurrent validity, and predictive validity of a curricular sampling approach to curriculum-based measurement in mathematics at kindergarten.* Research in progress.

50

PERFORMANCE ASSESSMENT

SUZANNE LANE AND SEAN T. TIERNEY
University of Pittsburgh

This chapter begins with an introduction to performance assessments. Performance assessments mirror the performance that is of interest, require students to construct or perform an original response, and use predetermined criteria to evaluate students' work. The different uses of performance assessments will then be discussed, including the use of performance assessments in large-scale testing as a vehicle for educational reform and for making important decisions about individual students, schools, or systems and the use of performance assessments by classroom teachers as an instructional tool. Following this, there is a discussion on the nature of performance assessments as well as topics related to the design of performance assessments and associated scoring methods. The chapter ends with a discussion on how to ensure the appropriateness and validity of the inferences we draw from performance assessment results.

Introduction

Educational reform in the 1980s was based on research suggesting that too many students knew how to repeat facts and concepts, but were unable to apply those facts and concepts to solve meaningful problems. Because assessment plays an integral role in instruction, it was not only instruction that was the target of change but also assessment. Proponents of the educational reform argued that assessments needed to better reflect students' competencies in applying

their knowledge and skills to solve real tasks. Advances in the 1980s in the study of both student cognition and measurement also prompted individuals to think differently about how students process and reason with information and, as a result, how assessments can be designed to capture meaningful aspects of students' thinking and learning. Additionally, advocates of curriculum reform considered performance assessments a valuable tool for educational reform in that they were considered to be useful vehicles to initiate changes in instruction and student learning. It was assumed that if large-scale assessments incorporated performance assessments it would signal important goals for educators and students to pursue.

Performance assessments are well-suited to measuring students' problem-solving and reasoning skills and the ability to apply knowledge to solve meaningful problems. Performance assessments are intended to "emulate the context or conditions in which the intended knowledge or skills are actually applied" (American Educational Research Association, [AERA], American Psychological Association [APA], & National Council on Measurement in Education [NCME], 1999, p. 137). The unique characteristic of a performance assessment is the close similarity between the performance on the assessment and the performance that is of interest (Kane, Crooks, & Cohen, 1999). Consequently, performance assessments provide more direct measures of student achievement and learning than multiple-choice tests (Frederiksen & Collins, 1989). Direct assessments of writing that require students to write persuasive letters to the local newspaper or the school board provide instances of the tasks we would like students to perform. Most performance assessments require a student to perform an activity such as conducting a laboratory experiment or constructing an original report based on the experiment. In the former, the process of solving the task is of interest, and in the latter, the product is of interest.

Typically, performance assessments assess higher-level thinking and problem-solving skills, afford multiple solutions or strategies, and require the application of knowledge or skills in relatively novel real-life situations or contexts (Baron, 1991; Stiggins, 1987). Performance assessments like conducting laboratory experiments, performing musical and dance routines, writing an informational article, and providing explanations for mathematical solutions may also provide opportunities for students to self-reflect, collaborate with peers, and have a choice in the task they are to complete (Baker, O'Neil, & Linn, 1993; Baron, 1991). Providing opportunities for self-reflection, such as asking students to explain in writing the thinking process they used to solve a task, allows students to evaluate their own thinking. Some believe that choice allows examinees to select a task that has a context they are familiar with, which may lead to better performance. Others argue that choice introduces an irrelevant feature into the assessment because choice not only measures a student's proficiency in a given subject area but also their ability to make a smart choice (Wainer & Thissen, 1994).

Performance assessments require carefully designed scoring procedures that are tailored to the nature of the task and the skills and knowledge being assessed. The scoring procedure for evaluating the performance of students when conducting an experiment would necessarily differ from the scoring procedure for evaluating the quality of a report based on the experiment. Scoring procedures for performance assessments require some judgment because the student's response is evaluated using predetermined criteria.

Uses of Performance Assessments

Performance Assessments for Use in Large-Scale Assessment and Accountability Systems

The use of performance assessments in large-scale assessment programs, such as state assessments, has been a valuable tool for standards-based educational reform (Resnick & Resnick, 1992). A few appealing assumptions underlie the use of performance assessments: (a) they serve as motivators in improving student achievement and learning, (b) they allow for better connections between assessment practices and curriculum, and (c) they encourage teachers to use instructional strategies that promote reasoning, problem solving, and communication (Frederiksen & Collins, 1989; Shepard, 2000). It is important, however, to ensure that these perceived benefits of performance assessments are realized.

Performance assessments are used for monitoring students' progress toward meeting state and local content standards, promoting standards-based reform, and holding schools accountable for student learning (Linn, Baker, & Dunbar, 1991). Most state assessment and accountability programs include some performance assessments, although in recent years there has been a steady decline in the use of performance assessments in state assessments due, in part, to limited resources and the amount of testing that had to be implemented in a short period of time under the No Child Left Behind (NCLB) Act of 2001. As of the 2005–06 school year, NCLB requires states to test all students in reading and mathematics annually in Grades 3 through 8 and at least once in high school. By 2007–08, states must assess students in science annually in one grade in elementary, middle, and high school. While the intent of NCLB is admirable—to provide better, more demanding instruction to all students with challenging content standards, to provide the same educational opportunities to all students, and to strive for all students to reach the same levels of achievement—the burden put on the assessment system has resulted in less of an emphasis on performance assessments. This is partly due to the amount of time and resources it takes to develop performance tasks and scoring procedures, and the time it takes to administer and score performance assessments.

The most common state performance assessment is a writing assessment, and in some states performance tasks have been used in reading, mathematics, and science assessments. Typically, performance tasks are used in conjunction with multiple-choice items to ensure that the assessment represents the content domain and that the assessment results allow for inferences about student performance within the broader content domain. An exception was the Maryland School Performance Assessment Program (MSPAP), which was entirely performance-based and was implemented from 1993 to 2002. On MSPAP, students developed written responses to interdisciplinary performance tasks that required the application of skills and knowledge to real-life problems (Maryland State Board of Education, 1995). Students worked collaboratively on some of the tasks, and then submitted their own written responses to the tasks. MSPAP provided school-level scores, not individual student scores. Students received only a small sample of performance tasks, but all of the tasks were administered within a school. This allowed for the school score to be based on a representative set of tasks, allowing one to make inferences about the performance of the school within the broader content domain. The goal of MSPAP was to promote performance-based instruction and classroom assessment. The National Assessment of Educational Progress (NAEP) uses performances tasks in conjunction with multiple-choice items. As an example, NAEP's mathematics assessment is composed of multiple-choice items as well as constructed-response items that require students to explain their mathematical thinking.

Many of the uses of large-scale assessments require reporting scores that are comparable over time, which require standardization of the content, administration, and scoring of the assessment. Features of performance assessments, such as extended time periods, collaborative work, and choice of task, pose challenges to the standardization and administration of performance assessments.

Performance Assessments for Classroom Use

Educators have argued that classroom instruction should, as often as possible, engage students in learning activities that promote the attainment of important and needed skills (Shepard et al., 2005). If the goal of instruction is to help students reason with and use scientific knowledge, then students should have the opportunity to conduct experiments and use scientific equipment so that they can explain how the process and outcomes of their investigations relate to theories they learn from textbooks (Shepard et al., 2005). The use of meaningful learning activities in the classroom requires that assessments be adapted to align to these instructional techniques. Further, students learn more when they receive feedback about particular qualities of their work, and are then able to improve their own learning (Black & Wiliam, 1998). Performance assessments allow for a direct alignment between important instructional and assessment activities, and for providing meaningful feedback to students regarding particular aspects of their work (Lane & Stone, 2006). Classroom performance assessments have the potential to better simulate the desired criterion performance as compared to large-scale assessments because the time students can spend on performance assessments for classroom use may range from several minutes to sustained work over a number of days or weeks.

Classroom performance assessments provide information about students' knowledge and skills to guide instruction, provide feedback to students so as to monitor their learning, and can be used to evaluate instruction. In addition to eliciting complex thinking skills, classroom performance assessments can assess processes and products that are important across subject areas, such as those involved in writing a position paper on an environmental issue (Wiggins, 1989). The assessment of performances across disciplines allows teachers of different subjects to collaborate on projects that ask students to make connections across content. Students who are asked to use scientific procedures to investigate the effects of toxicity levels on fish populations in different rivers may also be asked to use their social studies knowledge to describe what these levels mean for different communities whose economy is dependent on the fishing industry (Taylor & Nolen, 2005). Teachers may ask students to write an article for the local newspaper informing the community of the effects of toxicity levels in rivers. The realistic nature of these connections and tasks themselves may help motivate students to learn.

Similarity between simulated tasks and real-world performances is not the only characteristic that makes performance assessments motivational for students. Having the freedom to choose how they will approach certain problems and engage in certain performances allows students to use their strengths while examining an assignment from a variety of standpoints. For example, students required to write a persuasive essay may be allowed to choose the topic they wish to address. Furthermore, if one of the tasks is to gather evidence that supports one's claims, students could choose the means by which they obtain that information. Some students may feel more comfortable researching on the Internet, while others may choose to interview individuals whose comments support their position (Taylor & Nolen, 2005). Allowing choice ensures that most students will perceive at least some freedom and control over their own work, which is inherently motivational. When designing performance assessments, however, teachers need to ensure that the choices they provide will allow for a fair assessment of all students' work (Taylor & Nolen, 2005). Tasks that students choose should allow them to demonstrate what they know and can do. Providing a clear explanation of each task, its requirements or directions, and the criteria by which students will be evaluated will help ensure a fair assessment of all students. Students' understanding of the criteria and what constitutes successful performance will provide an equitable opportunity for students to demonstrate their knowledge. Providing appropriate feedback at different points in the assessment will also help ensure a fair assessment.

Although performance assessments can be beneficial when incorporated into classroom instruction, they are not always necessary. If a teacher is interested in assessing a student's ability to recall factual information, a different form of assessment would be more appropriate. Before designing any assessment, teachers need to ask themselves two questions: What do I want my students to know and be able to do, and what is the most appropriate way for them to demonstrate what they know and can do?

Nature of Performance Tasks

Performance tasks may assess the process used by students to solve the task or a product, such as a sculpture. They may involve the use of hands-on activities, such as building a model or using scientific equipment, or they may require students to produce an original response to a constructed-response item, write an essay, or write a position paper. Constructed-response items and essays provide students with the opportunity to "give explanations, articulate reasoning, and express their own approaches toward solving a problem" (Nitko, 2004, p. 240). Constructed-response items can be used to assess the process that students employ to solve a problem by requiring them to explain how they solved it.

The National Assessment of Educational Progress (NAEP) includes hands-on performance tasks in their science assessment. These tasks require students to conduct experiments, and to record their observations and conclusions by answering constructed-response items and multiple-choice items. As an example, a public release eigth-grade task provides students with a pencil with a thumb tack in the eraser, red marker, paper towels, a plastic bowl, graduated cylinder, and bottles of fresh water, salt water, and mystery water. Students are asked to perform a series of investigations that allow them to investigate the properties of freshwater and salt water, and are asked to determine whether a bottle of mystery water is freshwater or salt water. After each step, students respond to questions regarding the investigation. Some of the constructed-response items require students to provide their reasoning and to explain their answers (U.S. Department of Education, 1996).

NAEP also includes constructed-response items in their mathematics assessment. An eighth-grade sample NAEP constructed-response item requires student to use a ruler to determine how many boxes of tiles are needed to cover a diagram of a floor. The diagram of the floor is represented as a 3 ½- × 5 ¼-inch rectangle with a given scale of 1 inch equals 4 feet. The instructions are:

> The floor of a room shown in the figure above is to be covered with tiles. One box of floor tiles will cover 25 square feet. Use your ruler to determine how many whole boxes of these tiles must be bought to cover the entire floor. (U.S. Department of Education, 1997)

Performance tasks may also require students to write an essay, story, poem, or other piece of writing. On the Maryland School Performance Assessment Program (MSPAP), the assessment of writing would have taken place over a number of days. First the student would engage in some prewriting activity; then the student would write a draft; and finally the student would revise the draft, perhaps considering feedback from a peer. Consider this example of a 1996 Grade 8 writing prompt from MSPAP:

> Suppose your class has been asked to create a literary magazine to be placed in the library for you schoolmates to read. You are to write a story, play, poem, or any other piece of creative writing about any topic you choose. Your writing will be published in the literary magazine. (Maryland State Department of Education, 1996)

This task allows student to choose both the form and topic of writing. Only the revised writing was evaluated using a scoring rubric.

Design and Scoring of Performance Assessments

The design of classroom performance assessments follows the same guidelines as the design of performance assessments for large-scale purposes (see for example, Lane & Stone, 2006). Because of differences in the stakes associated with performance assessments that are used for classroom purposes, however, they do not need to meet the same level of standardization and reliability as do large-scale performance assessments. In large-scale assessments, performance is examined over time so the content of the assessment and procedures for administration and for scoring need to be the same across students and time—they need to be standardized. This ensures that the interpretations of the results are appropriate and fair.

Design of Performance Assessments

Performance assessment design begins with a description of the purpose of the assessment; construct or content domain (i.e., skills, knowledge, and their applications) to be measured; and the intended inferences to be drawn from the results. Delineating the domain to be measured ensures that the performance tasks and scoring procedures are aligned appropriately with the content standards. Whenever possible, assessments should be grounded in theories and models of student cognition and learning. Researchers have suggested that the assessment of students' understanding of matter and atomic-molecular theory can draw on research on how students learn and develop understandings of the nature of matter and materials, how matter and materials change, and the atomic structure of matter (National Research Council, 2006). An assessment within this domain may be able to reflect students' learning progressions—the path that students may follow from a novice understanding to a sophisticated understanding of atomic molecular theory. Assessments that are designed to capture the developmental nature of student learning can provide valuable information about a student's level of understanding.

To define the domain to be assessed, test specifications are developed that provide information regarding the assessment. For large-scale assessments, test specifications provide detailed information regarding the content and cognitive processes, format of tasks, time requirements for each task, materials needed to complete each task, scoring procedures, and desired statistical characteristics of the tasks (AERA, APA, & NCME, 1999). Explicit specifications of the content of the tasks are essential in designing performance assessments because they include fewer tasks and they tend to be more unique than multiple-choice items. Test specifications will help ensure that the tasks being developed are representative of the intended domain. Specifications for classroom assessments may not be as comprehensive as those for large-scale assessments; however, they are a valuable tool to classroom teachers for aligning their assessment with instruction. There are excellent sources for step-by-step guidelines for designing performance tasks and scoring rubrics, including Nitko (2004), Taylor and Nolen (2005), and Welch (2006).

Scoring Procedures for Performance Assessments

The evaluation of student performance requires scoring procedures based on expert judgment. Clearly defined scoring procedures are essential for developing performance assessments from which valid interpretations can be made. The first step is to delineate the performance criteria. Performance criteria reflect important characteristics of successful performance. At the classroom level, teachers use performance criteria developed by the state or may develop their own criteria. Defining the performance criteria deserves careful consideration, and informing students of the criteria safeguards a fair evaluation of student performance.

For classroom performance assessments, scoring rubrics, rating scales, or checklists are used to evaluate students. Scoring rubrics are rating scales that consist of pre-established performance criteria at each score level. The criteria specified at each score level are linked to the construct being assessed and depend on a number of factors, including whether a product or process is being assessed, the demands of the tasks, the nature of the student population, and the purpose of the assessment and the intended score interpretations (Lane & Stone, 2006). The number of score levels used depends on the extent to which the criteria across the score levels can meaningfully distinguish among student work. The performance reflected at each score level should differ distinctly from the performance at other score levels.

Designing scoring rubrics is an iterative process. A general scoring rubric that serves as a conceptual outline of the skills and knowledge underlying the given performance may be developed first. Performance criteria are specified for each score level. The general rubric can then be used to guide the design of each task-specific rubric. The performance criteria for the specific rubrics would reflect the criteria of the general rubric but also include criteria representing unique aspects of the individual task. Typically, the assessment of a particular genre of writing (e.g., persuasive writing) may have only a general rubric because the performance criteria at each score level are very similar across writing prompts within a genre. In mathematics, science, or history, performance assessment may have a general scoring rubric in addition to specific rubrics for each task. Specific rubrics guarantee accuracy in applying the criteria to student work, and facilitate generalizing from the performance on the assessment to the larger content domain of interest. Figure 50.1 shows a general and a specific rubric for a history performance task that assesses declarative knowledge. The specific rubric was designed for item 3 in the following performance task:

President Harry S. Truman has requested that you serve on a White House task force. The goal is to decide how to force the unconditional surrender of Japan, yet provide a secure post-war world. You are now a member of a committee of four and have reached the point at which you are trying to decide whether to drop the bomb.

1. Identify the alternatives you are considering and the criteria you are using to make the decision.

Figure 50.1 General and Specific Scoring Rubric for a History Standard

General Rubric

Score Level	Performance Criteria
4	Displays a thorough understanding of the generalizations, concepts, and facts specific to the task or situation. Provides new insights to some aspect of that information.
3	Displays a complete and accurate understanding of the generalizations, concepts, and facts specific to the task or situation.
2	Displays an incomplete understanding of the generalizations, concepts, and facts specific to the task or situation. Includes considerable misconceptions.
1	Displays severe misconceptions about the generalizations, concepts, and facts specific to the task or situation.

Specific Rubric

Score Level	Performance Criteria
4	Displays a thorough understanding of the generalization that war forces sensitive issues to surface and causes people to confront inherent conflicts of values. Provides new insights into people's behavior during wartime.
3	Displays a complete and accurate understanding of the generalization that war forces sensitive issues to surface and causes people to confront inherent conflicts of values.
2	Displays an incomplete understanding of the generalization that war forces sensitive issues to surface and causes people to confront inherent conflicts of values. Includes some notable misconceptions about this generalization.
1	Displays severe misconceptions about the generalization that war forces sensitive issues to surface and causes people to confront inherent conflicts of values.

SOURCE: Adapted from Marzano, R. J., Pickering, R. J., & McTighe, J. (1993). *Assessing student outcomes: Performance assessment using the dimensions of learning model.* Alexandria, VA: Association for Supervision and Curriculum Dimension.

2. Explain the values that influence the selection of the criteria and the weights you placed on each.

3. Explain how your decision has helped you better understand this statement: War forces people to confront inherent conflicts of values. (Marzano, Pickering, & McTighe, 1993, p. 28, note that numbers 1, 2, and 3 are added)

The specific rubric in Figure 50.1 could be expanded to provide examples of student misconceptions that are unique to question 3.

In addition to the distinction between general and specific rubrics, scoring rubrics may be either holistic or analytic. A holistic rubric requires the evaluation of the process or product as a whole. In other words, raters make a single, holistic judgment regarding the quality of the work, and they assign a single score using a rubric rather than evaluating the component parts separately. Figure 50.2 provides a holistic general scoring rubric for a mathematics performance assessment.

Analytic rubrics require the evaluation of component parts of the product or performance, and separate scores are assigned to those parts. If students are required to write a persuasive essay, rather than evaluate all aspects for their work as a whole, students may be evaluated separately on a few components such as strength of argument, organization, and writing mechanics. Each of these components would have a scoring rubric with distinct performance

---

Figure 50.2   Holistic General Scoring Rubric for Mathematics Constructed-Response Items

---

Performance Criteria

---

4   Shows understanding of the problem's mathematical concepts and principles; uses appropriate mathematical terminology and notations; executes algorithms completely and correctly.

Identifies all the important elements of the problem and shows understanding of the relationships among them; reflects an appropriate and systematic strategy for solving the problem; gives clear evidence of a solution process, and solution process is complete and systematic.

Gives a complete response with a clear, unambiguous explanation and/or description; may include an appropriate and complete diagram; communicates effectively to the identified audience; presents strong supporting arguments which are logically sound and complete; may include examples and counter-examples.

3   Shows nearly complete understanding of the problem's mathematical concepts and principles; uses nearly correct mathematical terminology and notations; executes algorithms completely; and computations are generally correct but may contain minor errors.

Identifies the most important elements of the problem and shows general understanding of the relationships among them; and gives clear evidence of a solution process, and solution process is complete or nearly complete and systematic.

Gives a fairly complete response with reasonably clear explanations or descriptions; may include a nearly complete, appropriate diagram; generally communicates effectively to the identified audience; presents strong supporting arguments which are logically sound but may contain some minor gaps.

2   Shows understanding of some of the problem's mathematical concepts and principles; and may contain computational errors.

Identifies some important elements of the problem but shows only limited understanding of the relationships among them; and gives some evidence of a solution process, but solution process may be incomplete or somewhat unsystematic.

Makes significant progress toward completion of the problem, but the explanation or description may be somewhat ambiguous or unclear; may include a diagram which is flawed or unclear; communication may be somewhat vague or difficult to interpret; and arguments may be incomplete or may be based on a logically unsound premise.

1   Shows very limited understanding of some of the problem's mathematical concepts and principles; may misuse or fail to use mathematical terms; and may make major computational errors.

Fails to identify important elements or places too much emphasis on unimportant elements; may reflect an inappropriate strategy for solving the problem; gives incomplete evidence of a solution process; solution process may be missing, difficult to identify, or completely unsystematic.

Has some satisfactory elements but may fail to complete or may omit significant parts of the problem; explanation or description may be missing or difficult to follow; may include a diagram, which incorrectly represents the problem situation, or diagram may be unclear and difficult to interpret.

0   Shows no understanding of the problem's mathematical concepts and principles.

Fails to indicate which elements of the problem are appropriate, copies part of the problem but without attempting a solution.

Communicates ineffectively; words do not reflect the problem; may include drawings which completely misrepresent the problem situation.

SOURCE: Adapted from Lane, S. (1993). The conceptual framework for the development of a mathematics performance assessment. *Educational Measurement: Issues and Practice, 12*(2), 23.

criteria at each score level. Analytic rubrics have the potential to provide meaningful information about students' strengths and weaknesses and the effectiveness of instruction on each of these components. Individual scores from an analytic rubric can also be summed to obtain a total score for the student.

Although rubrics are most commonly associated with scoring performance assessments, checklists and rating scales are sometimes used by classroom teachers. Checklists are lists of specific performance criteria expected to be present in a student's performance (Taylor & Nolen, 2005). Checklists only allow the option of indicating whether each criterion was present or absent in the student's work. They are best used to provide students with a quick and general indication of their strengths and weaknesses. Checklists tend to be easy to construct and simple to use; however, they are not appropriate for many performance assessments because no judgment is made as to the quality of the observation. If a teacher indicates that the criterion "grammar is correct" is present in a student's response, there is no indication of the degree to which the student's grammar was correct (see Taylor & Nolen, 2005).

Rating scales allow teachers to indicate the degree to which a student exhibits a particular characteristic or skill. A rating scale can be used if the teacher wants to differentiate the degree to which students use grammar correctly or incorrectly. Figure 50.3 provides an example of a rating scale for a persuasive essay.

In this rating scale, the rating labels are not the same across the performance criteria (e.g., clear, understand-able, and unfocused versus strong, adequate, and weak). This may pose a problem if teachers are hoping to combine the various ratings into a single, meaningful score for students. For some tasks, rating scales can be developed that have the same rating labels across items, which would allow for combining the ratings to produce a single score. When using rating scales, teachers must make explicit distinctions between the rating labels, such as few errors and many errors. If these distinctions are not made, scoring will be inconsistent and, as a result, accurate inferences about students' learning will be jeopardized. Teachers should strive to use scoring procedures that have explicitly defined performance criteria. Often, this is best achieved with using scoring rubrics to evaluate student performance.

Evaluating the Validity of Performance Assessments

Assessments are used in conjunction with other information to make important inferences and decisions about students, schools, and districts; and it is important to obtain evidence about the appropriateness of those inferences and decisions. Validity refers to the appropriateness, meaningfulness, and usefulness of the inferences drawn from assessment results (AERA, APA, & NCME, 1999). Evidence is needed therefore to help support the interpretation and use of assessment results. Validity criteria that are specific to performance assessments have been proposed, including, but not limited to, content representation, cognitive complexity, meaningfulness and transparency, transfer and generalizability, fairness, and consequences (Linn et al., 1991; Messick, 1995). A brief discussion of these validity criteria is presented in this section.

Content Representation

Because performance assessments consist of a small number of tasks, the ability to generalize from the student's performance on the assessment to the broader domain of interest may be hindered. It is important to consider carefully which tasks will compose a performance assessment. Test specifications will contribute to the development of tasks that systematically represent the content domain. For large-scale assessments that have high stakes associated with individual student

Figure 50.3   Rating Scale for the First Draft of a Persuasive Essay

Circle a rating for each characteristic that is present in the student's essay.

Persuasive Writing: Content and Ideas

Shows understanding of the issue	Clear	Understandable	Not focused
Position is stated and is related to the issue	Strong	Adequate	Weak
Reasons support the position	Strong	Adequate	Weak
Factual evidence supports the reasons	Accurate	Mostly Adequate	Little Accuracy
Descriptive examples support the reasons	Strong	Adequate	Weak
Conclusion urges action or agreement	Strong	Adequate	Weak

Organization and Language

Ideas are organized	Strong	Adequate	Weak
Language is appropriate for the audience	Strong	Adequate	Weak

Writing Conventions

Words are spelled correctly	All	Few Errors	Many Errors
Capitalization is correct	All	Few Errors	Many Errors
Punctuation is correct	All	Few Errors	Many Errors
Grammar is correct	All	Few Errors	Many Errors

SOURCE: Adapted from Taylor and Nolen (2005).

scores, multiple-choice items are typically used in conjunction with performance assessments to better represent the content domain and to help ensure accurate inferences regarding student performance. Classroom assessments can be tailored to the instructional material, allowing for a wide variety of assessment formats to capture the breadth of the content.

Cognitive Complexity

Some performance tasks may not require complex thinking skills. If the performance of interest is whether students can use a ruler accurately, then a performance task aligned to this skill requires the use of a ruler for measuring and does not require students to engage in complex thinking. Many performance assessments, however, are intended to assess students' reasoning and problem-solving skills. In fact, one of the promises of performance assessments is that they can assess these higher-order, complex skills. One cannot assume that complex thinking skills are being used by students when working on performance assessments; validity evidence is needed to establish that performance assessments do indeed evoke complex thinking skills (Linn et al., 1991). First, in assessment design it is important to consider how the task's format, content, and context may affect the cognitive processes used by students to solve the task. Second, the underlying cognitive demands of performance assessments, such as inference, integration, and reasoning, can be verified. Analyses of the strategies and processes that students use in solving performance tasks can provide such evidence. Students may be asked to think aloud as they respond to the task, or they may be asked to explain, in writing, reasons for their responses to tasks. If the purpose of a mathematics task is to determine whether students can solve it with a nonroutine solution strategy, but most students apply a strategy that they recently learned in instruction, then the task is not eliciting the intended cognitive skills and should be revised. The cognitive demands of performance tasks need to be considered in their design and then verified.

Meaningfulness and Transparency

If performance assessments are to improve instruction and student learning, both teachers and students should consider the tasks meaningful and of value to the instructional and assessment process (Frederiksen & Collins, 1989). Performance assessments also need to be transparent to both teachers and students—each party needs to know what is being assessed, by what methods, the criteria used to evaluate performances, and what constitutes successful performance. For large-scale assessments that have high-stakes associated with them, students need to be familiar with the task format and the performance criteria of the general scoring rubric. This will help ensure that all students have the opportunity to demonstrate what they know and can do. Throughout the instructional year, teach-

ers can use performance tasks with their students, and engage them in discussions about what the tasks are assessing and the nature of the criteria used for scoring student performances. Teachers can also engage students in using scoring rubrics to evaluate their own work and the work of their peers. These activities will provide opportunities for students to become familiar with the nature of the tasks and the criteria used in evaluating their work. It is best to embed these activities within the instructional process rather than treat them as test preparation activities. Research has shown that students who have had the opportunity to become familiar with the format of the performance assessment and the nature of the scoring criteria perform better than those who were not provided with such opportunities (Fuchs et al., 2000).

Transfer and Generalizability

An assessment is only a sample of tasks that measure some portion of the content domain of interest. Results from the assessment are then used to make inferences about student performance within that domain. The intent is to generalize from student performance on a sample of tasks to the broader domain of interest. The better the sample represents the domain, the more accurate the generalizations of student performance on the assessment to the broader domain of interest. It is necessary, then, to consider which tasks and how many tasks are needed within an assessment to give us confidence that we are making accurate inferences about student performance. For a writing assessment, generalizations about student performance across the writing domain may be of interest. Consequently, the sample of writing prompts should elicit various types of writing, such as narrative, persuasive, and expository. A student skilled in narrative writing may not be as skilled in persuasive writing. To generalize performance on an assessment to the entire writing domain, students would need to write essays across various types of writing. This is more easily accomplished in classroom performance assessments because samples of students' writing can be collected over a period of weeks.

An investigation of the generalizability of a performance assessment also requires examining the extent to which one can generalize the results across trained raters. Raters affect the extent to which accurate generalizations can be made about the assessment results because raters may differ in their appraisal of the quality of a student's response. Generalizability results across trained raters are typically much better than generalizability results across tasks in science, mathematics, and writing (e.g., Hieronymus & Hoover, 1987; Lane, Liu, Ankenmann, & Stone, 1996; Shavelson, Baxter, & Gao, 1993). To help achieve accuracy among raters in large-scale assessments, care is needed in designing precise scoring rubrics, selecting and training raters, and checking rater performance throughout the scoring process. Classroom performance assessments that are accompanied by scoring rubrics with clearly defined performance criteria will help ensure the accuracy of teachers' assigned scores to student work.

Fairness

Some proponents of performance assessments in the 1980s believed that performance assessments would help reduce the performance differences between subgroups of students—students with different cultural, ethnic, and socioeconomic backgrounds. As Linn et al. (1991) cautioned, however, it would be unreasonable to assume that group differences that are exhibited on multiple-choice tests would be smaller or alleviated by using performance assessments. Differences among groups are not necessarily due to test format, but are due to differences in learning opportunities, differences with the familiarity of the assessment format, and differences in student motivation. Closing the achievement gap for subgroups of students regardless of the format of the assessment requires that all students have the opportunity to learn the subject matter covered by the assessment (AERA, APA, & NCME, 1999). An integrated instruction and assessment system, as well as highly qualified teachers, are requisite for closing the achievement gap. Performance assessments can play an important role in closing the performance gap only if all students have opportunities to be engaged in meaningful learning.

Consequences

An assumption underlying the use of performance assessments is that they serve as motivators in improving student achievement and learning, and that they encourage the use of instructional strategies that promote students' reasoning, problem-solving, and communication skills. It is particularly important to obtain evidence about the consequences of performance assessments because particular intended consequences, such as fostering reasoning and thinking skills in instruction, are an essential part of the assessment system's rationale (Linn, 1993; Messick, 1995). Performance assessments are intended to promote student engagement in reasoning and problem solving in the classroom, so evidence of this intended consequence would support the validity of their use. Evaluation of both the intended and unintended consequences of assessments is fundamental to the validation of test use and the interpretation of the assessment results (Messick, 1995). To identify potential negative consequences, one needs to examine whether the purpose of the assessment is being compromised, such as teaching only the content standards that are on state assessments rather than to the entire set of content standards deemed important.

When some states relied more heavily on performance assessments in the early 1990s, there was evidence that many teachers revised their own instruction and classroom assessment accordingly. Teachers used more performance tasks and constructed-response items for classroom purposes. In a study examining the consequences of Washing-

ton's state assessment program, approximately two-thirds of teachers reported that the state's content standards and extended-response items on the state assessment were influential in promoting better instruction and student learning (Stecher, Barron, Chun, & Ross, 2000). Further, observations of classroom instruction in exemplary schools in Washington revealed that teachers were using reform-oriented strategies in meaningful ways (Borko, Wolf, Simone, & Uchiyama, 2003). Teachers and students were using scoring rubrics similar to those on the state assessment in the classroom, and their use of these rubrics promoted meaningful learning. In a study examining the consequences of Maryland's state performance assessment (MSPAP), teacher's reported use of reform-oriented instructional strategies was associated with positive changes in school performance on MSPAP in reading and writing over time (Stone & Lane, 2003). Schools in which teachers indicated that they had used more reform-oriented instructional strategies in reading and writing were associated with greater rates of change in school performance on MSPAP over a 5-year period. Further, teacher perceived effect of MSPAP on math and science instructional practices was also found to explain differences in changes in MSPAP school performance in math and science. The more impact MSPAP had on science and math instruction, the greater the gains in MSPAP school performance in math and science over a 5-year period.

Recently, however, many states have relied more heavily on multiple-choice items and short-answer formats, and as a consequence, teachers in some of these states are using fewer constructed-response items for classroom purposes (Hamilton et al., 2007). If extended constructed-response items that require students to explain their reasoning are not on the high-stakes state assessments, instruction may focus more on computation and less on complex math problems and teachers may rely less on constructed-response items on their classroom assessments.

Conclusion

Performance assessments are useful tools for initiating changes in instruction and student learning. Large-scale assessments that incorporate performance tasks can signal important goals for educators and students to pursue, which can have a positive effect on instruction and student learning. A balanced, coordinated assessment and instructional system is needed to help foster student learning. Coherency among content standards, instruction, large-scale assessments, and classroom assessments is necessary if we are committed to the goal of enhancing student achievement and learning. Because an important role for both large-scale and classroom performance assessments is to serve as models of good instruction, performance assessments should be grounded in current theories of student cognition and learning, be capable of evoking meaningful reasoning and problem-solving skills, and provide results that help guide instruction.

References and Further Readings

American Educational Research Association, American Psychological Association, & National Council on Measurement in Education. (1999). *Standards for educational and psychological testing.* Washington, DC: American Educational Research Association.

Baker, E. L., O'Neil, H. F., & Linn, R. L. (1993). Policy and validity prospects for performance-based assessment. *American Psychologist, 1210–1218.*

Baron, J. B. (1991). Strategies for the development of effective performance exercises. *Applied Measurement in Education, 4*(4), 305–318.

Black, P., & Wiliam, D. (1998). Inside the black box: Raising standards through classroom assessment. *Phi Delta Kappan, 80*(2), 139–148.

Borko, H., Wolf, S. A., Simone, G., & Uchiyama, K. (2003). Schools in transition: Reform efforts in exemplary schools of Washington. *Educational Evaluation and Policy Analysis, 25*(2), 171–202.

Frederiksen, J. R., & Collins, A. (1989). A systems approach to educational testing. *Educational Researcher, 18*(9), 27–32.

Fuchs, L. S., Fuchs, D., Karns, K., Hamlett, C. L., Dutka, S., & Katzaroff, M. (2000). The importance of providing background information on the structure and scoring of performance assessments. *Applied Measurement in Education, 13*(1), 1–34.

Hamilton, L. S., Stecher, B. M., Marsh, J. A., McCombs, J. S., Robyn, A., Russell, J. L., et al. (2007), *Standards-based accountability under No Child Left Behind.* Pittsburgh, PA: RAND.

Hieronymus, A. N., & Hoover, H. D. (1987). *Iowa tests of basic skills: Writing supplement teacher's guide.* Chicago: Riverside.

Kane, M., Crooks, T., & Cohen, A. (1999). Validating measures of performance. *Educational Measurement: Issues and Practice, 18*(2), 5–17.

Lane, S. (1993). The conceptual framework for the development of a mathematics performance assessment instrument. *Educational Measurement: Issues and Practice, 12*(3), 16–23.

Lane, S., Liu, M., Ankenmann, R. D., & Stone, C. A. (1996). Generalizability and validity of a mathematics performance assessment. *Journal of Educational Measurement, 33*(1), 71–92.

Lane, S., & Stone, C. A. (2006). Performance assessments. In B. Brennan (Ed.), *Educational Measurement* (pp. 387–432). Westport, CT: Praeger.

Linn, R. L. (1993). Educational assessment: Expanded expectations and challenges. *Educational Evaluation and Policy Analysis, 15,* 1–16.

Linn, R. L., Baker, E. L., & Dunbar, S. B. (1991). Complex performance assessment: Expectations and validation criteria. *Educational Researcher, 20*(8), 15–21.

Maryland State Board of Education. (1995). *Maryland school performance report: State and school systems.* Baltimore: Author.

Maryland State Department of Education. (1996). *1996 MSPAP public release task: Choice in reading and writing.* Baltimore: Author.

Marzano, R. J., Pickering, R. J., & McTighe, J. (1993). *Assessing student outcomes: Performance assessment using the dimensions of learning model.* Alexandria, VA: Association for Supervision and Curriculum Development.

Messick, S. (1995). Standards of validity and the validity of standards in performance assessment. *Educational Measurement: Issues and Practice, 14*(4), 5–8.

National Research Council. (2006). *Systems for state science assessment.* In M. R. Wilson & M. W. Bertenthal (Eds.), *Committee on test design for K–12 science achievement.* Washington, DC: National Academies Press.

Nitko, A. J. (2004). *Educational assessment of students* (4th ed.). Upper Saddle River, NJ: Pearson.

Resnick, L. B., & Resnick, D. P. (1992). Assessing the thinking curriculum: New tools for educational reform. In B. G. Gifford & M. C. O'Conner (Eds.), *Changing assessment: Alternative views of aptitude, achievement, and instruction* (pp. 37–55). Boston: Kluwer Academic.

Schmeiser, C. B., & Welch, C. J. (2007). Test development. In B. Brennan (Ed.), *Educational Measurement* (pp. 307–354). Westport, CT: Praeger.

Shavelson, R. J., Baxter, G. P., & Gao, X. (1993). Sampling variability of performance assessments. *Journal of Educational Measurement, 30*(3), 215–232.

Shepard, L. A. (2000). The role of assessment in a learning culture. *Educational Researcher, 29*(7), 4–14.

Shepard, L., Hammerness, K., Darling-Hammond, L., Rust, F., with Snowdon, J. B., Gordon, E., Gutierrez, C., & Pacheco, A. (2005). Assessment. In L. Darling-Hammond & J. Bransford (Eds.), *Preparing teachers for a changing world: What teachers should learn and be able to do.* San Francisco: Jossey-Bass.

Stecher, B., Barron, S., Chun, T., & Ross, K. (2000, August). *The effects of the Washington state education reform in schools and classrooms* (CSE Tech. Rep. NO. 525). Los Angeles: University of California, National Center for Research on Evaluation, Standards and Student Testing.

Stiggins, R. J. (1987). Design and development of performance assessments. *Educational Measurement: Issues and Practice, 6*(1), 33–42.

Stone, C. A., & Lane, S. (2003). Consequences of a state accountability program: Examining relationships between school performance gains and teacher, student and school variables. *Applied Measurement in Education, 16*(1), 1–26.

Taylor, C. S., & Nolen, S. B. (2005). *Classroom assessment: Supporting teaching and learning in real classrooms.* Upper Saddle River, NJ: Pearson.

U.S. Department of Education. (1996). *The Nations Report Card: 1996 assessment science public release Grade 8.* Washington, DC: Author. Retrieved June 1, 2007, from http://nces.ed.gov/nationsreportcard/itmrls/sampleq/

U.S. Department of Education. (1997). *The Nations Report Card: 1997 assessment mathematics public release Grade 8.* Washington, DC: Author. Retrieved from http://nces.ed.gov/nationsreportcard/ITMRLS/itemdisplay.asp

Wainer, H., & Thissen, D. (1994). On examinee choice in educational testing. *Review of Educational Research, 64,* 159–195.

Welch, C. (2006). Item and prompt development in performance testing. In S. M. Downing & T. M. Haladyna (Eds.), *Handbook of test development* (pp. 303–329). Mahwah, NJ: Lawrence Erlbaum Associates.

Wiggins, G. (1989, April). Teaching to the (authentic) test. *Educational Leadership,* 41–47.